DATE

MILESTONE DOCUMENTS IN AMERICAN HISTORY

Exploring the Primary Sources That Shaped America

MILESTONE DOCUMENTS IN AMERICAN HISTORY

Exploring the Primary Sources That Shaped America

Volume 4: 1956 – 2003

Paul Finkelman
Editor in Chief

Bruce A. Lesh
Consulting Editor

Schlager Group

Milestone Documents in American History
Copyright © 2008 by Schlager Group Inc.

Schlager Group Inc.
2501 Oak Lawn Avenue, Suite 245
Dallas, Tex. 75219
USA

You can find Schlager Group on the World Wide Web at
http://www.schlagergroup.com
http://www.milestonedocuments.com
Text and cover design by Patricia Moritz

Printed in the United States of America

10 9 8 7 6 5 4 3 2 1

ISBN: 978-0-9797758-0-2

This book is printed on acid-free paper.

Contents

Volume 1: 1763–1823

VOLUME 2: 1824–1887

Volume 3: 1888–1955

Volume 4: 1956–2003

MILESTONE DOCUMENTS
IN AMERICAN HISTORY

Exploring the Primary Sources
That Shaped America

Strom Thurmond was the principal instigator behind the Southern Manifesto. (AP Photo)

SOUTHERN MANIFESTO

"This unwarranted exercise of power by the Court ... is destroying the amicable relations between the white and Negro races."

Overview

On March 12, 1956, as the second anniversary of the Supreme Court case *Brown v. Board of Education* (1954) approached, Senator Walter F. George rose to the speaker's podium in the U.S. Senate to announce the creation of the latest weapon in the segregationist arsenal—the Southern Manifesto. It was a bold, brazen document, signed by 101 of the South's 128 congressional members. The Southern Manifesto, formally titled a Declaration of Constitutional Principles, denounced the Supreme Court's *Brown v. Board of Education* decision, calling it an "unwarranted exercise of power." The Southern Manifesto's signers pledged to "use all lawful means" to "bring about a reversal" of the *Brown* decision.

The declaration of the Southern Manifesto was not the first act in the South's massive resistance campaign against school desegregation. It was, however, one of the most important. As *New York Times* columnist and leading intellectual Anthony Lewis wrote, "The true meaning of the Manifesto was to make defiance of the Supreme Court and the Constitution socially acceptable to the South—to give resistance to the law the approval of the Southern Establishment" (qtd. in Aucoin, p. 176). Indeed, the Southern Manifesto's signers hoped to provide an ideological foundation for the white South's resistance movement. Rather than focusing on standard southern arguments about black racial inferiority or miscegenation, the Southern Manifesto concentrated on historical and constitutional issues. At base, it was a rear-guard action meant to preserve an entrenched but discriminatory system of education, which had existed in the South since the Supreme Court's *Plessy v. Ferguson* (1896) decision.

Context

Although many white southerners had established independent schools for their children before the Civil War, the first formal public education systems emerged in the South in the late nineteenth century. Each southern state created

its own Department of Education, with full power to draft curricula and enforce standards. In every case, however, southern schools segregated black and white students. The U.S. Supreme Court recognized the constitutional legitimacy of state-enforced racial segregation in *Plessy v. Ferguson*. This infamous decision cemented the "separate but equal" doctrine in American law, holding that racial segregation did not violate the Fourteenth Amendment's equal protection clause.

In 1954, as the Supreme Court considered *Brown v. Board of Education*, the "separate but equal" doctrine still governed race relations in America. Restaurants, restrooms, train cars, and taverns were segregated. In addition, seventeen southern and border states legally barred African Americans from white public schools, four western states allowed local school districts to determine segregation policy, and almost every other state in the nation practiced some form of de facto public school segregation. The Supreme Court's unanimous decision in *Brown* challenged the status quo and overturned the *Plessy* precedent. Chief Justice Earl Warren wrote, "In the field of public education the doctrine of 'separate but equal' has no place. Separate educational facilities are inherently unequal" (http://caselaw.lp.findlaw.com/scripts/getcase.pl?court=US&vol=347&involl=483). A year later, in *Brown II* (1955), Warren announced that public school districts must desegregate with "all deliberate speed" (http://caselaw.lp.findlaw.com/scripts/getcase.pl?court=us&vol=349&invol=294). Yet, of course, it was not that easy.

In the mid-1950s white southern Democrats launched a legal and political campaign against *Brown v. Board of Education*. On May 17, 1954—the day that the decision appeared—Senator Harry F. Byrd of Virginia condemned the Supreme Court's school desegregation order. He warned of dangers that would result from racial mixing in the schools. Georgia's Governor Herman Talmadge took a different approach. He said that the Supreme Court had ignored precedent and overstepped the boundaries of its authority.

Powerful southern senator James Eastland of Mississippi took yet another approach. Eastland portrayed racial segregation as a natural, self-evident truth. "Separation promotes racial harmony," he told the Senate, ten days

1896

■ May 18
The U.S. Supreme Court issues its decision for *Plessy v. Ferguson*, which holds that state-enforced racial segregation does not violate the Fourteenth Amendment's equal protection clause; based on this decision, school administrators in the South segregate white and black children into separate schools, which are terribly unequal.

1954

■ May 17
The U.S. Supreme Court hands down its *Brown v. Board of Education* decision, which overturns the "separate but equal" doctrine that had permitted legalized segregation in the United States since *Plessy v. Ferguson*.

■ June 26
Senator Harry F. Byrd, the political boss of Virginia, declares that he will use all legal means to continue segregating Virginia schools.

■ July 11
Robert Patterson and his associates found the White Citizens Council in Indianola, Mississippi.

1955

■ May 31
The U.S. Supreme Court issues its decision in *Brown v. Board of Education II*, which states that school desegregation must proceed with "all deliberate speed."

■ August
Emmett Till is murdered in Tallahatchie County, Mississippi, for allegedly whistling at a white woman; the accused assailants—two white men—are acquitted by an all-white jury.

■ December 1
Rosa Parks refuses to vacate her seat on a bus in Montgomery, Alabama, which sparks the Montgomery Bus Boycott.

1956

■ February 24
Senator Byrd of Virginia calls for massive resistance to *Brown v. Board of Education* and school desegregation.

after the *Brown* decision. "It permits each race to follow its own pursuits, and its own civilization. Segregation is not discrimination.... It is the law of nature, it is the law of God, that every race has both the right and the duty to perpetuate itself. All free men have the right to associate exclusively with members of their own race, free from governmental interference, if they so desire" (Commager, p. 70).

Robert Patterson, a plantation manager from Indianola, Mississippi, agreed with Eastland. Patterson and a dozen friends formed the first White Citizens' Council in July 1954. Their organization consisted primarily of white-collar, middle-class southern business leaders and professionals who used economic and legal means to discourage African Americans from pursuing court-ordered desegregation. By October 1954 twenty White Citizens' Councils had appeared across Mississippi. Within two years the organization could boast more than 250,000 supporters throughout the South.

Although southern politicians and members of the White Citizens' Councils often rejected base appeals to racism and violence, other southern whites commonly used these tactics to intimidate African Americans in the South. In 1955, for instance, four African Americans—including a young man named Emmett Till—were brutally murdered in separate cases of racial violence in Mississippi without one white person ever being convicted. Whites used threats of racial violence to keep African Americans from voting booths and courthouses, where they might most successfully challenge white supremacy.

As the South's white political leaders struggled to unite disparate segregationist organizations, they drew on the region's deep-rooted political traditions. No one was more successful in this endeavor than Senator Byrd of Virginia, who in 1956 called for massive resistance to the *Brown* decision. Byrd's most powerful arguments against the *Brown* decision were based on the writings of James J. Kilpatrick, the conservative editor of the *Richmond News Leader*. Kilpatrick argued that the *Brown* decision represented a federal violation of states' rights and that the southern states should interpose themselves between their citizens and the federal government, if it attempted to enforce the decision.

Senator Strom Thurmond of South Carolina, an outspoken critic of *Brown v. Board of Education*, showed keen interest in the interposition doctrine. In February 1956 Thurmond approached Byrd with an idea for a Southern Manifesto that might unite the South. He suggested that the document be constitutional and historical in nature and that it emphasize interposition. He wrote three drafts of the document in February 1956. In uncompromising, bombastic tones, Thurmond spoke publicly against the Supreme Court for violating the Constitution and the principles of federalism.

Thurmond's work on the manifesto secured the support of Byrd, a soft-spoken Virginia reactionary who controlled his state's political system through an elaborate network known as the Byrd machine. With Byrd's assistance, Thurmond circulated drafts of the Southern Manifesto on Capitol Hill in the hope of winning support from other southern delegates. While a few die-hard segregationists were willing to sign on to Thurmond's initiative, it proved far too radical for most southern congressmen to approve. Undeterred, Thurmond and Byrd threatened to issue the document with as many signatures as they could get.

At this point, the Senate's southern leadership intervened. Walter F. George, the eighty-year-old senior member of the Georgia delegation, called a meeting of the Southern Caucus. Attendees agreed that Sam Ervin, Jr., of North Carolina would revise the manifesto with assistance from Richard Russell, Jr., of Georgia and John Stennis of Mississippi. Ervin's draft of the manifesto tempered Thurmond's rhetoric, highlighting the historical and judicial precedents that the Supreme Court had supposedly ignored in the *Brown* decision. Still, Ervin's draft remained hard-hitting.

Leading southern moderates in the Senate, including J. William Fulbright of Arkansas, were discouraged by the Ervin draft. Although they wanted to demonstrate their fidelity to the southern cause of segregation, the moderates remained wary of the Southern Manifesto. As the historian Randall Woods has shown, Senator Fulbright rejected the idea that the states or the people could declare Supreme Court decisions unconstitutional. In March 1956, for instance, Fulbright wrote to a Little Rock constituent, "Under our system of government, the Supreme Court is specifically given the authority to interpret the Constitution, and no matter how wrong we think they are, there is no appeal from their decision unless you rebel as the South tried to do in 1860" (Woods, pp. 208–209).

In an effort to temper the manifesto's most dramatic and troublesome phrases, Fulbright worked with his staff and a coalition of other southern senators, including Lister Hill, John Sparkman, and Price Daniel, to draft an updated, fifth version of the document. As Randall Woods shows, Fulbright's new edition of the manifesto excised previous statements, which declared that the Supreme Court's decision in *Brown* was "illegal and unconstitutional." In place of these statements, Fulbright called the decision "unwarranted." In addition, he encouraged southerners to "scrupulously refrain from disorder and lawlessness" (Woods, p. 209).

Fulbright's draft proved too moderate for Thurmond and other hardliners. They wanted a dramatic denunciation of the *Brown* decision. Therefore, a committee of five senators including Thurmond, Russell, Stennis, Fulbright, and Daniel compiled a sixth and final draft of the manifesto. The committee completed its work in early March 1956.

About the Author

The Southern Manifesto was the product of many minds. The document, originally proposed by Senator Strom Thurmond of South Carolina, went through six revisions. Strom Thurmond (1902–2003) was the principal

Time Line	
1956	■ **March 12** One hundred and one southern congressmen sign the Southern Manifesto, which declares their opposition to *Brown v. Board of Education*. ■ **April** Alabama, Georgia, Mississippi, South Carolina, Tennessee, and Virginia pass interposition resolutions opposing *Brown v. Board of Education*. ■ **August–September** Violence erupts at Mansfield, Texas, and Clinton, Tennessee, as school desegregation occurs; in Texas, Governor Allan Shivers uses the Texas Rangers to uphold segregation; and in Tennessee, the National Guard intervenes to enforce desegregation.
1957	■ **January** Martin Luther King, Jr., and his associates found the Southern Christian Leadership Conference to pursue desegregation and equal rights for African Americans. ■ **September** Racial violence erupts at Little Rock, Arkansas, as school desegregation occurs; President Dwight D. Eisenhower dispatches troops to quell the violence.
1958– 1959	■ **September 1958– February 1959** Virginia closes nine schools in different localities to prevent integration.
1959	■ **February 3** Desegregation begins in Virginia.
1960	■ **February 1** Four college men from North Carolina Agricultural and Technological State University, frustrated by the slow pace of desegregation, lead a sit-in at a Woolworth's department store in downtown Greensboro, North Carolina; their action sparks a national movement, which would lead to the founding of the Student Nonviolent Coordinating Committee.

Walter F. George (Library of Congress)

instigator behind the Southern Manifesto. He was born in Edgefield, South Carolina, and he graduated from Clemson College before serving as a school superintendent, a senator, a judge, and governor. In 1948 Thurmond rose to national prominence when he ran for president as head of the Dixiecrat Party. Although he won only four states and thirty-nine electoral votes, this was a remarkable showing for a third-party candidate. Thurmond's willingness to stand firm on racial segregation and his ability to muster inventive constitutional arguments in its defense made him a popular hero among many white South Carolinians. With their support, Thurmond won an election to the U.S. Senate in 1954 as a write-in candidate. He was the only person to accomplish such a feat. That same year, the Supreme Court helped define the course of Thurmond's early senatorial career with its *Brown v. Board of Education* decision. Thurmond opposed the decision and its enforcement. In 1956 he proposed the Southern Manifesto to desist the Court's decision.

Harry F. Byrd (1887–1966) was Virginia's most powerful political figure during the mid-twentieth century. He grew up in Winchester, Virginia, a small town in the Shenandoah Valley, where his father operated a local newspaper and an apple orchid. In 1915 Byrd parlayed a prosperous business career at the Valley Turnpike Company into a successful political career. He was elected to the Virginia state senate in 1915, the chairmanship of the Virginia Democratic Committee in 1922, and the governor's office in 1926. As governor, Byrd formed a coalition to control the state's political life for more than three decades. He advocated strict construction of the Constitution, racial segregation, and a pay-as-you-go economic policy that limited taxes and government spending. In 1933 Byrd was elected to the U.S. Senate, beginning a long political tenure that included key debates on school desegregation. Byrd's most infamous statement on the matter came in February 1956, when he called for organized massive resistance in the South.

Richard Russell, Jr. (1897–1971), was the most influential southern senator in 1956. He was born in Winder, Georgia, where he followed in his father's footsteps as a lawyer and legislator. He received a law degree from the University of Georgia School of Law in 1918 and, three years later, won an election to the state house of representatives. After a ten-year legislative stint, Russell was elected governor of Georgia and then U.S. senator. He served in the Senate from 1933 to 1971, leading the conservative coalition that dominated Congress from 1937 to 1963. Russell was a key figure in the drafting of the Southern Manifesto.

Sam Ervin, Jr. (1896–1985), was one of the most powerful and influential southern senators of the mid-twentieth century. Ervin, a native of Morgantown, North Carolina, attended the University of North Carolina at Chapel Hill and Harvard Law School. Ervin parlayed a distinguished service record in World War I into a successful political career as a Democratic North Carolina state assemblyman, criminal court judge, and state supreme court justice. In 1946 Ervin was elected to finish the remainder of his brother's term in the U.S. House of Representatives. Ervin quickly gained reelection in his own right and, after four terms as a congressman, received an interim appointment to the Senate in 1954. As a congressman, Ervin strongly opposed civil rights reforms. He condemned the *Brown v. Board of Education* decision in 1954 and helped to draft the Southern Manifesto two years later. But Erwin carefully cloaked his opposition to desegregation in terms of his dislike of big government. He thus avoided the blatantly racist argument commonly used by other southern politicians at the time to oppose civil rights initiatives.

John C. Stennis (1901–1995) was a long-serving Mississippi senator well known for his segregationist views. Stennis was born in Kemper County, Mississippi, and graduated from Mississippi State University and the University of Virginia Law School. While still enrolled in law school, Stennis won a seat in the Mississippi House of Representatives. He pursued successful careers as a prosecutor and a circuit court judge before winning a special election to the U.S. Senate, convened following the death of Mississippi senator and die-hard segregationist Theodore Bilbo. Stennis spoke out openly against the civil rights movement and helped to draft the Southern Manifesto in 1956.

J. William Fulbright (1905–1995) was one of the most well-known, controversial figures in twentieth-century American political history. Fulbright, a native of Sumner, Mississippi, graduated from the University of Arkansas before attending Oxford University in England as a Rhodes Scholar and obtaining a law degree from George Washington University. He began his career in public service as a Justice Department attorney. Fulbright then served as a professor and later as president of the University of

Arkansas. In 1942 Fulbright was elected to Congress, where he promoted support for the eventual creation of the United Nations. In 1944 Arkansas voters elected Fulbright to the Senate, where he helped establish the Fulbright Scholar Program. Fulbright also earned a reputation as an opponent of Republican Senator Joseph McCarthy. Early in his career, Fulbright was a dedicated supporter of segregation. He opposed the Supreme Court decision in *Brown v. Board of Education* but urged fellow southerners to pursue a moderate opposition to the civil rights movement. In 1956 he toned down much of the hyperbolic tone found in the first draft of the Southern Manifesto to produce a more moderate but still thoroughly pro-segregationist document.

Price Daniel (1910–1988) was a Democratic senator from Texas and early opponent of the civil rights movement. He was raised in Dayton, Texas, and obtained a law degree from Baylor University. In 1939 Daniel was elected to the Texas House of Representatives, where he gained fame as an opponent of a state sales tax. After a brief stint as speaker of the house, Daniel enlisted in the army to serve in World War II. After the war, Daniel returned to Texas and was elected state attorney general in 1946. He unsuccessfully defended the University of Texas's segregation policies in the landmark Supreme Court case of *Sweatt v. Painter* (1950). Although Daniel was a moderate politician in many areas, he opposed civil rights reforms and was the last leading southern senator to participate in the drafting of the Southern Manifesto in 1956.

Explanation and Analysis of the Document

The Southern Manifesto, in the first three paragraphs of its "Declaration of Constitutional Principles," denounces the "unwarranted" decision in *Brown v. Board of Education* as a "clear abuse of judicial power." According to the manifesto, the Supreme Court ignored important constitutional precedents in the *Brown* decision. The manifesto states (in paragraph 11) that rather than following a traditional, strict-constructionist view of the Constitution, which had dominated school-segregation law for five decades, the Supreme Court justices "substituted their personal, political, and social ideas for the established law of the land." The manifesto declares that in doing so the justices overstepped their bounds and invaded the realm of states' rights.

The manifesto's signers challenge the *Brown* decision's most controversial finding: that segregated education deprives African Americans of their Fourteenth Amendment equal protection rights. The manifesto rejects this idea outright. It declares (in paragraph 4) that the Fourteenth Amendment's framers never intended to "affect the system of education maintained by the States." Indeed, the manifesto presents evidence to the contrary. It argues (in paragraphs 4–7) that the Fourteenth Amendment does not mention education. Indeed, the Congress that proposed it "subsequently provided for segregated schools in the District of Columbia," and twenty-six of the thirty-seven states that considered ratification of the amendment either possessed or developed segregated systems of public education. The manifesto's authors consider these points conclusive evidence that the Fourteenth Amendment does not provide legal justification for school desegregation.

The manifesto also claims (in paragraphs 8 and 9) that the *Brown* decision rejects a series of well-known legal precedents, including *Roberts v. City of Boston* (1849), *Plessy v. Ferguson* (1896), and *Gong Lum v. Rice* (1927). These cases each recognized the constitutionality of state-enforced segregation. *Gong Lum v. Rice* was perhaps the most powerful precedent in the group. In this case, the U.S. Supreme Court had declared that public school segregation was "within the discretion of the States … and does not conflict with the Fourteenth Amendment" (http://caselaw.lp.findlaw.com/cgi-bin/getcase.pl?friend=public&court=us&vol=275&invol=78). The manifesto's authors argue in the following paragraphs that this decision and others like it confirm the "habits, traditions, and way of life" in the South. Now, however, without any "constitutional amendment or act of Congress," the Supreme Court was "changing this established legal principle," which had existed for almost a century. Southerners would not abide by the Court's decision. On the contrary, they would use "all lawful means to bring about a reversal of this decision."

The Southern Manifesto's constitutional argument sidesteps the base appeals to racism and violence that so many segregationists relied upon. In fact, the manifesto's authors blame (in paragraph 12) the Supreme Court for "destroying the amicable relations between the white and Negro races" in the South. This self-serving, fallacious interpretation of the Jim Crow era would become a standard political ploy in the segregationist argument against the *Brown* decision. Segregationists argued that it was the Supreme Court, not the white South, that treated African Americans unfairly. For in its *Brown* decision, the Court had "planted hatred and suspicion" where previously there had been "friendship and understanding."

Despite the manifesto's defiant tone, the document concludes with a hint of moderation. The document's signers "appeal to the States and people … to consider the constitutional principles involved" in the school desegregation debate. No program of interposition or nullification is proposed. On the contrary, the manifesto's signers pledge to use "lawful means" to seek a reversal of the *Brown* decision. In addition, they request the people of the South to "scrupulously refrain from disorder and lawless acts."

Audience

The Southern Manifesto was a unique document in twentieth-century American politics. In many ways it hearkened back to the legislative petitions or memorials of the nineteenth century. Such documents often expressed a particular constituency's strongly felt sentiments but carried no formal legal weight. Although it was primarily a statement of purpose by white southerners engaged in massive resistance, a manifesto that criticized a landmark Supreme

Senator Harry F. Byrd of Virginia. (AP Photo)

Court decision signed by eighty-two representatives and nineteen senators could not be easily dismissed, which, of course, was what the manifesto's framers intended.

As a statement read from the Senate floor and entered into the *Congressional Record*, the Southern Manifesto was aimed at all Americans but also appealed to some groups in particular. On a basic level the manifesto lent emotional support to southern white school board members, local governmental officials, and others actively opposing the desegregation of public schools. By adding the prestige of national political figures, the manifesto gave massive resistance a veneer of social legitimacy, at least in the southern political climate. It also invoked a common southern argument used since the antebellum period, namely, that the South was a distinct region that could settle its unique racial problems only without outside pressure.

The manifesto, more broadly, went through several rewrites specifically designed to appeal to nonsoutherners and moderates. By invoking history to place the segregationist cause on the same moral side as the Kentucky and Virginia Resolutions or as the political thought of James Madison, the manifesto's authors sought to appeal to conservatives and opponents of big government in all sections of the country. Furthermore, the manifesto sought to remind northern Democrats that the white South was united in its defiance of integration and would split the party if necessary to achieve this goal. By the same token, the Southern Manifesto's authors sent a strong message to the Eisenhower administration (and presumably to all those who aspired to the White House in the future) that the Solid South would not back a presidential candidate that supported desegregation. The Southern Manifesto also reminded the U.S. Supreme Court to tread lightly on the issue of civil rights, as it needed the voluntary support of lower federal courts staffed by southern judges, as well as state and local government officials, to carry out its decisions.

Impact

The Southern Manifesto had an immediate impact in the South, where it unified legislators and encouraged resistance to desegregation. The most obvious example of the manifesto's success occurred in state legislatures. There, six southern states passed interposition resolutions in April 1956. Four states—Alabama, Mississippi, Georgia, and Florida—actually declared the *Brown* decision null and void within their borders. Even moderate states such as North Carolina and Tennessee joined the chorus of protest in 1957.

State legislatures in the South also pursued other, more pragmatic tactics to avoid school desegregation. One such method was the passage of pupil-placement acts, which required African American students to complete applications, tests, and in some cases personal interviews before their request for transfer would be considered by the state. Another legislative tactic pursued in a handful of states empowered the governors to cut funding for public schools should the federal courts order desegregation.

The legal posturing of southern legislatures was put to the test in a series of school-desegregation conflicts that erupted in the mid-1950s. In Mansfield, Texas, Governor Alan Shivers called the Texas Rangers to halt the desegregation of Mansfield High School. In Clinton, Tennessee, John Kasper and Asa Carter stirred up segregationists who attempted to halt the integration of Clinton High School. In Little Rock, Arkansas, Governor Orval Faubus deployed the Arkansas National Guard to uphold segregation. Although his efforts were thwarted by President Eisenhower and the federal court system in 1957, the following year, Faubus and the state legislature closed the high schools in Little Rock for the year to prevent integration. In Virginia, a similar story developed when Governor J. Lindsay Almond closed nine schools in four localities to prevent desegregation in September 1958. The federal courts intervened again, however, and massive resistance in Virginia ended in February 1959.

Although the Southern Manifesto encouraged resistance to the *Brown* decision, it is difficult to determine the document's long-term significance. It is well known that school desegregation proceeded slowly in the South during the 1960s, but the degree to which this related to the Southern Manifesto is questionable. The document remained of symbolic, rather than legal, significance. It provided southern segregationists with a popular rallying cry by which they continued to resist integration.

Related Documents

"Brown v. Board of Education, 347 U.S. 483 (1954)." Findlaw Web site. http://caselaw.lp.findlaw.com/scripts/getcase.pl?court=US&vol=

"*The unwarranted decision of the Supreme Court in the public school cases is now bearing the fruit always produced when men substitute naked power for established law.*"

(Paragraph 1)

"*We regard the decisions of the Supreme Court in the school cases as a clear abuse of judicial power. It climaxes a trend in the Federal Judiciary undertaking to legislate, in derogation of the authority of Congress, and to encroach upon the reserved rights of the States and the people.*"

(Paragraph 3)

"*This unwarranted exercise of power by the Court, contrary to the Constitution, is creating chaos and confusion in the States principally affected. It is destroying the amicable relations between the white and Negro races that have been created through 90 years of patient effort by the good people of both races. It has planted hatred and suspicion where there has been heretofore friendship and understanding.*"

(Paragraph 12)

"*We pledge ourselves to use all lawful means to bring about a reversal of this decision which is contrary to the Constitution and to prevent the use of force in its implementation.*"

(Paragraph 20)

"*In this trying period, as we all seek to right this wrong, we appeal to our people not to be provoked by the agitators and troublemakers invading our States and to scrupulously refrain from disorder and lawless acts.*"

(Paragraph 21)

347&invol=483. Accessed on February 22, 2008. The Supreme Court's decision in *Brown v. Board of Education* declared that school desegregation in America was unconstitutional.

"Brown v. Board of Education, 349 U.S. 294 (1955)" Findlaw Web site. http://caselaw.lp.findlaw.com/scripts/getcase.pl?court=us&vol=349&invol=294. Accessed on February 22, 2008. The Supreme Court's decision in *Brown v. Board of Education II* declared that school districts must desegregate with "all deliberate speed."

"Interposition Resolution in Response to Brown v. Board of Education (1957)." Florida Memory Project Web site. http://www.floridamemory.com/FloridaHighlights/collins/. Accessed on February 22, 2008. The Florida state legislature passed an interposition resolution in 1957 in which it attempted to intervene between the citizens of Florida and the federal government.

"Executive Order No. 10730: Desegregation of Central High School (1957)." National Archives "Our Documents" Web site. http://

www.ourdocuments.gov/doc.php?flash=true&doc=89. Accessed on February 22, 2008. President Dwight Eisenhower issued Executive Order 10730, which required the desegregation of Central High School in Little Rock, Arkansas.

Bibliography

■ Articles

Aucoin, Brent. "The Southern Manifesto and Southern Opposition to Desegregation." *Arkansas Historical Quarterly* 55, no. 2 (1996): 173–193.

Badger, Tony. "The Southern Manifesto: White Southerners and Civil Rights, 1956." *European Contributions to American Studies* 15 (1988): 77–99.

■ Books

Bartley, Numan. *The Rise of Massive Resistance: Race and Politics in the South During the 1950s.* Baton Rouge: Louisiana State University Press, 1969.

Cohodas, Nadine. *Strom Thurmond and the Politics of Southern Change.* New York: Simon and Schuster, 1993.

Commager, Henry, comp. *The Struggle for Racial Equality: A Documentary Record.* New York: Harper and Row, 1967.

Lassiter, Matthew D., and Andrew B. Lewis, eds. *The Moderates' Dilemma: Massive Resistance to School Desegregation in Virginia.* Charlottesville: University Press of Virginia, 1998.

Lewis, George. *Massive Resistance: The White Response to the Civil Rights Movement.* New York: Oxford University Press, 2006.

Patterson, James T. *Brown v. Board of Education: A Civil Rights Milestone and Its Troubled Legacy.* New York: Oxford University Press, 2001.

Webb, Clive, ed. *Massive Resistance: Southern Opposition to the Second Reconstruction.* New York: Oxford University Press, 2005.

Woods, Randall B. *Fulbright: A Biography.* New York: Cambridge University Press, 1995.

■ Web Sites

"Brown v. Board of Education." University of Michigan Library "Digital Archive" Web site.
   http://www.lib.umich.edu/exhibits/brownarchive/. Accessed on February 22, 2008.

"The Civil Rights Movement in Virginia: Massive Resistance." Virginia Historical Society Web site.
   http://www.vahistorical.org/civilrights/massiveresistance.htm. Accessed on February 22, 2008.

"Gong Lum v. Rice, 275 U.S. 78 (1927)." FindLaw Web site.
   http://caselaw.lp.findlaw.com/cgi-bin/getcase.pl?friend=public &court=us&vol=275&invol=78. Accessed on February 22, 2008.

"Television News of the Civil Rights Era, 1950–1970." University of Virginia Web site.
   http://www.vcdh.virginia.edu/civilrightstv. Accessed on February 22, 2008.

—By Jeffrey L. Littlejohn

Questions for Further Study

1. Compare the presentation of the Fourteenth Amendment found in *Brown v. Board of Education* with that enunciated by the Southern Manifesto's authors. Which interpretation do you find most convincing?

2. In what ways did the Southern Manifesto's authors invoke the states' rightist tradition of the eighteenth and nineteenth centuries?

3. Why would the Southern Manifesto's signers adopt the platform of "interposition," knowing its historical limitations?

4. Did the Southern Manifesto's signers legitimately believe that it would halt the implementation of *Brown v. Board of Education*, or did they see it merely as a short-term measure to delay school desegregation?

5. To what extent was the Southern Manifesto successful in delaying the enforcement of *Brown v. Board of Education*?

6. After the massive resistance campaign failed, how did the Southern Manifesto's signers react to the increasing success of the civil rights movement?

Glossary

checks and balances	the ability of separate federal branches to limit each other's powers
dual system of government	the division of sovereignty between the state and federal governments
rights reserved to the States	rights held exclusively by the states under a system of federalism and guaranteed by the Tenth Amendment to the Constitution
separate but equal	a phrase describing the system of segregated facilities in American society

SOUTHERN MANIFESTO

Declaration of Constitutional Principles

The unwarranted decision of the Supreme Court in the public school cases is now bearing the fruit always produced when men substitute naked power for established law.

The Founding Fathers gave us a Constitution of checks and balances because they realized the inescapable lesson of history that no man or group of men can be safely entrusted with unlimited power. They framed this Constitution with its provisions for change by amendment in order to secure the fundamentals of government against the dangers of temporary popular passion or the personal predilections of public officeholders.

We regard the decisions of the Supreme Court in the school cases as a clear abuse of judicial power. It climaxes a trend in the Federal Judiciary undertaking to legislate, in derogation of the authority of Congress, and to encroach upon the reserved rights of the States and the people.

The original Constitution does not mention education. Neither does the 14th Amendment nor any other amendment. The debates preceding the submission of the 14th Amendment clearly show that there was no intent that it should affect the system of education maintained by the States.

The very Congress which proposed the amendment subsequently provided for segregated schools in the District of Columbia.

When the amendment was adopted in 1868, there were 37 States of the Union....

Every one of the 26 States that had any substantial racial differences among its people, either approved the operation of segregated schools already in existence or subsequently established such schools by action of the same law-making body which considered the 14th Amendment.

As admitted by the Supreme Court in the public school case (*Brown v. Board of Education*), the

doctrine of separate but equal schools "apparently originated in *Roberts v. City of Boston* (1849), upholding school segregation against attack as being violative of a State constitutional guarantee of equality." This constitutional doctrine began in the North, not in the South, and it was followed not only in Massachusetts, but in Connecticut, New York, Illinois, Indiana, Michigan, Minnesota, New Jersey, Ohio, Pennsylvania and other northern states until they, exercising their rights as states through the constitutional processes of local self-government, changed their school systems.

In the case of *Plessy v. Ferguson* in 1896 the Supreme Court expressly declared that under the 14th Amendment no person was denied any of his rights if the States provided separate but equal facilities. This decision has been followed in many other cases. It is notable that the Supreme Court, speaking through Chief Justice Taft, a former President of the United States, unanimously declared in 1927 in *Lum v. Rice* that the "separate but equal" principle is "within the discretion of the State in regulating its public schools and does not conflict with the 14th Amendment."

This interpretation, restated time and again, became a part of the life of the people of many of the States and confirmed their habits, traditions, and way of life. It is founded on elemental humanity and commonsense, for parents should not be deprived by Government of the right to direct the lives and education of their own children.

Though there has been no constitutional amendment or act of Congress changing this established legal principle almost a century old, the Supreme Court of the United States, with no legal basis for such action, undertook to exercise their naked judicial power and substituted their personal political and social ideas for the established law of the land.

This unwarranted exercise of power by the Court, contrary to the Constitution, is creating chaos and confusion in the States principally affected. It is destroying the amicable relations between the white and Negro races that have been created through 90 years of patient effort by the good people of both races. It has planted hatred and suspicion where there has been heretofore friendship and understanding.

Without regard to the consent of the governed, outside mediators are threatening immediate and revolutionary changes in our public schools systems. If done, this is certain to destroy the system of public education in some of the States.

With the gravest concern for the explosive and dangerous condition created by this decision and inflamed by outside meddlers:

We reaffirm our reliance on the Constitution as the fundamental law of the land.

We decry the Supreme Court's encroachment on the rights reserved to the States and to the people, contrary to established law, and to the Constitution.

We commend the motives of those States which have declared the intention to resist forced integration by any lawful means.

We appeal to the States and people who are not directly affected by these decisions to consider the constitutional principles involved against the time when they too, on issues vital to them may be the victims of judicial encroachment.

Even though we constitute a minority in the present Congress, we have full faith that a majority of the American people believe in the dual system of government which has enabled us to achieve our greatness and will in time demand that the reserved rights of the States and of the people be made secure against judicial usurpation.

We pledge ourselves to use all lawful means to bring about a reversal of this decision which is contrary to the Constitution and to prevent the use of force in its implementation.

In this trying period, as we all seek to right this wrong, we appeal to our people not to be provoked by the agitators and troublemakers invading our States and to scrupulously refrain from disorder and lawless acts.

Signed by:

◆ Members of the United States Senate

Walter F. George, Richard B. Russell, John Stennis, Sam J. Ervin, Jr., Strom Thurmond, Harry F. Byrd, A. Willis Robertson, John L. McClellan, Allen J. Ellender, Russell B. Long, Lister Hill, James O. Eastland, W. Kerr Scott, John Sparkman, Olin D. Johnston, Price Daniel, J.W. Fulbright, George A. Smathers, Spessard L. Holland.

◆ Members of the United States House of Representatives

Alabama: Frank W. Boykin, George M. Grant, George W. Andrews, Kenneth A. Roberts, Albert Rains, Armistead I. Selden, Jr., Carl Elliott, Robert E. Jones, George Huddleston, Jr.

Arkansas: E.C. Gathings, Wilbur D. Mills, James W. Trimble, Oren Harris, Brooks Hays, W.F. Norrell.

Florida: Charles E. Bennett, Robert L.F. Sikes, A.S. Herlong, Jr., Paul G. Rogers, James A. Haley, D.R. Matthews.

Georgia: Prince H. Preston, John L. Pilcher, E.L. Forrester, John James Flynt, Jr., James C. Davis, Carl Vinson, Henderson Lanham, Iris F. Blitch, Phil M. Landrum, Paul Brown.

Louisiana: F. Edward Hebert, Hale Boggs, Edwin E. Willis, Overton Brooks, Otto E. Passman, James H. Morrison, T. Ashton Thompson, George S. Long.

Mississippi: Thomas G. Abernathy, Jamie L. Whitten, Frank E. Smith, John Bell Williams, Arthur Winstead, William M. Colmer.

North Carolina: Herbert C. Bonner, L.H. Fountain, Graham A. Barden, Carl T. Durham, F. Ertel Carlyle, Hugh Q. Alexander, Woodrow W. Jones, George A. Shuford.

South Carolina: L. Mendel Rivers, John J. Riley, W.J. Bryan Dorn, Robert T. Ashmore, James P. Richards, John L. McMillan.

Tennessee: James B. Frazier, Jr., Tom Murray, Jere Cooper, Clifford Davis.

[PUBLIC LAW __627__]

[CHAPTER __462__]

Eighty-fourth Congress of the United States of America

AT THE SECOND SESSION

Begun and held at the City of Washington on Tuesday, the third day of January,
one thousand nine hundred and fifty-six

An Act

To amend and supplement the Federal-Aid Road Act approved July 11, 1916, to authorize appropriations for continuing the construction of highways; to amend the Internal Revenue Code of 1954 to provide additional revenue from the taxes on motor fuel, tires, and trucks and buses; and for other purposes.

Be it enacted by the Senate and House of Representatives of the United States of America in Congress assembled,

TITLE I—FEDERAL-AID HIGHWAY ACT OF 1956

SEC. 101. SHORT TITLE FOR TITLE I.

This title may be cited as the "Federal-Aid Highway Act of 1956".

SEC. 102. FEDERAL-AID HIGHWAYS.

(a) (1) AUTHORIZATION OF APPROPRIATIONS.—For the purpose of carrying out the provisions of the Federal-Aid Road Act approved July 11, 1916 (39 Stat. 355), and all Acts amendatory thereof and supplementary thereto, there is hereby authorized to be appropriated for the fiscal year ending June 30, 1957, $125,000,000 in addition to any sums heretofore authorized for such fiscal year; the sum of $850,000,-000 for the fiscal year ending June 30, 1958; and the sum of $875,-000,000 for the fiscal year ending June 30, 1959. The sums herein authorized for each fiscal year shall be available for expenditure as follows:

(A) 45 per centum for projects on the Federal-aid primary highway system.

(B) 30 per centum for projects on the Federal-aid secondary highway system.

(C) 25 per centum for projects on extensions of these systems within urban areas.

(2) APPORTIONMENTS.—The sums authorized by this section shall be apportioned among the several States in the manner now provided by law and in accordance with the formulas set forth in section 4 of the Federal-Aid Highway Act of 1944, approved December 20, 1944 (58 Stat. 838): *Provided,* That the additional amount herein authorized for the fiscal year ending June 30, 1957, shall be apportioned immediately upon enactment of this Act.

(b) AVAILABILITY FOR EXPENDITURE.—Any sums apportioned to any State under this section shall be available for expenditure in that State for two years after the close of the fiscal year for which such sums are authorized, and any amounts so apportioned remaining unexpended at the end of such period shall lapse: *Provided,* That such funds shall be deemed to have been expended if a sum equal to the total of the sums herein and heretofore apportioned to the State is covered by formal agreements with the Secretary of Commerce for construction, reconstruction, or improvement of specific projects as provided in this title and prior Acts: *Provided further,* That in the case of those sums heretofore, herein, or hereafter apportioned to any State for projects on the Federal-aid secondary highway system, the Secretary of Commerce may, upon the request of any State, discharge his responsibility relative to the plans, specifications, estimates, surveys, contract awards, design, inspection, and construction of such secondary road projects by his receiving and approving a certified statement by the State highway department setting forth that the plans, design, and construction for such projects are in accord with the standards and procedures of such State applicable

The Federal-Aid Highway Act (National Archives and Records Administration)

"It is ... in the national interest to accelerate the construction of the Federal-aid highway systems."

Overview

The Federal-Aid Highway Act of 1956, more popularly known as the National Interstate and Defense Highways Act, was the culmination of numerous acts dating as far back as 1916. It called for a $25 billion appropriate for the construction of forty thousand miles of interstate highway over a ten-year period. Earlier in the twentieth century, various groups had recognized the need for a national system of highways. However, these efforts were often hindered by lack of funding and pressing world events, including the Great Depression, World War II, and the conflict in Korea. The Federal-Aid Highway Act of 1956, however, incorporated the previous acts and added a new mechanism for funding the new roads. The bill passed the Senate in a vote of 89 to 1, and later that same day the act was approved by the House of Representatives in a voice vote. President Dwight D. Eisenhower signed the bill on June 29 from his hospital bed at Walter Reed Army Medical Center, changing the American landscape forever.

To pay for the roads, taxes would be raised on certain transportation items: The tax on gasoline would increase from two cents to three cents, tires would cost three cents more per pound, and the excise tax on new trailers, trucks, and buses would rise to 10 percent. All of the monies collected through these new taxes would go into a trust that would pay 90 percent of all costs, with the individual states paying only 10 percent. The Federal-Aid Highway Act of 1956 was the largest public works project in American history.

Context

The 1950s were a time of nuclear families, suburbia, television, the cold war, the baby boom, and rock-and-roll music. Not since the 1920s had the United States experienced such a marked growth in the economy. With the end of World War II, soldiers and sailors returned home to take advantage of the GI Bill, which provided money for veterans to attend college. Returning military personnel also settled down and started families, creating the baby boom, a period of increasing birth rates. In 1954 alone over four million babies were born in the United States.

As the economy and population grew, so did the number of car owners in America. The government had noticed a need for a regulated series of highways as early as 1916 and authorized $75 million dollars for new roads. State governments were supposed to match the funding dollar for dollar, but many could not. A similar bill passed again in 1921, and in 1938 the Senate rejected a bill that would have created toll roads. Further, none of these bills called for a national network of roads for a large number of travelers operating at high speeds. The 1940s brought similar bills, but the country was soon entangled in World War II, and building roads took a backseat to defeating the Axis powers.

Then, in 1952, the former five-star general Dwight D. Eisenhower was elected as president. Even though he was immediately concerned with the conflict in Korea, roads were on his mind—and had been since 1919, when he participated in the army's first transcontinental convoy. Just after the end of Word War I the army sent eighty-one vehicles on a cross-country tour from Washington, D.C., to San Francisco to road-test the vehicles and to ascertain how quickly the army could travel across the country. It took the convoy sixty-two days to make the trip over dirt roads and wooden bridges and through extreme weather. Later, Eisenhower would experience firsthand what a good system of roads could mean, as he watched German leader Adolf Hitler take advantage of the German autobahn in World War II. Upon being elected president, Eisenhower wasted little time in calling for a national system of highways.

About the Author

The Federal-Aid Highway Act of 1956 combined two acts. The first (actually called the Federal-Aid Highway Act of 1956), written by Senator Albert Gore, Sr., of Tennessee and revised by Representative George Hyde Fallon of Maryland, would become Title I of the 1956 bill; the second part, Title II, was written as the Highway Revenue Act of 1956 by Louisiana Representative Thomas Hale Boggs.

Albert Arnold Gore, Sr., was born in Jackson County, Tennessee, on December 26, 1907, and worked his way

1919

■ **Summer**
Lieutenant Colonel Dwight D. Eisenhower participates in the army's Transcontinental Motor Convoy.

1938

■ **June 8**
The Federal-Aid Highway Act charges the chief of the Bureau of Public Roads with conducting a feasibility study for toll network passes as a means for raising revenue to pay for the roads.

1939

■ Norman Bel Geddes's "Futurama" exhibit at the World's Fair in New York wows visitors with its fourteen-lane transcontinental superhighways and speeds of over a hundred miles per hour.

1941

■ **April 14**
President Franklin D. Roosevelt appoints the National Interregional Highway Committee to investigate the need for a system of highways.

1943

■ **July 13**
The Federal-Aid Highway Amendment is approved, directing the commissioner of public roads to determine the number of highways needed and the cost of their construction.

1944

■ **January 12**
President Roosevelt submits the interregional highways report from the commissioner of public roads to Congress.

■ **December 20**
President Roosevelt signs the Federal-Aid Highway Act of 1944.

1956

■ **March 19**
The House Ways and Means Committee presents the Highway Revenue Act of 1956, written by Representative Hale Boggs. This act becomes Title II of the Federal-Aid Highway Act of 1956.

---

through Middle Tennessee State College by teaching, playing the fiddle, and pitching for the baseball team. He graduated in 1932. After teaching in rural Smith County, Tennessee, Gore ran for Smith County superintendent of schools. He lost the election, but when the elected superintendent died, Gore was appointed to finish the term. He began to study law and graduated from the YMCA Law School in 1936. Just one year later, in 1937, Tennessee's governor, Gordon Browning, appointed Gore the state's first commissioner of labor. That same year Gore married Pauline LaFon, who was working her way through law school as a waitress. In 1939, Gore was elected to Congress, where he served as a representative from 1939 to 1952 and as a senator from 1953 to 1970. He was progressive and liberal, often supporting civil rights legislation. Gore was also one of three southern Democrats who refused to sign the Southern Manifesto, which condemned integration. After losing the 1970 election, Gore practiced law with the Occidental Petroleum Company and taught law at Vanderbilt University in Nashville, Tennessee. He died on December 5, 1998.

Born in Baltimore, Maryland, on July 24, 1902, George Hyde Fallon attended public schools before moving on to Calvert Business College and Johns Hopkins University. After graduation, he worked in his father's advertising sign business. Fallon's first taste of politics was as chairman of the Democratic State Central Committee of Baltimore and then in the Baltimore City Council, where he served until being elected to the Senate in 1944, where he served until 1971. As chairman of the Subcommittee on Roads in the Committee on Public Works, Fallon's advocacy and dedication earned him the title "the father of the interstate highway system." In 1954, Fallon was one of five representatives wounded when four Puerto Rican nationalists fired automatic pistols from a visitors' balcony in the U.S. Capitol during a debate on immigration. Losing in the 1970 election, Fallon retired to Baltimore, where he died on March 21, 1980.

Thomas Hale Boggs was born in Long Beach, Mississippi, on February 15, 1914, but he was educated in Louisiana parochial schools and attended Tulane University, where he received his bachelor's degree in journalism (1934) and a law degree (1937). Boggs began practicing law in New Orleans but soon became swept up in Louisiana politics, winning his first congressional seat in 1941 at just twenty-six years of age. Losing his reelection bid, Boggs joined the navy in 1942 and served throughout World War II. After the war he returned to Congress in 1946 and won thirteen reelections. While Boggs signed the Southern Manifesto condemning integration, he supported the Voting Rights Act of 1965 and the Fair Housing Act of 1968. In addition, he served as majority whip from 1961 to 1970 and then as majority leader from 1971 until his disappearance. On October 16, 1972, while on a campaign trip for Nick Begich of Alaska, Boggs's plane disappeared over the Alaskan wilderness. Despite an intensive search-and-rescue effort by the military for thirty-nine days, the wreckage was never found. After the accident Congress passed a law requiring all civil aircraft to have emergency locator transmitters.

Explanation and Analysis of the Document

◆ Title I

Title I of the Federal-Aid Highway Act of 1956 is the combination of two bills written by Representative George Hyde Fallon of Maryland and Senator Albert Arnold Gore, Sr., of Tennessee.

Section 101 provides the short title for Title I as the "Federal-Aid Highway Act of 1956." The next six sections are concerned with authorizations and appropriations as outlined in past acts. Section 102 outlines the authorizations and appropriations for "Federal-Aid highways" as provided for in the Federal-Aid Road Act of 1916. The section allocates $125 million for the first year and over $800,000 over the next two years. The section goes on to outline what percentage of monies should be spent on the primary and secondary highways as well as how long individual states had to complete the project.

Section 103 seeks to carry out the provision of section 23 of the "Federal Highway Act of 1921," which covers forest highways and forest development. Over $30 million was designated for the first fiscal year. Section 104 turns to roads and trails in areas administered by the National Park Service, including Indian reservations. Section 105 was written to carry out the provision of section 10 of the Federal-Aid Highway Act of 1950 covering public lands, allocating $2 million the first fiscal year to survey, construct, and maintain roads on public land. Section 106 covers special provisions for federal domain roads. Any funds authorized for forest highways, parks, trails, Indian roads, or public lands were to be available for contract upon apportionment. Section 107 covers roads for the territory of Alaska, which would not become a state until 1959.

Section 108 outlines the National System of Interstate and Defense Highways. Here the interstate system is tied to national defense and named the "Interstate System." Congress authorizes at least $1 billion a year for the next thirteen years toward the interstate system. The sum is to be apportioned to the states based on the estimated cost of completing the roads in that state. This section also states that the federal government will pay 90 percent of the cost of building the roads. Paragraph (i) of the section outlines the standards for building the interstates. The standards were developed based on the estimated types and volume of traffic for 1975. Further, these standards were to be followed by all the states as they built their sections of the interstate.

Section 109 concerns the acquisition of rights-of-way. This section allows the secretary of commerce to acquire land needed for the interstate system by purchase, donation, condemnation, or other means. Section 110 continues to deal with rights-of-way and outlines the availability of funds for states to acquire them. Section 111 states that if states need to relocate public, private, or cooperative utility facilities that they may be reimbursed with federal funds. Section 112 returns to the topic of rights-of-way by stating that any individual state will not add any points of access to or exit from the project unless approved by the secretary of commerce. Further, states were not allowed to

Time Line

1956

■ **April 27**
The Federal-Aid Highway Act of 1956 (popularly known as the National Interstate and Defense Highways Act) passes the House by a vote of 388 to 91.

■ **June 29**
President Dwight Eisenhower signs the Federal-Aid Highway Act of 1956 to create a forty-thousand-mile system of highways.

1990

■ President George H. W. Bush signs the bill renaming the National System of Interstate and Defense Highways the "Dwight D. Eisenhower National System of Interstate and Defense Highways."

1993

■ **July 29**
The standard road sign, designed by the American Association of State Highway and Transportation Officials and the Federal Highway Administration, for the Dwight D. Eisenhower National System of Interstate and Defense Highways is unveiled.

permit the building of service stations or other businesses on the rights-of-way. Section 113 allows the secretary of commerce to build toll roads, bridges, and tunnels if such construction would benefit the interstate system.

Section 114 declares that the federal government may reimburse a state for a portion of road built on the interstate system prior to August 2, 1947, if the road meets certain conditions. For instance, to qualify for reimbursement, the road must meet the standards of the Federal-Aid Highway Act of 1956. Section 115 charges the secretary of commerce with ensuring that all laborers and mechanics are paid wages that meet the rates of their locality.

Section 116 is a declaration of the government's policy with regard to the Federal-Aid Highway Program. The section declares it to be in the national interest to accelerate construction on the highway systems because the current system is inadequate for commerce and national defense. The secretary of commerce is charged with providing a progress report no later than February 1, 1959. This section also provides for public hearings in the event the highway project is going to either bypass or go through a city, town, or village. Section 117 requires the secretary of commerce to investigate, study, and make recommendations for highway safety. The section outlines six items for the secretary to consider: federal enforcement assistance for maintaining safety and speed limits, support of uniform state safety and speed regulations, promotion of highway safety in the manufacture of vehicles, programs to educate about highway safety, design and physical characteristics of highways, and other matters as appropriate.

Section 118 establishes an emergency fund for the repair or reconstruction of highways and bridges. Section 119 defines "construction" for the Federal-Aid Highway Act of 1956. Section 120 authorizes funds for archeological and paleontological salvage in accordance with the Act for the Preservation of American Antiquities of 1906. Section 121 authorizes the secretary of commerce to employ photogrammetric methods to map areas for the highway system. Section 222 covers the relationship of the Federal-Aid Highway Act of 1956 to all the other preceding acts. All aspects of the Federal-Aid Road Act of 1916 and all its amendatory acts remain in force unless they are inconsistent with the 1956 act, in which case the inconsistent parts are repealed.

◆ **Title II**

Title II of the Federal-Aid Highway Act of 1956 consists of Louisiana Representative Thomas Hale Boggs's Highway Revenue Act of 1956.

Section 201 provides the short title for the act and declares that any amendment mentioned relating to another provision refers to the Internal Revenue Code of 1954. Section 202 outlines the tax increase on diesel and other special motor fuels. The taxes on both diesel fuel and other special fuels are raised from two cents to three cents.

Section 203 raises the tax on trucks, trailers, and buses to 10 percent until July 1, 1972, when the price is to drop to 5 percent. Section 204 addressed the increase of taxes on tires used on highway vehicles, tread rubber, and tubes. Highway tires are to be taxed at eight cents per pound and other tires at five cents per pound; inner tubes at nine cents a pound, and tread rubber at three cents a pound. The section also defines the materials being taxed. Section 205 covers the tax increase of three cents a gallon on gasoline. After July 1, 1972, the gas tax was supposed to be decreased to a cent and a half. Section 206 explains the tax increase on certain vehicles. For instance, any vehicle with a gross weight of more than 26,000 pounds was to be taxed $1.50 per thousand pounds. Exemptions are also outlined in this section. For example, state and local vehicles are exempt from this tax.

Section 207 deals with floor stock, or the inventory of car dealers. For instance, each dealer would pay 2 percent of the purchase price of the vehicle. Dealers also are required to pay a three-cent tax on the tires and tread rubber on their stock but not on the tires they held for sale, and the gas in their stock was charged at one cent per gallon. Section 208, one of the longer sections in the act, outlines the rules for the credit or refund of taxes. For instance, people could get at least a partial refund of the gas tax if the gas was for non-highway purposes.

Section 209 creates the trust fund where the all the tax money will put in order for the federal government to pay its 90 percent of the cost of the interstate highway system.

The section also lays out the rules and regulations for managing the trust fund. Section 210 authorizes the secretary of commerce to conducts investigations and studies in order to provide Congress with the information needed to disperse the tax burden equitability. Section 211, the last section in Title II, provides the effective date of the Federal Highway Act of 1956 and any exceptions to that date.

◆ **Title III**

Title III simply states that if any section, subsection, or other part of the Federal-Aid Highway Act of 1956 is held to be invalid, that does not mean the entire document is invalid.

Audience

The Federal-Aid Highway Act of 1956 was written for the American people. More specifically, however, it was written for the parties directly involved with building the interstate system, such as state governments and engineers. Another audience for this act would be any potential military foe.

Impact

In the twenty-first century, the national interstate system consists of more than 160,000 thousand miles of roadway. It can move military vehicles and supplies easily and quickly across the county, just as Eisenhower had hoped. The interstate system had a deep and lasting impact on society. People moved out of cities and into suburbs and the countryside. No longer were people required to live where they worked; commuting to work became the norm for many. As the ease of mobility increased, so did the ability of people to travel for business or vacation. As increasing numbers of people took to the roads, more and more businesses grew up along interstate routes. For instance, tens of thousands of new motels that included restaurants sprouted up along the interstate routes to accommodate weary and hungry travelers. The interstate helped to create a highly mobile society centered on the automobile.

The interstate also aided the economy by allowing goods and services to be obtained from far-flung places. Refrigerated trailers could deliver fresh fruit and vegetables all over the country with relative ease. This flexibility increased competition and lowered prices but also hurt the small local businesspeople, who could not compete with larger businesses. Further, the interstate system produced a lessening of dependence on mass transit and a growing reliance on cars. In many areas mass transit would be left for those who were unable to afford a car. This dependence on cars also has helped make America dependent on foreign sources of petroleum, which can have a huge impact on the nation— as evidenced by the 1973 Arab oil embargo, when Middle Eastern countries stopped exporting oil to Western nations.

The interstate system has been criticized for its negative impact on the environment, for instance, by the

> "It is hereby declared essential to the national interest to provide for the early completion, of the 'National System of Interstate Highways,' as authorized and designated in accordance with section 7 of the Federal-Aid Highway Act of 1944."
>
> (Section 108)

> "The Federal share payable on account of any project on the Interstate System provided for by finds made available under the provisions of this section shall be increased 90 per centum of the total cost thereof."
>
> (Section 108)

> "It is hereby declared to be in the national interest to accelerate the construction of the Federal-aid highway systems, including the Interstate System, since many of such highways, or portions thereof, are in fact inadequate to meet the needs of local and interstate commerce, the national and the civil defense."
>
> (Section 116)

building of roads over and through national parks and other scenic areas. Also, as fewer and fewer people used mass transit and relied more on cars for transport, pollution became a growing problem. Moreover, since the interstate system was designed to get motorists to their destinations quickly, they bypassed much of what the nation has to offer, prompting the writer John Steinbeck to say that soon it would "be possible to drive from New York to California without seeing a single thing" (p. 90).

Related Documents

Eisenhower, Dwight. *At Ease: Stories I Tell to Friends*. Garden City, N.Y.: Doubleday, 1967. This engaging book includes a chapter, "Through Darkest America with Truck and Tank," about Eisenhower's experience during the army's 1919 Transcontinental Motor Convoy.

National Highway Program: Message from the President of the United States Relative to a National Highway Program. Washington, D.C.: Government Printing Office, 1955. This work is a report from the President's Advisory Committee on a National Highway Program from January 1955.

Nixon, Richard M. *Stepping Up U.S. Aid to Inter-American Highway*. Washington, D.C.: Government Printing Office, 1955. This is President Eisenhower's letter, written by his vice president, to Congress regarding the status of the interstate highway system.

Bibliography

■ Articles

Barrett, Paul, and Mark H. Rose. "Street Smarts: The Politics of Transportation Statistics in the American City, 1900–1990." *Journal of Urban History* 25, no. 3 (1999): 405–433.

Harstad, Peter T., and Diana J. Fox. "Dusty Doughboys on the Lincoln Highway: The 1919 Army Convoy in Iowa." *Palimpsest* 56, no. 3 (1975): 66–87.

Heppenheimer, T. A. "The Rise of the Interstates: How America Built the Largest Network of Engineered Structures on Earth." *American Heritage of Invention and Technology* 7, no. 2 (1991): 8–17.

Lichter, Daniel T., and Glenn V. Fuguitt. "Demographic Response to Transportation Innovation: The Case of the Interstate Highway." *Social Forces* 59, no. 2 (1980): 492–512.

Patton, Phil. "A Quick Way from Here to There Was Also a Frolic." *Smithsonian* 21, no. 7 (1990): 96–108.

Pfeiffer, David A. "Ike's Interstates at 50: Anniversary of the Highway System Recalls Eisenhower's Role as Catalyst." *Prologue* 38, no. 2 (Summer 2006): 2–12, 19.

Rose, Mark H., and Bruce E. Seely. "Getting the Interstate System Built: Road Engineers and the Implementation of Public Policy, 1955–1985." *Journal of Policy History* 2, no. 1 (1990): 23–56.

Weber, Joe. "Everyday Places on the American Freeway System." *Journal of Cultural Geography* 21, no. 2 (2004): 1–26.

■ Books

Gutfreund, Owen D. *Twentieth-Century Sprawl: Highways and the Reshaping of the American Landscape*. New York: Oxford University Press, 2004.

Kaszynski, William. *The American Highway: The History and Culture of Roads in the United States*. Jefferson, N.C.: McFarland, 2000.

Kelley, Ben. *The Pavers and the Paved*. New York: D. W. Brown, 1971.

Leavitt, Helen. *Superhighway-Superhoax*. Garden City, N.Y.: Doubleday, 1970.

Lewis, David L. *The Interstate Highway System: Issues and Options*. Washington, D.C.: Government Printing Office, 1982.

Lewis, Tom. *Divided Highways: Building the Interstate Highways, Transforming American Life*. New York: Viking, 1997.

McNichol, Dan. *The Roads That Built America: The Incredible Story of the U.S. Interstate System*. New York: Sterling, 2006.

Rose, Mark H. *Interstate: Express Highway Politics, 1941–1956*. Lawrence: Regents Press of Kansas, 1979.

———. *Interstate: Express Highway Politics, 1939–1989*. Knoxville: University of Tennessee Press, 1990.

Seely, Bruce Edsall. *Building the American Highway System: Engineers as Policy Makers*. Philadelphia: Temple University Press, 1987.

Spangenburg, Ray, and Diane K. Moser. *Connecting a Continent: The Story of America's Roads*. New York: Facts On File, 1992.

Steinbeck, John. *Travels with Charley: In Search of America*. New York: Penguin, 1980.

■ Web Sites

"History of the Interstate Highway System." U.S. Department of Transportation, Federal Highway Administration Web site.
   http://www.fhwa.dot.gov/interstate/history.htm. Accessed on January 15, 2008.

"The Interstate Is 50." American Association of State Highway Officials Web site.
   http://www.interstate50th.org. Accessed on January 15, 2008.

Weingroff, Richard F. "Federal-Aid Highway Act of 1956: Creating the Interstate System." U.S. Department of Transportation, Federal Highway Administration Web site.
   http://www.tfhrc.gov/pubrds/summer96/p96su10.htm. Accessed on January 15, 2008.

———. "The Greatest Decade 1956–1966." U.S. Department of Transportation, Federal Highway Administration Web site.
   http://www.fhwa.dot.gov/infrastructure/50interstate.cfm. Accessed on January 15, 2008.

—By Lisa A. Ennis

Questions for Further Study

1. Why was the Federal-Aid Highway Act of 1956 successful when other attempts at creating legislation for a national system of highways were not? What was different about the Federal-Aid Highway Act of 1956? What was similar to the other bills?

2. How did the interstate system lead to the creation of suburbia? Was this good or bad for downtown areas? Explain your answer.

3. How did the Federal-Aid Highway Act of 1956 create new businesses?

4. What are some of the pros of the interstate highway system? What are some of the negatives? Be specific.

Glossary

apportionment	distribution or allotment in shares
per centum	percent
photogrammetric	the first remote-sensing technology, through which geometric properties are determined from photographs
public lands	lands held by federal, state, or local government
right-of-way	the right to use land that another person owns, such as through an easement
tread rubber	the part of the tire that comes in contact with the road and is designed to provide traction

FEDERAL-AID HIGHWAY ACT

An Act: To amend and supplement the Federal-Aid Road Act approved July 11, 1916, to authorize appropriations for continuing the construction of highways; to amend the Internal Revenue Code of 1954 to provide additional revenue from the taxes on motor fuel, tires, and trucks and buses; and for other purposes.

Be it enacted by the Senate and House of Representatives of the United States of America in Congress assembled,

Title I— Federal-Aid Highway Act of 1956

◆ **Sec. 101. Short Title For Title I.**

This title may be cited as the "Federal-Aid Highway Act of 1956".

◆ **Sec. 102. Federal-Aid highways.**

(a) (1) AUTHORIZATION OF APPROPRIATIONS— For the purpose of carrying out the provisions of the Federal-Aid Road Act approved July 11, 1916 (39 Stat 355), and all Acts amendatory thereof and supplementary thereto, there is hereby authorized to be appropriated for the fiscal year ending June 30,1957, $125,000,000 in addition to any sums heretofore authorized for such fiscal year; the sum of $850,000,000 for the fiscal year ending June 30, 1958; and the sum of $875,000,000 for the fiscal year ending June 30, 1959. The sums herein authorized for each fiscal year shall be available for expenditure as follows:

(A) 45 per centum for projects on the Federal-aid primary highway system.

(B) 30 per centum for projects on the Federal-aid secondary highway system.

(C) 25 per centum for projects on extensions of these systems within urban areas

(2) APPORTIONMENTS— The sums authorized by this section shall be apportioned among the several States in the manner now provided by law and in

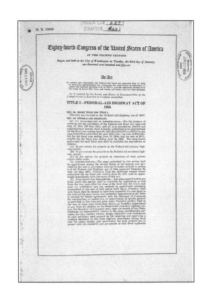

accordance with the formulas set forth in section 4 of the Federal-Aid Highway Act of 1944, approved December 20, 1944 (58 Stat. 838): *Provided,* That the additional amount herein authorized for the fiscal year ending June 30, 1957, shall be apportioned immediately upon enactment of this Act.

(b) AVAILABILITY FOR EXPENDITURE— Any sums apportioned to any State under this section shall be available for expenditure in that State for two years after the close of the fiscal year for which such sums are authorized, and any amounts so apportioned remaining unexpended at the end of such period shall lapse: *Provided,* That such funds shall be deemed to have been expended if a sum equal to the total of the sums herein and heretofore apportioned to the State is covered by formal agreements with the Secretary of Commerce for construction, reconstruction, or improvement of specific projects as provided in this title and prior Acts: *Provided further,* That in the case of those sums heretofore, herein, or hereafter apportioned to any State for projects on the Federal-aid secondary highway system, the Secretary of Commerce may, upon the request of any State, discharge his responsibility relative to the plans, specifications, estimates, surveys, contract awards, design, inspection, and construction of such secondary road projects by his receiving and approving a certified statement by the State highway department setting forth that the plans, design, and construction for such projects are in accord with the standards and procedures of such State applicable to projects in this category approved by him: *Provided further,* That such approval shall not be given unless such standards and procedures are in accordance with the objectives set forth in section 1 (b) of the Federal-Aid Highway Act of 1950: *And provided further,* That nothing contained in the foregoing provisos shall be construed to relieve any State of its obligation now provided by law relative to maintenance, nor to relieve the Secretary of Commerce of his obligation with respect to the selection of the secondary system or the location of projects thereon, to make a final inspection after construction of each project, and to require an adequate showing of the estimated and actual cost of construction of each project Any Federal-aid primary, secondary, or urban funds released by the payment of the final voucher or by modification of the formal project agreement shall be credited to the same class of funds, primary, secondary, or urban, previously apportioned to the State and be immediately available for expenditure.

(c) TRANSFERS OF APPORTIONMENTS— Not more than 20 per centum of the respective amounts apportioned to a State for any fiscal year from funds made available for expenditure under clause (A), clause (B), or clause (C) of subsection (a) (1) of this section, may be transferred to the apportionment made to such State under any other of such clauses, except that no such apportionment may be increased by more than 20 per centum by reason of transfers to it under this subsection: *Provided* That such transfer is requested by the State highway department and is approved by the Governor of such State and the Secretary of Commerce as being in the public interest: *Provided further*, That the transfers hereinabove permitted for funds authorized to be appropriated for the fiscal years ending June 30, 1958, and June 30, 1959, shall likewise be permitted on the same basis for funds which may be hereafter authorized to be appropriated for any subsequent fiscal year: *And provided further*, That nothing herein contained shall be deemed to alter or impair the authority contained in the last proviso to paragraph (b) of section 3 of the Federal-Aid Highway Act of 1944.

◆ Sec. 103. Forest Highways and Forest Development Roads and Trails.

(a) AUTHORIZATION OF APPROPRIATIONS— For the purpose of carrying out the provisions of section 23 of the Federal Highway Act of 1921 (42 Stat. 218), as amended and supplemented, there is hereby authorized to be appropriated (1) for forest highways the sum of $30,000,000 for the fiscal year ending June 30. 1958, and a like sum for the fiscal year ending June 30,1959; and (2) for forest development roads and trails the sum of $27,000,000 for the fiscal year ending June 30, 1958, and a like sum for the fiscal year ending June 30, 1959: *Provided*, That with respect to any proposed construction or reconstruction of a timber access road, advisory public hearings shall be held at a place convenient or adjacent to the

area of construction or reconstruction with notice and reasonable opportunity for interested persons to present their views as to the practicability and feasibility of such construction or reconstruction: *Provided further*, That hereafter funds available for forest highways and forest development roads and trails shall also be available for adjacent vehicular parking areas and for sanitary, water, and fire control facilities: *And provided further*, That the appropriation herein authorized for forest highways shall be apportioned by the Secretary of Commerce for expenditure in the several States, Alaska, and Puerto Rico in accordance with the provision of section 3 of the Federal-Aid Highway Act of 1950.

(b) REPEAL OF CERTAIN APPORTIONMENT PROCEDURES.— The provision of section 23 of the Federal Highway Act of 1921, as amended and supplemented, requiring apportionment of funds authorized for forest development roads and trails among the several States, Alaska, and Puerto Rico is hereby repealed.

◆ Sec. 104. Roads and Trails in National Parks, Etc.

(a) NATIONAL PARKS, ETC.— For the construction, reconstruction, and improvement of roads and trails, inclusive of necessary bridges, in national parks, monuments, and other areas administered, by the National Park Service, including areas authorized to be established as national parks and monuments, and national park and monument approach roads authorized by the Act of January 31, 1931 (46 Stat. 1053), as amended, there is hereby authorized to be appropriated the sum of $16,000,000 for the fiscal year ending June 30,1958, and a like sum for the fiscal year ending June 30,1959.

(b) PARKWAYS.— For the construction, reconstruction, and improvement of parkways, authorized by Acts of Congress, on lands to which title is vested in the United States, there is hereby authorized to be appropriated the sum of $16,000,000 for the fiscal year ending June 30, 1958, and a like sum for the fiscal year ending June 30, 1959.

(c) INDIAN RESERVATIONS AND LANDS.— For the construction, improvement, and maintenance of Indian reservation roads and bridges and roads and bridges to provide access to Indian reservations and Indian lands under the provisions of the Act approved May 26,1928 (45 Stat. 750), there is hereby authorized to be appropriated the sum of $12,000,000 for the fiscal year ending June 30,1958, and a like sum for the fiscal year ending June 30, 1959: *Provided*, That the location, type, and design of all roads and bridges constructed shall be approved by the Secretary of Commerce before any expenditures are made thereon, and all such construction shall be under the general supervision of the Secretary of Commerce.

◆ Sec. 105. Public Lands Highways.

For the purpose of carrying out the provisions of section 10 of the Federal-Aid Highway Act of 1950 (64 Stat. 785), there is hereby authorized to be appropriated for the survey, construction, reconstruction, and maintenance of main roads through unappropriated or unreserved public lands, nontaxable Indian lands, or other Federal reservations the additional sum of $2,000,000 for the fiscal year ending June 30, 1957, and the sum of $2,000,000 for the fiscal year ending June 30,1958, and a like sum for the fiscal year ending June 30,1959.

◆ Sec. 106. Special Provisions for Federal Domain Roads, Etc.

Any funds authorized herein for forest highways, forest development roads and trails, park roads and trails, parkways, Indian roads, and public lands highways shall be available for contract upon apportionment, or a date not earlier than one year preceding the beginning of the fiscal year for which authorized if no apportionment is required: *Provided*, That any amount remaining unexpended two years after the close of the fiscal year for which authorized shall lapse. The Secretary of the department charged with the administration of such funds is hereby granted authority to incur obligations, approve projects, and enter into contracts under such authorizations, and his action in doing so shall be deemed a contractual obligation of the Federal Government for the payment of the cost thereof, and such funds shall be deemed to have been expended when so obligated. Any funds heretofore, herein, or hereafter authorized for any fiscal year for forest highways, forest development roads and trails, park roads and trails, parkways, Indian roads, and public lands highways shall be deemed to have been expended if a sum equal to the total of the sums authorized for such fiscal year and previous fiscal years since and including the fiscal year ending June 30, 1955, shall have been obligated. Any of such funds released by payment of final voucher or modification of project authorizations shall be credited to the balance of unobligated authorizations and be immediately available for expenditure.

◆ Sec. 107. Highways for Alaska.

(a) APPORTIONMENT; MATCHING; SELECTION OF SYSTEMS.— The Territory of Alaska shall be entitled to share in funds herein or after authorized for expenditure for projects on the Federal-aid primary and secondary highway systems, and extensions thereof within urban areas, under the Federal-Aid Road Act approved July 11, 1916 (39 Stat. 355), and Acts amendatory thereof or supplementary thereto, upon the same terms and conditions as the several States and Hawaii and Puerto Rico, and the Territory of Alaska shall be included in the calculations to determine the basis of apportionment of such funds, except that one-third only of the area of Alaska shall be used in the calculations to determine the area factor in the apportionment of such funds: *Provided*, That the Territory of Alaska shall contribute funds each fiscal year in an amount that shall be not less than 10 per centum of the Federal funds apportioned to it for such fiscal year, such contribution to be deposited in a special account in the Federal Treasury for use in conjunction with the Federal funds apportioned to the Territory. The system or systems of roads on which Federal-aid apportionments to the Territory of Alaska are to be expended shall be determined and agreed upon by the Governor of Alaska, the Territorial Highway Engineer of Alaska, and the Secretary of Commerce, without regard to the limitations contained in section 6 of the Federal Highway Act (42 Stat 212), as amended and supplemented. The Federal funds apportioned to the Territory of Alaska and the funds contributed by such Territory in accordance herewith may be expended by the Secretary of Commerce either directly or in cooperation with the Territorial Board of Road Commissioners of Alaska, and may be so expended separately or in combination and without regard to the matching provisions of the Federal Highway Act (42 Stat. 212); and both such funds may be expended for the maintenance of roads within the system or systems of roads agreed upon under the same terms and conditions as for the construction of such roads.

(b) TRANSFER OF FUNCTIONS.— Effective not more than ninety days after the approval of this Act, the functions, duties, and authority pertaining to the construction, repair, and maintenance of roads, tramways, ferries, bridges, trails, and other works in Alaska, conferred upon the Department of the Interior and heretofore administered by the Secretary of the Interior under the Act of June 30,1932 (47 Stat. 446; 48 U. S. C, sec. 321a and following), are hereby transferred to the Department of Commerce, and thereafter shall be administered by the Secretary of Commerce, or under his direction, by such officer, or officers, as may be designated by him.

(c) TRANSFER OF PERSONNEL, ETC.— There are hereby transferred ˆto the Department of Commerce, to be employed and expended in connection with the functions, duties, and authority transferred to said Department by subsection (b) hereof, all personnel employed in connection with any such functions, duties, or authority, and the unexpended balances of appropriations, allocations, or other funds now available, or that hereafter may be made available, for use in connection with such functions, duties, or authority; and the Department of the Interior is directed to turn over to the Secretary of Commerce all equipment, materials, supplies, papers, maps, and documents, or other property (real or personal, and including office equipment and records) used or held in connection with such functions, duties, and authority.

(d) EFFECTUATION OF TRANSFER.— The Secretary of the Interior and the Secretary of Commerce shall take such steps as may be necessary or appropriate to effect the transfer from the Department of the Interior to the Department of Commerce of the functions, duties, and authority, and the funds and property, as herein provided for.

(e) DISTRIBUTION OF FUNCTIONS.— The Secretary of Commerce shall have power, by order or regulations, to distribute the functions, duties, and authority hereby transferred, and appropriations pertaining thereto, as he may deem proper to accomplish the economical and effective organization and administration thereof.

◆ Sec. 108. National System of Interstate and Defense Highways.

(a) INTERSTATE SYSTEM.— It is hereby declared to be essential to the national interest to provide for the early completion, of the "National System of Interstate Highways", as authorized and designated in accordance with section 7 of the Federal-Aid Highway Act of 1944 (58 Stat. 838). It is the intent of the Congress that the Interstate System be completed as nearly as practicable over a thirteen-year period and that the entire System in all the States be brought to simultaneous completion. Because of its primary importance to the national defense, the name of such system is hereby changed to the "National System of Interstate and Defense Highways". Such National System of Interstate and Defense Highways is hereinafter in this Act referred to as the "Interstate System".

(b) AUTHORIZATION OF APPROPRIATIONS.— For the purpose of expediting the construction, reconstruction or improvement, inclusive of necessary bridges and tunnels, of the Interstate System, including exten-

sions thereof through urban areas, designated in accordance with the provisions of section 7 of the Federal-Aid Highway Act of 1944 (58 Stat. 838), there is hereby authorized to be appropriated the additional sum of $1,000,000,000; for the fiscal year ending June 30, 1957, which sum shall be m addition to the authorization heretofore made for that year, the additional sum of $1,700,000,000 for the fiscal year ending June 30, 1958, the additional sum of $2,000,000,000 for the fiscal year ending June 30, 1959, the additional sum of $2,200,000,000 for the fiscal year ending June 30, 1960, the additional sum of $2,200,000,000 for the fiscal year ending June 30, 1961, the additional sum of $2,200,000,000 for the fiscal year ending June 30, 1962, the additional sum of $2,200,000,000 for the fiscal year ending June 30, 1963, the additional sum of $2,200,000,000 for the fiscal year ending June 30,1964, the additional sum of $2,200,000,000 for the fiscal year ending June 30, 1965, the additional sum of $2,200,000,000 for the fiscal year ending June 30,1966, the additional sum of $2,200,000,000 for the fiscal year ending June 30, 1967, the additional sum of $1,500,000,000 for the fiscal year ending June 30, 1968, and the additional sum of $1,025,000,000 for the fiscal year ending: June 30, 1969.

(c) APPORTIONMENTS FOR 1957, 1958, AND 1959.— The additional sums herein authorized for the fiscal years ending June 30, 1957, June 30, 1958, and June 30, 1959, shall be apportioned among the several States in the following manner: one-half in the ratio which the population of each State bears to the total population of all the States, as shown by the latest available Federal census: *Provided*, That no State shall receive less than three-fourths of 1 per centum of the money so apportioned; and one-half in the manner now provided by law for the apportionment of funds for the Federal-aid primary system. The additional sum herein authorized for the fiscal year ending June 30, 1957, shall be apportioned immediately upon enactment of this Act. The additional sums herein authorized for the fiscal years ending June 30, 1958, and June 30, 1959, shall be apportioned on a date not less than six months and not more than twelve months in advance of the beginning of the fiscal year for which authorized.

(d) APPORTIONMENTS FOR SUBSEQUENT YEARS BASED UPON REVISED ESTIMATES OF COST.— All sums authorized by this section to be appropriated for the fiscal years 1960 through 1969, inclusive, shall be apportioned among the several States in the ratio which the estimated cost of completing the Interstate System in each State, as determined and approved in the manner provided in this subsection, bears to the sum of the estimated cost of completing the Interstate System in all of the States. Each apportionment herein authorized for the fiscal years 1960 through 1969, inclusive, shall be made on a date as far in advance of the beginning of the fiscal year for which authorized as practicable but in no case more than eighteen months prior to the beginning of the fiscal year for which authorized. As soon as the standards provided for in subsection (i) have been adopted, the Secretary of Commerce, in cooperation with the State highway departments, shall make a detailed estimate of the cost of completing the Interstate System as then designated, after taking into account all previous apportionments made under this section, based upon such standards and in accordance with rules and regulations adopted by him and applied uniformly to all of the States. The Secretary of Commerce shall transmit such estimate to the Senate and the House of Representatives within ten days subsequent to January 2, 1958. Upon approval of such estimate by the Congress by concurrent resolution, the Secretary of Commerce shall use such approved estimate in making apportionments for the fiscal years ending June 30, 1960, June 30, 1961, and June 30, 1962. The Secretary of Commerce shall make a revised estimate of the cost of completing the then designated Interstate System, after taking into account all previous apportionments made under this section, in the same manner as stated above, and transmit the same to the Senate and the House of Representatives within ten days subsequent to January 2, 1962. Upon approval of such estimate by the Congress by concurrent resolution, the Secretary of Commerce shall use such approved estimate in making apportionments for the fiscal years ending June 30, 1963, June 30, 1964, June 30, 1965, and June 30, 1966. The Secretary of Commerce shall make a revised estimate of the cost of completing the then designated Interstate System, after taking into account all previous apportionments made under this section, in the same manner as stated above, and transmit the same to the Senate and time House of Representatives within ten days subsequent to January 2, 1966, and annually thereafter through and including January 2, 1968. Upon approval of any such estimate by the Congress by concurrent resolution, the Secretary of Commerce shall use such approved estimate in making apportionments for the fiscal year which begins next following the fiscal year in which such report is transmitted to the Senate and

the House of Representatives. Whenever the Secretary of Commerce, pursuant to this subsection, requests and receives estimates of cost from the State highway departments, he shall furnish copies of such estimates at the same time to the Senate and the House of Representatives.

(e) FEDERAL SHARE.— The Federal share payable on account of any project on the Interstate System provided for by funds made available under the provisions of this section shall be increased to 90 per centum of the total cost thereof, plus a percentage of the remaining 10 per centum of such cost in any State containing unappropriated and unreserved public lands and nontaxable Indian lands, individual and tribal, exceeding 5 per centum of the total area of all lands therein, equal to the percentage that the area of such lands in such State is its total area: *Provided*, That such Federal share payable on any project in any State shall not exceed 95 per centum of the total cost of such project.

(f) AVAILABILITY FOR EXPENDITURE.— Any sums apportioned to any State under the provisions of this section shall be available for expenditure in that State for two years after the close of the fiscal year for which such sums are authorized: *Provided*, That such funds for any fiscal year shall be deemed to be expended if a sum equal to the total of the sums apportioned to the State specifically for the Interstate System for such fiscal year and previous fiscal years is covered by formal agreements with the Secretary of Commerce for the construction, reconstruction, or improvement of specific projects under this section.

(g) LAPSE OF AMOUNTS APPORTIONED.— Any amount apportioned to the States under the provisions of this section unexpended at the end of the period during which it is available for expenditure under the terms of subsection (f) of this section shall lapse, and shall immediately be reapportioned among the other States in accordance with the provisions of subsection (d) of this section: *Provided*, That any Interstate System funds released by the payment of the final voucher or by the modification of the formal project agreement shall be credited to the Interstate System funds previously apportioned to the State and be immediately available for expenditure.

(h) CONSTRUCTION BY STATES IN ADVANCE OF APPORTIONMENT.— In any case in which a State has obligated all funds apportioned to it under this section and proceeds, subsequent to the date of enactment of this Act, to construct (without the aid of Federal funds) any project (including one or more parts of any project) on the Interstate System, as designated at that time, in accordance with all procedures and all requirements applicable to projects financed under the provisions of this section (except insofar as such procedures and requirements limit a State to the construction of projects with the aid of Federal funds previously apportioned to it), the Secretary of Commerce, upon application by such State and his approval of such application, is authorized, whenever additional funds are apportioned to such State under this section, to pay to such State from such funds the Federal share of the costs of construction of such project: *Provided*, That prior to construction of any such project, the plans and specifications therefor shall have been approved by the Secretary of Commerce in the same manner as other projects on the Interstate System: *Provided further*, That any such project shall conform to the standards adopted under subsection (i). In determining the apportionment for any fiscal year under the provisions of subsection (d) of this section, any such project constructed by a State without the aid of Federal funds shall not be considered completed until an application under the provisions of this subsection with respect to such project has been approved by the Secretary of Commerce.

(i) STANDARDS.— The geometric and construction standards to be adopted for the Interstate System shall be those approved by the Secretary of Commerce in cooperation with the State highway departments. Such standards shall be adequate to accommodate the types and volumes of traffic forecast for the year 1975. The right-of-way width of the Interstate System shall be adequate to permit construction of projects on the Interstate System up to such standards. The Secretary of Commerce shall apply such standards uniformly throughout the States. Such standard shall be adopted by the Secretary of Commerce in cooperation with the State highway departments as soon as practicable after the enactment of this Act.

(j) MAXIMUM WEIGHT AND WIDTH LIMITATIONS.— No funds authorized to be appropriated for any fiscal year by this section shall be apportioned to any State within the boundaries of which the Interstate System may lawfully be used by vehicles with weight in excess of eighteen thousand pounds carried on any one axle, or with a tandem-axle weight in excess of thirty-two thousand pounds, or with an overall gross weight in excess of 73,280 pounds, or with a width in excess of 96 inches, or the corresponding maximum weights or maximum widths permitted for vehi-

cles using the public highways of such State under laws or regulations established by appropriate State authority in effect on July 1, 1956, whichever is the greater. Any amount which is withheld from apportionment to any State pursuant to die foregoing provisions shall lapse: *Provided, however*, That nothing herein shall be construed to deny apportionment to any State allowing the operation within such State of any vehicles or combinations thereof that could be lawfully operated within such State on July 1, 1956.

(k) TESTS TO DETERMINE MAXIMUM DESIRABLE DIMENSIONS AND WEIGHTS.— The Secretary of Commerce is directed to take all action possible to expedite the conduct of a series of tests now planned or being conducted by the Highway Research Board of the National Academy of Sciences, in cooperation with the Bureau of Public Roads, the several States, and other persons and organizations, for the purpose of determining the maximum desirable dimensions and weights for vehicles operated on the Federal-aid highway systems, including the Interstate System, and, after the conclusion of such tests, but not later than March 1, 1959, to make recommendations to the Congress with respect to such maximum desirable dimensions and weights.

(l) INCREASE IN MILEAGE.— Section 7 of the Federal-Aid Highway Act of 1944 (58 Stat, 838), relating to the Interstate System, is hereby amended by striking out "forty thousand", and inserting in lieu thereof "forty-one thousand": *Provided*, That the cost of completing any mileage designated from the one thousand additional miles authorized by this subsection shall be excluded in making the estimates of cost for completing the Interstate System as provided in subsection (d) of this section.

◆ Sec. 109. Acquisition of Rights-Of-Way for Interstate System.

(a) FEDERAL ACQUISITION FOR STATES.— In any case in which the Secretary of Commerce is requested by any State to acquire any lands or interests in lands (including within the term "interests in lands", the control of access thereto from adjoining lands) required by such State for right-of-way or other purposes in connection with the prosecution of any project for the construction, reconstruction, or improvement of any section of the Interstate System, the Secretary of Commerce is authorized, in the name of the United States and prior to the approval of title by the Attorney General, to acquire, enter upon, and take possession of such lands or interests in lands by purchase, donation, condemnation, or otherwise in accordance with the laws of the United States (including the Act of February 26, 1931, 46 Stat, 1421), if—

(1) the Secretary of Commerce has determined either that such State is unable to acquire necessary lands or interests in lands, or is unable to acquire such lands or interests in lands with sufficient promptness; and

(2) such State has agreed with the Secretary of Commerce to pay, at such time as may be specified by the Secretary of Commerce, an amount equal to 10 per centum of the costs incurred by the Secretary of Commerce, in acquiring such lands or interests in lands, or such lesser percentage which represents the State's pro rata share of project costs as determined in accordance with section 108 (e) of this title.

The authority granted by this section shall also apply to lands and interests in lands received as grants of land from the United States and owned or held by railroads or other corporations.

(b) Costs of Acquisition.— The costs incurred by the Secretary of Commerce in acquiring any such lands or interests in lands may include the cost of examination and abstract of title, certificate of title, advertising, and any fees incidental to such acquisition. All costs incurred by the Secretary of Commerce in connection with the acquisition of any such lands or interests in lands shall be paid from the funds for construction, reconstruction, or improvement of the Interstate System apportioned to the State upon the request of which such lands or interests in lands are acquired, and any sums paid to the Secretary of Commerce by such State as its share of the costs of acquisition of such lands or interests in lands shall be deposited in the Treasury to the credit of the appropriation for Federal-aid highways and shall be credited to the amount apportioned to such State as its apportionment of funds for construction, reconstruction, or improvement of the Interstate System, or shall be deducted from other moneys due the State for reimbursement under section 108 of this title.

(c) Conveyance of Acquired Lands to the States.— The Secretary of Commerce is further authorized and directed by proper deed, executed in the name of the United States, to convey any such lands or interests in lands acquired in any State under the provisions of this section, except the outside fire feet of any such right-of-way in any State which does not provide control of access, to the State highway department of such State or such political subdivisions thereof as its laws may provide, upon such terms and conditions as to such lands or interests in lands as may be agreed upon by the Secretary of Commerce and the State highway department or political subdivisions to which the conveyance is to be made. Whenever the State makes provision for control of access satisfactory to the Secretary of Commerce, the outside five feet then shall be conveyed to the State by the Secretary of Commerce, as herein provided.

(d) Rights-of-Way Over Public Lands.— Whenever rights-of-way, including control or access, on the Interstate System are required over public lands or reservations of the United States, the Secretary of Commerce may make such arrangements with the agency having jurisdiction over such lands as may be necessary to give the State or other person constructing the projects on such lands adequate rights-of-way and control of access thereto from adjoining lands, and any such agency is hereby directed to cooperate with the Secretary of Commerce in this connection.

◆ Sec. 110. Availability of Funds to Acquire Rights-of-Way and to Make Advances to the States.

(a) Advance Right-of-Way Acquisitions.— For the purpose of facilitating the acquisition of rights-of-way on any of the Federal-aid highway systems, including the Interstate System, in the most expeditious and economical manner, and recognizing that the acquisition of rights-of-way requires lengthy planning and negotiations if it is to be done at a reasonable cost, the Secretary of Commerce is hereby authorized, upon request of a State highway department, to make available to such State for acquisition of rights-of-way, in anticipation of construction and under such rules and regulations as the Secretary, of Commerce may prescribe, the funds apportioned to such State for expenditure on any of the Federal-aid highway systems, including the Interstate System: *Provided*, That the agreement between the Secretary of Commerce and the State highway department for the reimbursement of the cost of such rights-of-way shall provide for the actual construction of a road on such rights-of-way within a period not exceeding five years following the fiscal year in which such request is made: *Provided further*, That Federal participation in the cost of rights-of-way so acquired shall not exceed the Federal pro rata share applicable to the class of funds from which Federal reimbursement is made.

(b) Advances to States.— Section 6 of the Federal-Aid Highway Act of 1944 is hereby amended to read as follows:

"Sec. 6. If the Secretary of Commerce shall determine that it is necessary for the expeditious completion of projects on any of the Federal-aid highway systems, including the Interstate System, he may advance to any State out of any existing appropriations the Federal share of the cost of construction thereof to enable the State highway department to make prompt payments for acquisition of rights-of-way, and for construction as it progresses. The sums so advanced shall be deposited in a special revolving trust fund, by the State official authorized under the laws of the State to receive Federal-aid highway funds, to be disbursed solely upon vouchers approved by the State highway department for rights-of-way which have been or are being acquired, and for construction which has been actually performed and approved by the Secretary of Commerce. Upon determination by the Secretary of Commerce that any part of the funds advanced to any State under the provisions of this section are no longer required, the amount of the advance which is determined to be in excess of current requirements of the State shall be repaid upon his demand, and such repayments shall be returned to the credit of the appropriation from which the funds were advanced. Any sums advanced and not repaid on demand shall be deducted from sums due the State for the Federal pro rata share of the cost of construction of Federal-aid projects."

◆ Sec. 111. Relocation of Utility Facilities.

(a) AVAILABILITY OF FEDERAL FUNDS FOR REIMBURSEMENT TO STATES.— Subject to the conditions contained in this section, whenever a State shall pay for the cost of relocation of utility facilities necessitated by the construction of a project on the Federal-aid primary or secondary systems or on the Interstate System, including extensions thereof within urban areas, Federal funds may be used to reimburse the State for such cost in the same proportion as Federal funds are expended on the project: *Provided*, That Federal funds shall not be apportioned to, the States under this section when the payment to the utility violates the law of the State or violates a legal contract between the utility and the State.

(b) UTILITY DEFINED.— For the purposes of this section, the term "utility" shall include publicly, privately, and cooperatively owned utilities.

(c) COST OF RELOCATION DEFINED.— For the purposes of this section, the term "cost of relocation" shall include the entire amount paid by such utility properly attributable to such relocation after deducting therefrom any increase in the value of the new facility and any salvage value derived from the old facility.

◆ Sec. 112. Agreements Relating to Use of and Access to Rights-of-Way.

All agreements between the Secretary of Commerce and the State highway department for the construction of projects on the Interstate System shall contain a clause providing that the State will not add any points of access to, or exit from, the project in addition to those approved by the Secretary in the plans for such project, without the prior approval of the Secretary. Such agreements shall also contain a clause providing that the State will not permit automotive service stations or other commercial establishments for serving motor vehicle users to be constructed or located on the rights-of-way of the Interstate System. Such agreements may, however, authorize a State or political subdivision thereof to use the air space above and below the established grade line of the highway pavement for the parking of motor vehicles provided such use does not interfere in any way with the free flow of traffic on the Interstate System.

◆ Sec. 113. Toll Roads, Bridges, and Tunnels.

(a) APPROVAL AS PART OF INTERSTATE SYSTEM.— Upon a finding by the Secretary of Commerce that such action will promote the development of an integrated Interstate System, the Secretary is authorized to approve as part of the Interstate System any toll road, bridge, or tunnel, now or hereafter constructed which meets the standards adopted for the improvement of projects located on the Interstate System, whenever such toll road, bridge, or tunnel is located on a route heretofore or hereafter designated as a part of the Interstate System: *Provided*, That no Federal-aid highway funds shall be expended for the construction, reconstruction, or improvement of any such toll road except to the extent hereafter permitted by law: *Provided further*, That no Federal-aid highway funds shall be expended for the construction, reconstruction, or improvement of any such toll bridge or tunnel except to the extent now or hereafter permitted by law.

(b) APPROACHES HAVING OTHER USE.— The funds authorized under this title, or under prior Acts, shall be available for expenditure on projects approaching any toll road, bridge, or tunnel to a point where such project will have some use irrespective of its use for such toll road, bridge, or tunnel

(c) APPROACHES HAVING NO OTHER USE.— The funds authorized under section 108 (b) of this title, or under prior Acts, shall be available for expenditure on Interstate System projects approaching any toll road on the Interstate System, even though the project has no use other than as an approach to such toll road: *Provided*, That agreement satisfactory to the Secretary of Commerce has been reached with the State prior to approval of any such project (1) that the section of toll road will become free to the public upon the collection of tolls sufficient to liquidate the cost of the toll road or any bonds outstanding at the time constituting a valid lien against said section of toll road covered in the agreement and their maintenance and operation and debt service during the period of toll collections, and (2) that there is one or more reasonably satisfactory alternate free routes available to traffic by which the toll section of the System may be bypassed.

(d) EFFECT ON CERTAIN PRIOR ACTS.— Nothing in this title shall be deemed to repeal the Act approved March 3, 1927 (44 Stat. 1398), or subsection (g) of section 204 of the National Industrial Recovery Act (48 Stat. 200), and such Acts are hereby amended to include tunnels as well as bridges.

◆ Sec. 114. Determination of Policy with Respect to Reimbursement for Certain Highways.

It is hereby declared to be the intent and policy of the Congress to determine whether or not the Federal Government should equitably reimburse any State for a portion of a highway which is on the Interstate System, whether toll or free, the construction of which has been completed subsequent to August 2, 1947, or which is either in actual use or under construction by contract, for completion, awarded not later than June 30, 1957: *Provided*, That such highway meets the standards required by this title for the Interstate System. The time, method, and amounts of such reimbursement, if any, shall be determined by the Congress following a study which the Secretary of Commerce is hereby authorized and directed to conduct, in cooperation with the State highway departments, and other agencies as may be required, to determine which highways in the Interstate System measure up to the standards required by this title, including all related factors of cost, depreciation, participation of Federal funds, and any other items relevant thereto. A complete report of the results of such Study shall be submitted to the Congress within ten days subsequent to January 2, 1958.

◆ Sec. 115. Prevailing Rate of Wage

(a) APPLICATION OF DAVIS-BACON ACT.— The Secretary of Commerce shall take such action as may be necessary to insure that all laborers and mechanics employed by contractors or subcontractors on the initial construction work performed on highway projects on the Interstate System authorized under section 108 of this title shall be paid wages at rates not less than those prevailing on the same type of work on similar construction in the immediate locality as determined by the Secretary of Labor in accordance with the Act of August 30,1935, known as the Davis-Bacon Act (40 U. S. C, sec, 276-a).

(b) CONSULTATION WITH STATE HIGHWAY DEPARTMENTS; PREDETERMINATION OF RATES.— In carrying out the duties of the foregoing subsection, the Secretary of Labor shall consult with the highway department of the State in which a project on the Interstate System is to be performed. After giving due regard to the information thus obtained, he shall make a predetermination of the minimum wages to be paid laborers and mechanics in accordance with the provisions pf the foregoing subsection which shall be set out in each project Advertisement for bids and in each bid proposal form and shall be made a part of the contract covering the project.

◆ Sec. 116. Declarations of Policy with Respect to Federal-Aid Highway Program.

(a) ACCELERATION OF PROGRAM.— It is hereby declared to be in the national interest to accelerate the construction of the Federal-aid highway systems, including the Interstate System, since many of such highways, or portions thereof, are in fact inadequate to meet the needs of local and interstate commerce, the national and the civil defense.

(b) COMPLETION OF INTERSTATE SYSTEM; PROGRESS REPORT ON FEDERAL-AID HIGHWAY PROGRAM.— It is further declared that one of the most important objectives of this Act is the prompt completion of the Interstate System. Insofar as possible in consonance with this objective, existing highways located on an interstate route shall be used to the extent that such use is practicable, suitable, and feasible, it being the intent that local needs, to the extent practicable, suitable, and feasible, shall be given equal consideration with the needs of interstate commerce. The Secretary of Commerce is hereby directed to submit to the Congress not later than February 1, 1959, a report on the progress made in attaining the objectives set forth in this subsection and in subsection (a), together with recommendations.

(c) PUBLIC HEARINGS.— Any State highway department which submits plans for a Federal-aid highway project involving the bypassing of, or going through, any city, town, or village, either incorporated or unincorporated, shall certify to the Commissioner of Public Roads that it had public hearing, or has afforded the opportunity for such hearing, and has considered the economic effects of such a location: *Provided*, That, if such hearing have been held, a copy of the transcript of said hearings shall be submitted to the Commissioner of Public Roads, together with the certification.

(d) PARTICIPATION BY SMALL BUSINESS ENTERPRISES.—It is hereby declared to be in the national interest to encourage and develop the actual and potential capacity of small business and to utilize this important segment of our economy to the fullest practicable extent in construction of the Federal-aid highway systems, including the Interstate System. In order to carry out that intent and encourage full and free competition, the Secretary of Commerce should assist, insofar as feasible, small business enterprises in obtaining contracts in connection with the prosecution of the highway program.

◆ Sec. 117. Highway Safety Study.

The Secretary of Commerce is authorized and directed to make a full and complete investigation and study for the purpose of determining what action can be taken by the Federal Government to promote the public welfare by increasing highway safety in the United States. In making such investigation and study the Secretary of Commerce shall give consideration to—

(1) the need for Federal assistance to State and local governments in the enforcement of necessary highway safety and speed requirements and the forms such assistance should take;

(2) the advisability and practicability of uniform State and local highway safety and speed laws and what steps should be taken by the Federal Government to promote the adoption of such uniform laws;

(3) possible means of promoting highway safety in the manufacture of the various types of vehicles used on the highways;

(4) educational programs to promote highway safety;

(5) the design and physical characteristics of highways; and

(6) such other matters as it may deem advisable and appropriate.

The Secretary of Commerce shall report his findings, together with such recommendations as he may deem advisable, to the Congress not later than March 1, 1959. The Secretary of Commerce shall conduct such study and investigation under the general author-

ity contained in section 10 of the Federal-Aid Highway Act of 1954; except that the amount expended for the purposes of this section shall not exceed $200,000.

◆ Sec. 118. Emergency Fund.

Section 7 of the Federal-Aid Highway Act of 1952 (66 Stat. 158) is hereby amended to read as follows:

"SEC. 7. There is hereby authorized an emergency fund in the amount of $30,000,000 for expenditure by the Secretary of Commerce, in accordance with the provisions of the Federal-Aid Road Act approved July 11, 1916, as amended and supplemented, after receipt of an application therefor from the highway department of any State, in the repair or reconstruction of highways and bridges on the Federal-aid highway systems, including the Interstate System, which he shall find have suffered serious damage as the result of disaster over a wide area, such as by floods, hurricanes, tidal waves, earthquakes, severe storms, landslides, or other catastrophes in any part of the United States. The appropriation of such moneys as may be necessary for the establishment of the fund in accordance with the provisions of this section and for its replenishment on an annual basis is hereby authorized: *Provided*, That pending the appropriation of such sum, or its replenishment, the Secretary of Commerce may expend, from existing Federal-aid highway appropriations, such sums as may be necessary for the immediate prosecution of the work herein authorized, such appropriations to be reimbursed from the appropriation herein authorized when made: *Provided further*, That no expenditures shall be made hereunder with respect to any such catastrophe in any State unless an emergency has been declared by the Governor of such State and concurred in by the Secretary of Commerce: *Provided further*, That the Federal share payable on account of any repair or reconstruction project provided for by funds made available under this section shall not exceed 50 per centum of the cost thereof: *And provided further*, That the funds herein authorized shall be available for use on any projects programed and approved at any time during the fiscal year ending June 30, 1956, and thereafter, which meet the provisions of this section, including projects which may have been previously approved during the fiscal year ending June 30, 1956, from any other category of funds under the Federal-Aid Road Act approved July 11, 1916, as amended and supplemented."

◆ Sec. 119. Definition of Construction.

The definition of the term "construction" in section 1 of the Federal-Aid Highway Act of 1944 is hereby amended by inserting after "mapping" the following: "(including the establishment of temporary and permanent geodetic markers in accordance with specifications of the Coast and Geodetic Survey in the Department of Commerce)".

◆ Sec. 120. Archeological and Paleontological Salvage.

Funds authorized by this title to be appropriated, to the extent approved as necessary by the highway department of any State, may be used for archeological and paleontological salvage in that State in compliance with the Act entitled "An Act for the preservation of American antiquities", approved June 8, 1906 (34 Stat. 225), and State laws where applicable.

◆ Sec. 121. Mapping

In carrying out the provisions of this title the Secretary of Commerce may, wherever practicable, authorize the use of photogram-metric methods in mapping, and the utilization of commercial enterprise for such services.

◆ Sec. 122. Relationship of This Title to Other Acts; Effective Date.

All provisions of the Federal-Aid Road Act approved July 11, 1916, together with all Acts amendatory thereof or supplementary thereto, not inconsistent with this title, shall remain in full force and effect and be applicable hereto. All Acts or parts of Acts in any way inconsistent with the provisions of this title are hereby repealed. This title shall take effect on the date of the enactment of this Act.

Title II— Highway Revenue Act of 1956

◆ Sec. 201. Short Title For Title II.

(a) Short Title.— This title may be cited as the "Highway Revenue Act of 1956".

(b) Amendment of 1954 Code.— Whenever in this title an amend-mentis expressed in terms of an amendment to a section or other provision, the reference shall be considered to be made to a section or other provision of the Internal Revenue Code of 1954.

◆ Sec. 202. Increase in Taxes on Diesel Fuel and on Special Motor Fuels.

(a) Diesel Fuel.— Subsection (a) of section 4041 (relating to tax on diesel fuel) is amended by striking out "2 cents a gallon" and inserting in lieu thereof "3 cents a gallon", and by adding after paragraph (2) the following:

"In the case of a liquid taxable under this subsection sold for use or used as a fuel in a diesel-powered highway vehicle (A) which (at the time of such sale or use) is not registered, and is not required to be registered, for highway use under the laws of any State or foreign country, or (B) which, in the case of a diesel-powered highway vehicle owned by the United States, is not used on the highway, the tax imposed by paragraph (1) or by paragraph (2) shall be 2 cents a gallon in lieu of 3 cents a gallon. If a liquid on which tax was imposed by paragraph (1) at the rate of 2 cents a gallon by reason of the preceding sentence is used as a fuel in a diesel-powered highway vehicle (A) which (at the time of such use) is registered, or is required to be registered, for highway use under the laws of any State or foreign country, or (B) which, in the case of a diesel-powered highway vehicle owned by the United States, is used on the highway, a tax of 1 cent a gallon shall be imposed under paragraph (2)."

(b) Special Motor Fuels.— Subsection (b) of section 4041 (relating to Special motor fuels) is amended by striking out "2 cents a gallon" and inserting in lieu thereof "3 cents a gallon", and by adding after paragraph (2) the following:

"In the case of a liquid taxable under this subsection sold for use or used otherwise than as a fuel for the propulsion of a highway vehicle (A) which (at the time of such sale or use) is registered, or is required to be registered, for highway use under the laws of any State or foreign country, or (B) which, in the case of a highway vehicle owned by the United States, is used on the highway, the tax imposed by paragraph (1) or by paragraph (2) shall be 2 cents a gallon in lieu of 3 cents a gallon. If a liquid on which tax was imposed by paragraph (1) at the rate of 2 cents a gallon by reason of the preceding sentence is used as a fuel for the propulsion of a highway vehicle (A) which (at the time of such use) is registered, or is required to be registered, for highway use under the laws of any State or foreign country, or (B) which, in the case of a highway vehicle owned by the United States, is used on the highway, a tax of 1 cent a gallon shall be imposed under paragraph (2)."

(c) Rate Reduction.— Subsection (c) of section 4041 (relating to rate reduction) is amended to read as follows:

"(c) Rate Reduction.— On and after July 1, 1972—

"(1) the taxes imposed by this section shall be 1 1/2 cents a gallon; and

"(2) the second and third sentences of subsections (a) and (b) shall not apply."

◆ Sec. 203. Increase in Tax on Trucks, Truck Trailers, Buses, Etc.

So much of paragraph (1) of section 4061 (a) (relating to tax on trucks, truck trailers, buses, etc.) as precedes "Automobile truck chassis" is amended to read as follows:

"(1) Articles taxable at 10 percent, except that on and after July 1, 1972, the rate shall be 5 percent—".

◆ Sec. 204. Increase in Taxes on Tires of the Type Used On Highway Vehicles; Tax on Tread Rubber, Etc.

(a) IN GENERAL.— Section 4071 (relating to tax on tires and tubes) is amended to read as follows:

"Sec. 4071. Imposition of Tax.

"(a) IMPOSITION AND RATE OF TAX.— There is hereby imposed upon the following articles, if wholly or in part of rubber, sold by the manufacturer, producer, or importer, a tax at the following rates:

"(1) Tires of the type used on highway vehicles, 8 cents a pound.

"(2) Other tires, 5 cents a pound.

"(3) Inner tubes for tires, 9 cents a pound

"(4) Tread rubber, 3 cents a pound.

"(b) DETERMINATION OF WEIGHT.— For purposes of this section, weight shall be based on total weight, except that in the case of tire such total weight shall be exclusive of metal rims or rim bases. Total weight of the articles shall be determined under regulations prescribed by the Secretary or his delegate.

"(c) RATE REDUCTION.— On and after July 1,1972—

"(1) the tax imposed by paragraph (1) of subsection (a) shall be 5 cents a pound; and

"(2) paragraph (4) of subsection (a) shall not apply."

(b) TREAD RUBBER DEFINED.— Section 4072 (defining the term "rubber") is amended to read as follows:

"Sec. 4072. Definitions.

"(a) RUBBER.— For purposes of this chapter, the term 'rubber' includes Synthetic and substitute rubber.

"(b) TREAD RUBBER.— For purposes of this chapter, the term 'tread rubber' means any material—

"(1) which is commonly or commercially known as tread rubber or camelback; or

"(2) which is a substitute for a material described in paragraph (1) and is of a type used in recapping or retreading tires.

(c) EXEMPTION OF CERTAIN TREAD RUBBER FROM TAX.— Section 4073 (relating to exemptions) is amended by adding at the end thereof the following new subsection:

"(c) EXEMPTION FROM TAX ON TREAD RUBBER IN CERTAIN CASES.— Under regulations prescribed by the Secretary or his delegate, the tax imposed by section 4071 (a) (4) shall not apply to tread rubber sold by the manufacturer, producer, or importer, to any person for use by such person otherwise than in the recapping or retreading of tires of the type used on highway vehicles."

(d) TECHNICAL AMENDMENT.— The table of sections for part II of subchapter A of chapter 32 is amended by striking out

"Sec. 4072. Definition of rubber."

and inserting in lieu thereof

"Sec 4072. Definitions."

◆ Sec. 205. Increase in Tax on Gasoline.

Section 4081 (relating to tax on gasoline) is amended to read as follows:

"Sec. 4081. Imposition of Tax.

"(a) IN GENERAL.— There is hereby imposed on gasoline sold by the producer or importer thereof, or by any producer of gasoline, a tax of 3 cents a gallon.

"(b) RATE REDUCTION.— On and after July 1,1972, the tax imposed by this section shall be 1 1/2 cents a gallon."

◆ Sec. 206. Tax on Use of Certain Vehicles.

(a) IMPOSITION OF TAX.— Chapter 36 (relating to certain other excise taxes) is amended by adding at the end thereof the following new subchapter:

"Subchapter D— Tax on Use of Certain Vehicles

"Sec. 4481. Imposition of tax.

"Sec. 4482. Definitions.

"Sec. 4483. Exemptions.

"Sec. 4484. Cross reference.

"Sec. 4481. Imposition of Tax.

"(a) IMPOSITION OF TAX.— A tax is hereby imposed on the use of any highway motor vehicle which (together with the semitrailers and trailers customarily used in connection with highway motor vehicles of the same type as such highway motor vehicle) has a taxable gross weight of more than 26,000 pounds, at the rate of $1.50 a year for each 1,000 pounds of taxable gross weight or fraction thereof.

"(b) BY WHOM PAID.— The tax imposed by this section shall be paid by the person in whose name the highway motor vehicle is, or is required to be, registered under the law of the State in which such vehicle is, or is required to be, registered, or, in case the highway motor vehicle is owned by the United

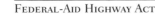

States, by the agency or instrumentality of the United States operating such vehicle.

"(c) PRORATION OF TAX.— If in any year the first use of the highway motor vehicle is after July 31, the tax shall be reckoned proportionately from the first day of the month in which such use occurs to and including the 30th day of June following.

"(d) ONE PAYMENT PER YEAR.— If the tax imposed by this section is paid with respect to any highway motor vehicle for any year, no further tax shall be imposed by this section for such year with respect to such vehicle.

"(e) PERIOD TAX IN EFFECT.— The tax imposed by this section shall apply only to use after June 30, 1956, and before July 1, 1972.

"Sec. 4482. Definitions.

"(a) HIGHWAY MOTOR VEHICLE.— For purposes of this subchapter, the term 'highway motor vehicle' means any motor vehicle which is a highway vehicle.

"(b) TAXABLE GROSS WEIGHT.— For purposes of this subchapter, the term 'taxable gross weight', when used with respect to any highway motor vehicle, means the sum of—

"(l) the actual unloaded weight of—

"(A) such highway motor vehicle fully equipped for service, and

"(B) the semitrailers and trailers (fully equipped for service) customarily used in connection with highway motor vehicles of the same type as such highway motor vehicle, and

"(2) the weight of the maximum load customarily carried on highway motor vehicles of the same type as such highway motor vehicle and on the semitrailers and trailers referred to in paragraph (1) (B).

Taxable gross weight shall be determined under regulations prescribed by the Secretary or his delegate (which regulations may include formulas or other methods for determining the taxable gross weight of vehicles by classes, specifications, or otherwise).

"(c) OTHER DEFINITIONS.— For purposes of this subchapter—

"(1) STATE.— The term 'State' means a State, a Territory of the United States and the District of Columbia.

"(2) YEAR.— The term 'year' means the one-year period beginning on July 1.

"(3) USE.— The term 'use' means use in the United States on the public highways.

"Sec. 4483. Exemptions

"(a) STATE AND LOCAL GOVERNMENTAL EXEMPTION.— Under regulations prescribed by the Secretary or his delegate, no tax shall be imposed by section 4481 on the use of any highway motor vehicle by any State or any political subdivision of a State.

"(b) EXEMPTION FOR UNITED STATES.— The Secretary may authorize exemption from the tax imposed by section 4481 as to the use by the United States of any particular highway motor vehicle, or class of highway motor vehicles, if he determines that the imposition of such tax with respect to such use will cause substantial burden or expense which can be avoided by granting tax exemption and that full benefit of such exemption, if granted, will accrue to the United States.

"(c) CERTAIN TRANSIT-TYPE BUSES.— Under regulations prescribed by the Secretary or his delegate, no tax shall be imposed by section 4481 on the use of any bus which is of the transit type (rather than of the intercity type) by a person who, for the last 3 months of the preceding year (or for such other period as the Secretary or his delegate may by regulations prescribe for purposes of this subsection), met the 60-percent passenger fare revenue test set forth in section 6421 (b) (2) as applied to the period prescribed for purposes of this subsection.

"Sec. 4484. Cross Reference.

"For penalties and administrative provisions applicable to this subchapter, see subtitle F."

(b) MODE AND TIME OF COLLECTION OF TAX.— Section 6302 (b) (relating to discretion as to method of collecting tax) is amended by inserting "section 4481 of chapter 36," after "33,".

(c) TECHNICAL AMENDMENT.— The table of subchapters for chapter 36 is amended by adding at the end thereof the following:

"Subchapter D, Tax on use of certain vehicles."

◆ **Sec. 207. Floor Stocks Taxes.**

(a) IMPOSITION OF TAXES.— Subchapter F of chapter 32 (special provisions applicable to manufacturers excise taxes) is amended by renumbering section 4226 as 4227 and by inserting after section 4225 the following new section:

"Sec. 4226. Floor Stocks Taxes.

"(a) IN GENERAL.—

"(1) 1956 TAX ON TRUCKS, TRUCK TRAILERS, BUSES, ETC.— On any article subject to tax under section 4061 (a) (1) (relating to tax on trucks, truck trailers, buses, etc.) which, on July 1, 1956, is held by a dealer for sale, there is hereby imposed a floor stocks tax at the rate of 2 percent of the price for which the article was purchased by such dealer. If the price for which the article was sold by the manufacturer, producer, or importer is established to the satisfaction of the Secretary or his delegate, then in lieu of the amount specified in the preceding sentence, the tax imposed by this paragraph shall be at the rate of 2 percent of the price for which the article was sold by the manufacturer, producer, or importer.

"(2) 1956 TAX ON TIRES OF THE TYPE USED ON HIGHWAY VEHICLES.— On tires subject to tax under section 4071 (a) (1) (as amended by the Highway Revenue Act of 1956) which, on July 1,1956, are held—

"(A) by a dealer for sale,

"(B) for sale on, or in connection with, other articles held by the manufacturer, producer, or importer of such other articles, or

"(c) for use in the manufacture or production of other articles, there is hereby imposed a floor stocks tax at the rate of 3 cents a pound. The tax imposed by this paragraph shall not apply to any tire which is held for sale by the manufacturer, producer, or importer of such tire or which will be subject under section 4218 (a) (2) or 4219 to the manufacturers excise tax on tires.

"(3) 1956 TAX ON TREAD RUBBER.— On tread rubber subject to tax under section 4071 (a) (4) (as amended by the Highway Revenue Act of 1956) which, on July 1, 1956, is held by a dealer, there is hereby imposed a floor stocks tax at the rate of 3 cents a pound. The tax imposed by this paragraph shall not apply in the case of any person if such person establishes, to the satisfaction of the Secretary or his delegate, that all tread rubber held by him on July 1, 1956, will be used otherwise than in the recapping or retreading of tires of the type used on highway vehicles (as defined in section 4072 (c)).

"(4) 1956 TAX ON GASOLINE.— On gasoline subject to tax under section 4081 which, on July 1, 1956, is held by a dealer for sale, there is hereby imposed a floor stocks tax at the rate of 1 cent a gallon. The tax imposed by this paragraph shall not apply to gasoline in retail stocks held at the place where intended to be sold at retail, nor to gasoline held for sale by a producer or importer of gasoline.

"(b) OVERPAYMENT OF FLOOR STOCKS TAXES.— Section 6416 shall apply in respect of the floor stocks taxes imposed by this section, so as to entitle, subject to all provisions of section 6416, any person paying such floor stocks taxes to a credit or refund thereof for any of the reasons specified in section 6416.

"(c) MEANING OF TERMS.— For purposes of subsection (a), the terms 'dealer' and 'held by a dealer' have the meaning assigned to them by section 6412 (a) (3).

"(d) DUE DATE OF TAXES.— The taxes imposed by subsection (a) shall be paid at such time after September 30,1956, as may be prescribed by the Secretary or his delegate."

(b) TECHNICAL AMENDMENT.— The table of sections for subchapter F of chapter 32 is amended by striking out

"Sec. 4226, Cross references."
and inserting in lieu thereof
"Sec. 4226. Floor stocks taxes."
"Sec. 4227. Cross references,"

◆ **Sec. 208. Credit or Refund of Tax.**

(a) FLOOR STOCKS REFUNDS.— So much of section 6412 (relating to floor stocks refunds) as precedes subsection (d) is amended to read as follows:

"Sec. 6412. Floor Stocks Refunds.

"(a) IN GENERAL.—

"(1) PASSENGER AUTOMOBILES, ETC.— Where before April 1, 1957, any article subject to the tax imposed by section 4061 (a) (2) has been, sold by the manufacturer, producer, or importer and on such date is held by a dealer and has not been used and is intended for sale, there shall be credited or refunded (without interest) to the manufacturer, producer, or importer an amount equal to the difference between the tax paid by such manufacturer, producer, or importer on his sale of the article and the amount of tax made applicable to such article on and after April 1, 1957, if claim for such credit or refund is filed with the Secretary or his delegate on or before August 10, 1957, based upon a request submitted to the manufacturer, producer, or importer before July 1, 1957, by the dealer who held the article in respect of which the credit or refund is claimed, and, on or before August 10, 1957, reimbursement has been made to such dealer by such manufacturer, producer, or importer for the tax reduction on such article or written consent has been obtained from such dealer to allowance of such credit or refund.

"(2) TRUCKS AND BUSES, TIRES, TREAD RUBBER, AND GASOLINE.— Where before July 1, 1972, any article subject to the tax imposed by section 4061 (a) (1), 4071 (a) (l)or (4), or 4081 has been sold by the manufacturer, producer, or importer and on such date is held by a dealer and has not been used and is intended for sale (or, in the case of tread rubber, is intended for sale or is held for use), there shall be credited or refunded (without interest) to the manufacturer, producer, or importer an amount equal to the difference between the tax paid by such manufacturer, producer, or importer on his sale of the article and the amount of tax made applicable to such article on and after July 1, 1972, if claim for such credit or refund is filed with the Secretary or his delegate on or before November 10, 1972, based upon a request submitted to the manufacturer, producer, or importer before October 1, 1972, by the dealer who held the article in respect of which the credit or refund is claimed, and, on or before November 10, 1972, reimbursement has been made to such dealer by such manufacturer, producer, or importer for the tax reduction on such article or written consent has been obtained from such dealer to allowance of such credit or refund. No credit or refund shall be allowable under this paragraph with respect to gasoline in retail stocks held at the place where intended to be sold at retail, nor with respect to gasoline held for sale by a producer or importer of gasoline.

"(3) DEFINITIONS.— For purposes of this section—

"(A) The term 'dealer' includes a wholesaler, jobber, distributor, or retailer, or, in the case of tread rubber subject to tax tinder section 4071 (a) (4), includes any person (other than the manufacturer, producer, or importer thereof) who holds such tread rubber for sale or use.

"(B) An article shall be considered as 'held by a dealer' if title thereto has passed to such dealer (whether or not delivery to him has been made), and if for purposes of consumption title to such article or possession thereof has not at any time been transferred to any person other than a dealer.

"(b) LIMITATION ON ELIGIBILITY FOR CREDIT OR REFUND.— No manufacturer, producer, or importer shall be entitled to credit; or refund under subsection (a) unless he has in his possession such evidence of the inventories with respect to which the credit or refund is claimed as may be required by regulations prescribed under this section.

"(c) OTHER LAWS APPLICABLE.— All provisions of law, including penalties, applicable in respect of the taxes imposed by sections 4061,4071, and 4081 shall, insofar as applicable and not inconsistent with subsections (a) and (b) of this section, apply in respect of the credits and refunds provided for in subsection (a) to the same extent as if such credits or refunds constituted overpayments of such taxes."

(b) SPECIAL CASES.— Section 6414 (b) (2) (special cases in which tax payments considered overpayments) is amended by striking out the period at the end of subparagraph (I) and inserting in lieu thereof a semicolon, and by adding at the end thereof the following:

"(J) In the case of a liquid in respect of which tax was paid under section 4041 (a) (1) at the rate of 3 cents a gallon, used or resold for use as a fuel in a diesel-powered highway vehicle (i) which (at the time of such use or resale) is not registered, and is not required to be registered, for highway use under the laws of any State or foreign country, or (ii) which, in the case of a diesel-powered highway vehicle owned by the United States, is not used on the highway; except that the amount of any overpayment by reason of this subparagraph shall not exceed an amount computed at the rate of 1 cent a gallon;

"(K) In the case of a liquid in respect of which tax was paid under section 4041 (b) (1) at the rate of 3 cents a gallon, used or resold for use otherwise than as a fuel for the propulsion of a highway vehicle (i) which (at the time of such use or resale) is registered, or is required to be registered, for highway use under the laws of any State or foreign country, or (ii) which, in the case of a highway vehicle owned by the United States, is used on the highway; except that the amount of any overpayment by reason of this subparagraph shall not exceed an amount computed at the rate of 1 cent a gallon;

"(L) In the case of a liquid in respect of which tax was paid under section 4041 at the rate of 3 cents a gallon, used during any calendar quarter in vehicles while engaged in furnishing scheduled common carrier public passenger land transportation service along regular routes; except that (i) this subparagraph shall apply only if the 60 percent passenger fare revenue test set forth in section 6421 (b) (2) is met with respect to such quarter, and (ii) the amount of such overpayment for such quarter shall be an amount determined by multiplying 1 cent for each gallon of liquid so used by the percentage which such person's tax-exempt passenger fare revenue (as defined in section 6421 (d) (2)) derived from such scheduled service during such quarter was of his total passenger fare revenue (not including the tax imposed by section 4261, relating to the tax on transportation of persons) derived from such scheduled service during such quarter;

"(M) In the case of tread rubber in respect of which tax was paid under section 4071 (a) (4), used or resold for use otherwise than in the recapping or retreading of tires of the type used on highway vehicles (as defined in section 4072 (c)), unless credit or refund of such tax is allowable under subsection (b) (3)."

(c) PAYMENTS TO ULTIMATE PURCHASES.— Subchapter B of chapter 65 (relating to rules of special application for abatements, credits, and refunds) is amended by renumbering section 6421 as 6422 and by inserting after section 6420 the following new section:

"Sec. 6421. Gasoline Used for Certain Nonhighway Purposes or by Local Transit Systems.

"(a) NONHIGHWAY USES.— If gasoline is used otherwise than as a fuel in a highway vehicle (1) which (at the time of such use) is registered, or is required to be registered, for highway use under the laws of any State or foreign country, or (2) which, in the case of a highway vehicle owned by the United States, is used on the highway, the Secretary or his delegate shall pay (without interest) to the ultimate purchaser of such gasoline an amount equal to 1 cent for each gallon of gasoline so used.

"(b) LOCAL TRANSIT SYSTEMS.—

"(1) ALLOWANCE— If gasoline is used during any calendar quarter in vehicles while engaged in furnishing scheduled common carrier public passenger land transportation service alone regular routes, the Secretary or his delegate shall, subject to the provisions of paragraph (2), pay (without interest) to the ultimate purchaser of such gasoline the amount determined by multiplying—

"(A) 1 cent for each gallon of gasoline so used, by

"(B) the percentage which the ultimate purchaser's tax-exempt passenger fare revenue derived from such scheduled service during such quarter was of his total passenger fare revenue (not including the tax imposed by section 4261, relating to the tax on transportation of persons) derived from such scheduled service during such quarter.

"(2) LIMITATION.— Paragraph (1) shall apply in respect of gasoline used during any calendar quarter only if at least 60 per-cent of the total passenger fare revenue (not including the tax imposed by section 4261, relating to the tax on transportation of persons) derived during such quarter from scheduled service described in paragraph (1) by the person filing the claim was attributable to tax-exempt passenger fare revenue derived during such quarter by such person from such scheduled service.

"(c) TIME FOR FILLING CLAIM; PERIOD COVERED.— Not more than one claim may be tiled under subsection (a), and not more than one claim may be filed under subsection (b), by any person with respect to gasoline used during the one-year period ending on June 30 of any year. No claim shall be allowed under this section with respect to any one-year period unless filed on or before September 30 of the year in which such one-year period ends.

"(d) DEFINITIONS.— For purposes of this section—

"(1) GASOLINE.— The term 'gasoline' has the meaning given to such term by section 4082 (b).

"(2) TAX-EXEMPT PASSENGER FARE REVENUE.— The term 'tax-exempt passenger fare revenue' means revenue attributable to fares which were exempt from the tax imposed by section 4261 by reason of section 4262 (b) (relating to the exemption for commutation travel, etc.).

"(e) EXEMPT SALES; OTHER PAYMENTS OR REFUNDS AVAILABLE.—

"(1) EXEMPT SALES.— No amount shall be paid under this section with respect to any gasoline which the Secretary or his delegate determines was exempt from the tax imposed by section 4081. The amount which (but for this sentence) would be payable under this section with respect to any gasoline shall be reduced by any other amount which the Secretary or his delegate determines is payable under this section, or is refundable under any provision of this title, to any person with respect to such gasoline.

"(2) GASOLINE USED ON FARMS.— This section shall not apply m respect of gasoline which was (within the meaning of paragraphs (1), (2), and (3) of section 6420 (c)) used on a farm for farming purposes.

"(f) APPLICABLE LAWS.—

"(1) IN GENERAL.— AII provisions of law, including penalties, applicable in respect of the tax imposed by section 4081 shall, insofar as applicable and not inconsistent with this section, apply in respect of the payments provided for in this section to the same extent as if such payments constituted refunds of overpayments of the tax so imposed.

"(2) EXAMINATION OF BOOKS AND WITNESSES.— For the purpose of ascertaining the correctness of any claim made under this section, or correctness of any payment made in respect of any claim, the Secretary or his delegate shall have the authority granted by paragraphs (1), (2), and (3) of section 7602 (relating to examination of books and witnesses) as if the claimant were the person liable for tax.

"(g) REGULATIONS.— The Secretary or his delegate may be regulations prescribe the conditions, not inconsistent with the provisions of this section, under which payments may be made under this section.

"(h) EFFECTIVE DATE.— This section shall apply only with respect to gasoline purchased after June 30, 1956, and before July 1, 1972.

"(i) CROSS REFERENCES.—

"(1) For reduced rate of tax in case of diesel fuel and special motor fuels used for certain nonhighway purposes, see subsections (a) and (b) of section 4041.

"(2) For partial refund of tat in case of diesel fuel and special motor fuels used for certain non-highway purposes, see section 6416 (b) (2) (J) and (K).

"(3) For partial refund of tax in case of diesel fuel and special motor fuels used by local transit systems, see section 6416 (b) (2) (L).

"(4) For civil penalty for excessive claims under this section, see section 6675.

"(5) For fraud penalties, etc, see chapter 75 (section 7201 and following, relating to crimes, other offenses, and forfeitures)."

(d) TECHNICAL AMENDMENTS.—

(1) Section 6206 (relating to special rules applicable to excessive claims) is amended—

(A) by striking out "SECTION 6420" in the heading and inserting in lieu thereof "SECTTONS 6420 AND 6421"

(B) by inserting after "6420" in the first sentence thereof "or 6421"; and

(C) by inserting after "6420" in the second sentence thereof "or 6421, as the case may be".

(2) Section 6675 (relating to excessive claims for gasoline used on farms) is amended—

(A) by striking out "FOR GASOLINE USED ON FARMS" in the heading and inserting in lieu thereof "WITH RESPECT TO THE USE OF CERTAIN GASOLINE";

(B) by inserting after "6420 (relating to gasoline used on farms)" in subsection (a) thereof "or 6421 (relating to gasoline used for certain nonhighway purposes or by local transit systems)"; and

(C) by inserting after "6420" in subsection (b) thereof "or 6421, as the case may be,".

(3) Section 7210 (relating to failure to obey summons) is amended by inserting after "sections 6420 (e) (2)," the following: "6421 (f) (2),".

(4) Section 7603 (relating to service of summons) and 7604 (relating to enforcement of summons) and the first sentence of section 7605 (relating to time and place of examination) are each amended by inserting after "section 6420 (e) (2)" wherever it appears a comma and the following: "6421 (f) (2),". The second sentence of section 7605 is amended by inserting after "section 6420 (e) (2)" the following: "or 6421 (f) (2)".

(e) CLERICAL AMENDMENTS.—

(1) Section 4084 is amended to read as follows:
"Sec. 4084. Cross References.

"(1) For provisions to relieve farmers from excise tax in the case of gasoline used on the farm for farming purposes, see section 6420.

"(2) For provisions to relieve purchasers of gasoline from excise tax in the case of gasoline used for certain nonhighway purposes or by local transit systems, see section 6421."

(2) The table of sections for subpart A of part III of sub-chapter A of chapter 32 is amended by striking out
"Sec. 4084. Belief of farmers from tax in case of gasoline used on the farm,"
and inserting in lieu thereof
"Sec. 4084. Cross references."

(3) The table of sections for subchapter A of chapter 63 is amended by striking out
"Sec. 6206. Special rules applicable to excessive claims under section 6420."
and inserting in lieu thereof
"Sec. 6206. Special rules applicable to excessive claims under sections 6420 and 6421."

(4) The table of sections for subchapter B of chapter 65 is amended by striking out
"Sec. 6421. Cross references."
and inserting in lieu thereof
"Sec. 6421. Gasoline used for certain nonhignway purposes or by local transit systems.
"Sec. 6422. Cross references."

(5) Section 6504 is amended by adding at the end thereof the following:
"(14) Assessments to recover excessive amounts paid under section 6421 (relating to gasoline used for certain nonhighway purposes or by local transit systems) and assessments of civil penalties under section 6675 for excessive claims under section 6121, see section 6206."

(6) Section 6511 (f) is amended by adding at the end thereof the following:
"(6) For limitations in case of payments under section 6421 (relating to gasoline used for certain nonhighway purposes or by local transit systems), see section 6421 (c)."

(7) Section 6612 (c) is amended by striking out "and" before "6420" and by inserting before the period at the end thereof the following: ", and 6421 (relating to payments in the case of gasoline used for certain nonhighway purposes or by local transit systems)".

(8) The table of sections for subchapter B of chapter 68 is amended by striking out
"Sec. 6675. Excessive claims for gasoline used on farms."
and inserting in lieu thereof
"Sec. 6675. Excessive claims with respect to the use of certain gasoline."

◆ Sec. 209. Highway Trust Fund.

(a) CREATION OF TRUST FUND.— There is hereby established in the Treasury of the United States a trust fund to be known as the "Highway Trust Fund" (hereinafter in this section called the "Trust Fund"). The Trust Fund shall consist of such amounts as may be appropriated or credited to the Trust Fund as provided in this section.

(b) DECLARATION OF POLICY.— It is hereby declared to be the policy of the congress that if it hereafter appears—

(1) that the total receipts of the Trust Fund (exclusive of advances under subsection (d)) will be less than the total expenditure from such Fund (exclusive of repayments of such advances); or

(2) that the distribution of the tax burden among the various classes of persons using the Federal-aid highways, or otherwise deriving benefits from such highways, is not equitable, the Congress shall enact legislation in order to bring about a balance of total receipts and total expenditures, or such equitable distribution, as the casee may be

(c) TRANSFER TO TRUST FUND OF AMOUNTS EQUIVALENT TO CERTAIN TAXES.—

(1) IN GENERAL.— There is hereby appropriated to the Trust Fund, out of any money in the Treasury not otherwise appropriated, amounts equivalent to the following percentages of the taxes received in the Treasury before July 1, 1972, under the following provisions of the Internal Revenue Code of 1954 (or under the corresponding provisions of prior revenue laws)—

(A) 100 percent of the taxes received after June 30, 1956, under sections 4041 (taxes on diesel fuel and special motor fuels), 4071 (a) (4) (tax on tread rubber), and 4081 (tax on gasoline);

(B) 20 percent of the tax received after June 30, 1956, and before July 1, 1957, under section 4061 (a) (1) (tax on trucks, buses, etc.);

(C) 50 percent of the tax received after June 30, 1957, under section 4061 (a) (1) (tax on trucks, buses, etc.);

(D) 37 1/2 percent of the tax received after June 30, 1956, and before July 1, 1957, under section 4071 (a) (1) (tax on tires of the type used on highway vehicles);

(E) 100 percent of the taxes received after June 30, 1957, under section 4071 (a) (1), (2), and (3) (taxes on tires of the type used on highway vehicles, other tires, and inner tubes);

(F) 100 percent of the tax received under section 4481 (tax on use of certain vehicles); and

(G) 100 percent of the floor stocks taxes imposed by section 4226 (a).

In the case of any tax described in subparagraph (A), (B), or (D), amounts received during the fiscal year ending June 30, 1957, shall be taken into account only to the extent attributable to liability for tax incurred after June 30, 1956.

(2) LIABILITIES INCURRED BEFORE JULY 1, 1972, FOR NEW OR INCREASED TAXES.— There is hereby appropriated to the Trust Fund, out of any money in the Treasury not otherwise appropriated, amounts equivalent to the following percentages of the taxes which are received in the Treasury after June 30, 1972, and before July 1, 1973, and which are attributable to liability for tax incurred before July 1, 1972, under the following provisions of the Internal Revenue Code of 1954—

(A) 100 percent of the taxes under sections 4041 (taxes on diesel fuel and special motor fuels) 4071 (a) (4) (tax on tread rubber), and 4081 (tax on gasoline);

(B) 20 percent of the tax under section 4061 (a) (1) (tax on trucks, buses, etc.);

(C) 37 1/2 percent of the tax under section 4071 (a) (1) (tax on tires of the type used on highway vehicles); and

(D) 100 percent of the tax under section 4481 (tax on use of certain vehicles).

(3) METHOD OF TRANSFER.— The amounts appropriated by paragraphs (1) and (2) shall be transferred at least monthly from the general fund of the Treasury to the Trust Fund on the basis of estimates by the Secretary of the Treasury of the amounts, referred to in paragraphs (1) and (2), received in the Treasury. Proper adjustments shall be made in the amounts subsequently transferred to the extent prior estimates were in excess of or less than the amounts required to be transferred.

(d) ADDITIONAL APPROPRIATIONS TO TRUST FUND.— There are hereby authorized to be appropriated to the Trust fund, as repayable advances, such additional sums as may be required to make the expenditures referred to in subsection (f).

(e) MANAGEMENT OF TRUST FUND.—

(1) IN GENERAL.— It shall be the duty of the Secretary of the Treasury to hold the Trust Fund, and (after consultation with the Secretary of Commerce) to report to the Congress not later than the first day of March of each year on the financial condition and the results of the operations of the Trust Fund during the preceding fiscal year and on its expected condition and operations during each fiscal year thereafter up to and including the fiscal year ending June

30, 1973. Such report shall be printed as a House document of the session of the Congress to which the report is made.

(2) INVESTMENT.— It shall be the duty of the Secretary of the Treasury to invest such portion of the Trust Fund as is not, in his judgment, required to meet current withdrawals. Such investments may be made only in interest-bearing obligations of the United States or in obligations guaranteed as to both principal and interest by the United States. For such purpose such obligations may be acquired (A) on original issue at par, or (B) by purchase of outstanding obligations at the market price. The purposes for which obligations of the United States may be issued under the Second Liberty Bond Act, as amended, are hereby extended to authorize the issuance at par of special obligations exclusively to the Trust Fund. Such special obligations shall bear interest at a rate equal to the average rate of interest, computed as to the end of the calendar month next preceding the date of such issue, borne by all marketable interest-bearing obligations of the United States then forming a part of the Public Debt; except that where such average rate is not a multiple of one-eighth of 1 percent, the rate of interest of such special obligations shall be the multiple of one-eighth of 1 percent next lower than such average rate. Such special obligations shall be issued only if the Secretary of the Treasury determines that the purchase of other interest-bearing obligations of the United States, or of obligations guaranteed as to both principal and interest by the United States on original issue or at the market price, is not in the public interest. Advances to the Trust Fund pursuant to subsection (d) shall not be invested.

(3) SALE OF OBLIGATIONS.— Any obligation acquired by the Trust Fund (except special obligations issued exclusively to the Trust Fund) maybe sold by the Secretary of the Treasury at the market price, and such special obligations may be redeemed at par plus, accrued interest.

(4) INTEREST AND CERTAIN PROCEEDS.— The interest on, and the proceeds from the sale or redemption of, any obligations held in the Trust Fund shall be credited to and form a part of the Trust Fund.

(f) EXPENDITURES FROM TRUST FUND.—

(1) FEDERAL AID HIGHWAY PROGRAM.—Amounts in the Trust Fund shall be available, as provided by appropriation Acts, for making expenditures after June 30, 1956, and before July 1, 1972, to meet those obligations of the United States heretofore or hereafter incurred under the Federal-Aid Road Act approved July 11, 1916, as amended and supplemented, which are attributable to Federal-aid highways (including those portions of general administrative expenses of the Bureau of Public Roads payable from such appropriations).

(2) REPAYMENT OF ADVANCES FROM GENERAL FUND.— Advances made pursuant to subsection (d) shall be repaid, and interest on such advances shall be paid, to the general fund of the Treasury when the Secretary of the Treasury determines that moneys are available in the Trust Fund for such purposes. Such interest shall be at rates computed in the same manner as provided in subsection (e) (2) for special obligations and shall be compounded annually.

(3) TRANSFERS FROM TRUST FUND FOR GASOLINE USED ON FARMS AND FOR CERTAIN OTHER PURPOSES.— The Secretary of the Treasury shall pay from time to time from the Trust Fund into the general fund of the Treasury amounts equivalent to the amounts paid before July 1, 1973, under sections 6420 (relating to amounts paid in respect or gasoline used on farms) and 6421 (relating to amounts paid in respect of gasoline used for certain nonhighway purposes or by local transit systems) of the Internal Revenue Code of 1954 on the basis of claims filed for periods beginning after June 30, 1956, and ending before July 1, 1972.

(4) FLOOR STOCKS REFUNDS.— The Secretary of the Treasury shall pay from time to time from the Trust Fund into the general fund of the Treasury amounts equivalent to the following percentages of the floor stocks refunds made before July 1, 1973, under section 6412 (a) (2) of the Internal Revenue Code of 1954—

(A) 40 percent of the refunds in respect of articles subject to the tax imposed by section 4061 (a) (1) of such Code (trucks, buses, etc.);

(B) 100 percent of the refunds in respect of articles subject to tax under section 4071 (a) (1) or (4) of such Code (tires of the type used on highway vehicles and tread rubber); and

(C) 66 2/3 percent of the refunds in respect of gasoline subject to tax under section 4081 of such Code.

(g) ADJUSTEMENTS OF APPORTIONMENTS.— The Secretary of the Treasury shall from time to time, after consultation with the Secretary of Commerce, estimate the amounts which will be available in the Highway Trust Fund (excluding repayable advances) to defray the expenditures which will be required to be made from such fund. In any case in which the Secretary of the Treasury determines that, after all other expenditures required to be made from the Highway Trust Fund have teen defrayed, the amounts which will be available in such fund (excluding repayable advances) will be insufficient to defray the expenditures which will be required as a result of the apportionment to the States of the amounts authorized to be appropriated for any fiscal year for the construction, reconstruction, or improvement of the Interstate System, he shall so advise the Secretary of Commerce and shall further advise the Secretary of Commerce as to the amount which, after all other expenditures required to be made from such fund have been defrayed, will be available in such fund (excluding repayable advances) to defray the expenditures required as a result of apportionment to the States of Federal-aid highway funds for the Interstate System for such fiscal year. The Secretary of Commerce shall determine the percentage which such amount is of the amount authorized to be appropriated for such fiscal year for the construction, reconstruction, or improvement of the Interstate System and, notwithstanding any other provision of law, shall thereafter apportion to the States for such fiscal year for the construction, reconstruction, or improvement of the Interstate System, in lieu of the amount which but for the provisions of this subsection would be so apportioned, the amount obtained by multiplying the amount authorized to be appropriated for such fiscal year by such percentage. Whenever the Secretary of the Treasury determines that there will be available in the Highway Trust Fund (excluding repayable advances) amounts which, after all other expenditures, required to be made from such fund have been defrayed, will be available to defray the expenditures required as a result of the apportionment of any Federal-aid highway funds for the Interstate System previously withheld from apportionment for any fiscal year, he shall so advise the Secretary of Commerce and the Secretary of Commerce shall apportion to the States such portion of the funds so withheld from apportionment as the Secretary of the Treasury has advised him may be so apportioned without causing expenditures from the Highway Trust Fund for the Interstate System to exceed amounts available in such fund (excluding repayable advances) to defray such expenditures. Any funds apportioned pursuant to the provisions of the preceding sentence shall remain available for expenditure until the close of the third fiscal year following that in which apportioned.

◆ Sec. 210. Investigation and Report to Congress.

(a) PURPOSE.— The purpose of this section is to make available to the Congress information on the basis of which it may determine what taxes should be imposed by the United States, and in what amounts, in order to assure, insofar as practicable, an equitable distribution of the tax burden among the various classes of persons using the Federal-aid highways or otherwise deriving benefits from such highways.

(b) STUDY AND INVESTIGATION.— In order to carry out the purpose of this section, the Secretary of Commerce is hereby authorized and directed, in cooperation with other Federal officers and agencies (particularly the Interstate Commerce Commission) and with the State highway departments, to make a study and investigation of—

(1) the effects on design, construction, and maintenance of Federal-aid highways of (A) the use of vehicles of different dimensions, weights, and other specifications, and (B) the frequency of occurrences of such vehicles in the traffic stream,

(2) the proportionate share of the design, construction, and maintenance costs of the Federal-aid highways attributable to each class of persons using such highways, such proportionate share to be based on the effects referred to in paragraph (1) and the benefits derived from the use of such highways, and

(3) any direct and indirect benefits accruing to any class which derives benefits from Federal-aid highways, in addition to benefits from actual use of such highways, which are attributable to public expenditures for such highways.

(c) COORDINATION WITH OTHER STUDIES.— The Secretary of Commerce shall coordinate the study and investigation required by this section with—

(1) the research and other activities authorized by section 10 of the Federal-Aid Highway Act of 1954, and

(2) the tests referred to in section 108 (k) of this Act.

(d) REPORTS ON STUDY AND INVESTIGATION.— The Secretary of Commerce shall report to the Congress the results of the study and investigation required by this section. The final report shall be made as soon as possible but in no event later than March 1, 1959. On or before March 1, 1957, and on or before March 1, 1958, the Secretary of Commerce shall report to the Congress the progress that has been made in carrying out the study and investigation required by this section. Each such report shall be printed as a House document of the session of the Congress to which the report is made

(e) FUNDS FOR STUDY AND INVESTIGATION.— There are hereby authorized to be appropriated out of the Highway Trust Fund such sums as may be necessary to enable the Secretary of Commerce to carry out the provisions of this section.

◆ Sec. 211. Effective Date of Title.

This title shall take effect on the date of its enactment, except that the amendments made by sections 202, 203, 204, and 205 shall take effect on July 1, 1956.

Title III— Separability

◆ Sec. 301. Separability.

If any section, subsection, or other provision of this Act or the application thereof to any person or circumstance is held invalid, the remainder of this Act and the application of such section, subsection, or other provision to other persons or circumstances shall not be affected thereby.

EXECUTIVE ORDER

PROVIDING ASSISTANCE FOR THE REMOVAL OF AN OBSTRUCTION OF JUSTICE WITHIN THE STATE OF ARKANSAS

WHEREAS on September 23, 1957, I issued Proclamation No. 3204 reading in part as follows:

> "WHEREAS certain persons in the State of Arkansas, individually and in unlawful assemblages, combinations, and conspiracies, have wilfully obstructed the enforcement of orders of the United States District Court for the Eastern District of Arkansas with respect to matters relating to enrollment and attendance at public schools, particularly at Central High School, located in Little Rock School District, Little Rock, Arkansas; and

> "WHEREAS such wilful obstruction of justice hinders the execution of the laws of that state and of the United States, and makes it impracticable to enforce such laws by the ordinary course of judicial proceedings; and

> "WHEREAS such obstruction of justice constitutes a denial of the equal protection of the laws secured by the Constitution of the United States and impedes the course of justice under those laws:

> "NOW, THEREFORE, I, DWIGHT D. EISENHOWER, President of the United States, under and by virtue of the authority vested in me by the Constitution and statutes of the United States, including Chapter 15 of Title 10 of the United States Code, particularly sections 332, 333 and 334 thereof, do command all persons engaged in such obstruction of justice to cease and desist therefrom, and to disperse forthwith;" and

WHEREAS the command contained in that Proclamation has not been obeyed and wilful obstruction of enforcement of said court orders still exists and threatens to continue:

Executive Order 10730

"The Secretary of Defense is authorized to use such of the armed forces of the United States as he may deem necessary."

Overview

By issuing Executive Order 10730 on September 24, 1957, President Dwight D. Eisenhower sent federal troops to Little Rock, Arkansas, where unruly crowds had prevented the desegregation of all-white Central High School. Not since the period of Reconstruction after the Civil War had federal troops gone to the South to maintain law and order. Many southern leaders angrily protested and said that the federal government was intervening in a matter for which state and local officials had exclusive responsibility. Even though Eisenhower's executive order had the effect of advancing integration, the president was not a strong supporter of civil rights. Instead, he acted because the mob at Central High was interfering with a federal court order to carry out a decision of the U.S. Supreme Court about school desegregation. He declared, "There must be respect for the Constitution—which means the Supreme Court's interpretation of the Constitution—or we shall have chaos" (qtd. in Galambos and van Ee, 2001, vol. 18, p. 322).

Context

Racial segregation and discrimination were common and ugly realities of American life when Eisenhower became president in January 1953. In most southern states, African Americans could not register to vote or serve on juries. Laws and customs barred African Americans from all-white restaurants, hotels, or swimming pools. Public schools were for blacks or whites only. In 1896, in Plessy v. Ferguson, the U.S. Supreme Court decided that these racially separate facilities were constitutional, provided they were equal. Rarely if ever, however, were they equal. Outside the South, racial discrimination was also common, even though it was usually the result of long-standing practice rather than legal requirement. There were segregated schools in Kansas, Delaware, and Massachusetts, just as there were in Mississippi, Virginia, and Texas. In his first State of the Union address in February 1953, Eisenhower declared that "discrimination against minorities" was a national problem arising from the "persistence of distrust and of fear" (Eisenhower, vol. 1953, p. 30).

On May 17, 1954, the Supreme Court struck a major blow against racial segregation in *Brown v. Board of Education*. In a unanimous ruling, the Court reversed the decision in *Plessy v. Ferguson* and declared that "separate but equal" schools were unconstitutional (qtd. in Pach and Richardson, p. 141). A year later, in May 1955, the court issued a second ruling, popularly known as *Brown II*, which called for the desegregation of public schools "with all deliberate speed" (qtd. in Pach and Richardson, p. 143). This instruction was confusing and contradictory, since "deliberate" contradicts "speed." The language was the result of an uneasy compromise among the justices, who hoped that by not imposing a deadline for compliance, they would encourage communities with segregated schools to accept their decision and carry it out within a reasonable period of time.

Despite this hope, many white southerners were furious. On March 12, 1956, nineteen U.S. senators and seventy-seven members of the House of Representatives signed the "Southern Manifesto," which condemned the Supreme Court for using "naked power" to intervene in a matter of states' rights and called for the reversal of the *Brown* decision. The Southern Manifesto also asserted that the Court's decision was "destroying the amicable relations between the white and Negro races that have been created through ninety years of patient effort by the good people of both races" (http://www.strom.clemson.edu/strom/manifesto.html). White citizens councils organized throughout the South to mobilize resistance to the Court's ruling and to intimidate local officials who did comply. As a result, most local school boards emphasized "deliberate" rather than "speed." They moved slowly, if at all, to desegregate all-white schools.

Little Rock, Arkansas, was one community that did comply, by preparing a plan for the gradual integration of its schools. In 1955 the local school board proposed to admit blacks to previously all-white schools in stages over a period of five to seven years. The first step would be the desegregation of Central High School in September 1957. The board members hoped that this plan for gradual action would satisfy African Americans, who wanted an end to racial discrimination, as well as most whites, who said they needed time to adjust to a major social change.

The plan, however, produced opposition. The local chapter of the National Association for the Advancement of Col-

Time Line

1896

■ **May 18**
In *Plessy v. Ferguson* the U.S. Supreme Court upholds the constitutionality of "separate but equal" public facilities for blacks and whites.

1954

■ **May 17**
The Supreme Court rules in the case of *Brown v. Board of Education* that racial segregation in public schools is unconstitutional.

1955

■ **May 31**
In the *Brown II* decision the Supreme Court instructs district courts to implement the 1954 decision to desegregate public schools.

1956

■ **March 12**
Members of the U.S. House and Senate release the Southern Manifesto.

■ **August 28**
A federal district judge rejects the NAACP challenge to the Little Rock school desegregation plan.

1957

■ **April 26**
A U.S. Circuit Court of Appeals affirms the district court ruling.

■ **September 4**
Arkansas National Guard troops surround Central High School and prevent its desegregation.

■ **September 14**
Eisenhower and Governor Faubus meet in Newport, Rhode Island, and seem to reach agreement about how to handle the Little Rock crisis.

■ **September 20**
Faubus removes the National Guard from Central High.

■ **September 23**
A violent mob forces African Americans to leave Central High.

■ **September 24**
President Eisenhower issues Executive Order 10730.

ored People (NAACP) filed a lawsuit to force more rapid integration of Little Rock's schools. On August 28, 1956, a federal district judge ruled against the NAACP. A U.S. Circuit Court of Appeals affirmed that decision on April 26, 1957. As the beginning of the school year approached, a local citizens council charged that "white and Negro revolutionaries" from the NAACP were responsible for the plan to desegregate Central High and threatened to "shed blood if necessary to stop this work of Satan" (Freyer, p. 81).

Governor Orval Faubus met secretly with the leaders of the citizens councils and decided to support them. Faubus had been a moderate on racial issues, and he said publicly that school issues were local matters. But he concluded that he could not win a third term as governor in 1958 without the support of white segregationists, whose voices were increasingly prominent in the aftermath of the *Brown* decisions. The governor maintained that he was concerned about the possibility of violence at Central High and so favored a delay in implementing the Little Rock desegregation plan. But after a judge for the U.S. District Court for the Eastern District of Arkansas rejected that argument, Faubus ordered the Arkansas National Guard to Little Rock. On September 4, the troops prevented the nine African American students who were supposed to start classes at Central High from entering the school.

The governor's actions created a constitutional crisis. Faubus was a state official who had defied a federal court. Eisenhower informed the governor that he had taken an oath when he became president to defend the Constitution and would do so "by every legal means" available (Eisenhower, vol. 1957, p. 659). Eisenhower, however, wished to avoid a showdown. Although he believed in the principles of equal opportunity and equality before the law, he did not support the *Brown* decision. He thought that the Supreme Court, in trying to achieve "school integration," might also cause "social disintegration" if white supporters of segregation resorted to violence (qtd. in Pach and Richardson, p. 143). He insisted that segregation and discrimination could not be eradicated by government action; what was necessary instead was a change in people's hearts and minds. Because of this outlook, Eisenhower offered very limited support to the civil rights movement. Because of his commitment to gradual change, he wished to avoid a confrontation in Little Rock between federal and state authorities.

Faubus, too, sought a negotiated solution to the crisis. On September 14, he met with Eisenhower, who was vacationing in Newport, Rhode Island. The president knew that federal authority would ultimately prevail over state power, but he thought the crisis could be resolved more easily if Faubus avoided a humiliating, public defeat. He suggested that the governor change the orders of the National Guard from preventing desegregation to preserving public order at Central High. Faubus seemed to accept this solution but, after returning to Arkansas, decided instead to remove the National Guard from the school. Eisenhower was irate that Faubus appeared to have broken his word. The police in Little Rock were no match for the angry mob of over a thousand people that gathered at Central High on September 23. The mob forced the nine black students, who had entered through a side door, to return home because of the danger of violence. Later that day, Eisenhower released a proclamation requiring the members of these "unlawful assemblages" to "cease and desist." But the next morning, an even larger mob surrounded Central High. Eisenhower then issued Executive Order 10730 authorizing the dispatch of federal troops to Little Rock.

About the Author

Dwight David Eisenhower was born in Denison, Texas, on October 14, 1890, and grew up in Abilene, Kansas, where his family had moved only months after he was born. He graduated from the U.S. Military Academy at West Point in 1915, but his career as an officer in the U.S. Army began slowly. It took almost a decade until he gained recognition from his superiors. He served as a military aide in the 1920s to General John J. Pershing, the commander of U.S. forces in World War I, and in the 1930s to General Douglas MacArthur in the Philippines. He returned to the United States in 1939, earned a promotion to brigadier general two years later, and then went to Washington, D.C., shortly after the Japanese attack on Pearl Harbor in 1941 to help in planning U.S. strategy in World War II.

During the war, Eisenhower led Allied forces to victory. He commanded the invasions of North Africa in 1942 and of Italy in 1943. As Supreme Allied Commander, he gave the order for the D-day invasion on June 6, 1944, that began the liberation of Nazi-occupied France. By the time he accepted the German surrender in Europe on May 8, 1945, he had become one of the greatest war leaders in American history.

After the war, Eisenhower served as army chief of staff (1945–1948) and president of Columbia University (1948–1950). In 1951, after the outbreak of the Korean War, he returned to active duty as the first commander of the armed forces of the North Atlantic Treaty Organization. In 1952, he decided to leave that command to campaign for the Republican nomination for president. He capitalized on his reputation as a war hero and his winning personality to win the nomination and the election in November. Millions of voters agreed with his campaign slogan: "I like Ike."

As president, Eisenhower gave highest priority to fighting the cold war. He believed that the Soviet Union posed a threat not only to U.S. security but also to U.S. values and principles. To meet this global challenge, he increased U.S. nuclear strength, ordered the Central Intelligence Agency to overthrow governments in Iran, Guatemala, and Indonesia that he considered hostile or dangerous, and launched a vigorous campaign to win the hearts and minds of peoples in the emerging third world nations of Africa and Asia to prevent them from turning to Communism. He agreed to an armistice in July 1953 that ended the fighting in Korea, and he was determined to avoid major wars that would strain the U.S. economy and weaken American efforts to contain Soviet influence. While making vigorous efforts to stop the spread of Communism, Eisenhower also hoped to improve

Time Line

1958

■ **May 27**
Ernest Green becomes the first African American graduate of Central High School.

■ **September 29**
In *Cooper v. Aaron* the Supreme Court rejects the Little Rock school board's appeal for a postponement of its school desegregation plan; Governor Faubus closes the Little Rock high schools for the 1958–1959 school year.

Soviet-American relations and to curb the arms race between the two nations. He met with the Soviet leader, Nikita Khrushchev, in Geneva in July 1955—the first U.S.-Soviet summit since the end of World War II—and held two more meetings with the Soviet premier in 1959 and 1960. But the president's hopes for a nuclear test ban treaty evaporated when the Soviets shot down an American U-2 spy plane over their territory on May 1, 1960, just days before Eisenhower and Khrushchev met in Paris.

In domestic affairs, the president's approach was "middle-way Republicanism." Eisenhower was a moderate conservative at a time when the Republican Party had many strong conservatives who wished to severely reduce or even eliminate programs for social welfare or regulation of the economy enacted during the New Deal of President Franklin D. Roosevelt (1933–1945) or the Fair Deal of President Harry S. Truman (1945–1953). Although Eisenhower worried that "big government" programs might diminish individual freedom and personal responsibility, he also feared that political conflict and even social chaos might occur if the federal government did not provide for Americans in need. While Eisenhower was president, Social Security benefits were expanded to cover payments to disabled workers. In 1956 the president signed legislation that established the interstate highway system. In 1957 and 1960, Eisenhower approved new civil rights acts—the first such legislation since Reconstruction—and he also ordered an end to racial discrimination in federal facilities in Washington, D.C. But he opposed vigorous government efforts to end segregation in public schools or other discriminatory practices and instead favored gradual change.

Eisenhower was an extremely popular president. He easily won reelection in 1956, and his approval rating in the polls never fell below 60 percent. After leaving the White House in 1961, he retired to his farm at Gettysburg, Pennsylvania. He died on March 28, 1969.

Explanation and Analysis of the Document

An executive order is an official directive from the president that has the force of law and that describes certain

President Dwight Eisenhower is shown here in a 1958 photograph with several African American civil rights leaders, including Martin Luther King, Jr. (on Eisenhower's right) and A. Philip Randolph (on Eisenhower's left).
(AP Photo)

actions that members of the executive branch should take to enforce the law. Because it is primarily a legal document, an executive order usually lacks the inspiring language that a president might use in a speech to try to explain issues to the American people or to win their support for a program. Instead, it contains references to the specific legal basis for the president's actions and precise instructions about how to carry them out.

Eisenhower begins with a reference to a proclamation he had issued the previous day about the riots that occurred after nine African American students entered Central High School in Little Rock. Once word spread that the students were inside the school, the mob became violent and attacked four African American journalists. School authorities sent the students home in the middle of the day so that they, too, would not become the victims of mob violence. Eisenhower issued his proclamation at the end of that harrowing day and also released a public statement. In the statement, he expressed his distress over the day's "disgraceful occurrences" and pledged that he would not let a

"mob of extremists" obstruct law and order in Little Rock. He also promised to use "the full power of the United States," including "whatever force might be necessary … to carry out the orders of the Federal Court." He added, however, "It will be a sad day for this country—both at home and abroad—if school children can safely attend their classes only under the protection of armed guards" (Eisenhower, vol. 1957, p. 689).

Eisenhower continues (paragraphs 2–4) by quoting the proclamation that explains the reasons for the action he is about to take. He uses precise, legal language in these paragraphs that begin with "whereas." He makes clear that the crowd that had driven the nine African American students from Central High had not conducted a legitimate, legal demonstration. The Constitution guarantees the right to peaceful protest. What happened in Little Rock, however, was an "unlawful" assemblage that had engaged in "obstruction of justice." Those who had participated in the mob that surrounded Central High had violated federal and state law, Eisenhower declares. Their actions had also

> "I hereby authorize and direct the Secretary of Defense to order into active military service of the United States as he may deem appropriate to carry out the purposes of this Order, any or all units of the National Guard of the United States and of the Air National Guard of the United States within the State of Arkansas to serve in the active military service of the United States for an indefinite period and until relieved by appropriate orders."
>
> (Paragraph 8)

> "The Secretary of Defense is authorized and directed to take all appropriate steps to enforce any orders of the United States District Court for the Eastern District of Arkansas for the removal of obstruction of justice in the State of Arkansas with respect to matters relating to enrollment and attendance at public schools in the Little Rock School District, Little Rock, Arkansas."
>
> (Paragraph 9)

> "In furtherance of the enforcement of the aforementioned orders of the United States District Court for the Eastern District of Arkansas, the Secretary of Defense is authorized to use such of the armed forces of the United States as he may deem necessary."
>
> (Paragraph 10)

denied to the black students the constitutional guarantee of "the equal protection of the laws." That last phrase comes from the Fourteenth Amendment to the Constitution, adopted in 1868 and designed to ensure that African Americans, most of whom had lived in slavery until the end of the Civil War in 1865, would enjoy the rights of citizenship and "the equal protection of the laws."

In paragraph 5, the president quotes the action that he had taken in the previous day's proclamation. He refers to specific sections of the U.S. Code, a compilation of federal law. The sections that Eisenhower cites deal with the president's authority to protect the rights of citizens in states where violations of law and order, such as domestic violence or insurrection, prevent the enforcement of federal or state law. Title 10, section 334 of the U.S. Code requires the president to issue a proclamation ordering those people who are obstructing justice through their violent actions to stop immediately. That is precisely what

Eisenhower does when he commands those persons "to cease and desist therefrom, and to disperse forthwith."

Further action, however, was necessary. As Eisenhower explains in paragraph 6, his proclamation had not ended the mob violence at Central High. On September 24, the morning after he issued the proclamation, there were even more people at the Little Rock high school who were determined to prevent its desegregation. As a result, Eisenhower was taking further action on the basis of specific sections in the U.S. Code that he cites in paragraph 7. Section 332 gives him authority to use the armed forces to restore order. Section 333 provides authorization to act if state authorities "are unable, fail, or refuse" to ensure people's constitutional and legal rights (http://caselaw.lp.findlaw.com/casecode/uscodes/10/subtitles/a/parts/i/chapters/15/sections/section_333.html). Because Faubus had not met his obligation to protect the rights of the African American students, Eisenhower was using his powers under federal law

Members of the so-called Little Rock Nine gather on the steps of Central High School in Little Rock in 1997 along with President Bill Clinton, top right; Arkansas governor Mike Huckabee, center; and Little Rock mayor Jim Daley.
(AP Photo/Danny Johnston)

to do so. Throughout his executive order, the president uses the exact language of the sections of the U.S. Code on which he is relying.

In paragraphs 8–11, Eisenhower orders military forces to Arkansas. Their mission is to prevent interference with the U.S. district court order concerning Central High School. Eisenhower gives the secretary of defense the authority to rely on National Guard troops as well as units of the U.S. Army. The secretary used that authority to dispatch to Little Rock soldiers from the 101st Airborne Division, a combat unit that had served in the D-day invasion of Nazi-occupied France during World War II. The soldiers in the 101st Airborne left their base at Fort Campbell, Kentucky, and arrived in Little Rock just hours after the president issued his executive order. Eisenhower places no time limit on the deployment of these troops; his executive order allows them to serve for "an indefinite period."

Audience

Eisenhower wrote for both a limited and a large audience. His executive order was an official document that gave authorization to the secretary of defense and other government officials to dispatch federal troops and National Guard units to Little Rock to enforce the law. It was also a public document that informed millions of Americans—and people around the world—that the president was taking strong action to ensure compliance with the law. Eisenhower worried that the Soviets were exploiting the turmoil in Little Rock to gain a propaganda advantage in the cold war by arguing that the realities of American life fell far short of the ideals of freedom and equality. Extensive television and newspaper coverage of the vicious mobs in Little Rock made people around the world keenly aware of American racism. Eisenhower hoped that his executive order would help restore America's tarnished image. The Voice of America broadcast news about the executive order and the deployment of troops to dozens of nations.

Impact

On the evening of September 24, Eisenhower gave a televised address to explain why he had issued his executive order. He said that he had no alternative to sending in troops because of the "disorderly mobs" led by "demagogic extremists" and the failure of local authorities to restore law and order. If he had not acted in these "extraordinary and compelling circumstances," the result would have been "anarchy." Eisenhower emphasized that the troops' mission was not to speed integration but to make sure that "mob rule" would not "override the decisions of our courts" (http://historymatters.gmu.edu/d/6335/).

Eisenhower did not say that school desegregation was a matter of civil rights or equal rights. Instead, he complained that events in Little Rock had damaged America's international prestige in the cold war competition with communism. "Our enemies are gloating over this incident and using it everywhere to misrepresent our whole nation," he asserted. "We are portrayed as a violator of those standards of conduct which the peoples of the world united to proclaim in the Charter of the United Nations." He called on the people of Arkansas to help in ending the trouble at Central High so that the federal troops could be withdrawn and the "blot upon the fair name and high honor of our nation in the world will be removed" (Eisenhower, vol. 1957, pp. 689–694). While some Americans praised Eisenhower's actions, there was also furious criticism. Faubus maintained that Arkansas was "occupied territory." Senator Richard Russell, a Democrat from Georgia, claimed that the soldiers in Little Rock were using the same tactics as "Hitler's storm troopers" (qtd. in Pach and Richardson, p. 154).

The troops restored order, but the situation did not return to normal at Central High during 1957–1958. Troops escorted the African American students to class. The soldiers of the 101st Airborne Division left Central High in late November, but National Guard troops under federal command remained until the end of the school year. The Little Rock Nine, as the black students were known, attracted international attention for their courage and commitment. In May 1958, Ernest Green, the only senior in the Little Rock Nine, became the first African American graduate of Central High.

Central High and all the other public high schools in Little Rock were closed during the 1958–1959 school year. The local school board asked for a delay of two years before continuing its desegregation plan. In *Cooper v. Aaron* the Supreme Court unanimously rejected its petition for delay on September 29. Faubus instead closed all four Little Rock high schools during 1958–1959. His decision helped him win reelection in 1958 and again in the next three elections. Eisenhower took no action to reopen the schools because there were no disorderly mobs or angry protests. Once more his goal was to preserve public order, not to promote integration. The Little Rock schools reopened in September 1959, and a few African American students attended two local high schools. Some parents, however, enrolled their children in a new, private all-white high school. The pace of school desegregation in Little Rock and in the South was extremely slow while Eisenhower was president. When he left the White House, less than 1 percent of African American students in the Deep South attended integrated schools. The percentage did not rise significantly until the last half of the 1960s.

It is ironic that Eisenhower used federal troops to enforce a court order concerning school desegregation. Eisenhower was not a vigorous supporter of civil rights. He had lived much of his life in states where racial segregation was common. Until the very end of his military career, the U.S. Army had separate black and white units. Eisenhower was uncomfortable in dealing with racial issues. He never spoke out in favor of civil rights as an urgent national issue; he thought the federal government had only limited powers to eliminate racial injustice. He was sympathetic to white southerners who said that advocates of equal rights under the law were demanding too much too soon. In the fall of 1956, when the governor of Texas used the National Guard to remove African-American students from previously all-white schools in Texarkana and Mansfield, Eisenhower condemned "extremists on both sides" but refused to take further action. When discussing civil rights at a news conference in July 1957—just weeks before the Little Rock crisis—Eisenhower declared, "I can't imagine any set of circumstances that would ever induce me to send Federal troops … into any area to enforce the orders of a Federal court, because I believe [the] common sense of America will never require it" (qtd. in Pach and Richardson, p. 150).

Still, by issuing his executive order, Eisenhower became the first president since Reconstruction to do precisely that. He took this step because he knew that he had taken an oath as president "to preserve, protect, and defend the Constitution." Although he had reservations about the *Brown* decision, he understood that the Supreme Court was the final authority in interpreting the Constitution. Failure to abide by the Supreme Court's decision would produce chaos. He issued the executive order not to promote desegregation but to insure that the order of a federal court and the laws of the land were faithfully executed.

Related Documents

Eisenhower, Dwight David. *Public Papers of the President of the United States: Dwight D. Eisenhower*. 8 vols. Washington, D.C.: U.S. Government Printing Office, 1958–1961. These annual volumes contain Eisenhower's speeches, remarks at news conferences, messages to Congress, and other public documents of his presidency.

Galambos, Louis, and Daun van Ee, eds. *The Papers of Dwight D. Eisenhower*. Vols. 14–17: *The Presidency: The Middle Way*. Baltimore: Johns Hopkins University Press, 1996. These volumes contain the letters, memoranda, and diary entries that Eisenhower wrote during his first term as president.

———. *The Papers of Dwight D. Eisenhower*. Vols. 18–21: *The Presidency: Keeping the Peace*. Baltimore: Johns Hopkins University Press, 2001. These volumes contain the letters, memoranda, and diary entries that Eisenhower wrote during his second term as president.

"The Integration of Little Rock Central." Vanity Fair Web site. http://www.vanityfair.com/politics/features/2007/09/littlerock_slide

show200709. Accessed on January 10, 2008. This photographic essay focuses on Elizabeth Eckford, one of the nine African American students who attended Central High in 1957, and what the school year was like before and after the deployment of federal troops.

"The Southern Manifesto." March 12, 1956. Strom Thurmond Institute of Government and Public Affairs, Clemson University Web site. http://www.strom.clemson.edu/strom/manifesto.html. Accessed on January 10, 2008. This manifesto, signed by 101 of the South's 128 congressional members, denounced the Supreme Court's decision in *Brown v. Board of Education* and pledged to bring about a reversal of the decision.

U.S. Army. "Guardians of Freedom: 50th Anniversary of Operation Arkansas." http://www.army.mil/arkansas/index.html. Accessed on January 10, 2008. This Web site contains a variety of documents related to the Little Rock crisis, including messages from President Eisenhower and Governor Faubus and reports from U.S. Army officials in Little Rock.

Bibliography

■ Books

Ambrose, Stephen E. *Eisenhower*. Vol. 2: *The President*. New York: Simon and Schuster, 1984.

Burk, Robert Frederick. *The Eisenhower Administration and Black Civil Rights*. Knoxville: University of Tennessee Press, 1984.

Duram, James. C. *A Moderate among Extremists: Dwight D. Eisenhower and the School Desegregation Crisis*. Chicago: Nelson-Hall, 1981.

Freyer, Tony A. *Little Rock on Trial*: Cooper v. Aaron *and School Desegregation*. Lawrence: University Press of Kansas, 2007.

Jacoway, Elizabeth. *Turn Away Thy Son: Little Rock, the Crisis That Shocked the Nation*. New York: Free Press, 2007.

Pach, Chester J., Jr., and Elmo Richardson. *The Presidency of Dwight D. Eisenhower*, rev. ed. Lawrence: University Press of Kansas, 1991.

Patterson, James T. Brown v. Board of Education: *A Civil Rights Milestone and Its Troubled Legacy*. New York: Oxford University Press, 2001.

■ Web Sites

The Dwight D. Eisenhower Presidential Library and Museum Web site.
    http://www.eisenhower.archives.gov. Accessed on January 10, 2008.

"Dwight David Eisenhower (1890–1969)." Miller Center of Public Affairs "American President: An Online Reference Resource" Web site.
    http://www.millercenter.virginia.edu/academic/americanpresident/eisenhower. Accessed on January 10, 2008.

The Little Rock Nine Web site.
    http://www.centralhigh57.org/The_Little_Rock_Nine.html#index.html. Accessed on January 10, 2008.

Margolick, David. "Through a Lens, Darkly." Vanity Fair Web site. http://www.vanityfair.com/politics/features/2007/09/littlerock200709. Accessed on February 27, 2008.

"'Mob Rule Cannot Be Allowed to Override the Decisions of Our Courts': President Dwight D. Eisenhower's 1957 Address on Little Rock, Arkansas." History Matters Web site.
    http://historymatters.gmu.edu/d/6335/. Accessed on February 27, 2008.

"U.S. Code. Title 10. Section 333: Interference with State and Federal Law." FindLaw Web site.
    http://caselaw.lp.findlaw.com/casecode/uscodes/10/subtitles/a/parts/i/chapters/15/sections/section_333.html. Accessed on February 27, 2008.

—By Chester Pach

Questions for Further Study

1. Why did Eisenhower send troops to Little Rock? How important were each of the following: his desire to maintain public order, his commitment to civil rights, his understanding of his responsibilities as president, his concern about the international effects of the disturbances at Central High? What do you think was the primary reason for his decision?

2. Eisenhower insisted that government action could not eliminate racial discrimination unless there was a change in public attitudes and people accepted the idea of equal rights. Do you think he was right? What should government do to eliminate racial injustice? How important are individual attitudes on racial issues in ensuring fairness and equality for all Americans?

3. Eisenhower's decision to send troops to Little Rock was extremely controversial; it elicited praise and provoked angry denunciations. Explain how you think each of the following reacted to Eisenhower's action and the reasons for their views: Arkansas governor Orval Faubus, a member of the Little Rock Nine, a white student at Central High, and a member of the 101st Airborne Division.

4. The school year of 1957–1958 was an extraordinary one for the Little Rock Nine. Use the documents, Web sites, and books and articles in the bibliography to gather information about what the school year was like for members of the Little Rock Nine. What were their most difficult experiences? What were their most rewarding experiences? What lessons did they learn from that school year? How did their experiences affect the rest of their lives?

Glossary

assemblages	gatherings of people
cease and desist	a legal term meaning "to stop an activity and not to engage in it in the future"
conspiracies	a group of persons that join together for illegal purposes
forthwith	right now; immediately
impracticable	impossible to effect or do
obstruction of justice	the crime of interfering with the work of law officers or legal authorities
United States Code	a compilation of federal law arranged by subject
whereas	in view of the fact that; considering that

EXECUTIVE ORDER 10730

Providing assistance for the removal of an obstruction of justice within the state of Arkansas.

WHEREAS on September 23, 1957, I issued Proclamation No. 3204 reading in part as follows:

WHEREAS certain persons in the state of Arkansas, individually and in unlawful assemblages, combinations, and conspiracies, have willfully obstructed the enforcement of orders of the United States District Court for the Eastern District of Arkansas with respect to matters relating to enrollment and attendance at public schools, particularly at Central High School, located in Little Rock School District, Little Rock, Arkansas; and

WHEREAS such willful obstruction of justice hinders the execution of the laws of that State and of the United States, and makes it impracticable to enforce such laws by the ordinary course of judicial proceedings; and

WHEREAS such obstruction of justice constitutes a denial of the equal protection of the laws secured by the Constitution of the United States and impedes the course of justice under those laws:

NOW, THEREFORE, I, DWIGHT D. EISENHOWER, President of the United States, under and by virtue of the authority vested in me by the Constitution and Statutes of the United States, including Chapter 15 of Title 10 of the United States Code, particularly sections 332, 333 and 334 thereof, do command all persons engaged in such obstruction of justice to cease and desist therefrom, and to disperse forthwith; and

WHEREAS the command contained in that Proclamation has not been obeyed and willful obstruction of enforcement of said court orders still exists and threatens to continue:

NOW, THEREFORE, by virtue of the authority vested in me by the Constitution and Statutes of the

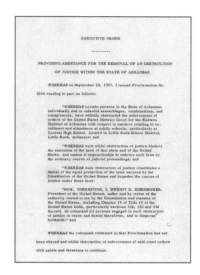

United States, including Chapter 15 of Title 10, particularly sections 332, 333 and 334 thereof, and section 301 of Title 3 of the United States Code, It is hereby ordered as follows:

SECTION 1. I hereby authorize and direct the Secretary of Defense to order into the active military service of the United States as he may deem appropriate to carry out the purposes of this Order, any or all of the units of the National Guard of the United States and of the Air National Guard of the United States within the State of Arkansas to serve in the active military service of the United States for an indefinite period and until relieved by appropriate orders.

SEC. 2. The Secretary of Defense is authorized and directed to take all appropriate steps to enforce any orders of the United States District Court for the Eastern District of Arkansas for the removal of obstruction of justice in the State of Arkansas with respect to matters relating to enrollment and attendance at public schools in the Little Rock School District, Little Rock, Arkansas. In carrying out the provisions of this section, the Secretary of Defense is authorized to use the units, and members thereof, ordered into the active military service of the United States pursuant to Section 1 of this Order.

SEC. 3. In furtherance of the enforcement of the aforementioned orders of the United States District Court for the Eastern District of Arkansas, the Secretary of Defense is authorized to use such of the armed forces of the United States as he may deem necessary.

SEC. 4. The Secretary of Defense is authorized to delegate to the Secretary of the Army or the Secretary of the Air Force, or both, any of the authority conferred upon him by this Order.

Dwight D. Eisenhower

The White House, September 24, 1957.

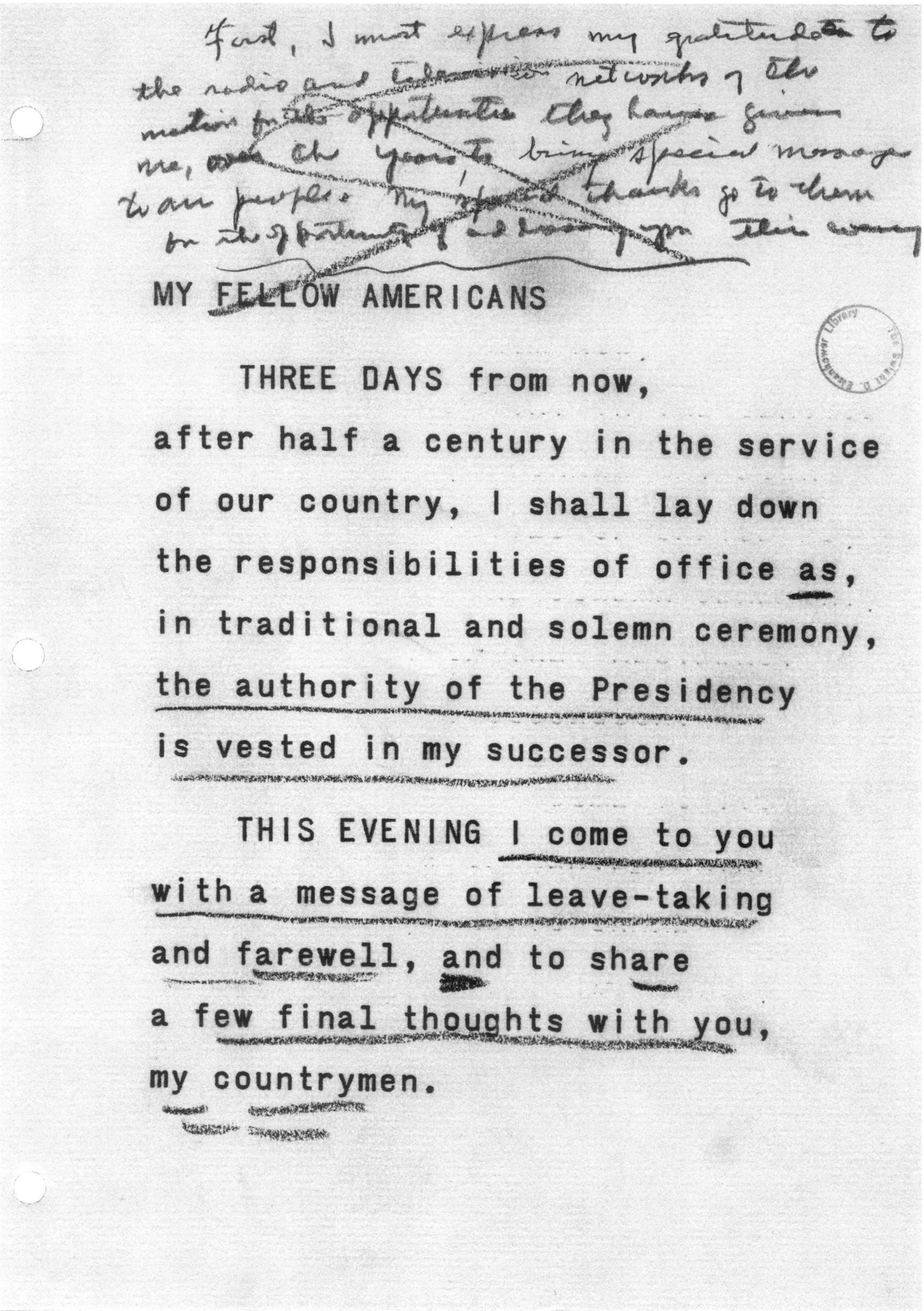

[handwritten text, partially struck through]
First, I must express my gratitude to
the radio and television networks of the
nation for the opportunities they have given
me, over the years to bring special messages
to our people. My special thanks go to them
for the opportunity of addressing you this evening

MY FELLOW AMERICANS

THREE DAYS from now,
after half a century in the service
of our country, I shall lay down
the responsibilities of office as,
in traditional and solemn ceremony,
the authority of the Presidency
is vested in my successor.

THIS EVENING I come to you
with a message of leave-taking
and farewell, and to share
a few final thoughts with you,
my countrymen.

Dwight D. Eisenhower's Farewell Address (National Archives and Records Administration)

DWIGHT D. EISENHOWER'S FAREWELL ADDRESS

"We must guard against the acquisition of unwarranted influence ... by the military-industrial complex."

Overview

On January 17, 1961, President Dwight D. Eisenhower, the onetime five-star general who had by then honed his skills and charisma as a consummate television communicator, gave his final televised speech from the Oval Office. One main purpose of his address was to powerfully remind the nation that of four catastrophic wars in the twentieth century, three had seen the United States embroiled in the conflict. This Eisenhower conversation piece came to be known as the "military-industrial complex" speech, as that term became popularized by his use of it here. The eye-catching and headline-grabbing portions of the speech focus on the cold war, on the confrontational positioning of the United States and the Iron Curtain countries, and on American, free-world democracy needing to strongly confront the threats and challenges of Communism.

Less publicized, and thus much less well known, in this farewell speech are fragments that read as being more applicable to the twenty-first century than to the twentieth. The notion of protecting American resources—"We cannot mortgage the material assets of our grandchildren"—is modernistic and could be interpreted as being related to conservation and ecological issues. Also of interest are Eisenhower's musings on battling fear and hate with trust and respect. Coming from a distinguished soldier and war leader, his demand that disarmament be seen as a "continuing imperative" is especially noteworthy.

Context

During President Eisenhower's two terms of office, Communism was seen not as some distant political storm cloud but as a menacing presence that threatened the American way of life. In early 1954 the Wisconsin senator Joseph R. McCarthy became a mass-media sensation as he launched a series of attacks on and investigations into members of the Communist Party of United States of America. While McCarthy quickly earned infamy, Congress nevertheless proceeded to outlaw the Communist Party in America.

To strengthen American's posture in opposition to the Union of Soviet Socialist Republics (USSR), Eisenhower and his secretary of state, John Foster Dulles, effectively created a geographic Communist buffer zone with the setting up of the Southeast Asia Treaty Organization in September 1954. This organization comprised the United States, France, Great Britain, Australia, New Zealand, the Philippines, Thailand, and Pakistan. Earlier that year, Eisenhower, with nearly forty years of military experience under his belt, had cautiously avoided providing military support for France in the battle of Dien Bien Phu; France lost its imperial colony of Indochina when Ho Chi Minh and his guerillas triumphed in May.

Technological and scientific advances accomplished by the Soviet Union led to its taking the lead in space exploration; on October 4, 1957, the USSR successfully launched the first man-made satellite to orbit the earth, *Sputnik 1*. The United States responded vigorously, with the National Aeronautics and Space Administration being established in 1958 under Eisenhower's watch. America's catching up with and eventually surpassing Soviet expertise in space technology can be traced to the reactive role of this organization.

The tension between the United States and the Soviet Union seemingly eased in 1959 with the Soviet premier Nikita S. Khrushchev's visit to Camp David, Maryland. However, Fidel Castro's rise to power in Cuba in 1959, his eventual embrace of Communism, and the Soviet shooting down of a U.S. spy plane over the USSR in May 1960 escalated tensions. These and other events set the scene for an early 1960s standoff situation between the United States and the Soviet Union. Eisenhower was unequivocal in deeming Communism a pernicious influence, remarking in his farewell speech, "We face a hostile ideology."

About the Author

Dwight David Eisenhower, later nicknamed "Ike," was born in Denison, Texas, and brought up in Abilene, Kansas. He was the third of seven sons. A childhood passion for sports led to his becoming a well-regarded athlete at Abilene High School, where he graduated in 1909.

1956

- **October 23–November 10**
Hungarian Revolution of 1956, led by students and workers; an estimated twenty-five thousand Hungarians and seven thousand Russians are killed.

1957

- **October 4**
Sputnik I, the first man-made satellite to orbit the earth, is launched by the Soviet Union, essentially extending the cold war to outer space.

1959

- **January 1**
General Fulgencio Batista y Zaldívar flees from Cuba to refuge in the Dominican Republic after being defeated by leftist guerillas led by Fidel Castro.

- **February 16**
Castro becomes prime minister of Cuba.

- **March 28**
Having crushed the Tibetan revolt, Chinese Communists dissolve the government of Tibet.

- **May 24**
John Foster Dulles, Dwight D. Eisenhower's secretary of state, dies; Eisenhower subsequently assumes a more assertive diplomatic role, visiting some twenty-seven countries before his 1961 retirement.

1960

- **May 1**
A U-2 reconnaissance plane piloted by Francis Gary Powers, of the United States, is shot down over the Soviet Union.

- **July 5**
Crisis unfolds in Congo following that country's gaining independence from Belgium as black soldiers mutiny against white officers.

1961

- **January 17**
Eisenhower gives his Farewell Address.

Athletics, particularly football, sustained Eisenhower at West Point, where in his 1915 graduating class he was only sixty-first in academic standing; of note is the fact that this graduating class produced no fewer than fifty-nine future generals. Eisenhower later demonstrated his full education potential at the Command and General Staff College, at Fort Leavenworth, Kansas, where as a major in 1926 he graduated first in a class of 275. In 1933 he became an aide to General Douglas MacArthur, chief of staff of the U.S. Army, eventually serving with MacArthur in the Philippines. By March 1941 Eisenhower was a full colonel, and later that year he was made chief of staff to the commander of the Third U.S. Army. He caught the eye of General George C. Marshall, chief of staff of the U.S. Army during World War II, who in 1942 selected Eisenhower to be commander of U.S. troops in Europe. This directed Eisenhower toward his crowning military glory as commander of the Allied troops and architect of the Normandy invasion, which was launched on June 6, 1944.

After the war, Eisenhower served for two years as army chief of staff, followed by a stint as president of Columbia University. In 1952 the famous soldier, helped by his wife, Mamie, and his cheerful, homespun personality, entered the political arena and won the presidency by an electoral vote of 442–89. Four years later Eisenhower had little difficulty retaining his position in the White House, comfortably garnering 57 percent of the popular vote.

Eisenhower's presidential terms fell in the thick of the cold war with the Soviet Union and were thus marked by a philosophy, robustly shaped by Secretary of State John Foster Dulles, aimed at combating Communist expansion, in part by rattling the saber of nuclear deterrent. Eisenhower's internal policies were relatively modest, featuring some expansion of the Social Security System but very limited progress with respect to civil rights. Upon his retirement Congress reestablished his rank of general, and he retired to Gettysburg, Pennsylvania, where he wrote several books.

In his later years, Eisenhower received mixed reviews from political commentators and analysts. While his war achievements were considerable, the arrival on the American stage of John F. Kennedy recast the ideal persona of the American president as one of youthful charisma and physicality. Nevertheless, Eisenhower's reputation waxed into the twenty-first century. Interestingly, the structure and syntax of his farewell speech shows him to have ever remained a master strategist, maintaining a hard-line position against the Soviet Union while having avoided the pitfalls of precipitous military action. Eisenhower died of heart failure at Walter Reed Army Hospital on March 28, 1969, at the age of seventy-eight.

Explanation and Analysis of the Document

In his Farewell Address, Eisenhower very much casts himself as a senior statesman and wise old soldier in a performance devoid of bells and whistles. His speech pattern is untheatrical, and his prose is sparse, workmanlike, and designed to communicate to, not uplift, America. Eisenhower could not draw upon the Bostonian twang or the rhetorical elegance that would make President Kennedy's Inaugural Address a piece of superbly staged drama, designed to energize a presidency and embrace a people. Nor could Eisenhower draw upon the fire, zeal, visionary splendor, and biblical oratory that Martin Luther King, Jr., would memorably present in his "I Have a Dream" Speech. What is extraordinary about Eisenhower's swan song is the spare prose and the impression produced by a military man relieved that his eight years as commander in chief had allowed the country to find "essential agreement on issues of great moment."

Introduction

In the introduction to the address, Eisenhower sets the stage for an evening television talk to a nation captivated by the celebrity appeal of John F. Kennedy, the incoming president. The nation was enjoying a reasonable standard of living yet was apprehensive about the confrontational posturing of the United States and the Soviet Union.

Eisenhower's first paragraphs are neither laudatory nor self-serving. He speaks of Congress, whence more than half a century earlier a senator had appointed him to West Point, with which he enjoyed a close relationship during World War II, and which carried on a partnership with the White House that he describes as "mutually interdependent." Eisenhower's speeches frequently contain elements of good-natured optimism and feature more cheerfulness than cynicism or skepticism. He states here, without caveat, that his administration and Congress cooperated well, "to serve the national good rather than mere partisanship, and so have assured that the business of the Nation should go forward."

◆ From Military Strength to Human Betterment

While the introduction to Eisenhower's address is a word canvas on which he gently and carefully sketches the overall picture of his departure, Section 2 is a single solid paragraph consisting of four dramatic sentences. Throughout his tenure, he was as much a graduate of West Point as he was the president, and while he sat and spoke in the Oval Office, his sphere of influence was both national and global. Here, without melodrama or the mincing of words, he speaks of great nations being embroiled in major wars in the twentieth century.

His deployment, in an essentially military allusion, of the key word *holocausts* is adroit and riveting; while the horrific Nazi slaughter of Jews and other groups in the 1930s and 1940s is traditionally referred to as the Holocaust, Eisenhower was categorizing World War I, World War II, and the Korean War as all being holocausts in which America suffered significant losses. Indeed, the actual numbers of Americans wounded and killed in those three conflicts were considerable and reflect the propriety of Eisenhower's reference to great destruction and loss of life: In World War I over one hundred fifteen thousand Americans died, and

Time Line

1961

■ **April 12**
The Soviet cosmonaut Yuri Gagarin becomes the first man to orbit the earth.

■ **August 13**
Communist East Germany begins construction on the Berlin Wall to thwart the refugee exodus to West Berlin.

more than two hundred thousand were wounded; in World War II over four hundred thousand died, and more than six hundred seventy thousand were wounded; and in the Korean War over thirty-five thousand died, and more than one hundred thousand were wounded. Eisenhower rounds off this forceful paragraph by first acknowledging that his country proudly enjoyed prestige as the "most influential and most productive nation in the world" and then sagely adding that America's real challenge would be to parlay its "unmatched material progress, riches and military strength" into "world peace and human betterment."

◆ Hostile Ideology

In Section 3 of his address, Eisenhower begins by extolling the cornerstones of the American way of life, listing "liberty, dignity and integrity" as stemming from "America's adventure in free government." For Eisenhower, the United States is essentially "a free and religious people." These remarks serve as a preamble to a discussion around one of Eisenhower's central themes, that of the world being in conflict and rent asunder. The culprit, Eisenhower asserts, is Communism, which he labels "the hostile ideology." His depiction of that ideology is bold, attention catching, and chilling and fully communicates the intensity and divisiveness of the cold war circa 1961: Communism is "global in scope, atheistic in character, ruthless in purpose, and insidious in method."

Nevertheless, the voice of the temperate and cautious soldier and statesman does not waver in this Farewell Address. As president, Eisenhower oversaw the establishment of peace in Korea in 1953, stayed out of the conflict in Indochina in 1954, and avoided U.S. excursions into Egypt and Hungary in 1956. While advocating a clenched-fist brand of diplomacy, he saw that fist as being used not for punitive action but as a symbol of resoluteness tempered with restraint. Eisenhower perceived that countering Communism did not call for military action at every turn; he repudiated "the emotional and transitory sacrifices of crisis." He cautions his audience about the "recurring temptation to feel that some spectacular and costly action could become the miraculous solution to all current difficulties," and he posits that large increases in defense spending would not prove to be the answer. As far as Eisenhower was concerned, solutions would be brought about through sanity, reason, and doing the right things for the right reasons. His ethos holds that "good judgment seeks balance and progress; lack of it eventually finds imbalance and frustration."

President Dwight D. Eisenhower reads from his notes during his Farewell Address to the nation. (AP Photo)

◆ The Military-Industrial Complex

In every respect the fourth section of Eisenhower's Farewell Address is the most important; indeed, many historians and journalists have described the whole piece as the "military-industrial complex" speech. This fragment of the whole essay was held up as an Eisenhower benchmark by which armed preparedness was to be the antidote to Communism and the bulwark for Western democracy in the time of the cold war. Still, Eisenhower presents extensive caveats in this regard. In *American Decades: 1960–1969*, the historian Richard Layman states that this portion of the address was "a warning that reverberated throughout the decade" and that Eisenhower's prophetic insight on the possible excessive influences of the military-industrial complex became "quoted more frequently than any other words that he spoke during his presidency" (p. 185).

Eisenhower makes the point that up until the Korean War, the United States had no permanent armaments industry. (Eisenhower does not mention Germany, but the long history of arms and munitions in that country offers an interesting contrast.) Recent events, the president notes, necessitated the building of "a permanent armaments industry of vast proportions," employing some 3.5

million workers. Eisenhower powerfully punctuates his plain speech with a thought-provoking figure: "We annually spend on military security more than the net income of all United States corporations."

Eisenhower's script here is somewhat reminiscent of George Orwell's *1984*, as he points to the emergence of the "conjunction of an immense military establishment and a large arms industry" and then admits that because of this development, the United States finds itself symbolically situated—morally and ethically—on shifting sands. Quite simply, might is needed, but in the headlong pursuit of victory, right could be vanquished. Eisenhower addresses the military-industrial complex's gaining in power thus: "We recognize the imperative need for this development. Yet we must not fail to comprehend its grave implications." Arguably, the two lines of Eisenhower's address that have the greatest resonance—they have stood the test of time remarkably well—are the ones that open the following paragraph: "In the councils of government, we must guard against the acquisition of unwarranted influence, whether sought or unsought, by the military-industrial complex. The potential for the disastrous rise of misplaced power exists and will persist."

To counter the potential excesses of the military-industrial complex, Eisenhower calls for Americans to be ever vigilant, so that security and liberty may flourish. His words have a Jeffersonian ring to them as he benevolently admonishes the nation, advising Americans that the ship of state need be steered by "an alert and knowledgeable citizenry."

Continuing to caution and warn about the threats posed by the machinations of an overly eager military-industrial complex, Eisenhower artfully contrasts the motivations of the spirited, independent, freethinking individuals with those of corporate "task forces of scientists." He laments that "the free university," the historical cornerstone of American education, and the role of "the solitary inventor" are on the verge of being co-opted by governmental and financial interests. His worst-case scenario is marked by the "domination of the nation's scholars by Federal employment, project allocations, and the power of money." In concluding this section, he reverts to terms of compromise and the search for common ground: "It is the task of statesmanship to mold, to balance."

In discussing this address in his two-volume biography of the president, Stephen Ambrose reiterates Eisenhower's thesis regarding the need for balance, for the preservation of both peace and personal freedoms, and spotlights the irony of the development of the military-industrial complex: "A huge military [was] established, [yet] the cost of building it threatened to create a garrison state in which there would be no freedom." In his overview, Ambrose nicely captures the soul and spirit of Eisenhower's message: "They were the words of a soldier-prophet, a general who had given his life to the defense of freedom and the achievement of peace" (p. 612).

◆ Precious Resources

In Section 5 of the address, which is nearly as concise as Section 2, Eisenhower continues his call for balance and

"Throughout America's adventure in free government, our basic purposes have been to keep the peace; to foster progress in human achievement, and to enhance liberty, dignity and integrity among people and among nations."

(Section 3, Paragraph 1)

"In the councils of government, we must guard against the acquisition of unwarranted influence, whether sought or unsought, by the military-industrial complex."

(Section 4, Paragraph 5)

"Only an alert and knowledgeable citizenry can compel the proper meshing of huge industrial and military machinery of defense with our peaceful methods and goals, so that security and liberty may prosper together."

(Section 4, Paragraph 6)

"We cannot mortgage the material assets of our grandchildren without risking the loss also of their political and spiritual heritage."

(Section 5, Paragraph 1)

"Together we must learn how to compose difference, not with arms, but with intellect and decent purpose."

(Section 6, Paragraph 3)

persists in warning Americans about the threats to "the precious resources of tomorrow." With other presidents, such a statement might be tied to concerns about conservation, ecology, and natural resources; in Eisenhower's case, the remark is more of a philosophical aside—a reminder that the United States should husband its various "material assets" so as to ensure a vibrant political and spiritual legacy. He notes, "We want democracy to survive for all generations to come, not to become the insolvent phantom of tomorrow."

◆ **Trust, Respect, and Disarmament**

In the penultimate section Eisenhower shifts his focus, moving from the American scene to a global stage. Interestingly, in terms of repeated sound bites, Eisenhower's Farewell Address has always been recognized for the *Brave New World*–style warning on potential abuse from the military-industrial complex; as such, scant attention has been paid to the clever and elegant remarks on the issues of cooperation, peace, and disarmament. Eisenhower's sentences are never long, and major issues are not belabored; in this section, such brevity highlights some memorable prose. Eisenhower hopes for the world to be not "a community of dreadful fear and hate" but rather "a proud confederation of mutual trust and respect." Earlier, Eisenhower calls disarmament "a continuing imperative" and asserts that peaceful cooperation would be forged through "intellect and decent purpose." Ultimately, he positions himself as a pragmatist, acknowledging that lasting peace is not in plain sight while nevertheless articulating a central tenet of survival and compromise. Regarding his experience as president, he declares, "I can say that war has been avoided."

◆ Thank You and Good Night

The conclusion to Eisenhower's address is marked by the same generalities that have marked other, similar presidential talks to the nation; the speech must be wrapped up, ideally in a manner that somehow reaches out to and connects with every constituency. Eisenhower embraces the spiritual over the secular and ties in the notion that freedom brings with it spiritual blessings, praying that "the scourges of poverty, disease and ignorance will be made to disappear from the earth." While perhaps consisting of platitudes and sentimentalized dreams, the extended prayer in no way detracts from the overall narrative. President Dwight D. Eisenhower's concluding wishes reflect that he is a man, a statesman, forever a general, and an individual who mostly favors good cheer and humankind's better qualities. He prays that "all peoples will come to live together in a peace guaranteed by the binding force of mutual respect and love."

Audience

Eisenhower's Farewell Address was designed to reach and connect with a vast audience from all walks of life. The population of the United States in January 1961 was a little over 181 million, and with 88 percent of American households owning televisions the potential audience for the Eisenhower address was colossal. Using his 8:30–9:00 PM time slot, Eisenhower knew that he was reaching a very significant number of Americans. On that particular Tuesday evening, Eisenhower's address came after the following programs on ABC, CBS, and NBC, respectively: *The Life and Legend of Wyatt Earp*, *The Many Loves of Dobie Gillis*, and *Alfred Hitchcock Presents*. One of Eisenhower's many charms was his genuine self-deprecating wit. This comment from Eisenhower can be found in the editor Janet Wasko's *Companion to Television*: "I can think of nothing more boring for the American people than to sit in their living rooms for a whole half hour looking at my face on their television screens" (p. 9). That notion notwithstanding, Eisenhower pioneered the presidential broadcast, and in *Eisenhower and the Mass Media*, Craig Allen does not label him a soldier-statesman but instead uses the telling words "televised photo opportunities" to make the case that Eisenhower was the first television president (p. 8). Allen claims that while Eisenhower was relatively unknown even to those who felt they personally understood him, he was part of the national family of 180 million Americans, and his acceptance and recognition came about in part because of the medium of television.

In his address of January 17, 1961, Eisenhower was neither entertainer nor curmudgeon. He spoke directly, and while he presented several complex and even essentially novel word associations—such as "military-industrial complex"—the majority of his discourse was matter of fact and full of plain speech. The opening paragraph sounded like the gracious goodbye of a well-regarded company chairman stepping down from office, while the conclusion would not have been out of place delivered from a Midwestern pulpit.

Less than a week after Eisenhower's Farewell Address, the *New York Times* presented an analysis of the military-industrial complex, authored by Jack Raymond. Raymond describes a 1960 House committee that determined that 726 former military top brass were working for the nation's 100 leading defense contractors. Reports of this type clearly gave heft and credibility to Eisenhower's argument. His concerns were substantial.

Impact

President Eisenhower's standing as a global figure in the days leading up to his Farewell Address was indicative of how his words would be received. The London *Times*, in an editorial of January 12, 1961, called him "the most friendly and agreeable of all American presidents" and highlighted his supreme achievement as maintaining peace with a management style based on tactical restraint while forming leadership decisions on information from relevant officials. "These are all aspects internal to his January 17 speech."

The *New York Times* editorial responding to Eisenhower's address, entitled "Vigilance Urged," focused on the necessity of American leaders—with Eisenhower passing the baton to Kennedy—to stand firm against Communism yet press for disarmament. Felix Belair, Jr., in this editorial, commented that Eisenhower's warning about the military-industrial complex "came as a surprise to many in the capital," especially since "a more sentimental leave taking had been expected from the old soldier."

In fact, two months after Eisenhower's Farewell Address, the *New York Times* observed that Washington seemed to have forgotten the outgoing president's stern warning on the potential excessive influence of the military and its industries. The article in that newspaper of March 26, 1961, titled "Drive to Expand Defense Persists," pointed to the shrewd accuracy of some of Eisenhower's claims, describing the "high-powered drive of the armed services, their contractors, and members of Congress" to get a sizable stake in the national defense budget of $40 million.

Nearly a year and a half after his Farewell Address, Eisenhower spoke at a Republican fund-raising dinner in Washington, D.C. Walter Trohan of the *Chicago Tribune* reacted favorably to Eisenhower's pointing out that more defense spending would indeed increase national security and strength. Reflecting on Eisenhower's 1961 Farewell Address, Trohan remarks, "It took honest courage for Gen. Eisenhower to call the attention of the people to the facts of life about the profession in which he spent his life."

In the twenty-first century, the case can be made that Eisenhower's warnings have largely been ignored. Regarding the might and influence of the military-industrial complex, contemporary vested economic interests have transformed it into a juggernaut. In turn, patience, caution, and the close budgeting of spending have not been governmental priorities. In the occasionally harrowing post-9/11 global landscape, the U.S. military-industrial complex has been marked by senses of excess and extremes, with few students of Eisenhower arguing for restraint and scrutiny. Irrespective of his own professional background, Eisenhower made every effort to avoid military entanglements, however minor they might have seemed. The extent of modern American armed involvement in Afghanistan and Iraq, to the contrary, indicates that the Eisenhower doctrine arguably had very little long-term impact.

Richard Willing, writing in a 2007 issue of *USA Today*, comments on the fact that the Defense Department was then paying private contractors more than $1 billion simply to collect and analyze intelligence for the four military services. Willing quotes Steven Aftergood, a government secrecy specialist with a Washington think tank, as saying, "We're starting to create a new kind of intelligence bureaucracy, one that is more expensive and less accountable."

Related Documents

Ambrose, Stephen E. *Eisenhower*. 2 vols. New York: Simon and Schuster, 1983–1984. Ambrose had a lifelong passion for writing about soldiers and history, and in this exhaustive study he wonderfully profiles one of the great organizers in armed history.

Boyle, Peter G. *Eisenhower*. New York: Longman/Pearson, 2005. Boyle's biography—a short read at only 151 pages—shows how revisionist historians of the 1970s and 1980s came to regard Eisenhower as astute, street-smart, and politically shrewd.

D'Este, Carlo. *Eisenhower: A Soldier's Life* New York: Henry Holt, 2002. As the title indicates, this book treats Eisenhower's military career.

Lyon, Peter. *Eisenhower: Portrait of the Hero*. Boston: Little, Brown, 1974. Lyon's work is especially helpful for a close reading of the Farewell Address and for a discussion of the coinage of the phrase *military-industrial complex*.

Vexler, Robert I., ed. *Dwight D. Eisenhower, 1890–1969: Chronology, Documents, Bibliographical Aids*. Dobbs Ferry, N.Y.: Oceana Publications, 1970. Vexler provides a practical and helpful listing of Eisenhower's major political speeches from January 20, 1953, to January 17, 1961.

Bibliography

■ Articles

Belair, Felix, Jr. "Vigilance Urged," *New York Times*, January 18, 1961.

"Drive to Expand Defense Persists." *New York Times*, March 26, 1961.

Editorial. *Times* (London), January 12, 1961. January 12, 1961.

Raymond, Jack. "The 'Military-Industrial Complex': An Analysis." *New York Times*, January 22, 1961.

Trohan, Walter. "Report from Washington." *Chicago Tribune*, July 11, 1962.

Willing, Richard. "Defense Department Pays $1B to Outside Analysts." *USA Today*, August 30, 2007.

■ Books

Allen, Craig. *Eisenhower and the Mass Media: Peace, Prosperity, and Prime-Time TV*. Chapel Hill: University of North Carolina Press, 1993.

Burk, Robert F. *Dwight D. Eisenhower, Hero and Politician*. Boston: Twayne Publishers, 1986.

Greenstein, Fred I. *The Hidden-Hand Presidency: Eisenhower as Leader*. New York: Basic Books, 1982.

Larson, Arthur. *Eisenhower: The President Nobody Knew*. New York: Scribner, 1968.

Lasby, Clarence G. *Eisenhower's Heart Attack: How Ike Beat Heart Disease and Held On to the Presidency*. Lawrence: University Press of Kansas, 1997.

Layman, Richard, ed. *American Decades, 1960–1969* Detroit: Gale Research, 1995.

Medhurst, Martin J. *Dwight D. Eisenhower: Strategic Communicator*. Westport, Conn.: Greenwood Press, 1993.

Wasko, Janet, ed. *A Companion to Television*. Malden, Mass.: Blackwell Publishing, 2005.

■ Web Sites

"Dwight David Eisenhower (1890–1969)." Miller Center of Public Affairs "American President: An Online Reference Resource" Web site.
http://www.millercenter.virginia.edu/academic/americanpresident/eisenhower. Accessed on March 3, 2008.

The Dwight D. Eisenhower Presidential Library & Museum Web site.
http://www.eisenhower.archives.gov/. Accessed on March 3, 2008.

The Eisenhower Foundation Web site.
http://www.eisenhowerfoundation.org/index.php. Accessed on March 3, 2008.

"Eisenhower National Historic Site." National Park Service Web site.
http://www.nps.gov/eise/. Accessed on March 3, 2008.

—By Scott A. G. M. Crawford

Questions for Further Study

1. In many respects President Dwight D. Eisenhower's Farewell Address was a series of warnings. Eisenhower cautioned against the spread of Communism, but his harshest criticism was reserved for the excesses of military spending and connections with big business. Robert F. Burk, in *Dwight D. Eisenhower, Hero and Politician*, makes the case that Eisenhower's concerns warranted reexamination during the Kennedy years. In modern times, in light of significant U.S. involvement in Iraq and Afghanistan, Eisenhower's focus on the military-industrial complex seems especially relevant. Examine the role and scope of the military-industrial complex in the twentieth century.

2. Eisenhower has been described as the "television president." Compare and contrast the television personae of American presidents from Eisenhower to George W. Bush. If possible, consult the various presidential libraries, which have archives of audiovisual material that provide insight on character, intellect, and charisma.

3. Conduct a content analysis of the farewell addresses of the presidents from Eisenhower to Bill Clinton. Read the various narratives, and in terms of prose, style, and overall writing, argue which make for greater and which for lesser enduring literature.

4. Televised speeches can reveal much about messaging, communication, and language. In the space of three years, between 1961 and 1963, America witnessed three very different leaders deploying extraordinarily diverse approaches as they addressed America. Compare and contrast the methods of Eisenhower, John F. Kennedy, and Martin Luther King, Jr.

5. Eisenhower talked of world peace and betterment in 1961. The first years of the twenty-first century were marked by continuing violence in the Middle East and the containment of global terrorism. What might modern politicians learn from Eisenhower's presidency and farewell address that would allow for the development of a cooperating, collegial word? When Eisenhower left office he was able to say "war has been avoided." How did he skillfully navigate a political terrain fraught with various tensions?

6. Retrospectively discussing his Farewell Address, Eisenhower said that he had thought long and hard about his final talk to the nation. His decision was to offer a stark and sober address that confronted life's harsh realities rather than a lighthearted farewell to friends. Identify and analyze key phrases in the address that underscore the grave nature of his warnings.

Glossary

atheistic	characterized by a disbelief in the existence of a deity
charity	feeling of good will
confederation	a group of states or countries joined in alliance
fountainhead	primary source
holocausts	events characterized by great destruction and loss of life
ideology	total complex of beliefs, such as one that directs a political group
insidious	treacherous and deceitful
knowledgeable citizenry	informed and educated members of a country
military-industrial complex	the conjunction of the military arm of the government and the collection of corporate businesses that provide key military materials
partisanship	strong support for one side
phantom	ghost
plundering	robbing by force
pre-eminence	superiority over others
provocation	action eliciting anger

Dwight D. Eisenhower's Farewell Address

My fellow Americans:

Three days from now, after half a century in the service of our country, I shall lay down the responsibilities of office as, in traditional and solemn ceremony, the authority of the Presidency is vested in my successor.

This evening I come to you with a message of leave-taking and farewell, and to share a few final thoughts with you, my countrymen.

Like every other citizen, I wish the new President, and all who will labor with him, Godspeed. I pray that the coming years will be blessed with peace and prosperity for all.

Our people expect their President and the Congress to find essential agreement on issues of great moment, the wise resolution of which will better shape the future of the Nation.

My own relations with the Congress, which began on a remote and tenuous basis when, long ago, a member of the Senate appointed me to West Point, have since ranged to the intimate during the war and immediate post-war period, and, finally, to the mutually interdependent during these past eight years.

In this final relationship, the Congress and the Administration have, on most vital issues, cooperated well, to serve the national good rather than mere partisanship, and so have assured that the business of the Nation should go forward. So, my official relationship with the Congress ends in a feeling, on my part, of gratitude that we have been able to do so much together.

Section 2

We now stand ten years past the midpoint of a century that has witnessed four major wars among great nations. Three of these involved our own country. Despite these holocausts America is today the strongest, the most influential and most productive nation in the world. Understandably proud of this pre-eminence, we yet realize that America's leadership and prestige depend, not merely upon our unmatched material progress, riches and military strength, but on how we use our power in the interests of world peace and human betterment.

Section 3

Throughout America's adventure in free government, our basic purposes have been to keep the peace; to foster progress in human achievement, and to enhance liberty, dignity and integrity among people and among nations. To strive for less would be unworthy of a free and religious people. Any failure traceable to arrogance, or our lack of comprehension or readiness to sacrifice would inflict upon us grievous hurt both at home and abroad.

Progress toward these noble goals is persistently threatened by the conflict now engulfing the world. It commands our whole attention, absorbs our very beings. We face a hostile ideology—global in scope, atheistic in character, ruthless in purpose, and insidious in method. Unhappily the danger it poses promises to be of indefinite duration. To meet it successfully, there is called for, not so much the emotional and transitory sacrifices of crisis, but rather those which enable us to carry forward steadily, surely, and without complaint the burdens of a prolonged and complex struggle—with liberty at stake. Only thus shall we remain, despite every provocation, on our charted course toward permanent peace and human betterment.

Crises there will continue to be. In meeting them, whether foreign or domestic, great or small, there is a recurring temptation to feel that some spectacular and costly action could become the miraculous solution to all current difficulties. A huge increase in newer elements of our defense; development of unrealistic programs to cure every ill in agriculture; a dramatic expansion in basic and applied research— these and many other possibilities, each possibly promising in itself, may be suggested as the only way to the road we which to travel.

But each proposal must be weighed in the light of a broader consideration: the need to maintain balance in and among national programs—balance between the private and the public economy, balance between cost and hoped for advantage—balance between the clearly necessary and the comfortably desirable; balance between our essential requirements as a nation and the duties imposed by the nation upon the individual; balance between action of the moment and the national welfare of the future. Good judgment seeks balance and progress; lack of it eventually finds imbalance and frustration.

The record of many decades stands as proof that our people and their government have, in the main, understood these truths and have responded to them well, in the face of stress and threat. But threats, new in kind or degree, constantly arise. I mention two only.

Section 4

A vital element in keeping the peace is our military establishment. Our arms must be mighty, ready for instant action, so that no potential aggressor may be tempted to risk his own destruction.

Our military organization today bears little relation to that known by any of my predecessors in peace time, or indeed by the fighting men of World War II or Korea.

Until the latest of our world conflicts, the United States had no armaments industry. American makers of plowshares could, with time and as required, make swords as well. But now we can no longer risk emergency improvisation of national defense; we have been compelled to create a permanent armaments industry of vast proportions. Added to this, three and a half million men and women are directly engaged in the defense establishment. We annually spend on military security more than the net income of all United States corporations.

This conjunction of an immense military establishment and a large arms industry is new in the American experience. The total influence—economic, political, even spiritual—is felt in every city, every state house, every office of the Federal government. We recognize the imperative need for this development. Yet we must not fail to comprehend its grave implications. Our toil, resources and livelihood are all involved; so is the very structure of our society.

In the councils of government, we must guard against the acquisition of unwarranted influence, whether sought or unsought, by the military-industrial complex. The potential for the disastrous rise of misplaced power exists and will persist.

We must never let the weight of this combination endanger our liberties or democratic processes. We should take nothing for granted only an alert and knowledgeable citizenry can compel the proper meshing of huge industrial and military machinery of defense with our peaceful methods and goals, so that security and liberty may prosper together.

Akin to, and largely responsible for the sweeping changes in our industrial-military posture, has been the technological revolution during recent decades.

In this revolution, research has become central; it also becomes more formalized, complex, and costly. A steadily increasing share is conducted for, by, or at the direction of, the Federal government.

Today, the solitary inventor, tinkering in his shop, has been over shadowed by task forces of scientists in laboratories and testing fields. In the same fashion, the free university, historically the fountainhead of free ideas and scientific discovery, has experienced a revolution in the conduct of research. Partly because of the huge costs involved, a government contract becomes virtually a substitute for intellectual curiosity. For every old blackboard there are now hundreds of new electronic computers.

The prospect of domination of the nation's scholars by Federal employment, project allocations, and the power of money is ever present and is gravely to be regarded.

Yet, in holding scientific research and discovery in respect, as we should, we must also be alert to the equal and opposite danger that public policy could itself become the captive of a scientific-technological elite.

It is the task of statesmanship to mold, to balance, and to integrate these and other forces, new and old, within the principles of our democratic system—ever aiming toward the supreme goals of our free society.

Section 5

Another factor in maintaining balance involves the element of time. As we peer into society's future, we—you and I, and our government—must avoid the impulse to live only for today, plundering, for our own ease and convenience, the precious resources of tomorrow. We cannot mortgage the material assets of our grandchildren without risking the loss also of their political and spiritual heritage. We want democracy to survive for all generations to come, not to become the insolvent phantom of tomorrow.

Section 6

Down the long lane of the history yet to be written America knows that this world of ours, ever growing smaller, must avoid becoming a community of dreadful fear and hate, and be, instead, a proud confederation of mutual trust and respect.

Such a confederation must be one of equals. The weakest must come to the conference table with the same confidence as do we, protected as we are by our moral, economic, and military strength. That table, though scarred by many past frustrations, cannot be abandoned for the certain agony of the battlefield.

Disarmament, with mutual honor and confidence, is a continuing imperative. Together we must learn how to compose difference, not with arms, but with intellect and decent purpose. Because this need is so sharp and apparent I confess that I lay down my official responsibilities in this field with a definite sense of disappointment. As one who has witnessed the horror and the lingering sadness of war—as one who knows that another war could utterly destroy this civilization which has been so slowly and painfully built over thousands of years—I wish I could say tonight that a lasting peace is in sight.

Happily, I can say that war has been avoided. Steady progress toward our ultimate goal has been made. But, so much remains to be done. As a private citizen, I shall never cease to do what little I can to help the world advance along that road.

Section 7

So—in this my last good night to you as your President—I thank you for the many opportunities you have given me for public service in war and peace. I trust that in that service you find some things worthy; as for the rest of it, I know you will find ways to improve performance in the future.

You and I—my fellow citizens—need to be strong in our faith that all nations, under God, will reach the goal of peace with justice. May we be ever unswerving in devotion to principle, confident but humble with power, diligent in pursuit of the Nation's great goals.

To all the peoples of the world, I once more give expression to America's prayerful and continuing inspiration:

We pray that peoples of all faiths, all races, all nations, may have their great human needs satisfied; that those now denied opportunity shall come to enjoy it to the full; that all who yearn for freedom may experience its spiritual blessings; that those who have freedom will understand, also, its heavy responsibilities; that all who are insensitive to the needs of others will learn charity; that the scourges of poverty, disease and ignorance will be made to disappear from the earth, and that, in the goodness of time, all peoples will come to live together in a peace guaranteed by the binding force of mutual respect and love.

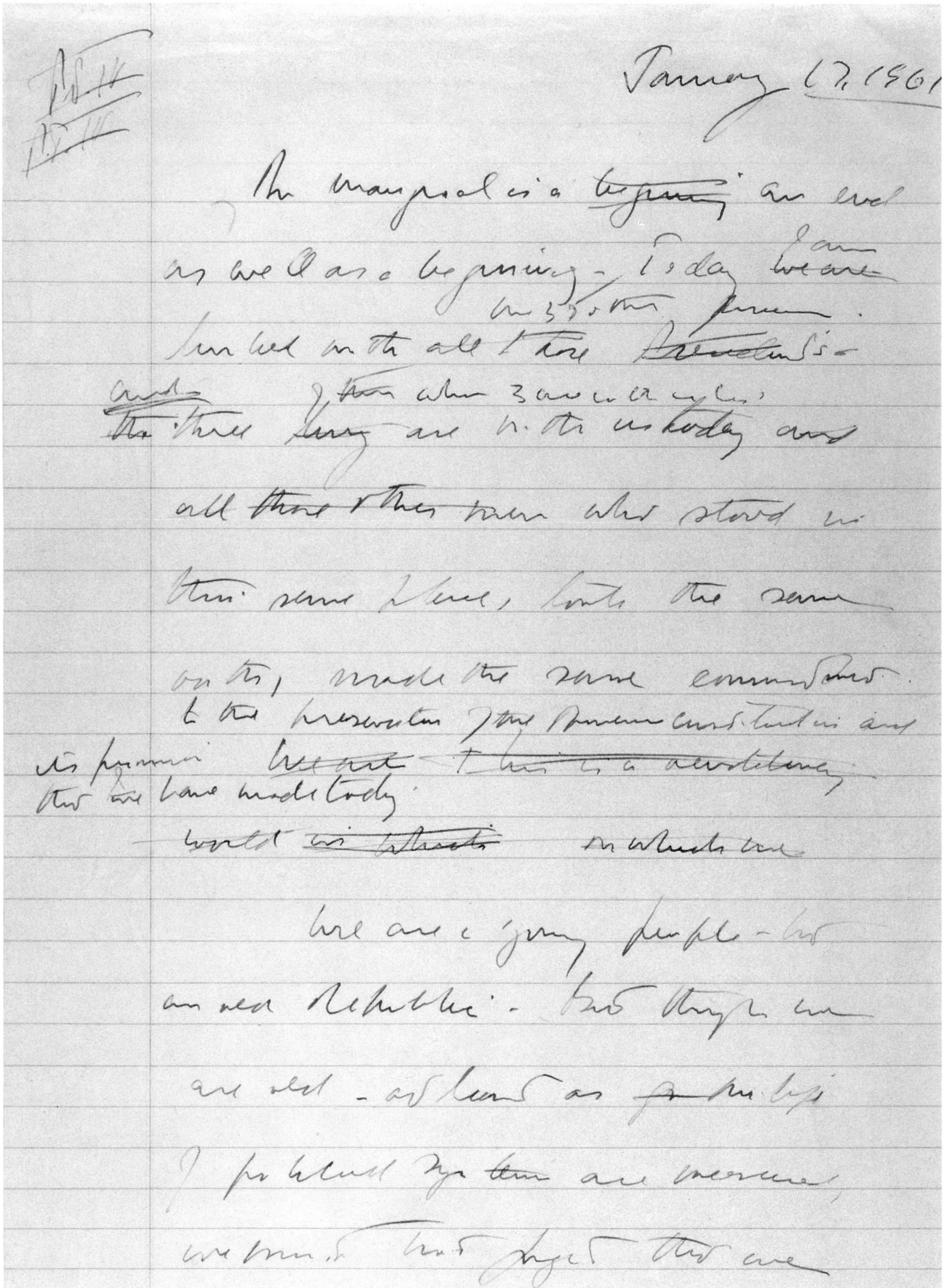

John F. Kennedy's Inaugural Address (National Archives and Records Administration)

JOHN F. KENNEDY'S INAUGURAL ADDRESS

*"Ask not what your country can do for you—
ask what you can do for your country."*

Overview

Only rarely do speeches reverberate through the decades, remaining as fresh and hopeful as has John F. Kennedy's Inaugural Address. The speech is as laden with quotable lines as Abraham Lincoln's Gettysburg Address and the wartime speeches of Winston Churchill. Each year Kennedy's address is included in more than twenty anthologies; it is one of the most quoted inaugural addresses. Since Kennedy's inauguration as the nation's thirty-fifth president, the speech has served as a comparative standard for subsequent inaugural speeches.

As was typical with Kennedy, he called upon numerous advisers to provide ideas for the address. Shortly after his election, Kennedy was already deciding on certain parameters for the speech: It was to remain short, focus on foreign affairs, and demonstrate a strong stance against the Soviet Union. In fact, at the start of the twenty-first century, it was the fourth-shortest inaugural address in American history. John F. Kennedy's first words as president were a succinct call to Americans to help achieve the New Frontier and other political proposals through sacrifice and service and to take up the "burdens" of freedom.

Context

Although the country was not fighting an actual battle when Kennedy was elected, it was at war. The cold war was a direct result of World War II and a major concern to the incoming president. Soon after the end of the war in Europe, the enemy became the Union of Soviet Socialist Republics, and Kennedy predicted that the United States could be at war with the Soviets within fifteen years. His forewarnings about the growing power of the Soviet Union proved true, and by 1960 the Soviet Union had extended its influence in Asia and Europe. In his speech of January 2, 1960, announcing his candidacy for president, Kennedy said, "I have developed an image of America as fulfilling a noble and historical role as the defender of freedom in a time of maximum peril" (qtd. in Clarke, p. 35).

Indeed, relations with the Soviet Union were not cordial, as evidenced by various unpleasant encounters during the presidency of Dwight D. Eisenhower with the Soviet leader Nikita Khrushchev. When the Soviets captured an American U-2 surveillance plane flying over Soviet territory on a spy mission in May 1960, trust between the two countries was destroyed. In September 1960, at the United Nations, Khrushchev's aggressive attitude toward the United States took the form of his removing a shoe and pounding it on the table to make his point. Khrushchev saw the United States as a declining power. Two weeks before Kennedy's inauguration, Khrushchev proclaimed the imminent triumph of Communism through the Soviet support of "national liberation wars" in third-world countries (qtd. in Clarke, p. 33).

Kennedy had no illusions about America's need and ability to engage in world problems, such as those in Laos, Vietnam, and the Congo. In Laos, a Communist-backed insurgency was fighting the U.S.-backed regime; in South Vietnam, the Viet Cong had the U.S.-supported government on the defensive; and in Africa, in the newly independent Congo, Soviet supporters were moving into positions of power. The Communist regime in Cuba was also a threat.

Another concern that grew directly out of World War II was the use of nuclear weapons. In 1945, after the atomic bombs dropped on Japan by the United States ended the war in the Pacific, Kennedy stated, "Humanity cannot afford another war" (qtd. in Silvestri, p. 3). The Soviets, in fact, not only had nuclear weapons but also were winning the space race. The Soviet launch of the first man-made satellite, *Sputnik I*, on October 4, 1957, and other developments indicated that the United States was no longer first in the world in armaments, in science, or in technology. Kennedy stressed in his campaign that the United States needed to recommit to a strong sense of national purpose. President Eisenhower, however, continually denied that the United States was falling behind the Soviet Union.

As far as civil rights were concerned, the government seemed oblivious to the developing movement, but the increasing numbers of sit-in, stand-ins, and other activist activities could not be ignored. Consequently, Kennedy, on August 2, 1960, formed a committee to work on the civil rights section of his campaign, not to secure the votes of

Time Line

1917	**■ May 29** John Fitzgerald Kennedy is born.
1940	**■ June** Kennedy graduates cum laude from Harvard.
1943	**■ August 2** USS *PT-109*, commanded by Kennedy, is rammed and sinks in the South Pacific.
1946	**■ November** Kennedy is elected to the U.S. House of Representatives.
1952	**■ November** Kennedy is elected to the U.S. Senate.
1953	**■ September 12** Senator Kennedy marries Jacqueline Bouvier.
1960	**■ January 2** From Washington, D.C., Kennedy announces his candidacy for president. **■ July 13** The Democratic Party presidential nomination is awarded to Kennedy. **■ November 8** Kennedy wins the presidential election, defeating Vice President Richard M. Nixon.
1961	**■ January 20** John F. Kennedy is sworn in as the thirty-fifth president of the United States and delivers his Inaugural Address. **■ April 17** Bay of Pigs invasion, sponsored by the United States to overthrow Fidel Castro, is unsuccessfully attempted in Cuba.
1962	**■ October 14–28** Cuban missile crisis; the Kennedy administration manages to avert open conflict with the Soviet Union and Cuba.

African Americans for the election but to focus on the civil rights of all people. During the campaign Kennedy repeatedly stated that if he were elected, he would use presidential power to promote equality for African Americans and support the strong civil rights position in the Democratic Party's 1960 platform. When Martin Luther King, Jr., head of the Southern Christian Leadership Conference, was jailed in Atlanta, Georgia, for an alleged minor traffic infraction (he was actually trying to integrate a department store) in October 1960, Kennedy called King's wife, Coretta Scott King, offering help in securing her husband's safe release. After Robert Kennedy successfully pressured the judge for the case to release King, Kennedy's presidency was endorsed by King's father. As a result, the African American vote went solidly for Kennedy (at over 70 percent), providing a winning edge in several key states.

About the Author

John Fitzgerald Kennedy was born in Brookline, Massachusetts, on May 29, 1917, to Joseph Patrick Kennedy, a businessman and later a diplomat, and Rose Fitzgerald Kennedy. He was brought up with his three brothers and five sisters in an atmosphere of intellectual stimulation and affluence. Kennedy attended the Choate preparatory school in Connecticut and graduated from Harvard in 1940. He traveled extensively throughout Europe and Latin America. Uncertain of what career to pursue but certain of America's future involvement in World War II, he enlisted in the U.S. Navy. Frustrated by office work in navy intelligence, he pressed for active duty; in 1942 he was assigned to motor torpedo boat training, and in March 1943 he assumed the command of his own patrol torpedo (PT) boat in the South Pacific. On August 2, 1943, the Japanese destroyer *Amagiri* rammed Kennedy's boat. His leadership and physical efforts to save a crewman by towing him to safety made Kennedy a war hero, and he received U.S. Navy and Marine Corps medals. The majority of the crew was rescued, but Kennedy had aggravated a chronic back injury and saw no more active duty. He was retired from the service in March 1945 with the rank of full lieutenant.

Although Kennedy began pursuing a career in journalism, his father encouraged him to enter politics. In 1946 he sought the Democratic nomination for Congress in the eleventh Massachusetts district. Hard campaigning, his war record, and family support resulted in his nomination and subsequent victory in November, when he was elected to the Eightieth Congress. After three terms in the House, he ran for the Senate in 1952 and defeated the incumbent, Henry Cabot Lodge, Jr. Kennedy married Jacqueline Lee Bouvier on September 12, 1953. They had four children, but only two survived infancy.

As a senator, Kennedy served on a number of key committees. His back problems required surgeries, however, and he spent months recuperating, during which he wrote *Profiles in Courage* (1956). Back in Congress, he supported social welfare legislation and sponsored several bills, including one for federal financial aid to education. His work in Congress and his book attracted national attention, and he was narrowly defeated at the 1956 Democratic National Convention by Estes Kefauver in the race to become the running mate of the Democratic presidential nominee, Adlai E. Stevenson. Encouraged by his increasing national visibility, Kennedy began planning his own presidential campaign. Reelected to the Senate in 1958 by a huge majority, he began a program of speaking at various venues around the country. He declared his candidacy on January 2, 1960, and on July 13, 1960, at the Democratic National Convention in Los Angeles, he was nominated for president on the first ballot. As with previous campaigns, Kennedy's run for the presidency was driven by hard work and the extensive resources, in both people and funds, of the Kennedy family. The campaign also featured the first televised presidential debates. During the four debates, Kennedy's youth, wit, and use of language bested his Republican opponent, Richard M. Nixon. Kennedy won the general election by only one-tenth of 1 percent of the popular vote; the margin in the Electoral College was more decisive: Kennedy earned 303 electoral votes, Nixon 219.

On January 20, 1961, Kennedy, the youngest man and first Roman Catholic ever elected president, was sworn into office by Chief Justice Earl Warren. In his Inaugural Address, Kennedy emphasized America's global role and obligation to humanitarian concerns. Begun on a high note, Kennedy's presidency lasted just over a thousand days. He had some successes, such as with the establishment of the Peace Corps and the signing of the Nuclear Test Ban Treaty (1963), but failures as well, such as with the Bay of Pigs invasion and his inability to downsize American involvement in Vietnam. His biggest challenge was the Cuban missile crisis, which brought America to the brink of war when a U.S. spy plane took reconnaissance photographs of missile bases being constructed in Cuba. Kennedy worked for civil rights by issuing various executive orders, and he appointed an unprecedented number of African Americans to public office. On November 22, 1963, Kennedy was assassinated by Lee Harvey Oswald in Dallas, Texas. He was buried at Arlington National Cemetery.

Explanation and Analysis of the Document

Although debate has continued as to who actually wrote his Inaugural Address, Kennedy himself is understood as the author, with contributions of suggestions from Theodore Sorensen, his special counsel, in particular, as well as ideas and phrases from Arthur Schlesinger, Jr.; John Kenneth Galbraith; Adlai Stevenson; and others. From his earliest years, Kennedy was an avid reader and a collector of important or catchy quotations. Often confined to bed because of illness, he read. Writing was another passion. His senior thesis at Harvard, "Appeasement at Munich," was published as *Why England Slept* (1940); reviews were positive, and the book became a best seller. In 1957 his *Profiles in Courage* won the Pulitzer Prize for Biography.

Time Line

1963

■ **June 26**
Kennedy delivers a speech at the Berlin Wall (in which he famously utters the words "Ich bin ein Berliner" "I am a Berliner").

■ **November 22**
Kennedy is assassinated by Lee Harvey Oswald in Dallas, Texas.

Kennedy's Inaugural Address demonstrates his skill as a writer and an editor. Kennedy began work on the speech following his election. He instructed Sorensen to research previous inaugural addresses and Lincoln's Gettysburg Address, seeking to discover why each was a success or failure. He determined that his address would not be long; in fact, it was less than 1400 words in length and lasted fourteen minutes. Taking the cue from Lincoln's address, Kennedy used comparatively simple language, both for impact and in consideration of the fact that the speech would be translated into many languages across the globe. Straightforward language would lessen chances for misunderstandings. The tone of the speech was largely positive. Negative elements were discarded through the various drafts, and the first person "I" was omitted in favor of "we," underlying the point that all Americans were to be involved in the new endeavors of the Kennedy presidency. Of the speech's twenty-seven paragraphs, eleven focus on peace and eight on freedom.

The speech underwent a number of drafts, as Kennedy, writing on sheets of yellow legal paper, incorporated suggestions from Sorensen and others, crafting them into a document that was still in progress as he spoke the words at the inauguration itself. As he read from the final draft, Kennedy made thirty-two small but significant changes, such as changing individual words and tightening sentences for sharper impact. Only an author supremely confident in his message and in his skill with words could have so "improved" his work before a live audience.

The salutation addresses "fellow citizens," as was customary since George Washington's First Inaugural Address (1789), and, in a second tradition initiated by Franklin Delano Roosevelt in his fourth inaugural address (1945), recognizes the individuals sitting on the inauguration platform by name; Kennedy acknowledges the specific people first and ends with "fellow citizens." The first sentence of the speech itself shows the balance characteristic of the whole, hailing "not a victory of party, but a celebration of freedom" in echoes of the language of Winston Churchill. Kennedy had read Churchill extensively and memorized passages when he was recuperating from surgery in 1955. The next paragraph focuses on human beings' power for doing good as well as their capacity for destruction, a specific reference to the nuclear threat. The possibility of nuclear annihilation was a concern expressed by Kennedy in his first campaign in 1946, when he stated, "We have a world which has unleashed the powers of atomic energy … a world capable of destroying itself" (qtd. in Tofel, p. 95). He reiterated this concern throughout his presidential campaign and in his 1960 acceptance speech at the Democratic National Convention.

The following paragraph sums up what Kennedy had been saying for years and also reflects his personal history as one of the "new generation of Americans." Kennedy was the first president "born in this century," and he, too, was tempered by war, through both the fighting and the witnessing of it. The image of passing the torch may originate from the Olympics and has been used over the ages. It is a classic symbol of heroism, invoked in this instance by a war hero, and also represents the passing of the duties of president of the United States from the oldest president yet, Eisenhower, to the youngest, Kennedy, intimating a change from a tired "runner" to someone newer and fresher. The paragraph concludes with a statement of commitment to human rights "at home and around the world." The insertion of the words "at home" is the sole acknowledgment of civil rights or any other domestic issues in the address. In considering the potential scope of the address, Kennedy did not want to allude to any partisan concerns. He felt that references to domestic policy might be too divisive and told Sorensen, "Let's drop out the domestic stuff altogether" (qtd. in Sorensen, p. 242). However, Kennedy later responded to the suggestion by advisers that the final six words of the third paragraph be added, acknowledging the support that he had received from African Americans during the election.

The next paragraph, rewritten to replace the word "enemy" with "foe," is a strong statement of what America was prepared to do to guarantee liberty. It has, in fact, been criticized as being warlike. In his delivery, Kennedy paused between each of these five pledges to stress their gravity. Like Churchill, he repeated a key word. Churchill had famously used "fight" in his speech to the House of Commons on June 4, 1940, following the British evacuation of Dunkirk in World War II: "We shall fight on the beaches, we shall fight on the landing grounds, we shall fight in the fields and in the streets, we shall fight in the hills; we shall never surrender" (http://www.winstonchurchill.org/i4a/pages/index.cfm?pageid=393). Here, Kennedy uses "any" before each noun, and in speaking he omitted several words from the reading copy of the speech, tightening up the sentence and creating an almost drumlike cadence.

The next sentence, "This much we pledge—and more," serves as a transition to the next six paragraphs, a series of promises to different audiences around the world. Kennedy first addresses "those old allies," stressing the importance of continuing to stand together. To former colonies that have become nations, he vows to protect their new freedom and specifically warns against "a far more iron tyranny," an allusion to Soviet incursions into new nations. His use of the metaphor of the tiger, originally from the limerick "There was a young lady of Niger," resulted in the only instance of laughter from the audience. Churchill had used

the metaphor in 1938 after the Munich agreement, referring to dictators: "Dictators ride to and fro upon tigers which they dare not dismount. And the tigers are getting hungry" (Clarke, p. 130).The Munich agreement had allowed the Germans to take over part of Czechoslovakia without going to war, basically appeasing the German chancellor Adolph Hitler. Kennedy uses the metaphor to warn against those seeking power through the guise of helping newly emancipated nations. Concerning those in developing countries who are still living in "huts and villages," Kennedy simply states that the nation must help "because it is right."

Kennedy refers to the countries south of the U.S. border, constituting Latin America, as "sister republics," intimating a strong bond. Here he uses the phrase "alliance for progress," naming for the first time a program that would be part of his presidency. Again he warns of "hostile powers," though he does not specifically name Communism. His reference to the United Nations as "our last best hope" echoes the language of Thomas Jefferson and of Lincoln, who, in addressing Congress in 1862, had remarked, "We shall nobly save, or meanly lose, the last best hope of earth" (qtd. in Tofel, p. 105). To close out this series of addresses, Kennedy reserves words for the nation's enemies, using again not the word *enemy* but the more conciliatory word *adversary*; he does not offer a "pledge" but "requests" that both sides work together to avoid nuclear destruction.

Paragraph 12 functions as a bridge to a series of proposals aimed at decreasing tensions in the cold war. His statement concerning weakness shows his understanding of history, both from his reading and from his experience, as he watched the beginnings of and finally was involved in World War II. The line "We dare not tempt them with weakness" was offered by Adlai Stevenson. Sorensen had changed "them" to "you," but Kennedy, again in an effort to soften the address, changed "you" back to "them." The perceived necessity of being adequately armed was indicative of Kennedy's foreign policy during his presidency. In September 1960, Kennedy stated that the only way to have Khrushchev agree to disarmament was "by our strength of armaments, enough to stop the next war before it starts" (http://www.presidency.ucsb.edu/ws/index.php?pid=25654&st=&st1=).

In the paragraph that opens "So let us begin anew," the reference to civility refers to a specific incident during Eisenhower's presidency when Secretary of State John Foster Dulles refused to shake hands with the Chinese envoy Zhou Enlai in Geneva during negotiations concerning the war in Indochina. The next sentences—"Let us never negotiate out of fear. But let us never fear to negotiate."—were contributed by Galbraith and offer an example of Kennedy's use of antithesis, word choice emphasizing a contrast. Such sentences illustrate the seeking of a balance between equal but opposite forces. The device of antithesis can be effective for the expression of conflicting ideas in a concise and memorable way. Kennedy used antithesis in almost every paragraph of the address.

The ensuing proposals for cooperation between the two opposing forces of the cold war are constructive, looking toward the future rather than back at the past. Specific proposals include "the inspection and control of arms," the exploration of the world (including space), the eradication of disease, the promotion of trade, and even the development of the arts. The following paragraph includes the first of the address's two quotes from the Bible, with words of Isaiah from the Old Testament urging aid to the oppressed. Continuing his invitation to the Soviets to reduce cold war tensions, he proposes "a new endeavor, not a new balance of power."

In retrospect, the next paragraph is full of sad irony, as Kennedy states, "All this will not be finished in the first one hundred days … nor in the life of this Administration." The truth of this statement became clear on November 22, 1963, when Kennedy was assassinated.

Again ironically, the statement "In your hands, my fellow citizens, more than mine" foreshadows the future, as Kennedy's programs would ultimately need to be carried forward by others; his civil rights bill would be promoted and signed into law by his successor, Lyndon B. Johnson, but his Alliance for Progress became a failure. The opening phrase here comes directly from Lincoln's First Inaugural Address, in which Lincoln was trying to dissuade action on the part of the southern states. Kennedy, on the other hand, is introducing a call to action. The next sentence, referring to the generation of Americans who have "answered the call to service," illustrates the concept of Americans "giving testimony" by doing. In previous addresses, as he reflected on his older brother (who had died in World War II) and his *PT-109* crew members, Kennedy's voice filled with emotion, speaking of those dead in graves or memorials around the globe.

A sounding trumpet has long been a call to arms and to revitalization. In this address, it represents a call to "struggle against the common enemies of man." The language is reminiscent of Handel's *Messiah* ("The trumpet shall sound"), with the excitement of the image and sound intended to stir Americans into battle with those "common enemies of man: tyranny, poverty, disease and war itself." The quote "rejoicing in hope, patient in tribulation" is from St. Paul's Epistle to the Romans, in the Bible's New Testament. Kennedy's rhetorical questions as to whether nations can join together to provide "a more fruitful life for all mankind" and whether "you"—each individual—will help were answered by hundreds of voices shouting, "Yes."

Paragraph 24 again refers to the present as a time of "maximum danger," reflecting the concern over nuclear war that Kennedy had expressed throughout his campaign. Unlike in the rest of the address, Kennedy here uses the first-person "I." When he avowed to the nation that he would not "shrink from this responsibility" of "defending freedom," he dropped his voice, to then raise it to "welcome" the challenge in the second part of the sentence. The image of a fire lighting the world has been used in other speeches, including Washington's First Inaugural Address. Many believe that the image inspired the eternal flame on Kennedy's grave.

John F. Kennedy (Library of Congress)

The master sentence in Kennedy's Inaugural Address, presented in the form of an antithesis, comes near the close: "And so, my fellow Americans: ask not what your country can do for you—ask what you can do for your country." These are undoubtedly the address's most remembered words. With the casual opening "And so," Kennedy leads up to the noble request that his listeners look into themselves and discover what they could do for the United States—how they might selflessly commit to implementing the proposals presented by their new president. The phrase is reminiscent of one uttered by the Supreme Court justice Oliver Wendell Holmes, who in an 1884 Memorial Day address had stated, "It is now the moment when by common consent we pause to become conscious of our national life and to rejoice in it, to recall what our country has done for each of us, and to ask ourselves what we can do for our country in return" (qtd. in Tofel, pp. 123–124). Some consider Kennedy's second use of the "ask not" phrasing here to be anticlimactic.

In the final paragraph, the conclusion, Kennedy fully broadens his message to address all those around the globe, calling his worldwide audience to action. The inaugural addresses of American presidents have customarily invoked God for his blessing and aid, and Kennedy's does so here. Using moving alliteration, he urges his listeners "to lead the land we love," making the conclusion both a prayer and a poem. In closing, President Kennedy reminds people, in less poetic language, that "God's work" must be accomplished by humankind.

> "We observe today not a victory of party but a celebration of freedom."
>
> (Paragraph 1)

> "Let the word go forth from this time and place, to friend and foe alike, that the torch has been passed to a new generation of Americans."
>
> (Paragraph 3)

> "Let us never negotiate out of fear. But let us never fear to negotiate."
>
> (Paragraph 14)

> "And so, my fellow Americans: ask not what your country can do for you—ask what you can do for your country."
>
> (Paragraph 25)

Audience

Kennedy delivered his Inaugural Address before an audience of twenty thousand people sitting on seats swept free of snow. The address was televised, and eighty million Americans watched; it was also broadcast over radios around the world. Being aware of the extensive audience, Kennedy consciously spoke not only to Americans but to the people around the globe as well. Beyond the initial audience of people who heard the original speech can be added those who subsequently read it in newspapers or texts, those who heard recordings of the speech, and those who studied the speech in classrooms.

Impact

The immediate impact of the speech was applause; Kennedy was interrupted by such appreciation fourteen times during his delivery. Another result of the speech was tears from many of those attending. The event was also a graphic signaling of the change that the election ushered in, as Kennedy, standing in freezing weather without a topcoat, with his tanned face and his youth, symbolized a new generation of Americans.

Both Democrats and Republicans praised the speech, and many of those who had not voted for Kennedy changed their opinion of him following the address. In fact, shortly after the inauguration, a poll showed his approval rating at 72 percent. Newspapers praised the speech, particularly his "olive branch" approach to engaging with the Soviet Union. After hearing the speech, Nikita Khrushchev sent Kennedy a conciliatory telegram, setting the tone for a series of positive steps in working cooperatively toward a number of issues. By the time of his death, Kennedy had achieve détente with the Soviet Union and had negotiated the Nuclear Test Ban Treaty.

Through the speech, Kennedy conveyed a sense of hope and purpose that made an impression on the public, particularly on the young. With its stress on American involvement in bettering the world, it was a literal call to action, and soon after, through Executive Order 10924, Kennedy would direct the creation of the Peace Corps. Kennedy had originally suggested such an organization on October 14, 1960, at a speech at the University of Michigan. The first Peace Corps class numbered five hundred. By Kennedy's death, the number of volunteers had grown to nine hundred. As early as 1965, Peace Corps volunteers numbered some twelve thousand, and twenty-three other countries had developed their own peace corps. A future member of President Bill Clinton's cabinet, Donna Shalala, credited Kennedy's Inaugural Address with inspiring her to pursue a career in public service.

Millions of people across the world heard the address, either in English or translated into their own languages. For many of these people, Kennedy became a legend, and bridges, schools, and roads were named for him. The words with which he announced to every nation the commitment "to assure the survival and the success of liberty" are inscribed on a plaque in Runnymede, England, the site of the signing of the Magna Carta.

As Arthur Schlesinger stated in *A Thousand Days* (1965), his memoir of the Kennedy administration, "The energies Kennedy released, the purposes he inspired, the goals he established would guide the land he loved for years to come" (qtd. in Clarke, p. 7). The sense of idealism extolled by Kennedy in his opening address as president of the United States—of what was possible for individuals to accomplish in attempting to bring freedom from tyranny and from want to others—created an atmosphere of hope for millions of Americans of that generation and for generations to come.

Related Documents

"Address of President-Elect John F. Kennedy Delivered to a Joint Convention of the General Court of the Commonwealth of Massachusetts. State House, Boston, Mass., January 9, 1961." John F. Kennedy Presidential Library & Museum Web site. http://www.jfklibrary.org/Historical+Resources/Archives/Reference+Desk/Speeches/JFK/003POF03GeneralCourt01091961.htm. Accessed on March 3, 2008. In his "farewell to Massachusetts" speech, Kennedy discusses the state's contributions to "national greatness." As in other speeches, he refers to the United States as sailing though hazardous times.

"Address of Senator John F. Kennedy Accepting the Democratic Party Nomination for the Presidency of the United States—Memorial Coliseum, Los Angeles." The American Presidency Project Web site. http://www.presidency.ucsb.edu/ws/index.php?pid=25966. Accessed on March 4, 2008. In this speech Kennedy acknowledges the "risk" taken in nominating a Roman Catholic but, as he did throughout his campaign, stresses that his religion and his office, should he achieve it, will not conflict; other themes include "new and more terrible weapons," new nations, human rights, and "a New Frontier."

"Announcement of Candidacy for President: Statement of Senator John F. Kennedy January 2, 1960 Washington, D.C." John F. Kennedy Presidential Library & Museum Web site. http://www.jfklibrary.org/Historical+Resources/Archives/Reference+Desk/Announcement+of+Candidacy+for+President.htm. Accessed on March 4, 2008. In declaring his candidacy, Kennedy spoke of "the burdensome arms race" and, using the same words as he would in his Inaugural Address, described the present as "a time of maximum peril."

Bibliography

■ Articles

Golden, James L. "John F. Kennedy and the 'Ghosts.'" *Quarterly Journal of Speech* 52, no. 4 (December 1966): 348–357.

Hahn, Dan F. "Ask Not What a Youngster Can Do for You: Kennedy's Inaugural Address." *Presidential Studies Quarterly* 12, no. 4 (1982): 610–614.

Kenny, Edward B. "Another Look at Kennedy's Inaugural Address." *Today's Speech* 13, no. 4 (November 1965): 17–19.

Menand, Louis. "Ask Not, Tell Not: Anatomy of an Inaugural." *New Yorker*, November 8, 2004: 110–119.

Meyer, Sam. "The John F. Kennedy Inauguration Speech: Function and Importance of Its 'Address System.'" *Rhetoric Society Quarterly* 12, no. 4 (Fall 1982): 239–250.

Silvestri, Vito N. "Background Perspectives on John F. Kennedy's Inaugural Address." *Political Communication and Persuasion* 8 (1991): 1–15.

Wolfarth, Donald L. "John F. Kennedy in the Tradition of Inaugural Speeches." *Quarterly Journal of Speech* 47 (April 1961): 124–132.

■ Books

Clarke, Thurston. *Ask Not: The Inauguration of John F. Kennedy and the Speech That Changed America*. New York: Henry Holt, 2005.

Fairlie, Henry. *The Kennedy Promise: The Politics of Expectation*. Garden City, N.Y.: Doubleday, 1973.

Giglio, James N. *The Presidency of John F. Kennedy*. 2nd ed. Lawrence: University Press of Kansas, 2006.

O'Brien, Michael. *John F. Kennedy: A Biography*. New York: Thomas Dunne Books/St. Martin's Press, 2005.

Schlesinger, Arthur M., Jr. *A Thousand Days: John F. Kennedy in the White House*. Boston: Houghton Mifflin, 1965.

Sorensen, Theodore C. *Kennedy*. New York: Harper & Row, 1965.

Tofel, Richard J. *Sounding the Trumpet: The Making of John F. Kennedy's Inaugural Address*. Chicago: Ivan R. Dee, 2005.

White, Theodore H. *The Making of the President, 1960*. New York: Atheneum Publishers, 1961.

■ Web Sites

"John F. Kennedy." PBS "American Experience: The Presidents" Web site.
http://www.pbs.org/wgbh/amex/presidents/35_kennedy/index.html. Accessed on March 4, 2008.

"John Fitzgerald Kennedy (1917–1963)." Miller Center of Public Affairs "American President: An Online Reference Resource" Web site.
http://www.millercenter.virginia.edu/academic/americanpresident/kennedy. Accessed on March 4, 2008.

John F. Kennedy Presidential Library and Museum Web site.
http://www.jfklibrary.org. Accessed on October 25, 2007.

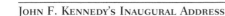

"Speech of Senator John F. Kennedy, Civic Auditorium, Seattle, WA, September 6th, 1960." The American Presidency Project Web site.
http://www.presidency.ucsb.edu/ws/index.php?pid=25654&st= &st1=. Accessed on March 5, 2008.

"Speeches and Quotes: 'We Shall Fight on the Beaches.'" The Churchill Centre Web site.
http://www.winstonchurchill.org/i4a/pages/index.cfm?pageid=3 93. Accessed on March 3, 2008.

—By Marcia B. Dinneen

Questions for Further Study

1. Trace the origins of the Peace Corps and discuss its validity in the modern world.

2. Compare and contrast the context and language of Lincoln's Second Inaugural Address with those of Kennedy's Inaugural Address.

3. Discuss the effectiveness of Kennedy's Alliance for Progress as carried out during his presidency.

4. Although Kennedy's Inaugural Address does not specifically address civil rights issues, how did Kennedy subsequently begin to develop the civil rights legislation that would culminate in the Civil Rights Act of 1964? Does his Inaugural Address contain any ideas that he carried through to his work on civil rights?

Glossary

absolute	complete and unconditional
asunder	into separate parts or groups
alliance	formal pact of confederation between nations for a common cause
beachhead	a position opening the way for further development
belaboring	harping on
civility	courtesy
colonial	relating to lands settled by an imperial country and subject to the laws of that country
embattled	engaged in combat
endeavor	concerted effort toward a given end
forebears	ancestors
instruments	implements (in this case, weapons)
invective	abusive or denunciatory expression
mortal	liable or subject to death
republics	political powers whose heads of state are not monarchs and usually are instead presidents
sovereign	self-governing
subversion	the undermining of character, morals, or allegiance
tempered	modified by the addition of an agent or quality
this Hemisphere	the Western Hemisphere, including North, Central, and South America
tyranny	a government in which a single ruler is vested with absolute power
writ	a written court order

JOHN F. KENNEDY'S INAUGURAL ADDRESS

Vice President Johnson, Mr. Speaker, Mr. Chief Justice, President Eisenhower, Vice President Nixon, President Truman, Reverend Clergy, fellow citizens:

We observe today not a victory of party but a celebration of freedom—symbolizing an end as well as a beginning—signifying renewal as well as change. For I have sworn before you and Almighty God the same solemn oath our forbears prescribed nearly a century and three-quarters ago.

The world is very different now. For man holds in his mortal hands the power to abolish all forms of human poverty and all forms of human life. And yet the same revolutionary beliefs for which our forebears fought are still at issue around the globe—the belief that the rights of man come not from the generosity of the state but from the hand of God.

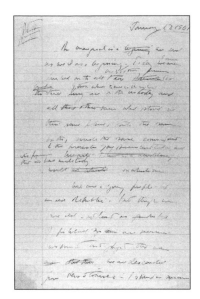

We dare not forget today that we are the heirs of that first revolution. Let the word go forth from this time and place, to friend and foe alike, that the torch has been passed to a new generation of Americans—born in this century, tempered by war, disciplined by a hard and bitter peace, proud of our ancient heritage—and unwilling to witness or permit the slow undoing of those human rights to which this nation has always been committed, and to which we are committed today at home and around the world.

Let every nation know, whether it wishes us well or ill, that we shall pay any price, bear any burden, meet any hardship, support any friend, oppose any foe to assure the survival and the success of liberty.

This much we pledge—and more.

To those old allies whose cultural and spiritual origins we share, we pledge the loyalty of faithful friends. United there is little we cannot do in a host of cooperative ventures. Divided there is little we can do—for we dare not meet a powerful challenge at odds and split asunder.

To those new states whom we welcome to the ranks of the free, we pledge our word that one form of colonial control shall not have passed away merely to be replaced by a far more iron tyranny. We shall not always expect to find them supporting our view. But we shall always hope to find them strongly supporting their own freedom—and to remember that, in the past, those who foolishly sought power by riding the back of the tiger ended up inside.

To those people in the huts and villages of half the globe struggling to break the bonds of mass misery, we pledge our best efforts to help them help themselves, for whatever period is required—not because the communists may be doing it, not because we seek their votes, but because it is right. If a free society cannot help the many who are poor, it cannot save the few who are rich.

To our sister republics south of our border, we offer a special pledge—to convert our good words into good deeds—in a new alliance for progress—to assist free men and free governments in casting off the chains of poverty. But this peaceful revolution of hope cannot become the prey of hostile powers. Let all our neighbors know that we shall join with them to oppose aggression or subversion anywhere in the Americas. And let every other power know that this Hemisphere intends to remain the master of its own house.

To that world assembly of sovereign states, the United Nations, our last best hope in an age where the instruments of war have far outpaced the instruments of peace, we renew our pledge of support—to prevent it from becoming merely a forum for invective—to strengthen its shield of the new and the weak—and to enlarge the area in which its writ may run.

Finally, to those nations who would make themselves our adversary, we offer not a pledge but a request: that both sides begin anew the quest for peace, before the dark powers of destruction unleashed by science engulf all humanity in planned or accidental self-destruction.

We dare not tempt them with weakness. For only when our arms are sufficient beyond doubt can we be certain beyond doubt that they will never be employed.

But neither can two great and powerful groups of nations take comfort from our present course—both sides overburdened by the cost of modern weapons, both rightly alarmed by the steady spread of the deadly atom, yet both racing to alter that uncertain balance of terror that stays the hand of mankind's final war.

So let us begin anew—remembering on both sides that civility is not a sign of weakness, and sincerity is always subject to proof. Let us never negotiate out of fear. But let us never fear to negotiate.

Let both sides explore what problems unite us instead of belaboring those problems which divide us.

Let both sides, for the first time, formulate serious and precise proposals for the inspection and control of arms—and bring the absolute power to destroy other nations under the absolute control of all nations.

Let both sides seek to invoke the wonders of science instead of its terrors. Together let us explore the stars, conquer the deserts, eradicate disease, tap the ocean depths and encourage the arts and commerce.

Let both sides unite to heed in all corners of the earth the command of Isaiah—to "undo the heavy burdens … (and) let the oppressed go free."

And if a beachhead of cooperation may push back the jungle of suspicion, let both sides join in creating a new endeavor, not a new balance of power, but a new world of law, where the strong are just and the weak secure and the peace preserved.

All this will not be finished in the first one hundred days. Nor will it be finished in the first one thousand days, nor in the life of this Administration, nor even perhaps in our lifetime on this planet. But let us begin.

In your hands, my fellow citizens, more than mine, will rest the final success or failure of our course. Since this country was founded, each generation of Americans has been summoned to give testimony to its national loyalty. The graves of young Americans who answered the call to service surround the globe.

Now the trumpet summons us again—not as a call to bear arms, though arms we need—not as a call to battle, though embattled we are—but a call to bear the burden of a long twilight struggle, year in and year out, "rejoicing in hope, patient in tribulation"—a struggle against the common enemies of man: tyranny, poverty, disease and war itself.

Can we forge against these enemies a grand and global alliance, North and South, East and West, that can assure a more fruitful life for all mankind? Will you join in that historic effort?

In the long history of the world, only a few generations have been granted the role of defending freedom in its hour of maximum danger. I do not shrink from this responsibility—I welcome it. I do not believe that any of us would exchange places with any other people or any other generation. The energy, the faith, the devotion which we bring to this endeavor will light our country and all who serve it—and the glow from that fire can truly light the world.

And so, my fellow Americans: ask not what your country can do for you—ask what you can do for your country.

My fellow citizens of the world: ask not what America will do for you, but what together we can do for the freedom of man.

Finally, whether you are citizens of America or citizens of the world, ask of us here the same high standards of strength and sacrifice which we ask of you. With a good conscience our only sure reward, with history the final judge of our deeds, let us go forth to lead the land we love, asking His blessing and His help, but knowing that here on earth God's work must truly be our own.

EXECUTIVE ORDER

ESTABLISHMENT AND ADMINISTRATION OF THE PEACE CORPS IN THE DEPARTMENT OF STATE

By virtue of the authority vested in me by the Mutual Security Act of 1954, 68 Stat. 832, as amended (22 U.S.C. 1750 et seq.), and as President of the United States, it is hereby ordered as follows:

Section 1. Establishment of the Peace Corps. The Secretary of State shall establish an agency in the Department of State which shall be known as the Peace Corps. The Peace Corps shall be headed by a Director.

Section 2. Functions of the Peace Corps. (a) The Peace Corps shall be responsible for the training and service abroad of men and women of the United States in new programs of assistance to nations and areas of the world, and in conjunction with or in support of existing economic assistance programs of the United States and of the United Nations and other international organizations.

(b) The Secretary of State shall delegate, or cause to be delegated, to the Director of the Peace Corps such of the functions under the Mutual Security Act of 1954, as amended, vested in the President and delegated to the Secretary, or vested in the Secretary, as the Secretary shall deem necessary for the accomplishment of the purposes of the Peace Corps.

Section 3. Financing of the Peace Corps. The Secretary of State shall provide for the financing of the Peace Corps with funds available

Executive Order 10924 (National Archives and Records Administration)

"The Peace Corps shall be responsible for the training and service abroad of men and women of the United States."

Overview

During his presidential campaign against Richard M. Nixon, John F. Kennedy attacked the foreign policy practices of Eisenhower's 1952 to 1960 Republican administration. Kennedy advocated an increase in the nation's military might and flexibility through the development of new weapons programs to compete with Communism. In the competitive cold war atmosphere, he also depicted the United States as falling behind the Soviet Union in its effort to win new and developing countries to the side of democracy. In his eyes, American diplomacy was stifled by bureaucracy and an inept staff who did not understand, much less respond to, the needs of the people they served. He resolved to put a fresh face on American aid to Africa, Asia, and Latin America.

Kennedy uncovered, almost by accident, a ready and eager talent pool for his projects—the youth of America. At two o'clock in the morning of October 14, 1960, the weary candidate arrived at the University of Michigan. He spoke spontaneously to an audience of ten thousand students, casually joked with them about the late hour, vigorously presented his challenge, and asked how many of them were willing to dedicate a few years of their lives to the service of their country by providing manpower and skill in developing nations. That brief and sketchy call to action marked the birth of the Peace Corps. Students across the country answered the challenge, meeting to develop plans and proposing their agendas to the candidate. Less than one month later, Kennedy called for the establishment of "a peace corps of talented young men and women, willing and able to serve their country" (http://www.presidency.ucsb.edu/ws/index.php?pid=2592 8). After his election, thousands of young men and women volunteered for service. He did not keep them waiting. His staff worked tirelessly and conceived the plan for the new volunteer-abroad service program. Just six weeks after taking office, the president issued Executive Order 10924, the Establishment and Administration of the Peace Corps in the Department of State.

Context

Many cite Senator Henry Reuss as the Peace Corps's father, John Kennedy as its icon, and Sargent Shriver as its driving force, but the organization also sprang from an age and a set of philosophical and social circumstances that made the time ripe for American volunteerism. The Peace Corps was a child of World War II and the cold war. The Holocaust, global war, and nuclear annihilation philosophically inspired a view that life itself was absurd. In response, a person could create meaning and morality only through individual action—the more heroic and self-sacrificing the better. It was determined that effort, not results, mattered.

Unlike the "Greatest Generation" that fought the war, the "New Generation," which the Peace Corps would tap, was searching for serious purpose and significant work. Writers of the time captured the male malaise in such books as *Growing Up Absurd*, *The Organization Man*, and *The Lonely Crowd*, all describing colorless, deadening work and empty lives. *The Feminine Mystique* depicted the constraints and frustration felt by American women. Across the globe, young people were sensing the same need for a release into meaningful lives, with many of them finding fulfillment in missionary-like volunteering in foreign countries.

Meanwhile, the United States felt the impact of a cold war with the Soviet Union that was corroding U.S. prestige and self-image. While Americans sought the comforts of modern life, the country was allowing racism and injustice to tear at its national fabric of freedom. On the other hand, throughout the 1950s Communism spread to new nations, including Cuba—just ninety miles from the United States. To that insult to American hemispheric sovereignty, the Russians added the indignity of Sputnik, the 1956 rocket that sent the first man into space. For the first time, nations were openly criticizing the perceived imperialism of the world's leading democracy. In Kennedy's view, America's "ill-chosen, ill-equipped, and ill-briefed" ambassadors created an "Ugly American" image abroad (Hoffman, p. 41). The cold war was going the wrong way. Citizens wondered where the vaunted American ingenuity, creativity, kindness, vigor, and drive had gone, and the pioneering spirit that marked the founding of the country, the opening of the frontier, and building of international stature and leadership.

1960

January
The Democratic congressman Henry S. Reuss of Wisconsin proposes a bill in the House for a formal examination of the feasibility of a Point Four Youth Corps, similar in purpose to the Peace Corps; it is not approved. Later, the Democratic senator Richard L. Neuberger of Oregon incorporates the Reuss proposal as part of a proposed amendment to the Mutual Security Act of 1960, calling for a nongovernmental study of the feasibility of a Point Four Youth Corps that would allow American citizens to serve as technical advisers to developing countries.

June 16
The Democratic senator Hubert Humphrey of Minnesota proposes the creation of a five thousand to ten-thousand-member volunteer peace corps.

July 15
Senator John F. Kennedy accepts the Democratic presidential nomination at the Democratic National Convention and delivers his New Frontier speech.

October 14
At two o'clock in the morning, after his third debate against his rival, Richard Nixon, Kennedy arrives at the University of Michigan, where the Democratic candidate speaks to ten thousand students with the congressional initiatives in mind, challenging them with America's need for foreign service.

November 2
Kennedy, while speaking at the Cow Palace in San Francisco, promises that if elected he will create a "Peace Corps" as one remedy for U.S. failings in foreign diplomacy and service.

November
Immediately after Kennedy's election, more than one hundred students from across the country meet at Princeton University to discuss ways for serving the country through the Peace Corps.

Young Americans, however, were already responding to the questions and the crises. On college campuses, students were demanding free speech and working as civil rights volunteers. Leaders such as Senator Ruess and Senator Hubert Humphrey already saw altruistic volunteerism as one way to satisfy the aspirations of young people for heroic action and significance in their lives. President Kennedy responded by empowering his brother-in-law Sargent Shriver to create a Peace Corps that would embody the New Frontier spirit and Americans' love for size, speed, and action. (The "New Frontier" was a term coined by Kennedy in his acceptance speech at the Democratic National Convention. It soon became a descriptor of his administration's domestic and foreign programs.) It would be big, bold, ambitious, and mobile and would set in motion even before Congress could deliberate. In his proposal for the Peace Corps, called "A Towering Task," Warren W. Wiggins outlined three goals: "To help interested countries meet their need for trained men and women. To promote better understanding of America on the part of the people served. To promote better understanding of other people on the part of Americans" (http://www.rpcv.org/A ToweringTaskbyWarrenWigginsFeb1961.pdf). The Peace Corps would provide an avenue for the altruism of the country's youth and an answer for the diplomatic needs of its government. Those twin functions would create an enduring tension of giving and getting at the heart of the Peace Corps.

About the Author

John Fitzgerald Kennedy, America's thirty-fifth president, seemed to be destined for politics from his birth in Brookline, Massachusetts, on May 29, 1917. His mother, Rose, was the daughter of the legendary Boston mayor John "Honey Fitz" Fitzgerald. His father, Joseph P. Kennedy, Sr., served in the late 1930s as ambassador to the Court of St. James's—the royal court of Great Britain. Kennedy, reared in both Boston and New York City, attended various schools and graduated from the Choate School in 1935. As a Harvard College senior, Kennedy toured Europe from February to September 1939, gathering information for his thesis, which was later published as the book *Why England Slept*. In spring 1941, one year after his graduation, the navy overlooked Kennedy's history of bad health and recurring back problems and accepted him into the Reserve Officers Training Corps. In World War II, while commanding torpedo boat PT-109, Lieutenant Kennedy saw his ship rammed by a Japanese destroyer. He rescued his crewmates and earned the Navy and Marine Corps Medal, which cited his outstanding courage, endurance, and leadership that saved several lives.

Once he was home, Kennedy launched his political career in 1946 with election to the House of Representatives, where he served until 1953, when he was elected to the Senate. He remained in the Senate until 1960. On September 12, 1946, he married Jacqueline Bouvier. In 1956

Kennedy, still in his thirties, almost won the Democratic Party's nomination for vice president. The near miss indicated that the junior senator from Massachusetts had acquired the respect of his party. That same year, while recuperating from spinal surgery, he enhanced his recognition by writing *Profiles in Courage*, a series of eight short biographies of U.S. senators who had displayed that virtue. The best-selling book earned him the Pulitzer Prize for Biography. As a senator, Kennedy manifested the disposition that would help change American foreign diplomacy and add the Peace Corps to its tools. He championed the cause of new relationships with emerging nations and told his colleagues, "Call it internationalism, call it anti-colonialism, call it what you will, the word is out and spreading like wild fire in nearly a thousand languages and dialects—that it is no longer necessary to remain forever in bondage" (Hoffman, p. 90).

In 1960 the senator won his party's nomination for the presidency in part by convincing voters that his Catholicism would not dictate his decisions as president. Kennedy then waged a vigorous battle for the presidency against Republican Vice President Richard Nixon. The campaign was marked by the first televised presidential debates, constituting a milestone in American history. Kennedy won the November presidential election by the narrowest of margins.

Kennedy, the youngest man ever elected to the presidency, asked the nation, especially its young people, to join him in facing the domestic and international challenges of the time. He spoke of Americans as pioneers facing a new frontier that would call on them for courage and sacrifice. On the home front, the country would renew efforts to eliminate poverty and racism. In the midst of a cold war that pitted democracy against Communism, Kennedy asked his countrymen to help ensure America's preeminence as a benign world power, one that would surpass the Soviet Union militarily while at the same time extending cooperation and assistance to all nations, especially to those struggling to find peace and security in a free world.

In addition to starting the Peace Corps, Kennedy's brief term in office was marked by the Bay of Pigs invasion (1961), a failed effort attempt to overthrow Cuba's dictator, Fidel Castro; the Cuban missile crisis (1962), which almost launched nuclear war against the Soviets; efforts to thwart Communist inroads in Latin America; and growing U.S. military involvement in Vietnam. On June 23, 1963, the president visited the Berlin Wall and cited it as an indication of the failure of Communism. With almost the entire Berlin population in the street, he delivered one of his most famous lines—"Ich bin ein Berliner" ("I am a Berliner"). Kennedy also pushed for and, in August 1963, signed with Britain and the Soviet Union the Nuclear Test Ban Treaty.

At home, Kennedy became progressively more supportive of the civil rights movement and more active in the expanding immigration opportunities, which he viewed as an extension of his civil rights policies. The president also urged a national commitment to space exploration and the goal of putting a man on the moon, as happened in 1969.

Time Line

1961

■ **February 6**
At a meeting with Sargent Shriver, Warren Wiggins, the deputy director for Far East Operations in the International Cooperation Administration, presents "The Towering Task"—the basic plan for creating the Peace Corps.

■ **February 28**
Shriver presents the final plan to the president, which calls for an immediate executive order to establish the Peace Corps.

■ **March 1**
President Kennedy signs Executive Order 10924, which establishes the Peace Corps as an agency of the Department of State.

■ **March 4**
Kennedy appoints Sargent Shriver as the director of the Peace Corps.

■ **September 22**
Congress approves legislation and passes the Peace Corps Act (Public Law 87-293), which formally establishes the Peace Corps and declares that its purpose is "to promote world peace and friendship through a Peace Corps which shall make available to interested countries and areas men and women of the United Sates qualified for service abroad and willing to serve, under conditions of hardship if necessary, to help the peoples of such countries and areas in meeting their needs for trained manpower" (http://www.peacecorps.gov/multimedia/pdf/policies/ms101.pdf).

1971

■ **June 30**
President Nixon issues Executive Order 11603, which transfers the Peace Corps and makes it a component within ACTION, an organization that embraces several volunteer agencies.

1982

■ **February 22**
Congress reestablishes the Peace Corps as a separate agency outside ACTION.

President John F. Kennedy hands a pen to his brother-in-law R. Sargent Shriver, after he signed legislation at the White House giving the Peace Corps permanent status, September 22, 1961. (AP Photo)

Kennedy's charisma and his wife's glamour added a youthful vigor and elegance to the White House that was home to two very young children, Caroline and John. Then, on November 23, 1963, in Dallas, Texas, Lee Harvey Oswald assassinated Kennedy. He was pronounced dead at one o'clock in the afternoon. On March 14, 1967, his body was moved to a permanent resting place in Arlington National Cemetery and marked by an eternal flame.

Explanation and Analysis of the Document

In issuing an executive order, a president must proceed cautiously lest he offend the legislative branch by usurping their lawmaking powers or overstepping the bounds of his office. Kennedy's winning the election by such a slim margin added motive for political discretion. Prior to sending out this executive order, the former representative and senator had to ensure congressional support for the Peace Corps, which he did. In light of the delicate balance of executive and legislative powers, the tone and content of the executive order merit scrutiny as the new president moved his agenda even while calming Congress.

In its opening line, the executive order reflects a clear respect for the legislative process that his order would seem to bypass. By citing the Mutual Security Act of 1954, Kennedy places the Peace Corps program within the framework of an already existing law, and, later in the document, he employs the same act to provide a familiar structure for placing the Peace Corps director under the secretary of state. In section 2, the rhetoric continues the theme of connecting the new order to the old law by tying the Peace Corps to "existing economic assistance programs" and by citing functions already allowed by the Mutual Security Act as the jobs of the Peace Corps director.

Section 3 seems to assure the Congress that little will change. The executive order requests no new funds. It instead allows the already allocated Mutual Security Act budget to provide old contingency monies to support the new program's start. To this judicious framing of the order, Kennedy appended a note to Congress that further alleviated apprehension by saying that the order would establish the Peace Corp on a temporary basis.

In section 4 the president again seems to limit the plan, this time by citing an executive order of his Republican predecessor. Dwight Eisenhower, just before leaving office, issued Executive Order 10893, Administration of Foreign Assistance and Related Functions. This final section of Executive Order 10924 reminds Congress, especially Republicans, of that recent precedent for issuing executive orders on foreign policy. Kennedy then places the Peace Corps establishment within the boundaries of Executive Order 10893, neither superseding it nor derogating from any of its provisions.

Kennedy, explaining the need for the executive order, again downplays its significance by depicting a test run for the Peace Corps and the chance to permit several hundred volunteers to be selected, trained, and sent to serve by the end of 1961. The president's note and the executive order's pervasive minimizing of the changes in establishing the Peace Corps hardly hint at the reality that would soon follow. The Peace Corps would evolve into an independent agency with thousands of volunteers in scores of countries serving millions of people and would endure into the twenty-first century.

Audience

Congress is the primary audience of "The Towering Task" and Executive Order 10924. Shriver and his committee's plan proposed a Peace Corps that would have five thousand volunteers serving in fifty countries by 1964. They argued that this size would have enormous psychological impact on American youth and developing nations. Kennedy, however, faced the skepticism of politicians, including Eisenhower, who ironically and prophetically suggested sending volunteers to the moon, and Nixon, who saw the Peace Corps as a potential haven for draft dodgers. In using the executive order and depicting the Peace Corps as a pilot plan, Kennedy allowed time for popular support to grow; for volunteers to be recruited, trained, and sent; and for Shriver and former Speaker of the House and current Vice President Lyndon Baines Johnson to convince Congress. The executive order reassured Congress. Shriver and Johnson persuaded Congress to turn the order into a law—the pilot program became an independent, funded agency. The combination of Johnson's prestige, Shriver's visit to each senator and representative, and the public's enthusiasm carried the day with lawmakers.

Executive Order 10924, despite seeming tentative, showed prospective volunteers that the Peace Corps promised during the heat of a political campaign was now being

"The Secretary of State shall establish an agency in the Department of State which shall be known as the Peace Corps."

(Section 1)

"The Peace Corps shall be responsible for the training and service abroad of men and women of the United States in new programs of assistance to nations and areas of the world."

(Section 2)

"Ask not what your country can do for you—ask what you can do for your country.... Finally, whether you are citizens of America or citizens of the world, ask of us the same high standards of strength and sacrifice which we ask of you."

("Inaugural Address of John F. Kennedy," http://www.yale.edu/lawweb/avalon/presiden/inaug/kennedy.htm)

"Our role is essential and unavoidable in the construction of a sound and expanding economy for the entire non-communist world, helping other nations build the strength to meet their own problems.... The problems in achieving this goal are towering and unprecedented—the response must be towering and unprecedented as well, much as Lend-Lease and the Marshall Plan were in earlier years, which brought such fruitful results."

("Annual Message to the Congress on the State of the Union: January 30, 1961," http://www.presidency.ucsb.edu/ws/index.php?pid=8045)

"To help the peoples of such countries and areas in meeting their needs for trained manpower ... and to help promote a better understanding of the American people on the part of the peoples served and a better understanding of other peoples on the part of the American people."

("MS 101: The Peace Corps Act," http://www.peacecorps.gov/multimedia/pdf/policies/ms101.pdf)

delivered to them as an opening act of the new administration. The order was also a beacon for the American public, showing that the country was facing a new frontier with a "new generation" ready, as Kennedy later said, to meet its "rendezvous with destiny" (Hoffman, p. 39). Finally, the order sent a signal to friend and foe alike of America's humane willingness to help other nations help themselves.

Impact

While Executive Order 10924 opened the way for the start of the Peace Corps, neither the executive order nor Congress's Peace Corps Act set the table for the agency. Both delegated that duty to Sargent Shriver, the new director. "Sarge," a well-traveled Chicago businessman with a

Yale law degree, proved to be a buoyant, shrewd, hard-driving organizer and a galvanizing leader. Having advised the president to issue Executive Order 10924, Shriver used Kennedy's and his own charisma to recruit a high-powered administrative board and hundreds of tireless volunteers for his staff. Shriver, aided by Vice President Johnson, who was equally impatient with endless protocol of Capitol Hill, kept the Peace Corps outside the organizational charts of the Agency for International Development and established it as a semiautonomous agency of the Department of State. The Peace Corps then won the approval of Congress and procured a budget of $30 million in contingency funds.

Meanwhile, Shriver had started designing and promoting the agency. Size, speed, and agility were key images in creating and publicizing the Peace Corps. The large scale would impress Congress as well as host countries and would persuade young people to commit themselves to this epic venture. Speed would convey the youthful vigor of the new frontier and the distain of the program for fearful hesitation and strangling red tape. "Our country and our times have had plenty of experience with programs that were too little too late" (Shriver, 1963, p. 700). The Peace Corps would be neither, but flaws would follow from the haste and the magnitude of the agency's birth.

With advertising companies donating their services and his staff developing public relations, Shriver launched a publicity campaign that depicted the gratifications to be found in hard work, daring, and self-sacrifice. Ads featured a shovel and slogans such as "The toughest job you'll ever love" and "The human care package." The mud hut stood as an icon of the mission. Within months, half of the country could identify the Peace Corps and its purposes, and youth were applying by the thousands. In that sense, the Peace Corps grew out of popular demand. By June a training-selection program was ready and waiting for the 1961 college graduates. When Congress approved the Peace Corps in September, hundred of volunteers were already serving abroad.

The volunteers, an elite 20 percent of all applicants, were generally white, middle-class, college graduates; nearly 85 percent were younger than twenty-five years old. Women made up 40 percent of the corps, and despite intense recruiting efforts, minorities represented fewer than 10 percent of the early classes. The rigorous sixteen weeks of "boot camp" combined academic, psychological, and physical training, including the daunting Outward Bound Program. Many volunteers complained about the overdoses of pro-America and anti-Communist propaganda courses, the stress induced by constant psychological evaluations, and the lack of practical training for teaching. The instruction did not always fit the needs they faced, but the volunteers received ten times the language training and twice the medical training as their counterparts in other countries.

While the image showed Peace Corps volunteers living in the wild and building bridges, most of them were teachers because that was the most available and often the most needed job. Many of them lived comfortably, some even with servants that depended on them for jobs. Based on numbers, the Peace Corps impact was huge. By 1961 America had 2,816 people serving, while Canada had 100 and England had 85. By 1966 the number had grown to nearly 14,000, supported by a budget of over $104 million. Nearly fifty countries were hosting the volunteers.

The Peace Corps paid for its size and haste but would incrementally improve its selection, training, and placement of volunteers. The well-intentioned program also may have suffered from an idealism that needed a harder look at realities. The effective volunteers, however, learned to accept the difference between program aspirations and in-field realities. Just because they meant well did not mean they would be loved or successful. Volunteers soon realized their host countries' people and problems were too complicated and complex for instant, friendly relationships and quick remedies. American policies sometimes seemed to thwart their work. By the late 1960s, for example, many of the volunteers, like young people back home, could not reconcile an America that burned villages (in Vietnam) with a Peace Corps that wanted to build them. Their numbers dropped from 11,210 in 1966 to 5,650 in 1969. They would grow again, especially after 1989 when the former cold war adversaries Poland, China, and Russia started to request volunteers.

In retrospect, the Peace Corps can point to achievements in education, medicine, and infrastructures that continue to serve appreciative host countries. The agency can also celebrate what it did for its volunteers. In the mid-1990s there were 145,000 returnees; 94 percent said they would do it again and recommend it to a friend. As volunteers, they balanced America's power with its moral and humanitarian impulse. In coming home, they brought with them exactly what the founders had hoped for: a deeper understanding and appreciation of other countries, cultures, and peoples. They fostered a new sensitive rhetoric that condemned negative terms such as "third world" and "natives." They advanced a resistance to racial and ethnic stereotyping. Subsequently, the returnees assumed leadership roles in all walks of life, including politics, education, business, and journalism. Their ranks include the Democratic Senator Chris Dodd of Connecticut, the CNBC anchor Chris Matthews, the Netflix founder Reed Hastings, and the Levi-Strauss board chair Robert Haas. The Peace Corps mission continued to thrive in the early twenty-first century, fulfilling President Kennedy's dream and perpetuating the vision voiced by one former corpsman: "If the right men and women are chosen—persons of understanding, imagination, and courage—the Peace Corps' moment in history can become a long and valuable one" (Ashabranner, p. 381).

Related Documents

"Address of President-Elect John F. Kennedy Delivered to a Joint Convention of the General Court of the Commonwealth of Massachusetts." John F. Kennedy Presidential Library and Museum

Web site. http://www.jfklibrary.org/Historical+Resources/Archives/ Reference+Desk/Speeches/JFK/. Accessed on February 27, 2008. In this speech delivered just before his inauguration, Kennedy alludes to the guidance he has taken from the first governor of Massachusetts, John Winthrop, in the forming of his own administration.

"Address of Senator John F. Kennedy Accepting the Democratic Party Nomination for the Presidency of the United States." John F. Kennedy Presidential Library and Museum Web site. http://www.jfklibrary.org/Historical+Resources/Archives/Reference+Desk/Speeches/JFK/JFK+Pre-Pres/Address+of+Senator+ John+F.+Kennedy+Accepting+the+Democratic+Party+Nomination+for+the+Presidency+of+t.htm. Accessed on October 8, 2007. In this speech Kennedy accepts the nomination and describes the "New Frontier" facing the country as a turning point in its history.

"Annual Message to the Congress on the State of the Union: January 30, 1961." The American Presidency Project Web site. http://www.presidency.ucsb.edu/ws/index.php?pid=8045. Accessed on October 8, 2007. In the cold war context, Kennedy's speech promises military preparedness and international goodwill through programs like a national Peace Corps.

"Executive Order 11041: Continuance and Administration of the Peace Corps in the Department of State." University of Michigan Library Web site. http://www.lib.umich.edu/govdocs/jfkeo/eo/ 11041.htm. Accessed on February 26, 2008. With the one-year trial period over, Kennedy ordered the secretary of state to continue the Peace Corps pursuant to Executive Order 10924 and the act of Congress.

"Executive Order 11063—Equal Opportunity in Housing." The National Archives "Federal Register" Web site. http://www. archives.gov/federal-register/codification/executive-order/11063. html. Accessed on February 26, 2008. President Nixon, who once derided the idea of the Peace Corps, removed its independence by assigning it as an additional function of the director of ACTION.

"Executive Order 12137—The Peace Corps." The National Archives "Federal Register" Web site. URL: http://www.archives. gov/federal-register/codification/executive-order/12137.html. Accessed on February 26, 2008. President Jimmy Carter restored autonomy to the Peace Corps, making it answerable to the director of the Peace Corps. Three years later Congress restored its full independence.

"Inaugural Address of John F. Kennedy." The Avalon Project at Yale Law School. http://www.yale.edu/lawweb/avalon/presiden/inaug/ kennedy.htm. Accessed on February 26, 2008. Kennedy challenges his countrymen to serve their country and asks other nations to join in fighting the tyranny of war and disease with strength and sacrifice.

"MS 101: The Peace Corps Act." Peace Corps Web site. http:// www.peacecorps.gov/multimedia/pdf/policies/ms101.pdf. Accessed on February 27, 2008. After being established by Executive Order 10924, the Peace Corps was authorized by act of Congress on September 22, 1961.

Bibliography

■ Articles

Colmen, Joseph G. "A Discovery of Commitment." *Annals of the American Academy of Political and Social Science* 365 (May 1966): 12–20.

Shriver, Sargent. "Two Years in the Peace Corps." *Foreign Affairs* (July 1963): 694–707.

■ Books

Ashabranner, Brent. *A Moment in History: The First Ten Years of the Peace Corps.* Garden City, N.Y.: Doubleday, 1971.

Fischer, Fritz. *Making Them Like Us: Peace Corps Volunteers in the 1960s.* Washington, D.C.: Smithsonian Institution Press, 1998.

Hoffman, Elizabeth Cobbs. *All You Need Is Love: The Peace Corps and the Spirit of the 1960s.* Cambridge, Mass.: Harvard University, 1998.

Hoopes, Roy. *The Peace Corps Experience.* New York: Clarkson N Potter, 1968.

Lederer, William, and Eugene Burdick. *The Ugly American.* New York: W. W. Norton, 1958.

Reeves, T. Zane. *The Politics of the Peace Corps and Vista.* Tuscaloosa: University of Alabama, 1988.

Schwarz, Karen. *What You Can Do for Your Country: An Oral History of the Peace Corps.* New York: William Morrow, 1991.

Shriver, Sargent. *Point of the Lance.* New York: Harper and Row, 1964.

■ Web Sites

John F. Kennedy Presidential Library and Museum Web site. http://www.jfklibrary.org/. Accessed on February 27, 2008.

"The Peace Corps Is Born, 1960–1962." Peace Corps Online Web site. http://peacecorpsonline.org/messages/messages/2629/4098.html. Accessed on March 10, 2008.

Peace Corps Web site. http://www.peacecorps.gov/. Accessed on February 27, 2008.

"Speech of Senator John F. Kennedy, Cow Palace, San Francisco, CA." The American Presidency Project Web site. http://www.presidency.ucsb.edu/ws/index.php?pid=25928. Accessed on March 10, 2008.

Wiggins, Warren W. "A Towering Task." National Peace Corps Association Web site. http://www.rpcv.org/AToweringTaskbyWarrenWigginsFeb1961. pdf. Accessed on March 10, 2008.

—By Gerard Molyneaux and J. Christopher Chamberlain

1. Eleven days before his inauguration, President Kennedy, in a speech to a Joint Convention of the General Court of the Commonwealth of Massachusetts, quoted John Winthrop's 1630 oration "A Modell of Christian Charity," saying, "We must always consider … that we shall be as a city upon a hill—the eyes of all people are upon us" (http://www.jfklibrary.org/Historical+Resources/Archives/Reference+Desk/Speeches/JFK/). To what extent does the Peace Corps' mission imply a notion of America as a morally superior and, therefore, globally responsible nation (that is, "a city upon a hill")? Contrast the concept of "city upon a hill" to realpolitik (the idea that a government should pursue only the most practical means of satisfying national interest, regardless of what it considers morally right). How does the Peace Corps' mission embrace or renounce the tenets of each concept?

2. Presidents often use executive orders for crisis management. In what ways does Executive Order 10924 meet this condition? Because executive orders infringe on the legislative process, they can be controversial and must be used with caution. What steps did Kennedy take to assuage congressional misgivings and to make sure his bill would pass? What role should national crises and citizen sentiment play in determining the use of an executive order? For Executive Order 10924, did national needs justify the use of an executive order?

3. Imagine that you are Nicholas Hobbs, the first director of selection for the Peace Corps. You have been charged with creating the first-ever set of recruitment guidelines by which Peace Corps volunteers will be chosen. Do you target a group of individuals with technical and professional training or prioritize native intelligence and ingenuity? Considering the goals of the Peace Corps and the availability of prospective volunteers, describe the perfect Peace Corps.

4. Executive Order 10924 constitutes Kennedy's first step into America's New Frontier—a frontier full of "unsolved problems of peace and war … ignorance and prejudice … poverty and surplus" (http://www.jfklibrary.org/Historical+Resources/Archives/Reference+Desk/Speeches/JFK/JFK+Pre-Pres/Address+of+Senator+John+F.+Kennedy+Accepting+the+Democratic+Party+Nomination+for+the+Presidency+of+t.htm). Kennedy challenged America's youth to become the pioneers of this new political, economic, and geographic territory. These national images, though popular, failed to inspire America's minority population, specifically blacks and Native Americans. What may have caused this lack of enthusiasm? Think of new national images that would galvanize today's youth to tackle contemporary global issues, for example, environment, health care, and city crime.

5. Nixon, among others, criticized the Peace Corps for creating "a haven for draft dodgers" (http://peacecorps online.org/messages/messages/2629/4098.html). Shriver's response was to offer young men draft deferment but not exemption. Should a peaceful national service such as the Peace Corps provide exemption or deferment from required military service? Should the United States require, as other nations do, a term of national service, peaceful or military, from all its citizens?

Glossary

deemed	considered
delegated	entrusted to another, assigned responsibility
derogate	to detract or deviate from
Executive Order	a declaration issued by the president or by a governor that has the force of law, usually based on existing statutory authority and requiring no action by Congress or the state legislature to become effective
pursuant	in accordance, in conformity with
supersede	to cause to be set aside
vested	fully and unconditionally guaranteed as a legal right or privilege

EXECUTIVE ORDER 10924

Establishment and Administration of the Peace Corps in the Department of State

By virtue of the authority vested in me by the Mutual Security Act of 1954, 68 Stat. 832, as amended (22 U.S.C. 1750 et seq.), and as President of the United States, it is hereby ordered as follows:

SECTION 1. Establishment of the Peace Corps. The Secretary of State shall establish an agency in the Department of State which shall be known as the Peace Corps. The Peace Corps shall be headed by a Director.

SEC. 2. Functions of the Peace Corps. (a) The Peace Corps shall be responsible for the training and service abroad of men and women of the United States in new programs of assistance to nations and areas of the world, and in conjunction with or in support of existing economic assistance programs of the United States and of the United Nations and other international organizations.

(b) The Secretary of State shall delegate, or cause to be delegated, to the Director of the Peace Corps

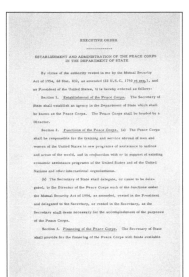

such of the functions under the Mutual Security Act of 1954, as amended, vested in the President and delegated to the Secretary, or vested in the Secretary, as the Secretary shall deem necessary for the accomplishment of the purposes of the Peace Corps.

SEC. 3. Financing of the Peace Corps. The Secretary of State shall provide for the financing of the Peace Corps with funds available to the Secretary for the performance of functions under the Mutual Security Act of 1954, as amended.

SEC. 4. Relation to Executive Order No. 10893. This order shall not be deemed to supersede or derogate from any provision of Executive Order No. 10893 of November 8, 1960, as amended, and any delegation made by or pursuant to this order shall, unless otherwise specifically provided therein, be deemed to be in addition to any delegation made by or pursuant to that order.

JOHN F. KENNEDY
THE WHITE HOUSE, March 1, 1961.

04 36 56	0.4	CC	Roger.
04 37 00	9.6	P	There is quite a bit of cloud cover down in this area. I can, ah, right on track, I can only see certain areas. I can see quite a bit on up to the north, however.
04 37 18	2.4	P	This is Friendship 7, going to manual control.
04 37 21	1.3	CC	Ah, Roger, Friendship 7.
04 37 23	2.7	P	This is banging in and out here; I'll just control it manually.
04 37 25	0.4	CC	Roger.
04 37 48	3.1	CC	Friendship 7, Guaymas Cap Com, reading you loud and clear.
04 37 51	2.1	P	Roger, Guaymas, read you loud and clear also.

TEXAS

04 38 06	4.0	CT	Friendship 7, Friendship 7, this is Texas Com Tech. Do you read? Over.
04 38 10	1.3	P	Roger, Texas, go ahead.
04 38 13	3.9	CT	Ah, Roger. Reading you 5 square. Standby for Texas Cap Com.
04 38 16	0.4	P	Roger.
04 38 25	23.8	CC	This is Texas Cap Com, Friendship 7. We are recommending that you leave the retropackage on through the entire reentry. This means that you will have to override the 05g switch which is expected to occur at 04 43 _3. This also means that you will have to manually retract the scope. Do you read?
04 38 49	4.0	P	This is Friendship 7. What is the reason for this? Do you have any reason? Over.
04 38 53	3.6	CC	Not at this time; this is the judgement of Cape Flight.
04 38 58	2.6	P	Ah, Roger. Say again your instructions please. Over.
04 39 01	22.1	CC	We are recommending that the retropackage not, I say again, not be jettisoned. This means that you will have to override the 05g switch which is expected to occur at 04 43 53. This is approximately 4-1/2 minutes from now. This also means that you will have to retract the scope manually. Do you understand?

John Glenn's Official Communication with the Command Center (National Archives and Records Administration)

JOHN GLENN'S OFFICIAL COMMUNICATION WITH THE COMMAND CENTER

"This is Friendship 7. I think the pack just let go.... A real fireball outside."

Overview

On February 20, 1962, Marine Lieutenant Colonel John Glenn became the first American to orbit the earth in a space capsule. His official communication with the National Aeronautics and Space Administration's Mission Control center at Cape Canaveral, Florida, recorded his skillful manual piloting of his capsule, *Friendship 7*, after the autopilot device failed during reentry. In addition, after the second orbit, the heat shield, designed to prevent the capsule from burning up during reentry, was reported to be loose. In spite of these obstacles, Glenn was able to orbit the earth three times and safely return to Cape Canaveral almost five hours after launch. Glenn's flight came during the cold war, characterized by intense ideological and military competition between the United States and the Soviet Union. The exploration of space and its use for strategic purposes were crucial aspects of such competition. In the late 1950s and early 1960s, the Soviets had made spectacular advances in their space program, and the United States appeared to be behind the Communist superpower.

Glenn's successful mission restored confidence in the nation's ability to rival the Soviet Union in the race for space exploration. The enthusiasm that followed Glenn's flight encouraged the Kennedy administration to develop its Apollo program and the president's commitment to land an American on the moon by the end of the 1960s. The successful orbiting and reentry of *Friendship 7* thus represented a remarkable political and a scientific achievement for the United States and a turning point in the space race between the two superpowers.

Context

To understand the political and scientific impact of John Glenn's orbit around the earth, it is important to place the flight in the context of the cold war and the space race of the late 1950s and the 1960s. Before the *Friendship 7* mission, the United States was perceived to be lagging behind the Soviet Union in the space race. In 1957 the Soviet Union launched *Sputnik I* and *Sputnik II* the first earth-orbiting satellites. The successful launch was considered a Soviet triumph and challenged American military and technological superiority. Concerns spread throughout the country as well as through the Western bloc about national safety. If the Soviets were able to orbit satellites, they might also be capable of delivering atomic warheads on American soil as well as against American allies. The *Sputnik* satellites were effective propaganda tools for the Soviet Union in its quest for new allies in third world countries, which constituted the new important battlefields of the cold war after the division of Western and Eastern Europe. As the cultural historian Dale Carter reports, the Indian prime minister Jawaharlal Nehru described the launch as a "great scientific advancement," and Radio Cairo pointed out that the *Sputnik* satellites would "make countries think twice before tying themselves to the imperialist policy led by the United States" (p. 120). The triumph of the *Sputnik* satellites resonated even more because of the U.S. failure to launch a small satellite onboard a *Vanguard* rocket, which exploded shortly after its takeoff in December 1957.

Democratic politicians blamed the Russian space triumphs on President Dwight Eisenhower's bland leadership and stubborn commitment to fiscal conservatism. Supported by unanimous opinion polls in which Americans asked for higher spending on defense and military weapons, Democrats demanded more investments in missile programs to repair the blow to American military prestige represented by *Sputnik*. In their attacks against the administration in view of the congressional elections of 1958 and the presidential election of 1960, Democrats were helped by Eisenhower's apparent lack of reaction to the Russian advances. Eisenhower remained convinced of American superiority and was skeptical about devoting financial resources to the space race, which he considered of secondary importance. His major commitment was to a balanced budget, and he was concerned about the effects on inflation that increased military spending on space might have. However, confronted with congressional pressure, Eisenhower agreed to the creation of a new federal agency, the National Aeronautics and Space Administration (NASA), which was to devise more effective space pro-

1957

■ September 23–24
Escorted by the police, a group of African American students enter Little Rock's Central High School following the partial desegregation of the institution. The riot that ensues causes the temporary removal of the pupils. The next morning the students are escorted inside the school by the 327th Airborne Battle Group of the U.S. Army's 101st Airborne Division.

■ October 4
The Soviet Union launches *Sputnik I*, the first artificial satellite to orbit the earth.

■ November 3
Launched by the Soviets, *Sputnik II* carries the first living passenger into space, a dog called Laika.

■ December 6
The United States fails to launch a small satellite onboard the *Vanguard* rocket, which explodes shortly after takeoff.

1958

■ July 29
The National Aeronautics and Space Act establishes the National Aeronautics and Space Administration, the government agency responsible for the U.S. space program.

1960

■ November 8
John F. Kennedy defeats Richard Nixon and becomes the thirty-fifth president of the United States.

1961

■ April 12
The Russian astronaut Yuri Gagarin is the first man to fly into space.

■ April 17–21
The CIA launches the failed Bay of Pigs invasion to assassinate Castro and replace his Communist regime with a government loyal to the United States.

■ May 5
American astronaut Alan Shepard becomes the second man and the first American to travel into space.

grams. Eisenhower also proposed the National Defense and Education Act, which, once passed by Congress, authorized $887 million in loans and grants to aid college students studying sciences and languages.

In the late 1950s, American national confidence as well as the image of a unified nation were also greatly shaken in the aftermath of the desegregation of public schools following the U.S. Supreme Court ruling in *Brown v. Board of Education of Topeka* (1954). In open opposition to the ruling, in September 1957 Arkansas's governor Orval E. Faubus summoned the state's National Guard to block the entry of black students at Little Rock's Central High School. Eisenhower did not attempt to stop Faubus, but the governor had to withdraw the national guardsmen in the wake of a federal judge's order. Nine black students made their entry to the school escorted by soldiers of the U.S. Army. Fearing bloodshed, Eisenhower had federalized the Arkansas National Guard and dispatched paratroopers to Little Rock to ensure the students' safety. Troops guarded the school for the rest of the year, and city officials preferred to close public high schools during the 1958–1959 school year rather than desegregate them. These events suggested a racially divided country.

The perceived military superiority of the Soviet Union and the racial conflicts of the late 1950s challenged the entire record of the Eisenhower administration. They contributed to the victory of the Democratic ticket formed by John F. Kennedy and Lyndon B. Johnson in the 1960 presidential election, one of the closest and most hard-fought in twentieth-century politics. In contrast to the conservative and staid image of Eisenhower, Kennedy presented himself as an injection of youth and modernity into American politics. He was able to use the media to his advantage in ways that his Republican opponent, Richard Nixon, was not. Nixon had been Eisenhower's vice president for two terms, yet Eisenhower gave him only a timid endorsement, a fact that further damaged him. Kennedy was also skillful at exploiting the negative record of Eisenhower and Nixon on the space race and civil rights. When Nixon challenged Kennedy's ability to deal with the Soviets, the Democrat easily countered that during the previous administration American prestige in the face of the Soviet Union had declined. During his campaign, Kennedy endorsed investments in the space race, "the symbol of the twentieth century" in which, "to insure peace and freedom," the United States could not afford to be second to the Soviet Union (Carter, p. 154). As for civil rights, Kennedy could afford to court African American voters, for he was sure that his Texan running mate, Johnson, would keep the southern states loyal to the Democratic Party.

Despite Kennedy's claim that he would defeat Communism in the 1960s, his own administration opened with international crises that seriously undermined the credibility of his statement. In August 1961, after Kennedy refused to negotiate the end of the Western occupation of Berlin, Soviet and East German authorities erected a concrete and barbed-wire barrier, the Berlin Wall, to stop the flight of East Germans into West Berlin. Cuba, where the 1959

Communist revolution led by Fidel Castro had ousted the regime of Fulgencio Batista, a long-time American ally, provoked the most serious confrontations between the United States and the Soviet Union. In April 1961, the Central Intelligence Agency (CIA) launched the Bay of Pigs invasion, an operation designed to assassinate Castro and restore a government more favorable to American political and economic interests. The CIA carried more than one thousand armed exiled Cuban leaders to the island to foster an uprising against Castro, but they did not draw support from the population. The invasion failed almost before it started, with boats running against coral reefs and the equipment malfunctioning. Following the unsuccessful invasion, the CIA devised Operation Mongoose to disrupt Cuban commerce and plot the assassination of Castro. This continued American hostility toward Cuba would lead to the Cuban missile crisis of October 1962, bringing the world to the brink of nuclear warfare.

During the early months of the Kennedy administration, the Soviet Union continued to appear to be ahead of the United States in the space race. In April 1961, the Russian astronaut Yuri Gagarin became the first man to fly into space, aboard the *Vostok 3KA-2*. Speaking on Radio Moscow, Gagarin emphasized the political significance of his flight, dedicating it "to the people of a communist society, the society which our Soviet people are already entering, and which, I am convinced, all the people on earth will enter" (Carter, p. 156). In response to Gagarin's flight, Kennedy asked Vice President Johnson to examine the status of the American space program. The vice president suggested that the United States was not doing enough to oppose the Soviet Union in the space race. He concluded that the stated goal of NASA's Apollo program, a planned manned moon landing before the end of the 1960s, was far enough in the future to make it possible for the United States to achieve it first. Listening to Johnson's suggestion, Kennedy confidently endorsed the Apollo program. In the meantime, the United States answered Gagarin's mission with the successful suborbital flights of Alan Shepard and Virgil Grissom in May and July 1961, respectively. Yet these missions were soon obscured by the daylong seventeen-orbit flight of Gherman Titov in August 1961. Thus, when John Glenn successfully orbited the earth in February 1962, his mission was considered a triumph that could finally rival the Soviet achievements and restore American national pride.

About the Author

John Herschel Glenn, Jr., was born in Cambridge, Ohio, on July 18, 1921. He attended public schools in New Concord, Ohio, and later graduated from Muskingum College. Glenn served in the U.S. Marine Corps from 1942 to 1965. He was awarded six Distinguished Flying Crosses and seventeen Air Medals for his service in World War II and the Korean War. In July 1957, he established a new coast-to-coast flying speed record for the U.S. Navy. This event brought Glenn into the media spotlight.

Time Line

1961

■ **May 25**
President Kennedy addresses a joint session of Congress and announces his support for NASA's Apollo program, designed to take American astronauts to the moon before the end of the decade.

■ **July 21**
Virgil Grissom commands a suborbital flight on the *Liberty Bell 7*.

■ **August 6**
Soviet astronaut Gherman Titov accomplishes seventeen earth orbits.

■ **August 13**
Soviets and East Germans begin the construction of the Berlin Wall, which separates West Berlin from Communist East Berlin and the rest of East Germany.

1962

■ **February 20**
John Glenn becomes the first American to orbit the earth in a space capsule.

1963

■ **November 22**
President John F. Kennedy is assassinated in Dallas, Texas. Vice President Lyndon B. Johnson succeeds him.

1969

■ **July 20**
Neil Armstrong and Buzz Aldrin successfully conclude the *Apollo 11* mission by landing on the moon.

Because of these accomplishments and media attention, Glenn was the best known of the original seven trainees selected by NASA for its Mercury program, which aimed to put a man in orbit around the earth. In February 1962, Glenn became the first American to achieve that goal, orbiting the earth three times. His successful landing in adverse conditions made him an object of adulation, and he soon attained the status of a national hero. He was flooded by congratulatory telegrams, and President Kennedy presented him with NASA's Distinguished Service Medal. In February 1962, Glenn was received at the White House and addressed a joint session of Congress. He was welcomed to Washington by 250,000 people, and at the White House reception he was given the keys to the city.

After the *Friendship 7* mission, Glenn worked for NASA's publicity operations but was not allowed to take

John H. Glenn is shown on January 26, 1962, during final phases of his training at Cape Canaveral, Florida, for his upcoming three-orbit flight around the Earth.
(AP Photo/NASA)

part to space missions, for it was thought that the eventual loss of such a national hero on a future mission would threaten the very existence of the agency's space program. Thus, Glenn resigned from the Marine Corps and turned to public affairs. He decided to run for the Democratic Senate primaries in 1964 and 1970 but was unsuccessful both times. However, he started a career in the corporate world as an executive for Royal Crown Cola and as a member of several boards. In November 1974, he was elected to the U.S. Senate, where he remained until 1999, when he did not seek reelection. As a senator, Glenn was the chief author of the 1978 Nuclear Non-Proliferation Act and served as chairman of the Committee on Governmental Affairs from 1987 until 1995.

Glenn made a bid to run as vice president with Jimmy Carter in 1976, but Carter selected Minnesota senator Walter Mondale. In 1984 Glenn ran as a candidate in the Democratic presidential primaries. Early on, Glenn polled well, coming in a strong second to Mondale, but his bid was eventually unsuccessful. In the early 1990s, Glenn was involved in the Keating Five scandal after accepting financial contributions from Charles Keating, the American banker convicted for fraud after the bankruptcy of the American Continental Corporation in 1989. In the end, however, Glenn was

exonerated, and the Senate committee investigating the matter found him guilty only of exercising poor judgment.

He returned to space aboard the space shuttle *Discovery* from October 29 to November 7, 1998, becoming, at age seventy-seven, the oldest human to travel into space. Glenn married his high school sweetheart, Anna Margaret Castor, in April 1943. The couple had two children, David and Carolyn.

In 1990, Glenn was inducted into the Astronaut Hall of Fame. On March 1, 1999, NASA renamed its Cleveland center the "John H. Glenn Research Center at Lewis Field" in his honor. Dale Carter has described John Glenn as the quintessential American self-made man "whose personal experiences confirmed the promises of freedom his 1962 flight had been commissioned to extend." He rose from an undistinguished small-town childhood to "personal wealth, political influence, and presidential aspiration" through "distinguished military service and national heroism." As the typical self-made man, he recovered from "setbacks, disadvantages, and disappointments through hard work and personal initiative" (p. 192).

Explanation and Analysis of the Document

The document records communication between John Glenn and NASA's command center at Cape Canaveral during the last twenty minutes of the *Friendship* 7 mission. The exchange focuses on the defective operation of the heat shield and the necessary maneuvers for Glenn to make safe reentry. When Glenn entered the second orbit, the Mission Control Center received a signal that the heat shield, whose function was to prevent the capsule from burning up during reentry, was becoming loose. This could have been a faulty signal, as in fact it was later shown to be, but the command center advises Glenn not to jettison the retropackage after the rockets are fired to slow the capsule for reentry, as the normal procedure would have required. In this case, Mission Control tells Glenn to retain the retropack for the entire duration of reentry, to keep the heat shield in its place. The purpose of this maneuver was to protect Glenn during the early part of entry into the atmosphere. Although the pack would eventually burn away, the team felt that by that time the aerodynamic pressures would hold the shield in place, protecting the astronaut. Glenn is not told the reason for this decision. Although Glenn asks the reason for this change of plans, Mission Control only vaguely replies that "Cape flight will give you the reasons for this action when you are in view."

After four hours and forty minutes of the flight, the command center advises Glenn to go to reentry attitude. They restate that they are not sure the heat shield and the landing bag are still locked into position but reassure Glenn that it is possible to reenter safely with the retropack on. They also remind him that he might have to deploy the landing bag manually. Because he is retaining the retropackage, Glenn is advised to retract the periscope

> "We are recommending that you leave the retropackage on through the entire reentry. This means that you will have to override the 05g switch which is expected to occur at 04 43 _3. This also means that you will have to manually retract the scope. Do you read?"
>
> (Mission Control to John Glenn, 4 hours, 38 minutes, 25 seconds after launch)

> "This is Friendship 7. I think the pack just let go.... A real fireball outside."
>
> (John Glenn to Mission Control, 4 hours, 43 minutes, 16 seconds after launch)

> "Ah, Seven, this is Cape. What's your general condition? Are you feeling pretty well?" "My condition is good, but that was a real fireball, boy.... I had great chunks of that retropack breaking off all the way through."
>
> (Exchange between Mission Control and John Glenn, 4 hours, 47 minutes, 55 seconds after launch)

manually. Glenn then communicates to control that he is down to 15 percent fuel on manual control. The operations team then tells Glenn that the weather in his landing area is excellent and that visibility is good. The exchange that follows records the most difficult and suspenseful moment during the flight. The astronaut struggles to maintain control of the spacecraft and notices huge lumps breaking off from the capsule. He announces that the retropack has come loose and that the capsule is experiencing peak reentry heating. The heat shield, however, holds. If it had not, Glenn and his capsule would have been reduced to ashes. For a few seconds communications break down, and for almost three minutes Glenn does not receive replies from Cape Canaveral. Yet when Mission Control finally responds, Glenn reassures them that he is feeling well despite the "fireball" he has witnessed as the retropack burned down. *Friendship* 7 splashed down in the Atlantic about forty miles from the planned landing zone southeast of Bermuda. The destroyer USS *Noa* spotted the spacecraft while it was descending and arrived at Glenn's recovery site seventeen minutes later.

Audience

The audience of John Glenn's flight was primarily the fifty thousand spectators who had gathered at Cape Canaveral in Florida to witness the launch. The countdown was also broadcast on television, reaching millions

of people. But the effective audience of the flight was a much larger one, and the political significance of the orbit of *Friendship* 7 reached well beyond national borders. Because the Soviets had been ahead of the United States in the space race, their propaganda had promoted the missions of their astronauts as examples of the better prospects that a Socialist society reserved for the common man. So, too, for the common woman: In February 1962, a few days before Glenn's flight, Valentina Tereshkova was selected for the *Vostok VI* mission, and in June 1963 she became the first woman in space. In addition, the Soviets used their space program to promote the multiracial nature of Socialist society. When Andriyan Nikolayev was selected for the *Vostok III* mission, his Chuvash ethnic background was stressed, to illustrate the equal opportunities afforded to everyone. The famous words of the Russian premier Nikita Khrushchev in his telephone call to Gagarin upon the astronaut's return to the earth resonated as a challenge difficult to meet: "Let the capitalist countries catch up with our country!" (Carter, p. 157).

Glenn's flight was the evidence that "the capitalist countries" were catching up with the Communist bloc in the space race. The audience of Glenn's mission therefore extended to U.S. allies, who were increasingly concerned about Soviet military and technological advances. It also included those third world countries that were still not aligned with either superpower or where Communist movements were developing. To both American and Soviet political and military leaders, the third world was the new front of the cold war. The Mercury and Apollo programs were to demonstrate, in Dale Carter's words, that "the United States and its free enterprise system" were still "the recognized instruments of liberation" (p. 157).

Impact

John Glenn's flight helped rescue the political fortunes of the Kennedy administration and restore American prestige internationally after Yuri Gagarin's flight and the fiasco at the Bay of Pigs. Kennedy became increasingly convinced of the domestic electoral benefits and the international clout potentially connected with space exploration. As the *Washington Post* editor Benjamin Bradlee pointed out, the president was eager to identify with the astronauts selected for the Mercury program, with "the glamour surrounding them, and the courage and skill it [took] to do their job" (p. 191). Kennedy was particularly keen on Glenn and came to see him as the embodiment of the spirit of his New Frontier social and political program.

Glenn's mission was given spectacular resonance by national media and by the NASA publicity machine. An estimated crowd of fifty thousand spectators gathered at Cape Canaveral to watch the launch. The countdown was also broadcast on television for an audience of approximately one hundred million. Once back on the ground, Glenn was immediately treated as a national hero, and his mission was memorialized with special events and museum exhibitions. The astronaut's first footsteps on the recovery ship USS *Noa* were highlighted with white paint for exhibition at the Smithsonian Institution. The U.S. Post Office immediately designed commemorative stamps. As the flight was meant to restore confidence in American scientific and military technology both nationally and internationally, the capsule was taken on a tour to seventeen countries. It was then put next to Glenn's footprints at the Smithsonian Institution. As Dale Carter notes, the "rarely equaled campaign of adulation" devoted to Glenn was "intended to counter the renewed claims of the Russians in space and also to overwhelm the obstacles erected by the Russians across Berlin in the weeks after Titov's return" (p. 187).

Related Documents

Kennedy, John F. "Address at Rice University on the Nation's Space Effort." In *The Greatest Speeches of President John F. Kennedy*, ed. Brian R. Dudley. West Vancouver, Canada: Titan Publishing, 2004. Delivered on September 12, 1962, in Houston, Texas, this speech announced the intention of landing an American on the moon by the end of the 1960s.

Mailer, Norman. *Of a Fire on the Moon*. New York: New American Library, 1971. In this nonfiction book, Mailer assesses the impact of the moon landing in American history. The book is an interest-

ing encounter between two opposites: NASA's patriotic discourse and Mailer's countercultural approach.

"National Aeronautics and Space Act of 1958." National Aeronautics and Space Administration Web site. http://history.nasa.gov/spaceact.html. Accessed on February 28, 2008. With this 1958 act, President Eisenhower created the National Aeronautics and Space Administration (NASA) to compete more effectively with the Soviets in the space race.

Wolfe, Tom. *The Right Stuff*. London: Jonathan Cape, 1979. A nonfiction novel, *The Right Stuff* tells the story of the seven astronauts selected by NASA for the Mercury program, including John Glenn. The narrative places strong emphasis on the personal stories of the astronauts and their wives rather than on the technical aspects of space exploration. *The Right Stuff* also addresses the political reasons for putting people into space, assessing the propaganda impact of the seven astronauts.

Bibliography

■ Books

Bizony, Piers. *The Man Who Ran the Moon: James E. Webb, NASA, and the Secret History of Project Apollo*. New York: Thunder's Mouth Press, 2006.

Bradlee, Benjamin. *Conversations with Kennedy*. New York: W. W. Norton, 1975.

Brzezinski, Matthew. *Red Moon Rising: Sputnik and the Hidden Rivalries That Ignited the Space Age*. New York: Times Books, 2007.

Cadbury, Deborah. *Space Race: The Epic Battle between America and the Soviet Union for Dominion of Space*. New York: Harper Perennial, 2006.

Carter, Dale. *The Final Frontier: The Rise and Fall of the American Rocket State*. London: Verso, 1988.

Glenn, John, and Nick Taylor. *John Glenn: A Memoir*. New York: Bantam, 2000.

Green, Robert. *John Glenn: Astronaut and Senator*. New York: Ferguson, 2000.

Launius, Roger D., and Howard E. McCurdy, eds. *Spaceflight and the Myth of Presidential Leadership*. Champaign: University of Illinois Press, 1997.

McDougall, Walter A. *The Heavens and the Earth: A Political History of the Space Age*. Baltimore: Johns Hopkins University Press, 1997.

Raum, Elizabeth. *John Glenn*. Chicago: Heinemann Library, 2005.

Schlesinger, Arthur, Jr. *A Thousand Days: John F. Kennedy in the White House*. Boston: Mariner Books, 2003.

Sorensen, Theodore. *Kennedy*. London: Hodder and Stoughton, 1965.

■ **Web Sites**

The John and Annie Glenn Historic Site and Exploration Center Web site.
> http://www.johnglennhome.org/index.shtml. Accessed on January 14, 2008.

National Aeronautics and Space Administration "Mercury 7 Archives" Web site.
> http://science.ksc.nasa.gov/history/mercury/. Accessed on January 14, 2008.

National Aeronautics and Space Administration "NASA History Division" Web site.
> http://history.nasa.gov/. Accessed on January 14, 2008.

"Speech and the Following Discussion at the Munich Conference on Security Policy." President of Russia Web site.
> http://president.kremlin.ru/eng/speeches/2007/02/10/0138_type82912type82914type82917type84779_118123.shtml. Accessed on February 28, 2008.

—By Luca Prono

1. After more than a decade of peaceful relations following the fall of the Berlin Wall, newspaper headlines around the globe talked about a new cold war as Russia's president Vladimir Putin addressed the Forty-third Munich Conference on Security Policy in February 2007. Putin complained about the global dominance of the United States, often achieved with an "almost uncontained hyper use of force in international relations." Putin made clear that the "arms race" engineered by the U.S. attitude was leading to a new militarization of space: "Star wars is no longer a fantasy—it is a reality." (The entire speech by Putin is available online at http://president.kremlin.ru/eng/speeches/2007/02/10/0138_type82912type82914type82917type84779_118123.shtml.) Compare and contrast the historical and political context of the *Friendship 7* mission with our contemporary situation, which seems to have sparked a renewed interest in the military use of outer space.

2. After more than thirty-five years, John Glenn returned into space in 1998. Compare the two eras of his space flights and the two missions in terms of their scientific and ideological functions.

3. Since his flight, John Glenn has been hailed as an "All-American hero." Dale Carter, however, has offered an alternative view of Glenn as produced by the state's mechanisms of "engineering and propaganda, and advanced … within its capitalist precepts" (p. 192). Assess the definition of Glenn as a hero, taking into account his corporate and political career as well as the ways in which he was used as propaganda.

4. Compare the space policies of the Eisenhower and Kennedy administrations and explain why the exploration of space became such an important part of Kennedy's political program. Do not focus exclusively on foreign relations but attempt to address the domestic consequences of developing a more aggressive space program.

5. *Destination Moon* (1950) by Irving Pichel and *Dr. Strangelove* (1964) by Stanley Kubrick are two films that resonate with anxieties of the space and the nuclear arms race. Compare how the two films exploit the cold war rhetoric within their narratives.

Glossary

attitude	mode
Cape	Cape Canaveral Air Force Station, NASA's space-launch facility on the East Coast.
fly-by-wire	electrically signaled control system
Friend	*Friendship 7*
read	hear
retropackage	part of the spacecraft strapped onto its heat shield
Roger	"got your message" or "heard you"
Seven	*Friendship 7*
scope	periscope

JOHN GLENN'S OFFICIAL COMMUNICATION WITH THE COMMAND CENTER

04 36 56 0.4 … *Command Center*—Roger.

04 37 00 9.6 … *Pilot*—There is quite a bit of cloud cover down in this area. I can, ah, right on track, I can only see certain areas. I can see quite a bit on up to the north, however.

04 37 18 2.4 … *P*—This is Friendship 7, going to manual control.

04 37 21 1.3 … *CC*—Ah, Roger, Friendship 7.

04 37 23 2.7 … *P*—This is banging in and out here; I'll just control it manually.

04 37 25 0.4 … *CC*—Roger.

04 37 48 3.1 … *CC*—Friendship 7, Guaymas Cap Com, reading you loud and clear.

04 37 51 2.1 … *P*—Roger, Guaymas, read you loud and clear also.

◆ TEXAS

04 38 06 4.0 … *Com Tech*—Friendship 7, Friendship 7, this is Texas Com Tech. Do you read? Over.

04 38 10 1.3 … *P*—Roger, Texas, go ahead.

04 38 13 3.9 … *CT*—Ah, Roger. Reading you 5 square. Standby for Texas Cap Com.

04 38 16 0.4 … *P*—Roger.

04 38 25 23.8 … *CC*—This is Texas Cap Com, *Friendship* 7. We are recommending that you leave the retropackage on through the entire reentry. This means that you will have to override the 05g switch which is expected to occur at 04 43 _3. Tis also means that you will have to manually retract the scope. Do you read?

04 38 49 4.0 … *P*—This is *Friendship* 7. What is the reason for this? Do you have any reason? Over.

04 38 53 3.6 … *CC*—Not at this time; this is the judgement of Cape Flight.

04 38 58 2.6 … *P*—Ah, Roger. Say again your instructions please. Over.

04 39 01 22.1 … *CC*—We are recommending that the retropackage not, I say again, not be jettisoned. This means that you will have to override the 05g switch which is expected to occur at 04 43 53.

This is approximately 4-1/2 minutes from now. This also means that you will have to retract the scope manually. Do you understand?

04 39 25 9.7 … *P*—Ah, Roger, understand. I will have to make a manual 05g entry when it occurs, and bring the scope in, ah, manually. Is that affirm?

04 39 35 2.5 … *CC*—That is affirmative, *Friendship* 7.

04 39 39 0.6 … *P*—Ah, Roger.

04 39 42 3.6 … *P*—This is *Friendship* 7, going to reentry attitude, then, in that case.

04 40 00 3.8 … *CC*—*Friendship* 7, Cape flight will give you the reasons for this action when you are in view.

04 40 06 2.6 … *P*—Ah, Roger. Ah, Roger. *Friendship* 7.

04 40 09 2.5 … *CC*—Everything down here on the ground looks okay.

04 40 12 1.5 … *P*—Ah, Roger. This is *Friendship* 7.

04 40 14 1.4 … *CC*—Confirm your attitudes.

04 40 16 0.4 … *P*—Roger.

◆ CANAVERAL

04 40 23 1.7 … *CC*—Ah, *Friendship* 7, this is Cape. Over.

04 40 25 1.5 … *P*—Go ahead, Cape. Friend 7.

04 40 27 4.9 … *CC*—Ah, recommend you go to reentry attitude and retract the scope manually at this time.

04 40 32 1.9 … *P*—Ah, Roger, retracting scope manually.

04 40 36 14.6 … *CC*—While you're doing that, we are not sure whether or not your landing bag has deployed. We feel it is possible to reenter with the retropackage on. Ah, we see no difficulty at this time in that type of reentry. Over.

04 40 51 1.6 … *P*—Ah, Roger, understand.

04 41 10 1.4 … *CC*—Seven, this is Cape. Over.

04 41 12 1.5 … *P*—Go ahead, Cape. *Friendship* 7.

04 41 15 5.4 … *CC*—Estimating 05g at 04 44.

04 41 21 0.6 … P—Ah, Roger.

04 41 23 3.0 … CC—You override 05g at that time.

04 41 31 2.7 … P—Ah, Roger. *Friendship* 7.

04 41 33 13.2 … P—This is *Friendship* 7. I'm on straight manual control at present time. This was, ah, still kicking in and out of orientation mode, mainly in yaw, ah, following retrofire, so I am on straight manual now. I'll back it up—

04 41 45 0.8 … CC——on reentry.

04 41 47 0.9 … P—Say again.

04 41 50 0.6 … CC—Standby.

04 41 53 6.2 … P—This is *Friendship* 7. Ah, going to fly-by-wire. I'm down to about 15 percent on manual.

04 42 00 8.9 … CC—Ah, Roger. You're going to use fly-by-wire for reentry and we recommend that you do the best you can to keep a zero angle during reentry. Over.

04 42 09 1.2 … P—Ah, Roger. *Friendship* 7.

04 42 13 3.4 … P—This is *Friendship* 7. I'm on fly-by-wire, back-it up with manual. Over.

04 42 18 1.1 … CC—Roger, understand.

04 42 29 9.2 … CC—Ah, Seven, this is Cape. The weather in the recovery area is excellent, 3-foot waves, only one-tenth cloud coverage, 10 miles visibility.

04 42 39 1.2 … P—Ah, Roger. *Friendship* 7.

04 42 47 1.4 … CC—Ah, Seven, this is Cape. Over.

04 42 49 2.5 … P—Go ahead, Cape, you're ground, you are going out.

04 42 52 1.8 … CC—We recommend that you—

04 43 16 2.9 … P—This is *Friendship* 7. I think the pack just let go.

04 43 39 2.4 … P—This is *Friendship* 7. A real fireball outside.

04 44 20 1.9 … P—Hello, Cape. *Friendship* 7. Over.

04 45 18 1.9 … P—Hello, Cape. *Friendship* 7. Over.

04 45 43 2.3 … P—Hello, Cape. *Friendship* 7. Do you receive? Over.

04 46 20 2.0 … P—Hello, Cape. *Friendship* 7. Do you receive? Over.

04 47 18 1.2 … CC——How do you read? Over.

04 47 20 1.5 … P—Loud and clear; how me?

04 47 22 1.6 … CC—Roger, reading you loud and clear. How are you doing?

04 47 25 1.0 … P—Oh, pretty good.

04 47 30 3.8 … CC—Roger. Your impact point is within one mile of the up-range destroyer.

04 47 34 0.5 … P—Ah, Roger.

04 47 35 0.2 … CC——Over.

04 47 36 0.3 … P—Roger.

04 47 44 3.4 … CC—This is Cape, estimating 4 50. Over.

04 47 48 1.5 … P—Roger, 04 50.

04 47 53 1.6 … P—Okay, we're through the peak g now.

04 47 55 4.0 … CC—Ah, Seven, this is Cape. What's your general condition? Are you feeling pretty well?

04 47 59 2.8 … P—My condition is good, but that was a real fireball, boy.

04 48 05 3.2 … P—I had great chunks of that retropack breaking off all the way through.

04 48 08 2.1 … CC—Very good; it did break off, is that correct?

04 48 11 3.4 … P—Roger. Altimeter off the peg indicating 80 thousand.

04 48 15 1.7 … CC—Roger, reading you loud and clear.

04 48 17 0.3 … P—Roger.

Martin Luther King, Jr. (Library of Congress)

Martin Luther King, Jr.'s "Letter from Birmingham Jail"

"Freedom is never voluntarily given by the oppressor; it must be demanded by the oppressed."

Overview

In his "Letter from Birmingham Jail," Martin Luther King, Jr., delivered an important statement on civil rights and civil disobedience. The 1963 racial crisis in Birmingham, Alabama, was a critical turning point in the struggle for African American civil rights. Nonviolent protestors led by King faced determined opposition from hard-core segregationists. King and his organization, the Southern Christian Leadership Conference (SCLC), needed a victory to sustain the momentum of their movement. The integration of downtown stores and lunch counters was the primary focus of SCLC's "Project C"—the "C" stood for *confrontation*. Demonstrations began one day after a new city government was elected. Many observers criticized King for protesting at a time when Birmingham's race relations appeared to be moving in a more positive direction. These critics included eight prominent white clergymen who published a statement characterizing these protests as "unwise and untimely" and asking African Americans to withdraw their support from King's efforts (http://www.stanford.edu/group/King/frequentdocs/clergy.pdf).

The SCLC timed its campaign to coincide with the Easter shopping season. Its strategy involved using economic pressure to force white businesses to remove segregated facilities, extend more courteous treatment to African American customers, and hire black salespeople. King was arrested on Good Friday in 1963 and remained imprisoned for eight days. He used his jail time to compose a response to the clergymen. In his "Letter from Birmingham Jail," King articulated a moral and philosophical defense of his tactics and delivered a stinging rebuke to those who counseled caution on civil rights. Although King's letter was not published until after the Birmingham crisis was resolved, it is widely regarded as the most important written document of the modern civil rights movement and a classic text on civil disobedience.

Context

Birmingham had long had a reputation as one of the most racist and violent cities in the South. Starting in 1947 a series of bombings targeted the homes of African Americans who had moved into previously all-white neighborhoods. The Ku Klux Klan operated openly and was widely believed to be responsible for these attacks. When the outspoken black minister the Reverend Fred Shuttlesworth formed the Alabama Christian Movement for Human Rights to press for civil rights, the terrorists struck his home and church. Because no one was apprehended for any of the more than fifty explosions, Birmingham blacks concluded that the police were in league with the bombers. Public Safety Commissioner Eugene "Bull" Connor, an outspoken segregationist, used all resources at his disposal to preserve the Jim Crow system (laws and social practices that segregated and discriminated against African Americans).

Connor's heavy-handed methods aroused the ire of more temperate civic leaders, who hoped to create a more favorable image for their city. These leaders spearheaded an effort to oust Connor by shifting the form of city government from three commissioners to a mayor and a city council. On April 2, 1963, Birmingham voters rejected Connor and elected Albert Boutwell, a moderate segregationist, as their mayor. The losers immediately sued to prevent the new administration from taking office. For a time Birmingham had two competing city governments.

In January 1963 the SCLC decided to make Birmingham the site of its next major civil rights drive. The SCLC had suffered a serious setback the previous year in Albany, Georgia, where, despite months of nonviolent struggle and hundreds of arrests, African Americans were unable to wrest any concessions from an intransigent city government. Shuttlesworth, the most prominent Birmingham civil rights activist, assured the SCLC board that his city would be different; Connor could be counted on to react in his usual heavy-handed fashion. King also had a larger objective in mind: He hoped that by creating a crisis in Birmingham, he could force President John F. Kennedy to take much-needed action on civil rights.

After a delay in demonstrations until the Boutwell-Connor runoff election was resolved, protests began on April 3 with sit-ins and picketing at downtown department stores. On April 10 Judge W. A. Jenkins issued an injunction prohibiting King and other civil rights leaders from participating in or encouraging any civil disobedience. King decided

1963

January 10
The Southern Christian Leadership Conference targets Birmingham for civil rights demonstrations during the pre-Easter shopping season.

April 2
Albert Boutwell defeats Eugene "Bull" Connor in a runoff election for mayor of Birmingham.

April 3
Birmingham demonstrations begin.

April 12
Martin Luther King, Jr., is arrested, refuses bail, and is placed in solitary confinement; "A Call for Unity" by eight Birmingham clergymen appears in the *Birmingham News.*

April 16
The text of "Letter from Birmingham Jail" is smuggled out of jail.

April 20
King is released from jail.

May 3
Connor orders fire hoses and police dogs to be turned on young demonstrators. Television coverage creates a groundswell of support for King's movement.

May 9
King announces an agreement with Birmingham business leaders to desegregate their establishments, ending the demonstrations.

May 28
"Letter from Birmingham Jail" is published by the American Friends Service Committee.

June 11
President John F. Kennedy proposes a comprehensive civil rights bill.

August 28
King delivers his "I Have a Dream" Speech at the March on Washington for Jobs and Freedom.

September 15
Birmingham's 16th Street Baptist Church is bombed, killing four young girls attending Sunday school.

to defy the court order, and on Good Friday, April 12, he, the Reverend Ralph Abernathy, and more than fifty other demonstrators were arrested. They were taken to the Birmingham City Jail, where King was placed in solitary confinement.

On April 12 a statement by eight white clergymen—a rabbi, a Catholic bishop, and six prominent Protestant leaders—appeared in the *Birmingham News* under the title "A Call for Unity." They characterized the demonstrations as "unwise and untimely" and claimed that the protests were likely "incite to hatred and violence" (http://www.stanford.edu/group/King/frequentdocs/clergy.pdf). The authors praised the Birmingham media and police for the "calm manner" in which they handled the civil rights forces and urged blacks to withdraw their support from King's efforts. They implied that King should return to Atlanta and allow local residents to resolve their differences without outside interference.

King probably read the churchmen's declaration in a newspaper smuggled into his cell. Taylor Branch, author of *Parting the Waters: America in the King Years, 1954–63,* credits Harvey Shapiro, an editor for the *New York Times Magazine,* for planting the idea that King write a letter from prison during the Albany campaign. That message never materialized, but now King realized the time was right. Almost immediately he began formulating a response. When King's lawyer, Clarence Jones, visited him on April 16, the jailed civil rights leader handed Jones the newspaper with his notes scribbled in the margins. S. Jonathan Bass, author of *Blessed Are the Peacemakers: Martin Luther King, Jr., Eight White Religious Leaders, and the "Letter from Birmingham Jail",* describes what happened next. The Reverend Wyatt T. Walker, SCLC executive director, deciphered King's "chicken scratch" handwriting and dictated to his secretary, Willie Pearl Mackey, who typed the first rough copy. Lawyers returned the draft to King, who continued writing on scraps of paper provided by a black jail trustee. When he was released from jail on April 20, the bulk of the letter was composed, but King, according to Bass, "continued writing, editing, and revising drafts several days after the date on the manuscript" (p. 135).

The SCLC sent the letter to national media in early May, but there was little immediate reaction. The *New York Post* printed excerpts in its May 19 edition. The American Friends Service Committee published the full text of the letter as a pamphlet on May 28. It subsequently appeared in *Christian Century,* the *New Leader, Atlantic Monthly,* and *Ebony.* A slightly revised version was included in King's 1964 book *Why We Can't Wait.*

About the Author

Martin Luther King, Jr., was the preeminent leader of the modern civil rights movement. His philosophy of nonviolent direct action and inspirational oratory helped overthrow the Jim Crow system of racial segregation and win greater rights for African Americans.

King was born in Atlanta, Georgia, on January 15, 1929, the son, grandson, and great-grandson of Baptist ministers. He was educated at Morehouse College and Crozier Theological Seminary. He studied philosophy at Boston University, receiving his doctorate in 1955.

In 1953 he married Coretta Scott. They had four children. Also in 1953 he accepted the pastorate of Dexter Avenue Baptist Church in Montgomery, Alabama. After Rosa Parks was arrested on December 1, 1955, for refusing to give up her bus seat to a white passenger, King was persuaded to head the Montgomery Improvement Association, an organization formed to coordinate the 381-day boycott of city buses. King's successful leadership of the boycott and his application of Gandhian nonviolence to civil rights issues thrust him into national prominence.

King and other African American ministers formed the SCLC in 1957 to expand the struggle against racial segregation in the South. In 1962 King and the SCLC suffered a major defeat in Albany, Georgia, where months of demonstrations had failed to desegregate any public facilities. Mass protests in Birmingham produced a more successful outcome. In response to growing pressure for legislative action, President John F. Kennedy introduced a comprehensive civil rights bill. On August 28, 1963, King delivered his "I Have a Dream" Speech before 250,000 people assembled for the March on Washington. He was named *Time* magazine's "Man of the Year" for 1963 and was awarded the Nobel Peace Prize in 1964.

King and the SCLC focused on voting rights in 1965. Selma, Alabama, was targeted for demonstrations because of white authorities' determined opposition to African American voter registration. A vicious attack by Alabama state troopers on nonviolent protesters drew national attention. King then led marchers from Selma to Montgomery to press for national voting rights legislation. President Lyndon B. Johnson responded by sponsoring the Voting Rights Act, which became law that summer. In subsequent years King extended his crusade beyond the South, tackling slum housing in Chicago in 1966, declaring his opposition to the Vietnam War in 1967, and calling for a Poor People's Campaign for economic justice in 1968.

King was assassinated in Memphis, Tennessee, on April 4, 1968, while supporting a strike by sanitation workers. In 1983 Congress declared King's birthday a national holiday.

Explanation and Analysis of the Document

King establishes a tone of rational dialogue as he begins his letter to the eight clergymen. He explains that he rarely responds to critics, but since they are "men of genuine good will" who are sincere in their criticism, he is making an exception. He hopes that they will find his remarks "patient and reasonable." Because they had questioned his presence in Birmingham, he relates that he was invited to their city by the Alabama Christian Movement for Human Rights. A more compelling reason, however, was the pervasive racial oppression in Birmingham. King compares him-

Time Line

1964	■ **July 2** President Lyndon B. Johnson signs the Civil Rights Act of 1964.
	■ **December 10** King is awarded the Nobel Peace Prize in Oslo, Norway.
1968	■ **April 4** King is assassinated in Memphis, Tennessee.
1983	■ **November 2** King's birthday is declared a national holiday.

self to the apostle Paul, who spread the Christian faith among the Gentiles. Paul traveled more widely than any of the early Christian missionaries, preaching and establishing churches throughout Greece and Asia Minor. The "Macedonian call" mentioned in the third paragraph refers to Acts 16:9, in which a man appears to Paul in a dream, asking him to "come over into Macedonia, and help us." During his journeys Paul was persecuted for spreading unpopular beliefs and spent more than four years in prison before being executed by Roman authorities. Three of his famous epistles were written from jail. King justifies his arrest by invoking Paul's sufferings—an example that the Christian ministers could appreciate. He further defends his presence in Alabama by citing the "interrelatedness of all communities." King asserts that people living outside Alabama cannot ignore blatant racism in Birmingham. Every citizen has an obligation to act against injustice wherever it may be found, King explains. Those who consider him an "outside agitator" reveal their own "narrow, provincial" outlook.

King takes the clergymen to task for their statement deploring the Birmingham demonstrations. Instead of worrying about threats to public order, they should be concerned about racism and inequality in their city—the "underlying causes" that gave rise to the African American protests. Because the white leadership had been unresponsive to repeated appeals to dismantle the Jim Crow system, King contends that black citizens of Birmingham had "no alternative" other than to take to the streets.

King goes on to outline the stages of his nonviolent crusade. Fact finding was the first phase. Among the damaging information uncovered were Birmingham's long history of unpunished attacks on its black citizens and the failure of city fathers to negotiate in good faith with civil rights advocates. King reminds the clergymen that Birmingham merchants had not honored an earlier agreement to remove Jim Crow signs from their stores. African American activists also were mindful of the need to defeat Connor and thus delayed their demonstrations until the conclusion of the runoff election. Now the merchants must deal with the economic consequences of protests timed to coincide with the Easter shopping season. These actions were not irresponsible, King insists. Rather, black leaders exercised great restraint in the face of numerous provocations.

The second stage was negotiation. The clergymen had criticized King for resorting to confrontation instead of negotiating to achieve his goals. King claims that he, too, desires negotiation but explains that sometimes pressure must be applied to bring reluctant parties to the bargaining table. Rather than avoiding conflict and tension, he freely admits his intention to create a crisis in order to expose the evils of segregation. In support of his position, he cites Socrates, who maintained that mental tension stimulates intellectual growth.

The eight Birmingham clerics had claimed that the Birmingham demonstrations were "untimely." They were not the only observers voicing this objection. Attorney General Robert Kennedy and the *Washington Post*, among others, had complained that the new Boutwell administration should be given a chance to show that it was more open to change than the outgoing Connor regime. King rejects this reasoning. He maintains that those in positions of power cannot be expected to surrender their privileges voluntarily; they must be persuaded forcefully to do the right thing. In this assertion, he echoes the words of the great abolitionist Frederick Douglass, who said, "Power concedes nothing without a demand. It never did and it never will" (http://www.buildingequality.us/Quotes/Frederick_Douglass.htm). He also cites the Protestant theologian Reinhold Niebuhr to support his contention that change is more difficult for groups than for individuals.

King points out that any action disrupting the status quo is likely to be considered poorly timed by those who are comfortable with existing arrangements. For those suffering from oppression, however, change cannot come soon enough. He then launches into an eloquent defense of his movement by concentrating on the word *wait*. Whites who counsel patience in the quest for civil rights, he asserts, have not personally experienced the harsh sting of discrimination. King explains why he and other African Americans are unwilling to slow the pace of their crusade. He quotes the nineteenth-century British jurist and prime minister William Gladstone, saying that "'justice ... delayed is justice denied.'" To drive home the devastating impact of segregation, he recites a weary litany of potent examples of the injuries inflicted by racism. These range from lynch mobs to whites' refusal to use courtesy titles when addressing African Americans. Perhaps the most poignant is the plight of a black father who must explain to his young daughter why she cannot attend the amusement park she has seen advertised on television. One wonders whether this girl is one of King's own children. At the conclusion of this powerful passage, he pleads with the clergymen to understand the "legitimate and unavoidable impatience" felt by African Americans.

King next addresses the most difficult question raised by the Birmingham clergymen: How can he encourage his fol-

lowers to violate some laws and at the same time urge whites to observe such legal decisions as *Brown v. Board of Education*? Here he draws on the concept of "natural law" developed by Saint Thomas Aquinas and other Catholic philosophers. A man-made law is just if it accords with the divinely established code to uplift the human spirit. All such laws should be obeyed. King cites the Jewish philosopher Martin Buber and the Protestant theologian Paul Tillich to give ecumenical sanction to his contention that segregation laws are immoral and therefore should not be obeyed. Other examples of unjust laws are those applied to one group (African Americans) but not another (whites) and laws adopted by legislatures, such as Alabama's, that exclude participation by large numbers of their citizens. Laws also may be unjust if used to deprive citizens of their constitutionally guaranteed rights.

King maintains that those who advocate civil disobedience do not contribute to anarchy. In the tradition of Henry David Thoreau and Mahatma Gandhi, he asserts that those who violate unjust laws must do so "openly, lovingly, and with a willingness to accept the penalty." Rather than expressing defiance, the protestor shows respect for the law by acting to remove injustice from a community. King cites several well-known examples of civil disobedience of which the eight clergymen would most certainly approve. These include the biblical story from the book of Daniel in which Shadrach, Meshach, and Abednego are cast into a fiery furnace for refusing to worship the golden idol erected by the Babylonian king Nebuchadnezzar. King contends that in the modern era, religious people have a moral duty to confront Hitler's anti-Semitic codes and the atheistic decrees of Communist regimes.

The longest section of the letter addresses the role of the white moderate in the struggle for civil rights. King hits hard at the clergymen who objected to the Birmingham demonstrations, expressing his frustration with liberals who claimed to support the goal of equal rights while objecting to the methods of the movement. He accuses them of being almost as harmful as members of the Ku Klux Klan or the White Citizens' Council, a supremacist organization. The main reason for King's impatience is the moderates' frequently expressed insistence that change must be peaceful and orderly. These critics of the movement fail to understand the true source of the conflicts that surface during civil rights protests. These conflicts are not caused by those participating in civil disobedience; rather, the demonstrations bring to the surface long-standing community tensions. If they are to be resolved, they must first be exposed to public scrutiny.

Many detractors also denounced civil rights activists for precipitating violence from those opposed to integration. King has no patience with this line of reasoning. Accusing nonviolent demonstrators of causing violence is a classic example of blaming the victim. According to King, these critics suffer from distorted vision; they should defend those being attacked and condemn their attackers.

White moderates frequently argued that civil rights advocates like King were pressing too hard to transform south-

"Injustice anywhere is a threat to justice everywhere. We are caught in an inescapable network of mutuality, tied in a single garment of destiny. Whatever affects one directly, affects all indirectly."

(Paragraph 4)

"Nonviolent direct action seeks to create such a crisis and foster such a tension that a community that has constantly refused to negotiate is forced to confront the issue. It seeks to so dramatize the issue that it can no longer be ignored."

(Paragraph 10)

"We have not made a single gain in civil rights without determined legal and nonviolent pressure. Lamentably, it is an historical fact that privileged groups seldom give up their privileges voluntarily."

(Paragraph 12)

"We know through painful experience that freedom is never voluntarily given by the oppressor; it must be demanded by the oppressed. Frankly, I have yet to engage in a direct-action campaign that was 'well timed' in the view of those who have not suffered unduly from the disease of segregation. For years now I have heard the word 'Wait!' It rings in the ear of every Negro with piercing familiarity. This 'Wait' has almost always meant 'Never.'"

(Paragraph 13)

"One who breaks an unjust law must do so openly, lovingly, and with a willingness to accept the penalty. I submit that an individual who breaks a law that conscience tells him is unjust, and who willingly accepts the penalty of imprisonment in order to arouse the conscience of the community over its injustice, is in reality expressing the highest respect for law."

(Paragraph 20)

"I must confess that over the past few years I have been gravely disappointed with the white moderate,… who is more devoted to 'order' than to justice."

(Paragraph 23)

ern society. If only African Americans could be more patient, they insisted, change would come in time. King forcefully rebuts this argument. Time is neutral, King insists; it can be used for good or evil. There is nothing inevitable about progress; the passage of time does not guarantee the solution of social problems. People of goodwill cannot afford to be silent in the face of injustice; they must "use time creatively" to realize "the promise of democracy."

The eight clergymen had described the Birmingham protestors as extremists. King at first repudiates this label. Rather than viewing himself as an extremist, he claims that he is a moderate caught between Uncle Toms who have acquiesced to segregation and the Black Muslims who charge that the white man is "the devil." In this context, the true extremists are those advocating separation from American society. Believers in nonviolent, direct action seek inclusion in the larger community, not its destruction. To call them extremists is an error. King even argues that demonstrations against segregation have therapeutic value. They allow African Americans to release their many "pent-up resentments and latent frustrations." Whites should not see them as a threat to the status quo but as a creative alternative to mass violence.

After considering the extremist label, however, King reverses course and embraces it. "Was not Jesus an extremist?" he asks. He then recites a long list of heroic figures who could be considered extremists: the Old Testament prophet Amos; the New Testament evangelist Paul; the Christian reformer Martin Luther; the English preacher and writer John Bunyan; Abraham Lincoln, who ended slavery; and Thomas Jefferson, author of the Declaration of Independence. All of these men were seen as extremists in their time. King implies that the United States needs more visionaries of this sort.

Although King harshly criticizes those moderates who had failed to defend the civil rights movement, he praises a handful of southern whites who risked persecution and ostracism by their public support of the movement. These include the Atlanta editor Ralph McGill, the Georgia novelist Lillian Smith, the North Carolina writer Harry Golden, the South Carolina author James McBride Dabbs, the Alabama journalist Anne Braden, and Sarah Patton Boyle, who advocated racial integration in Virginia schools.

King then launches a sustained critique of established religion in the South. He acknowledges a few instances of courageous action by white churches, but these are "notable exceptions." During the Montgomery bus boycott, for example, the leaders of white congregations remained silent or actively opposed the protest. The same was true in Birmingham, where King's organization reached out to white denominations but was consistently rebuffed. King scorns the view that religion should focus solely on the hereafter and avoid involvement in social issues. He squarely embraces the Social Gospel tradition that calls upon Christians to work for the welfare of their fellow humans. The South was known for its strong religious institutions, yet King notes the ironic correlation of high rates of church membership and the popularity of racist governors, like Mississippi's Ross Barnett and Alabama's George Wallace. As the scion of a long line of Baptist ministers, King confesses his love of the church and, at the same time, his deep disappointment in it. He calls upon his white brethren to emulate early Christians who were not afraid to become "disturbers of the peace" while following their divine calling. A few members of the clergy had joined the movement in confronting segregation in the South, but not nearly enough. Nevertheless, despite the opposition of organized religion, King expresses confidence that the movement he leads eventually will be victorious because both the principles of American democracy and the "eternal will of God" require it.

King's final paragraphs dwell on the clergymen's ironic praise of the Birmingham police force for keeping order during the demonstrations. Three weeks after their statement was published, Connor ordered his men to turn police dogs and fire hoses on peaceful demonstrators, revealing to the world the lengths to which Alabama segregationists were willing to go in defense of the Jim Crow system. King points out that the police may have been restrained in public but were harsh in their treatment of jailed activists. He faults the ministers for not praising the discipline and courage of the African American protestors, who remained nonviolent in the face of great provocation. King's clerical critics reveal their one-sided perspective when they defend the white guardians of racial privilege and consistently find fault with those who seek to change this oppressive system.

King closes his letter on a brotherly note, apologizing for the length of his missive and asking for understanding. He expresses the hope that one day they may be able to meet person to person without the antagonism and misunderstanding that currently surround them.

Audience

Although the "Letter from Birmingham Jail" was nominally addressed to the eight white clergymen who had publicly urged African Americans to curtail their Birmingham demonstrations, King had a much wider audience in mind; his letter was produced for national consumption. Specifically, his letter was intended to answer his critics, especially white liberals who questioned the timing of his decision to initiate sit-ins, pickets, and marches following the electoral defeat of Connor. More generally, King hoped to explain the religious and philosophical foundations of nonviolent, direct action to all who shared his Judeo-Christian beliefs.

Impact

King's "Letter from Birmingham Jail" had no direct effect on his Birmingham campaign, since most issues were resolved prior to its publication. The eight white clergymen felt that King had singled them out unfairly. For the rest of their lives they would be known as the men who publicly chastised King. As the letter reached a larger audience, support for civil rights legislation began to swell. Liberal white religious organizations, especially the National Council of Churches, responded by unequivocally endorsing the movement's goals. Religious groups played a critical role in lobbying Congress on behalf of the 1964 Civil Rights Act. When King called upon church leaders to join him for the 1965 march from Selma to Montgomery, hundreds of ministers, rabbis, priests, and nuns came to Alabama to participate in the protest. Their consciences no doubt had been pricked by King's letter.

King's "Letter from Birmingham Jail" has been hailed as the most important written document of the modern civil rights struggle. In it King set forth in prophetic language the aspirations of African Americans to be accepted as human beings entitled to the same respect and rights as other Americans. He articulated the objectives of his movement and offered an eloquent defense of civil disobedience and nonviolent, direct action. His letter has been included in anthologies alongside the classic works of Thoreau and Gandhi. King's words and example have inspired people fighting for freedom around the world, from workers in Poland's Solidarity movement to Chinese students in Beijing's Tiananmen Square.

Related Documents

"Civil Rights Act (1964)." National Archives "Our Documents Web site. http://www.ourdocuments.gov/doc.php?flash=true&doc=97. Accessed on March 3, 2008. This is the text of the law introduced by President John F. Kennedy in 1963 and passed by Congress in July 1964.

"I Have a Dream, Address Delivered at the March on Washington for Jobs and Freedom." The Martin Luther King, Jr., Research and Education Institute Web site. http://www.stanford.edu/group/King/publications/speeches/address_at_march_on_washington.pdf. Accessed on March 3, 2008. This is the text of King's address at the March on Washington, August 28, 1963.

King, Martin Luther, Jr. *Why We Can't Wait*. New York: Signet Books, 1964. This book gives King's account of the Birmingham campaign.

"Statement by Alabama Clergymen." The Martin Luther King, Jr., Research and Education Institute Web site. http://www.stanford.edu/group/King/frequentdocs/clergy.pdf. Accessed on January 22, 2008. "Letter from Birmingham Jail" was King's response to this statement—published as "A Call for Unity" in the *Birmingham News*—which urged him to postpone demonstrations in Birmingham.

Thoreau, Henry David. "On Civil Disobedience." The Thoreau Reader Web site. http://thoreau.eserver.org/civil.html. Accessed on January 22, 2008. This is Thoreau's classic essay in defense of principled civil disobedience.

Bibliography

■ Articles

Colaiaco, James A. "The American Dream Unfulfilled: Martin Luther King, Jr., and the 'Letter from Birmingham Jail.'" *Phylon* 45 (1984): 1–18.

Mott, Wesley T. "The Rhetoric of Martin Luther King, Jr.: Letter from Birmingham Jail." *Phylon* 36 (1975): 411–421.

■ Books

Bass, S. Jonathan. *Blessed Are the Peacemakers: Martin Luther King, Jr., Eight White Clergymen, and the "Letter from Birmingham Jail"*. Baton Rouge: Louisiana State University Press, 2001.

Branch, Taylor. *Parting the Waters: America in the King Years, 1954–63*. New York: Simon & Schuster, 1988.

Durham, Michael S. *Powerful Days: The Civil Rights Photography of Charles Moore*. New York: Stewart, Tabori & Chang, 1991.

Eskew, Glenn T. *But for Birmingham: The Local and National Movements in the Civil Rights Struggle*. Chapel Hill: University of North Carolina Press, 1997.

Garrow, David J. *Bearing the Cross: Martin Luther King, Jr., and the Southern Christian Leadership Conference, 1955–1968*. New York: William Morrow, 1986.

———, ed. *Birmingham, Alabama, 1956–1963: The Black Struggle for Civil Rights*. New York: Carlson Publishing, 1989.

Manis, Andrew M. *A Fire You Can't Put Out: The Civil Rights Life of Birmingham's Reverend Fred Shuttlesworth*. Tuscaloosa: University of Alabama Press, 1999.

McWhorter, Diane. *Carry Me Home: Birmingham, Alabama—The Climactic Battle of the Civil Rights Revolution*. New York: Simon & Schuster, 2001.

Washington, James M., ed. *A Testament of Hope: The Essential Writings of Martin Luther King, Jr.* San Francisco: Harper & Row, 1986.

■ Web Sites

Douglass, Frederick. "The Significance of Emancipation." The International Endowment for Democracy Web site. http://www.iefd.org/manifestos/significance_of_emancipation.php. Accessed on March 3, 2008.

"King Encyclopedia: Birmingham Campaign." Stanford University "Martin Luther King, Jr., Papers Project" Web site. http://www.stanford.edu/group/King/about_king/encyclopedia/birmingham_campaign.htm. Accessed on January 22, 2008.

—By Paul T. Murray

Questions for Further Study

1. King argues that a person is justified in breaking unjust laws, but how does one distinguish between just and unjust laws? What are some examples of unjust laws in contemporary society?

2. In Birmingham nonviolent demonstrators repeatedly confronted the police, who eventually responded with police dogs and fire hoses. In this case, were the demonstrators guilty of provoking the police? To what extent, if any, were the demonstrators responsible for this violence?

3. King's critics often said that he pushed too hard for change and that he should have allowed his opponents more time to adjust to the social changes he advocated. Why did King reject these arguments? In his opinion, who should determine the timetable for social change? Why?

4. King often was accused of being an "extremist." Is this charge accurate? Explain why or why not. Why did King both reject and embrace this label?

5. In his letter, King takes white churches to task for not openly denouncing the evil of segregation, yet many ministers maintain that religious organizations should not take sides in partisan political issues. What is the proper role of the church in social issues? Should churches become involved in movements for social change? Why or why not?

Glossary

black nationalism	the belief that blacks should live separately from whites
concoct	to invent
cognizant	aware
complacency	a feeling of contentment or self-satisfaction
ekklesia	Greek term for a congregation of believers
gainsaying	contradicting
inevitability	the impossibility of avoiding or preventing
lamentably	with regret
latent	hidden; unseen
moratorium	a temporary halt or cessation of activity
query	a question
paradoxical	inconsistent; contradictory
paternalistically	in a fatherly manner exercised authoritatively
precipitate	to cause to happen suddenly
reiterate	to repeat
sanctimonious	pretending to be pious or righteous
Zeitgeist	German term for "spirit of the times"

MARTIN LUTHER KING, JR.'S "LETTER FROM BIRMINGHAM JAIL"

My Dear Fellow Clergymen:

While confined here in the Birmingham city jail, I came across your recent statement calling my present activities "unwise and untimely." Seldom do I pause to answer criticism of my work and ideas. If I sought to answer all the criticisms that cross my desk, my secretaries would have little time for anything other than such correspondence in the course of the day, and I would have no time for constructive work. But since I feel that you are men of genuine good will and that your criticisms are sincerely set forth, I want to try to answer your statements in what I hope will be patient and reasonable terms.

I think I should indicate why I am here In Birmingham, since you have been influenced by the view which argues against "outsiders coming in." I have the honor of serving as president of the Southern Christian Leadership Conference, an organization operating in every southern state, with headquarters in Atlanta, Georgia. We have some eighty-five affiliated organizations across the South, and one of them is the Alabama Christian Movement for Human Rights. Frequently we share staff, educational and financial resources with our affiliates. Several months ago the affiliate here in Birmingham asked us to be on call to engage in a nonviolent direct-action program if such were deemed necessary. We readily consented, and when the hour came we lived up to our promise. So I, along with several members of my staff, am here because I was invited here I am here because I have organizational ties here.

But more basically, I am in Birmingham because injustice is here. Just as the prophets of the eighth century B.C. left their villages and carried their "thus saith the Lord" far beyond the boundaries of their home towns, and just as the Apostle Paul left his village of Tarsus and carried the gospel of Jesus Christ to the far corners of the Greco-Roman world, so am I compelled to carry the gospel of freedom beyond my own home town. Like Paul, I must constantly respond to the Macedonian call for aid.

Moreover, I am cognizant of the interrelatedness of all communities and states. I cannot sit idly by in Atlanta and not be concerned about what happens in Birmingham. Injustice anywhere is a threat to justice everywhere. We are caught in an inescapable network of mutuality, tied in a single garment of destiny. Whatever affects one directly, affects all indirectly. Never again can we afford to live with the narrow, provincial "outside agitator" idea. Anyone who lives inside the United States can never be considered an outsider anywhere within its bounds.

You deplore the demonstrations taking place in Birmingham. But your statement, I am sorry to say, I fails to express a similar concern for the conditions that brought about the demonstrations. I am sure that none of you would want to rest content with the superficial kind of social analysis that deals merely with effects and does not grapple with underlying causes. It is unfortunate that demonstrations are taking place in Birmingham, but it is even more unfortunate that the city's white power structure left the Negro community with no alternative.

In any nonviolent campaign there are four basic steps: collection of the facts to determine whether injustices exist; negotiation; self-purification; and direct action. We have gone through all these steps in Birmingham. There can be no gainsaying the fact that racial injustice engulfs this community. Birmingham is probably the most thoroughly segregated city in the United States. Its ugly record of brutality is widely known. Negroes have experienced grossly unjust treatment in the courts. There have been more unsolved bombings of Negro homes and churches in Birmingham than in any other city in the nation. These are the hard, brutal facts of the case. On the basis of these conditions, Negro leaders sought to negotiate with the city fathers. But the latter consistently refused to engage in good-faith negotiation

Then, last September, came the opportunity to talk with leaders of Birmingham's economic community. In the course of the negotiations, certain promises were made by the merchants—for example, to remove the stores' humiliating racial signs. On the basis of these promises, the Reverend Fred Shuttlesworth and the leaders of the Alabama Christian Movement for Human Rights agreed to a moratorium on all demonstrations. As the weeks and months went by, we realized that we were the victims of a broken promise. A few signs, briefly removed, returned; the others remained.

As in so many past experiences, our hopes had been blasted, and the shadow of deep disappointment settled upon us. We had no alternative except to prepare for direct action, whereby we would present our very bodies as a means of laying our case before the conscience of the local and the national community. Mindful of the difficulties involved, we decided to undertake a process of self-purification. We began a series of workshops on nonviolence, and we repeatedly asked ourselves: "Are you able to accept blows without retaliating?" "Are you able to endure the ordeal of jail?" We decided to schedule our direct-action program for the Easter season, realizing that except for Christmas, this is the main shopping period of the year. Knowing that a strong economic withdrawal program would be the by-product of direct action, we felt that this would be the best time to bring pressure to bear on the merchants for the needed change.

Then it occurred to us that Birmingham's mayoralty election was coming up in March, and we speedily decided to postpone action until after election day. When we discovered that the Commissioner of Public Safety, Eugene "Bull" Connor, had piled up enough votes to be in the run-off, we decided again to postpone action until the day after the run-off so that the demonstrations could not be used to cloud the issues. Like many others, we waited to see Mr. Connor defeated, and to this end we endured postponement after postponement. Having aided in this community need, we felt that our direct-action program could be delayed no longer.

You may well ask: "Why direct action? Why sit-ins, marches and so forth? Isn't negotiation a better path?" You are quite right in calling for negotiation. Indeed, this is the very purpose of direct action. Nonviolent direct action seeks to create such a crisis and foster such a tension that a community which has constantly refused to negotiate is forced to confront the issue. It seeks so to dramatize the issue that

it can no longer be ignored. My citing the creation of tension as part of the work of the nonviolent-resister may sound rather shocking. But I must confess that I am not afraid of the word "tension." I have earnestly opposed violent tension, but there is a type of constructive, nonviolent tension which is necessary for growth. Just as Socrates felt that it was necessary to create a tension in the mind so that individuals could rise from the bondage of myths and half-truths to the unfettered realm of creative analysis and objective appraisal, so must we see the need for nonviolent gadflies to create the kind of tension in society that will help men rise from the dark depths of prejudice and racism to the majestic heights of understanding and brotherhood.

The purpose of our direct-action program is to create a situation so crisis-packed that it will inevitably open the door to negotiation. I therefore concur with you in your call for negotiation. Too long has our beloved Southland been bogged down in a tragic effort to live in monologue rather than dialogue.

One of the basic points in your statement is that the action that I and my associates have taken in Birmingham is untimely. Some have asked: "Why didn't you give the new city administration time to act?" The only answer that I can give to this query is that the new Birmingham administration must be prodded about as much as the outgoing one, before it will act. We are sadly mistaken if we feel that the election of Albert Boutwell as mayor will bring the millennium to Birmingham. While Mr. Boutwell is a much more gentle person than Mr. Connor, they are both segregationists, dedicated to maintenance of the status quo. I have hope that Mr. Boutwell will be reasonable enough to see the futility of massive resistance to desegregation. But he will not see this without pressure from devotees of civil rights. My friends, I must say to you that we have not made a single gain in civil rights without determined legal and nonviolent pressure. Lamentably, it is an historical fact that privileged groups seldom give up their privileges voluntarily. Individuals may see the moral light and voluntarily give up their unjust posture; but, as Reinhold Niebuhr has reminded us, groups tend to be more immoral than individuals.

We know through painful experience that freedom is never voluntarily given by the oppressor; it must be demanded by the oppressed. Frankly, I have yet to engage in a direct-action campaign that was "well timed" in the view of those who have not suffered unduly from the disease of segregation. For years now I have heard the word "Wait!" It rings in the ear of every Negro with piercing familiarity. This "Wait" has almost always meant "Never." We must come to see, with one of our distinguished jurists, that "justice too long delayed is justice denied."

We have waited for more than 340 years for our constitutional and God-given rights. The nations of Asia and Africa are moving with jetlike speed toward gaining political independence, but we still creep at horse-and-buggy pace toward gaining a cup of coffee at a lunch counter. Perhaps it is easy for those who have never felt the stinging darts of segregation to say, "Wait." But when you have seen vicious mobs lynch your mothers and fathers at will and drown your sisters and brothers at whim; when you have seen hate-filled policemen curse, kick and even kill your black brothers and sisters; when you see the vast majority of your twenty million Negro brothers smothering in an airtight cage of poverty in the midst of an affluent society; when you suddenly find your tongue twisted and your speech stammering as you seek to explain to your six-year-old daughter why she can't go to the public amusement park that has just been advertised on television, and see tears welling up in her eyes when she is told that Funtown is closed to colored children, and see ominous clouds of inferiority beginning to form in her little mental sky, and see her beginning to distort her personality by developing an unconscious bitterness toward white people; when you have to concoct an answer for a five-year-old son who is asking: "Daddy, why do white people treat colored people so mean?"; when you take a cross-county drive and find it necessary to sleep night after night in the uncomfortable corners of your automobile because no motel will accept you; when you are humiliated day in and day out by nagging signs reading "white" and "colored"; when your first name becomes "nigger," your middle name becomes "boy" (however old you are) and your last name becomes "John," and your wife and mother are never given the respected title "Mrs."; when you are harried by day and haunted by night by the fact that you are a Negro, living constantly at tiptoe stance, never quite knowing what to expect next, and are plagued with inner fears and outer resentments; when you are forever fighting a degenerating sense of "nobodiness"—then you will understand why we find it difficult to wait. There comes a time when the cup of endurance runs over, and men are no longer willing to be plunged into the abyss of despair. I hope, sirs, you can understand our legitimate and unavoidable impatience.

You express a great deal of anxiety over our willingness to break laws. This is certainly a legitimate concern. Since we so diligently urge people to obey the Supreme Court's decision of 1954 outlawing segregation in the public schools, at first glance it may seem rather paradoxical for us consciously to break laws. One may well ask: "How can you advocate breaking some laws and obeying others?" The answer lies in the fact that there are two types of laws: just and unjust. I would be the first to advocate obeying just laws. One has not only a legal but a moral responsibility to obey just laws. Conversely, one has a moral responsibility to disobey unjust laws. I would agree with St. Augustine that "an unjust law is no law at all."

Now, what is the difference between the two? How does one determine whether a law is just or unjust? A just law is a man-made code that squares with the moral law or the law of God. An unjust law is a code that is of harmony with the moral law. To put it in the terms of St. Thomas Aquinas: An unjust law is a human law that is not rooted in eternal law and natural law. Any law that uplifts human personality is just. Any law that degrades human personality is unjust. All segregation statutes are unjust because segregation distorts the soul and damages the personality. It gives the segregator a false sense of superiority and the segregated a false sense of inferiority. Segregation, to use the terminology of the Jewish philosopher Martin Buber, substitutes an "I-it" relationship for an "I-thou" relationship and ends up relegating persons to the status of things. Hence segregation is not only politically, economically and sociologically unsound, it is morally wrong and sinful. Paul Tillich has said that sin is separation. Is not segregation an existential expression of man's tragic separation, his awful estrangement, his terrible sinfulness? Thus it is that I can urge men to obey the 1954 decision of the Supreme Court, for it is morally right; and I can urge them to disobey segregation ordinances, for they are morally wrong.

Let us consider a more concrete example of just and unjust laws. An unjust law is a code that a numerical or power majority group compels a minority group to obey but does not make binding on itself. This is *difference* made legal. By the same token, a just law is a code that a majority compels a minority to follow and that it is willing to follow itself. This is *sameness* made legal.

Let me give another explanation. A law is unjust if it is inflicted on a minority that, as a result of being denied the right to vote, had no part in enacting or devising the law. Who can say that the legislature of

Alabama which set up that state's segregation laws was democratically elected? Throughout Alabama all sorts of devious methods are used to prevent Negroes from becoming registered voters, and there are some counties in which, even though Negroes constitute a majority of the population, not a single Negro is registered. Can any law enacted under such circumstances be considered democratically structured?

Sometimes a law is just on its face and unjust in its application. For instance, I have been arrested on a charge of parading without a permit. Now, there is nothing wrong in having an ordinance which requires a permit for a parade. But such an ordinance becomes unjust when it is used to maintain segregation and to deny citizens the First-Amendment privilege of peaceful assembly and protest.

I hope you are able to see the distinction I am trying to point out. In no sense do I advocate evading or defying the law, as would the rabid segregationist. That would lead to anarchy. One who breaks an unjust law must do so openly, lovingly, and with a willingness to accept the penalty. I submit that an individual who breaks a law that conscience tells him is unjust, and who willingly accepts the penalty of imprisonment in order to arouse the conscience of the community over its injustice, is in reality expressing the highest respect for law.

Of course, there is nothing new about this kind of civil disobedience. It was evidenced sublimely in the refusal of Shadrach, Meshach and Abednego to obey the laws of Nebuchadnezzar, on the ground that a higher moral law was at stake. It was practiced superbly by the early Christians, who were willing to face hungry lions and the excruciating pain of chopping blocks rather than submit to certain unjust laws of the Roman Empire. To a degree, academic freedom is a reality today because Socrates practiced civil disobedience. In our own nation, the Boston Tea Party represented a massive act of civil disobedience.

We should never forget that everything Adolf Hitler did in Germany was "legal" and everything the Hungarian freedom fighters did in Hungary was "illegal." It was "illegal" to aid and comfort a Jew in Hitler's Germany. Even so, I am sure that, had I lived in Germany at the time, I would have aided and comforted my Jewish brothers. If today I lived in a Communist country where certain principles dear to the Christian faith are suppressed, I would openly advocate disobeying that country's antireligious laws.

I must make two honest confessions to you, my Christian and Jewish brothers. First, I must confess that over the past few years I have been gravely disappointed with the white moderate. I have almost reached the regrettable conclusion that the Negro's great stumbling block in his stride toward freedom is not the White Citizens Counciler or the Ku Klux Klanner, but the white moderate, who is more devoted to "order" than to justice; who prefers a negative peace which is the absence of tension to a positive peace which is the presence of justice; who constantly says: "I agree with you in the goal you seek, but I cannot agree with your methods of direct action"; who paternalistically believes he can set the timetable for another man's freedom; who lives by a mythical concept of time and who constantly advises the Negro to wait for a "more convenient season." Shallow understanding from people of good will is more frustrating than absolute misunderstanding from people of ill will. Lukewarm acceptance is much more bewildering than outright rejection.

I had hoped that the white moderate would understand that law and order exist for the purpose of establishing justice and that when they fail in this purpose they become the dangerously structured dams that block the flow of social progress. I had hoped that the white moderate would understand that the present tension in the South is a necessary phase of the transition from an obnoxious negative peace, in which the Negro passively accepted his unjust plight, to a substantive and positive peace, in which all men will respect the dignity and worth of human personality Actually, we who engage in nonviolent direct action are not the creators of tension. We merely bring to the surface the hidden tension that is already alive. We bring it out in the open, where it can be seen and dealt with. Like a boil that can never be cured so long as it is covered up but must be opened with all its ugliness to the natural medicines of air and light, injustice must be exposed, with all the tension its exposure creates, to the light of human conscience and the air of national opinion before it can be cured.

In your statement you assert that our actions, even though peaceful, must be condemned because they precipitate violence. But is this a logical assertion? Isn't this like condemning a robbed man because his possession of money precipitated the evil act of robbery? Isn't this like condemning Socrates because his unswerving commitment to truth and his philosophical inquiries precipitated the act by the misguided populace in which they made him drink hemlock? Isn't this like condemning Jesus because his unique God-consciousness and never-ceasing devotion to God's will precipitated the evil act of crucifixion? We must come to see that, as the federal courts have consistently affirmed, it is wrong to urge an individual to cease his efforts to gain his basic constitutional rights because the quest may precipitate violence. Society must protect the robbed and punish the robber.

I had also hoped that the white moderate would reject the myth concerning time in relation to the struggle for freedom. I have just received a letter from a white brother in Texas. He writes: "All Christians know that the colored people will receive equal rights eventually, but it is possible that you are in too great a religious hurry. It has taken Christianity almost two thousand years to accomplish what it has. The teachings of Christ take time to come to earth." Such an attitude stems from a tragic misconception of time, from the strangely irrational notion that there is something in the very flow of time that will inevitably cure all ills. Actually, time itself is neutral; it can be used either destructively or constructively. More and more I feel that the people of ill will have used time much more effectively than have the people of good will. We will have to repent in this generation not merely for the hateful words and actions of the bad people but for the appalling silence of the good people. Human progress never rolls in on wheels of inevitability; it comes through the tireless efforts of men willing to be co-workers with God, and without this hard work, time itself becomes an ally of the forces of social stagnation. We must use time creatively, in the knowledge that the time is always ripe to do right. Now is the time to make real the promise of democracy and transform our pending national elegy into a creative psalm of brotherhood. Now is the time to lift our national policy from the quicksand of racial injustice to the solid rock of human dignity.

You speak of our activity in Birmingham as extreme At first I was rather disappointed that fellow clergymen would see my nonviolent efforts as those of an extremist. I began thinking about the fact that I stand in the middle of two opposing forces in the Negro community. One is a force of complacency, made up in part of Negroes who, as a result of long years of oppression, are so drained of self-respect and a sense of "somebodiness" that they have adjusted to segregation; and in part of a few middle-class Negroes who, because of a degree of academic and economic security and because in some ways they profit by segregation, have become insensitive to the problems of the masses. The other force is one of bitterness and hatred, and it comes perilously close to advocating violence. It is expressed in the various black nationalist groups that are springing up across the nation, the largest and best-known being Elijah Muhammad's Muslim movement. Nourished by the Negro's frustration over the continued existence of racial discrimination, this movement is made up of people who have lost faith in America, who have absolutely repudiated Christianity, and who have concluded that the white man is an incorrigible "devil."

I have tried to stand between these two forces, saying that we need emulate neither the "do-nothingism" of the complacent nor the hatred and despair of the black nationalist. For there is the more excellent way of love and nonviolent protest I am grateful to God that, through the influence of the Negro church, the way of nonviolence became an integral part of our struggle.

If this philosophy had not emerged, by now many streets of the South would, I am convinced, be flowing with blood. And I am further convinced that if our white brothers dismiss as "rabble-rousers" and "outside agitators" those of us who employ nonviolent direct action, and if they refuse to support our nonviolent efforts, millions of Negroes will, out of frustration and despair, seek solace and security in black-nationalist ideologies—a development that would inevitably lead to a frightening racial nightmare.

Oppressed people cannot remain oppressed forever. The yearning for freedom eventually manifests itself, and that is what has happened to the American Negro. Something within has reminded him of his birthright of freedom, and something without has reminded him that it can be gained. Consciously or unconsciously, he has been caught up by the *Zeitgeist* and with his black brothers of Africa and his brown and yellow brothers of Asia, South America and the Caribbean, the United States Negro is moving with a sense of great urgency toward the promised land of racial justice. If one recognizes this vital urge that has engulfed the Negro community, one should readily understand why public demonstrations are taking place. The Negro has many pent-up resentments and latent frustrations, and he must release them. So let him march; let him make prayer pilgrimages to the city hall; let him go on freedom rides—and try to understand why he must do so. If his repressed emotions are not released in nonviolent ways, they will seek expression through violence; this is not a threat but a fact of history. So I have not said to my people: "Get rid of your discontent." Rather, I have tried to say that this normal and healthy discontent can be channeled into the creative outlet of nonviolent direct action. And now this approach is being termed extremist.

But though I was initially disappointed at being categorized as an extremist, as I continued to think about the matter I gradually gained a measure of satisfaction from the label. Was not Jesus an extremist for love: "Love your enemies, bless them that curse you, do good to them that hate you, and pray for them which despitefully use you, and persecute you." Was not Amos an extremist for justice: "Let justice roll down like waters and righteousness like an ever-flowing stream." Was not Paul an extremist for the Christian gospel: "I bear in my body the marks of the Lord Jesus." Was not Martin Luther an extremist: "Here I stand; I cannot do otherwise, so help me God." And John Bunyan: "I will stay in jail to the end of my days before I make a butchery of my conscience." And Abraham Lincoln: "This nation cannot survive half slave and half free." And Thomas Jefferson: "We hold these truths to be self-evident, that all men are created equal..." So the question is not whether we will be extremists, but what kind of extremists we will be. Will we be extremists for hate or for love? Will we be extremist for the preservation of injustice or for the extension of justice? In that dramatic scene on Calvary's hill three men were crucified. We must never forget that all three were crucified for the same crime—the crime of extremism. Two were extremists for immorality, and thus fell below their environment. The other, Jesus Christ, was an extremist for love, truth and goodness, and thereby rose above his environment. Perhaps the South, the nation and the world are in dire need of creative extremists.

I had hoped that the white moderate would see this need. Perhaps I was too optimistic; perhaps I expected too much. I suppose I should have realized that few members of the oppressor race can understand the deep groans and passionate yearnings of the oppressed race, and still fewer have the vision to see that injustice must be rooted out by strong, persistent and determined action. I am thankful, however, that some of our white brothers in the South have grasped the meaning of this social revolution and committed themselves to it. They are still too few in quantity, but they are big in quality. Some—such as Ralph McGill, Lillian Smith, Harry Golden, James McBride Dabbs, Ann Braden and Sarah Patton Boyle—have written about our struggle in eloquent and prophetic terms. Others have marched with us down nameless streets of the South. They have languished in filthy, roach-infested jails, suffering the abuse and brutality of policemen who view them as "dirty nigger-lovers" Unlike so many of their moderate brothers and sisters, they have recognized the urgency of the moment and sensed the need for powerful "action" antidotes to combat the disease of segregation.

Let me take note of my other major disappointment. I have been so greatly disappointed with the white church and its leadership. Of course, there are some notable exceptions. I am not unmindful of the fact that each of you has taken some significant stands on this issue. I commend you, Reverend Stallings, for your Christian stand on this past Sunday, in welcoming Negroes to your worship service on a nonsegregated basis. I commend the Catholic leaders of this state for integrating Spring Hill College several years ago.

But despite these notable exceptions, I must honestly reiterate that I have been disappointed with the church. I do not say this as one of those negative critics who can always find something wrong with the church. I say this as a minister of the gospel, who loves the church; who was nurtured in its bosom; who has been sustained by its spiritual blessings and who will remain true to it as long as the cord of life shall lengthen.

When I was suddenly catapulted into the leadership of the bus protest in Montgomery, Alabama, a few years ago, I felt we would be supported by the white church. I felt that the white ministers, priests and rabbis of the South would be among our strongest allies. Instead, some have been outright opponents, refusing to understand the freedom movement and misrepresenting its leaders; all too many others have been more cautious than courageous and have remained silent behind the anesthetizing security of stained-glass windows.

In spite of my shattered dreams, I came to Birmingham with the hope that the white religious leadership of this community would see the justice of our cause and, with deep moral concern, would serve as the channel through which our just grievances could reach the power structure. I had hoped that each of you would understand. But again I have been disappointed.

I have heard numerous southern religious leaders admonish their worshipers to comply with a desegregation decision because it is the law, but I have longed to hear white ministers declare: "Follow this decree because integration is morally right and because the Negro is your brother." In the midst of blatant injustices inflicted upon the Negro, I have watched white churchmen stand on the sideline and mouth pious irrelevancies and sanctimonious trivialities. In the midst of a mighty struggle to rid our nation of racial and economic injustice, I have heard many ministers say: "Those are social issues, with which the gospel has no real concern." And I have watched many churches commit themselves to a completely other-worldly religion which makes a strange, un-Biblical distinction between body and soul, between the sacred and the secular.

I have traveled the length and breadth of Alabama, Mississippi and all the other southern states. On sweltering summer days and crisp autumn mornings I have looked at the South's beautiful churches with their lofty spires pointing heavenward. I have beheld the impressive outlines of her massive religious-education buildings. Over and over I have found myself asking: "What kind of people worship here? Who is their God? Where were their voices when the lips of Governor Barnett dripped with words of interposition and nullification? Where were they when Governor Wallace gave a clarion call for defiance and hatred? Where were their voices of support when bruised and weary Negro men and women decided to rise from the dark dungeons of complacency to the bright hills of creative protest?"

Yes these questions are still in my mind. In deep disappointment I have wept over the laxity of the church. But be assured that my tears have been tears of love. There can be no deep disappointment where there is not deep love. Yes, I love the church. How could I do otherwise? I am in the rather unique position of being the son, the grandson and the great-grandson of preachers. Yes, I see the church as the body of Christ. But oh! How we have blemished and scarred that body through social neglect and through fear of being nonconformists.

There was a time when the church was very powerful—in the time when the early Christians rejoiced at being deemed worthy to suffer for what they believed. In those days the church was not merely a thermometer that recorded the ideas and principles of popular opinion; it was a thermostat that transformed the mores of society. Whenever the early Christians entered a town, the people in power became disturbed and immediately sought to convict the Christians for being "disturbers of the peace" and "outside agitators'" But the Christians pressed on, in the conviction that they were "a colony of heaven," called to obey God rather than man. Small in number, they were big in commitment. They were too God-intoxicated to be "astronomically intimidated." By their effort and example they brought an end to such ancient evils as infanticide and gladiatorial contests.

Things are different now. So often the contemporary church is a weak, ineffectual voice with an uncertain sound. So often it is an archdefender of the status quo. Far from being disturbed by the presence of the church, the power structure of the average community is consoled by the church's silent—and often even vocal—sanction of things as they are.

But the judgment of God is upon the church as never before. If today's church does not recapture the sacrificial spirit of the early church, it will lose its authenticity, forfeit the loyalty of millions, and be dismissed as an irrelevant social club with no meaning for the twentieth century. Every day I meet young people whose disappointment with the church has turned into outright disgust.

Perhaps I have once again been too optimistic. Is organized religion too inextricably bound to the status quo to save our nation and the world? Perhaps I must turn my faith to the inner spiritual church, the church within the church, as the true *ekklesia* and the hope of the world. But again I am thankful to God that some noble souls from the ranks of organized religion have broken loose from the paralyzing chains of conformity and joined us as active partners in the struggle for freedom. They have left their secure congregations and walked the streets of Albany, Georgia, with us. They have gone down the highways of the South on tortuous rides for freedom. Yes, they have gone to jail with us. Some have been dismissed from their churches, have lost the support of their bishops and fellow ministers. But they have acted in the faith that right defeated is stronger than evil triumphant. Their witness has been the spiritual salt that has preserved the true meaning of the gospel in these troubled times. They have carved a tunnel of hope through the dark mountain of disappointment.

I hope the church as a whole will meet the challenge of this decisive hour. But even if the church does not come to the aid of justice, I have no despair about the future. I have no fear about the outcome of our struggle in Birmingham, even if our motives are at present misunderstood. We will reach the goal of freedom in Birmingham and all over the nation, because the goal of America is freedom. Abused and scorned though we may be, our destiny is tied up with America's destiny. Before the pilgrims landed at Plymouth, we were here. Before the pen of Jefferson etched the majestic words of the Declaration of Independence across the pages of history, we were here. For more than two centuries our forebears labored in this country without wages; they made cotton king; they built the homes of their masters while suffering gross injustice and shameful humiliation—and yet out of a bottomless vitality they continued to thrive and develop. If the inexpressible cruelties of slavery could not stop us, the opposition we now face will surely fail. We will win our freedom because the sacred heritage of our nation and the eternal will of God are embodied in our echoing demands.

Before closing I feel impelled to mention one other point in your statement that has troubled me profoundly. You warmly commended the Birmingham police force for keeping "order" and "preventing violence." I doubt that you would have so warmly commended the police force if you had seen its dogs sinking their teeth into unarmed, nonviolent Negroes. I doubt that you would so quickly commend the policemen if you were to observe their ugly and inhumane treatment of Negroes here in the city jail; if you were to watch them push and curse old Negro women and young Negro girls; if you were to see them slap and kick old Negro men and young boys; if you were to observe them, as they did on two occasions, refuse to give us food because we wanted to sing our grace together. I cannot join you in your praise of the Birmingham police department.

It is true that the police have exercised a degree of discipline in handling the demonstrators. In this sense they have conducted themselves rather "nonviolently" in public. But for what purpose? To preserve the evil system of segregation. Over the past few years I have consistently preached that nonviolence demands that the means we use must be as pure as the ends we seek. I have tried to make clear that it is wrong to use immoral means to attain moral ends. But now I must affirm that it is just as wrong, or perhaps even more so, to use moral means to preserve immoral ends. Perhaps Mr. Connor and his policemen have been rather nonviolent in public, as was Chief Pritchett in Albany, Georgia, but they have used the moral means of nonviolence to maintain the immoral end of racial injustice. As T. S. Eliot has said: "The last temptation is the greatest treason: To do the right deed for the wrong reason."

I wish you had commended the Negro sit-inners and demonstrators of Birmingham for their sublime courage, their willingness to suffer and their amazing discipline in the midst of great provocation. One day the South will recognize its real heroes. They will be the James Merediths, with the noble sense of purpose that enables them to face jeering, and hostile mobs, and with the agonizing loneliness that characterizes the life of the pioneer. They will be old, oppressed, battered Negro women, symbolized in a seventy-two-year-old woman in Montgomery, Alabama, who rose up with a sense of dignity and with her people decided not to ride segregated buses, and who responded with ungrammatical profundity to one who inquired about her weariness: "My feets is tired, but my soul is at rest." They will be the young high school and college students, the young ministers of the gospel and a host of their elders, courageously and nonviolently sitting in at lunch counters and willingly going to jail for conscience' sake. One day the South will know that when these disinherited children of God sat down at lunch counters, they were in reality standing up for what is best in the American dream and for the most sacred values in our Judaeo-Christian heritage, thereby bringing our nation back to those great wells of democracy which were dug deep by the founding fathers in their formulation of the Constitution and the Declaration of Independence.

Never before have I written so long a letter. I'm afraid it is much too long to take your precious time. I can assure you that it would have been much shorter if I had been writing from a comfortable desk, but what else can one do when he is alone in a narrow jail cell, other than write long letters, think long thoughts and pray long prayers?

I have said anything in this letter that overstates the truth and indicates an unreasonable impatience, I beg you to forgive me. If I have said anything that understates the truth and indicates my having a patience that allows me to settle for anything less than brotherhood, I beg God to forgive me.

I hope this letter finds you strong in the faith. I also hope that circumstances will soon make it possible for me to meet each of you, not as an integrationist or a civil rights leader but as a fellow clergyman and a Christian brother. Let us all hope that the dark clouds of racial prejudice will soon pass away and the deep fog of misunderstanding will be lifted from our fear-drenched communities, and in some not too distant tomorrow the radiant stars of love and brotherhood will shine over our great nation with all their scintillating beauty.

Yours for the cause of Peace and Brotherhood,
Martin Luther King, Jr.

JOHN F. KENNEDY'S CIVIL RIGHTS ADDRESS

"We face ... a moral crisis as a country and as a people."

Overview

The modern American civil rights movement, which began with the Montgomery bus boycott in 1955, was aimed at regaining the ground that had been achieved in the aftermath of the Civil War, such as through the enactment of the Fourteenth and Fifteenth Amendments to the Constitution and of civil rights laws in 1866 and 1875, and moving toward the complete elimination of racial inequality in all its forms. Civil rights organizations pursued a variety of tactics, including lawsuits, boycotts, lobbying, sit-ins, freedom rides, street demonstrations, and marches, in attempts to demand freedom, equality, jobs, dignity, and an end to racial segregation, disfranchisement, and second-class citizenship.

President John F. Kennedy's Civil Rights Address, delivered to the nation by radio and television, marked the first time that a president called on Americans to recognize civil rights as a lofty moral cause to which all persons should contribute, so that the nation might fully end discrimination against and provide equal treatment to African Americans. In 1963, the centennial year of President Abraham Lincoln's Emancipation Proclamation, to which Kennedy alludes in his speech, the movement led by African Americans and their allies for civil rights reached the center stage of American politics. Although Kennedy had hesitated to seek progress with regard to civil rights during his first two years in the White House because of the strength of southern Democratic opponents in Congress, he now added the moral weight of the presidency to the demand for civil rights, and he emerged as an ally of the movement. Kennedy explained the economic, educational, and moral dimensions of racial discrimination and announced that he would be submitting legislation to ensure equal access to public accommodations and to address other aspects of ongoing discrimination. On July 2, 1964, seven months after Kennedy was assassinated, the Civil Rights Act of 1964, abolishing discrimination in public accommodations, employment, and federally funded programs, became law.

Context

Two sets of events in Alabama in the spring of 1963 brought the civil rights movement a new level of public attention. Television viewers witnessed the Birmingham sheriff Eugene "Bull" Connor's use of water hoses and dogs against demonstrators as young as nine years old who were seeking equal access to public accommodations as well as Governor George Wallace's campaign pledge to "stand in the schoolhouse door" to prevent the integration of any Alabama school. On June 11, 1963, President Kennedy ended Wallace's resistance by federalizing the Alabama National Guard to support the court-mandated entry of Vivian J. Malone and James A. Hood to the University of Alabama. The determination of civil rights demonstrators, the violent and repressive actions of Alabama authorities, the solidarity protests galvanized by national civil rights organizations, and widespread public sympathy for the cause led Kennedy to take dramatic action to support civil rights.

In taking to the television and radio airwaves later that same day (June 11, 1963) to support the civil rights cause, Kennedy abandoned his previous go-slow approach to the issue. Moreover, he departed radically from the silence held by the Republican president Dwight D. Eisenhower when the Supreme Court handed down the historic 1954 *Brown v. Board of Education* decision, overturning the *Plessy v. Ferguson* separate-but-equal precedent of 1896. Kennedy's speech was momentous because he called on the nation to support civil rights as a moral cause.

About the Author

John Fitzgerald Kennedy was born in Massachusetts in 1917, the second of nine children of Joseph P. and Rose Fitzgerald Kennedy. John Kennedy's maternal grandfather had served as mayor of Boston, while his father was a successful business person and had served President Franklin Roosevelt as head of the Securities and Exchange Commission and then as ambassador to Great Britain. Kennedy's childhood was shaped by his family's great wealth, his parents' aloofness, attendance at boarding schools beginning in the seventh grade, and frequent illnesses. Kennedy

1954

■ **May 17**
Supreme Court decision in *Brown v. Board of Education* overturns the *Plessy v. Ferguson* separate-but-equal ruling and renews the protection of civil rights under the Fourteenth Amendment.

1955–1956

■ **December 1, 1955–December 20, 1956**
Montgomery bus boycott.

1957

Founding of Southern Christian Leadership Conference, headed by Martin Luther King, Jr.

1960

■ **February 1**
First civil rights sit-in demonstration takes place in Greensboro, North Carolina.

■ **April 15–17**
Founding of the Student Nonviolent Coordinating Committee at Shaw University, in Raleigh, North Carolina.

■ **December 5**
Supreme Court decision in *Boynton v. Virginia* bars discrimination against interstate bus passengers in station restaurants.

1961

Congress of Racial Equality renews Freedom Rides, a tactic previously used in 1947.

1962

■ **November 20**
President John F. Kennedy signs Executive Order 11063, providing for the desegregation of new federal housing.

1963

■ **June 10**
Kennedy delivers a commencement address at American University on rethinking the cold war.

■ **June 11**
Kennedy federalizes the Alabama National Guard to prevent the Alabama governor George Wallace's interference with the admission of Vivian Malone and James Hood to the University of Alabama. Kennedy later addresses the nation regarding civil rights on television and radio.

would contend with physical pain and a variety of illnesses throughout his life.

Rose Kennedy's focus on caring for her mentally retarded daughter, Rosemary, who was one year younger than John, led all the children to emulate their mother's example of caring. Kennedy graduated from Harvard College in 1940. Thanks to his father's prominence and the assistance of the *New York Times* columnist Arthur Krock, Kennedy succeeded in having his senior thesis published as a book, *Why England Slept*.

Kennedy and his older brother, Joseph Kennedy, Jr., both served in World War II, John as a PT boat commander; only John returned home safely. Their father had been grooming Joseph, Jr., for a political career that might culminate in the presidency. When John Kennedy decided to enter politics after a brief stint as a journalist, he received his father's financial and political backing. Kennedy was elected to the U.S. House of Representatives in 1946 and served as a member of the Committee on Education and Labor. His principal interests were foreign and defense policies. He was strongly anti-Communist and critical of the Truman administration for being insufficiently aggressive. In 1952 he won election to the U.S. Senate.

Kennedy married Jacqueline Bouvier in 1953. The couple had three children, one of whom died in infancy. Kennedy had been promiscuous prior to his marriage, and this behavior continued during the marriage and during his presidency, but in this era the press customarily declined to focus on the private lives of officeholders.

Kennedy's stance on domestic economic issues was liberal, but he failed to join in the 1954 Senate vote to censure Senator Joseph McCarthy. In 1956 Kennedy gained national attention with his unsuccessful bid to win the Democratic nomination for vice president. Kennedy's second book, *Profiles in Courage*, was awarded a Pulitzer Prize in 1957. The book highlights the careers of members of Congress who took principled stands, often in opposition to what was politically prudent. In the Senate, Kennedy served on a special committee on labor and on the Foreign Relations Committee. He was elected to a second term in the Senate in 1958, won the Democratic nomination for president in 1960, and claimed a narrow victory over the Republican candidate, Vice President Richard Nixon, in the general election later that year. Civil rights became a key issue in the campaign when Martin Luther King, Jr., was sentenced to four months of hard labor on a misdemeanor traffic charge, leading some civil rights leaders to fear that King would be killed in prison. Kennedy called Coretta King, King's wife, to express his sympathy, and his brother Robert called the judge and persuaded him to release King on bail. Kennedy won 70 percent of the black vote, 30 percent higher than the Democratic percentage in the 1956 election.

As president, Kennedy initially disappointed civil rights partisans by proceeding slowly with civil rights initiatives and appointing segregationist judges in the South. Kennedy had criticized the Eisenhower administration for failing to ban discrimination in federal housing via an executive order but then delayed the issuance of his own limited executive order addressing the matter until November 1962. Kennedy thought that an assertive approach to civil rights would hurt his chances for spurring legislative action on medical insurance, federal aid to education, and other initiatives, but he failed to achieve gains in these areas even with his go-slow approach to civil rights. His main focus was on an aggressive cold war foreign policy. The failure of the Bay of Pigs invasion in Cuba (in an attempt to overthrow the Communist regime of Fidel Castro) in 1961 and the October 1962 crisis with the Soviet Union over the placement of nuclear missiles in Cuba were key events in his presidency. He was also involved in increasing the number of U.S. military advisers in South Vietnam, where the U.S.-backed government was increasingly unpopular.

In the third and last year of his presidency, Kennedy moved toward rethinking the cold war and affirmative leadership on civil rights. He negotiated the Nuclear Test Ban Treaty with the Soviet Union and Great Britain, spoke out forcefully for civil rights, and submitted a major civil rights proposal to Congress. Kennedy was a popular president, and his assassination on November 22, 1963, shocked the nation. President Lyndon B. Johnson was able to carry to fruition Kennedy's domestic civil rights program.

Explanation and Analysis of the Document

After an initial greeting to his "fellow citizens"—marking the familiar tone the president adopted throughout the address—Kennedy reports on the day's events at the University of Alabama, where he had acted to enforce a U.S. district court decision for the admission of two African American students, Vivian Malone and James Hood. By federalizing the Alabama National Guard, the president overcame the resistance of Governor George Wallace and ended Alabama's status as the only remaining state with state universities closed to African Americans. In contrast to the president's similar experience with the desegregation of the University of Mississippi the previous year, no violence occurred. The president takes note of this fact and praises students at the University of Alabama "who met their responsibilities in a constructive way." In highlighting the good behavior of students, the president introduces one of the important themes of the address, the need for individual citizens to contribute to the solution of the civil rights crisis.

In the third paragraph the president begins to emphasize the key theme of the address, the morality of the civil rights cause, which he links to the responsibility of each American to act in accord with the nation's values and the principle of basic fairness. In an allusion to President Abraham Lincoln's Gettysburg Address, Kennedy notes that the nation was "founded on the principle that all men are created equal." He implicitly criticizes racist concepts regarding the nation's origins when he affirms that "this Nation was founded by men of many nations and backgrounds." In asserting that "the rights of every man are diminished when the rights of one man are threatened," the president alludes

to a long-standing labor movement slogan, "An injury to one is the concern of all." Organized labor was a central constituency of the Democratic Party, and its leaders strongly supported the enactment of civil rights legislation.

In paragraphs 4–6, Kennedy introduces an important theme of the address—that the "worldwide struggle to promote and protect the rights of all who wish to be free" was connected with the successful practice of the ideal of freedom for all in America. During World War II, many civil rights partisans raised the idea that eliminating racial discrimination at home was a logical and practical counterpart to the struggle against fascism abroad, particularly against the Nazi ideology of Aryan racial superiority. In the ensuing cold war between the United States and the Soviet Union, the issue of the connection between freedom at home and freedom abroad loomed in a new way. The Soviet Union, and indeed the world Communist movement, had long criticized racial oppression in the United States and the imperialist oppression of peoples in the developing world. In advocating a heightened struggle against Communism and for the U.S. concept of freedom around the world in his Inaugural Address, Kennedy was aware of the need for the United States to improve its civil rights record at home and the quality of its interactions with nations in the developing world. In his commencement address at the American University (delivered on June 10, 1963—the day before his Civil Rights Speech), in which he promoted a new approach to the cold war, Kennedy called on Americans to "examine our attitude towards peace and freedom here at home. The quality and spirit of our own society must justify and support our efforts abroad.... Wherever we are, we must all, in our daily lives, live up to the age-old faith that peace and freedom walk together. In too many of

Time Line

1963

■ **June 12**
Assassination of Medgar Evers, leader of the National Association for the Advancement of Colored People, in Mississippi.

■ **June 19**
Kennedy submits civil rights bill to Congress.

1964

■ **June 21**
During the Freedom Summer voting campaign, organized by the Student Nonviolent Coordinating Committee, the civil rights workers Michael Schwerner, Andrew Goodman, and James Chaney are murdered.

■ **July 2**
President Lyndon Johnson signs the Civil Rights Act of 1964.

President John F. Kennedy discusses civil rights with more than 200 lawyers on June 21, 1963, in the White House.
(AP Photo/Bob Schutz)

our cities today, the peace is not secure because freedom is incomplete" (http://www.americanrhetoric.com/speeches/jfkamericanuniversityaddress.html).

Noting in paragraph 4 that "we do not ask for whites only" when "Americans are sent to Viet-Nam or West Berlin," Kennedy then argues that Americans "of any color" should be able to attend any public university without needing backup from troops, to register to vote without "interference or fear of reprisal," and to receive "equal service" in public places. In the sixth paragraph, Kennedy couples the theme of equal rights with an allusion to the Golden Rule: "Every American ought to have the right to be treated as he would wish to be treated." A secular person, Kennedy nevertheless included in the address a few spiritual references.

In paragraphs 7 and 8, the president summarizes statistics on the vast economic, educational, and health gaps between blacks and whites and expresses concern about "a rising tide of discontent that threatens the public safety." The perception within the Kennedy administration that deterioration in the Birmingham situation could lead to "uncontrollable" outbursts by African Americans was, indeed, a major factor in the president's deciding to take to the public airwaves on the spur of the moment (Dallek, p. 598).

The president stresses in paragraph 8 that the issue of civil rights is neither a sectional nor a partisan issue. Although the central issue of equal access to public accommodations was primarily a problem in southern states, in keeping with his sense of responsibility as the leader of the entire country, the president asserts that "difficulties over segregation and discrimination" exist in every city and state. His references to the nationwide racial gap and to discontent in cities throughout the country place the issue of southern segregation in its larger national context—perhaps to reduce white southerners' feeling that their section was being unfairly targeted. Kennedy's emphasis on nonpartisanship reflected the reality that the strongest opponents of civil rights were white southerners in his own party and evinced his determination to work with Republican leaders in Congress on his civil rights legislative proposal.

Paragraphs 9–11 are among the most important passages in the speech. After stating in paragraph 9 that the country is "confronted primarily with a moral issue," the president calls on all Americans to do the right thing, to put fairness above partisanship, sectionalism, and comfort with the racial status quo. Kennedy makes clear that the basis of his moral appeal is fairness and a concern for others and their rights when he links a religious reference with an allusion to a central secular document of the U.S. polity: "It is as old as the scriptures and is as clear as the American Constitution." As a secular politician, Kennedy personally confronted the issue of anti-Catholic prejudice in his run for the presidency in 1960 when he spoke before Protestant ministers in Houston, Texas, and assured them that he advocated "an America where the separation of church and state is absolute" (Dallek, pp. 283–284). In this instance, Kennedy used a nondenominational appeal to religious values to reinforce his attempt to inspire the country on a moral issue. Kennedy, like other presidents, had referred to God in his Inaugural Address.

In paragraph 10, Kennedy refers to the obligations of the Golden Rule—"The heart of the question is … whether we are going to treat our fellow Americans as we want to be treated"—and issues a creative call for white people to imagine how they would feel if they were black. What would you think, he asks, about being denied service at restaurants, access to the best public schools, the right to vote, and "the full and free life which all of us want"? The paragraph closes with an incisive critique of the moderate approach that he himself had earlier followed and which Martin Luther King, Jr., had so sharply criticized two months earlier in his "Letter from Birmingham Jail." The president asks, "Who among us would then be content with the counsels of patience and delay?" Kennedy is asking Americans to look beyond the sometimes disconcerting and disruptive means used by civil rights activists to see the justice of their cause. As the president himself had only recently come to perceive, the time for incremental changes that essentially left the Jim Crow system intact had passed. Those who saw the issue as a struggle between two extremes, violent racists and civil rights activists, were mistaken. Rather, the struggle was between justice and injustice.

To reinforce the notion that the time for ending racial equality had come, Kennedy notes in paragraph 11 that one hundred years had passed "since President Lincoln freed the slaves," yet "their heirs … are not fully free." A few years prior to the anniversary of the Emancipation Proclamation, the National Association for the Advancement of Colored People had begun a "Free by '63" campaign. On the occasion of Lincoln's birthday in 1963, the president and the first lady hosted a reception for African American leaders and their spouses and distributed to the guests the U.S. Commission on Civil Rights report *Freedom to the Free: Century of Emancipation, 1863–1963*. In Paragraph 11 Kennedy also reiterates the opening theme from paragraph 3, the interconnection of one person's freedom with another, remarking that the nation "will not be fully free until all its citizens are free."

Paragraph 12 focuses on the interconnection between the consequences for the U.S. advocacy of "freedom around the world" and for U.S. foreign policy brought about by the treatment of African Americans as "second-class citizens." As concerned as he was about foreign policy, the president maintains that a bigger problem is that people can "say … to each other that this is the land of the free except for the Negroes." Kennedy emphasizes the heinousness of this situation by alluding to Nazi ideology with the use of the term "master race." For Kennedy, who had fought in World War II, and for all those over the age of thirty-five or so, memories of the struggle against Nazi Germany and the other Axis powers were still vivid.

In paragraphs 13–17, Kennedy emphasizes that crisis conditions are at hand, calling for immediate action. The "cries for equality" are too great to ignore; the president declares in paragraph 14 that with "legal remedies" unavailable, people are taking to the streets in protests that "create tensions and threaten violence and threaten lives." The opponents of civil rights, of course, were the ones who committed the acts of violence. Although civil rights activists' decisions to violate the laws of segregation and to protest in the streets certainly contributed to confrontations, they were committed to nonviolence. Kennedy was worried, however, that spontaneous eruptions of anger among members of the black community could lead to violence. This is the only moment in the speech where the president seems to tilt against the civil rights movement. In the next paragraph he returns to the underlying positive theme of the address, asserting, "We face, therefore, a moral crisis as a country and as a people." He notes that he opposes "repressive police action." While the president says that the situation "cannot be left to increased demonstrations in the streets," he also calls for substantive action, not "token moves or talk," at all levels of society.

In paragraph 16, Kennedy calls on the nation to avoid sectionalism and attempts to place blame. He characterizes the vast change needed as a "revolution" but notes that it should be "peaceful and constructive for all."

In paragraphs 18–21, Kennedy focuses on the need for civil rights legislation and announces that he will submit a proposal to Congress for equal access to public accommodations, which he characterizes as "an elementary right." Kennedy notes that without legislation, the only remedy that African American citizens have for wrongs inflicted on them "is in the street"; "in too many communities, in too many parts of the country," no "remedies at law" could be found. Kennedy maintains that the denial of access is "an arbitrary indignity that no American in 1963 should have to endure, but many do," thus appealing once again to white viewers and listeners to empathize with African Americans and to see that the recognition of equal rights is long overdue.

In paragraph 22 the president reports that he has met with many business leaders and is pleased that they have responded to his call for "voluntary action" to end discrimination in public accommodations. Kennedy comments that despite progress in over seventy-five cities in the past two weeks, legislation is nevertheless needed because "many are unwilling to act alone."

In paragraphs 23–26, Kennedy outlines additional features of the civil rights legislation that he will propose, including federal government involvement in lawsuits to promote desegregation in schools and "greater protection for the right to vote." He notes that "too many" black students who entered segregated grade schools at the time of the *Brown v. Board of Education* Supreme Court decision "will enter segregated high schools this fall." Only a small percentage of black students had yet moved from segregated to desegregated schools. The consequence of this delayed desegregation, the president argues, is lost job opportunities.

In paragraph 26, the president again emphasizes the need for action "in the homes of every American in every community," while in paragraphs 27 and 28 he praises the "honor" and "courage" of those working for civil rights. Kennedy asserts that these individuals have acted "out of a sense of human decency" and compares them with "our soldiers and sailors" because "they are meeting freedom's challenge on the firing line." This was high praise, indeed, given the importance Kennedy attached to foreign policy and the stress that he placed on political and moral courage in his book *Profiles in Courage*.

In paragraph 29, the president highlights the economic gap between blacks and whites throughout the country. Kennedy argues that this is a problem that "faces us all," in "the North as well as the South." Describing in detail the crisis facing the nation, Kennedy again calls on "every citizen" to care and to act.

In paragraphs 30 and 31, Kennedy makes an appeal based on cultural pluralism, national unity, and equality: The United States "has become one country because all of us and all of the people who came here had an equal chance to develop their talents." He reiterates the need to give the "10 percent of the population" constituted by African Americans alternatives to discrimination and to demonstrations as the only means of gaining rights. The issue, he insists, is one of basic fairness and in the interests of all: "I think we owe them and we owe ourselves a better country than that."

In paragraph 32 the president makes an explicit appeal for people's help and reiterates the theme of treating people as one would want to be treated. In this and the following paragraph, the president emphasizes the theme of equality of opportunity and the importance of treating children right—"to give a chance for every child to be educated to the limit of his talents." Kennedy uses exclusively male pronouns here and throughout most of the address.

In paragraph 34 Kennedy speaks of the reciprocal obligation to be held by black citizens ("be responsible ... uphold the law") and by society ("the law will be fair ... the Constitution will be color blind"). In advocating a color-blind Constitution, Kennedy alludes to John Marshall Harlan's use of this terminology in his dissent in the *Plessy v. Ferguson* separate-but-equal Supreme Court decision of 1896. In the closing paragraph, the president states that basic principles are at stake—what the country "stands for"—and again asks for the support of "all our citizens."

Audience

President Kennedy's audience for his Civil Rights Speech was the entire population of the United States. The address was carried on television and radio, so the vast majority of the population was in a position to hear the president's words. He asked the three major television networks for airtime for the address, and all readily agreed. As part of their licenses to use the public airwaves, the broadcast companies in the period prior to deregulation were expected to be responsive to such requests.

Although the president was speaking to all "fellow Americans," he was particularly addressing white Americans. For example, he asks people to put themselves in the place of a black person and imagine how they would feel about having their rights denied. Kennedy also says that "we" expect things of the black community but that "they" expect to have equal rights.

Kennedy directed his remarks to people of both parties, of all regions, and of all classes. His remarks included praise for businesspeople responding to his call for voluntary action to desegregate as well as for those working on the front lines of the struggle for racial justice. By appealing to fairness, Kennedy hoped to expand support for his civil rights initiative beyond the ranks of liberals and the left.

In using male language at several points, the president addresses himself primarily to men (as in "one-third as much chance of becoming a professional man," "law alone cannot make men see right," and "if an American, because his skin is dark"). In referring to the effort to secure the admission of two African American students to the University of Alabama, one of whom was female, the president uses gender-neutral language ("clearly qualified young Alabama residents"). In referring to student potential in the close of the address, he shifts between male ("his talents") and gender-neutral language ("their talent").

Impact

Civil rights movement leaders and activists were thrilled by President Kennedy's national address of June 11, 1963. Martin Luther King, Jr., immediately sent Kennedy a message praising the speech. The Kennedy administration had been lending assistance to the civil rights movement and was now staking its own political success on the achievement of fundamental reform in the civil rights arena; the administration acted as a good if imperfect ally of the movement. In fact, when civil rights leaders met with the president on June 22, 1963, the president acknowledged that he did not think that the planned march on Washington, D.C., was a good idea. The difference of opinion was resolved, and Kennedy ended up supporting the march. Although the Student Nonviolent Coordinating Committee leader John Lewis was pressured into modifying his address, the march of 250,000 people from the Washington Monument to the Lincoln Memorial was a great success and further expanded positive public attention for the movement.

The Kennedy administration did experience some immediate negative political repercussions after the address, as southern Congress members withdrew support from other administration proposals. Also, disagreements with the National Association for the Advancement of Colored People occurred over the details of the civil rights bill, with the administration seeking a more moderate version than was sought by the civil rights coalition. Kennedy met

"Today we are committed to a worldwide struggle to promote and protect the rights of all who wish to be free. And when Americans are sent to Viet-Nam or West Berlin, we do not ask for whites only. It ought to be possible, therefore, for American students of any color to attend any public institution they select without having to be backed up by troops."

(Paragraph 4)

"It ought to be possible, in short, for every American to enjoy the privileges of being American without regard to his race or his color. In short, every American ought to have the right to be treated as he would wish to be treated, as one would wish his children to be treated. But this is not the case."

(Paragraph 6)

"We are confronted primarily with a moral issue. It is as old as the scriptures and is as clear as the American Constitution."

(Paragraph 9)

"The heart of the question is whether all Americans are to be afforded equal rights and equal opportunities, whether we are going to treat our fellow Americans as we want to be treated. If an American, because his skin is dark, cannot eat lunch in a restaurant open to the public, if he cannot send his children to the best public school available, if he cannot vote for the public officials who will represent him, if, in short, he cannot enjoy the full and free life which all of us want, then who among us would be content to have the color of his skin changed and stand in his place? Who among us would then be content with the counsels of patience and delay?"

(Paragraph 10)

"We face, therefore, a moral crisis as a country and as a people. It cannot be met by repressive police action. It cannot be left to increased demonstrations in the streets. It cannot be quieted by token moves or talk. It is time to act in the Congress, in your State and local legislative body and, above all, in all of our daily lives."

(Paragraph 15)

with Democratic and Republican House leaders on October 23 to craft a compromise that proved stronger than the administration's bill. The House Judiciary Committee approved the civil rights bill on November 20, 1963, but whether the bill would be successfully processed by the House Rules Committee, chaired by the segregationist Howard W. Smith, was uncertain. Kennedy would not have the opportunity to work on that problem because of his assassination. President Lyndon B. Johnson took up the banner, however, and worked effectively to secure the passage of the Civil Rights Act of 1964. As vice president, Johnson had urged Kennedy to take a moral stance on civil rights. As segregationists left the Democratic Party in the wake of the passage of the Civil Rights Act and the Voting Rights Act of 1965, the party's stance as an ally of the civil rights movement and of African Americans became a permanent fixture of the political landscape.

Related Documents

Hampton, Henry, and Steve Fayer, eds. *Voices of Freedom: An Oral History of the Civil Rights Movement from the 1950s through the 1980s*. New York: Bantam Books, 1990. This is a companion volume to the *Eyes on the Prize* documentary series.

"John F. Kennedy: American University Commencement Address." American Rhetoric "Top 100 Speeches" Web site. http://www.americanrhetoric.com/speeches/jfkamericanuniversityaddress.html. Accessed on February 26, 2008. In his commencement address delivered at American University in Washington, D.C., the day before his Civil Rights Speech, Kennedy urges rethinking of the cold war with the Soviet Union and calls for peace and disarmament.

Kennedy, John F. *Public Papers of the Presidents of the United States: John F. Kennedy*. Washington, D.C.: U.S. Government Printing Office, 1962–1964. This is a three-volume record of Kennedy's statements.

King, Martin Luther, Jr. "Letter from the Birmingham Jail." In *Why We Can't Wait*. New York: Harper & Row, 1964. This letter of April 16, 1963, was King's response to a call by a group of moderate white Protestant ministers for an end to civil rights demonstrations in Birmingham. It can be found on the Web at http://www.stanford.edu/group/King/popular_requests/frequentdocs/birmingham.pdf.

Sorensen, Theodore C., ed. *"Let the Word Go Forth": The Speeches, Statements, and Writings of John F. Kennedy*. New York: Delacorte Press, 1988. This is a selection of important Kennedy documents edited by his principal speech writer.

Strober, Deborah Hart, and Gerald S. Strober. *The Kennedy Presidency: An Oral History of the Era*. Washington, D.C.: Brassey's, 2003. Organized topically, this volume includes a chapter on civil

rights featuring interviews with key individuals both inside and outside the Kennedy administration.

Bibliography

■ Books

Branch, Taylor. *Parting the Waters: America in the King Years, 1954–63*. New York: Simon & Schuster, 1988.

———. *Pillar of Fire: America in the King Years, 1963–65*. New York: Simon & Schuster, 1988.

Bryant, Nick. *The Bystander: John F. Kennedy and the Struggle for Black Equality*. New York: Basic Books, 2006.

Dallek, Robert. *An Unfinished Life: John F. Kennedy, 1917–1963*. Boston: Little, Brown, 2003.

Giglio, James N. *The Presidency of John F. Kennedy*. 2nd ed. Lawrence: University Press of Kansas, 2006.

Lawson, Steven F. *Running for Freedom: Civil Rights and Black Politics in America since 1941*. 2nd ed. New York: McGraw-Hill, 1997.

Rorabaugh, W. J. *Kennedy and the Promise of the Sixties*. Cambridge, U.K.: Cambridge University Press, 2002.

Sorensen, Theodore C. *Kennedy*. New York: Perennial Library, 1988.

U.S. Commission on Civil Rights. *Freedom to the Free: Century of Emancipation, 1863–1963; A Report to the President*. Washington, D.C.: U.S. Government Printing Office, 1963.

Watson, Denton L. *Lion in the Lobby: Clarence Mitchell, Jr.'s Struggle for the Passage of Civil Rights Laws*. New York: Morrow, 1990.

Wofford, Harris. *Of Kennedys and Kings: Making Sense of the Sixties*. Pittsburgh: University of Pittsburgh Press, 1992.

■ Web Sites

John F. Kennedy Presidential Library and Museum Web site. http://www.jfklibrary.org/. Accessed on October 25, 2007.

"Martin Luther King, Jr. Papers Project." The Martin Luther King, Jr., Research and Education Institute Web site. http://www.stanford.edu/group/King/mlkpapers/. Accessed on October 25, 2007.

—By Martin Halpern

Questions for Further Study

1. Compare Kennedy's responses to civil rights crises with those of President Dwight D. Eisenhower to the Supreme Court's *Brown v. Board of Education* decision, to the rise of massive resistance, and to the 1957 Little Rock crisis.

2. In referring to the Supreme Court justice John Marshall Harlan's concept of a color-blind Constitution, was President Kennedy concerned with ending systematic discrimination against African Americans or with eliminating any reference to race in American law and practice, or with both?

3. Kennedy highlighted economic disparities between whites and African Americans in his address. Overcoming economic privation was one of the goals of the March on Washington for Jobs and Freedom of August 28, 1963, and the goal of the Poor People's Campaign, which Martin Luther King, Jr., was leading at the time of his assassination. Examine the extent of economic disparities in society today. To what degree would the universal implementation of affirmation action or a program of reparations contribute to substantially closing racial socioeconomic gaps? Might a modern-day president committed to civil rights take other initiatives to eliminate such gaps?

4. In the 1990s a trend toward the resegregation of public schools began taking place. The 2007 Supreme Court decision in *Parents Involved in Community Schools v. Seattle School District No. 1* against the use of race in assigning students to schools further undermined the promise of the *Brown v. Board of Education* decision that schools would be equal and integrated. What measures might be taken today to restore the goal of establishing equal educational opportunity championed by Kennedy in his June 11, 1963, address to the nation?

Glossary

caste system	rigid hereditary separation of social groups
deplore	condemn
equity law	the application of principles of fairness in the absence of rules
ghettoes	sections of cities where groups that are discriminated against reside
harassment	persecution
oppression	subjugation
public accommodation	facilities serving the public
redress	correct
remedy	fix
scriptures	sacred religious texts

John F. Kennedy's Civil Rights Address

Good evening my fellow citizens:

This afternoon, following a series of threats and defiant statements, the presence of Alabama National Guardsmen was required on the University of Alabama to carry out the final and unequivocal order of the United States District Court of the Northern District of Alabama. That order called for the admission of two clearly qualified young Alabama residents who happened to have been born Negro.

That they were admitted peacefully on the campus is due in good measure to the conduct of the students of the University of Alabama, who met their responsibilities in a constructive way.

I hope that every American, regardless of where he lives, will stop and examine his conscience about this and other related incidents. This Nation was founded by men of many nations and backgrounds. It was founded on the principle that all men are created equal, and that the rights of every man are diminished when the rights of one man are threatened.

Today we are committed to a worldwide struggle to promote and protect the rights of all who wish to be free. And when Americans are sent to Viet-Nam or West Berlin, we do not ask for whites only. It ought to be possible, therefore, for American students of any color to attend any public institution they select without having to be backed up by troops.

It ought to be possible for American consumers of any color to receive equal service in places of public accommodation, such as hotels and restaurants and theaters and retail stores, without being forced to resort to demonstrations in the street, and it ought to be possible for American citizens of any color to register to vote in a free election without interference or fear of reprisal.

It ought to be possible, in short, for every American to enjoy the privileges of being American without regard to his race or his color. In short, every American ought to have the right to be treated as he would wish to be treated, as one would wish his children to be treated. But this is not the case.

The Negro baby born in America today, regardless of the section of the Nation in which he is born, has about one-half as much chance of completing a high school as a white baby born in the same place on the same day, one-third as much chance of completing

college, one-third as much chance of becoming a professional man, twice as much chance of becoming unemployed, about one-seventh as much chance of earning $10,000 a year, a life expectancy which is 7 years shorter, and the prospects of earning only half as much.

This is not a sectional issue. Difficulties over segregation and discrimination exist in every city, in every State of the Union, producing in many cities a rising tide of discontent that threatens the public safety. Nor is this a partisan issue. In a time of domestic crisis men of good will and generosity should be able to unite regardless of party or politics. This is not even a legal or legislative issue alone. It is better to settle these matters in the courts than on the streets, and new laws are needed at every level, but law alone cannot make men see right.

We are confronted primarily with a moral issue. It is as old as the scriptures and is as clear as the American Constitution.

The heart of the question is whether all Americans are to be afforded equal rights and equal opportunities, whether we are going to treat our fellow Americans as we want to be treated. If an American, because his skin is dark, cannot eat lunch in a restaurant open to the public, if he cannot send his children to the best public school available, if he cannot vote for the public officials who will represent him, if, in short, he cannot enjoy the full and free life which all of us want, then who among us would be content to have the color of his skin changed and stand in his place? Who among us would then be content with the counsels of patience and delay?

One hundred years of delay have passed since President Lincoln freed the slaves, yet their heirs, their grandsons, are not fully free. They are not yet freed from the bonds of injustice. They are not yet freed from social and economic oppression. And this Nation, for all its hopes and all its boasts, will not be fully free until all its citizens are free.

We preach freedom around the world, and we mean it, and we cherish our freedom here at home, but are we to say to the world, and much more importantly, to each other that this is the land of the free except for the Negroes; that we have no second-class citizens except Negroes; that we have no class or caste system, no ghettoes, no master race except with respect to Negroes?

Now the time has come for this Nation to fulfill its promise. The events in Birmingham and elsewhere have so increased the cries for equality that no city or State or legislative body can prudently choose to ignore them.

The fires of frustration and discord are burning in every city, North and South, where legal remedies are not at hand. Redress is sought in the streets, in demonstrations, parades, and protests which create tensions and threaten violence and threaten lives.

We face, therefore, a moral crisis as a country and as a people. It cannot be met by repressive police action. It cannot be left to increased demonstrations in the streets. It cannot be quieted by token moves or talk. It is time to act in the Congress, in your State and local legislative body and, above all, in all of our daily lives.

It is not enough to pin the blame of others, to say this a problem of one section of the country or another, or deplore the fact that we face. A great change is at hand, and our task, our obligation, is to make that revolution, that change, peaceful and constructive for all.

Those who do nothing are inviting shame as well as violence. Those who act boldly are recognizing right as well as reality.

Next week I shall ask the Congress of the United States to act, to make a commitment it has not fully made in this century to the proposition that race has no place in American life or law. The Federal judiciary has upheld that proposition in the conduct of its affairs, including the employment of Federal personnel, the use of Federal facilities, and the sale of federally financed housing.

But there are other necessary measures which only the Congress can provide, and they must be provided at this session. The old code of equity law under which we live commands for every wrong a remedy, but in too many communities, in too many parts of the country, wrongs are inflicted on Negro citizens and there are no remedies at law. Unless the Congress acts, their only remedy is in the street.

I am, therefore, asking the Congress to enact legislation giving all Americans the right to be served in facilities which are open to the public—hotels, restaurants, theaters, retail stores, and similar establishments.

This seems to me to be an elementary right. Its denial is an arbitrary indignity that no American in 1963 should have to endure, but many do.

I have recently met with scores of business leaders urging them to take voluntary action to end this discrimination and I have been encouraged by their response, and in the last 2 weeks over 75 cities have seen progress made in desegregating these kinds of facilities. But many are unwilling to act alone, and for this reason, nationwide legislation is needed if we are to move this problem from the streets to the courts.

I am also asking the Congress to authorize the Federal Government to participate more fully in lawsuits designed to end segregation in public education. We have succeeded in persuading many districts to desegregate voluntarily. Dozens have admitted Negroes without violence. Today a Negro is attending a State-supported institution in every one of our 50 States, but the pace is very slow.

Too many Negro children entering segregated grade schools at the time of the Supreme Court's decision 9 years ago will enter segregated high schools this fall, having suffered a loss which can never be restored. The lack of an adequate education denies the Negro a chance to get a decent job.

The orderly implementation of the Supreme Court decision, therefore, cannot be left solely to those who may not have the economic resources to carry the legal action or who may be subject to harassment.

Other features will also be requested, including greater protection for the right to vote. But legislation, I repeat, cannot solve this problem alone. It must be solved in the homes of every American in every community across our country.

In this respect I want to pay tribute to those citizens North and South who have been working in their communities to make life better for all. They are acting not out of a sense of legal duty but out of a sense of human decency.

Like our soldiers and sailors in all parts of the world they are meeting freedom's challenge on the firing line, and I salute them for their honor and their courage.

My fellow Americans, this is a problem which faces us all—in every city of the North as well as the South. Today there are Negroes unemployed, two or three times as many compared to whites, inadequate in education, moving into the large cities, unable to find work, young people particularly out of work without hope, denied equal rights, denied the opportunity to eat at a restaurant or lunch counter or go to a movie theater, denied the right to a decent education, denied almost today the right to attend a State university even though qualified. It seems to me that these are matters which concern us all, not merely Presidents or Congressmen or Governors, but every citizen of the United States.

This is one country. It has become one country because all of us and all the people who came here had an equal chance to develop their talents.

We cannot say to 10 percent of the population that you can't have that right; that your children cannot have the chance to develop whatever talents they have; that the only way that they are going to get their rights is to go into the streets and demonstrate. I think we owe them and we owe ourselves a better country than that.

Therefore, I am asking for your help in making it easier for us to move ahead and to provide the kind of equality of treatment which we would want ourselves; to give a chance for every child to be educated to the limit of his talents.

As I have said before, not every child has an equal talent or an equal ability or an equal motivation, but they should have an equal right to develop their talent and their ability and their motivation, to make something of themselves.

We have a right to expect that the Negro community will be responsible, will uphold the law, but they have a right to expect that the law will be fair, that the Constitution will be color blind, as Justice Harlan said at the turn of the century.

This is what we are talking about and this is a matter which concerns this country and what it stands for, and in meeting it I ask the support of all our citizens.

Thank you very much.

Martin Luther King, Jr., addresses marchers during his "I Have a Dream" Speech in 1963. (AP Photo)

MARTIN LUTHER KING, JR.'S "I HAVE A DREAM" SPEECH

"From every mountainside, let freedom ring."

Overview

On August 28, 1963, nearly a quarter of a million people arrived in the District of Columbia for the March on Washington for Jobs and Freedom. They had been summoned by the veteran African American labor leader A. Philip Randolph to urge the federal government to broaden economic opportunities for low-income families and to pressure Congress to pass the Civil Rights Act, which was then being debated. Delegations of civil rights supporters from cities across the United States thus joined together for a massive one-day protest.

The orderly crowd assembled in front of the Lincoln Memorial and listened as representatives of labor, religious, and civil rights organizations delivered short addresses. The day's final speaker was Martin Luther King, Jr., the nation's preeminent civil rights leader. The demonstrations against segregation led by King in Birmingham, Alabama, four months earlier had raised the issue of racial equality to the top of the national agenda. Sensing a changing mood in the country, President John F. Kennedy responded by proposing comprehensive civil rights legislation.

King reminded his listeners that day of African Americans' legitimate grievances and promised that they would not rest until full equality was won. As he neared the end of his speech, King departed from his prepared text to deliver his most memorable words: "I have a dream," he thundered, in the powerful preaching cadence of the black Baptist tradition. Using a series of riveting images, King shared his vision of a country free of racial hatred, in which black and white Americans would live as equals. His oration eclipsed the remarks of all other speakers that day and is among the most quoted American public addresses. The "I Have a Dream" Speech has come to epitomize the aspirations of the modern civil rights movement.

Context

Gathering in the nation's capital to petition Congress is a time-honored tradition of American political movements. In 1894 Jacob Coxey led an army of unemployed workers to Washington, demanding that the government create more jobs. Thirty thousand World War I veterans seeking early bonuses for their military service camped outside Washington for forty days in 1932, until routed by army troops. In 1941 A. Philip Randolph, the president of the Brotherhood of Sleeping Car Porters, threatened to lead one hundred thousand African Americans down Pennsylvania Avenue, forcing President Franklin D. Roosevelt to act against racial discrimination in defense industries.

As civil rights protests gained momentum in the early 1960s, Randolph revived the idea of a march on Washington. Because he was concerned primarily about African American poverty and unemployment, Randolph proposed a two-day demonstration for jobs to be held in October 1963. He maintained that a massive assembly of black citizens was needed to prod a reluctant President Kennedy into action. Randolph's idea initially drew a lukewarm response from other black leaders—until Martin Luther King, Jr., lent his support. King had just finished a successful campaign to desegregate stores and lunch counters in Birmingham, Alabama. Nationally televised scenes of police dogs and fire hoses battering youthful demonstrators roused public sympathy behind the crusade for equal rights. King was looking for a way to sustain the energy of his movement and press for needed civil rights legislation. When he announced his intention to participate in the march, rival civil rights leaders felt compelled to join. After Kennedy submitted his civil rights bill to Congress, the event was renamed the "March for Jobs and Freedom," the date was changed to late August, and the emphasis shifted from economic issues to support for the proposed legislation.

At a meeting at the White House in June, Kennedy tried to convince march organizers that a mass protest would actually derail support for his civil rights bill. When Randolph and King declared their determination to go ahead with the demonstration, the president offered the assistance of federal agencies to ensure that the march proceeded smoothly. In the weeks leading up to the event, Randolph's chief aide, Bayard Rustin, worked around the clock to nail down the smallest details. Marchers would arrive by chartered buses and trains on the morning of August 28 and depart that afternoon; they would carry only signs approved by the march committee; no sit-ins or civil disobedience would be staged; thousands of sandwiches

1963

January
A. Philip Randolph announces plans for a demonstration in Washington, D.C., to force legislative action on economic problems facing African Americans.

April–May
Police attacks on civil rights demonstrators in Birmingham, Alabama, capture the attention of the nation and increase pressure for federal civil rights legislation.

June 11
In a nationally televised address, President John F. Kennedy announces that he will send a comprehensive civil rights bill to Congress.

June 18
Kennedy delivers what will become the Civil Rights Act to Congress.

June 22
Civil rights leaders meet with Kennedy, who tries to persuade them to drop plans for their march.

June 23
Martin Luther King, Jr., leads 125,000 marchers through the streets of Detroit in a "dress rehearsal" for the March on Washington.

July 2
Bayard Rustin presents a detailed plan for the march. To ensure that the march will be racially integrated, four prominent whites are added as cochairmen of the event.

August 27
King toils late into the night preparing his address for the march.

August 28
Some 250,000 demonstrators arrive in Washington, D.C. King delivers his "I Have a Dream" Speech, which is broadcast live by all of the major television networks.

November 22
Kennedy is assassinated in Dallas, Texas. Lyndon B. Johnson becomes president.

would be prepared to feed the hungry throngs; and security would be provided by off-duty New York City police officers and federal personnel.

King began composing his speech four days before the march, asking advisers to prepare drafts for his consideration. When King arrived in Washington on August 27, he still did not have a version that he felt was satisfactory. That evening he retired to his room at the Willard Hotel to work on revisions; at four o'clock the next morning King handed his final handwritten text to aides for typing and distribution to the press.

The day's events began with a program of entertainment on a stage erected near the Washington Monument. Musicians performed, and celebrities were introduced to the well-dressed marchers, but the crowd grew restive. Around eleven o'clock people spontaneously began moving toward the Lincoln Memorial, and the assembled dignitaries had to scramble to catch up with the people they were supposed to be leading. As the huge crowd congregated on either side of the memorial's Reflecting Pool, the speakers took their turns at the podium in the shadow of the Great Emancipator's statue. John Lewis, the young head of the Student Nonviolent Coordinating Committee, delivered the day's most militant address, calling for a "great revolution" to "splinter the segregated south into a thousand pieces." Mahalia Jackson roused the crowd when she sang the traditional spiritual "I've Been 'Buked and I've Been Scorned." Then, Randolph introduced "the moral leader of our nation," Dr. Martin Luther King, Jr., whose address sounded the climactic final note for the day's celebration (Hansen, p. 50).

When King concluded his speech, the throngs quickly dispersed, carrying a message of hope back to their home communities. Leaders of the march, in turn, adjourned to the White House, where they ate a hastily prepared lunch and were congratulated by President Kennedy, who was relieved and delighted that the event had gone off without serious controversy or disorder of any kind.

About the Author

Martin Luther King, Jr., was born and raised in Atlanta, Georgia, where both his father and grandfather pastored the Ebenezer Baptist Church. At the age of fifteen he entered Morehouse College to study sociology. He prepared for the ministry at Crozier Theological Seminary, in Pennsylvania, and then earned a doctorate in philosophy from Boston University. While in Boston he met and married Coretta Scott, an aspiring concert singer from Marion, Alabama.

In 1953 King returned to the South to become pastor of the Dexter Avenue Baptist Church in Montgomery, Alabama. When Rosa Parks was arrested in 1955 for refusing to give up her seat to a white passenger, King emerged as the leader of a year-long boycott of city buses. His application of Gandhian nonviolent resistance to fight Jim Crow laws and the successful outcome of the Montgomery protest thrust him into the national spotlight. In 1957 he founded the Southern Christian Leadership Conference to carry his fight for civil rights to other southern communities. Over the next decade King remained at the forefront of the rapidly growing civil rights movement. In 1963 he led a campaign of civil disobedience against segregation in Birmingham, Alabama—one of the most violent southern cities. His "Letter from Birmingham Jail," written following his arrest while leading a demonstration, is an eloquent defense of his nonviolent tactics.

King's "I Have a Dream" Speech at the March on Washington helped build public support for the landmark Civil Rights Act that was passed by Congress in 1964. In turn, the Voting Rights Act that became law the following year was enacted largely because of his efforts to dramatize the disenfranchisement of African American citizens in Selma, Alabama. In 1966 King turned his attention to the North, where he attacked slum conditions and segregated housing in Chicago. King's growing opposition to the Vietnam War put him in the front ranks of the antiwar movement. At the time of his assassination in 1968, he was preparing to lead the Poor People's Campaign, a multiracial effort to spur government action against poverty.

King received the Nobel Peace Prize in 1964. His birthday is commemorated by a national holiday, and his bust stands in the U.S. Capitol.

Explanation and Analysis of the Document

After a brief salutation, King reminds his listeners of the symbolic importance of the ground they occupy. By locating their rally in the shadow of the Great Emancipator's memorial, march organizers hoped to call attention to Abraham Lincoln's unfinished agenda; a century after the end of slavery, African Americans still were not free. King's use of the archaic "fivescore years ago" is an obvious echo of Lincoln's Gettysburg Address. He briefly mentions the triple problems of segregation, discrimination, and poverty that mark the unequal status of black Americans. King emphasizes the long gap between the Emancipation Proclamation's promise of equality and the lingering reality of pervasive racism by repeating "one hundred years" four times.

Using the words of the Declaration of Independence, King advises his listeners that African Americans are seeking only the rights guaranteed to all citizens. He accuses the United States of bad faith in delivering its pledge of freedom. The Constitution, then, can be viewed as a "promissory note" that has not yet been redeemed for people of color. King employs the metaphor of a bad check to describe the unrealized assurance of full citizenship. In the only trace of humor in this otherwise solemn declamation, he claims that the government's check has bounced due to "insufficient funds." King does not dwell on past injustices, however. Rather, he concludes this passage on a hopeful note, stating his belief that the United States will soon honor its commitment to its black citizens.

Time Line

1964

- **July 2**
  Congress passes the Civil Rights Act, which Johnson signs into law.

- **December 10, 1964**
  King is awarded the Nobel Peace Prize in Oslo, Norway.

1968

- **April 4**
  King is assassinated in Memphis, Tennessee. Riots follow in more than one hundred cities, including Washington, D.C.

1983

- **November 2**
  Bill establishing a national holiday to commemorate King's birthday is signed by President Ronald Reagan.

King proceeds to assert that America cannot afford to wait any longer; its black citizens are demanding change now. Many critics were accusing the civil rights movement of impatience, of pressing too hard for reform, but King rejects this argument. He underscores the urgency of African American demands for equal rights by reiterating "now is the time" four times. The United States cannot afford to continue "business as usual," as the stakes are too great. He threatens that "there will be neither rest nor tranquility" until these demands are granted.

Lest he be accused of fomenting violence, King abruptly changes gears and admonishes his fellow African Americans to refrain from bitterness and a desire for revenge. They must conduct themselves with dignity and self-restraint; nonviolence must continue to be the hallmark of their movement. He acknowledges the presence of white supporters, estimated to be about 10 percent of the march's participants. White allies are essential for the movement's success, he insists, because "we cannot walk alone."

King then resumes a more militant tone, listing some of the top priorities of the civil rights movement: an end to police brutality, access to public accommodations, the elimination of housing segregation, the removal of Jim Crow signs, voting rights, and meaningful participation in political affairs. He repeats "we cannot be satisfied" or "we can never be satisfied" seven times as he enumerates black grievances. King then enlists biblical support for his position, ending this litany by paraphrasing the Old Testament prophet Amos in saying that blacks will not be satisfied until "justice rolls down like waters and righteousness like a mighty stream."

This section illustrates King's favorite literary device, anaphora—a frequently repeated word or phrase. Drew Hansen, in his text *The Dream: Martin Luther King, Jr.,*

A view of the crowd that gathered for the March on Washington on April 28, 1963 (Library of Congress)

and the Speech That Inspired a Nation, observes that by using anaphora, "King could create a series of parallel images, which allowed him to suggest connections between seemingly unrelated topics" (p. 106).

King next turns his attention to those battle-scarred veterans of the civil rights movement in the audience; those who have suffered beatings and imprisonment for the sake of freedom. He salutes their sacrifices and courage. Some of them have questioned the effectiveness of Gandhian civil disobedience, but King encourages them to keep faith in nonviolence. They should return to the South to continue their work with confidence that victory is in sight.

If King had concluded at this point, as he had planned, his address probably would have been little remembered. As Drew Hansen remarks, "There was nothing particularly unusual about the substance of the first ten minutes of King's speech" (p. 151). Many other politicians and activists had covered the same ground. Here, however, King departs from his prepared text to deliver an extemporaneous oration describing his vision for the future of America. David Garrow quotes King's recollection of this moment: "I started out reading the speech … and all of a sudden this thing came to me that I have used—I'd used it many times before, that thing about 'I have a dream'—and I just felt I wanted to use

it here" (p. 31). This is a set piece he had used several times previously—most recently in Birmingham in April and in Detroit in June—but never more effectively than on this day. Indeed, the speech metamorphoses into a sermon at this point, with King switching to his role as preacher and with the massive audience as his spirited congregation. Using the distinctive call-and-response style perfected by his Baptist forbearers, he enlists the crowd as a chorus to affirm and endorse his prophecy. Every time King reveals a new facet of his dream, the crowd replies with affirmation, clamoring for more. Each response sends King to a higher level of emotional intensity.

In the first glimpse of his dream, King refers again to the Declaration of Independence, asserting his belief that one day Americans truly will honor the words "all men are created equal." King then presents a series of vivid images describing what this new reality will look like. In outlining his vision, he utilizes a series of paired contrasting ideas: slavery and brotherhood; oppression and freedom; segregation and integration; despair and hope; and "jangling discord" and "a beautiful symphony." He foresees a society where the barriers of segregation dividing the races no longer will be enforced—where blacks and whites will be able to sit down and eat together. Jim Crow laws and southern custom widely prohibited the sharing of meals by black and white people at the same table because this sharing would symbolize equal status and inclusion. King thus anticipates the day when blacks and whites in his native Georgia will be able to break bread together.

King's dream also extends to the state of Mississippi, home to some of the most violent defenders of white supremacy. King does not need to remind the assembled marchers of past injustices committed in the Magnolia State; they well know the names of African Americans lynched for alleged transgressions of the Jim Crow code, including fourteen-year-old Emmett Till, who was abducted from his uncle's home and then beaten and drowned, and Medgar Evers, the martyred leader of the National Association for the Advancement of Colored People, who was shot in the back with a high-powered rifle just ten weeks earlier. Despite this sorry record, King asserts that Mississippi will become "an oasis of freedom and justice."

King next makes the dream very personal by including his four young children. He maintains that one day, instead of being considered inferior beings and denied opportunities to develop their full human potential because of the color of their skin, they will be judged by "the content of their character."

Alabama will also be transformed in this renewed nation. King knew very well how difficult it was to bring change to this state, having led the Montgomery bus boycott and, more recently, having defeated hard-core segregationists in the streets of Birmingham. Without mentioning him by name, King attacks the state's governor, George C. Wallace, who made national headlines earlier that summer with his futile defiance of the federal government while trying to prevent black students from enrolling at the University of Alabama. King offers a vision of a time when "little black boys and black girls" will not be isolated from their white peers. Not only will they see each other as equals, but they will also join hands "as sisters and brothers." The physical intimacy King suggests by this simple act was no doubt offensive to rabid racists but presented a powerful image of innocent fraternity to those in his audience.

King turns back to the Old Testament for the next facet of his vision. Quoting the book of Isaiah, he recalls the prophet's description of the kingdom of God. It is a place where earthly imperfections will disappear; where the mighty will be humbled and the lowly will be exalted; and where "the glory of the Lord shall be revealed" for all to see. King embraces the prophetic role, testifying that the quest for civil rights is part of God's divine plan for America and equating the coming victory over segregation with the arrival of the millennium.

At this point King briefly returns to his prepared text for a few sentences affirming his faith in this vision. This faith gives him strength to resume the struggle for freedom in the South with hope for victory despite entrenched opposition; it gives him confidence that America can overcome its bitter divisions and emerge "into a beautiful symphony of brotherhood." Then, improvising again, he claims that the knowledge that "we will be free one day" is enough to sustain him and other civil rights activists through the difficult battles that undoubtedly lie ahead.

King continues spontaneously, describing a coming era when "all of God's children" will win their freedom. On that day, African Americans will be able to sing the patriotic hymn "America the Beautiful," confident at last that the verses apply to them. Here, King paraphrases a well-known address delivered by the Chicago minister Archibald Carey at the 1952 Republican National Convention. He seizes on the refrain "from every mountainside, let freedom ring," once again using anaphora to launch a series of references to specific geographic regions of the United States. The first five are mountain ranges outside of the South—in New Hampshire, New York, Pennsylvania, Colorado, and California. The final three, then, are more poignant because they locate the need for freedom in the Deep South: King speaks of Georgia's Stone Mountain, Lookout Mountain in Tennessee, and even "every hill and molehill of Mississippi," a state without notable mountain ranges.

At this point the crowd in front of the Lincoln Memorial was cheering wildly. King's rhetoric had brought them to the emotional peak of his oration. He summons a vision of the day when freedom will ring "from every village and every hamlet" and when this message will be embraced by "all of God's children." He offers a closing image of blacks and whites, Jews and Gentiles, Protestants and Catholics all joining hands in brotherhood. Finally—as he spoke, he raised his arm in a blessing—King invokes an African American spiritual for his benediction: "Free at last, free at last, thank God Almighty, we are free at last."

The final seven minutes were what made King's speech a triumph of American oratory. These are the words that schoolchildren memorize, because King "added something completely fresh to the way that Americans thought about race and civil rights. He gave the nation a vision of what it could look like if all things were made new" (Hansen, p. 156).

Audience

The immediate audience for King's speech was the approximately 250,000 people gathered on August 28, 1963, in front of the Lincoln Memorial and around the nearby Reflecting Pool. Additional millions listened on the radio and watched on television. King's words were aimed at all Americans. For black listeners they carried a message of hope with the promise that the goals of freedom and equality were within reach. For whites, King articulated the aspirations of African Americans, placing them squarely in the context of the American dream. Each year, on the national holiday commemorating his life, King's message is passed on to new generations.

Impact

King's words were broadcast live by the three major television networks into homes across the United States. Millions of people for whom King had been only a name in the news were thus able to witness the power of his oratory firsthand. One of the many who were impressed was President Kennedy, who remarked while viewing coverage of the march in the White House, "That guy is really good" (Garrow, p. 677). Despite his privately expressed admiration, however, the chief executive was unwilling to praise King in public for fear of drawing the ire of die-hard segregationists.

Public reaction to the speech was largely favorable. The next day's edition of the *New York Times* was generous in its praise, with a front-page headline reading, "Peroration by Dr. King Sums Up a Day the Capital Will Remember." The Motown Company released an unauthorized recording of King's speech that sold briskly in African American record stores. A few black militants, however, chided march organizers for not taking a more critical stance toward the Kennedy administration. One of these naysayers was Malcolm X, who acidly lampooned the day's events as "the Farce in Washington" (http://www.stanford.edu/group/King/about_king/encyclopedia/march_washington.html).

King's powerful message undoubtedly helped build support for Kennedy's pending civil rights legislation. According to Drew Hansen, "by delivering a message of hope, and not something that was likely to be labeled as angry or extremist, King's speech could only help the civil rights bill" (p. 175). Nonetheless, while the success of the march boosted the morale of civil rights backers, it probably did not influence any congressional votes. The historian Lerone Bennett has pointed to the lack of concrete accomplishments flowing from the march. In his *Confrontation: Black and White*, he states, "It led nowhere and was not intended to lead anywhere. It was not planned as an event with a coherent plan of action. As a result, the march was a stimulating but detached and iso-

"Now is the time to make real the promises of democracy. Now is the time to rise from the dark and desolate valley of segregation to the sunlit path of racial justice. Now is the time to lift our nation from the quicksands of racial injustice to the solid rock of brotherhood. Now is the time to make justice a reality for all of God's children."

(Paragraph 6)

"No, we are not satisfied and we will not be satisfied until 'justice rolls down like waters and righteousness like a mighty stream.'"

(Paragraph 10)

"I have a dream that my four little children will one day live in a nation where they will not be judged by the color of their skin but by the content of their character."

(Paragraph 16)

"I have a dream that one day down in Alabama ... little black boys and black girls will be able to join hands with little white boys and white girls as sisters and brothers."

(Paragraph 17)

"Let freedom ring from Stone Mountain of Georgia. Let freedom ring from Lookout Mountain of Tennessee. Let freedom ring from every hill and molehill of Mississippi. From every mountainside, let freedom ring."

(Paragraphs 26–29)

"When we allow freedom [to] ring ... we will be able to speed up that day when all of God's children, black men and white men, Jews and Gentiles, Protestants and Catholics, will be able to join hands and sing in the words of the old Negro spiritual, 'Free at last! Free at last! Thank God Almighty, we are free at last!'"

(Paragraph 30)

lated episode" (p. 285). It would take ten months of bitter partisan wrangling and skillful political maneuvering by President Lyndon B. Johnson to secure the passage of the Civil Rights Act in July 1964.

King's heightened public profile following the March on Washington inflamed the Federal Bureau of Investigation director J. Edgar Hoover's animus toward the civil rights leader. Where others saw eloquence, Hoover perceived demagoguery. Richard Gid Powers speaks of the "campaign to utterly discredit King, to destroy him personally and as a public figure" that was touched off by the "I Have a Dream" Speech (p. 43). The bureau had been monitoring King's activities for several years, but "after the March the Bureau shifted from a hostile but relatively passive surveillance of King to an aggressive—at times violently aggressive—campaign to destroy him" (p. 44). The bureau's wiretaps, bugging of hotel rooms, and leaks to the press would continue until King's 1968 assassination in Memphis.

Although King's speech was widely hailed in the days following the march, by the time of his death, in Hansen's words, it "had nearly vanished from public view" (p. 167). In his cogent historical analysis of the speech, Hansen maintains that between 1963 and 1968 "few people spent substantial time talking or thinking about what King had said at the march" (p. 167). One reason for this was the increasingly militant stance taken by the black liberation movement. The Watts riot of 1965 and the periods of urban revolt that followed made the interracial harmony prophesied by King seem increasingly unattainable. Whites were offended in 1966 when the young radical Stokely Carmichael proclaimed that "Black Power" should replace "Freedom Now" as the motto of the movement. King himself also became more radical in his views. Faced with the intractable problems of poverty and the Vietnam War in addition to pervasive racism, he also grew increasingly pessimistic. In speeches after 1965 King began saying that his dream had turned into a nightmare. By the time of his death in 1968, the upbeat spirit of the "I Have a Dream" Speech seemed hopelessly out of date. Only after King's murder was his speech elevated to the exalted position it now occupies.

According to Hansen, politicians focused on the "I Have a Dream" Speech because it helped them "forget King's post-1965 career" (p. 213). Although the speech twice mentions racial problems in the North, its major emphasis is on the Jim Crow discrimination of the South. By the time a national holiday in King's name was declared in 1983, corresponding with his mid-January birthday, "whites only" signs had disappeared, and discriminatory voting laws were safely in the past. The recycling of King's speech thus allowed the nation to celebrate the elimination of legally sanctioned segregation while ignoring the widespread racial inequality that remained unaffected by civil rights legislation. In an ironic twist, conservative commentators began to quote King's admonition to judge people not by the color of their skin but by "the content of their character" in arguing against affirmative action, a program King himself endorsed.

Related Documents

"Civil Rights Act; July 2, 1964." The Avalon Project at Yale Law School Web site. http://www.yale.edu/lawweb/avalon/statutes/civil_rights_1964.htm. Accessed on February 29, 2008. This is the text of the act passed by Congress and signed into law by President Lyndon Johnson.

"I've Been to the Mountaintop." The Martin Luther King, Jr., Research and Education Institute Web site. http://www.stanford.edu/group/King/publications/speeches/I%27ve_been_to_the_mountaintop.pdf. Accessed on February 29, 2008. The text of Martin Luther King's last public address, delivered in Memphis, Tennessee, on April 3, 1968, on the evening before his assassination.

"Letter from Birmingham Jail." The Martin Luther King, Jr., Research and Education Institute Web site. http://www.stanford.edu/group/King/popular_requests/frequentdocs/birmingham.pdf. Accessed on February 29, 2008. This letter is King's eloquent defense of his nonviolent tactics, written on April 16, 1963, in response to a call by a group of moderate white Protestant ministers for an end to civil rights demonstrations in Birmingham.

"Patience is a Dirty and Nasty Word." PBS "American Experience: Eyes on the Prize" Web site. http://www.pbs.org/wgbh/amex/eyesontheprize/sources/ps_washington.html. Accessed on February 29, 2008. John Lewis, chairman of the Student Nonviolent Coordinating Committee, delivered this speech at the March on Washington for Jobs and Freedom.

"Radio and Television Report to the American People on Civil Rights." John F. Kennedy Presidential Library and Museum. http://www.jfklibrary.org/Historical+Resources/Archives/Reference+Desk/Speeches/JFK/003POF03CivilRights06111963.htm. Accessed on February 29, 2008. In this speech President John F. Kennedy identifies racial discrimination as a moral problem and announces that he soon will submit a comprehensive civil rights bill to Congress.

Bibliography

■ Articles

Alvarez, Alexandra. "Martin Luther King's 'I Have a Dream': The Speech Event as Metaphor." *Journal of Black Studies* 18, no. 3 (March 1988): 337–357.

Garrow, David J. "King: The Man, the March, the Dream." *American History* 38, no. 3 (August 2003): 26–35.

Mills, Nicholas. "Heard and Unheard Speeches: What Really Happened at the March on Washington?" *Dissent* 35 (Summer 1988): 285–291.

Powers, Richard Gid. "The FBI Marches on the Dreamer." *American History* 38, no. 3 (August 2003): 42–47.

Reed, Harry A. "Martin Luther King, Jr.: History and Memory, Reflections on Dreams and Silences." *Journal of Negro History* 84, no. 2 (Spring 1999): 150–166.

■ **Books**

Bennett, Lerone. *Confrontation: Black and White*. Chicago: Johnson Publishing, 1965.

Garrow, David J. *Bearing the Cross: Martin Luther King, Jr., and the Southern Christian Leadership Conference*. New York: Vintage Books, 1986.

Hansen, Drew D. *The Dream: Martin Luther King, Jr., and the Speech That Inspired a Nation*. New York: HarperCollins, 2003.

Johnson, Charles, and Bob Adelman. *King: The Photobiography of Martin Luther King, Jr.* New York: Viking Studio, 2000.

Lischer, Richard. *The Preacher King: Martin Luther King, Jr. and the Word That Moved America*. New York: Oxford University Press, 1995.

Miller, Keith D. *Voice of Deliverance: The Language of Martin Luther King, Jr., and Its Sources*. New York: Free Press, 1992.

■ **Web Sites**

"March on Washington for Jobs and Freedom (1963)." King Encyclopedia Web site.
    http://www.stanford.edu/group/King/about_king/encyclopedia/march_washington.html. Accessed on March 5, 2008.

1. On April 3, 1968, the day before he was assassinated, Martin Luther King, Jr., delivered a speech in support of striking Memphis sanitation workers. Known as his "I See the Promised Land" Speech, or "the mountaintop speech," it is second only to the "I Have a Dream" Speech in popularity among King's speeches. Compare the two addresses. How do they differ in tone? How do they differ in content?

2. There is no substitute for actually watching a film of King's "I Have a Dream" Speech. View the speech and closely observe the interaction between King and his audience. At what points of the speech do his listeners react most enthusiastically? How does the audience's response affect King's delivery? In what ways does the impact of the film version differ from the effect of the written document?

3. John Lewis also delivered an important address at the March on Washington. Both King and Lewis were working in the southern civil rights movement, and both came from strong religious backgrounds, yet their speeches are quite different. After reading Lewis's words, compare the two documents. How do they differ? What are the points of agreement? Why is King's speech remembered today while Lewis's is largely forgotten?

4. In 1895 the African American educator Booker T. Washington delivered a memorable speech—the Atlanta Exposition Address—at the Cotton States and International Exposition in Atlanta. Following his address, Washington was hailed—as King would be—as the unquestioned leader of his people. The thrust of Washington's words, however, is almost totally contradictory to that of King's. Compare the two speeches and identify the different historical circumstances that shaped them.

5. In 1852 the black abolitionist Frederick Douglass spoke at a rally commemorating the Declaration of Independence. This speech, his "Fourth of July" Speech, explored several of the same themes covered by Martin Luther King, Jr.'s "I Have a Dream" Speech. Compare these two documents and discuss the historical circumstances that produced them.

Glossary

curvaceous	endowed with ample curves, such as an attractive woman
hallowed	sacred
interposition and nullification	a discredited legal theory holding that states can nullify federal laws that they consider unconstitutional, as used by segregationists trying to reverse the Supreme Court's *Brown v. Board of Education* decision
promissory note	a written promise to pay a specific amount on demand or at a specific time
fivescore	one hundred—a "score" being twenty

MARTIN LUTHER KING, JR.'S "I HAVE A DREAM" SPEECH

I am happy to join with you today in what will go down in history as the greatest demonstration for freedom in the history of our nation.

Fivescore years ago, a great American, in whose symbolic shadow we stand today, signed the Emancipation Proclamation. This momentous decree came as a great beacon light of hope to millions of Negro slaves who had been seared in the flames of withering injustice. It came as a joyous daybreak to end the long night of their captivity.

But one hundred years later, the Negro still is not free. One hundred years later, the life of the Negro is still sadly crippled by the manacles of segregation and the chains of discrimination. One hundred years later, the Negro lives on a lonely island of poverty in the midst of a vast ocean of material prosperity. One hundred years later the Negro is still languished in the corners of American society and finds himself an exile in his own land. And so we've come here today to dramatize a shameful condition.

In a sense we've come to our nation's capital to cash a check. When the architects of our republic wrote the magnificent words of the Constitution and the Declaration of Independence, they were signing a promissory note to which every American was to fall heir. This note was a promise that all men, yes, black men as well as white men, would be guaranteed the "unalienable Rights of Life, Liberty, and the pursuit of Happiness." It is obvious today that America has defaulted on this promissory note insofar as her citizens of color are concerned. Instead of honoring this sacred obligation, America has given the Negro people a bad check, a check which has come back marked "insufficient funds."

But we refuse to believe that the bank of justice is bankrupt. We refuse to believe that there are insufficient funds in the great vaults of opportunity of this nation. And so we've come to cash this check, a check that will give us upon demand the riches of freedom and the security of justice.

We have also come to this hallowed spot to remind America of the fierce urgency of now. This is no time to engage in the luxury of cooling off or to take the tranquilizing drug of gradualism. Now is the time to make real the promises of democracy. Now is the time to rise from the dark and desolate valley of segregation to the sunlit path of racial justice. Now is the time to lift our nation from the quicksands of racial injustice to the solid rock of brotherhood. Now is the time to make justice a reality for all of God's children.

It would be fatal for the nation to overlook the urgency of the moment. This sweltering summer of the Negro's legitimate discontent will not pass until there is an invigorating autumn of freedom and equality. Nineteen sixty-three is not an end, but a beginning. And those who hope that the Negro needed to blow off steam and will now be content will have a rude awakening if the nation returns to business as usual, There will be neither rest nor tranquility in America until the Negro is granted his citizenship rights. The whirlwinds of revolt will continue to shake the foundations of our nation until the bright day of justice emerges.

But there is something that I must say to my people, who stand on the warm threshold which leads into the palace of justice: In the process of gaining our rightful place, we must not be guilty of wrongful deeds. Let us not seek to satisfy our thirst for freedom by drinking from the cup of bitterness and hatred. We must forever conduct our struggle on the high plane of dignity and discipline. We must not allow our creative protest to degenerate into physical violence. Again and again, we must rise to the majestic heights of meeting physical force with soul force. The marvelous new militancy which has engulfed the Negro community must not lead us to a distrust of all white people, for many of our white brothers, as evidenced by their presence here today, have come to realize that their destiny is tied up with our destiny. And they have come to realize that their freedom is inextricably bound to our freedom. We cannot walk alone.

And as we walk, we must make the pledge that we shall always march ahead. We cannot turn back. There are those who are asking the devotees of civil rights, "When will you be satisfied?"

We can never be satisfied as long as the Negro is the victim of the unspeakable horrors of police brutality. We can never be satisfied as long as our bodies, heavy with the fatigue of travel, cannot gain lodging in the motels of the highways and the hotels of the cities. We cannot be satisfied as long as the Negro's basic mobility is from a smaller ghetto to a larger one. We can never be satisfied as long as our children are stripped of their selfhood and robbed of their dignity by signs stating "for whites only." We cannot be satisfied as long as a Negro in Mississippi cannot vote and a Negro in New York believes he has nothing for which to vote. No, no, we are not satisfied and we will not be satisfied until "justice rolls down like waters and righteousness like a mighty stream."

I am not unmindful that some of you have come here out of great trials and tribulations. Some of you have come fresh from narrow jail cells. Some of you have come from areas where your quest for freedom left you battered by the storms of persecution and staggered by the winds of police brutality. You have been the veterans of creative suffering. Continue to work with the faith that unearned suffering is redemptive. Go back to Mississippi, go back to Alabama, go back to South Carolina, go back to Georgia, go back to Louisiana, go back to the slums and ghettos of our northern cities, knowing that somehow this situation can and will be changed. Let us not wallow in the valley of despair.

I say to you today, my friends so even though we face the difficulties of today and tomorrow, I still have a dream. It is a dream deeply rooted in the American dream.

I have a dream that one day this nation will rise up and live out the true meaning of its creed: "We hold these truths to be self-evident, that all men are created equal."

I have a dream that one day on the red hills of Georgia, the sons of former slaves and the sons of former slave owners will be able to sit down together at the table of brotherhood.

I have a dream that one day even the state of Mississippi, a state sweltering with the heat of injustice, sweltering with the heat of oppression, will be transformed into an oasis of freedom and justice.

I have a dream that my four little children will one day live in a nation where they will not be judged by the color of their skin but by the content of their character. I have a dream today

I have a dream that one day down in Alabama, with its vicious racists, with its governor having his lips dripping with the words of "interposition" and "nullification," one day right there in Alabama little black boys and black girls will be able to join hands with little white boys and white girls as sisters and brothers. I have a dream today.

I have a dream that one day "every valley shall be exalted, and every hill and mountain shall be made low; the rough places will be made plain, and the crooked places will be made straight; and the glory of the Lord shall be revealed, and all flesh shall see it together."

This is our hope. This is the faith that I go back to the South with. With this faith we will be able to hew out of the mountain of despair a stone of hope. With this faith we will be able to transform the jangling discords of our nation into a beautiful symphony of brotherhood. With this faith we will be able to work together, to pray together, to struggle together, to go to jail together, to stand up for freedom together, knowing that we will be free one day. This will be the day, this will be the day when all of God's children will be able to sing with new meaning:

My Country, 'tis of thee, sweet land of liberty, of thee I Sing.

Land where my fathers died, land of the pilgrim's pride

From every mountainside, let freedom ring!

And if America is to be a great nation, this must become true.

And so let freedom ring from the prodigious hilltops of New Hampshire.

Let freedom ring from the mighty mountains of New York.

Let freedom ring from the heightening Alleghenies of Pennsylvania.

Let freedom ring from the snowcapped Rockies of Colorado.

Let freedom ring from the curvaceous slopes of California.

But not only that: Let freedom ring from Stone Mountain of Georgia.

Let freedom ring from Lookout Mountain of Tennessee.

Let freedom ring from every hill and molehill of Mississippi.

From every mountainside, let freedom ring.

And when this happens, when we allow freedom ring, when we let it ring from every village and every hamlet, from every state and every city; we will be able to speed up that day when all of God's children, black men and white men, Jews and Gentiles, Protestants and Catholics, will be able to join hands and sing in the words of the old Negro spiritual:

Free at last! Free at last!

Thank God Almighty, we are free at last!

Eighty-eighth Congress of the United States of America

AT THE SECOND SESSION

Begun and held at the City of Washington on Tuesday, the seventh day of January,
one thousand nine hundred and sixty-four

An Act

To enforce the constitutional right to vote, to confer jurisdiction upon the district courts of the United States to provide injunctive relief against discrimination in public accommodations, to authorize the Attorney General to institute suits to protect constitutional rights in public facilities and public education, to extend the Commission on Civil Rights, to prevent discrimination in federally assisted programs, to establish a Commission on Equal Employment Opportunity, and for other purposes.

Be it enacted by the Senate and House of Representatives of the United States of America in Congress assembled, That this Act may be cited as the "Civil Rights Act of 1964".

TITLE I—VOTING RIGHTS

Sec. 101. Section 2004 of the Revised Statutes (42 U.S.C. 1971), as amended by section 131 of the Civil Rights Act of 1957 (71 Stat. 637), and as further amended by section 601 of the Civil Rights Act of 1960 (74 Stat. 90), is further amended as follows:

(a) Insert "1" after "(a)" in subsection (a) and add at the end of subsection (a) the following new paragraphs:

"(2) No person acting under color of law shall—

"(A) in determining whether any individual is qualified under State law or laws to vote in any Federal election, apply any standard, practice, or procedure different from the standards, practices, or procedures applied under such law or laws to other individuals within the same county, parish, or similar political subdivision who have been found by State officials to be qualified to vote;

"(B) deny the right of any individual to vote in any Federal election because of an error or omission on any record or paper relating to any application, registration, or other act requisite to voting, if such error or omission is not material in determining whether such individual is qualified under State law to vote in such election; or

"(C) employ any literacy test as a qualification for voting in any Federal election unless (i) such test is administered to each individual and is conducted wholly in writing, and (ii) a certified copy of the test and of the answers given by the individual is furnished to him within twenty-five days of the submission of his request made within the period of time during which records and papers are required to be retained and preserved pursuant to title III of the Civil Rights Act of 1960 (42 U.S.C. 1974–74e; 74 Stat. 88): *Provided, however,* That the Attorney General may enter into agreements with appropriate State or local authorities that preparation, conduct, and maintenance of such tests in accordance with the provisions of applicable State or local law, including such special provisions as are necessary in the preparation, conduct, and maintenance of such tests for persons who are blind or otherwise physically handicapped, meet the purposes of this subparagraph and constitute compliance therewith.

"(3) For purposes of this subsection—

"(A) the term 'vote' shall have the same meaning as in subsection (e) of this section;

"(B) the phrase 'literacy test' includes any test of the ability to read, write, understand, or interpret any matter."

(b) Insert immediately following the period at the end of the first sentence of subsection (c) the following new sentence: "If in any such proceeding literacy is a relevant fact there shall be a rebuttable

The Civil Rights Act of 1964 (National Archives and Records Administration)

CIVIL RIGHTS ACT OF 1964

"All persons shall be entitled to the full and equal enjoyment ... of any place of public accommodation."

Overview

Enacted on July 2, 1964—in the year after President John F. Kennedy's assassination; the bloody campaign to integrate Birmingham, Alabama; and the first March on Washington, which featured Martin Luther King, Jr.'s "I Have a Dream" Speech—the Civil Rights Act of 1964 was the most important piece of civil rights legislation passed since the Reconstruction era. It outlawed discrimination on a number of bases, including race, color, religion, national origin, and, with respect to employment, sex. Also of importance was the breadth of areas in which discrimination was outlawed, as the act prohibited discrimination in places of public accommodations, public facilities, federally assisted programs, employment, and voting. It also pushed for the full desegregation of schools and expanded the U.S. Commission on Civil Rights, which had been created by the Civil Rights Act of 1957. Last, the 1964 act created institutions for monitoring and facilitating the advancement of civil rights, such as the Equal Employment Opportunity Commission, to enforce Title VII of the act, and the Community Relations Service, to assist "communities and persons therein in resolving disputes, disagreements, or difficulties relating to discriminatory practices based on race, color, or national origin."

In requiring equality, the Civil Rights Act of 1964 arguably provided many of the freedoms that African Americans should have already enjoyed as a result of the Fourteenth Amendment, extending that amendment close to its logical limit. However, the act went further than Fourteenth Amendment doctrine allowed in regulating purely private conduct in some instances. The regulation of private conduct required that the act be based on Congress's commerce clause power in addition to whatever authority Congress had under its Fourteenth Amendment enforcement power. The act's continual mention of interstate commerce is a nod to that requirement. In truth, without the regulation of private conduct, the act would not be nearly as important as it was and continues to be. Simply put, it remains the broadest, most effective, and most important civil rights bill passed since Reconstruction.

The 1964 act and the debate around it signaled a changing of the guard: Discrimination was officially repudiated, and equality was required in more places than previously imagined. The filibuster of the act by southern senators arguably represented the last-ditch efforts of desperate men who wished to hew to a bygone era. Those who wished to protect and perpetuate the old order were duly told to stand aside, as the United States entered a new era in which all of its citizens were to be treated as equal under the law and as full members of the polity.

Context

The Civil Rights Act of 1964 was passed in the middle of the turmoil and upheaval in American society of the 1950s and 1960s. Seminal events such as the Montgomery bus boycott, the Supreme Court case *Brown v. Board of Education of Topeka*, the integration of Little Rock Central High School, and the March on Washington for Jobs and Freedom had already occurred. Many other events—including the attacks in Selma, Alabama; the passage of the Voting Rights Act of 1965; the assassinations of Martin Luther King, Jr., and Malcolm X; and the riots in major American cities—were yet on the horizon.

The events that immediately precipitated the 1964 act's introduction in Congress and its eventual passage are fairly clear. President Kennedy originally sent the bill that would become the act to Congress on June 19, 1963, as a reaction to the violence that accompanied the civil rights movement's attempt to integrate Birmingham. The bill had not moved far at the time of President Kennedy's assassination in November 1963. In the immediate aftermath of Kennedy's death, President Lyndon B. Johnson called on Congress to pass the law as a fitting tribute to his predecessor. During the legislative debate on the bill, President Johnson used many of the favors he was owed from his longtime service in Congress to move the bill forward. In addition to Johnson's favors, the supporters of the civil rights legislation used many parliamentary maneuvers, voting power, and sheer will to shepherd the bill through Congress. The need for resolve intensified when the bill was significantly strengthened in the House Judiciary Committee after prodding by civil rights

Time Line

1947

■ **December**
The President's Committee on Civil Rights issues *To Secure These Rights*, urging Congress to pass civil rights legislation.

1954

■ **May 17**
In *Brown v. Board of Education*, the Supreme Court outlaws segregation in public schools.

1955

■ **December 1**
Rosa Parks refuses to vacate her seat for a white person, sparking the Montgomery bus boycott.

1957

■ **September 4–25**
Central High School in Little Rock, Arkansas, is integrated in a process that requires that federal troops protect African American students and escort them to classes.

■ **September 9**
The Civil Rights Act of 1957, the first civil rights act since 1875, is signed by President Dwight D. Eisenhower, creating the Commission on Civil Rights and attempting—fairly weakly—to protect the voting rights of African Americans.

1960

■ **May 6**
The Civil Rights Act of 1960 is signed by President Eisenhower.

■ **November 8**
John F. Kennedy is elected president of the United States.

1963

■ **April–June**
Civil rights groups attempt to integrate Birmingham, Alabama, and are met with police dogs and fire hoses.

■ **June 11**
The University of Alabama is integrated.

■ **June 12**
Medgar Evers, Mississippi director of the National Association for the Advancement of Colored People, is slain.

---

groups. Following passage in the House of Representatives, the bill was sent to the Senate on February 17, 1964; after the longest filibuster on record in the U.S. Senate—eighty-two days—the act passed in amended form by a vote of 73–27. The Senate bill then passed unamended in the House of Representatives by a vote of 289–126. President Johnson signed the bill on July 2, 1964.

About the Author

The Civil Rights Act of 1964 was shaped by a host of people. The original bill was crafted and drafted in the Department of Justice, headed by Attorney General Robert Kennedy. The drafting group almost certainly included Robert Kennedy and his assistant attorneys general, Burke Marshall and Nicholas Katzenbach, as well as the Justice Department lawyer Harold Greene (who later became a judge). As the bill moved through the committee process in the House of Representatives, it was significantly redrafted and strengthened by members and staff of the House Judiciary Committee, including Representatives Emanuel Celler (D-N.Y.) and William McCulloch (R-Ohio) and their aides. Many amendments were added from the floor of the House, with one of the most momentous being offered by Howard W. Smith (D-Va.), chairman of the House Rules Committee. Smith added the provision including sex discrimination to Title VII of the act as a prohibited mode of discrimination, apparently in an effort to derail the bill. The amendment passed, and the bill ultimately passed the House. On the Senate side, a number of amendments were offered and passed, but the bill was not overwhelmingly altered in substance; Everett Dirksen (R-Ill.) was the Senate's most active amender of the bill.

Explanation and Analysis of the Document

The Civil Rights Act of 1964 begins with a simple recitation of its purpose, indicating the range of substantive areas it touches, the federal commissions it creates, and the methods of enforcement it provides.

Title I (Voting Rights) is an amendment of the Civil Rights Acts of 1957 and 1960. It applies to federal elections, requiring that all voters be held to the same qualification standards and prohibiting discrimination on the basis of race, color, religion, or national origin. However, this title does not outlaw some of the methods that were being used to discriminate against African Americans, including literacy tests. Regarding such tests, Title I instead attempts to ensure that they are applied as equally as possible. For example, it requires that literacy tests be administered in writing and allows the attorney general to negotiate with state and local authorities regarding their use. This title also allows the attorney general to request that a three-judge panel hear allegations of voting rights violations arising under its statutes. Appeals from the three-judge panel would be directed to the Supreme Court.

Title I was largely superseded by the Voting Rights Act of 1965, which generally prohibited methods of discriminating against minorities, including literacy tests, and strengthened the right to vote in general. The Voting Rights Act was passed pursuant to the Fifteenth Amendment rather than to the Fourteenth Amendment.

Title II (Injunctive Relief against Discrimination in Places of Public Accommodation) prohibits discrimination on the basis of race, color, religion, or national origin in the provision of goods, services, facilities, privileges, advantages, and accommodations at any place of public accommodations. Title II also prohibits attempts to prevent any persons from attempting to enjoy their rights under its terms. Places of public accommodations are held to include lodging places of all kinds other than owner-occupied establishments with five or fewer rooms for rent or hire. Also included under the title's terms are restaurants, theaters, sports arenas, and all establishments located inside of such places if they serve the customers of those places. The title does not cover private clubs and other places not open to the public.

Title II was one of the act's most controversial titles because it struck at the heart of what some thought were the legitimate prerogatives of business owners. By elevating the right of minority patrons to receive equal treatment above the right of business owners to refuse service to anyone, the title became a public expression of the nation's new equality—and made sit-ins at lunch counters unnecessary.

Rights granted under Title II may be vindicated in a number of different ways. If rights have been violated or are about to be violated, aggrieved individuals may directly sue for injunctive relief, and under certain circumstances the attorney general may intervene in support of the plaintiff. However, if the activity held to be a violation occurs in a state or locality that allows local officials to "grant or seek relief from such practice or to institute criminal proceedings with respect thereto," those local officials must be given the opportunity to address the issue before an action for federal injunctive relief may be brought. If the violation occurs in a state or locality that does not authorize local officials to redress the activity, the aggrieved person may sue, although the court may refer the matter to the Community Relations Service, established in Title X of the act, to see if voluntary compliance is a possibility.

Title II tracks the public accommodations provisions of the Civil Rights Act of 1875, which were deemed unconstitutional in the *Civil Rights Cases* (1883), although the 1964 act's provisions are somewhat narrower. In the 1964 act, Congress limited actionable discrimination to discrimination that involves state action or involves establishments whose operations affect commerce. In doing so, Congress guaranteed that the title was clearly within either Congress's Fourteenth Amendment enforcement power or its commerce clause power. Nonetheless, two challenges to Title II arose immediately after the 1964 act was passed, with both *Heart of Atlanta Motel v. United States* and *Katzenbach v. McClung* challenging the constitutionality of Title II that same year. In both cases, the Supreme Court

Time Line

1963

■ **June 19**
President Kennedy sends the civil rights bill that would become the Civil Rights Act of 1964 to Congress.

■ **August 28**
Martin Luther King, Jr., leads the March on Washington and delivers his "I Have a Dream" Speech.

■ **November 22**
President Kennedy is assassinated in Dallas, Texas.

■ **November 27**
President Lyndon B. Johnson calls for the passage of the civil rights bill to honor President Kennedy's memory.

1964

■ **July 2**
The Civil Rights Act of 1964 is signed by President Johnson.

■ **November 3**
Lyndon B. Johnson is popularly elected president.

1965

■ **February 21**
Malcolm X is assassinated in New York City.

■ **March 7**
The march from Selma to Montgomery for voting rights ends with Alabama state troopers attacking marchers.

■ **August 6**
The Voting Rights Act of 1965 becomes law.

1968

■ **April 4**
Martin Luther King, Jr., is assassinated in Memphis, Tennessee.

■ **June 5**
Robert F. Kennedy is assassinated in Los Angeles.

■ **November 5**
Richard M. Nixon is elected president of the United States.

determined that Title II was an acceptable exercise of Congress' commerce clause power. Once those cases were settled, the constitutionality of the 1964 act was not in doubt, and the task of fully integrating the country could begin.

Title III (Desegregation of Public Facilities) authorizes the attorney general to file suit on behalf of the United

States against a state or locality under certain circumstances when the attorney general has received a complaint from an individual indicating that he or she is being denied equal protection rights because he or she is being denied equal use of a public facility. If the individual is unable to litigate the case fully or properly and if suit by the United States "will materially further the orderly progress of desegregation in public facilities," the attorney general may intervene. This title simply puts the resources of the federal government behind those who attempt to integrate public facilities that should have already been desegregated.

Title IV (Desegregation of Public Education) provides technical and financial assistance to school districts that experience problems with desegregation. It also provides help to those persons whose children are being denied the equal protection of the law because of race, color, religion, or national origin by a school board or public college and who are unable to fully and adequately prosecute the litigation. However, the title makes clear that it is not to apply to cases in which busing is sought to resolve issues of racial imbalance in schools. As with Title III, the resources of the federal government are being made available so that established constitutional requirements, in this case the desegregation of schools, can be met.

Title V (Commission on Civil Rights) renews and retools the mandate of the Commission on Civil Rights, which was created by the Civil Rights Act of 1957. The commission is authorized to investigate allegations related to voting rights and voting fraud allegations. In addition, it is tasked with studying and collecting information and appraising the laws and policies of the federal government regarding denials of equal protection based on race, color, religion, or national origin in the administration of justice. Last, the commission is to "serve as a national clearinghouse for information in respect to denials of equal protection of the laws because of race, color, religion or national origin, including but not limited to the fields of voting, education, housing, employment, the use of public facilities, and transportation, or in the administration of justice." However, the commission is restricted from investigating the membership practices of fraternal organizations, fraternities, sororities, private clubs, and religious organizations.

Title V's passage was not without problems, as debate occurred regarding whether merely to extend the life of the Commission on Civil Rights or to make it permanent. The 1964 act simply extended the life of the commission, but it has continued to exist through various extensions and reauthorizations.

Title VI (Nondiscrimination in Federally Assisted Programs) focuses on guaranteeing that federal tax money does not go to programs that discriminate on the basis of race, color, or national origin. It directs federal agencies and departments to issue rules and regulations consistent with the principles underlying Title VI and the act as a whole. Title VI was largely intended to discontinue the funds that were being provided to segregated schools in the South. However, the title clearly applies to all sorts of programs that receive federal funding, including hospitals, building projects, and road construction. Indeed, regulations stemming from Title VI may have been the biggest benefit to minority contractors in the country's history.

Title VII (Equal Employment Opportunity) is by far the longest title of the 1964 Civil Rights Act and possibly the act's most controversial. As originally submitted by the Kennedy administration, Title VII merely allowed the president to establish a commission on equal employment opportunity to regulate companies with government contracts. As finally enacted, the title dealt with guaranteeing equality in employment, an area that was historically thought to have been controlled by the prerogative of the employer. The limitation on how employment decisions could be made was arguably second only to the requirement that public accommodations be equal in its effect on the psyche of those whose actions were regulated by the act. The title restricts not only how employers can fill jobs but also how employment agencies can refer people for employment and how labor organizations can include and exclude people from membership. Simply put, under the terms of the act, none of these entities may discriminate against people and employees based on their race, color, religion, sex, or national origin. In addition, none of the entities may retaliate against those who formally or informally oppose employment practices made unlawful by Title VII.

The most momentous aspect of Title VII was its inclusion of sex discrimination as a prohibited ground for discrimination. Sex was added as an amendment by Representative Howard Smith (D-Va.). Although he was the powerful chairman of the House Rules Committee, he was outmaneuvered and overruled by those who were determined to pass the 1964 act. As one of his final attempts to derail the bill, he proposed the addition of sex to the terms. Rather than reject the proposal, the House, with the support of most of its female members, accepted the amendment and eventually the entire act. However, because sex was added to the terms near the very end of the legislative process, little legislative history exists to interpret what constitutes the clause. Consequently, courts have had a more difficult time determining what constitutes sex discrimination under Title VII than what constitutes race discrimination under Title VII.

Title VII also creates the Equal Employment Opportunity Commission and gives it primary responsibility for investigating and processing discrimination claims, although the process of adjudicating such claims is largely left to the federal courts. In addition, the commission is to provide technical assistance to those employers and others who wish to properly discharge their responsibilities and duties under Title VII.

Title VII was controversial not only for what it did but for what some believed it would do. Many claimed that Title VII's provisions would eventually require that businesses maintain quotas to ensure the racial balance of the workforce. A number of congressmen and senators disputed this reading of the bill. Nevertheless, specific language was added to the bill to make clear that Title VII would never require a preference for one race based solely on a racial imbalance in the workplace.

Title VIII (Registration and Voting Statistics) authorizes the secretary of commerce to gather voting data on populations and parse the data based on race, color, and national origin. Rather than parsing data for the entire country, the data is to be gathered for whatever geographic areas are suggested by the Commission on Civil Rights. Given that the Bureau of the Census gathers statistics and is a part of the Department of Commerce, the act unsurprisingly tasks the commerce secretary with the responsibility outlined here.

Title IX (Intervention and Procedure after Removal in Civil Rights Cases) is purely procedural in nature. It dictates what is to occur when a case that was filed in state court and then removed to federal court is sent back to the state court. It also addresses when the federal government may intervene in a civil rights case and the implications of the intervention.

Title X (Establishment of Community Relations Service) creates the Community Relations Service to provide conciliation and mediation in local communities when issues of equality arise that can be solved through means more informal that court filings. The service is purely a problem-solving entity; it is not supposed to be involved in any litigation that might arise out of the matters it handles. The Community Relations Service can be thought of as a mechanism to turn down the heat on a community dispute before it boils over into discord or violence.

Title XI (Miscellaneous), as its title suggests, addresses various issues not dealt with anywhere else in the statute. For example, it addresses rules for criminal contempt in cases brought pursuant to the act. It also notes that nothing in the act should be construed to affect the ability of the attorney general or anyone acting in his stead from intervening in cases based on laws passed prior to the act. Last, the final title notes the severability of any part of the act found to be invalid.

Audience

The intended audience for the 1964 act was the country as a whole. The message was to be sent to all citizens of the United States that discrimination would no longer be acceptable if the government could prevent it. Although the government could not change the hearts and minds of its citizens, it could guarantee equality in the most important spheres of life. People cannot be required to think in a certain way; however, they can be influenced in their thinking by the country's collective thoughts on an issue as expressed in its laws.

Of course, many of the nation's citizens did not need to have their mindsets changed by the act. According to Gallup and Harris polls taken in 1964, the bill had the support of more than half of the American public as it was moving toward passage. Consequently, the act did not have to be sold wholesale to the American people. Rather, the sale needed to be made to certain parts of the country—

President Lyndon Johnson signs into law the Civil Rights Act in ceremonies on July 2, 1964, in the East Room of the White House. (AP Photo)

and perhaps to certain segments in every part of the country—that were quite vocal in their opposition to equality. Eventually, the chorus for equality drowned out the voices for inequality.

Impact

The Civil Rights Act of 1964 changed the landscape of American race relations forever by indicating that discrimination would no longer be the order of the day. The symbolic significance of the act cannot be overstated. By delving into the realm of private conduct and requiring equality in areas that many thought Congress would never regulate, the 1964 act made equality in public areas the new paradigm. The law afforded African Americans everyday dignities that had been owed but not granted to such citizens. The act did not cure racial strife, but it helped make American life significantly more hospitable for minorities. The law may not have altered mindsets as much as it gave voice to the attitudes of the more progressive among the citizenry. Equally important, it removed the cover of law for those with discriminatory views. In the end, the law was accepted,

"An Act: To enforce the constitutional right to vote, to confer jurisdiction upon the district courts of the United States to provide injunctive relief against discrimination in public accommodations, to authorize the Attorney General to institute suits to protect constitutional rights in public facilities and public education, to extend the Commission on Civil Rights, to prevent discrimination in federally assisted programs, to establish a Commission on Equal Employment Opportunity, and for other purposes."

(Introduction)

"All persons shall be entitled to the full and equal enjoyment of the goods, services, facilities, and privileges, advantages, and accommodations of any place of public accommodation, as defined in this section, without discrimination or segregation on the ground of race, color, religion, or national origin."

(Section 201)

"It shall be an unlawful employment practice for an employer—(1) to fail or refuse to hire or to discharge any individual, or otherwise to discriminate against any individual with respect to his compensation, terms, conditions, or privileges of employment, because of such individual's race, color, religion, sex, or national origin; or (2) to limit, segregate, or classify his employees in any way which would deprive or tend to deprive any individual of employment opportunities or otherwise adversely affect his status as an employee, because of such individual's race, color, religion, sex, or national origin."

(Section 703[a])

grudgingly or not, and most calls to obey were heeded. Indeed, the law and its sanctions made it almost impossible for businesses to fail to comply.

In many ways, the 1964 act finished much of the work of the Reconstruction amendments. Those amendments provided a constitutional structure that was supposed to make all citizens equal before the law and full members of American society. While the Reconstruction amendments made minority Americans legal citizens, the 1964 act helped allow those citizens to enjoy their full rights of citizenship. Equality finally became the glue that is supposed to hold all Americans together.

The 1964 act was a powerful sequel to the Civil Rights Acts of 1957 and 1960. The 1957 act had been the first significant civil rights bill passed since the Reconstruction-era Civil Rights Act of 1875. However, the 1957 act focused on voting rights and did not have nearly the breadth and importance that the 1964 act would have. Similarly, the Civil Rights Act of 1960 was fairly weak. The 1964 act, to the contrary, opened the floodgates of change. In its immediate wake, Congress passed the Voting Rights Act of 1965, and additional strong antidiscrimination measures were passed soon after. Some, like the Age Discrimination in Employment Act of 1967, targeted the hiring practices of businesses. Others, such as the Fair Housing Act of 1968 and the Equal Credit Opportunity Act of 1974, targeted discrimination more broadly. Beyond the wake of the 1960s civil rights era, antidiscrimination legislation continued to get passed, both in the form of revisions, such as those to the 1964 act that occurred in 1972 and 1991, and in the form of new acts, such as the Americans with Disabilities Act of 1990. Thus, the Civil Rights Act of 1964 paved the way for many other laws that have made America even more hospitable to all of her people.

Related Documents

Brown v. Board of Education of Topeka, 347 U.S. 483 (1954). In this case, the Supreme Court decided that the segregation of public schools is unconstitutional. Although the case was not the first to challenge segregation in schools, it was the most heralded and the clearest signal that official state-sanctioned inequality was to end.

Civil Rights Act of 1875, U.S. *Statutes at Large* 18 (1875): 335. This Reconstruction-era law is known primarily for requiring equal public accommodations for African Americans with respect to railroads, theaters, and hotels. That provision was deemed unconstitutional in the Civil Rights Cases (1883), *but the public accommodations provision was largely revived as Title II of the Civil Rights Act of 1964.*

Civil Rights Act of 1957, Public Law 85-315, U.S. *Statutes at Large* 71 (1957) 637. This fairly weak voting rights bill was shepherded to passage by Lyndon Johnson when he was a U.S. senator from Texas. Some have argued that Johnson traded away too many strong provisions in exchange for the acquiescence of southerners.

Civil Rights Cases, 109 U.S. 3 (1883). This consolidated Supreme Court case deemed portions of the Civil Rights Act of 1875 requiring equality in public accommodations to be unconstitutional in that they exceeded Congress's power under the Fourteenth Amendment. The case was the primary reason why the Civil Rights Act of 1964 had to be passed pursuant to Congress's commerce clause power rather than to its Fourteenth Amendment enforcement power alone.

Heart of Atlanta Motel v. United States, 379 U.S. 241 (1964). In this case, the motel held that the public accommodations provision of the Civil Rights Act of 1964 was unconstitutional because it exceeded Congress's commerce clause power. The Court, however, noted that the hotel did affect interstate commerce and concluded that the 1964 act's provisions were in this case constitutional.

Katzenbach v. McClung, 379 U.S. 294 (1964). This case addressed a claim by an Alabama restaurant serving almost exclusively local clientele that the public accommodations provisions of the 1964 act were unconstitutional. The Court held that the provisions applied to a restaurant when most of the food served by the restaurant had traveled via interstate commerce.

King, Martin Luther, Jr. "'I Have a Dream': Address Delivered at the March on Washington for Jobs and Freedom." The Martin

Luther King, Jr., Research and Education Institute Web site. http://stanford.edu/group/King/publications/speeches/address_at_march_on_washington.pdf. This speech of August 28, 1963 became the rallying cry for equality from the moment it was given and stands as one of the clearest expositions of principles supporting equal rights for all persons that the nation has ever heard.

———. "Letter from Birmingham Jail." The Martin Luther King, Jr., Research and Education Institute Web site. http://www.stanford.edu/group/King/popular_requests/frequentdocs/birmingham.pdf. Accessed on February 27, 2008. King wrote this letter, addressed to his fellow clergymen, in the midst of the struggle to desegregate Birmingham. In the letter (written on April 16, 1963), King explains why African Americans deserve equality based on biblical and democratic principles and why he is comfortable using the nonviolent but provocative methods that he uses to gain freedom for all.

Voting Rights Act of 1965, Public Law 89-110, U.S. *Statutes at Large* 79 (1965): 437. Passed in the wake of the Civil Rights Act of 1964, this law strengthened and superseded Title I of that act. Passed pursuant to the Fifteenth Amendment, it provides more powerful protection for voting rights by outlawing some of the tactics used to disfranchise minority citizens, such as the literacy test.

Bibliography

■ Books

Gillon, Steven M. *That's Not What We Meant to Do: Reform and Its Unintended Consequences in Twentieth-Century America*. New York: W. W. Norton, 2000.

Grofman, Bernard, ed. *Legacies of the 1964 Civil Rights Act*. Charlottesville: University Press of Virginia, 2000.

Halpern, Stephen C. *On the Limits of the Law: The Ironic Legacy of Title VI of the 1964 Civil Rights Act*. Baltimore: Johns Hopkins University Press, 1995.

Klarman, Michael J. *From Jim Crow to Civil Rights: The Supreme Court and the Struggle for Racial Equality*. New York: Oxford University Press, 2004.

Kotz, Nick. *Judgment Days: Lyndon Baines Johnson, Martin Luther King, Jr., and the Laws That Changed America*. Boston: Houghton Mifflin, 2005.

Loevy, Robert D., ed. *The Civil Rights Act of 1964: The Passage of the Law That Ended Racial Segregation*. Albany: State University of New York Press, 1997.

Sokol, Jason. *There Goes My Everything: White Southerners in the Age of Civil Rights, 1945–1975*. New York: Alfred A. Knopf, 2006.

Whalen, Charles, and Barbara Whalen. *The Longest Debate: A Legislative History of the 1964 Civil Rights Act*. Cabin John, Md.: Seven Locks Press, 1985.

Zietlow, Rebecca E. *Enforcing Equality: Congress, the Constitution, and the Protection of Individual Rights*. New York: New York University Press, 2006.

■ Web Sites

Rhodes, Henry A. "An Analysis of the Civil Rights Act of 1964: A Legislated Response to Racial Discrimination in the U.S." Yale–New Haven Teachers Institute Web site.
   http://www.yale.edu/ynhti/curriculum/units/1982/3/82.03.04.x. html. Accessed on February 2, 2008.

"Teaching with Documents: The Civil Rights Act of 1964 and the Equal Employment Opportunity Commission." National Archives "Educators and Students" Web site.
   http://www.archives.gov/education/lessons/civil-rights-act/. Accessed on February 2, 2008.

—By Henry L. Chambers, Jr.

1. The Civil Rights Act of 1964 was justified both as an extension of the Fourteenth Amendment and as a proper application of the commerce clause. Would the Civil Rights Act of 1964 have been reasonable law if it had been passed during the Reconstruction era? How similar are some of its sections to laws passed during Reconstruction?

2. To ensure passage, the Civil Rights Act of 1964 underwent significant changes. In fact, the act as finalized proved stronger than the civil rights bill sent to Congress by President Kennedy in 1963. Does this circumstance reveal anything about President Kennedy's commitment to civil rights, or does it reveal his ability to divine Congress's tolerance for a strong civil rights bill, or does it reveal something entirely different?

3. What effect, if any, do you believe the Civil Rights Act of 1964 has had on the electoral results of the Democratic Party in the South from the 1960s to the present?

4. What would the United States have come to look like had the Civil Rights Act of 1964 not been passed? Would the act have passed had President Kennedy not been assassinated?

5. Arguably, the Civil Rights Act of 1964 was the culmination of the first stage of the civil rights era. Which act was more important to civil rights, the Civil Rights Act of 1964 or the Voting Rights Act of 1965?

Glossary

civil action	a lawsuit that seeks relief for a wrong
complaint	the opening plea filed in a lawsuit that seeks relief for a wrong
equal protection of the laws	concept drawn from the Fourteenth Amendment that all persons should be treated equally by and under the laws of the government
executive session	the convening of a public body that is closed to the public because of the subject matter to be discussed
injunction	equitable relief granted to a party that requires that the opposing party perform a specific act or refrain from performing specific acts; also called injunctive relief
literacy test	test of reading or comprehension, such as those that have historically been given to prospective voters specifically to prevent African Americans and members of other minority groups from voting
rebuttable presumption	presumption that arises after specific facts are proved and that can be disproved if contrary evidence is presented
restraining order	order from a court stopping a party from doing a particular act, usually until an action on an injunction is heard
State action	behavior that is done by or on behalf of the state and is required to trigger the protections of the Fourteenth Amendment
subpoena	document requiring that a witness provide evidence in a court case or proceeding

Civil Rights Act of 1964

An Act: To enforce the constitutional right to vote, to confer jurisdiction upon the district courts of the United States to provide injunctive relief against discrimination in public accommodations, to authorize the Attorney General to institute suits to protect constitutional rights in public facilities and public education, to extend the Commission on Civil Rights, to prevent discrimination in federally assisted programs, to establish a Commission on Equal Employment Opportunity, and for other purposes.

Be it enacted by the Senate and House of Representatives of the United States of America in Congress assembled, That this Act may be cited as the "Civil Rights Act of 1964".

Title I—Voting Rights

SEC. 101. Section 2004 of the Revised Statutes (42 U.S.C. 1971), as amended by section 131 of the Civil Rights Act of 1957 (71 Stat. 637), and as further amended by section 601 of the Civil Rights Act of 1960 (74 Stat. 90), is further amended as follows:

(a) Insert "1" after "(a)" in subsection (a) and add at the end of subsection (a) the following new paragraphs:

"(2) No person acting under color of law shall—

"(A) in determining whether any individual is qualified under State law or laws to vote in any Federal election, apply any standard, practice, or procedure different from the standards, practices, or procedures applied under such law or laws to other individuals within the same county, parish, or similar political subdivision who have been found by State officials to be qualified to vote;

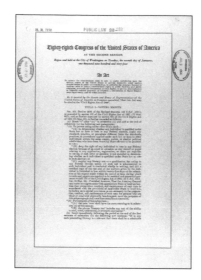

"(B) deny the right of any individual to vote in any Federal election because of an error or omission on any record or paper relating to any application, registration, or other act requisite to voting, if such error or omission is not material in determining whether such individual is qualified under State law to vote in such election; or

"(C) employ any literacy test as a qualification for voting in any Federal election unless (i) such test is administered to each individual and is conducted wholly in writing, and (ii) a certified copy of the test and of the answers given by the individual is furnished to him within twenty-five days of the submission of his request made within the period of time during which records and papers are required to be retained and preserved pursuant to title III of the Civil Rights Act of 1960 (42 U.S.C. 1974-74e; 74 Stat. 88): Provided, however, That the Attorney General may enter into agreements with appropriate State or local authorities that preparation, conduct, and maintenance of such tests in accordance with the provisions of applicable State or local law, including such special provisions as are necessary in the preparation, conduct, and maintenance of such tests for persons who are blind or otherwise physically handicapped, meet the purposes of this subparagraph and constitute compliance therewith.

"(3) For purposes of this subsection—

"(A) the term 'vote' shall have the same meaning as in subsection (e) of this section;

"(B) the phrase 'literacy test' includes any test of the ability to read, write, understand, or interpret any matter."

(b) Insert immediately following the period at the end of the first sentence of subsection (c) the following new sentence: "If in any such proceeding literacy is a relevant fact there shall be a rebuttable presumption that any person who has not been adjudged an incompetent and who has completed the sixth grade in a public school in, or a private school accredited by, any State or territory, the District of Columbia, or the Commonwealth of Puerto Rico where instruction is carried on predominantly in the English language, possesses sufficient literacy, comprehension, and intelligence to vote in any Federal election."

(c) Add the following subsection "(f)" and designate the present subsection "(f)" as subsection "(g)": "(f) When used in subsection (a) or (c) of this section, the words 'Federal election' shall mean any general, special, or primary election held solely or in part for the purpose of electing or selecting any candidate for the office of President, Vice President, presidential elector, Member of the Senate, or Member of the House of Representatives."

(d) Add the following subsection "(h)":

"(h) In any proceeding instituted by the United States in any district court of the United States under this section in which the Attorney General requests a finding of a pattern or practice of discrimination pursuant to subsection (e) of this section the Attorney General, at the time he files the complaint, or any defendant in the proceeding, within twenty days after service upon him of the complaint, may file with the clerk of such court a request that a court of three judges be convened to hear and determine the entire case. A copy of the request for a three-judge court shall be immediately furnished by such clerk to the chief judge of the circuit (or in his absence, the presiding circuit judge of the circuit) in which the case is pending. Upon receipt of the copy of such request it shall be the duty of the chief justice of the circuit or the presiding circuit judge, as the case may be, to designate immediately three judges in such circuit, of whom at least one shall be a circuit judge and another of whom shall be a district judge of the court in which the proceeding was instituted, to hear and determine such case, and it shall be the duty of the judges so designated to assign the case for hearing at the earliest practicable date, to participate in the hearing and determi-

nation thereof, and to cause the case to be in every way expedited.

An appeal from the final judgment of such court will lie to the Supreme Court.

"In any proceeding brought under subsection (c) of this section to enforce subsection (b) of this section, or in the event neither the Attorney General nor any defendant files a request for a three-judge court in any proceeding authorized by this subsection, it shall be the duty of the chief judge of the district (or in his absence, the acting chief judge) in which the case is pending immediately to designate a judge in such district to hear and determine the case. In the event that no judge in the district is available to hear and determine the case, the chief judge of the district, or the acting chief judge, as the case may be, shall certify this fact to the chief judge of the circuit (or, in his absence, the acting chief judge) who shall then designate a district or circuit judge of the circuit to hear and determine the case.

"It shall be the duty of the judge designated pursuant to this section to assign the case for hearing at the earliest practicable date and to cause the case to be in every way expedited."

Title II—Injunctive Relief against Discrimination in Places of Public Accommodation

SEC. 201. (a) All persons shall be entitled to the full and equal enjoyment of the goods, services, facilities, and privileges, advantages, and accommodations of any place of public accommodation, as defined in this section, without discrimination or segregation on the ground of race, color, religion, or national origin.

(b) Each of the following establishments which serves the public is a place of public accommodation within the meaning of this title if its operations affect commerce, or if discrimination or segregation by it is supported by State action:

(1) any inn, hotel, motel, or other establishment which provides lodging to transient guests, other than an establishment located within a building which contains not more than five rooms for rent or hire and which is actually occupied by the proprietor of such establishment as his residence;

(2) any restaurant, cafeteria, lunchroom, lunch counter, soda fountain, or other facility principally engaged in selling food for consumption on the premises, including, but not limited to, any such facility located on the premises of any retail establishment; or any gasoline station;

(3) any motion picture house, theater, concert hall, sports arena, stadium or other place of exhibition or entertainment; and

(4) any establishment (A)(i) which is physically located within the premises of any establishment otherwise covered by this subsection, or (ii) within the premises of which is physically located any such covered establishment, and (B) which holds itself out as serving patrons of such covered establishment.

(c) The operations of an establishment affect commerce within the meaning of this title if (1) it is one of the establishments described in paragraph (1) of subsection (b); (2) in the case of an establishment described in paragraph (2) of subsection (b), it serves or offers to serve interstate travelers or a substantial portion of the food which it serves, or gasoline or other products which it sells, has moved in commerce; (3) in the case of an establishment described in paragraph (3) of subsection (b), it customarily presents films, performances, athletic teams, exhibitions, or other sources of entertainment which move in commerce; and (4) in the case of an establishment described in paragraph (4) of subsection (b), it is physically located within the premises of, or there is physically located within its premises, an establishment the operations of which affect commerce within the meaning of this subsection. For purposes of this section, "commerce" means travel, trade, traffic, commerce, transportation, or communication among the several States, or between the District of Columbia and any State, or between any foreign country or any territory or possession and any State or the District of Columbia, or between points in the same State but through any other State or the District of Columbia or a foreign country.

(d) Discrimination or segregation by an establishment is supported by State action within the meaning of this title if such discrimination or segregation (1) is carried on under color of any law, statute, ordinance, or regulation; or (2) is carried on under color of any custom or usage required or enforced by officials of the State or political subdivision thereof; or (3) is required by action of the State or political subdivision thereof.

(e) The provisions of this title shall not apply to a private club or other establishment not in fact open to the public, except to the extent that the facilities of such establishment are made available to the customers or patrons of an establishment within the scope of subsection (b).

SEC. 202. All persons shall be entitled to be free, at any establishment or place, from discrimination or segregation of any kind on the ground of race, color, religion, or national origin, if such discrimination or segregation is or purports to be required by any law, statute, ordinance, regulation, rule, or order of a State or any agency or political subdivision thereof.

SEC. 203. No person shall (a) withhold, deny, or attempt to withhold or deny, or deprive or attempt to deprive, any person of any right or privilege secured by section 201 or 202, or (b) intimidate, threaten, or coerce, or attempt to intimidate, threaten, or coerce any person with the purpose of interfering with any right or privilege secured by section 201 or 202, or (c) punish or attempt to punish any person for exercising or attempting to exercise any right or privilege secured by section 201 or 202.

SEC. 204. (a) Whenever any person has engaged or there are reasonable grounds to believe that any person is about to engage in any act or practice prohibited by section 203, a civil action for preventive relief, including an application for a permanent or temporary injunction, restraining order, or other order, may be instituted by the person aggrieved and, upon timely application, the court may, in its discretion, permit the Attorney General to intervene in such civil action if he certifies that the case is of general public importance. Upon application by the complainant and in such circumstances as the court may deem just, the court may appoint an attorney for such complainant and may authorize the commencement of the civil action without the payment of fees, costs, or security.

(b) In any action commenced pursuant to this title, the court, in its discretion, may allow the prevailing party, other than the United States, a reasonable attorney's fee as part of the costs, and the United States shall be liable for costs the same as a private person.

(c) In the case of an alleged act or practice prohibited by this title which occurs in a State, or political subdivision of a State, which has a State or local law prohibiting such act or practice and establishing or authorizing a State or local authority to grant or seek relief from such practice or to institute criminal proceedings with respect thereto upon receiving notice thereof, no civil action may be brought under subsection (a) before the expiration of thirty days after written notice of such alleged act or practice has been given to the appropriate State or local authority by registered mail or in person, provided that the court may stay proceedings in such civil action pending the termination of State or local enforcement proceedings.

(d) In the case of an alleged act or practice prohibited by this title which occurs in a State, or political subdivision of a State, which has no State or local law prohibiting such act or practice, a civil action may be brought under subsection (a): Provided, That the court may refer the matter to the Community Relations Service established by title X of this Act for as long as the court believes there is a reasonable possibility of obtaining voluntary compliance, but for not more than sixty days: Provided further, That upon expiration of such sixty-day period, the court may extend such period for an additional period, not to exceed a cumulative total of one hundred and twenty days, if it believes there then exists a reasonable possibility of securing voluntary compliance.

SEC. 205. The Service is authorized to make a full investigation of any complaint referred to it by the court under section 204(d) and may hold such hearings with respect thereto as may be necessary. The Service shall conduct any hearings with respect to any such complaint in executive session, and shall not release any testimony given therein except by agreement of all parties involved in the complaint with the permission of the court, and the Service shall endeavor to bring about a voluntary settlement between the parties.

SEC. 206. (a) Whenever the Attorney General has reasonable cause to believe that any person or group of persons is engaged in a pattern or practice of resistance to the full enjoyment of any of the rights secured by this title, and that the pattern or practice is of such a nature and is intended to deny the full exercise of the rights herein described, the Attorney General may bring a civil action in the appropriate district court of the United States by filing with it a complaint (1) signed by him (or in his absence the Acting Attorney General), (2) setting forth facts pertaining to such pattern or practice, and (3) requesting such preventive relief, including an application for a permanent or temporary injunction, restraining order or other order against the person or persons responsible for such pattern or practice, as he deems necessary to insure the full enjoyment of the rights herein described.

(b) In any such proceeding the Attorney General may file with the clerk of such court a request that a court of three judges be convened to hear and determine the case. Such request by the Attorney General shall be accompanied by a certificate that, in his opinion, the case is of general public importance. A copy of the certificate and request for a three-judge court shall be immediately furnished by such clerk to the chief judge of the circuit (or in his absence, the presiding circuit judge of the circuit) in which the case is pending. Upon receipt of the copy of such request it shall be the duty of the chief judge of the circuit or the presiding circuit judge, as the case may be, to designate immediately three judges in such circuit, of whom at least one shall be a circuit judge and another of whom shall be a district judge of the court in which the proceeding was instituted, to hear and determine such case, and it shall be the duty of the judges so designated to assign the case for hearing at the earliest practicable date, to participate in the hearing and determination thereof, and to cause the case to be in every way expedited. An appeal from the final judgment of such court will lie to the Supreme Court.

In the event the Attorney General fails to file such a request in any such proceeding, it shall be the duty of the chief judge of the district (or in his absence, the acting chief judge) in which the case is pending immediately to designate a judge in such district to hear and determine the case. In the event that no judge in the district is available to hear and determine the case, the chief judge of the district, or the acting chief judge, as the case may be, shall certify this fact to the chief judge of the circuit (or in his absence, the acting chief judge) who shall then designate a district or circuit judge of the circuit to hear and determine the case.

It shall be the duty of the judge designated pursuant to this section to assign the case for hearing at the earliest practicable date and to cause the case to be in every way expedited.

SEC. 207. (a) The district courts of the United States shall have jurisdiction of proceedings instituted pursuant to this title and shall exercise the same without regard to whether the aggrieved party shall have exhausted any administrative or other remedies that may be provided by law.

(b) The remedies provided in this title shall be the exclusive means of enforcing the rights based on this title, but nothing in this title shall preclude any individual or any State or local agency from asserting any right based on any other Federal or State law not inconsistent with this title, including any statute or ordinance requiring nondiscrimination in public establishments or accommodations, or from pursuing any remedy, civil or criminal, which may be available for the vindication or enforcement of such right.

Title III—Desegregation of Public Facilities

SEC. 301. (a) Whenever the Attorney General receives a complaint in writing signed by an individual to the effect that he is being deprived of or threatened with the loss of his right to the equal protection of the laws, on account of his race, color, religion, or national origin, by being denied equal utilization of any public facility which is owned, operated, or managed by or on behalf of any State or subdivision thereof, other than a public school or public college as defined in section 401 of title IV hereof, and the Attorney General believes the complaint is meritorious and certifies that the signer or signers of such complaint are unable, in his judgment, to initiate and maintain appropriate legal proceedings for relief and that the institution of an action will materially further the orderly progress of desegregation in public facilities, the Attorney General is authorized to institute for or in the name of the United States a civil action in any appropriate district court of the United States against such parties and for such relief as may be appropriate, and such court shall have and shall exercise jurisdiction of proceedings instituted pursuant to this section. The Attorney General may implead as defendants such additional parties as are or become necessary to the grant of effective relief hereunder.

(b) The Attorney General may deem a person or persons unable to initiate and maintain appropriate legal proceedings within the meaning of subsection

(a) of this section when such person or persons are unable, either directly or through other interested persons or organizations, to bear the expense of the litigation or to obtain effective legal representation; or whenever he is satisfied that the institution of such litigation would jeopardize the personal safety, employment, or economic standing of such person or persons, their families, or their property.

SEC. 302. In any action or proceeding under this title the United States shall be liable for costs, including a reasonable attorney's fee, the same as a private person.

SEC. 303. Nothing in this title shall affect adversely the right of any person to sue for or obtain relief in any court against discrimination in any facility covered by this title.

SEC. 304. A complaint as used in this title is a writing or document within the meaning of section 1001, title 18, United States Code.

Title IV—Desegregation of Public Education Definitions

SEC. 401. As used in this title—(a) "Commissioner" means the Commissioner of Education.

(b) "Desegregation" means the assignment of students to public schools and within such schools without regard to their race, color, religion, or national origin, but "desegregation" shall not mean the assignment of students to public schools in order to overcome racial imbalance.

(c) "Public school" means any elementary or secondary educational institution, and "public college" means any institution of higher education or any technical or vocational school above the secondary school level, provided that such public school or public college is operated by a State, subdivision of a State, or governmental agency within a State, or operated wholly or predominantly from or through the use of governmental funds or property, or funds or property derived from a governmental source.

(d) "School board" means any agency or agencies which administer a system of one or more public schools and any other agency which is responsible for the assignment of students to or within such system.

Survey and Report of Educational Opportunities

SEC. 402. The Commissioner shall conduct a survey and make a report to the President and the Congress, within two years of the enactment of this title, concerning the lack of availability of equal educational opportunities for individuals by reason of race, color, religion, or national origin in public educational institutions at all levels in the United States, its territories and possessions, and the District of Columbia.

◆ Technical Assistance

SEC. 403. The Commissioner is authorized, upon the application of any school board, State, municipality, school district, or other governmental unit legally responsible for operating a public school or schools, to render technical assistance to such applicant in the preparation, adoption, and implementation of plans for the desegregation of public schools. Such technical assistance may, among other activities, include making available to such agencies information regarding effective methods of coping with special educational problems occasioned by desegregation, and making available to such agencies personnel of the Office of Education or other persons specially equipped to advise and assist them in coping with such problems.

◆ **Training Institutes**

SEC. 404. The Commissioner is authorized to arrange, through grants or contracts, with institutions of higher education for the operation of short-term or regular session institutes for special training designed to improve the ability of teachers, supervisors, counselors, and other elementary or secondary school personnel to deal effectively with special educational problems occasioned by desegregation. Individuals who attend such an institute on a full-time basis may be paid stipends for the period of their attendance at such institute in amounts specified by the Commissioner in regulations, including allowances for travel to attend such institute.

◆ **Grants**

SEC. 405. (a) The Commissioner is authorized, upon application of a school board, to make grants to such board to pay, in whole or in part, the cost of—

(1) giving to teachers and other school personnel inservice training in dealing with problems incident to desegregation, and

(2) employing specialists to advise in problems incident to desegregation.

(b) In determining whether to make a grant, and in fixing the amount thereof and the terms and conditions on which it will be made, the Commissioner shall take into consideration the amount available for grants under this section and the other applications which are pending before him; the financial condition of the applicant and the other resources available to it; the nature, extent, and gravity of its problems incident to desegregation; and such other factors as he finds relevant.

◆ **Payments**

SEC. 406. Payments pursuant to a grant or contract under this title may be made (after necessary adjustments on account of previously made overpayments or underpayments) in advance or by way of reimbursement, and in such installments, as the Commissioner may determine.

◆ **Suits By the Attorney General**

SEC. 407. (a) Whenever the Attorney General receives a complaint in writing—

(1) signed by a parent or group of parents to the effect that his or their minor children, as members of a class of persons similarly situated, are being deprived by a school board of the equal protection of the laws, or

(2) signed by an individual, or his parent, to the effect that he has been denied admission to or not permitted to continue in attendance at a public college by reason of race, color, religion, or national origin, and the Attorney General believes the complaint is meritorious and certifies that the signer or signers of such complaint are unable, in his judgment, to initiate and maintain appropriate legal proceedings for relief and that the institution of an action will materially further the orderly achievement of desegregation in public education, the Attorney General is authorized, after giving notice of such complaint to the appropriate school board or college authority and after certifying that he is satisfied that such board or authority has had a reasonable time to adjust the conditions alleged in such complaint, to institute for or in the name of the United States a civil action in any appropriate district court of the United States against such parties and for such relief as may be appropriate, and such court shall have and shall exercise jurisdiction of proceedings instituted pursuant to this section, provided that nothing herein shall empower any official or court of the United States to issue any order seeking to achieve a racial balance in any school by requiring the transportation of pupils or students from one school to another or one school district to another in order to achieve such racial balance, or otherwise enlarge the existing power of the court to insure compliance with constitutional standards. The Attorney General may implead as defendants such additional parties as are or become necessary to the grant of effective relief hereunder.

(b) The Attorney General may deem a person or persons unable to initiate and maintain appropriate legal proceedings within the meaning of subsection

(a) of this section when such person or persons are unable, either directly or through other interested persons or organizations, to bear the expense of the litigation or to obtain effective legal representation; or whenever he is satisfied that the institution of such litigation would jeopardize the personal safety, employment, or economic standing of such person or persons, their families, or their property.

(c) The term "parent" as used in this section includes any person standing in loco parentis. A "complaint" as used in this section is a writing or document within the meaning of section 1001, title 18, United States Code.

SEC. 408. In any action or proceeding under this title the United States shall be liable for costs the same as a private person.

SEC. 409. Nothing in this title shall affect adversely the right of any person to sue for or obtain relief in any court against discrimination in public education.

SEC. 410. Nothing in this title shall prohibit classification and assignment for reasons other than race, color, religion, or national origin.

Title V—Commission on Civil Rights

SEC. 501. Section 102 of the Civil Rights Act of 1957 (42 U.S.C. 1975a; 71

Stat. 634) is amended to read as follows:

"Rules of Procedure of the Commission Hearings: SEC. 102. (a) At least thirty days prior to the commencement of any hearing, the Commission shall cause to be published in the Federal Register notice of the date on which such hearing is to commence, the place at which it is to be held and the subject of the hearing. The Chairman, or one designated by him to act as Chairman at a hearing of the Commission, shall announce in an opening statement the subject of the hearing.

"(b) A copy of the Commission's rules shall be made available to any witness before the Commission, and a witness compelled to appear before the Commission or required to produce written or other matter shall be served with a copy of the Commission's rules at the time of service of the subpoena.

"(c) Any person compelled to appear in person before the Commission shall be accorded the right to be accompanied and advised by counsel, who shall have the right to subject his client to reasonable examination, and to make objections on the record and to argue briefly the basis for such objections. The Commission shall proceed with reasonable dispatch to conclude any hearing in which it is engaged. Due

regard shall be had for the convenience and necessity of witnesses.

"(d) The Chairman or Acting Chairman may punish breaches of order and decorum by censure and exclusion from the hearings.

"(e) If the Commission determines that evidence or testimony at any hearing may tend to defame, degrade, or incriminate any person, it shall receive such evidence or testimony or summary of such evidence o testimony in executive session. The Commission shall afford any person defamed, degraded, or incriminated by such evidence or testimony an opportunity to appear and be heard in executive session, with a reasonable number of additional witnesses requested by him, before deciding to use such evidence or testimony. In the event the Commission determines to release or use such evidence or testimony in such manner as to reveal publicly the identity of the person defamed, degraded, or incriminated, such evidence or testimony, prior to such public release or use, shall be given at a public session, and the Commission shall afford such person an opportunity to appear as a voluntary witness or to file a sworn statement in his behalf and to submit brief and pertinent sworn statements of others. The Commission shall receive and dispose of requests from such person to subpoena additional witnesses.

"(f) Except as provided in sections 102 and 105 (f) of this Act, the Chairman shall receive and the Commission shall dispose of requests to subpoena additional witnesses.

"(g) No evidence or testimony or summary of evidence or testimony taken in executive session may be released or used in public sessions without the consent of the Commission. Whoever releases or uses in public without the consent of the Commission such evidence or testimony taken in executive session shall be fined not more than $1,000, or imprisoned for not more than one year.

"(h) In the discretion of the Commission, witnesses may submit brief and pertinent sworn statements in writing for inclusion in the record. The Commission shall determine the pertinency of testimony and evidence adduced at its hearings.

"(i) Every person who submits data or evidence shall be entitled to retain or, on payment of lawfully prescribed costs, procure a copy or transcript thereof, except that a witness in a hearing held in executive session may for good cause be limited to inspection of the official transcript of his testimony. Transcript copies of public sessions may be obtained by the public upon the payment of the cost thereof. An accurate transcript shall be made of the testimony of all witnesses at all hearings, either public or executive sessions, of the Commission or of any subcommittee thereof.

"(j) A witness attending any session of the Commission shall receive $6 for each day's attendance and for the time necessarily occupied in going to and returning from the same, and 10 cents per mile for going from and returning to his place of residence. Witnesses who attend at points so far removed from their respective residences as to prohibit return thereto from day to day shall be entitled to an additional allowance of $10 per day for expenses of subsistence including the time necessarily occupied in going to and returning from the place of attendance. Mileage payments shall be tendered to the witness upon service of a subpoena issued on behalf of the Commission or any subcommittee thereof.

"(k) The Commission shall not issue any subpoena for the attendance and testimony of witnesses or for the production of written or other matter which would require the presence of the party subpoenaed at a hearing to be held outside of the State wherein the witness is found or resides or is domiciled or transacts business, or has appointed an agent for receipt of service of process except that, in any event, the Commission may issue subpoenas for the attendance and testimony of witnesses and the production of written or other matter at a hearing held within fifty miles of the place where the witness is found or resides or is domiciled or transacts business or has appointed an agent for receipt of service of process.

"(l) The Commission shall separately state and currently publish in the Federal Register (1) descriptions of its central and field organization including the established places at which, and methods whereby, the public may secure information or make requests; (2) statements of the general course and method by which its functions are channeled and determined, and (3) rules adopted as authorized by law. No person shall in any manner be subject to or required to resort to rules, organization, or procedure not so published."

SEC. 502. Section 103(a) of the Civil Rights Act of 1957 (42 U.S.C. 1975b(a); 71 Stat. 634) is amended to read as follows:

"SEC. 103. (a) Each member of the Commission who is not otherwise in the service of the Government of the United States shall receive the sum of $75 per day for each day spent in the work of the Commission, shall be paid actual travel expenses, and per diem in lieu of subsistence expenses when away from his usual place of residence, in accordance with section 5 of the Administrative Expenses Act of 1946, as amended (5 U.S.C 73b-2; 60 Stat. 808)."

SEC. 503. Section 103(b) of the Civil Rights Act of 1957 (42 U.S.C. 1975(b); 71 Stat. 634) is amended to read as follows:

"(b) Each member of the Commission who is otherwise in the service of the Government of the United States shall serve without compensation in addition to that received for such other service, but while engaged in the work of the Commission shall be paid actual travel expenses, and per diem in lieu of subsistence expenses when away from his usual place of residence, in accordance with the provisions of the Travel Expenses Act of 1949, as amended (5 U.S.C. 835-42; 63 Stat. 166)."

SEC. 504. (a) Section 104(a) of the Civil Rights Act of 1957 (42 U.S.C. 1975c(a); 71 Stat. 635), as amended, is further amended to read as follows:

"Duties of the Commission: SEC. 104. (a) The Commission shall—

"(1) investigate allegations in writing under oath or affirmation that certain citizens of the United States are being deprived of their right to vote and have that vote counted by reason of their color, race, religion, or national origin; which writing, under oath or affirmation, shall set forth the facts upon which such belief or beliefs are based;

"(2) study and collect information concerning legal developments constituting a denial of equal protection of the laws under the Constitution because of race, color, religion or national origin or in the administration of justice;

"(3) appraise the laws and policies of the Federal Government with respect to denials of equal protection of the laws under the Constitution because of race, color, religion or national origin or in the administration of justice;

"(4) serve as a national clearinghouse for information in respect to denials of equal protection of the laws because of race, color, religion or national origin, including but not limited to the fields of voting, education, housing, employment, the use of public facilities, and transportation, or in the administration of justice;

"(5) investigate allegations, made in writing and under oath or affirmation, that citizens of the United States are unlawfully being accorded or denied the right to vote, or to have their votes properly counted, in any election of presidential electors, Members of the United States Senate, or of the House of Representatives, as a result of any patterns or practice of fraud or discrimination in the conduct of such election; and

"(6) Nothing in this or any other Act shall be construed as authorizing the Commission, its Advisory Committees, or any person under its supervision or control to inquire into or investigate any membership practices or internal operations of any fraternal organization, any college or university fraternity or sorority, any private club or any religious organization."

(b) Section 104(b) of the Civil Rights Act of 1957 (42 U.S.C. 1975c(b); 71 Stat. 635), as amended, is further amended by striking out the present subsection "(b)" and by substituting therefore:

"(b) The Commission shall submit interim reports to the President and to the Congress at such times as

the Commission, the Congress or the President shall deem desirable, and shall submit to the President and to the Congress a final report of its activities, findings, and recommendations not later than January 31, 1968."

SEC. 505. Section 105(a) of the Civil Rights Act of 1957 (42 U.S.C. 1975d(a); 71 Stat. 636) is amended by striking out in the last sentence thereof "$50 per diem" and inserting in lieu thereof "$75 per diem."

SEC. 506. Section 105(f) and section 105(g) of the Civil Rights Act of 1957 (42 U.S.C. 1975d (f) and (g); 71 Stat. 636) are amended to read as follows:

"(f) The Commission, or on the authorization of the Commission any subcommittee of two or more members, at least one of whom shall be of each major political party, may, for the purpose of carrying out the provisions of this Act, hold such hearings and act at such times and places as the Commission or such authorized subcommittee may deem advisable. Subpoenas for the attendance and testimony of witnesses or the production of written or other matter may be issued in accordance with the rules of the Commission as contained in section 102 (j) and (k) of this Act, over the signature of the Chairman of the Commission or of such subcommittee, and may be served by any person designated by such Chairman. The holding of hearings by the Commission, or the appointment of a subcommittee to hold hearings pursuant to this subparagraph, must be approved by a majority of the Commission, or by a majority of the members present at a meeting at which at least a quorum of four members is present.

"(g) In case of contumacy or refusal to obey a subpoena, any district court of the United States or the United States court of any territory or possession, or the District Court of the United States for the District of Columbia, within the jurisdiction of which the inquiry is carried on or within the jurisdiction of which said person guilty of contumacy or refusal to obey is found or resides or is domiciled or transacts business, or has appointed an agent for receipt of service of process, upon application by the Attorney General of the United States shall have jurisdiction to issue to such person an order requiring such person to appear before the Commission or a subcommittee thereof, there to produce pertinent, relevant and nonprivileged evidence if so ordered, or there to give testimony touching the matter under investigation; and any failure to obey such order of the court may be punished by said court as a contempt thereof."

SEC. 507. Section 105 of the Civil Rights Act of 1957 (42 U.S.C. 1975d; 71 Stat. 636), as amended by section 401 of the Civil Rights Act of 1960 (42 U.S.C. 1975d(h); 74 Stat. 89), is further amended by adding a new subsection at the end to read as follows:

"(i) The Commission shall have the power to make such rules and regulations as are necessary to carry out the purposes of this Act."

Title VI—Nondiscrimination in Federally Assisted Programs

SEC. 601. No person in the United States shall, on the ground of race, color, or national origin, be excluded from participation in, be denied the benefits of, or be subjected to discrimination under any program or activity receiving Federal financial assistance.

SEC. 602. Each Federal department and agency which is empowered to extend Federal financial assistance to any program or activity, by way of grant, loan, or contract other than a contract of insurance or guaranty, is authorized and directed to effectuate the provisions of section 601 with respect to such program or activity by issuing rules, regulations, or orders of general applicability which shall be consistent with achievement of the objectives of the statute authorizing the financial assistance in connection with which the action is taken. No such rule, regulation, or order shall become effective unless and until approved by the President. Compliance with any requirement adopted pursuant to this section may be effected (1) by the termination of or refusal to grant or to continue assistance under such program or activity to any recipient as to whom there has been an express finding on the record, after opportunity for hearing, of a failure to comply with such requirement, but such termination or refusal shall be limited to the particular political entity, or part thereof, or other recipient as to whom such a finding has been made and, shall be limited in its effect to the particular program, or part thereof, in which such noncompliance has been so found, or (2) by any other

means authorized by law: Provided, however, That no such action shall be taken until the department or agency concerned has advised the appropriate person or persons of the failure to comply with the requirement and has determined that compliance cannot be secured by voluntary means. In the case of any action terminating, or refusing to grant or continue, assistance because of failure to comply with a requirement imposed pursuant to this section, the head of the federal department or agency shall file with the committees of the House and Senate having legislative jurisdiction over the program or activity involved a full written report of the circumstances and the grounds for such action. No such action shall become effective until thirty days have elapsed after the filing of such report.

SEC. 603. Any department or agency action taken pursuant to section 602 shall be subject to such judicial review as may otherwise be provided by law for similar action taken by such department or agency on other grounds. In the case of action, not otherwise subject to judicial review, terminating or refusing to grant or to continue financial assistance upon a finding of failure to comply with any requirement imposed pursuant to section 602, any person aggrieved (including any State or political subdivision thereof and any agency of either) may obtain judicial review of such action in accordance with section 10 of the Administrative Procedure Act, and such action shall not be deemed committed to unreviewable agency discretion within the meaning of that section.

SEC. 604. Nothing contained in this title shall be construed to authorize action under this title by any department or agency with respect to any employment practice of any employer, employment agency, or labor organization except where a primary objective of the Federal financial assistance is to provide employment.

SEC. 605. Nothing in this title shall add to or detract from any existing authority with respect to any program or activity under which Federal financial assistance is extended by way of a contract of insurance or guaranty.

Title VII—Equal Employment Opportunity Definitions

SEC. 701. For the purposes of this title—
(a) The term "person" includes one or more individuals, labor unions, partnerships, associations, cor-

porations, legal representatives, mutual companies, joint-stock companies, trusts, unincorporated organizations, trustees, trustees in bankruptcy, or receivers.

(b) The term "employer" means a person engaged in an industry affecting commerce who has twenty-five or more employees for each working day in each of twenty or more calendar weeks in the current or preceding calendar year, and any agent of such a person, but such term does not include (1) the United States, a corporation wholly owned by the Government of the United States, an Indian tribe, or a State or political subdivision thereof, (2) a bona fide private membership club (other than a labor organization) which is exempt from taxation under section 501(c) of the Internal Revenue Code of 1954: Provided, That during the first year after the effective date prescribed in subsection (a) of section 716, persons having fewer than one hundred employees (and their agents) shall not be considered employers, and, during the second year after such date, persons having fewer than seventy-five employees (and their agents) shall not be considered employers, and, during the third year after such date, persons having fewer than fifty employees (and their agents) shall not be considered employers: Provided further, That it shall be the policy of the United States to insure equal employment opportunities for Federal employees without discrimination because of race, color, religion, sex or national origin and the President shall utilize his existing authority to effectuate this policy.

(c) The term "employment agency" means any person regularly undertaking with or without compensation to procure employees for an employer or to procure for employees opportunities to work for an employer and includes an agent of such a person; but shall not include an agency of the United States, or an agency of a State or political subdivision of a State, except that such term shall include the United States Employment Service and the system of State and local employment services receiving Federal assistance.

(d) The term "labor organization" means a labor organization engaged in an industry affecting commerce, and any agent of such an organization, and includes any organization of any kind, any agency, or employee representation committee, group, association, or plan so engaged in which employees participate and which exists for the purpose, in whole or in part, of dealing with employers concerning grievances, labor disputes, wages, rates of pay, hours, or other terms or conditions of employment, and any conference, general committee, joint or system board, or joint council so engaged which is subordinate to a national or international labor organization.

(e) A labor organization shall be deemed to be engaged in an industry affecting commerce if (1) it maintains or operates a hiring hall or hiring office which procures employees for an employer or procures for employees opportunities to work for an employer, or (2) the number of its members (or, where it is a labor organization composed of other labor organizations or their representatives, if the aggregate number of the members of such other labor organization) is (A) one hundred or more during the first year after the effective date prescribed in subsection (a) of section 716, (B) seventy-five or more during the second year after such date or fifty or more during the third year, or (C) twenty-five or more thereafter, and such labor organization—

(1) is the certified representative of employees under the provisions of the National Labor Relations Act, as amended, or the Railway Labor Act, as amended;

(2) although not certified, is a national or international labor organization or a local labor organization recognized or acting as the representative of employees of an employer or employers engaged in an industry affecting commerce; or

(3) has chartered a local labor organization or subsidiary body which is representing or actively seeking to represent employees of employers within the meaning of paragraph (1) or (2); or

(4) has been chartered by a labor organization representing or actively seeking to represent employees within the meaning of paragraph (1) or (2) as the local or subordinate body through which such employees may enjoy membership or become affiliated with such labor organization; or

(5) is a conference, general committee, joint or system board, or joint council subordinate to a national or international labor organization, which includes a labor organization engaged in an industry affecting commerce within the meaning of any of the preceding paragraphs of this subsection.

(f) The term "employee" means an individual employed by an employer.

(g) The term "commerce" means trade, traffic, commerce, transportation, transmission, or communication among the several States; or between a State and any place outside thereof; or within the District of Columbia, or a possession of the United States; or between points in the same State but through a point outside thereof.

(h) The term "industry affecting commerce" means any activity, business, or industry in commerce or in which a labor dispute would hinder or obstruct commerce or the free flow of commerce and includes any activity or industry "affecting commerce" within the meaning of the Labor-Management Reporting and Disclosure Act of 1959.

(i) The term "State" includes a State of the United States, the District of Columbia, Puerto Rico, the Virgin Islands, American Samoa, Guam, Wake Island, The Canal Zone, and Outer Continental Shelf lands defined in the Outer Continental Shelf Lands Act.

◆ Exemption

SEC. 702. This title shall not apply to an employer with respect to the employment of aliens outside any State, or to a religious corporation, association, or society with respect to the employment of individuals of a particular religion to perform work connected with the carrying on by such corporation, association, or society of its religious activities or to an educational institution with respect to the employment of individuals to perform work connected with the educational activities of such institution.

◆ Discrimination Because of Race, Color, Religion, Sex, or National Origin

SEC. 703. (a) It shall be an unlawful employment practice for an employer—

(1) to fail or refuse to hire or to discharge any individual, or otherwise to discriminate against any individual with respect to his compensation, terms, conditions, or privileges of employment, because of such individual's race, color, religion, sex, or national origin; or

(2) to limit, segregate, or classify his employees in any way which would deprive or tend to deprive any individual of employment opportunities or otherwise adversely affect his status as an employee, because of such individual's race, color, religion, sex, or national origin.

(b) It shall be an unlawful employment practice for an employment agency to fail or refuse to refer for employment, or otherwise to discriminate against, any individual because of his race, color, religion, sex, or national origin, or to classify or refer for employment any individual on the basis of his race, color, religion, sex, or national origin.

(c) It shall be an unlawful employment practice for a labor organization—

(1) to exclude or to expel from its membership, or otherwise to discriminate against, any individual because of his race, color, religion, sex, or national origin;

(2) to limit, segregate, or classify its membership, or to classify or fail or refuse to refer for employment any individual, in any way which would deprive or tend to deprive any individual of employment opportunities, or would limit such employment opportunities or otherwise adversely affect his status as an employee or as an applicant for employment, because of such individual's race, color, religion, sex, or national origin; or

(3) to cause or attempt to cause an employer to discriminate against an individual in violation of this section.

(d) It shall be an unlawful employment practice for any employer, labor organization, or joint labor-management committee controlling apprenticeship or other training or retraining, including on-the-job training programs to discriminate against any individual because of his race, color, religion, sex, or national origin in admission to, or employment in, any program established to provide apprenticeship or other training.

(e) Notwithstanding any other provision of this title, (1) it shall not be an unlawful employment practice for an employer to hire and employ employees, for an employment agency to classify, or refer for employment any individual, for a labor organization to classify its membership or to classify or refer for employment any individual, or for an employer, labor organization, or joint labor-management committee controlling apprenticeship or other training or retraining programs to admit or employ any individual in any such program, on the basis of his religion, sex, or national origin in those certain instances where religion, sex, or national origin is a bona fide occupational qualification reasonably necessary to the normal operation of that particular business or enterprise, and (2) it shall not be an unlawful employment practice for a school, college, university, or other educational institution or institution of learning to hire and employ employees of a particular religion if such school, college, university, or other educational institution or institution of learning is, in whole or in substantial part, owned, supported, controlled, or managed by a particular religion or by a particular religious corporation, association, or society, or if the curriculum of such school, college, university, or other educational institution or institution of learning is directed toward the propagation of a particular religion.

(f) As used in this title, the phrase "unlawful employment practice" shall not be deemed to include any action or measure taken by an employer, labor organization, joint labor-management committee, or employment agency with respect to an individual who is a member of the Communist Party of the United States or of any other organization required to register as a Communist-action or Communist-front organization by final order of the Subversive Activities Control Board pursuant to the Subversive Activities Control Act of 1950.

(g) Notwithstanding any other provision of this title, it shall not be an unlawful employment practice for an employer to fail or refuse to hire and employ any individual for any position, for an employer to discharge any individual from any position, or for an employment agency to fail or refuse to refer any individual for employment in any position, or for a labor organization to fail or refuse to refer any individual for employment in any position, if—

(1) the occupancy of such position, or access to the premises in or upon which any part of the duties of such position is performed or is to be performed, is subject to any requirement imposed in the interest of the national security of the United States under any security program in effect pursuant to or administered under any statute of the United States or any Executive order of the President; and

(2) such individual has not fulfilled or has ceased to fulfill that requirement.

(h) Notwithstanding any other provision of this title, it shall not be an unlawful employment practice for an employer to apply different standards of compensation, or different terms, conditions, or privileges of employment pursuant to a bona fide seniority or merit system, or a system which measures earnings by quantity or quality of production or to employees who work in different locations, provided that such differences are not the result of an intention to discriminate because of race, color, religion, sex, or national origin, nor shall it be an unlawful employment practice for an employer to give and to act upon the results of any professionally developed ability test provided that such test, its administration or action upon the results is not designed, intended or used to discriminate because of race, color, religion, sex or national origin. It shall not be an unlawful employment practice under this title for any employer to differentiate upon the basis of sex in determining the amount of the wages or compensation paid or to be paid to employees of such employer if such differentiation is authorized by the provisions of section 6(d) of the Fair Labor Standards Act of 1938, as amended (29 U.S.C. 206(d)).

(i) Nothing contained in this title shall apply to any business or enterprise on or near an Indian reservation with respect to any publicly announced employment practice of such business or enterprise under which a preferential treatment is given to any individual because he is an Indian living on or near a reservation.

(j) Nothing contained in this title shall be interpreted to require any employer, employment agency, labor organization, or joint labor-management committee subject to this title to grant preferential treatment to any individual or to any group because of the race, color, religion, sex, or national origin of such individual or group on account of an imbalance which may exist with respect to the total number or percentage of persons of any race, color, religion, sex, or national origin employed by any employer, referred or classified for employment by any employment agency or labor organization, admitted to membership or classified by any labor organization, or admitted to, or employed in, any apprenticeship or other training program, in comparison with the total number or percentage of persons of such race, color, religion, sex, or national origin in any community, State, section, or other area, or in the available work force in any community, State, section, or other area.

◆ **Other Unlawful Employment Practices**

SEC. 704. (a) It shall be an unlawful employment practice for an employer to discriminate against any of his employees or applicants for employment, for an employment agency to discriminate against any individual, or for a labor organization to discriminate against any member thereof or applicant for membership, because he has opposed, any practice made an unlawful employment practice by this title, or because he has made a charge, testified, assisted, or participated in any manner in an investigation, proceeding, or hearing under this title.

(b) It shall be an unlawful employment practice for an employer, labor organization, or employment agency to print or publish or cause to be printed or published any notice or advertisement relating to employment by such an employer or membership in or any classification or referral for employment by such a labor organization, or relating to any classification or referral for employment by such an employment agency, indicating any preference, limitation, specification, or discrimination, based on race, color, religion, sex, or national origin, except that such a notice or advertisement may indicate a preference, limitation, specification, or discrimination based on religion, sex, or national origin when religion, sex, or national origin is a bona fide occupational qualification for employment.

◆ Equal Employment Opportunity Commission

SEC. 705. (a) There is hereby created a Commission to be known as the Equal Employment Opportunity Commission, which shall be composed of five members, not more than three of whom shall be members of the same political party, who shall be appointed by the President by and with the advice and consent of the Senate. One of the original members shall be appointed for a term of one year, one for a term of two years, one for a term of three years, one for a term of four years, and one for a term of five years, beginning from the date of enactment of this title, but their successors shall be appointed for terms of five years each, except that any individual chosen to fill a vacancy shall be appointed only for the unexpired term of the member whom he shall succeed. The President shall designate one member to serve as Chairman of the Commission, and one member to serve as Vice Chairman. The Chairman shall be responsible on behalf of the Commission for the administrative operations of the Commission, and shall appoint, in accordance with the civil service laws, such officers, agents, attorneys, and employees as it deems necessary to assist it in the performance of its functions and to fix their compensation in accordance with the Classification Act of 1949, as amended. The Vice Chairman shall act as Chairman in the absence or disability of the Chairman or in the event of a vacancy in that office.

(b) A vacancy in the Commission shall not impair the right of the remaining members to exercise all the powers of the Commission and three members thereof shall constitute a quorum.

(c) The Commission shall have an official seal which shall be judicially noticed.

(d) The Commission shall at the close of each fiscal year report to the Congress and to the President concerning the action it has taken; the names, salaries, and duties of all individuals in its employ and the moneys it has disbursed; and shall make such further reports on the cause of and means of eliminating discrimination and such recommendations for further legislation as may appear desirable.

(e) The Federal Executive Pay Act of 1956, as amended (5 U.S.C. 2201-2209), is further amended—

(1) by adding to section 105 thereof (5 U.S.C. 2204) the following clause:

"(32) Chairman, Equal Employment Opportunity Commission"; and

(2) by adding to clause (45) of section 106(a) thereof (5 U.S.C. 2205(a)) the following: "Equal Employment Opportunity Commission (4)."

(f) The principal office of the Commission shall be in or near the District of Columbia, but it may meet or exercise any or all its powers at any other place. The Commission may establish such regional or State offices as it deems necessary to accomplish the purpose of this title.

(g) The Commission shall have power—

(1) to cooperate with and, with their consent, utilize regional, State, local, and other agencies, both public and private, and individuals;

(2) to pay to witnesses whose depositions are taken or who are summoned before the Commission or any of its agents the same witness and mileage fees as are paid to witnesses in the courts of the United States;

(3) to furnish to persons subject to this title such technical assistance as they may request to further their compliance with this title or an order issued thereunder;

(4) upon the request of (i) any employer, whose employees or some of them, or (ii) any labor organization, whose members or some of them, refuse or threaten to refuse to cooperate in effectuating the provisions of this title, to assist in such effectuation by conciliation or such other remedial action as is provided by this title;

(5) to make such technical studies as are appropriate to effectuate the purposes and policies of this title and to make the results of such studies available to the public;

(6) to refer matters to the Attorney General with recommendations for intervention in a civil action brought by an aggrieved party under section 706, or for the institution of a civil action by the Attorney General under section 707, and to advise, consult, and assist the Attorney General on such matters.

(h) Attorneys appointed under this section may, at the direction of the Commission, appear for and represent the Commission in any case in court.

(i) The Commission shall, in any of its educational or promotional activities, cooperate with other departments and agencies in the performance of such educational and promotional activities.

(j) All officers, agents, attorneys, and employees of the Commission shall be subject to the provisions of section 9 of the Act of August 2, 1939, as amended (the Hatch Act), notwithstanding any exemption contained in such section.

◆ Prevention of Unlawful Employment Practices

SEC. 706. (a) Whenever it is charged in writing under oath by a person claiming to be aggrieved, or a written charge has been filed by a member of the Commission where he has reasonable cause to believe a violation of this title has occurred (and such charge sets forth the facts upon which it is based) that an employer, employment agency, or labor organization has engaged in an unlawful employment practice, the Commission shall furnish such employer, employment agency, or labor organization (hereinafter referred to as the "respondent") with a copy of such charge and shall make an investigation of such charge, provided that such charge shall not be made public by the Commission. If the Commission shall determine, after such investigation, that there is reasonable cause to believe that the charge is true, the Commission shall endeavor to eliminate any such alleged unlawful employment practice by informal methods of conference, conciliation, and persuasion. Nothing said or done during and as a part of such endeavors may be made public by the Commission without the written consent of the parties, or used as evidence in a subsequent proceeding. Any officer or employee of the Commission, who shall make public in any manner whatever any information in violation of this subsection shall be deemed guilty of a misdemeanor and upon conviction thereof shall be fined not more than $1,000 or imprisoned not more than one year.

(b) In the case of an alleged unlawful employment practice occurring in a State, or political subdivision of a State, which has a State or local law prohibiting the unlawful employment practice alleged and establishing or authorizing a State or local authority to grant or seek relief from such practice or to institute criminal proceedings with respect thereto upon receiving notice thereof, no charge may be filed under subsection (a) by the person aggrieved before the expiration of sixty days after proceedings have been commenced under the State or local law, unless such proceedings have been earlier terminated, provided that such sixty-day period shall be extended to one hundred and twenty days during the first year after the effective date of such State or local law. If any requirement for the commencement of such proceedings is imposed by a State or local authority other than a requirement of the filing of a written and signed statement of the facts upon which

the proceeding is based, the proceeding shall be deemed to have been commenced for the purposes of this subsection at the time such statement is sent by registered mail to the appropriate State or local authority.

(c) In the case of any charge filed by a member of the Commission alleging an unlawful employment practice occurring in a State or political subdivision of a State, which has a State or local law prohibiting the practice alleged and establishing or authorizing a State or local authority to grant or seek relief from such practice or to institute criminal proceedings with respect thereto upon receiving notice thereof, the Commission shall, before taking any action with respect to such charge, notify the appropriate State or local officials and, upon request, afford them a reasonable time, but not less than sixty days (provided that such sixty-day period shall be extended to one hundred and twenty days during the first year after the effective day of such State or local law), unless a shorter period is requested, to act under such State or local law to remedy the practice alleged.

(d) A charge under subsection (a) shall be filed within ninety days after the alleged unlawful employment practice occurred, except that in the case of an unlawful employment practice with respect to which the person aggrieved has followed the procedure set out in subsection (b), such charge shall be filed by the person aggrieved within two hundred and ten days after the alleged unlawful employment practice occurred, or within thirty days after receiving notice that the State or local agency has terminated the proceedings under the State or local, law, whichever is earlier, and a copy of such charge shall be filed by the Commission with the State or local agency.

(e) If within thirty days after a charge is filed with the Commission or within thirty days after expiration of any period of reference under subsection (c) (except that in either case such period may be extended to not more than sixty days upon a determination by the Commission that further efforts to secure voluntary compliance are warranted), the Commission has been unable to obtain voluntary compliance with this title, the Commission shall so notify the person aggrieved and a civil action may, within thirty days thereafter, be brought against the respondent named in the charge (1) by the person claiming to be aggrieved, or (2) if such charge was filed by a member of the Commission, by any person whom the charge alleges was aggrieved by the alleged unlawful employment practice. Upon application by the complainant and in such circumstances as the court may deem just, the court may appoint an attorney for such complainant and may authorize the commencement of the action without the payment of fees, costs, or security. Upon timely application, the court may, in its discretion, permit the Attorney General to intervene in such civil action if he certifies that the case is of general public importance. Upon request, the court may, in its discretion, stay further proceedings for not more than sixty days pending the termination of State or local proceedings described in subsection (b) or the efforts of the Commission to obtain voluntary compliance.

(f) Each United States district court and each United States court of a place subject to the jurisdiction of the United States shall have jurisdiction of actions brought under this title. Such an action may be brought in any judicial district in the State in which the unlawful employment practice is alleged to have been committed, in the judicial district in which the employment records relevant to such practice are maintained and administered, or in the judicial district in which the plaintiff would have worked but for the alleged unlawful employment practice, but if the respondent is not found within any such district, such an action may be brought within the judicial district in which the respondent has his principal office. For purposes of sections 1404 and 1406 of title 28 of the United States Code, the judicial district in which the respondent has his principal office shall in all cases be considered a district in which the action might have been brought.

(g) If the court finds that the respondent has intentionally engaged in or is intentionally engaging in an unlawful employment practice charged in the complaint, the court may enjoin the respondent from engaging in such unlawful employment practice, and order such affirmative action as may be appropriate, which may include reinstatement or hiring of employees, with or without back pay (payable by the employer, employment agency, or labor organization, as the case may be, responsible for the unlawful employment practice). Interim earnings or amounts earnable with reasonable diligence by the person or persons discriminated against shall operate to reduce the back pay otherwise allowable. No order of the court shall require the admission or reinstatement of an individual as a member of a union or the hiring, reinstatement, or promotion of an individual as an employee, or the payment to him of any back pay, if such individual was refused admission, suspended, or expelled or was refused employment or advancement or was suspended or discharged for any reason

other than discrimination on account of race, color, religion, sex or national origin or in violation of section 704(a).

(h) The provisions of the Act entitled "An Act to amend the Judicial Code and to define and limit the jurisdiction of courts sitting in equity, and for other purposes," approved March 23, 1932 (29 U.S.C. 101-115), shall not apply with respect to civil actions brought under this section.

(i) In any case in which an employer, employment agency, or labor organization fails to comply with an order of a court issued in a civil action brought under subsection (e), the Commission may commence proceedings to compel compliance with such order.

(j) Any civil action brought under subsection (e) and any proceedings brought under subsection (i) shall be subject to appeal as provided in sections 1291 and 1292, title 28, United States Code.

(k) In any action or proceeding under this title the court, in its discretion, may allow the prevailing party, other than the Commission or the United States, a reasonable attorney's fee as part of the costs, and the Commission and the United States shall be liable for costs the same as a private person.

SEC. 707. (a) Whenever the Attorney General has reasonable cause to believe that any person or group of persons is engaged in a pattern or practice of resistance to the full enjoyment of any of the rights secured by this title, and that the pattern or practice is of such a nature and is intended to deny the full exercise of the rights herein described, the Attorney General may bring a civil action in the appropriate district court of the United States by filing with it a complaint (1) signed by him (or in his absence the Acting Attorney General), (2) setting forth facts pertaining to such pattern or practice, and (3) requesting such relief, including an application for a permanent or temporary injunction, restraining order or other order against the person or persons responsible for such pattern or practice, as he deems necessary to insure the full enjoyment of the rights herein described.

(b) The district courts of the United States shall have and shall exercise jurisdiction of proceedings instituted pursuant to this section, and in any such proceeding the Attorney General may file with the clerk of such court a request that a court of three judges be convened to hear and determine the case. Such request by the Attorney General shall be accompanied by a certificate that, in his opinion, the case is of general public importance. A copy of the certificate and request for a three-judge court shall be immediately furnished by such clerk to the chief judge of the circuit (or in his absence, the presiding circuit judge of the circuit) in which the case is pending. Upon receipt of such request it shall be the duty of the chief judge of the circuit or the presiding circuit judge, as the case may be, to designate immediately three judges in such circuit, of whom at least one shall be a circuit judge and another of whom shall be a district judge of the court in which the proceeding was instituted, to hear and determine such case, and it shall be the duty of the judges so designated to assign the case for hearing at the earliest practicable date, to participate in the hearing and determination thereof, and to cause the case to be in every way expedited. An appeal from the final judgment of such court will lie to the Supreme Court.

In the event the Attorney General fails to file such a request in any such proceeding, it shall be the duty of the chief judge of the district (or in his absence, the acting chief judge) in which the case is pending immediately to designate a judge in such district to hear and determine the case. In the event that no judge in the district is available to hear and determine the case, the chief judge of the district, or the acting chief judge, as the case may be, shall certify this fact to the chief judge of the circuit (or in his absence, the acting chief judge) who shall then designate a district or circuit judge of the circuit to hear and determine the case.

It shall be the duty of the judge designated pursuant to this section to assign the case for hearing at the earliest practicable date and to cause the case to be in every way expedited.

◆ Effect on State Laws

SEC. 708. Nothing in this title shall be deemed to exempt or relieve any person from any liability, duty, penalty, or punishment provided by any present or future law of any State or political subdivision of a State, other than any such law which purports to require or permit the doing of any act which would be an unlawful employment practice under this title.

◆ Investigations, Inspections, Records, State Agencies

SEC. 709. (a) In connection with any investigation of a charge filed under section 706, the Commission or its designated representative shall at all reasonable times have access to, for the purposes of examination, and the right to copy any evidence of any person being investigated or proceeded against that relates to unlawful employment practices covered by this title and is relevant to the charge under investigation.

(b) The Commission may cooperate with State and local agencies charged with the administration of State fair employment practices laws and, with the consent of such agencies, may for the purpose of carrying out its functions and duties under this title and within the limitation of funds appropriated specifically for such purpose, utilize the services of such agencies and their employees and, notwithstanding any other provision of law, may reimburse such agencies and their employees for services rendered to assist the Commission in carrying out this title. In furtherance of such cooperative efforts, the Commission may enter into written agreements with such State or local agencies and such agreements may include provisions under which the Commission shall refrain from processing a charge in any cases or class of cases specified in such agreements and under which no person may bring a civil action under section 706 in any cases or class of cases so specified, or under which the Commission shall relieve any person or class of persons in such State or locality from requirements imposed under this section. The Commission shall rescind any such agreement whenever it determines that the agreement no longer serves the interest of effective enforcement of this title.

(c) Except as provided in subsection (d), every employer, employment agency, and labor organization subject to this title shall (1) make and keep such records relevant to the determinations of whether unlawful employment practices have been or are being committed, (2) preserve such records for such periods, and (3) make such reports therefrom, as the Commission shall prescribe by regulation or order, after public hearing, as reasonable, necessary, or appropriate for the enforcement of this title or the regulations or orders thereunder. The Commission shall, by regulation, require each employer, labor organization, and joint labor-management committee subject to this title which controls an apprenticeship or other training program to maintain such records as are reasonably necessary to carry out the purpose of this title, including, but not limited to, a list of applicants who wish to participate in such program, including the chronological order in which such applications were received, and shall furnish to the Commission, upon request, a detailed description of the manner in which persons are selected to participate in the apprenticeship or other training program. Any employer, employment agency, labor organization, or joint labor-management committee which believes that the application to it of any regulation or order issued under this section would result in undue hardship may (1) apply to the Commission for an exemption from the application of such regulation or order, or (2) bring a civil action in the United States district court for the district where such records are kept. If the Commission or the court, as the case may be, finds that the application of the regulation or order to the employer, employment agency, or labor organization in question would impose an undue hardship, the Commission or the court, as the case may be, may grant appropriate relief.

(d) The provisions of subsection (c) shall not apply to any employer, employment agency, labor organization, or joint labor-management committee with respect to matters occurring in any State or political subdivision thereof which has a fair employment practice law during any period in which such employer, employment agency, labor organization, or joint labor-management committee is subject to such law, except that the Commission may require such notations on records which such employer, employment agency, labor organization, or joint labor-management committee keeps or is required to keep as are necessary because of differences in coverage or methods of enforcement between the State or local law and the provisions of this title. Where an employer is required by Executive Order 10925, issued March 6, 1961, or by any other Executive order prescribing fair employment practices for Government contractors and subcontractors, or by rules or regulations issued thereunder, to file reports relating to his employment practices with any Federal agency or committee, and he is substantially in compliance with such requirements, the Commission shall not require him to file additional reports pursuant to subsection (c) of this section.

(e) It shall be unlawful for any officer or employee of the Commission to make public in any manner whatever any information obtained by the Commission pursuant to its authority under this section prior to the institution of any proceeding under this title involving such information. Any officer or employee of the Commission who shall make public in any manner whatever any information in violation of this subsection shall be guilty of a misdemeanor and upon conviction thereof, shall be fined not more than $1,000, or imprisoned not more than one year.

◆ Investigatory Powers

SEC. 710. (a) For the purposes of any investigation of a charge filed under the authority contained in section 706, the Commission shall have authority to examine witnesses under oath and to require the production of documentary evidence relevant or material to the charge under investigation.

(b) If the respondent named in a charge filed under section 706 fails or refuses to comply with a demand of the Commission for permission to examine or to copy evidence in conformity with the provisions of section 709(a), or if any person required to comply with the provisions of section 709 (c) or (d) fails or refuses to do so, or if any person fails or refuses to comply with a demand by the Commission to give testimony under oath, the United States district court for the district in which such person is found, resides, or transacts business, shall, upon application of the Commission, have jurisdiction to issue to such person an order requiring him to comply with the provisions of section 709 (c) or (d) or to comply with the demand of the Commission, but the attendance of a witness may not be required outside the State where he is found, resides, or transacts business and the production of evidence may not be required outside the State where such evidence is kept.

(c) Within twenty days after the service upon any person charged under section 706 of a demand by the Commission for the production of documentary evidence or for permission to examine or to copy evidence in conformity with the provisions of section 709(a), such person may file in the district court of the United States for the judicial district in which he resides, is found, or transacts business, and serve upon the Commission a petition for an order of such court modifying or setting aside such demand. The time allowed for compliance with the demand in whole or in part as deemed proper and ordered by the court shall not run during the pendency of such petition in the court. Such petition shall specify each ground upon which the petitioner relies in seeking such relief, and may be based upon any failure of such demand to comply with the provisions of this title or with the limitations generally applicable to compulsory process or upon any constitutional or other legal right or privilege of such person. No objection which is not raised by such a petition may be urged in the defense to a proceeding initiated by the Commission under subsection (b) for enforcement of such a demand unless such proceeding is commenced by the Commission prior to the expiration of the twenty-day period, or unless the court determines that the defendant could not reasonably have been aware of the availability of such ground of objection.

(d) In any proceeding brought by the Commission under subsection (b), except as provided in subsection (c) of this section, the defendant may petition the court for an order modifying or setting aside the demand of the Commission.

SEC. 711. (a) Every employer, employment agency, and labor organization, as the case may be, shall post and keep posted in conspicuous places upon its premises where notices to employees, applicants for employment, and members are customarily posted a notice to be prepared or approved by the Commission setting forth excerpts from or, summaries of, the pertinent provisions of this title and information pertinent to the filing of a complaint.

(b) A willful violation of this section shall be punishable by a fine of not more than $100 for each separate offense.

◆ Veterans' Preference

SEC. 712. Nothing contained in this title shall be construed to repeal or modify any Federal, State, territorial, or local law creating special rights or preference for veterans.

◆ Rules and Regulations

SEC. 713. (a) The Commission shall have authority from time to time to issue, amend, or rescind suitable procedural regulations to carry out the provisions of this title. Regulations issued under this section shall be in conformity with the standards and limitations of the Administrative Procedure Act.

(b) In any action or proceeding based on any alleged unlawful employment practice, no person shall be subject to any liability or punishment for or on account of (1) the commission by such person of an unlawful employment practice if he pleads and proves that the act or omission complained of was in good faith, in conformity with, and in reliance on any written interpretation or opinion of the Commission, or (2) the failure of such person to publish and file any information required by any provision of this title if he pleads and proves that he failed to publish and file such information in good faith, in conformity with the instructions of the Commission issued under this title regarding the filing of such information. Such a defense, if established, shall be a bar to the action or proceeding, notwithstanding that (A) after such act or omission, such interpretation or opinion is modified or rescinded or is determined by judicial authority to be invalid or of no legal effect, or (B) after publishing or filing the description and annual reports, such publication or filing is determined by judicial authority not to be in conformity with the requirements of this title.

◆ Forcibly Resisting the Commission or Its Representatives

SEC. 714. The provisions of section 111, title 18, United States Code, shall apply to officers, agents, and employees of the Commission in the performance of their official duties.

◆ Special Study by Secretary of Labor

SEC. 715. The Secretary of Labor shall make a full and complete study of the factors which might tend to result in discrimination in employment because of age and of the consequences of such discrimination on the economy and individuals affected. The Secretary of Labor shall make a report to the Congress not later than June 30, 1965, containing the results of such study and shall include in such report such recommendations for legislation to prevent arbitrary discrimination in employment because of age as he determines advisable.

◆ Effective Date

SEC. 716. (a) This title shall become effective one year after the date of its enactment.

(b) Notwithstanding subsection (a), sections of this title other than sections 703, 704, 706, and 707 shall become effective immediately.

(c) The President shall, as soon as feasible after the enactment of this title, convene one or more conferences for the purpose of enabling the leaders of groups whose members will be affected by this title to become familiar with the rights afforded and obligations imposed by its provisions, and for the purpose of making plans which will result in the fair and effective administration of this title when all of its provisions become effective. The President shall invite the participation in such conference or conferences of (1) the members of the President's Committee on Equal Employment Opportunity, (2) the members of the Commission on Civil Rights, (3) representatives of State and local agencies engaged in furthering equal employment opportunity, (4) representatives of private agencies engaged in furthering equal employment opportunity, and (5) representatives of employers, labor organizations, and employment agencies who will be subject to this title.

Title VIII—Registration and Voting Statistics

SEC. 801. The Secretary of Commerce shall promptly conduct a survey to compile registration and voting statistics in such geographic areas as may be recommended by the Commission on Civil Rights. Such a survey and compilation shall, to the extent recommended by the Commission on Civil Rights, only include a count of persons of voting age by race, color, and national origin, and determination of the extent to which such persons are registered to vote, and have voted in any statewide primary or general election in which the Members of the United States House of Representatives are nominated or elected, since January 1, 1960. Such information shall also be collected and compiled in connection with the Nineteenth Decennial Census, and at such other times as the Congress may prescribe. The provisions of section 9 and chapter 7 of title 13, United States Code, shall apply to any survey, collection, or compilation of registration and voting statistics carried out under this title: Provided, however, That no person shall be compelled to disclose his race, color, national origin, or questioned about his political party affiliation, how he voted, or the reasons therefore, nor shall any penalty be imposed for his failure or refusal to make such disclosure. Every person interrogated orally, by written survey or questionnaire or by any other means with respect to such information shall be fully advised with respect to his right to fail or refuse to furnish such information.

Title IX—Intervention and Procedure after Removal in Civil Rights Cases

SEC. 901. Title 28 of the United States Code, section 1447(d), is amended to read as follows:

"An order remanding a case to the State court from which it was removed is not reviewable on appeal or otherwise, except that an order remanding a case to the State court from which it was removed pursuant to section 1443 of this title shall be reviewable by appeal or otherwise."

SEC. 902. Whenever an action has been commenced in any court of the United States seeking relief from the denial of equal protection of the laws under the fourteenth amendment to the Constitution on account of race, color, religion, or national origin, the Attorney General for or in the name of the United States may intervene in such action upon timely application if the Attorney General certifies that the case is of general public importance. In such action the United States shall be entitled to the same relief as if it had instituted the action.

Title X—Establishment of Community Relations Service

SEC. 1001. (a) There is hereby established in and as a part of the Department of Commerce a Community Relations Service (hereinafter referred to as the "Service"), which shall be headed by a Director who shall be appointed by the President with the advice and consent of the Senate for a term of four years. The Director is authorized to appoint, subject to the civil service laws and regulations, such other personnel as may be necessary to enable the Service to carry out its functions and duties, and to fix their compensation in accordance with the Classification Act of 1949, as amended. The Director is further authorized to procure services as authorized by section 15 of the Act of August 2, 1946 (60 Stat. 810; 5 U.S.C. 55(a)), but at rates for individuals not in excess of $75 per diem.

(b) Section 106(a) of the Federal Executive Pay Act of 1956, as amended (5 U.S.C. 2205(a)), is further amended by adding the following clause thereto:

"(52) Director, Community Relations Service."

SEC. 1002. It shall be the function of the Service to provide assistance to communities and persons therein in resolving disputes, disagreements, or difficulties relating to discriminatory practices based on race, color, or national origin which impair the rights of persons in such communities under the Constitution or laws of the United States or which affect or may affect interstate commerce. The Service may offer its services in cases of such disputes, disagreements, or difficulties whenever, in its judgment, peaceful relations among the citizens of the community involved are threatened thereby, and it may offer its services either upon its own motion or upon the request of an appropriate State or local official or other interested person.

SEC. 1003. (a) The Service shall, whenever possible, in performing its functions, seek and utilize the cooperation of appropriate State or local, public, or private agencies.

(b) The activities of all officers and employees of the Service in providing conciliation assistance shall be conducted in confidence and without publicity, and the Service shall hold confidential any information acquired in the regular performance of its duties upon the understanding that it would be so held. No officer or employee of the Service shall engage in the performance of investigative or prosecuting functions of any department or agency in any litigation arising out of a dispute in which he acted on behalf of the Service. Any officer or other employee of the Service, who shall make public in any manner whatever any information in violation of this subsection, shall be deemed guilty of a misdemeanor and, upon conviction thereof, shall be fined not more than $1,000 or imprisoned not more than one year.

SEC. 1004. Subject to the provisions of sections 205 and 1003(b), the Director shall, on or before January 31 of each year, submit to the Congress a report of the activities of the Service during the preceding fiscal year.

Title XI—Miscellaneous

SEC. 1101. In any proceeding for criminal contempt arising under title II, III, IV, V, VI, or VII of this Act, the accused, upon demand therefore, shall be entitled to a trial by jury, which shall conform as near as may be to the practice in criminal cases. Upon conviction, the accused shall not be fined more than $1,000 or imprisoned for more than six months.

This section shall not apply to contempts committed in the presence of the court, or so near thereto as to obstruct the administration of justice, nor to the misbehavior, misconduct, or disobedience of any officer of the court in respect to writs, orders, or process of the court. No person shall be convicted of criminal contempt hereunder unless the act or omission constituting such contempt shall have been intentional, as required in other cases of criminal contempt.

Nor shall anything herein be construed to deprive courts of their power, by civil contempt proceedings, without a jury, to secure compliance with or to prevent obstruction of, as distinguished from punishment for violations of, any lawful writ, process, order, rule, decree, or command of the court in accordance with the prevailing usages of law and equity, including the power of detention.

SEC. 1102. No person should be put twice in jeopardy under the laws of the United States for the same act or omission. For this reason, an acquittal or conviction in a prosecution for a specific crime under the laws of the United States shall bar a proceeding for criminal contempt, which is based upon the same act or omission and which arises under the provisions of this Act; and an acquittal or conviction in a proceeding for criminal contempt, which arises under the provisions of this Act, shall bar a prosecution for a specific crime under the laws of the United States based upon the same act or omission.

SEC. 1103. Nothing in this Act shall be construed to deny, impair, or otherwise affect any right or authority of the Attorney General or of the United States or any agency or officer thereof under existing law to institute or intervene in any action or proceeding.

SEC. 1104. Nothing contained in any title of this Act shall be construed as indicating an intent on the part of Congress to occupy the field in which any such title operates to the exclusion of State laws on the same subject matter, nor shall any provision of this Act be construed as invalidating any provision of State law unless such provision is inconsistent with any of the purposes of this Act, or any provision thereof.

SEC. 1105. There are hereby authorized to be appropriated such sums as are necessary to carry out the provisions of this Act.

SEC. 1106. If any provision of this Act or the application thereof to any person or circumstances is held invalid, the remainder of the Act and the application of the provision to other persons not similarly situated or to other circumstances shall not be affected thereby.

PUBLIC LAW 88-408

Eighty-eighth Congress of the United States of America

AT THE SECOND SESSION

Begun and held at the City of Washington on Tuesday, the seventh day of January, one thousand nine hundred and sixty-four

Joint Resolution

To promote the maintenance of international peace and security in southeast Asia.

Whereas naval units of the Communist regime in Vietnam, in violation of the principles of the Charter of the United Nations and of international law, have deliberately and repeatedly attacked United States naval vessels lawfully present in international waters, and have thereby created a serious threat to international peace; and

Whereas these attacks are part of a deliberate and systematic campaign of aggression that the Communist regime in North Vietnam has been waging against its neighbors and the nations joined with them in the collective defense of their freedom; and

Whereas the United States is assisting the peoples of southeast Asia to protect their freedom and has no territorial, military or political ambitions in that area, but desires only that these peoples should be left in peace to work out their own destinies in their own way: Now, therefore, be it

Resolved by the Senate and House of Representatives of the United States of America in Congress assembled, That the Congress approves and supports the determination of the President, as Commander in Chief, to take all necessary measures to repel any armed attack against the forces of the United States and to prevent further aggression.

Sec. 2. The United States regards as vital to its national interest and to world peace the maintenance of international peace and security in southeast Asia. Consonant with the Constitution of the United States and the Charter of the United Nations and in accordance with its obligations under the Southeast Asia Collective Defense Treaty, the United States is, therefore, prepared, as the President determines, to take all necessary steps, including the use of armed force, to assist any member or protocol state of the Southeast Asia Collective Defense Treaty requesting assistance in defense of its freedom.

Sec. 3. This resolution shall expire when the President shall determine that the peace and security of the area is reasonably assured by international conditions created by action of the United Nations or otherwise, except that it may be terminated earlier by concurrent resolution of the Congress.

Speaker of the House of Representatives.

Acting President pro tempore of the Senate.

APPROVED

AUG 10 1964

Lyndon B. Johnson

The Gulf of Tonkin Resolution (National Archives and Records Administration)

GULF OF TONKIN RESOLUTION

"The United States regards as vital to its national interest ... the maintenance of international peace ... in southeast Asia."

Overview

The Gulf of Tonkin Resolution, approved by the U.S. Congress by an almost unanimous vote, marked the beginning of the Vietnam War, authorizing American military intervention "to promote the maintenance of international peace and security in southeast Asia." Thus, after years of providing indirect help to the South Vietnamese government against the Vietcong—Communist rebels supported by the North Vietnamese regime of Ho Chi Minh—the United States directly entered the conflict. The military escalation that followed the approval of the resolution led America into its longest armed conflict, in which the world's most powerful nation would fail to curb the resistance of a peasant people in spite of the enormous losses those people suffered.

President Lyndon B. Johnson and his administration managed to push the resolution through Congress with virtually no debate on August 7, 1964, following two alleged North Vietnamese attacks against the American destroyer *Maddox*; the second attack, in fact, never took place. In approving the resolution, Congress surrendered its control of American foreign policy into the hands of the president, allowing Johnson and his military aides to design and apply the military strategies that they considered most appropriate for conducting the war. The Gulf of Tonkin Resolution was repealed in June 1970, after nationwide protests against President Richard M. Nixon's decision to extend the conflict into Cambodia.

Context

After the end of the Second World War, despite American military and financial assistance, the French colonial regime in Vietnam faced a series of important defeats at the hands of the Vietminh, the Communist guerillas headed by Ho Chi Minh. These engagements culminated in early 1954 with the battle of Dien Bien Phu, between Ho Chi Minh's forces and the French troops stationed at the northwestern outpost of Dien Bien Phu. The battle lasted for several months, finally ending in May with a Vietminh victory. Later that year,

France and Ho Chi Minh's Democratic Republic of Vietnam signed the Geneva Accords of 1954, which divided Vietnam into two states at the seventeenth parallel. North Vietnam would be controlled by Ho Chi Minh's Communist forces, while South Vietnam would be governed by Bao Dai, the former emperor of Vietnam. This was a provisional agreement, and the whole country was to be unified after a national election scheduled for 1956. Neither the United States nor Bao Dai signed the Geneva Accords, fearing that they would amount to a Communist victory.

Bao Dai was soon replaced by Ngo Dinh Diem, a nationalist and anti-Communist. However, as a wealthy Catholic, he was not particularly popular in a nation of poor Buddhist peasants, and his dictatorial ways earned him further enemies. Because Diem was aware of his scant following, he refused, supported by the administration of President Dwight D. Eisenhower, to take part in the national election called by North Vietnam according to the Geneva Accords. American financial and military aid continued to pour into South Vietnam in the following years, and the country became dependent on the United States for its very existence. At the end of the 1950s, Diem's unpopularity prompted southern Communists to organize the National Liberation Front, known as the Vietcong. The rebels, drawing support from North Vietnam as well as from other anti-Diem organizations in South Vietnam, started a massive campaign of terror and assassination against government officials.

Seeking to counterbalance the cold war fiascos of the Bay of Pigs and the Berlin Wall, the administration of President John F. Kennedy continued to lend support to South Vietnam, ordering more financial aid and more American military personnel into the country in the hope of taming Diem's totalitarian methods. As Diem failed to adopt more democratic reforms and discontent for the regime peaked, the U.S. government authorized Central Intelligence Agency personnel to work with Vietnamese generals to stage a coup against Diem. Although Diem's assassination was initially welcomed by South Vietnamese, the event effectively left the country without a leader and with a weak and divided government. When Johnson became the new president, he committed himself to preventing the victory of Communism in Vietnam.

1954

April 26–July 21
Geneva Conference is attended by France and North Vietnam, with each nation signing the resulting Geneva Accords.

1955

January 1
The United States begins direct aid to South Vietnam, training its army and creating a national guard.

October 23
A rigged referendum, staged with the help of the United States, ousts the South Vietnamese emperor Bao Dai and gives control of the country to Ngo Dinh Diem.

1960

November 8
John F. Kennedy defeats Richard Nixon and becomes the thirty-fifth president of the United States.

December 20
The National Front for the Liberation of South Vietnam is established with the support of the Communist regime of North Vietnam.

1961

October 18
Diem declares a state of national emergency, assuming special powers and asking U.S. troops to be dispatched to South Vietnam.

1963

November 2
Diem is murdered during a coup organized by his generals with the support of the Central Intelligence Agency.

November 22
President John F. Kennedy is murdered in Dallas, Texas; Vice President Lyndon B. Johnson succeeds him.

1964

August 2
USS *Maddox* is attacked by North Vietnamese patrol boats while gathering intelligence in the Gulf of Tonkin off the coast of North Vietnam.

The Gulf of Tonkin incident of August 1964 occurred at a particularly crucial moment for President Johnson, who was concentrating on his Great Society reforms, intended to reduce poverty, improve education, extend civil rights, and prevent war. Johnson had also just begun his campaign for reelection against the Republican senator Barry Goldwater. He did not want the civil war between North and South Vietnam to turn into a larger conflict replicating what had happened in Korea ten years earlier. President Johnson was doubtful about how to act, but at the same time he could not appear weak and unpatriotic in comparison with Goldwater's staunch anti-Communism.

About the Author

The Gulf of Tonkin Resolution is a government act for which the identification of a specific author is impossible. Nevertheless, the secretaries of defense and state at the time, Robert McNamara and Dean Rusk, respectively, as well as Senator J. William Fulbright played key roles in encouraging Congress to pass the resolution without changes and with very little debate.

Both Rusk and McNamara appeared as witnesses before Congress to urge the passage of the resolution in the face of national emergency. President Johnson had retained Rusk and McNamara in the same positions that they had held in the Kennedy administration. Johnson was awed by the academic credentials of his advisers, and his feelings of educational inferiority toward them led him to rely heavily on their opinions, particularly in the arena of foreign policy.

Rusk was born in Cherokee County, Georgia, in 1909 and graduated from North Carolina's Davidson College in 1931. He was a Rhodes Scholar at St. John's College, Oxford, where he obtained an MA in philosophy, politics, and economics in 1934. After teaching at Mills College, in Oakland, California, for six years, he served as deputy chief of staff for the China-Burma-India theater during World War II. Upon leaving the military in 1946, he entered the State Department, where he held a variety of posts before President Kennedy appointed him head of the department. As secretary of state from 1961 to 1968, Rusk had to face several cold war emergencies, including the Cuban missile crisis, which precipitated the world to the brink of nuclear war. Rusk remained a convinced defender of American involvement in Vietnam, thus becoming a target of the antiwar demonstrations that spread throughout the country in the latter half of the 1960s. Rusk's reputation as a cold war warrior is confirmed by his vehement opposition to diplomatic recognition of Communist China. After stepping down as secretary of state in January 1969, Rusk accepted a professorship in international law at the University of Georgia, which he held until his retirement in 1984. He died in Athens, Georgia, in 1994.

Robert S. McNamara was born in 1916 in San Francisco. He graduated from the University of California, Berkeley, in 1937 and two years later earned a graduate degree at the Harvard Business School, then becoming a member of the Harvard faculty. After the Second World War, he was hired to revitalize Ford Motor Company, where his plans met with immediate success and allowed him to advance quickly through the corporate ranks. His career at Ford climaxed in 1960 when he became the first person outside the Ford family to assume the presidency of the company, a position that he resigned soon after to accept the role of secretary of defense, offered by President Kennedy. McNamara proved a successful innovator of military bureaucracy and a modernizer of the armed forces. At the time of the Gulf of Tonkin Resolution, McNamara strongly supported American intervention in Vietnam, and he continued to advocate the prosecution of the war until 1966. By then, he had grown disillusioned with the conflict and began to voice his doubts to Johnson in private; nevertheless, he publicly supported Johnson until 1968, when he left the administration to become the president of the World Bank. He retired from the World Bank in 1981 and worked on his memoir, *In Retrospect: The Tragedy and Lessons of Vietnam*, which was published in 1995. Therein, McNamara decries the policies that the Kennedy and Johnson administrations followed in Vietnam.

As the chairman of the Foreign Relations Committee and the floor manager for the Gulf of Tonkin Resolution, the Democratic senator J. William Fulbright was the most influential member of Congress to engineer the passage of the resolution. Although he would later be remembered for his opposition to the Vietnam War, Fulbright was one of the most vigorous supporters of the administration's approach in the early days of August 1964. He used his highly respected authority on foreign policy to convince senators with little knowledge of Vietnam that the resolution was necessary to restore order in the area. Fulbright refused the request by the Democratic senator Wayne Morse to hold regular hearings to explain to the Senate and to the American public the complex political and military situation in Vietnam; he insisted that a state of national emergency existed and thus opted for abbreviated hearings. Although he later regarded the Gulf of Tonkin Resolution as the biggest mistake in his long career, Senator Fulbright consistently defended it during the abbreviated Senate hearings of August 1964 and guided it toward passage.

James William Fulbright was born in Sumner, Missouri, in 1905. He graduated from the University of Arkansas and was then a Rhodes Scholar at Oxford. Back in the United States, he earned a law degree from George Washington University in 1934. Fulbright began his political career in 1942, winning a seat in the House of Representatives as a Democrat. His Fulbright Resolution committed the United States to taking part in the United Nations. In 1944 Fulbright was elected to the Senate, where he introduced the Fulbright Act in 1946, establishing an exchange program for scholars. He also played a crucial role in the downfall of Senator Joseph McCarthy and his Communist witch hunt. According to Arthur Schlesinger's memoir *A Thousand Days: John F. Kennedy in the White House*, that president considered Fulbright, a recognized authority on foreign policy, for the role of secretary of state. However, his

www.milestonedocuments.com

Time Line

1964

■ **August 4**
The *Maddox* and another destroyer, the *Turner Joy*, report a second attack by North Vietnamese patrols that, in fact, never took place; President Johnson announces on television that the United States would retaliate against the unprovoked attacks.

■ **August 7**
The House of Representatives and the Senate approve almost unanimously the Gulf of Tonkin Resolution.

■ **November 3**
Lyndon Johnson defeats the Republican senator Barry Goldwater in the presidential election, garnering 61 percent of the popular vote, one of the highest percentages in American history.

1965–1968

■ **March 2, 1965– November 1, 1968**
After the North Vietnamese attack the American military base at Pleiku, killing nine soldiers, the United States begins Operation Rolling Thunder, a massive but ultimately ineffectual campaign of aerial bombardment.

1965

■ **March 8**
American ground troops begin operations in South Vietnam.

1968

■ **January 30**
The North Vietnamese launch a vast military offensive during Tet, the holiday for the lunar new year, which has a shocking effect on American public opinion.

■ **March 16**
My Lai massacre takes place; more than three hundred Vietnamese civilians, most of them women and children, are tortured and killed by U.S. soldiers in the hamlet of My Lai.

■ **March 31**
Johnson announces on television a reduction of American troops in Vietnam and his decision not to run for reelection.

Time Line

1969

■ **November 12**
The freelance journalist
Seymour Hersh breaks the My
Lai story despite a military
cover-up, leading public
opposition against the war to
mount in the United States
and worldwide.

hostility to civil rights disqualified him; Senator Fulbright opposed measures for the integration of African Americans and the desegregation of American society throughout his career. From 1966 onward, Fulbright became an advocate for the suspension of American bombing in North Vietnam and for the beginning of peace talks. He remained in the U.S. Senate until 1974, when he lost the Democratic primary and retired. He died in 1995 in Washington, D.C.

Explanation and Analysis of the Document

The Gulf of Tonkin Resolution is grounded in the cold war rhetoric of the domino theory, which had become a cornerstone of American policies in Southeast Asia since the days of the Eisenhower administration. While the immediate concern of the resolution is the nation of South Vietnam, the overall focus is much broader; the wording of the document consistently relates the fate of South Vietnam to that of all of Southeast Asia. As such, the resolution fostered fears that Vietnam would be only the first of many countries to fall into Communist hands if Ho Chi Minh's North Vietnam were not effectively stopped.

The three paragraphs of the preamble define the Communist threat to the peace of Southeast Asia and are instrumental in justifying the operative sections that form the second part of the document. The first paragraph describes the North Vietnamese attacks against American ships as deliberate and repeated. Such attacks are in violation of "international law" and constitute a "threat to international peace." The second paragraph situates these attacks in the wider campaign of territorial expansion pursued by North Vietnam in Southeast Asia. The third paragraph states the purpose of American policy in the area: The United States does not seek colonies in Southeast Asia but simply wishes to help the people of the region maintain their freedom. The cold war rhetoric of the preamble makes clear that the future of South Vietnam is indissolubly linked to that of the wider region of Southeast Asia and to that of international peace in general. In the starkly divided world of the preamble, the United States is portrayed as the last rampart of freedom and democracy against the Communist regime of North Vietnam. Unlike North Vietnam, the United States does not aim to expand its influence in the area but simply wants to let the people decide their own future. This depiction contrasts with the recent history of heavy U.S. intervention in South Vietnam,

which had limited the country's self-determination; For example, support had been given to Ngo Dinh Diem to rig the referendum against Bao Dai and to refuse the 1956 election, which should have unified North and South Vietnam.

In fact, the preamble and, as a consequence, the whole document are based on incorrect premises. Although the United States is identified with legality and North Vietnam with aggression, the assertion that the American ships were lawfully present in international waters is not true. In his statement before the Senate's Committee on Armed Services and Committee on Foreign Relations on August 6, 1964, Secretary of Defense Robert McNamara stated that the *Maddox* was engaged "in a routine patrol in International waters of the Gulf of Tonkin off the North Viet Nam coast" (Siff, p. 117). Subsequent evidence, including McNamara's memoir, would show that the *Maddox* was in fact on an intelligence-gathering assignment, not a routine patrol. In addition, as Senator Morse pointed out in the brief debate that preceded the approval of the resolution, also uncertain was whether the ship was in international waters. Both North and South Vietnam recognized their territorial boundaries as extending twelve miles out to sea, and the *Maddox* had likely transgressed this perimeter. Some commentators, including Senator Morse, also stressed from the beginning of the incident the role of provocateur that U.S. destroyers often played in the area, acting as backups for South Vietnamese naval vessels attacking North Vietnamese territory. In addition, contrary to the text of the preamble, no coordinated attack against U.S. forces took place, and, as has been revealed by successive evidence, the second attack against the *Maddox* actually never happened at all.

The three operative sections of the resolution announce the unconditional approval by Congress of the military choices that the president may make as commander in chief to prevent further aggression against American forces (Section 1) and to protect from Communist aggression any member or protocol state of the Southeast Asia Collective Defense Treaty (Section 2). This treaty, which created the Southeast Asia Treaty Organization, had been signed in Manila in 1954 by Australia, France, New Zealand, Pakistan, the Philippines, Thailand, the United Kingdom, and the United States, granting military aid to the signatories against Communist aggression. Vietnam, Laos, and Cambodia, though not among the original signatories, were granted help by a protocol. As does the preamble, Section 2 makes clear that the Communist threat is casting its shadow on the whole region, not only on South Vietnam. The citation of the Southeast Asia Collective Defense Treaty is a curious choice, since, as the debate in the Senate made apparent, the United States was acting unilaterally, without consulting the other signatories of the treaty. Sections 1 and 2, the former authorizing the president to "repel any armed attack against the forces of the United States," effectively contemplate the use of preventive war. The resolution ends with the third operative section, which gives no precise expiration for the application of the resolution. In accordance with the wide latitude of powers given to the president, he is assigned the responsibility of deciding when peace and stability have been sufficiently reestablished in the area, such that the resolution can be terminated. The third section also states that the resolution can alternatively be terminated by Congress, and this is what happened on June 24, 1970, when the Senate voted overwhelmingly to repeal it.

Two passages of these final operative sections seemed troublesome to some senators at the time. The president was authorized "to take all necessary measures" to prevent further aggression against U.S. forces and "to take all necessary steps, including the use of armed force," to assist the countries of Southeast Asia in preserving their freedom. The wording is very vague, which has led commentators to speculate that Johnson wanted the support of the Senate without having a clear strategy in mind with regard to the development of war. At the time, Johnson insisted that he was not seeking an escalation of the ongoing Vietnamese conflict, and during his electoral campaign he reassured the American public that U.S. soldiers would not be employed to fight an Asian war. Using such strategies proved rewarding, as the president succeeded in painting himself as a moderate and reliable commander in chief. He also effectively characterized his Republican opponent, Barry Goldwater, as an extremist whose statements on the potential use of nuclear weapons to solve the Vietnam crisis disqualified him as a dependable leader. The famous "Daisy Girl" political commercial played effectively on fears that Goldwater might begin a nuclear war. (The ad, aired only once, featured a little girl counting out as she plucks daisy petals. When she reaches the number 9, a male voice takes over, counting down a missile launch to zero, after which the screen goes black and is replaced by a mushroom cloud.)

At the same time, President Johnson and his administration refused to clarify what taking "all necessary measures" and "all necessary steps, including the use of armed force," really entailed. The brief Senate debate that preceded the vote on the resolution hinged precisely on these two passages. Senator Wayne Morse criticized them as unconstitutional, as they would allow the president to conduct war almost unilaterally. Morse asserted that Article I of the Constitution gave the power to declare war to Congress, not to the president. Secretary of State Dean Rusk directly answered this criticism in his statement, explaining that the same authority was given to the president in the Formosa Resolution of 1955, the Middle East Resolution of 1957 (also known as the Eisenhower Doctrine), and the Cuba Resolution of 1962. In addition, he argued that the president had the constitutional right to take a limited degree of armed action to protect American interests, as was generally accepted, and that this had occurred in at least 85 instances. The resolution's vague reference to the use of armed force also stirred concerns about the possible intervention of land troops, as many senators feared another Korean War. To the concerns of Senator Daniel Brewster about the use of land troops, Senator Fulbright replied that nothing in the resolution contemplated such intervention,

The USS Maddox (AP Photo/DOD)

but, equally, nothing prevented it: "It would authorize whatever the Commander in Chief feels is necessary" (qtd. in Siff, p. 27).

Senator Gaylord Nelson was the only member of Congress to suggest an amendment to the resolution, limiting the powers of the president with regard to military intervention. The proposed amendment clearly stated that the "United States, seeking no extension of the present military conflict, will respond to provocation in a manner that is 'limited and fitting'" (qtd. in Siff, p. 36). The proposed change also unmistakably asserted that Congress held that the United States "should continue to attempt to avoid a direct military involvement in the Southeast Asian conflict" (qtd. in Siff, p. 36). Senator Fulbright refused the amendment not because he objected to it as a statement of policy but because its eventual approval would require a conference, and the state of national emergency made this unacceptable. Fulbright also contended that the views of the president were similar to those expressed in the amendment anyway; considering the military escalation that indeed followed the Gulf of Tonkin Resolution, this was a tragic misjudgment on Fulbright's part.

Audience

The audience for the Gulf of Tonkin Resolution was exceptionally wide, including all of the starkly divided world of the cold war. The United States was posing as a model and example to follow for its allies, with the resolution indicating that in difficult times, the American people, through their representatives in Congress, unite behind the president and overcome political divisions. This aspect of the situation was also alluded to by Lyndon Johnson himself in his televised address of August 4, 1964, following the alleged second attack against the *Maddox*. The president announced to the nation that he had been given "encouraging assurance" by leaders of both parties that "a resolution will be promptly introduced … and passed with

> "The Congress approves and supports the determination of the President, as Commander in Chief, to take all necessary measures to repel any armed attack against the forces of the United States and to prevent further aggression."
>
> (Section 1)

> "The United States regards as vital to its national interest and to world peace the maintenance of international peace and security in southeast Asia.... The United States is, therefore, prepared, as the President determines, to take all necessary steps, including the use of armed force, to assist any member or protocol state of the Southeast Asia Collective Defense Treaty requesting assistance in defense of its freedom."
>
> (Section 2)

> "We cannot tell what steps may in the future be required to meet Communist aggression in Southeast Asia. The unity and determination of the American people, through their Congress, should be declared in terms so firm that they cannot possibly be mistaken by other nations. The world has learned over fifty years of history that aggression is invited if there is doubt about the response. Let us leave today's aggressors in no doubt whatever."
>
> (Secretary of State Dean Rusk, qtd. in Siff, p. 125)

overwhelming support" (Siff, p. 114). He also explicitly thanked his Republican opponent in the presidential race, Senator Barry Goldwater, for supporting the statement that the president was making on television. The Gulf of Tonkin Resolution was also addressed to America's enemies from the Communist bloc, warning them that the United States was vigilant against aggression aimed at reducing the freedom of its allies, which was considered a national interest.

Impact

The Gulf of Tonkin Resolution had a tragic impact on American society. It led the United States into a cruel and expensive conflict that, in the end, the nation realized could not be won. Through the determined and firm resolution, Johnson effectively eliminated Vietnam as a topic of the campaign for the 1964 presidential election. However, the escalation of the war allowed by the resolution perma-

nently etched the tragedy of Vietnam into Johnson's second administration, drawing attention away from his vast and ambitious program for social reforms and civil rights, the Great Society. Estimates hold that more than 50,000 Americans died in Vietnam, while Vietnamese victims numbered over 2 million.

At first, Americans overwhelmingly supported the Gulf of Tonkin Resolution and the escalation of the conflict. The House approved the bill unanimously with only Representative Eugene Siler "pairing" against it (that is, leaving the chamber when the vote took place). The Senate voted 88–2 in favor of the resolution, with Wayne Morse and Ernest Gruening casting the only opposing votes. Over the years, the resolution became synonymous with "the arrogance of power," an expression used by Senator Fulbright as the title of the book in which he retracts his support for the resolution and the war. As subsequent evidence showed, Johnson and his administration used the Gulf of Tonkin Resolution to "inflate the incidental, almost non-event, into a major crisis" (Siff, p. xvi). They purposefully withheld information on the true nature of the mission of the *Maddox*, and they chose to ignore the legitimate doubts that surrounded the alleged second attack against the American destroyer from the very beginning.

A document once hailed as an example of patriotism, the Gulf of Tonkin Resolution is today considered a typical illustration of President Johnson's ability to manipulate Congress into passing his desired legislation. Critics of President George W. Bush's war in Iraq disparagingly branded his resolution to escalate the conflict against Saddam Hussein a second Gulf of Tonkin Resolution.

Related Documents

Siff, Ezra Y. *Why the Senate Slept: The Gulf of Tonkin Resolution and the Beginning of America's Vietnam War.* Westport, Conn.: Praeger, 1999. This volume contains a number of enlightening appendices, including President Johnson's television announcement of the resolution of August 4, 1964; the statements given by McNamara and Rusk before the Senate committees on August 6, 1964; President Johnson's speech at Johns Hopkins University of April 7, 1965, given a month after the beginning of Operation Rolling Thunder; and the text of the presidential message accompanying H. J. Resolution 447, of May 1965, effectively again asking Congress to grant the president wide powers to conduct the war.

Bibliography

■ Books

Beschloss, Michael, ed. *Taking Charge: The Johnson White House Tapes, 1963–1964.* New York: Simon & Schuster, 1997.

Fulbright, J. William. *The Arrogance of Power.* New York: Random House, 1966.

McNamara, Robert. *In Retrospect: The Tragedy and Lessons of Vietnam.* New York: Times Books, 1995.

Moïse, Edward E. *Tonkin Gulf and the Escalation of the Vietnam War.* Chapel Hill: University of North Carolina Press, 1996.

Schlesinger, Arthur, Jr. *A Thousand Days: John F. Kennedy in the White House.* Boston: Houghton Mifflin, 1965.

Sobel, Richard. *The Impact of Public Opinion on U.S. Foreign Policy since Vietnam: Constraining the Colossus.* New York: Oxford University Press, 2001.

■ Web Sites

"The Gulf of Tonkin Incident, 40 Years Later: Flawed Intelligence and the Decision for War in Vietnam." National Security Archive, George Washington University Web site.
http://www.gwu.edu/~nsarchiv/NSAEBB/NSAEBB132. Accessed on October 22, 2007.

McNamara, Robert S. "In Retrospect: The Tragedy and Lessons of Vietnam." Times Books Web site.
http://archives.obs-us.com/obs/english/books/mcnamara/ir0xv.htm. Accessed on February 27, 2008.

"Vietnam: 1954–1968." CNN "Cold War" Web site.
http://www.cnn.com/SPECIALS/cold.war/episodes/11/. Accessed on October 22, 2007.

"The Wars for Viet Nam: 1945 to 1975." Vassar College Web site.
http://vietnam.vassar.edu/index.html. Accessed on October 22, 2007.

—By Luca Prono

1. After the overwhelming vote by Congress in favor of the Gulf of Tonkin Resolution, Senator Wayne Morse declared that history would judge it to be an enormous mistake. Although several other senators, including George McGovern and Gaylord Nelson, shared Morse's concerns, they still voted for the resolution. Explain why the majority of the senators decided to cast their doubts aside and vote in favor of the resolution, and debate whether their behavior was justified.

2. In the preface to his 1995 memoir *In Retrospect*, the former defense secretary Robert McNamara notes, "We of the Kennedy and Johnson administrations who participated in the decisions on Vietnam acted according to what we thought were the principles and traditions of this nation. We made our decisions in light of those values. Yet we were wrong, terribly wrong. We owe it to future generations to explain why" (http://archives.obs-us.com/obs/english/books/mcnamara/ir0xv.htm). McNamara suggests that there is continuity between the Kennedy and Johnson administrations that was also evoked at the time of the Gulf of Tonkin Resolution. Comment on the accuracy of this suggestion, which McNamara himself seems to contradict later in his memoir, and explain why the Johnson administration felt the need to be perceived as continuing Kennedy's policies in the region.

3. In his statement before the Senate, Secretary of State Dean Rusk compared the Gulf of Tonkin Resolution to the Cuba Resolution of 1962, approved by Congress on October 3, 1962, less than two weeks before the Cuban missile crisis. Compare the political contexts and historical facts that led to the approval of the two documents as well as the role reserved for the president in each resolution to assess the correctness of Rusk's analogy.

4. Compare and contrast the Gulf of Tonkin Resolution with the Authorization for Use of Military Force against Iraq Resolution of 2002. Why have so many political and military commentators drawn parallels between the two documents? In addressing the question, comparatively analyze the nature of the events and evidence that prompted the resolutions, the role of the president contemplated in both documents, and the events that followed their approval.

Glossary

Charter of the United Nations	the 1945 treaty that established the United Nations, in which its members pledged to work for international peace
concurrent	having equal authority
consonant with	according to
deliberate	intentional
protest	assert
systematic	planned
thereby	by that means
vessels	ships
whereas	in view of the fact that

GULF OF TONKIN RESOLUTION

Joint Resolution: To Promote the Maintenance of International Peace and Security in Southeast Asia

Whereas naval units of the Communist regime in Vietnam, in violation of the principles of the Charter of the United Nations and of international law, have deliberately and repeatedly attacked United Stated naval vessels lawfully present in international waters, and have thereby created a serious threat to international peace; and

Whereas these attackers are part of deliberate and systematic campaign of aggression that the Communist regime in North Vietnam has been waging against its neighbors and the nations joined with them in the collective defense of their freedom; and

Whereas the United States is assisting the peoples of southeast Asia to protest their freedom and has no territorial, military or political ambitions in that area, but desires only that these people should be left in peace to work out their destinies in their own way: Now, therefore be it

Resolved by the Senate and House of Representatives of the United States of America in Congress assembled, That the Congress approves and supports the determination of the President, as Commander in Chief, to take all necessary measures to repel any armed attack against the forces of the United States and to prevent further aggression.

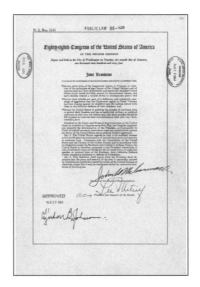

Section 2. The United States regards as vital to its national interest and to world peace the maintenance of international peace and security in southeast Asia. Consonant with the Constitution of the United States and the Charter of the United Nations and in accordance with its obligations under the Southeast Asia Collective Defense Treaty, the United States is, therefore, prepared, as the President determines, to take all necessary steps, including the use of armed force, to assist any member or protocol state of the Southeast Asia Collective Defense Treaty requesting assistance in defense of its freedom.

Section 3. This resolution shall expire when the President shall determine that the peace and security of the area is reasonably assured by international conditions created by action of the United Nations or otherwise, except that it may be terminated earlier by concurrent resolution of the Congress.

S. 1564

Eighty-ninth Congress of the United States of America

AT THE FIRST SESSION

Begun and held at the City of Washington on Monday, the fourth day of January,
one thousand nine hundred and sixty-five

An Act

To enforce the fifteenth amendment to the Constitution of the United States,
and for other purposes.

Be it enacted by the Senate and House of Representatives of the
United States of America in Congress assembled, That this Act shall
be known as the "Voting Rights Act of 1965".

SEC. 2. No voting qualification or prerequisite to voting, or standard,
practice, or procedure shall be imposed or applied by any State or
political subdivision to deny or abridge the right of any citizen of
the United States to vote on account of race or color.

SEC. 3. (a) Whenever the Attorney General institutes a proceeding
under any statute to enforce the guarantees of the fifteenth amendment in any State or political subdivision the court shall authorize
the appointment of Federal examiners by the United States Civil
Service Commission in accordance with section 6 to serve for such
period of time and for such political subdivisions as the court shall
determine is appropriate to enforce the guarantees of the fifteenth
amendment (1) as part of any interlocutory order if the court determines that the appointment of such examiners is necessary to enforce
such guarantees or (2) as part of any final judgment if the court finds
that violations of the fifteenth amendment justifying equitable relief
have occurred in such State or subdivision: *Provided,* That the court
need not authorize the appointment of examiners if any incidents of
denial or abridgement of the right to vote on account of race or color
(1) have been few in number and have been promptly and effectively
corrected by State or local action, (2) the continuing effect of such
incidents has been eliminated, and (3) there is no reasonable probability of their recurrence in the future.

(b) If in a proceeding instituted by the Attorney General under
any statute to enforce the guarantees of the fifteenth amendment in
any State or political subdivision the court finds that a test or device
has been used for the purpose or with the effect of denying or abridging the right of any citizen of the United States to vote on account
of race or color, it shall suspend the use of tests and devices in such
State or political subdivisions as the court shall determine is appropriate and for such period as it deems necessary.

(c) If in any proceeding instituted by the Attorney General under
any statute to enforce the guarantees of the fifteenth amendment in
any State or political subdivision the court finds that violations of the
fifteenth amendment justifying equitable relief have occurred within
the territory of such State or political subdivision, the court, in
addition to such relief as it may grant, shall retain jurisdiction for
such period as it may deem appropriate and during such period no
voting qualification or prerequisite to voting, or standard, practice,
or procedure with respect to voting different from that in force or
effect at the time the proceeding was commenced shall be enforced
unless and until the court finds that such qualification, prerequisite,
standard, practice, or procedure does not have the purpose and will
not have the effect of denying or abridging the right to vote on
account of race or color: *Provided,* That such qualification, prerequisite, standard, practice, or procedure may be enforced if the
qualification, prerequisite, standard, practice, or procedure has been
submitted by the chief legal officer or other appropriate official of
such State or subdivision to the Attorney General and the Attorney
General has not interposed an objection within sixty days after such

The Voting Rights Act of 1965 (National Archives and Records Administration)

"No voting qualification ... shall ... deny or abridge the right of any citizen of the United States to vote on account of race or color."

Overview

The Voting Rights Act of 1965 has been described as one of the most successful pieces of civil rights legislation ever adopted by the U.S. Congress. Coming at a time when, despite decades of reform efforts, African Americans were still substantially disenfranchised in many southern states, the act employed various measures and procedures to restore suffrage to excluded minority voters in the South and later in the nation as a whole. In doing this, the Voting Rights Act permitted, and even required, the federal government to intrude in matters previously reserved to the individual states, significantly reworking the balance between state and federal powers. Furthermore, the act gave reformers the tools they needed to radically transform election laws and procedures. The result was the rapid integration of African Americans and, later on, members of language minorities, into the electoral process. In time, the act brought about a transformation in politics and the election of thousands of African Americans, Hispanics, and Asian Americans to political office. The outcome, in the words of the sociologist Chandler Davidson and the political scientist Bernard Grofman, was nothing less than a "quiet revolution," a reshaping of politics first in the South and later across the nation.

Context

By the 1960s, southern efforts to disenfranchise African American voters had been in place for the better part of a century; blacks had been denied the vote by southern election officials through means both fair and foul. Among the obstacles placed before black voters were unfairly applied literacy and comprehension tests, in which voters had to read, understand, or interpret sections of state constitutions to the satisfaction of white (and usually hostile) election officials; complicated registration requirements that excluded minority voters on technical grounds; and financial barriers such as poll taxes. Intimidation and threats of violence were also effective means of keeping southern blacks from attending the polls. One of the simplest ways of undermin-

ing the black vote involved setting up polling places in areas inconvenient for blacks. Many polling places were placed in distant locations or in the middle of white sections of the town or county; similarly, some were put in businesses owned by known opponents of African American suffrage. Finally, in efforts to ensure that blacks had as little voice as possible in government through the election process, state legislatures across the South implemented rules prohibiting blacks from voting in the politically dominant Democratic Party primaries. Since Democratic candidates almost always won in the general elections, this particular method of exclusion was extraordinarily effective.

The South's system of race-based vote denial, which was well entrenched by the start of the twentieth century, came under increasing attack from the 1930s onward. By 1944 the National Association for the Advancement of Colored People (NAACP), a leader in the fight against race-based disenfranchisement via the courts, had pushed the Supreme Court to declare the all-white Democratic primary held in Texas—and by implication, similar institutions in other southern states—to be unconstitutional. Political pressure from the civil rights movement in the 1950s, along with further litigation by the NAACP, led to the passage of two civil rights acts—one in 1957 and the other in 1960—each of which empowered the Justice Department to bring suit against unconstitutional vote-denial techniques. Finally, the Civil Rights Act of 1964 sped up the ability of three-judge courts to hear voting rights cases, required that any literacy tests employed be given entirely in writing, demanded that black registration be based upon the same voter qualifications as those applied to whites, and allowed for the temporary appointment of federal voting registrars.

Still, despite the best efforts of leaders of the civil rights movement and the federal government, African American disenfranchisement remained largely intact as the 1960s approached the midway point. As late as 1964, black voter registration in the Deep South state of Mississippi stood at only 6.7 percent—which was at least an increase from the rate of 2 percent of a mere two years earlier. Conditions were admittedly better in other states; African American registration throughout the Deep South, where the majority of blacks lived, stood at 22.5 percent in 1964, while in the border-state region, which included such states as

1868

■ **July 9**
Ratification of the Fourteenth Amendment, which would become one of the foundations of vote expansion.

1870

■ **February 3**
Ratification of the Fifteenth Amendment, prohibiting any discrimination in voting based on race, color, or previous condition of slavery; Congress passed the Voting Rights Act in 1965 under this amendment.

1898

■ Louisiana imposes a literacy test as a prerequisite for voting.

1900

■ North Carolina imposes a poll tax and adopts literacy tests administered by local registrars (who had full discretion as to which parts of the state constitution applicants had to read) as its primary tool of vote denial.

1907

Georgia imposes a literacy test as a prerequisite for voting.

1944

■ **April 3**
Supreme Court invalidates the all-white primary in Texas and by implication those across the South in *Smith v. Allwright.*

1949

■ The Georgia state legislature passes a law under which those who fail to vote for two years are removed from voter rolls, while those registering or re-registering have to pass either a literacy test or a citizenship test administered by local election registrars; this law effectively excludes most blacks from the polls.

1957

■ The Alabama state legislature gerrymanders the municipal boundaries of Tuskegee to exclude all but four or five of the city's four hundred or so qualified black voters from city elections.

Florida, Texas, Tennessee, and Arkansas, registration rates averaged 43 percent. Regardless, come Election Day, the majority of southern blacks were yet unable to cast ballots.

The root of this problem lay in white southerners' extreme unwillingness to accept any court orders or administrative programs reversing disenfranchisement laws. Every time the courts or Justice Department overturned laws aimed at disenfranchising southern black voters, southern election officials turned to new (or, at the least, different) techniques to achieve the same discriminatory end—techniques not covered by the courts' orders and thus still permissible until invalidated by another court proceeding. Whenever the courts seemed about to invalidate these new procedures, southern election officials simply adopted still other methods of disenfranchisement, starting the whole process over once more. In consequence, opponents of black vote denial were forced to initiate court case after court case in their efforts to gain the vote and to do so with very few practical gains.

The Voting Rights Act, which passed in 1965, was expressly designed to attack the sources of delay in the case-by-case litigation approach, as the nineteen sections of the act imposed a completely new enforcement methodology with respect to voting rights violations. The act not only outlawed vote denial based on race or color—and later ethnicity—but also gave both the executive branch and the federal courts powerful new abilities and regulations. Among them were the power to appoint federal examiners and observers in whatever numbers the president felt necessary, prohibitions on literacy tests and poll taxes, and rules outlawing any action "under color of the law" that prevented qualified citizens from voting or having their votes fairly counted. Most important of all, the Voting Rights Act froze all southern election laws in place as of its passage. If local or state officials wanted to change laws or procedures, they would have to receive clearance from the Justice Department or the federal courts beforehand. In this way, the southern strategy of using ever-shifting techniques of voter denial to derail election reforms was effectively ended.

About the Author

Pressure for reform of voting rights legislation had been growing for years. In 1963 the federal Commission on Civil Rights announced that the only way to guarantee all citizens the right to vote was through federal legislation that spelled out clear and uniform voter standards. When the Civil Rights Act of 1964 did not go far enough to protect black voting, the Southern Christian Leadership Conference took the risky step of staging a voting registration drive that featured an organized march in Selma, Alabama, in early 1965; their hope was that the expected violent response to the march by local officials would increase public pressure for a voting rights act. The state police indeed produced a public spectacle under the leadership of the racist Selma sheriff, Jim Clark, using excessive and unjustified violence against the protesters, including frequent beatings of demonstrators and mass arrests. The leaders of the drive were thus successful in putting pressure on President Lyndon B. Johnson to address the need for an effective voting rights act.

The bill that would become the Voting Rights Act of 1965 was sent to Congress by President Johnson on March 15, 1965. Johnson noted in his message to Congress as he submitted the bill, "Every device of which human ingenuity is capable has been used to deny" blacks their right to vote. He continued: "It is wrong—deadly wrong—to deny any of your fellow Americans the right to vote in this country" (http://millercenter.org/scripps/digitalarchive/speeches/spe_1965_0315_johnson). The Senate passed the bill on May 11, after a successful cloture vote on March 23, by a vote of 77 to 19; the House then passed it by a vote of 333 to 85 on July 10; over the following three weeks, the differences between the two bills were resolved in conference. The House passed the conference report on August 3 by a vote of 328 to 74 and the Senate on August 4 by a vote of 79 to 18. President Johnson signed the Voting Rights Act into law on August 6, 1965.

Explanation and Analysis of the Document

Totaling nineteen sections, the Voting Rights Act of 1965 includes both permanent rule changes regulating the voting process nationwide and temporary special provisions designed to attack specific racial injustices in the South (and after 1970, nationwide with respect to language minorities). Before 1980 the temporary provisions—found primarily in sections 4 to 9 and renewed and amended in 1970, 1974, 1982, and 2006—had the greatest impact on minority voting rights. Designed in direct response to the ongoing problems faced by African Americans and the Justice Department in combating southern disenfranchisement, these sections provide for direct federal intervention in the South to protect minority voting rights and place authority to enforce these rights directly in the hands of the executive branch. This dual objective was implemented in three ways.

First, section 4 creates a triggering formula that imposes federal executive authority over any state that employs such voter-limiting devices as literacy tests to determine voter qualifications and in which, as of November 1, 1964, less than 50 percent of voting-age residents are registered. Those states that meet these criteria—between 1965 and 1975, this group included six southern states in whole and parts of another—automatically fall under the jurisdiction of the act's various temporary requirements.

Second, later in section 4, comes a direct assault on the tools of vote denial then in use across the South. This portion of the act abolishes the most significant barriers to black voting: literacy tests, exams measuring "good moral character" and "ability to … understand," and the requirement that a registered voter vouch for a potential voter. Extended by Congress for another five years in 1970, these prohibitions were made permanent in 1975, at which time another triggering formula was added, applying to states that discriminated against language-minority groups, such as Texas.

1957

■ **September 9**
President Dwight D. Eisenhower signs into law a civil rights act granting the Justice Department authority to intervene in voting rights matters.

1960

■ **May 6**
President Eisenhower signs into law a civil rights act increasing the powers of the Justice Department in voting rights suits.

1964

■ **July 2**
President Lyndon B. Johnson signs into law the Civil Rights Act of 1964, which aggressively attacks most forms of race-based discrimination; voting rights, however, are not explicitly covered by the new law.

1965

■ **August 6**
President Johnson signs the Voting Rights Act into law.

1966

■ **March 7**
In *South Carolina v. Katzenbach*, the Supreme Court upholds the Voting Rights Act as a valid exercise of Congress's plenary power to enforce the Fifteenth Amendment.

■ **March 24**
In *Harper v. Virginia Board of Elections*, the Court declares poll taxes unconstitutional. In separate cases, district courts order state officials in Mississippi and Louisiana to provide illiterate voters with any assistance needed to cast ballots.

1969

■ **March 3**
In *Allen v. State Board of Elections*, the Supreme Court holds that the Voting Rights Act prohibits discrimination by vote dilution as well as by vote denial; invoking the "one person, one vote" requirement of *Reynolds v. Sims* (377 U.S. 533 [1964]), the Court rules that laws seeking to dilute the voting strength of minorities are constitutionally impermissible.

1969

■ **June 2**
The Supreme Court declares literacy tests unconstitutional in *Gaston County v. United States*.

1970

■ Congress reauthorizes the Voting Rights Act.

■ **December 21**
The Supreme Court upholds the act's suspension of literacy tests in *Oregon v. Mitchell*.

1975

■ Congress renews the Voting Rights Act, amending it to include members of minorities such as Hispanics and Asian Americans within the special provisions.

1980

■ **April 22**
In *City of Mobile v. Bolden*, the Supreme Court demands that plaintiffs must prove willful discrimination in voting-dilution matters, throwing a shadow over voting rights litigation.

1982

■ Congress renews the Voting Rights Act, amending it so that proof of discriminatory effect alone, rather than proof of intent to discriminate, would be necessary to overturn laws; this revision allowed for the immediate filing of hundreds of vote-dilution suits.

1986

■ **June 30**
In *Thornburg v. Gingles*, the Supreme Court imposes a new standard in vote-dilution cases, demanding that "the minority group ... demonstrate that it is sufficiently large and geographically compact to constitute a majority in a single-member district"; otherwise, the "form of the district cannot be responsible for minority voters' inability to elect candidates" (478 U.S. 30 [1986]).

Third, sections 5 through 9 expand the federal government's power and authority to implement these and other reforms. Most important in this regard is section 5, designed expressly to check the seemingly endless cycle by which southern states replaced one discriminatory law with another every time the old requirements were suspended or declared unconstitutional. To achieve this end, all state voting statutes and procedures in place as of November 1, 1964, are frozen pending federal approval for proposed changes. This meant that any state or county covered by the act's triggering formula that sought to modify its voting laws would first have to gain approval for the changes by submitting proposed revisions to the Justice Department and proving that they did "not have the purpose and ... [would] not have the effect of denying or abridging the right to vote on account of race or color." All changes not cleared ahead of time by the Justice Department, which had sixty days to object, were legally barred from implementation. Alternately, a state could file for a declaratory judgment from the district court for the District of Columbia, whose positive response served the same result as preclearance by the Justice Department.

Of lesser importance than section 5 but still significant in promoting change, sections 6 and 7 grant the attorney general jurisdiction to appoint voting examiners to certify that legally qualified voters are free to register. Section 8 permits the attorney general to assign, as needed, federal observers to oversee the actual voting process in those areas covered by the triggering formula. Elsewhere, passages define the terms *vote* and *voting* for the purposes of the act (section 14), set out criminal penalties for violating the act (section 12), prohibit voter fraud and outlaw any action "under color of law" preventing qualified voters from voting or having their votes fairly counted (section 11), and suggest to the attorney general that he bring suit challenging the poll taxes still in use in four states (section 10). At the beginning of the document, section 2 accomplishes the fundamental justice of prohibiting discrimination in voting based on race or color.

Audience

As with most forms of legislation, the intended audience of the Voting Rights Act of 1965 was twofold. The first category included the judicial and executive offices that made up the enforcement arm of the federal government—in particular, the federal courts of the South and the Justice Department. The act was expressly designed to attack the perceived sources of delay in the case-by-case litigation approach, including obstructionist southern federal judges and the ability of southern governments to come up with unending series of inventive new ways to deny blacks the vote. The nineteen sections of the act imposed a completely new enforcement methodology for voting rights, outlawing vote denial in any form based on race or color and giving both the executive branch and the courts powerful new means to enforce the right to vote. In a very real sense, the

Voting Rights Act was a call to arms to the federal courts and the federal bureaucracy to finally act to fully protect, preserve, and even enhance the voting rights of minorities.

The second intended audience encompassed the many levels of southern government involved in creating and maintaining race-based disenfranchisement. As the president's comments at the issuing of the act made clear, race-based vote denial was incompatible with evolving visions of American democracy. The act's nineteen sections made clear this incompatibility and stressed the need—and the methods that would be used—to reform this unacceptable situation.

Impact

In the years following its passage, the Voting Rights Act of 1965 became one of the most effective tools in the advancement of racial integration across the South. As cited in literally hundreds of separate litigations, the act's provisions forced major changes in the ways that southern states ran their elections. Most states and municipalities were forced to shift away from at-large election formats, whereby all candidates for a similar office (such as county commissioner) ran against one another no matter where they resided in the county, and the top vote-getters countywide were declared the winners. Further, where possible, every effort was taken to encourage the creation of minority-majority districts, in which minorities made up the majorities. The result in terms of minority officeholding was explosive. In 1965 the number of black public officials nationwide, of any level or significance, numbered fewer than 100. By 1989 the number of African American elected officials stood at 3,265, or 9.8 percent of all offices. By 2000 the number of minority officeholders in any category had increased to almost five thousand. Given that as late as 1944 only about 3 percent of southern blacks were even registered to vote and that none had held elective office since the turn of the century, the changes in southern politics generated by the Voting Rights Act were truly extraordinary. These changes amounted to a reconstruction of southern political power so profound and extensive that it was, in Davidson and Grofman's words, nothing less than a "quiet revolution" in southern politics.

Related Documents

"Allen v. State Board of Elections, 393 U.S. 544 (1969)." U.S. Supreme Court Media "Oyez" Web site. http://www.oyez.org/cases/1960-1969/1968/1968_3/. Accessed on March 5, 2008. In this later important case, the Supreme Court extended the reach of the Voting Rights Act from prohibiting clear-cut cases of vote denial to also prohibiting the much more ambiguous problem of vote dilution.

Civil Rights Act of 1964, Public Law 88-352, *U.S. Statutes at Large* 241 (1964): 78. National Archives "Our Documents" Web site. http://www.ourdocuments.gov/doc.php?flash=true&doc=97. Accessed on March 5, 2008. The Civil Rights Act of 1964 was the

Time Line

1993

June 28
Supreme Court rules in *Shaw v. Reno* that districts cannot be reapportioned specifically to concentrate minority populations in certain districts.

2006

July
Congress reauthorizes the Voting Rights Act.

other great civil rights law passed under the urging of President Lyndon Johnson; in a very real sense, this act and the Voting Rights Act of 1965 were companion works of lawmaking.

"Reynolds v. Sims, 377 U.S. 533 (1964)." FindLaw Web site. http://caselaw.lp.findlaw.com/scripts/getcase.pl?court=US&vol=377&invol=533. Accessed on March 5, 2008. In this case, the Supreme Court held that the equal protection clause of the Constitution required that one person's vote be worth as much as another's.

"South Carolina v. Katzenbach, 383 U.S. 301 (1966)." U.S. Supreme Court Media "Oyez" Web site. http://www.oyez.org/cases/1960-1969/1965/1965_22_orig/. Accessed on March 5, 2008. In the first test of the Voting Rights Act in the Supreme Court, with Chief Justice Earl Warren presiding, the justices upheld the act and all of its procedures, including the controversial preclearance requirement.

"Thornburg v. Gingles, 478 U.S. 30 (1986)." FindLaw Web site. http://caselaw.lp.findlaw.com/scripts/getcase.pl?navby=case&court=US&vol=478&page=30. Accessed on March 5, 2008. In this case, the Supreme Court imposed a new standard in vote-dilution cases, demanding that "the minority group ... demonstrate that it is sufficiently large and geographically compact to constitute a majority in a single-member district."

Bibliography

■ Articles

Binion, Gayle. "The Implementation of Section 5 of the 1965 Voting Rights Act: A Retrospective on the Role of Courts." *Western Political Quarterly* 32, no. 2 (1979): 154–173.

■ Books

Ball, Howard, Dale Krane, and Thomas P. Lauth. *Compromised Compliance: Implementation of the 1965 Voting Rights Act*. Westport, Conn.: Greenwood Press, 1982.

Davidson, Chandler, and Bernard Grofman, eds. *Quiet Revolution in the South: The Impact of the Voting Rights Act, 1965–1990*. Princeton, N.J.: Princeton University Press, 1994.

www.milestonedocuments.com

President Lyndon B. Johnson signs the Voting Rights Act in a ceremony in the President's Room near the Senate chambers in Washington, D.C., August 6, 1965. (AP Photo)

Grofman, Bernard, and Chandler Davidson, eds., *Controversies in Minority Voting: The Voting Rights Act in Perspective*. Washington, D.C.: Brookings Institution, 1992.

Landsberg, Brian K. *Free at Last to Vote: The Alabama Origins of the 1965 Voting Rights Act*. Lawrence: University Press of Kansas, 2007.

Lawson, Steven F. *In Pursuit of Power: Southern Blacks and Electoral Politics, 1965–1982*. New York: Columbia University Press, 1985.

———. *Black Ballots: Voting Rights in the South, 1944–1969*. Lanham, Md.: Lexington Books, 1999.

Perman, Michael. *Struggle for Mastery: Disfranchisement in the South, 1888–1908*. Chapel Hill: University of North Carolina Press, 2001.

Valelly, Richard M., ed. *The Voting Rights Act: Securing the Ballot*. Washington, D.C.: CQ Press, 2006.

■ Web Sites

"The Civil Rights Era: Sit-ins, Freedom Rides, and Demonstrations." Library of Congress "African American Odyssey" Web site.
    http://memory.loc.gov/ammem/aaohtml/exhibit/aopart9b.html. Accessed on March 5, 2008.

Conroy, Terrye. "The Voting Rights Act of 1965: A Selected Annotated Bibliography." American Association of Law Libraries Web site.
    http://www.aallnet.org/products/pub_llj_v98n04/2006-39.pdf. Accessed on March 5, 2008.

"Fact Sheet: Voting Rights Act Reauthorization and Amendments Act of 2006." The White House Web site.
    http://www.whitehouse.gov/news/releases/2006/07/20060727-1.html. Accessed on March 5, 2008.

"Introduction to Federal Voting Rights Laws: The Voting Rights Act of 1965." United States Department of Justice Web site.
    http://www.usdoj.gov/crt/voting/intro/intro_b.htm. Accessed on March 5, 2008.

"Lyndon B. Johnson Speeches: Speech before Congress on Voting Rights Act (March 15, 1965)." Miller Center of Public Affairs Web site.
    http://millercenter.org/scripps/digitalarchive/speeches/spe_1965_0315_johnson. Accessed on March 5, 2008.

"Primer: The Voting Rights Act." PBS "NOW" Web site.
    http://www.pbs.org/now/shows/235/voting-rights-act.html. Accessed on March 5, 2008.

"Protect Voting Rights: Renew the VRA." Renew the VRA Web site.
    http://www.renewthevra.org/. Accessed on March 5, 2008.

"No voting qualification or prerequisite to voting, or standard, practice, or procedure shall be imposed or applied by any State or political subdivision to deny or abridge the right of any citizen of the United States to vote on account of race or color."

(Section 2)

"To assure that the right of citizens of the United States to vote is not denied or abridged on account of race or color, no citizen shall be denied the right to vote in any Federal, State, or local election because of his failure to comply with any test or device."

(Section 4a)

"At times history and fate meet at a single time in a single place to shape a turning point in man's unending search for freedom.... So it was last week in Selma, Alabama."

(Lyndon B. Johnson, "Speech before Congress on Voting Rights," http://millercenter.org/scripps/digitalarchive/speeches/spe_1965_0315_johnson)

"Every American citizen must have an equal right to vote.... Yet the harsh fact is that in many places in this country men and women are kept from voting simply because they are Negroes.... It is wrong—deadly wrong—to deny any of your fellow Americans the right to vote in this country. There is no issue of States' rights or national rights. There is only the struggle for human rights."

(Lyndon B. Johnson, "Speech before Congress on Voting Rights," http://millercenter.org/scripps/digitalarchive/speeches/spe_1965_0315_johnson)

"We here hold that the portions of the Voting Rights Act properly before us are a valid means for carrying out the commands of the Fifteenth Amendment. Hopefully, millions of non-white Americans will now be able to participate for the first time on an equal basis in the government under which they live."

(Chief Justice Earl Warren, Opinion of the Court in *South Carolina v. Katzenbach*, 383 U.S. 301 [1966])

"The Act was drafted to make the guarantees of the Fifteenth Amendment finally a reality for all citizens."

(Chief Justice Earl Warren, Majority Opinion in *Allen v. State Board of Elections*, 393 U.S. 544 [1969])

Simon, Scott. "Andrew Young and the Voting Rights Act of 1965." NPR Web site.
   http://www.npr.org/templates/story/story.php?storyId=4788074. Accessed on March 5, 2008.

"Voting Rights Act of 1965." The Dirksen Congressional Center "CongressLink" Web site.
   http://www.congresslink.org/print_basics_histmats_votingrights_contents.htm. Accessed on March 5, 2008.

—By Charles L. Zelden

Questions for Further Study

1. The Voting Rights Act of 1965 was designed to attack the perceived sources of delay in the reform of southern voting procedures. Through the act, Congress sought to combat the vote-denial problem in various ways, empowering officials at different levels of government. Why do you think that Congress distributed authority for enforcement between the executive and judicial branches? Which branch do you think Congress intended to carry the primary enforcement burden here, and why? Is this the way events played out? Why or why not?

2. Why was preclearance viewed as a substantially novel—even radical—approach to the enforcement of minority voting rights? What legal or constitutional doctrines does this approach come into conflict with? Is preclearance compatible with federalism?

3. In what ways was the Voting Rights Act of 1965 similar to and different from other civil rights legislation of the era? In particular, how do its focus and approach to enforcement compare and contrast with those of the Civil Rights Act of 1964?

Glossary

affidavits	written statements made under oath before an authorized official
American-flag schools	schools located in the United States or in U.S. territories
poll tax	a tax requiring a person to pay a fee before being allowed to vote

Voting Rights Act of 1965

An Act to Enforce the Fifteenth Amendment to the Constitution of the United States, and For Other Purposes

Be it enacted by the Senate and House of Representatives of the United States of America in Congress assembled, That this Act shall be known as the "Voting Rights Act of 1965."

SEC. 2. No voting qualification or prerequisite to voting, or standard, practice, or procedure shall be imposed or applied by any State or political subdivision to deny or abridge the right of any citizen of the United States to vote on account of race or color.

SEC. 3. (a) Whenever the Attorney General institutes a proceeding under any statute to enforce the guarantees of the fifteenth amendment in any State or political subdivision the court shall authorize the appointment of Federal examiners by the United States Civil Service Commission in accordance with section 6 to serve for such period of time and for such political subdivisions as the court shall determine is appropriate to enforce the guarantees of the fifteenth amendment (1) as part of any interlocutory order if the court determines that the appointment of such examiners is necessary to enforce such guarantees or (2) as part of any final judgment if the court finds that violations of the fifteenth amendment justifying equitable relief have occurred in such State or subdivision: Provided, That the court need not authorize the appointment of examiners if any incidents of denial or abridgement of the right to vote on account of race or color (1) have been few in number and have been promptly and effectively corrected by State or local action, (2) the continuing effect of such incidents has been eliminated, and (3) there is no reasonable probability of their recurrence in the future.

(b) If in a proceeding instituted by the Attorney General under any statute to enforce the guarantees of the fifteenth amendment in any State or political subdivision the court finds that a test or device has

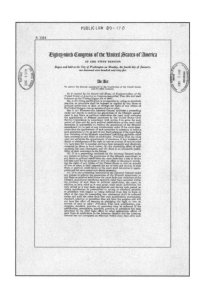

been used for the purpose or with the effect of denying or abridging the right of any citizen of the United States to vote on account of race or color, it shall suspend the use of tests and devices in such State or political subdivisions as the court shall determine is appropriate and for such period as it deems necessary.

(c) If in any proceeding instituted by the Attorney General under any statute to enforce the guarantees of the fifteenth amendment in any State or political subdivision the court finds that violations of the fifteenth amendment justifying equitable relief have occurred within the territory of such State or political subdivision, the court, in addition to such relief as it may grant, shall retain jurisdiction for such period as it may deem appropriate and during such period no voting qualification or prerequisite to voting, or standard, practice, or procedure with respect to voting different from that in force or effect at the time the proceeding was commenced shall be enforced unless and until the court finds that such qualification, prerequisite, standard, practice, or procedure does not have the purpose and will not have the effect of denying or abridging the right to vote on account of race or color: Provided, That such qualification, prerequisite, standard, practice, or procedure may be enforced if the qualification, prerequisite, standard, practice, or procedure has been submitted by the chief legal officer or other appropriate official of such State or subdivision to the Attorney General and the Attorney General has not interposed an objection within sixty days after such submission, except that neither the court's finding nor the Attorney General's failure to object shall bar a subsequent action to enjoin enforcement of such qualification, prerequisite, standard, practice, or procedure.

SEC. 4. (a) To assure that the right of citizens of the United States to vote is not denied or abridged on account of race or color, no citizen shall be denied the right to vote in any Federal, State, or local election because of his failure to comply with any test or device in any State with respect to which the determinations have been made under subsection (b) or in any political subdivision with respect to which such determinations have been made as a separate unit, unless the United States District Court for the District of Columbia in an action for a declaratory judgment brought by such State or subdivision against the United States has determined that no such test or device has been used during the five years preceding the filing of the action for the purpose or with the effect of denying or abridging the right to vote on account of race or color: Provided, That no such declaratory judgment shall issue with respect to any plaintiff for a period of five years after the entry of a final judgment of any court of the United States, other than the denial of a declaratory judgment under this section, whether entered prior to or after the enactment of this Act, determining that denials or abridgments of the right to vote on account of race or color through the use of such tests or devices have occurred anywhere in the territory of such plaintiff. An action pursuant to this subsection shall be heard and determined by a court of three judges in accordance with the provisions of section 2284 of title 28 of the United States Code and any appeal shall lie to the Supreme Court. The court shall retain jurisdiction of any action pursuant to this subsection for five years after judgment and shall reopen the action upon motion of the Attorney General alleging that a test or device has been used for the purpose or with the effect of denying or abridging the right to vote on account of race or color.

If the Attorney General determines that he has no reason to believe that any such test or device has been used during the five years preceding the filing of the action for the purpose or with the effect of denying or abridging the right to vote on account of race or color, he shall consent to the entry of such judgment

(b) The provisions of subsection (a) shall apply in any State or in any political subdivision of a state which (1) the Attorney General determines maintained on November 1, 1964, any test or device, and with respect to which (2) the Director of the Census determines that less than 50 percentum of the persons of voting age residing therein were registered on November 1, 1964, or that less than 50 percentum of such persons voted in the presidential election of November 1964.

A determination or certification of the Attorney General or of the Director of the Census under this section or under section 6 or section 13 shall not be reviewable in any court and shall be effective upon publication in the Federal Register.

(c) The phrase "test or device" shall mean any requirement that a person as a prerequisite for voting or registration for voting (1) demonstrate the ability to read, write, understand, or interpret any matter, (2) demonstrate any educational achievement or his knowledge of any particular subject, (3) possess good moral character, or (4) prove his qualifications by the voucher of registered voters or members of any other class.

(d) For purposes of this section no State or political subdivision shall be determined to have engaged in the use of tests or devices for the purpose or with the effect of denying or abridging the right to vote on account of race or color if (1) incidents of such use have been few in number and have been promptly and effectively corrected by State or local action, (2) the continuing effect of such incidents has been eliminated, and (3) there is no reasonable probability of their recurrence in the future.

(e) (1) Congress hereby declares that to secure the rights under the fourteenth amendment of persons educated in American-flag schools in which the predominant classroom language was other than English, it is necessary to prohibit the States from conditioning the right to vote of such persons on ability to read, write, understand, or interpret any matter in the English language. (2) No person who demonstrates that he has successfully completed the sixth primary grade in a public school in, or a private school accredited by, any State or territory, the District of Columbia, or the Commonwealth of Puerto Rico in which the predominant classroom language was other than English, shall be denied the right to vote in any Federal, State, or local election because of his inability to read, write, understand, or interpret any matter in the English language, except that, in States in which State law provides that a different level of education is presumptive of literacy, he shall demonstrate that he has successfully completed an equivalent level of education in a public school in, or a private school accredited by, any State or territory, the District of Columbia, or the Commonwealth of Puerto Rico in which the predominant classroom language was other than English.

SEC. 5. Whenever a State or political subdivision with respect to which the prohibitions set forth in section 4(a) are in effect shall enact or seek to administer any voting qualification or prerequisite to voting, or standard, practice, or procedure with respect to voting different from that in force or effect on November 1, 1964, such State or subdivision may institute an action in the United States District Court for the District of Columbia for a declaratory judgment that such qualification, prerequisite, standard, practice, or procedure does not have the purpose and will not have the effect of denying or abridging the right to vote on account of race or color, and unless and until the court enters such judgment no person shall be denied the right to vote for failure to comply with such qualification, prerequisite, standard, practice, or procedure: Provided, That such qualification, prerequisite, standard, practice, or procedure may be enforced without such proceeding if the qualification, prerequisite, standard, practice, or procedure has been submitted by the chief legal officer or other appropriate official of such State or subdivision to the Attorney General and the Attorney General has not interposed an objection within sixty days after such submission, except that neither the Attorney General's failure to object nor a declaratory judgment entered under this section shall bar a subsequent action to enjoin enforcement of such qualification, prerequisite, standard, practice, or procedure. Any action under this section shall be heard and determined by a court of three judges in accordance with the provisions of section 2284 of title 28 of the United States Code and any appeal shall lie to the Supreme Court.

SEC. 6. Whenever (a) a court has authorized the appointment of examiners pursuant to the provisions of section 3(a), or (b) unless a declaratory judgment has been rendered under section 4(a), the Attorney General certifies with respect to any political subdivision named in, or included within the scope of, determinations made under section 4(b) that (1) he has received complaints in writing from twenty or more residents of such political subdivision alleging that they have been denied the right to vote under color of law on account of race or color, and that he believes such complaints to be meritorious, or (2) that, in his judgment (considering, among other factors, whether the ratio of nonwhite persons to white persons registered to vote within such subdivision appears to him to be reasonably attributable to violations of the fifteenth amendment or whether substantial evidence exists that bona fide efforts are being made within such subdivision to comply with the fifteenth amendment), the appointment of examiners is otherwise necessary to enforce the guarantees of the fifteenth amendment, the Civil Service Commission shall appoint as many examiners for

such subdivision as it may deem appropriate to prepare and maintain lists of persons eligible to vote in Federal, State, and local elections. Such examiners, hearing officers provided for in section 9(a), and other persons deemed necessary by the Commission to carry out the provisions and purposes of this Act shall be appointed, compensated, and separated without regard to the provisions of any statute administered by the Civil Service Commission, and service under this Act shall not be considered employment for the purposes of any statute administered by the Civil Service Commission, except the provisions of section 9 of the Act of August 2, 1939, as amended (5 U.S.C. 118i), prohibiting partisan political activity: Provided, That the Commission is authorized, after consulting the head of the appropriate department or agency, to designate suitable persons in the official service of the United States, with their consent, to serve in these positions. Examiners and hearing officers shall have the power to administer oaths.

SEC. 7. (a) The examiners for each political subdivision shall, at such places as the Civil Service Commission shall by regulation designate, examine applicants concerning their qualifications for voting. An application to an examiner shall be in such form as the Commission may require and shall contain allegations that the applicant is not otherwise registered to vote.

(b) Any person whom the examiner finds, in accordance with instructions received under section 9(b), to have the qualifications prescribed by State law not inconsistent with the Constitution and laws of the United States shall promptly be placed on a list of eligible voters. A challenge to such listing may be made in accordance with section 9(a) and shall not be the basis for a prosecution under section 12 of this Act. The examiner shall certify and transmit such list, and any supplements as appropriate, at least once a month, to the offices of the appropriate election officials, with copies to the Attorney General and the attorney general of the State, and any such lists and supplements thereto transmitted during the month shall be available for public inspection on the last business day of the month and, in any event, not later than the forty-fifth day prior to any election. The appropriate State or local election official shall place such names on the official voting list. Any person whose name appears on the examiner's list shall be entitled and allowed to vote in the election district of his residence unless and until the appropriate election officials shall have been notified that such person has been removed from such list in accordance with subsection (d): Provided, That no person shall be entitled to vote in any election by virtue of this Act unless his name shall have been certified and transmitted on such a list to the offices of the appropriate election officials at least forty-five days prior to such election.

(c) The examiner shall issue to each person whose name appears on such a list a certificate evidencing his eligibility to vote.

(d) A person whose name appears on such a list shall be removed therefrom by an examiner if (1) such person has been successfully challenged in accordance with the procedure prescribed in section 9, or (2) he has been determined by an examiner to have lost his eligibility to vote under State law not inconsistent with the Constitution and the laws of the United States.

SEC. 8. Whenever an examiner is serving under this Act in any political subdivision, the Civil Service Commission may assign, at the request of the Attorney General, one or more persons, who may be officers of the United States, (1) to enter and attend at any place for holding an election in such subdivision for the purpose of observing whether persons who are entitled to vote are being permitted to vote, and (2) to enter and attend at any place for tabulating the votes cast at any election held in such subdivision for the purpose of observing whether votes cast by persons entitled to vote are being properly tabulated. Such persons so assigned shall report to an examiner appointed for such political subdivision, to the Attorney General, and if the appointment of examiners has been authorized pursuant to section 3(a), to the court.

SEC. 9. (a) Any challenge to a listing on an eligibility list prepared by an examiner shall be heard and determined by a hearing officer appointed by and responsible to the Civil Service Commission and under such rules as the Commission shall by regulation prescribe. Such challenge shall be entertained only if filed at such office within the State as the Civil Service Commission shall by regulation designate, and within ten days after the listing of the challenged person is made available for public inspection, and if supported by (1) the affidavits of at least two persons having personal knowledge of the facts constituting grounds for the challenge, and (2) a certification that a copy of the challenge and affidavits have been served by mail or in person upon the person challenged at his place of residence set out in the application. Such challenge shall be determined

within fifteen days after it has been filed. A petition for review of the decision of the hearing officer may be filed in the United States court of appeals for the circuit in which the person challenged resides within fifteen days after service of such decision by mail on the person petitioning for review but no decision of a hearing officer shall be reversed unless clearly erroneous. Any person listed shall be entitled and allowed to vote pending final determination by the hearing officer and by the court.

(b) The times, places, procedures, and form for application and listing pursuant to this Act and removals from the eligibility lists shall be prescribed by regulations promulgated by the Civil Service Commission and the Commission shall, after consultation with the Attorney General, instruct examiners concerning applicable State law not inconsistent with the Constitution and laws of the United States with respect to (1) the qualifications required for listing, and (2) loss of eligibility to vote.

(c) Upon the request of the applicant or the challenger or on its own motion the Civil Service Commission shall have the power to require by subpoena the attendance and testimony of witnesses and the production of documentary evidence relating to any matter pending before it under the authority of this section. In case of contumacy or refusal to obey a subpoena, any district court of the United States or the United States court of any territory or possession, or the District Court of the United States for the District of Columbia, within the jurisdiction of which said person guilty of contumacy or refusal to obey is found or resides or is domiciled or transacts business, or has appointed an agent for receipt of service of process, upon application by the Attorney General of the United States shall have jurisdiction to issue to such person an order requiring such person to appear before the Commission or a hearing officer, there to produce pertinent, relevant, and nonprivileged documentary evidence if so ordered, or there to give testimony touching the matter under investigation, and any failure to obey such order of the court may be punished by said court as a contempt thereof.

SEC. 10. (a) The Congress finds that the requirement of the payment of a poll tax as a precondition to voting (i) precludes persons of limited means from voting or imposes unreasonable financial hardship upon such persons as a precondition to their exercise of the franchise, (ii) does not bear a reasonable relationship to any legitimate State interest in the conduct of elections, and (iii) in some areas has the purpose or effect of denying persons the right to vote because of race or color. Upon the basis of these findings, Congress declares that the constitutional right of citizens to vote is denied or abridged in some areas by the requirement of the payment of a poll tax as a precondition to voting.

(b) In the exercise of the powers of Congress under section 5 of the fourteenth amendment and section 2 of the fifteenth amendment, the Attorney General is authorized and directed to institute forthwith in the name of the United States such actions, including actions against States or political subdivisions, for declaratory judgment or injunctive relief against the enforcement of any requirement of the payment of a poll tax as a precondition to voting, or substitute therefor enacted after November 1, 1964, as will be necessary to implement the declaration of subsection (a) and the purposes of this section.

(c) The district courts of the United States shall have jurisdiction of such actions which shall be heard and determined by a court of three judges in accordance with the provisions of section 2284 of title 28 of the United States Code and any appeal shall lie to the Supreme Court. It shall be the duty of the judges designated to hear the case to assign the case for hearing at the earliest practicable date, to participate in the hearing and determination thereof, and to cause the case to be in every way expedited.

(d) During the pendency of such actions, and thereafter if the courts, notwithstanding this action by the Congress, should declare the requirement of the payment of a poll tax to be constitutional, no citizen of the United States who is a resident of a State or political subdivision with respect to which determinations have been made under subsection 4(b) and a declaratory judgment has not been entered under subsection 4(a), during the first year he becomes otherwise entitled to vote by reason of registration by State or local officials or listing by an examiner, shall be denied the right to vote for failure to pay a poll tax if he tenders payment of such tax for the current year to an examiner or to the appropriate State or local official at least forty-five days prior to election, whether or not such tender would be timely or adequate under State law. An examiner shall have authority to accept such payment from any person authorized by this Act to make an application for listing, and shall issue a receipt for such payment. The examiner shall transmit promptly any such poll tax payment to the office of the State or local official authorized to receive such payment under State law, together with the name and address of the applicant.

SEC. 11. (a) No person acting under color of law shall fail or refuse to permit any person to vote who is entitled to vote under any provision of this Act or is otherwise qualified to vote, or willfully fail or refuse to tabulate, count, and report such person's vote.

(b) No person, whether acting under color of law or otherwise, shall intimidate, threaten, or coerce, or attempt to intimidate, threaten, or coerce any person for voting or attempting to vote, or intimidate, threaten, or coerce, or attempt to intimidate, threaten, or coerce any person for urging or aiding any person to vote or attempt to vote, or intimidate, threaten, or coerce any person for exercising any powers or duties under section 3(a), 6, 8, 9, 10, or 12(e).

(c) Whoever knowingly or willfully gives false information as to his name, address, or period of residence in the voting district for the purpose of establishing his eligibility to register or vote, or conspires with another individual for the purpose of encouraging his false registration to vote or illegal voting, or pays or offers to pay or accepts payment either for registration to vote or for voting shall be fined not more than $10,000 or imprisoned not more than five years, or both: Provided, however, That this provision shall be applicable only to general, special, or primary elections held solely or in part for the purpose of selecting or electing any candidate for the office of President, Vice President, presidential elector, Member of the United States Senate, Member of the United States House of Representatives, or Delegates or Commissioners from the territories or possessions, or Resident Commissioner of the Commonwealth of Puerto Rico.

(d) Whoever, in any matter within the jurisdiction of an examiner or hearing officer knowingly and willfully falsifies or conceals a material fact, or makes any false, fictitious, or fraudulent statements or representations, or makes or uses any false writing or document knowing the same to contain any false, fictitious, or fraudulent statement or entry, shall be fined not more than $10,000 or imprisoned not more than five years, or both.

SEC. 12. (a) Whoever shall deprive or attempt to deprive any person of any right secured by section 2, 3, 4, 5, 7, or 10 or shall violate section 11(a) or (b), shall be fined not more than $5,000, or imprisoned not more than five years, or both.

(b) Whoever, within a year following an election in a political subdivision in which an examiner has been appointed (1) destroys, defaces, mutilates, or otherwise alters the marking of a paper ballot which has been cast in such election, or (2) alters any official record of voting in such election tabulated from a voting machine or otherwise, shall be fined not more than $5,000, or imprisoned not more than five years, or both

(c) Whoever conspires to violate the provisions of subsection (a) or (b) of this section, or interferes with any right secured by section 2, 3 4, 5, 7, 10, or 11(a) or (b) shall be fined not more than $5,000, or imprisoned not more than five years, or both.

(d) Whenever any person has engaged or there are reasonable grounds to believe that any person is about to engage in any act or practice prohibited by section 2, 3, 4, 5, 7, 10, 11, or subsection (b) of this section, the Attorney General may institute for the United States, or in the name of the United States, an action for preventive relief, including an application for a temporary or permanent injunction, restraining order, or other order, and including an order directed to the State and State or local election officials to require them (1) to permit persons listed under this Act to vote and (2) to count such votes.

(e) Whenever in any political subdivision in which there are examiners appointed pursuant to this Act any persons allege to such an examiner within forty-eight hours after the closing of the polls that notwithstanding (1) their listing under this Act or registration by an appropriate election official and (2) their eligibility to vote, they have not been permitted to vote in such election, the examiner shall forthwith notify the Attorney General if such allegations in his opinion appear to be well founded. Upon receipt of such notification, the Attorney General may forthwith file with the district court an application for an order providing for the marking, casting, and counting of the ballots of such persons and requiring the inclusion of their votes in the total vote before the results of such election shall be deemed final and any force or effect given thereto. The district court shall hear and determine such matters immediately after the filing of such application. The remedy provided in this subsection shall not preclude any remedy available under State or Federal law.

(f) The district courts of the United States shall have jurisdiction of proceedings instituted pursuant to this section and shall exercise the same without regard to whether a person asserting rights under the provisions of this Act shall have exhausted any administrative or other remedies that may be provided by law

SEC. 13. Listing procedures shall be terminated in any political subdivision of any State (a) with

respect to examiners appointed pursuant to clause (b) of section 6 whenever the Attorney General notifies the Civil Service Commission, or whenever the District Court for the District of Columbia determines in an action for declaratory judgment brought by any political subdivision with respect to which the Director of the Census has determined that more than 50 percentum of the nonwhite persons of voting age residing therein are registered to vote, (1) that all persons listed by an examiner for such subdivision have been placed on the appropriate voting registration roll, and (2) that there is no longer reasonable cause to believe that persons will be deprived of or denied the right to vote on account of race or color in such subdivision, and (b), with respect to examiners appointed pursuant to section 3(a), upon order of the authorizing court. A political subdivision may petition the Attorney General for the termination of listing procedures under clause (a) of this section, and may petition the Attorney General to request the Director of the Census to take such survey or census as may be appropriate for the making of the determination provided for in this section. The District Court for the District of Columbia shall have jurisdiction to require such survey or census to be made by the Director of the Census and it shall require him to do so if it deems the Attorney General's refusal to request such survey or census to be arbitrary or unreasonable.

SEC. 14. (a) All cases of criminal contempt arising under the provisions of this Act shall be governed by section 151 of the Civil Rights Act of 1957 (42 U.S.C.1995).

(b) No court other than the District Court for the District of Columbia or a court of appeals in any proceeding under section 9 shall have jurisdiction to issue any declaratory judgment pursuant to section 4 or section 5 or any restraining order or temporary or permanent injunction against the execution or enforcement of any provision of this Act or any action of any Federal officer or employee pursuant hereto.

(c) (1) The terms "vote" or "voting" shall include all action necessary to make a vote effective in any primary, special, or general election, including, but not limited to, registration, listing pursuant to this Act, or other action required by law prerequisite to voting, casting a ballot, and having such ballot counted properly and included in the appropriate totals of votes cast with respect to candidates for public or party office and propositions for which votes are received in an election. (2) The term "political subdivision" shall mean any county or parish, except that, where registration for voting is not conducted under the supervision of a county or parish, the term shall include any other subdivision of a State which conducts registration for voting.

(d) In any action for a declaratory judgment brought pursuant to section 4 or section 5 of this Act, subpoenas for witnesses who are required to attend the District Court for the District of Columbia may be served in any judicial district of the United States: Provided, That no writ of subpoena shall issue for witnesses without the District of Columbia at a greater distance than one hundred miles from the place of holding court without the permission of the District Court for the District of Columbia being first had upon proper application and cause shown.

SEC. 15. Section 2004 of the Revised Statutes (42 U.S.C.1971), as amended by section 131 of the Civil Rights Act of 1957 (71 Stat. 637), and amended by section 601 of the Civil Rights Act of 1960 (74 Stat. 90), and as further amended by section 101 of the Civil Rights Act of 1964 (78 Stat. 241), is further amended as follows:

(a) Delete the word "Federal" wherever it appears in subsections (a) and (c);

(b) Repeal subsection (f) and designate the present subsections (g) and (h) as (f) and (g), respectively.

SEC. 16. The Attorney General and the Secretary of Defense, jointly, shall make a full and complete study to determine whether, under the laws or practices of any State or States, there are preconditions to voting, which might tend to result in discrimination against citizens serving in the Armed Forces of the United States seeking to vote. Such officials shall, jointly, make a report to the Congress not later than June 30, 1966, containing the results of such study, together with a list of any States in which such preconditions exist, and shall include in such report such recommendations for legislation as they deem advisable to prevent discrimination in voting against citizens serving in the Armed Forces of the United States.

SEC. 17. Nothing in this Act shall be construed to deny, impair, or otherwise adversely affect the right to vote of any person registered to vote under the law of any State or political subdivision.

SEC. 18. There are hereby authorized to be appropriated such sums as are necessary to carry out the provisions of this Act

SEC 19. If any provision of this Act or the application thereof to any person or circumstances is held invalid, the remainder of the Act and the application of the provision to other persons not similarly situated or to other circumstances shall not be affected thereby.

Approved August 6, 1965.

Chief Justice Earl Warren wrote the Court's decision in **Miranda v. Arizona.** (AP Photo)

> *"The accused who does not know his rights and therefore does not make a request may be the person who most needs counsel."*

Overview

The U.S. Supreme Court dramatically reshaped the nation's criminal justice system in the 1960s. As presided over by Chief Justice Earl Warren until mid-1969, the Court broadly interpreted rights that the Fourth, Fifth, and Sixth Amendments afford persons accused of crimes. Through the process of selective incorporation, the Court used the Fourteenth Amendment to apply elements of these amendments, historically restricting federal but not state infringement of individual rights, to the states.

Miranda v. Arizona, decided in 1966, is a major landmark in the Warren Court's expansion of rights of the accused. The decision reversed criminal convictions and threw out statements made by the defendant while in police custody. The accused, the Court wrote, had not been apprised of his right not to incriminate himself or of his right to consult an attorney and have one present during interrogation. This violation of constitutional rights made his confession to the police, the major piece of evidence upon which the state relied for his conviction, inadmissible.

Context

The Constitution places value on both crime control and the rights of the accused. To the state and federal governments, the Constitution extends the authority to protect citizens' safety and to provide for the general security of the public. To an individual accused of crimes, it extends rights upon which governments may not infringe while investigating and prosecuting. The balance between government mandates and individual rights is delineated in the policies and practices employed by police and followed in court proceedings.

The Warren Court revolutionized the law of criminal procedure during the 1960s. Certain decisions increased the scope and reach of the constitutional rights of accused persons and established national standards for criminal procedures, applying across all states. Among the many cases that created this legacy, four stand out: *Mapp v. Ohio*

(1961), *Gideon v. Wainwright* (1963), *Escobedo v. Illinois* (1964), and *Miranda v. Arizona* (1966). In the first three cases, the Court traveled a great distance in a very short time. These decisions spurred loud disapproval from advocates of crime control. In many quarters of the nation, the Court and especially the chief justice, Earl Warren, were roundly criticized, even vilified. But the decisions, as they piled up, also signaled to defendants convicted in lower courts and their attorneys that, where possible constitutional violations had occurred, the Warren Court was willing to hear pleas for reversal.

Ernesto Miranda was one of these defendants. The case unfolded as follows: A young woman in Phoenix reported to the police that she had been abducted and raped. Based on a description of the assailant's car, the police tracked down Miranda and, with his approval, brought him to the station at 10:30 AM for a lineup and questioning. At 1:30 PM, Miranda wrote and signed a statement admitting to the abduction and rape. The subsequent trial proceeded quickly, with the written confession entered as evidence. The jury quickly returned unanimous guilty verdicts for kidnapping and rape.

On appeal to the Arizona State Supreme Court, Miranda's convictions were upheld, but that decision caught the attention of attorneys in Phoenix, who then made an appeal to the U.S. Supreme Court on Miranda's behalf. In the spring of 1966, the case was argued before the Supreme Court, as consolidated with appeals of three other lower-court decisions, all folded into the same case.

About the Author

Earl Warren, chief justice of the Supreme Court from 1953 to 1969, authored the Court's opinion in *Miranda v. Arizona*. Joining him were Justices Hugo Black, William O. Douglas, William Brennan, and Abe Fortas. These five formed a reliable liberal voting bloc that pushed for constitutional reforms in many areas during the 1960s. (Justice Fortas, replaced by Arthur Goldberg in 1965, and Thurgood Marshall, who joined the Court in 1967, were also members of this bloc.) By custom, the chief justice, when voting in the majority, assigns the authorship of the Court's

Time Line

1961

■ **June 19**
The Warren Court announces its decision in *Mapp v. Ohio*, establishing that evidence obtained in violation of the Fourth Amendment must be excluded from state courts.

1963

■ **March 13**
At a Phoenix police station, after a period of in-custody interrogation, Ernesto Miranda writes and signs a confession. He is charged with kidnapping and rape.

■ **March 18**
The Court announces its decision in *Gideon v. Wainwright*, establishing the right of impoverished defendants to be provided with state-appointed counsel for defense in state courts.

■ **June 20**
Miranda is brought to trial, where he is represented by counsel. He is convicted of both of the crimes in question and is returned to custody.

1964

■ **June 22**
The Court announces its decision in *Escobedo v. Illinois*, establishing the right to counsel during police questioning.

1965

■ **April 22**
The Arizona State Supreme Court affirms the convictions of Miranda. His appeal to the U.S. Supreme Court follows.

1966

■ **June 13**
The Warren Court's decision in *Miranda v. Arizona* is announced.

1968

■ **June 13**
Earl Warren informs President Lyndon B. Johnson of his intent to resign as chief justice. Johnson had announced his intention not to seek reelection ten weeks earlier, and Senate Republicans successfully put off the nomination of the next chief justice until after the next presidential election; Warren continues indefinitely as chief justice.

---

opinion; in this case, to write an opinion sure to stir controversy, Warren chose himself.

President Dwight Eisenhower appointed Earl Warren as chief justice in 1953. A Republican, Warren had served California as attorney general and three times was elected the state's governor. Eisenhower expressed surprise and disappointment when his choice for chief justice became the strong leader of a Court that boldly took American society in progressive directions in areas of race relations, legislative apportionment, free speech, and rights of the accused.

Dissenting opinions in *Miranda* were written by Tom Clark, appointed by President Harry Truman, for whom Clark had served as U.S. attorney general; by John Harlan, another Eisenhower appointee and grandson of Justice John Marshall Harlan, who famously dissented in *Plessy v. Ferguson* (1896); and by Byron White, appointed by President John F. Kennedy. These justices, along with Potter Stewart, who joined the dissents of Harlan and White—who also joined each other's dissents—often took conservative positions when casting votes in cases decided by the Warren Court.

Explanation and Analysis of the Document

◆ Chief Justice Earl Warren's Majority Opinion

In the first paragraph of the majority opinion—which was joined by Black, Douglas, Brennan, and Fortas—Warren places the four cases in question securely in the province of the constitutional rights of the accused, or "the restraints society must observe consistent with the Federal Constitution in prosecuting individuals for crime." The tone Warren adopts in this first paragraph foreshadows the Court's decision—it concerns not a suspected criminal who is questioned by the police but rather "an individual who is subjected to custodial police interrogation." In these cases the Court deals with "the necessity for procedures which assure that the individual is accorded his privilege under the Fifth Amendment to the Constitution not to be compelled to incriminate himself." At this point, the reader clearly may anticipate that Miranda has won on appeal.

Warren next aligns the cases in *Miranda* with the Court's decision two years earlier in *Escobedo v. Illinois*. In that case, the defendant, who had been arrested and was under interrogation at the police station, asked to see his lawyer. The police refused the request and subsequently obtained from Escobedo a confession that was used at trial to successfully prosecute him. Warren does not recount the basis on which the Supreme Court overturned this case on appeal: The Sixth Amendment right to counsel applies as soon as police focus on a particular suspect; the confession, because it was obtained in violation of this right, was inadmissible at trial.

The results in *Escobedo*, Warren explains, allowed for interpretation, debate, and speculation regarding issues on "applying the privilege of self-incrimination to in-custody interrogation." Thus, Warren fashions the ruling in *Escobedo* to play down the right to counsel (from the Sixth Amendment) and instead emphasizes self-incrimination (as addressed in the Fifth Amendment), the issue on which *Miranda* will turn. A holding based on the privilege against self-incrimination during in-custody interrogation, Warren assures, does not break new ground. It is "an application of principles long recognized and applied in other settings." (On this point, the dissenters to this decision strongly disagree.)

In part I, Warren writes that because the four cases under review all involve "incommunicado interrogation of individuals in a police-dominated atmosphere," this section will survey police methods in that setting. A factual study of police operations and police manuals is quoted at length. Warren stresses that "the modern practice of in-custody interrogation is psychologically rather than physically oriented." The manuals teach police to isolate the suspect in a setting chosen by authorities, to conduct extended questioning during which the suspect's guilt is assumed, and to deflect requests by the suspect for legal representation. In the cases under consideration, Warren admits, the records contain no evidence of "physical coercion or patent psychological ploys." The dissenting justices believe that the matter properly turns on whether evidence exists that a particular defendant's statements were made involuntarily. Warren, however, is building a more general case against in-custody questioning. To him, "the very fact of custodial interrogation exacts a heavy toll on individual liberty and trades on the weaknesses of individuals." He sees "an intimate connection between the privilege against self-incrimination and police custodial questioning."

The privilege against self-incrimination is lodged in venerable traditions of English law, Warren says in part II, and was given constitutional status by the framers. "We cannot depart from this noble heritage," he declares. In the third paragraph, Warren establishes this heritage further: Arising from a right to privacy and "founded on a complex of values," the privilege against self-incrimination strikes a fair balance between the individual and the state.

These are fine ideals, stated strongly. But because these ideals are expansive and general, it is difficult to make the argument that they require the highly specific *Miranda* rules that the Court is about to impose on police. These ideals could just as logically and reasonably support rules that do not go as far as those laid down in *Miranda* or rules that go even further. To support these particular practices, Warren examines the case law to determine "whether the privilege is fully applicable during a period of custodial interrogation." Predictably, the answer that he will arrive at is that it is applicable.

Warren writes that in *Bram v. United States* (1897), the Court reasoned that the Fifth Amendment requires that an admissible statement must be voluntary—that is, made by a defendant not compelled by improper influences to make the statement. In *Malloy v. Hogan* (1964), as Warren notes, the Court reasoned that the voluntariness doctrine "encompasses all interrogation practices which are likely to exert such pressure upon an individual as to disable him from making a free and rational choice." Finally, in *Escobedo v. Illinois*, when the defendant chose to speak to the police, Warren writes, "the abdication of the constitutional

www.milestonedocuments.com

Time Line

1968

■ **June 19**
President Johnson signs the Omnibus Crime Control and Safe Streets Act of 1968; Section 3501 contains language overruling *Miranda v. Arizona*. In 2000, in *Dickerson v. United States*, the Supreme Court would rule that Congress may not legislatively supersede the constitutional rule established in *Miranda*.

■ **August 8**
Richard Nixon, accepting the Republican Party's presidential nomination, criticizes courts that have weakened law-enforcement efforts; in the general campaign in the fall, he will run on a law and order platform.

■ **September 4**
Warren Burger, a judge sitting on the U.S. Court of Appeals for the District of Columbia Circuit, makes a speech to the Ohio Judicial Conference in which he criticizes Warren Court rulings expanding the rights of the accused.

■ **November 5**
Richard Nixon is elected president.

1969

■ **January 20**
Nixon takes office.

■ **May 21**
President Nixon announces his nomination of Warren Burger to be chief justice of the U.S. Supreme Court.

■ **June 23**
Burger takes over the position of chief justice from Earl Warren.

privilege—the choice on his part to speak to the police—was not made knowingly or competently because of the failure to apprise him his rights; the compelling atmosphere of the in-custody interrogation, and not an independent decision on his part, caused the defendant to speak."

Thus, for the second time, Warren has cast the Court's holding in *Escobedo* in a way that smoothly anticipates the result to be arrived at in *Miranda*. The defendant in *Escobedo*, during custodial interrogation, asked for an attorney and was denied the request; the constitutional violation in question concerned the Sixth Amendment. As such, Fifth Amendment privilege as delineated in *Miranda* does not flow as directly from *Escobedo*, as Warren would have it.

Ernesto Miranda (AP Photo)

Still, the right to an attorney—what Warren calls "a protective device to dispel the compelling atmosphere of the interrogation"—does apply to both *Escobedo* and *Miranda*. The presence of counsel "would be the adequate protective device necessary to make the process of police interrogation conform to the dictates of the privilege."

In part III, Warren states the law that goes forward in *Miranda v. Arizona*. The first paragraph offers, in general terms, what the Court holds to be required by the Constitution. In the second paragraph, Warren writes that the Court encourages "Congress and the States to continue their laudable search for increasingly effective ways of protecting the rights of the individual while promoting efficient enforcement of our criminal laws." The invitation can be read two ways: It is modest and amenable but also, at the same time, critical and imperious. On one hand, under

the Constitution, Congress and the States are recognized as having the power to pass laws governing police procedures. On the other hand, the Court's ruling in *Miranda* is intended to correct failures to observe the individual's privilege against self-incrimination, especially such failures by state police. In addition, the Court, because it exercises the power to interpret the Constitution, will pass judgment on any "possible alternatives for protecting the privilege which might be devised by Congress or the States in the exercise of their creative rule-making capacities."

The remainder of this section fleshes out the warnings that comprise the "*Miranda* warnings" that defendants are given by police. Warren emphasizes that these warnings are necessary anytime "a person in custody is to be subjected to interrogation." The capacity or background of the defendant does not matter; rather, the "warning is an absolute prerequisite in overcoming the inherent pressures of the interrogation process." The warning of the right to remain silent, "accompanied by the explanation that anything said can and will be used against the individual in Court," puts the defendant on alert "that he is faced with a phase of the adversary system." The presence of counsel at the interrogation is "indispensable to the protection of the Fifth Amendment privilege" and will sharpen the record of the interrogation to be reported at trial. A defendant may waive his right to counsel, but that waiver is effective only when "made after the warnings we here delineate have been given." Finally, "the financial ability of the individual has no relationship to the scope of the rights involved here." An express explanation to an indigent person that a lawyer will be appointed for him is necessary to assure that person that he is in a position to exercise the right to have counsel present during interrogation.

Warren next lays down additional ground rules: An individual, once given the warnings, may assert the rights at any time prior to or during questioning. If he waives his rights and speaks with the police, he may stop at any time and exercise his right to remain silent or his right to have counsel. In either instance, police are required to cease interrogation. Where an individual waives his rights and interrogation follows, "a heavy burden rests on the government to demonstrate that the defendant knowingly and intelligently waived" his rights. Silence from the defendant in response to any question does not constitute a waiver.

In part IV, Warren addresses critics who will claim—or who, in the case of justices dissenting to the decision, do claim—that with its holding in *Miranda*, the Court is hindering the ability of society, through the efforts of its police, to control crime. He cites the experiences of other law-enforcement agencies employing rules protecting against self-incrimination—the Federal Bureau of Investigation, criminal justice systems in other nations, and the U.S. military—to buttress his view that the *Miranda* warnings will not unduly hamper police.

Warren's opinion for the Court in *Miranda v. Arizona* is remarkable for many reasons. The discussion of the Fifth Amendment privilege is so expansive as to constitute an essay on the rights of the individual. The warnings that the

Court dictates must be given to defendants by police are highly specific; the Court rarely prescribes policy in such a detailed way. Regarding the actual cases under review, not until part V does Warren finally address the facts of the four cases collected under the rubric of *Miranda*.

In fact, discussion of the four cases may not appear until the final section for good reason. An important point *Miranda* makes is that the Court will not consider, case by case, whether a defendant's confession was voluntary. The intent of *Miranda* is that, absent the necessary warnings or a permissible equivalent, a Fifth Amendment violation has occurred, and statements made by the defendant are inadmissible. As time would tell, however, *Miranda* did not provide total resolution for questions about the privilege against self-incrimination during police questioning. To close the opinion, in quick order, the Court announces the findings in the four separate cases.

◆ Justice Tom Clark's Dissenting Opinion

Justice Clark's dissent is short and focused. He objects to the majority's use of police manuals to explain its findings, as "not one is shown by the record here to be the official manual of any political department, much less in universal use in crime detection." Also, the Court has "not fairly characterized" the efforts made by city and state police to enforce the law. In part I, Clark criticizes the Court's innovation in *Miranda*, holding that the ruling goes "too far too fast." In part II, Clark criticizes the Court for "the promulgation of doctrinaire rules" that police must follow when conducting in-custody interrogation. The prior rule to determine whether a statement admitting guilt was voluntary, Clark writes, "depended upon 'a totality of circumstances.'" He declares in Part III, "I would continue to follow that rule." He does not object to having police inform detained persons, prior to custodial interrogation, that they have a right to counsel and that counsel will be appointed if they cannot afford one. "In the absence of warnings … the confession was clearly voluntary."

◆ Justice John Marshall Harlan II's Dissenting Opinion

In this dissent, which was joined by Justices Potter Stewart and Byron White, Harlan expresses deep and fundamental disagreement with the Court's reasoning and results in *Miranda*. To Harlan, "the thrust of the new rules is to negate all pressures, to reinforce the nervous or ignorant suspect, and ultimately to discourage any confession at all." The decision, he says, is not supported by the Constitution, nor does it make good public policy.

With the *Miranda* rules, Harlan writes in part II, the Court travels far from the due process clause of the Fourteenth Amendment and its "voluntariness" test as a way to determine the admissibility of a statement made during police questioning. A string of Supreme Court cases had fine-tuned the "voluntariness" standard, resulting in "an elaborate, sophisticated, and sensitive approach to admissibility of confessions." Cases were considered one at a time, the standard was "flexible in its ability to respond to the endless mutations of fact presented," and lower courts knew how to use the standard. Furthermore, the cases attached ample value "to society's interest in suspect questioning as an instrument of law enforcement." For Harlan, no precedents exist in cases prior to *Miranda* supporting the view that the Fifth and Sixth Amendments protect defendants during police interrogation.

The *Miranda* rules, writes Harlan in part III, are not supported by concerns of public policy, such as by being "plainly desirable in the context of our society." The rules impair and may even frustrate police interrogation. He notes, "There can be little doubt that the Court's new code would markedly decrease the number of confessions." With this "hazardous experimentation," the Court is reaching far ahead of other societal forces that might lay claim to having a say in the determination of proper police practices. Harlan reasons that "this Court's too rapid departure from existing constitutional standards" will discourage criminal law reform that might otherwise occur elsewhere in the political system, particularly in the legislative branches, where the initiative "truly belongs."

◆ Justice Byron White's Dissenting Opinion

White's dissent, which was joined by Justices Harlan and Stewart, differs in perspective and tone from Harlan's but comes to the same conclusions. White seemingly accepts the application of the Fifth Amendment privilege against self-incrimination during police questioning. However, he reasons that *Bram v. United States*, which is cited by Warren, supports only "whether a confession, obtained during custodial interrogation, had been compelled." White shares with Harlan the conviction that a version of the voluntariness standard, where the question becomes whether the confession was compelled, is better than the *Miranda* rules, where the question is whether the warnings were given. In part II, White does not dismiss out of hand the Court's innovation in *Miranda* but asserts that when the Court forges new law and policy, that act invites close examination.

The rules that the Court announces, writes White, are aimed at reducing confessions and guilty pleas. As such, the system of criminal law and "society's interest in the general security" will suffer. Although the Court's rules might appear to give clear-cut guidance as to when a statement is not admissible, White believes otherwise. He predicts that the decision will leave open

> questions as to whether the accused was in custody, whether his statements were spontaneous or the product of interrogation, whether the accused has effectively waived his rights, and whether nontestimonial evidence introduced at trial is the fruit of statements made during a prohibited interrogation, all of which are certain to prove productive of uncertainty during investigation and litigation during prosecution.

White indeed writes presciently here; later Supreme Court cases on self-incrimination following *Miranda* probed exactly these issues.

"The current practice of incommunicado interrogation is at odds with one of our Nation's most cherished principles—that the individual may not be compelled to incriminate himself. Unless adequate protective devices are employed to dispel the compulsion inherent in custodial surroundings, no statement obtained from the defendant can truly be the product of his free choice."

(Chief Justice Earl Warren's Majority Opinion, Part I)

"The accused who does not know his rights and therefore does not make a request may be the person who most needs counsel."

(Chief Justice Earl Warren's Majority Opinion, Part III)

Audience

Miranda v. Arizona speaks to many audiences. First, the justices address one another. In the majority opinion, Warren often writes to answer or head off objections drawn by the dissenters, just as those objections speak directly to the Court's holding. Warren also replies to concerns of Justice William Brennan, who joined him in the majority, in issuing the invitation to Congress and the states to continue their efforts to develop criminal law. Those legislative bodies are a second audience addressed by the document. A third audience, also governmental, is larger: police departments and their personnel throughout the nation, to whose daily actions the *Miranda* rules apply directly. Lower courts, a fourth audience, are expected to apply the findings of *Miranda* going forward.

A fifth audience is society at large. The legal scholar Morton Horwitz has noted that the Warren Court "regularly handed down opinions that have transformed American constitutional doctrine and, in turn, profoundly affected American society" (p. 3). Much of the majority opinion is written in a style that is easily accessible to a nonlegal audience; Warren often wrote this way. The four cases' defendants, who won reversals of their convictions, constitute a sixth audience. Ernesto Miranda, in particular, was granted a retrial in Arizona, at which his confession was inadmissible. Nevertheless, the state won convictions again, based on new evidence: Miranda's common-law wife testified that while he was in jail after confessing to the police, Miranda confessed to her that he committed the kidnapping and rape. Against a number of objections, that evidence was admitted, and Miranda was found guilty of the two crimes. The Arizona Supreme Court turned down his subsequent request for appeal.

Impact

The impact of *Miranda v. Arizona*, measured purely as a legal standard, began to dissipate shortly after it was handed down. Congress announced its displeasure with the *Miranda* rules in the Omnibus Crime Control and Safe Streets Act of 1968. As led by Chief Justice Warren Burger from 1969 to 1986, the Supreme Court never overruled *Miranda* but instead chipped away at it by developing, in cases where defendants claimed a *Miranda* violation, exceptions to the requirement that the warnings always be given. Other cases required the Court to confront issues created by *Miranda* but not settled there, including the questions raised by Justice White in his dissent. Clearly, *Miranda* was not the last word on the right against self-incrimination during in-custody interrogation.

Nonetheless, the general impact of the case cannot be denied, for, as noted in a *Los Angeles Times* editorial by the constitutional law scholar Akhil Reed Amar, "*Miranda* has been woven into the fabric of daily life" (http://www.law.yale.edu/documents/pdf/1999Right.pdf). Police departments incorporate the *Miranda* rules into their training and practices, sometimes printing the *Miranda* rights on cards for officers to hand to suspects. Americans are likely more familiar with the particulars of the holding in this case than in any other ever heard by the Supreme Court, for the *Miranda* warnings are common parlance on television and in crime fiction. Thus, the clamor trailing this case through American culture more than a half century after its disposition has instructed people, in a simplified manner, about important constitutional rights.

Dire predictions that *Miranda* would hinder or hobble efforts to fight crime, made by *Miranda*'s dissenters and repeated by law-enforcement officials when the decision became known, did not pan out. The legal scholar Stephen Schulhofer reviewed relevant empirical research and concluded that those studies show that *Miranda* did not seriously affect conviction rates or the ability of police to interrogate suspects and obtain statements that proved useful in convictions.

Overall, the Warren Court's decision in *Miranda*, as well as the decisions in prior cases that championed rights of the accused, undoubtedly set in motion political forces that helped shape the nation's future. Richard Nixon, accepting the Republican Party's presidential nomination on August 8, 1968, told delegates "that some of our courts in their decisions have gone too far in weakening the peace forces as against the criminal forces in this country and we must act to restore that balance" (http://www.4president.org/speeches/nixon1968acceptance.htm). Nixon was elected that fall on a campaign that stressed "law and order." Meanwhile, Warren Burger, a U.S. appeals court judge, had become well known as a vocal critic of the Warren Court's expansion of the rights of the accused, especially the *Miranda* decision. Months after taking office, President Nixon selected Burger to replace the retiring Earl Warren as chief justice. The Burger Court (1969–1986) and the Court led by Chief Justice William Rehnquist (1986–2005) would try to undo the progressive steps taken by the Warren Court in many areas of the law.

Related Documents

Dickerson v. United States, 530 U.S. 428 (2000). In this case the Supreme Court ruled that Congress did not legitimately overrule *Miranda* in the Omnibus Crime Control and Safe Streets Act of 1968.

Escobedo v. Illinois, 378 U.S. 478 (1964). In a 5–4 opinion, the Supreme Court applied the Sixth Amendment to make inadmissible a confession made in the absence of counsel, where the defendant had requested counsel.

Omnibus Crime Control and Safe Streets Act of 1968, Public Law 90-351, *U.S. Statutes at Large* 82 (1968): 197. The portion of the act codified at 18 U.S.C. §3501, which was intended to overrule *Miranda* and reinstate the "voluntariness" standard, states that a confession is "admissible in evidence if it is voluntarily given."

"United States Constitution." Cornell University Law School Web site. http://www.law.cornell.edu/constitution/constitution.billof rights.html. Accessed on February 27, 2008. Amendment V contains the privilege against self-incrimination, on which the Supreme Court grounded its decision in *Miranda*.

Bibliography

■ Articles

Amar, Akhil Reed. "OK, All Together Now: 'You Have the Right To ...'" *Los Angeles Times*, December 12, 1999.

■ Books

Baker, Liva. *Miranda: Crime, Law and Politics*. New York: Atheneum, 1983.

Belknap, Michal R. *The Supreme Court under Earl Warren, 1953–1969*. Columbia: University of South Carolina Press, 2004.

Horwitz, Morton J. *The Warren Court and the Pursuit of Justice: A Critical Issue*. New York: Hill and Wang, 1998.

Schulhofer, Stephen. "*Miranda v. Arizona*: A Modest but Important Legacy." In *Criminal Procedure Stories*, ed. Carol Steiker. New York: Foundation Press/Thomson/West, 2006.

Stuart, Gary L. *Miranda: The Story of America's Right to Remain Silent*. Tucson: University of Arizona Press, 2004.

■ Web Sites

"Gideon v. Wainwright." U.S. Supreme Court Media "Oyez" Web site.
    http://www.oyez.org/cases/1960-1969/1962/1962_155/. Accessed on February 28, 2008.

"Mapp v. Ohio." U.S. Supreme Court Media "Oyez" Web site.

    http://www.oyez.org/cases/1960-1969/1960/1960_236/. Accessed on February 28, 2008.

"Miranda v. Arizona—Oral Argument." U.S. Supreme Court Media "Oyez" Web site.
    http://www.oyez.org/cases/1960-1969/1965/1965_759/argument/. Accessed on August 30, 2007.

"Richard M. Nixon: Presidential Nomination Acceptance Speech." 4President.org Web site.
    http://www.4president.org/speeches/nixon1968acceptance.htm. Accessed on February 27, 2008.

—By Randy Wagner

1. Review the standards set by the Court in *Miranda* for determining whether a defendant has "waived his privilege against self-incrimination and his right to retained or appointed counsel" (part III). Has the Court backed into another "voluntariness" standard here? Why did Chief Justice Warren not expressly rule that any in-custody interrogation require the presence of counsel? And why would a defendant agree to waive his rights? (In fact, many do.)

2. At retrial, Arizona convicted Miranda after presenting testimony by his common-law wife that he had confessed to her that he had committed the abduction and rape. She stated that the confession had been made to her when she visited Miranda in jail, three days after he confessed to the police, and after she confirmed, upon Miranda's inquiry, that police had informed her of his confession to them. Did the use of this evidence actually violate the Supreme Court's ruling in *Miranda*? Think carefully about Miranda's conversation with his common-law wife. Why did he confess to her?

3. The three dissenting opinions in *Miranda* criticize the Court for moving ahead of the rest of the political system. Does the Supreme Court's making new law and policy constitute a problem? Consider cases since *Miranda* in which courts have ruled in innovative ways, regarding, for example, abortion (*Roe v. Wade*, decided by the U.S. Supreme Court in 1973) or same-sex marriage (*Goodridge v. Department of Public Health*, decided by the Massachusetts Supreme Judicial Court in 2004).

4. Should the rights of the accused be applied on a sliding scale, based on the type of crime? Might, for example, a robbery suspect, undergoing police interrogation, deserve more rights than a murder suspect or than someone detained for suspicion of international terrorism? Why or why not?

Glossary

adversary system	legal system, as in the United States, in which opposing parties contest each other before an independent judge
amicus curiae	literally, "friend of the court," a nonparty in the proceedings who files a brief arguing issues to be settled in the case
certiorari	a writ issued by an appellate court calling up a lower court case for review; the way most cases reach the U.S. Supreme Court
exculpatory	regarding evidence, tending to establish innocence
inculpatory	regarding evidence, tending to show guilt or involvement in a crime
inquisitorial system	legal system used in much of the world outside the United States and Britain, in which the judge directs most facets of the inquiry, including the collection of evidence and the questioning of witnesses
Solicitor General	Justice Department official who conducts all litigation on behalf of the United States in the Supreme Court

MIRANDA V. ARIZONA

Mr. Chief Justice Warren Delivered the Opinion of the Court

The cases before us raise questions which go to the roots of our concepts of American criminal jurisprudence: the restraints society must observe consistent with the Federal Constitution in prosecuting individuals for crime. More specifically, we deal with the admissibility of statements obtained from an individual who is subjected to custodial police interrogation and the necessity for procedures which assure that the individual is accorded his privilege under the Fifth Amendment to the Constitution not to be compelled to incriminate himself.

We dealt with certain phases of this problem recently in *Escobedo v. Illinois*, 378 U.S. 478 (1964). There, as in the four cases before us, law enforcement officials took the defendant into custody and interrogated him in a police station for the purpose of obtaining a confession. The police did not effectively advise him of his right to remain silent or of his right to consult with his attorney. Rather, they confronted him with an alleged accomplice who accused him of having perpetrated a murder. When the defendant denied the accusation and said "I didn't shoot Manuel, you did it," they handcuffed him and took him to an interrogation room. There, while handcuffed and standing, he was questioned for four hours until he confessed. During this interrogation, the police denied his request to speak to his attorney, and they prevented his retained attorney, who had come to the police station, from consulting with him. At his trial, the State, over his objection, introduced the confession against him. We held that the statements thus made were constitutionally inadmissible.

This case has been the subject of judicial interpretation and spirited legal debate since it was decided two years ago. Both state and federal courts, in assessing its implications, have arrived at varying conclusions. A wealth of scholarly material has been written tracing its ramifications and underpinnings.

Police and prosecutor have speculated on its range and desirability. We granted certiorari in these cases, 382 U.S. 924, 925, 937, in order further to explore some facets of the problems, thus exposed, of applying the privilege against self-incrimination to in-custody interrogation, and to give concrete constitutional guidelines for law enforcement agencies and courts to follow.

We start here, as we did in Escobedo, with the premise that our holding is not an innovation in our jurisprudence, but is an application of principles long recognized and applied in other settings. We have undertaken a thorough re-examination of the Escobedo decision and the principles it announced, and we reaffirm it. That case was but an explication of basic rights that are enshrined in our Constitution—that "No person ... shall be compelled in any criminal case to be a witness against himself," and that "the accused shall ... have the Assistance of Counsel"—rights which were put in jeopardy in that case through official overbearing. These precious rights were fixed in our Constitution only after centuries of persecution and struggle. And in the words of Chief Justice Marshall, they were secured "for ages to come, and ... designed to approach immortality as nearly as human institutions can approach it," *Cohens v. Virginia*, 6 Wheat. 264, 387 (1821).

Over 70 years ago, our predecessors on this Court eloquently stated:

"The maxim nemo tenetur seipsum accusare had its origin in a protest against the inquisitorial and manifestly unjust methods of interrogating accused persons, which [have] long obtained in the continental system, and, until the expulsion of the Stuarts from the British throne in 1688, and the erection of additional barriers for the protection of the people against the exercise of arbitrary power, [were] not uncommon even in England. While the admissions or confessions of the prisoner, when voluntarily and freely made, have always ranked high in the scale of incriminating evidence, if an accused person be asked to explain his apparent connection with a crime under investigation, the ease with which the questions put to him may assume an inquisitorial character, the temptation to press the witness unduly, to browbeat him if he be timid or reluctant, to push him into a corner, and to entrap him into fatal contradictions, which is so painfully evident in many of the earlier state trials, notably in those of Sir Nicholas Throckmorton, and Udal, the Puritan minister, made the system so odious as to give rise to a demand for its total abolition. The change in the English criminal procedure in that particular seems to be founded upon no statute and no judicial opinion, but upon a general and silent acquiescence of the courts in a popular demand. But, however adopted, it has become firmly embedded in English, as well as in American jurisprudence. So deeply did the iniquities of the ancient system impress themselves upon the minds of the American colonists that the States, with one accord, made a denial of the right to question an accused person a part of their fundamental law, so that a maxim, which in England was a mere rule of evidence, became clothed in this country with the impregnability of a constitutional enactment." *Brown v. Walker*, 161 U.S. 591, 596-597 (1896).

In stating the obligation of the judiciary to apply these constitutional rights, this Court declared in *Weems v. United States*, 217 U.S. 349, 373 (1910):

"… our contemplation cannot be only of what has been but of what may be. Under any other rule a constitution would indeed be as easy of application as it would be deficient in efficacy and power. Its general principles would have little value and be converted by precedent into impotent and lifeless formulas. Rights declared in words might be lost in reality. And this has been recognized. The meaning and vitality of the Constitution have developed against narrow and restrictive construction."

This was the spirit in which we delineated, in meaningful language, the manner in which the constitutional rights of the individual could be enforced against overzealous police practices. It was necessary in Escobedo, as here, to insure that what was proclaimed in the Constitution had not become but a "form of words," *Silverthorne Lumber Co. v. United States*, 251 U.S. 385, 392 (1920), in the hands of government officials. And it is in this spirit, consistent with our role as judges, that we adhere to the principles of Escobedo today.

Our holding will be spelled out with some specificity in the pages which follow but briefly stated it is this: the prosecution may not use statements, whether exculpatory or inculpatory, stemming from custodial interrogation of the defendant unless it demonstrates the use of procedural safeguards effective to secure the privilege against self-incrimination. By custodial interrogation, we mean questioning initiated by law enforcement officers after a person has been taken into custody or otherwise deprived of his freedom of action in any significant way. As for the procedural safeguards to be employed, unless other fully effective means are devised to inform accused persons of their right of silence and to assure a continuous opportunity to exercise it, the following measures are required. Prior to any questioning, the person must be warned that he has a right to remain silent, that any statement he does make may be used as evidence against him, and that he has a right to the presence of an attorney, either retained or appointed. The defendant may waive effectuation of these rights, provided the waiver is made voluntarily, knowingly and intelligently. If, however, he indicates in any manner and at any stage of the process that he wishes to consult with an attorney before speaking there can be no questioning. Likewise, if the individual is alone and indicates in any manner that he does not wish to be interrogated, the police may not question him. The mere fact that he may have answered some questions or volunteered some statements on his own does not deprive him of the right to refrain from answering any further inquiries until he has consulted with an attorney and thereafter consents to be questioned.

◆ I

The constitutional issue we decide in each of these cases is the admissibility of statements obtained from a defendant questioned while in custody or otherwise deprived of his freedom of action in any significant way. In each, the defendant was questioned by police officers, detectives, or a prosecuting attorney in a room in which he was cut off from the outside world. In none of these cases was the defendant given a full and effective warning of his rights at the outset of the interrogation process. In all the cases, the questioning elicited oral admissions, and in three of them, signed statements as well which were admitted at their trials. They all thus share salient features—incommunicado interrogation of individuals in a police-dominated atmosphere, resulting in self-incriminating statements without full warnings of constitutional rights.

An understanding of the nature and setting of this in-custody interrogation is essential to our decisions today. The difficulty in depicting what transpires at such interrogations stems from the fact that in this country they have largely taken place incommunicado. From extensive factual studies undertaken in the early 1930's, including the famous Wickersham Report to Congress by a Presidential Commission, it is clear that police violence and the "third degree" flourished at that time. In a series of cases decided by this Court long after these studies, the police resorted to physical brutality—beating, hanging, whipping—and to sustained and protracted questioning incommunicado in order to extort confessions. The Commission on Civil Rights in 1961 found much evidence to indicate that "some policemen still resort to physical force to obtain confessions," 1961 Comm'n on Civil Rights Rep., Justice, pt. 5, 17. The use of physical brutality and violence is not, unfortunately, relegated to the past or to any part of the country. Only recently in Kings County, New York, the police brutally beat, kicked and placed lighted cigarette butts on the back of a potential witness under interrogation for the purpose of securing a statement incriminating a third party. *People v. Portelli*, 15 N. Y. 2d 235, 205 N. E. 2d 857, 257 N. Y. S. 2d 931 (1965).

The examples given above are undoubtedly the exception now, but they are sufficiently widespread to be the object of concern. Unless a proper limitation upon custodial interrogation is achieved—such as these decisions will advance—there can be no assurance that practices of this nature will be eradicated in the foreseeable future. The conclusion of the Wickersham Commission Report, made over 30 years ago, is still pertinent:

"To the contention that the third degree is necessary to get the facts, the reporters aptly reply in the language of the present Lord Chancellor of England (Lord Sankey): 'It is not admissible to do a great right by doing a little wrong.... It is not sufficient to do justice by

obtaining a proper result by irregular or improper means.' Not only does the use of the third degree involve a flagrant violation of law by the officers of the law, but it involves also the dangers of false confessions, and it tends to make police and prosecutors less zealous in the search for objective evidence. As the New York prosecutor quoted in the report said, 'It is a short cut and makes the police lazy and unenterprising.' Or, as another official quoted remarked: 'If you use your fists, you are not so likely to use your wits.' We agree with the conclusion expressed in the report, that 'The third degree brutalizes the police, hardens the prisoner against society, and lowers the esteem in which the administration of justice is held by the public.'" IV National Commission on Law Observance and Enforcement, Report on Lawlessness in Law Enforcement 5 (1931).

Again we stress that the modern practice of in-custody interrogation is psychologically rather than physically oriented. As we have stated before, "Since *Chambers v. Florida*, 309 U.S. 227, this Court has recognized that coercion can be mental as well as physical, and that the blood of the accused is not the only hallmark of an unconstitutional inquisition." *Blackburn v. Alabama*, 361 U.S. 199, 206 (1960). Interrogation still takes place in privacy. Privacy results in secrecy and this in turn results in a gap in our knowledge as to what in fact goes on in the interrogation rooms. A valuable source of information about present police practices, however, may be found in various police manuals and texts which document procedures employed with success in the past, and which recommend various other effective tactics. These texts are used by law enforcement agencies themselves as guides. It should be noted that these texts professedly present the most enlightened and effective means presently used to obtain statements through custodial interrogation. By considering these texts and other data, it is possible to describe procedures observed and noted around the country.

The officers are told by the manuals that the "principal psychological factor contributing to a successful interrogation is privacy—being alone with the person under interrogation." The efficacy of this tactic has been explained as follows:

"If at all practicable, the interrogation should take place in the investigator's office or at least in a room of his own choice. The subject should be deprived of every psychological advantage. In his own home he may be confident, indignant, or recalcitrant. He is more keenly aware of his rights and more reluctant to tell of his indiscretions or criminal behavior within the walls of his home. Moreover his family and other friends are nearby, their presence lending moral support. In his own office, the investigator possesses all the advantages. The atmosphere suggests the invincibility of the forces of the law."

To highlight the isolation and unfamiliar surroundings, the manuals instruct the police to display an air of confidence in the suspect's guilt and from outward appearance to maintain only an interest in confirming certain details. The guilt of the subject is to be posited as a fact. The interrogator should direct his comments toward the reasons why the subject committed the act, rather than court failure by asking the subject whether he did it. Like other men, perhaps the subject has had a bad family life, had an unhappy childhood, had too much to drink, had an unrequited desire for women. The officers are instructed to minimize the moral seriousness of the offense, to cast blame on the victim or on society. These tactics are designed to put the subject in a psychological state where his story is but an elaboration of what the police purport to know already—that he is guilty. Explanations to the contrary are dismissed and discouraged.

The texts thus stress that the major qualities an interrogator should possess are patience and perseverance. One writer describes the efficacy of these characteristics in this manner:

"In the preceding paragraphs emphasis has been placed on kindness and stratagems. The investigator will, however, encounter many situations where the sheer weight of his personality will be the deciding factor. Where emotional appeals and tricks are employed to no avail, he must rely on an oppressive atmosphere of dogged persistence. He must interrogate steadily and without relent, leaving the subject no prospect of surcease. He must dominate his subject and overwhelm him with his inexorable will to obtain the truth. He should interrogate for a spell of several hours pausing only for the subject's necessities in acknowledgment of the need to avoid a charge of duress that can be technically substantiated.

In a serious case, the interrogation may continue for days, with the required intervals for food and sleep, but with no respite from the atmosphere of domination. It is possible in this way to induce the subject to talk without resorting to duress or coercion. The method should be used only when the guilt of the subject appears highly probable."

The manuals suggest that the suspect be offered legal excuses for his actions in order to obtain an initial admission of guilt. Where there is a suspected revenge-killing, for example, the interrogator may say:

"Joe, you probably didn't go out looking for this fellow with the purpose of shooting him. My guess is, however, that you expected something from him and that's why you carried a gun—for your own protection. You knew him for what he was, no good. Then when you met him he probably started using foul, abusive language and he gave some indication that he was about to pull a gun on you, and that's when you had to act to save your own life. That's about it, isn't it, Joe?"

Having then obtained the admission of shooting, the interrogator is advised to refer to circumstantial evidence which negates the self-defense explanation. This should enable him to secure the entire story. One text notes that "Even if he fails to do so, the inconsistency between the subject's original denial of the shooting and his present admission of at least doing the shooting will serve to deprive him of a self-defense 'out' at the time of trial."

When the techniques described above prove unavailing, the texts recommend they be alternated with a show of some hostility. One ploy often used has been termed the "friendly-unfriendly" or the "Mutt and Jeff" act:

"… In this technique, two agents are employed. Mutt, the relentless investigator, who knows the subject is guilty and is not going to waste any time. He's sent a dozen men away for this crime and he's going to send the subject away for the full term. Jeff, on the other hand, is obviously a kindhearted man. He has a family himself. He has a brother who was involved in a little scrape like this. He disapproves of Mutt and his tactics and will arrange to get him off the case if the subject will cooperate. He can't hold Mutt off for very long. The subject would be wise to make a quick decision. The technique is applied by having both investigators present while Mutt acts out his role. Jeff may stand by quietly and demur at some of Mutt's tactics. When Jeff makes his plea for cooperation, Mutt is not present in the room."

The interrogators sometimes are instructed to induce a confession out of trickery. The technique here is quite effective in crimes which require identification or which run in series. In the identification situation, the interrogator may take a break in his questioning to place the subject among a group of men in a line-up. "The witness or complainant (previously coached, if necessary) studies the line-up and confidently points out the subject as the guilty party." Then the questioning resumes "as though there were now no doubt about the guilt of the subject." A variation on this technique is called the "reverse line-up":

> "The accused is placed in a line-up, but this time he is identified by several fictitious witnesses or victims who associated him with different offenses. It is expected that the subject will become desperate and confess to the offense under investigation in order to escape from the false accusations."

The manuals also contain instructions for police on how to handle the individual who refuses to discuss the matter entirely, or who asks for an attorney or relatives. The examiner is to concede him the right to remain silent. "This usually has a very undermining effect. First of all, he is disappointed in his expectation of an unfavorable reaction on the part of the interrogator. Secondly, a concession of this right to remain silent impresses the subject with the apparent fairness of his interrogator." After this psychological conditioning, however, the officer is told to point out the incriminating significance of the suspect's refusal to talk:

> "Joe, you have a right to remain silent. That's your privilege and I'm the last person in the world who'll try to take it away from you. If that's the way you want to leave this, O. K. But let me ask you this. Suppose you were in my shoes and I were in yours and you called me in to ask me about this and I told you, 'I don't want to answer any of your questions.' You'd

think I had something to hide, and you'd probably be right in thinking that. That's exactly what I'll have to think about you, and so will everybody else. So let's sit here and talk this whole thing over."

Few will persist in their initial refusal to talk, it is said, if this monologue is employed correctly.

In the event that the subject wishes to speak to a relative or an attorney, the following advice is tendered:

> "[T]he interrogator should respond by suggesting that the subject first tell the truth to the interrogator himself rather than get anyone else involved in the matter. If the request is for an attorney, the interrogator may suggest that the subject save himself or his family the expense of any such professional service, particularly if he is innocent of the offense under investigation. The interrogator may also add, 'Joe, I'm only looking for the truth, and if you're telling the truth, that's it. You can handle this by yourself.'"

From these representative samples of interrogation techniques, the setting prescribed by the manuals and observed in practice becomes clear. In essence, it is this: To be alone with the subject is essential to prevent distraction and to deprive him of any outside support. The aura of confidence in his guilt undermines his will to resist. He merely confirms the preconceived story the police seek to have him describe. Patience and persistence, at times relentless questioning, are employed. To obtain a confession, the interrogator must "patiently maneuver himself or his quarry into a position from which the desired objective may be attained." When normal procedures fail to produce the needed result, the police may resort to deceptive stratagems such as giving false legal advice. It is important to keep the subject off balance, for example, by trading on his insecurity about himself or his surroundings. The police then persuade, trick, or cajole him out of exercising his constitutional rights.

Even without employing brutality, the "third degree" or the specific stratagems described above, the very fact of custodial interrogation exacts a heavy toll on individual liberty and trades on the weakness of individuals. This fact may be illustrated simply by referring to three confession cases decided by this Court in the Term immediately preceding our Escobedo decision. In *Townsend v. Sain*, 372 U.S. 293 (1963), the defendant was a 19-year-old heroin addict, described as a "near mental defective," id., at 307-310. The defendant in *Lynumn v. Illinois*, 372 U.S. 528 (1963), was a woman who confessed to the arresting officer after being importuned to "cooperate" in order to prevent her children from being taken by relief authorities. This Court as in those cases reversed the conviction of a defendant in *Haynes v. Washington*, 373 U.S. 503 (1963), whose persistent request during his interrogation was to phone his wife or attorney. In other settings, these individuals might have exercised their constitutional rights. In the incommunicado police-dominated atmosphere, they succumbed.

In the cases before us today, given this background, we concern ourselves primarily with this interrogation atmosphere and the evils it can bring. In No. 759, *Miranda v. Arizona*, the police arrested the defendant and took him to a special interrogation room where they secured a confession. In No. 760, *Vignera v. New York*, the defendant made oral admissions to the police after interrogation in the afternoon, and then signed an inculpatory statement upon being questioned by an assistant district attorney later the same evening. In No. 761, *Westover v. United States*, the defendant was handed over to the Federal Bureau of Investigation by local authorities after they had detained and interrogated him for a lengthy period, both at night and the following morning. After some two hours of questioning, the federal officers had obtained signed statements from the defendant. Lastly, in No. 584, *California v. Stewart*, the local police held the defendant five days in the station and interrogated him on nine separate occasions before they secured his inculpatory statement.

In these cases, we might not find the defendants' statements to have been involuntary in traditional terms. Our concern for adequate safeguards to protect precious Fifth Amendment rights is, of course, not lessened in the slightest. In each of the cases, the defendant was thrust into an unfamiliar atmosphere and run through menacing police interrogation procedures. The potentiality for compulsion is forcefully apparent, for example, in Miranda, where the indigent Mexican defendant was a seriously disturbed individual with pronounced sexual fantasies, and in Stewart, in which the defendant was an indigent Los Angeles Negro who had dropped out of school in the sixth grade. To be sure, the records do not evince overt physical coercion or patent psychological ploys. The fact remains that in none of these cases did the officers undertake to afford appropriate safeguards at the outset of the interrogation to insure that the statements were truly the product of free choice.

It is obvious that such an interrogation environment is created for no purpose other than to subjugate the individual to the will of his examiner. This atmosphere carries its own badge of intimidation. To be sure, this is not physical intimidation, but it is equally destructive of human dignity. The current practice of incommunicado interrogation is at odds with one of our Nation's most cherished principles—that the individual may not be compelled to incriminate himself. Unless adequate protective devices are employed to dispel the compulsion inherent in custodial surroundings, no statement obtained from the defendant can truly be the product of his free choice.

From the foregoing, we can readily perceive an intimate connection between the privilege against self-incrimination and police custodial questioning. It is fitting to turn to history and precedent underlying the Self-Incrimination Clause to determine its applicability in this situation.

◆ II

We sometimes forget how long it has taken to establish the privilege against self-incrimination, the sources from which it came and the fervor with which it was defended. Its roots go back into ancient times. Perhaps the critical historical event shedding light on its origins and evolution was the trial of one John Lilburn, a vocal anti-Stuart Leveller, who was made to take the Star Chamber Oath in 1637. The oath would have bound him to answer to all questions posed to him on any subject. The Trial of John Lilburn and John Wharton, 3 How. St. Tr. 1315 (1637). He resisted the oath and declaimed the proceedings, stating:

"Another fundamental right I then contended for, was, that no man's conscience ought to be racked by oaths imposed, to answer to questions concerning himself in matters criminal, or pretended to be so." Haller & Davies, The Leveller Tracts 1647-1653, p. 454 (1944).

On account of the Lilburn Trial, Parliament abolished the inquisitorial Court of Star Chamber and went further in giving him generous reparation. The lofty principles to which Lilburn had appealed during his trial gained popular acceptance in England. These sentiments worked their way over to the Colonies and were implanted after great struggle into the Bill of Rights. Those who framed our Constitution and the Bill of Rights were ever aware of subtle encroachments on individual liberty. They knew that "illegitimate and unconstitutional practices get their first footing ... by silent approaches and slight deviations from legal modes of procedure." *Boyd v. United States*, 116 U.S. 616, 635 (1886). The privilege was elevated to constitutional status and has always been "as broad as the mischief against which it seeks to guard." *Counselman v. Hitchcock*, 142 U.S. 547, 562 (1892). We cannot depart from this noble heritage.

Thus we may view the historical development of the privilege as one which groped for the proper scope of governmental power over the citizen. As a "noble principle often transcends its origins," the privilege has come rightfully to be recognized in part as an individual's substantive right, a "right to a private enclave where he may lead a private life. That right is the hallmark of our democracy." *United States v. Grunewald*, 233 F.2d 556, 579, 581-582 (Frank, J., dissenting), rev'd, 353 U.S. 391 (1957). We have recently noted that the privilege against self-incrimination—the essential mainstay of our adversary system—is founded on a complex of values, *Murphy v. Waterfront Comm'n*, 378 U.S. 52, 55-57, n. 5 (1964); *Tehan v. Shott*, 382 U.S. 406, 414-415, n. 12 (1966). All these policies point to one overriding thought: the constitutional foundation underlying the privilege is the respect a government—state or federal—must accord to the dignity and integrity of its citizens. To maintain a "fair state-individual balance," to require the government "to shoulder the entire load," 8 Wigmore, Evidence 317 (McNaughton rev. 1961), to respect the inviolability of the human personality, our accusatory system of criminal justice demands that the government seeking to punish an individual produce the evidence against him by its own independent labors, rather than by the cruel, simple expedient of compelling it from his own mouth. *Chambers v. Florida*, 309 U.S. 227, 235-238 (1940). In sum, the privilege is fulfilled only when the person is guaranteed the right "to remain silent unless he chooses to speak in the unfettered exercise of his own will." *Malloy v. Hogan*, 378 U.S. 1, 8 (1964).

The question in these cases is whether the privilege is fully applicable during a period of custodial interrogation. In this Court, the privilege has consistently been accorded a liberal construction. *Albertson v. SACB*, 382 U.S. 70, 81 (1965); *Hoffman v. United States*, 341 U.S. 479, 486 (1951); *Arndstein v. McCarthy*, 254 U.S. 71, 72-73 (1920); *Counselman v. Hitchcock*, 142 U.S. 547, 562 (1892). We are satisfied that all the principles embodied in the privilege apply to informal compulsion exerted by law-enforcement officers during in-custody questioning. An individual swept from familiar surroundings into police custody, surrounded by antagonistic forces, and subjected to the techniques of persuasion described above cannot be otherwise than under compulsion to speak. As a practical matter, the compulsion to speak in the isolated setting of the police station may well be greater than in courts or other official investigations, where there are often impartial observers to guard against intimidation or trickery.

This question, in fact, could have been taken as settled in federal courts almost 70 years ago, when, in *Bram v. United States*, 168 U.S. 532, 542 (1897), this Court held:

"In criminal trials, in the courts of the United States, wherever a question arises whether a confession is incompetent because not voluntary, the issue is controlled by that portion of the Fifth Amendment ... commanding that no person 'shall be compelled in any criminal case to be a witness against himself.'"

In Bram, the Court reviewed the British and American history and case law and set down the Fifth Amendment standard for compulsion which we implement today:

"Much of the confusion which has resulted from the effort to deduce from the adjudged cases what would be a sufficient quantum of proof to show that a confession was or was not voluntary, has arisen from a misconception of the subject to which the proof must address itself. The rule is not that in order to render a statement admissible the proof must be adequate to establish that the particular communications contained in a statement were voluntarily made, but it must be sufficient to establish that the making of the statement was voluntary; that is to say, that from the causes, which the law treats as legally sufficient to engender in the mind of the accused hope or fear in respect to the crime charged, the accused was not involuntarily impelled to make a statement, when but for the improper influences he would have remained silent...." 168 U.S., at 549. And see, id., at 542.

The Court has adhered to this reasoning. In 1924, Mr. Justice Brandeis wrote for a unanimous

Court in reversing a conviction resting on a compelled confession, *Wan v. United States*, 266 U.S. 1. He stated:

"In the federal courts, the requisite of voluntariness is not satisfied by establishing merely that the confession was not induced by a promise or a threat. A confession is voluntary in law if, and only if, it was, in fact, voluntarily made. A confession may have been given voluntarily, although it was made to police officers, while in custody, and in answer to an examination conducted by them. But a confession obtained by compulsion must be excluded whatever may have been the character of the compulsion, and whether the compulsion was applied in a judicial proceeding or otherwise. *Bram v. United States*, 168 U.S. 532." 266 U.S., at 14-15.

In addition to the expansive historical development of the privilege and the sound policies which have nurtured its evolution, judicial precedent thus clearly establishes its application to incommunicado interrogation. In fact, the Government concedes this point as well established in No. 761, *Westover v. United States*, stating: "We have no doubt … that it is possible for a suspect's Fifth Amendment right to be violated during in-custody questioning by a law-enforcement officer."

Because of the adoption by Congress of Rule 5 (a) of the Federal Rules of Criminal Procedure, and this Court's effectuation of that Rule in *McNabb v. United States*, 318 U.S. 332 (1943), and *Mallory v. United States*, 354 U.S. 449 (1957), we have had little occasion in the past quarter century to reach the constitutional issues in dealing with federal interrogations. These supervisory rules, requiring production of an arrested person before a commissioner "without unnecessary delay" and excluding evidence obtained in default of that statutory obligation, were nonetheless responsive to the same considerations of Fifth Amendment policy that unavoidably face us now as to the States. In McNabb, 318 U.S., at 343-344, and in Mallory, 354 U.S., at 455-456, we recognized both the dangers of interrogation and the appropriateness of prophylaxis stemming from the very fact of interrogation itself.

Our decision in *Malloy v. Hogan*, 378 U.S. 1 (1964), necessitates an examination of the scope of the privilege in state cases as well. In Malloy, we squarely held the privilege applicable to the States, and held that the substantive standards underlying the privilege applied with full force to state court proceedings. There, as in *Murphy v. Waterfront Comm'n*, 378 U.S. 52 (1964), and *Griffin v. California*, 380 U.S. 609 (1965), we applied the existing Fifth Amendment standards to the case before us. Aside from the holding itself, the reasoning in Malloy made clear what had already become apparent—that the substantive and procedural safeguards surrounding admissibility of confessions in state cases had become exceedingly exacting, reflecting all the policies embedded in the privilege, 378 U.S., at 7-8. The voluntariness doctrine in the state cases, as Malloy indicates, encompasses all interrogation practices which are likely to exert such pressure upon an individual as to disable him from making a free and rational choice. The implications of this proposition were elaborated in our decision in *Escobedo v. Illinois*, 378 U.S. 478, decided one week after Malloy applied the privilege to the States.

Our holding there stressed the fact that the police had not advised the defendant of his constitutional privilege to remain silent at the outset of the interrogation, and we drew attention to that fact at several points in the decision, 378 U.S., at 483, 485, 491. This was no isolated factor, but an essential ingredient in our decision. The entire thrust of police interrogation there, as in all the cases today, was to put the defendant in such an emotional state as to impair his capacity for rational judgment. The abdication of the constitutional privilege—the choice on his part to speak to the police—was not made knowingly or competently because of the failure to apprise him of his rights; the compelling atmosphere of the in-custody interrogation, and not an independent decision on his part, caused the defendant to speak.

A different phase of the Escobedo decision was significant in its attention to the absence of counsel during the questioning. There, as in the cases today, we sought a protective device to dispel the compelling atmosphere of the interrogation. In Escobedo, however, the police did not relieve the defendant of the anxieties which they had created in the interrogation rooms. Rather, they denied his request for the assistance of counsel, 378 U.S., at 481, 488, 491. This heightened his dilemma, and made his later statements the product of this compulsion. Cf. *Haynes v. Washington*, 373 U.S. 503, 514 (1963). The denial of the defendant's request for his attorney thus undermined his ability to exercise the privilege—to remain silent if he chose or to speak without any intimidation, blatant or subtle. The presence of counsel, in all the cases before us today, would be the adequate protective device necessary to make the process of police interrogation conform to the dictates of the privilege. His presence would insure that statements made in the government-established atmosphere are not the product of compulsion.

It was in this manner that Escobedo explicated another facet of the pre-trial privilege, noted in many of the Court's prior decisions: the protection of rights at trial. That counsel is present when statements are taken from an individual during interrogation obviously enhances the integrity of the fact-finding processes in court. The presence of an attorney, and the warnings delivered to the individual, enable the defendant under otherwise compelling circumstances to tell his story without fear, effectively, and in a way that eliminates the evils in the interrogation process. Without the protections flowing from adequate warnings and the rights of counsel, "all the careful safeguards erected around the giving of testimony, whether by an accused or any other witness, would become empty formalities in a procedure where the most compelling possible evidence of guilt, a confession, would have already been obtained at the unsupervised pleasure of the police." *Mapp v. Ohio*, 367 U.S. 643, 685 (1961) (HARLAN, J., dissenting). Cf. *Pointer v. Texas*, 380 U.S. 400 (1965).

◆ III

Today, then, there can be no doubt that the Fifth Amendment privilege is available outside of criminal court proceedings and serves to protect persons in all settings in which their freedom of action is curtailed in any significant way from being compelled to incriminate themselves. We have concluded that without proper safeguards the process of in-custody interrogation of persons suspected or accused of crime contains inherently compelling pressures which work to undermine the individual's will to resist and to compel him to speak where he would not otherwise do so freely. In order to combat these pressures and to permit a full opportunity to exercise the privilege against self-incrimination, the accused must be adequately and effectively apprised of his rights and the exercise of those rights must be fully honored.

It is impossible for us to foresee the potential alternatives for protecting the privilege which might be devised by Congress or the States in the exercise of their creative rule-making capacities. Therefore we cannot say that the Constitution necessarily requires adherence to any particular solution for the inherent compulsions of the interrogation process as

it is presently conducted. Our decision in no way creates a constitutional straitjacket which will handicap sound efforts at reform, nor is it intended to have this effect. We encourage Congress and the States to continue their laudable search for increasingly effective ways of protecting the rights of the individual while promoting efficient enforcement of our criminal laws. However, unless we are shown other procedures which are at least as effective in apprising accused persons of their right of silence and in assuring a continuous opportunity to exercise it, the following safeguards must be observed.

At the outset, if a person in custody is to be subjected to interrogation, he must first be informed in clear and unequivocal terms that he has the right to remain silent. For those unaware of the privilege, the warning is needed simply to make them aware of it—the threshold requirement for an intelligent decision as to its exercise. More important, such a warning is an absolute prerequisite in overcoming the inherent pressures of the interrogation atmosphere. It is not just the subnormal or woefully ignorant who succumb to an interrogator's imprecations, whether implied or expressly stated, that the interrogation will continue until a confession is obtained or that silence in the face of accusation is itself damning and will bode ill when presented to a jury. Further, the warning will show the individual that his interrogators are prepared to recognize his privilege should he choose to exercise it.

The Fifth Amendment privilege is so fundamental to our system of constitutional rule and the expedient of giving an adequate warning as to the availability of the privilege so simple, we will not pause to inquire in individual cases whether the defendant was aware of his rights without a warning being given. Assessments of the knowledge the defendant possessed, based on information as to his age, education, intelligence, or prior contact with authorities, can never be more than speculation; a warning is a clearcut fact. More important, whatever the background of the person interrogated, a warning at the time of the interrogation is indispensable to overcome its pressures and to insure that the individual knows he is free to exercise the privilege at that point in time.

The warning of the right to remain silent must be accompanied by the explanation that anything said can and will be used against the individual in court. This warning is needed in order to make him aware not only of the privilege, but also of the consequences of forgoing it. It is only through an awareness of these consequences that there can be any assurance of real understanding and intelligent exercise of the privilege. Moreover, this warning may serve to make the individual more acutely aware that he is faced with a phase of the adversary system—that he is not in the presence of persons acting solely in his interest.

The circumstances surrounding in-custody interrogation can operate very quickly to overbear the will of one merely made aware of his privilege by his interrogators. Therefore, the right to have counsel present at the interrogation is indispensable to the protection of the Fifth Amendment privilege under the system we delineate today. Our aim is to assure that the individual's right to choose between silence and speech remains unfettered throughout the interrogation process. A once-stated warning, delivered by those who will conduct the interrogation, cannot itself suffice to that end among those who most require knowledge of their rights. A mere warning given by the interrogators is not alone sufficient to accomplish that end. Prosecutors themselves claim that the admonishment of the right to remain silent without more "will benefit only the recidivist and the professional." Brief for the National District Attorneys Association as amicus curiae, p. 14. Even preliminary advice given to the accused by his own attorney can be swiftly overcome by the secret interrogation process. Cf. *Escobedo v. Illinois*, 378 U.S. 478, 485, n. 5. Thus, the need for counsel to protect the Fifth Amendment privilege comprehends not merely a right to consult with counsel prior to questioning, but also to have counsel present during any questioning if the defendant so desires.

The presence of counsel at the interrogation may serve several significant subsidiary functions as well. If the accused decides to talk to his interrogators, the assistance of counsel can mitigate the dangers of untrustworthiness. With a lawyer present the likelihood that the police will practice coercion is reduced, and if coercion is nevertheless exercised the lawyer can testify to it in court. The presence of a lawyer can also help to guarantee that the accused gives a fully accurate statement to the police and that the statement is rightly reported by the prosecution at trial. See *Crooker v. California*, 357 U.S. 433, 443-448 (1958) (DOUGLAS, J., dissenting).

An individual need not make a pre-interrogation request for a lawyer. While such request affirmatively secures his right to have one, his failure to ask for a lawyer does not constitute a waiver. No effective waiver of the right to counsel during interrogation can be recognized unless specifically made after the warnings we here delineate have been given. The accused who does not know his rights and therefore does not make a request may be the person who most needs counsel. As the California Supreme Court has aptly put it:

"Finally, we must recognize that the imposition of the requirement for the request would discriminate against the defendant who does not know his rights. The defendant who does not ask for counsel is the very defendant who most needs counsel. We cannot penalize a defendant who, not understanding his constitutional rights, does not make the formal request and by such failure demonstrates his helplessness. To require the request would be to favor the defendant whose sophistication or status had fortuitously prompted him to make it." *People v. Dorado*, 62 Cal. 2d 338, 351, 398 P.2d 361, 369-370, 42 Cal. Rptr. 169, 177-178 (1965) (Tobriner, J.).

In *Carnley v. Cochran*, 369 U.S. 506, 513 (1962), we stated: "[I]t is settled that where the assistance of counsel is a constitutional requisite, the right to be furnished counsel does not depend on a request." This proposition applies with equal force in the context of providing counsel to protect an accused's Fifth Amendment privilege in the face of interrogation. Although the role of counsel at trial differs from the role during interrogation, the differences are not relevant to the question whether a request is a prerequisite.

Accordingly we hold that an individual held for interrogation must be clearly informed that he has the right to consult with a lawyer and to have the lawyer with him during interrogation under the system for protecting the privilege we delineate today. As with the warnings of the right to remain silent and that anything stated can be used in evidence against him, this warning is an absolute prerequisite to interrogation. No amount of circumstantial evidence that the person may have been aware of this right will suffice to stand in its stead: Only through such a warning is there ascertainable assurance that the accused was aware of this right.

If an individual indicates that he wishes the assistance of counsel before any interrogation occurs, the authorities cannot rationally ignore or deny his request on the basis that the individual does not have or cannot afford a retained attorney. The financial ability of the individual has no relationship to the scope of the rights involved here. The privilege against self-incrimination secured by the Constitution applies to all individuals. The need for counsel in order to protect the privilege exists for the indigent as well as the affluent. In fact, were we to limit these constitutional rights to those who can retain an attorney, our decisions today would be of little significance. The cases before us as well as the vast majority of confession cases with which we have dealt in the past involve those unable to retain counsel. While authorities are not required to relieve the accused of his poverty, they have the obligation not to take advantage of indigence in the administration of justice. Denial of counsel to the indigent at the time of interrogation while allowing an attorney to those who can afford one would be no more supportable by reason or logic than the similar situation at trial and on appeal struck down in *Gideon v. Wainwright*, 372 U.S. 335 (1963), and *Douglas v. California*, 372 U.S. 353 (1963).

In order fully to apprise a person interrogated of the extent of his rights under this system then, it is necessary to warn him not only that he has the right to consult with an attorney, but also that if he is indigent a lawyer will be appointed to represent him. Without this additional warning, the admonition of the right to consult with counsel would often be understood as meaning only that he can consult with a lawyer if he has one or has the funds to obtain one. The warning of a right to counsel would be hollow if not couched in terms that would convey to the indigent—the person most often subjected to interrogation—the knowledge that he too has a right to have counsel present. As with the warnings of the right to remain silent and of the general right to counsel, only by effective and express explanation to the indigent of this right can there be assurance that he was truly in a position to exercise it.

Once warnings have been given, the subsequent procedure is clear. If the individual indicates in any manner, at any time prior to or during questioning, that he wishes to remain silent, the interrogation must cease. At this point he has shown that he intends to exercise his Fifth Amendment privilege; any statement taken after the person invokes his privilege cannot be other than the product of compulsion, subtle or otherwise. Without the right to cut off questioning, the setting of in-custody interrogation operates on the individual to overcome free choice in producing a statement after the privilege has been once invoked. If the individual states that he wants an attorney, the interrogation must cease until an attorney is present. At that time, the individual must have an opportunity to confer with the attorney and to have him present during any subsequent questioning. If the individual cannot obtain an attorney and he indicates that he wants one before speaking to police, they must respect his decision to remain silent.

This does not mean, as some have suggested, that each police station must have a "station house lawyer" present at all times to advise prisoners. It does mean, however, that if police propose to interrogate a person they must make known to him that he is entitled to a lawyer and that if he cannot afford one, a lawyer will be provided for him prior to any interrogation. If authorities conclude that they will not provide counsel during a reasonable period of time in which investigation in the field is carried out, they may refrain from doing so without violating the person's Fifth Amendment privilege so long as they do not question him during that time.

If the interrogation continues without the presence of an attorney and a statement is taken, a heavy burden rests on the government to demonstrate that the defendant knowingly and intelligently waived his privilege against self-incrimination and his right to retained or appointed counsel. *Escobedo v. Illinois*, 378 U.S. 478, 490, n. 14. This Court has always set high standards of proof for the waiver of constitutional rights, *Johnson v. Zerbst*, 304 U.S. 458 (1938), and we re-assert these standards as applied to in-custody interrogation. Since the State is responsible for establishing the isolated circumstances under which the interrogation takes place and has the only means of making available corroborated evidence of warnings given during incommunicado interrogation, the burden is rightly on its shoulders.

An express statement that the individual is willing to make a statement and does not want an attorney followed closely by a statement could constitute a waiver. But a valid waiver will not be presumed simply from the silence of the accused after warnings are given or simply from the fact that a confession was in fact eventually obtained. A statement we made in *Carnley v. Cochran*, 369 U.S. 506, 516 (1962), is applicable here:

> "Presuming waiver from a silent record is impermissible. The record must show, or there must be an allegation and evidence which show, that an accused was offered counsel but intelligently and understandingly rejected the offer. Anything less is not waiver."

See also *Glasser v. United States*, 315 U.S. 60 (1942). Moreover, where in-custody interrogation is involved, there is no room for the contention that the privilege is waived if the individual answers some questions or gives some information on his own prior to invoking his right to remain silent when interrogated.

Whatever the testimony of the authorities as to waiver of rights by an accused, the fact of lengthy interrogation or incommunicado incarceration before a statement is made is strong evidence that the accused did not validly waive his rights. In these circumstances the fact that the individual eventually made a statement is consistent with the conclusion that the compelling influence of the interrogation finally forced him to do so. It is inconsistent with any notion of a voluntary relinquishment of the privilege. Moreover, any evidence that the accused was threatened, tricked, or cajoled into a waiver will, of course, show that the defendant did not voluntarily waive his privilege. The requirement of warnings and waiver of rights is a fundamental with respect to the Fifth Amendment privilege and not simply a preliminary ritual to existing methods of interrogation.

The warnings required and the waiver necessary in accordance with our opinion today are, in the absence of a fully effective equivalent, prerequisites to the admissibility of any statement made by a defendant. No distinction can be drawn between statements which are direct confessions and statements which amount to "admissions" of part or all of an offense. The privilege against self-incrimination protects the individual from being compelled to incriminate himself in any manner; it does not distinguish degrees of incrimination. Similarly, for precisely the same reason, no distinction may be drawn between inculpatory statements and statements alleged to be merely "exculpatory." If a statement made were in fact truly exculpatory it would, of course, never be used by the prosecution. In fact, statements merely intended to be exculpatory by the defendant are often used to impeach his testimony at trial or to demonstrate untruths in the statement given under interrogation and thus to prove guilt by implication. These statements are incriminating in any meaningful sense of the word and may not be used without the full warnings and effective waiver required for any other statement. In Escobedo itself, the defendant fully intended his accusation of another as the slayer to be exculpatory as to himself.

The principles announced today deal with the protection which must be given to the privilege against self-incrimination when the individual is first subjected to police interrogation while in custody at the station or otherwise deprived of his freedom of action in any significant way. It is at this point that our adversary system of criminal proceedings commences, distinguishing itself at the outset from the inquisitorial system recognized in some countries. Under the system of warnings we delineate today or under any other system which may be devised and found effective, the safeguards to be erected about the privilege must come into play at this point.

Our decision is not intended to hamper the traditional function of police officers in investigating crime. See *Escobedo v. Illinois*, 378 U.S. 478, 492. When an individual is in custody on probable cause, the police may, of course, seek out evidence in the field to be used at trial against him. Such investigation may include inquiry of persons not under restraint. General on-the-scene questioning as to facts surrounding a crime or other general questioning of citizens in the fact-finding process is not affected by our holding. It is an act of responsible citizenship for individuals to give whatever information they may have to aid in law enforcement. In such situations the compelling atmosphere inherent in the process of in-custody interrogation is not necessarily present.

In dealing with statements obtained through interrogation, we do not purport to find all confessions inadmissible. Confessions remain a proper element in law enforcement. Any statement given freely and voluntarily without any compelling influences is, of course, admissible in evidence. The fundamental import of the privilege while an individual is in custody is not whether he is allowed to talk to the police without the benefit of warnings and counsel, but whether he can be interrogated. There is no requirement that police stop a person who enters a police station and states that he wishes to confess to a crime, or a person who calls the police to offer a confession or any other statement he desires to make. Volunteered statements of any kind are not barred by the Fifth Amendment and their admissibility is not affected by our holding today.

To summarize, we hold that when an individual is taken into custody or otherwise deprived of his freedom by the authorities in any significant way and is subjected to questioning, the privilege against self-incrimination is jeopardized. Procedural safeguards must be employed to protect the privilege, and unless other fully effective means are adopted to notify the person of his right of silence and to assure that the exercise of the right will be scrupulously honored, the following measures are required. He must be warned prior to any questioning that he has the right to remain silent, that anything he says can be used against him in a court of law, that he has the right to the presence of an attorney, and that if he cannot afford an attorney one will be appointed for him prior to any questioning if he so desires. Opportunity to exercise these rights must be afforded to him throughout the interrogation. After such warnings have been given, and such opportunity afforded him, the individual may knowingly and intelligently waive these rights and agree to answer questions or make a statement. But unless and until such warnings and waiver are demonstrated by the prosecution at trial, no evidence obtained as a result of interrogation can be used against him.

◆ IV

A recurrent argument made in these cases is that society's need for interrogation outweighs the privilege. This argument is not unfamiliar to this Court. See, e. g., *Chambers v. Florida*, 309 U.S. 227, 240-241 (1940). The whole thrust of our foregoing discussion demonstrates that the Constitution has prescribed the rights of the individual when confronted with the power of government when it provided in the Fifth Amendment that an individual cannot be compelled to be a witness against himself. That right cannot be abridged. As Mr. Justice Brandeis once observed:

"Decency, security and liberty alike demand that government officials shall be subjected to the same rules of conduct that are commands to the citizen. In a government of laws, existence of the government will be imperilled if it fails to observe the law scrupulously. Our Government is the potent, the omnipresent teacher. For good or for ill, it teaches the whole people by its example. Crime is contagious. If the Government becomes a lawbreaker, it breeds contempt for law; it invites every man to become a law unto himself; it invites anarchy. To declare that in the administration of the criminal law the end justifies the means … would bring terrible retribution. Against that pernicious doctrine this Court should resolutely set its face." *Olmstead v. United States*, 277 U.S. 438, 485 (1928) (dissenting opinion).

In this connection, one of our country's distinguished jurists has pointed out: "The quality of a nation's civilization can be largely measured by the methods it uses in the enforcement of its criminal law."

If the individual desires to exercise his privilege, he has the right to do so. This is not for the authorities to decide. An attorney may advise his client not to talk to police until he has had an opportunity to investigate the case, or he may wish to be present with his client during any police questioning. In doing so an attorney is merely exercising the good professional judgment he has been taught. This is not cause for considering the attorney a menace to law enforcement. He is merely carrying out what he is sworn to do under his oath—to protect to the extent of his ability the rights of his client. In fulfilling this responsibility the attorney plays a vital role in the administration of criminal justice under our Constitution.

In announcing these principles, we are not unmindful of the burdens which law enforcement officials must bear, often under trying circumstances. We also fully recognize the obligation of all citizens to aid in enforcing the criminal laws. This Court, while protecting individual rights, has always given ample latitude to law enforcement agencies in the legitimate exercise of their duties. The limits we have placed on the interrogation process should not constitute an undue interference with a proper system of law enforcement. As we have noted, our decision does not in any way preclude police from carrying out their traditional investigatory functions. Although confessions may play an important role in some convictions, the cases before us present graphic examples of the overstatement of the "need" for confessions. In each case authorities conducted interrogations ranging up to five days in duration despite the presence, through standard investigating practices, of considerable evidence against each defendant. Further examples are chronicled in our prior cases. See, e. g., *Haynes v. Washington*, 373 U.S. 503, 518-519 (1963); *Rogers v. Richmond*, 365 U.S. 534, 541 (1961); *Malinski v. New York*, 324 U.S. 401, 402 (1945).

It is also urged that an unfettered right to detention for interrogation should be allowed because it will often redound to the benefit of the person questioned. When police inquiry determines that there is no reason to believe that the person has committed any crime, it is said, he will be released without need for further formal procedures. The person who has committed no offense, however, will be better able to clear himself after warnings with counsel present than without. It can be assumed that in such circumstances a lawyer would advise his client to talk freely to police in order to clear himself.

Custodial interrogation, by contrast, does not necessarily afford the innocent an opportunity to clear themselves. A serious consequence of the present practice of the interrogation alleged to be beneficial for the innocent is that many arrests "for investigation" subject large numbers of innocent persons to detention and interrogation. In one of the cases before us, No. 584, *California v. Stewart*, police held four persons, who were in the defendant's house at the time of the arrest, in jail for five days until defendant confessed. At that time they were finally released. Police stated that there was "no evidence to connect them with any crime." Available statistics on the extent of this practice where it is condoned indicate that these four are far from alone in being subjected to arrest, prolonged detention, and interrogation without the requisite probable cause.

Over the years the Federal Bureau of Investigation has compiled an exemplary record of effective law enforcement while advising any suspect or arrested person, at the outset of an interview, that he is not required to make a statement, that any statement may be used against him in court, that the individual may obtain the services of an attorney of his own choice and, more recently, that he has a right to free counsel if he is unable to pay. A letter received from the Solicitor General in response to a question from the Bench makes it clear that the present pattern of warnings and respect for the rights of the individual followed as a practice by the FBI is consistent with the procedure which we delineate today. It states:

> "At the oral argument of the above cause, Mr. Justice Fortas asked whether I could provide certain information as to the practices followed by the Federal Bureau of Investigation. I have directed these questions to the attention of the Director of the Federal Bureau of Investigation and am submitting herewith a statement of the questions and of the answers which we have received.
>
> "'(1) When an individual is interviewed by agents of the Bureau, what warning is given to him?
>
> "'The standard warning long given by Special Agents of the FBI to both suspects and persons under arrest is that the person has a right to say nothing and a right to counsel, and that

any statement he does make may be used against him in court. Examples of this warning are to be found in the Westover case at 342 F.2d 684 (1965), and *Jackson v. U.S.*, 337 F.2d 136 (1964), cert. den. 380 U.S. 935.

"'After passage of the Criminal Justice Act of 1964, which provides free counsel for Federal defendants unable to pay, we added to our instructions to Special Agents the requirement that any person who is under arrest for an offense under FBI jurisdiction, or whose arrest is contemplated following the interview, must also be advised of his right to free counsel if he is unable to pay, and the fact that such counsel will be assigned by the Judge. At the same time, we broadened the right to counsel warning to read counsel of his own choice, or anyone else with whom he might wish to speak.

"'(2) When is the warning given?

"'The FBI warning is given to a suspect at the very outset of the interview, as shown in the Westover case, cited above. The warning may be given to a person arrested as soon as practicable after the arrest, as shown in the Jackson case, also cited above, and in *U.S. v. Konigsberg*, 336 F.2d 844 (1964), cert. den. 379 U.S. 933, but in any event it must precede the interview with the person for a confession or admission of his own guilt.

"'(3) What is the Bureau's practice in the event that (a) the individual requests counsel and (b) counsel appears?

"'When the person who has been warned of his right to counsel decides that he wishes to consult with counsel before making a statement, the interview is terminated at that point, *Shultz v. U.S.*, 351 F.2d 287 (1965). It may be continued, however, as to all matters other than the person's own guilt or innocence. If he is indecisive in his request for counsel, there may be some question on whether he did or did not waive counsel. Situations of this kind must necessarily be left to the judgment of the interviewing Agent. For example, in *Hiram v. U.S.*, 354 F.2d 4 (1965), the Agent's conclusion that the person arrested had waived his right to counsel was upheld by the courts.

"'A person being interviewed and desiring to consult counsel by telephone must be permitted to do so, as shown in *Caldwell v. U.S.*, 351 F.2d 459 (1965). When counsel appears in person, he is permitted to confer with his client in private.

"'(4) What is the Bureau's practice if the individual requests counsel, but cannot afford to retain an attorney?

"'If any person being interviewed after warning of counsel decides that he wishes to consult with counsel before proceeding further the interview is terminated, as shown above. FBI Agents do not pass judgment on the ability of the person to pay for counsel. They do, however, advise those who have been arrested for an offense under FBI jurisdiction, or whose arrest is contemplated following the interview, of a right to free counsel if they are unable to pay, and the availability of such counsel from the Judge.'"

The practice of the FBI can readily be emulated by state and local enforcement agencies. The argument that the FBI deals with different crimes than are dealt with by state authorities does not mitigate the significance of the FBI experience.

The experience in some other countries also suggests that the danger to law enforcement in curbs on interrogation is overplayed. The English procedure since 1912 under the Judges' Rules is significant. As recently strengthened, the Rules require that a cautionary warning be given an accused by a police officer as soon as he has evidence that affords reasonable grounds for suspicion; they also require that any statement made be given by the accused without questioning by police. The right of the individual to consult with an attorney during this period is expressly recognized.

The safeguards present under Scottish law may be even greater than in England. Scottish judicial decisions bar use in evidence of most confessions obtained through police interrogation. In India, confessions made to police not in the presence of a magistrate have been excluded by rule of evidence since 1872, at a time when it operated under British law. Identical provisions appear in the Evidence Ordinance of Ceylon, enacted in 1895. Similarly, in our country the Uniform Code of Military Justice has long provided that no suspect may be interrogated without first being warned of his right not to make a statement and that any statement he makes may be used against him. Denial of the right to consult counsel during interrogation has also been proscribed by military tribunals. There appears to have been no marked detrimental effect on criminal law enforcement in these jurisdictions as a result of these rules. Conditions of law enforcement in our country are sufficiently similar to permit reference to this experience as assurance that lawlessness will not result from warning an individual of his rights or allowing him to exercise them. Moreover, it is consistent with our legal system that we give at least as much protection to these rights as is given in the jurisdictions described. We deal in our country with rights grounded in a specific requirement of the Fifth Amendment of the Constitution, whereas other jurisdictions arrived at their conclusions on the basis of principles of justice not so specifically defined.

It is also urged upon us that we withhold decision on this issue until state legislative bodies and advisory groups have had an opportunity to deal with these problems by rule making. We have already pointed out that the Constitution does not require any specific code of procedures for protecting the privilege against self-incrimination during custodial interrogation. Congress and the States are free to develop their own safeguards for the privilege, so long as they are fully as effective as those described above in informing accused persons of their right of silence and in affording a continuous opportunity to exercise it. In any event, however, the issues presented are of constitutional dimensions and must be determined by the courts. The admissibility of a statement in the face of a claim that it was obtained in violation of the defendant's constitutional rights is an issue the resolution of which has long since been undertaken by this Court. See *Hopt v. Utah*, 110 U.S. 574 (1884). Judicial solutions to problems of constitutional dimension have evolved decade by decade. As courts have been presented with the need to enforce constitutional rights, they have found means of doing so. That was our responsibility when Escobedo was before us and it is our responsibility today. Where rights secured by the Constitution are involved, there can be no rule making or legislation which would abrogate them.

◆ V

Because of the nature of the problem and because of its recurrent significance in numerous cases, we have to this point discussed the relationship of the Fifth Amendment privilege to police interrogation without specific concentration on the facts of the cases before us. We turn now to these facts to consider the application to these cases of the constitutional principles discussed above. In each instance, we have concluded that statements were obtained from the defendant under circumstances that did not meet constitutional standards for protection of the privilege.

No. 759. *Miranda v. Arizona.*

On March 13, 1963, petitioner, Ernesto Miranda, was arrested at his home and taken in custody to a Phoenix police station. He was there identified by the complaining witness. The police then took him to "Interrogation Room No. 2" of the detective bureau. There he was questioned by two police officers. The officers admitted at trial that Miranda was not advised that he had a right to have an attorney present. Two hours later, the officers emerged from the interrogation room with a written confession signed by Miranda. At the top of the statement was a typed paragraph stating that the confession was made voluntarily, without threats or promises of immunity and "with full knowledge of my legal rights, understanding any statement I make may be used against me."

At his trial before a jury, the written confession was admitted into evidence over the objection of defense counsel, and the officers testified to the prior oral confession made by Miranda during the interrogation. Miranda was found guilty of kidnapping and rape. He was sentenced to 20 to 30 years' imprisonment on each count, the sentences to run concurrently. On appeal, the Supreme Court of Arizona held that Miranda's constitutional rights were not violated in obtaining the confession and affirmed the conviction. 98 Ariz. 18, 401 P.2d 721. In reaching its decision, the court emphasized heavily the fact that Miranda did not specifically request counsel.

We reverse. From the testimony of the officers and by the admission of respondent, it is clear that Miranda was not in any way apprised of his right to consult with an attorney and to have one present during the interrogation, nor was his right not to be compelled to incriminate himself effectively protected in any other manner. Without these warnings the statements were inadmissible. The mere fact that he signed a statement which contained a typed-in clause stating that he had "full knowledge" of his "legal rights" does not approach the knowing and intelligent waiver required to relinquish constitutional rights. Cf. *Haynes v. Washington*, 373 U.S. 503, 512-513 (1963); *Haley v. Ohio*, 332 U.S. 596, 601 (1948) (opinion of MR. JUSTICE DOUGLAS).

No. 760. *Vignera v. New York.*

Petitioner, Michael Vignera, was picked up by New York police on October 14, 1960, in connection with the robbery three days earlier of a Brooklyn dress shop. They took him to the 17th Detective Squad headquarters in Manhattan. Sometime thereafter he was taken to the 66th Detective Squad. There a detective questioned Vignera with respect to the robbery. Vignera orally admitted the robbery to the detective. The detective was asked on cross-examination at trial by defense counsel whether Vignera was warned of his right to counsel before being interrogated. The prosecution objected to the question and the trial judge sustained the objection. Thus, the defense was precluded from making any showing that warnings had not been given. While at the 66th Detective Squad, Vignera was identified by the store owner and a saleslady as the man who robbed the dress shop. At about 3 p. m. he was formally arrested. The police then transported him to still another station, the 70th Precinct in Brooklyn, "for detention." At 11 p. m. Vignera was questioned by an assistant district attorney in the presence of a hearing reporter who transcribed the questions and Vignera's answers. This verbatim account of these proceedings contains no statement of any warnings given by the assistant district attorney. At Vignera's trial on a charge of first degree robbery, the detective testified as to the oral confession. The transcription of the statement taken was also introduced in evidence. At the conclusion of the testimony, the trial judge charged the jury in part as follows:

"The law doesn't say that the confession is void or invalidated because the police officer didn't advise the defendant as to his rights. Did you hear what I said? I am telling you what the law of the State of New York is."

Vignera was found guilty of first degree robbery. He was subsequently adjudged a third-felony offender and sentenced to 30 to 60 years' imprisonment. The conviction was affirmed without opinion by the Appellate Division, Second Department, 21 App. Div. 2d 752, 252 N. Y. S. 2d 19, and by the Court of Appeals, also without opinion, 15 N. Y. 2d 970, 207 N. E. 2d 527, 259 N. Y. S. 2d 857, remittitur amended, 16 N. Y. 2d 614, 209 N. E. 2d 110, 261 N. Y. S. 2d 65. In argument to the Court of Appeals, the State contended that Vignera had no constitutional right to be advised of his right to counsel or his privilege against self-incrimination.

We reverse. The foregoing indicates that Vignera was not warned of any of his rights before the questioning by the detective and by the assistant district attorney. No other steps were taken to protect these rights. Thus he was not effectively apprised of his Fifth Amendment privilege or of his right to have counsel present and his statements are inadmissible.

No. 761. *Westover v. United States.*

At approximately 9:45 p. m. on March 20, 1963, petitioner, Carl Calvin Westover, was arrested by local police in Kansas City as a suspect in two Kansas City robberies. A report was also received from the FBI that he was wanted on a felony charge in California. The local authorities took him to a police station and placed him in a line-up on the local charges, and at about 11:45 p. m. he was booked. Kansas City police interrogated Westover on the night of his arrest. He denied any knowledge of criminal activities. The next day local officers interrogated him again throughout the morning. Shortly before noon they informed the FBI that they were through interrogating Westover and that the FBI could proceed to interrogate him. There is nothing in the record to indicate that Westover was ever given any warning as to his rights by local police. At noon, three special agents of the FBI continued the interrogation in a private interview room of the Kansas City Police Department, this time with respect to the robbery of a savings and loan association and a bank in Sacramento, California. After two or two and one-half hours, Westover signed separate confessions to each of these two robberies which had been prepared by one of the agents during the interrogation. At trial one of the agents testified, and a paragraph on each of the statements states, that the agents advised Westover that he did not have to make a statement, that any statement he made could be used against him, and that he had the right to see an attorney.

Westover was tried by a jury in federal court and convicted of the California robberies. His statements were introduced at trial. He was sentenced to 15 years' imprisonment on each count, the sentences to run consecutively. On appeal, the conviction was affirmed by the Court of Appeals for the Ninth Circuit. 342 F.2d 684.

We reverse. On the facts of this case we cannot find that Westover knowingly and intelligently waived his right to remain silent and his right to consult with counsel prior to the time he made the statement. At the time the FBI agents began questioning Westover, he had been in custody for over 14 hours and had been interrogated at length during that period. The FBI interrogation began immediately upon the conclusion of the interrogation by Kansas City police and was conducted in local police headquarters. Although the two law enforcement authorities are legally distinct and the crimes for which they interrogated Westover were different, the impact on him was that of a continuous period of questioning. There is no evidence of any warning given prior to the FBI interrogation nor is there any evidence of an articulated waiver of rights after the FBI commenced its interrogation. The record simply shows that the defendant did in fact confess a short time after being turned over to the FBI following interrogation by local police. Despite the fact that the FBI agents gave warnings at the outset of their interview, from Westover's point of view the warnings came at the end of the interrogation process. In these circumstances an intelligent waiver of constitutional rights cannot be assumed.

We do not suggest that law enforcement authorities are precluded from questioning any individual who has been held for a period of time by other authorities and interrogated by them without appropriate warnings. A different case would be presented if an accused were taken into custody by the second authority, removed both in time and place from his original surroundings, and then adequately advised of his rights and given an opportunity to exercise them. But here the FBI interrogation was conducted immediately following the state interrogation in the same police station—in the same compelling surroundings. Thus, in obtaining a confession from Westover the federal authorities were the beneficiaries of the pressure applied by the local in-custody interrogation. In these circumstances the giving of warnings alone was not sufficient to protect the privilege.

In the course of investigating a series of purse-snatch robberies in which one of the victims had died of injuries inflicted by her assailant, respondent, Roy Allen Stewart, was pointed out to Los Angeles police as the endorser of dividend checks taken in one of the robberies. At about 7:15 p. m., January 31, 1963, police officers went to Stewart's house and arrested him. One of the officers asked Stewart if they could search the house, to which he replied, "Go ahead." The search turned up various items taken from the five robbery victims. At the time of Stewart's arrest, police also arrested Stewart's wife and three other persons who were visiting him. These four were jailed along with Stewart and were interrogated. Stewart was taken to the University Station of the Los Angeles Police Department where he was placed in a cell. During the next five days, police interrogated Stewart on nine different occasions. Except during the first interrogation session, when he was confronted with an accusing witness, Stewart was isolated with his interrogators.

During the ninth interrogation session, Stewart admitted that he had robbed the deceased and stated that he had not meant to hurt her. Police then brought Stewart before a magistrate for the first time. Since there was no evidence to connect them with any crime, the police then released the other four persons arrested with him.

Nothing in the record specifically indicates whether Stewart was or was not advised of his right to remain silent or his right to counsel. In a number of instances, however, the interrogating officers were asked to recount everything that was said during the interrogations. None indicated that Stewart was ever advised of his rights.

Stewart was charged with kidnapping to commit robbery, rape, and murder. At his trial, transcripts of the first interrogation and the confession at the last interrogation were introduced in evidence. The jury found Stewart guilty of robbery and first degree murder and fixed the penalty as death. On appeal, the Supreme Court of California reversed. 62 Cal. 2d 571, 400 P.2d 97, 43 Cal. Rptr. 201. It held that under this Court's decision in Escobedo, Stewart should have been advised of his right to remain silent and of his right to counsel and that it would not presume in the face of a silent record that the police advised Stewart of his rights.

We affirm. In dealing with custodial interrogation, we will not presume that a defendant has been effectively apprised of his rights and that his privilege against self-incrimination has been adequately safeguarded on a record that does not show that any warnings have been given or that any effective alternative has been employed. Nor can a knowing and intelligent waiver of these rights be assumed on a silent record. Furthermore, Stewart's steadfast denial of the alleged offenses through eight of the nine interrogations over a period of five days is subject to no other construction than that he was compelled by persistent interrogation to forgo his Fifth Amendment privilege.

Therefore, in accordance with the foregoing, the judgments of the Supreme Court of Arizona in No. 759, of the New York Court of Appeals in No. 760, and of the Court of Appeals for the Ninth Circuit in No. 761 are reversed. The judgment of the Supreme Court of California in No. 584 is affirmed.

It is so ordered.

Mr. Justice Clark, Dissenting in Nos. 759, 760, and 761, and Concurring in the Result in No. 584

It is with regret that I find it necessary to write in these cases. However, I am unable to join the majority because its opinion goes too far on too little, while my dissenting brethren do not go quite far enough. Nor can I join in the Court's criticism of the present practices of police and investigatory agencies as to custodial interrogation. The materials it refers to as "police manuals" are, as I read them, merely writings in this field by professors and some police officers. Not one is shown by the record here to be the official manual of any police department, much less in universal use in crime detection. Moreover, the examples of police brutality mentioned by the Court are rare exceptions to the thousands of cases that appear every year in the law reports. The police agencies—all the way from municipal and state forces to the federal bureaus—are responsible for law enforcement and public safety in this country. I am proud of their efforts, which in my view are not fairly characterized by the Court's opinion.

♦ I

The ipse dixit of the majority has no support in our cases. Indeed, the Court admits that "we might not find the defendants' statements [here] to have been involuntary in traditional terms." Ante, p. 457. In short, the Court has added more to the requirements that the accused is entitled to consult with his lawyer and that he must be given the traditional warning that he may remain silent and that anything that he says may be used against him. Escobedo v. Illinois, 378 U.S. 478, 490-491 (1964). Now, the Court fashions a constitutional rule that the police may engage in no custodial interrogation without additionally advising the accused that he has a right under the Fifth Amendment to the presence of counsel during interrogation and that, if he is without funds, counsel will be furnished him. When at any point during an interrogation the accused seeks affirmatively or impliedly to invoke his rights to silence or counsel, interrogation must be forgone or postponed. The Court further holds that failure to follow the new procedures requires inexorably the exclusion of any statement by the accused, as well as the fruits thereof. Such a strict constitutional specific inserted at the nerve center of crime detection may well kill the patient. Since there is at this time a paucity of information and an almost total lack of empirical knowledge on the practical operation of requirements truly comparable to those announced by the majority, I would be more restrained lest we go too far too fast.

◆ II

Custodial interrogation has long been recognized as "undoubtedly an essential tool in effective law enforcement." *Haynes v. Washington*, 373 U.S. 503, 515 (1963). Recognition of this fact should put us on guard against the promulgation of doctrinaire rules. Especially is this true where the Court finds that "the Constitution has prescribed" its holding and where the light of our past cases, from *Hopt v. Utah*, 110 U.S. 574, (1884), down to *Haynes v. Washington*, supra, is to the contrary. Indeed, even in Escobedo the Court never hinted that an affirmative "waiver" was a prerequisite to questioning; that the burden of proof as to waiver was on the prosecution; that the presence of counsel—absent a waiver—during interrogation was required; that a waiver can be withdrawn at the will of the accused; that counsel must be furnished during an accusatory stage to those unable to pay; nor that admissions and exculpatory statements are "confessions." To require all those things at one gulp should cause the Court to choke over more cases than *Crooker v. California*, 357 U.S. 433 (1958), and *Cicenia v. Lagay*, 357 U.S. 504 (1958), which it expressly overrules today.

The rule prior to today—as Mr. Justice Goldberg, the author of the Court's opinion in Escobedo, stated it in *Haynes v. Washington*—depended upon "a totality of circumstances evidencing an involuntary ... admission of guilt." 373 U.S., at 514. And he concluded:

> "Of course, detection and solution of crime is, at best, a difficult and arduous task requiring determination and persistence on the part of all responsible officers charged with the duty of law enforcement. And, certainly, we do not mean to suggest that all interrogation of witnesses and suspects is impermissible. Such questioning is undoubtedly an essential tool in effective law enforcement. The line between proper and permissible police conduct and techniques and methods offensive to due process is, at best, a difficult one to draw, particularly in cases such as this where it is necessary to make fine judgments as to the effect of psychologically coercive pressures and inducements on the mind and will of an accused.... We are here impelled to the conclusion, from all of the facts presented, that

the bounds of due process have been exceeded." Id., at 514-515.

◆ III

I would continue to follow that rule. Under the "totality of circumstances" rule of which my Brother Goldberg spoke in Haynes, I would consider in each case whether the police officer prior to custodial interrogation added the warning that the suspect might have counsel present at the interrogation and, further, that a court would appoint one at his request if he was too poor to employ counsel. In the absence of warnings, the burden would be on the State to prove that counsel was knowingly and intelligently waived or that in the totality of the circumstances, including the failure to give the necessary warnings, the confession was clearly voluntary.

Rather than employing the arbitrary Fifth Amendment rule which the Court lays down I would follow the more pliable dictates of the Due Process Clauses of the Fifth and Fourteenth Amendments which we are accustomed to administering and which we know from our cases are effective instruments in protecting persons in police custody. In this way we would not be acting in the dark nor in one full sweep changing the traditional rules of custodial interrogation which this Court has for so long recognized as a justifiable and proper tool in balancing individual rights against the rights of society. It will be soon enough to go further when we are able to appraise with somewhat better accuracy the effect of such a holding.

I would affirm the convictions in *Miranda v. Arizona*, No. 759; *Vignera v. New York*, No. 760; and *Westover v. United States*, No. 761. In each of those cases I find from the circumstances no warrant for reversal. In *California v. Stewart*, No. 584, I would dismiss the writ of certiorari for want of a final judgment, 28 U.S.C. 1257 (3) (1964 ed.); but if the merits are to be reached I would affirm on the ground that the State failed to fulfill its burden, in the absence of a showing that appropriate warnings were given, of proving a waiver or a totality of circumstances showing voluntariness. Should there be a retrial, I would leave the State free to attempt to prove these elements.

Mr. Justice Harlan, whom Mr. Justice Stewart and Mr. Justice White Join, Dissenting

I believe the decision of the Court represents poor constitutional law and entails harmful consequences for the country at large. How serious these consequences may prove to be only time can tell. But the basic flaws in the Court's justification seem to me readily apparent now once all sides of the problem are considered.

◆ Introduction

At the outset, it is well to note exactly what is required by the Court's new constitutional code of rules for confessions. The foremost requirement, upon which later admissibility of a confession depends, is that a fourfold warning be given to a person in custody before he is questioned, namely, that he has a right to remain silent, that anything he says may be used against him, that he has a right to have present an attorney during the questioning, and that if indigent he has a right to a lawyer without charge. To forgo these rights, some affirmative statement of rejection is seemingly required, and threats, tricks, or cajolings to obtain this waiver are forbidden. If before or during questioning the suspect seeks to invoke his right to remain silent, interrogation must be forgone or cease; a request for counsel brings about the same result until a lawyer is procured. Finally, there are a miscellany of minor directives, for example, the burden of proof of waiver is on the State, admissions and exculpatory statements are treated just like confessions, withdrawal of a waiver is always permitted, and so forth.

While the fine points of this scheme are far less clear than the Court admits, the tenor is quite apparent. The new rules are not designed to guard against police brutality or other unmistakably banned forms of coercion. Those who use third-degree tactics and deny them in court are equally able and destined to lie as skillfully about warnings and waivers. Rather, the thrust of the new rules is to negate all pressures, to reinforce the nervous or ignorant suspect, and ultimately to discourage any confession at all. The aim in short is toward "voluntariness" in a utopian sense, or to view it from a different angle, voluntariness with a vengeance.

To incorporate this notion into the Constitution requires a strained reading of history and precedent and a disregard of the very pragmatic concerns that alone may on occasion justify such strains. I believe that reasoned examination will show that the Due Process Clauses provide an adequate tool for coping with confessions and that, even if the Fifth Amendment privilege against self-incrimination be invoked, its precedents taken as a whole do not sustain the present rules. Viewed as a choice based on pure pol-

icy, these new rules prove to be a highly debatable, if not one-sided, appraisal of the competing interests, imposed over widespread objection, at the very time when judicial restraint is most called for by the circumstances.

◆ II. Constitutional Premises

It is most fitting to begin an inquiry into the constitutional precedents by surveying the limits on confessions the Court has evolved under the Due Process Clause of the Fourteenth Amendment. This is so because these cases show that there exists a workable and effective means of dealing with confessions in a judicial manner; because the cases are the baseline from which the Court now departs and so serve to measure the actual as opposed to the professed distance it travels; and because examination of them helps reveal how the Court has coasted into its present position.

The earliest confession cases in this Court emerged from federal prosecutions and were settled on a nonconstitutional basis, the Court adopting the common-law rule that the absence of inducements, promises, and threats made a confession voluntary and admissible. *Hopt v. Utah*, 110 U.S. 574; *Pierce v. United States*, 160 U.S. 355. While a later case said the Fifth Amendment privilege controlled admissibility, this proposition was not itself developed in subsequent decisions. The Court did, however, heighten the test of admissibility in federal trials to one of voluntariness "in fact," *Wan v. United States*, 266 U.S. 1, 14 (quoted, ante, p. 462), and then by and large left federal judges to apply the same standards the Court began to derive in a string of state court cases.

This new line of decisions, testing admissibility by the Due Process Clause, began in 1936 with *Brown v. Mississippi*, 297 U.S. 278, and must now embrace somewhat more than 30 full opinions of the Court. While the voluntariness rubric was repeated in many instances, e. g., *Lyons v. Oklahoma*, 322 U.S. 596, the Court never pinned it down to a single meaning but on the contrary infused it with a number of different values. To travel quickly over the main themes, there was an initial emphasis on reliability, e. g., *Ward v. Texas*, 316 U.S. 547, supplemented by concern over the legality and fairness of the police practices, e. g., *Ashcraft v. Tennessee*, 322 U.S. 143, in an "accusatorial" system of law enforcement, *Watts v. Indiana*, 338 U.S. 49, 54, and eventually by close attention to the individual's state of mind and capacity for effective choice, e. g., *Gallegos v. Colorado*, 370 U.S. 49. The outcome was a continuing re-evaluation on the facts of each case of how much pressure on the suspect was permissible.

Among the criteria often taken into account were threats or imminent danger, e. g., *Payne v. Arkansas*, 356 U.S. 560, physical deprivations such as lack of sleep or food, e. g., *Reck v. Pate*, 367 U.S. 433, repeated or extended interrogation, e. g., *Chambers v. Florida*, 309 U.S. 227, limits on access to counsel or friends, *Crooker v. California*, 357 U.S. 433; *Cicenia v. Lagay*, 357 U.S. 504, length and illegality of detention under state law, e. g., *Haynes v. Washington*, 373 U.S. 503, and individual weakness or incapacities, *Lynumn v. Illinois*, 372 U.S. 528. Apart from direct physical coercion, however, no single default or fixed combination of defaults guaranteed exclusion, and synopses of the cases would serve little use because the overall gauge has been steadily changing, usually in the direction of restricting admissibility. But to mark just what point had been reached before the Court jumped the rails in *Escobedo v. Illinois*, 378 U.S. 478, it is worth capsulizing the then-recent case of *Haynes v. Washington*, 373 U.S. 503. There, Haynes had been held some 16 or more hours in violation of state law before signing the disputed confession, had received no warnings of any kind, and despite requests had been refused access to his wife or to counsel, the police indicating that access would be allowed after a confession. Emphasizing especially this last inducement and rejecting some contrary indicia of voluntariness, the Court in a 5-to-4 decision held the confession inadmissible.

There are several relevant lessons to be drawn from this constitutional history. The first is that with over 25 years of precedent the Court has developed an elaborate, sophisticated, and sensitive approach to admissibility of confessions. It is "judicial" in its treatment of one case at a time, see *Culombe v. Connecticut*, 367 U.S. 568, 635 (concurring opinion of THE CHIEF JUSTICE), flexible in its ability to respond to the endless mutations of fact presented, and ever more familiar to the lower courts. Of course, strict certainty is not obtained in this developing process, but this is often so with constitutional principles, and disagreement is usually confined to that borderland of close cases where it matters least.

The second point is that in practice and from time to time in principle, the Court has given ample recognition to society's interest in suspect questioning as an instrument of law enforcement. Cases countenancing quite significant pressures can be cited without difficulty, and the lower courts may often have been yet more tolerant. Of course the lim-itations imposed today were rejected by necessary implication in case after case, the right to warnings having been explicitly rebuffed in this Court many years ago. *Powers v. United States*, 223 U.S. 303; *Wilson v. United States*, 162 U.S. 613. As recently as *Haynes v. Washington*, 373 U.S. 503, 515, the Court openly acknowledged that questioning of witnesses and suspects "is undoubtedly an essential tool in effective law enforcement." Accord, *Crooker v. California*, 357 U.S. 433, 441.

Finally, the cases disclose that the language in many of the opinions overstates the actual course of decision. It has been said, for example, that an admissible confession must be made by the suspect "in the unfettered exercise of his own will," *Malloy v. Hogan*, 378 U.S. 1, 8, and that "a prisoner is not 'to be made the deluded instrument of his own conviction,'" *Culombe v. Connecticut*, 367 U.S. 568, 581 (Frankfurter, J., announcing the Court's judgment and an opinion). Though often repeated, such principles are rarely observed in full measure. Even the word "voluntary" may be deemed somewhat misleading, especially when one considers many of the confessions that have been brought under its umbrella. See, e. g., supra, n. 5. The tendency to overstate may be laid in part to the flagrant facts often before the Court; but in any event one must recognize how it has tempered attitudes and lent some color of authority to the approach now taken by the Court.

I turn now to the Court's asserted reliance on the Fifth Amendment, an approach which I frankly regard as a trompe l'oeil. The Court's opinion in my view reveals no adequate basis for extending the Fifth Amendment's privilege against self-incrimination to the police station. Far more important, it fails to show that the Court's new rules are well supported, let alone compelled, by Fifth Amendment precedents. Instead, the new rules actually derive from quotation and analogy drawn from precedents under the Sixth Amendment, which should properly have no bearing on police interrogation.

The Court's opening contention, that the Fifth Amendment governs police station confessions, is perhaps not an impermissible extension of the law but it has little to commend itself in the present circumstances. Historically, the privilege against self-incrimination did not bear at all on the use of extra-legal confessions, for which distinct standards evolved; indeed, "the history of the two principles is wide apart, differing by one hundred years in origin, and derived through separate lines of precedents...." 8 Wigmore, Evidence 2266, at 401 (McNaughton rev.

1961). Practice under the two doctrines has also differed in a number of important respects. Even those who would readily enlarge the privilege must concede some linguistic difficulties since the Fifth Amendment in terms proscribes only compelling any person "in any criminal case to be a witness against himself." Cf. Kamisar, Equal Justice in the Gatehouses and Mansions of American Criminal Procedure, in Criminal Justice in Our Time 1, 25-26 (1965).

Though weighty, I do not say these points and similar ones are conclusive, for, as the Court reiterates, the privilege embodies basic principles always capable of expansion. Certainly the privilege does represent a protective concern for the accused and an emphasis upon accusatorial rather than inquisitorial values in law enforcement, although this is similarly true of other limitations such as the grand jury requirement and the reasonable doubt standard. Accusatorial values, however, have openly been absorbed into the due process standard governing confessions; this indeed is why at present "the kinship of the two rules [governing confessions and self-incrimination] is too apparent for denial." McCormick, Evidence 155 (1954). Since extension of the general principle has already occurred, to insist that the privilege applies as such serves only to carry over inapposite historical details and engaging rhetoric and to obscure the policy choices to be made in regulating confessions.

Having decided that the Fifth Amendment privilege does apply in the police station, the Court reveals that the privilege imposes more exacting restrictions than does the Fourteenth Amendment's voluntariness test. It then emerges from a discussion of Escobedo that the Fifth Amendment requires for an admissible confession that it be given by one distinctly aware of his right not to speak and shielded from "the compelling atmosphere" of interrogation. See ante, pp. 465-466. From these key premises, the Court finally develops the safeguards of warning, counsel, and so forth. I do not believe these premises are sustained by precedents under the Fifth Amendment.

The more important premise is that pressure on the suspect must be eliminated though it be only the subtle influence of the atmosphere and surroundings. The Fifth Amendment, however, has never been thought to forbid all pressure to incriminate one's self in the situations covered by it. On the contrary, it has been held that failure to incriminate one's self can result in denial of removal of one's case from state to federal court, *Maryland v. Soper*, 270 U.S. 9; in refusal of a military commission, *Orloff v.*

Willoughby, 345 U.S. 83; in denial of a discharge in bankruptcy, *Kaufman v. Hurwitz*, 176 F.2d 210; and in numerous other adverse consequences. See 8 Wigmore, Evidence 2272, at 441-444, n. 18 (McNaughton rev. 1961); Maguire, Evidence of Guilt 2.062 (1959). This is not to say that short of jail or torture any sanction is permissible in any case; policy and history alike may impose sharp limits. See, e. g., *Griffin v. California*, 380 U.S. 609. However, the Court's unspoken assumption that any pressure violates the privilege is not supported by the precedents and it has failed to show why the Fifth Amendment prohibits that relatively mild pressure the Due Process Clause permits.

The Court appears similarly wrong in thinking that precise knowledge of one's rights is a settled prerequisite under the Fifth Amendment to the loss of its protections. A number of lower federal court cases have held that grand jury witnesses need not always be warned of their privilege, e. g., *United States v. Scully*, 225 F.2d 113, 116, and Wigmore states this to be the better rule for trial witnesses. See 8 Wigmore, Evidence 2269 (McNaughton rev. 1961). Cf. *Henry v. Mississippi*, 379 U.S. 443, 451-452 (waiver of constitutional rights by counsel despite defendant's ignorance held allowable). No Fifth Amendment precedent is cited for the Court's contrary view. There might of course be reasons apart from Fifth Amendment precedent for requiring warning or any other safeguard on questioning but that is a different matter entirely. See infra, pp. 516-517.

A closing word must be said about the Assistance of Counsel Clause of the Sixth Amendment, which is never expressly relied on by the Court but whose judicial precedents turn out to be linchpins of the confession rules announced today. To support its requirement of a knowing and intelligent waiver, the Court cites *Johnson v. Zerbst*, 304 U.S. 458, ante, p. 475; appointment of counsel for the indigent suspect is tied to *Gideon v. Wainwright*, 372 U.S. 335, and *Douglas v. California*, 372 U.S. 353, ante, p. 473; the silent-record doctrine is borrowed from *Carnley v. Cochran*, 369 U.S. 506, ante, p. 475, as is the right to an express offer of counsel, ante, p. 471. All these cases imparting glosses to the Sixth Amendment concerned counsel at trial or on appeal. While the Court finds no pertinent difference between judicial proceedings and police interrogation, I believe the differences are so vast as to disqualify wholly the Sixth Amendment precedents as suitable analogies in the present cases.

The only attempt in this Court to carry the right to counsel into the station house occurred in Escobedo, the Court repeating several times that that stage was no less "critical" than trial itself. See 378 U.S., 485-488. This is hardly persuasive when we consider that a grand jury inquiry, the filing of a certiorari petition, and certainly the purchase of narcotics by an undercover agent from a prospective defendant may all be equally "critical" yet provision of counsel and advice on that score have never been thought compelled by the Constitution in such cases. The sound reason why this right is so freely extended for a criminal trial is the severe injustice risked by confronting an untrained defendant with a range of technical points of law, evidence, and tactics familiar to the prosecutor but not to himself. This danger shrinks markedly in the police station where indeed the lawyer in fulfilling his professional responsibilities of necessity may become an obstacle to truthfinding. See infra, n. 12. The Court's summary citation of the Sixth Amendment cases here seems to me best described as "the domino method of constitutional adjudication ... wherein every explanatory statement in a previous opinion is made the basis for extension to a wholly different situation." Friendly, supra, n. 10, at 950.

◆ III. Policy Considerations

Examined as an expression of public policy, the Court's new regime proves so dubious that there can be no due compensation for its weakness in constitutional law. The foregoing discussion has shown, I think, how mistaken is the Court in implying that the Constitution has struck the balance in favor of the approach the Court takes. Ante, p. 479. Rather, precedent reveals that the Fourteenth Amendment in practice has been construed to strike a different balance, that the Fifth Amendment gives the Court little solid support in this context, and that the Sixth Amendment should have no bearing at all. Legal history has been stretched before to satisfy deep needs of society. In this instance, however, the Court has not and cannot make the powerful showing that its new rules are plainly desirable in the context of our society, something which is surely demanded before those rules are engrafted onto the Constitution and imposed on every State and county in the land.

Without at all subscribing to the generally black picture of police conduct painted by the Court, I think it must be frankly recognized at the outset that police questioning allowable under due process precedents may inherently entail some pressure on the suspect and may seek advantage in his ignorance or weaknesses. The atmosphere and questioning techniques, proper and fair though they be, can in themselves exert a tug on the suspect to confess, and in this light "[t]o speak of any confessions of crime made after arrest as being 'voluntary' or 'uncoerced' is somewhat inaccurate, although traditional. A confession is wholly and incontestably voluntary only if a guilty person gives himself up to the law and becomes his own accuser." *Ashcraft v. Tennessee*, 322 U.S. 143, 161 (Jackson, J., dissenting). Until today, the role of the Constitution has been only to sift out undue pressure, not to assure spontaneous confessions.

The Court's new rules aim to offset these minor pressures and disadvantages intrinsic to any kind of police interrogation. The rules do not serve due process interests in preventing blatant coercion since, as I noted earlier, they do nothing to contain the policeman who is prepared to lie from the start. The rules work for reliability in confessions almost only in the Pickwickian sense that they can prevent some from being given at all. In short, the benefit of this new regime is simply to lessen or wipe out the inherent compulsion and inequalities to which the Court devotes some nine pages of description. Ante, pp. 448-456.

What the Court largely ignores is that its rules impair, if they will not eventually serve wholly to frustrate, an instrument of law enforcement that has long and quite reasonably been thought worth the price paid for it. There can be little doubt that the Court's new code would markedly decrease the number of confessions. To warn the suspect that he may remain silent and remind him that his confession may be used in court are minor obstructions. To require also an express waiver by the suspect and an end to questioning whenever he demurs must heavily handicap questioning. And to suggest or provide counsel for the suspect simply invites the end of the interrogation. See, supra, n. 12.

How much harm this decision will inflict on law enforcement cannot fairly be predicted with accuracy. Evidence on the role of confessions is notoriously incomplete, see Developments, supra, n. 2, at 941-944, and little is added by the Court's reference to the FBI experience and the resources believed wasted in interrogation. See infra, n. 19, and text. We do know that some crimes cannot be solved without confessions, that ample expert testimony attests to their importance in crime control, and that the Court is taking a real risk with society's welfare in imposing its new regime on the country. The social costs of crime are too great to call the new rules anything but a hazardous experimentation.

While passing over the costs and risks of its experiment, the Court portrays the evils of normal police questioning in terms which I think are exaggerated. Albeit stringently confined by the due process standards interrogation is no doubt often inconvenient and unpleasant for the suspect. However, it is no less so for a man to be arrested and jailed, to have his house searched, or to stand trial in court, yet all this may properly happen to the most innocent given probable cause, a warrant, or an indictment. Society has always paid a stiff price for law and order, and peaceful interrogation is not one of the dark moments of the law.

This brief statement of the competing considerations seems to me ample proof that the Court's preference is highly debatable at best and therefore not to be read into the Constitution. However, it may make the analysis more graphic to consider the actual facts of one of the four cases reversed by the Court. *Miranda v. Arizona* serves best, being neither the hardest nor easiest of the four under the Court's standards.

On March 3, 1963, an 18-year-old girl was kidnapped and forcibly raped near Phoenix, Arizona. Ten days later, on the morning of March 13, petitioner Miranda was arrested and taken to the police station. At this time Miranda was 23 years old, indigent, and educated to the extent of completing half the ninth grade. He had "an emotional illness" of the schizophrenic type, according to the doctor who eventually examined him; the doctor's report also stated that Miranda was "alert and oriented as to time, place, and person," intelligent within normal limits, competent to stand trial, and sane within the legal definition. At the police station, the victim picked Miranda out of a lineup, and two officers then took him into a separate room to interrogate him, starting about 11:30 a. m. Though at first denying his guilt, within a short time Miranda gave a detailed oral confession and then wrote out in his own hand and signed a brief statement admitting and describing the crime. All this was accomplished in two hours or less without any force, threats or promises and—I will assume this though the record is uncertain, ante, 491-492 and nn. 66-67—without any effective warnings at all.

Miranda's oral and written confessions are now held inadmissible under the Court's new rules. One is entitled to feel astonished that the Constitution can be read to produce this result. These confessions were obtained during brief, daytime questioning con-

ducted by two officers and unmarked by any of the traditional indicia of coercion. They assured a conviction for a brutal and unsettling crime, for which the police had and quite possibly could obtain little evidence other than the victim's identifications, evidence which is frequently unreliable. There was, in sum, a legitimate purpose, no perceptible unfairness, and certainly little risk of injustice in the interrogation. Yet the resulting confessions, and the responsible course of police practice they represent, are to be sacrificed to the Court's own finespun conception of fairness which I seriously doubt is shared by many thinking citizens in this country.

The tenor of judicial opinion also falls well short of supporting the Court's new approach. Although Escobedo has widely been interpreted as an open invitation to lower courts to rewrite the law of confessions, a significant heavy majority of the state and federal decisions in point have sought quite narrow interpretations. Of the courts that have accepted the invitation, it is hard to know how many have felt compelled by their best guess as to this Court's likely construction; but none of the state decisions saw fit to rely on the state privilege against self-incrimination, and no decision at all has gone as far as this Court goes today.

It is also instructive to compare the attitude in this case of those responsible for law enforcement with the official views that existed when the Court undertook three major revisions of prosecutorial practice prior to this case, *Johnson v. Zerbst*, 304 U.S. 458, *Mapp v. Ohio*, 367 U.S. 643, and *Gideon v. Wainwright*, 372 U.S. 335. In Johnson, which established that appointed counsel must be offered the indigent in federal criminal trials, the Federal Government all but conceded the basic issue, which had in fact been recently fixed as Department of Justice policy. See Beaney, Right to Counsel 29-30, 36-42 (1955). In Mapp, which imposed the exclusionary rule on the States for Fourth Amendment violations, more than half of the States had themselves already adopted some such rule. See 367 U.S., at 651. In Gideon, which extended *Johnson v. Zerbst* to the States, an amicus brief was filed by 22 States and Commonwealths urging that course; only two States besides that of the respondent came forward to protest. See 372 U.S., at 345. By contrast, in this case new restrictions on police questioning have been opposed by the United States and in an amicus brief signed by 27 States and Commonwealths, not including the three other States which are parties. No State in the country has urged this Court to impose the newly announced rules, nor has any State chosen to go nearly so far on its own.

The Court in closing its general discussion invokes the practice in federal and foreign jurisdictions as lending weight to its new curbs on confessions for all the States. A brief resume will suffice to show that none of these jurisdictions has struck so one-sided a balance as the Court does today. Heaviest reliance is placed on the FBI practice. Differing circumstances may make this comparison quite untrustworthy, but in any event the FBI falls sensibly short of the Court's formalistic rules. For example, there is no indication that FBI agents must obtain an affirmative "waiver" before they pursue their questioning. Nor is it clear that one invoking his right to silence may not be prevailed upon to change his mind. And the warning as to appointed counsel apparently indicates only that one will be assigned by the judge when the suspect appears before him; the thrust of the Court's rules is to induce the suspect to obtain appointed counsel before continuing the interview. See ante, pp. 484-486. Apparently American military practice, briefly mentioned by the Court, has these same limits and is still less favorable to the suspect than the FBI warning, making no mention of appointed counsel. Developments, supra, n. 2, at 1084-1089.

The law of the foreign countries described by the Court also reflects a more moderate conception of the rights of the accused as against those of society when other data are considered. Concededly, the English experience is most relevant. In that country, a caution as to silence but not counsel has long been mandated by the "Judges' Rules," which also place other somewhat imprecise limits on police cross-examination of suspects. However, in the court's discretion confessions can be and apparently quite frequently are admitted in evidence despite disregard of the Judges' Rules, so long as they are found voluntary under the common-law test. Moreover, the check that exists on the use of pretrial statements is counterbalanced by the evident admissibility of fruits of an illegal confession and by the judge's often-used authority to comment adversely on the defendant's failure to testify.

India, Ceylon and Scotland are the other examples chosen by the Court. In India and Ceylon the general ban on police-adduced confessions cited by the Court is subject to a major exception: if evidence is uncovered by police questioning, it is fully admissible at trial along with the confession itself, so far as it relates to the evidence and is not blatantly coerced. See Developments, supra, n. 2, at 1106-1110; *Reg. v. Ramasamy* 1965. A. C. 1 (P. C.). Scotland's limits on interrogation do measure up to the Court's; however, restrained comment at trial on the defendant's failure to take the stand is allowed the judge, and in many other respects Scotch law redresses the prosecutor's disadvantage in ways not permitted in this country. The Court ends its survey by imputing added strength to our privilege against self-incrimination since, by contrast to other countries, it is embodied in a written Constitution. Considering the liberties the Court has today taken with constitutional history and precedent, few will find this emphasis persuasive.

In closing this necessarily truncated discussion of policy considerations attending the new confession rules, some reference must be made to their ironic untimeliness. There is now in progress in this country a massive re-examination of criminal law enforcement procedures on a scale never before witnessed. Participants in this undertaking include a Special Committee of the American Bar Association, under the chairmanship of Chief Judge Lumbard of the Court of Appeals for the Second Circuit; a distinguished study group of the American Law Institute, headed by Professors Vorenberg and Bator of the Harvard Law School; and the President's Commission on Law Enforcement and Administration of Justice, under the leadership of the Attorney General of the United States. Studies are also being conducted by the District of Columbia Crime Commission, the Georgetown Law Center, and by others equipped to do practical research. There are also signs that legislatures in some of the States may be preparing to re-examine the problem before us.

It is no secret that concern has been expressed lest long-range and lasting reforms be frustrated by this Court's too rapid departure from existing constitutional standards. Despite the Court's disclaimer, the practical effect of the decision made today must inevitably be to handicap seriously sound efforts at reform, not least by removing options necessary to a just compromise of competing interests. Of course legislative reform is rarely speedy or unanimous, though this Court has been more patient in the past. But the legislative reforms when they come would have the vast advantage of empirical data and comprehensive study, they would allow experimentation and use of solutions not open to the courts, and they would restore the initiative in criminal law reform to those forums where it truly belongs.

◆ IV. Conclusions

All four of the cases involved here present express claims that confessions were inadmissible, not because of coercion in the traditional due process sense, but solely because of lack of counsel or lack of warnings concerning counsel and silence. For the reasons stated in this opinion, I would adhere to the due process test and reject the new requirements inaugurated by the Court. On this premise my disposition of each of these cases can be stated briefly.

In two of the three cases coming from state courts, *Miranda v. Arizona* (No. 759) and *Vignera v. New York* (No. 760), the confessions were held admissible and no other errors worth comment are alleged by petitioners. I would affirm in these two cases. The other state case is *California v. Stewart* (No. 584), where the state supreme court held the confession inadmissible and reversed the conviction. In that case I would dismiss the writ of certiorari on the ground that no final judgment is before us, 28 U.S.C. 1257 (1964 ed.); putting aside the new trial open to the State in any event, the confession itself has not even been finally excluded since the California Supreme Court left the State free to show proof of a waiver. If the merits of the decision in Stewart be reached, then I believe it should be reversed and the case remanded so the state supreme court may pass on the other claims available to respondent.

In the federal case, *Westover v. United States* (No. 761), a number of issues are raised by petitioner apart from the one already dealt with in this dissent. None of these other claims appears to me tenable, nor in this context to warrant extended discussion. It is urged that the confession was also inadmissible because not voluntary even measured by due process standards and because federal-state cooperation brought the McNabb-Mallory rule into play under *Anderson v. United States*, 318 U.S. 350. However, the facts alleged fall well short of coercion in my view, and I believe the involvement of federal agents in petitioner's arrest and detention by the State too slight to invoke Anderson. I agree with the Government that the admission of the evidence now protested by petitioner was at most harmless error, and two final contentions—one involving weight of the evidence and another improper prosecutor comment—seem to me without merit. I would therefore affirm Westover's conviction.

In conclusion: Nothing in the letter or the spirit of the Constitution or in the precedents squares with the heavy-handed and one-sided action that is so precipitously taken by the Court in the name of fulfilling its constitutional responsibilities. The foray which the Court makes today brings to mind the wise and farsighted words of Mr. Justice Jackson in *Dou-glas v. Jeannette*, 319 U.S. 157, 181 (separate opinion): "This Court is forever adding new stories to the temples of constitutional law, and the temples have a way of collapsing when one story too many is added."

Mr. Justice White, with Whom Mr. Justice Harlan and Mr. Justice Stewart Join, Dissenting

◆ I

The proposition that the privilege against self-incrimination forbids in-custody interrogation without the warnings specified in the majority opinion and without a clear waiver of counsel has no significant support in the history of the privilege or in the language of the Fifth Amendment. As for the English authorities and the common-law history, the privilege, firmly established in the second half of the seventeenth century, was never applied except to prohibit compelled judicial interrogations. The rule excluding coerced confessions matured about 100 years later, "[b]ut there is nothing in the reports to suggest that the theory has its roots in the privilege against self-incrimination. And so far as the cases reveal, the privilege, as such, seems to have been given effect only in judicial proceedings, including the preliminary examinations by authorized magistrates." Morgan, The Privilege Against Self-Incrimination, 34 Minn. L. Rev. 1, 18 (1949).

Our own constitutional provision provides that no person "shall be compelled in any criminal case to be a witness against himself." These words, when "[c]onsidered in the light to be shed by grammar and the dictionary ... appear to signify simply that nobody shall be compelled to give oral testimony against himself in a criminal proceeding under way in which he is defendant." Corwin, The Supreme Court's Construction of the Self-Incrimination Clause, 29 Mich. L. Rev. 1, 2. And there is very little in the surrounding circumstances of the adoption of the Fifth Amendment or in the provisions of the then existing state constitutions or in state practice which would give the constitutional provision any broader meaning. Mayers, The Federal Witness' Privilege Against Self-Incrimination: Constitutional or Common-Law? 4 American Journal of Legal History 107 (1960). Such a construction, however, was considerably narrower than the privilege at common law, and when eventually faced with the issues, the Court extended the constitutional privilege to the compulsory production of books and papers, to the ordinary witness before the grand jury and to witnesses generally. *Boyd v. United States*, 116 U.S. 616, and *Counselman v. Hitchcock*, 142 U.S. 547. Both rules had solid support in common-law history, if not in the history of our own constitutional provision.

A few years later the Fifth Amendment privilege was similarly extended to encompass the then well-established rule against coerced confessions: "In criminal trials, in the courts of the United States, wherever a question arises whether a confession is incompetent because not voluntary, the issue is controlled by that portion of the Fifth Amendment to the Constitution of the United States, commanding that no person 'shall be compelled in any criminal case to be a witness against himself.'" *Bram v. United States*, 168 U.S. 532, 542. Although this view has found approval in other cases, *Burdeau v. McDowell*, 256 U.S. 465, 475; *Powers v. United States*, 223 U.S. 303, 313; *Shotwell v. United States*, 371 U.S. 341, 347, it has also been questioned, see *Brown v. Mississippi*, 297 U.S. 278, 285; *United States v. Carignan*, 342 U.S. 36, 41; *Stein v. New York*, 346 U.S. 156, 191, n. 35, and finds scant support in either the English or American authorities, see generally *Regina v. Scott*, Dears. & Bell 47; 3 Wigmore, Evidence 823 (3d ed. 1940), at 249 ("a confession is not rejected because of any connection with the privilege against self-crimination"), and 250, n. 5 (particularly criticizing Bram); 8 Wigmore, Evidence 2266, at 400-401 (McNaughton rev. 1961). Whatever the source of the rule excluding coerced confessions, it is clear that prior to the application of the privilege itself to state courts, *Malloy v. Hogan*, 378 U.S. 1, the admissibility of a confession in a state criminal prosecution was tested by the same standards as were applied in federal prosecutions. Id., at 6-7, 10.

Bram, however, itself rejected the proposition which the Court now espouses. The question in Bram was whether a confession, obtained during custodial interrogation, had been compelled, and if such interrogation was to be deemed inherently vulnerable the Court's inquiry could have ended there. After examining the English and American authorities, however, the Court declared that:

"In this court also it has been settled that the mere fact that the confession is made to a police officer, while the accused was under arrest in or out of prison, or was drawn out by his questions, does not necessarily render the confession involuntary, but, as one of the circumstances, such imprisonment or interrogation may be taken into account in determining whether or not the statements of the prisoner were voluntary." 168 U.S., at 558.

In this respect the Court was wholly consistent with prior and subsequent pronouncements in this Court.

Thus prior to Bram the Court, in *Hopt v. Utah*, 110 U.S. 574, 583-587, had upheld the admissibility of a confession made to police officers following arrest, the record being silent concerning what conversation had occurred between the officers and the defendant in the short period preceding the confession. Relying on Hopt, the Court ruled squarely on the issue in Sparf and *Hansen v. United States*, 156 U.S. 51, 55 :

"Counsel for the accused insist that there cannot be a voluntary statement, a free open confession, while a defendant is confined and in irons under an accusation of having committed a capital offence. We have not been referred to any authority in support of that position. It is true that the fact of a prisoner being in custody at the time he makes a confession is a circumstance not to be overlooked, because it bears upon the inquiry whether the confession was voluntarily made or was extorted by threats or violence or made under the influence of fear. But confinement or imprisonment is not in itself sufficient to justify the exclusion of a confession, if it appears to have been voluntary, and was not obtained by putting the prisoner in fear or by promises. Wharton's Cr. Ev. 9th ed. 661, 663, and authorities cited."

Accord, *Pierce v. United States*, 160 U.S. 355, 357.

And in *Wilson v. United States*, 162 U.S. 613, 623, the Court had considered the significance of custodial interrogation without any antecedent warnings regarding the right to remain silent or the right to counsel. There the defendant had answered questions posed by a Commissioner, who had failed to advise him of his rights, and his answers were held admissible over his claim of involuntariness. "The fact that [a defendant] is in custody and manacled does not necessarily render his statement involuntary, nor is that necessarily the effect of popular excitement shortly preceding.... And it is laid down that it is not essential to the admissibility of a confession that it should appear that the person was warned that what he said would be used against him, but on the contrary, if the confession was voluntary, it is sufficient though it appear that he was not so warned."

Since Bram, the admissibility of statements made during custodial interrogation has been frequently reiterated. *Powers v. United States*, 223 U.S. 303, cited Wilson approvingly and held admissible as voluntary statements the accused's testimony at a preliminary hearing even though he was not warned that what he said might be used against him. Without any discussion of the presence or absence of warnings, presumably because such discussion was deemed unnecessary, numerous other cases have declared that "[t]he mere fact that a confession was made while in the custody of the police does not render it inadmissible," *McNabb v. United States*, 318 U.S. 332, 346; accord, *United States v. Mitchell*, 322 U.S. 65, despite its having been elicited by police examination, *Wan v. United States*, 266 U.S. 1, 14; *United States v. Carignan*, 342 U.S. 36, 39. Likewise, in *Crooker v. California*, 357 U.S. 433, 437, the Court said that "the bare fact of police 'detention and police examination in private of one in official state custody' does not render involuntary a confession by the one so detained." And finally, in *Cicenia v. Lagay*, 357 U.S. 504, a confession obtained by police interrogation after arrest was held voluntary even though the authorities refused to permit the defendant to consult with his attorney. See generally *Culombe v. Connecticut*, 367 U.S. 568, 587-602 (opinion of Frankfurter, J.); 3 Wigmore, Evidence 851, at 313 (3d ed. 1940); see also Joy, Admissibility of Confessions 38, 46 (1842).

Only a tiny minority of our judges who have dealt with the question, including today's majority, have considered in-custody interrogation, without more, to be a violation of the Fifth Amendment. And this Court, as every member knows, has left standing literally thousands of criminal convictions that rested at least in part on confessions taken in the course of interrogation by the police after arrest.

♦ **II**

That the Court's holding today is neither compelled nor even strongly suggested by the language of the Fifth Amendment, is at odds with American and English legal history, and involves a departure from a long line of precedent does not prove either that the Court has exceeded its powers or that the Court is wrong or unwise in its present reinterpretation of the Fifth Amendment. It does, however, underscore the obvious—that the Court has not discovered or found the law in making today's decision, nor has it derived it from some irrefutable sources; what it has done is to make new law and new public policy in much the same way that it has in the course of interpreting other great clauses of the Constitution. This is what the Court historically has done. Indeed, it is what it must do and will continue to do until and unless there is some fundamental change in the constitutional distribution of governmental powers.

But if the Court is here and now to announce new and fundamental policy to govern certain aspects of our affairs, it is wholly legitimate to examine the mode of this or any other constitutional decision in this Court and to inquire into the advisability of its end product in terms of the long-range interest of the country. At the very least the Court's text and reasoning should withstand analysis and be a fair exposition of the constitutional provision which its opinion interprets. Decisions like these cannot rest alone on syllogism, metaphysics or some ill-defined notions of natural justice, although each will perhaps play its part. In proceeding to such constructions as it now announces, the Court should also duly consider all the factors and interests bearing upon the cases, at least insofar as the relevant materials are available; and if the necessary considerations are not treated in the record or obtainable from some other reliable source, the Court should not proceed to formulate fundamental policies based on speculation alone.

♦ **III**

First, we may inquire what are the textual and factual bases of this new fundamental rule. To reach the result announced on the grounds it does, the Court must stay within the confines of the Fifth Amendment, which forbids self-incrimination only if compelled. Hence the core of the Court's opinion is that because of the "compulsion inherent in custodial surroundings, no statement obtained from [a] defendant [in custody] can truly be the product of his free choice," ante, at 458, absent the use of adequate protective devices as described by the Court. However, the Court does not point to any sudden inrush of new knowledge requiring the rejection of 70 years' experience. Nor does it assert that its novel conclusion reflects a changing consensus among state courts, see *Mapp v. Ohio*, 367 U.S. 643, or that a succession of cases had steadily eroded the old rule and proved it unworkable, see *Gideon v. Wainwright*, 372 U.S. 335. Rather than asserting new knowledge, the Court concedes that it cannot truly know what occurs during custodial questioning, because of the innate secrecy of such proceedings. It extrapolates a picture of what it conceives to be the norm from police investigatorial manuals, published in 1959 and 1962 or earlier, without any attempt to allow for adjustments in police practices that may have occurred in the wake of more recent decisions of state appellate tribunals or this Court. But even if the relentless application of the described procedures could lead to involuntary confessions, it most assuredly does not follow that each and every case will disclose this kind of interrogation or this kind of consequence. Insofar as appears from the Court's opinion, it has not examined a single transcript of any police interrogation, let alone the interrogation that took place in any one of these cases which it decides today. Judged by any of the standards for empirical investigation utilized in the social sciences the factual basis for the Court's premise is patently inadequate.

Although in the Court's view in-custody interrogation is inherently coercive, the Court says that the spontaneous product of the coercion of arrest and detention is still to be deemed voluntary. An accused, arrested on probable cause, may blurt out a confession which will be admissible despite the fact that he is alone and in custody, without any showing that he had any notion of his right to remain silent or of the consequences of his admission. Yet, under the Court's rule, if the police ask him a single question such as "Do you have anything to say?" or "Did you kill your wife?" his response, if there is one, has somehow been compelled, even if the accused has been clearly warned of his right to remain silent. Common sense informs us to the contrary. While one may say that the response was "involuntary" in the sense the question provoked or was the occasion for the response and thus the defendant was induced to speak out when he might have remained silent if not arrested and not questioned, it is patently unsound to say the response is compelled.

Today's result would not follow even if it were agreed that to some extent custodial interrogation is inherently coercive. See *Ashcraft v. Tennessee*, 322 U.S. 143, 161 (Jackson, J., dissenting). The test has been whether the totality of circumstances deprived the defendant of a "free choice to admit, to deny, or to refuse to answer," *Lisenba v. California*, 314 U.S. 219, 241, and whether physical or psychological coercion was of such a degree that "the defendant's will was overborne at the time he confessed," *Haynes v. Washington*, 373 U.S. 503, 513; *Lynumn v. Illinois*, 372 U.S. 528, 534. The duration and nature of incommunicado custody, the presence or absence of advice concerning the defendant's constitutional rights, and the granting or refusal of requests to communicate with lawyers, relatives or friends have all been rightly regarded as important data bearing on the basic inquiry. See, e. g., *Ashcraft v. Tennessee*, 322 U.S. 143; *Haynes v. Washington*, 373 U.S. 503. But it has never been suggested, until today, that such questioning was so coercive and accused persons so lacking in hardihood that the very first response to the very first question following the commencement of custody must be conclusively presumed to be the product of an overborne will.

If the rule announced today were truly based on a conclusion that all confessions resulting from custodial interrogation are coerced, then it would simply have no rational foundation. Compare *Tot v. United States*, 319 U.S. 463, 466; *United States v. Romano*, 382 U.S. 136. A fortiori that would be true of the extension of the rule to exculpatory statements, which the Court effects after a brief discussion of why, in the Court's view, they must be deemed incriminatory but without any discussion of why they must be deemed coerced. See *Wilson v. United States*, 162 U.S. 613, 624. Even if one were to postulate that the Court's concern is not that all confessions induced by police interrogation are coerced but rather that some such confessions are coerced and present judicial procedures are believed to be inadequate to identify the confessions that are coerced and those that are not, it would still not be essential to impose the rule that the Court has now fashioned. Transcripts or observers could be required, specific time limits, tailored to fit the cause, could be imposed, or other devices could be utilized to reduce the chances that otherwise indiscernible coercion will produce an inadmissible confession.

On the other hand, even if one assumed that there was an adequate factual basis for the conclusion that all confessions obtained during in-custody interrogation are the product of compulsion, the rule propounded by the Court would still be irrational, for, apparently, it is only if the accused is also warned of his right to counsel and waives both that right and the right against self-incrimination that the inherent compulsiveness of interrogation disappears. But if the defendant may not answer without a warning a question such as "Where were you last night?" without having his answer be a compelled one, how can the Court ever accept his negative answer to the question of whether he wants to consult his retained counsel or counsel whom the court will appoint? And why if counsel is present and the accused nevertheless confesses, or counsel tells the accused to tell the truth, and that is what the accused does, is the situation any less coercive insofar as the accused is concerned? The Court apparently realizes its dilemma of foreclosing questioning without the necessary warnings but at the same time permitting the accused, sitting in the same chair in front of the same policemen, to waive his right to consult an attorney. It expects, however, that the accused will not often waive the right; and if it is claimed that he has, the State faces a severe, if not impossible burden of proof.

All of this makes very little sense in terms of the compulsion which the Fifth Amendment proscribes. That amendment deals with compelling the accused himself. It is his free will that is involved. Confessions and incriminating admissions, as such, are not forbidden evidence; only those which are compelled are banned. I doubt that the Court observes these distinctions today. By considering any answers to any interrogation to be compelled regardless of the content and course of examination and by escalating the requirements to prove waiver, the Court not only prevents the use of compelled confessions but for all practical purposes forbids interrogation except in the presence of counsel. That is, instead of confining itself to protection of the right against compelled self-incrimination the Court has created a limited Fifth Amendment right to counsel—or, as the Court expresses it, a "need for counsel to protect the Fifth Amendment privilege...." Ante, at 470. The focus then is not on the will of the accused but on the will of counsel and how much influence he can have on the accused. Obviously there is no warrant in the Fifth Amendment for thus installing counsel as the arbiter of the privilege.

In sum, for all the Court's expounding on the menacing atmosphere of police interrogation procedures, it has failed to supply any foundation for the conclusions it draws or the measures it adopts.

◆ IV

Criticism of the Court's opinion, however, cannot stop with a demonstration that the factual and textual bases for the rule it propounds are, at best, less than compelling. Equally relevant is an assessment of the rule's consequences measured against community values. The Court's duty to assess the consequences of its action is not satisfied by the utterance of the truth that a value of our system of criminal justice is "to respect the inviolability of the human personality" and to require government to produce the evidence against the accused by its own independent labors. Ante, at 460. More than the human

dignity of the accused is involved; the human personality of others in the society must also be preserved. Thus the values reflected by the privilege are not the sole desideratum; society's interest in the general security is of equal weight.

The obvious underpinning of the Court's decision is a deep-seated distrust of all confessions. As the Court declares that the accused may not be interrogated without counsel present, absent a waiver of the right to counsel, and as the Court all but admonishes the lawyer to advise the accused to remain silent, the result adds up to a judicial judgment that evidence from the accused should not be used against him in any way, whether compelled or not. This is the not so subtle overtone of the opinion—that it is inherently wrong for the police to gather evidence from the accused himself. And this is precisely the nub of this dissent. I see nothing wrong or immoral, and certainly nothing unconstitutional, in the police's asking a suspect whom they have reasonable cause to arrest whether or not he killed his wife or in confronting him with the evidence on which the arrest was based, at least where he has been plainly advised that he may remain completely silent, see *Escobedo v. Illinois*, 378 U.S. 478, 499 (dissenting opinion). Until today, "the admissions or confessions of the prisoner, when voluntarily and freely made, have always ranked high in the scale of incriminating evidence." *Brown v. Walker*, 161 U.S. 591, 596; see also *Hopt v. Utah*, 110 U.S. 574, 584-585. Particularly when corroborated, as where the police have confirmed the accused's disclosure of the hiding place of implements or fruits of the crime, such confessions have the highest reliability and significantly contribute to the certitude with which we may believe the accused is guilty. Moreover, it is by no means certain that the process of confessing is injurious to the accused. To the contrary it may provide psychological relief and enhance the prospects for rehabilitation.

This is not to say that the value of respect for the inviolability of the accused's individual personality should be accorded no weight or that all confessions should be indiscriminately admitted. This Court has long read the Constitution to proscribe compelled confessions, a salutary rule from which there should be no retreat. But I see no sound basis, factual or otherwise, and the Court gives none, for concluding that the present rule against the receipt of coerced confessions is inadequate for the task of sorting out inadmissible evidence and must be replaced by the per se rule which is now imposed. Even if the new concept can be said to have advantages of some sort over the present law, they are far outweighed by its likely undesirable impact on other very relevant and important interests.

The most basic function of any government is to provide for the security of the individual and of his property. *Lanzetta v. New Jersey*, 306 U.S. 451, 455. These ends of society are served by the criminal laws which for the most part are aimed at the prevention of crime. Without the reasonably effective performance of the task of preventing private violence and retaliation, it is idle to talk about human dignity and civilized values.

The modes by which the criminal laws serve the interest in general security are many. First the murderer who has taken the life of another is removed from the streets, deprived of his liberty and thereby prevented from repeating his offense. In view of the statistics on recidivism in this country and of the number of instances in which apprehension occurs only after repeated offenses, no one can sensibly claim that this aspect of the criminal law does not prevent crime or contribute significantly to the personal security of the ordinary citizen.

Secondly, the swift and sure apprehension of those who refuse to respect the personal security and dignity of their neighbor unquestionably has its impact on others who might be similarly tempted. That the criminal law is wholly or partly ineffective with a segment of the population or with many of those who have been apprehended and convicted is a very faulty basis for concluding that it is not effective with respect to the great bulk of our citizens or for thinking that without the criminal laws, or in the absence of their enforcement, there would be no increase in crime. Arguments of this nature are not borne out by any kind of reliable evidence that I have seen to this date.

Thirdly, the law concerns itself with those whom it has confined. The hope and aim of modern penology, fortunately, is as soon as possible to return the convict to society a better and more law-abiding man than when he left. Sometimes there is success, sometimes failure. But at least the effort is made, and it should be made to the very maximum extent of our present and future capabilities.

The rule announced today will measurably weaken the ability of the criminal law to perform these tasks. It is a deliberate calculus to prevent interrogations, to reduce the incidence of confessions and pleas of guilty and to increase the number of trials. Criminal trials, no matter how efficient the police

are, are not sure bets for the prosecution, nor should they be if the evidence is not forthcoming. Under the present law, the prosecution fails to prove its case in about 30% of the criminal cases actually tried in the federal courts. See Federal Offenders: 1964, supra, note 4, at 6 (Table 4), 59 (Table 1); Federal Offenders: 1963, supra, note 4, at 5 (Table 3); District of Columbia Offenders: 1963, supra, note 4, at 2 (Table 1). But it is something else again to remove from the ordinary criminal case all those confessions which heretofore have been held to be free and voluntary acts of the accused and to thus establish a new constitutional barrier to the ascertainment of truth by the judicial process. There is, in my view, every reason to believe that a good many criminal defendants who otherwise would have been convicted on what this Court has previously thought to be the most satisfactory kind of evidence will now, under this new version of the Fifth Amendment, either not be tried at all or will be acquitted if the State's evidence, minus the confession, is put to the test of litigation.

I have no desire whatsoever to share the responsibility for any such impact on the present criminal process.

In some unknown number of cases the Court's rule will return a killer, a rapist or other criminal to the streets and to the environment which produced him, to repeat his crime whenever it pleases him. As a consequence, there will not be a gain, but a loss, in human dignity. The real concern is not the unfortunate consequences of this new decision on the criminal law as an abstract, disembodied series of authoritative proscriptions, but the impact on those who rely on the public authority for protection and who without it can only engage in violent self-help with guns, knives and the help of their neighbors similarly inclined. There is, of course, a saving factor: the next victims are uncertain, unnamed and unrepresented in this case.

Nor can this decision do other than have a corrosive effect on the criminal law as an effective device to prevent crime. A major component in its effectiveness in this regard is its swift and sure enforcement. The easier it is to get away with rape and murder, the less the deterrent effect on those who are inclined to attempt it. This is still good common sense. If it were not, we should posthaste liquidate the whole law enforcement establishment as a useless, misguided effort to control human conduct.

And what about the accused who has confessed or would confess in response to simple, noncoercive questioning and whose guilt could not otherwise be proved? Is it so clear that release is the best thing for him in every case? Has it so unquestionably been resolved that in each and every case it would be better for him not to confess and to return to his environment with no attempt whatsoever to help him? I think not. It may well be that in many cases it will be no less than a callous disregard for his own welfare as well as for the interests of his next victim.

There is another aspect to the effect of the Court's rule on the person whom the police have arrested on probable cause. The fact is that he may not be guilty at all and may be able to extricate himself quickly and simply if he were told the circumstances of his arrest and were asked to explain. This effort, and his release, must now await the hiring of a lawyer or his appointment by the court, consultation with counsel and then a session with the police or the prosecutor. Similarly, where probable cause exists to arrest several suspects, as where the body of the victim is discovered in a house having several residents, compare *Johnson v. State*, 238 Md. 140, 207 A. 2d 643 (1965), cert. denied, 382 U.S. 1013, it will often be true that a suspect may be cleared only through the results of interrogation of other suspects. Here too the release of the innocent may be delayed by the Court's rule.

Much of the trouble with the Court's new rule is that it will operate indiscriminately in all criminal cases, regardless of the severity of the crime or the circumstances involved. It applies to every defendant, whether the professional criminal or one committing a crime of momentary passion who is not part and parcel of organized crime. It will slow down the investigation and the apprehension of confederates in those cases where time is of the essence, such as kidnapping, see *Brinegar v. United States*, 338 U.S. 160, 183 (Jackson, J., dissenting); *People v. Modesto*, 62 Cal. 2d 436, 446, 398 P.2d 753, 759 (1965), those involving the national security, see

United States v. Drummond, 354 F.2d 132, 147 (C. A. 2d Cir. 1965) (en banc) (espionage case), pet. for cert. pending, No. 1203, Misc., O. T. 1965; cf. *Gessner v. United States*, 354 F.2d 726, 730, n. 10 (C. A. 10th Cir. 1965) (upholding, in espionage case, trial ruling that Government need not submit classified portions of interrogation transcript), and some of those involving organized crime. In the latter context the lawyer who arrives may also be the lawyer for the defendant's colleagues and can be relied upon to insure that no breach of the organization's security takes place even though the accused may feel that the best thing he can do is to cooperate.

At the same time, the Court's per se approach may not be justified on the ground that it provides a "bright line" permitting the authorities to judge in advance whether interrogation may safely be pursued without jeopardizing the admissibility of any information obtained as a consequence. Nor can it be claimed that judicial time and effort, assuming that is a relevant consideration, will be conserved because of the ease of application of the new rule. Today's decision leaves open such questions as whether the accused was in custody, whether his statements were spontaneous or the product of interrogation, whether the accused has effectively waived his rights, and whether nontestimonial evidence introduced at trial is the fruit of statements made during a prohibited interrogation, all of which are certain to prove productive of uncertainty during investigation and litigation during prosecution. For all these reasons, if further restrictions on police interrogation are desirable at this time, a more flexible approach makes much more sense than the Court's constitutional straitjacket which forecloses more discriminating treatment by legislative or rule-making pronouncements.

Applying the traditional standards to the cases before the Court, I would hold these confessions voluntary. I would therefore affirm in Nos. 759, 760, and 761, and reverse in No. 584.

Illinois governor Otto Kerner, foreground, and New York mayor John Lindsay meet with reporters in October 1967.
(AP Photo/Bob Daughtery)

"White society is deeply implicated in the ghetto."

Overview

There have been many presidential commissions, but few have been more famous—or more controversial—than the National Advisory Commission on Civil Disorders, popularly known as the Kerner Commission. Appointed by President Lyndon B. Johnson in July 1967, as a series of deadly riots convulsed African American neighborhoods in many U.S. cities, the commission had the task of explaining why the violence was occurring and what to do about it. Johnson was a strong supporter of black rights and a champion of social reform to help the poor and minorities. The Kerner Commission proposed many reforms to augment the Johnson administration's efforts, but the president was cool to the recommendations because the Vietnam War had become so expensive that the country could no longer afford costly new social programs. In addition, the president worried that the commission's report, which asserted that white racism was the primary cause of inner-city problems, would alienate white, middle-class support for the programs it proposed. As a result, even though the Kerner Commission asserted that racial problems were about to fracture American society, many of its recommendations went unheeded.

Context

During the Johnson presidency (1963–1969), Americans experienced several summers of racial strife. Most people called these civil disturbances "riots"—frightening eruptions of violence that ended only when the police, National Guard, or even U.S. Army troops restored order. Some people considered them rebellions—uprisings against discriminatory institutions and practices that were forcing millions of African Americans in inner cities to endure poverty and second-class citizenship. Whatever one termed these disturbances, they were destructive, deadly, and common. During the summer of 1967 alone, 136 civil disturbances took place in all parts of the country.

These disturbances surprised, puzzled, and even outraged Johnson because of the notable advances in civil rights that had preceded them. The civil rights movement had achieved its greatest victories just as violence was beginning to plague America's cities. Tens of thousands of courageous citizens took enormous risks to protest against the racial segregation that prevented African Americans from voting, securing decent employment, buying or renting housing in many communities, and attending all-white schools. This grassroots movement for racial justice had many leaders, but the most prominent was Martin Luther King, Jr., who inspired blacks and whites alike with his commitment to using nonviolent action to achieve his dream of a harmonious, colorblind society. Johnson supported racial integration, and in July 1964 he signed the Civil Rights Act, which outlawed racial discrimination in public accommodations, such as restaurants and movie theaters, and in employment. A year later, he signed the Voting Rights Act, which gave the federal government new power to prevent states and localities from denying people of color the right to register to vote.

Eliminating racial injustice was an important step toward the creation of the Great Society, an ambitious effort, as Johnson explained, "to enrich and elevate our national life" (Johnson, vol. 2, p. 704). A thriving national economy, popular confidence in federal efforts to improve American society, and large Democratic majorities in Congress gave Johnson, a Democrat, an unusual opportunity to secure the passage of one of the most remarkable programs of social reform in U.S. history. In 1964 and 1965 Congress approved many new Great Society initiatives that Johnson thought would benefit all Americans, including a War on Poverty, aid for elementary and secondary schools as well as colleges and universities, Medicare for senior citizens, and a Model Cities program to revitalize inner cities and improve housing.

Only five days after the president signed the 1965 Voting Rights Act, one of the worst racial disturbances in U.S. history began in Los Angeles in the predominantly African American neighborhood of Watts. On August 11, 1965, a small event—a white police officer's arrest of an African American driver for a traffic violation—triggered a huge explosion. In six days of violence, thirty-four people died, and $45 million in property damage occurred. The arson, looting, and killing in Watts stunned President Johnson and millions of other Americans. "How is it possible after

Time Line

1964

■ **July 2**
Johnson signs the Civil Rights
Act of 1964.

1965

■ **March 8**
The first U.S. combat troops
arrive in South Vietnam.

■ **August 6**
Johnson signs the Voting
Rights Act.

■ **August 11**
A civil disturbance begins in
the Watts section of Los
Angeles.

1967

■ **July 12**
Rioting starts in Newark, New
Jersey.

■ **July 23**
Riots begin in Detroit and last
for five days; forty-three
people die.

■ **July 27**
President Johnson speaks to
the nation about the civil
disorders and announces the
appointment of a special
commission to study the
disorders.

■ **December 31**
Some 485,600 Americans are
engaged in fighting in the
Vietnam War.

1968

■ **February 29**
The Kerner Commission issues
its report.

■ **April 4**
Martin Luther King, Jr., is
murdered in Memphis,
Tennessee.

Seale even carried guns in public to show that they rejected nonviolent protest in favor of self-defense. These new, aggressive leaders said that civil rights and voting rights legislation and Great Society reforms had not changed the basic conditions of life for the millions of African Americans who lived in segregated inner-city neighborhoods where poverty was pervasive, job opportunities were limited, and municipal services were ineffective and unreliable. They also had grown tired of waiting for change. Some even advocated separatism; they said that African Americans should not make integration their goal but should instead establish separate communities and institutions.

The rising racial tensions divided the American people. Many whites, alarmed by what they considered the disintegration of law and order, blamed Black Power advocates for violence in the streets. Great Society programs became increasingly controversial, as conservatives charged that they were wasteful and ineffective or provided benefits to militants who defied the law. Liberals also attacked Johnson because they thought that the president's commitment to the expanding and costly war in Vietnam was draining funds from the War on Poverty and other Great Society programs. King declared regretfully, "The promises of the Great Society have been shot down on the battlefield of Vietnam" (Hill, p. 1). Radical black leaders offered even more scathing criticism, as they alleged that the Great Society was just another example of tokenism rather than a genuine effort to eliminate poverty and racism.

America's inner cities exploded once more during the summer of 1967. In June violence flared in Tampa, Florida; Cincinnati, Ohio; and Atlanta, Georgia. On July 12, after six days of gunfire, arson, and street violence, major disorder left twenty-three dead in Newark, New Jersey. The worst disturbance occurred in Detroit, Michigan, beginning on July 23. Once again a small incident—a raid on an illegal drinking establishment known as a "blind pig"—started a wave of violence that resulted in forty-three deaths. To quell this disturbance, Johnson ordered U.S. Army troops, some of whom had served in Vietnam, to Detroit.

On July 27, as the violence in Detroit ended, President Johnson delivered an address to the American people. He condemned the lawlessness that had devastated Detroit and other cities and stated bluntly that "looting, arson, plunder, and pillage" had nothing to do with the quest for civil rights. Yet while he called for those who had committed these crimes to be brought to justice, he asserted that "the only genuine, long-range solution" to the problem of civil disorders was "an attack ... upon the conditions that breed despair and violence...: ignorance, discrimination, slums, poverty, disease, not enough jobs" (Johnson, vol. 2, pp. 721–724). He also announced the appointment of a special National Advisory Commission on Civil Disorders, made up of eleven members led by the Democratic Illinois governor Otto Kerner and the Republican New York City mayor John Lindsay, to determine the causes of the riots and what to do to prevent new ones. People commonly called this group the Kerner Commission.

all we've accomplished?" he wondered. "How could it be?" (Woods, p. 591).

Part of the answer, according to a new group of black leaders, was that the Great Society programs provided too little too late. Stokely Carmichael (later known as Kwame Turé) gained prominence in 1966 by calling for Black Power, a slogan with many possible meanings, including racial pride, self-reliance, and unity. Yet Black Power also suggested a new militancy; as Carmichael declared, "I'm not going to beg the white man for anything I deserve; I'm going to take it" (Pach, p. xv). For Huey Newton and Bobby Seale, who established the Black Panther Party for Self-Defense in 1966, Black Power meant revolutionary action. Newton and

About the Author

No single individual wrote the Kerner Commission Report. The document was the product of a collective effort that included dozens of staff assistants as well as the eleven members of the committee. The chair of the commission was Otto Kerner, and the vice chair was John Lindsay.

Otto Kerner, Jr., who was born in Chicago on August 15, 1908, graduated from Brown University in 1930 and earned a law degree from Northwestern University in 1934. His father was a prominent lawyer who served as attorney general of Illinois. Kerner started working for his father's law firm in 1934, the same year he married Helena Cermak Kenlay, the daughter of the late Democratic mayor of Chicago Anton Cermak. Political connections helped Kerner secure an appointment in 1947 as U.S. attorney for the Northern District of Illinois. After twice being elected as a circuit court judge in Cook County (which includes Chicago) during the 1950s, Kerner won the governorship of Illinois as a Democrat in 1960. He proved popular with voters, gaining reelection in 1964. Illinois experienced strong economic growth while Kerner was in the statehouse, and he championed many reforms, including increased state aid to education and an improved mental health program. Kerner resigned as governor in May 1968 after President Johnson nominated him to serve on the U.S. Court of Appeals for the Seventh Circuit. In 1973, he was convicted on corruption charges for providing political favors when he was governor in return for financial benefits. He served eight months in jail and died not long after, on May 9, 1976.

John Vliet Lindsay was born on November 24, 1921, in New York City into a prosperous family. He graduated from Yale University in 1944, served in the U.S. Navy during World War II, and earned a degree from Yale Law School in 1948. Running as a Republican in 1958, he won the first of four terms in the House of Representatives from a district in Manhattan. In Congress, he earned a reputation as a liberal reformer. In 1965 he was elected mayor of New York City, and he won a second term four years later. He was sensitive to the concerns of African Americans and Hispanics but lost the support of many white, middle-class voters because of rising welfare costs and the increasing crime rate. In 1971 he became a Democrat, and he made an unsuccessful bid for that party's presidential nomination in 1972. After he left the mayor's office in 1973, he practiced law. He died on December 19, 2000.

The Kerner Commission had nine other members. I. W. Abel was the president of the United Steelworkers of America and a strong supporter of civil rights. Edward Brooke, a Republican senator from Massachusetts, was the first African American to be elected to the Senate since Reconstruction. James C. Corman was a Democratic member of the House from California who helped secure the passage of the Civil Rights Act of 1964.

Fred R. Harris, a Democratic senator from Oklahoma, was known for his support of civil rights and Indian rights. Herbert Jenkins was the police chief of Atlanta, serving longer than any previous occupant of the position. William M. McCulloch was a Republican member of the House who was conservative on most issues but a supporter of the Civil Rights Acts and the Voting Rights Act. Katherine Graham Peden was Kentucky's commissioner of commerce and had also served on the President's Commission on the Status of Women from 1961 to 1963. Charles B. Thornton was one of the founders of Litton Industries and its chief executive officer. Roy Wilkins was the executive director of the National Association for the Advancement of Colored People and a critic of the Black Power movement who believed that the best way to advance African American interests was through legal and political action.

Explanation and Analysis of the Document

◆ Introduction

The introduction quickly sets the tone for the summary of the Kerner Commission Report: It is blunt, direct, and unsettling. After a few preliminary sentences, the commissioners state their basic conclusion in stark and alarming language: "Our nation is moving toward two societies, one black, one white—separate and unequal." By placing this finding so early in the report, the commissioners call attention to the gravity and urgency of America's racial problems. They later emphasize that they completed the report four months before the deadline. The speed with which they performed the work underlined their belief that there was "no higher priority for national action and no higher claim on the nation's conscience" than addressing the issues causing the violent disturbances in America's cities. The commissioners also wanted to finish the study as quickly as possible so that it might help in formulating policies that could head off another "long, hot summer" in 1968.

Dealing with the problem of civil disorders, however, would require confronting some unpleasant truths, the commissioners believed. For many whites in comfortable suburbs, small towns, and rural communities, the problems of predominantly black inner cities seemed remote, the product of circumstances for which they bore no responsibility and in which they may have had little interest. The Kerner Commission challenged that outlook, asserting in the report, "What white Americans have never fully understood but what the Negro can never forget—is that white society is deeply implicated in the ghetto." Preventing new explosions of violence would require more than effective law enforcement or new programs to alleviate poverty or teach job skills. What would also be necessary on the part of "every American" were "new attitudes, new understanding, and, above all, new will." The report establishes at the outset that the riots of the 1960s were not an urban problem or a black problem but a national problem of the greatest magnitude and urgency.

◆ Part I—What Happened?

This section of the report summary provides brief accounts of the disturbances in several cities during the summer of 1967. The Kerner Commission Report moves beyond the details of each disorder, however, to find patterns in the violence. While there was no "'typical' riot," the instances of disorder shared some important common characteristics. The central conclusion of this section of the report is that the civil disorders involved "Negroes acting against local symbols of white American society, authority, and property in Negro neighborhoods—rather than against white persons." Especially powerful were grievances about police practices, lack of employment, and poor housing.

The Kerner Commission found no evidence to support the widespread belief that inner-city disturbances were the result of a domestic or foreign plot. J. Edgar Hoover, the director of the Federal Bureau of Investigation, thought that Communists were somehow involved in the violence. Hoover was extremely suspicious of black leaders, including mainstream advocates of civil rights like Martin Luther King, Jr. Hoover insisted that King took advice from Communists and was so convinced that King was a dangerous radical that he even carried on a secret campaign to destroy King's reputation. Hoover also thought that Black Power advocates were treacherous enemies of law and order. Some did espouse socialist principles or urge African Americans to rise up against white oppression. Nonetheless, the Kerner Commission looked carefully at many sources of information, including Federal Bureau of Investigation documents, and found no proof that any group or individuals had planned the inner-city violence. Conspiracy did not explain the turbulent summer of 1967. Rather, a combination of national problems and local conditions produced an inflammatory mixture that ignited in dozens of American cities.

◆ Part II—Why Did It Happen?

Explaining the historical roots of the racial problems of the 1960s is the goal of the next part of the report. The commissioners assert that white racism was the most fundamental reason for the "explosive mixture" in American cities. In this section of the report, as in the introduction, the most important finding appears near the beginning. Once more, the conclusion is alarming and unsettling, especially for white readers.

The report uses history to explain that the development of large, segregated communities in urban areas—commonly called "ghettos" in the 1960s—was a fairly recent phenomenon. In 1910, 91 percent of the nation's black population lived in the South. Black migration out of the South accelerated during World War I and increased even more during World War II, as the growth of defense industries created job opportunities in northern factories. The movement to northern cities continued when peace came in 1945, in part because the mechanization of southern agriculture reduced the demand for farm labor. By the time the Kerner Commission was established, about 45 percent of African Americans lived outside the South, mainly in central cities. During the 1950s and 1960s, cities like Detroit, Chicago, Cleveland, and Philadelphia became increasingly black, since most of the growth in white population during those decades was in suburbs. "White exodus" increased the proportion of African Americans in

these cities and in certain neighborhoods within them. Discriminatory practices, including unwillingness among owners to rent or sell housing to blacks in some areas and among banks to make home loans to qualified black buyers who wished to move into predominantly white neighborhoods, confined the bulk of the black population to segregated, inner city districts, or ghettos.

Deprivation combined with segregation to create bitterness and resentment that could eventually lead to explosive violence. Conditions of life in many inner cities were horrendous. The report provides statistical measures of the pervasiveness of poverty and the severity of unemployment and underemployment. Blacks were almost four times more likely than whites to live in poverty and more than twice as likely to be unemployed. A nonwhite baby had a 58 percent greater chance than a white baby of dying during the first month of life. Far more frequently than other Americans, inner-city residents became victims of crime or unfair commercial or financial practices, such as high food prices and credit scams.

African Americans endured these deplorable conditions of life while the economy was thriving and while more and more people were achieving their American dream of success and prosperity. Inner-city residents heard government officials praise the achievements of the civil rights movement, the advances in desegregation, and the progress in making equality of opportunity a reality for all Americans. The report explains how this combination of rising expectations and frustrated hopes produced intense, widespread bitterness.

Disillusionment and alienation, according to the Kerner Commission, led some African Americans to embrace Black Power in the hope of advancing racial unity and achieving independent economic and political power. The report provides a scathing critique of those who thought Black Power should lead to separatism. Their ideas were not really new, the commissioners maintain, but echoed those of the late-19th-century African American leader Booker T. Washington. The comparison to Washington was devastating. Washington had urged blacks not to challenge segregation but instead to concentrate on economic self-improvement. In a similar manner, black separatists of the 1960s, according to the report, backed away from confronting white racism by not demanding further integration.

At the end of this section, the commissioners address a common question: Why was it more difficult for African Americans than for European immigrants "to escape from the ghetto and from poverty?" The report offers several reasons, but especially important is the assertion that Europeans never faced as intense and widespread discrimination as did blacks.

◆ Part III—What Can Be Done?

The Kerner Commission studied a severe national problem, but their recommendations for dealing with it begin with local action. Many suggestions concern improving communication so that inner-city problems do not go neglected until they lead to violence. The commissioners deem especially important the bettering of police-community relations so as to strengthen law enforcement, avoid the "indiscriminate and excessive use of force," and prevent incidents like those that had occurred in Detroit from triggering civil disturbance. They also consider necessary changes in local court systems, which suffered from "long-standing structural deficiencies," and the preparation of emergency plans, formulated with "broad community participation," to deal with civil disturbances.

The report warns that the future of many large cities with growing African American populations is "grim" and that a continuation of current policies would have "ominous consequences for our society." To do nothing different would "make permanent the division" between a predominantly black and poor society in inner cities and a white and affluent society concentrated in suburbs. The report asserts that integration is essential; that new programs must help blacks move out of inner cities; and that the most important goal "must be a single society, in which every citizen will be free to live and work according to his capabilities and desires, not his color."

Specific proposals for federal action concentrate on employment, education, the welfare system, and housing. The commissioners urge "immediate action" to create two million new jobs over the coming three years and to eliminate racial barriers in hiring and promotion. Also considered essential are dramatic efforts to improve education, including federal action to eliminate segregation in schools and increased aid for new and better programs serving disadvantaged students. The commissioners recommend substantial reforms in the welfare system, including increased federal funds to raise benefits in the short term and the creation of a new system of income supplementation over the long term. Changes in housing programs are also held to be crucial because existing federal efforts had done "comparatively little" to help the disadvantaged. Especially important would be the passage of a federal open housing law, to ban discrimination in the sale or rental of housing on account of race, and new efforts to build more low-income housing outside predominantly black inner cities.

The Kerner Commission concludes its report by reiterating that Americans could not continue to delay in confronting these pressing problems. The commissioners admit that they have "uncovered no startling truths, no unique insights"; as the distinguished and perceptive scholar Kenneth Clark pointed out, investigations after earlier riots had produced similar analyses and similar recommendations. Those previous studies had produced few, if any, changes, however, and the Kerner Commission warns of the dangers of inaction yet again. Improving conditions in inner cities would be expensive and require "national action on an unprecedented scale." Just as important as money would be the need "to generate new will." Only such a widespread and wholehearted commitment, the commission concludes, could "end the destruction and the violence, not only in the streets … but in the lives of people."

The worst riots in the summer of 1967 occurred in Detroit. Here, rioters charge down 12th Street on Detroit's west side on July 23, 1967, throwing stones and bottles at store fronts and looting them. (AP Photo/file)

Audience

In the body of their report, the commissioners explain that they address their study to the institutions of government. They hoped that their analysis and recommendations would help the president and Congress take action to deal with the problems contributing to civil disturbances. They were also writing for local and state officials—those who made policies and provided funding for schools, police, welfare programs, and other social services that had such profound effects on the lives of inner-city residents.

The audience, however, was far larger than government officials. The Kerner Commission hoped to touch "the conscience of the nation" and "the minds and hearts of each citizen" (National Advisory Commission on Civil Disorders, p. 34). The increasing racial polarization of the 1960s affected all Americans; only a national commitment to alleviate the underlying causes could reverse the trend. The commissioners declare in their report, "The responsibility for decisive action, never more clearly demanded in the history of our country, rests on all of us" (National Advisory Commission on Civil Disorders, p. 34).

Impact

The report of the Kerner Commission produced strong but divided reactions. The *New York Times* (March 2, 1968) praised it for making a powerful case for "escalation of the war against poverty and discrimination at home." The *Washington Star* (as quoted in the *New York Times*, March 10, 1968), however, complained that the report "does not put as much emphasis on forthrightly condemning riots and rioters as it does on offering excuses for them." Seven mayors whose cities had experienced civil disturbances endorsed the commission's recommendations. Richard Nixon, who was campaigning for the Republican nomination for president, reached the opposite con-

> "This is our basic conclusion: our nation is moving toward two societies, one black, one white—separate and unequal."
>
> (Introduction)

> "What white Americans have never fully understood but what the Negro can never forget—is that white society is deeply implicated in the ghetto. White institutions created it, white institutions maintain it, and white society condones it."
>
> (Introduction)

> "White racism is essentially responsible for the explosive mixture which has been accumulating in our cities since the end of World War II."
>
> (Part II, Chapter 4)

> "No American—white or black—can escape the consequences of the continuing social and economic decay of our major cities. Only a commitment to national action on an unprecedented scale can shape a future compatible with the historic ideals of American society."
>
> (Part III, Chapter 17)

clusion and declared that the commission's report "blames everybody for the riots except the rioters" (Woods, p. 821).

President Johnson at first made no public comment. In private, he was angry because he thought that the report gave insufficient credit to his administration for its many efforts to end discrimination and alleviate poverty. Nonetheless, the president agreed that social and economic deprivation created the conditions for urban violence, and he knew that the Great Society, however ambitious, had by no means done enough to prevent another riot-filled summer. He also worried that the emphasis on white racism would undermine the support of middle-class and working-class white Americans for essential social reforms. An even bigger obstacle to new social programs was the rising cost of the Vietnam War, in which more than 500,000 Americans were engaged in battle by early 1968. The Kerner Commission's report did not state the costs of the programs it proposed. The White House estimated that $75 to $100 billion would be needed over several years to implement the commission's recommendations, at a time when the entire federal budget was about $180 billion. Even with

a tax increase, which the president approved in June 1968, Congress was determined to reduce new expenditures to cut the federal deficit.

Johnson did persuade Congress to approve two important new reforms. On April 11, the president signed the new Civil Rights Act of 1968, which banned racial discrimination in the sale and rental of most of the nation's housing. Johnson had proposed the legislation even before the Kerner Commission endorsed that reform in its report. Still, only after another national tragedy—the assassination of Martin Luther King, Jr., on April 4, 1968, and rioting in more than one hundred cities—did the House of Representatives pass the measure. On August 1, a new housing program became law, one that authorized funds to build or renovate 1.7 million housing units and also provided mortgage assistance to low-income families who wanted to buy their own homes.

On several occasions over the next thirty years, study groups reviewed the nation's progress in dealing with the problems of inner cities and reached pessimistic conclusions. The first assessment occurred only a year after the

Kerner Commission's report and concluded that "the nation has not reversed the movement apart. Blacks and whites remain deeply divided" (Urban America, p. 116). Twenty years afterward, the 1988 Commission on the Cities, a nongovernmental group of experts that included the Kerner Commission member Fred Harris, warned that America "is *again* becoming two separate societies," one white, one black and Hispanic (Harris and Wilkins, p. 177). Ten years later, the Milton S. Eisenhower Foundation sponsored another look back at the Kerner Commission. This study concluded that a greater percentage of Americans lived in poverty in 1998 than in 1968 and that "inner cities have become America's poorhouses from which many, now, have little hope of escape" (Harris and Curtis, p. 152). These different assessments seemed to confirm what Kenneth Clark had told the Kerner Commission about efforts to improve the conditions of life in inner cities: "the same analysis, the same recommendations, and the same inaction."

Related Documents

Harris, Fred R., and Lynn A. Curtis, eds. *Locked in the Poorhouse: Cities, Race, and Poverty in the United States*. Lanham, Md.: Rowman & Littlefield, 1998. These essays provide a pessimistic assessment of America's response to the Kerner Commission report over three decades.

Harris, Fred R., and Roger W. Wilkins, eds. *Quiet Riots: Race and Poverty in the United States*. New York: Pantheon Books, 1988. The essays in this book grew out of a conference in 1988 to assess urban poverty and race twenty years after the Kerner Commission.

Johnson, Lyndon. *Public Papers of the Presidents of the United States: Lyndon Johnson*. 5 vols. in 10 parts. Washington, D.C.: U.S. Government Printing Office, 1965–1970. These annual volumes contain Johnson's speeches, remarks at news conferences, and messages to Congress, as well as other public documents of his presidency.

National Advisory Commission on Civil Disorders. *Report of the National Advisory Commission on Civil Disorders*. New York: Bantam Books, 1968. The volume contains the full text of the Kerner Commission's report, including the summary and several lengthy appendices.

Urban America. *One Year Later: An Assessment of the Nation's Response to the Crisis Described by the National Advisory Commission on Civil Disorders*. New York: Frederick A. Praeger, 1969. This study, completed one year after the Kerner Commission report, concludes that "the nation's response to the crisis of the cities has been perilously inadequate" (p. v).

Bibliography

■ Articles
"Another Opinion: Attack on the Kerner Report." *New York Times*, March 10, 1968.

Hill, Gladwin. "Dr. King Advocates Quitting Vietnam." *New York Times*, February 26, 1967.

"'Separate and Unequal.'" *New York Times*, March 3, 1968.

■ Books
Blum, John Morton. *Years of Discord: American Politics and Society, 1961–1974*. New York: W. W. Norton, 1991.

Crump, Spencer. *Black Riot in Los Angeles: The Story of the Watts Tragedy*. Los Angeles: Trans-Anglo Books, 1966.

Dallek, Robert. *Flawed Giant: Lyndon Johnson and His Times, 1961–1973*. New York: Oxford University Press, 1998.

Lemann, Nicholas. *The Promised Land: The Great Black Migration and How It Changed America*. New York: Vintage Books, 1992.

Lytle, Mark Hamilton. *America's Uncivil Wars: The Sixties Era from Elvis to the Fall of Richard Nixon*. New York: Oxford University Press, 2006.

Pach, Chester. *The Johnson Years*. New York: Facts On File, 2006.

Woods, Randall B. *LBJ: Architect of American Ambition*. New York: Free Press, 2006.

■ Web Sites
Lyndon Baines Johnson Library and Museum Web site. http://www.lbjlib.utexas.edu/. Accessed on March 4, 2008.

"Lyndon Baines Johnson (1908–1973)." Miller Center of Public Affairs "American President: An Online Reference Resource" Web site. http://www.millercenter.virginia.edu/academic/americanpresident/lbjohnson. Accessed on March 4, 2008.

—By Chester Pach

Questions for Further Study

1. The Kerner Commission issued a controversial report about a difficult and divisive subject. Explain how each of the following persons probably would have reacted to the report's analysis and conclusions: 1) an African American female living below the poverty line in the inner city, 2) a white male working-class laborer living in the same city as the African American female, 3) a white liberal Democrat female in a northern city who supported the civil rights movement and had voted for Lyndon Johnson in 1964, and 4) a male Black Power advocate living in the inner city. Be sure to explain which of the report's main conclusions or recommendations each would have approved and which ones each would have criticized and why.

2. Although the Kerner Commission proposed many new government programs and policies, it also maintained that "new attitudes" were necessary on the part of every American. What new attitudes do you think were required? How important were changes in outlook, thinking, or attitude in resolving the problems of poverty and racism?

3. Many years have passed since the Kerner Commission issued its report and warned that America was moving toward two separate societies divided by race. Do you think that America today still faces that danger? How would you compare fundamental conditions of life in inner cities now and in the 1960s? What improvements have occurred? What problems remain? Have conditions in inner cities deteriorated?

4. Americans continue to differ over how to deal with poverty, racism, discrimination, and inequality. Discuss your views about the role of each of the following in dealing with these issues: individual responsibility; family; community organizations; local government; the news media; the federal government; social activists.

Glossary

de facto segregation	segregation that exists not because of law or government requirement but because of residential patterns or other social practices
exodus	the emigration, departure, or movement of a large group of people
Molotov cocktail	an improvised firebomb thrown by hand and usually consisting of a bottle filled with a liquid that will burn and a rag for a wick
Negro	common term for an African American in the 1960s
nihilism	the view that destroying existing society is necessary to bring about social improvement
polemics	controversial arguments
underemployment	inadequate employment in a part-time instead of full-time job, labor in a low-paying position, or work that requires skills that are less than the worker possesses

KERNER COMMISSION REPORT SUMMARY

Summary of Report

◆ Introduction

The summer of 1967 again brought racial disorders to American cities, and with them shock, fear and bewilderment to the nation.

The worst came during a two-week period in July, first in Newark and then in Detroit. Each set off a chain reaction in neighboring communities.

On July 28, 1967, the President of the United States established this Commission and directed us to answer three basic questions:

What happened?

Why did it happen?

What can be done to prevent it from happening again?

To respond to these questions, we have undertaken a broad range of studies and investigations. We have visited the riot cities; we have heard many witnesses; we have sought the counsel of experts across the country.

This is our basic conclusion: Our nation is moving toward two societies, one black, one white—separate and unequal.

Reaction to last summer's disorders has quickened the movement and deepened the division. Discrimination and segregation have long permeated much of American life; they now threaten the future of every American.

This deepening racial division is not inevitable. The movement apart can be reversed. Choice is still possible. Our principal task is to define that choice and to press for a national resolution.

To pursue our present course will involve the continuing polarization of the American community and, ultimately, the destruction of basic democratic values.

The alternative is not blind repression or capitulation to lawlessness. It is the realization of common opportunities for all within a single society.

This alternative will require a commitment to national action—compassionate, massive and sus-

tained, backed by the resources of the most powerful and the richest nation on this earth. From every American it will require new attitudes, new understanding, and, above all, new will.

The vital needs of the nation must be met; hard choices must be made, and, if necessary, new taxes enacted.

Violence cannot build a better society. Disruption and disorder nourish repression, not justice. They strike at the freedom of every citizen. The community cannot—it will not—tolerate coercion and mob rule.

Violence and destruction must be ended—in the streets of the ghetto and in the lives of people.

Segregation and poverty have created in the racial ghetto a destructive environment totally unknown to most white Americans.

What white Americans have never fully understood but what the Negro can never forget—is that white society is deeply implicated in the ghetto. White institutions created it, white institutions maintain it, and white society condones it.

It is time now to turn with all the purpose at our command to the major unfinished business of this nation. It is time to adopt strategies for action that will produce quick and visible progress. It is time to make good the promises of American democracy to all citizens-urban and rural, white and black, Spanish-surname, American Indian, and every minority group.

Our recommendations embrace three basic principles:

To mount programs on a scale equal to the dimension of the problems:

To aim these programs for high impact in the immediate future in order to close the gap between promise and performance;

To undertake new initiatives and experiments that can change the system of failure and frustration that now dominates the ghetto and weakens our society.

These programs will require unprecedented levels of funding and performance, but they neither probe deeper nor demand more than the problems which called them forth. There can be no higher priority for national action and no higher claim on the nation's conscience.

We issue this Report now, four months before the date called for by the President. Much remains that can be learned. Continued study is essential.

As Commissioners we have worked together with a sense of the greatest urgency and have sought to compose whatever differences exist among us. Some differences remain. But the gravity of the problem and the pressing need for action are too clear to allow further delay in the issuance of this Report.

Part I—What Happened?

Chapter I—Profiles of Disorder

The report contains profiles of a selection of the disorders that took place during the summer of 1967. These profiles are designed to indicate how the disorders happened, who participated in them, and how local officials, police forces, and the National Guard responded. Illustrative excerpts follow:

Newark

… It was decided to attempt to channel the energies of the people into a nonviolent protest. While Lofton promised the crowd that a full investigation would be made of the Smith incident, the other Negro leaders began urging those on the scene to form a line of march toward the city hall.

Some persons joined the line of march. Others milled about in the narrow street. From the dark grounds of the housing project came a barrage of rocks. Some of them fell among the crowd. Others hit persons in the line of march. Many smashed the windows of the police station. The rock throwing, it was believed, was the work of youngsters; approximately 2,500 children lived in the housing project.

Almost at the same time, an old car was set afire in a parking lot. The line of march began to disintegrate. The police, their heads protected by World War I-type helmets, sallied forth to disperse the crowd. A fire engine, arriving on the scene, was pelted with rocks. As police drove people away from the station, they scattered in all directions.

A few minutes later a nearby liquor store was broken into. Some persons, seeing a caravan of cabs appear at city hall to protest Smith's arrest, interpreted this as evidence that the disturbance had been organized, and generated rumors to that effect. However, only a few stores were looted. Within a short period of time, the disorder appeared to have run its course.

* * *

… On Saturday, July 15, [Director of Police Dominick] Spina received a report of snipers in a housing project. When he arrived he saw approximately 100 National Guardsmen and police officers crouching behind vehicles, hiding in corners and lying on the ground around the edge of the courtyard.

Since everything appeared quiet and it was broad daylight, Spina walked directly down the middle of the street. Nothing happened. As he came to the last building of the complex, he heard a shot. All around him the troopers jumped, believing themselves to be under sniper fire. A moment later a young Guardsman ran from behind a building.

The Director of Police went over and asked him if he had fired the shot. The soldier said yes, he had fired to scare a man away from a window; that his orders were to keep everyone away from windows.

Spina said he told the soldier: "Do you know what you just did? You have now created a state of hysteria. Every Guardsman up and down this street and every state policeman and every city policeman that is present thinks that somebody just fired a shot and that it is probably a sniper."

A short time later more "gunshots" were heard. Investigating, Spina came upon a Puerto Rican sitting on a wall. In reply to a question as to whether he knew "where the firing is coming from?" the man said:

"That's no firing. That's fireworks. If you look up to the fourth floor, you will see the people who are throwing down these cherry bombs."

By this time four truckloads of National Guardsmen had arrived and troopers and policemen were again crouched everywhere looking for a sniper. The Director of Police remained at the scene for three hours, and the only shot fired was the one by the Guardsman.

Nevertheless, at six o'clock that evening two columns of National Guardsmen and state troopers were directing mass fire at the Hayes Housing Project in response to what they believed were snipers.…

Detroit

… A spirit of carefree nihilism was taking hold. To riot and destroy appeared more and more to become ends in themselves. Late Sunday afternoon it appeared to one observer that the young people were "dancing amidst the flames."

A Negro plainclothes officer was standing at an intersection when a man threw a Molotov cocktail into a business establishment at the corner... In the heat of the afternoon, fanned by the 20 to 25 m.p.h. winds of both Sunday and Monday, the fire reached the home next door within minutes. As residents uselessly sprayed the flames with garden hoses, the fire jumped from roof to roof of adjacent two- and three-story buildings. Within the hour the entire block was in flames. The ninth house in the burning row belonged to the arsonist who had thrown the Molotov cocktail....

* * *

... Employed as a private guard, 55-year-old Julius L. Dorsey, a Negro, was standing in front of a market when accosted by two Negro men and a woman. They demanded he permit them to loot the market. He ignored their demands. They began to berate him. He asked a neighbor to call the police. As the argument grew more heated, Dorsey fired three shots from his pistol into the air.

The police radio reported: "Looters, they have rifles." A patrol car driven by a police officer and carrying three National Guardsmen arrived. As the looters fled, the law enforcement personnel opened fire. When the firing ceased, one person lay dead.

He was Julius L. Dorsey ...

* * *

... As the riot alternately waxed and waned, one area of the ghetto remained insulated. On the northeast side the residents of some 150 square blocks inhabited by

21,000 persons had, in 1966, banded together in the Positive Neighborhood Action Committee (PNAC). With professional help from the Institute of Urban Dynamics, they had organized block clubs and made plans for the improvement of the neighborhood....

When the riot broke out, the residents, through the block clubs, were able to organize quickly. Youngsters, agreeing to stay in the neighborhood, participated in detouring traffic. While many persons reportedly sympathized with the idea of a rebellion against the "system," only two small fires were set—one in an empty building.

* * *

... According to Lt. Gen. Throckmorton and Col. Bolling, the city, at this time, was saturated with fear. The National Guardsmen were afraid, the residents were afraid, and the police were afraid. Numerous persons, the majority of them Negroes, were being injured by gunshots of undetermined origin. The general and his staff felt that the major task of the troops was to reduce the fear and restore an air of normalcy.

In order to accomplish this, every effort was made to establish contact and rapport between the troops and the residents. The soldiers—20 percent of whom were Negro—began helping to clean up the streets, collect garbage, and trace persons who had disappeared in the confusion. Residents in the neighborhoods responded with soup and sandwiches for the troops. In areas where the National Guard tried to establish rapport with the citizens, there was a smaller response.

New Brunswick

... A short time later, elements of the crowd—an older and rougher one than the night before—appeared in front of the police station. The participants wanted to see the mayor.

Mayor [Patricia] Sheehan went out onto the steps of the station. Using a bullhorn, she talked to the people and asked that she be given an opportunity to correct conditions. The crowd was boisterous. Some persons challenged the mayor. But, finally, the opinion, "She's new! Give her a chance!" prevailed.

A demand was issued by people in the crowd that all persons arrested the previous night be released. Told that this already had been done, the people were suspicious. They asked to be allowed to inspect the jail cells.

It was agreed to permit representatives of the people to look in the cells to satisfy themselves that everyone had been released.

The crowd dispersed. The New Brunswick riot had failed to materialize ...

Chapter 2—Patterns of Disorder

The "typical" riot did not take place. The disorders of 1967 were unusual, irregular, complex and unpredictable social processes. Like most human events, they did not unfold in an orderly sequence. However, an analysis of our survey information leads to some conclusions about the riot process. In general:

- The civil disorders of 1967 involved Negroes acting against local symbols of white American society, authority and property in Negro neighborhoods—rather than against white persons.
- Of 164 disorders reported during the first nine months of 1967, eight (5 percent) were major in terms of violence and damage; 33 (20 percent) were serious but not major; 123 (75 percent) were minor and undoubtedly would not have received national attention as "riots" had the nation not been sensitized by the more serious outbreaks.

- In the 75 disorders studied by a Senate subcommittee, 83 deaths were reported. Eighty-two percent of the deaths and more than half the injuries occurred in Newark and Detroit. About 10 percent of the dead and 38 percent of the injured were public employees, primarily law officers and firemen. The overwhelming majority of the persons killed or injured in all the disorders were Negro civilians.

- Initial damage estimates were greatly exaggerated. In Detroit, newspaper damage estimates at first ranged from $200 million to $500 million; the highest recent estimate is $45 million. In Newark, early estimates ranged from $15 to $25 million. A month later damage was estimated at $10.2 million, over 80 percent in inventory losses.

In the 24 disorders in 23 cities which we surveyed:

- The final incident before the outbreak of disorder, and the initial violence itself, generally took place in the evening or at night at a place in which it was normal for many people to be on the streets.

- Violence usually occurred almost immediately following the occurrence of the final precipitating incident, and then escalated rapidly. With but few exceptions, violence subsided during the day, and flared rapidly again at night. The night-day cycles continued through the early period of the major disorders.

- Disorder generally began with rock and bottle throwing and window breaking. Once store windows were broken, looting usually followed.

- Disorder did not erupt as a result of a single "triggering" or "precipitating" incident. Instead, it was generated out of an increasingly disturbed social atmosphere, in which typically a series of tension-heightening incidents over a period of weeks or months became linked in the minds of many in the Negro community with a reservoir of underlying grievances. At some point in the mounting tension, a further incident-in itself often routine or trivial-became the breaking point and the tension spilled over into violence.

- "Prior" incidents, which increased tensions and ultimately led to violence, were police actions in almost half the cases; police actions were "final" incidents before the outbreak of violence in 12 of the 24 surveyed disorders.

- No particular control tactic was successful in every situation. The varied effectiveness of control techniques emphasizes the need for advance training, planning, adequate intelligence systems, and knowledge of the ghetto community.

- Negotiations between Negroes—including your militants as well as older Negro leaders—and white officials concerning "terms of peace" occurred during virtually all the disorders surveyed. In many cases, these negotiations involved discussion of underlying grievances as well as the handling of the disorder by control authorities.

- The typical rioter was a teenager or young adult, a lifelong resident of the city in which he rioted, a high school dropout; he was, nevertheless, somewhat better educated than his nonrioting Negro neighbor, and was usually underemployed or employed in a menial job. He was proud of his race, extremely hostile to both whites and middle-class Negroes and, although informed about politics, highly distrustful of the political system.

- A Detroit survey revealed that approximately 11 percent of the total residents of two riot areas admitted participation in the rioting, 20 to 25 percent identified themselves as "bystanders," over 16 percent identified themselves as "counter-rioters" who urged rioters to "cool it," and the remaining 48 to 53 percent said they were at home or elsewhere and did not participate. In a survey of Negro males between the ages of 15 and 35 residing in the disturbance area in Newark, about 45 percent identified themselves as rioters, and about 55 percent as "noninvolved."

- Most rioters were young Negro males. Nearly 53 percent of arrestees were between 15 and 24 years of age; nearly 81 percent between 15 and 35.

- In Detroit and Newark about 74 percent of the rioters were brought up in the North. In contrast, of the noninvolved, 36 percent in Detroit and 52 percent in Newark were brought up in the North.

- What the rioters appeared to be seeking was fuller participation in the social order and the material benefits enjoyed by the majority of American citizens. Rather than rejecting the American system, they were anxious to obtain a place for themselves in it.

- Numerous Negro counter-rioters walked the streets urging rioters to "cool it." The typical counter-rioter was better educated and had higher income than either the rioter or the noninvolved.

- The proportion of Negroes in local government was substantially smaller than the Negro proportion of population. Only three of the 20 cities studied had more than one Negro legislator; none had ever had a Negro mayor or city manager. In only four cities did Negroes hold other important policy-making positions or serve as heads of municipal departments.

- Although almost all cities had some sort of formal grievance mechanism for handling citizen complaints, this typically was regarded by Negroes as ineffective and was generally ignored.

- Although specific grievances varied from city to city, at least 12 deeply held grievances can be identified and ranked into three levels of relative intensity: '

  FIRST LEVEL OF INTENSITY

    1. Police practices
    2. Unemployment and underemployment
    3. Inadequate housing

  SECOND LEVEL OF INTENSITY

    4. Inadequate education
    5. Poor recreation facilities and programs
    6. Ineffectiveness of the political structure and grievance mechanisms

  THIRD LEVEL OF INTENSITY

    7. Disrespectful white attitudes
    8. Discriminatory administration of justice
    9. Inadequacy of federal programs
    10. Inadequacy of municipal services
    11. Discriminatory consumer and credit practices
    12. Inadequate welfare programs

- The results of a three-city survey of various federal programs—manpower, education, housing, welfare and community action—indicate that, despite substantial expenditures, the number of persons assisted constituted only a fraction of those in need.

The background of disorder is often as complex and difficult to analyze as the disorder itself. But we find that certain general conclusions can be drawn:

- Social and economic conditions in the riot cities constituted a clear pattern of severedisadvantage for Negroes compared with whites, whether the Negroes lived in the area where the riot took place or outside it. Negroes had completed fewer years of education and fewer had attended high school. Negroes were twice as likely to be unemployed and three times as likely to be in unskilled and service jobs. Negroes averaged 70 percent of the income earned by whites and were more than twice as likely to be living in poverty. Although housing cost Negroes relatively more, they had worse housing-three times as likely to be overcrowded and substandard. When compared to white suburbs, the relative disadvantage is even more pronounced.

A study of the aftermath of disorder leads to disturbing conclusions. We find that, despite the institution of some postriot programs:

- Little basic change in the conditions underlying the outbreak of disorder has taken place. Actions to ameliorate Negro grievances have been limited and sporadic; with but few exceptions, they have not significantly reduced tensions.

- In several cities, the principal official response has been to train and equip the police with more sophisticated weapons. In several cities, increasing polarization is evident, with continuing breakdown of inter-racial communication, and growth of white segregationist or black separatist groups.

Chapter 3—Organized Activity

The President directed the Commission to investigate "to, what extent, if any, there has been planning or organization in any of the riots."

To carry out this part of the President's charge, the Commission established a special investigative staff supplementing the field teams that made the general examination of the riots in 23 cities. The unit examined data collected by federal agencies and congressional committees, including thousands of documents supplied by the Federal Bureau of Investigation, gathered and evaluated information from local and state law enforcement agencies and officials, and conducted its own field investigation in selected cities.

On the basis of all the information collected, the Commission concludes that:

The urban disorders of the summer of 1967 were not caused by, nor were they the consequence of, any organized plan or "conspiracy."

Specifically, the Commission has found no evidence that all or any of the disorders or the incidents that led to them were planned or directed by any organization or group, international, national or local.

Militant organizations, local and national, and individual agitators, who repeatedly forecast and called for violence, were active in the spring and summer of 1967. We believe that they sought to encourage violence, and that they helped to create an atmosphere that contributed to the outbreak of disorder.

We recognize that the continuation of disorders and the polarization of the races would provide fertile ground for organized exploitation in the future.

Investigations of organized activity are continuing at all levels of government, including committees of Congress. These investigations relate not only to the disorders of 1967 but also to the actions of groups and individuals, particularly in schools and colleges, during this last fall and winter. The Commission has cooperated in these investigations. They should continue.

Part II—Why Did It Happen?

Chapter 4—The Basic Causes

In addressing the question "Why did it happen?" we shift our focus from the local to the national scene, from the particular events of the summer of 1967 to the factors within the society at large that created a mood of violence among many urban Negroes.

These factors are complex and interacting; they vary significantly in their effect from city to city and from year to year; and the consequences of one disorder, generating new grievances and new demands, become the causes of the next. Thus was created the "thicket of tension, conflicting evidence and extreme opinions" cited by the President.

Despite these complexities, certain fundamental matters are clear. Of these, the most fundamental is the racial attitude and behavior of white Americans toward black Americans.

Race prejudice has shaped our history decisively; it now threatens to affect our future.

White racism is essentially responsible for the explosive mixture which has been accumulating in our cities since the end of World War II. Among the ingredients of this mixture are:

- Pervasive discrimination and segregation in employment, education and housing, which have resulted in the continuing exclusion of great numbers of Negroes from the benefits of economic progress.
- Black in-migration and white exodus, which have produced the massive and growing concentrations of impoverished Negroes in our major cities, creating a growing crisis of deteriorating facilities and services and unmet human needs.
- The black ghettos where segregation and poverty converge on the young to destroy opportunity and enforce failure. Crime, drug addiction, dependency on welfare, and bitterness and resentment against society in general and white society in particular are the result.

At the same time, most whites and some Negroes outside the ghetto have prospered to a degree unparalleled in the history of civilization. Through television and other media, this affluence has been flaunted before the eyes of the Negro poor and the jobless ghetto youth.

Yet these facts alone cannot be said to have caused the disorders. Recently, other powerful ingredients have begun to catalyze the mixture:

- Frustrated hopes are the residue of the unfulfilled expectations aroused by the great judicial and legislative victories of the Civil Rights Movement and the dramatic struggle for equal rights in the South.
- A climate that tends toward approval and encouragement of violence as a form of protest has been created by white terrorism directed against nonviolent protest; by the open defiance of law and federal authority by state and local officials resisting desegregation; and by some protest groups engaging in civil disobedience who turn their backs on nonviolence, go beyond the constitutionally protected rights of petition and free assembly, and resort to violence to attempt to compel alteration of laws and policies with which they disagree.
- The frustrations of powerlessness have led some Negroes to the conviction that there is no effective alternative to violence as a means of achieving redress of grievances, and of "moving the system." These frustrations are reflected in alienation and hostility toward the institutions of law and government and the white society which controls them, and in the reach toward racial consciousness and solidarity reflected in the slogan "Black Power."
- A new mood has sprung up among Negroes, particularly among the young, in which self-esteem and enhanced racial pride are replacing apathy and submission to "the system."
- The police are not merely a "spark" factor. To some Negroes police have come to symbolize white power, white racism and white repression. And the fact is that many police do reflect and express these white attitudes. The atmosphere of hostility and cynicism is reinforced by a widespread belief among Negroes in the existence of police brutality and in a "double standard" of justice and protection—one for Negroes and one for whites.

To this point, we have attempted to identify the prime components of the "explosive mixture." In the chapters that follow we seek to analyze them in the perspective of history. Their meaning, however, is clear:

In the summer of 1967, we have seen in our cities a chain reaction of racial violence. If we are heedless, none of us shall escape the consequences.

Chapter 5—Rejection and Protest: An Historical Sketch

The causes of recent racial disorders are embedded in a tangle of issues and circumstances—social, economic, political and psychological which arise out of the historic pattern of Negro-white relations in America.

In this chapter we trace the pattern, identify the recurrent themes of Negro protest and, most importantly, provide a perspective on the protest activities of the present era.

We describe the Negro's experience in America and the development of slavery as an institution. We show his persistent striving for equality in the face of rigidly maintained social, economic and educational barriers, and repeated mob violence. We portray the ebb and flow of the doctrinal tides—accommodation, separatism, and self-help—and their relationship to the current theme of Black Power. We conclude:

The Black Power advocates of today consciously feel that they are the most militant group in the Negro protest movement. Yet they have retreated from a direct confrontation with American society on the issue of integration and, by preaching separatism, unconsciously function as an accommodation to white racism. Much of their economic program, as well as their interest in Negro history, self-help, racial solidarity and separation, is reminiscent of Booker T. Washington. The rhetoric is different, but the ideas are remarkably similar.

Chapter 6—The Formation Of the Racial Ghettos

Throughout the 20th century the Negro population of the United States has been moving steadily from rural areas to urban and from South to North and West. In 1910, 91 percent of the nation's 9.8 million Negroes lived in the South and only 27 percent of American Negroes lived in cities of 2,500 persons or more. Between 1910 and 1966 the total Negro population more than doubled, reaching 21.5 million, and the number living in metropolitan areas rose more than fivefold (from 2.6 million to 14.8 million). The number outside the South rose eleven-fold (from 880,000 to 9.7 million).

Negro migration from the South has resulted from the expectation of thousands of new and high-ly paid jobs for unskilled workers in the North and the shift to mechanized farming in the South. However, the Negro migration is small when compared to earlier waves of European immigrants. Even between 1960 and 1966, there were 1.8 million immigrants from abroad compared to the 613,000 Negroes who arrived in the North and West from the South.

As a result of the growing number of Negroes in urban areas, natural increase has replaced migration as the primary source of Negro population increase in the cities. Nevertheless, Negro migration from the South will continue unless economic conditions there change dramatically.

Basic data concerning Negro urbanization trends indicate that:

- Almost all Negro population growth (98 percent from 1950 to 1966) is occurring within metropolitan areas, primarily within central cities.
- The vast majority of white population growth (78 percent from 1960 to 1966) is occurring in suburban portions of metropolitan areas. Since 1960, white central-city population has declined by 1.3 million.
- As a result, central cities are becoming more heavily Negro while the suburban fringes around them remain almost entirely white.
- The twelve largest central cities now contain over two-thirds of the Negro population outside the South, and one-third of the Negro total in the United States.

Within the cities, Negroes have been excluded from white residential areas through discriminatory practices. Just as significant is the withdrawal of white families from, or their refusal to enter, neighborhoods where Negroes are moving or already residing. About 20 percent of the urban population of the United States changes residence every year. The refusal of whites to move into "changing" areas when vacancies occur means that most vacancies eventually are occupied by Negroes.

The result, according to a recent study, is that in 1960 the average segregation index for 207 of the largest United States cities was 86.2. In other words, to create an unsegregated population distribution, an average of over 86 percent of all Negroes would have to change their place of residence within the city.

Chapter 7—Unemployment, Family Structure, and Social Disorganization

Although there have been gains in Negro income nationally, and a decline in the number of Negroes below the "poverty level," the condition of Negroes ill the central city remains in a state of crisis. Between

2 and 2.5 million Negroes-16 to 20 percent of the total Negro population of all central cities live in squalor and deprivation in ghetto neighborhoods.

Employment is a key problem. It not only controls the present for the Negro American but, in a most profound way, it is creating the future as well. Yet, despite continuing economic growth and declining national unemployment rates, the unemployment rate for Negroes in 1967 was more than double that for whites …

Equally important is the undesirable nature of many jobs open to Negroes and other minorities. Negro men are more than three times as likely as white men to be in low paying, unskilled or service jobs. This concentration of male Negro employment at the lowest end of the occupational scale is the single most important cause of poverty among Negroes.

In one study of low-income neighborhoods, the "subemployment rate," including both unemployment and underemployment, was about 33 percent, or 8.8 times greater than the overall unemployment rate for all United States workers.

Employment problems, aggravated by the constant arrival of new unemployed migrants, many of them from depressed rural areas, create persistent poverty in the ghetto. In 1966, about 11.9 percent of the nation's whites and 40.6 percent of its nonwhites were below the "poverty level" defined by' the Social Security Administration (currently $3,335 per year for an urban family of four). Over 40 percent of the nonwhites below the poverty level live in the central cities.

Employment problems have drastic social impact in the ghetto. Men who are chronically unemployed or employed in the lowest status jobs are often unable or unwilling to remain with their families. The handicap imposed on children growing up without fathers in an atmosphere of poverty and deprivation is increased as mothers are forced to work to provide support.

The culture of poverty that results from unemployment and family breakup generates a system of ruthless, exploitative relationships within the ghetto. Prostitution, dope addiction, and crime create an environmental "jungle" characterized by personal insecurity and tension. Children growing up under such conditions are likely participants in civil disorder.

Chapter 8—Conditions of Life In the Racial Ghetto

A striking difference in environment from that of white, middle-class Americans profoundly influences the lives of residents of the ghetto.

Crime rates, consistently higher than in other areas, create a pronounced sense of insecurity. For example, in one city one low-income Negro district had 35 times as many serious crimes against persons as a high-income white district. Unless drastic steps are taken, the crime problems in poverty areas are likely to continue to multiply as the growing youth and rapid urbanization of the population outstrip police resources.

Poor health and sanitation conditions in the ghetto result in higher mortality rates, a higher incidence of major diseases, and lower availability and utilization of medical services. The infant mortality rate for nonwhite babies under the age of one month is 58 percent higher than for whites; for one to 12 months it is almost three times as high. The level of sanitation in the ghetto is far below that in high income areas. Garbage collection is often inadequate. Of an estimated 14,000 cases of rat bite in the United States in 1965, most were in ghetto neighborhoods.

Ghetto residents believe they are "exploited" by local merchants; and evidence substantiates some of these beliefs. A study conducted in one city by the Federal Trade Commission showed that distinctly higher prices were charged for goods sold in ghetto stores than in other areas.

Lack of knowledge regarding credit purchasing creates special pitfalls for the disadvantaged. In many states garnishment practices compound these difficulties by allowing creditors to deprive individuals of their wages without hearing or trial.

Chapter 9—Comparing the Immigrant and Negro Experience

In this chapter, we address ourselves to a fundamental question that many white Americans are asking: why have so many Negroes, unlike the European immigrants, been unable to escape from the ghetto and from poverty. We believe the following factors play a part:

- The Maturing Economy: When the European immigrants arrived, they gained an economic foothold by providing the unskilled labor needed by industry. Unlike the immigrant, the Negro migrant found little opportunity in the city. The economy, by then matured, had little use for the unskilled labor he had to offer.
- The Disability of Race: The structure of discrimination has stringently narrowed opportunities for the Negro and restricted his prospects. European immigrants suffered from discrimination, but never so pervasively.
- Entry into the Political System: The immigrants usually settled in rapidly growing cities with

powerful and expanding political machines, which traded economic advantages for political support. Ward-level grievance machinery, as well as personal representation, enabled the immigrant to make his voice heard and his power felt. By the time the Negro arrived, these political machines were no longer so powerful or so well equipped to provide jobs or other favors, and in many cases were unwilling to share their influence with Negroes.

- Cultural Factors: Coming from societies with a low standard of living and at a time when job aspirations were low, the immigrants sensed little deprivation in being forced to take the less desirable and poorer-paying jobs. Their large and cohesive families contributed to total income. Their vision of the future—one that led to a life outside of the ghetto—provided the incentive necessary to endure the present.

Although Negro men worked as hard as the immigrants, they were unable to support their families. The entrepreneurial opportunities had vanished. As a result of slavery and long periods of unemployment, the Negro family structure had become matriarchal; the males played a secondary and marginal family role—one which offered little compensation for their hard and unrewarding labor. Above all, segregation denied Negroes access to good jobs and the opportunity to leave the ghetto. For them, the future seemed to lead only to a dead end.

Today, whites tend to exaggerate how well and quickly they escaped from poverty. The fact is that immigrants who came from rural backgrounds, as many Negroes do, are only now, after three generations, finally beginning to move into the middle class.

By contrast, Negroes began concentrating in the city less than two generations ago, and under much less favorable conditions. Although some Negroes have escaped poverty, few have been able to escape the urban ghetto.

Part III—What Can Be Done?

Chapter 10—The Community Response

Our investigation of the 1967 riot cities establishes that virtually every major episode of violence was foreshadowed by an accumulation of unresolved grievances and by widespread dissatisfaction among Negroes with the unwillingness or inability of local government to respond.

Overcoming these conditions is essential for community support of law enforcement and civil order. City governments need new and more vital channels of communication to the residents of the ghetto; they need to improve their capacity to respond effectively to community needs before they become community grievances; and they need to provide opportunity for, meaningful involvement of ghetto residents in shaping policies and programs which affect the community.

The Commission recommends that local governments:

- Develop Neighborhood Action Task Forces as joint community government efforts through which more effective communication can be achieved, and the delivery of city services to ghetto residents improved.
- Establish comprehensive grievance-response mechanisms in order to bring all public agencies under public scrutiny.
- Bring the institutions of local government closer to the people they serve by establishing neighborhood outlets for local, state and federal administrative and public service agencies.
- Expand opportunities for ghetto residents to participate in the formulation of public policy and the implementation of programs affecting them through improved political representation, creation of institutional channels for community action, expansion of legal services, and legislative hearings on ghetto problems.

In this effort, city governments will require state and federal support.

The Commission recommends:

- State and federal financial assistance for mayors and city councils to support the research, consultants, staff and other resources needed to respond effectively to federal program initiatives.
- State cooperation in providing municipalities with the jurisdictional tools needed to deal with their problems; a fuller measure of financial aid to urban areas; and the focusing of the interests of suburban communities on the physical, social and cultural environment of the central city.

Chapter 11—Police and the Community

The abrasive relationship between the police and the minority communities has been a major—and explosive—source of grievance, tension and disorder. The blame must be shared by the total society.

The police are faced with demands for increased protection and service in the ghetto. Yet the aggressive patrol practices thought necessary to meet these demands themselves create tension and hostility. The resulting grievances have been further aggravated by the lack of effective mechanisms for handling complaints against the police. Special programs for bettering police-community relations have been instituted, but these alone are not enough. Police administrators, with the guidance of public officials, and the support of the entire community, must take vigorous action to improve law enforcement arid to decrease the potential for disorder.

The Commission recommends that city government and police authorities:

- Review police operations in the ghetto to ensure proper conduct by police officers, and eliminate abrasive practices.
- Provide more adequate police protection to ghetto residents to eliminate their high sense of insecurity, and the belief of many Negro citizens in the existence of a dual standard of law enforcement.
- Establish fair and effective mechanisms for the redress of grievances against the police, and other municipal employees.
- Develop and adopt policy guidelines to assist officers in making critical decisions in areas where police conduct can create tension.
- Develop and use innovative programs to ensure widespread community support for law enforcement.
- Recruit more Negroes into the regular police force, and review promotion policies to ensure fair promotion for Negro officers.
- Establish a "Community Service Officer" program to attract ghetto youths between the ages of 17 and 21 to police work. These junior officers would perform duties in ghetto neighborhoods, but would not have full police authority. The federal government should provide support equal to 90 percent of the costs of employing CSOs on the basis of one for every ten regular officers.

Chapter 12—Control of Disorder

Preserving civil peace is the first responsibility of government. Unless the rule of law prevails, our society will lack not only order but also the environment essential to social and economic progress.

The maintenance of civil order cannot be left to the police alone. The police need guidance, as well as support, from mayors and other public officials. It is the responsibility of public officials to determine proper police policies, support adequate police standards for personnel and performance, and participate in planning for the control of disorders.

To maintain control of incidents which could lead to disorders, the Commission recommends that local officials:

- Assign seasoned, well-trained policemen and supervisory officers to patrol ghetto areas, and to respond to disturbances.
- Develop plans which will quickly muster maximum police man power and highly qualified senior commanders at the outbreak of disorders.
- Provide special training in the prevention of disorders, and prepare police for riot control and for operation in units, with adequate command and control and field communication for proper discipline and effectiveness.
- Develop guidelines governing the use of control equipment and provide alternatives to the use of lethal weapons. Federal support for research in this area is needed.
- Establish an intelligence system to provide police and other public officials with reliable information that may help to prevent the outbreak of a disorder and to institute effective control measures in the event a riot erupts.
- Develop continuing contacts with ghetto residents to make use of the forces for order which exist within the community.
- Establish machinery for neutralizing rumors, and enabling Negro leaders and residents to obtain the facts. Create special rumor details to collect, evaluate, and dispel rumors that may lead to a civil disorder.

The Commission believes there is a grave danger that some communities may resort to the indiscriminate and excessive use of force. The harmful effects of overreaction are incalculable. The Commission condemns moves to equip police departments with mass destruction weapons, such as automatic rifles, machine guns and tanks. Weapons which are designed to destroy, not to control, have no place in densely populated urban communities.

The Commission recognizes the sound principle of local authority and responsibility in law enforcement, but recommends that the federal government share, in the financing of programs for improvement of police forces, both in their normal law enforcement activities as well as in their response to civil disorders.

To assist government authorities in planning their response to civil disorder, this report contains a Supplement on Control of Disorder. It deals with specific problems encountered during riot-control operations, and includes:

- Assessment of the present capabilities of police, National Guard and Army forces to control major riots, and recommendations for improvement;
- Recommended means by which the control operations of those forces may be coordinated with the response of other agencies, such as fire departments, and with the community at large;
- Recommendations for review and revision of federal, state and local laws needed to provide the framework for control efforts and for the call-up and interrelated action of public safety forces.

Chapter 13—The Administration of Justice Under Emergency Conditions

In many of the cities which experienced disorders last summer, there were recurring breakdowns in the mechanisms for processing, prosecuting and protecting arrested persons. These resulted mainly from long-standing structural deficiencies in criminal court systems, and from the failure of communities to anticipate and plan for the emergency demands of civil disorders.

In part, because of this, there were few successful prosecutions for serious crimes committed during the riots. In those cities where mass arrests occurred many arrestees were deprived of basic legal rights.

The Commission recommends that the cities and states:

- Undertake reform of the lower courts so as to improve the quality of justice rendered under normal conditions.
- Plan comprehensive measures by which the criminal justice system may be supplemented during civil disorders so that its deliberative functions are protected, and the quality of justice is maintained.

Such emergency plans require broad community participation and dedicated leadership by the bench and bar. They should include:

- Laws sufficient to deter and punish riot conduct.
- Additional judges, bail and probation officers, and clerical staff.
- Arrangements for volunteer lawyers to help prosecutors and to represent riot defendants at every stage of proceedings.
- Policies to ensure proper and individual bail, arraignment, pre-trial, trial and sentencing proceedings.
- Procedures for processing arrested persons, such as summons and release, and release on personal recognizance, which permit separation of minor offenders from those dangerous to the community, in order that serious offenders may be detained and prosecuted effectively.
- Adequate emergency processing and detention facilities.

Chapter 14—Damages: Repair and Compensation

The Commission recommends that the federal government:

- Amend the Federal Disaster Act-which now applies only to natural disasters—to permit federal emergency food and medical assistance to cities during major civil disorders, and provide long-term economic assistance afterwards.
- With the cooperation of the states, create incentives for the private insurance industry to provide more adequate property-insurance coverage in inner-city areas.

The Commission endorses the report of the National Advisory Panel on Insurance in Riot-Affected Areas: "Meeting the Insurance Crisis of our Cities."

Chapter 15—The News Media and the Disorders

In his charge to the Commission, the President asked: "What effect do the mass media have on the riots?"

The Commission determined that the answer to the President's question did not lie solely in the performance of the press and broadcasters in reporting the riots. Our analysis had to consider also the overall treatment by the media of the Negro ghettos, community relations, racial attitudes, and poverty-day by day and month by month, year in and year out. A wide range of interviews with government officials, law enforcement authorities, media personnel and other citizens, including ghetto residents, as well as a quantitative analysis of riot coverage and a special conference with industry representatives, leads us to conclude that:

- Despite instances of sensationalism, inaccuracy and distortion, newspapers, radio and television tried on the whole to give a balanced, factual account of the 1967 disorders.
- Elements of the news media failed to portray accurately the scale and character of the violence that occurred last summer. The overall effect was, we believe, an exaggeration of both mood and event.
- Important segments of the media failed to report adequately on the causes and consequences of civil disorders and on the underlying problems of race relations. They have not com-

municated to the majority of their audience—
which is white—a sense of the degradation,
misery and hopelessness of life in the ghetto.

These failings must be corrected, and the
improvement must come from within the industry.
Freedom of the press is not the issue. Any effort to
impose governmental restrictions would be inconsistent with fundamental constitutional precepts.

We have seen evidence that the news media are
becoming aware of and concerned about their performance in this field. As that concern grows, coverage will improve. But much more must be done, and
it must be done soon.

The Commission recommends that the media:

- Expand coverage of the Negro community and
  of race problems through permanent assignment of reporters familiar with urban and racial
  affairs, and through establishment of more and
  better links with the Negro community.
- Integrate Negroes and Negro activities into all
  aspects of coverage and content, including
  newspaper articles and television programming. The news media must publish newspapers and produce programs that recognize the
  existence and activities of Negroes as a group
  within the community and as a part of the larger community.
- Recruit more Negroes into journalism and
  broadcasting and promote those who are qualified to positions of significant responsibility.
  Recruitment should begin in high schools and
  continue through college; where necessary, aid
  for training should be provided.
- Improve coordination with police in reporting
  riot news through advance planning, and cooperate with the police in the designation of police
  information officers, establishment of information centers, and development of mutually
  acceptable guidelines for riot reporting and the
  conduct of media personnel.
- Accelerate efforts to ensure accurate and
  responsible reporting of pot and racial news,
  through adoption by all news gathering organizations of stringent internal staff guidelines.
- Cooperate in the establishment of a privately
  organized and funded Institute of Urban Communications to train and educate journalists in
  urban affairs, recruit and train more Negro journalists, develop methods for improving police-
  press relations, review coverage of riots and
  racial issues, and support continuing research in
  the urban field.

Chapter 16—The Future of the Cities

By 1985, the Negro population in central cities is
expected to increase by 72 percent to approximately
20.8 million. Coupled with the continued exodus of
white families to the suburbs, this growth will produce majority Negro populations in many of the
nation's largest cities.

The future of these cities, and of their burgeoning
Negro populations, is grim. Most new employment
opportunities are being created in suburbs and outlying areas. This trend will continue unless important changes in public policy are made.

In prospect, therefore, is further deterioration of
already inadequate municipal tax bases in the face of
increasing demands for public services, and continuing unemployment and poverty among the urban
Negro population.

Three choices are open to the nation:

- We can maintain present policies, continuing
  both the proportion of the nation's resources
  now allocated to programs for the unemployed
  and the disadvantaged, and the inadequate and
  failing effort to achieve an integrated society.
- We can adopt a policy of "enrichment" aimed at
  improving dramatically the quality of ghetto life
  while abandoning integration as a goal.
- We can pursue integration by combining ghetto
  "enrichment" with policies which will encourage Negro movement out of central city areas.

The first choice, continuance of present policies,
has ominous consequences for our society. The share of
the nation's resources now allocated to programs for the
disadvantaged is insufficient to arrest the deterioration
of life in central city ghettos. Under such conditions, a
rising proportion of Negroes may come to see in the
deprivation and segregation they experience, a justification for violent protest, or for extending support to now
isolated extremists who advocate civil disruption. Large-
scale and continuing violence could result, followed by
white retaliation, and, ultimately, the separation of the
two communities in a garrison state.

Even if violence does not occur, the consequences are unacceptable. Development of a racially
integrated society, extraordinarily difficult today, will
be virtually impossible when the present black ghetto population of 12.5 million has grown to almost 21
million.

To continue present policies is to make permanent the division of our country into two societies;
one, largely Negro and poor, located in the central
cities; the other, predominantly white and affluent,
located in the suburbs and in outlying areas.

The second choice, ghetto enrichment coupled with abandonment of integration, is also unacceptable. It is another way of choosing a permanently divided country. Moreover, equality cannot be achieved under conditions of nearly complete separation. In a country where the economy, and particularly the resources of employment, are predominantly white, a policy of separation can only relegate Negroes to a permanently inferior economic status.

We believe that the only possible choice for America is the third—a policy which combines ghetto enrichment with programs designed to encourage integration of substantial numbers of Negroes into the society outside the ghetto.

Enrichment must be an important adjunct to integration, for no matter how ambitious or energetic the program, few Negroes now living in central cities can be quickly integrated. In the meantime, large-scale improvement in the quality of ghetto life is essential.

In the meantime, large-scale improvement in the quality of ghetto life is essential.

But this can be no more than an interim strategy. Programs must be developed which will permit substantial Negro movement out of the ghettos. The primary goal must be a single society, in which every citizen will be free to live and work according to his capabilities and desires, not his color.

Chapter 17—Recommendations For National Action

Introduction

No American—white or black—can escape the consequences of the continuing social and economic decay of our major cities.

Only a commitment to national action on an unprecedented scale can shape a future compatible with the historic ideals of American society.

The great productivity of our economy, and a federal revenue system which is highly responsive to economic growth, can provide the resources.

The major need is to generate new will—the will to tax ourselves to the extent necessary, to meet the vital needs of the nation.

We have set forth goals and proposed strategies to reach those goals. We discuss and recommend programs not to commit each of us to specific parts of such programs but to illustrate the type and dimension of action needed.

The major goal is the creation of a true union—a single society and a single American identity. Toward that goal, we propose the following objectives for national action:

- Opening up opportunities to those who are restricted by racial segregation and discrimination, and eliminating all barriers to their choice of jobs, education and housing.
- Removing the frustration of powerlessness among the disadvantaged by providing the means for them to deal with the problems that affect their own lives and by increasing the capacity of our public and private institutions to respond to these problems.
- Increasing communication across racial lines to destroy stereotypes, to halt polarization, end distrust and hostility, and create common ground for efforts toward public order and social justice.

We propose these aims to fulfill our pledge of equality and to meet the fundamental needs of a democratic and civilized society—domestic peace and social justice.

Employment

Pervasive unemployment and underemployment are the most persistent and serious grievances in minority areas. They are inextricably linked to the problem of civil disorder.

Despite growing federal expenditures for manpower development and training programs, and sustained general economic prosperity and increasing demands for skilled workers, about two million—white and nonwhite—are permanently unemployed. About ten million are underemployed, of whom 6.5 million work full time for wages below the poverty line.

The 500,000 "hard-core" unemployed in the central cities who lack a basic education and are unable to hold a steady job are made up in large part of Negro males between the ages of 18 and 25. In the riot cities which we surveyed, Negroes were three times as likely as whites to hold unskilled jobs, which are often part time, seasonal, low-paying and "dead end."

Negro males between the ages of 15 and 25 predominated among the rioters. More than 20 percent of the rioters were unemployed, and many who were employed held intermittent, low status, unskilled jobs which they regarded as below their education and ability.

The Commission recommends that the federal government:

- Undertake joint efforts with cities and states to consolidate existing manpower programs to avoid fragmentation and duplication.
- Take immediate action to create 2,000,000 new jobs over the next three years—one million in the public sector and one million in the private

sector—to absorb the hard-core unemployed and materially reduce the level of underemployment for all workers, black and white. We propose 250,000 public sector and 300,000 private sector jobs in the first year.

- Provide on-the-job training by both public and private employers with reimbursement to private employers for the extra costs of training the hard-core unemployed, by contract or by tax credits.
- Provide tax and other incentives to investment in rural as well as urban poverty areas in order to offer to the rural poor an alternative to migration to urban centers.
- Take new and vigorous action to remove artificial barriers to employment and promotion, including not only racial discrimination but, in certain cases, arrest records or lack of a high school diploma. Strengthen those agencies such as the Equal Employment Opportunity Commission, charged with eliminating discriminatory practices, and provide full support for Title VI of the 1964 Civil Rights Act allowing federal grant-in-aid funds to be withheld from activities which discriminate on grounds of color or race.

The Commission commends the recent public commitment of the National Council of the Building and Construction Trades Unions, AFL-CIO, to encourage and recruit Negro membership in apprenticeship programs. This commitment should be intensified and implemented.

Education

Education in a democratic society must equip children to develop their potential and to participate fully in American life. For the community at large, the schools have discharged this responsibility well. But for many minorities, and particularly for the children of the ghetto, the schools have failed to provide the educational experience which could overcome the effects of discrimination and deprivation.

This failure is one of the persistent sources of grievance and resentment within the Negro community. The hostility of Negro parents and students toward the school system is generating increasing conflict and causing disruption within many city school districts. But the most dramatic evidence of the relationship between educational practices and civil disorders lies in the high incidence of riot participation by ghetto youth who have not completed high school.

The bleak record of public education for ghetto children is growing worse. In the critical skills—verbal and reading ability—Negro students are falling further behind whites with each year of school completed. The high unemployment and underemployment rate for Negro youth is evidence, in part, of the growing educational crisis.

We support integration as the priority education strategy; it is essential to the future of American society. In this last summer's disorders we have seen the consequences of racial isolation at all levels, and of attitudes toward race, on both sides, produced by three centuries of myth, ignorance and bias. It is indispensable that opportunities for interaction between the races be expanded.

We recognize that the growing dominance of pupils from disadvantaged minorities in city school populations will not soon be reversed. No matter how great the effort toward desegregation, many children of the ghetto will not, within their school careers, attend integrated schools.

If existing disadvantages are not to be perpetuated, we must drastically improve the quality of ghetto education. Equality of results with all-white schools must be the goal.

To implement these strategies, the Commission recommends:

- Sharply increased efforts to eliminate de facto segregation in our schools through substantial federal aid to school systems seeking to desegregate either within the system or in cooperation with neighboring school systems.
- Elimination of racial discrimination in Northern as well as Southern schools by vigorous application of Title VI of the Civil Rights Act of 1964.
- Extension of quality early childhood education to every disadvantaged child in the country.
- Efforts to improve dramatically schools serving disadvantaged children through substantial federal funding of year-round compensatory education programs, improved teaching, and expanded experimentation and research.
- Elimination of illiteracy through greater federal support for adult basic education.
- Enlarged opportunities for parent and community participation in the public schools.
- Reoriented vocational education emphasizing work-experience training and the involvement of business and industry.
- Expanded opportunities for higher education through increased federal assistance to disadvantaged students.
- Revision of state aid formulas to assure more per student aid to districts having a high proportion of disadvantaged school-age children.

The Welfare System

Our present system of public welfare is designed to save money instead of people, and tragically ends up doing neither. This system has two critical deficiencies:

First, it excludes large numbers of persons who are in great need, and who, if provided a decent level of support, might be able to become more productive and self-sufficient. No federal funds are available for millions of men and women who are needy but neither aged, handicapped nor the parents of minor children.

Second, for those included, the system provides assistance well below the minimum necessary for a decent level of existence, and imposes restrictions that encourage continued dependency on welfare and undermine self-respect.

A welter of statutory requirements and administrative practices and regulations operate to remind recipients that they are considered untrustworthy, promiscuous and lazy. Residence requirements prevent assistance to people in need who are newly arrived in the state. Regular searches of recipients' homes violate privacy. Inadequate social services compound the problems.

The Commission recommends that the federal government, acting with state and local governments where necessary, reform the existing welfare system to:

- Establish uniform national standards of assistance at least as high as the annual "poverty level" of income, now set by the Social Security Administration at $3,335 per year for an urban family of four.
- Require that all states receiving federal welfare contributions participate in the Aid to Families with Dependent Children Unemployed Parents program (AFDC-UP) that permits assistance to families with both father and mother in the home, thus aiding the family while it is still intact.
- Bear a substantially greater portion of all welfare costs—at least 90 percent of total payments.
- Increase incentives for seeking employment and job training, but remove restrictions recently enacted by the Congress that would compel mothers of young children to work.
- Provide more adequate social services through neighborhood centers and family-planning programs.
- Remove the freeze placed by the 1967 welfare amendments on the percentage of children in a state that can be covered by federal assistance.
- Eliminate residence requirements.

As a long-range goal, the Commission recommends that the federal government seek to develop a national system of income supplementation based strictly on need with two broad and basic purposes:

- To provide, for those who can work or who do work, any necessary supplements in such a way as to develop incentives for fuller employment;
- To provide, for those who cannot work and for mothers who decide to remain with their children, a minimum standard of decent living, and to aid in the saving of children from the prison of poverty that has held their parents.

A broad system of implementation would involve substantially greater federal expenditures than anything now contemplated. The cost will range widely depending on the standard of need accepted as the "basic allowance" to individuals and families, and on the rate at which additional income above this level is taxed. Yet if the deepening cycle of poverty and dependence on welfare can be broken, if the children of the poor can be given the opportunity to scale the wall that now separates them from the rest of society, the return on this investment will be great indeed.

Housing

After more than three decades of fragmented and grossly underfunded federal housing programs, nearly six million substandard housing units remain occupied in the United States.

The housing problem is particularly acute in the minority ghettos. Nearly two-thirds of all non-white families living in the central cities today live in neighborhoods marked with substandard housing and general urban blight. Two major factors are responsible.

First: Many ghetto residents simply cannot pay the rent necessary to support decent housing. In Detroit, for example, over 40 percent of the non-white occupied units in 1960 required rent of over 35 percent of the tenants' income.

Second: Discrimination prevents access to many non-slum areas, particularly the suburbs, where good housing exists. In addition, by creating a "back pressure" in the racial ghettos, it makes it possible for landlords to break up apartments for denser occupancy, and keeps prices and rents of deteriorated ghetto housing higher than they would be in a truly free market.

To date, federal programs have been able to do comparatively little to provide housing for the disadvantaged. In the 31-year history of subsidized federal housing, only about 800,000 units have been constructed, with recent production averaging about

50,000 units a year. By comparison, over a period only three years longer, FHA insurance guarantees have made possible the construction of over ten million middle and upper-income units.

Two points are fundamental to the Commission's recommendations:

First: Federal housing programs must be given a new thrust aimed at overcoming the prevailing patterns of racial segregation. If this is not done, those programs will continue to concentrate the most impoverished and dependent segments of the population into the central-city ghettos where there is already a critical gap between the needs of the population and the public resources to deal with them.

Second: The private sector must be brought into the production and financing of low and moderate rental housing to supply the capabilities and capital necessary to meet the housing needs of the nation.

The Commission recommends that the federal government:

- Enact a comprehensive and enforceable federal open housing law to cover the sale or rental of all housing, including single family homes.
- Reorient federal housing programs to place more low and moderate income housing outside of ghetto areas.
- Bring within the reach of low and moderate income families within the next five years six million new and existing units of decent housing, beginning with 600,000 units in the next year.

To reach this goal we recommend:

- Expansion and modification of the rent supplement program to permit use of supplements for existing housing, thus greatly increasing the reach of the program.
- Expansion and modification of the below-market interest rate program to enlarge the interest subsidy to all sponsors and provide interest-free loans to nonprofit sponsors to cover pre-construction costs, and permit sale of projects to nonprofit corporations, cooperatives, or condominiums.
- Creation of an ownership supplement program similar to present rent supplements, to make home ownership possible for low-income families.

- Federal writedown of interest rates on loans to private builders constructing moderate-rent housing.
- Expansion of the public housing program, with emphasis on small units on scattered sites, and leasing and "turnkey" programs.
- Expansion of the Model Cities program.
- Expansion and reorientation of the urban renewal program to give priority to projects directly assisting low-income households to obtain adequate housing.

Conclusion

One of the first witnesses to be invited to appear before this Commission was Dr. Kenneth B. Clark, a distinguished and perceptive scholar. Referring to the reports of earlier riot commissions, he said:

I read that report ... of the 1919 riot in Chicago, and it is as if I were reading the report of the investigating committee on the Harlem riot of '35, the report of the investigating committee on the Harlem riot of '43, the report of the McCone Commission on the Watts riot.

I must again in candor say to you members of this Commission—it is a kind of Alice in Wonderland—with the same moving picture re-shown over and over again, the same analysis, the same recommendations, and the same inaction.

These words come to our minds as we conclude this report.

We have provided an honest beginning. We have learned much. But we have uncovered no startling truths, no unique insights, no simple solutions. The destruction and the bitterness of racial disorder, the harsh polemics of black revolt and white repression have been seen and heard before in this country.

It is time now to end the destruction and the violence, not only in the streets of the ghetto but in the lives of people.

Alice Paul, 1915 (AP Photo)

"Equality of rights under the law shall not be denied ... on account of sex."

Overview

The Equal Rights Amendment (ERA), originally written by Alice Paul in 1921 and first proposed to Congress in 1923, was intended to guarantee full rights for women under the law. Following the passage of the Nineteenth Amendment, which extended suffrage to women, in August 1920, some believed that the U.S. Constitution should be amended to guarantee full rights for women in all aspects of life, from employment to education to divorce to property ownership. In fact, not all feminists agreed that such a constitutional amendment was necessary. Nevertheless, Alice Paul and other members of the National Woman's Party (NWP) discussed language for the proposed ERA. In the ensuing years the fight over the amendment waxed and waned, with the proposed legislation being introduced to every session of Congress from 1923 onward but remaining bottled up in committees. Paul rewrote the ERA into the current language in 1943, aiming to echo the language of the Fifteenth Amendment (which bars governments from preventing a person from voting on the basis of race or previous slave status) and the Nineteenth Amendment.

With the revitalization of the women's movement in the 1960s, the demand for the passage of the ERA gained new life. Feminists, male and female, recognized that inequities still existed under American law, despite the passage of such landmark legislation as the Equal Pay Act of 1963 and Title VII of the Civil Rights Act of 1964 (protecting people against discrimination in the workplace on the basis of race or national origin or gender). The revised version of the ERA was finally pushed through Congress and presented to the states for ratification on March 22, 1972. The amendment's proponents saw it as the culmination of the long struggle for women's rights that began with the American Revolution and the adoption of the U.S. Constitution.

Context

When the NWP proposed the first version of the ERA, the Nineteenth Amendment to the U.S. Constitution had just been passed, giving women the right to vote. This major victory spurred some feminists to seek further legal guarantees for women's equality. The 1920s, however, marked the beginning of an era of conservatism, with business-minded politicians controlling Congress and the White House. Generally, Americans were tired of war, weary of the radicalism of the immediate post–World War I years, and longing for a return to "normalcy," as Warren G. Harding put it in a speech given in Boston in 1920. The popular image of the 1920s is of the Jazz Age, when women bobbed their hair, shortened their skirts, danced the Charleston until dawn, and drank bootleg gin with handsome young men, making out in the backseat of, say, a Stutz Bearcat when appropriate. In the eyes of their late-Victorian-period mothers, the women of this new era were liberated and free.

In reality, however, most people did not live the life of F. Scott Fitzgerald's bon vivant literary character Jay Gatsby and his friends: African Americans were subject to the brutalities of racism; the Ku Klux Klan revitalized and added immigrants, Catholics, and Jews to its hate list; and the typical American woman was hardly a liberated flapper in the model of the actress and sex symbol Clara Bow. Indeed, women were still subject to inequities in employment, divorce law, property rights, and other matters of daily life. Still, the feminists who sought equal rights under the law had a difficult time finding allies in their quest for justice. With the arrival of the Great Depression in the late 1920s, more pressing matters than women's rights occupied the nation. Despite the national presence in the 1930s of First Lady Eleanor Roosevelt, who championed the cause of women, such as by trying to ensure that they were given fair treatment in her husband Franklin's New Deal programs, few were concerned about trying to gain passage for the ERA. With World War II coming on the heels of the Great Depression, other issues again pushed women's rights far into the background.

The post–World War II years gave birth to the complacent "Eisenhower fifties" (under President Dwight D. Eisenhower). While women had made extraordinary contributions to the American war effort, society in general demanded that most now return home and proceed with the business of finding husbands and raising families. While the popular image of the 1950s became one of con-

Time Line

1919

■ **June 28**
Treaty of Versailles is signed, officially ending World War I, with provision for the establishment of the League of Nations.

1920

■ **March 19**
U.S. Senate rejects the Treaty of Versailles; United States does not join League of Nations.

■ **August 18**
Nineteenth Amendment to the U.S. Constitution, granting women the right to vote, is ratified; women nationwide will help elect the Republican Warren G. Harding to the presidency the following November.

1923

■ **December 10**
Equal Rights Amendment is first introduced into the U.S. Senate.

1929

■ **October 29**
Stock market crashes, precipitating the Great Depression.

1933

■ **March 4**
Inauguration of President Franklin D. Roosevelt, who begins instituting his New Deal programs to aid in recovery from the depression.

1943

■ Equal Rights Amendment is rewritten into current language.

1948

■ **July 26**
President Harry S. Truman signs Executive Order 9981, ending segregation in the U.S. armed forces; he also signs Executive Order 9980, outlawing discrimination in federal employment.

1954

■ **May 17**
The U.S. Supreme Court, under Chief Justice Earl Warren, hands down its decision in the case of *Brown v. Board of Education*, forever outlawing segregation in the nation's schools.

sumerism-driven Americans living in neat suburban houses, going to malt shops, and dancing to the new "rock and roll," the reality again was quite different; the 1950s were generally prosperous but were still a time when America was more turbulent than the mythology indicates. The decade opened with undeclared war in Korea, where U.S. and United Nations troops fought the Chinese and their allies. The cold war, which had begun at the end of World War II, raged on, as the United States and its allies faced off against Communism. In one of the bitterest episodes in American history, the Wisconsin senator Joseph McCarthy instigated a witch hunt against people over a broad spectrum of American society who he believed to be Communists or Communist sympathizers. The allegations, rumors, and outright lies put forth during the McCarthy hearings ruined many lives. Actors, politicians, labor leaders, academicians, writers, musicians, and many others consequently lost their livelihoods and good names.

The 1950s also saw the rise of the civil rights movement, which in turn sparked a new women's rights movement. While some people had long supported equal rights for African Americans, they amounted to a small minority. Black men did get the right to vote after the Civil War, but few proved able to actually exercise the right, especially in the segregated South. At the beginning of the twentieth century, organizations such as the National Association for the Advancement of Colored People and the National Urban League formed to fight for the rights of African Americans. For many years, these were voices crying out in the wilderness, as African Americans continued to be systematically denied basic rights, such as equal access to employment and to decent schools. Furthermore, African Americans who dared to challenge the system were intimidated and risked their very lives, with lynching becoming widespread.

At the end of World War II, many African Americans came home after bravely serving their deeply segregated nation and realized that the time to systematically fight back had come. After President Harry S. Truman took the courageous step of desegregating the armed forces in 1948, which nearly cost him the subsequent election, African Americans were further encouraged to stand up for themselves. One of the first major episodes in the modern civil rights movement came in 1954, when the U.S. Supreme Court declared segregation unconstitutional in public schools in the landmark decision in *Brown v. Board of Education*. This case paved the way for the desegregation of the nation in other aspects of life. The following year, Rosa Parks, secretary of the Montgomery branch of the National Association for the Advancement of Colored People, further fueled the movement when she refused to relinquish her bus seat to a white person in Montgomery, Alabama. Parks's actions sparked the Montgomery bus boycott, in which African Americans refused to ride city buses until the buses were desegregated in 1956. Dr. Martin Luther King, Jr., first established his name and reputation by leading the Montgomery bus boycott.

Over the next decade, men and women of conscience battled discrimination in numerous ways, on the streets and in the halls of Congress and state legislatures. Young people, such as the African American students who desegregated Central High School in Little Rock, Arkansas, in 1956 and who sometimes feared for their very lives in the classroom, were an important part of the movement. The U.S. Congress finally saw the need to pass legislation guaranteeing equal protection under the law regardless of the color of one's skin. The first piece of landmark legislation in this respect was the Civil Rights Act of 1964, which forbade discrimination on the basis of race, religion, or national origin. Title VII of that act also became important for the nascent women's movement, since it outlawed discrimination on the basis of gender as well. The Twenty-fourth Amendment to the U.S. Constitution, also passed in 1964, finally abolished the poll tax, which had prevented many poor and working-class people from casting ballots. The Voting Rights Act of 1965 made it easier for people to register to vote without having to take literacy tests.

The turmoil over civil rights for African Americans inspired American women to demand equal treatment as well. Impetus for the women's movement came from a number of sources. Generally, middle-class women in the 1950s were better educated than previous generations, with many earning college degrees. Still, society dictated that every woman's goal in life should be to find a husband, settle down, and raise a family as the perfect housewife and mother. The trouble was that not all women were happy in the restrictive role dictated by society. While these women loved their families, being the domestic wife and mother was sometimes not fulfilling enough. In 1963 Betty Freidan published her seminal work *The Feminine Mystique*, which questioned the popular vision that women could find true happiness only in the domestic realm. Freidan referred to the discontent many women felt as the problem without a name. *The Feminine Mystique* became a best seller and is considered one of the major works of the modern feminist canon. Around the time of this book's appearance, the President's Commission on the Status of Women, which President John F. Kennedy had appointed in 1961 and which was originally headed by Eleanor Roosevelt, issued its report on women in American society. The report noted that women still faced enormous discrimination in the workplace, including lower pay, denial of promotions, and other unfair labor practices. The report led to the passage of the Equal Pay Act in 1963, making it illegal for employers to pay women less than they paid men for the same job.

While the federal commission's report retained societal notions regarding women's responsibility for family life, it was revolutionary for the era, calling for an end to discriminatory practices based on gender in realms such as divorce law, eligibility for jury duty, and property rights of married women. The commission also triggered the establishment of a number of state commissions on the status of women. Most of the members of the federal commission, however, saw no need for the ERA, assuming that other legislation would eventually give women equal rights, such as with Title VII of the Civil Rights Act of 1964, which ended discriminatory labor practices based on gender. However, the

Time Line

1955

■ **December 1**
Rosa Parks, an African American, refuses to give up her bus seat to a white person in Montgomery, Alabama, leading to the Montgomery bus boycott.

1961

■ **December 14**
President John F. Kennedy issues Executive Order 10980, establishing the President's Commission on the Status of Women, chaired by Eleanor Roosevelt.

1963

■ **June 10**
Passage of the Equal Pay Act of 1963, aimed at ending discrimination on the basis of gender in employment.

■ **October**
Report of the President's Commission on the Status of Women is published.

1964

■ **July 2**
Congress passes the Civil Rights Act of 1964, which includes a provision for prohibiting discrimination in employment on the basis of gender, race, color, creed, or national origin; the act creates the Equal Employment Opportunity Commission to enforce the legislation.

■ **October 1**
Beginnings of Free Speech Movement at University of California, Berkeley, which escalates into student protests against the Vietnam War.

1966

■ **October 29–30**
National Organization for Women is organized in Washington, D.C.

1967

■ NOW endorses support for the ERA.

1972

■ **March 22**
Congress passes the Equal Rights Amendment and sends it to the states for ratification, with a seven-year deadline for passage.

Time Line

1972

■ **June 23**
Congress passes Title IX of the Education Amendments of 1972, banning sex discrimination in schools.

1973

■ **January 22**
The U.S. Supreme Court reaches a 7–2 decision in the case *Roe v. Wade*, upholding a woman's right to a safe and legal abortion.

1982

■ **June 30**
After the deadline for passage of the ERA was extended in 1978 to 1982, the amendment falls three states short of the thirty-eight needed for ratification.

Equal Employment Opportunity Commission, created to enforce the Civil Rights Act, was lackadaisical in addressing women's complaints about work situations. Betty Freidan and other feminist leaders, such as Pauli Murray, a member of the President's Commission on the Status of Women, were particularly incensed by the commission's obstinacy in refusing to end sex-segregated advertisements for wanted help.

At the third annual conference of the Commission on the Status of Women, held in 1966, Freidan, Murray, and twenty-six other participants set up what they thought at the time was a temporary organization to fight for women's rights. This group became the National Organization for Women (NOW). At the first organizational meeting, the members adopted a lengthy statement of purpose, which was drafted by Freidan. At the core of the statement of purpose is NOW's mission: "to take action to bring women into full participation in the mainstream of American society now, exercising all the rights and responsibilities thereof in truly equal partnership with men" (http://www.now.org/history/purpos66.html). At the second national conference the following year, NOW adopted the passage of the ERA as one of its major goals.

The formation of NOW owed much to the civil rights movement. As inspired by the activism of African Americans and other justice-minded people, the women and men who formed NOW believed that women deserved to be given an equal place in society. The general air of liberalism in the 1960s, coupled with the rise of the anti–Vietnam War movement, also affected the development of the contemporary women's rights movement. In this atmosphere the revised ERA was introduced into Congress and in 1972 passed the Senate by a vote of 84–8. By 1977, thirty-five of the needed thirty-eight states had ratified the proposed twenty-seventh amendment. At the time of its introduction,

the ERA was given a seven-year limit for ratification; in 1978, ratification was still needed from three more states, and the limit was extended to 1982. By 1982 the United States had become a more conservative country than it had been ten years earlier, as exemplified by the election of the Republican Ronald Reagan to the presidency in 1980. The anti-ERA forces, playing on fears that the amendment would cause the downfall of society and other such propaganda, were remarkably well organized and successfully pressured politicians to allow the amendment's defeat.

Despite setbacks, progress has been made in the protection of women's hard-won rights, such as the passage of Title IX of the Education Amendments of 1972, which guarantees equal access to education for women, including in athletics. NOW and other feminist organizations are still committed to the passage of the ERA and continue to work for the empowerment of women.

About the Author

Alice Paul was born on January 11, 1885, in Mount Laurel, New Jersey, to Tacie Parry and William Mickle Paul. Alice's father was a successful banker and businessman. The Pauls were Quakers, and Alice received her earliest education at the Moorestown Friends School, where she graduated in 1901. The young Alice Paul's Quaker upbringing instilled in her the principle of equality of the sexes. She went on to Swarthmore College, where she received a BA in 1905. She then attended the New York School of Philanthropy to train for social work and later received an MA in sociology from the University of Pennsylvania. After attending the London School of Economics and the University of Birmingham in England, she returned to the United States and earned a doctorate in political science in 1912 from the University of Pennsylvania. She later received a master of laws and a doctorate in civil law from American University's Washington College of Law.

Paul's sojourn in England exposed her to the ideas of the British suffragette Christabel Pankhurst. She joined the radical Women's Social and Political Union, which advocated aggressive action in the fight for women's rights, including hunger strikes, rock throwing, and window breaking. Paul brought these tactics home to the United States, where she joined the National American Woman Suffrage Association (NAWSA), to be appointed head of the group's Congressional Committee and lead the campaign for a federal suffrage amendment. Paul and her friends Crystal Eastman and Lucy Burns traveled to Washington, D.C., to work on their cause, organizing a parade up Pennsylvania Avenue in March 1913 that coincided with President Woodrow Wilson's inauguration. While the march began peacefully, male onlookers quickly turned verbally abusive and physically violent, insulting, jeering at, and assaulting the suffragists. The police did nothing to help the marchers.

Although she was a member of NAWSA, Paul did not agree with all of the organization's tactics. In 1914 Paul and

An estimated 10,000 marchers descend on the Capitol building in Springfield, Illinois, to demonstrate for the passage of the Equal Rights Amendment, May 16, 1976. (AP Photo)

her followers formed the Congressional Union for Woman Suffrage, which was technically an arm of NAWSA but eventually separated, becoming the National Woman's Party (NWP) in 1916. As did their British sisters, the NWP held the party in power responsible for the failure to get the women's suffrage amendment passed. Despite the fact that the United States was engaged in the Great War, the NWP picketed the White House, going so far as to chain themselves to the fence. The NWP members' actions led to their imprisonment and outraged many who felt that they had gone too far while America was at war. While in prison, Paul and others went on hunger strikes but were forcibly fed in an exceedingly cruel manner; the harsh treatment they received in prison did gain the women much sympathy.

The contributions of women to the war effort, in conjunction with the hard work of the various suffrage camps and perhaps even the sympathy generated by the imprisonment of Paul and her allies, finally led to women's gaining the vote when the Nineteenth Amendment to the U.S. Con-

stitution was ratified on August 18, 1920. When the idea of suffrage for women finally became a reality, some American feminists were unsure as to what their next goal would be. NAWSA morphed into the League of Women Voters, a non-partisan organization dedicated to fostering an informed electorate. Paul, aware of the fact that in spite of having the vote women were still victimized by discrimination in most areas of life, believed that women still needed a federal amendment guaranteeing all of their rights. In 1923, on the seventy-fifth anniversary of the Seneca Falls Convention, Paul and the NWP proposed the ERA. Paul dubbed it the "Lucretia Mott Amendment" in honor of that pioneer feminist, one of the organizers of the Seneca Falls Convention.

Throughout her life, Alice Paul tirelessly sought to secure passage of the ERA, which was rewritten in 1943 and later redubbed the "Alice Paul Amendment" in her honor. She traveled widely and even started the World Woman's Party in Geneva, Switzerland, in 1938, to work for worldwide gender equality. Upon the formation of the

United Nations in 1945, Paul worked to ensure that the charter would include a call for equal rights for women and helped establish the United Nations' Commission on the Status of Women. Paul was one of the people who pushed for the inclusion of gender in Title VII of the Civil Rights Act of 1964. She supported the ratification of the ERA as a twenty-seventh amendment to the Constitution but did not live to see it become law. Paul died on July 9, 1977, in Moorestown, New Jersey, having given her long life to the cause of equal rights for women.

Explanation and Analysis of the Document

The text of both versions of the ERA is relatively short. Alice Paul's original 1921 text is deceptively simple, stating that both genders shall have equal rights under the law. The revised version is subtly different, dropping the word *men* and stating that women's rights shall not be denied by the federal government or by any of its states. The revised version also includes two additional clauses, one stating that Congress shall have the right to enforce the law and one giving the time frame for compliance. Ostensibly, Paul revised the ERA to conform the language to that of the Fifteenth and Nineteenth Amendments to the U.S. Constitution. The Fifteenth Amendment, passed in 1870, states that "the right of citizens of the United States to vote shall not be denied or abridged by the United States or by any State on account of race, color, or previous condition of servitude" and that "Congress shall have power to enforce this article by appropriate legislation." The language of the Nineteenth Amendment is nearly identical, with "sex" replacing the wording on racial considerations; the enforcement clause is the same.

The simplicity of the language in both versions of the ERA actually triggered opposition to the amendment. Indeed, the ERA was a source of controversy and division even among feminists from the outset of its introduction in 1923. Many women feared that such an amendment would negate various pieces of labor legislation, particularly laws designed to "protect" female workers. Organized labor was especially opposed to the ERA, largely because of the protective labor laws, well into the late 1960s. Paul and other supporters felt that some of the labor legislation ostensibly protecting women was actually harmful, in that employers often used the legislation as an excuse to pay women less, not promote them, or not hire them at all. From the 1920s to the 1960s this was one of the biggest arguments against the ERA. Even Eleanor Roosevelt, one of the staunchest supporters of women's rights, felt that the ERA was unnecessary, believing that other legislation would eliminate legal inequities based on gender.

In 1972, after Congress finally approved the ERA, the amendment seemed on the verge of sailing through to ratification by the needed thirty-eight states, with thirty-five ratifying within five years. However, ERA opponents led by Phyllis Schlafly marshaled their forces and launched an attack on the proposed amendment. The simplicity of the language left the amendment open to all sorts of interpretations as to what would happen should it be adopted. Schlafly's group—Stop ERA, which became the Eagle Forum—and other right-wing pundits argued that the ERA would allow for same-sex marriages, the drafting of women into the armed forces, the creation of unisex public restrooms, and the negation of other "privileges" granted to American women. Despite the fact that the pro-ERA forces—led by NOW, ERAmerica, and more than eighty other mainstream organizations—were also well organized and well funded, the amendment was not ratified by the needed number of states, and it is still not a part of the U.S. Constitution.

Audience

The audience for the ERA was the population of the United States of America, gender notwithstanding. For proponents to get the ERA passed, of course, they needed to gain the support of both men and women; the same was true with the women's suffrage movement, where the suffragists needed men as well as women to support the cause. Especially since so very few women held political positions in 1923, when the ERA was first introduced in Congress, its original supporters had to appeal to as many people as possible.

Impact

When Alice Paul and the NWP began discussing what is now called the ERA, M. Carey Thomas, the president of Bryn Mawr College, offered her support for the legislation, stating, "How much better by one blow to do away with discriminating against women in work, salaries, promotion and opportunities to compete with men in a fair field with no favor on either side!" (Cott, p. 125). While the need for the ERA may have been self-evident to women like Paul and Thomas, many longtime supporters of women's rights were in the opposite camp. The whole issue of protective labor legislation for women was thorny; feminists who tried to look out for the interests of working-class women in particular believed protective legislation to be necessary, especially for women engaged in industrial labor. In the 1920s, the NWP's insistence on a federal amendment addressing women's equality divided the ranks of American feminists. Many leading women's organizations, such as the League of Women Voters (the successor to the National American Woman Suffrage Association), the National Consumers League (led by the feminist Florence Kelley), and the Women's Trade Union League, believed that the ERA was not necessary and could in fact be detrimental to women workers, especially in the area of protectionist legislation.

By the late 1960s, with the revitalization of the feminist movement, the ERA had become a cornerstone of women's rights issues. With NOW urging its ratification as early as 1967, the ERA came to symbolize the cause of feminism in the United States. Instead of dividing supporters of women's rights at this time, the cause of the ERA proved to have a galvanizing effect. As part of the liberal, reformist

"Men and women shall have equal rights throughout the United States and every place subject to its jurisdiction."

(Original ERA)

"Equality of rights under the law shall not be denied or abridged by the United States or by any State on account of sex."

(Revised ERA, Section 1)

"The Congress shall have the power to enforce, by appropriate legislation, the provisions of this article."

(Revised ERA, Section 2)

"This amendment shall take effect two years after the date of ratification."

(Revised ERA, Section 3)

spirit of the 1960s and early 1970s, other legislation affecting the lives of women was enacted. Beginning with the Equal Pay Act of 1963 and Title VII of the Civil Rights Act of 1964, much progress was made in the elimination of legal barriers to women in the United States.

Despite the fact that the ERA has not been adopted as part of the U.S. Constitution, the movement that coalesced around it raised consciousness about women's second-class status in American society. The women's movement sparked many women's desires to enter the professions, politics, and other areas of employment not traditionally considered "feminine." Partly because of the women's movement, the Democrats nominated the first woman vice presidential candidate in 1984, the New York representative Geraldine Ferraro. In the run-up to the 2008 presidential election, a woman, Senator Hillary Rodham Clinton, was considered one of the leading contenders for the Democratic nomination. While women like Clinton have been very visible, many more women not in the public eye have also benefited from the feminist movement, even without the ERA. Women throughout the nation have gone to college on athletic scholarships thanks to Title IX; have won sex discrimination lawsuits against employers who broke labor laws regarding equal employment; and have become stay-at-home mothers because they chose to be, not because society dictated that they do so. While gender inequities still exist—and the ERA remains unratified—American women have made gains in most aspects of life.

Related Documents

Civil Rights Act of 1964, Public Law 88-352, U.S. *Statutes at Large* 78 (1964): 241. National Archives "Our Documents" Web site. http://www.ourdocuments.gov/doc.php?flash=true&doc=97. Accessed on March 4, 2008. Title VII of this landmark legislation forbade discrimination against employees based on gender as well as on race, creed, color, or national origin.

"The Constitution of the United States of America." Cornell University Law School Web site. http://www.law.cornell.edu/constitution/constitution.table.html#amendments. Accessed on March 4, 2008. The Fifteenth Amendment gave black men the right to vote, while the Nineteenth Amendment is the women's suffrage amendment.

Equal Pay Act of 1963, Public Law 88-38, U.S. *Code* 29 (1963), section 206(d). The U.S. Equal Employment Opportunity Commission Web site. http://www.eeoc.gov/policy/epa.html. Accessed on March 4, 2008. One of the first pieces of legislation to deal with women's rights, this act forbade discrimination in women's salaries, legally establishing the principle of equal pay for equal work.

"The National Organization for Women's 1966 Statement of Purpose." National Organization for Women Web site. http://www.now.org/history/purpos66.html. Accessed on March 4, 2008. This lengthy document lays out NOW's original purpose and issues strong statements on gender equity.

"1998 Declaration of Sentiments of the National Organization for Women." National Organization for Women Web site. http://www.now.org/organization/conference/1998/vision98.html. Accessed on March 4, 2008. In keeping with changes in language and with a deeper awareness of the needs of women globally, NOW issued its Declaration of Sentiments on July 12, 1998, the 150th anniversary of the Declaration of Sentiments of the Seneca Falls Convention.

Title IX of the Education Amendments of 1972, Public Law 92-318, *U.S. Code* 20 (1972), sections 1681–1688. U.S. Department of Labor Web site. http://www.dol.gov/oasam/regs/statutes/titleix.htm. Accessed on March 4, 2008. This is the landmark legislation guaranteeing gender equity in education.

Bibliography

■ Books

Barakso, Maryann. *Governing NOW: Grassroots Activism in the National Organization for Women*. Ithaca, N.Y.: Cornell University Press, 2004.

Butler, Amy E. *Two Paths to Equality: Alice Paul and Ethel M. Smith in the ERA Debate, 1921–1929*. Albany: State University of New York Press, 2002.

Chafe, William H. *The American Woman: Her Changing Social, Economic, and Political Roles, 1920–1970*. New York: Oxford University Press, 1972.

———. *The Paradox of Change: American Women in the Twentieth Century*. New York: Oxford University Press, 1991.

Cott, Nancy F. *The Grounding of Modern Feminism*. New Haven, Conn.: Yale University Press, 1987.

Echols, Alice. *Daring to Be Bad: Radical Feminism in America, 1967–1975*. Minneapolis: University of Minnesota Press, 1989.

Evans, Sara M. *Born for Liberty: A History of Women in America*. New York: Free Press, 1989.

———. *Tidal Wave: How Women Changed America at Century's End*. New York: Free Press, 2003.

Friedan, Betty. *The Feminine Mystique*. New York: W. W. Norton, 1963.

Lunardini, Christine. *From Equal Suffrage to Equal Rights: Alice Paul and the National Woman's Party, 1910–1928*. New York: New York University Press, 1986.

Woloch, Nancy. *Women and the American Experience*. New York: Knopf, 1984.

■ Web Sites

Alice Paul Institute Web site.
    http://www.alicepaul.org/. Accessed on March 4, 2008.

The Equal Rights Amendment Web site.
    http://www.equalrightsamendment.org/. Accessed on March 4, 2008.

National Organization for Women Web site.
    http://www.now.org/. Accessed on March 4, 2008.

National Women's History Project Web site.
    http://www.nwhp.org/. Accessed on March 4, 2008.

—Donna M. DeBlasio

Questions for Further Study

1. Compare and contrast the two versions of the ERA. Look at the context for both, consider the wording, and discuss the significance of the differences.

2. Imagine that you are a member of the International Ladies Garment Workers Union in 1925. Write an argument opposing the proposed ERA.

3. Why do you think the ERA is still not a part of the U.S. Constitution? Be specific and use examples in your answer.

Glossary

abridged	lessened, diminished, or curtailed
ratification	approval or confirmation; formal sanction

EQUAL RIGHTS AMENDMENT

Section 1. Equality of rights under the law shall not be denied or abridged by the United States or by any State on account of sex.

Section 2. The Congress shall have the power to enforce, by appropriate legislation, the provisions of this article.

Section 3. This amendment shall take effect two years after the date of ratification.

*"This involves ... a lot of hanky-panky that
we have nothing to do with ourselves."*

Overview

By the time of Richard Nixon's reelection to a second term as president in November 1972, Nixon and his White House staff were deeply involved in covering up a crime that led eventually to his resignation in August 1974. Early in the morning of June 17, 1972, five men employed by Nixon's Committee to Re-Elect the President (CREEP) were arrested at the Democratic Party's national headquarters at the Watergate Hotel in Washington, D.C. At the time of their arrest the burglars were attempting to replace defective listening devices they had installed previously on the Democrats' telephones in an attempt to gather information they could use against Nixon's opponent in the 1972 general election, Senator George S. McGovern of South Dakota.

Although it appears that Nixon did not directly order the Watergate break-in, he quickly understood the potential political damage it could do to his reelection campaign. Thus, within six days of the break-in, in a June 23 Oval Office meeting with chief of staff H. R. Haldeman, Nixon initiated an effort that included key members of his administration to cover up any White House connection to the crime. Over the next twenty months, however, the cover-up steadily unraveled. Because the June 23 meeting—like all Oval Office conversations in Nixon's administration—was recorded, it provided proof of Nixon's role in the cover-up when it was released to investigators in July 1974 via an order from the Supreme Court. Ultimately, to avoid impeachment on charges of obstruction of justice, Nixon resigned the presidency on August 8, 1974.

Context

When Nixon was elected president in 1968, the nation was sharply divided by the Vietnam War and by a counterculture rebellion. The Vietnam War was by far the most polarizing issue. When the United States first became militarily involved in Southeast Asia in the early 1950s, it was widely seen as part of the ongoing U.S. effort to contain Communism and thus as essential to national security. But

by 1968, with the United States seemingly no closer to victory and with U.S. casualties exceeding sixteen thousand, many Americans had lost faith in the war and the leaders responsible for it. Antiwar protests swept across the nation, culminating with a massive and violent demonstration at the 1968 Democratic National Convention in Chicago.

By 1968 a counterculture rebellion was also dividing the nation. Although Americans were initially united in their celebration of the prosperous society that emerged after World War II, by 1968 that consensus had broken apart. Counterculture rebels protested against the materialistic values of the post–World War II consumer culture and what they regarded as the bland, conformist lifestyle of middle-class suburban Americans. Through alternative lifestyles, psychedelic drugs, free love, and rock music, the rebels sought to recapture the American individualistic tradition.

Americans were deeply troubled by these divisions, and Nixon used them effectively to win the 1968 election. By promising that he would achieve an honorable peace and that he would bring the nation together, Nixon portrayed himself as a political moderate who would repair the national consensus. However, Nixon also campaigned in 1968 on darker themes meant to exploit the divisions in society for his political advantage. In his acceptance speech at the Republican National Convention in August, he promised that he would restore "law and order" (http://www.watergate.info/nixon/acceptance-speech-1968.shtml), thereby implicitly criticizing both the antiwar protestors and the counterculture rebels. Once in the White House, however, Nixon became the symbol of the establishment protestors held responsible for the Vietnam War and the affluent society. Thus, when ending the Vietnam War proved to be an intractable problem for him, and as protests mounted, Nixon increasingly turned to these darker campaign tactics to silence his critics.

Protests and civil unrest are difficult problems for any president, but for a man with Nixon's temperament the national divisions of the late 1960s were particularly troublesome. An insecure person by nature, Nixon compensated for his worries through almost obsessive overachievement. His defeat by John F. Kennedy in the 1960 presidential election by one of the narrowest margins in history and his razor-thin victory in the 1968 presidential election

1970

■ **July 10**
Richard Nixon approves a plan to utilize the FBI and the CIA to gather intelligence on Vietnam War protestors and political opponents.

1971

■ **June 24**
Nixon creates the White House Special Investigations Unit, known as the "plumbers," to staunch the leaks of classified government information.

■ **September 9**
The White House "plumbers" break into the office of Dr. Lewis J. Fielding, the psychiatrist of Daniel Ellsberg, the man who had leaked the *Pentagon Papers* to the *New York Times*.

1972

■ **June 17**
Five men are arrested for attempting to plant listening devices on the telephones in the Democratic Party's national headquarters in the Watergate Hotel in Washington, D.C.

■ **June 23**
The White House cover-up of the Watergate break-in begins when Nixon and H. R. Haldeman discuss ways to short-circuit the FBI investigation. The recording of this conversation is the so-called Smoking Gun Tape.

■ **November 11**
Nixon is reelected to a second term as president.

1973

■ **January 30**
Two Watergate burglars, G. Gordon Liddy and James W. McCord, Jr., are convicted of conspiracy, burglary, and wiretapping in U.S. district court.

■ **May 18**
The Senate Watergate Committee opens televised hearings into the Watergate incident.

heightened his insecurities. Thus, when confronted with nationwide protests during his presidency, Nixon saw them not as legitimate forms of political expression but as threats to the viability of his leadership. In June 1970 Nixon approved a secret plan developed by his aide Tom Charles Huston that proposed using the Federal Bureau of Investigation (FBI) and Central Intelligence Agency (CIA) to spy on antiwar protestors. When in 1971 the *New York Times* published the *Pentagon Papers*, a top-secret history of America's war in Vietnam leaked by the security analyst Daniel Ellsberg, Nixon approved the creation of the White House Special Investigations Unit, known popularly as the "plumbers," to stop the leaks of classified information. Later that year, in an effort to help Nixon's reelection, the chief White House plumber, former FBI agent G. Gordon Liddy, developed Operation Gemstone, which proposed a series of covert operations including the installation of listening devices on the Democratic National Committee's telephones, the incapacitation of the air-conditioning system at the Democratic Party's 1972 convention, and the kidnapping of radical Americans to prevent demonstrations at the Republican Party's 1972 convention. A scaled-down version of Gemstone was approved later that year by Attorney General John N. Mitchell. The Watergate scandal that led to Nixon's resignation originated ironically, then, in a covert plan intended to secure his reelection.

Throughout his presidency Nixon met frequently in the Oval Office with his chief of staff, Haldeman. Among other duties, the White House chief of staff supervises the president's daily schedule and controls access to the chief executive. However, because Haldeman had worked for Nixon in a variety of political capacities stretching back to 1956, the president also relied heavily on his aide for advice. Their Oval Office meeting on June 23, 1972, was thus part of their normal daily routine. One item on the agenda, however, the break-in at the Watergate Hotel six days earlier, was of particular concern to them.

When five men were arrested in the early morning hours of June 17, 1972, at the Democratic Party's national headquarters at the Watergate Hotel in Washington, D.C., they carried with them a variety of items suggesting that they were not ordinary burglars. One of them carried $2,400 in cash, including thirteen new, sequentially numbered $100 bills. Another had an address book containing the cryptic entry "Howard E. Hunt—W. House" with an attached phone number that proved to be for the White House switchboard. The burglars also carried expensive cameras and sophisticated electronic eavesdropping equipment. Because the eavesdropping equipment raised the possibility of a violation of federal wiretapping laws, the arresting Washington, D.C., policemen called in the FBI. The preliminary FBI investigation and the arraignment of the burglars later on June 17 turned up additional evidence that suggested a possible connection between the Watergate break-in and Nixon's reelection campaign. Four of the burglars were Cuban nationals who had been employed previously by the CIA in a variety of covert activities, including the failed 1961 Bay of Pigs invasion, in which the CIA attempted to have the Cuban leader Fidel Castro overthrown. In the hotel room of the Cuban nationals the FBI found a check signed by E. Howard Hunt, a former CIA agent who had helped organize the Bay of Pigs invasion. The fifth man proved to be James W. McCord, Jr., also a former CIA operative who at the time of his arrest was the chief of security for CREEP, Nixon's main campaign organization.

Although Nixon publicly dismissed the Watergate break-in as a minor burglary with no connection whatsoever to his reelection campaign, privately he understood almost immediately the potential damage it could do. His campaign's chief of security had been arrested, and, as Nixon and Haldeman both knew, Hunt was part of a secret White House unit created in 1971 to engage in "dirty tricks" against the president's political opponents. Moreover, by the time of his meeting with Haldeman on the morning of June 23, 1972, the FBI investigation also had discovered that a $25,000 campaign contribution solicited by Kenneth H. Dahlberg, a fund-raiser for Nixon's reelection campaign, had been deposited in the bank account of Bernard Barker, one of the Cubans arrested in the Watergate burglary. Moreover, the FBI had traced the $25,000 through a Mexican bank back to CREEP and its finance chairman, Maurice Stans, who had earlier served as Nixon's secretary of commerce. In their meeting on the morning of June 23, 1972, Nixon and Haldeman contemplated how to keep the FBI from discovering evidence that would undermine the president's reelection.

About the Author

Richard Nixon was born in Yorba Linda, California, on January 9, 1913; he was the second of five sons of Frank and Hannah Nixon. His parents were devout Quakers of modest means who instilled in their son a powerful work ethic, a characteristic that was evident throughout Nixon's life. He excelled at school and graduated second in his class in 1934 from Whittier College, a Quaker school in Whittier, California. He won a full scholarship to Duke University Law School, graduated third in his class in 1937, and returned to Whittier to begin his law career. Despite his Quaker upbringing, Nixon served several years in a noncombat position in the South Pacific during World War II. Following the war Nixon was recruited by Republican businessmen in Whittier to run for Congress in California's twelfth district, a seat then occupied by the five-term incumbent Democrat Jerry Voorhis. Taking advantage of the growing fear of internal subversion during the early cold war, Nixon mounted a campaign that branded Voorhis as a Communist sympathizer because of his ardent support of Franklin Roosevelt's New Deal. Nixon won the election, but his smear tactics polarized voters. While some saw him as a fearless patriot confronting the Communist menace, others saw him as a vicious opportunist willing to do anything to win. This duel public image followed Nixon throughout the remainder of his life.

■ **July 13**
During Senate Watergate hearings Alexander Butterfield, a White House aide, reveals the existence of Nixon's secret system to record conversations in the Oval Office.

■ **July 23**
Citing executive privilege, Nixon refuses to release his Oval Office tapes.

1974

■ **February 6**
The House of Representatives adopts Resolution 803 by a vote of 410–4 authorizing the Judiciary Committee to begin impeachment hearings on Nixon.

■ **March 1**
Nixon aides John N. Mitchell, H. R. Haldeman, John Ehrlichman, Charles Colson, Robert Mardian, Kenneth Parkinson, and Gordon Strachan are indicted on charges of conspiracy to impede the Watergate investigation. Nixon is named as an unindicted co-conspirator.

■ **July 24**
The U.S. Supreme Court rules unanimously in *United States v. Nixon* that the president must turn over the White House tapes to investigators.

■ **July 27**
The House Judiciary Committee approves the first article of impeachment, claiming that Nixon obstructed justice.

■ **August 8**
Nixon resigns, and Vice President Gerald Ford becomes the thirty-eighth president.

Congressman Nixon rose quickly to national prominence through the 1948 House Un-American Activities Committee investigation of Alger Hiss, a former prominent member of the U.S. State Department accused of passing secret government documents to the Soviets. Nixon's aggressive questioning throughout the hearings was widely credited with a playing a key role in Hiss's eventual conviction on perjury charges. Nixon used his anti-Communist reputation to win a seat in the U.S. Senate in 1950, defeating the actress Helen Gahagan Douglas in another cam-

President Nixon gestures toward transcripts of White House tapes after announcing he would turn them over to House impeachment investigators and make them public in April of 1974. (AP Photo)

paign dominated by smear tactics. Nixon's political star continued its rapid ascent with his election in 1952 as Dwight D. Eisenhower's vice president, but again, controversy surrounded his campaign. This time Nixon was accused of benefiting from a secret "slush fund" created by wealthy businessmen. Although Nixon preserved his place on the GOP presidential ticket, the slush fund incident added to the questions about his integrity. Thus, long before the Watergate scandal ended his political career, Nixon had developed a reputation as a cold-blooded politician who valued winning above all else.

As vice president, Nixon regularly advised Eisenhower on both political and national security issues and served as the nation's goodwill ambassador to the world. The vice presidency broadened Nixon's experience and raised his public profile so that he easily won the Republican Party's presidential nomination in 1960. He was defeated by John F. Kennedy in one of the closest elections in U.S. political history. Following his defeat Nixon resumed his career as a lawyer, but he also remained active in politics, running unsuccessfully for governor of California in 1962 and also campaigning on behalf of numerous GOP candidates throughout the nation. Although he was a private citizen after 1960, his hard work in the political trenches enabled him to secure the 1968 Republican presidential nomina-

tion, and this time he narrowly defeated the Democratic candidate, Hubert H. Humphrey.

Nixon became president of a nation deeply divided over the war in Vietnam. Although there were more than five hundred thousand U.S. troops in Vietnam by 1968, many Americans believed the nation was no closer to resolving the conflict. Large, vocal antiwar protests roiled the nation during the election year, and Nixon as president promised an end to the war honorably. To this end he promoted a policy of "Vietnamization," which gradually withdrew U.S. troops from Vietnam. Nixon and his national security adviser, Henry Kissinger, also sought an end to the Vietnam War by improving American relations with its cold war enemy the Soviet Union and with China in a strategy called détente. They believed that a combination of economic and military incentives offered to the Communist superpowers would enable the United States to safeguard its national security while spending less money on national defense. It would also give the United States a chance to persuade these superpowers to reduce their support to North Vietnam, thereby accelerating peace talks to end the war. Détente led to Nixon's historic visit to China in 1972 and the first Strategic Arms Limitation Treaty (SALT I) with the Soviet Union in 1972, but it failed to hasten a peace treaty with North Vietnam.

Nixon was finally able to conclude a treaty in January 1973 only by widening the war into neighboring Cambodia and intensifying the bombing of North Vietnam, ending America's long war in Vietnam.

While the focus of his presidency was foreign policy, some of Nixon's domestic policies continued to affect the nation into the twenty-first century. In 1971 he ended the Bretton Woods monetary system under which the United States had agreed since 1944 to redeem all its dollars for gold at the fixed rate of $35 per ounce. This action allowed the value of the dollar to be determined by the world currency market. Nixon also established the Environmental Protection Agency in 1970 and signed into law the Clean Air Act in 1970 and the Clean Water Act in 1972. But after five employees of his reelection campaign were arrested at the Watergate Hotel in June 1972, most of Nixon's time and energy were devoted to covering up White House involvement in the crime. When the American people learned the extent of his involvement in the cover-up through the release of the Smoking Gun Tape, Nixon resigned on August 8, 1974, to avoid impeachment. After his resignation, Nixon continued to try to influence national affairs through a series of books on American politics and national security. He died on April 22, 1994.

Explanation and Analysis of the Document

In their June 23, 1972, meeting, Nixon and Haldeman discuss how to prevent the FBI investigation from uncovering still more evidence that could undermine the president's reelection, and they agree upon a strategy to cover up White House involvement in the Watergate break-in. Their discussion begins with an idea proposed by John N. Mitchell, Nixon's campaign director at CREEP and his former attorney general, and by White House counsel John Dean. Because FBI agents working on the case believed that their Watergate investigation had uncovered a covert CIA operation, Mitchell and Dean propose in the Smoking Gun Tape that the president simply halt the investigation on national security grounds. When Haldeman says to Nixon that "the way to handle this now is for us to have Walters call Pat Gray and just say, 'Stay the hell out of this ... this is ah, business here we don't want you to go any further on,'" he suggests that the president ask the CIA deputy director, Vernon A. Walters, to urge the FBI director, L. Patrick Gray, to halt his agency's Watergate investigation because it had uncovered a covert CIA operation. Nixon quickly agrees with this strategy ("All right. Fine"), understanding that this would effectively prevent the FBI from following any additional leads that might connect CREEP more deeply to Watergate or that might uncover additional "dirty tricks" initiated by the White House. During this part of the conversation, Haldeman and Nixon reference Mark Felt—then associate director of the FBI—by expressing their confidence that he will support his boss, Gray, in halting the FBI's investigation of the break-in. However, Felt would later play a key role in Nixon's downfall by leaking confidential information about the Watergate cover-up to the *Wash-*

H. R. Haldeman, 1973 (AP Photo)

ington Post journalists Bob Woodward and Carl Bernstein. Their stories about the cover-up kept the issue in front of the public. Dubbed "Deep Throat" by the two journalists in order to keep his identity a secret, Felt confirmed that he was Woodward and Bernstein's source in 2005.

As the two men continue to discuss the cover-up, Nixon points out the vulnerabilities of the CIA and its director, Richard Helms. "We protected Helms from one hell of a lot of things," Nixon tells his chief of staff. Then, rehearsing the case that could be made to Helms to call off the FBI investigation, the president maintains,

> Of course ... this is a Hunt ... that will uncover a lot of things. You open up that scab there's a hell of a lot of things and that we just feel that it would be very detrimental to have this thing go any further. This involves these Cubans, Hunt, and a lot of hanky-panky that we have nothing to do with ourselves.

In this passage, Nixon raises the possibility of subtle blackmail if the spy agency balks at the cover-up. Because Cuban nationals and CIA agents were involved in the Watergate break-in, Helms would be warned that if the FBI investigation continued, it was likely to uncover CIA covert actions against Cuba. The "scab" and "hanky-panky" Nixon mentions was the CIA's Operation Mongoose, a top-secret plan initiated by President John F. Kennedy in late 1961 to topple the Cuban dictator Castro from power following the failure of the Bay of Pigs invasion. Under Operation Mongoose the CIA tried and failed throughout the 1960s to remove Castro through the use of political propaganda, the

"*That the way to handle this now is for us to have Walters call Pat Gray and just say, 'Stay the hell out of this ... this is ah, business here we don't want you to go any further on it.'*"

(Richard Nixon)

"*You open that scab there's a hell of a lot of things and that we just feel that it would be very detrimental to have this thing go any further. This involves these Cubans, [E. Howard] Hunt, and a lot of hanky-panky that we have nothing to do with ourselves.*"

(Richard Nixon)

"*Good deal! Play it tough. That's the way they [Nixon's opponents] play it and that's the way we are going to play it.*"

(Richard Nixon)

"*'Look, the problem is that this will open ... the whole Bay of Pigs thing, and the President just feels that' ah, without going into the details ... don't, don't lie to them to the extent to say there is no [White House] involvement, but just say this is sort of a comedy of errors, bizarre, without getting into it, 'the President believes that it is going to open the whole Bay of Pigs thing up again. And, ah because these people [Nixon's opponents] are plugging for, for keeps and that they should call the FBI in and say that we wish for the country, don't go any further into this case,' period!*"

(Richard Nixon)

funding of insurgent guerrilla forces, and various assassination plots that included poisoned cigars and bombs concealed in seashells. Nixon clearly believed that Helms could be persuaded to cooperate with the Watergate cover-up to protect the spy agency from the public outcry that would surely follow the revelation that it had attempted to assassinate a foreign leader.

With the basic strategy to halt the FBI investigation agreed upon, Nixon then seeks to understand who or what is responsible for the break-in. "Well what the hell, did Mitchell know about this thing to any much of a degree?" he asks, referring to his campaign director, John N. Mitchell. When Haldeman ventures that Mitchell had only general knowledge of the Watergate operation, Nixon presses on, trying to determine who had concocted the scheme by which

funds donated to CREEP had been funneled to the Watergate burglars through a Mexican bank. "Is it Liddy?" he asks, referring to G. Gordon Liddy, then the head of the White House Special Investigations Unit, or "plumbers," Nixon had established in 1971 to halt the leak of classified information to anti-administration forces. Haldeman confirms that Liddy was responsible, adding that as Mitchell pressured him "to get more information" to aid the president's reelection, Liddy "pushed the people harder to move harder on ... Gemstone." Haldeman's answer thus reveals that the Watergate break-in originated in the secret plan Operation Gemstone, developed by Liddy and approved by Mitchell in 1971, to engage in a series of covert "dirty tricks" against Nixon's political opponents. Nixon's reply to Haldeman, "All right, fine, I understand it all," indicates that even though the president had not approved the Watergate break-in, he was fully aware of the illegal activities that led to it.

Later on the tape, Haldeman's report that White House Special Counsel Charles W. (Chuck) Colson's interview with the FBI on June 22 had gone well bolsters their confidence that the cover-up will succeed. As they both knew, Colson was deeply involved in Watergate and other illicit campaign activities. He had a hand in the creation of the "plumbers" and in the White House discussions that led to Operation Gemstone. Despite his involvement, his FBI interrogators concluded that the Watergate break-in had not involved CREEP but was, as Haldeman notes, "a CIA thing." With this knowledge, Nixon decides to go forward with the plan. He tells Haldeman to call in Helms and Walters:

> When you … get these people in, say: "Look, the problem is that this will open … the whole Bay of Pigs thing, and the President just feels that" ah, without going into the details … don't, don't lie to them to the extent to say there is no [White House] involvement, but just say this is sort of a comedy of errors, bizarre, without getting into it, "the President believes that it is going to open the whole Bay of Pigs thing up again. And, ah because these people [Nixon's political opponents] are plugging for, for keeps and that they should call the FBI in and say that we wish for the country, don't go any further into this case," period!

By setting in motion this plan to use the CIA to turn off the FBI investigation into the Watergate break-in, Nixon attempted to obstruct justice, an action the House Judiciary Committee later determined to be an impeachable offense.

Audience

The Smoking Gun Tape was intended for only two men: Nixon and Haldeman. A record of this private conversation exists only because Nixon installed a voice-activated system to record conversations in the Oval Office. The taping system remained a secret until the White House aide Alexander Butterfield revealed its existence on July 13, 1973, during the Senate Watergate investigation. The tape recording was not heard by individuals outside Nixon's private circle of advisers until the U.S. Supreme Court ordered the president on July 24, 1974, to turn over sixty-four White House tapes to the Watergate special prosecutor.

Impact

The public release of the Smoking Gun Tape following the unanimous Supreme Court decision in *United States v. Nixon* on July 24, 1974, was the beginning of the end of the Watergate saga. For more than two years after the break-in on June 17, 1972, Nixon had doggedly denied any involvement in the crime. As evidence of illicit White House activ-

ities mounted, however, the nation divided over the famous question posed by Senator Howard Baker of Tennessee: "What did the President know and when did he know it?" (http://bakercenter.utk.edu/main/howardbaker. php). Many believed that the president was complicit at least to some degree in Watergate. But others continued to believe in Nixon's innocence out of respect for the office of the presidency or because it seemed improbable that the president, whose reelection was all but certain, would spy on his opponent. The Smoking Gun Tape erased all doubts about Nixon's guilt by demonstrating that within six days of the Watergate break-in, the president had initiated a plan to cover up White House involvement, thereby obstructing justice. Release of the tape forged a national consensus that the president was guilty of "high crimes and misdemeanors," and, to avoid certain impeachment and trial in the U.S. Senate, Nixon resigned on August 8, 1974.

The Smoking Gun Tape, by providing irrefutable evidence that Nixon, notwithstanding his repeated denials, had lied to the American people, did much to tarnish the presidency and contributed to the long-term erosion of presidential power. Throughout the twentieth century and especially during Franklin D. Roosevelt's New Deal in the 1930s, the presidency was transformed from an office designed primarily to execute the laws enacted by Congress into one that initiated legislation and that dominated the national government. The Watergate scandal helped to end this trend, however. After the mid-1970s Congress reasserted its power in a number of areas, and although the office of the presidency did not revert to a primarily administrative post, it was by the early twenty-first century a less powerful branch of government than it had been in the mid-twentieth century.

By demonstrating conclusively that the president had lied and had abused his power, the Smoking Gun Tape also damaged the nation's self-image in the late twentieth century. Because such heroic figures as George Washington, Thomas Jefferson, and Abraham Lincoln had once been president, generations of Americans had developed a reverence for the office. That reverence was burnished considerably by Franklin D. Roosevelt, who guided the nation successfully through the Great Depression and World War II. But the Smoking Gun Tape and other White House tapes that revealed a president who abused his power and who frequently used coarse language and occasional racial and ethnic epithets made it difficult for many Americans to maintain reverence for the office. As the nation grappled with the ignominious end of the Vietnam War and the decline of the economy in the 1970s, the Watergate scandal added considerably to a pervasive cynicism and pessimism that continued to affect the nation in the twenty-first century.

Related Documents

Haldeman, H. R. *The Haldeman Diaries: Inside the Nixon White House.* New York: G. P. Putnam's Sons, 1994. This is a fascinating and unvarnished account of the Nixon presidency from the perspective of the most reclusive member of the administration.

Kutler, Stanley I. *Abuse of Power: The New Nixon Tapes*. New York: Free Press, 1997. After Nixon released the transcripts of sixty-four White House conversations to the House Judiciary Committee in 1974, he fought against the release of the remaining tapes, nearly 3,700 hours, for the remainder of his life. These tapes were finally released in 1996, and the first portion of them, dealing with Watergate, was transcribed by Kutler, a leading Nixon scholar.

Nixon, Richard M. *The White House Transcripts*. New York: Viking Press, 1974. This volume contains the transcripts of the White House tapes that Nixon submitted to the House Judiciary Committee on April 30, 1974. These transcripts were edited heavily by Nixon and his staff and often do not provide a full account of the conversations.

———. *RN: The Memoirs of Richard Nixon*. New York: Grosset & Dunlap, 1978. Nixon provided his own version of his life and presidency in this volume. It is of interest for how he described key events and often for what he chose not to say.

Bibliography

■ Books

Ambrose, Stephen E. *Nixon*. 3 vols. New York: Simon & Schuster, 1987–1991.

Emery, Fred. *Watergate: The Corruption of American Politics and the Fall of Richard Nixon*. New York: Times Books, 1994.

Gellman, Irwin F. *The Contender, Richard Nixon: The Congress Years, 1946–1952*. New York: Free Press, 1999.

Kutler, Stanley I. *The Wars of Watergate: The Last Crisis of Richard Nixon*. New York: Knopf, 1990.

Nixon, Richard M. *Six Crises*. Garden City, N.Y.: Doubleday, 1962.

Reeves, Richard. *President Nixon: Alone in the White House*. New York: Simon & Schuster, 2001.

Wicker, Tom. *One of Us: Richard Nixon and the American Dream*. New York: Random House, 1991.

■ Web Sites

"Howard H. Baker, Jr., 1925–." Howard Baker Jr. Center for Public Policy Web site.
http://bakercenter.utk.edu/main/howardbaker.php. Accessed on March 6, 2008.

"Nixon's Acceptance of the Republican Party Nomination for President: August 8, 1968." Watergate.info Web site.
http://www.watergate.info/nixon/acceptance-speech-1968.shtml. Accessed on March 6, 2008.

"Nixon Tapes." Miller Center of Public Affairs Web site.
http://millercenter.org/index.php/academic/presidentialrecordings/pages/tapes_rmn. Accessed on March 6, 2008.

"Nixon White House Tapes–Online." Nixon Presidential Library and Museum Web site.
http://nixon.archives.gov/virtuallibrary/tapeexcerpts/index.php. Accessed on March 6, 2008.

"Special Collections: Nixon Tapes." U.S. Social Security Administration Web site.
http://www.ssa.gov/history/Nixon/nixontapes.html. Accessed on March 6, 2008.

—By John W. Malsberger

1. Release of the Smoking Gun Tape led Nixon to resign to escape certain impeachment. Only two presidents in American history, Andrew Johnson and Bill Clinton, have been impeached. How do Nixon's crimes compare with Johnson's and Clinton's?

2. Some have argued that the Watergate scandal was a less serious abuse of power than the Iran-Contra scandal that occurred during Ronald Reagan's presidency. How are the two scandals similar? How are they different? Why was Reagan's punishment far less severe than Nixon's?

3. Many have argued that Nixon's resignation proved that the system of checks and balances worked as intended by the framers of the U.S. Constitution to protect our democracy. Others have argued that the nation was saved only by luck. Had it not been for the White House tapes, Nixon would have remained in office. Which claim is more persuasive?

4. Given the significant achievements in foreign and domestic policy of Nixon's presidency, how much weight should be given to the Watergate scandal in determining his place in history? Do you believe that future historians who were not alive during Nixon's presidency will regard him more positively than contemporary historians?

Glossary

Barker	Bernard L. Barker, a former CIA operative arrested in the Watergate break-in
Bay of Pigs	covert CIA plan approved by President John F. Kennedy to invade Cuba and remove Fidel Castro from power
Colson	Charles W. (Chuck) Colson, White House special counsel to Nixon
Gemstone	covert operation developed by the White House operative G. Gordon Liddy to gather intelligence on Nixon's opponents
Helms	Richard Helms, director of the CIA from 1966 to 1973
Hunt	E. Howard Hunt, a former CIA agent and White House "plumber" arrested in the Watergate break-in
John Dean	White House counsel to Nixon
Ken Dahlberg	a fund-raiser for Nixon's reelection committee
Liddy	G. Gordon Liddy, chief White House "plumber" and the person who developed Operation Gemstone
Mark Felt	associate director of the FBI from 1972 to 1974; known as "Deep Throat" for leaking information about the Watergate investigation to Bob Woodward and Carl Bernstein of the *Washington Post*
Mitchell	John N. Mitchell, U.S. attorney general from 1969 to 1972 and director of Nixon's 1972 reelection campaign
Pat Gray	acting director of the FBI from 1972 to 1973
Stans	Maurice H. Stans, U.S. secretary of commerce from 1969 to 1972 and finance director of Nixon's 1972 reelection campaign
Walters	Vernon A. Walters, deputy director of the CIA from 1972 to 1976

RICHARD NIXON'S SMOKING GUN TAPE

Haldeman: Okay—that's fine. Now, on the investigation, you know, the Democratic break-in thing, we're back to the—in the, the problem area because the FBI is not under control, because Gray doesn't exactly know how to control them, and they have, their investigation is now leading into some productive areas, because they've been able to trace the money, not through the money itself, but through the bank, you know, sources—the banker himself. And, and it goes in some directions we don't want it to go. Ah, also there have been some things, like an informant came in off the street to the FBI in Miami, who was a photographer or has a friend who is a photographer who developed some films through this guy, Barker, and the films had pictures of Democratic National Committee letter head documents and things. So I guess, so it's things like that that are gonna, that are filtering in. Mitchell came up with yesterday, and John Dean analyzed very carefully last night and concludes, concurs now with Mitchell's recommendation that the only way to solve this, and we're set up beautifully to do it, ah, in that and that...the only network that paid any attention to it last night was NBC...they did a massive story on the Cuban...

Nixon: That's right.

Haldeman: thing.

Nixon: Right.

Haldeman: That the way to handle this now is for us to have Walters call Pat Gray and just say, "Stay the hell out of this...this is ah, business here we don't want you to go any further on it." That's not an unusual development,...

Nixon: Um huh.

Haldeman: ...and, uh, that would take care of it.

Nixon: What about Pat Gray, ah, you mean he doesn't want to?

Haldeman: Pat does want to. He doesn't know how to, and he doesn't have, he doesn't have any basis for doing it. Given this, he will then have the basis. He'll call Mark Felt in, and the two of them ...and Mark Felt wants to cooperate because...

Nixon: Yeah.

Haldeman: he's ambitious...

Nixon: Yeah.

Haldeman: Ah, he'll call him in and say, "We've got the signal from across the river to, to put the hold on this." And that will fit rather well because the FBI agents who are working the case, at this point, feel that's what it is. This is CIA.

Nixon: But they've traced the money to 'em.

Haldeman: Well they have, they've traced to a name, but they haven't gotten to the guy yet.

Nixon: Would it be somebody here?

Haldeman: Ken Dahlberg.

Nixon: Who the hell is Ken Dahlberg?

Haldeman: He's ah, he gave $25,000 in Minnesota and ah, the check went directly in to this, to this guy Barker.

Nixon: Maybe he's a ...bum.

Nixon: He didn't get this from the committee though, from Stans.

Haldeman: Yeah. It is. It is. It's directly traceable and there's some more through some Texas people in—that went to the Mexican bank which they can also trace to the Mexican bank...they'll get their names today. And (pause)

Nixon: Well, I mean, ah, there's no way... I'm just thinking if they don't cooperate, what do they say? They they, they were approached by the Cubans. That's what Dahlberg has to say, the Texans too. Is that the idea?

Haldeman: Well, if they will. But then we're relying on more and more people all the time. That's the problem. And ah, they'll stop if we could, if we take this other step.

Nixon: All right. Fine.

Haldeman: And, and they seem to feel the thing to do is get them to stop?

Nixon: Right, fine.

Haldeman: They say the only way to do that is from White House instructions. And it's got to be to Helms and, ah, what's his name…? Walters.

Nixon: Walters.

Haldeman: And the proposal would be that Ehrlichman (coughs) and I call them in

Nixon: All right, fine.

Haldeman: and say, ah…

Nixon: How do you call him in, I mean you just, well, we protected Helms from one hell of a lot of things.

Haldeman: That's what Ehrlichman says.

Nixon: Of course, this is a, this is a Hunt, you will—that will uncover a lot of things. You open that scab there's a hell of a lot of things and that we just feel that it would be very detrimental to have this thing go any further. This involves these Cubans, Hunt, and a lot of hanky-panky that we have nothing to do with ourselves. Well what the hell, did Mitchell know about this thing to any much of a degree?

Haldeman: I think so. I don 't think he knew the details, but I think he knew.

Nixon: He didn't know how it was going to be handled though, with Dahlberg and the Texans and so forth? Well who was the asshole that did? (Unintelligible) Is it Liddy? Is that the fellow? He must be a little nuts.

Haldeman: He is.

Nixon: I mean he just isn't well screwed on is he? Isn't that the problem?

Haldeman: No, but he was under pressure, apparently, to get more information, and as he got more pressure, he pushed the people harder to move harder on…

Nixon: Pressure from Mitchell?

Haldeman: Apparently.

Nixon: Oh, Mitchell, Mitchell was at the point that you made on this, that exactly what I need from you is on the—

Haldeman: Gemstone, yeah.

Nixon: All right, fine, I understand it all. We won't second-guess Mitchell and the rest. Thank God it wasn't Colson.

Haldeman: The FBI interviewed Colson yesterday. They determined that would be a good thing to do.

Nixon: Um hum.

Haldeman: Ah, to have him take a…

Nixon: Um hum.

Haldeman: An interrogation, which he did, and that, the FBI guys working the case had concluded that there were one or two possibilities, one, that this was a White House, they don't think that there is anything at the Election Committee, they think it was either a White House operation and they had some obscure reasons for it, non political,…

Nixon: Uh huh.

Haldeman: or it was a…

Nixon: Cuban thing—

Haldeman: Cubans and the CIA. And after their interrogation of, of…

Nixon: Colson.

Haldeman: Colson, yesterday, they concluded it was not the White House, but are now convinced it is a CIA thing, so the CIA turn off would…

Nixon: Well, not sure of their analysis, I'm not going to get that involved. I'm (unintelligible).

Haldeman: No, sir. We don't want you to.

Nixon: You call them in.

Nixon: Good. Good deal! Play it tough. That's the way they play it and that's the way we are going to play it.

Haldeman: O.K. We'll do it.

Nixon: Yeah, when I saw that news summary item, I of course knew it was a bunch of crap, but I thought ah, well it's good to have them off on this wild hair thing because when they start bugging us, which they have, we'll know our little boys will not know how to handle it. I hope they will though. You never know. Maybe, you think about it. Good!

* * * * * * * * * *

Nixon: When you get in these people when you…get these people in, say: "Look, the problem is that this will open the whole, the whole Bay of Pigs thing, and the President just feels that" ah, without going into the details… don't, don't lie to them to the extent to say there is no involvement, but just say this is sort of a comedy of errors, bizarre, without getting into it, "the President believes that it is going to open the whole Bay of Pigs thing up again. And, ah because these people are plugging for, for keeps and that they should call the FBI in and say that we wish for the country, don't go any further into this case," period!

Haldeman: OK

Nixon: That's the way to put it, do it straight (Unintelligible)

Haldeman: Get more done for our cause by the opposition than by us at this point.

Nixon: You think so?

Haldeman: I think so, yeah.

ROE V. WADE

"This right of privacy ... is broad enough to encompass a woman's decision whether or not to terminate her pregnancy."

Overview

Abortion, or the deliberate termination of unwanted pregnancy, has occurred in some form in human society since ancient times. Nevertheless, amid the Victorian morals of the mid-nineteenth century, it became one of Western society's most contentious issues, sparking bitter religious and ethical debates that continued into the twenty-first century. In 1973 the Supreme Court case known as *Roe v. Wade* became the most pivotal moment for the issue in the history of the United States.

In *Roe v. Wade*, the Supreme Court for the first time established abortion as a fundamental right guaranteed in the U.S. Constitution, albeit with some qualifications. Regardless, the case brought a virtual end to illegal, unsanitary "back-alley" abortions and, in broader terms, established new parameters for the concept of a constitutional right to privacy. Far from settling the debate on abortion, however, *Roe v. Wade* further stoked Americans' passions over the issue. Subsequently, legal battles continually swirled around the abortion right, and changes to the composition of the Supreme Court during the presidency of George W. Bush raised the question of whether the right to abortion would continue to erode—or perhaps be reversed at the federal level and thus revert to the states for regulation.

Context

Before the nineteenth century, abortion was fairly widely available to women in the United States, though it was extremely hazardous because of the lack of advanced medical procedures and knowledge concerning the need for sterilization. Starting in the 1820s, many states began to restrict access to abortion. The Comstock Act (1873), a federal law named for the nineteenth-century anti-obscenity crusader Anthony Comstock, restricted the dissemination of birth control devices and information. Twenty-four states passed similar laws, likewise prohibiting the distribution of birth control information and materials. Women continued to seek illegal abortions when poverty, domestic

abuse, or other circumstances made pregnancy unwanted; they often suffered grievous injury or death as a result. In 1950 authorities estimated that from 200,000 to 1.3 million illegal abortions were performed in the United States that year.

To some, the abortion debate hinged on whether women should be forced to surrender control of their own bodies to their states of residence. Others held the religious view that life begins at conception, such that abortion is nothing short of murder. Laws varied from state to state, creating a situation that many decried as fundamentally unfair: A woman's ability to obtain an abortion depended upon where she happened to live as well as upon whether she had the wealth to travel to wherever facilities were available.

In the years leading up to *Roe v. Wade*, a series of Supreme Court precedents began relaxing restrictions on contraception and paved the way for a claim of a right to privacy under the Constitution. The most significant acknowledgement of a privacy right came in the 1965 case of *Griswold v. Connecticut*, which struck down a statute outlawing the use of birth control by married couples. Estelle Griswold, the executive director of Planned Parenthood of Connecticut, had been prosecuted by the state for giving contraceptives to a married couple. In her appeal, the Supreme Court determined that the Constitution presupposes a class of fundamental rights, among which is privacy in matters of marriage, family, and sex. *Griswold* would be a key precedent for *Roe*. Relying on that and other precedent cases, the attorneys Linda Coffee and Sarah Weddington teamed with the plaintiff Norma McCorvey, a former carnival worker and mother of two previous children—who would be named as Jane Roe—to file the original 1970 lawsuit against the Texas district attorney Henry Wade.

About the Author

Roe v. Wade was the defining case of Associate Justice Harry Blackmun's twenty-four-year career on the Supreme Court, which stretched from 1970 to 1994. When President Richard Nixon nominated Blackmun for the Court in April 1970, following the Senate rejection of two southern conservative nominees, Blackmun seemed poised to adhere

Time Line

2600 BCE
- Estimated date of the first recorded recipe for an herbal drug used to induce abortion.

1821
- Connecticut passes the first U.S. law prohibiting abortions after "quickening," or fetal movement.

1869
- October 12
Pope Pius IX forbids all abortions, a stance the Catholic Church would maintain into the twenty-first century.

1873
- March 3
Congresses passes the Comstock Act, which bans distribution through the mails of "obscene" materials, including contraceptive devices and information.

1916
- October 16
Margaret Sanger opens the first U.S. birth control clinic.

1942
- Planned Parenthood Federation of America, formerly the American Birth Control League, is organized and begins lobbying for reforms in abortion law.

1965
- June 7
The U.S. Supreme Court issues its opinion in *Griswold v. Connecticut*, establishing the constitutional right to privacy that would later be the foundation for *Roe v. Wade*.

1970
- March 3
Roe v. Wade is filed in U.S. District Court in Texas.

1971
- December 13
Initial arguments are made before the Supreme Court for *Roe v. Wade*.

1972
- October 11
Roe is reargued before the Court.

to conventional Republican principles. He and Chief Justice Warren Burger were friends, and newspapers dubbed them the "Minnesota twins" because of their shared history in the state. As Blackmun's career progressed, however, particularly after the *Roe* decision, his opinions drifted toward the Court's liberal side, as he often sided with Justices William Brennan and Thurgood Marshall in finding constitutional protection for individual rights.

Born in Illinois on November 12, 1908, and reared in Minnesota, Blackmun was a 1932 graduate of Harvard Law School. He married Dorothy Clark in 1941 and fathered three daughters. Perhaps the most influential phase of his career before he sat on the federal bench was his service as resident counsel for the Mayo Clinic in Rochester, Minnesota, from 1950 to 1959. That pioneering era for heart surgery exhilarated Blackmun and inspired in him an almost reverential respect for physicians. After joining the Eighth Circuit Court of Appeals upon President Dwight Eisenhower's nomination, he continued to serve on the board of directors of the Rochester Methodist Hospital until ascending to the Supreme Court. He would later state that if he had had the chance to pursue his career over again, he would have become a physician. In the summer of 1972, he did much of his work on the *Roe* opinion from the Mayo Clinic's library.

Blackmun's interest in the practice of medicine resonates throughout the *Roe* opinion, particularly in his examination of the Hippocratic oath and in his footnote citation of medical texts such as Arturo Castiglioni's *History of Medicine*. Blackmun's opinion reflected the Court's 7–2 majority ruling, with Justices Burger, Brennan, William Douglas, Marshall, Lewis Powell, and Potter Stewart joining and with Justices Byron White and William Rehnquist dissenting. After *Roe*, Blackmun received a flood of public response and letters, including some death threats.

Another significant issue addressed by Blackmun during his Supreme Court career was the death penalty. Although he often voted to uphold capital punishment in his early cases, he reversed himself shortly before his retirement in a dissenting opinion in 1994's *Callins v. Collins*, declaring the death penalty unconstitutional in all circumstances. At the time of his retirement from the Court in 1994, he was considered one of the Court's most liberal justices. Blackmun died on March 4, 1999, following complications from hip surgery.

Explanation and Analysis of the Document

Three appellants came before the Court challenging Texas abortion statutes. The first was Jane Roe (Norma McCorvey), a single woman who was pregnant and had been unable to procure a legal abortion at the time she filed action against the Dallas County district attorney Henry Wade in 1970. The second appellant was the licensed physician James Hubert Hallford, who had faced two state prosecutions for performing abortions and argued that the Texas statute was unconstitutionally vague and violated his own and his patients' rights. The third was the married couple John and Mary Doe (David and Marsha King). Mary Doe suffered from a medical disorder that left her unable to use birth control pills and made pregnancy a medical danger; the couple sued on the grounds of potential injury resulting from possible contraceptive failure and pregnancy.

Justice Harry Blackmun's Majority Opinion

The majority ruling, authored by Blackmun and joined by Justices Burger, Brennan, Douglas, Marshall, Powell, and Stewart, holds that only Roe had the standing to sue. The ruling establishes that the end of Roe's pregnancy—she gave birth and allowed the child to be adopted—did not render the case moot; that Hallford's arguments could be asserted in his defense in state courts and therefore did not belong in federal court; and that the Does' complaint was too "speculative … to present an actual case or controversy." Then—the part that those in the courtroom in January 1973 were waiting to hear—the ruling declares that abortion is constitutionally protected by the right to privacy implicit in the Fourteenth Amendment. In her cultural and legal history of the case, Marian Faux states, "A palpable sigh of relief went through the courtroom. That was the crux of the opinion—the victory for pro-choice forces, as it were" (p. 308).

The Court does apply some qualifications to the right to abortion, enumerating them as based on three stages of pregnancy. During the first trimester, the abortion decision is left to the woman and her attending physician; between the end of that trimester and the point where the fetus becomes viable, states may regulate abortion "in ways that are reasonably related to maternal health"; and after fetal viability, states may prohibit abortion except when the procedure is necessary to protect the life or health of the mother.

In the initial paragraphs of his opinion, Blackmun acknowledges the controversial nature of the abortion issue and the need to "resolve the issue by constitutional measurement, free of emotion and of predilection." The first four parts following the brief introduction deal with the issues of jurisdiction, standing, and mootness, dismissing the claims of Hallford and the Does. Blackmun rejects the appellee's argument that the case was moot because Roe was no longer pregnant; because of the 266-day length of the normal human gestation period, virtually no pregnancy-related appellate review could be conducted before the natural end of the pregnancy. Blackmun declares, "Our law should not be that rigid."

After a brief paragraph laying out the appellant's argument, Blackmun embarks in part VI on a lengthy history of abortion laws. He begins with the Persian Empire and the classical Greek and Roman eras, when abortion was commonly practiced and not barred by ancient religion. He reviews the history of the Hippocratic oath, an ethical guide to the medical profession that proscribes abortion. Blackmun concludes, based on his research, that the oath's rigidity represented a small minority of Greek opinion. He

Time Line

1973

■ **January 22**
The *Roe v. Wade* decision legalizes abortion with some qualifications.

■ **June**
National Right to Life Committee holds its first meeting in Detroit and begins expansion that will produce chapters in all fifty states devoted to lobbying for restrictions on abortion rights.

1989

■ **July 3**
The Supreme Court case *Webster v. Reproductive Health Services* gives states new authority to regulate abortions but stops short of reversing Roe.

1992

■ **June 29**
Planned Parenthood v. Casey upholds the foundation of Roe v. Wade but allows states to establish further new abortion restrictions.

2000

■ **September 28**
The U.S. Food and Drug Administration approves the use of RU-486 (mifepristone) for medical abortion.

2006

■ **August 24**
The U.S. Food and Drug Administration approves the use of the post-intercourse emergency contraception Plan B—also known as the "morning-after pill"—for nonprescription access to women aged eighteen and older.

then examines the treatment of abortion across the centuries under English law, common law, and historic American law. He notes that most states did not have laws proscribing abortion until the Civil War era. Thus, until the mid-nineteenth century, he writes, "a woman enjoyed a substantially broader right to terminate a pregnancy than she does in most States today." He then summarizes the stances of the American Medical Association, the American Public Health Association, and the American Bar Association, all of which accepted abortion to varying degrees.

In part VII, Blackmun raises three legislative purposes for the enactment of criminal abortion laws: the discouragement of illicit sexual conduct for moral reasons; the

Norma McCorvey, the "Jane Roe" of the Roe v. Wade *decision, is seen in 1990.* (AP Photo)

protection of maternal health, in light of the medical hazards of abortion procedures that preceded the advent of sterilization; and the protection of prenatal life. Blackmun also introduces the concept of "potential life," which had not been raised by any parties in the case; the appellees argued that life begins at conception, and the appellants disputed that claim. The historian Faux states that the term "appeared to be the Court's own creation" (p. 309) and raised the question of whether fetuses might have some rights of personhood.

Blackmun begins addressing the constitutional contentions of the case in part VIII. He traces the line of Supreme Court decisions establishing a right of personal privacy, notably including *Griswold v. Connecticut*, and concludes that the constitutional right of privacy found in the Fourteenth Amendment "is broad enough to encompass a woman's decision whether or not to terminate her pregnancy." However, he continues, the right is not unqualified and must be balanced against state interests in its regulation.

In part IX, Blackmun turns his attention to the definition of "person" under the law. Despite the questions raised by his earlier use of the term "potential life," Blackmun states that his duty for the case does not entail answering the question of when human life begins. He concludes that nowhere in the Constitution is the term "person" intended to apply before birth.

Part X delineates the framework for how states will be permitted to regulate abortion, based on the stage of pregnancy involved. As Faux notes, this idea as well had not been raised in either the briefs or the oral arguments and appears to be Blackmun's own creation. He chose to permit abortion during the first trimester of pregnancy based on medical evidence that mortality from abortion during that stage is lower than mortality from normal childbirth. Therefore, he writes, the state cannot claim maternal health as a compelling interest. He establishes that the state's interest in regulation becomes compelling at the point of viability of the fetus outside the mother's womb and that states may

proscribe abortion during that period "except when it is necessary to preserve the life or health of the mother."

In the final two parts, Blackmun summarizes and repeats his key findings about the stages of pregnancy. He notes that states may prohibit anyone who is not a physician from performing an abortion. Justice Blackmun instructs that the opinion in the companion case *Doe v. Bolton* should be read together with *Roe* and concludes that the Texas statute must fall.

Audience

In the majority opinion, Blackmun is speaking, of course, to more than just the government of Texas; his ruling was aimed at instilling uniformity in the patchwork of abortion restrictions that then varied from state to state. The care he took in researching the medical and historical aspects of the issue enfolded the medical community into his audience along with the legal community—and made physicians' judgments key to the enforcement of the rulings' provisions. His opinion also gave lower courts a framework to use in their continuing review of challenges to aspects of the regulation of abortion across the nation.

Impact

On a personal level, the case in fact had no impact on the outcome of its plantiff's pregnancy; Norma McCorvey wrote in her autobiography *I Am Roe: My Life,* Roe v. Wade, *and Freedom of Choice* that she learned of the decision only upon reading about it in the newspaper at home the following day. After more than two decades lobbying in favor of abortion rights, she experienced a religious conversion in 1995 and shifted her efforts to antiabortion causes.

The uniform legalization of abortion, of course, had far-reaching political and social consequences. The 1973 ruling galvanized the nation's political and religious right wing, sparking the formation of the National Right to Life Committee that same year. Under President Ronald Reagan, a Republican Party platform plank called for a constitutional amendment banning abortions, but the issue was a low priority during the Reagan administration. Antiabortion forces gained traction with the 1988 election of George H. W. Bush—who, ironically, began his political career as a supporter of Planned Parenthood. His successor, Bill Clinton, vetoed several attempts to further restrict abortion, but the 2000 election of President George W. Bush put abortion policies—and nominations for Supreme Court justices—back under right-wing control.

The issue of abortion was indeed revealed to be far from settled as the composition of the Supreme Court evolved. Subsequent decisions barred the use of public hospitals and clinics for abortions and upheld certain restrictions that were held not to impose undue burdens on women. On April 18, 2007, the Court voted to uphold a ban on the late-term abortion procedure of intact dila-

"We forthwith acknowledge our awareness of the sensitive and emotional nature of the abortion controversy, of the vigorous opposing views, even among physicians, and of the deep and seemingly absolute convictions that the subject inspires. One's philosophy, one's experiences, one's exposure to the raw edges of human existence, one's religious training, one's attitudes toward life and family and their values, and the moral standards one establishes and seeks to observe, are all likely to influence and to color one's thinking and conclusions about abortion."

(Justice Harry Blackmun's Majority Opinion, Introduction)

"It is thus apparent that, at common law, at the time of the adoption of our Constitution, and throughout the major portion of the 19th century, abortion was viewed with less disfavor than under most American statutes currently in effect. Phrasing it another way, a woman enjoyed a substantially broader right to terminate a pregnancy than she does in most States today."

(Justice Harry Blackmun's Majority Opinion, Part VI)

"This right of privacy, whether it be founded in the Fourteenth Amendment's concept of personal liberty and restrictions upon state action, as we feel it is, or, as the District Court determined, in the Ninth Amendment's reservation of rights to the people, is broad enough to encompass a woman's decision whether or not to terminate her pregnancy."

(Justice Harry Blackmun's Majority Opinion, Part VIII)

"We need not resolve the difficult question of when life begins. When those trained in the respective disciplines of medicine, philosophy, and theology are unable to arrive at any consensus, the judiciary, at this point in the development of man's knowledge, is not in a position to speculate as to the answer."

(Justice Harry Blackmun's Majority Opinion, Part IX)

"Perfection of the interests involved, again, has generally been contingent upon live birth. In short, the unborn have never been recognized in the law as persons in the whole sense."

(Justice Harry Blackmun's Majority Opinion, Part IX)

Members of the 1972 Supreme Court. Chief Justice Warren E. Burger is third from left in the front row; Harry A. Blackmun is third from left in the back row.
(AP Photo/John Rous)

tion and extraction, also known as partial-birth abortion, in *Gonzales v. Carhart.*

Estimates hold that in the years following *Roe v. Wade*, up to 1.6 million women per year underwent surgical abortions in the United States. As of the mid-1990s, an estimated one-fifth of American women over the age of fifteen had had an abortion. In 2006 the Food and Drug Administration approved over-the-counter access to Plan B emergency contraception, which is taken after intercourse to prevent the implantation of a fertilized egg. Whether this advancement would result in decreases in the numbers of surgical abortions was uncertain.

Related Documents

"Doe v. Bolton, 410 U.S. 179 (1973)." FindLaw Web site. http://caselaw.lp.findlaw.com/scripts/getcase.pl?court=US&vol=410&invol=179. Accessed on March 5, 2008. In this companion case to Roe v. Wade, the Court struck down Georgia's less-restrictive abortion statute.

"Griswold v. Connecticut, 381 U.S. 479 (1965)." FindLaw Web site. http://caselaw.lp.findlaw.com/scripts/getcase.pl?court=US&vol=381&invol=479. Accessed on March 5, 2008. By a 7–2 vote, the Supreme Court invalidated a Connecticut law prohibiting the dissemination of birth control to married couples on the ground that it violated a constitutional right to marital privacy. This would later become a key precedent for Roe v. Wade.

"Planned Parenthood of Southeastern Pa. v. Casey, 505 U.S. 833 (1992)." FindLaw Web site. http://caselaw.lp.findlaw.com/scripts/getcase.pl?court=US&vol=505&invol=833. Accessed on March 5,

2008. In this challenge to several Pennsylvania state restrictions on abortion, the Court ruled in a 5–4 vote to uphold the central right to have an abortion but changed the standard for restricting that right.

"Webster v. Reproductive Health Services, 492 U.S. 490 (1989)." FindLaw Web site. http://caselaw.lp.findlaw.com/scripts/getcase.pl?court=US&vol=492&invol=490. Accessed on March 5, 2008. This decision upheld a Missouri law imposing restrictions on the use of state funds, facilities, and employees in performing, assisting with, or counseling about abortions. This was widely viewed as an infringement on the precedent of Roe.

Bibliography

■ Books

Faux, Marion. *Roe v. Wade*: Marking the 20th Anniversary of the Landmark Supreme Court Decision That Made Abortion Legal. *New York: Penguin Books, 1993.*

Garrow, David J. *Liberty and Sexuality: The Right to Privacy and the Making of* Roe v. Wade. Berkeley: University of California Press, 1998.

Gordon, Linda. *Woman's Body, Woman's Right: Birth Control in America*. New York: Penguin Books, 1990.

Landis, Jacquelyn, ed. *Abortion*. San Diego: Greenhaven Press, 2007.

McCorvey, Norma, with Andy Meisler. *I Am Roe: My Life*, Roe v. Wade *and Freedom of Choice*. New York: HarperCollins Publishers, 1994.

———, with Gary Thomas. *Won by Love: Norma McCorvey, Jane Roe of* Roe v. Wade, *Speaks Out for the Unborn as She Shares Her New Conviction for Life*. Nashville, Tenn.: Thomas Nelson Publishers, 1997.

Tompkins, Nancy. Roe v. Wade *and the Fight over Life and Liberty*. New York: Franklin Watts, 1996.

■ Web Sites

"Justice Harry Blackmun's Papers." NPR Web site. http://www.npr.org/news/specials/blackmun/. Accessed on March 5, 2008.

"Roe vs. Wade: 25 Years Later." CNN Web site. http://www.cnn.com/SPECIALS/1998/roe.wade/. Accessed on March 5, 2008.

—By Leigh Dyer

Questions for Further Study

1. *Roe v. Wade* and *Brown v. Board of Education*, a 1954 ruling that ended racial segregation in public schools, are considered two of the Supreme Court's most significant landmark cases of the twentieth century. Compare and contrast the social impact of each. Which case do you think has had more importance in American society?

2. For centuries, philosophers and theologians have debated the question of when human life begins. The Supreme Court has examined the question of when human life is constitutionally protected on numerous occasions. In the modern era, scientific advancements have pushed the boundaries regarding what is considered a viable fetus. Consider the perspectives from each of these realms of knowledge. When, in your view, does human life begin?

3. The Supreme Court is integral to the constitutional system of checks and balances instituted in the executive, legislative, and judicial branches of the U.S. government. Examine *Roe v. Wade* in the context of this system and discuss the positions of each of the three branches of government on the abortion issue both before the decision and since the decision was handed down.

Glossary

abortion	voluntary termination of a pregnancy
contraception	deliberate prevention of pregnancy by drugs, techniques, or devices; also known as birth control
embryo	the fertilized egg as implanted in the womb through the first two months of development
fetus	the developing human after the second month of gestation
gestation	pregnancy
Hippocratic Oath	an oath embodying the duties and obligations of physicians
precedents	legal decisions that serve as rules or patterns for future similar cases
quickening	stage of pregnancy at which fetal movement first occurs
trimester	a period of three months
viable	capable of living outside a uterus

ROE V. WADE

Mr. Justice Blackmun delivered the opinion of the Court.

This Texas federal appeal and its Georgia companion, *Doe v. Bolton*, post, p. 179, present constitutional challenges to state criminal abortion legislation. The Texas statutes under attack here are typical of those that have been in effect in many States for approximately a century. The Georgia statutes, in contrast, have a modern cast, and are a legislative product that, to an extent at least, obviously reflects the influences of recent attitudinal change, of advancing medical knowledge and techniques, and of new thinking about an old issue.

We forthwith acknowledge our awareness of the sensitive and emotional nature of the abortion controversy, of the vigorous opposing views, even among physicians, and of the deep and seemingly absolute convictions that the subject inspires. One's philosophy, one's experiences, one's exposure to the raw edges of human existence, one's religious training, one's attitudes toward life and family and their values, and the moral standards one establishes and seeks to observe, are all likely to influence and to color one's thinking and conclusions about abortion.

In addition, population growth, pollution, poverty, and racial overtones tend to complicate and not to simplify the problem.

Our task, of course, is to resolve the issue by constitutional measurement, free of emotion and of predilection. We seek earnestly to do this, and, because we do, we have inquired into, and in this opinion place some emphasis upon, medical and medical-legal history and what that history reveals about man's attitudes toward the abortion procedure over the centuries. We bear in mind, too, Mr. Justice Holmes' admonition in his now-vindicated dissent in *Lochner v. New York*, 198 U.S. 45, 76 (1905):

[The Constitution] is made for people of fundamentally differing views, and the accident of our finding certain opinions natural and familiar or novel and even shocking ought not to conclude our judgment upon the question whether statutes embodying them conflict with the Constitution of the United States.

I

The Texas statutes that concern us here are Arts. 1191-1194 and 1196 of the State's Penal Code. These make it a crime to "procure an abortion," as therein defined, or to attempt one, except with respect to "an abortion procured or attempted by medical advice for the purpose of saving the life of the mother." Similar statutes are in existence in a majority of the States.

Texas first enacted a criminal abortion statute in 1854. Texas Laws 1854, c. 49, § 1, set forth in 3 H. Gammel, Laws of Texas 1502 (1898). This was soon modified into language that has remained substantially unchanged to the present time. See Texas Penal Code of 1857, c. 7, Arts. 531-536; G. Paschal, Laws of Texas, Arts. 2192-2197 (1866); Texas Rev.Stat., c. 8, Arts. 536-541 (1879); Texas Rev.Crim.Stat., Arts. 1071-1076 (1911). The final article in each of these compilations provided the same exception, as does the present Article 1196, for an abortion by "medical advice for the purpose of saving the life of the mother."

II

Jane Roe, a single woman who was residing in Dallas County, Texas, instituted this federal action in March 1970 against the District Attorney of the county. She sought a declaratory judgment that the Texas criminal abortion statutes were unconstitutional on their face, and an injunction restraining the defendant from enforcing the statutes.

Roe alleged that she was unmarried and pregnant; that she wished to terminate her pregnancy by an abortion "performed by a competent, licensed physician, under safe, clinical conditions"; that she was unable to get a "legal" abortion in Texas because her life did not appear to be threatened by the continuation of her pregnancy; and that she could not afford to travel to another jurisdiction in order to secure a legal abortion under safe conditions. She claimed that the Texas statutes were unconstitutionally vague and that they abridged her right of personal privacy, protected by the First, Fourth, Fifth, Ninth, and Fourteenth

Amendments. By an amendment to her complaint, Roe purported to sue "on behalf of herself and all other women" similarly situated.

James Hubert Hallford, a licensed physician, sought and was granted leave to intervene in Roe's action. In his complaint, he alleged that he had been arrested previously for violations of the Texas abortion statutes, and that two such prosecutions were pending against him. He described conditions of patients who came to him seeking abortions, and he claimed that for many cases he, as a physician, was unable to determine whether they fell within or outside the exception recognized by Article 1196. He alleged that, as a consequence, the statutes were vague and uncertain, in violation of the Fourteenth Amendment, and that they violated his own and his patients' rights to privacy in the doctor-patient relationship and his own right to practice medicine, rights he claimed were guaranteed by the First, Fourth, Fifth, Ninth, and Fourteenth Amendments.

John and Mary Doe, a married couple, filed a companion complaint to that of Roe. They also named the District Attorney as defendant, claimed like constitutional deprivations, and sought declaratory and injunctive relief. The Does alleged that they were a childless couple; that Mrs. Doe was suffering from a "neural-chemical" disorder; that her physician had "advised her to avoid pregnancy until such time as her condition has materially improved" (although a pregnancy at the present time would not present "a serious risk" to her life); that, pursuant to medical advice, she had discontinued use of birth control pills; and that, if she should become pregnant, she would want to terminate the pregnancy by an abortion performed by a competent, licensed physician under safe, clinical conditions. By an amendment to their complaint, the Does purported to sue "on behalf of themselves and all couples similarly situated."

The two actions were consolidated and heard together by a duly convened three-judge district court. The suits thus presented the situations of the pregnant single woman, the childless couple, with the wife not pregnant, and the licensed practicing physician, all joining in the attack on the Texas criminal abortion statutes. Upon the filing of affidavits, motions were made for dismissal and for summary judgment. The court held that Roe and members of her class, and Dr. Hallford, had standing to sue and presented justiciable controversies, but that the Does had failed to allege facts sufficient to state a present controversy, and did not have standing. It

concluded that, with respect to the requests for a declaratory judgment, abstention was not warranted. On the merits, the District Court held that the

fundamental right of single women and married persons to choose whether to have children is protected by the Ninth Amendment, through the Fourteenth Amendment,

and that the Texas criminal abortion statutes were void on their face because they were both unconstitutionally vague and constituted an overbroad infringement of the plaintiffs' Ninth Amendment rights. The court then held that abstention was warranted with respect to the requests for an injunction. It therefore dismissed the Does' complaint, declared the abortion statutes void, and dismissed the application for injunctive relief. 314 F.Supp. 1217, 1225 (ND Tex.1970).

The plaintiffs Roe and Doe and the intervenor Hallford, pursuant to 28 U.S.C. § 1253 have appealed to this Court from that part of the District Court's judgment denying the injunction. The defendant District Attorney has purported to cross-appeal, pursuant to the same statute, from the court's grant of declaratory relief to Roe and Hallford. Both sides also have taken protective appeals to the United States Court of Appeals for the Fifth Circuit. That court ordered the appeals held in abeyance pending decision here. We postponed decision on jurisdiction to the hearing on the merits. 402 U.S. 941 (1971)

III

It might have been preferable if the defendant, pursuant to our Rule 20, had presented to us a petition for certiorari before judgment in the Court of Appeals with respect to the granting of the plaintiffs' prayer for declaratory relief. Our decisions in *Mitchell v. Donovan*, 398 U.S. 427 (1970), and *Gunn v. University Committee*, 399 U.S. 383 (1970), are to the effect that § 1253 does not authorize an appeal to this Court from the grant or denial of declaratory relief alone. We conclude, nevertheless, that those decisions do not foreclose our review of both the injunctive and the declaratory aspects of a case of this kind when it is properly here, as this one is, on appeal under 1253 from specific denial of injunctive relief, and the arguments as to both aspects are necessarily identical. See *Carter v. Jury Comm'n*, 396 U.S. 320 (1970); *Florida Lime Growers v. Jacobsen*, 362 U.S.

73, 80-81 (1960). It would be destructive of time and energy for all concerned were we to rule otherwise. Cf. *Doe v. Bolton*, post, p. 179.

IV

We are next confronted with issues of justiciability, standing, and abstention. Have Roe and the Does established that "personal stake in the outcome of the controversy," *Baker v. Carr*, 369 U.S. 186, 204 (1962), that insures that

the dispute sought to be adjudicated will be presented in an adversary context and in a form historically viewed as capable of judicial resolution,

Flast v. Cohen, 392 U.S. 83, 101 (1968), and *Sierra Club v. Morton*, 405 U.S. 727, 732 (1972)? And what effect did the pendency of criminal abortion charges against Dr. Hallford in state court have upon the propriety of the federal court's granting relief to him as a plaintiff-intervenor?

A. Jane Roe. Despite the use of the pseudonym, no suggestion is made that Roe is a fictitious person. For purposes of her case, we accept as true, and as established, her existence; her pregnant state, as of the inception of her suit in March 1970 and as late as May 21 of that year when she filed an alias affidavit with the District Court; and her inability to obtain a legal abortion in Texas.

Viewing Roe's case as of the time of its filing and thereafter until as late a May, there can be little dispute that it then presented a case or controversy and that, wholly apart from the class aspects, she, as a pregnant single woman thwarted by the Texas criminal abortion laws, had standing to challenge those statutes. *Abele v. Markle*, 452 F.2d 1121, 1125 (CA2 1971); *Crossen v. Breckenridge*, 446 F.2d 833, 838-839 (CA6 1971); *Poe v. Menghini*, 339 F.Supp. 986, 990-991 (Kan.1972). See *Truax v. Raich*, 239 U.S. 33 (1915). Indeed, we do not read the appellee's brief as really asserting anything to the contrary. The "logical nexus between the status asserted and the claim sought to be adjudicated," *Flast v. Cohen*, 392 U.S. at 102, and the necessary degree of contentiousness, *Golden v. Zwickler*, 394 U.S. 103 (1969), are both present.

The appellee notes, however, that the record does not disclose that Roe was pregnant at the time of the District Court hearing on May 22, 1970, or on the following June 17 when the court's opinion and judg-

ment were filed. And he suggests that Roe's case must now be moot because she and all other members of her class are no longer subject to any 1970 pregnancy.

The usual rule in federal cases is that an actual controversy must exist at stages of appellate or certiorari review, and not simply at the date the action is initiated. *United States v. Munsingwear, Inc.*, 340 U.S. 36 (1950); *Golden v. Zwickler*, supra; *SEC v. Medical Committee for Human Rights*, 404 U.S. 403 (1972).

But when, as here, pregnancy is a significant fact in the litigation, the normal 266-day human gestation period is so short that the pregnancy will come to term before the usual appellate process is complete. If that termination makes a case moot, pregnancy litigation seldom will survive much beyond the trial stage, and appellate review will be effectively denied. Our law should not be that rigid. Pregnancy often comes more than once to the same woman, and in the general population, if man is to survive, it will always be with us. Pregnancy provides a classic justification for a conclusion of nonmootness. It truly could be "capable of repetition, yet evading review." *Southern Pacific Terminal Co. v. ICC*, 219 U.S. 498, 515 (1911). See *Moore v. Ogilvie*, 394 U.S. 814, 816 (1969); *Carroll v. Princess Anne*, 393 U.S. 175, 178-179 (1968); *United States v. W. T. Grant Co.*, 345 U.S. 629, 632-633 (1953).

We, therefore, agree with the District Court that Jane Roe had standing to undertake this litigation, that she presented a justiciable controversy, and that the termination of her 1970 pregnancy has not rendered her case moot.

B. Dr. Hallford. The doctor's position is different. He entered Roe's litigation as a plaintiff-intervenor, alleging in his complaint that he:

[I]n the past has been arrested for violating the Texas Abortion Laws and at the present time stands charged by indictment with violating said laws in the Criminal District Court of Dallas County, Texas to-wit: (1) The State of Texas vs. James H. Hallford, No. C-69-5307-IH, and (2) The State of Texas vs. James H. Hallford, No. C-692524-H. In both cases, the defendant is charged with abortion....

In his application for leave to intervene, the doctor made like representations as to the abortion charges pending in the state court. These representations were also repeated in the affidavit he executed and filed in support of his motion for summary judgment.

Dr. Hallford is, therefore, in the position of seeking, in a federal court, declaratory and injunctive relief with respect to the same statutes under which he stands charged in criminal prosecutions simultaneously pending in state court. Although he stated that he has been arrested in the past for violating the State's abortion laws, he makes no allegation of any substantial and immediate threat to any federally protected right that cannot be asserted in his defense against the state prosecutions. Neither is there any allegation of harassment or bad faith prosecution. In order to escape the rule articulated in the cases cited in the next paragraph of this opinion that, absent harassment and bad faith, a defendant in a pending state criminal case cannot affirmatively challenge in federal court the statutes under which the State is prosecuting him, Dr. Hallford seeks to distinguish his status as a present state defendant from his status as a "potential future defendant," and to assert only the latter for standing purposes here.

We see no merit in that distinction. Our decision in *Samuels v. Mackell*, 401 U.S. 66 (1971), compels the conclusion that the District Court erred when it granted declaratory relief to Dr. Hallford instead of refraining from so doing. The court, of course, was correct in refusing to grant injunctive relief to the doctor. The reasons supportive of that action, however, are those expressed in *Samuels v. Mackell*, supra, and in *Younger v. Harris*, 401 U.S. 37 (1971); *Boyle v. Landry*, 401 U.S. 77 (1971); *Perez v. Ledesma*, 401 U.S. 82 (1971); and *Byrne v. Karaleis*, 401 U.S. 216 (1971). See also *Dombrowski v. Pfister*, 380 U.S. 479 (1965). We note, in passing, that Younger and its companion cases were decided after the three-judge District Court decision in this case.

Dr. Hallford's complaint in intervention, therefore, is to be dismissed. He is remitted to his defenses in the state criminal proceedings against him. We reverse the judgment of the District Court insofar as it granted Dr. Hallford relief and failed to dismiss his complaint in intervention.

C. The Does. In view of our ruling as to Roe's standing in her case, the issue of the Does' standing in their case has little significance. The claims they assert are essentially the same as those of Roe, and they attack the same statutes. Nevertheless, we briefly note the Does' posture.

Their pleadings present them as a childless married couple, the woman not being pregnant, who have no desire to have children at this time because of their having received medical advice that Mrs. Doe should avoid pregnancy, and for "other highly personal reasons." But they "fear… they may face the prospect of becoming parents." And if pregnancy ensues, they "would want to terminate" it by an abortion. They assert an inability to obtain an abortion legally in Texas and, consequently, the prospect of obtaining an illegal abortion there or of going outside Texas to some place where the procedure could be obtained legally and competently.

We thus have as plaintiffs a married couple who have, as their asserted immediate and present injury, only an alleged "detrimental effect upon [their] marital happiness" because they are forced to "the choice of refraining from normal sexual relations or of endangering Mary Doe's health through a possible pregnancy." Their claim is that, sometime in the future, Mrs. Doe might become pregnant because of possible failure of contraceptive measures, and, at that time in the future, she might want an abortion that might then be illegal under the Texas statutes.

This very phrasing of the Does' position reveals its speculative character. Their alleged injury rests on possible future contraceptive failure, possible future pregnancy, possible future unpreparedness for parenthood, and possible future impairment of health. Any one or more of these several possibilities may not take place, and all may not combine. In the Does' estimation, these possibilities might have some real or imagined impact upon their marital happiness. But we are not prepared to say that the bare allegation of so indirect an injury is sufficient to present an actual case or controversy. *Younger v. Harris*, 401 U.S. at 41-42; *Golden v. Zwickler*, 394 U.S. at 109-110; *Abele v. Markle*, 452 F.2d at 1124-1125; *Crossen v. Breckenridge*, 446 F.2d at 839. The Does' claim falls far short of those resolved otherwise in the cases that the Does urge upon us, namely, *Investment Co. Institute v. Camp*, 401 U.S. 617 (1971); *Data Processing Service v. Camp*, 397 U.S. 150 (1970); and *Epperson v. Arkansas*, 393 U.S. 97 (1968). See also *Truax v. Raich*, 239 U.S. 33 (1915).

The Does therefore are not appropriate plaintiffs in this litigation. Their complaint was properly dismissed by the District Court, and we affirm that dismissal.

V

The principal thrust of appellant's attack on the Texas statutes is that they improperly invade a right, said to be possessed by the pregnant woman, to choose to terminate her pregnancy. Appellant would discover this right in the concept of personal "liberty" embodied in the Fourteenth Amendment's Due Process Clause; or in personal, marital, familial, and sexual privacy said to be protected by the Bill of Rights or its penumbras, see *Griswold v. Connecticut*, 381 U.S. 479 (1965); *Eisenstadt v. Baird*, 405 U.S. 438 (1972); id. at 460 (WHITE, J., concurring in result); or among those rights reserved to the people by the Ninth Amendment, *Griswold v. Connecticut*, 381 U.S. at 486 (Goldberg, J., concurring). Before addressing this claim, we feel it desirable briefly to survey, in several aspects, the history of abortion, for such insight as that history may afford us, and then to examine the state purposes and interests behind the criminal abortion laws.

VI

It perhaps is not generally appreciated that the restrictive criminal abortion laws in effect in a majority of States today are of relatively recent vintage. Those laws, generally proscribing abortion or its attempt at any time during pregnancy except when necessary to preserve the pregnant woman's life, are not of ancient or even of common law origin. Instead, they derive from statutory changes effected, for the most part, in the latter half of the 19th century.

1. Ancient attitudes. These are not capable of precise determination. We are told that, at the time of the Persian Empire, abortifacients were known, and that criminal abortions were severely punished. We are also told, however, that abortion was practiced in Greek times as well as in the Roman Era, and that "it was resorted to without scruple." The Ephesian, Soranos, often described as the greatest of the ancient gynecologists, appears to have been generally opposed to Rome's prevailing free-abortion practices. He found it necessary to think first of the life of the mother, and he resorted to abortion when, upon this standard, he felt the procedure advisable. Greek and Roman law afforded little protection to the unborn. If abortion was prosecuted in some places, it seems to have been based on a concept of a violation of the father's right to his offspring. Ancient religion did not bar abortion.

2. The Hippocratic Oath. What then of the famous Oath that has stood so long as the ethical guide of the medical profession and that bears the name of the great Greek (460(?)-377(?) B. C.), who has been described as the Father of Medicine, the "wisest and the greatest practitioner of his art," and the "most important and most complete medical personality of antiquity," who dominated the medical schools of his time, and who typified the sum of the medical knowledge of the past? The Oath varies somewhat according to the particular translation, but in any translation the content is clear:

I will give no deadly medicine to anyone if asked, nor suggest any such counsel; and in like manner, I will not give to a woman a pessary to produce abortion,

or

I will neither give a deadly drug to anybody if asked for it, nor will I make a suggestion to this effect. Similarly, I will not give to a woman an abortive remedy.

Although the Oath is not mentioned in any of the principal briefs in this case or in *Doe v. Bolton*, post, p. 179, it represents the apex of the development of strict ethical concepts in medicine, and its influence endures to this day. Why did not the authority of Hippocrates dissuade abortion practice in his time and that of Rome? The late Dr. Edelstein provides us with a theory: [n16] The Oath was not uncontested even in Hippocrates' day; only the Pythagorean school of philosophers frowned upon the related act of suicide. Most Greek thinkers, on the other hand, commended abortion, at least prior to viability. See Plato, Republic, V, 461; Aristotle, Politics, VII, 1335b 25. For the Pythagoreans, however, it was a matter of dogma. For them, the embryo was animate from the moment of conception, and abortion meant destruction of a living being. The abortion clause of the Oath, therefore, "echoes Pythagorean doctrines," and "[i]n no other stratum of Greek opinion were such views held or proposed in the same spirit of uncompromising austerity."

Dr. Edelstein then concludes that the Oath originated in a group representing only a small segment of Greek opinion, and that it certainly was not accepted by all ancient physicians. He points out that medical writings down to Galen (A.D. 130-200) "give evidence of the violation of almost every one of its injunctions." But with the end of antiquity, a decided change took place. Resistance against suicide and against abortion became common. The Oath came to be popular. The emerging teachings of

Christianity were in agreement with the Pythagorean ethic. The Oath "became the nucleus of all medical ethics," and "was applauded as the embodiment of truth." Thus, suggests Dr. Edelstein, it is "a Pythagorean manifesto, and not the expression of an absolute standard of medical conduct."

This, it seems to us, is a satisfactory and acceptable explanation of the Hippocratic Oath's apparent rigidity. It enables us to understand, in historical context, a long-accepted and revered statement of medical ethics.

3. The common law. It is undisputed that, at common law, abortion performed before "quickening"—the first recognizable movement of the fetus in utero, appearing usually from the 16th to the 18th week of pregnancy—was not an indictable offense. The absence of a common law crime for pre-quickening abortion appears to have developed from a confluence of earlier philosophical, theological, and civil and canon law concepts of when life begins. These disciplines variously approached the question in terms of the point at which the embryo or fetus became "formed" or recognizably human, or in terms of when a "person" came into being, that is, infused with a "soul" or "animated." A loose consensus evolved in early English law that these events occurred at some point between conception and live birth. This was "mediate animation." Although Christian theology and the canon law came to fix the point of animation at 40 days for a male and 80 days for a female, a view that persisted until the 19th century, there was otherwise little agreement about the precise time of formation or animation. There was agreement, however, that, prior to this point, the fetus was to be regarded as part of the mother, and its destruction, therefore, was not homicide. Due to continued uncertainty about the precise time when animation occurred, to the lack of any empirical basis for the 40-80-day view, and perhaps to Aquinas' definition of movement as one of the two first principles of life, Bracton focused upon quickening as the critical point. The significance of quickening was echoed by later common law scholars, and found its way into the received common law in this country.

Whether abortion of a quick fetus was a felony at common law, or even a lesser crime, is still disputed. Bracton, writing early in the 13th century, thought it homicide. But the later and predominant view, following the great common law scholars, has been that it was, at most, a lesser offense. In a frequently cited passage, Coke took the position that abortion of a woman "quick with childe" is "a great misprision,

and no murder." Blackstone followed, saying that, while abortion after quickening had once been considered manslaughter (though not murder), "modern law" took a less severe view. A recent review of the common law precedents argues, however, that those precedents contradict Coke, and that even post-quickening abortion was never established as a common law crime. This is of some importance, because, while most American courts ruled, in holding or dictum, that abortion of an unquickened fetus was not criminal under their received common law, others followed Coke in stating that abortion of a quick fetus was a "misprision," a term they translated to mean "misdemeanor." That their reliance on Coke on this aspect of the law was uncritical and, apparently in all the reported cases, dictum (due probably to the paucity of common law prosecutions for post-quickening abortion), makes it now appear doubtful that abortion was ever firmly established as a common law crime even with respect to the destruction of a quick fetus.

4. The English statutory law. England's first criminal abortion statute, Lord Ellenborough's Act, 43 Geo. 3, c. 58, came in 1803. It made abortion of a quick fetus, § 1, a capital crime, but, in § 2, it provided lesser penalties for the felony of abortion before quickening, and thus preserved the "quickening" distinction. This contrast was continued in the general revision of 1828, 9 Geo. 4, c. 31, § 13. It disappeared, however, together with the death penalty, in 1837, 7 Will. 4 & 1 Vict., c. 85. § 6, and did not reappear in the Offenses Against the Person Act of 1861, 24 & 25 Vict., c. 100, § 59, that formed the core of English anti-abortion law until the liberalizing reforms of 1967. In 1929, the Infant Life (Preservation) Act, 19 & 20 Geo. 5, c. 34, came into being. Its emphasis was upon the destruction of "the life of a child capable of being born alive." It made a willful act performed with the necessary intent a felony. It contained a proviso that one was not to be found guilty of the offense

> unless it is proved that the act which caused the death of the child was not done in good faith for the purpose only of preserving the life of the mother.

A seemingly notable development in the English law was the case of *Rex v. Bourne*, [1939] 1 K.B. 687. This case apparently answered in the affirmative the question whether an abortion necessary to preserve the life of the pregnant woman was excepted from the criminal penalties of the 1861 Act. In his instructions to the jury, Judge Macnaghten referred to the 1929 Act, and observed that that Act related to "the case where a child is killed by a willful act at the time when it is being delivered in the ordinary course of nature." Id. at 691. He concluded that the 1861 Act's use of the word "unlawfully," imported the same meaning expressed by the specific proviso in the 1929 Act, even though there was no mention of preserving the mother's life in the 1861 Act. He then construed the phrase "preserving the life of the mother" broadly, that is, "in a reasonable sense," to include a serious and permanent threat to the mother's health, and instructed the jury to acquit Dr. Bourne if it found he had acted in a good faith belief that the abortion was necessary for this purpose. Id. at 693-694. The jury did acquit.

Recently, Parliament enacted a new abortion law. This is the Abortion Act of 1967, 15 & 16 Eliz. 2, c. 87. The Act permits a licensed physician to perform an abortion where two other licensed physicians agree (a)

that the continuance of the pregnancy would involve risk to the life of the pregnant woman, or of injury to the physical or mental health of the pregnant woman or any existing children of her family, greater than if the pregnancy were terminated,

or (b)

that there is a substantial risk that, if the child were born it would suffer from such physical or mental abnormalities as to be seriously handicapped.

The Act also provides that, in making this determination, "account may be taken of the pregnant woman's actual or reasonably foreseeable environment." It also permits a physician, without the concurrence of others, to terminate a pregnancy where he is of the good faith opinion that the abortion "is immediately necessary to save the life or to prevent grave permanent injury to the physical or mental health of the pregnant woman."

5. The American law. In this country, the law in effect in all but a few States until mid-19th century was the preexisting English common law. Connecticut, the first State to enact abortion legislation, adopted in 1821 that part of Lord Ellenborough's Act that related to a woman "quick with child." The death penalty was not imposed. Abortion before quickening was made a crime in that State only in 1860. In 1828, New York enacted legislation that, in two respects, was to serve as a model for early antiabortion statutes. First, while barring destruction of an unquickened fetus as well as a quick fetus, it made the former only a misdemeanor, but the latter second-degree manslaughter. Second, it incorporated a concept of therapeutic abortion by providing that an abortion was excused if it shall have been necessary to preserve the life of such mother, or shall have been advised by two physicians to be necessary for such purpose.

By 1840, when Texas had received the common law, only eight American States had statutes dealing with abortion. It was not until after the War Between the States that legislation began generally to replace the common law. Most of these initial statutes dealt severely with abortion after quickening, but were lenient with it before quickening. Most punished attempts equally with completed abortions. While many statutes included the exception for an abortion thought by one or more physicians to be necessary to save the mother's life, that provision soon disappeared, and the typical law required that the procedure actually be necessary for that purpose. Gradually, in the middle and late 19th century, the quickening distinction disappeared from the statutory law of most States and the degree of the offense and the penalties were increased. By the end of the 1950's, a large majority of the jurisdictions banned abortion, however and whenever performed, unless done to save or preserve the life of the mother. The exceptions, Alabama and the District of Columbia, permitted abortion to preserve the mother's health. Three States permitted abortions that were not "unlawfully" performed or that were not "without lawful justification," leaving interpretation of those standards to the courts. In the past several years, however, a trend toward liberalization of abortion statutes has resulted in adoption, by about one-third of the States, of less stringent laws, most of them patterned after the ALI Model Penal Code, § 230.3, set forth as Appendix B to the opinion in *Doe v. Bolton*, post, p. 205.

It is thus apparent that, at common law, at the time of the adoption of our Constitution, and throughout the major portion of the 19th century, abortion was viewed with less disfavor than under most American statutes currently in effect. Phrasing it another way, a woman enjoyed a substantially broader right to terminate a pregnancy than she does in most States today. At least with respect to the early stage of pregnancy, and very possibly without such a limitation, the opportunity to make this choice was present in this country well into the 19th century. Even later, the law continued for some time to treat less punitively an abortion procured in early pregnancy.

6. The position of the American Medical Association. The anti-abortion mood prevalent in this country in the late 19th century was shared by the medical profession. Indeed, the attitude of the profession may have played a significant role in the enactment of stringent criminal abortion legislation during that period.

An AMA Committee on Criminal Abortion was appointed in May, 1857. It presented its report, 12 Trans. of the Am.Med.Assn. 778 (1859), to the Twelfth Annual Meeting. That report observed that the Committee had been appointed to investigate criminal abortion "with a view to its general suppression." It deplored abortion and its frequency and it listed three causes of "this general demoralization":

The first of these causes is a widespread popular ignorance of the true character of the crime—a belief, even among mothers themselves, that the foetus is not alive till after the period of quickening.

The second of the agents alluded to is the fact that the profession themselves are frequently supposed careless of foetal life....

The third reason of the frightful extent of this crime is found in the grave defects of our laws, both common and statute, as regards the independent and actual existence of the child before birth, as a living being. These errors, which are sufficient in most instances to prevent conviction, are based, and only based, upon mistaken and exploded medical dogmas. With strange inconsistency, the law fully acknowledges the foetus in utero and its inherent rights, for civil purposes; while personally and as criminally affected, it fails to recognize it, and to its life as yet denies all protection.

Id. at 776. The Committee then offered, and the Association adopted, resolutions protesting "against such unwarrantable destruction of human life," calling upon state legislatures to revise their abortion laws, and requesting the cooperation of state medical societies "in pressing the subject." Id. at 28, 78.

In 1871, a long and vivid report was submitted by the Committee on Criminal Abortion. It ended with the observation,

We had to deal with human life. In a matter of less importance, we could entertain no compromise. An honest judge on the bench would

call things by their proper names. We could do no less.

22 Trans. of the Am.Med.Assn. 268 (1871). It proffered resolutions, adopted by the Association, id. at 38-39, recommending, among other things, that it

be unlawful and unprofessional for any physician to induce abortion or premature labor without the concurrent opinion of at least one respectable consulting physician, and then always with a view to the safety of the child—if that be possible,

and calling

the attention of the clergy of all denominations to the perverted views of morality entertained by a large class of females—aye, and men also, on this important question.

Except for periodic condemnation of the criminal abortionist, no further formal AMA action took place until 1967. In that year, the Committee on Human Reproduction urged the adoption of a stated policy of opposition to induced abortion except when there is "documented medical evidence" of a threat to the health or life of the mother, or that the child "may be born with incapacitating physical deformity or mental deficiency," or that a pregnancy "resulting from legally established statutory or forcible rape or incest may constitute a threat to the mental or physical health of the patient," two other physicians "chosen because of their recognized professional competence have examined the patient and have concurred in writing," and the procedure "is performed in a hospital accredited by the Joint Commission on Accreditation of Hospitals." The providing of medical information by physicians to state legislatures in their consideration of legislation regarding therapeutic abortion was "to be considered consistent with the principles of ethics of the American Medical Association." This recommendation was adopted by the House of Delegates. Proceedings of the AMA House of Delegates 40-51 (June 1967).

In 1970, after the introduction of a variety of proposed resolutions and of a report from its Board of Trustees, a reference committee noted "polarization of the medical profession on this controversial issue"; division among those who had testified; a difference of opinion among AMA councils and.committees; "the remarkable shift in testimony" in six months, felt to be influenced "by the rapid changes in state laws and by the judicial decisions which tend to make abortion more freely available;" and a feeling "that this trend will continue." On June 25, 1970, the House of Delegates adopted preambles and most of the resolutions proposed by the reference committee. The preambles emphasized "the best interests of the patient," "sound clinical judgment," and "informed patient consent," in contrast to "mere acquiescence to the patient's demand." The resolutions asserted that abortion is a medical procedure that should be performed by a licensed physician in an accredited hospital only after consultation with two other physicians and in conformity with state law, and that no party to the procedure should be required to violate personally held moral principles. Proceedings of the AMA House of Delegates 220 (June 1970). The AMA Judicial Council rendered a complementary opinion.

7. The position of the American Public Health Association. In October, 1970, the Executive Board of the APHA adopted Standards for Abortion Services. These were five in number:

a. Rapid and simple abortion referral must be readily available through state and local public health departments, medical societies, or other nonprofit organizations.

b. An important function of counseling should be to simplify and expedite the provision of abortion services; it should not delay the obtaining of these services.

c. Psychiatric consultation should not be mandatory. As in the case of other specialized medical services, psychiatric consultation should be sought for definite indications, and not on a routine basis.

d. A wide range of individuals from appropriately trained, sympathetic volunteers to highly skilled physicians may qualify as abortion counselors.

e. Contraception and/or sterilization should be discussed with each abortion patient.
Recommended Standards for Abortion Services, 61 Am.J.Pub.Health 396 (1971). Among factors pertinent to life and health risks associated with abortion were three that "are recognized as important":

a. the skill of the physician,

b. the environment in which the abortion is performed, and above all

c. the duration of pregnancy, as determined by uterine size and confirmed by menstrual history.

Id. at 397.
It was said that "a well equipped hospital" offers more protection

to cope with unforeseen difficulties than an office or clinic without such resources.... The factor of gestational age is of overriding importance.

Thus, it was recommended that abortions in the second trimester and early abortions in the presence of existing medical complications be performed in hospitals as inpatient procedures. For pregnancies in the first trimester, abortion in the hospital with or without overnight stay "is probably the safest practice." An abortion in an extramural facility, however, is an acceptable alternative "provided arrangements exist in advance to admit patients promptly if unforeseen complications develop." Standards for an abortion facility were listed. It was said that, at present, abortions should be performed by physicians or osteopaths who are licensed to practice and who have "adequate training." Id. at 398.

8. The position of the American Bar Association. At its meeting in February, 1972, the ABA House of Delegates approved, with 17 opposing votes, the Uniform Abortion Act that had been drafted and approved the preceding August by the Conference of Commissioners on Uniform State Laws. 58 A.B.A.J. 380 (1972). We set forth the Act in full in the margin. The Opinion of the Court Conference has appended an enlightening Prefatory Note.

VII

Three reasons have been advanced to explain historically the enactment of criminal abortion laws in the 19th century and to justify their continued existence.

It has been argued occasionally that these laws were the product of a Victorian social concern to discourage illicit sexual conduct. Texas, however, does not advance this justification in the present case, and it appears that no court or commentator has taken the argument seriously. The appellants and amici contend, moreover, that this is not a proper state purpose, at all and suggest that, if it were, the Texas statutes are overbroad in protecting it, since the law fails to distinguish between married and unwed mothers.

A second reason is concerned with abortion as a medical procedure. When most criminal abortion laws were first enacted, the procedure was a hazardous one for the woman. This was particularly true prior to the development of antisepsis. Antiseptic techniques, of course, were based on discoveries by Lister, Pasteur, and others first announced in 1867, but were not generally accepted and employed until about the turn of the century. Abortion mortality was high. Even after 1900, and perhaps until as late as the development of antibiotics in the 1940's, standard modern techniques such as dilation and curettage were not nearly so safe as they are today. Thus, it has been argued that a State's real concern in enacting a criminal abortion law was to protect the pregnant woman, that is, to restrain her from submitting to a procedure that placed her life in serious jeopardy.

Modern medical techniques have altered this situation. Appellants and various amici refer to medical data indicating that abortion in early pregnancy, that is, prior to the end of the first trimester, although not without its risk, is now relatively safe. Mortality rates for women undergoing early abortions, where the procedure is legal, appear to be as low as or lower than the rates for normal childbirth. Consequently, any interest of the State in protecting the woman from an inherently hazardous procedure, except when it would be equally dangerous for her to forgo it, has largely disappeared. Of course, important state interests in the areas of health and medical standards do remain. The State has a legitimate interest in seeing to it that abortion, like any other medical procedure, is performed under circumstances that insure maximum safety for the patient. This interest obviously extends at least to the performing physician and his staff, to the facilities involved, to the availability of after-care, and to adequate provision for any complication or emergency that might arise. The prevalence of high mortality rates at illegal "abortion mills" strengthens, rather than weakens, the State's interest in regulating the conditions under which abortions are performed. Moreover, the risk to the woman increases as her pregnancy continues. Thus, the State retains a definite interest in protecting the woman's own health and safety when an abortion is proposed at a late stage of pregnancy.

The third reason is the State's interest—some phrase it in terms of duty—in protecting prenatal life. Some of the argument for this justification rests on the theory that a new human life is present from the moment of conception. The State's interest and general obligation to protect life then extends, it is argued, to prenatal life. Only when the life of the pregnant mother herself is at stake, balanced against the life she carries within her, should the interest of the embryo or fetus not prevail. Logically, of course, a legitimate state interest in this area need not stand or fall on acceptance of the belief that life begins at conception or at some other point prior to live birth. In assessing the State's interest, recognition may be given to the less rigid claim that as long as at least potential life is involved, the State may assert interests beyond the protection of the pregnant woman alone.

Parties challenging state abortion laws have sharply disputed in some courts the contention that a purpose of these laws, when enacted, was to protect prenatal life. Pointing to the absence of legislative history to support the contention, they claim that most state laws were designed solely to protect the woman. Because medical advances have lessened this concern, at least with respect to abortion in early pregnancy, they argue that with respect to such abortions the laws can no longer be justified by any state interest. There is some scholarly support for this view of original purpose. The few state courts called upon to interpret their laws in the late 19th and early 20th centuries did focus on the State's interest in protecting the woman's health, rather than in preserving the embryo and fetus. Proponents of this view point out that in many States, including Texas, by statute or judicial interpretation, the pregnant woman herself could not be prosecuted for self-abortion or for cooperating in an abortion performed upon her by another. They claim that adoption of the "quickening" distinction through received common law and state statutes tacitly recognizes the greater health hazards inherent in late abortion and impliedly repudiates the theory that life begins at conception.

It is with these interests, and the eight to be attached to them, that this case is concerned.

VIII

The Constitution does not explicitly mention any right of privacy. In a line of decisions, however, going back perhaps as far as *Union Pacific R. Co. v. Botsford*, 141 U.S. 250, 251 (1891), the Court has recognized that a right of personal privacy, or a guarantee of certain areas or zones of privacy, does exist under the Constitution. In varying contexts, the Court or individual Justices have, indeed, found at least the roots of that right in the First Amendment, *Stanley v. Georgia*, 394 U.S. 557, 564 (1969); in the Fourth and Fifth Amendments, *Terry v. Ohio*, 392 U.S. 1, 8-9 (1968), *Katz v. United States*, 389 U.S. 347, 350 (1967), *Boyd v. United States*, 116 U.S. 616 (1886), see *Olmstead v. United States*, 277 U.S. 438, 478 (1928) (Brandeis, J., dissenting); in the penumbras of the Bill of Rights, *Griswold v. Connecticut*, 381 U.S. at 484-485; in the Ninth Amendment, id. at 486 (Goldberg, J., concurring); or in the concept of liberty guaranteed by the first section of the Fourteenth Amendment, see *Meyer v. Nebraska*, 262 U.S. 390, 399 (1923). These decisions make it clear that only personal rights that can be deemed "fundamental" or "implicit in the concept of ordered liberty," *Palko v. Connecticut*, 302 U.S. 319, 325 (1937), are included in this guarantee of personal privacy. They also make it clear that the right has some extension to activities relating to marriage, *Loving v. Virginia*, 388 U.S. 1, 12 (1967); procreation, *Skinner v. Oklahoma*, 316 U.S. 535, 541-542 (1942); contraception, *Eisenstadt v. Baird*, 405 U.S. at 453-454; id. at 460, 463-465 (WHITE, J., concurring in result); family relationships, *Prince v. Massachusetts*, 321 U.S. 158, 166 (1944); and childrearing and education, *Pierce v. Society of Sisters*, 268 U.S. 510, 535 (1925), *Meyer v. Nebraska*, supra.

This right of privacy, whether it be founded in the Fourteenth Amendment's concept of personal liberty and restrictions upon state action, as we feel it is, or, as the District Court determined, in the Ninth Amendment's reservation of rights to the people, is broad enough to encompass a woman's decision whether or not to terminate her pregnancy. The detriment that the State would impose upon the pregnant woman by denying this choice altogether is apparent. Specific and direct harm medically diagnosable even in early pregnancy may be involved. Maternity, or additional offspring, may force upon the woman a distressful life and future. Psychological harm may be imminent. Mental and physical health may be taxed by child care. There is also the distress, for all concerned, associated with the unwanted child, and there is the problem of bringing a child into a family already unable, psychologically and otherwise, to care for it. In other cases, as in this one, the additional difficulties and continuing stigma of unwed motherhood may be involved. All these are factors the woman and her responsible physician necessarily will consider in consultation.

On the basis of elements such as these, appellant and some amici argue that the woman's right is absolute and that she is entitled to terminate her pregnancy at whatever time, in whatever way, and for whatever reason she alone chooses. With this we do not agree. Appellant's arguments that Texas either has no valid interest at all in regulating the abortion decision, or no interest strong enough to support any limitation upon the woman's sole determination, are unpersuasive. The Court's decisions recognizing a right of privacy also acknowledge that some state regulation in areas protected by that right is appropriate. As noted above, a State may properly assert important interests in safeguarding health, in maintaining medical standards, and in protecting potential life. At some point in pregnancy, these respective interests become sufficiently compelling to sustain regulation of the factors that govern the abortion decision. The privacy right involved, therefore, cannot be said to be absolute. In fact, it is not clear to us that the claim asserted by some amici that one has an unlimited right to do with one's body as one pleases bears a close relationship to the right of privacy previously articulated in the Court's decisions. The Court has refused to recognize an unlimited right of this kind in the past. *Jacobson v. Massachusetts*, 197 U.S. 11 (1905) (vaccination); *Buck v. Bell*, 274 U.S. 200 (1927) (sterilization).

We, therefore, conclude that the right of personal privacy includes the abortion decision, but that this right is not unqualified, and must be considered against important state interests in regulation.

We note that those federal and state courts that have recently considered abortion law challenges have reached the same conclusion. A majority, in addition to the District Court in the present case, have held state laws unconstitutional, at least in part, because of vagueness or because of overbreadth and abridgment of rights. *Abele v. Markle*, 342 F.Supp. 800 (Conn.1972), appeal docketed, No. 72-56; *Abele v. Markle*, 351 F.Supp. 224 (Conn.1972), appeal docketed, No. 72-730; *Doe v. Bolton*, 319 F.Supp. 1048 (ND Ga.1970), appeal decided today, post, p. 179; *Doe v. Scott*, 321 F.Supp. 1385 (ND Ill.1971), appeal docketed, No. 70-105; *Poe v. Menghini*, 339 F.Supp. 986 (Kan.1972); *YWCA v. Kuler*, 342 F.Supp. 1048 (NJ 1972); *Babbitz v. McCann*, 310 F.Supp. 293 (ED Wis.1970), appeal dismissed, 400 U.S. 1 (1970); *People v. Belous*, 71 Cal.2d 954, 458 P.2d 194 (1969), cert. denied, 397 U.S. 915 (1970); *State v. Barquet*, 262 So.2d 431 (Fla.1972).

Others have sustained state statutes. *Crossen v. Attorney General*, 344 F.Supp. 587 (ED Ky.1972), appeal docketed, No. 72-256; *Rosen v. Louisiana State Board of Medical Examiners*, 318 F.Supp. 1217 (ED La.1970), appeal docketed, No. 70-42; *Corkey v. Edwards*, 322 F.Supp. 1248 (WDNC 1971), appeal docketed, No. 71-92; *Steinberg v. Brown*, 321 F.Supp. 741 (ND Ohio 1970); *Doe v. Rampton* (Utah 1971), appeal docketed, No. 71-5666; *Cheaney v. State*, ___ Ind. ___, 285 N.E.2d 265 (1972); *Spears v. State*, 257 So.2d 876 (Miss. 1972); *State v. Munson*, 86 S.D. 663, 201 N.W.2d 123 (1972), appeal docketed, No. 72-631.

Although the results are divided, most of these courts have agreed that the right of privacy, however based, is broad enough to cover the abortion decision; that the right, nonetheless, is not absolute, and is subject to some limitations; and that, at some point, the state interests as to protection of health, medical standards, and prenatal life, become dominant. We agree with this approach.

Where certain "fundamental rights" are involved, the Court has held that regulation limiting these rights may be justified only by a "compelling state interest," *Kramer v. Union Free School District*, 395 U.S. 621, 627 (1969); *Shapiro v. Thompson*, 394 U.S. 618, 634 (1969), *Sherbert v. Verner*, 374 U.S. 398, 406 (1963), and that legislative enactments must be narrowly drawn to express only the legitimate state interests at stake. *Griswold v. Connecticut*, 381 U.S. at 485; *Aptheker v. Secretary of State*, 378 U.S. 500, 508 (1964); *Cantwell v. Connecticut*, 310 U.S. 296, 307-308 (1940); see *Eisenstadt v. Baird*, 405 U.S. at 460, 463-464 (WHITE, J., concurring in result).

In the recent abortion cases cited above, courts have recognized these principles. Those striking down state laws have generally scrutinized the State's interests in protecting health and potential life, and have concluded that neither interest justified broad limitations on the reasons for which a physician and his pregnant patient might decide that she should have an abortion in the early stages of pregnancy. Courts sustaining state laws have held that the State's determinations to protect health or prenatal life are dominant and constitutionally justifiable.

IX

The District Court held that the appellee failed to meet his burden of demonstrating that the Texas statute's infringement upon Roe's rights was necessary to support a compelling state interest, and that, although the appellee presented "several compelling justifications for state presence in the area of abortions," the statutes outstripped these justifications and swept "far beyond any areas of compelling state interest." 314 F.Supp. at 1222-1223. Appellant and appellee both contest that holding. Appellant, as has been indicated, claims an absolute right that bars any state imposition of criminal penalties in the area. Appellee argues that the State's determination to recognize and protect prenatal life from and after conception constitutes a compelling state interest. As noted above, we do not agree fully with either formulation.

A. The appellee and certain amici argue that the fetus is a "person" within the language and meaning of the Fourteenth Amendment. In support of this, they outline at length and in detail the well known facts of fetal development. If this suggestion of personhood is established, the appellant's case, of course, collapses, for the fetus' right to life would then be guaranteed specifically by the Amendment. The appellant conceded as much on reargument. On the other hand, the appellee conceded on reargument that no case could be cited that holds that a fetus is a person within the meaning of the Fourteenth Amendment.

The Constitution does not define "person" in so many words. Section 1 of the Fourteenth Amendment contains three references to "person." The first, in defining "citizens," speaks of "persons born or naturalized in the United States." The word also appears both in the Due Process Clause and in the Equal Protection Clause. "Person" is used in other places in the Constitution: in the listing of qualifications for Representatives and Senators, Art. I, § 2, cl. 2, and § 3, cl. 3; in the Apportionment Clause, Art. I, § 2, cl. 3; in the Migration and Importation provision, Art. I, § 9, cl. 1; in the Emolument Clause, Art. I, § 9, cl. 8; in the Electors provisions, Art. II, § 1, cl. 2, and the superseded cl. 3; in the provision outlining qualifications for the office of President, Art. II, § 1, cl. 5; in the Extradition provisions, Art. IV, § 2, cl. 2, and the superseded Fugitive Slave Clause 3; and in the Fifth, Twelfth, and Twenty-second Amendments, as well as in §§ 2 and 3 of the Fourteenth Amendment. But in nearly all these instances, the use of the word is such that it has application only post-natally. None indicates, with any assurance, that it has any possible pre-natal application.

All this, together with our observation, supra, that, throughout the major portion of the 19th century, prevailing legal abortion practices were far freer than they are today, persuades us that the word "person," as used in the Fourteenth Amendment, does not include the unborn. This is in accord with the results reached in those few cases where the issue has been squarely presented. *McGarvey v. Magee-Womens Hospital*, 340 F.Supp. 751 (WD Pa.1972); *Byrn v. New York City Health & Hospitals Corp.*, 31 N.Y.2d 194, 286 N.E.2d 887 (1972), appeal docketed, No. 72-434; *Abele v. Markle*, 351 F.Supp. 224 (Conn.1972), appeal docketed, No. 72-730. Cf. *Cheaney v. State*, ___ Ind. at ___, 285 N.E.2d at 270; *Montana v. Rogers*, 278 F.2d 68, 72 (CA7 1960), affs' d sub nom. *Montana v. Kennedy*, 366 U.S. 308 (1961); *Keeler v. Superior Court*, 2 Cal.3d 619, 470 P.2d 617 (1970); *State v. Dickinson*, 28 Ohio St.2d 65, 275 N.E.2d 599 (1971). Indeed, our decision in *United States v. Vuitch*, 402 U.S. 62 (1971), inferentially is to the same effect, for we there would not have indulged in statutory interpretation favorable to abortion in specified circumstances if the necessary consequence was the termination of life entitled to Fourteenth Amendment protection.

This conclusion, however, does not of itself fully answer the contentions raised by Texas, and we pass on to other considerations.

B. The pregnant woman cannot be isolated in her privacy. She carries an embryo and, later, a fetus, if one accepts the medical definitions of the developing young in the human uterus. See Dorland's Illustrated Medical Dictionary 478-479, 547 (24th ed.1965). The situation therefore is inherently different from marital intimacy, or bedroom possession of obscene material, or marriage, or procreation, or education, with which Eisenstadt and Griswold, Stanley, Loving, Skinner, and Pierce and Meyer were respectively concerned. As we have intimated above, it is reasonable and appropriate for a State to decide that, at some point in time another interest, that of health of the mother or that of potential human life, becomes significantly involved. The woman's privacy is no longer sole and any right of privacy she possesses must be measured accordingly.

Texas urges that, apart from the Fourteenth Amendment, life begins at conception and is present throughout pregnancy, and that, therefore, the State has a compelling interest in protecting that life from and after conception. We need not resolve the difficult question of when life begins. When those trained in the respective disciplines of medicine, philosophy, and theology are unable to arrive at any consensus, the judiciary, at this point in the development of man's knowledge, is not in a position to speculate as to the answer.

It should be sufficient to note briefly the wide divergence of thinking on this most sensitive and difficult question. There has always been strong support for the view that life does not begin until live birth. This was the belief of the Stoics. It appears to be the predominant, though not the unanimous, attitude of the Jewish faith. It may be taken to represent also the position of a large segment of the Protestant community, insofar as that can be ascertained; organized groups that have taken a formal position on the abortion issue have generally regarded abortion as a matter for the conscience of the individual and her family. As we have noted, the common law found greater significance in quickening. Physician and their scientific colleagues have regarded that event with less interest and have tended to focus either upon conception, upon live birth, or upon the interim point at which the fetus becomes "viable," that is, potentially able to live outside the mother's womb, albeit with artificial aid. Viability is usually placed at about seven months (28 weeks) but may occur earlier, even at 24 weeks. The Aristotelian theory of "mediate animation," that held sway throughout the Middle Ages and the Renaissance in Europe, continued to be official Roman Catholic dogma until the 19th century, despite opposition to this "ensoulment" theory from those in the Church who would recognize the existence of life from the moment of conception. The latter is now, of course, the official belief of the Catholic Church. As one brief amicus discloses, this is a view strongly held by many non-Catholics as well, and by many physicians. Substantial problems for precise definition of this view are posed, however, by new embryological data that purport to indicate that conception is a "process" over time, rather than an event, and by new medical techniques such as menstrual extraction, the "morning-after" pill, implantation of embryos, artificial insemination, and even artificial wombs.

In areas other than criminal abortion, the law has been reluctant to endorse any theory that life, as we recognize it, begins before live birth, or to accord legal rights to the unborn except in narrowly defined situations and except when the rights are contingent upon live birth. For example, the traditional rule of tort law denied recovery for prenatal injuries even though the child was born alive. That rule has been changed in almost every jurisdiction. In most States, recovery is said to be permitted only if the fetus was viable, or at least quick, when the injuries were sustained, though few courts have squarely so held. In a recent development, generally opposed by the commentators, some States permit the parents of a stillborn child to maintain an action for wrongful death because of prenatal injuries. Such an action, however, would appear to be one to vindicate the parents' interest and is thus consistent with the view that the fetus, at most, represents only the potentiality of life. Similarly, unborn children have been recognized as acquiring rights or interests by way of inheritance or other devolution of property, and have been represented by guardians ad litem. Perfection of the interests involved, again, has generally been contingent upon live birth. In short, the unborn have never been recognized in the law as persons in the whole sense.

X

In view of all this, we do not agree that, by adopting one theory of life, Texas may override the rights of the pregnant woman that are at stake. We repeat, however, that the State does have an important and legitimate interest in preserving and protecting the health of the pregnant woman, whether she be a resident of the State or a nonresident who seeks medical consultation and treatment there, and that it has still another important and legitimate interest in protecting the potentiality of human life. These interests are separate and distinct. Each grows in substantiality as the woman approaches term and, at a point during pregnancy, each becomes "compelling."

With respect to the State's important and legitimate interest in the health of the mother, the "compelling" point, in the light of present medical knowledge, is at approximately the end of the first trimester. This is so because of the now-established medical fact, referred to above at 149, that, until the end of the first trimester mortality in abortion may be less than mortality in normal childbirth. It follows that, from and after this point, a State may regulate the abortion procedure to the extent that the regulation reasonably relates to the preservation and protection of maternal health. Examples of permissible state regulation in this area are requirements as to the qualifications of the person who is to perform the abortion; as to the licensure of that person; as to the facility in which the procedure is to be performed, that is, whether it must be a hospital or may be a clinic or some other place of less-than-hospital status; as to the licensing of the facility; and the like.

This means, on the other hand, that, for the period of pregnancy prior to this "compelling" point, the attending physician, in consultation with his patient, is free to determine, without regulation by the State, that, in his medical judgment, the patient's pregnancy should be terminated. If that decision is reached, the judgment may be effectuated by an abortion free of interference by the State.

With respect to the State's important and legitimate interest in potential life, the "compelling" point is at viability. This is so because the fetus then presumably has the capability of meaningful life outside the mother's womb. State regulation protective of fetal life after viability thus has both logical and biological justifications. If the State is interested in protecting fetal life after viability, it may go so far as to proscribe abortion during that period, except when it is necessary to preserve the life or health of the mother.

Measured against these standards, Art. 1196 of the Texas Penal Code, in restricting legal abortions to those "procured or attempted by medical advice for the purpose of saving the life of the mother," sweeps too broadly. The statute makes no distinction between abortions performed early in pregnancy and those performed later, and it limits to a single reason, "saving" the mother's life, the legal justification for the procedure. The statute, therefore, cannot survive the constitutional attack made upon it here.

This conclusion makes it unnecessary for us to consider the additional challenge to the Texas statute asserted on grounds of vagueness. See *United States v. Vuitch*, 402 U.S. at 67-72.

XI

To summarize and to repeat:

1. A state criminal abortion statute of the current Texas type, that excepts from criminality only a lifesaving procedure on behalf of the mother, without regard to pregnancy stage and without recognition of the other interests involved, is violative of the Due Process Clause of the Fourteenth Amendment.

(a) For the stage prior to approximately the end of the first trimester, the abortion decision and its effectuation must be left to the medical judgment of the pregnant woman's attending physician.

(b) For the stage subsequent to approximately the end of the first trimester, the State, in promoting its interest in the health of the mother, may, if it chooses, regulate the abortion procedure in ways that are reasonably related to maternal health.

(c) For the stage subsequent to viability, the State in promoting its interest in the potentiality of human life may, if it chooses, regulate, and even proscribe, abortion except where it is necessary, in appropriate medical judgment, for the preservation of the life or health of the mother.

2. The State may define the term "physician," as it has been employed in the preceding paragraphs of this Part XI of this opinion, to mean only a physician currently licensed by the State, and may proscribe any abortion by a person who is not a physician as so defined.

In *Doe v. Bolton*, post, p. 179, procedural requirements contained in one of the modern abortion statutes are considered. That opinion and this one, of course, are to be read together.

This holding, we feel, is consistent with the relative weights of the respective interests involved, with the lessons and examples of medical and legal history, with the lenity of the common law, and with the demands of the profound problems of the present day. The decision leaves the State free to place increasing restrictions on abortion as the period of pregnancy lengthens, so long as those restrictions are tailored to the recognized state interests. The decision vindicates the right of the physician to administer medical treatment according to his professional judgment up to the points where important state interests provide compelling justifications for intervention. Up to those points, the abortion decision in all its aspects is inherently, and primarily, a medical decision, and basic responsibility for it must rest with the physician. If an individual practitioner abuses the privilege of exercising proper medical judgment, the usual remedies, judicial and intra-professional, are available.

XII

Our conclusion that Art. 1196 is unconstitutional means, of course, that the Texas abortion statutes, as a unit, must fall. The exception of Art. 1196 cannot be struck down separately, for then the State would be left with a statute proscribing all abortion procedures no matter how medically urgent the case.

Although the District Court granted appellant Roe declaratory relief, it stopped short of issuing an injunction against enforcement of the Texas statutes. The Court has recognized that different considerations enter into a federal court's decision as to declaratory relief, on the one hand, and injunctive relief, on the other. *Zwickler v. Koota*, 389 U.S. 241, 252-255 (1967); *Dombrowski v. Pfister*, 380 U.S. 479 (1965). We are not dealing with a statute that, on its face, appears to abridge free expression, an area of particular concern under Dombrowski and refined in *Younger v. Harris*, 401 U.S. at 50.

We find it unnecessary to decide whether the District Court erred in withholding injunctive relief, for we assume the Texas prosecutorial authorities will give full credence to this decision that the present criminal abortion statutes of that State are unconstitutional.

The judgment of the District Court as to intervenor Hallford is reversed, and Dr. Hallford's complaint in intervention is dismissed. In all other respects, the judgment of the District Court is affirmed. Costs are allowed to the appellee.

It is so ordered.

Lewis F. Powell, Jr. (AP Photo)

"Preferring members of any one group for no reason other than race or ethnic origin is discrimination for its own sake."

Overview

Regents of the University of California v. Bakke was the first important U.S. Supreme Court decision to test Title VI of the 1964 Civil Rights Act, prohibiting racial discrimination in public education and other endeavors receiving federal funds. In the 1970s, the University of California at Davis School of Medicine had what amounted to dual admission standards based on race. Each year one hundred students were admitted to the medical program, but a number of them were subject to different, more lenient admissions requirements. Sixteen spaces were reserved for "disadvantaged" students, who could identify themselves on the application form as belonging to a minority group or as disadvantaged either economically or educationally. Candidates in this group did not have to meet the same minimum grade point average, and they were compared with one another rather than with the entire pool of applicants.

Allan Bakke, a white male applicant, was rejected by the regular admissions program in 1973 and again in 1974. Both years, applicants with grade-point averages and admissions-test scores lower than Bakke's were admitted under the rules for disadvantaged students. After he was rejected a second time, Bakke sued the university, asking that the court compel his admission. Bakke based his case on his right to equal protection under the laws, as guaranteed by the Fourteenth Amendment; he also claimed that the university violated Title VI because it had rejected him owing to his race. The Supreme Court ruled in Bakke's favor, ordering the university to admit him, but the Court also held that while Title VI disallowed educational institutions from making racial quotas part of their admissions policies, giving race some special consideration was permissible in order to achieve the important goal of diversity in institutions of higher education and—beyond that—at all levels of society. Thus *Bakke* became, as the Court later characterized it in *Grutter v. Bollinger* (2003), the "touchstone for constitutional analysis of race-conscious admissions policies" (http://www.oyez.org/cases/2000-2009/2002/2002_02_241).

Context

The history of what is known as affirmative action began in March 1961, when President John F. Kennedy, shortly after assuming office, issued Executive Order 10925, establishing the President's Committee on Equal Employment Opportunity. The committee's purpose was to end discrimination in the federal government and any body or organization funded by the federal government. Accordingly, Executive Order 10925 required those contracting with the government to pledge that "the contractor will not discriminate against any employee or applicant for employment because of race, creed, color, or national origin. The contractor will take affirmative action to ensure that applicants are employed, and that employees are treated during employment, without regard to their race, creed, color, or national origin" (http://www.eeoc.gov/abouteeoc/35th/thelaw/eo-10925.html).

Three years later, Title VI of the Civil Rights Act of 1964 expanded upon the original goal of ending discrimination in employment with the following words: "No person in the United States shall, on the ground of race, color or national origin, be excluded from participation in, be denied the benefits of, or be subjected to discrimination under any program or activity receiving federal financial assistance" (http://www.ourdocuments.gov/doc.php?doc=97&page=transcript). The Civil Rights Act of 1964 was a product of the civil rights movement that grew out of an education case, *Brown v. Board of Education*, in which the Supreme Court made it clear that racial segregation was no longer the law of the land. *Brown*, decided shortly after Earl Warren took his seat at chief justice, was the first of many socially progressive decisions handed down during Warren's fifteen-year tenure.

The atmosphere of social unrest that characterized the United States in the 1960s had as much to do with the nation's discontent with the conduct of war in Vietnam as it did with the Warren Court, but the turbulent times gave rise to a conservative "silent majority" that in 1968 elected Republican Richard M. Nixon as the thirty-seventh president of the United States. Nixon had run on a platform that emphasized law and order, and when Warren retired in 1969, Nixon nominated another law-and-order Republican,

1954

■ **May 17**
U.S. Supreme Court decides
Brown v. Board of Education.

1961

■ **March 6**
President John F. Kennedy
issues Executive Order 10925,
establishing the President's
Committee on Equal
Employment Opportunity.

1963

■ **November 22**
Lyndon B. Johnson is sworn in
as president after the
assassination of Kennedy.

1964

■ **July 2**
President Johnson signs the
Civil Rights Act of 1964 into law.

1965

■ **September 24**
President Johnson signs
Executive Order 11246,
requiring equal employment
opportunity.

1967

■ **October 13**
President Johnson amends
Executive Order 11246 to include
affirmative action requirements
benefiting women.

1969

■ **January 20**
Richard M. Nixon is
inaugurated as thirty-seventh
president of the United States.

■ **June 23**
Warren Burger takes the oath
of office as chief justice of the
Supreme Court.

■ **December 23**
Nixon issues a statement
endorsing congressional action
on the "Philadelphia Plan,"
requiring potential federal
contractors to submit affirmative
action goals and timetables.

1971

■ **March 8**
U.S. Supreme Court decides
Griggs v. Duke Power Co.,
holding that hiring and
promotion requirements of
federal contractors, no matter
how seemingly neutral, are
per se illegal if they
disparately affect
disadvantaged people.

Warren Burger, as the next chief justice. Burger's mission was to help curtail many of the reforms enabled by decisions of the previous Court. He was only marginally successful in achieving this goal, but *Bakke* clearly represented at least a partial retreat from what had up to that time been steady expansion of the doctrine of affirmative action.

Four years before *Bakke*, the Court agreed to hear *DeFunis v. Odegaard*, another education case concerning what came to be known as "reverse discrimination." Marco DeFunis, a white applicant to the University of Washington law school, protested his rejection on ground that his academic record was superior to that of all but one of the African Americans admitted the year he applied. Interim court orders forced the school to admit DeFunis, so that by the time his case was decided by the Supreme Court, he had almost finished his program. The Court declared his case moot, making Bakke's case the first one obliging the justices to struggle with the issue of racial preference in publicly funded education.

About the Author

Lewis Franklin Powell, Jr., was born on November 19, 1907, in Suffolk, Virginia, into a family that traced its roots in the state back to the Jamestown colony. He obtained his undergraduate and law degrees from Washington and Lee University in Lexington, Virginia, finally leaving his home state to work on a master of laws degree at Harvard. There, he studied administrative law under Felix Frankfurter, who would leave Harvard shortly thereafter, when President Franklin D. Roosevelt appointed him a U.S. Supreme Court justice.

Powell returned to Virginia, where he practiced law privately until his legal career was interrupted by World War II, when he enlisted in the Army Air Corps. Serving as an intelligence officer, he rose to the rank of colonel before being demobilized as a decorated veteran. After the war, Powell resumed his legal practice in Richmond, but he became more involved in civic and national affairs, helping the Richmond school board comply with the desegregation requirements spelled out in *Brown v. Board of Education II* (1955) and advising a number of presidential commissions.

When Richard Nixon nominated Powell to the Supreme Court in 1971, he did so in part to fulfill his aim to appoint a southerner to the Court, a goal that had been frustrated when two previous appointments, of the southerners Clement Haynsworth and G. Harold Carswell, were defeated. On December 6, 1971, Powell was confirmed by a nearly unanimous vote in the Senate, becoming, at sixty-four, the second-oldest junior associate justice in Supreme Court history.

Powell was one of the few individuals to come to the Court directly from private practice, and his long years of practice disciplined him to take a pragmatic, lawyerly approach on the high bench, one that included adherence to legal precedents even when he personally disagreed with them. He became a centrist, and he often acted as a swing vote on a Court divided between activist holdovers from the Warren years and more conservative recent appointees. This was the role he played in the *Bakke* case, where he cast the deciding vote and wrote an opinion for the plurality that remains a definitive statement about affirmative action as it pertains to public education. After retiring from the Court in 1987, Powell served occasionally on federal appellate courts until his death in Richmond on August 25, 1998, at the age of ninety.

Explanation and Analysis of the Document

◆ Headnotes

Modern recorded legal opinions all follow a similar format. *Regents of the University of California v. Bakke* opens with headnotes, written by the individual or individuals who recorded the case. Headnotes summarize a case but are not part of the Court's official opinion. The first paragraph contains a summary of the facts of the case and is followed by the holding of the case, the legal principle that is binding on all subsequent similar cases. In *Bakke* the holding is especially complex, not to say confusing, because the case was decided by a plurality; that is to say, while a majority of the justices agreed on the outcome of the case (the vote was five to four), the opinion itself was endorsed by fewer than a majority. Here, the reporter says, the decision of the court below, the California Supreme Court, was upheld in its decision that Allan Bakke should be admitted to the University of California at Davis School of Medicine and in the decision that the university's special admissions policy was invalid. However, a majority of the justices also reversed the California Supreme Court's ruling that the university could not take race into account in future admissions.

Justice Powell's opinion setting forth the judgment of the divided Court is summarized, followed by brief summaries of two other opinions. The first of these, written by Justice William J. Brennan, Jr., and endorsed by Justices Byron R. White, Thurgood Marshall, and Harry A. Blackmun, agree with parts of the Court's judgment while disagreeing with others. In addition, White, Marshall, and Blackmun each filed his own written opinion. Another opinion, written by Justice John Paul Stevens and endorsed by Chief Justice Warren Burger, Justice Potter Stewart, and Justice William H. Rehnquist, likewise agreed with some of what Justice Powell wrote while disagreeing with other parts.

Legal representatives of both the petitioner (the University of California) and the respondent (Bakke) are listed, as are those responsible for an enormous number of amicus curiae, or "friend of the court" briefs, urging the Court to rule one way or the other.

◆ Powell's Opinion Announcing the Judgment of the Court

Justice Powell first restates the essential facts of the case, including the decisions of the lower courts that had heard *Bakke* before it reached the Supreme Court. He also states that Burger, Stewart, Rehnquist, and Stevens agree

(albeit in a separate opinion) with his view that the university's admissions policy is unlawful and that Bakke must be admitted to the medical school. Powell's view that the lower court's decision that race cannot play a role in the university's admissions policy is joined (again, in separate opinions) by Brennan, White, Marshall, and Blackmun.

Part I of Powell's opinion details the facts of the case at great length, starting with the history of the University of California Davis School of Medicine and its attempts to diversify its student body, and concluding with the Court's decision to grant the university's petition for certiorari (a term that essentially means that the Court has agreed to hear the case) because of the important constitutional question raised by the case: Are affirmative action programs such as the medical school's permissible under the Fourteenth Amendment and Title VI?

Part II concerns the applicability of Title VI to the case. Although the question of whether a private individual such as Bakke can bring an action under Title VI has not been legally settled, Powell declines to take up this issue, assuming for purposes of this case that Bakke has this right. Powell then revisits the legislative history of Title VI, which was intended to combat discrimination against African Ameri-

Allan Bakke (AP Photo)

cans by entities in receipt of federal funds, actions that congressional backers of the proposed legislation clearly viewed as unconstitutional. In view of this intent, Powell declares, Title VI must be seen as ruling out only such racial classifications as would violate the Fifth Amendment or the equal protection clause of the Fourteenth Amendment.

Part III opens with the observation that while the university accepts that decisions based on race or ethnic heritage are subject to legal review, and while Bakke agrees that not all considerations of race and ethnicity are not illegal on their face, the two sides disagree about what level of judicial scrutiny should be applied in determining the constitutionality of these categories as used in admissions considerations. In addition, while the university asserts that its special admissions program serves the goal of minority representation in the medical school, Bakke claims that the program promotes a racial quota. Powell declares this last a distinction without a difference, saying that although racial classification is not necessarily illegal, any use of such categorization is subject to "the most exacting judicial examination."

Powell next reviews the history of the equal protection clause. Originally meant to protect African Americans, it was suppressed after the Civil War by a reactionary judiciary. By the time it resumed it proper place in American jurisprudence, the nation had become one made up of many minorities, and over the three decades prior to *Bakke* the Court had interpreted the equal protection clause as a means of extending equal protection of the laws to all persons. The university's contention that discrimination against white applicants to its medical school is not suspect because its purpose is benign must therefore be discarded as outmoded and legally unworkable. The university's contention that the Court has applied a lesser degree of scrutiny when approving preferential classifications is brushed aside, as the cases it cites to support these contentions all concern clear constitutional or statutory violations that can be corrected only through such means. The university, however, was under no legal mandate to preference certain groups over others. "When a classification denies an individual opportunities or benefits enjoyed by others solely because of his race or ethnic background, it must be regarded as suspect"—and subject to strict scrutiny.

In Part IV, Powell states that in order to sanction the use of a suspect classification, the state must be able to demonstrate that it is doing so to advance a goal that is both legal and necessary to achieve a vital interest. The university's interest in maintaining a certain percentage of disadvantaged individuals in its student body is inherently discriminatory and unconstitutional. Remedying the effects of "societal discrimination," which the university declares to be one of its goals, is too unclear to justify discriminating against innocent persons solely because of race. And the university has failed to prove that its stated goal of delivering more and better medical care to minority communities will be achieved through its admissions policies. Furthermore, the university's claim that its pursuit of a diverse student body—and thus a truly free exchange of ideas—is protected by the First Amendment in no way offsets the potential damage its policies can inflict on the equal protection of the rights of such individuals as Allan Bakke.

In Part V, Powell addresses the idea that the university's use of racial quotas is meant to achieve a desirable level of ethnic diversity and then discards it because he refuses to accept the university's argument that quotas are the only means of achieving this goal. While an admissions program that considers race as only one factor might achieve the same goal, the university's special admissions program is purposely racially discriminatory, totally excluding applicants who are not African American, Asian, or Latino from consideration for a set number of places in the medical school, regardless of their qualifications. At the same time, preferred applicants are free to compete for every seat in each entering class. The university's special admissions scheme is for these reasons invalid under the Fourteenth Amendment, although the university is not enjoined from taking race into consideration when weighing applicants.

In Part VI, Powell takes up Bakke's request that the university be ordered to admit him. Because the university admits that absent the requirements of its special admissions program it would have no grounds on which to deny Bakke's application, the Court upholds the lower court's judgment granting Bakke's injunction.

◆ Brennan's Opinion, Concurring in Part and Dissenting in Part

Brennan opens with the statement that the Court's judgment reinforces the constitutional mandate empowering state and federal governments to seek equal opportunity for all citizens. Despite the many and differing opinions recorded in the case, he adds, the fundamental meaning of *Bakke* is that the government may take race into account when seeking to redress past inequality. Justices Burger, Stewart, Rehnquist, and Stevens all agree that the university's special admissions program, however, is impermissible under Title VI and that therefore Bakke must be admitted. Justice Powell looks beyond Title VI to the Constitution, finding the university's program unnecessary to achieve its stated goals. These five form a majority upholding the California Supreme Court's ruling that Bakke must be admitted. The four signatories to this opinion, however, have concluded that the university's program is constitutional and therefore vote to reverse the lower court's opinion in its entirety. But because Powell agrees with these four justices that some consideration of race in admissions policies is permissible, a majority of the Court also votes to reverse the opinion below insofar as it prohibits the university from establishing race-conscious admissions policies in the future.

In Part I, Brennan, like Powell, rehearses the history of the Fourteenth Amendment. In light of its goals and the manner in which they were perverted after the Civil War, Brennan finds it unrealistic and unhelpful to assume that discrimination is a thing of the past and the law color-blind.

Brennan begins Part II of his opinion by declaring that Title VI does not violate the Fourteenth Amendment if it is used to remedy past inequality via methods consonant with the amendment. And the legislative history of Title VI indicates that its whole purpose was to lend government the authority to terminate federal funding when a private program disadvantages members of a minority, just as the Fourteenth Amendment prohibits government from performing in such a manner. Brennan, however, finds that this history does not support Bakke's contention that Title VI was intended to bar affirmative action programs. Instead, he says, Title VI was meant to stop federal funding of programs disadvantaging minority groups through segregation. As support for his contention that Title VI does not require racial neutrality, Brennan cites three reasons: (1) The Court has never said that the Constitution is color-blind; (2) Congress clearly intended to use all remedies, including racial factors, to eliminate unconstitutional discrimination; (3) in drafting Title VI, Congress deliberately avoided defining "discrimination," thus affording considerable latitude in enforcing the legislation as society and the law evolve. Literal application of the plain language of Title VI could, as in the present case, lead to results diametrically opposed to those the Congress intended. Regulations intended as interpretations of Title VI make it clear that race-conscious actions are not only tolerated but also required to fulfill the goals of the statute. Finally, congressional action—as well as decisions of the Court—taken in the aftermath of its pas-

sage clearly indicate that racial preferences are an acceptable means of remedying past inequality.

Part III opens with Brennan's assertion that for the Court, human equality has never meant that race is constitutionally irrelevant. Starting with the proposition that racial classifications are not per se invalid under the Fourteenth Amendment, Brennan indicates that "strict scrutiny" of laws compelling affirmative action is necessary only if they violate a fundamental right or contain "suspect classifications." No such right has been violated by the university. What is more, whites do not constitute a group with a history of the kind of unequal treatment the Fourteenth Amendment and Title VI were meant to undo.

The facts in *Bakke*, however, call for something more than the "rational basis" minimal standard of review applied in all affirmative action cases. Instead, Brennan says, gender-discrimination cases suggest a standard that is appropriate here: "Racial classifications designed to further remedial purposes 'must serve important governmental objectives and must be substantially related to achievement of those objectives.'" Racial classifications developed for supposedly benign purposes can and have been misused, so a third, intermediate level of scrutiny is required.

Part IV opens with an endorsement of the university's intention of using racial classifications as a means of redressing long-standing minority underrepresentation in the medical school. Inaction or neutrality in the face of such inequality is insufficient. Brennan cites numerous legal precedents for the proposition that state educational institutions may constitutionally adopt measures—even measures explicitly taking race into account—designed to remedy past racial inequality.

Bakke has asserted that but for the university's special admissions program, he would have been admitted to the medical school. Brennan disputes this claim, adding that the disruption of settled expectations of nonminorities is no argument against affirmative action. Indeed, these expectations are themselves the product of discrimination and therefore "tainted." The special admission program at the medical school was designed to remove pervasive, long-standing inequality; a single admissions standard would only perpetuate underrepresentation of blacks in medicine born of "the habit of discrimination and the cultural tradition of race prejudice."

"The habit of discrimination and the cultural tradition of race prejudice" constitute the type of indirect, unintentional harm the law calls "disparate impact," and it is often cited as validation for programs like Davis's. In cases such as this, affirmative action that can reasonably be expected to counteract factors that have stigmatized particular groups or individuals are legally permissible. On the other hand, Davis's program has not harmed nonminority groups. It cannot even be said to have harmed Allan Bakke, who probably will not suffer long from having been rejected.

Brennan agrees with the university's assertion that there is no real alternative to special admissions as a means of resolving minority underrepresentation in the medical school. He disagrees with Powell's assertion that there is a qualitative difference between setting aside a fixed number of places for minority applicants and simply using race as one among many considerations determining acceptance. The less-specific Harvard plan for attaining diversity, endorsed by Powell, is to Brennan's way of thinking not superior—only less straightforward. He and his fellow signatories therefore believe that the opinion of the California Supreme Court, declaring the Davis program unconstitutional and ordering Bakke's admission to the medical school, should be reversed in its entirety.

◆ White's Opinion

Justice White chose to write a separate opinion regarding the question of whether or not Title VI allows for private causes of action such as Bakke's suit. While all of the other justices believe it does—either in general or for purposes of this case—White disagrees with this assumption, for if its premise is invalid, then the courts have no jurisdiction to hear *Bakke*. For his part, White feels that private lawsuits brought under Title VI are contrary to legislative intent, owing to the existence of an individual's right to bring suit for discrimination under preexisting laws. Congress would therefore have no reason to—and did not—include such a right as part of Title VI. Termination of funding is the sanction provided for violating Title VI, and allowing an individual to sue to cut off funds sabotages all of the carefully spelled out procedural safeguards intended to promote voluntary compliance. Just because Congress intended Title VI to combat discrimination in both public and private programs, it does not follow that the legislature silently allowed a private right of enforcement. Congress has always required that an inferred private cause of action to enforce a statute be both backed by clear legislative intent and in line with the purposes of the statute. Neither of these requirements is satisfied in this case.

◆ Marshall's Opinion

Justice Marshall agrees with the other members of the Court that the university should be permitted to take race into account in its admissions policy; he does not agree that this policy is unconstitutional. Marshall then rehearses the history of slavery in America, noting the irony of the Founding Fathers' assertion in the Declaration of Independence that "all men are created equal" and "endowed … with certain unalienable rights." The implicit protection of slavery found in the Declaration of Independence was reiterated in the Constitution, which counted a slave as three-fifths of a person. Emancipation finally came as a result of the Civil War, but despite passage of the Thirteenth, Fourteenth, and Fifteenth Amendments, African Americans were far from equal to white citizens. The Supreme Court worsened this situation when it began interpreting the Civil Rights amendments in ways that distorted their intended protections, finally declaring in *Plessy v. Ferguson* (1896) that "separate but equal" was the law of the land. And, Marshall maintains, the legacy of this past is still alive in the disfavored position of blacks in American society.

The Fourteenth Amendment was designed to remedy such discrimination, not stand in the way of measures intended to redress long-standing inequality. The Court has in the past endorsed race-conscious remedial measures, and it is ironic that after several hundred years of class-based discrimination against blacks, it is unwilling to uphold a class-based remedy for that discrimination. This case affects far more than one individual and one institution. Marshall fears that just as *Plessy* stopped the movement toward equality after the Civil War, this case will stop the progress *Brown v. Board of Education* jump-started in 1954.

◆ Blackmun's Opinion

Justice Blackmun fears that the goal of racial equality may never be achieved if institutions of higher learning are not permitted to preference disadvantaged applicants. He notes the irony of general approval of preferences given college athletes. The original intent of the Fourteenth Amendment, he says, is essentially that of affirmative action. For Blackmun, the Davis program is not unconstitutional. In order to get beyond racism, he says, we must consider race.

◆ Stevens's Opinion, Joined by Burger, Stewart, and Rehnquist, Concurring in the Judgment in Part and Dissenting in Part

The question of racial considerations should not be a part of this case, which concerns a dispute between an individual and an institution of higher learning, which the lower court decided on grounds other than race. As there is no outstanding issue concerning whether race can be used as a factor in an admissions decision, it is also unnecessary to consider the constitutional issue of whether the admissions policy violated the equal protection clause of the Fourteenth Amendment, as resolution of the dispute between the parties rests on interpretation of statute. Because the act in question clearly prohibits the exclusion of anyone from a federally funded program on the ground of race, Allan Bakke must be admitted to the university's medical program.

Audience

Powell's opinion in *Bakke,* like all Court opinions, was intended to reach the entire nation. Few things have more influence on the lives of Americans than Supreme Court decisions and the rationales behind them. In 1978, when *Bakke* was handed down, sectors of American society were beginning to react to the changes wrought by the civil rights movement, and this decision was an attempt to balance two countervailing forces, which were, in a sense, the same ones that had been with us from the inception of the nation. Bakke's suit was at bottom a reverse-discrimination suit, and it roused so much interest and passion because it involved a well-documented claim by a white man that his rights had been violated by those seeking to advance the rights of a whole class of people whose rights had been long thwarted. How to balance two compelling and competing interests? The justices, as much at odds with one another as the larger

> "The guarantees of the Fourteenth Amendment extend to all persons. Its language is explicit: 'No State shall ... deny to any person within its jurisdiction the equal protection of the laws.' It is settled beyond question that the 'rights created by the first section of the Fourteenth Amendment are, by its terms, guaranteed to the individual. The rights established are personal rights.' ... The guarantee of equal protection cannot mean one thing when applied to one individual and something else when applied to a person of another color. If both are not accorded the same protection, then it is not equal."

(Lewis Franklin Powell, Majority Opinion, Part III)

> "If petitioner's purpose is to assure within its student body some specified percentage of a particular group merely because of its race or ethnic origin, such a preferential purpose must be rejected not as insubstantial but as facially invalid. Preferring members of any one group for no reason other than race or ethnic origin is discrimination for its own sake. This the Constitution forbids."

(Lewis Franklin Powell, Majority Opinion, Part IV)

> "The diversity that furthers a compelling state interest encompasses a far broader array of qualifications and characteristics of which racial or ethnic origin is but a single though important element."

(Lewis Franklin Powell, Majority Opinion, Part V)

society, could not reach consensus, and it was left to Lewis Powell basically to split the difference, granting Bakke his rights even while clearing a path for African Americans to make their way to medical school and other institutions of higher learning by granting schools some latitude in making their own decisions about rectifying the past.

Impact

Bakke was far from a definitive statement on affirmative action, and when William Rehnquist took over from Warren Burger as chief justice, the Court, guided by its new leader's conservative agenda, seemed determined—and empowered—to roll back affirmative action. In cases such as *Richmond v. J.A. Croson* (1989), for example, the Court applied a more stringent standard in scrutinizing state plans for job set-asides than had been employed to evaluate similar plans at the federal level. And in *Adarand Constructors v. Pena* (1995), the Court retreated even farther from endorsing the use of minority set-asides as a remedy for past discrimination. Clearly, after *Bakke*, anything resembling a quota was suspect.

Because Powell had written alone, with none of the other justices signing on to his opinion and several writing their own, many legal commentators doubted that the plurality decision in *Bakke* would hold much sway as precedent. But when the Rehnquist Court revisited the issue of affirmative action in the academy and promoting a color-blind society through equality of education, the justices followed the bifurcated path Powell laid out a quarter century earlier.

Bakke's flexible criteria had not been bent so far as to break. When two cases with similar facts, *Gratz v. Bollinger* and *Grutter v. Bollinger*, reached the Court in

2003, the rationale carefully explicated by Lewis Powell in the earlier decision held up well. While striking down in *Gratz* the rigid point system used to promote affirmative action at the undergraduate level at the University of Michigan, in *Grutter* the Court upheld the university law school's use of race as one factor in admissions deliberations. In addition, the Court amplified the spirit of the *Bakke* decision by holding for the first time that diversity in a student body is a compelling state interest justifying the use of race in university admissions.

Related Documents

"Brown v. Board of Education, 347 U.S. 483 (1954)." FindLaw Web site. http://caselaw.lp.findlaw.com/scripts/getcase.pl?court=US&vol=347&invol=483. Accessed on March 6, 2008. This seminal Supreme Court case, which delineated the academy as the primary venue for working toward a color-blind society, marked a crucial turning point in the civil rights movement.

"Executive Order 10925: Establishing the President's Committee on Equal Employment Opportunity." EEOC Web site. http://www.eeoc.gov/abouteeoc/35th/thelaw/eo-10925.html. Accessed on March 6, 2008. This executive order established the President's Committee on Equal Employment Opportunity, whose purpose was to end discrimination in the federal government and any body or organization funded by the federal government.

"Gratz v. Bollinger, 539 U.S. 244 (2003)" (http://www.oyez.org/cases/2000-2009/2002/2002_02_516/) and "Grutter v. Bollinger, 539 U.S. 306 (2003)" (http://www.oyez.org/cases/2000-2009/2002/2002_02_241). U.S. Supreme Court Media "Oyez" Web site. Accessed on March 6, 2008. This pair of cases about admissions policies at the University of Michigan demonstrates how the affirmative action policies spelled out in *Bakke* have both lasted and evolved over the past quarter century.

"Transcript of Civil Rights Act (1964)." National Archives "Our Documents" Web site. http://www.ourdocuments.gov/doc.php?doc=97&page=transcript. Accessed on March 6, 2008. Title VI of the act expanded upon the original goal of ending discrimination in employment by banning "discrimination under any program or activity receiving federal financial assistance."

"U.S. Constitution: Fourteenth Amendment." FindLaw Web site. http://caselaw.lp.findlaw.com/data/constitution/amendment14/. Accessed on March 6, 2008. In this, perhaps the most important of the Civil War amendments, Congress spelled out its intent that all persons born or naturalized in the United States, including former slaves, are citizens endowed with equal protection under the laws.

Bibliography

■ Books

Anderson, Terry H. *The Pursuit of Fairness: A History of Affirmative Action*. New York: Oxford University Press, 2004.

Ball, Howard. *The Bakke Case: Race, Education, and Affirmative Action*. Lawrence: University Press of Kansas, 2000.

Kellough, J. Edward. *Understanding Affirmative Action: Politics, Discrimination, and the Search for Justice*. Washington, D.C.: Georgetown University Press, 2006.

Paddock, Lisa. *Facts about the Supreme Court of the United States*. New York: H. W. Wilson, 1996.

Schwartz, Bernard. *A History of the Supreme Court*. New York: Oxford University Press, 1993.

Wilkinson, J. Harvie. *From Brown to Bakke: The Supreme Court and School Integration, 1954–1978*. New York: Oxford University Press, 1981.

■ Web Sites

"The Bakke Case and Affirmative Action, 1978." PBS "American Experience" Web site.
   http://www.pbs.org/wgbh/amex/eyesontheprize/story/22_bakke.html. Accessed on March 6, 2008.

"Regents of the University of California v. Bakke (1978): Background Summary and Questions." Landmark Supreme Court Cases Web site.
   http://www.landmarkcases.org/bakke/background2.html. Accessed on March 6, 2008.

Questions for Further Study

1. Although his administration submitted an amicus brief supporting both of the petitioners in the Michigan cases, President George W. Bush's response to the Court's decisions in *Grutter* and *Gratz* stressed his hope that America will become a color-blind society. Is it possible to realize this hope if affirmative action were to be outlawed in the education arena?

2. Do you agree that the Harvard plan for achieving student body diversity that Powell holds up as a model is preferable to that of the University of California at Davis Medical School? Why or why not?

3. Do you agree with Justice Brennan that Powell's separation of racial quotas from consideration of race in admissions policies is a distinction without a difference? Why or why not?

Glossary

due process	a portion of the Fifth and, later, the Fourteenth Amendment preventing the federal and state governments from depriving any person of life, liberty, or property "without due process of law"
equal protection	clause from the Fourteenth Amendment ensuring that no individual or class of individuals can be denied rights enjoyed by others who exist in similar circumstances
jurisdiction	power to hear and decide cases

REGENTS OF THE UNIVERSITY OF CALIFORNIA V. BAKKE

The Medical School of the University of California at Davis (hereinafter Davis) had two admissions programs for the entering class of 100 students—the regular admissions program and the special admissions program. Under the regular procedure, candidates whose overall under-graduate grade point averages fell below 2.5 on a scale of 4.0 were summarily rejected. About one out of six applicants was then given an interview, following which he was rated on a scale of 1 to 100 by each of the committee members (five in 1973 and six in 1974), his rating being based on the interviewers' summaries, his overall grade point average, his science courses grade point average, his Medical College Admissions Test (MCAT) scores, letters of recommendation, extracurricular activities, and other biographical data, all of which resulted in a total "benchmark score." The full admissions committee then made offers of admission on the basis of their review of the applicant's file and his score, considering and acting upon applications as they were received. The committee chairman was responsible for placing names on the waiting list and had discretion to include persons with "special skills." A separate committee, a majority of whom were members of minority groups, operated the special admissions program. The 1973 and 1974 application forms, respectively, asked candidates whether they wished to be considered as "economically and/or educationally disadvantaged" applicants and members of a "minority group" (blacks, Chicanos, Asians, American Indians). If an applicant of a minority group was found to be "disadvantaged," he would be rated in a manner similar to the one employed by the general admissions committee. Special candidates, however, did not have to meet the 2.5 grade point cutoff and were not ranked against candidates in the general admissions process. About one-fifth of the special applicants were invited for interviews in 1973 and 1974, following which they were given benchmark scores, and the top choices were then given to the general admissions committee, which could reject special candidates for failure to meet course requirements or other specific deficiencies. The special committee continued to recommend candidates until 16 special admission selections had been made. During a four-year period 63 minority students were admitted to Davis under the special program and 44 under the general program. No disadvantaged whites were admitted under the special program, though many applied. Respondent, a white male, applied to Davis in 1973 and 1974, in both years being considered only under the general admissions program. Though he had a 468 out of 500 score in 1973, he was rejected since no general applicants with scores less than 470 were being accepted after respondent's application, which was filed late in the year, had been processed and completed. At that time four special admission slots were still unfilled. In 1974 respondent applied early, and though he had a total score of 549 out of 600, he was again rejected. In neither year was his name placed on the discretionary waiting list. In both years special applicants were admitted with significantly lower scores than respondent's. After his second rejection, respondent filed this action in state court for mandatory, injunctive, and declaratory relief to compel his admission to Davis, alleging that the special admissions program operated to exclude him on the basis of his race in violation of the Equal Protection Clause of the Fourteenth Amendment, a provision of the California Constitution, and 601 of Title VI of the Civil Rights Act of 1964, which provides, inter alia, that no person shall on the ground of race or color be excluded from participating in any program receiving federal financial assistance. Petitioner cross-claimed for a declaration that its special admissions program was lawful. The trial court found that the special program operated as a racial quota, because minority applicants in that program were rated only against one another, and 16 places in the class of 100 were reserved for them. Declaring that petitioner could not take race into account in making admissions decisions, the program was held to violate the Federal and State Constitutions and Title VI. Respondent's admission was not ordered, however, for lack of proof that he would have been admitted but for the special program. The California Supreme Court, applying a strict-scrutiny standard, concluded that the special admissions program was not the least intrusive means of achieving the goals of the admittedly compelling state interests of integrating the medical profession and increasing the number of doctors willing to serve minority patients. Without passing on the state constitutional or federal statutory grounds the court held that petitioner's special admissions program violated the Equal Protection Clause. Since petitioner could not satisfy its burden of demonstrating that respondent, absent the special program, would not have been admitted, the court ordered his admission to Davis.

Held: The judgment below is affirmed insofar as it orders respondent's admission to Davis and invalidates petitioner's special admissions program, but is reversed insofar as it prohibits petitioner from taking race into account as a factor in its future admissions decisions.

18 Cal. 3d 34, 553 P.2d 1152, affirmed in part and reversed in part.

MR. JUSTICE POWELL, concluded:

1. Title VI proscribes only those racial classifications that would violate the Equal Protection Clause if employed by a State or its agencies. Pp. 281-287.

2. Racial and ethnic classifications of any sort are inherently suspect and call for the most exacting judicial scrutiny. While the goal of achieving a diverse student body is sufficiently compelling to justify consideration of race in admissions decisions under some circumstances, petitioner's special admissions program, which forecloses consideration to persons like respondent, is unnecessary to the achievement of this compelling goal and therefore invalid under the Equal Protection Clause. Pp. 287-320.

3. Since petitioner could not satisfy its burden of proving that respondent would not have been admitted even if there had been no spe-

cial admissions program, he must be admitted. P. 320.

MR. JUSTICE BRENNAN, MR. JUSTICE WHITE, MR. JUSTICE MARSHALL, and MR. JUSTICE BLACKMUN concluded:

1. Title VI proscribes only those racial classifications that would violate the Equal Protection Clause if employed by a State or its agencies. Pp. 328-355.

2. Racial classifications call for strict judicial scrutiny. Nonetheless, the purpose of overcoming substantial, chronic minority underrepresentation in the medical profession is sufficiently important to justify petitioner's remedial use of race. Thus, the judgment below must be reversed in that it prohibits race from being used as a factor in university admissions. Pp. 355-379.

MR. JUSTICE STEVENS, joined by THE CHIEF JUSTICE, MR. JUSTICE STEWART, and MR. JUSTICE REHNQUIST, being of the view that whether race can ever be a factor in an admissions policy is not an issue here; that Title VI applies; and that respondent was excluded from Davis in violation of Title VI, concurs in the Court's judgment insofar as it affirms the judgment of the court below ordering respondent admitted to Davis. Pp. 408-421.

POWELL, J., announced the Court's judgment and filed an opinion expressing his views of the case, in Parts I, III-A, and V-C of which WHITE, J., joined; and in Parts I and V-C of which BRENNAN, MARSHALL, and BLACKMUN, JJ., joined. BRENNAN, WHITE, MARSHALL, and BLACKMUN, JJ., filed an opinion concurring in the judgment in part and dissenting in part, post, p. 324. WHITE, J., post, p. 379, MARSHALL, J., post, p. 387, and BLACKMUN, J., post, p. 402, filed separate opinions. STEVENS, J., filed an opinion concurring in the judgment in part and dissenting in part, in which BURGER, C. J., and STEWART and REHNQUIST, JJ., joined, post, p. 408.

Archibald Cox argued the cause for petitioner. With him on the briefs were Paul J. Mishkin, Jack B. Owens, and Donald L. Reidhaar.

Reynold H. Colvin argued the cause and filed briefs for respondent.

Solicitor General McCree argued the cause for the United States as amicus curiae. With him on the briefs were Attorney General Bell, Assistant Attorney General Days, Deputy Solicitor General Wallace, Brian K. Landsberg, Jessica Dunsay Silver, Miriam R. Eisenstein, and Vincent F. O'Rourke.

MR. JUSTICE POWELL announced the judgment of the Court.

This case presents a challenge to the special admissions program of the petitioner, the Medical School of the University of California at Davis, which is designed to assure the admission of a specified number of students from certain minority groups. The Superior Court of California sustained respondent's challenge, holding that petitioner's program violated the California Constitution, Title VI of the Civil Rights Act of 1964, 42 U.S.C. 2000d et seq., and the Equal Protection Clause of the Fourteenth Amendment. The court enjoined petitioner from considering respondent's race or the race of any other applicant in making admissions decisions. It refused, however, to order respondent's admission to the Medical School, holding that he had not carried his burden of proving that he would have been admitted but for the constitutional and statutory violations. The Supreme Court of California affirmed those portions of the trial court's judgment declaring the special admissions program unlawful and enjoining petitioner from considering the race of any applicant. It modified that portion of the judgment denying respondent's requested injunction and directed the trial court to order his admission.

For the reasons stated in the following opinion, I believe that so much of the judgment of the California court as holds petitioner's special admissions program unlawful and directs that respondent be admitted to the Medical School must be affirmed. For the reasons expressed in a separate opinion, my Brothers THE CHIEF JUSTICE, MR. JUSTICE STEWART, MR. JUSTICE REHNQUIST, and MR. JUSTICE STEVENS concur in this judgment.

I also conclude for the reasons stated in the following opinion that the portion of the court's judgment enjoining petitioner from according any consideration to race in its admissions process must be reversed. For reasons expressed in separate opinions, my Brothers MR. JUSTICE BRENNAN, MR. JUSTICE WHITE, MR. JUSTICE MARSHALL, and MR. JUSTICE BLACKMUN concur in this judgment.

Affirmed in part and reversed in part.

I

The Medical School of the University of California at Davis opened in 1968 with an entering class of 50 students. In 1971, the size of the entering class was increased to 100 students, a level at which it remains. No admissions program for disadvantaged or minority students existed when the school opened, and the first class contained three Asians but no blacks, no Mexican-Americans, and no American Indians. Over the next two years, the faculty devised a special admissions program to increase the representation of "disadvantaged" students in each Medical School class. The special program consisted of a separate admissions system operating in coordination with the regular admissions process.

Under the regular admissions procedure, a candidate could submit his application to the Medical School beginning in July of the year preceding the academic year for which admission was sought. Record 149. Because of the large number of applications, the admissions committee screened each one to select candidates for further consideration. Candidates whose overall undergraduate grade point averages fell below 2.5 on a scale of 4.0 were summarily rejected. Id., at 63. About one out of six applicants was invited for a personal interview. Ibid. Following the interviews, each candidate was rated on a scale of 1 to 100 by his interviewers and four other members of the admissions committee. The rating embraced the interviewers' summaries, the candidate's overall grade point average, grade point average in science courses, scores on the Medical College Admissions Test (MCAT), letters of recommendation, extracurricular activities, and other biographical data. Id., at 62. The ratings were added together to arrive at each candidate's "benchmark" score. Since five committee members rated each candidate in 1973, a perfect score was 500; in 1974, six members rated each candidate, so that a perfect score was 600. The full committee then reviewed the file and scores of each applicant and made offers of admission on a "rolling" basis. The chairman was responsible for placing names on the waiting list. They were not placed in strict numerical order; instead, the chairman had discretion to include persons with "special skills." Id., at 63-64.

The special admissions program operated with a separate committee, a majority of whom were members of minority groups. Id., at 163. On the 1973 application form, candidates were asked to indicate whether they wished to be considered as "economically and/or educationally disadvantaged" applicants; on the 1974 form the question was whether they wished to be considered as members of a "minority group," which the Medical School apparently viewed as "Blacks," "Chicanos," "Asians," and "American Indians." Id., at 65-66, 146, 197, 203-205, 216-218. If these questions were answered affirmatively, the application was forwarded to the special admissions committee. No formal definition of "disadvantaged" was ever produced, id., at 163-164, but the chairman of the special committee screened each application to see whether it reflected economic or educational deprivation. Having passed this initial hurdle, the applications then were rated by the special committee in a fashion similar to that used by the general admissions committee, except that special candidates did not have to meet the 2.5 grade point average cutoff applied to regular applicants. About one-fifth of the total number of special applicants were invited for interviews in 1973 and 1974. Following each interview, the special committee assigned each special applicant a benchmark score. The special committee then presented its top choices to the general admissions committee. The latter did not rate or compare the special candidates against the general applicants, id., at 388, but could reject recommended special candidates for failure to meet course requirements or other specific deficiencies. Id., at 171-172. The special committee continued to recommend special applicants until a number prescribed by faculty vote were admitted. While the overall class size was still 50, the prescribed number was 8; in 1973 and 1974, when the class size had doubled to 100, the prescribed number of special admissions also doubled, to 16. Id., at 164, 166.

From the year of the increase in class size—1971—through 1974, the special program resulted in the admission of 21 black students, 30 Mexican-Americans, and 12 Asians, for a total of 63 minority students. Over the same period, the regular admissions program produced 1 black, 6 Mexican-Americans, and 37 Asians, for a total of 44 minority students. Although disadvantaged whites applied to the special program in large numbers, see n. 5, supra, none received an offer of admission through that process. Indeed, in 1974, at least, the special committee explicitly considered only "disadvantaged" special applicants who were members of one of the designated minority groups. Record 171.

Allan Bakke is a white male who applied to the Davis Medical School in both 1973 and 1974. In both years Bakke's application was considered under the general admissions program, and he received an interview. His 1973 interview was with Dr. Theodore C. West, who considered Bakke "a very desirable applicant to [the] medical school." Id., at 225. Despite a strong benchmark score of 468 out of 500, Bakke was rejected. His application had come late in the year, and no applicants in the general admissions process with scores below 470 were accepted after Bakke's application was completed. Id., at 69. There were four special admissions slots unfilled at that time, however, for which Bakke was not considered. Id., at 70. After his 1973 rejection, Bakke wrote to Dr. George H. Lowrey, Associate Dean and Chairman of the Admissions Committee, protesting that the special admissions program operated as a racial and ethnic quota. Id., at 259.

Bakke's 1974 application was completed early in the year. Id., at 70. His student interviewer gave him an overall rating of 94, finding him "friendly, well tempered, conscientious and delightful to speak with." Id., at 229. His faculty interviewer was, by coincidence, the same Dr. Lowrey to whom he had written in protest of the special admissions program. Dr. Lowrey found Bakke "rather limited in his approach" to the problems of the medical profession and found disturbing Bakke's "very definite opinions which were based more on his personal viewpoints than upon a study of the total problem." Id., at 226. Dr. Lowrey gave Bakke the lowest of his six ratings, an 86; his total was 549 out of 600. Id., at 230. Again, Bakke's application was rejected. In neither year did the chairman of the admissions committee, Dr. Lowrey, exercise his discretion to place Bakke on the waiting list. Id., at 64. In both years, applicants were admitted under the special program with grade point averages, MCAT scores, and benchmark scores significantly lower than Bakke's.

After the second rejection, Bakke filed the instant suit in the Superior Court of California. He sought mandatory, injunctive, and declaratory relief compelling his admission to the Medical School. He alleged that the Medical School's special admissions program operated to exclude him from the school on the basis of his race, in violation of his rights under the Equal Protection Clause of the Fourteenth Amendment, Art. I, 21, of the California Constitution, and 601 of Title VI of the Civil Rights Act of 1964, 78 Stat. 252, 42 U.S.C. 2000d. The University cross-complained for a declaration that its special admissions program was lawful. The trial court found that the special program operated as a racial quota, because minority applicants in the special program were rated only against one another, Record 388, and 16 places in the class of 100 were reserved for them. Id., at 295-296. Declaring that the University could not take race into account in making admissions decisions, the trial court held the challenged program violative of the Federal Constitution, the State Constitution, and Title VI. The court refused to order Bakke's admission, however, holding that he had failed to carry his burden of proving that he would have been admitted but for the existence of the special program.

Bakke appealed from the portion of the trial court judgment denying him admission, and the University appealed from the decision that its special admissions program was unlawful and the order enjoining it from considering race in the processing of applications. The Supreme Court of California transferred the case directly from the trial court, "because of the importance of the issues involved." 18 Cal. 3d 34, 39, 553 P.2d 1152, 1156 (1976). The California court accepted the findings of the trial court with respect to the University's program. Because the special admissions program involved a racial classification, the Supreme Court held itself bound to apply strict scrutiny. Id., at 49, 553 P.2d, at 1162-1163. It then turned to the goals the University presented as justifying the special program. Although the court agreed that the goals of integrating the medical profession and increasing the number of physicians willing to serve members of minority groups were compelling state interests, id., at 53, 553 P.2d, at 1165, it concluded that the special admissions program was not the least intrusive means of achieving those goals. Without passing on the state constitutional or the federal statutory grounds cited in the trial court's judgment, the California court held that the Equal Protection Clause of the Fourteenth Amendment required that "no applicant may be rejected because of his race, in favor of another who is less qualified, as measured by standards applied without regard to race." Id., at 55, 553 P.2d, at 1166.

Turning to Bakke's appeal, the court ruled that since Bakke had established that the University had discriminated against him on the basis of his race, the burden of proof shifted to the University to demonstrate that he would not have been admitted even in the absence of the special admissions program. Id., at 63-64, 553 P.2d, at 1172. The court analogized Bakke's situation to that of a plaintiff under Title VII of the Civil Rights Act of 1964, 42 U.S.C. 2000e-17 (1970 ed., Supp. V), see, e. g., *Franks v. Bowman Transportation Co.*, 424 U.S. 747,

772 (1976). 18 Cal. 3d, at 63-64, 553 P.2d, at 1172. On this basis, the court initially ordered a remand for the purpose of determining whether, under the newly allocated burden of proof, Bakke would have been admitted to either the 1973 or the 1974 entering class in the absence of the special admissions program. App. A to Application for Stay 48. In its petition for rehearing below, however, the University conceded its inability to carry that burden. App. B to Application for Stay A19-A20. The California court thereupon amended its opinion to direct that the trial court enter judgment ordering Bakke's admission to the Medical School. 18 Cal. 3d, at 64, 553 P.2d, at 1172. That order was stayed pending review in this Court. 429 U.S. 953 (1976). We granted certiorari to consider the important constitutional issue. 429 U.S. 1090 (1977).

II

In this Court the parties neither briefed nor argued the applicability of Title VI of the Civil Rights Act of 1964. Rather, as had the California court, they focused exclusively upon the validity of the special admissions program under the Equal Protection Clause. Because it was possible, however, that a decision on Title VI might obviate resort to constitutional interpretation, see *Ashwander v. TVA*, 297 U.S. 288, 346-348 (1936) (concurring opinion), we requested supplementary briefing on the statutory issue. 434 U.S. 900 (1977).

◆ A

At the outset we face the question whether a right of action for private parties exists under Title VI. Respondent argues that there is a private right of action, invoking the test set forth in *Cort v. Ash*, 422 U.S. 66, 78 (1975). He contends that the statute creates a federal right in his favor, that legislative history reveals an intent to permit private actions, that such actions would further the remedial purposes of the statute, and that enforcement of federal rights under the Civil Rights Act generally is not relegated to the States. In addition, he cites several lower court decisions which have recognized or assumed the existence of a private right of action. Petitioner denies the existence of a private right of action, arguing that the sole function of 601, see n. 11, supra, was to establish a predicate for administrative action under 602, 78 Stat. 252, 42 U.S.C. 2000d-1. In its view, administrative curtailment of federal funds under that section was the only sanction to be imposed upon recipients that violated 601. Petitioner also points out that Title VI contains no explicit grant of a private right of action, in contrast to Titles II, III, IV, and VII, of the same statute, 42 U.S.C. 2000a-3 (a), 2000b-2, 2000c-8, and 2000e-5 (f) (1970 ed. and Supp. V).

We find it unnecessary to resolve this question in the instant case. The question of respondent's right to bring an action under Title VI was neither argued nor decided in either of the courts below, and this Court has been hesitant to review questions not addressed below. *McGoldrick v. Compagnie Generale Transatlantique*, 309 U.S. 430, 434-435 (1940). See also *Massachusetts v. Westcott*, 431 U.S. 322 (1977); *Cardinale v. Louisiana*, 394 U.S. 437, 439 (1969). Cf. *Singleton v. Wulff*, 428 U.S. 106, 121 (1976). We therefore do not address this difficult issue. Similarly, we need not pass upon petitioner's claim that private plaintiffs under Title VI must exhaust administrative remedies. We assume, only for the purposes of this case, that respondent has a right of action under Title VI. See *Lau v. Nichols*, 414 U.S. 563, 571 n. 2 (1974) (STEWART, J., concurring in result).

◆ **B**

The language of 601, 78 Stat. 252, like that of the Equal Protection Clause, is majestic in its sweep:

> "No person in the United States shall, on the ground of race, color, or national origin, be excluded from participation in, be denied the benefits of, or be subjected to discrimination under any program or activity receiving Federal financial assistance."

The concept of "discrimination," like the phrase "equal protection of the laws," is susceptible of varying interpretations, for as Mr. Justice Holmes declared, "[a] word is not a crystal, transparent and unchanged, it is the skin of a living thought and may vary greatly in color and content according to the circumstances and the time in which it is used." *Towne v. Eisner*, 245 U.S. 418, 425 (1918). We must, therefore, seek whatever aid is available in determining the precise meaning of the statute before us. Train v. Colorado Public Interest Research Group, 426 U.S. 1, 10 (1976), quoting *United States v. American Trucking Assns.*, 310 U.S. 534, 543-544 (1940). Examination of the voluminous legislative history of Title VI reveals a congressional intent to halt federal funding of entities that violate a prohibition of racial

discrimination similar to that of the Constitution. Although isolated statements of various legislators, taken out of context, can be marshaled in support of the proposition that 601 enacted a purely color-blind scheme, without regard to the reach of the Equal Protection Clause, these comments must be read against the background of both the problem that Congress was addressing and the broader view of the statute that emerges from a full examination of the legislative debates.

The problem confronting Congress was discrimination against Negro citizens at the hands of recipients of federal moneys. Indeed, the color blindness pronouncements cited in the margin at n. 19, generally occur in the midst of extended remarks dealing with the evils of segregation in federally funded programs. Over and over again, proponents of the bill detailed the plight of Negroes seeking equal treatment in such programs. There simply was no reason for Congress to consider the validity of hypothetical preferences that might be accorded minority citizens; the legislators were dealing with the real and pressing problem of how to guarantee those citizens equal treatment.

In addressing that problem, supporters of Title VI repeatedly declared that the bill enacted constitutional principles. For example, Representative Celler, the Chairman of the House Judiciary Committee and floor manager of the legislation in the House, emphasized this in introducing the bill:

> "The bill would offer assurance that hospitals financed by Federal money would not deny adequate care to Negroes. It would prevent abuse of food distribution programs whereby Negroes have been known to be denied food surplus supplies when white persons were given such food. It would assure Negroes the benefits now accorded only white students in programs of high[er] education financed by Federal funds. It would, in short, assure the existing right to equal treatment in the enjoyment of Federal funds. It would not destroy any rights of private property or freedom of association." 110 Cong. Rec. 1519 (1964).

Other sponsors shared Representative Celler's view that Title VI embodied constitutional principles.

In the Senate, Senator Humphrey declared that the purpose of Title VI was "to insure that Federal funds are spent in accordance with the Constitution and the moral sense of the Nation." Id., at 6544. Senator Ribicoff agreed that Title VI embraced the constitutional standard: "Basically, there is a constitutional restriction against discrimination in the use of federal funds; and title VI simply spells out the procedure to be used in enforcing that restriction." Id., at 13333. Other Senators expressed similar views.

Further evidence of the incorporation of a constitutional standard into Title VI appears in the repeated refusals of the legislation's supporters precisely to define the term "discrimination." Opponents sharply criticized this failure, but proponents of the bill merely replied that the meaning of "discrimination" would be made clear by reference to the Constitution or other existing law. For example, Senator Humphrey noted the relevance of the Constitution:

"As I have said, the bill has a simple purpose. That purpose is to give fellow citizens— Negroes—the same rights and opportunities that white people take for granted. This is no more than what was preached by the prophets, and by Christ Himself. It is no more than what our Constitution guarantees." Id., at 6553.

In view of the clear legislative intent, Title VI must be held to proscribe only those racial classifications that would violate the Equal Protection Clause or the Fifth Amendment.

III

◆ A

Petitioner does not deny that decisions based on race or ethnic origin by faculties and administrations of state universities are reviewable under the Fourteenth Amendment. See, e. g., *Missouri ex rel. Gaines v. Canada*, 305 U.S. 337 (1938); *Sipuel v. Board of Regents*, 332 U.S. 631 (1948); *Sweatt v. Painter*, 339 U.S. 629 (1950); *McLaurin v. Oklahoma State Regents*, 339 U.S. 637 (1950). For his part, respondent does not argue that all racial or ethnic classifications are per se invalid. See, e. g., *Hirabayashi v. United States*, 320 U.S. 81 (1943); *Korematsu v. United States*, 323 U.S. 214 (1944); *Lee v. Washington*, 390 U.S. 333, 334 (1968) (Black, Harlan, and STEWART, JJ., concurring); *United Jewish Organizations v. Carey*, 430 U.S. 144 (1977). The parties do disagree as to the level of judicial scrutiny to be applied to the special admissions program. Petitioner argues that the court below erred in applying strict scrutiny, as

this inexact term has been applied in our cases. That level of review, petitioner asserts, should be reserved for classifications that disadvantage "discrete and insular minorities." See *United States v. Carolene Products Co.*, 304 U.S. 144, 152 n. 4 (1938). Respondent, on the other hand, contends that the California court correctly rejected the notion that the degree of judicial scrutiny accorded a particular racial or ethnic classification hinges upon membership in a discrete and insular minority and duly recognized that the "rights established [by the Fourteenth Amendment] are personal rights." *Shelley v. Kraemer*, 334 U.S. 1, 22 (1948).

En route to this crucial battle over the scope of judicial review, the parties fight a sharp preliminary action over the proper characterization of the special admissions program. Petitioner prefers to view it as establishing a "goal" of minority representation in the Medical School. Respondent, echoing the courts below, labels it a racial quota.

This semantic distinction is beside the point: The special admissions program is undeniably a classification based on race and ethnic background. To the extent that there existed a pool of at least minimally qualified minority applicants to fill the 16 special admissions seats, white applicants could compete only for 84 seats in the entering class, rather than the 100 open to minority applicants. Whether this limitation is described as a quota or a goal, it is a line drawn on the basis of race and ethnic status.

The guarantees of the Fourteenth Amendment extend to all persons. Its language is explicit: "No State shall ... deny to any person within its jurisdiction the equal protection of the laws." It is settled beyond question that the "rights created by the first section of the Fourteenth Amendment are, by its terms, guaranteed to the individual. The rights established are personal rights," *Shelley v. Kraemer*, supra, at 22. Accord, *Missouri ex rel. Gaines v. Canada*, supra, at 351; *McCabe v. Atchison, T. & S. F. R. Co.*, 235 U.S. 151, 161-162 (1914). The guarantee of equal protection cannot mean one thing when applied to one individual and something else when applied to a person of another color. If both are not accorded the same protection, then it is not equal.

Nevertheless, petitioner argues that the court below erred in applying strict scrutiny to the special admissions program because white males, such as respondent, are not a "discrete and insular minority" requiring extraordinary protection from the majoritarian political process. Carolene Products Co., supra, at 152-153, n. 4. This rationale, however, has never been invoked in our decisions as a prerequisite to subjecting racial or ethnic distinctions to strict scrutiny. Nor has this Court held that discreteness and insularity constitute necessary preconditions to a holding that a particular classification is invidious. See, e. g., *Skinner v. Oklahoma ex rel. Williamson*, 316 U.S. 535, 541 (1942); *Carrington v. Rash*, 380 U.S. 89, 94-97 (1965). These characteristics may be relevant in deciding whether or not to add new types of classifications to the list of "suspect" categories or whether a particular classification survives close examination. See, e. g., *Massachusetts Board of Retirement v. Murgia*, 427 U.S. 307, 313 (1976) (age); *San Antonio Independent School Dist. v. Rodriguez*, 411 U.S. 1, 28 (1973) (wealth); *Graham v. Richardson*, 403 U.S. 365, 372 (1971) (aliens). Racial and ethnic classifications, however, are subject to stringent examination without regard to these additional characteristics. We declared as much in the first cases explicitly to recognize racial distinctions as suspect:

> "Distinctions between citizens solely because of their ancestry are by their very nature odious to a free people whose institutions are founded upon the doctrine of equality." Hirabayashi, 320 U.S., at 100.

> "[A]ll legal restrictions which curtail the civil rights of a single racial group are immediately suspect. That is not to say that all such restrictions are unconstitutional. It is to say that courts must subject them to the most rigid scrutiny." Korematsu, 323 U.S., at 216.

The Court has never questioned the validity of those pronouncements. Racial and ethnic distinctions of any sort are inherently suspect and thus call for the most exacting judicial examination.

◆ B

This perception of racial and ethnic distinctions is rooted in our Nation's constitutional and demographic history. The Court's initial view of the Fourteenth Amendment was that its "one pervading purpose" was "the freedom of the slave race, the security and firm establishment of that freedom, and the protection of the newly-made freeman and citizen from the oppressions of those who had formerly exercised dominion over him." Slaughter-House Cases, 16 Wall. 36, 71 (1873). The Equal Protection Clause, however, was "[v]irtually strangled in infancy by post-civil-war judicial reactionism." It was relegated to decades of relative desuetude while the Due Process Clause of the Fourteenth Amendment, after a short germinal period, flourished as a cornerstone in the Court's defense of property and liberty of contract. See, e. g., *Mugler v. Kansas*, 123 U.S. 623, 661 (1887); *Allgeyer v. Louisiana*, 165 U.S. 578 (1897); *Lochner v. New York*, 198 U.S. 45 (1905). In that cause, the Fourteenth Amendment's "one pervading purpose" was displaced. See, e. g., *Plessy v. Ferguson*, 163 U.S. 537 (1896). It was only as the era of substantive due process came to a close, see, e. g., *Nebbia v. New York*, 291 U.S. 502 (1934); *West Coast Hotel Co. v. Parrish*, 300 U.S. 379 (1937), that the Equal Protection Clause began to attain a genuine measure of vitality, see, e. g., *United States v. Carolene Products*, 304 U.S. 144 (1938); *Skinner v. Oklahoma ex rel. Williamson*, supra.

By that time it was no longer possible to peg the guarantees of the Fourteenth Amendment to the struggle for equality of one racial minority. During the dormancy of the Equal Protection Clause, the United States had become a Nation of minorities. Each had to struggle—and to some extent struggles still—to overcome the prejudices not of a monolithic majority, but of a "majority" composed of various minority groups of whom it was said—perhaps unfairly in many cases—that a shared characteristic was a willingness to disadvantage other groups. As the Nation filled with the stock of many lands, the reach of the Clause was gradually extended to all ethnic groups seeking protection from official discrimination. See *Strauder v. West Virginia*, 100 U.S. 303, 308 (1880) (Celtic Irishmen) (dictum); *Yick Wo v. Hopkins*, 118 U.S. 356 (1886) (Chinese); *Truax v. Raich*, 239 U.S. 33, 41 (1915) (Austrian resident aliens); Korematsu, supra (Japanese); *Hernandez v. Texas*, 347 U.S. 475 (1954) (Mexican-Americans). The guarantees of equal protection, said the Court in Yick Wo, "are universal in their application, to all persons within the territorial jurisdiction, without regard to any differences of race, of color, or of nationality; and the equal protection of the laws is a pledge of the protection of equal laws." 118 U.S., at 369.

Although many of the Framers of the Fourteenth Amendment conceived of its primary function as bridging the vast distance between members of the Negro race and the white "majority," Slaughter-House Cases, supra, the Amendment itself was framed in universal terms, without reference to color, ethnic origin, or condition of prior servitude.

As this Court recently remarked in interpreting the 1866 Civil Rights Act to extend to claims of racial discrimination against white persons, "the 39th Congress was intent upon establishing in the federal law a broader principle than would have been necessary simply to meet the particular and immediate plight of the newly freed Negro slaves." *McDonald v. Santa Fe Trail Transportation Co.*, 427 U.S. 273, 296 (1976). And that legislation was specifically broadened in 1870 to ensure that "all persons," not merely "citizens," would enjoy equal rights under the law. See *Runyon v. McCrary*, 427 U.S. 160, 192-202 (1976) (WHITE, J., dissenting). Indeed, it is not unlikely that among the Framers were many who would have applauded a reading of the Equal Protection Clause that states a principle of universal application and is responsive to the racial, ethnic, and cultural diversity of the Nation. See, e. g., Cong. Globe, 39th Cong., 1st Sess., 1056 (1866) (remarks of Rep. Niblack); id., at 2891-2892 (remarks of Sen. Conness); id., 40th Cong., 2d Sess., 883 (1868) (remarks of Sen. Howe) (Fourteenth Amendment "protect[s] classes from class legislation"). See also Bickel, The Original Understanding and the Segregation Decision, 69 Harv. L. Rev. 1, 60-63 (1955).

Over the past 30 years, this Court has embarked upon the crucial mission of interpreting the Equal Protection Clause with the view of assuring to all persons "the protection of equal laws," Yick Wo, supra, at 369, in a Nation confronting a legacy of slavery and racial discrimination. See, e. g., *Shelley v. Kraemer*, 334 U.S. 1 (1948); *Brown v. Board of Education*, 347 U.S. 483 (1954); *Hills v. Gautreaux*, 425 U.S. 284 (1976). Because the landmark decisions in this area arose in response to the continued exclusion of Negroes from the mainstream of American society, they could be characterized as involving discrimination by the "majority" white race against the Negro minority. But they need not be read as depending upon that characterization for their results. It suffices to say that "[o]ver the years, this Court has consistently repudiated '[d]istinctions between citizens solely because of their ancestry' as being 'odious to a free people whose institutions are founded upon the doctrine of equality.'" *Loving v. Virginia*, 388 U.S. 1, 11 (1967), quoting Hirabayashi, 320 U.S., at 100.

Petitioner urges us to adopt for the first time a more restrictive view of the Equal Protection Clause and hold that discrimination against members of the white "majority" cannot be suspect if its purpose can be characterized as "benign." The clock of our liberties, however, cannot be turned back to 1868. *Brown v. Board of Education*, supra, at 492; accord, *Loving v. Virginia*, supra, at 9. It is far too late to argue that the guarantee of equal protection to all persons permits the recognition of special wards entitled to a degree of protection greater than that accorded others. "The Fourteenth Amendment is not directed solely against discrimination due to a 'two-class theory'—that is, based upon differences between 'white' and Negro." Hernandez, 347 U.S., at 478.

Once the artificial line of a "two-class theory" of the Fourteenth Amendment is put aside, the difficulties entailed in varying the level of judicial review according to a perceived "preferred" status of a particular racial or ethnic minority are intractable. The concepts of "majority" and "minority" necessarily reflect temporary arrangements and political judgments. As observed above, the white "majority" itself is composed of various minority groups, most of which can lay claim to a history of prior discrimination at the hands of the State and private individuals. Not all of these groups can receive preferential treatment and corresponding judicial tolerance of distinctions drawn in terms of race and nationality, for then the only "majority" left would be a new minority of white Anglo-Saxon Protestants. There is no principled basis for deciding which groups would merit "heightened judicial solicitude" and which would not. Courts would be asked to evaluate the extent of the prejudice and consequent harm suffered by various minority groups. Those whose societal injury is thought to exceed some arbitrary level of tolerability then would be entitled to preferential classifications at the expense of individuals belonging to other groups. Those classifications would be free from exacting judicial scrutiny. As these preferences began to have their desired effect, and the consequences of past discrimination were undone, new judicial rankings would be necessary. The kind of variable sociological and political analysis necessary to produce such rankings simply does not lie within the judicial competence—even if they otherwise were politically feasible and socially desirable.

Moreover, there are serious problems of justice connected with the idea of preference itself. First, it may not always be clear that a so-called preference is in fact benign. Courts may be asked to validate burdens imposed upon individual members of a particular group in order to advance the group's general interest. See *United Jewish Organizations v. Carey*, 430 U.S., at 172-173 (BRENNAN, J., concurring in part). Nothing in the Constitution supports the notion that individuals may be asked to suffer otherwise impermissible burdens in order to enhance the societal standing of their ethnic groups. Second, preferential programs may only reinforce common stereotypes holding that certain groups are unable to achieve success without special protection based on a factor having no relationship to individual worth. See *DeFunis v. Odegaard*, 416 U.S. 312, 343 (1974) (Douglas, J., dissenting). Third, there is a measure of inequity in forcing innocent persons in respondent's position to bear the burdens of redressing grievances not of their making.

By hitching the meaning of the Equal Protection Clause to these transitory considerations, we would be holding, as a constitutional principle, that judicial scrutiny of classifications touching on racial and ethnic background may vary with the ebb and flow of political forces. Disparate constitutional tolerance of such classifications well may serve to exacerbate racial and ethnic antagonisms rather than alleviate them. United Jewish Organizations, supra, at 173-174 (BRENNAN, J., concurring in part). Also, the mutability of a constitutional principle, based upon shifting political and social judgments, undermines the chances for consistent application of the Constitution from one generation to the next, a critical feature of its coherent interpretation. *Pollock v. Farmers' Loan & Trust Co.*, 157 U.S. 429, 650-651 (1895) (White, J., dissenting). In expounding the Constitution, the Court's role is to discern "principles sufficiently absolute to give them roots throughout the community and continuity over significant periods of time, and to lift them above the level of the pragmatic political judgments of a particular time and place." A. Cox, The Role of the Supreme Court in American Government 114 (1976).

If it is the individual who is entitled to judicial protection against classifications based upon his racial or ethnic background because such distinctions impinge upon personal rights, rather than the individual only because of his membership in a particular group, then constitutional standards may be applied consistently. Political judgments regarding the necessity for the particular classification may be weighed in the constitutional balance, *Korematsu v. United States*, 323 U.S. 214 (1944), but the standard of justification will remain constant. This is as it should be, since those political judgments are the product of rough compromise struck by contending groups within the democratic process. When they touch upon an individual's race or ethnic background, he is entitled to a judicial determination that

the burden he is asked to bear on that basis is precisely tailored to serve a compelling governmental interest. The Constitution guarantees that right to every person regardless of his background. *Shelley v. Kraemer*, 334 U.S., at 22; *Missouri ex rel. Gaines v. Canada*, 305 U.S., at 351.

◆ **C**

Petitioner contends that on several occasions this Court has approved preferential classifications without applying the most exacting scrutiny. Most of the cases upon which petitioner relies are drawn from three areas: school desegregation, employment discrimination, and sex discrimination. Each of the cases cited presented a situation materially different from the facts of this case.

The school desegregation cases are inapposite. Each involved remedies for clearly determined constitutional violations. E. g., *Swann v. Charlotte-Mecklenburg Board of Education*, 402 U.S. 1 (1971); *McDaniel v. Barresi*, 402 U.S. 39 (1971); *Green v. County School Board*, 391 U.S. 430 (1968). Racial classifications thus were designed as remedies for the vindication of constitutional entitlement. Moreover, the scope of the remedies was not permitted to exceed the extent of the violations. E. g., *Dayton Board of Education v. Brinkman*, 433 U.S. 406 (1977); *Milliken v. Bradley*, 418 U.S. 717 (1974); see *Pasadena City Board of Education v. Spangler*, 427 U.S. 424 (1976). See also *Austin Independent School Dist. v. United States*, 429 U.S. 990, 991-995 (1976) (POWELL, J., concurring). Here, there was no judicial determination of constitutional violation as a predicate for the formulation of a remedial classification.

The employment discrimination cases also do not advance petitioner's cause. For example, in *Franks v. Bowman Transportation Co.*, 424 U.S. 747 (1976), we approved a retroactive award of seniority to a class of Negro truckdrivers who had been the victims of discrimination—not just by society at large, but by the respondent in that case. While this relief imposed some burdens on other employees, it was held necessary "to make [the victims] whole for injuries suffered on account of unlawful employment discrimination.'" Id., at 763, quoting *Albemarle Paper Co. v. Moody*, 422 U.S. 405, 418 (1975). The Courts of Appeals have fashioned various types of racial preferences as remedies for constitutional or statutory violations resulting in identified, race-based injuries to individuals held entitled to the preference. E. g., *Bridgeport Guardians, Inc. v. Bridgeport Civil Service Commission*, 482 F.2d 1333 (CA2

1973); *Carter v. Gallagher*, 452 F.2d 315 (CA8 1972), modified on rehearing en banc, id., at 327. Such preferences also have been upheld where a legislative or administrative body charged with the responsibility made determinations of past discrimination by the industries affected, and fashioned remedies deemed appropriate to rectify the discrimination. E. g., *Contractors Association of Eastern Pennsylvania v. Secretary of Labor*, 442 F.2d 159 (CA3), cert. denied, 404 U.S. 854 (1971); *Associated General Contractors of Massachusetts, Inc. v. Altshuler*, 490 F.2d 9 (CA1 1973), cert. denied, 416 U.S. 957 (1974); cf. *Katzenbach v. Morgan*, 384 U.S. 641 (1966). But we have never approved preferential classifications in the absence of proved constitutional or statutory violations.

Nor is petitioner's view as to the applicable standard supported by the fact that gender-based classifications are not subjected to this level of scrutiny. E. g., *Califano v. Webster*, 430 U.S. 313, 316-317 (1977); *Craig v. Boren*, 429 U.S. 190, 211 n. (1976) (POWELL, J., concurring). Gender-based distinctions are less likely to create the analytical and practical problems present in preferential programs premised on racial or ethnic criteria. With respect to gender there are only two possible classifications. The incidence of the burdens imposed by preferential classifications is clear. There are no rival groups which can claim that they, too, are entitled to preferential treatment. Classwide questions as to the group suffering previous injury and groups which fairly can be burdened are relatively manageable for reviewing courts. See, e. g., *Califano v. Goldfarb*, 430 U.S. 199, 212-217 (1977); *Weinberger v. Wiesenfeld*, 420 U.S. 636, 645 (1975). The resolution of these same questions in the context of racial and ethnic preferences presents far more complex and intractable problems than gender-based classifications. More importantly, the perception of racial classifications as inherently odious stems from a lengthy and tragic history that gender-based classifications do not share. In sum, the Court has never viewed such classification as inherently suspect or as comparable to racial or ethnic classifications for the purpose of equal protection analysis.

Petitioner also cites *Lau v. Nichols*, 414 U.S. 563 (1974), in support of the proposition that discrimination favoring racial or ethnic minorities has received judicial approval without the exacting inquiry ordinarily accorded "suspect" classifications. In Lau, we held that the failure of the San Francisco school system to provide remedial English instruction for some 1,800 students of oriental ancestry who spoke no English amounted to a violation of Title VI of the Civil Rights Act of 1964, 42 U.S.C. 2000d, and the regulations promulgated thereunder. Those regulations required remedial instruction where inability to understand English excluded children of foreign ancestry from participation in educational programs. 414 U.S., at 568. Because we found that the students in Lau were denied "a meaningful opportunity to participate in the educational program," ibid., we remanded for the fashioning of a remedial order.

Lau provides little support for petitioner's argument. The decision rested solely on the statute, which had been construed by the responsible administrative agency to reach educational practices "which have the effect of subjecting individuals to discrimination," ibid. We stated: "Under these state-imposed standards there is no equality of treatment merely by providing students with the same facilities, textbooks, teachers, and curriculum; for students who do not understand English are effectively foreclosed from any meaningful education." Id., at 566. Moreover, the "preference" approved did not result in the denial of the relevant benefit—"meaningful opportunity to participate in the educational program"—to anyone else. No other student was deprived by that preference of the ability to participate in San Francisco's school system, and the applicable regulations required similar assistance for all students who suffered similar linguistic deficiencies. Id., at 570-571 (STEWART, J., concurring in result).

In a similar vein, petitioner contends that our recent decision in *United Jewish Organizations v. Carey*, 430 U.S. 144 (1977), indicates a willingness to approve racial classifications designed to benefit certain minorities, without denominating the classifications as "suspect." The State of New York had redrawn its reapportionment plan to meet objections of the Department of Justice under 5 of the Voting Rights Act of 1965, 42 U.S.C. 1973c (1970 ed., Supp. V). Specifically, voting districts were redrawn to enhance the electoral power of certain "nonwhite" voters found to have been the victims of unlawful "dilution" under the original reapportionment plan. United Jewish Organizations, like Lau, properly is viewed as a case in which the remedy for an administrative finding of discrimination encompassed measures to improve the previously disadvantaged group's ability to participate, without excluding individuals belonging to any other group from enjoyment of the relevant opportunity—meaningful participation in the electoral process.

In this case, unlike Lau and United Jewish Organizations, there has been no determination by the legislature or a responsible administrative agency that the University engaged in a discriminatory practice requiring remedial efforts. Moreover, the operation of petitioner's special admissions program is quite different from the remedial measures approved in those cases. It prefers the designated minority groups at the expense of other individuals who are totally foreclosed from competition for the 16 special admissions seats in every Medical School class. Because of that foreclosure, some individuals are excluded from enjoyment of a state-provided benefit—admission to the Medical School—they otherwise would receive. When a classification denies an individual opportunities or benefits enjoyed by others solely because of his race or ethnic background, it must be regarded as suspect. E. g., *McLaurin v. Oklahoma State Regents*, 339 U.S., at 641-642.

IV

We have held that in "order to justify the use of a suspect classification, a State must show that its purpose or interest is both constitutionally permissible and substantial, and that its use of the classification is 'necessary … to the accomplishment' of its purpose or the safeguarding of its interest." In re Griffiths, 413 U.S. 717, 721-722 (1973) (footnotes omitted); *Loving v. Virginia*, 388 U.S., at 11; *McLaughlin v. Florida*, 379 U.S. 184, 196 (1964). The special admissions program purports to serve the purposes of: (i) "reducing the historic deficit of traditionally disfavored minorities in medical schools and in the medical profession," Brief for Petitioner 32; (ii) countering the effects of societal discrimination; (iii) increasing the number of physicians who will practice in communities currently underserved; and (iv) obtaining the educational benefits that flow from an ethnically diverse student body. It is necessary to decide which, if any, of these purposes is substantial enough to support the use of a suspect classification.

◆ A

If petitioner's purpose is to assure within its student body some specified percentage of a particular group merely because of its race or ethnic origin, such a preferential purpose must be rejected not as insubstantial but as facially invalid. Preferring members of any one group for no reason other than race or ethnic origin is discrimination for its own sake.

This the Constitution forbids. E. g., *Loving v. Virginia*, supra, at 11; *McLaughlin v. Florida*, supra, at 196; *Brown v. Board of Education*, 347 U.S. 483 (1954).

◆ B

The State certainly has a legitimate and substantial interest in ameliorating, or eliminating where feasible, the disabling effects of identified discrimination. The line of school desegregation cases, commencing with Brown, attests to the importance of this state goal and the commitment of the judiciary to affirm all lawful means toward its attainment. In the school cases, the States were required by court order to redress the wrongs worked by specific instances of racial discrimination. That goal was far more focused than the remedying of the effects of "societal discrimination," an amorphous concept of injury that may be ageless in its reach into the past.

We have never approved a classification that aids persons perceived as members of relatively victimized groups at the expense of other innocent individuals in the absence of judicial, legislative, or administrative findings of constitutional or statutory violations. See, e. g., *Teamsters v. United States*, 431 U.S. 324, 367-376 (1977); United Jewish Organizations, 430 U.S., at 155-156; *South Carolina v. Katzenbach*, 383 U.S. 301, 308 (1966). After such findings have been made, the governmental interest in preferring members of the injured groups at the expense of others is substantial, since the legal rights of the victims must be vindicated. In such a case, the extent of the injury and the consequent remedy will have been judicially, legislatively, or administrative defined. Also, the remedial action usually remains subject to continuing oversight to assure that it will work the least harm possible to other innocent persons competing for the benefit. Without such findings of constitutional or statutory violations, it cannot be said that the government has any greater interest in helping one individual than in refraining from harming another. Thus, the government has no compelling justification for inflicting such harm.

Petitioner does not purport to have made, and is in no position to make, such findings. Its broad mission is education, not the formulation of any legislative policy or the adjudication of particular claims of illegality. For reasons similar to those stated in Part III of this opinion, isolated segments of our vast governmental structures are not competent to make those decisions, at least in the absence of legislative mandates and legislatively determined criteria. Cf. *Hampton v. Mow*

Sun Wong, 426 U.S. 88 (1976); n. 41, supra. Before relying upon these sorts of findings in establishing a racial classification, a governmental body must have the authority and capability to establish, in the record, that the classification is responsive to identified discrimination. See, e. g., *Califano v. Webster*, 430 U.S., at 316-321; *Califano v. Goldfarb*, 430 U.S., at 212-217. Lacking this capability, petitioner has not carried its burden of justification on this issue.

Hence, the purpose of helping certain groups whom the faculty of the Davis Medical School perceived as victims of "societal discrimination" does not justify a classification that imposes disadvantages upon persons like respondent, who bear no responsibility for whatever harm the beneficiaries of the special admissions program are thought to have suffered. To hold otherwise would be to convert a remedy heretofore reserved for violations of legal rights into a privilege that all institutions throughout the Nation could grant at their pleasure to whatever groups are perceived as victims of societal discrimination. That is a step we have never approved. Cf. *Pasadena City Board of Education v. Spangler*, 427 U.S. 424 (1976).

◆ C

Petitioner identifies, as another purpose of its program, improving the delivery of health-care services to communities currently underserved. It may be assumed that in some situations a State's interest in facilitating the health care of its citizens is sufficiently compelling to support the use of a suspect classification. But there is virtually no evidence in the record indicating that petitioner's special admissions program is either needed or geared to promote that goal. The court below addressed this failure of proof:

> "The University concedes it cannot assure that minority doctors who entered under the program, all of whom expressed an 'interest' in practicing in a disadvantaged community, will actually do so. It may be correct to assume that some of them will carry out this intention, and that it is more likely they will practice in minority communities than the average white doctor. (See Sandalow, Racial Preferences in Higher Education: Political Responsibility and the Judicial Role (1975) 42 U. Chi. L. Rev. 653, 688.) Nevertheless, there are more precise and reliable ways to identify applicants who are genuinely interested in the medical problems of minorities than by race. An applicant of whatever race who has demonstrated

his concern for disadvantaged minorities in the past and who declares that practice in such a community is his primary professional goal would be more likely to contribute to alleviation of the medical shortage than one who is chosen entirely on the basis of race and disadvantage. In short, there is no empirical data to demonstrate that any one race is more selflessly socially oriented or by contrast that another is more selfishly acquisitive." 18 Cal. 3d, at 56, 553 P.2d, at 1167.

Petitioner simply has not carried its burden of demonstrating that it must prefer members of particular ethnic groups over all other individuals in order to promote better health-care delivery to deprived citizens. Indeed, petitioner has not shown that its preferential classification is likely to have any significant effect on the problem.

◆ D

The fourth goal asserted by petitioner is the attainment of a diverse student body. This clearly is a constitutionally permissible goal for an institution of higher education. Academic freedom, though not a specifically enumerated constitutional right, long has been viewed as a special concern of the First Amendment. The freedom of a university to make its own judgments as to education includes the selection of its student body. Mr. Justice Frankfurter summarized the "four essential freedoms" that constitute academic freedom:

> "It is the business of a university to provide that atmosphere which is most conductive to speculation, experiment and creation. It is an atmosphere in which there prevail 'the four essential freedoms' of a university—to determine for itself on academic grounds who may teach, what may be taught, how it shall be taught, and who may be admitted to study." *Sweezy v. New Hampshire*, 354 U.S. 234, 263 (1957) (concurring in result).

Our national commitment to the safeguarding of these freedoms within university communities was emphasized in *Keyishian v. Board of Regents*, 385 U.S. 589, 603 (1967):

> "Our Nation is deeply committed to safeguarding academic freedom which is of transcendent value to all of us and not merely to the teach-

ers concerned. That freedom is therefore a special concern of the First Amendment…. The Nation's future depends upon leaders trained through wide exposure to that robust exchange of ideas which discovers truth 'out of a multitude of tongues, [rather] than through any kind of authoritative selection.' *United States v. Associated Press*, 52 F. Supp. 362, 372."

The atmosphere of "speculation, experiment and creation"—so essential to the quality of higher education—is widely believed to be promoted by a diverse student body. As the Court noted in Keyishian, it is not too much to say that the "nation's future depends upon leaders trained through wide exposure" to the ideas and mores of students as diverse as this Nation of many peoples.

Thus, in arguing that its universities must be accorded the right to select those students who will contribute the most to the "robust exchange of ideas," petitioner invokes a countervailing constitutional interest, that of the First Amendment. In this light, petitioner must be viewed as seeking to achieve a goal that is of paramount importance in the fulfillment of its mission.

It may be argued that there is greater force to these views at the undergraduate level than in a medical school where the training is centered primarily on professional competency. But even at the graduate level, our tradition and experience lend support to the view that the contribution of diversity is substantial. In *Sweatt v. Painter*, 339 U.S., at 634, the Court made a similar point with specific reference to legal education:

> "The law school, the proving ground for legal learning and practice, cannot be effective in isolation from the individuals and institutions with which the law interacts. Few students and no one who has practiced law would choose to study in an academic vacuum, removed from the interplay of ideas and the exchange of views with which the law is concerned."

Physicians serve a heterogeneous population. An otherwise qualified medical student with a particular background—whether it be ethnic, geographic, culturally advantaged or disadvantaged—may bring to a professional school of medicine experiences, outlooks, and ideas that enrich the training of its student body and better equip its graduates to render with understanding their vital service to humanity.

Ethnic diversity, however, is only one element in a range of factors a university properly may consider in attaining the goal of a heterogeneous student body. Although a university must have wide discretion in making the sensitive judgments as to who should be admitted, constitutional limitations protecting individual rights may not be disregarded. Respondent urges—and the courts below have held—that petitioner's dual admissions program is a racial classification that impermissibly infringes his rights under the Fourteenth Amendment. As the interest of diversity is compelling in the context of a university's admissions program, the question remains whether the program's racial classification is necessary to promote this interest. In re Griffiths, 413 U.S., at 721-722.

V

◆ A

It may be assumed that the reservation of a specified number of seats in each class for individuals from the preferred ethnic groups would contribute to the attainment of considerable ethnic diversity in the student body. But petitioner's argument that this is the only effective means of serving the interest of diversity is seriously flawed. In a most fundamental sense the argument misconceives the nature of the state interest that would justify consideration of race or ethnic background. It is not an interest in simple ethnic diversity, in which a specified percentage of the student body is in effect guaranteed to be members of selected ethnic groups, with the remaining percentage an undifferentiated aggregation of students. The diversity that furthers a compelling state interest encompasses a far broader array of qualifications and characteristics of which racial or ethnic origin is but a single though important element. Petitioner's special admissions program, focused solely on ethnic diversity, would hinder rather than further attainment of genuine diversity.

Nor would the state interest in genuine diversity be served by expanding petitioner's two-track system into a multitrack program with a prescribed number of seats set aside for each identifiable category of applicants. Indeed, it is inconceivable that a university would thus pursue the logic of petitioner's two-track program to the illogical end of insulating each category of applicants with certain desired qualifications from competition with all other applicants.

The experience of other university admissions programs, which take race into account in achieving the educational diversity valued by the First Amendment, demonstrates that the assignment of a fixed number of places to a minority group is not a necessary means toward that end. An illuminating example is found in the Harvard College program:

"In recent years Harvard College has expanded the concept of diversity to include students from disadvantaged economic, racial and ethnic groups. Harvard College now recruits not only Californians or Louisianans but also blacks and Chicanos and other minority students....

"In practice, this new definition of diversity has meant that race has been a factor in some admission decisions. When the Committee on Admissions reviews the large middle group of applicants who are 'admissible' and deemed capable of doing good work in their courses, the race of an applicant may tip the balance in his favor just as geographic origin or a life spent on a farm may tip the balance in other candidates' cases. A farm boy from Idaho can bring something to Harvard College that a Bostonian cannot offer. Similarly, a black student can usually bring something that a white person cannot offer.... [See Appendix hereto.]

"In Harvard College admissions the Committee has not set target-quotas for the number of blacks, or of musicians, football players, physicists or Californians to be admitted in a given year.... But that awareness [of the necessity of including more than a token number of black students] does not mean that the Committee sets a minimum number of blacks or of people from west of the Mississippi who are to be admitted. It means only that in choosing among thousands of applicants who are not only 'admissible' academically but have other strong qualities, the Committee, with a number of criteria in mind, pays some attention to distribution among many types and categories of students." App. to Brief for Columbia University, Harvard University, Stanford University, and the University of Pennsylvania, as Amici Curiae 2-3.

In such an admissions program, race or ethnic background may be deemed a "plus" in a particular applicant's file, yet it does not insulate the individual

from comparison with all other candidates for the available seats. The file of a particular black applicant may be examined for his potential contribution to diversity without the factor of race being decisive when compared, for example, with that of an applicant identified as an Italian-American if the latter is thought to exhibit qualities more likely to promote beneficial educational pluralism. Such qualities could include exceptional personal talents, unique work or service experience, leadership potential, maturity, demonstrated compassion, a history of overcoming disadvantage, ability to communicate with the poor, or other qualifications deemed important. In short, an admissions program operated in this way is flexible enough to consider all pertinent elements of diversity in light of the particular qualifications of each applicant, and to place them on the same footing for consideration, although not necessarily according them the same weight. Indeed, the weight attributed to a particular quality may vary from year to year depending upon the "mix" both of the student body and the applicants for the incoming class.

This kind of program treats each applicant as an individual in the admissions process. The applicant who loses out on the last available seat to another candidate receiving a "plus" on the basis of ethnic background will not have been foreclosed from all consideration for that seat simply because he was not the right color or had the wrong surname. It would mean only that his combined qualifications, which may have included similar nonobjective factors, did not outweigh those of the other applicant. His qualifications would have been weighed fairly and competitively, and he would have no basis to complain of unequal treatment under the Fourteenth Amendment.

It has been suggested that an admissions program which considers race only as one factor is simply a subtle and more sophisticated—but no less effective—means of according racial preference than the Davis program. A facial intent to discriminate, however, is evident in petitioner's preference program and not denied in this case. No such facial infirmity exists in an admissions program where race or ethnic background is simply one element—to be weighed fairly against other elements—in the selection process. "A boundary line," as Mr. Justice Frankfurter remarked in another connection, "is none the worse for being narrow." *McLeod v. Dilworth*, 322 U.S. 327, 329 (1944). And a court would not assume that a university, professing to employ a facially nondiscriminatory admissions policy, would operate it as a cover for the functional equivalent of a quota system. In short, good faith would be presumed in the absence of a showing to the contrary in the manner permitted by our cases. See, e. g., *Arlington Heights v. Metropolitan Housing Dev. Corp.*, 429 U.S. 252 (1977); *Washington v. Davis*, 426 U.S. 229 (1976); *Swain v. Alabama*, 380 U.S. 202 (1965).

◆ B

In summary, it is evident that the Davis special admissions program involves the use of an explicit racial classification never before countenanced by this Court. It tells applicants who are not Negro, Asian, or Chicano that they are totally excluded from a specific percentage of the seats in an entering class. No matter how strong their qualifications, quantitative and extracurricular, including their own potential for contribution to educational diversity, they are never afforded the chance to compete with applicants from the preferred groups for the special admissions seats. At the same time, the preferred applicants have the opportunity to compete for every seat in the class.

The fatal flaw in petitioner's preferential program is its disregard of individual rights as guaranteed by the Fourteenth Amendment. *Shelley v. Kraemer*, 334 U.S., at 22. Such rights are not absolute. But when a State's distribution of benefits or imposition of burdens hinges on ancestry or the color of a person's skin, that individual is entitled to a demonstration that the challenged classification is necessary to promote a substantial state interest. Petitioner has failed to carry this burden. For this reason, that portion of the California court's judgment holding petitioner's special admissions program invalid under the Fourteenth Amendment must be affirmed.

◆ C

In enjoining petitioner from ever considering the race of any applicant, however, the courts below failed to recognize that the State has a substantial interest that legitimately may be served by a properly devised admissions program involving the competitive consideration of race and ethnic origin. For this reason, so much of the California court's judgment as enjoins petitioner from any consideration of the race of any applicant must be reversed.

VI

With respect to respondent's entitlement to an injunction directing his admission to the Medical School, petitioner has conceded that it could not carry its burden of proving that, but for the existence of its unlawful special admissions program, respondent still would not have been admitted. Hence, respondent is entitled to the injunction, and that portion of the judgment must be affirmed.

MR. JUSTICE BRENNAN, MR. JUSTICE WHITE, MR. JUSTICE MARSHALL, and MR. JUSTICE BLACKMUN join Parts I and V-C of this opinion. MR. JUSTICE WHITE also joins Part III-A of this opinion.

RONALD REAGAN'S "EVIL EMPIRE" SPEECH

"They are the focus of evil in the modern world."

Overview

When President Ronald Reagan spoke to the National Association of Evangelicals (NAE) in Orlando, Florida, on March 8, 1983, he used the term *evil empire* to describe the Soviet Union. Millions of Americans heard or read the phrase and remembered it for years; it was powerful language that in Reagan's view explained why the United States had been locked in a cold war with the Union of Soviet Socialist Republics since the end of World War II. The speech was not mainly about the cold war, the Soviet Union, or international affairs, however. It was about moral values, particularly how they underlay American democracy and how political disagreements were often, at bottom, moral conflicts. Reagan delivered the speech at a time when his defense and foreign policies divided the American people. He was hoping to enlist the members of the NAE and other Christian conservatives to support his national security policies as they had his social policies. His language in this speech, however, touched a nerve and produced divided reactions. During Reagan's second term as president, as he sought to improve U.S.-Soviet relations, the words *evil empire* became an awkward reminder of an earlier time of international tension. By 1988, as the cold war was starting to end, Reagan said that the term no longer applied.

Context

Ronald Reagan was a popular president, with his approval ratings in the polls usually registering above 60 percent. In early 1983, however, Reagan's popularity was at a low point, with only 37 percent of Americans approving of his performance as president. The severe recession of 1981 and 1982, from which the economy had only begun to recover, accounted for much of the discontent. Critics also complained about the big increases in defense spending during Reagan's first two years in office, especially since the president had simultaneously cut the budgets for some social programs for the poor and needy. Reagan maintained that the sharp increases in defense appropriations

were essential because the Soviets had carried out an enormous buildup of their military forces during the past decade. Still, many people worried about the arms race and maintained that both the Americans and Soviets had far more nuclear weapons than they needed to protect national security. A proposal to freeze the nuclear arsenals of both sides as a first step in controlling the arms race gained the support of two-thirds of the American people, according to polls. The Reagan administration nonetheless opposed a nuclear freeze, which in the president's view would have locked in Soviet advantages in some categories of weapons. The president also worried that the popularity of such a freeze might prevent Congress from approving the administration's defense budget.

Reagan also endured criticism for his blunt condemnations of Communism and of Soviet policy. Soviet-American relations sharply deteriorated during the last year of Jimmy Carter's presidency and the first two years in which Reagan occupied the White House. Gone were the days of détente, which began in the early 1970s during the presidency of Richard Nixon, when U.S. officials hoped that negotiations on arms control and trade would lead to the relaxation of tensions with the Soviet Union. Although he himself was a staunch anti-Communist, Nixon refrained from the public condemnations of Communism that had been common in the cold war rhetoric of earlier presidents. Détente, however, had many opponents, and the policy ended when the Soviets invaded Afghanistan on December 25, 1979. When Reagan became president, he was determined to pursue tough policies against Soviet expansion. His harsh denunciations of Soviet actions and Communist principles seemed an abrupt return to the language of the early cold war. Reagan's hard-line policies won considerable praise, but they also produced anxiety and even alarm, especially as arms-control negotiations stalled, the U.S. military buildup continued, and international tensions rose. By the beginning of 1983, polls showed that the American people were almost evenly divided over whether Reagan was effectively handling relations with the Soviets.

Some of Reagan's advisers thought the president needed to energize supporters to counter the growing support for a nuclear freeze as well as the mounting discontent with his Soviet policies. The speechwriter Anthony Dolan

1962

■ **June 25**
The Supreme Court rules in *Engel v. Vitale* that mandatory prayer in public schools is unconstitutional.

1973

■ **January 22**
In the case of *Roe v. Wade*, the Supreme Court rules that a woman has a right to secure an abortion during the first three months of her pregnancy.

1981

■ **January 29**
President Reagan holds his first news conference and asserts that Soviet leaders reserve "the right to commit any crime, to lie, to cheat" to achieve their goal of world revolution (Reagan, *Public Papers: 1981*, p. 57).

1982

■ **June 8**
Reagan speaks to the British Parliament and declares that Marxism-Leninism will end up "on the ashheap of history" (Cannon, p. 272).

1983

■ **March 8**
President Reagan gives his "Evil Empire" Speech at the annual convention of the National Association of Evangelicals in Orlando, Florida.

■ **May 4**
By a vote of 278–148, the House of Representatives approves a resolution asking President Reagan to negotiate with the Soviet Union a freeze in nuclear weapons as a first step in reducing those armaments.

1984

■ **January 16**
Reagan gives a televised address on Soviet-American relations and states that while there are many differences between the two nations, they share a common interest in avoiding war and reducing armaments.

encouraged the president to accept an invitation to speak at the annual meeting of the NAE. Dolan argued that Reagan could mobilize an important constituency—conservative Christians, who had backed him in the election of 1980 and supported his social policies. Some of these Christian conservatives were members of the NAE, and Reagan could reassure them that he would continue to work for the causes they endorsed, such as restricting abortion and allowing prayer in public schools, and also urge them to make a similar commitment to the success of the administration's national security policies. The NAE, which had more than three million members, could be a formidable ally in the battle over a nuclear freeze; the organization's support could offset the endorsement of a nuclear freeze by other church groups.

Dolan wrote drafts of the president's NAE speech, but Reagan put his own stamp on the final version. The president was extremely adept at using his skills as an actor to establish rapport with his audience. He was also responsible for many of the actual lines he delivered, as he wrote or revised substantial portions of his own speeches. Reagan eliminated references in Dolan's draft to liberal antagonists, instead characterizing the principal opponents of administration policies as those who wanted to remove religious values from public affairs. He reworded an opening joke and added a story about a father who imagined what life would be like if his daughters lived under Communist rule. The most memorable part of the speech was about Communism and the Soviet Union, but most of the text revolved around hot-button social issues of the early 1980s. The goal was to enlist social conservatives in what would be one of the last battles of the cold war.

About the Author

Ronald Reagan was born on February 6, 1911, in Tampico, Illinois, into a poor family that moved several times before settling in Dixon, Illinois. Despite the hardships of his youth, Reagan developed a strong sense of optimism that he carried with him throughout his life. His mother, a member of the Christian Church (Disciples of Christ), taught him that everything occurred according to God's plan. Reagan graduated from Eureka College in 1932, when the Great Depression was most severe, yet he still found a job as a sports announcer at a radio station in Davenport, Iowa. Sports announcing soon allowed Reagan to embark on a movie career. In 1937, he signed a contract with Warner Bros. Pictures, and he gave solid performances mainly in what were then called B movies: low-budget films that were the second halves of the double features that commonly played in theaters. Between April 1942 and December 1945, Reagan served in the Army Air Forces, making official films connected to the U.S. war effort during World War II.

After the war, as his film career declined, Reagan became involved in politics. Between 1947 and 1952, he was president of the Screen Actors Guild, a union representing performers in film and television. As the cold war emerged and fears about Communist influence in the motion picture industry rose, Reagan testified before the House Un-American Activities Committee in 1947 and provided names of alleged Communists to the Federal Bureau of Investigation. Although he had been a liberal Democrat, his politics became more conservative, especially after he began working for General Electric in 1954. He was the host of the weekly television drama series *General Electric Theater*, and he also spoke at General Electric plants around the country. His talks became increasingly political, and he developed a few basic ideas that shaped his thinking on public issues for the rest of his life. He denounced high taxes; he believed that the government had grown so big that it interfered too much in the economy and undermined personal responsibility; and he called for stronger efforts to stop the spread of international Communism. In 1962, he registered as a Republican. Two years later, he gave a famous speech in support of the Republican candidate for president, Barry Goldwater.

After Goldwater's defeat, Reagan made his first run for political office, winning the governorship of California in 1966 by appealing to voter discontent with rising crime rates, urban riots, and anti–Vietnam War protests. In 1975, at the end of his second term, Reagan left the governor's mansion and challenged President Gerald R. Ford for the Republican nomination for president. Ford won a narrow victory over Reagan but lost the election to Jimmy Carter. Four years later, Reagan easily secured his party's nomination and overwhelmed Carter in November.

As president, Reagan proposed sweeping changes in both domestic and foreign policy. Reagan's first priority when he took office on January 20, 1981, was to lift the nation's economy out of stagflation, a severe and persistent combination of high inflation and unemployment. Believing that government was the source of the nation's economic problems, not the solution to them, Reagan secured cuts in income tax rates, reductions in federal economic regulations, and decreases in the rate of spending on social welfare programs. Although the economy fell in 1981 into a severe recession that lasted through 1982, it recovered the following year, with inflation falling to its lowest level in more than a decade. Reagan also made drastic changes in national security policies. He secured sharp increases in defense spending, which he said were necessary to protect against Soviet efforts to gain power and influence around the world. Reagan easily won reelection in 1984, and his second term witnessed a remarkable improvement in Soviet-American relations after Mikhail Gorbachev came to power in Moscow in 1985. Reagan and Gorbachev held several meetings, established a cooperative relationship, negotiated important treaties, and made progress in ending the cold war. Despite the notorious Iran-Contra scandal over the provision of arms to secure the release of hostages in the Middle East and the illegal support of counterrevolutionaries in Nicaragua, Reagan left office a popular president in January 1989. He died of complications related to Alzheimer's disease on June 5, 2004.

Time Line

1985

■ **March 11**
Mikhail Gorbachev becomes General Secretary of the Central Committee of the Communist Party of the Soviet Union.

■ **November 19–21**
Reagan and Gorbachev meet for the first time in Geneva, Switzerland; at the end of the summit Reagan states that the meeting provided a fresh start in U.S.-Soviet relations.

1988

■ **May 31–June 2**
Reagan visits the Soviet Union and declares that the "evil empire" was part of "another time, another era" (Reagan, *Public Papers: 1988*, p. 709).

Explanation and Analysis of the Document

As president, Reagan earned a reputation as "the Great Communicator," conveying ideas and connecting with listeners in original, striking, and memorable ways. In speaking to the NAE, which was founded in 1942 and four decades later had 3.5 million members with strong religious views, Reagan began by establishing a connection with the audience. In the first few paragraphs of the speech, Reagan explains that he, too, often prayed and was grateful for all the prayers for his success. He then uses humor, as he often did in his talks, to win over his audience; in this case the humor is partly at his own expense, as the joke is about the first politician who ever reached heaven. After the laughter ended, Reagan asserted that many political leaders, himself included, based their political thinking on religious conviction. At the end of this opening section, in paragraphs 8 and 9, Reagan introduces the speech's major idea, explaining that American democracy thrived because of widespread belief in God. He mentions the colonial leader William Penn; two of the founders of the American nation, Thomas Jefferson and George Washington; and the French traveler Alexis de Tocqueville, who traveled to the United States in the 1830s and wrote a remarkable account of American life entitled *Democracy in America*. Each of these historical figures confirms the president's central point: religious faith was the foundation of individual liberty and democratic rule in the United States.

In the next section of the address, Reagan warns that the traditional values that he and the members of the NAE cherish are facing formidable challenges. The president concentrates on three controversies to make his point. The first involves the provision of contraceptives to young women at federally funded clinics. Reagan presents this issue as one of federal "bureaucrats and social engineers" depriving parents of control of their children and, in so doing, turning sexual

President Ronald Reagan, 1983 (AP Photo/J. Scott Applewhite)

activity into a "purely physical" matter rather than a moral choice. As the president explains, Congress had started funding family planning clinics years ago, specifically, in 1970. Eight years later, additional legislation required that these clinics serve adolescents, since many members of Congress wanted to lower the high rate of unwanted teen pregnancy. The legislation encouraged parental involvement in young people's choices about birth control; however, it also emphasized the need to maintain confidentiality about any services provided to patients, since teens might not be willing to use such birth control services if clinics were to notify parents. In January 1983, the Department of Health and Human Services announced new regulations for these clinics reflecting the president's preference for parental notification. Only two weeks later, a federal court prevented these new rules from taking effect, holding that they were at odds with the main purpose of the legislation: to prevent unwanted teen pregnancy. In his "Evil Empire" Speech, Reagan challenges that court's reasoning. He even equates being "sexually active," which could mean having a relationship with only one partner, with promiscuity, which includes casual sex with a number of partners. Reagan's most important point here, though, is to connect this dispute to his larger concern about threats to moral values that are, in his view, the foundation of American society.

The president next discusses the controversy over the exclusion of prayer from public schools. The Supreme Court ruled in 1962 that mandatory school prayer was unconstitutional. Nevertheless, President Reagan and many evangelical Christians who supported him, including members of the NAE, wanted students to have the opportunity to participate in voluntary prayer during the school day. On May 17, 1982, the president submitted to Congress a constitutional amendment that would have allowed "individual or group prayer in public schools or other public institutions" while stipulating that "no person shall be required … to participate in prayer" ("The Politics of Prayer," http://www.time.com/time/magazine/article/0,9171, 925650,00.html). Congress took no action, so Reagan sent the proposed legislation to Capitol Hill once more on the same day as his speech to the NAE. Over a year later, on March 20, 1984, the Senate voted on the amendment, which did not secure the necessary two-thirds majority. In this speech, Reagan insists that the courts had gone far beyond protecting the division between church and state. He refers to the schools in Lubbock, Texas, that had allowed student religious groups to use school facilities for their meetings. A federal appeals court invalidated that policy, and the Supreme Court declined to hear the case in January 1983. The president states here that such rulings erected "a wall of hostility between government and the concept of religious belief itself."

Reagan's third example of declining morality concerns the volatile issue of abortion. On January 22, 1973, in the case of *Roe v. Wade*, the Supreme Court had ruled that a woman had a right to abortion during her first three months of pregnancy, while states could restrict access to abortion in later stages of pregnancy. For millions of Americans, abortion was a moral issue. Many insisted that abortion was a private choice for a woman, her family, and her physician that involved her health and well-being and control of her body. Many others, including the president and the NAE, maintained that abortion involved the taking of human life. Reagan asserts here that the availability of abortion is corrupting moral values and leading to infanticide, such as with the failure to keep alive infants with severe birth defects. He hopes that federal legislation will end such practices and overturn the decision in *Roe v. Wade*. For the time being, the issues of birth control for young women, school prayer, and abortion can be discouraging, Reagan observes, because they suggest a decline in the nation's morality.

Still, Reagan sees reason for hope. In the next section of his address (paragraphs 28–34), the president cites evidence of "a spiritual awakening." He concedes that racism and bigotry have been deplorable parts of American life, past and present, yet he believes that an American strength is "transcending the moral evils of our past." As he closes this part of his talk, Reagan declares that American history is a "story of hopes fulfilled and dreams made into reality." This idea was central to Reagan's understanding of the American nation and what it represented. He thought that the United States was a unique experiment in freedom, a beacon of hope to people around the world, and a society that allowed people to achieve their potential. As usual, when Reagan looked to the future, he was an optimist.

Reagan next shifts from domestic to international affairs, concentrating on the cold war struggle with the Soviet Union. He reminds his audience that he condemned the Soviets in his first presidential press conference, in January 1981, for rejecting religious morality and for insisting that whatever served their political and international goals was moral. This point was crucial, because Reagan believed that the U.S.-Soviet struggle was not merely a conflict over power or security or a competition between different economic or social systems. Here, he portrays this struggle as primarily a moral contest between two nations with fundamentally different values. Reagan remarks that the United States sought cooperation with the Soviets but not at the cost of "our principles and standards" or "our freedom." Reagan was replying to critics who complained that his strong condemnations of Communism had worsened Soviet-American relations and that his proposals for deep cuts in nuclear arsenals were unrealistic, as they required the Soviets, who had more land-based missiles, to make greater reductions. Reagan implies that those who disagree with his Soviet policies are like the appeasers of the 1930s who did not understand that Nazi Germany was a totalitarian nation with unlimited ambitions for aggressive expansion.

The proposal for a freeze of U.S. and Soviet nuclear arsenals jeopardized national security, according to the president. The nuclear freeze movement gathered momentum in the early 1980s, drawing support from members of Congress, concerned citizens, scientists, clergy, antinuclear activists, and security experts. On June 12, 1982, more than five hundred thousand people attended a nuclear freeze rally in Central Park in New York City. They thought that the United States and the Soviets should stop adding to their nuclear arsenals as a first step toward controlling the arms race. In this speech, Reagan asserts that the freeze proposal, while simple and appealing, is deceptive and dangerous. In the president's view, a freeze would allow the Soviets to retain superiority in some categories of nuclear weapons, advantages they had gained through the expansion of strategic forces over the previous fifteen years. In addition, a freeze could only lead to an illusory peace, since it would not change Soviet values, ideology, or ambitions. Reagan told his audience in Orlando something that he repeated often during his presidency: Peace would come only through strength.

Reagan next shifts back to a comparison of U.S. and Soviet morality. He uses the story about the young father, his daughters, and their future to assert that the spiritual matters more than the physical—that it was better, according to a famous cold war phrase, to be dead than Red. Reagan then uses language more reminiscent of a sermon than of a typical presidential speech as he calls for prayers for those living in "totalitarian darkness" in the Soviet Union and the Eastern European nations that it dominated. Those who enforced this totalitarian dominance, denying individual rights such as the freedom to worship, are described as "the focus of evil in the modern world."

Reagan continues this discussion of evil (paragraphs 45–47) until it culminates in the famous phrase that gave the address its popular title. Drawing on the writer C. S. Lewis, the president maintains that evil is usually the work not of brutish figures in sordid places but of seemingly ordinary people in comfortable offices. Their ideas and rhetoric, at least on the surface, can be appealing, even reassuring; but beneath this veneer can be found aggressive impulses and repugnant values. Reagan proceeds to call his immediate audience, as people of the church, to a moral crusade. Just as they fought evils at home—such as the exclusion of prayer from public schools and the corrupting effects of abortion—so they should rally against international evil by supporting administration efforts to defeat a nuclear freeze proposal that could benefit only the Soviet Union and the totalitarianism it sought to extend. He urges his listeners to place the debate about a nuclear freeze in the context of the cold war "struggle between right and wrong and good and evil." The United States and the Soviet Union are not morally equivalent or equally responsible for international tensions or the arms race. One nation, as Reagan previously explained, was an inspiration for freedom-loving people the world over. The other was "an evil empire."

Reagan ends his address on a hopeful note. He reiterates that the real battle in the United States and around the

President Ronald Reagan (left) shown with Soviet leader Mikhail Gorbachev in Geneva, Switzerland, 1985. (AP-Photo/mw/stf/Deugherty/11/19/1985)

world is a moral conflict. The victor will not be the side with superior military strength but the one with greater spiritual resolve. Vanquishing Communism will require maintaining religious faith. Reagan uses the example of Whittaker Chambers, a controversial figure who had been a Soviet agent during the 1930s but later repudiated Communism and testified in a famous trial that a former State Department official, Alger Hiss, had provided government secrets to the Soviets. Hiss maintained that he was innocent, but he was eventually convicted of perjury. During the 1950s, Chambers became increasingly gloomy about Communist threats and the strength of Western nations to resist them. Many conservatives endorsed his perspective, and Reagan thought that the connection Chambers saw between faith in God and resistance to Communism was as important in the 1980s as it had been thirty years earlier. Nevertheless, Reagan maintains that however vital and resilient it might seem, Communism is dying. He repeats an idea that he had included in a speech in June 1982 to the British Parliament, when he said that the eventual destination of Marxism-Leninism, the philosophical basis of Soviet Communism, would be "the ashheap of history" (Cannon, p. 272). Ultimately, religious conviction, cooperation, and common purpose, in the words of Thomas Paine, the famous writer from the era of the American Revolution, would enable Americans "to begin the world over again."

Audience

Reagan's audience for his "Evil Empire" Speech was the group whose meeting he was attending—the NAE. He also expected, of course, that his message would reach beyond the hotel ballroom in Orlando where he delivered the address. He particularly hoped that other Christian

conservatives who were especially concerned with social issues would also be encouraged to back his defense policies and oppose the nuclear freeze movement. Since the speech received extensive news coverage, he also thought that it could strengthen general support for the building up of U.S. military strength to deter war and oppose Soviet expansion.

Impact

"Evil empire" was one of the most sensational phrases that Reagan ever used as president, and those words became a convenient way of summarizing the president's views about the Soviet Union. Reactions were powerful and polarized. Supporters applauded Reagan's use of blunt language to describe a dangerous adversary and a system of values—Communism—that they abhorred. Many commentators complained that Reagan had given a sermon, rather than a speech, that had alienated many Americans who did not share his religious convictions. Others worried that by using a reckless phrase to frame U.S.-Soviet differences as an irreconcilable moral conflict, he had undermined the chances that negotiations would produce agreements on such vital issues as arms control.

Only two years after he delivered the address in Orlando, "evil empire" became an inconvenient phrase that the president wanted to avoid. Reagan never repudiated his words; he confirmed that they expressed his views about the Soviet system. Nonetheless, he told reporters in November 1985 that Soviet and American leaders would make more progress in settling issues of common concern if they avoided such inflammatory language. He was right: Just days later, he had his first meeting in Geneva, Switzerland, with Mikhail Gorbachev, who had become the Soviet leader in March 1985. Reagan quickly concluded that Gorbachev was different from previous Soviet leaders. When Gorbachev visited the United States in December 1987, the two leaders signed a treaty to eliminate their intermediate-range nuclear forces. The agreement symbolized the rapid—and unexpected—improvement in Soviet-American relations during Reagan's second term as president. When Reagan journeyed to the Soviet Union in May 1988, he told reporters who asked about the memorable phrase that he had used five years earlier that "evil empire" was part of "another time, another era" (Reagan, *Public Papers: 1988*, p. 709).

Long after Reagan left the White House, the term *evil empire* continued to elicit strong and divided reactions. The cold war came to end in 1991, as the Soviet Union collapsed and divided into many independent republics. Many people credit Reagan with ending—and winning—the cold war by aiming for victory and applying pressure—diplomatic, military, and rhetorical—to bring about the Soviet demise. Others maintain that the cold war ended mainly because of changes in the Soviet Union and that the "Evil Empire" Speech had little, if anything, to do with those larger developments. These assessments, while fundamen-

> "*Yes, let us pray for the salvation of all of those who live in that totalitarian darkness—pray they will discover the joy of knowing God. But until they do, let us be aware that while they preach the supremacy of the state, declare its omnipotence over individual man, and predict its eventual domination of all peoples on the Earth, they are the focus of evil in the modern world.*"
>
> (Paragraph 44)

> "*I urge you to beware the temptation of pride—the temptation of blithely declaring yourselves above it all and label both sides equally at fault, to ignore the facts of history and the aggressive impulses of an evil empire, to simply call the arms race a giant misunderstanding and thereby remove yourself from the struggle between right and wrong and good and evil.*"
>
> (Paragraph 47)

> "*I believe that communism is another sad, bizarre chapter in human history whose last pages even now are being written.*"
>
> (Paragraph 52)

tally different, still show the power of Reagan's words and the ways that they affected public thinking while he was president and long afterward as well.

Related Documents

Brinkley, Douglas, ed. *The Reagan Diaries*. New York: HarperCollins, 2007. Reagan kept a diary while he was president, and this book contains extensive excerpts. The diary provides glimpses of Reagan's White House activities as well as insights into his personal life.

Reagan, Ronald. *Public Papers of the Presidents of the United States: Ronald Reagan.* 8 vols. in 15 parts. Washington, D.C.: U.S. Government Printing Office, 1982–1991. These annual volumes contain Reagan's speeches, remarks at news conferences, messages to Congress and other public documents of his presidency.

Skinner, Kiron K., Annelise Anderson, and Martin Anderson, eds. *Reagan, in His Own Hand.* New York: Simon & Schuster, 2001. From 1975 to 1979, Reagan had a radio program during which he commented about a wide range of international and domestic issues five days each week. Reagan wrote most of the commen-

taries himself, and this book contains hundreds of them as well as a selection of other writings.

———. *Reagan: A Life in Letters.* New York: Free Press, 2003. Reagan was a prolific correspondent, and this collection contains letters he wrote throughout his life, though mainly while he was president.

Bibliography

■ Articles

Peterson, Jon R. "Words Will Never Hurt Me? The Evil Empire Speech and Ronald Reagan." Master's thesis, Ohio University, 2006.

■ Books

Brownlee, W. Elliot, and Hugh Davis Graham. *The Reagan Presidency: Pragmatic Conservatism and Its Legacies.* Lawrence: University Press of Kansas, 2003.

Cannon, Lou. *President Reagan: The Role of a Lifetime.* New York: Public Affairs, 2000.

Diggins, John Patrick. *Ronald Reagan: Fate, Freedom, and the Making of History*. New York: W. W. Norton, 2007.

FitzGerald, Frances R. *Way Out There in the Blue: Reagan, Star Wars, and the End of the Cold War*. New York: Simon & Schuster, 2000.

Pemberton, William E. *Exit with Honor: The Life and Presidency of Ronald Reagan*. Armonk, N.Y.: M. E. Sharpe, 1997.

Reeves, Richard. *President Reagan: The Triumph of Imagination*. New York: Simon & Schuster, 2005.

■ **Web Sites**

"The Politics of Prayer." Time Magazine Web site. August 9, 1982. http://www.time.com/time/magazine/article/0,9171,925650,00.html. Accessed on March 7, 2008.

Ronald Reagan Presidential Library Web site. http://www.reagan.utexas.edu/. Accessed on January 22, 2008.

"Ronald Wilson Reagan (1911–2004)." Miller Center of Public Affairs "American President: An Online Reference Resource" Web site. http://www.millercenter.virginia.edu/academic/americanpresident/reagan. Accessed on January 22, 2008.

—By Chester Pach

1. Ronald Reagan made hundreds of speeches as president, but "evil empire" was one of the most memorable phrases he ever used. Why do you think that these words had such a powerful effect in 1983 and in the following years? What about Reagan's language, the ideas he conveyed, the context of the speech, and the nature of the Soviet-American conflict during the cold war accounted for the power of his words?

2. In the "Evil Empire" Speech, Reagan states that "traditional values" are part of the foundation of American democracy and "that freedom prospers only where the blessings of God are avidly sought and humbly accepted." Do you agree with Reagan's assertions about the connections between religion and American democracy? In what ways do religious values strengthen or reinforce democratic practices or institutions? In what ways do religious values complicate or weaken democratic practices or institutions?

3. President Reagan presents the cold war as a conflict between a nation committed to freedom and an "evil empire" that recognizes no moral values except whatever advances its goal of world revolution. Do you think that Reagan was right to explain the cold war as fundamentally a moral conflict? Are there other ways of understanding the reasons for the international differences associated with the cold war? What role did security issues play? Economic conflicts? Ideological differences?

4. President Reagan called the Soviet Union an "evil empire" and explained the cold war with the Soviets as a conflict between good and evil. In his State of the Union address of January 29, 2002, President George W. Bush asserted that Iran, Iraq, and North Korea were parts of an "axis of evil." He also depicted the war on terror as a conflict between good and evil. What advantages are there to presenting international adversaries or enemies as "evil?" Are there disadvantages to using that term to describe American foes? Compare and contrast the ways Reagan and Bush used the term "evil" to generate support for their foreign policies.

Glossary

Evangelicals	Protestants who base their Christian faith on the Bible, believe that religious faith is the only way to achieve salvation, and strive to change the world based on their spiritual beliefs
infanticide	killing of an infant
intercessionary prayer	prayer to God to help another person
phenomenology	a view that reality is a part of human consciousness and does not exist outside of it
promiscuous	having a number of sexual partners, often chosen casually
salvation	delivery from evil or sin; redemption
secularism	a conviction that religious ideas should not be part of morality
strategic	regarding nuclear arms, descriptive of missiles or weapons that could be launched from Soviet or U.S. bases and delivered against targets on the opposite's soil

Ronald Reagan's "Evil Empire" Speech

Reverend clergy all, Senator Hawkins, distinguished members of the Florida congressional delegation, and all of you:

I can't tell you how you have warmed my heart with your welcome. I'm delighted to be here today.

Those of you in the National Association of Evangelicals are known for your spiritual and humanitarian work. And I would be especially remiss if I didn't discharge right now one personal debt of gratitude. Thank you for your prayers. Nancy and I have felt their presence many times in many ways. And believe me, for us they've made all the difference.

The other day in the East Room of the White House at a meeting there, someone asked me whether I was aware of all the people out there who were praying for the President. And I had to say, "Yes, I am. I've felt it. I believe in intercessionary prayer." But I couldn't help but say to that questioner after he'd asked the question that—or at least say to them that if sometimes when he was praying he got a busy signal, it was just me in there ahead of him. I think I understand how Abraham Lincoln felt when he said, "I have been driven many times to my knees by the overwhelming conviction that I had nowhere else to go."

From the joy and the good feeling of this conference, I go to a political reception. Now, I don't know why, but that bit of scheduling reminds me of a story—which I'll share with you.

An evangelical minister and a politician arrived at Heaven's gate one day together. And St. Peter, after doing all the necessary formalities, took them in hand to show them where their quarters would be. And he took them to a small, single room with a bed, a chair, and a table and said this was for the clergyman. And the politician was a little worried about what might be in store for him. And he couldn't believe it then when St. Peter stopped in front of a beautiful mansion with lovely grounds, many servants, and told him that these would be his quarters.

And he couldn't help but ask, he said, "But wait, how—there's something wrong—how do I get this mansion while that good and holy man only gets a single room?" And St. Peter said, "You have to understand how things are up here. We've got thousands and thousands of clergy. You're the first politician who ever made it."

But I don't want to contribute to a stereotype. So, I tell you there are a great many God-fearing, dedicated, noble men and women in public life, present company included. And, yes, we need your help to keep us ever mindful of the ideas and the principles that brought us into the public arena in the first place. The basis of those ideals and principles is a commitment to freedom and personal liberty that, itself, is grounded in the much deeper realization that freedom prospers only where the blessings of God are avidly sought and humbly accepted.

The American experiment in democracy rests on this insight. Its discovery was the great triumph of our Founding Fathers, voiced by William Penn when he said: "If we will not be governed by God, we must be governed by tyrants." Explaining the inalienable rights of men, Jefferson said, "The God who gave us life, gave us liberty at the same time." And it was George Washington who said that "of all the dispositions and habits which lead to political prosperity, religion and morality are indispensable supports."

And finally, that shrewdest of all observers of American democracy, Alexis de Tocqueville, put it eloquently after he had gone on a search for the secret of America's greatness and genius—and he said: "Not until I went into the churches of America and heard her pulpits aflame with righteousness did I understand the greatness and the genius of America.... America is good. And if America ever ceases to be good, America will cease to be great."

Well, I'm pleased to be here today with you who are keeping America great by keeping her good. Only through your work and prayers and those of millions of others can we hope to survive this perilous century and keep alive this experiment in liberty, this last, best hope of man.

I want you to know that this administration is motivated by a political philosophy that sees the greatness of America in you, her people, and in your families, churches, neighborhoods, communities—the institutions that foster and nourish values like concern for others and respect for the rule of law under God.

Now, I don't have to tell you that this puts us in opposition to, or at least out of step with, a prevailing attitude of many who have turned to a modern-day secularism, discarding the tried and time-tested values upon which our very civilization is based. No matter how well intentioned, their value system is radically different from that of most Americans. And while they proclaim that they're freeing us from superstitions of the past, they've taken upon themselves the job of superintending us by government rule and regulation. Sometimes their voices are louder than ours, but they are not yet a majority.

An example of that vocal superiority is evident in a controversy now going on in Washington. And since I'm involved, I've been waiting to hear from the parents of young America. How far are they willing to go in giving to government their prerogatives as parents?

Let me state the case as briefly and simply as I can. An organization of citizens, sincerely motivated and deeply concerned about the increase in illegitimate births and abortions involving girls well below the age of consent, sometime ago established a nationwide network of clinics to offer help to these girls and, hopefully, alleviate this situation. Now, again, let me say, I do not fault their intent. However, in their well-intentioned effort, these clinics have decided to provide advice and birth control drugs and devices to underage girls without the knowledge of their parents.

For some years now, the Federal Government has helped with funds to subsidize these clinics. In providing for this, the Congress decreed that every effort would be made to maximize parental participation. Nevertheless, the drugs and devices are prescribed without getting parental consent or giving notification after they've done so. Girls termed "sexually active"—and that has replaced the word "promiscuous"—are given this help in order to prevent illegitimate birth or abortion.

Well, we have ordered clinics receiving Federal funds to notify the parents such help has been given.

One of the Nation's leading newspapers has created the term "squeal rule" in editorializing against us for doing this, and we're being criticized for violating the privacy of young people. A judge has recently granted an injunction against an enforcement of our rule. I've watched TV panel shows discuss this issue, seen columnists pontificating on our error, but no one seems to mention morality as playing a part in the subject of sex.

Is all of Judeo-Christian tradition wrong? Are we to believe that something so sacred can be looked upon as a purely physical thing with no potential for emotional and psychological harm? And isn't it the parents' right to give counsel and advice to keep their children from making mistakes that may affect their entire lives?

Many of us in government would like to know what parents think about this intrusion in their family by government. We're going to fight in the courts. The right of parents and the rights of family take precedence over those of Washington-based bureaucrats and social engineers.

But the fight against parental notification is really only one example of many attempts to water down traditional values and even abrogate the original terms of American democracy. Freedom prospers when religion is vibrant and the rule of law under God is acknowledged. When our Founding Fathers passed the first amendment, they sought to protect churches from government interference. They never intended to construct a wall of hostility between government and the concept of religious belief itself.

The evidence of this permeates our history and our government. The Declaration of Independence mentions the Supreme Being no less than four times. "In God We Trust" is engraved on our coinage. The Supreme Court opens its proceedings with a religious invocation. And the Members of Congress open their sessions with a prayer. I just happen to believe the schoolchildren of the United States are entitled to the same privileges as Supreme Court Justices and Congressmen.

Last year, I sent the Congress a constitutional amendment to restore prayer to public schools. Already this session, there's growing bipartisan support for the amendment, and I am calling on the Congress to act speedily to pass it and to let our children pray.

Perhaps some of you read recently about the Lubbock school case, where a judge actually ruled that it was unconstitutional for a school district to give equal treatment to religious and nonreligious student groups, even when the group meetings were being held during the students' own time. The first amendment never intended to require government to discriminate against religious speech.

Senators Denton and Hatfield have proposed legislation in the Congress on the whole question of prohibiting discrimination against religious forms of student speech. Such legislation could go far to restore freedom of religious speech for public school students. And I hope the Congress considers these bills quickly. And with your help, I think it's possible we could also get the constitutional amendment through the Congress this year.

More than a decade ago, a Supreme Court decision literally wiped off the books of 50 States statutes protecting the rights of unborn children. Abortion on demand now takes the lives of up to 1.5 million unborn children a year. Human life legislation ending this tragedy will some day pass the Congress, and you and I must never rest until it does. Unless and until it can be proven that the unborn child is not a living entity, then its right to life, liberty, and the pursuit of happiness must be protected.

You may remember that when abortion on demand began, many, and, indeed, I'm sure many of you, warned that the practice would lead to a decline in respect for human life, that the philosophical premises used to justify abortion on demand would ultimately be used to justify other attacks on the sacredness of human life—infanticide or mercy killing. Tragically enough, those warnings proved all too true. Only last year a court permitted the death by starvation of a handicapped infant.

I have directed the Health and Human Services Department to make clear to every health care facility in the United States that the Rehabilitation Act of 1973 protects all handicapped persons against discrimination based on handicaps, including infants. And we have taken the further step of requiring that each and every recipient of Federal funds who provides health care services to infants must post and keep posted in a conspicuous place a notice stating that "discriminatory failure to feed and care for handicapped infants in this facility is prohibited by Federal law." It also lists a 24-hour, toll-free number so that nurses and others may report violations in time to save the infant's life.

In addition, recent legislation introduced in the Congress by Representative Henry Hyde of Illinois not only increases restrictions on publicly financed abortions, it also addresses this whole problem of infanticide. I urge the Congress to begin hearings and to adopt legislation that will protect the right of life to all children, including the disabled or handicapped.

Now, I'm sure that you must get discouraged at times, but you've done better than you know, perhaps. There's a great spiritual awakening in America, a renewal of the traditional values that have been the bedrock of America's goodness and greatness.

One recent survey by a Washington-based research council concluded that Americans were far more religious than the people of other nations; 95 percent of those surveyed expressed a belief in God and a huge majority believed the Ten Commandments had real meaning in their lives. And another study has found that an overwhelming majority of Americans disapprove of adultery, teenage sex, pornography, abortion, and hard drugs. And this same study showed a deep reverence for the importance of family ties and religious belief.

I think the items that we've discussed here today must be a key part of the Nation's political agenda. For the first time the Congress is openly and seriously debating and dealing with the prayer and abortion issues—and that's enormous progress right there. I repeat: America is in the midst of a spiritual awakening and a moral renewal. And with your Biblical keynote, I say today, "Yes, let justice roll on like a river, righteousness like a never-failing stream."

Now, obviously, much of this new political and social consensus I've talked about is based on a positive view of American history, one that takes pride in our country's accomplishments and record. But we must never forget that no government schemes are going to perfect man. We know that living in this world means dealing with what philosophers would call the phenomenology of evil or, as theologians would put it, the doctrine of sin.

There is sin and evil in the world, and we're enjoined by Scripture and the Lord Jesus to oppose it with all our might. Our nation, too, has a legacy of evil with which it must deal. The glory of this land has been its capacity for transcending the moral evils of our past. For example, the long struggle of minority citizens for equal rights, once a source of disunity and civil war, is now a point of pride for all Americans. We must never go back. There is no room for racism, anti-Semitism, or other forms of ethnic and racial hatred in this country.

I know that you've been horrified, as have I, by the resurgence of some hate groups preaching bigotry and prejudice. Use the mighty voice of your pulpits and the powerful standing of your churches to denounce and isolate these hate groups in our midst. The commandment given us is clear and simple: "Thou shalt love thy neighbor as thyself."

But whatever sad episodes exist in our past, any objective observer must hold a positive view of American history, a history that has been the story of hopes fulfilled and dreams made into reality. Especially in this century, America has kept alight the torch of freedom, but not just for ourselves but for millions of others around the world.

And this brings me to my final point today. During my first press conference as President, in answer to a direct question, I pointed out that, as good Marxist-Leninists, the Soviet leaders have openly and publicly declared that the only morality they recognize is that which will further their cause, which is world revolution. I think I should point out I was only quoting Lenin, their guiding spirit, who said in 1920 that they repudiate all morality that proceeds from supernatural ideas—that's their name for religion—or ideas that are outside class conceptions. Morality is entirely subordinate to the interests of class war. And everything is moral that is necessary for the annihilation of the old, exploiting social order and for uniting the proletariat.

Well, I think the refusal of many influential people to accept this elementary fact of Soviet doctrine illustrates an historical reluctance to see totalitarian powers for what they are. We saw this phenomenon in the 1930's. We see it too often today.

This doesn't mean we should isolate ourselves and refuse to seek an understanding with them. I intend to do everything I can to persuade them of our peaceful intent, to remind them that it was the West that refused to use its nuclear monopoly in the forties and fifties for territorial gain and which now proposes 50-percent cut in strategic ballistic missiles and the elimination of an entire class of land-based, intermediate-range nuclear missiles.

At the same time, however, they must be made to understand we will never compromise our principles and standards. We will never give away our freedom. We will never abandon our belief in God. And we will never stop searching for a genuine peace. But we can assure none of these things America stands for through the so-called nuclear freeze solutions proposed by some.

The truth is that a freeze now would be a very dangerous fraud, for that is merely the illusion of peace. The reality is that we must find peace through strength.

I would agree to a freeze if only we could freeze the Soviets' global desires. A freeze at current levels of weapons would remove any incentive for the Soviets to negotiate seriously in Geneva and virtually end our chances to achieve the major arms reductions which we have proposed. Instead, they would achieve their objectives through the freeze.

A freeze would reward the Soviet Union for its enormous and unparalleled military buildup. It would prevent the essential and long overdue modernization of United States and allied defenses and would leave our aging forces increasingly vulnerable. And an honest freeze would require extensive prior negotiations on the systems and numbers to be limited and on the measures to ensure effective verification and compliance. And the kind of a freeze that has been suggested would be virtually impossible to verify. Such a major effort would divert us completely from our current negotiations on achieving substantial reductions.

A number of years ago, I heard a young father, a very prominent young man in the entertainment world, addressing a tremendous gathering in California. It was during the time of the cold war, and communism and our own way of life were very much on people's minds. And he was speaking to that subject. And suddenly, though, I heard him saying, "I love my little girls more than anything." And I said to myself, "Oh, no, don't. You can't—don't say that." But I had underestimated him. He went on: "I would rather see my little girls die now, still believing in God, than have them grow up under communism and one day die no longer believing in God."

There were thousands of young people in that audience. They came to their feet with shouts of joy. They had instantly recognized the profound truth in what he had said, with regard to the physical and the soul and what was truly important.

Yes, let us pray for the salvation of all of those who live in that totalitarian darkness—pray they will discover the joy of knowing God. But until they do, let us be aware that while they preach the supremacy of the state, declare its omnipotence over individual man, and predict its eventual domination of all peoples on the Earth, they are the focus of evil in the modern world.

It was C. S. Lewis who, in his unforgettable "Screwtape Letters," wrote: "The greatest evil is not done now in those sordid 'dens of crime' that Dickens loved to paint. It is not even done in concentration camps and labor camps. In those we see its final result. But it is conceived and ordered (moved, seconded, carried and minuted) in clear, carpeted, warmed, and well-lighted offices, by quiet men with white collars and cut fingernails and smooth-shaven cheeks who do not need to raise their voice."

Well, because these "quiet men" do not "raise their voices," because they sometimes speak in soothing tones of brotherhood and peace, because, like other dictators before them, they're always making "their final territorial demand," some would have us accept them at their word and accommodate ourselves to their aggressive impulses. But if history teaches anything, it teaches that simple-minded appeasement or wishful thinking about our adversaries is folly. It means the betrayal of our past, the squandering of our freedom.

So, I urge you to speak out against those who would place the United States in a position of military and moral inferiority. You know, I've always believed that old Screwtape reserved his best efforts for those of you in the church. So, in your discussions of the nuclear freeze proposals, I urge you to beware the temptation of pride—the temptation of blithely declaring yourselves above it all and label both sides equally at fault, to ignore the facts of history and the aggressive impulses of an evil empire, to simply call the arms race a giant misunderstanding and thereby remove yourself from the struggle between right and wrong and good and evil.

I ask you to resist the attempts of those who would have you withhold your support for our efforts, this administration's efforts, to keep America strong and free, while we negotiate real and verifiable reductions in the world's nuclear arsenals and one day, with God's help, their total elimination.

While America's military strength is important, let me add here that I've always maintained that the struggle now going on for the world will never be decided by bombs or rockets, by armies or military might. The real crisis we face today is a spiritual one; at root, it is a test of moral will and faith.

Whittaker Chambers, the man whose own religious conversion made him a witness to one of the terrible traumas of our time, the Hiss-Chambers case, wrote that the crisis of the Western World exists to the degree in which the West is indifferent to God, the degree to which it collaborates in communism's attempt to make man stand alone without God. And then he said, for Marxism-Leninism is actually the second oldest faith, first proclaimed in the Garden of Eden with the words of temptation, "Ye shall be as gods."

The Western World can answer this challenge, he wrote, "but only provided that its faith in God and the freedom He enjoins is as great as communism's faith in Man."

I believe we shall rise to the challenge. I believe that communism is another sad, bizarre chapter in human history whose last pages even now are being written. I believe this because the source of our strength in the quest for human freedom is not material, but spiritual. And because it knows no limitation, it must terrify and ultimately triumph over those who would enslave their fellow man. For in the words of Isaiah: "He giveth power to the faint; and to them that have no might He increased strength.... But they that wait upon the Lord shall renew their strength; they shall mount up with wings as eagles; they shall run, and not be weary...."

Yes, change your world. One of our Founding Fathers, Thomas Paine, said, "We have it within our power to begin the world over again." We can do it, doing together what no one church could do by itself. God bless you, and thank you very much.

CÉSAR CHÁVEZ'S COMMONWEALTH ADDRESS

1984

"Our union will forever exist as an empowering force among Chicanos in the Southwest."

Overview

Through much struggle, the United Farm Workers of America leader César Chávez saw the hopes for better lives for Mexican, Mexican American, and Hispanic workers in the United States repeatedly raised, sunk, and revived again. Many factors contributed to this seemingly unending pendulum swing from hopefulness to despair, and the speech that Chávez delivered to the Commonwealth Club of California in 1984 highlights some of these factors. The address offers a window into Chávez's keen awareness of the plights of the farmworkers whom he represented as well as of Latinos in general.

Among the several issues addressed in this speech are the blunt disregard of growers for the provision of safe vehicles to transport farmworkers, the intimidation tactics used by growers to discourage unionization among farmworkers, child labor concerns, union survival, pesticides and environmental concerns, Chávez's nonviolence philosophy, and the role of the boycott in pressuring growers to acknowledge workers' needs. Chávez also highlights his view of how the political climate created by California's governor, George Deukmejian, discouraged and nearly prevented farmworkers from fulfilling the American dream of enjoying equal rights. Throughout the speech, Chávez's main drive to fulfill the tenets of La Causa—the farmworkers' movement he founded—resounds loud and clear.

Context

César Chávez's Commonwealth Address was delivered at the Commonwealth Club of California in San Francisco. The Commonwealth Club of California is a nonprofit, nonpartisan organization that was founded in 1903 with the principal goal of supporting independent thought, particularly cultural thought. The club has a program called Voices of Reform, aimed at fomenting understanding among policy makers in California. Many famous leaders have spoken at club events, including President Franklin Delano Roosevelt. The actress Shirley Temple Black was the presi-

dent of the club in 1984. That year, an admirer who very much respected what Chávez stood for sought him out to speak to members of the club in San Francisco. In this speech, given on November 9, 1984, Chávez discussed the changes that he underwent as a leader of farmworkers and as a man who advocated the causes of the oppressed of all races and walks of life.

At the time of this address, Chávez's peak years of grape boycotts, strikes, and marches of protest had diminished. However, according to the biographer Dan La Botz, Chávez knew that this was no time to retreat, especially since his "archenemy [had] moved into the White House" (p. 159). As governor of California, Ronald Reagan was a forthright opponent of the United Farm Workers of America. In addition, George Deukmejian, who had become governor of California in 1983, was a known enemy of farmworker unions and a friend of California growers. These factors were certainly uppermost in Chávez's mind as he addressed the audience at the Commonwealth Club in San Francisco.

About the Author

César Estrada Chávez was born on March 31, 1927, near Yuma, Arizona. He was raised on a 160-acre farm. Chávez's parents were originally from Mexico, where his grandfather had lived under the dictator Porfirio Díaz and had seen the poor and humble become only more deprived while the rich and powerful grew richer and more powerful. This motivated Chávez's grandfather to move his family to the United States. Chávez's father's hard work enabled him to homestead a large farm in Yuma, Arizona, but he was eventually denied the continuation of this homesteading. As they were unable to find another way to sustain a living, the Chávez family began the common practice of wandering from farm to farm for work, following the crops. In 1937 the family moved to California in search of better pastures.

In California, Chávez began learning more clearly the plight of the migrant farmworker. During the Great Depression, Mexicans and Mexican Americans in the state were made scapegoats; they were blamed and maligned for taking the few jobs available at low wages and were deported by the thousands. The Chávez family continued to expe-

1952

■ César Chávez begins to work for the Community Service Organization, organizing citizenship classes and voter registration drives among Mexican Americans.

1962

■ **March**
Chávez resigns from the Community Service Organization and moves to Delano, California, in the San Joaquin Valley, where he begins to organize farmworkers.

■ **September 30**
First convention of the National Farm Workers Association takes place.

1963

■ **September 17**
A truck that had been converted into a bus and which is carrying farmworkers overturns near Salinas; thirty-two people lose their lives.

1965

■ **September 8**
The first strike of the grape farmworkers (the Agricultural Workers Organizing Committee) begins. Chávez's union votes to join the strike on September 16; it would last five years.

1966

■ **March**
After Senate hearings on the plight of the farmworkers, Senator Robert Kennedy of New York lends his support to the strike.

■ **March–April**
In what is later referred to as a peregrination, Chávez and supporters of his cause march from Delano to Sacramento to protest growers' unfair practices toward farmworkers.

1967

■ Chávez leads a boycott whereby people are discouraged from buying grapes from growers who refuse to recognize the rights of workers to belong to unions; Chávez's union, then the United Farm Workers Organizing Committee, eventually reaches a settlement with the major grower Schenley, and the boycott is called off.

rience hardship as they moved from town to town. Chávez himself went to junior high school but never attended high school. Having experienced segregation in public facilities early on, he determined that Mexicans and Mexican Americans needed to assert their rights and value the cultural solidarity that united them. During World War II he spent two years in the U.S. Navy. La Botz notes that Chávez's experiences in the navy gave him a sense of entitlement and a newfound assertiveness, with which he intended to claim his rights as an American citizen.

Soon after his return to California, at the age of nineteen, Chávez joined his first union, the National Agricultural Workers Union. On October 22, 1948, he married Helen Fabela, whom he had met in Delano, California, and who would be the only woman to share his life. Chávez and his new wife first lived in Delano for a time and then later moved to a San Jose neighborhood called by the Spanish name Sal Si Puedes ("Escape if you can") Barrio. Helen and Cásar had eight children, five girls and three boys.

Chávez's deep spirituality played a key role in his life from the beginning of his career as a labor leader. His mother was a very religious woman, and La Botz credits her influence with drawing Chávez to the principles of fairness and justice for all. Father Donald McDonnell came to the barrio to organize a church, and Chávez initially became involved in religious efforts. McDonnell exposed Chávez to the principles found in *"Rerum novarum,"* a famous encyclical issued in 1891 by Pope Leo XIII denouncing the appalling conditions of the workers of the world. McDonnell instilled in Chávez a love of reading books about social justice. The lessons Chávez learned from such books became the core of his peaceful but assertive approach to fighting the legal battles in which he would engage throughout the rest of his life.

The labor leader Saul Alinsky of Chicago is credited with giving Chávez fundamental lessons on principles of community organization, principles that Chávez later applied in uniting farmworkers. In fact, in organizing the seemingly unorganizable farmworkers, Chávez single-handedly accomplished what many 1930s labor leaders, such as Pat Chambers, had tried and failed to do before. In 1962, almost thirty years after Chambers's efforts, Chávez organized the National Farm Workers Association, the precursor organization to the United Farm Workers of America. According to Marc Grossman, who was Chávez's press contact and speech writer in the 1970s and 1980s, Chávez always asserted that he sought improvements in the lives of the oppressed regardless of race. This philosophy ultimately made Chávez very appealing to people of all ethnicities and walks of life. The historian Peter Matthiessen asserts that "by the midsixties, he had become a beloved folk hero to the poor and to the boisterous student movement, and public enemy number one to conservative California businessmen and politicians" (p. xi). Regarding the bracero program, through which Mexican workers were admitted to the United States from the years 1942 to 1964, Chávez expressed strict opposition. He saw the program as one wherein the exploitation of farmworkers had been given legal sanction. During the 1960s, 1970s, and 1980s, Chávez continued to fight for the civil rights of farmworkers and against the use of pesticides on the fields of California, which extended his appeal to environmentalists.

In 1968 Chávez embraced the teachings of the Indian nationalist leader Mahatma Gandhi in a more concrete way by beginning a fast, so as to emphasize the notion that victory for the farmworkers needed to be won by pacific means. Through this fast, which lasted twenty-five days, Chávez lost thirty-five pounds. Afterward, his message was deemed ethically stronger, and his reputation as a serious nonviolent labor leader was reinforced. In 1984 Chávez began a new boycott on grapes to protest the harmful effects of the pesticides on farmworkers and on the people who consumed the grapes. Chávez fasted again in 1988, for thirty-six days, further protesting the use of pesticides.

After an unprecedented life of service, Chávez died on April 23, 1993. In 1994, in recognition of a lifetime dedicated to the farmworkers of America, Chávez was posthumously awarded the Presidential Medal of Freedom by Bill Clinton.

Explanation and Analysis of the Document

César Chávez's speech to the audience of the Commonwealth Club of California should be placed in the context of what the historians Richard J. Jensen and John C. Hammerback call "the difficult years": the period from 1984 to 1993 and its "conservative reaction," wherein George Bush succeeded Ronald Reagan as president and the governors of California were George Deukmejian and Pete Wilson (p. 125). These four conservative politicians were known for not being friends of the labor movement. Rather, Reagan and also Deukmejian were friends of the powerful growers' lobby in California.

Chávez begins his speech with what the scholar Joseph P. Zompetti calls an "appeal to sympathy," a technique that Zompetti cites as a chief component of the labor leader's rhetoric (p. 79). From the opening, then, Chávez captures the attention and sympathy of his audience regardless of their ethnicity, education, or financial status. In the first paragraph he narrates an incident that happened in 1963 near the California town of Salinas, wherein a truck carrying some thirty-two farmworkers was involved in an accident in which these workers lost their lives. Chávez related this story in front of the sophisticated club audience to vividly present the plight of the farmworker, which was perhaps very foreign to their lives and pursuits; he was banking on the humanity of his listeners, on the importance that human beings naturally assign to the lives of others.

In remarking, "The Braceros had been imported from Mexico," Chávez is saying that while human beings are not cattle, farmworkers are often transported as cattle, with little regard for their lives. He stresses the identity of the deceased workers as braceros, indicating that they were part of a program that he saw as legalized exploitation and which he opposed until its termination. Chávez emphasizes

Time Line

1968
- Chávez fasts for twenty-five days to highlight the nonviolent nature of the continuing farmworkers' strike against the grape growers.

1970
- **July 29**
The grape strike ends.

1972
- The United Farm Workers Organizing Committee is granted a national charter from its parent organization, the American Federation of Labor and Congress of Industrial Organizations; the name is changed to United Farm Workers of America.

1973
- A second grape strike is called to protest growers' shifting contracts to the Teamsters union; some 2,500 workers are jailed after refusing to stop picketing.

1975
- **June 5**
California governor Jerry Brown signs the Agricultural Labor Relations Act, guaranteeing farmworkers in California the right to bargain collectively. This marks the first time in American history that this right is given to farmworkers.

1977
- **March 10**
Chávez and the Teamsters agree that the United Farm Workers will exclusively represent all farmworkers.

1984
- **November 9**
Chávez speaks to the Commonwealth Club of California in San Francisco.

1993
- **April 23**
Chávez dies in San Luis, Arizona.

César Chávez, 1978 (AP Photo)

that unless workers were organized and had legal recourse, they were essentially dehumanized and defenseless; on this occasion, "most of the bodies lay unidentified for days." State laws, in fact, had been broken in this incident, as a flatbed truck had been converted to a bus with no governmental approval—and with no safety belts. Chávez asserts that this was not an isolated incident but a common occurrence in the farm communities of California.

In the fifth paragraph, Chávez continues his appeal to sympathy by bringing his audience to the present: "Today, thousands of farm workers live under savage conditions." Here, Chávez contrasts the state-of-the-art farm technologies in the fields with the appalling conditions that farmworkers live under. His description is graphic and persuasive. Chávez does not spare his sophisticated audience the harsh details of the farmworkers' lives—"Vicious rats gnaw on them as they sleep"—making his description both graphic and persuasive. He describes lives of hardship and exploitation, noting that farmworkers "walk miles to buy food at inflated prices." In fact, the local stores were usually run by the owners of the fields, such that workers often found themselves owing more to the growers than what the

growers paid them, producing a vicious circle of poverty that constituted a virtual peonage system.

Chávez next addresses child labor, stressing that it is not a thing of the past: "As much as 30 percent of Northern California's garlic harvesters are under-aged children." This topic was especially close to Chávez's heart, as he himself had experienced the hardships of the life of a child working in the fields. He knew of the absence of stability and of how it felt to move from town to town following the harvests, working many hours with a body that was not mature enough. He knew how attending many schools led to the lack of a solid education. In denouncing child labor in this speech, he further seeks the sympathy and understanding of his audience.

Over the next three paragraphs, Chávez discusses three more facts of farmworkers' lives: malnutrition, a high infant mortality rate, and short life expectancy. He emphasizes that farmworkers lack health insurance and the hygienic conditions necessary to ensure the survival of their children. In addition, the backbreaking nature of farmwork has a devastating effect upon the physical condition of the workers.

Chávez has now set the stage to present his dream of improving the life conditions endured by farmworkers. In the twelfth paragraph he makes the appeal personal, stating, "All my life, I have been driven by one dream." Borrowing a sentiment made famous by a man he greatly admired—the civil rights activist Martin Luther King, Jr.—and knowing that his audience was familiar with the broader dream of social justice, Chávez details his dream of justice for the lowest of the low, the farmworker. He dreams that someday farmworkers will be treated like "human beings." Over the previous decade, Chávez had experienced attacks from conservatives and even from people of his own circle who did not understand his dream. La Botz notes that the 1980 election of Ronald Reagan—Chávez's "arch-enemy" (p. 159)—to the presidency and the 1982 election of Deukmejian as governor of California had created a climate unfavorable to the cause of minorities and to civil rights in general.

In paragraph 16, Chávez defines his dream as a form of resistance to oppression, drawing an analogy between slavery and the conditions that he had experienced as a child. He chooses to speak to his audience in terms that most educated Americans would understand, stating that he and his people were treated like "chattel"—like slaves. He emphasizes that his dream grew out of a desire to see racism and prejudice eradicated. Throughout his rhetoric, Chávez reiterates his basic principle, namely, that all human beings owe respect to one another as human beings. In this paragraph Chávez makes himself somewhat vulnerable, exposing his core humanity in expressing that his dream rose from the frustration and anger that he had experienced as a child facing prejudice. He saw that violence did not bring any resolution to race-related problems in America. Through his quest for an answer that would work for his people, he had come to favor a pacifist approach. He tells his audience that at one time he made a choice not to embrace the frustration and anger he felt in trying to combat prejudice.

Reminiscing about his life in the 1950s, Chávez describes the Sal Si Puedes Barrio in San Jose, where he first began to understand the importance of organizing when he saw workers exploited because they were not unionized. From then on he decided to dedicate his life to labor organizing.

Chávez next addresses the need for farmworkers to become citizens and the importance of civic education. He tells his audience of his humble beginnings as a member of an immigrant family who had to learn the basic principles of citizenship before feeling ready to lead farmworkers' organizing efforts. He believed that he could not rightfully tell others to fight for their rights if he did not know his own. He notes that the fate of Hispanics in America, regardless of socioeconomic status, is linked to the fate of the farmworkers. According to Chávez, just as free African Americans in the antebellum period felt a bond with their brothers and sisters under the yoke of slavery, Hispanics in the twentieth century could not enjoy freedom and advancement in society while their farmworker brothers and sisters suffered humiliation and defeat. The answer to the dilemma was civic education, which would allow farmworkers to exercise citizenship. As citizens, farmworkers could, without fear, enjoy their rights to free speech and to labor organizing.

Paragraphs 28 through 37 offer a defense of Chávez's beloved union—the United Farm Workers of America, or the UFW—and of his approach to unionizing. Here Chávez wants his audience to see that his primary concern is the betterment of the farmworker community. His core efforts were aimed at ensuring that collective bargaining became a reality and that Hispanics gained positions of leadership through which they could help bring about positive outcomes for Hispanics in general.

In paragraph 35 Chávez's spirituality is made evident. Chávez alludes to biblical teachings that hold that in the eyes of God, the humble will rule the earth. Chávez had grown up in a spiritual home: His mother was a strong and devoted Catholic who lived her life in a very Christian manner. This greatly influenced Chávez, who became keenly aware of the important role that religion and religious icons, such as the Virgin of Guadalupe, played in the lives of farmworkers. His awareness, in conjunction with his upbringing, motivated Chávez to adopt a deeply rooted spiritual stance. The main theme of this segment of his address is that if the lowest of the low can be successful in America, that reality in itself will inspire and support the dreams of other Hispanics: The humble can own the earth! Here Chávez uses the rhetorical technique anaphora (which appears in most of his speeches of this period), the repetition of phrases for emphasis: The union's survival—its very existence—sent out a signal to all Hispanics that we were fighting for our dignity, that we were challenging and overcoming injustice, that we were empowering the least educated among us—the poorest among us."

In the next segment of the address, beginning with paragraph 40, Chávez delivers a series of statements aimed at defending the position of the UFW in the 1980s. He addresses the accusation that the numbers of workers belonging to the UFW had decreased significantly since that time. He states that the mere fact that the union was under attack, with agribusiness spending millions of dollars in this attack, testified to its strength. He wants his audience to become aware of the full relevance of the union: All farmworkers, unionized or not, are directly or indirectly benefiting from union efforts to better their lives. Chávez sees his clarification of the vitality of the union as a fundamental point.

Paragraph 47 marks a transition. Chávez begins by reporting on the successes that Hispanics have experienced as a result of the union's work. Following this account, he declares, "Two major trends give us hope and encouragement"; his speeches always present necessary improvements and changes but also offer pictures of hope. Following this pattern, he gives an optimistic analysis of what the UFW has accomplished. One reason for hope is found in the positive results of the boycott of 1970, which, among other benefits, brought about regulations to protect workers from pesticides. The second reason for hope is that in the companies where workers were unionized, child labor had been abolished, and miserable wages and living conditions had been ameliorated.

After presenting what the union has accomplished for farmworkers, Chávez relates what is impeding progress in 1984. The Agricultural Labor Relations Act, passed in California in 1975, had corrected the omission of farmworkers from the 1935 National Labor Relations Act. The California act gave farmworkers the right to vote in collective bargaining elections. In the early 1970s growers signed "sweetheart" contracts with the Teamsters, a predominantly white union that did not recognize any of the needs of farmworkers. Chávez understood that the growers wanted a union that had the growers' own interests at heart. The Teamsters pledged to protect workers from pesticides, but the contracts that workers were asked to sign lacked specific measures to protect them. Chávez points out that the gains of the California labor act were virtually lost when Governor Deukmejian came to power in 1983, as he persisted in not enforcing the law that granted agricultural workers the right to unionize and strike. This, in Chávez's view, was a mockery of the principles embedded in the labor act. Chávez wanted his audience to know that these were dangerous times for farmworkers. This part of his address is essentially a call to alarm, lest what had been won should be lost; Chávez goes as far as to assert that "the law that guarantees our right to organize ... doesn't work anymore." This statement specifically signifies that the act giving farmworkers the right to organize was violated when growers were allowed to choose which union should represent the farmworker. He denounces the financial contributions that Deukmejian had received from growers, exposing him as a man who had sold his soul, so to speak, to that lobby. In one of the most powerful statements of his speech, Chávez laments, "Deukmejian has paid back his debt to the growers with the blood and sweat of California farm workers."

First denouncing the governor's role in the setbacks to the unionization of farmworkers, Chávez then begins to detail what has been compromised. Here he uses anaphora again. He asks the rhetorical question "What does all this mean for farm workers?" and responds with a series of statements beginning with the words "It means," evoking a nightmarish landscape of poverty, deprivation, child labor, and oppression. He wants his audience to know that all that has been won could indeed be lost unless something is done to stop the conservative dominion over the rights of farmworkers, as held by conservative politicians in complicity with agribusiness.

Chávez follows with more rhetorical questions: "Are these make-believe threats? Are they exaggerations?" In a series of responses to his questions, he begins with the word "Ask": "Ask the farmworkers who are still waiting for growers to bargain in good faith and sign contracts! Ask the farm workers who've been fired from their jobs because they spoke out for the union. Ask the farm workers who've been threatened with physical violence because they support the UFW." He cites the threats and actual physical violence that farmworkers have endured as the price to pay for the right to belong to the UFW. He mentions a particular incident in Fresno where a worker lost his life to violence as a result of his union activities; Chávez himself had been to the funeral of Rene Lopez, a nineteen-year-old worker at Sikkema Dairy, near Fresno. In a statement related to Lopez's death, Chávez had noted, "Rene's first union card was also his last." (http://clnet.ucla.edu/research/chavez/themes/ufw/rene.htm). In mentioning this incident, Chávez communicates to his audience that agribusiness did not stop at murder to prevent farmworkers from belonging to the UFW.

Chávez next makes another appeal to sympathy. He knew that his listeners were primarily wealthy, educated people and that San Francisco, a city with a long progressive tradition, was bound to have an audience favorable to environmentalism and human rights. Thus, he makes another call to boycott grapes, to protest both environmental issues and the violations of human rights that agribusiness is continuing to commit. Here he acknowledges the importance of help from environmentally conscious nonminority people. His allies also included members of the baby boom generation who had supported civil rights and environmental consciousness twenty years earlier and who continued to fight for those causes. Keenly aware of his audience, Chávez speaks of environmental issues as they relate to middle- and upper-class professionals as well as to farmworkers.

Chávez next focuses on new forms of violations of farmworkers' rights, including sexual harassment and pesticides found to be carcinogenic. He wants his audience to know, however, that change is on the horizon. Jensen and Hammerback note that in his leadership of the UFW, Chávez recognized the need to modernize the way in which the union reached its audience; in the computer age, Chávez relates, the UFW has begun using technological means of making its messages known. He then enumerates a series of positive changes that have encouraged him, among them the rapid growth in the Hispanic population. As consistent with his lifelong belief in the power of suffrage, Chávez states that as Hispanics become registered voters, their numbers in political positions will increase as well.

Close to the end of his speech, Chávez's tone changes markedly, from one of hope to one of unapologetic indictment of agribusiness. He addresses the environmental damage that has been done to the land and the consequences of this damage, identifying the growers as clearly responsible. He cites the historical misuse of government handouts, probably referring to Agricultural Adjustment Administration policies during the Great Depression; growers had a long history of "special privileges," in the form of government subsidies originally designed to help the humble farmer, the historic "yeoman." The programs designed to help small farmers were not congruent with the reality of the giant California farms owned by very powerful men. Chávez notes that "rural lawmakers dominated the Legislature and the Congress" until the landmark Supreme Court decision in *Reynolds v. Sims* (1964), which he refers to as the "'one person, one vote' decision." This decision estab-

> *"All my life, I have been driven by one dream, one goal, one vision: To overthrow a farm labor system in this nation which treats farm workers as if they were not important human beings."*
>
> (Paragraph 12)

> *"Our union will forever exist as an empowering force among Chicanos in the Southwest. And that means our power and our influence will grow and not diminish."*
>
> (Paragraph 49)

lished that state districts were to be drawn with roughly equal divisions of population. This diminished the power that agribusiness had gained in scarcely populated rural areas, where a few growers could have as much political power as a more densely populated region.

Chávez refers to the awakening of urban taxpayers, who began to question why they should pay for the extravagancy of growers. Continuing to use religious terminology, he speaks of the "sins of the growers." Again employing anaphora, he states, "We did not poison the land. We did not...." The growers are in denial, however, as they refuse to acknowledge the sins they have committed against "brown people" and against the land. Chávez announces that even though Republicans are in power, he refuses to be pessimistic about the conservative trend that they have brought. He hopes that the general public can see that "corporate growers are the past," as they have been exposed as greedy, power-hungry individuals far from being the traditional yeomen whose privileges they claimed.

The last segment of Chávez's speech is optimistic and uplifting, as he predicts that social change is unstoppable. Drawing from principles that Martin Luther King, Jr., used to promote the uplifting of the African American race, Chávez declares that once the lowly and oppressed taste freedom, they cannot return to their former state; further, he asserts that education is the key to freedom, as has historically been the case. Once more, Chávez depends on his educated audience's knowledge of American history. He knows that most Americans are familiar with the history of slavery and with how masters opposed teaching slaves to read because they knew that "you cannot uneducate the person who has learned to read."

Chávez refers back to the basic principles of La Causa to posit that the UFW is more than a union; it is a way of life that teaches people who belong to it or who have been supported by it to walk tall and to help others do the same. The people who have experienced what the cause stands for—

namely, civil rights, decent living conditions, and equal rights for all—will not return to oppression. Their stand will make politicians acknowledge them, and Hispanics will receive treatment more congruent with their growing numbers. Chávez harks back to a statement he made at the beginning of his speech, when he recalled that while farmworkers were great in number, a select few were dictating their lot. At the end of his speech, Chávez declares that farmworkers have learned what representation means and will let their numbers speak of their political power. In a way again reminiscent of Martin Luther King, Jr., Chávez ends his speech by describing what he sees as the promised land—the land where equal rights reign. Echoing King, Chávez reminds his audience of Jesus's statement regarding the supper he will hold when he comes back after his Resurrection: "The last shall be first and the first shall be last." The lowly—the farmworker and his children—will be the first to sit at the table in a place of honor. He hopes that farmworkers' resilience will allow them a place of honor at the tables of America.

Audience

The primary audience for Chávez's speech was the Commonwealth Club of California in San Francisco. The club is a nonpartisan educational organization that promotes art and the free exchange of ideas through guest speakers and panels. Among the guest speakers that have spoken to the club are former presidents and other political leaders. According to Marc Grossman, the speech was also broadcast to approximately ninety radio stations.

Impact

The immediate significance of César Chávez's Commonwealth Address partly lay in the speaker's deep introspection, which allowed listeners a closer look not just at his philosophy but also at his feelings as a leader and as a man. The speech also broadcast his thoughts about the use of pesticides in crop fields. Chávez offered a bold denunciation of some of the practices of right-wing conservatives in the nation and more particularly in California, which served to prepare the public to understand the coming grape boycott.

Predictions that Chávez made regarding the ascendancy of Latinos to positions of political leadership in the United States indeed came true. The chant of *"Si se puede!"* ("It can be done!") in the May 2006 march held to protest racial discrimination against illegal aliens and the potential of impending legislation to do away with their human rights was a testament to Chávez's philosophy that anything is possible if one tries. Chávez's Commonwealth Address was a hymn of optimism and hope in the midst of difficulty, and it remains a testament to Chávez's resilience and to his idea that "it can be done"—*"Si se puede!"*

Related Documents

Jensen, Richard J., and John C. Hammerback, eds. *The Words of César Chávez.* College Station: Texas A&M University Press, 2002. Speeches of particular note in this volume include "César Chávez Talks about Organizing and about the History of the NFWA, December 1965"; "Martin Luther King, Jr.: He Showed Us the Way, April 1978"; "The Plan of Delano (English and Spanish Versions), 1966"; and "Wrath of Grapes Boycott Speech, 1986."

Bibliography

■ Articles

García, Richard A. "César Chávez: A Personal and Historical Testimony." *Pacific Historical Review* 63, no. 2 (May 1994): 225–233.

Gordon, Robert. "Poisons in the Fields: The United Farm Workers, Pesticides, and Environmental Politics." *Pacific Historical Review* 68, no. 1 (February 1999): 51–77.

"Gov. Brown Orders Full Probe of Train Bus Crash." *Salinas Californian*, September 18, 1963.

Martin, Phillip L., and Daniel L. Egan. "The Makewhole Remedy in California Agriculture." *Industrial and Labor Relations Review* 43, no. 1 (October 1989): 120–130.

Rivera, Alicia. "Solidarity in the San Joaquin Valley, California Cotton Strike of 1933." Master's thesis, California State University, Fresno, 2005.

Stavans, Ilan. "Reading Cesar." *Transition* 9, no. 4 (2000): 62–76.

Walsh, Edward J. "On the Interaction between a Movement and Its Environment." *American Sociological Review* 43, no. 1 (February 1978): 110–112.

Zompetti, Joseph P. "César Chávez's Rhetorical Strategies of Resistance." PhD dissertation, Wayne State University, 1998.

■ Books

Kushner, Sam. *Long Road to Delano.* New York: International Publishers, 1975.

La Botz, Dan. *César Chávez and La Causa.* New York: Pearson Longman, 2006.

Matthiessen, Peter. *Sal Si Puedes (Escape If You Can): Cesar Chavez and the New American Revolution.* Berkeley: University of California Press, 2000.

■ Web Sites

Commonwealth Club Web site.
    http://www.commonwealthclub.org. Accessed on March 10, 2008.

"Rene Lopez (1962–1983)." United Farm Workers Web site.
    http://clnet.ucla.edu/research/chavez/themes/ufw/rene.htm. Accessed on March 8, 2008.

"Rerum novarum: Encyclical of Pope Leo XIII on Capital and Labor." The Holy See Web site.
    http://www.vatican.va/holy_father/leo_xiii/encyclicals/documents/hf_l-xiii_enc_15051891_rerum-novarum_en.html. Accessed on March 10, 2008.

United Farm Workers Web site.
    http://www.ufw.org/. Accessed on March 10, 2008.

—By Alicia J. Rivera

Questions for Further Study

1. Consider how César Chávez's philosophy changed throughout his life by comparing his speeches from different periods.

2. How is Chávez's message of nonviolence presented in his various speeches?

3. What is the essence of Chávez's spiritual message?

4. How does Chávez use rhetoric to convey his messages both clearly and powerfully?

5. Which speech (or part of a speech) stands out to you as the most introspective? Support your contention with examples.

6. Examine and describe similarities between Chávez's and Martin Luther King's ideologies.

7. What were the fundamental ideas behind Chávez's fasting?

Glossary

braceros	Mexican workers, primarily peasants, imported by the U.S. government to fill the need for manual labor in crop fields in a program that ended in 1964

CÉSAR CHÁVEZ'S COMMONWEALTH ADDRESS

Twenty-one years ago last September, on a lonely stretch of railroad track paralleling U.S. Highway 101 near Salinas, 32 Bracero farm workers lost their lives in a tragic accident.

The Braceros had been imported from Mexico to work on California farms. They died when their bus, which was converted from a flatbed truck, drove in front of a freight train.

Conversion of the bus had not been approved by any government agency. The driver had "tunnel" vision.

Most of the bodies lay unidentified for days. No one, including the grower who employed the workers, even knew their names.

Today, thousands of farm workers live under savage conditions—beneath trees and amid garbage and human excrement—near tomato fields in San Diego County, tomato fields which use the most modern farm technology.

Vicious rats gnaw on them as they sleep. They walk miles to buy food at inflated prices. And they carry in water from irrigation pumps.

Child labor is still common in many farm areas.

As much as 30 percent of Northern California's garlic harvesters are under-aged children. Kids as young as six years old have voted in state-conducted union elections since they qualified as workers.

Some 800,000 under-aged children work with their families harvesting crops across America. Babies born to migrant workers suffer 25 percent higher infant mortality than the rest of the population.

Malnutrition among migrant worker children is 10 times higher than the national rate.

Farm workers' average life expectancy is still 49 years—compared to 73 years for the average American.

All my life, I have been driven by one dream, one goal, one vision: To overthrow a farm labor system in this nation which treats farm workers as if they were not important human beings.

Farm workers are not agricultural implements. They are not beasts of burden—to be used and discarded.

That dream was born in my youth. It was nurtured in my early days of organizing. It has flourished. It has been attacked.

I'm not very different from anyone else who has ever tried to accomplish something with his life. My motivation comes from my personal life—from watching what my mother and father went through when I was growing up; from what we experienced as migrant farm workers in California.

That dream, that vision, grew from my own experience with racism, with hope, with the desire to be treated fairly and to see my people treated as human beings and not as chattel.

It grew from anger and rage—emotions I felt 40 years ago when people of my color were denied the right to see a movie or eat at a restaurant in many parts of California.

It grew from the frustration and humiliation I felt as a boy who couldn't understand how the growers could abuse and exploit farm workers when there were so many of us and so few of them.

Later, in the '50s, I experienced a different kind of exploitation. In San Jose, in Los Angeles and in other urban communities, we—the Mexican American people—were dominated by a majority that was Anglo.

I began to realize what other minority people had discovered: That the only answer—the only hope—was in organizing. More of us had to become citizens. We had to register to vote. And people like me had to develop the skills it would take to organize, to educate, to help empower the Chicano people.

I spent many years—before we founded the union—learning how to work with people.

We experienced some successes in voter registration, in politics, in battling racial discrimination—successes in an era when Black Americans were just beginning to assert their civil rights and when political awareness among Hispanics was almost non-existent.

But deep in my heart, I knew I could never be happy unless I tried organizing the farm workers. I didn't know if I would succeed. But I had to try.

All Hispanics—urban and rural, young and old—are connected to the farm workers' experience. We had all lived through the fields—or our parents had. We shared that common humiliation.

How could we progress as a people, even if we lived in the cities, while the farm workers—men and women of our color—were condemned to a life without pride?

How could we progress as a people while the farm workers—who symbolized our history in this land—were denied self-respect?

How could our people believe that their children could become lawyers and doctors and judges and business people while this shame, this injustice was permitted to continue?

Those who attack our union often say, 'It's not really a union. It's something else: A social movement. A civil rights movement. It's something dangerous.'

They're half right. The United Farm Workers is first and foremost a union. A union like any other. A union that either produces for its members on the bread and butter issues or doesn't survive.

But the UFW has always been something more than a union—although it's never been dangerous if you believe in the Bill of Rights.

The UFW was the beginning! We attacked that historical source of shame and infamy that our people in this country lived with. We attacked that injustice, not by complaining; not by seeking hand-outs; not by becoming soldiers in the War on Poverty.

We organized!

Farm workers acknowledged we had allowed ourselves to become victims in a democratic society—a society where majority rule and collective bargaining are supposed to be more than academic theories or political rhetoric. And by addressing this historical problem, we created confidence and pride and hope in an entire people's ability to create the future.

The UFW's survival—its existence—was not in doubt in my mind when the time began to come—after the union became visible—when Chicanos started entering college in greater numbers, when Hispanics began running for public office in greater numbers—when our people started asserting their rights on a broad range of issues and in many communities across the country.

The union's survival—its very existence—sent out a signal to all Hispanics that we were fighting for our dignity, that we were challenging and overcoming injustice, that we were empowering the least educated among us—the poorest among us.

The message was clear: If it could happen in the fields, it could happen anywhere—in the cities, in the courts, in the city councils, in the state legislatures.

I didn't really appreciate it at the time, but the coming of our union signaled the start of great changes among Hispanics that are only now beginning to be seen.

I've travelled to every part of this nation. I have met and spoken with thousands of Hispanics from every walk of life—from every social and economic class.

One thing I hear most often from Hispanics, regardless of age or position—and from many non-Hispanics as well—is that the farm workers gave them hope that they could succeed and the inspiration to work for change.

From time to time you will hear our opponents declare that the union is weak, that the union has no support, that the union has not grown fast enough. Our obituary has been written many times.

How ironic it is that the same forces which argue so passionately that the union is not influential are the same forces that continue to fight us so hard.

The union's power in agriculture has nothing to do with the number of farm workers under union contract. It has nothing to do with the farm workers' ability to contribute to Democratic politicians. It doesn't even have much to do with our ability to conduct successful boycotts.

The very fact of our existence forces an entire industry—unionized and non-unionized—to spend millions of dollars year after year on improved wages, on improved working conditions, on benefits for workers.

If we're so weak and unsuccessful, why do the growers continue to fight us with such passion?

Because so long as we continue to exist, farm workers will benefit from our existence—even if they don't work under union contract.

It doesn't really matter whether we have 100,000 members or 500,000 members. In truth, hundreds of thousands of farm workers in Calfiornia—and in other states—are better off today because of our work.

And Hispanics across California and the nation who don't work in agriculture are better off today because of what the farm workers taught people about organization, about pride and strength, about seizing control over their own lives.

Tens of thousands of the children and grandchildren of farm workers and the children and grandchildren of poor Hispanics are moving out of the fields and out of the barrios—and into the professions and into business and into politics. And that movement cannot be reversed!

Our union will forever exist as an empowering force among Chicanos in the Southwest. And that means our power and our influence will grow and not diminish.

Two major trends give us hope and encouragement.

First, our union has returned to a tried and tested weapon in the farm workers' non-violent arsenal—the boycott!

After the Agricultural Labor Relations Act became law in California in 1975, we dismantled our boycott to work with the law.

During the early- and mid-'70s, millions of Americans supported our boycotts. After 1975, we redirected our efforts from the boycott to organizing and winning elections under the law.

The law helped farm workers make progress in overcoming poverty and injustice. At companies where farm workers are protected by union contracts, we have made progress in overcoming child labor, in overcoming miserable wages and working conditions, in overcoming sexual harassment of women workers, in overcoming dangerous pesticides which poison our people and poison the food we all eat.

Where we have organized, these injustices soon pass into history.

But under Republican Governor George Deukmejian, the law that guarantees our right to organize no longer protects farm workers. It doesn't work anymore.

In 1982, corporate growers gave Deukmejian one million dollars to run for governor of California. Since he took office, Deukmejian has paid back his debt to the growers with the blood and sweat of California farm workers.

Instead of enforcing the law as it was written against those who break it, Deukmejian invites growers who break the law to seek relief from the governor's appointees.

What does all this mean for farm workers?

It means that the right to vote in free elections is a sham. It means that the right to talk freely about the union among your fellow workers on the job is a cruel hoax. It means the right to be free from threats and intimidation by growers is an empty promise.

It means the right to sit down and negotiate with your employer as equals across the bargaining table—and not as peons in the field—is a fraud. It means that thousands of farm workers—who are owed millions of dollars in back pay because their employers broke the law—are still waiting for their checks.

It means that 36,000 farm workers—who voted to be represented by the United Farm Workers in free elections—are still waiting for contracts from growers who refuse to bargain in good faith.

It means that, for farm workers, child labor will continue. It means that infant mortality will continue. It means malnutrition among our children will continue. It means the short life expectancy and the inhuman living and working conditions will continue.

Are these make-believe threats? Are they exaggerations?

Ask the farm workers who are still waiting for growers to bargain in good faith and sign contracts. Ask the farm workers who've been fired from their jobs because they spoke out for the union. Ask the farm workers who've been threatened with physical violence because they support the UFW.

Ask the family of Rene Lopez, the young farm worker from Fresno who was shot to death last year because he supported the union.

These tragic events forced farm workers to declare a new international boycott of California table grapes. That's why we are asking Americans once again to join the farm workers by boycotting California grapes.

The Louis Harris poll revealed that 17 million American adults boycotted grapes. We are convinced that those people and that good will have not disappeared.

That segment of the population which makes our boycotts work are the Hispanics, the Blacks, the other minorities and our allies in labor and the church. But it is also an entire generation of young Americans who matured politically and socially in the 1960s and '70s—millions of people for whom boycotting grapes and other products became a socially accepted pattern of behavior.

If you were young, Anglo and on or near campus during the late '60s and early '70s, chances are you supported farm workers.

Fifteen years later, the men and women of that generation of are alive and well. They are in their mid-30s and '40s. They are pursuing professional careers. Their disposable income is relatively high. But they are still inclined to respond to an appeal from farm workers. The union's mission still has meaning for them.

Only today we must translate the importance of a union for farm workers into the language of the 1980s. Instead of talking about the right to organize, we must talk about protection against sexual harasasment in the fields. We must speak about the right to quality food—and food that is safe to eat.

I can tell you that the new language is working; the 17 million are still there. They are resonding—not to picketlines and leafletting alone, but to the high-tech boycott of today—a boycott that uses computers and direct mail and advertising techniques which have revolutionized business and politics in recent years.

We have achieved more success with the boycott in the first 11 months of 1984 that we achieved in the 14 years since 1970.

The other trend that gives us hope is the monumental growth of Hispanic influence in this country and what that means in increased population, increased social and economic clout, and increased political influence.

South of the Sacramento River in California, Hispanics now make up more than 25 percent of the population. That figure will top 30 percent by the year 2000.

There are 1.1 million Spanish-surnamed registered voters in California; 85 percent are Democrats; only 13 percent are Republicans.

In 1975, there were 200 Hispanic elected officials at all levels of government. In 1984, there are over 400 elected judges, city council members, mayors and legislators.

In light of these trends, it is absurd to believe or suggest that we are going to go back in time—as a union or as a people!

The growers often try to blame the union for their problems—to lay their sins off on us—sins for which they only have themselves to blame.

The growers only have themselves to blame as they begin to reap the harvest from decades of environmental damage they have brought upon the land—the pesticides, the herbicides, the soil fumigants, the fertilizers, the salt deposits from thoughtless irrigation—the ravages from years of unrestrained poisoning of our soil and water.

Thousands of acres of land in California have already been irrevocably damaged by this wanton abuse of nature. Thousands more will be lost unless growers understand that dumping more poisons on the soil won't solve their problems—on the short term or the long term.

Health authorities in many San Joaquin Valley towns already warn young children and pregnant women not to drink the water because of nitrates from fertilizers which have contaminated the groundwater.

The growers only have themselves to blame for an increasing demand by consumers for higher quality food—food that isn't tainted by toxics; food that doesn't result from plant mutations or chemicals which produce red, lucious-looking tomatos—that taste like alfalfa.

The growers are making the same mistake American automakers made in the '60s and '70s when they refused to produce small economical cars—and opened the door to increased foreign competition.

Growers only have themselves to blame for increasing attacks on their publicly-financed hand-outs and government welfare: Water subsidies; mechanization research; huge subsidies for not growing crops.

These special privileges came into being before the Supreme Court's one-person, one-vote decision—at a time when rural lawmakers dominated the Legislature and the Congress. Soon, those hand-outs could be in jeopardy as government searches for more revenue and as urban taxpayers take a closer look at farm programs—and who they really benefit.

The growers only have themselves to blame for the humiliation they have brought upon succeeding waves of immigrant groups which have sweated and sacrificed for 100 years to make this industry rich. For generations, they have subjugated entire races of dark-skinned farm workers.

These are the sins of the growers, not the farm workers. We didn't poison the land. We didn't open the door to imported produce. We didn't covet billions of dollars in government hand-outs. We didn't abuse and exploit the people who work the land.

Today, the growers are like a punch-drunk old boxer who doesn't know he's past his prime. The times are changing. The political and social environment has changed. The chickens are coming home to roost—and the time to account for past sins is approaching.

I am told, these days, why farm workers should be discouraged and pessimistic: The Republicans control the governor's office and the White House. They say there is a conservative trend in the nation.

Yet we are filled with hope and encouragement. We have looked into the future and the future is ours!

History and inevitability are on our side. The farm workers and their children—and the Hispanics and their children—are the future in California. And corporate growers are the past!

Those politicians who ally themselves with the corporate growers and against the farm workervs and the Hispanics are in for a big surprise. They want to make their careers in politics. They want to hold power 20 and 30 years from now.

But 20 and 30 years from now—in Modesto, in Salinas, in Fresno, in Bakersfield, in the Imperial Valley, and in many of the great cities of California—those communities will be dominated by farm workers and not by growers, by the children and randchildren of farm workers and not by the children and grandchildren of growers.

These trends are part of the forces of history that cannot be stopped. No person and no organization can resist them for very long. They are inevitable.

Once social change begins, it cannot be reversed.

You cannot uneducate the person who has learned to read. You cannot humiliate the person who feels pride. You cannot oppress the people who are not afraid anymore.

Our opponents must understand that it's not just a union we have built. Unions, like other institutions, can come and go.

But we're more than an institution. For nearly 20 years, our union has been on the cutting edge of a people's cause—and you cannot do away with an entire people; you cannot stamp out a people's cause.

Regardless of what the future holds for the union, regardless of what the future holds for farm workers, our accomplishments cannot be undone. "La Causa"—our cause—doesn't have to be experienced twice.

The consciousness and pride that were raised by our union are alive and thriving inside millions of young Hispanics who will never work on a farm!

Like the other immigrant groups, the day will come when we win the economic and political rewards which are in keeping with our numbers in society. The day will come when the politicians do the right thing by our people out of political necessity and not out of charity or idealism.

That day may not come this year. That day may not come during this decade. But it will come, someday!

And when that day comes, we shall see the fulfillment of that passage from the Book of Matthew in the New Testament, "That the last shall be first and the first shall be last."

And on that day, our nation shall fulfill its creed—and that fulfillment shall enrich us all.

Thank you very much.

President George H. W. Bush, 1991 (AP Photo/Doug Mills)

GEORGE H. W. BUSH'S ADDRESS TO CONGRESS ON THE PERSIAN GULF CRISIS

"Our world leadership and domestic strength are mutual and reinforcing."

Overview

Eleven years before another President Bush spoke on a day that Americans will always remember, the first President Bush addressed the American people on September 11, 1990, about a Middle Eastern threat to U.S. values and security. President George H. W. Bush discussed Iraq's military occupation of neighboring Kuwait and declared that this invasion would not stand. He spoke hopefully about how determined action by a broad coalition of nations not only would repel aggression but also would help create "a new world order" of peace and security. Bush also warned that economic problems at home threatened U.S. leadership abroad and appealed for public support for new legislation to reduce a growing budget deficit. As was often the case during his presidency, Bush enjoyed far more success in international affairs than in domestic matters. Even though the United States and its coalition partners achieved victory in the Persian Gulf War of 1991 that liberated Kuwait, Bush found that economic problems diminished his popularity and contributed to his defeat when he ran for a second term in 1992.

Context

Iraq's invasion of Kuwait on August 2, 1990, brought about a major international crisis. The invasion came as a surprise to most world leaders. Saddam Hussein, the president of Iraq, ordered military action for several reasons. Iraq had severe financial problems because of a long, costly war that it had fought with Iran from 1980 to 1988. Although Iraq was a major oil producer, falling petroleum prices in the late 1980s undermined Iraqi efforts to pay off its war debts. Although many oil-producing nations agreed to limit production to increase prices, Kuwait refused to do so. Finally, there had been border disputes ever since Kuwait achieved its independence from Great Britain in 1961. Hussein maintained that Kuwaiti territory that contained rich oil deposits really belonged to Iraq.

The United States had provided aid to Iraq during its war with Iran. U.S. officials were keenly aware that Hussein, who had become president in 1979, had started the war and commonly treated Iraqi citizens with brutality. But in the aftermath of the Iran hostage crisis of 1979 to 1981, when fifty-two Americans were held captive for 444 days after Iranian students seized the U.S. embassy in Tehran, any enemy of Iran had a common interest with the United States. The Bush administration continued to provide agricultural credits to Iraq. The president later explained that U.S. policy was to "work with Saddam Hussein and … bring him along into the family of nations" (Parmet, p. 446).

Once Iraqi forces invaded, however, Bush was outraged. He denounced the move into Kuwait as a violation of international law, and he quickly telephoned other world leaders to enlist their support. Concerned that Iraqi troops might move next into Saudi Arabia, one of the world's largest oil producers, Bush urged King Fahd to allow U.S. troops to help defend his country. On August 8, Bush spoke to the American people on national television and announced the beginning of Operation Desert Shield, the dispatch of U.S. forces to deter an attack against Saudi Arabia. Yet even before he made that announcement, the president said that U.S. objectives in the Persian Gulf went beyond preventing another Iraqi invasion. On August 5 he told reporters, "This will not stand, this aggression against Kuwait" (Parmet, p. 458). The next day, the United Nations (UN) Security Council approved economic sanctions to force Iraq to withdraw from Kuwait. Bush said he would give sanctions time to work, but in case they did not, U.S. military leaders made plans for war in the Persian Gulf.

The president also faced major economic problems as he dealt with this international crisis. During the 1980s the federal budget deficit had grown to record levels. Congress passed legislation in 1985, modified two years later, known as the Gramm-Rudman-Hollings Act, which set annual targets for the deficit in an effort to reduce it over several years. If the deficit exceeded the target, an automatic cut, known as a "sequester," would occur in most government programs.

In early 1990 the projected deficit for the fiscal year, which would begin on October 1, was greater than the annual target. The president quietly met with congressional leaders about reducing the deficit. Democrats controlled both houses of Congress, and their leaders asked the president if he would be willing to consider tax increases as part

1979

■ **July 16**
Saddam Hussein becomes the president of Iraq.

1988

■ **August 18**
President George H. W. Bush pledges that he will not raise taxes if elected and asserts that if Congress pressures him to do so, he will reply, "Read my lips: no new taxes."

1990

■ **August 2**
Iraqi military forces invade Kuwait, overthrow the government, and occupy that nation.

■ **August 2**
By a vote of fourteen to zero, the UN Security Council condemns the Iraqi invasion of Kuwait and demands the withdrawal of Iraqi military forces from that country; four days later the UN Security Council imposes economic sanctions against Iraq.

■ **August 5**
During a question-and-answer session with reporters, Bush declares, "This will not stand, this aggression against Kuwait."

■ **August 8**
Bush announces that he is sending U.S. troops to Saudi Arabia to protect that nation against Iraqi attack in what is known as Operation Desert Shield.

■ **September 11**
Bush gives a televised address before a joint session of Congress about the Persian Gulf crisis and the federal budget deficit.

■ **November 5**
Bush signs the Omnibus Budget Reconciliation Act of 1990, which increases some taxes in order to reduce the federal deficit by almost $500 billion dollars during the next five years.

■ **November 29**
The UN Security Council sets a deadline of January 15, 1991, for an Iraqi withdrawal from Kuwait and authorizes member states to use "all necessary means" against Iraq if it fails to comply.

of the solution to the deficit problem. Less than two years earlier, when he accepted the Republican nomination for president, Bush had pledged that he would not yield to pressure, no matter how great, to raise taxes. He said his response would be "Read my lips: no new taxes" (Greene, p. 37). Yet Bush knew that it would be all but impossible to control the deficit without raising taxes. The economy was slowing in 1990 and heading toward recession. In addition, severe problems with financial institutions called savings and loans (S&Ls) added to the federal deficit. Because of changes in government regulations in the 1980s, S&Ls had more freedom to make investments to earn money for their depositors. When many of those investments went bad and the S&Ls, in large numbers, went bankrupt, the federal government was left with a huge bill, about $150 billion, to reimburse depositors who had lost their savings. When the White House announced that budget negotiations were taking place without preconditions—that is, the president had not ruled out a tax increase—there was a storm of criticism that Bush had violated a promise to the American people. Bush continued to meet with congressional negotiators, but their talks made no progress. "I must say I hate dealing with Congress and these budget matters," the president wrote in his diary. "I much prefer foreign affairs" (Parmet, p. 430).

About the Author

George Herbert Walker Bush was born in Milton, Massachusetts, on June 12, 1924, and grew up in Greenwich, Connecticut, in a rich, privileged family. His father, Prescott Bush, was a partner in a prominent investment banking firm and later served from 1952 to 1963 as a Republican U.S. senator from Connecticut. After graduating from the Phillips Academy on his birthday in 1942, Bush enlisted that same day in the U.S. Navy. He became the youngest pilot in that service. He earned the Distinguished Flying Cross in 1944 when his plane was hit by anti-aircraft fire during a bombing mission in the western Pacific. He married Barbara Pierce in January 1945, enrolled at Yale University, and earned a degree in economics in 1948.

After graduation, Bush moved to Texas, where he established the Zapata Petroleum Company. By the 1960s his company and its affiliates were involved in oil production in many parts of the world, including the Persian Gulf. He entered Republican politics in Texas during the early 1960s and won election in 1966 to the U.S. House of Representatives. After two terms, he ran for the U.S. Senate in 1970, but he lost to Democrat Lloyd Bentsen. Following his defeat, Bush was appointed to several major positions, including U.S. ambassador to the UN from 1971 to 1972, chair of the Republican National Committee (1972–1974), U.S. representative to the People's Republic of China (1974–1975), and director of the Central Intelligence Agency (1976–1977). In 1980 Bush campaigned unsuccessfully for the Republican nomination for president. Ronald Reagan asked Bush to join the ticket as his vice presidential running mate, and he served two terms in that office (1981–1989). In 1988 he won the Republican nomination for president and then handily defeated his Democratic opponent, Michael Dukakis of Massachusetts, in November.

Bush's most significant achievements as president were in foreign affairs. During his first year in the White House, the cold war ended as the Soviet empire in Eastern Europe collapsed when popular revolutions drove Communist regimes from power. As the Berlin Wall tumbled on November 9, 1989, Bush avoided any triumphant declarations and instead established a cooperative relationship with the Soviet president, Mikhail Gorbachev, that reshaped international relations. The new U.S.–Soviet harmony contributed to concerted international opposition to the Iraqi invasion of Kuwait in 1990. Bush forged a broad international coalition that waged the Persian Gulf War in January to February 1991 to liberate Kuwait.

Bush had a much less successful record in domestic affairs. He signed the Americans with Disabilities Act and the Clean Air Act, but economic troubles persisted throughout his presidency. In 1991 a recession erased the gains in the public approval polls that he had made during the Persian Gulf War. Many conservative Republicans doubted that he shared their convictions, especially after he agreed to tax increases in 1990 to close the federal budget deficit. Liberals and moderates complained that he had no grand goals that he hoped to achieve as president. In a three-way contest for the presidency in 1992 that included independent candidate Ross Perot, Bush lost the election to the Democratic nominee, Bill Clinton. After leaving the presidency, Bush retired from politics. In 2001 he became the second former president—John Adams was the first—to see his son (George W. Bush) inaugurated as president.

Explanation and Analysis of the Document

Unlike Reagan, his predecessor in the White House, Bush did not have a reputation as a "Great Communicator." He was instead known for using words carelessly, ineffectively, and even strangely; his critics called these mistakes "Bushisms." But as he begins his speech on September 11, 1990, President Bush uses one of the most effective techniques of Reagan, the Great Communicator: He presents a complex and controversial issue in human terms. After providing the basic facts that had produced the crisis in the Persian Gulf, Bush concentrates in the first four paragraphs of his address on the American men and women in uniform who are meeting this international challenge. He praises their courage, dedication, and skill, and he emphasizes the sacrifices they are making, along with those of their family members, while serving far from home with little advance notice. Bush then puts a human face on the thousands of Americans in uniform in the Persian Gulf as he uses the example of Private Wade Merritt. Whatever differences there might be about how to deal with Iraqi aggression, the president emphasizes that Americans should unite in thanking U.S. troops and supporting them.

Time Line

1991

■ **January 17**
The first U.S. air strikes occur against Iraq in Operation Desert Storm as the Persian Gulf War begins.

■ **February 27**
Bush proclaims the liberation of Kuwait and orders the cessation of all offensive military actions.

2003

■ **March 19**
The armed forces of a U.S.-led coalition begin military action against Iraq.

2006

■ **December 30**
Hussein, who had been captured three years earlier, is executed by hanging after being found guilty in an Iraqi court of crimes against humanity for his role in a 1982 massacre.

The president then builds on this theme of national unity as he tries to capitalize on public approval of the steps he had taken in the aftermath of Iraq's invasion of Kuwait. He asks the American people to support not only the troops but also their mission. He also links the defense of U.S. interests and values abroad to economic strength at home. Polls showed that his approval rating had increased by twelve points, to 75 percent, after his decision to commit U.S. military forces to the Persian Gulf. Yet the same polls revealed that only a small plurality of Americans (49 to 41 percent) thought the current situation justified the United States' going to war. Most Americans (69 percent) also believed an economic recession would occur during the next year, and a smaller but still substantial majority (53 percent) disapproved of the president's handling of the economy. By linking the crisis in the Persian Gulf and the health of the economy, the president hoped to use his public approval on the first issue to increase support for his proposals to deal with the second issue.

In the next section of his address (paragraphs 5 to 8), Bush asserts that what is happening in the Persian Gulf could shape world affairs for years to come. He states four clear goals: the withdrawal of Iraqi military forces from Kuwait, the restoration of Kuwait's government, the preservation of security in the Persian Gulf, and the protection of American lives. These objectives, which he had announced a month earlier when sending U.S. troops to Saudi Arabia, rested on principles that most nations had accepted. International peace and stability could not exist if aggressors could conquer other nations. The members of the UN Security Council had agreed, when a month earlier they had condemned Iraq's invasion, demanded the withdrawal of its troops from Kuwait, and imposed economic sanctions on Iraq. Hussein had not just invaded one nation or challenged regional stability; he had violated principles that put him at odds with the world community. "It is Iraq against the world," the president asserts.

This crisis occurred at what Bush calls "a unique and extraordinary moment," since the end of the cold war less than a year earlier had fundamentally altered international relations. Bush had met during the past week with Soviet President Gorbachev in Helsinki, Finland, and he quotes the statement that he and Gorbachev had released denouncing Iraqi aggression. In previous international crises, the Soviet Union and the United States had usually been on opposite sides. U.S.–Soviet cooperation allowed the UN to act quickly to condemn Iraq's invasion of Kuwait and to impose economic sanctions. "No longer can a dictator count on East-West confrontation to stymie concerted United Nations action against aggression," Bush declares.

The president looks forward to the achievement of a fifth major objective in addition to the four he previously listed. The last goal, a new world order, is the most ambitious of all. Bush describes it as a sweeping and even revolutionary change in how nations dealt with each other. The new world order would allow nations to live in security and harmony, free from the danger of terror, and to cooperate to ensure international justice and respect for the rights of the weak. These are lofty and laudable goals, even if the president is more than a little optimistic in declaring that humanity is on the verge of achieving what had eluded a hundred previous generations. Yet Bush is justified in believing that the end of Soviet-American antagonism, which had shaped international affairs since the mid-1940s, creates new opportunities for nations to work together through the UN to prevent aggression or to punish nations that attack their neighbors.

Whether the nations of the world would achieve a new world order, according to the president, depends on how they respond to Iraq's invasion of Kuwait. Bush believes that he is confronting the first post–cold war crisis, or what he calls "the first test of our mettle." If the United States and the UN were resolute and successful in meeting this challenge, the new world order would not just be an inspiring dream but an emerging reality.

At stake are not just matters of principle, the president explains, but also important interests that require U.S. leadership. In the next section of his speech (paragraphs 9 to 14), Bush explains that the occupation of Kuwait enabled Saddam Hussein to double his control of the world's proven oil reserves. U.S. troops are in Saudi Arabia to prevent Hussein from doubling his share yet again, from the 20 percent then under his control to 40 percent, if Iraq were to occupy Saudi Arabia. At a time when the United States imported almost half the petroleum that it used each day, the president asserts, "We cannot permit a resource so vital to be dominated by one so ruthless."

Also critical was the release of Americans and other foreign nationals being detained in Iraq and Kuwait. Approximately three thousand foreign nationals, at least one-quarter of them Americans, were being held in Iraq against their will. Many were workers; a few were tourists who happened to be in the wrong place at the wrong time. Hussein referred to them as "guests," an outrageous description of civilians whom he planned to use as human shields to prevent attacks against Iraqi military forces. For the Bush administration and the American people, the detention of these foreign nationals evoked memories of the Iran hostage crisis a decade earlier. In his speech, Bush denounces the cruelty of seizing hostages and the cynicism of calling them "guests." He quotes the British prime minister Margaret Thatcher to make clear that he will not negotiate or pay blackmail to secure the hostages' freedom. Eventually, Iraq yielded to international pressure and released the last of the hostages in December 1990, four months after their detention.

While pledging that the United States would cooperate with other nations, Bush asserts the need for U.S. leadership. He energetically sought international partners who would join with the United States in forcing an Iraqi withdrawal from Kuwait. Eventually, he secured about three dozen coalition partners. Forging such a broad coalition required considerable diplomatic skill, and the president was pleased that armed forces from nations on four continents were helping to defend Saudi Arabia. While he welcomed these international partners, the president declares here, "There is no substitute for American leadership." He thought it essential to demonstrate that even though the cold war was over, the United States would take strong, quick, and effective action to meet international threats. "Let no one doubt American credibility and reliability," he proclaims. "Let no one doubt our staying power."

Bush then turns to the substantial costs of the international effort in the Persian Gulf (paragraphs 15 to 20). Although the United States was the leading member of the coalition, it lacked the financial resources to pay the costs of its increasing military commitment in the Persian Gulf. Coalition partners that did not supply troops, such as Germany and Japan, provided financial assistance. So did several Arab countries, as Bush explains in his speech. Saudi Arabia and other petroleum-rich countries were expanding oil production, a critical step because the United States depended so heavily on oil imports. Gas prices had risen after Iraqi forces struck Kuwait. The president's discussion of these steps to increase oil supplies helped ease popular fears about shortages at the pump in the event of a major war in the Middle East.

The United States would achieve its goals, whatever the cost, in the Persian Gulf, the president tells his audience. Bush states that sanctions would have sufficient time to work. While he does not explicitly threaten military action, his assertion that he would "continue to review all options with our allies" makes clear that he would use force, if necessary. The president briefly mentions that a major U.S. role in the Persian Gulf is not a new development. Ten years earlier, in what became known as the "Carter Doctrine," President Jimmy Carter had declared that any attempt by an outside force to control the Persian Gulf was

"*Our objectives in the Persian Gulf are clear, our goals defined and familiar: Iraq must withdraw from Kuwait completely, immediately, and without condition. Kuwait's legitimate government must be restored. The security and stability of the Persian Gulf must be assured. And American citizens abroad must be protected.*"

(Paragraph 5)

"*We stand today at a unique and extraordinary moment. The crisis in the Persian Gulf, as grave as it is, also offers a rare opportunity to move toward an historic period of cooperation. Out of these troubled times, our fifth objective—a new world order—can emerge: a new era—freer from the threat of terror, stronger in the pursuit of justice, and more secure in the quest for peace. An era in which the nations of the world, East and West, North and South, can prosper and live in harmony.*"

(Paragraph 7)

"*I cannot predict just how long it will take to convince Iraq to withdraw from Kuwait. Sanctions will take time to have their full intended effect. We will continue to review all options with our allies, but let it be clear: we will not let this aggression stand.*"

(Paragraph 18)

"*Iraq will not be permitted to annex Kuwait. That's not a threat, that's not a boast, that's just the way it's going to be.*"

(Paragraph 20)

"*Our world leadership and domestic strength are mutual and reinforcing; a woven piece, strongly bound as Old Glory.*"

(Paragraph 21)

a threat to vital U.S. interests that would require a response including military force, if necessary. Bush does not refer to this statement by his Democratic predecessor but instead reiterates his own basic policy in simple, straightforward language. "We will not let this aggression stand," he says. "That's not a threat, that's not a boast, that's just the way it's going to be."

In the last major section of his address (paragraphs 21 to 30), the president concentrates on the domestic economy and its effects on U.S. strength abroad. The focus of his discussion is the annual budget deficit, which had risen to a projected $232 billion. The Gramm-Rudman-Hollings legislation required a reduction in that projected shortfall, or there would be mandatory cuts—"the ax of sequester"—in most major programs, including defense at a time when such reductions could have a devastating effect. Time was running short for the White House and Congress to agree to a budget compromise, since the new fiscal year, which started on October 1, was less than three weeks away. Although the president refers to his "friends in Congress," his goal was to use the Persian Gulf crisis and public frustration about what he calls "endless battles" over financial matters to pressure the Democratic leadership on Capitol Hill to make concessions. It was now "time to produce" a long-term program that "truly solved the deficit problem" and to devise solutions to other economic problems, such as dependence on foreign oil. The president appeals for a resolution of differences at this moment of "adversity and challenge."

In the final paragraph, Bush ends as he began by framing the issues of security and the economy in human terms. Americans were saying painful goodbyes to serve in Operation Desert Shield. Soviets and Americans, "old adversaries," were making "common cause." Surely, he thinks, Democrats and Republicans, liberals and conservatives, could do the same.

Audience

Bush spoke before a joint session of Congress, but his audience was much larger than those in the House chamber. He hoped to influence members of Congress, who had to approve budget legislation or authorize military action, if necessary, in the Persian Gulf. He also wanted to impress the American people, millions of whom watched his speech on television or listened to it on radio. He aimed to bolster support for his handling of the Persian Gulf crisis as well as the deficit problem. He also was speaking to international leaders, especially Saddam Hussein, and conveying to them a message of U.S. firmness and resolve.

Impact

Bush's speech failed to solve the nation's economic problems or his own political problems that arose from them. Bush made concessions, the most important of which was agreeing to an increase in the gasoline tax, to reach agreement with congressional negotiators on a budget reduction plan in late September. But conservative Republicans, irate over the president's broken promise not to raise taxes, opposed the legislation. Joining with Democrats who had other objections, they defeated the budget bill. While the White House and Congress tried to hammer out a new agreement, the federal government shut down for three days because the new fiscal year had started without an approved budget. Eventually, both sides agreed to a new plan, which substituted higher income taxes on the wealthiest Americans for some of the gas tax increases. The president signed the Omnibus Budget Reconciliation Act on November 5 and praised it as "the

largest deficit reduction package in history" because it was supposed to reduce the shortfall in the budget by almost one-half trillion dollars during the coming five years (Bush, *Public Papers of the President: 1990*, vol. 2, p. 1553). But polls showed that the president's approval rating had declined more than twenty points, to 53 percent, mainly because of discontent with his handling of the deficit and the economy.

On international affairs, as usual, Bush was more successful. The speech he gave on September 11 was part of a continuing effort to build support for strong action to force Saddam Hussein to withdraw Iraqi forces from Kuwait. Bush wrote in his memoirs that he was not sure when he realized that only military force, not sanctions, would secure that objective. But he was clearly preparing for war when he announced on November 8 that he was substantially increasing U.S. forces in Saudi Arabia so they would have "an adequate offensive military option"(Parmet, p. 471). On November 29, the UN Security Council authorized member nations to use "all necessary means" against Iraq if it did not remove its troops from Kuwait by January 15, 1991 (Parmet, p. 474). When Saddam Hussein failed to comply, Operation Desert Shield became Operation Desert Storm when U.S. air attacks began on January 17. Coalition ground troops attacked Iraqi forces five weeks later. After only one hundred hours of fighting, Bush proclaimed the liberation of Kuwait and victory in the Persian Gulf War.

The president's approval in the polls soared to 87 percent, but his popularity did not last. A recession gripped the economy, and many discontented Americans blamed Bush for the hard times. Many people could not forget his reversal on raising taxes. These economic problems contributed to his defeat in the election of 1992.

What seemed in 1991 to a vast majority of Americans as a highly successful war that had achieved its fundamental objectives became an incomplete triumph, or even a failure, during the next twelve years. Hussein remained the president of Iraq. Although UN sanctions continued, Hussein challenged international efforts to curb his power and seemed to be carrying out programs to develop weapons of mass destruction, including nuclear bombs. After the attacks on September 11, 2001, President George W. Bush condemned Iraq as an outlaw nation, part of an international "axis of evil" that "continues to flaunt its hostility toward America and to support terror" (http://www.presidency.ucsb.edu/ws/?pid=29644). On March 19, 2003, the second President Bush authorized the beginning of military attacks on Iraq that drove Hussein's government from power in weeks but that led to a prolonged war between the United States and Iraqi resistance forces and among Iraqis themselves. The war generated enormous controversy over its origins, conduct, and results. It led to many comparisons between the two presidents Bush, their diplomatic skills, and their war leadership as well as the ways that the first war with Iraq contributed to a second one.

Related Documents

Bush, George H. W. *Public Papers of the President of the United States: George Bush*. 4 vols. Washington, D.C.: U.S. Government Printing Office, 1990–1993. These annual volumes contain Bush's speeches (including those on the Persian Gulf crisis), remarks at news conferences, messages to Congress, and other public documents of his presidency.

———. *All the Best, George Bush: My Life in Letters and Other Writings*. New York: Scribner, 1999. The former president tells his life story through these writings, which extend from his naval service in World War II through his presidency.

Bibliography

■ Books

Beschloss, Michael R., and Strobe Talbott. *At the Highest Levels: The Inside Story of the End of the Cold War*. Boston: Little, Brown, 1993.

Bush, George, and Brent Scowcroft. *A World Transformed*. New York: Knopf, 1998.

Freedman, Lawrence, and Efraim Karsh. *The Gulf Conflict, 1990–1991: Diplomacy and War in the New World Order*. Princeton, N.J.: Princeton University Press, 1993.

Greene, John Robert. *The Presidency of George Bush*. Lawrence: University Press of Kansas, 2000.

Parmet, Herbert S. *George Bush: The Life of a Lone Star Yankee*. New York: Scribner, 1997.

■ Web Sites

"Address before a Joint Session of Congress on the State of the Union." The American Presidency Project Web site.
http://www.presidency.ucsb.edu/ws/?pid=29644. Accessed on March 5, 2008.

George Bush Presidential Library and Museum Web site.
http://bushlibrary.tamu.edu. Accessed on March 4, 2008.

"George Herbert Walker Bush (1924–)." Miller Center of Public Affairs "American President: An Online Reference Resource" Web site.
http://www.millercenter.virginia.edu/academic/americanpresident/bush. Accessed on March 4, 2008.

Questions for Further Study

1. In recent years, the United States has been deeply involved in Middle Eastern affairs. To what extent was the United States engaged in the Middle East prior to Iraq's invasion of Kuwait? Provide examples of this earlier U.S. involvement. Did earlier American involvement in that region reflect economic, strategic, cultural, humanitarian, or military concerns? Do you think that the Persian Gulf War was a turning point in U.S. involvement in the Middle East?

2. In his speech, Bush said that a new world order was "struggling to be born." What did he mean by a new world order? Why do you think he believed it was possible in the early 1990s for such a change in international affairs to take place? Did a new world order emerge while Bush was in the White House? How do you account for the changes in international order, or lack of them, that occurred during the Persian Gulf War and its aftermath?

3. Bush declared in his speech, "Our ability to function effectively as a great power abroad depends on how we conduct ourselves at home." Explain what you think he meant by that statement. Do you think that he was right? Can you provide examples from recent years when the ways that Americans conducted themselves at home either strengthened or harmed U.S. leadership abroad?

4. The United States fought a second war with Iraq beginning in 2003 during the presidency of George W. Bush. Compare and contrast the origins of the Persian Gulf War with the origins of the second war with Iraq. Did the first war and the way it ended contribute to the coming of the second war? Which of the two presidents Bush was more effective in securing international support for the war he fought? How do you account for any differences in the success of each president in using diplomacy to build an international coalition?

Glossary

enterprise zones	depressed or distressed areas that government tries to revitalize by offering tax incentives to businesses that move into the areas
fiscal year	the year during which a government or business makes budgetary plans and spends annual appropriations; for the federal government, the fiscal year runs from October 1 to September 30
IRA	individual retirement account; different types of these accounts may provide individuals with certain federal tax advantages
proliferation	rapid growth or spread; in international affairs, the spread of weapons of mass destruction to nations not previously possessing them
sanctions	penalties that several nations or an international organization imposes on a nation that has violated a treaty or international law
sequester	an automatic cut in federal spending required by legislation prevailing from 1985 to 1990 in the event that the yearly budget deficit is greater than a predetermined amount

George H. W. Bush's Address to Congress on the Persian Gulf Crisis

Mr. President and Mr. Speaker and Members of the United States Congress, distinguished guests, fellow Americans, thank you very much for that warm welcome. We gather tonight, witness to events in the Persian Gulf as significant as they are tragic. In the early morning hours of August 2d, following negotiations and promises by Iraq's dictator Saddam Hussein not to use force, a powerful Iraqi army invaded its trusting and much weaker neighbor, Kuwait. Within 3 days, 120,000 Iraqi troops with 850 tanks had poured into Kuwait and moved south to threaten Saudi Arabia. It was then that I decided to act to check that aggression.

At this moment, our brave servicemen and women stand watch in that distant desert and on distant seas, side by side with the forces of more than 20 other nations. They are some of the finest men and women of the United States of America. And they're doing one terrific job. These valiant Americans were ready at a moment's notice to leave their spouses and their children, to serve on the front line halfway around the world. They remind us who keeps America strong: they do. In the trying circumstances of the Gulf, the morale of our service men and women is excellent. In the face of danger, they're brave, they're well-trained, and dedicated.

A soldier, Private First Class Wade Merritt of Knoxville, Tennessee, now stationed in Saudi Arabia, wrote his parents of his worries, his love of family, and his hope for peace. But Wade also wrote, "I am proud of my country and its firm stance against inhumane aggression. I am proud of my army and its men. I am proud to serve my country." Well, let me just say, Wade, America is proud of you and is grateful to every soldier, sailor, marine, and airman serving the cause of peace in the Persian Gulf. I also want to thank the Chairman of the Joint Chiefs of Staff, General Powell; the Chiefs here tonight; our commander in the Persian Gulf, General Schwartzkopf; and the men and women of the Department of Defense. What a magnificent job you all are doing. And thank you very, very much from a grateful people. I wish I could say that their work is done. But we all know it's not.

So, if there ever was a time to put country before self and patriotism before party, the time is now. And let me thank all Americans, especially those here in this Chamber tonight, for your support for our armed forces and for their mission. That support will be even more important in the days to come. So, tonight I want to talk to you about what's at stake—what we must do together to defend civilized values around the world and maintain our economic strength at home.

Our objectives in the Persian Gulf are clear, our goals defined and familiar: Iraq must withdraw from Kuwait completely, immediately, and without condition. Kuwait's legitimate government must be restored. The security and stability of the Persian Gulf must be assured. And American citizens abroad must be protected. These goals are not ours alone. They've been endorsed by the United Nations Security Council five times in as many weeks. Most countries share our concern for principle. And many have a stake in the stability of the Persian Gulf. This is not, as Saddam Hussein would have it, the United States against Iraq. It is Iraq against the world.

As you know, I've just returned from a very productive meeting with Soviet President Gorbachev. And I am pleased that we are working together to build a new relationship. In Helsinki, our joint statement affirmed to the world our shared resolve to counter Iraq's threat to peace. Let me quote: "We are united in the belief that Iraq's aggression must not be tolerated. No peaceful international order is possible if larger states can devour their smaller neighbors." Clearly, no longer can a dictator count on East-West confrontation to stymie concerted United Nations action against aggression. A new partnership of nations has begun.

We stand today at a unique and extraordinary moment. The crisis in the Persian Gulf, as grave as it is, also offers a rare opportunity to move toward an historic period of cooperation. Out of these troubled times, our fifth objective—a new world order—can emerge: a new era—freer from the threat of terror, stronger in the pursuit of justice, and more secure in the quest for peace. An era in which the nations of the world, East and West, North and South, can prosper and live in harmony. A hundred generations have searched for this elusive path to peace, while a thousand wars raged across the span of human endeavor. Today that new world is struggling to be born, a world quite different from the one we've known. A world where the rule of law supplants the rule of the jungle. A world in which nations recognize the shared responsibility for freedom and justice. A world where the strong respect the rights of the weak. This is the vision that I shared with President Gorbachev in Helsinki. He and other leaders from Europe, the Gulf, and around the world understand that how we manage this crisis today could shape the future for generations to come.

The test we face is great, and so are the stakes. This is the first assault on the new world that we seek, the first test of our mettle. Had we not responded to this first provocation with clarity of purpose, if we do not continue to demonstrate our determination, it would be a signal to actual and potential despots around the world. America and the world must defend common vital interests—and we will. America and the world must support the rule of law—and we will. America and the world must stand up to aggression—and we will. And one thing more: In the pursuit of these goals America will not be intimidated.

Vital issues of principle are at stake. Saddam Hussein is literally trying to wipe a country off the face of the Earth. We do not exaggerate. Nor do we exaggerate when we say Saddam Hussein will fail. Vital economic interests are at risk as well. Iraq itself controls some 10 percent of the world's proven oil reserves. Iraq plus Kuwait controls twice that. An Iraq permitted to swallow Kuwait would have the economic and military power, as well as the arrogance, to intimidate and coerce its neighbors—neighbors who control the lion's share of the world's remaining oil reserves. We cannot permit a resource so vital to be dominated by one so ruthless. And we won't.

Recent events have surely proven that there is no substitute for American leadership. In the face of tyranny, let no one doubt American credibility and reliability. Let no one doubt our staying power. We will stand by our friends. One way or another, the leader of Iraq must learn this fundamental truth. From the outset, acting hand in hand with others, we've sought to fashion the broadest possible international response to Iraq's aggression. The level of world cooperation and condemnation of Iraq is unprecedented. Armed forces from countries spanning four continents are there at the request of King Fahd of Saudi Arabia to deter and, if need be, to defend against attack. Moslems and non-Moslems, Arabs and non-Arabs, soldiers from many nations stand shoulder to shoulder, resolute against Saddam Hussein's ambitions.

We can now point to five United Nations Security Council resolutions that condemn Iraq's aggression. They call for Iraq's immediate and unconditional withdrawal, the restoration of Kuwait's legitimate government, and categorically reject Iraq's cynical and self-serving attempt to annex Kuwait. Finally, the United Nations has demanded the release of all foreign nationals held hostage against their will and in contravention of international law. It is a mockery of human decency to call these people "guests." They are hostages, and the whole world knows it.

Prime Minister Margaret Thatcher, a dependable ally, said it all: "We do not bargain over hostages. We will not stoop to the level of using human beings as bargaining chips ever." Of course, of course, our hearts go out to the hostages and to their families. But our policy cannot change, and it will not change. America and the world will not be blackmailed by this ruthless policy.

We're now in sight of a United Nations that performs as envisioned by its founders. We owe much to the outstanding leadership of Secretary-General Javier Perez de Cuellar. The United Nations is backing up its words with action. The Security Council has imposed mandatory economic sanctions on Iraq, designed to force Iraq to relinquish the spoils of its illegal conquest. The Security Council has also taken the decisive step of authorizing the use of all means necessary to ensure compliance with these sanctions. Together with our friends and allies, ships of the United States Navy are today patrolling Mideast waters. They've already intercepted more than 700 ships to enforce the sanctions. Three regional leaders I spoke with just yesterday told me that these sanctions are working. Iraq is feeling the heat. We continue to hope that Iraq's leaders will recalculate just what their aggression has cost them. They are cut off from world trade, unable to sell their oil. And only a tiny fraction of goods gets through.

The communique with President Gorbachev made mention of what happens when the embargo is so effective that children of Iraq literally need milk or the sick truly need medicine. Then, under strict international supervision that guarantees the proper destination, then food will be permitted.

At home, the material cost of our leadership can be steep. That's why Secretary of State Baker and Treasury Secretary Brady have met with many world leaders to underscore that the burden of this collective effort must be shared. We are prepared to do our share and more to help carry that load; we insist that others do their share as well.

The response of most of our friends and allies has been good. To help defray costs, the leaders of Saudi Arabia, Kuwait, and the UAE—the United Arab Emirates—have pledged to provide our deployed troops with all the food and fuel they need. Generous assistance will also be provided to stalwart front-line nations, such as Turkey and Egypt. I am also heartened to report that this international response extends to the neediest victims of this conflict—those refugees. For our part, we've contributed 28 million for relief efforts. This is but a portion of what is needed. I commend, in particular, Saudi Arabia, Japan, and several European nations who have joined us in this purely humanitarian effort.

There's an energy-related cost to be borne as well. Oil-producing nations are already replacing lost Iraqi and Kuwaiti output. More than half of what was lost has been made up. And we're getting superb cooperation. If producers, including the United States, continue steps to expand oil and gas production, we can stabilize prices and guarantee against hardship. Additionally, we and several of our allies always have the option to extract oil from our strategic petroleum reserves if conditions warrant. As I've pointed out before, conservation efforts are essential to keep our energy needs as low as possible. And we must then take advantage of our energy sources across the board: coal, natural gas, hydro, and nuclear. Our failure to do these things has made us more dependent on foreign oil than ever before. Finally, let no one even contemplate profiteering from this crisis. We will not have it.

I cannot predict just how long it will take to convince Iraq to withdraw from Kuwait. Sanctions will take time to have their full intended effect. We will continue to review all options with our allies, but let it be clear: we will not let this aggression stand.

Our interest, our involvement in the Gulf is not transitory. It predated Saddam Hussein's aggression and will survive it. Long after all our troops come home—and we all hope it's soon, very soon—there will be a lasting role for the United States in assisting the nations of the Persian Gulf. Our role then: to deter future aggression. Our role is to help our friends in their own self-defense. And something else: to curb the proliferation of chemical, biological, ballistic missile and, above all, nuclear technologies.

Let me also make clear that the United States has no quarrel with the Iraqi people. Our quarrel is with Iraq's dictator and with his aggression. Iraq will not be permitted to annex Kuwait. That's not a threat, that's not a boast, that's just the way it's going to be.

Our ability to function effectively as a great power abroad depends on how we conduct ourselves at home. Our economy, our Armed Forces, our energy dependence, and our cohesion all determine whether we can help our friends and stand up to our foes. For America to lead, America must remain strong and vital. Our world leadership and domestic strength are mutual and reinforcing; a woven piece, strongly bound as Old Glory. To revitalize our leadership, our leadership capacity, we must address our budget deficit—not after election day, or next year, but now.

Higher oil prices slow our growth, and higher defense costs would only make our fiscal deficit problem worse. That deficit was already greater than it should have been—a projected 232 billion for the coming year. It must—it will—be reduced.

To my friends in Congress, together we must act this very month—before the next fiscal year begins on October 1st—to get America's economic house in order. The Gulf situation helps us realize we are more economically vulnerable than we ever should be. Americans must never again enter any crisis, economic or military, with an excessive dependence on foreign oil and an excessive burden of Federal debt.

Most Americans are sick and tired of endless battles in the Congress and between the branches over budget matters. It is high time we pulled together and get the job done right. It's up to us to straighten this out. This job has four basic parts. First, the Congress should, this month, within a budget agreement, enact growth-oriented tax measures—to help avoid recession in the short term and to increase savings, investment, productivity, and competitiveness for the longer term. These measures include extending incentives for research and experimentation; expanding the use of IRA's for new homeowners; establishing tax-deferred family savings accounts; creating incentives for the creation of enterprise zones and initiatives to encourage more domestic drilling; and, yes, reducing the tax rate on capital gains.

And second, the Congress should, this month, enact a prudent multiyear defense program, one that reflects not only the improvement in East-West relations but our broader responsibilities to deal with the continuing risks of outlaw action and regional conflict. Even with our obligations in the Gulf, a sound defense budget can have some reduction in real terms; and we're prepared to accept that. But to go beyond such levels, where cutting defense would threaten our vital margin of safety, is something I will never accept. The world is still dangerous. And surely, that is now clear. Stability's not secure. American interests are far reaching. Interdependence has increased. The consequences of regional instability can be global. This is no time to risk America's capacity to protect her vital interests.

And third, the Congress should, this month, enact measures to increase domestic energy production and energy conservation in order to reduce dependence on foreign oil. These measures should include my proposals to increase incentives for domestic oil and gas exploration, fuel-switching, and to accelerate the development of the Alaskan energy resources without damage to wildlife. As you know, when the oil embargo was imposed in the early 1970's, the United States imported almost 6 million barrels of oil a day. This year, before the Iraqi invasion, U.S. imports had risen to nearly 8 million barrels per day. And we'd moved in the wrong direction. And now we must act to correct that trend.

And fourth, the Congress should, this month, enact a 5-year program to reduce the projected debt and deficits by 500 billion—that's by half a trillion dollars. And if, with the Congress, we can develop a satisfactory program by the end of the month, we can avoid the ax of sequester—deep across-the-board cuts that would threaten our military capacity and risk substantial domestic disruption. I want to be able to tell the American people that we have truly solved the deficit problem. And for me to do that, a budget agreement must meet these tests: It must include the measures I've recommended to increase economic growth and reduce dependence on foreign oil. It must be fair. All should contribute, but the burden should not be excessive for any one group of programs or people. It must address the growth of government's hidden liabilities. It must reform the budget process and, further, it must be real.

I urge Congress to provide a comprehensive 5-year deficit reduction program to me as a complete legislative package, with measures to assure that it can be fully enforced. America is tired of phony deficit reduction or promise-now, save-later plans. It is time for a program that is credible and real. And finally, to the extent that the deficit reduction program includes new revenue measures, it must avoid any measure that would threaten economic growth or turn us back toward the days of punishing income tax rates. That is one path we should not head down again.

I have been pleased with recent progress, although it has not always seemed so smooth. But now it's time to produce. I hope we can work out a responsible plan. But with or without agreement from the budget summit, I ask both Houses of the Congress to allow a straight up-or-down vote on a complete 500-billion deficit reduction package not later than September 28. If the Congress cannot get me a budget, then Americans will have to face a tough, mandated sequester. I'm hopeful, in fact, I'm confident that the Congress will do what it should. And I can assure you that we in the executive branch will do our part.

In the final analysis, our ability to meet our responsibilities abroad depends upon political will and consensus at home. This is never easy in democracies, for we govern only with the consent of the governed. And although free people in a free society are bound to have their differences, Americans traditionally come together in times of adversity and challenge.

Once again, Americans have stepped forward to share a tearful goodbye with their families before leaving for a strange and distant shore. At this very moment, they serve together with Arabs, Europeans, Asians, and Africans in defense of principle and the dream of a new world order. That's why they sweat and toil in the sand and the heat and the sun. If they can come together under such adversity, if old adversaries like the Soviet Union and the United States can work in common cause, then surely we who are so fortunate to be in this great Chamber—Democrats, Republicans, liberals, conservatives—can come together to fulfill our responsibilities here. Thank you. Good night. And God bless the United States of America.

BILL CLINTON'S RADIO ADDRESS ON THE WELFARE REFORM ACT

"I came to office determined to end welfare as we know it."

Overview

In 1992 Bill Clinton campaigned for president under the promise to "end welfare as we know it." Welfare, Franklin D. Roosevelt's depression-era assistance program to the needy, had grown into Aid to Families with Dependent Children (AFDC), which included food stamps, Medicare, and direct assistance to a clientele that increasingly consisted of divorced and unwed mothers. By the 1990s most Americans believed that the welfare system was broken, rife with abuse and fraud. Welfare reform, stalled for a number of political reasons, resurfaced as a key issue following the 1994 Republican sweep of the midterm elections. Clinton vetoed two Republican versions of welfare reform, concerned that they did not provide enough child care, job training, and health care support to successfully move aid recipients into the workforce. As President Clinton faced reelection in 1996, however, it became increasingly clear that the public would judge him poorly if he did not deliver welfare reform legislation. Clinton signed, with resolutions, the Personal Responsibility and Work Opportunity Reconciliation Act (PRWORA) on August 22, 1996. Following his reelection in November, Clinton gave a December 7 radio address in which he discussed welfare reform with the American people.

In his memoir, *My Life*, Clinton states, "Signing the welfare reform bill was one of the most important decisions of my presidency" (p. 721). He indeed did end welfare as Americans knew it. Low-income families were no longer entitled to public assistance. The new legislation cut overall spending on food stamps, limited lifetime welfare benefits to five years, imposed new work requirements on most recipients, and denied food stamps and medical care to legal immigrants. The law also renamed the AFDC program as Temporary Assistance to Needy Families (TANF) and replaced federal direct assistance with block grants to states. Finally, welfare reform emphasized personal behaviors, rewarding aid recipients for maintaining traditional marriages and limiting the number of children in their families and requiring single mothers to participate in the workforce. Clinton's support of the PRWORA reflected a more conservative American electorate, one unwilling to support a welfare system based on assumptions of federal guarantees and stay-at-home mothers.

Context

Roosevelt created the American welfare system with the 1935 Social Security Act. This legislation established a system of unemployment and retirement insurance funded by employer and employee contributions as well as federal grants to aid elderly, blind, and disabled adults and dependent children. The latter group was covered under Aid to Dependent Children (ADC), a minor component of the Social Security system. During the depression, most ADC recipients consisted of children of single-parent families headed by widows. By the late 1950s, however, ADC recipients outnumbered those receiving other assistance and were primarily divorced and unwed mothers or those who had been deserted by their spouses.

During the 1960s presidents John F. Kennedy and Lyndon B. Johnson expanded the reach and volume of public assistance started by Roosevelt. Under Kennedy's watch, the 1962 Public Welfare Amendments Act dedicated more federal funds to welfare. ADC was renamed the AFDC to recognize that adults were also receiving benefits. Johnson increased the resources and services available to the poor and created community groups that had authority to decide how funds would best be spent locally. State laws that set criteria for welfare eligibility were increasingly challenged, resulting in a relaxation of standards and expansion of benefits. The number of welfare recipients increased from three million in 1960 to 10.2 million in 1971.

As the welfare rolls soared, Americans increasingly moved toward the political right. The massive social upheavals of the 1960s and 1970s, including the war in Vietnam; race riots; legalization of abortion; rising rates of crime, divorce, and out-of-wedlock births; gay rights; and a growing drug culture, created a backlash. A series of Republican presidencies, interrupted briefly by Jimmy Carter after the Watergate scandal that forced the resignation of Richard Nixon in 1974, indicated that the country was ready for change: a return to fiscal and social conser-

1935

■ **August 14**
Franklin Roosevelt signs the Social Security Act.

1962

■ **July 25**
Congress approves the Public Welfare Amendments Act.

1968

■ **January 2**
Lyndon Johnson signs the Social Security Amendments of 1967, creating the Work Incentive Program for AFDC recipients.

1981

■ **August 13**
Ronald Reagan signs the Omnibus Budget Reconciliation Act, which limits the earnings disregarded for AFDC recipients.

1988

■ **October 13**
Reagan signs the Family Support Act, which requires welfare recipients to work, train, or be educated in order to receive benefits.

1992

■ Democratic presidential candidate Bill Clinton campaigns on a promise to reshape welfare.

1994

■ **September 27**
More than one hundred Republicans sign the "Contract with America," which is authored by Republican congressman Newt Gingrich of Georgia.

■ **November 8**
Republicans win control of the House and the Senate in the midterm election.

1995

■ **December 18**
A government shutdown begins with a budget dispute between the president and Congress.

1996

■ **January 9**
Clinton vetoes PRWORA.

vatism, including a reform of the welfare system. Charles Murray's book *Losing Ground: American Social Policy, 1950–1980*, published in 1984, served as the inspiration for President Ronald Reagan's changes to the welfare system. Murray characterized welfare (AFDC, food stamps, Medicare, and unemployment benefits) as rewarding irresponsible behavior. Reagan's cuts to AFDC reduced the percentage of poor families receiving aid from 88 percent in 1979 to 63 percent in 1984. Subsidized housing was cut more deeply, from $32 billion in 1981 to $6 billion in 1989. The Family Support Act of 1988 marked another important shift in welfare by establishing strong incentives for aid recipients to move into the workforce.

By the 1990s critics of AFDC focused on problems related to its incentive structure. A significant change to the welfare system under the Reagan administration was the reduction of so-called earning disregards. Previously, the government did not count low-income families' entire earnings in calculating eligibility for various benefits; a portion of the earnings was disregarded. After the reforms of the 1980s, welfare recipients who entered the workforce often found that, by the time they factored in lost cash benefits and medical coverage, they were actually worse off than if they had remained unemployed and on government aid. Without any incentive to leave AFDC and take low-wage jobs, many recipients understandably chose to remain within the system. Thus, although benefits in real dollar terms had declined over twenty years, the system itself seemed broken.

As Clinton entered the political scene in the early 1990s, he faced a changed electorate. The Reagan administration's focus on tax cuts, small government, and a return to traditional values resonated with voters. To win the 1992 presidential election and to stay in office, Clinton had to appeal to this more conservative electorate, and the broken AFDC system was one way to do so. In his 1992 election campaign, he promised to radically reshape the welfare system. However, health care reform, not welfare reform, was a priority after his election. The subject of welfare reform moved into the foreground again following the Republican sweep of the 1994 midterm elections. Speaker of the House Newt Gingrich led the Republican charge, introducing welfare reform legislation as part of the 1994 budget. Clinton vetoed the budget because it contained cuts in Medicare and Medicaid, two cornerstone programs in his emphasis on health care. The Republicans returned in 1995 with similar legislation titled the PRWORA, which was unattached to a budget. Clinton vetoed this as well, arguing that changes in the food stamp and school lunch programs were more focused on meeting budget goals than on implementing serious welfare reform. By the late summer of 1996, as Clinton faced reelection, the presidential adviser Dick Morris urged him to sign the bill; polls indicated that if Clinton did not, his fifteen-point advantage over the Republican candidate Bob Dole would plummet to a three-point deficit.

On August 22, 1996, Clinton signed the PRWORA in a Rose Garden ceremony. Clinton campaigned under the promise of welfare reform; although he despised several components of the bill, he delivered on his promise at the end of his first term as president of the United States. Clinton transformed America's welfare system from a federal cash aid program to one tied to work and other personal behaviors. His welfare reform speech exemplifies the way in which he sought to refashion the Democratic Party along more centrist lines, moving away from the party's traditional liberal policies. In Clinton's January 20, 1997, inaugural speech, he stated, "The preeminent mission of our Government is to give all Americans an opportunity, not a guarantee but a real opportunity, to build better lives" (http://millercenter.org/scripps/digitalarchive/speeches/spe_1997_0120_clinton).

About the Author

Clinton was born William Jefferson Blythe on August 19, 1946, in Hope, Arkansas. His father, William Blythe, was killed before Clinton was born. His mother, Virginia, married Roger Clinton, and Bill changed his name to William Jefferson Clinton at age sixteen. He graduated from Georgetown University with honors in 1968, attended Oxford University as a Rhodes Scholar, and earned a law degree from Yale.

Clinton's political career began when he volunteered for Democrat George McGovern's 1972 presidential campaign. He unsuccessfully ran for Congress in 1974, but he was elected as Arkansas attorney general in 1976 and governor in 1978. In 1975 he married Hillary Rodham. Clinton lost the reelection bid in 1980, but he regained the governor's office two years later and served for five consecutive terms. Clinton chaired the Democratic Leadership Council, an organization created in response to the defections of conservative southern Democrats from the party's traditional positions. The council pursued a more centrist agenda, including welfare and education reforms. Clinton was instrumental in organizing governors across the country to restructure welfare laws and to gain support for the Family Support Act.

Clinton defeated George H. W. Bush and the independent candidate Ross Perot in the 1992 presidential election. Although he campaigned under the banner of welfare reform, Clinton devoted much of his first term to an unsuccessful national health care reform program, passage of the North American Free Trade Agreement, and the Oslo Accords, during which Israeli Prime Minister Yitzhak Rabin and Palestine Liberation Organization chairman Yasser Arafat agreed to Palestinian self-rule in Gaza and the West Bank. In 1994 the Republicans took control of the House of Representatives and the Senate for the first time in forty years.

Dogged by investigations into the Clintons' investments in the Whitewater Land Development project in Arkansas as well as the looming sexual harassment lawsuit filed by Paula Corbin Jones, Clinton nonetheless was reelected to a second term in 1996, shortly after signing the PRWORA. Although partisan disagreements between the president

www.milestonedocuments.com

Time Line

1996

■ **January 23**
Clinton delivers his State of the Union address in which he indicates near agreement on "sweeping welfare reform" (http://www.presidency.ucsb.edu/ws/index.php?pid=53091).

■ **August 22**
Clinton signs PRWORA.

■ **November 5**
Clinton and Vice President Al Gore are reelected.

■ **December 7**
Clinton gives his Radio Address on the Welfare Reform Act.

and the Republican-controlled Congress hindered much progress on the domestic front, the economy improved dramatically in the late 1990s; in 1998 the federal budget had a surplus of $70 billion, the largest since the administration of Dwight D. Eisenhower in the 1950s.

Foreign policy matters dominated Clinton's second term, with problems in the Middle East and Bosnia presenting particular challenges. But the majority of his time was spent dealing with the investigation of his sexual relations with the White House intern Monica Lewinsky. In November 1998 the House Judiciary Committee began impeachment hearings, and in December, Bill Clinton became the second president in history to be impeached. The 1999 impeachment trial ended with neither the charge of obstruction of justice nor the charge of perjury sustaining enough votes to remove Clinton from office.

During the 2000 election Clinton's wife, Hillary Rodham Clinton, successfully ran for U.S. senator in New York. After leaving office, Clinton moved into an office in Harlem and published his memoirs, *My Life*, in 2004. Clinton played a prominent role in his wife's bid for the presidency in the 2008 election.

Explanation and Analysis of the Document

The president sets the tone of his speech in the first paragraph. He references the holiday season, noting that the time of year is about not just celebrating but also recognizing obligations and commitments. Clinton uses the holidays as a way to frame his discussion of welfare reform; he celebrates the PRWORA's passage, but he also wants the nation to acknowledge the unfinished business of ensuring its successful implementation.

After using the phrase "obligations to family and community" in the first paragraph, Clinton further describes welfare reform as a "moral obligation for our Nation." He carefully frames the legislation in terms of how it will help the poor. He characterizes the old welfare system as one

President Bill Clinton gives his weekly radio address in the Oval Office on November 18, 1995. (AP Photo/The White House, ho)

that failed Americans, blaming the welfare system itself rather than recipients of AFDC. This is an important detail; earlier presidents, such as Reagan, had often used the image of the "welfare queen," the stereotypical long-term abuser of the welfare system, as a reason for reform. Clinton does not stress that the new law will stop people from abusing the system; instead, he argues that it will prevent the system from abusing Americans. Clinton takes this a step further in paragraph 3, stating that welfare recipients themselves called for reform.

In paragraph 4, Clinton references his 1992 campaign promise to "end welfare as we know it." He also mentions that he gave states waivers before signing the reform bill. Beginning with the Reagan administration in the 1980s, states were encouraged to experiment with welfare reform. The Social Security Act allowed the Department of Health and Human Services to grant waivers to states that had programs which met the objectives of the AFDC. Under the Reagan administration, Health and Human Services had granted more waivers to states, but it was under the George H. W. Bush administration that waiver use truly increased. Bush, faced with a daunting reelection threat from Clinton, relaxed some of the standards required in the past, and more states began to initiate their own welfare reform programs. Clinton further expanded the waiver

process during his first term. In many ways, the PRWORA merely continued an existing trend toward state experimentation with welfare reform. Clinton notes the three primary components of most of the state-initiated programs: emphasis on immediate employment, time limits on benefits, and linkage of benefits to personal behaviors such as getting married or not having additional children.

In paragraph 5, Clinton comments on the success of the bill in terms of the drop in welfare rolls. Most historians, sociologists, and political scientists note that the extraordinary job growth during the 1990s provided opportunities for former welfare recipients that were not there during the 1980s. During the 1970s and 1980s economic shifts took many jobs, primarily those in the manufacturing sector, overseas. Manufacturing jobs represented 26 percent of the total economy in 1969 but just 19 percent in 1984 and 15 percent by 1998. These jobs were replaced with lower-paying, lower-skilled service jobs. Former welfare recipients, most of whom were single women, were qualified for this kind of work. As the economy recovered from the recession of the early 1980s, the economic expansion of the 1990s created more of these jobs, which were available for former welfare recipients.

In paragraph 6, Clinton points to Wisconsin and Indiana as two states with remarkable results in welfare reform.

> "*This law dramatically changes the Nation's welfare system so that no longer will it fail our people, trap so many families in a cycle of dependency, but instead will now help people to move from welfare to work.*"
>
> (Paragraph 2)

> "*I came to office determined to end welfare as we know it, to replace welfare checks with paychecks.*"
>
> (Paragraph 4)

> "*The door has now been opened to a new era of freedom and independence. And now it's up to us, to all of us, to help all the people who need it through that door, one family at a time.*"
>
> (Paragraph 12)

Wisconsin had developed its own welfare reform program through the waiver process beginning in 1986. Wisconsin Works, the state aid system, tied benefits to employment; recipients who could not find private sector jobs were provided with government work. Still, there was a generous system of child and health care to the working poor in the state. It was no accident that President Clinton highlighted such a program in his speech; he had reservations about signing the PRWORA, believing that welfare reform would happen only if recipients were given the tools and support to succeed, especially health benefits and child care.

Paragraph 7 marks the end of Clinton's "celebration" portion of his speech. He ends the paragraph with the word *celebrate* and then moves to the other point he wishes to make: the obligation of the American people to ensure the success of the PRWORA.

Clinton notes in paragraph 8 that the PRWORA will require "even more change" than the waiver reform efforts will. The PRWORA eliminated AFDC and replaced it with block grants to states under the name TANF. The primary focus of the new law was to set up welfare as a temporary assistance program, not as a way of life. TANF gave the states substantial leeway in terms of how they chose to use federal funds. In the past, families that could meet income eligibility received federal aid. Under the new legislation, states could impose work and other requirements to determine eligibility. The PRWORA prohibited states from providing aid to families for more than five years. States also received incentives for reducing TANF caseloads; there were annual work requirements for recipients. Noncitizens

were not eligible for assistance. The PRWORA also increased child support enforcement, reduced funds for food stamps and child nutrition, and enacted a number of provisions to encourage two-parent families.

Clinton emphasizes the end of federal welfare (AFDC) in paragraph 9, noting that it is up to the states to develop programs under the TANF block grants authorized by PRWORA. He also reinforces his personal concern (and one reason he previously had vetoed the legislation) that school lunch programs, child nutrition, health care, and child care programs be included in each state reform effort.

In paragraph 10, Clinton echoes Roosevelt's language, referring to the old welfare system as a "bad deal" and the legislation as the beginning of a "better deal"; this is reminiscent of Roosevelt's New Deal, which created the ADC program. Clinton notes the August 1996 congressional vote to increase the minimum wage and the expansion of the earned income tax credit. The earned income tax credit, begun in 1975, provided federal income tax relief for low-income earners. The program had expanded substantially since it began; real expenditures had grown almost six times between 1980 and 1996. Earned income tax credits encourage people to work yet still provide them with direct cash assistance in the form of tax relief; as such, they have proved to be politically popular with both Republican and Democratic legislators.

At the close of his speech, Clinton returns to his theme of the nation's moral obligation to the community, calling on the private and public sectors to create jobs for those currently receiving aid. He ends his speech with the statement that the success of welfare reform depends on "all of

President Clinton prepares to sign the Personal Responsibility and Work Opportunity Reconciliation Act on August 22, 1996. (AP Photo/J. Scott Applewhite)

us," on every American, to reinforce the message that the PRWORA is just one step in the process of change.

Audience

The president aimed his speech at the general public, with the primary goal of signaling the next steps needed to ensure the success of welfare reform. He also clearly wanted to indicate to the states some of his concerns about the bill itself as well as to convey ways in which state welfare programs might be set up effectively.

Clinton delivered his radio address one month after his reelection in 1996. Welfare reform had been one of the dominant issues of the campaign. Clinton had made the issue key in his 1992 bid for the presidency but had been sidetracked by other issues, notably health care reform. His adviser Dick Morris informed Clinton that the passage of welfare reform would strongly aid his reelection bid. Thus, political expediency played a major role in the passage of welfare reform. It is no accident that the president gave

this speech, rallying the nation around the issue, shortly after his reelection.

Beginning with the so-called Reagan revolution of the 1980s, the American public had moved noticeably to the center politically. One issue that appealed broadly to this new, more conservative electorate was the reduction of big government, and welfare fraud and abuse became the symbols of wasteful federal spending. Reagan invoked the image of the "welfare queen," collecting government checks for life while honest, hard-working Americans footed the bill. At the same time, Americans did not want to see all aid programs eliminated. They wanted, as the historian William Berman notes, the end of "'value-free' effort[s] to provide uplift and support for lazy and ungrateful welfare recipients" (p. 190). Clinton's address reflected this more centrist audience; he emphasized tough work requirements but also maintained a tone of sympathy for "trapped" families.

As the social policy analyst Alvin L. Schorr points out, AFDC was not designed for a 1990s society in which women were expected to work whether they wanted to or not. In 1935, and even during the 1960s, American women were viewed as homemakers and mothers, not breadwinners. Clinton's public audience, however, had different conceptions of gender roles; AFDC was unpopular with the public because it was based on outdated notions of women's role in society.

Not everyone was pleased with the president's decision to sign the PRWORA. The Democratic senator Daniel Patrick Moynihan of New York referred to the legislation as "the most brutal act of social policy since Reconstruction" (qtd. in Harris, p. 250). Health and Human Services secretary Donna Shalala was also against the bill, as was Robert Reich, the labor secretary, and Harold Ickes, the deputy chief of staff. Clinton himself was particularly concerned with the elimination of benefits for legal immigrants as well as other cuts in services. Thus, in this speech, he emphasized that passing the PRWORA was not the end of welfare reform; it was only one step in the process.

Impact

Clinton's welfare reform speech illustrates one of the most important results of his administration: the shift of the Democratic Party away from its traditional stance on social policy toward a more conservative position. While many embraced this new moderate outlook, others decried Clinton's centrism; the historian Robin D. G. Kelley referred to the PRWORA as "the most draconian measure of the late twentieth century … signed not by a Republican president but by a self-proclaimed liberal Democrat" (p. 82). Three officials in Health and Human Services resigned in protest over the president's decision to sign the bill. Clinton's welfare reform may have won him reelection, but it also cost him political capital with many in his own party.

The public reaction was somewhat muted. Most polls indicated strong support in general for welfare reform, although one poll showed that almost half of all Americans had not heard about the reform bill or had no opinion. However, the fact that the legislation had the support of a Democratic president and the Republican Congress seemed to convince most that this was a change for the better.

The most immediate impact of the PRWROA was a dramatic reduction in the number of people receiving welfare. As measured in TANF caseloads, the number of people receiving public assistance declined 59 percent between August 1996 and March 2006, the largest decline in history. Fueled by the economic expansion of the late 1990s, job growth helped former welfare recipients make the transition into the workforce. Welfare reform in part contributed to the dramatic increase in the number of single mothers who held jobs. Of single mothers who had received welfare in previous years, 30 percent obtained jobs in 1989; that number grew to 57 percent in 2000.

However, not all states experienced the same level of welfare case reductions. Some states saw dramatic reductions: Wisconsin witnessed an 84 percent drop from June 1995 to June 1998. Others, however, had quite different results: Hawaii experienced a 7 percent increase in TANF cases during the same period. Different implementation decisions as well as varying economic conditions affected the results in each state.

President George W. Bush reauthorized TANF under the Deficit Reduction Act of 2005. As part of that bill, Bush included new incentives for welfare recipients to marry and remain married. Part of the president's Healthy Marriage Initiative of 2002, the incentives provided $150 million to support programs for TANF grant recipients, with a particular emphasis on promoting responsible fatherhood. Although the PRWORA specified that the TANF grants should "encourage the formation and maintenance of two-parent families," most states focused on moving aid recipients into jobs in the early years of welfare reform (http://thomas.loc.gov/cgi-bin/query/z?c104:H.R.3734.ENR:). Under the George W. Bush administration, states were encouraged to emphasize family formation and retention.

The long-term impacts of welfare reform remain to be seen. Economic conditions, most notably a prolonged recession, could result in the elimination of job opportunities for welfare recipients or those formerly receiving aid. Several analysts argue that the PRWORA created a new class of working poor, as most of the jobs these people occupy are low-skilled, low-paying positions that do not allow people to move out of poverty and into self-sufficiency. Even if its true economic legacy remains a subject of debate, the PRWORA definitely reflects a change in the way Americans view public assistance. Whether one believes it was an astute political move or a long-held desire to truly reform a broken system, Clinton's decision to sign the Welfare Reform Act did indeed "end welfare as we know it." His radio address, like the Welfare Reform Act, reflects the ambivalence Americans feel about the poor: They are willing to help those that help themselves.

Related Documents

Armey, Dick, and Newt Gingrich. *Contract with America.* New York: Times Books, 1994. This blueprint for the Republican Party following the midterm election includes a discussion of welfare reform.

Clinton, Bill. *Between Hope and History.* New York: Times Books, 1996. Clinton gives his perspective on welfare reform and other key aspects of his administration.

Morris, Dick. *Behind the Oval Office: Getting Reelected against All Odds.* New York: Random House, 1997. A political insider, Morris discusses the 1996 Clinton reelection campaign, especially the controversy over welfare reform.

Moynihan, Daniel P. *Miles to Go: A Personal History of Social Policy.* Cambridge, Mass.: Harvard University Press, 1997. One of the sharpest critics of welfare reform provides his view of the process and its aftermath.

Murray, Charles A. *Losing Ground: American Social Policy, 1950–1980.* New York: Basic Books, 1984. Murray, one of the most influential writers for Republican administrations, challenges the very notion of the welfare state.

"H.R.3734: Personal Responsibility and Work Opportunity Reconciliation Act of 1996." Library of Congress Web site. http://thomas.loc.gov/cgi-bin/query/z?c104:H.R.3734.ENR:. Accessed on March 8, 2008. This federal law revamped U.S. welfare programs and was considered to be a fundamental change in the method and the goal of distributing federal cash assistance to the poor.

Bibliography

■ Books

Berkowitz, Edward, and Kim McQuaid. *Creating the Welfare State: The Political Economy of Twentieth-Century Reform*. New York: Praeger Publishers, 1988.

Berman, William C. *America's Right Turn: From Nixon to Clinton*. Baltimore, Md.: Johns Hopkins University Press, 1998.

Blank, Rebecca M., and Ron Haskins, eds. *The New World of Welfare*. Washington, D.C.: Brookings Institution Press, 2001.

Campbell, Colin, and Bert A. Rockman, eds. *The Clinton Presidency: First Appraisals*. Chatham, N.J.: Chatham House Publishers, 1996.

Clinton, Bill. *My Life*. New York: Vintage Books, 2004.

Denton, Robert E., Jr., and Rachel L. Holloway, eds. *The Clinton Presidency: Images, Issues, and Communication Strategies*. Westport, Conn.: Praeger Publishers, 1996.

Harris, John F. *The Survivor: Bill Clinton in the White House*. New York: Random House, 2005.

Kelley, Robin D. G. *Yo' Mama's Disfunktional! Fighting the Culture Wars in Urban America*. Boston: Beacon Press, 1997.

Kilty, Keith M., and Elizabeth A. Segal, eds. *The Promise of Welfare Reform: Political Rhetoric and the Reality of Poverty in the Twenty-first Century*. New York: Haworth Press, 2006.

Myers-Lipton, Scott J., ed. *Social Solutions to Poverty: America's Struggle to Build a Just Society*. Boulder, Colo.: Paradigm Publishers, 2006.

Reese, Ellen. *Backlash against Welfare Mothers: Past and Present*. Berkeley: University of California Press, 2005.

Schorr, Alvin L. *Welfare Reform: Failure and Remedies*. Westport, Conn.: Praeger Publishers, 2001.

Schram, Sanford F., Joe Soss, and Richard C. Fording, eds. *Race and the Politics of Welfare Reform*. Ann Arbor: University of Michigan Press, 2003.

Shields, Todd G., Jeannie M. Whayne, and Donald R. Kelley, eds. *The Clinton Riddle: Perspectives on the Forty-second President*. Fayetteville: University of Arkansas Press, 2004.

Warshaw, Shirley Anne. *Presidential Profiles: The Clinton Years*. New York: Facts On File, 2004.

Weaver, R. Kent. *Ending Welfare as We Know It*. Washington, D.C.: Brookings Institution Press, 2000.

■ Web Sites

"Address before a Joint Session of the Congress on the State of the Union January 23rd, 1996." The American Presidency Project Web site.
http://www.presidency.ucsb.edu/ws/index.php?pid=53091. Accessed on March 8, 2008.

The American Presidency Project Web site.
http://www.presidency.ucsb.edu. Accessed on September 16, 2007.

The United States Department of Health and Human Services Administration for Children and Families Web site.
http://www.acf.hhs.gov. Accessed on September 30, 2007.

William J. Clinton Presidential Library and Museum Web site.
http://www.clintonlibrary.gov. Accessed on September 16, 2007.

"William J. Clinton Speeches: Second Inaugural (January 20, 1997)." Miller Center of Public Affairs Web site.
http://millercenter.org/scripps/digitalarchive/speeches/spe_1997_0120_clinton. Accessed on March 7, 2008.

—By Karen Linkletter

Questions for Further Study

1. Compare Clinton's Radio Address on the Welfare Reform Act with Ronald Reagan's radio address of February 15, 1986, also on welfare reform. How is Reagan's address different from Clinton's? How much of this difference can be attributed to audience or context and how much to each man's disparate visions for reform?

2. How do most Americans form their opinions about welfare recipients? What exposure do they have to people on public assistance? Think in terms of different types of media (news programs, television series, movies, and political campaigns). How might public attitudes, correct or incorrect, shape public policy?

3. Historically, most recipients of TANF and AFDC have been women. How does welfare reform (the PRWORA) reflect changing gender expectations of single mothers or widows from the 1930s to the 1990s? How does the legislation reflect similar assumptions regarding the role of women in society today and during the Depression?

4. What would Franklin Roosevelt think about Clinton's radio address? What would he think about the changes made to welfare itself, including the expansion of the system in the 1960s?

Glossary

vexing	annoying, irritating, or puzzling
consigning	handing over
afoul	in trouble or conflict with someone or something
waivers	relinquishments of a right or claim

BILL CLINTON'S RADIO ADDRESS ON THE WELFARE REFORM ACT

Good morning. This week I had the honor of lighting both the national Christmas tree and the national menorah. Both are symbols of a time of year filled with joy, hope, and expectation, a time, too, when we reflect on what we've done and what is left to do, a time to honor our obligations to family and community.

Last summer we made a new beginning on one of our Nation's most vexing problems, the welfare system. When I signed the historic welfare reform law, we set out to honor a moral obligation for our Nation, to help many people in our national community to help themselves. This law dramatically changes the Nation's welfare system so that no longer will it fail our people, trap so many families in a cycle of dependency, but instead will now help people to move from welfare to work. It will do so by requiring work of every able-bodied person, by protecting children, by promoting parental responsibility through tougher child support enforcement.

We've worked a long time to reform welfare. Change was demanded by all the American people, especially those on welfare who bore the brunt of the system's failure. For decades now, welfare has too often been a trap, consigning generation after generation to a cycle of dependency. The children of welfare are more likely to drop out of school, to run afoul of the law, to become teen parents, to raise their own children on welfare. That's a sad legacy we have the power to prevent. And now we can.

I came to office determined to end welfare as we know it, to replace welfare checks with paychecks. Even before I signed the welfare reform bill, we were working with States to test reform strategies, giving 43 States waivers from Federal rules to experiment with reforms that required work, imposed time limits, and demanded personal responsibility. And we were toughening child support enforcement, increasing collections by 50 percent over the last 4 years. That's about $4 billion.

We were determined to move millions from welfare to work, and our strategy has worked. I am pleased to announce today that there are now 2.1 million fewer people on welfare than on the day I took the oath of office. That is the biggest drop in the welfare rolls in history.

Some of these reductions have been even more striking. The welfare rolls have dropped 41 percent in Wisconsin, 38 percent in Indiana—two States where we granted landmark waivers to launch welfare reform experiments.

Throughout the country we're working to make responsibility a way of life, not an option. That means millions of people are on their way to building lives with the structure, purpose, meaning, and dignity that work gives. And that is something to celebrate.

But this is just the beginning of welfare reform. We had a choice: We could have gone on as we had with a system that was failing, or start anew to create a system that could give everyone who's able-bodied a chance to work and a chance to be independent. We chose the right way: first, working over the last 4 years with the States to reform their own systems, then passing a new welfare reform law requiring even more change in every State and every community.

But there is still much to do, and it now falls to all of us to make sure this reform works. The next step is for the States to implement the new law by tailoring a reform plan that works for their communities. As required by the law, we have already certified new welfare reform plans for 14 States. Today I'm pleased to announce we're certifying welfare for four more States: California, Nebraska, South Dakota, and Alabama. All their plans will require and reward work, impose time limits, increase child care payments, and demand personal responsibility. And across the board, as we give welfare funds back to the States, we will protect the guarantees of health care, nutrition, and child care, all of which are critical to helping families move from welfare to work. And we'll continue to crack down on child support enforcement.

Welfare as we knew it was a bad deal for everyone. We're determined to create a better deal. We want to say to every American, work pays. We raised the minimum wage; we expanded the earned-income tax credit to allow the working poor to keep more of what they earn. Now we have to create a million jobs for people on welfare by giving businesses incentives to hire people off welfare and enlisting the private sector in a national effort to bring all Americans into the economic mainstream. We have to have help from the private sector.

Together we can make the permanent underclass a thing of the past. But we have a moral obligation to do that through welfare reform, working together in our communities, our businesses, our churches, and our schools. Every organization which employs people should consider hiring someone off welfare, and every State ought to give those organizations the incentives to do so, so that we can help families reclaim the right to know they can take care of themselves and their own obligations.

Our future does not have to be one with so many people living trapped lives. The door has now been opened to a new era of freedom and independence. And now it's up to us, to all of us, to help all the people who need it through that door, one family at a time.

Thanks for listening.

President Clinton makes a statement of contrition to the nation on December 11, 1998, just minutes before the House Judiciary Committee voted to approve the first article of impeachment against him. (AP Photo/Greg Gibson)

ARTICLES OF IMPEACHMENT OF WILLIAM JEFFERSON CLINTON

"William Jefferson Clinton has undermined the integrity of his office."

Overview

On October 5, 1998, the Judiciary Committee of the House of Representatives approved a resolution recommending an impeachment inquiry of President Bill Clinton. After debating the committee's four Articles of Impeachment, the House approved two and sent them to the Senate on December 19, 1998. An impeachment trial began in the Senate on January 7, 1999, and ended on February 12, 1999, with the president's acquittal.

Context

On May 6, 1994, Paula Jones filed a lawsuit against President Clinton for sexual harassment. Seeking $700,000 in damages, she claimed that Clinton, while he was governor of Arkansas, had made unwanted sexual advances that were later reported in such a way as to demean her reputation and hold her up to public ridicule. Although the lawsuit was eventually settled on November 13, 1998, for $850,000 without requiring Clinton to admit to wrongdoing or to issue an apology, the impression that he had lied about his sexual history continued to be the focus of stories in the press and criticism of the president in Congress and in the media.

The Jones lawsuit was the culmination of years of rumors that Clinton had had numerous affairs with Arkansas state employees and others. During his campaign for the presidency, Gennifer Flowers had come forward with testimony and tape recordings alleging a twelve-year intimate affair with Clinton. Although he admitted wrongdoing in his marriage, he successfully won the support of his wife and the American people.

But the Jones lawsuit erupted in the midst of Independent Counsel Kenneth Starr's investigation of other improprieties, including what came to be known as Whitewater, a real estate investment involving Morgan Guaranty, an Arkansas savings-and-loan association that engaged in speculative land deals, insider lending, and hefty commissions involving the Whitewater Development Corporation.

Although Bill and Hillary Clinton were never directly implicated in the scandal, several of their associates were convicted and sent to prison, and Congress continued to investigate Whitewater during the first two years of Clinton's presidency.

When Independent Counsel Kenneth Starr learned of Clinton's alleged involvement with a White House intern, Monica Lewinsky, he secured Attorney General Janet Reno's approval to expand his probe of the president to include these charges of sexual misconduct while in office. On January 17, 1998, Clinton testified under oath in the Paula Jones case, denying that he had had sexual relations with Lewinsky but admitting to having had an affair with Gennifer Flowers, a charge he had previously denied.

On January 22, Clinton made his first statement to the press denying his affair with Lewinsky and likewise denying that he had urged Lewinsky or others to lie about the affair. Then, in a March 12 interview (which aired on March 15), Kathleen Willey, a White House employee, told Ed Bradley of CBS's *60 Minutes* television newsmagazine program that the president had made unwelcome sexual advances to her.

On August 17, 1998, Clinton appeared on national television to acknowledge that he had misled the American people. He was admitting for the first time that the allegations of sexual misconduct with a White House intern, Monica Lewinsky, were true. On September 9, the House of Representatives received Starr's report. Amid mounting criticism from Democrats and Republicans that Clinton had not been truthful about the charges against him, the House Judiciary Committee released Starr's report to the public and, after an impeachment inquiry, voted to bring to the floor of the House four impeachment articles, accusing the president of perjury, obstruction of justice, and abuse of power. The Republican leadership in Congress demanded that Clinton resign and won endorsement from the Republican majority in the House of two Articles of Impeachment, which were sent to the Senate for a trial that began on January 7, 1999.

After arguments presented by representatives from both parties and from the White House and a question-and-answer period, the Senate acquitted Clinton on both Articles of Impeachment, voting 45–55 on perjury and 50–50 on obstruction of justice. In a brief White House Rose Gar-

1992

■ **November 3**
William Jefferson Clinton is elected president of the United States.

1994

■ **May 6**
Paula Jones files a lawsuit against Clinton.

1995

■ **July**
Monica S. Lewinsky begins a White House internship.

1996

■ **April 5**
Clinton begins sexual relationship with Lewinsky.

■ **November 5**
Clinton is reelected.

1997

■ **March 29**
Last intimate contact between the president and Lewinsky.

■ **December 5**
Lewinsky appears on Jones lawsuit witness list.

1998

■ **January 16**
Kenneth W. Starr is appointed to investigate Lewinsky liaison with Clinton.

■ **January 17**
President is deposed in Jones lawsuit

■ **January 21**
President denies allegations of a sexual relationship with Lewinsky and of suborning perjury

■ **July 28**
Immunity/cooperation agreement is reached between Lewinsky and the Office of Independent Counsel (Kenneth Starr).

■ **August 17**
President publicly acknowledges improper relationship with Lewinsky.

■ **December 19**
Two Articles of Impeachment are approved by the House of Representatives and sent to the Senate.

den speech, Clinton accepted the verdict and called on the nation to begin a period of "reconciliation and renewal" ("Clinton Impeachment," http://www.eagleton.rutgers.edu/e-gov/e-politicalarchive-Clintonimpeach.htm).

About the Author

From the beginning, control of the impeachment process was in the hands of the Republican majority in the House of Representatives. While the House minority leader, Dick Gephardt, and other Democrats acknowledged and deplored Clinton's disingenuous efforts to obscure his sexual misconduct, the Republican majority on the House Judiciary Committee under the leadership of Chairman Henry Hyde designed an impeachment inquiry very close in wording to the 1974 Watergate resolution that eventually led to President Richard Nixon's resignation from office. In formulating the Articles of Impeachment, Hyde was following the strategy of his predecessor, Peter Rodino, a Democrat who had chaired the Judiciary Committee during the Nixon investigation. To begin with, Hyde and his fellow Republicans placed no restrictions on the subject areas to be considered. But Democrats viewed this strategy as a way to carry on an endless investigation intended to dredge up every conceivable charge against the president. Democratic efforts to offer an alternative inquiry plan were voted down by the Republican majority. Under Hyde's leadership, the committee made Kenneth Starr the major witness and formulated eighty-one questions for Clinton to answer.

Starr's testimony was incorporated into Articles of Impeachment that focused on Clinton's efforts to cover up his affair with Monica Lewinsky. On Whitewater and other areas of investigation, Starr reported no impeachable offenses, and again his testimony weighed heavily in the decision of Hyde and other Republicans to focus on the president's efforts to obstruct inquiries into his sexual affairs.

Although the Articles of Impeachment had no single author, it is clear from all accounts that Hyde dominated the proceedings—rejecting, for example, a fellow Republican's argument that accepting the Democratic plan for an impeachment inquiry stood the best chance of making the process bipartisan. Peter Baker reports that Hyde believed that Starr would eventually submit evidence of other impeachable offenses that would be more difficult to investigate under the Democratic plan. Starr never did submit additional evidence of impeachable offenses.

Under Hyde's direction, Mitch Glazier, a thirty-two-year-old graduate of Vanderbilt University Law School, worked on the first draft of the impeachment articles. Glazier studied the articles accusing Nixon of obstruction of justice and abuse of power. He saw similarities between the Nixon and Clinton investigations insofar as the president's truthfulness and efforts to cover up wrongdoing were at issue. As far as possible, Glazier used Rodino's language, believing a precedent had been set that should be followed. (Andrew Johnson's impeachment articles in the nineteenth century had not been specified until after the House had voted an impeachment resolution.)

Glazier also received drafts of Articles of Impeachment from Republican Judiciary Committee members, including Bob Barr, one of the managers of the Republican case in the Senate trial. But Glazier avoided inflammatory words such as *perjury* in favor of Rodino's formulation of false or misleading statements. Although Hyde suggested some changes, committee members modified Glazier's language to focus on Clinton's improper relationship with Monica Lewinsky. Other suggested changes included references to Kathleen Willey and specific instances of Clinton's false or misleading statements. After several revisions, the Republicans reached a consensus on four Articles of Impeachment, which included references to the Paula Jones case and Monica Lewinsky, citing instances where Clinton had not been truthful under oath, and using the term "perjurious" to indicate testimony that contained perjury.

No true attempt was made to involve Democrats in the drafting of the impeachment articles, according to Peter Baker. Besides, Democrats were known to be in favor of some sort of censure resolution, stopping far short of impeachment. The impeachment articles as the Republican committee members had drafted them were passed in spite of the Democrats' efforts at amendment and disputes about procedure.

Explanation and Analysis of the Document

◆ Article I

The two Articles of Impeachment do not specify treason or bribery, the "high crimes and misdemeanors" identified in the U.S. Constitution. However, the Constitution recognizes "other high crimes and misdemeanors" without detailing what they might be. High crimes, as Richard Posner points out, may mean both serious crimes and those crimes committed by a high official. Misdemeanor, in the modern sense, would mean a minor crime, which clearly is not the intent of the Constitution's wording. Instead, *misdemeanor* has been construed to mean low crimes committed by high officials. The phrase *high crimes and misdemeanors* also suggests that impeachment arises out of complex illegal or unconstitutional actions.

Hence the formulation of Article I, which charges the president with violating his oath of office—meaning that he has violated the Constitution that he has sworn to uphold. By violating the Constitution, he has failed to "take care that the laws be faithfully executed." For personal gain he has corrupted the judicial process and impeded the administration of justice. Two key words in the articles—"manipulated" and "exoneration"—are used to claim that the president has not put his country first but rather has used the mechanisms of the law for selfish purposes. This is what his fellow Democrats Dick Gephardt and Thomas A. Daschle (minority leader of the Senate) had in mind when they issued statements on September 16, 1998, urging President Clinton to abandon legalisms

Time Line

1999

■ **February 12**
The Senate acquits Clinton on both Articles of Impeachment.

in his defense. Article I, then, is building a case that shows the president has used the tools of the legal system to undermine the legal system and, as a result, has committed an impeachable offense. Article I alleges that rather than preserving, protecting, and defending the Constitution, the president subverted it.

The first specific charge in Article I is that Clinton lied to a grand jury. The language of the charge, however, accuses him of "one or more" false, misleading, and perjurious statements. In other words, Article I does not definitively call each statement a lie but rather groups together testimony that in the aggregate amounts to a conscious decision not to tell the truth. The "subordinate Government employee" referred to in (1) is Monica Lewinsky. In his grand jury testimony the president barely acknowledged his sexual relationship with her, although he would later confess to having misled the American people. That Lewinsky was a White House intern, a "subordinate," implies that the president took advantage of her and thus abused his government office. In (2) and (3) Clinton is charged with lying about his affair with Gennifer Flowers. When he gave a deposition in the Paula Jones lawsuit (the "civil rights action" accusing him of sexual harassment), he denied an affair with Flowers, but when questioned under oath by the grand jury investigating his relationship with Lewinsky, he admitted to having had sex with Flowers. By allowing his attorney in the Jones case to repeat to a federal judge false and misleading statements, Clinton had, in effect, committed perjury and perverted the course of justice.

The culminating charge in (4) is that the president lied or gave misleading testimony about tampering with grand jury witnesses and impeding the gathering of evidence that would have uncovered his unconstitutional and unlawful behavior. This charge refers specifically to Clinton's vague grand jury testimony about whether he gave Monica Lewinsky gifts and his subsequent efforts to retrieve those gifts with the help of his secretary. Lewinsky also had been in contact with the attorney Vernon Jordan, who had offered her a job and who was under suspicion of having advised her about her grand jury testimony. Clinton alluded to this suspicion when he made public statements denying that he had told anyone to lie about their dealings with him.

Article I is designed to move from quite specific accusations of perjurious testimony before a grand jury and a federal judge to a broader characterization of the president's actions after his grand jury testimony. The last charge, (4), is quite broad in its implications, which is perhaps why the language of Article I includes the phrase "one or more" to characterize the president's perjurious statements. Thus, the president has dealt with the grand jury in a "corrupt"—

House Judiciary Committee chairman Henry Hyde, center, walks to the Senate chamber on January 7, 1999, to deliver his committee's articles of impeachment against President Clinton. (AP Photo/Khue Bui)

that is, dishonest and immoral—manner, a charge that leads to the conclusion that he "undermined the integrity of his office." In other words, he has brought into disrepute one of the major institutions of government, the executive branch, and "betrayed his trust as President"—words that signify that he is both unworthy of the office and of the American people's confidence. Indeed, his actions have done "manifest injury" to the people of the United States. The word *manifest* implies that the president's crimes have been obvious and public and ought not to be regarded merely as private sins. Clinton would use the word himself later when he confessed, "I have sinned" ("William Jefferson Clinton: Remarks at the 46th Annual Prayer Breakfast," http://www.americanrhetoric.com/speeches/wjclintonihavesinned.htm). In this case, it was not the sin but the cover-up of his sin, leading to illegal and unconstitutional actions, that warranted his removal from office. Because he is president, sworn to uphold the law, his corrupt actions have subverted the "rule of law and justice." His offenses, in other words, strike at the very core of government authority. Thus Article I concludes that President Clinton should be disqualified from holding any office "honor, trust, or profit under the United States."

◆ **Article II**

Article II builds on the case in Article I (4), which is tantamount to accusing Clinton of obstruction of justice. Article II spells out that charge as another example of the way Clinton has violated his oath to preserve, protect, and defend the Constitution and the laws of the United States. Article II focuses on the president's "conduct," a word used at the end of Article I to expand the case against him. He has impeded not merely grand jury investigations and Paula Jones's civil rights action but also the "administration of justice." He has concealed evidence, covered up his crimes, and delayed legal actions that would expose his corrupt conduct. He has also engaged others in abetting his efforts to impede the course of justice.

Paralleling the language in Article I, Article II then specifies "one or more" of the president's actions that demonstrate his scheme to conceal the evidence brought against him in the civil rights action. That names are never mentioned in either article has the effect of making the impeachment charges less personal and more public, so that Clinton stands accused not of having lied about sex with a White House intern, for example, but rather of obstructing and perverting a "civil rights action." The president's defenders wanted to make the distinction between lying about sexual affairs and other kinds of lies that might be deemed "high crimes and misdemeanors." Indeed, the House Judiciary Committee heard testimony from scholars objecting to the committee's effort to impeach Clinton on the basis of his misleading and false statements about his private conduct.

The first specific charges, (1) and (2), in Article II refer to a 2:00 AM telephone call Clinton made to Lewinsky. He was concerned about gifts he had given to Lewinsky, and he encouraged her to say she visited the White House to see his secretary, Betty Currie. The president's discussion with Lewinsky about her testimony and his suggestions about how she should testify form the basis of the charge that he had encouraged a witness to provide false and misleading testimony in an affidavit or in person.

Charge (3) is directly linked to charges (1) and (2). It refers to Lewinsky's meeting with Clinton in the White House. The president gave her several Christmas presents, including a stuffed animal, chocolates, and a pair of joke sunglasses. That afternoon, the president's secretary contacted Lewinsky and later drove to her apartment and collected a box containing some of the gifts. Currie hid the box under her bed at home. Involving his secretary and hiding gifts are what this charge refers to as Clinton's scheming to "conceal evidence that had been subpoenaed in a Federal civil rights action brought against him."

Charge (4) refers to contacts Lewinsky had with Vernon Jordan (contacts that are also alluded to in the last charge in Article 4), who responded to the president's request that Jordan find Lewinsky a job. Lewinsky and Jordan spoke several times on the phone, and he also met with her in person, not only to set up job interviews but also to discuss her relationship with Clinton. This close involvement of Clinton and Jordan in the job search of a White House intern is what led to the charge that the president was prejudicing the testimony of a witness in a civil rights action and thus corrupting a witness (Lewinsky) who could have given damaging testimony against him.

Charges (5) through (8) all center on Clinton's false and misleading statements not only about his own actions but also about those of others in order to obscure, obstruct, manipulate, and "corruptly influence" the testimony of others. In addition, he misled his own attorney, thus allowing his counsel to make "false and misleading statements to a Federal judge" (charge 5). The grand jury also received this false and misleading information.

The specific events alluded to in these charges include Clinton's statement in a deposition given in the Jones lawsuit. He denied having "sexual relations" with Lewinsky under a definition provided by her lawyers ("Clinton Impeachment," http://www.eagleton.rutgers.edu/e-gov/e-politicalarchive-Clintonimpeach.htm), and said he could not recall whether he had ever been alone with her. He also met with his secretary on January 18 and 20, 1998, and allegedly asked her leading questions designed to corroborate his version of events. At the second meeting he also went over with his secretary her testimony before the grand jury—another effort to tamper with a witness that is alluded to in charge (7).

The conclusion to Article II repeats word for word the conclusion of Article I: President Clinton has brought the presidency into disrepute, betrayed his trust as president, and subverted the rule of law and justice "to the manifest injury of the people of the United States." He is thus disqualified not only to be president but also to hold any office of "honor, trust, or profit under the United States."

As Speaker of the House of Representatives, Newt Gingrich signed the Articles of Impeachment that were passed in the House on December 19, 1998, and he had his signature witnessed by Robert H. Carle, clerk of the House of Representatives.

Audience

In the broadest sense, of course, the audience for the Articles of Impeachment was the American people. The Republican leadership in the House of Representatives hoped to demonstrate to the public that President Clinton deserved removal from office, primarily because he had abused their trust, subverted the law, and injured the institution of the presidency.

The partisan nature of the impeachment articles—almost all votes on the investigation of Clinton and on Articles of Impeachment were along party lines—meant that the audience for impeachment, strictly speaking, became the Republican Party and its efforts to destroy a president they believed was harming the national interest.

The House Republicans, however, also had to consider a more specific audience: their Republican colleagues in the Senate, who had the responsibility to consider whether Clinton should be removed from office. At least some Senate Republicans doubted the wisdom of such a drastic measure—even if they believed their House colleagues had a good case. The vote in the Senate was along party lines, and the failure of Senate Republicans to enlist even a few Democrats was telling and produced a far different outcome from the impeachment of Richard Nixon, who resigned rather than face a Senate trial. The case for impeachment—arguably a strong one—simple did not convince the American people once it was presented to them.

Impact

The impact of President Clinton's impeachment remains debatable and will depend on the judgments of historians and of the American people in generations to come. However the decision to impeach the president is ultimately viewed, it is unquestionable that Clinton's actions damaged the image, if not the substance, of the presidency. Presidents are moral as well as political leaders, and historians (regardless of their political views) recognize that Clinton demeaned his office by engaging in sex with a White House intern and then by making indisputably false

> "William Jefferson Clinton willfully provided perjurious, false and misleading testimony to the grand jury."
>
> (Article I)

> "William Jefferson Clinton has undermined the integrity of his office, has brought disrepute on the Presidency, has betrayed his trust as President, and has acted in a manner subversive of the rule of law and justice, to the manifest injury of the people of the United States."
>
> (Article I)

> "In his conduct while President of the United States, William Jefferson Clinton, in violation of his constitutional oath faithfully to execute the office of President of the United States and, to the best of his ability, preserve, protect, and defend the Constitution of the United States, and in violation of his constitutional duty to take care that the laws be faithfully executed, has prevented, obstructed, and impeded the administration of justice, and has to that end engaged personally, and through his subordinates and agents, in a course of conduct or scheme designed to delay, impede, cover up, and conceal the existence of evidence and testimony related to a Federal civil rights action brought against him in a duly instituted judicial proceeding."
>
> (Article II)

> "William Jefferson Clinton, by such conduct, warrants impeachment and trial, and removal from office and disqualification to hold and enjoy any office of honor, trust, or profit under the United States."
>
> (Article II)

and misleading statements. Indeed, two months after his acquittal, Judge Susan Webber Wright (presiding in the Paula Jones lawsuit) held the president in contempt for giving false testimony in his January 17, 1998, deposition when asked about Lewinsky. This was the first time a president had been held in contempt of court. The president had engaged in sexual relations with Monica Lewinsky and had seen her in private, and he had lied about both under oath, the judge affirmed, ordering him to pay $90,000 of Jones's lawyers' legal fees.

Why, then, did the American public not condemn President Clinton? To be sure, a sizable portion of the American people deplored his conduct, and some wanted him removed from office. But this was not the majority mood, and when Clinton left office he had very high approval ratings that have been sustained. It would seem that what Clinton lied about made the difference. He was not misleading the public about affairs of state. He had not interfered with other institutions of government, notwithstanding the language in the Articles of Impeachment claiming that he had injured the legal system. The American public did not feel "manifestly injured." Indeed, the unrelenting investigation of Kenneth Starr, which provoked considerable criticism of his invasion of the president's privacy, also had the effect of creating sympathy for Clinton. In at least some quarters, his lying about his affair with Monica Lewinsky was deemed a natural response to undue prying and an effort to preserve his family life. Even Clinton critics such as Richard Posner found Starr's brutal methods repugnant.

If impeachment was the only remedy for Clinton's misconduct, then the majority of the public simply was not prepared to endorse his removal from office. In all likelihood, Democratic proposals to censure the president would have received significant, perhaps majority support from the public, since no one—not even the president's staunchest defenders—declared him innocent of deceiving the American people. Indeed, the president himself acknowledged as much in a statement on television.

While President Nixon had his staunch defenders during the period he faced impeachment, in the end his resignation was inevitable, given that he could no longer command enough support from his own party, let alone from Democrats or the American people. Thus, whatever else future historians may conclude about the impeachment of President Clinton, the partisan nature of the process will have to be factored into their judgments. At the same time, the irrefutable evidence that a president lied under oath will certainly damage Bill Clinton's reputation, if not, in the end, the office of the presidency itself.

Related Documents

"Articles of Impeachment Adopted by the Committee on the Judiciary." Watergate.info Web site. http://watergate.info/impeachment/impeachment-articles.shtml. Accessed on March 6, 2008. The Watergate articles of impeachment served as a model for the drafting of the Clinton Articles of Impeachment.

"Proceedings of the Senate Sitting for the Trial of Andrew Johnson, President of the United States, on Articles of Impeachment Exhibited by the House of Representatives." University of Missouri–Kansas City School of Law "Famous Trials" Web site. http://www.law.umkc.edu/faculty/projects/ftrials/impeach/articles.html. Accessed on March 6, 2008. Drafters of the Clinton impeachment articles also consulted the articles of impeachment against President Andrew Johnson but found them less precise and thorough than the Nixon impeachment articles.

Bibliography

■ Books

Baker, Peter. *The Breach: Inside the Impeachment and Trial of William Jefferson Clinton*. New York: Scribner, 2000.

Clinton, Bill. *My Life*. New York: Knopf, 2004.

Dershowitz, Alan M. *Sexual McCarthyism: Clinton, Starr, and the Emerging Constitutional Crisis*. New York: Basic Books, 1998.

Gerhardt, Michael J. *The Federal Impeachment Process: A Constitutional and Historical Analysis*. 2nd ed. Chicago: University of Chicago Press, 2000.

Kalb, Marvin. *One Scandalous Story: Clinton, Lewinsky, and 13 Days That Tarnished American Journalism*. New York: Free Press, 2001.

McLoughlin, Merrill, ed. *The Impeachment and Trial of President Clinton: The Official Transcripts, from the House Judiciary Committee Hearings to the Senate Trial*. New York: Times Books, 1999.

Posner, Richard A. *An Affair of State: The Investigation, Impeachment, and Trial of President Clinton*. Cambridge, Mass.: Harvard University Press, 1999.

Starr, Kenneth. *The Starr Report: The Independent Counsel's Complete Report to Congress on the Investigations of President Clinton*. New York: Pocket Books, 1998.

■ Web Sites

"Clinton Impeachment." Eagleton Institute of Politics Web site. http://www.eagleton.rutgers.edu/e-gov/e-politicalarchive-Clintonimpeach.htm. Accessed on March 6, 2008.

"Famous Trials: The Impeachment Trial of President William Clinton, 1999." University of Missouri–Kansas City School of Law "Famous Trials" Web site. http://www.law.umkc.edu/faculty/projects/ftrials/clinton/clintonhome.html. Accessed on March 6, 2008.

"Impeachment of President William Jefferson Clinton." The University of Michigan Library Documents Center Web site. http://www.lib.umich.edu/govdocs/impeach.html. Accessed on March 6, 2008.

"William Jefferson Clinton: Remarks at the 46th Annual Prayer Breakfast." American Rhetoric Web site. http://www.americanrhetoric.com/speeches/wjclintonihavesinned.htm. Accessed on March 7, 2008.

—By Carl Rollyson

Questions for Further Study

1. Compare the circumstances and the language used in the Articles of Impeachment against Andrew Johnson and Clinton.

2. Compare the circumstances and the language used in the Articles of Impeachment against Richard Nixon and Clinton.

3. Although Clinton was acquitted of both Articles of Impeachment, the vote on obstruction of justice was closer than the vote on perjury. Explain why.

4. Compare the responses of Nixon and Clinton to the Articles of Impeachment against them.

5. Why did Nixon resign from office before a trial in the Senate? What were the consequences of his resignation?

6. Why did Clinton refuse to resign from office and decide to face a trial in the Senate?

7. What impact has the impeachment of three presidents had on American history?

Glossary

affidavit	a written declaration made under oath before somebody authorized to administer oaths, usually setting out the statement of a witness for court proceedings
deposition	testimony given under oath, especially a statement given by a witness that is read out in court in the witness's absence
impeachment	the first part of a legislative process enacted to remove a government official from office; a vote for an indictment leading to a trial in which the government official is either convicted or acquitted
high crimes	defined in the U. S. Constitution as treason and bribery, but in the phrase "other high crimes" implies yet other serious actions that may warrant impeachment and conviction
misdemeanors	according to several legal scholars, political crimes such as misconduct in office and abuse of power
perjurious	testimony in court or during a deposition that contains perjury (false statements)

ARTICLES OF IMPEACHMENT OF WILLIAM JEFFERSON CLINTON

Resolution

Impeaching William Jefferson Clinton, President of the United States, for high crimes and misdemeanors. Resolved, That William Jefferson Clinton, President of the United States, is impeached for high crimes and misdemeanors, and that the following articles of impeachment be exhibited to the United States Senate:

Articles of impeachment exhibited by the House of Representatives of the United States of America in the name of itself and of the people of the United States of America, against William Jefferson Clinton, President of the United States of America, in maintenance and support of its impeachment against him for high crimes and misdemeanors.

Article I

In his conduct while President of the United States, William Jefferson Clinton, in violation of his constitutional oath faithfully to execute the office of President of the United States and, to the best of his ability, preserve, protect, and defend the Constitution of the United States, and in violation of his constitutional duty to take care that the laws be faithfully executed, has willfully corrupted and manipulated the judicial process of the United States for his personal gain and exoneration, impeding the administration of justice, in that:

On August 17, 1998, William Jefferson Clinton swore to tell the truth, the whole truth, and nothing but the truth before a Federal grand jury of the United States. Contrary to that oath, William Jefferson Clinton willfully provided perjurious, false and misleading testimony to the grand jury concerning one or more of the following: (1) the nature and details of his relationship with a subordinate Government employee; (2) prior perjurious, false and misleading testimony he gave in a Federal civil rights action

brought against him; (3) prior false and misleading statements he allowed his attorney to make to a Federal judge in that civil rights action; and (4) his corrupt efforts to influence the testimony of witnesses and to impede the discovery of evidence in that civil rights action.

In doing this, William Jefferson Clinton has undermined the integrity of his office, has brought disrepute on the Presidency, has betrayed his trust as President, and has acted in a manner subversive of the rule of law and justice, to the manifest injury of the people of the United States.

Wherefore, William Jefferson Clinton, by such conduct, warrants impeachment and trial, and removal from office and disqualification to hold and enjoy any office of honor, trust, or profit under the United States.

Article II

In his conduct while President of the United States, William Jefferson Clinton, in violation of his constitutional oath faithfully to execute the office of President of the United States and, to the best of his ability, preserve, protect, and defend the Constitution of the United States, and in violation of his constitutional duty to take care that the laws be faithfully executed, has prevented, obstructed, and impeded the administration of justice, and has to that end engaged personally, and through his subordinates and agents, in a course of conduct or scheme designed to delay, impede, cover up, and conceal the existence of evidence and testimony related to a Federal civil rights action brought against him in a duly instituted judicial proceeding.

The means used to implement this course of conduct or scheme included one or more of the following acts:

(1) On or about December 17, 1997, William Jefferson Clinton corruptly encouraged a witness in a

Federal civil rights action brought against him to execute a sworn affidavit in that proceeding that he knew to be perjurious, false and misleading.

(2) On or about December 17, 1997, William Jefferson Clinton corruptly encouraged a witness in a Federal civil rights action brought against him to give perjurious, false and misleading testimony if and when called to testify personally in that proceeding.

(3) On or about December 28, 1997, William Jefferson Clinton corruptly engaged in, encouraged, or supported a scheme to conceal evidence that had been subpoenaed in a Federal civil rights action brought against him.

(4) Beginning on or about December 7, 1997, and continuing through and including January 14, 1998, William Jefferson Clinton intensified and succeeded in an effort to secure job assistance to a witness in a Federal civil rights action brought against him in order to corruptly prevent the truthful testimony of that witness in that proceeding at a time when the truthful testimony of that witness would have been harmful to him.

(5) On January 17, 1998, at his deposition in a Federal civil rights action brought against him, William Jefferson Clinton corruptly allowed his attorney to make false and misleading statements to a Federal judge characterizing an affidavit, in order to prevent questioning deemed relevant by the judge. Such false and misleading statements were subsequently acknowledged by his attorney in a communication to that judge.

(6) On or about January 18 and January 20-21, 1998, William Jefferson Clinton related a false and misleading account of events relevant to a Federal civil rights action brought against him to a potential witness in that proceeding, in order to corruptly influence the testimony of that witness.

(7) On or about January 21, 23, and 26, 1998, William Jefferson Clinton made false and misleading statements to potential witnesses in a Federal grand jury proceeding in order to corruptly influence the testimony of those witnesses. The false and misleading statements made by William Jefferson Clinton were repeated by the witnesses to the grand jury, causing the grand jury to receive false and misleading information.

In all of this, William Jefferson Clinton has undermined the integrity of his office, has brought disrepute on the Presidency, has betrayed his trust as President, and has acted in a manner subversive of the rule of law and justice, to the manifest injury of the people of the United States.

Wherefore, William Jefferson Clinton, by such conduct, warrants impeachment and trial, and removal from office and disqualification to hold and enjoy any office of honor, trust, or profit under the United States.

Sandra Day O'Connor (AP Photo/J. Scott Applewhite)

*"We deal here not with an ordinary election,
but with an election for the President of the United States."*

Overview

Traditionally, the federal courts have refused to become involved in "political question suits," or disputes arising from and revolving around the political process. Foremost among such disputes are questions over electoral outcomes. Election contests tend to be messy; by definition, such events speak directly to the divided will of the people. Especially where certain voting laws have been bent or broken, a "right" or "wrong" solution to a dispute often cannot be determined. Inevitably, judges have to make choices that seem to ignore the will of at least a part of the electorate. As Justice Felix Frankfurter noted in 1946's *Colegrove v. Green*, the democratic state simply presents some "demands on judicial power which ... [are] not met for judicial determination," for "it is hostile to a democratic system to involve the judiciary in the politics of the people." He concluded, "Courts ought not to enter this political thicket" (http://caselaw.lp.findlaw.com/cgi-bin/getcase.pl?navby=case&court=US&vol=328&invol=549).

In 2000, nevertheless, the U.S. Supreme Court was obligated to enter the political thicket of electoral outcomes. At issue was the winner of the 2000 presidential election, between the vice president, Albert Gore, Jr., and the Texas governor, George W. Bush. The two were separated by only some 200 votes—out of more than five million cast—in Florida, which held the decisive electoral college votes needed by each candidate to win the presidency. Al Gore had challenged the accuracy of the Florida vote totals, calling for selective hand recounts. George W. Bush defended these totals and challenged the validity of recounting votes by hand. Ultimately, the issues raised by the Florida recounts landed in the Supreme Court, which ruled by a 5–4 vote that Florida's methods of recounting votes were so disorganized and diverse from county to county that they amounted to an unconstitutional violation of the equal protection clauses of the Constitution and of the Fourteenth Amendment. In addition, the ruling held that as the time allowed for counting votes had expired, the Florida recounts were finished and the candidate ahead at that time, George W. Bush, was the winner of the Florida

vote—and hence became the forty-third president of the United States.

Context

Election Day was November 7, 2000. More than one hundred million Americans voted in this election, with tracking polls showing very close totals throughout the day. That evening, the television networks began to announce which candidates had won which states. As the night progressed, the race remained tight; midnight came and passed, but the election still remained too close to call. By early in the morning of November 8, it became clear that the presidential election between Al Gore and George W. Bush had deadlocked in a virtual tie.

The source of this tie was Florida. Out of some five million votes cast in the Sunshine State, about sixteen hundred votes separated the two candidates as of November 8; with less than a 0.005 percent difference between the two, state law required an automatic recount. The law also allowed the losing candidate to request hand recounts. Given that without Florida's twenty-five electoral college votes, neither candidate would have a majority of the all-important electoral votes, the ultimate outcome of the Florida recount would determine which candidate had won the presidency. When the automatic recount lessened the gap between the two candidates to just under two hundred votes, the candidate who was then losing, Al Gore, indeed requested hand recounts.

Gore's decision to contest the Florida vote count extended the 2000 election for weeks. The following thirty-six days of electoral crisis and chaos featured grand political theater, with local county officials attempting to hand recount ballots in an atmosphere of intense pressure, with more than forty separate court cases litigating all aspects of the recount process, and with some ten separate rulings being issued by the Florida Supreme Court, including a controversial order for a statewide recount more than three weeks after the election. At length, the U.S. Supreme Court heard cases on the matter on two occasions. With its ruling in *Bush v. Gore* on December 12, the Supreme Court finally ended the recounts in Florida and effectively named

November 7
Election Day.

November 8
With the two candidates separated by only some sixteen hundred votes, Florida initiates automatic recounts in all sixty-seven counties. By day's end, Bush's lead has shrunk to approximately four hundred votes.

November 9
Mandatory recounts continue. Bush's lead shrinks to 229 votes. Gore officially requests hand recounts in four heavily Democratic counties: Palm Beach, Miami-Dade, Broward, and Volusia.

November 11
The Bush campaign files a federal lawsuit in Miami (*Siegel v. LePore*) seeking declaratory and injunctive relief to halt all manual recounts. Palm Beach County begins a 1 percent sample recount to determine whether a countywide recount is necessary.

November 12
The Palm Beach County elections board votes in favor of a countywide recount. Volusia County begins a countywide recount.

November 13
The Florida secretary of state, Katherine Harris, a Republican and vice-chair of the Bush campaign in Florida, requires all counties to complete their recounts by 5:00 PM the next day, with no exceptions allowed. The Volusia County Canvassing Board sues Harris to withdraw the 5:00 PM vote certification and recount deadline, with lawyers for Palm Beach County and for the Gore campaign joining the suit. Bush joins the state of Florida (*McDermott v. Harris*) to block any extension. Meanwhile, the U.S. district court judge Donald Middlebrooks denies the Bush campaign's earlier request (*Siegel v. LePore*) for injunctive relief to halt a manual recount of Florida voters' ballots.

George W. Bush the forty-third president of the United States.

About the Author

Unlike most U.S. Supreme Court opinions, the ruling in *Bush v. Gore* was not signed by a single justice as author. Rather, the opinion was issued as a per curiam ruling, or an unsigned ruling—written by one or more justices but presented as merely being "from the court." Supreme Court justices often issue a per curiam ruling when they wish to express a result that enjoyed the full and total institutional support of all nine justices. At other times, they issue such a ruling when a case is so lacking in complexity that no member of the Court wishes to commit the time to draft and sign his or her own opinion. Per curiam rulings also can provide cover in politically sensitive cases, shielding the writing justice within the protecting arms of the whole Court. Last, a per curiam ruling, especially in a case featuring dissent among the nine justices, can be a means of expressing the barest measure of consensus.

Most likely, the Court adopted the per curiam approach to authorship in *Bush v. Gore* for all of these reasons. With little time to spare, the opinion was probably written in different chambers and later cobbled together to form a whole—in point of fact, the evidence that exists suggests that most of this ruling was written by Justices Anthony Kennedy and Sandra Day O'Connor working in tandem. The per curiam approach also served as a means to consensus, permitting the members of the 7–2 majority in agreement on equal protection to reach a rough accord on the basic proposition that the Florida recount was flawed and unconstitutional; with this accord expressed in the per curiam statement, the justices were free to write separate concurring and dissenting opinions further detailing their personal views. Of course, the per curiam ruling also spared one of the justices from having to sign his or her name to an opinion that, owing to severe time constraints, was less coherent than the authors might have wished. So, too, it provided protection from the ruling's politically explosive impact. Perhaps above all, the per curiam statement gave the Court's ruling an air of consensus that actually did not exist, implied that the ruling was of modest scope, and supported the assertion that the Court was only reluctantly entering the fray to fulfill its constitutional role.

Explanation and Analysis of the Document

◆ The Per Curiam Ruling

The per curiam statement begins by noting that Bush's petition to the Court presented three interrelated questions: "whether the Florida Supreme Court established new standards for resolving Presidential election contests, thereby violating Art. II, §1, cl. 2, of the United States Constitution and failing to comply with 3 U.S.C. §5, and whether the use of standardless manual recounts violates the Equal Protection and Due Process Clauses." The opinion, however, largely ignores the first two questions, almost immediately moving on to the third topic, equal protection and due process. In fact, other than drawing on Article II of the Constitution and Title 3 of the U.S. Code as a foundation for grounding the ruling on equal protection, the per curiam statement ignores these matters entirely.

The majority starts its discussion of equal protection and voting, ironically, by noting how "the individual citizen has no federal constitutional right to vote for electors for the President of the United States unless and until the state legislature chooses a statewide election as the means to implement its power to appoint members of the Electoral College." With this fundamental constitutional tenet understood, "the State legislature's power to select the manner for appointing electors" was undeniably supreme; if it so chose, the state legislature had the power and the right to "select the electors itself." However, "history has now favored the voter" in the selection of "Presidential electors." This extension of the right to vote was key in this matter. "When the state legislature vests the right to vote for President in its people," explains the per curiam statement, "the right to vote as the legislature has prescribed is fundamental; and one source of its fundamental nature lies in the equal weight accorded to each vote and the equal dignity owed to each voter." In fact, "the right to vote is protected in more than the initial allocation of the franchise": Equal protection applies as well "to the manner of its exercise." As the per curiam ruling makes clear, having granted to the people the right to vote on equal terms, the state could not, "by later arbitrary and disparate treatment, value one person's vote over that of another." Once granted, in other words, a citizen's right to vote is subject to the full protection of the law, including the equal protection clauses of the Constitution.

With this established, the per curiam statement moves to the issues raised by the Florida recounts, noting, "The question before us … is whether the recount procedures the Florida Supreme Court has adopted" were consistent with the voters' equal protection rights. The Court's consensus on this question is that the Florida courts had not met this burden. To be valid, notes the per curiam ruling, recounts had to be performed in a uniform manner, "to assure" that the determination of voters' intents was "equal [in] application." This had not been the case in Florida: "The standards for accepting or rejecting contested ballots might vary not only from county to county," notes the ruling, but also often "within a single county from one recount team to another." Since the intents of voters were sometimes difficult to determine, what one county called a valid ballot frequently was excluded in another county and vice versa. The Florida Supreme Court's order initiating a statewide recount, in turn, had improperly "ratified this uneven treatment."

Worse yet, continues the per curiam ruling, the recount procedures issued by the Florida court system were, if anything, just as bad as and perhaps worse than the preexisting state standards. The rules issued by the circuit court (under orders from the Florida Supreme Court) "did not

November 14
The judge Terry Lewis, of the Circuit Court of Leon County, upholds Harris's 5:00 PM deadline but cautions that he will allow supplemental or corrected presidential vote totals after the deadline, which totals Harris may or may not use under her discretion. Later that day, Harris issues vote totals as of 5 PM, with Bush holding a three-hundred-vote margin. Hand recounts continue in the counties of Palm Beach, Volusia, and now also Broward.

November 15
Harris announces that she has reviewed letters from the hand-counting counties and found their reasons for delay insufficient; she will not accept the results of any hand recounts when certifying the Florida vote on November 18.

November 16
Gore lawyers ask Judge Lewis to require Harris to include ballots counted by hand after the deadline of November 14.

November 17
Judge Lewis refuses to order Harris to accept late returns. Gore appeals this decision to the Florida Supreme Court. Hand recounting continues.

November 21
The Florida Supreme Court renders a unanimous decision in *Palm Beach County Canvassing Board v. Harris*, ordering that manual recounts must be added to the final certified count of presidential votes by Florida voters. The justices give the counties until 5:00 PM on Sunday, November 26, to send in the amended results.

November 22
Bush petitions the U.S. Supreme Court, seeking to have the decision of the Florida Supreme Court in *Palm Beach County Canvassing Board v. Harris* overruled. As the counting deadline of November 26 looms, Miami-Dade election officials abruptly halt the county's recount, saying all 600,000 ballots cannot be counted in time. Broward and Palm Beach counties continue counting.

November 24
In a historic decision, the U.S. Supreme Court decides to hear Bush's appeal of the Florida Supreme Court's November 21 decision.

November 26
Broward County completes and submits revised vote totals. Palm Beach County is unable to complete its recounts in time, submitting revised totals two hours after the 5:00 PM deadline. Florida Secretary of State Harris certifies George W. Bush as the Florida voters' choice for president, rejecting the Palm Beach County Canvassing Board's amended partial recounts. Harris's tally shows Bush ahead by 537 votes.

November 27
As permitted by Florida law, Gore formally contests the election outcome. He calls for a court-ordered and court-supervised recount of fourteen thousand disputed ballots.

December 2
Judge Sander Sauls holds a trial to consider Gore's request for a hand count of the fourteen thousand contested ballots (*Gore v. Harris*).

December 4
In *Bush v. Palm Beach County Canvassing Board*, the U.S. Supreme Court sets aside the Florida ruling that had extended the deadline for submitting returns, citing considerable uncertainty as to the grounds for the Florida Supreme Court's decision. Gore's plea for a recount of the undervote is rejected by Judge Sauls. Sauls declares that there is no evidence establishing a reasonable probability that Gore might win if granted a hand recount of the disputed ballots.

December 8
By a 4–3 majority, the Florida Supreme Court overturns Judge Sauls's decision in *Gore v. Harris* rejecting Gore's plea for a recount of the undervote in certain Florida counties. On its own motion, the majority rules that ballots for which no vote for president was recorded must be recounted in all sixty-seven Florida counties that have not already carried out hand recounts. Bush appeals the ruling to the U.S. Supreme Court.

specify who would recount the ballots." This omission forced the creation of ad hoc counting teams "who had no previous training in handling and interpreting ballots." Such informal procedures were constitutionally unacceptable, argues the per curiam statement, "inconsistent with the minimum procedures necessary to protect the fundamental right of each voter" in a statewide recount. Further, the state standard regarding the validity of votes simply cited "the intent of the voter" as determined by the totality of the circumstances as presented by the ballot; the deficiency of uniform rules regarding vote validity meant that the "recount mechanisms implemented in response to the decisions of the Florida Supreme Court do not satisfy the minimum requirement for non-arbitrary treatment of voters necessary to secure the fundamental right." Such had been the reason behind the Court's stay order of December 9. Lacking necessary procedural "safeguards," the contest provisions were simply "not well calculated to sustain the confidence that all citizens must have in the outcome of elections." As such, they were in direct violation of the equal protection clause of the Constitution.

Up to this point, the per curiam ruling had the support of seven of the nine justices; only Justices Ruth Bader Ginsburg and John Paul Stevens objected to the application of equal protection requirements to the Florida recounts. This consensus broke when the issue switched to the appropriate remedy for these violations. Only five of the Justices—William Rehnquist, Antonin Scalia, Clarence Thomas, O'Connor, and Kennedy—agreed that the recounts had to end. Thus, with little foundation of agreement to be presented in the rest of the opinion, the per curiam ruling simply states that the time for recounts has run out; the recounts are thus by necessity over and so is the election.

With its bombshell dropped, the per curiam statement ends with an intriguing attempt to minimize the Court's central role in this matter—despite the revolutionary potential of the ruling. The majority, in identifying equal protection as a fundamental entitlement guaranteeing the voters' right to have their votes counted in a manner that avoids "arbitrary and disparate treatment," had enunciated a new equal protection principle, one whose long-term implications for voting in America was explosive. With voting procedures differing not only between states but also within most states, the potential to revolutionize how Americans voted was enormous and intriguing, yet the majority seemed anxious to limit this principle almost as soon as they formulated it. Most explicit in this regard is the statement early in the ruling limiting the scope of the ruling to the current case alone: "Our consideration," writes the majority, "is limited to the present circumstances, for the problem of equal protection in election processes generally presents many complexities." Just why the ruling could so effectively overcome the many complexities of the 2000 postelection debacle and not be fit for application to future cases remains unstated. Nonetheless, with these words the per curiam ruling limited the use of equal protection as a precedent in future cases.

The per curiam statement's conclusion offers a more subtle and encompassing effort at distancing as well. In one of the most striking paragraphs of the opinion, the Court effectively asserts a limitation on its own judicial role:

> None are more conscious of the vital limits on judicial authority than are the members of this Court, and none stand more in admiration of the Constitution's design to leave the selection of the President to the people, through their legislatures, and to the political sphere. When contending parties invoke the process of the courts, however, it becomes our unsought responsibility to resolve the federal and constitutional issues the judicial system has been forced to confront.

Like the equal protection right that the majority created and then confined, this statement both asserts and rejects judicial power in these matters. The Court's opinion thus portrays the justices of the majority as reluctant decision makers, forced to resolve this case but unwilling and unable to extend their unsought authority beyond the minimum required to perform that task.

◆ The Concurrence

If the per curiam statement aims at deemphasizing the Court's powers—and authority—to act in this matter, Chief Justice Rehnquist's concurrence celebrates them. (The concurrence was joined by Justices Scalia and Thomas.) As far as the chief justice is concerned, "We deal here not with an ordinary election, but with an election for the President of the United States," and this made all the difference in the world. It is true, the chief justice explains, that "in most cases, comity and respect for federalism" lead the Supreme Court "to defer to the decisions of state courts on issues of state law." After all, the decisions of state courts are generally seen as "definitive pronouncements of the will of the States as sovereigns." But this situation was different: "In ordinary cases, the distribution of powers among the branches of a State's government raises no questions of federal constitutional law.... But there are a few exceptional cases in which the Constitution imposes a duty or confers a power on a particular branch of a State's government. This is one of them."

With the Court's power to rule established, the chief justice offers an additional—and, though unstated, presumably superior—reason to overturn the Florida Supreme Court's recount order. Article II, Section 1, Clause 2 of the Constitution places authority over presidential elections *exclusively* in the hands of the state legislatures. In Florida the legislature had set up a series of (admittedly inadequate) procedures for counting votes and determining the distribution of presidential electors. The Florida Supreme Court, in turn, had disrupted these legislatively mandated procedures by ordering a statewide recount so late in the vote-counting process. Moreover, federal law had created a "safe harbor" under which a state's determination of its electors could not be challenged so long as the rules

Time Line

2000

■ **December 9**
The U.S. Supreme Court halts the Florida recount. Oral arguments in *Bush v. Gore* are scheduled for Monday, December 11.

■ **December 12**
The U.S. Supreme Court reverses the Florida Supreme Court's decision by an effective 5–4 vote. In the per curiam opinion, the Court holds that differing vote-counting standards from county to county and the lack of a single judicial officer to oversee the recount violated the equal protection clause of the Constitution. Recounts are ordered to be ended.

2001

■ **January 20**
George W. Bush is sworn in as the forty-third president of the United States.

applied were set *before* the election and all disputes were settled by December 18, 2000. For its part, the Florida legislature had clearly sought to reach this safe harbor; the Florida Supreme Court's ruling, on the other hand, created new rules *after* the election. Therefore, the Florida Supreme Court's changing the method of determining presidential electors by calling for a statewide recount was tantamount to neglect of the safe harbor provisions and was thus a violation of Article II's grant of exclusive authority to the state legislature. Hence, the Florida recounts were unconstitutional.

◆ The Dissents

Four justices objected to the per curiam ruling. Justices Stevens and Ginsburg objected to the whole of the per curiam statement in strident terms. The other two, Justices Stephen Breyer and David Souter, agreed with the majority on the equal protection failures of the Florida electoral system but disagreed regarding the proposed remedy of halting all recounts.

Despite his agreement on the issue of equal protection, Justice Breyer complains that the majority is implementing the wrong remedy. "Of course, the selection of the President is of fundamental national importance," Breyer writes. "But that importance is political, not legal." The federal legal questions presented by this case, "with one exception," were "insubstantial." For this reason alone, "this Court should resist the temptation unnecessarily to resolve tangential legal disputes, where doing so threatens to determine the outcome of the election." As Breyer sees it, "The Court was wrong to take this case. It was wrong to grant a stay. It should now vacate that stay and permit the

Anthony Kennedy (AP Photo/J. Scott Applewhite)

Florida Supreme Court to decide whether the recount should resume." The benefits of the halting of the recounts were tainted by the questionable constitutionalism of the act, explains Breyer, and the costs of the Court acting were simply too great. Breyer writes,

> We run no risk of returning to the days when a President (responding to this Court's efforts to protect the Cherokee Indians) might have said, "John Marshall has made his decision; now let him enforce it!" … But we do risk a self-inflicted wound—a wound that may harm not just the Court, but the Nation. I fear that in order to bring this agonizingly long election process to a definitive conclusion we have not adequately attended to that necessary "check upon our own exercise of power," "our own sense of self-restraint."

Justice Souter is even more blunt in his conclusions about the majority's proposed remedies when he writes: "If this Court had allowed the State to follow the course indicated by the opinions of its own Supreme Court, it is entirely possible that there would ultimately have been no issue requiring our review, and political tension could have worked itself out in the Congress following the procedure provided in 3 U.S.C. § 15." Sadly, the situation had not been resolved in any such way. And with the Court having wrongly taken up the case, "its resolution by the majority" amounted to "another erroneous decision." The key problem in Souter's eyes is the per curiam ruling's remedy. Souter himself believes that the best option would have been to "remand the case to the courts of Florida with instructions to establish uniform standards for evaluating the several types of ballots that have prompted differing treatments." Unlike the majority, Souter sees "no warrant for this Court to assume that Florida could not possibly comply with this requirement before the date set for the meeting of electors, December 18." For Souter, there is simply "no justification for denying the State the opportunity to try to count all disputed ballots now."

Unlike Breyer and Souter, Justice John Paul Stevens objected to the majority's entire ruling. He asserts that "the Constitution assigns to the States the primary responsibility for determining the manner of selecting the Presidential electors." Hence, "when questions arise about the meaning of state laws, including election laws," it has been the Court's "settled practice to accept the opinions of the highest courts of the States as providing the final answers." This was decidedly not the case here. The per curiam statement's equal protection arguments also did not convince Justice Stevens of the need to act. "Admittedly, the use of differing substandards for determining voter intent in different counties employing similar voting systems may raise serious concerns," he says. However, notes Stevens, "those concerns are alleviated—if not eliminated—by the fact that a single impartial magistrate will ultimately adjudicate all objections arising from the recount process." Actually underlying the entire assault on the Florida election procedures, Justice Stevens argues, was "an unstated lack of confidence in the impartiality and capacity of the state judges who would make the critical decisions if the vote count were to proceed." This was a troubling view, one, he states, that can "only lend credence to the most cynical appraisal of the work of judges throughout the land." "Time will one day heal the wound to that confidence that will be inflicted by today's decision," Justice Stevens concludes. Still, "one thing … is certain. Although we may never know with complete certainty the identity of the winner of this year's Presidential election, the identity of the loser is perfectly clear. It is the Nation's confidence in the judge as an impartial guardian of the rule of law."

The most angry of the dissenters was Justice Ruth Bader Ginsburg. Ginsburg is especially malcontented with the lack of respect shown the Florida Supreme Court, noting, "The extraordinary setting of this case has obscured the ordinary principle that dictates its proper resolution: Federal courts defer to state high courts' interpretations of their state's own law." This principle was the foundation upon which federalism was built and to which all agreed. The five justices in the majority were normally among the strongest supporters of state authority under federalism. This role reversal frustrates Ginsburg:

The Chief Justice's solicitude for the Florida Legislature comes at the expense of the more fundamental solicitude we owe to the legislature's sovereign [the State and its people].... Were the other members of this Court as mindful as they generally are of our system of dual sovereignty, they would affirm the judgment of the Florida Supreme Court.

Ginsburg also questions the majority's equal protection logic. Ideally, she explains,

perfection would be the appropriate standard for judging the recount. But we live in an imperfect world, one in which thousands of votes have not been counted. I cannot agree that the recount adopted by the Florida court, flawed as it may be, would yield a result any less fair or precise than the certification that preceded that recount.

Lacking any respect for the majority's logic, and perhaps distrusting their motives, Justice Ginsburg breaks tradition by ending her views bluntly: "I dissent."

Audience

There is a certain art to writing a Supreme Court opinion. Judicial opinions are written to achieve particular goals and feature a specific structure, dictating what goes into the statement as well as what gets left out. A Supreme Court opinion must lay out in detail the unique situation underlying the legal dispute; set forth the key legal and constitutional questions raised by the case and then provide answers to these questions; and, finally, explain why the justices ruled as they did and make clear the scope and extent of the rulings. In a very real sense, a justice writing a Supreme Court opinion has several constituencies to satisfy with words: the litigants in the case, whose primary focus is winning and losing; the judges whence the case originated, who need to be informed of their errors; lower court judges hearing similar cases, who need a clear precedent as to the law's or Constitution's meaning in this particular context; and, last, the wider community of Americans, for whom a Supreme Court ruling can act as an important means of education on the workings of the constitutional system of government.

As with most Supreme Court decisions, the Court's ruling in *Bush v. Gore* was aimed at all of these audiences. As such, the decision had to operate on three levels. The first level was legal and constitutional, as the Court set out the legal parameters of the case. The second level was political; at the center of the case was the issue of who would become president, and the Court's ruling had to provide some sort of resolution to the ongoing political crisis. Finally, through its ruling the Court had to operate as a teacher, educating the American public on the meaning and content of the Constitution as applied in these matters.

Justice Ruth Bader Ginsburg was one of two justices who objected to the whole of the per curiam. (AP Photo/ J. Scott Applewhite)

Impact

More so than the average Supreme Court case, the ruling in *Bush v. Gore* had a very obvious and significant impact: the naming of a president. Hence, President George W. Bush was the one to face the crises of the following few years. In particular, President Bush, rather than President Gore, responded to the attacks of September 11, 2001; not just America but the world as well, then, might have become a very different place had the Court ruled differently.

On a constitutional level the impact of the case was more ambiguous. On the one hand, the application of equal protection to matters of electoral administration was a major expansion of the doctrine into the realm of voting rights. Florida was not alone in having electoral rules and procedures that permitted the nonstandardized counting of votes in elections; in fact, Florida was not even the worst state in this regard. The per curiam ruling's use of the equal protection doctrine thus promised a new future of ever-increasing federal involvement in the running of elections, as inequitable state voting procedures would seemingly have to be ended under federal supervision. On the other hand, little has come of the case or its promise of enhanced federal involve-

"Our consideration is limited to the present circumstances, for the problem of equal protection in election processes generally presents many complexities."

(Per Curiam Ruling)

"We deal here not with an ordinary election, but with an election for the President of the United States.... In most cases, comity and respect for federalism compel us to defer to the decisions of state courts on issues of state law. That practice reflects our understanding that the decisions of state courts are definitive pronouncements of the will of the States as sovereigns.... But there are a few exceptional cases in which the Constitution imposes a duty or confers a power on a particular branch of a State's government. This is one of them."

(Chief Justice William Rehnquist, Concurrence)

"In this highly politicized matter, the appearance of a split decision runs the risk of undermining the public's confidence in the Court itself.... We run no risk of returning to the days when a President (responding to this Court's efforts to protect the Cherokee Indians) might have said, 'John Marshall has made his decision; now let him enforce it!' ... But we do risk a self-inflicted wound—a wound that may harm not just the Court, but the Nation."

(Justice Stephen Breyer, Dissent)

"Time will one day heal the wound to that confidence that will be inflicted by today's decision. One thing, however, is certain. Although we may never know with complete certainty the identity of the winner of this year's Presidential election, the identity of the loser is perfectly clear. It is the Nation's confidence in the judge as an impartial guardian of the rule of law."

(Justice John Paul Stevens, Dissent)

ment in voting since the opinion's writing. The Supreme Court has not mentioned the case even once in any subsequent opinion. Similarly, the lower federal courts have seemed to avoid the case as precedent—even when matters have involved voting rights issues. As a result, while the opinion seemed to promise much, it effectively did nothing to change the existing structural relationship between the states and the national government on the issue of voting.

Related Documents

"Brief for Petitioners George W. Bush and Richard Cheney," and "Brief of Respondent Albert Gore, Jr.," *Bush et al. v. Gore et al.*, U.S. Supreme Court, Case No. 00-949 (December 10, 2000). FindLaw Web site. http://news.findlaw.com/legalnews/us/election/election2000.html. Accessed on March 10, 2008. These briefs, filed only two days before the Supreme Court handed down its decision in *Bush v. Gore*, lay out the arguments of both sides as they faced off before the Court.

Albert Gore, Jr., and Joseph I. Lieberman v. Katherine Harris et al. Florida Supreme Court, Case No. SC00-2431 (December 8, 2000). Florida Supreme Court Web site. http://www.floridasupremecourt.org/decisions/pre2004/ops/sc00-2431.pdf. Accessed on March 10, 2008. This opinion was the basis for the Supreme Court's ruling in *Bush v. Gore.* It was this monumental ruling that Bush appealed and which the Supreme Court justices reversed.

Bibliography

■ Books

Boies, David. *Courting Justice: From* NY Yankees v. Major League Baseball *to* Bush v. Gore, *1997–2000.* New York: Hyperion, 2004.

Gillman, Howard. *The Votes That Counted: How the Court Decided the 2000 Presidential Election.* Chicago: University of Chicago Press, 2001.

Greene, Abner. *Understanding the 2000 Election: A Guide to the Legal Battles That Decided the Presidency.* New York: New York University Press, 2001.

Kaplan, David A. *The Accidental President: How 413 Lawyers, 9 Supreme Court Justices, and 5,963,110 (Give or Take a Few) Floridians Landed George W. Bush in the White House.* New York: Morrow, 2001.

Merzer, Martin. *The Miami Herald Report: Democracy Held Hostage.* New York: St. Martin's Press, 2001.

Posner, Richard A. *Breaking the Deadlock: The 2000 Election, the Constitution, and the Courts.* Princeton, N.J.: Princeton University Press, 2001.

Sunstein, Cass R., and Richard A. Epstein, eds. *The Vote: Bush, Gore, and the Supreme Court.* Chicago: University of Chicago Press, 2001.

Tapper, Jake. *Down and Dirty: The Plot to Steal the Presidency.* Boston: Little, Brown, 2001.

Toobin, Jeffrey. *Too Close to Call: The Thirty-Six-Day Battle to Decide the 2000 Election.* New York: Random House, 2001.

United States Commission on Civil Rights. *Voting Irregularities in Florida during the 2000 Presidential Election.* Washington, D.C.: Government Printing Office, 2001.

Washington Post. *Deadlock: The Inside Story of America's Closest Election.* New York: PublicAffairs, 2001.

■ Web Sites

"Colgreve v. Green, 328 U.S. 549 (1946)." FindLaw Web site. http://caselaw.lp.findlaw.com/cgi-bin/getcase.pl?navby=case&court=US&vol=328&invol=549. Accessed on March 10, 2008.

"Election 2000." Stanford Law School "Robert Crown Law Library" Web site. http://election2000.stanford.edu/. Accessed on March 10, 2008.

"Election 2000: Recounts and Challenges." Washington Post Web site. http://www.washingtonpost.com/wp-srv/onpolitics/elections/postelection2000coverage.htm. Accessed on March 10, 2008.

"Election 2000: Special Coverage." FindLaw Web site. http://news.findlaw.com/legalnews/us/election/election2000.html. Accessed on March 10, 2008.

"Elections 2000." University of Michigan Library "Documents Center" Web site. http://www.lib.umich.edu/govdocs/elec2000.html. Accessed on March 10, 2008.

"Florida Election Cases." Supreme Court of the United States Web site. http://www.supremecourtus.gov/florida.html. Accessed on March 10, 2008.

"LII Backgrounder on Election 2000." Legal Information Institute Web site. http://www.law.cornell.edu/background/election/. Accessed on March 10, 2008.

"Presidential Election Law." Jurist Web site. http://jurist.law.pitt.edu/election2000.htm. Accessed on March 10, 2008.

—By Charles L. Zelden

1. Discuss possible reasons why the Supreme Court in *Bush v. Gore* decided (a) to accept the case, (b) to base the ruling on the concept of equal protection, and (c) to end the recounts by its own fiat.

2. In what ways is the Supreme Court's ruling in *Bush v. Gore* similar to and different from another key document in voting rights history, the Voting Rights Act of 1965?

3. Explore the validity of Justice Stevens's dissenting assertions: "Time will one day heal the wound to that confidence that will be inflicted by today's decision. One thing, however, is certain. Although we may never know with complete certainty the identity of the winner of this year's Presidential election, the identity of the loser is perfectly clear. It is the Nation's confidence in the judge as an impartial guardian of the rule of law." Do you agree with Stevens's assessment? Have perceptions of the Supreme Court and of judges in general changed since 2000? If so, why and how? If not, then how should Justice Stevens's comment be considered?

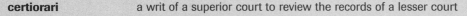

certiorari	a writ of a superior court to review the records of a lesser court
chads	in some voting technologies, the small pieces of paper pushed out of voting cards when a vote is cast
concurrence	a judicial opinion written in support of the result of a majority ruling but providing alternate reasons or justifications for action
dissents	judicial opinions written in objection to or in disagreement with a majority ruling
due process	the concept that all citizens should be treated equally under the law by the terms of a set of known and understandable rules and laws
election contests	procedures organized under state laws for recounting votes to determine the winner of an election
Electoral College	the system used to choose the president of the United States, by which states are proportionately assigned electors determined by popular vote, a majority of which are required to win the presidency
equal protection	legal and constitutional concept by which no state law or procedure can treat or affect one segment of the population any differently from any other population segment
overvotes	the results when a voter places marks next to the names of more than one candidate for the same office; such overvotes invalidate a ballot for that electoral race
per curiam	literally, "from the court" as a whole; said of a judicial opinion without a declared author
petitioner	one who asks an appellate court to hear a case; normally the first name listed in a court case title
Presidential electors	members of the Electoral College, assigned by popular vote in each state to determine the winner of the presidential election
safe harbor	provision for upholding a state's electoral votes without challenge in Congress, as set out by Title 3 of the U.S. Code, section 5
sub silentio	without comment
undervotes	the results when no mark is made by a voter for a particular electoral race; such undervotes are not counted in the final vote tallies

BUSH V. GORE

Per Curiam

On December 8, 2000, the Supreme Court of Florida ordered that the Circuit Court of Leon County tabulate by hand 9,000 ballots in Miami-Dade County. It also ordered the inclusion in the certified vote totals of 215 votes identified in Palm Beach County and 168 votes identified in Miami-Dade County for Vice President Albert Gore, Jr., and Senator Joseph Lieberman, Democratic Candidates for President and Vice President. The Supreme Court noted that petitioner, Governor George W. Bush asserted that the net gain for Vice President Gore in Palm Beach County was 176 votes, and directed the Circuit Court to resolve that dispute on remand. ___ So. 2d, at ___ (slip op., at 4, n. 6). The court further held that relief would require manual recounts in all Florida counties where so-called "undervotes" had not been subject to manual tabulation. The court ordered all manual recounts to begin at once. Governor Bush and Richard Cheney, Republican Candidates for the Presidency and Vice Presidency, filed an emergency application for a stay of this mandate. On December 9, we granted the application, treated the application as a petition for a writ of certiorari, and granted certiorari. Post, p. ___.

The proceedings leading to the present controversy are discussed in some detail in our opinion in *Bush v. Palm Beach County Canvassing Bd.*, ante, p. ____ (per curiam) (Bush I). On November 8, 2000, the day following the Presidential election, the Florida Division of Elections reported that petitioner, Governor Bush, had received 2,909,135 votes, and respondent, Vice President Gore, had received 2,907,351 votes, a margin of 1,784 for Governor Bush. Because Governor Bush's margin of victory was less than "one-half of a percent ... of the votes cast," an automatic machine recount was conducted under §102.141(4) of the election code, the results of which showed Governor Bush still winning the race but by a dimin-

ished margin. Vice President Gore then sought manual recounts in Volusia, Palm Beach, Broward, and Miami-Dade Counties, pursuant to Florida's election protest provisions. Fla. Stat. §102.166 (2000). A dispute arose concerning the deadline for local county canvassing boards to submit their returns to the Secretary of State (Secretary). The Secretary declined to waive the November 14 deadline imposed by statute. §§102.111, 102.112. The Florida Supreme Court, however, set the deadline at November 26. We granted certiorari and vacated the Florida Supreme Court's decision, finding considerable uncertainty as to the grounds on which it was based. Bush I, ante, at ___-___ (slip. op., at 6-7). On December 11, the Florida Supreme Court issued a decision on remand reinstating that date. ___ So. 2d ___, ___ (slip op. at 30-31).

On November 26, the Florida Elections Canvassing Commission certified the results of the election and declared Governor Bush the winner of Florida's 25 electoral votes. On November 27, Vice President Gore, pursuant to Florida's contest provisions, filed a complaint in Leon County Circuit Court contesting the certification. Fla. Stat. §102.168 (2000). He sought relief pursuant to §102.168(3)(c), which provides that "[r]eceipt of a number of illegal votes or rejection of a number of legal votes sufficient to change or place in doubt the result of the election" shall be grounds for a contest. The Circuit Court denied relief, stating that Vice President Gore failed to meet his burden of proof. He appealed to the First District Court of Appeal, which certified the matter to the Florida Supreme Court.

Accepting jurisdiction, the Florida Supreme Court affirmed in part and reversed in part. *Gore v. Harris*, ___ So. 2d. ____ (2000). The court held that the Circuit Court had been correct to reject Vice President Gore's challenge to the results certified in Nassau County and his challenge to the Palm Beach County Canvassing Board's determination that

3,300 ballots cast in that county were not, in the statutory phrase, "legal votes."

The Supreme Court held that Vice President Gore had satisfied his burden of proof under §102.168(3)(c) with respect to his challenge to Miami-Dade County's failure to tabulate, by manual count, 9,000 ballots on which the machines had failed to detect a vote for President ("undervotes"). ___ So. 2d., at ___ (slip. op., at 22-23). Noting the closeness of the election, the Court explained that "[o]n this record, there can be no question that there are legal votes within the 9,000 uncounted votes sufficient to place the results of this election in doubt." Id., at ___ (slip. op., at 35). A "legal vote," as determined by the Supreme Court, is "one in which there is a 'clear indication of the intent of the voter.'" Id., at ____ (slip op., at 25). The court therefore ordered a hand recount of the 9,000 ballots in Miami-Dade County. Observing that the contest provisions vest broad discretion in the circuit judge to "provide any relief appropriate under such circumstances," Fla. Stat. §102.168(8) (2000), the Supreme Court further held that the Circuit Court could order "the Supervisor of Elections and the Canvassing Boards, as well as the necessary public officials, in all counties that have not conducted a manual recount or tabulation of the undervotes… to do so forthwith, said tabulation to take place in the individual counties where the ballots are located." ___ So. 2d, at ____ (slip. op., at 38).

The Supreme Court also determined that both Palm Beach County and Miami-Dade County, in their earlier manual recounts, had identified a net gain of 215 and 168 legal votes for Vice President Gore. Id., at ___ (slip. op., at 33-34). Rejecting the Circuit Court's conclusion that Palm Beach County lacked the authority to include the 215 net votes submitted past the November 26 deadline, the Supreme Court explained that the deadline was not intended to exclude votes identified after that date through ongoing manual recounts. As to Miami-Dade County, the Court concluded that although the 168 votes identified were the result of a partial recount, they were "legal votes [that] could change the outcome of the election." Id., at (slip op., at 34). The Supreme Court therefore directed the Circuit Court to include those totals in the certified results, subject to resolution of the actual vote total from the Miami-Dade partial recount.

The petition presents the following questions: whether the Florida Supreme Court established new standards for resolving Presidential election con-

tests, thereby violating Art. II, §1, cl. 2, of the United States Constitution and failing to comply with 3 U. S. C. §5, and whether the use of standardless manual recounts violates the Equal Protection and Due Process Clauses. With respect to the equal protection question, we find a violation of the Equal Protection Clause.

◆ II

A

The closeness of this election, and the multitude of legal challenges which have followed in its wake, have brought into sharp focus a common, if heretofore unnoticed, phenomenon. Nationwide statistics reveal that an estimated 2% of ballots cast do not register a vote for President for whatever reason, including deliberately choosing no candidate at all or some voter error, such as voting for two candidates or insufficiently marking a ballot. See Ho, More Than 2M Ballots Uncounted, AP Online (Nov. 28, 2000); Kelley, Balloting Problems Not Rare But Only In A Very Close Election Do Mistakes And Mismarking Make A Difference, Omaha World-Herald (Nov. 15, 2000). In certifying election results, the votes eligible for inclusion in the certification are the votes meeting the properly established legal requirements.

This case has shown that punch card balloting machines can produce an unfortunate number of ballots which are not punched in a clean, complete way by the voter. After the current counting, it is likely legislative bodies nationwide will examine ways to improve the mechanisms and machinery for voting.

B

The individual citizen has no federal constitutional right to vote for electors for the President of the United States unless and until the state legislature chooses a statewide election as the means to implement its power to appoint members of the Electoral College. U. S. Const., Art. II, §1. This is the source for the statement in *McPherson v. Blacker*, 146 U. S. 1, 35 (1892), that the State legislature's power to select the manner for appointing electors is plenary; it may, if it so chooses, select the electors itself, which indeed was the manner used by State legislatures in several States for many years after the Framing of our Constitution. Id., at 28-33. History has now favored the voter, and in each of the several States the citizens themselves vote for Presidential electors. When the state legislature vests the right to vote for President in its people, the right to vote as the legislature has prescribed is fundamental; and one source of its fundamental nature lies in the equal weight accorded to each vote and the equal dignity owed to each voter. The State, of course, after granting the franchise in the special context of Article II, can take back the power to appoint electors. See id., at 35 ("[T]here is no doubt of the right of the legislature to resume the power at any time, for it can neither be taken away nor abdicated") (quoting S. Rep. No. 395, 43d Cong., 1st Sess.).

The right to vote is protected in more than the initial allocation of the franchise. Equal protection applies as well to the manner of its exercise. Having once granted the right to vote on equal terms, the State may not, by later arbitrary and disparate treatment, value one person's vote over that of another. See, e.g., *Harper v. Virginia Bd. of Elections*, 383 U. S. 663, 665 (1966) ("[O]nce the franchise is granted to the electorate, lines may not be drawn which are inconsistent with the Equal Protection Clause of the Fourteenth Amendment"). It must be remembered that "the right of suffrage can be denied by a debasement or dilution of the weight of a citizen's vote just as effectively as by wholly prohibiting the free exercise of the franchise." *Reynolds v. Sims*, 377 U. S. 533, 555 (1964).

There is no difference between the two sides of the present controversy on these basic propositions. Respondents say that the very purpose of vindicating the right to vote justifies the recount procedures now at issue. The question before us, however, is whether the recount procedures the Florida Supreme Court has adopted are consistent with its obligation to avoid arbitrary and disparate treatment of the members of its electorate.

Much of the controversy seems to revolve around ballot cards designed to be perforated by a stylus but which, either through error or deliberate omission, have not been perforated with sufficient precision for a machine to count them. In some cases a piece of the card—a chad—is hanging, say by two corners. In other cases there is no separation at all, just an indentation.

The Florida Supreme Court has ordered that the intent of the voter be discerned from such ballots. For purposes of resolving the equal protection challenge, it is not necessary to decide whether the Florida Supreme Court had the authority under the legislative scheme for resolving election disputes to define what a legal vote is and to mandate a manual recount implementing that definition. The recount mechanisms implemented in response to the deci-

sions of the Florida Supreme Court do not satisfy the minimum requirement for non-arbitrary treatment of voters necessary to secure the fundamental right. Florida's basic command for the count of legally cast votes is to consider the "intent of the voter." *Gore v. Harris*, ___ So. 2d, at ___ (slip op., at 39). This is unobjectionable as an abstract proposition and a starting principle. The problem inheres in the absence of specific standards to ensure its equal application. The formulation of uniform rules to determine intent based on these recurring circumstances is practicable and, we conclude, necessary.

The law does not refrain from searching for the intent of the actor in a multitude of circumstances; and in some cases the general command to ascertain intent is not susceptible to much further refinement. In this instance, however, the question is not whether to believe a witness but how to interpret the marks or holes or scratches on an inanimate object, a piece of cardboard or paper which, it is said, might not have registered as a vote during the machine count. The factfinder confronts a thing, not a person. The search for intent can be confined by specific rules designed to ensure uniform treatment.

The want of those rules here has led to unequal evaluation of ballots in various respects. See *Gore v. Harris*, ___ So. 2d, at ___ (slip op., at 51) (Wells, J., dissenting) ("Should a county canvassing board count or not count a 'dimpled chad' where the voter is able to successfully dislodge the chad in every other contest on that ballot? Here, the county canvassing boards disagree"). As seems to have been acknowledged at oral argument, the standards for accepting or rejecting contested ballots might vary not only from county to county but indeed within a single county from one recount team to another.

The record provides some examples. A monitor in Miami-Dade County testified at trial that he observed that three members of the county canvassing board applied different standards in defining a legal vote. 3 Tr. 497, 499 (Dec. 3, 2000). And testimony at trial also revealed that at least one county changed its evaluative standards during the counting process. Palm Beach County, for example, began the process with a 1990 guideline which precluded counting completely attached chads, switched to a rule that considered a vote to be legal if any light could be seen through a chad, changed back to the 1990 rule, and then abandoned any pretense of a per se rule, only to have a court order that the county consider dimpled chads legal. This is not a process with sufficient guarantees of equal treatment.

An early case in our one person, one vote jurisprudence arose when a State accorded arbitrary and disparate treatment to voters in its different counties. *Gray v. Sanders*, 372 U. S. 368 (1963). The Court found a constitutional violation. We relied on these principles in the context of the Presidential selection process in *Moore v. Ogilvie*, 394 U. S. 814 (1969), where we invalidated a county-based procedure that diluted the influence of citizens in larger counties in the nominating process. There we observed that "[t]he idea that one group can be granted greater voting strength than another is hostile to the one man, one vote basis of our representative government." Id., at 819.

The State Supreme Court ratified this uneven treatment. It mandated that the recount totals from two counties, Miami-Dade and Palm Beach, be included in the certified total. The court also appeared to hold sub silentio that the recount totals from Broward County, which were not completed until after the original November 14 certification by the Secretary of State, were to be considered part of the new certified vote totals even though the county certification was not contested by Vice President Gore. Yet each of the counties used varying standards to determine what was a legal vote. Broward County used a more forgiving standard than Palm Beach County, and uncovered almost three times as many new votes, a result markedly disproportionate to the difference in population between the counties.

In addition, the recounts in these three counties were not limited to so-called undervotes but extended to all of the ballots. The distinction has real consequences. A manual recount of all ballots identifies not only those ballots which show no vote but also those which contain more than one, the so-called overvotes. Neither category will be counted by the machine. This is not a trivial concern. At oral argument, respondents estimated there are as many as 110,000 overvotes statewide. As a result, the citizen whose ballot was not read by a machine because he failed to vote for a candidate in a way readable by a machine may still have his vote counted in a manual recount; on the other hand, the citizen who marks two candidates in a way discernable by the machine will not have the same opportunity to have his vote count, even if a manual examination of the ballot would reveal the requisite indicia of intent. Furthermore, the citizen who marks two candidates, only one of which is discernable by the machine, will have his vote counted even though it should have been read as an invalid ballot. The State Supreme Court's inclusion of vote counts based on

these variant standards exemplifies concerns with the remedial processes that were under way.

That brings the analysis to yet a further equal protection problem. The votes certified by the court included a partial total from one county, Miami-Dade. The Florida Supreme Court's decision thus gives no assurance that the recounts included in a final certification must be complete. Indeed, it is respondent's submission that it would be consistent with the rules of the recount procedures to include whatever partial counts are done by the time of final certification, and we interpret the Florida Supreme Court's decision to permit this. See _____ So. 2d, at _____, n. 21 (slip op., at 37, n. 21) (noting "practical difficulties" may control outcome of election, but certifying partial Miami-Dade total nonetheless). This accommodation no doubt results from the truncated contest period established by the Florida Supreme Court in Bush I, at respondents' own urging. The press of time does not diminish the constitutional concern. A desire for speed is not a general excuse for ignoring equal protection guarantees.

In addition to these difficulties the actual process by which the votes were to be counted under the Florida Supreme Court's decision raises further concerns. That order did not specify who would recount the ballots. The county canvassing boards were forced to pull together ad hoc teams comprised of judges from various Circuits who had no previous training in handling and interpreting ballots. Furthermore, while others were permitted to observe, they were prohibited from objecting during the recount.

The recount process, in its features here described, is inconsistent with the minimum procedures necessary to protect the fundamental right of each voter in the special instance of a statewide recount under the authority of a single state judicial officer. Our consideration is limited to the present circumstances, for the problem of equal protection in election processes generally presents many complexities.

The question before the Court is not whether local entities, in the exercise of their expertise, may develop different systems for implementing elections. Instead, we are presented with a situation where a state court with the power to assure uniformity has ordered a statewide recount with minimal procedural safeguards. When a court orders a statewide remedy, there must be at least some assurance that the rudimentary requirements of equal treatment and fundamental fairness are satisfied.

Given the Court's assessment that the recount process underway was probably being conducted in an unconstitutional manner, the Court stayed the order directing the recount so it could hear this case and render an expedited decision. The contest provision, as it was mandated by the State Supreme Court, is not well calculated to sustain the confidence that all citizens must have in the outcome of elections. The State has not shown that its procedures include the necessary safeguards. The problem, for instance, of the estimated 110,000 overvotes has not been addressed, although Chief Justice Wells called attention to the concern in his dissenting opinion. See ____ So. 2d, at ____, n. 26 (slip op., at 45, n. 26).

Upon due consideration of the difficulties identified to this point, it is obvious that the recount cannot be conducted in compliance with the requirements of equal protection and due process without substantial additional work. It would require not only the adoption (after opportunity for argument) of adequate statewide standards for determining what is a legal vote, and practicable procedures to implement them, but also orderly judicial review of any disputed matters that might arise. In addition, the Secretary of State has advised that the recount of only a portion of the ballots requires that the vote tabulation equipment be used to screen out undervotes, a function for which the machines were not designed. If a recount of overvotes were also required, perhaps even a second screening would be necessary. Use of the equipment for this purpose, and any new software developed for it, would have to be evaluated for accuracy by the Secretary of State, as required by Fla. Stat. §101.015 (2000).

The Supreme Court of Florida has said that the legislature intended the State's electors to "participat[e] fully in the federal electoral process," as provided in 3 U. S. C. §5. ____ So. 2d, at ____ (slip op. at 27); see also *Palm Beach Canvassing Bd. v. Harris*, 2000 WL 1725434, *13 (Fla. 2000). That statute, in turn, requires that any controversy or contest that is designed to lead to a conclusive selection of electors be completed by December 12. That date is upon us, and there is no recount procedure in place under the State Supreme Court's order that comports with minimal constitutional standards. Because it is evident that any recount seeking to meet the December 12 date will be unconstitutional for the reasons we have discussed, we reverse the judgment of the Supreme Court of Florida ordering a recount to proceed.

Seven Justices of the Court agree that there are constitutional problems with the recount ordered by the Florida Supreme Court that demand a remedy.

See post, at 6 (Souter, J., dissenting); post, at 2, 15 (Breyer, J., dissenting). The only disagreement is as to the remedy. Because the Florida Supreme Court has said that the Florida Legislature intended to obtain the safe-harbor benefits of 3 U. S. C. §5, Justice Breyer's proposed remedy—remanding to the Florida Supreme Court for its ordering of a constitutionally proper contest until December 18-contemplates action in violation of the Florida election code, and hence could not be part of an "appropriate" order authorized by Fla. Stat. §102.168(8) (2000).

* * * *

None are more conscious of the vital limits on judicial authority than are the members of this Court, and none stand more in admiration of the Constitution's design to leave the selection of the President to the people, through their legislatures, and to the political sphere. When contending parties invoke the process of the courts, however, it becomes our unsought responsibility to resolve the federal and constitutional issues the judicial system has been forced to confront.

The judgment of the Supreme Court of Florida is reversed, and the case is remanded for further proceedings not inconsistent with this opinion.

Pursuant to this Court's Rule 45.2, the Clerk is directed to issue the mandate in this case forthwith.

It is so ordered.

Chief Justice Rehnquist, with Whom Justice Scalia and Justice Thomas Join, Concurring

We join the per curiam opinion. We write separately because we believe there are additional grounds that require us to reverse the Florida Supreme Court's decision.

◆ I

We deal here not with an ordinary election, but with an election for the President of the United States. In *Burroughs v. United States*, 290 U. S. 534, 545 (1934), we said:

"While presidential electors are not officers or agents of the federal government (In re Green, 134 U. S. 377, 379), they exercise federal functions under, and discharge duties in virtue of authority conferred by, the Constitution of the United States. The President is vested with the executive power of the nation. The importance of his election and the vital character of its relationship to and effect upon the welfare and safety of the whole people cannot be too strongly stated."

Likewise, in *Anderson v. Celebrezze*, 460 U. S. 780, 794-795 (1983) (footnote omitted), we said: "[I]n the context of a Presidential election, state-imposed restrictions implicate a uniquely important national interest. For the President and the Vice President of the United States are the only elected officials who represent all the voters in the Nation."

In most cases, comity and respect for federalism compel us to defer to the decisions of state courts on issues of state law. That practice reflects our understanding that the decisions of state courts are definitive pronouncements of the will of the States as sovereigns. Cf. *Erie R. Co. v. Tompkins*, 304 U. S. 64 (1938). Of course, in ordinary cases, the distribution of powers among the branches of a State's government raises no questions of federal constitutional law, subject to the requirement that the government be republican in character. See U. S. Const., Art. IV, §4. But there are a few exceptional cases in which the Constitution imposes a duty or confers a power on a particular branch of a State's government. This is one of them. Article II, §1, cl. 2, provides that "[e]ach State shall appoint, in such Manner as the *Legislature* thereof may direct," electors for President and Vice President. (Emphasis added.) Thus, the text of the election law itself, and not just its interpretation by the courts of the States, takes on independent significance.

In *McPherson v. Blacker*, 146 U. S. 1 (1892), we explained that Art. II, §1, cl. 2, "convey[s] the broadest power of determination" and "leaves it to the legislature exclusively to define the method" of appointment. Id., at 27. A significant departure from the legislative scheme for appointing Presidential electors presents a federal constitutional question.

3 U. S. C. §5 informs our application of Art. II, §1, cl. 2, to the Florida statutory scheme, which, as the Florida Supreme Court acknowledged, took that statute into account. Section 5 provides that the State's selection of electors "shall be conclusive, and shall govern in the counting of the electoral votes" if the electors are chosen under laws enacted prior to election day, and if the selection process is completed six days prior to the meeting of the electoral college. As we noted in *Bush v. Palm Beach County Canvassing Bd.*, ante, at 6.

"Since §5 contains a principle of federal law that would assure finality of the State's determination if made pursuant to a state law in effect before the election, a legislative wish to take advantage of the 'safe harbor' would counsel against any construction of the Election Code that Congress might deem to be a change in the law."

If we are to respect the legislature's Article II powers, therefore, we must ensure that postelection state-court actions do not frustrate the legislative desire to attain the "safe harbor" provided by §5.

In Florida, the legislature has chosen to hold statewide elections to appoint the State's 25 electors. Importantly, the legislature has delegated the authority to run the elections and to oversee election disputes to the Secretary of State (Secretary), Fla. Stat. §97.012(1) (2000), and to state circuit courts, §§102.168(1), 102.168(8). Isolated sections of the code may well admit of more than one interpretation, but the general coherence of the legislative scheme may not be altered by judicial interpretation so as to wholly change the statutorily provided apportionment of responsibility among these various bodies. In any election but a Presidential election, the Florida Supreme Court can give as little or as much deference to Florida's executives as it chooses, so far as Article II is concerned, and this Court will have no cause to question the court's actions. But, with respect to a Presidential election, the court must be both mindful of the legislature's role under Article II in choosing the manner of appointing electors and deferential to those bodies expressly empowered by the legislature to carry out its constitutional mandate.

In order to determine whether a state court has infringed upon the legislature's authority, we necessarily must examine the law of the State as it existed prior to the action of the court. Though we generally defer to state courts on the interpretation of state law—see, e.g., *Mullaney v. Wilbur*, 421 U. S. 684 (1975)—there are of course areas in which the Constitution requires this Court to undertake an independent, if still deferential, analysis of state law.

For example, in *NAACP v. Alabama ex rel. Patterson*, 357 U. S. 449 (1958), it was argued that we were without jurisdiction because the petitioner had not pursued the correct appellate remedy in Alabama's state courts. Petitioners had sought a state-law writ of certiorari in the Alabama Supreme Court when a writ of mandamus, according to that court, was proper. We found this state-law ground inadequate to defeat our jurisdiction because we were "unable to reconcile the procedural holding of the Alabama Supreme Court" with prior Alabama precedent. Id., at 456. The purported state-law ground was so novel, in our independent estimation, that "petitioner could not fairly be deemed to have been apprised of its existence." Id., at 457.

Six years later we decided *Bouie v. City of Columbia*, 378 U. S. 347 (1964), in which the state court had held, contrary to precedent, that the state trespass law applied to black sit-in demonstrators who had consent to enter private property but were then asked to leave. Relying upon NAACP, we concluded that the South Carolina Supreme Court's interpretation of a state penal statute had impermissibly broadened the scope of that statute beyond what a fair reading provided, in violation of due process. See 378 U. S., at 361-362. What we would do in the present case is precisely parallel: Hold that the Florida Supreme Court's interpretation of the Florida election laws impermissibly distorted them beyond what a fair reading required, in violation of Article II.

This inquiry does not imply a disrespect for state courts but rather a respect for the constitutionally prescribed role of state legislatures. To attach definitive weight to the pronouncement of a state court, when the very question at issue is whether the court has actually departed from the statutory meaning, would be to abdicate our responsibility to enforce the explicit requirements of Article II.

◆ **II**

Acting pursuant to its constitutional grant of authority, the Florida Legislature has created a detailed, if not perfectly crafted, statutory scheme that provides for appointment of Presidential electors by direct election. Fla. Stat. §103.011 (2000). Under the statute, "[v]otes cast for the actual candidates for President and Vice President shall be counted as votes cast for the presidential electors supporting such candidates." Ibid. The legislature has designated the Secretary of State as the "chief election officer," with the responsibility to "[o]btain and maintain uniformity in the application, operation, and interpretation of the election laws." §97.012. The state legislature has delegated to county canvassing boards the duties of administering elections. §102.141. Those boards are responsible for providing results to the state Elections Canvassing Commission, comprising the Governor, the Secretary of State, and the Director of the Division of Elections. §102.111. Cf. *Boardman v. Esteva*, 323 So. 2d 259, 268, n. 5 (1975) ("The election process ... is committed to the executive branch of government through duly designated officials all charged with specific duties.... [The] judgments [of these officials] are entitled to be regarded by the courts as presumptively correct...").

After the election has taken place, the canvassing boards receive returns from precincts, count the votes, and in the event that a candidate was defeated by 5% or less, conduct a mandatory recount. Fla. Stat. §102.141(4) (2000). The county canvassing boards must file certified election returns with the Department of State by 5 p.m. on the seventh day following the election. §102.112(1). The Elections Canvassing Commission must then certify the results of the election. §102.111(1).

The state legislature has also provided mechanisms both for protesting election returns and for contesting certified election results. Section 102.166 governs protests. Any protest must be filed prior to the certification of election results by the county canvassing board. §102.166(4)(b). Once a protest has been filed, "the county canvassing board may authorize a manual recount." §102.166(4)(c). If a sample recount conducted pursuant to §102.166(5) "indicates an error in the vote tabulation which could affect the outcome of the election," the county canvassing board is instructed to: "(a) Correct the error and recount the remaining precincts with the vote tabulation system; (b) Request the Department of State to verify the tabulation software; or (c) Manually recount all ballots," §102.166(5). In the event a canvassing board chooses to conduct a manual recount of all ballots, §102.166(7) prescribes procedures for such a recount.

Contests to the certification of an election, on the other hand, are controlled by §102.168. The grounds for contesting an election include "[r]eceipt of a number of illegal votes or rejection of a number of legal votes sufficient to change or place in doubt the result of the election." §102.168(3)(c). Any contest must be filed in the appropriate Florida circuit court, Fla. Stat. §102.168(1), and the canvassing board or election board is the proper party defendant, §102.168(4). Section 102.168(8) provides that "[t]he circuit judge to whom the contest is presented may fashion such orders as he or she deems necessary to ensure that each allegation in the complaint is investigated, examined, or checked, to prevent or correct any alleged wrong, and to provide any relief appropriate under such circumstances." In Presidential elections, the contest period necessarily terminates on the date set by 3 U. S. C. §5 for concluding the State's "final determination" of election controversies.

In its first decision, *Palm Beach Canvassing Bd. v. Harris*, ___ So. 2d, ___ (Nov. 21, 2000) (Harris I), the Florida Supreme Court extended the 7-day statutory certification deadline established by the legislature. This modification of the code, by lengthening the protest period, necessarily shortened the contest period for Presidential elections. Underlying the extension of the certification deadline and the short-changing of the contest period was, presumably, the clear implication that certification was a matter of significance: The certified winner would enjoy presumptive validity, making a contest proceeding by the losing candidate an uphill battle. In its latest opinion, however, the court empties certification of virtually all legal consequence during the contest, and in doing so departs from the provisions enacted by the Florida Legislature.

The court determined that canvassing boards' decisions regarding whether to recount ballots past the certification deadline (even the certification deadline established by Harris I) are to be reviewed de novo, although the election code clearly vests discretion whether to recount in the boards, and sets strict deadlines subject to the Secretary's rejection of late tallies and monetary fines for tardiness. See Fla. Stat. §102.112 (2000). Moreover, the Florida court held that all late vote tallies arriving during the contest period should be automatically included in the certification regardless of the certification deadline (even the certification deadline established by Harris I), thus virtually eliminating both the deadline and the Secretary's discretion to disregard recounts that violate it.

Moreover, the court's interpretation of "legal vote," and hence its decision to order a contest-period recount, plainly departed from the legislative scheme. Florida statutory law cannot reasonably be thought to require the counting of improperly marked ballots. Each Florida precinct before election day provides instructions on how properly to cast a vote, §101.46; each polling place on election day contains a working model of the voting machine it uses, §101.5611; and each voting booth contains a sample ballot, §101.46. In precincts using punch-card ballots, voters are instructed to punch out the ballot cleanly:

AFTER VOTING, CHECK YOUR BALLOT CARD TO BE SURE YOUR VOTING SELECTIONS ARE CLEARLY AND CLEANLY PUNCHED AND THERE ARE NO CHIPS LEFT HANGING ON THE BACK OF THE CARD.

Instructions to Voters, quoted in *Touchston v. McDermott*, 2000 WL 1781942, *6 & n. 19 (CA11) (Tjoflat, J., dissenting). No reasonable person would call it "an error in the vote tabulation," Fla. Stat.

§102.166(5), or a "rejection of legal votes," Fla. Stat. §102.168(3)(c), when electronic or electromechanical equipment performs precisely in the manner designed, and fails to count those ballots that are not marked in the manner that these voting instructions explicitly and prominently specify. The scheme that the Florida Supreme Court's opinion attributes to the legislature is one in which machines are required to be "capable of correctly counting votes," §101.5606(4), but which nonetheless regularly produces elections in which legal votes are predictably not tabulated, so that in close elections manual recounts are regularly required. This is of course absurd. The Secretary of State, who is authorized by law to issue binding interpretations of the election code, §§97.012, 106.23, rejected this peculiar reading of the statutes. See DE 00-13 (opinion of the Division of Elections). The Florida Supreme Court, although it must defer to the Secretary's interpretations, see *Krivanek v. Take Back Tampa Political Committee*, 625 So. 2d 840, 844 (Fla. 1993), rejected her reasonable interpretation and embraced the peculiar one. See *Palm Beach County Canvassing Board v. Harris*, No. SC00-2346 (Dec. 11, 2000) (Harris III).

But as we indicated in our remand of the earlier case, in a Presidential election the clearly expressed intent of the legislature must prevail. And there is no basis for reading the Florida statutes as requiring the counting of improperly marked ballots, as an examination of the Florida Supreme Court's textual analysis shows. We will not parse that analysis here, except to note that the principal provision of the election code on which it relied, §101.5614(5), was, as the Chief Justice pointed out in his dissent from Harris II, entirely irrelevant. See *Gore v. Harris*, No. SC00-2431, slip op., at 50 (Dec. 8, 2000). The State's Attorney General (who was supporting the Gore challenge) confirmed in oral argument here that never before the present election had a manual recount been conducted on the basis of the contention that "undervotes" should have been examined to determine voter intent. Tr. of Oral Arg. in *Bush v. Palm Beach County Canvassing Bd.*, 39-40 (Dec. 1, 2000); cf. *Broward County Canvassing Board v. Hogan*, 607 So. 2d 508, 509 (Fla. Ct. App. 1992) (denial of recount for failure to count ballots with "hanging paper chads"). For the court to step away from this established practice, prescribed by the Secretary of State, the state official charged by the legislature with "responsibility to … [o]btain and maintain uniformity in the application, operation, and interpretation of the election laws," §97.012(1), was to depart from the legislative scheme.

◆ III

The scope and nature of the remedy ordered by the Florida Supreme Court jeopardizes the "legislative wish" to take advantage of the safe harbor provided by 3 U. S. C. §5. *Bush v. Palm Beach County Canvassing Bd.*, ante, at 6. December 12, 2000, is the last date for a final determination of the Florida electors that will satisfy §5. Yet in the late afternoon of December 8th—four days before this deadline—the Supreme Court of Florida ordered recounts of tens of thousands of so-called "undervotes" spread through 64 of the State's 67 counties. This was done in a search for elusive—perhaps delusive—certainty as to the exact count of 6 million votes. But no one claims that these ballots have not previously been tabulated; they were initially read by voting machines at the time of the election, and thereafter reread by virtue of Florida's automatic recount provision. No one claims there was any fraud in the election. The Supreme Court of Florida ordered this additional recount under the provision of the election code giving the circuit judge the authority to provide relief that is "appropriate under such circumstances." Fla. Stat. §102.168(8) (2000).

Surely when the Florida Legislature empowered the courts of the State to grant "appropriate" relief, it must have meant relief that would have become final by the cut-off date of 3 U. S. C. §5. In light of the inevitable legal challenges and ensuing appeals to the Supreme Court of Florida and petitions for certiorari to this Court, the entire recounting process could not possibly be completed by that date. Whereas the majority in the Supreme Court of Florida stated its confidence that "the remaining undervotes in these counties can be [counted] within the required time frame," ___ So. 2d. at ___, n. 22 (slip op., at 38, n. 22), it made no assertion that the seemingly inevitable appeals could be disposed of in that time. Although the Florida Supreme Court has on occasion taken over a year to resolve disputes over local elections, see, e.g., *Beckstrom v. Volusia County Canvassing Bd.*, 707 So. 2d 720 (1998) (resolving contest of sheriff's race 16 months after the election), it has heard and decided the appeals in the present case with great promptness. But the federal deadlines for the Presidential election simply do not permit even such a shortened process.

As the dissent noted:

"In [the four days remaining], all questionable ballots must be reviewed by the judicial officer appointed to discern the intent of the voter in a process open to the public. Fairness dictates that a provision be made for either party to object to how a particular ballot is counted. Additionally, this short time period must allow for judicial review. I respectfully submit this cannot be completed without taking Florida's presidential electors outside the safe harbor provision, creating the very real possibility of disenfranchising those nearly 6 million voters who are able to correctly cast their ballots on election day." ___ So. 2d, at ___ (slip op., at 55) (Wells, C. J., dissenting).

The other dissenters echoed this concern: "[T]he majority is departing from the essential requirements of the law by providing a remedy which is impossible to achieve and which will ultimately lead to chaos." Id., at ___ (slip op., at 67 (Harding, J., dissenting, Shaw, J. concurring).

Given all these factors, and in light of the legislative intent identified by the Florida Supreme Court to bring Florida within the "safe harbor" provision of 3 U. S. C. §5, the remedy prescribed by the Supreme Court of Florida cannot be deemed an "appropriate" one as of December 8. It significantly departed from the statutory framework in place on November 7, and authorized open-ended further proceedings which could not be completed by December 12, thereby preventing a final determination by that date.

For these reasons, in addition to those given in the per curiam, we would reverse.

Justice Stevens, with Whom Justice Ginsburg and Justice Breyer Join, Dissenting

The Constitution assigns to the States the primary responsibility for determining the manner of selecting the Presidential electors. See Art. II, §1, cl. 2. When questions arise about the meaning of state laws, including election laws, it is our settled practice to accept the opinions of the highest courts of the States as providing the final answers. On rare occasions, however, either federal statutes or the Federal Constitution may require federal judicial intervention in state elections. This is not such an occasion.

The federal questions that ultimately emerged in this case are not substantial. Article II provides that "[e]ach *State* shall appoint, in such Manner as the Legislature *thereof* may direct, a Number of Electors." Ibid. (emphasis added). It does not create state legislatures out of whole cloth, but rather takes them as they come—as creatures born of, and constrained by, their state constitutions. Lest there be any doubt, we stated over 100 years ago in *McPherson v. Blacker*, 146 U. S. 1, 25 (1892), that "[w]hat is forbidden or required to be done by a State" in the Article II context "is forbidden or required of the legislative power under state constitutions as they exist." In the same vein, we also observed that "[t]he [State's] legislative power is the supreme authority except as limited by the constitution of the State." Ibid.; cf. *Smiley v. Holm*, 285 U. S. 355, 367 (1932). The legislative power in Florida is subject to judicial review pursuant to Article V of the Florida Constitution, and nothing in Article II of the Federal Constitution frees the state legislature from the constraints in the state constitution that created it. Moreover, the Florida Legislature's own decision to employ a unitary code for all elections indicates that it intended the Florida Supreme Court to play the same role in Presidential elections that it has historically played in resolving electoral disputes. The Florida Supreme Court's exercise of appellate jurisdiction therefore was wholly consistent with, and indeed contemplated by, the grant of authority in Article II.

It hardly needs stating that Congress, pursuant to 3 U. S. C. §5, did not impose any affirmative duties upon the States that their governmental branches could "violate." Rather, §5 provides a safe harbor for States to select electors in contested elections "by judicial or other methods" established by laws prior to the election day. Section 5, like Article II, assumes the involvement of the state judiciary in interpreting state election laws and resolving election disputes under those laws. Neither §5 nor Article II grants federal judges any special authority to substitute their views for those of the state judiciary on matters of state law.

Nor are petitioners correct in asserting that the failure of the Florida Supreme Court to specify in detail the precise manner in which the "intent of the voter," Fla. Stat. §101.5614(5) (Supp. 2001), is to be determined rises to the level of a constitutional violation. We found such a violation when individual votes within the same State were weighted unequally, see, e.g., *Reynolds v. Sims*, 377 U. S. 533, 568 (1964), but we have never before called into question the substantive standard by which a State determines that a vote has been legally cast. And there is no reason to think that the guidance provided to the factfinders, specifically the various canvassing boards, by the "intent of the voter" standard is any

less sufficient—or will lead to results any less uniform—than, for example, the "beyond a reasonable doubt" standard employed everyday by ordinary citizens in courtrooms across this country.

Admittedly, the use of differing substandards for determining voter intent in different counties employing similar voting systems may raise serious concerns. Those concerns are alleviated—if not eliminated—by the fact that a single impartial magistrate will ultimately adjudicate all objections arising from the recount process. Of course, as a general matter, "[t]he interpretation of constitutional principles must not be too literal. We must remember that the machinery of government would not work if it were not allowed a little play in its joints." *Bain Peanut Co. of Tex. v. Pinson*, 282 U. S. 499, 501 (1931) (Holmes, J.). If it were otherwise, Florida's decision to leave to each county the determination of what balloting system to employ—despite enormous differences in accuracy—might run afoul of equal protection. So, too, might the similar decisions of the vast majority of state legislatures to delegate to local authorities certain decisions with respect to voting systems and ballot design.

Even assuming that aspects of the remedial scheme might ultimately be found to violate the Equal Protection Clause, I could not subscribe to the majority's disposition of the case. As the majority explicitly holds, once a state legislature determines to select electors through a popular vote, the right to have one's vote counted is of constitutional stature. As the majority further acknowledges, Florida law holds that all ballots that reveal the intent of the voter constitute valid votes. Recognizing these principles, the majority nonetheless orders the termination of the contest proceeding before all such votes have been tabulated. Under their own reasoning, the appropriate course of action would be to remand to allow more specific procedures for implementing the legislature's uniform general standard to be established.

In the interest of finality, however, the majority effectively orders the disenfranchisement of an unknown number of voters whose ballots reveal their intent—and are therefore legal votes under state law—but were for some reason rejected by ballot-counting machines. It does so on the basis of the deadlines set forth in Title 3 of the United States Code. Ante, at 11. But, as I have already noted, those provisions merely provide rules of decision for Congress to follow when selecting among conflicting slates of electors. Supra, at 2. They do not prohibit a

State from counting what the majority concedes to be legal votes until a bona fide winner is determined. Indeed, in 1960, Hawaii appointed two slates of electors and Congress chose to count the one appointed on January 4, 1961, well after the Title 3 deadlines. See Josephson & Ross, Repairing the Electoral College, 22 J. Legis. 145, 166, n. 154 (1996). Thus, nothing prevents the majority, even if it properly found an equal protection violation, from ordering relief appropriate to remedy that violation without depriving Florida voters of their right to have their votes counted. As the majority notes, "[a] desire for speed is not a general excuse for ignoring equal protection guarantees." Ante, at 10.

Finally, neither in this case, nor in its earlier opinion in *Palm Beach County Canvassing Bd. v. Harris*, 2000 WL 1725434 (Fla., Nov. 21, 2000), did the Florida Supreme Court make any substantive change in Florida electoral law. Its decisions were rooted in long-established precedent and were consistent with the relevant statutory provisions, taken as a whole. It did what courts do—it decided the case before it in light of the legislature's intent to leave no legally cast vote uncounted. In so doing, it relied on the sufficiency of the general "intent of the voter" standard articulated by the state legislature, coupled with a procedure for ultimate review by an impartial judge, to resolve the concern about disparate evaluations of contested ballots. If we assume—as I do—that the members of that court and the judges who would have carried out its mandate are impartial, its decision does not even raise a colorable federal question.

What must underlie petitioners' entire federal assault on the Florida election procedures is an unstated lack of confidence in the impartiality and capacity of the state judges who would make the critical decisions if the vote count were to proceed. Otherwise, their position is wholly without merit. The endorsement of that position by the majority of this Court can only lend credence to the most cynical appraisal of the work of judges throughout the land. It is confidence in the men and women who administer the judicial system that is the true backbone of the rule of law. Time will one day heal the wound to that confidence that will be inflicted by today's decision. One thing, however, is certain. Although we may never know with complete certainty the identity of the winner of this year's Presidential election, the identity of the loser is perfectly clear. It is the Nation's confidence in the judge as an impartial guardian of the rule of law.

I respectfully dissent.

Justice Souter, with Whom Justice Breyer Joins and with Whom Justice Stevens and Justice Ginsburg Join with Regard to All but Part C, Dissenting

The Court should not have reviewed either *Bush v. Palm Beach County Canvassing Bd.*, ante, p. ___ (per curiam), or this case, and should not have stopped Florida's attempt to recount all undervote ballots, see ante at ___, by issuing a stay of the Florida Supreme Court's orders during the period of this review, see *Bush v. Gore*, post at ____ (slip op., at 1). If this Court had allowed the State to follow the course indicated by the opinions of its own Supreme Court, it is entirely possible that there would ultimately have been no issue requiring our review, and political tension could have worked itself out in the Congress following the procedure provided in 3 U. S. C. §15. The case being before us, however, its resolution by the majority is another erroneous decision.

As will be clear, I am in substantial agreement with the dissenting opinions of Justice Stevens, Justice Ginsburg and Justice Breyer. I write separately only to say how straightforward the issues before us really are.

There are three issues: whether the State Supreme Court's interpretation of the statute providing for a contest of the state election results somehow violates 3 U. S. C. §5; whether that court's construction of the state statutory provisions governing contests impermissibly changes a state law from what the State's legislature has provided, in violation of Article II, §1, cl. 2, of the national Constitution; and whether the manner of interpreting markings on disputed ballots failing to cause machines to register votes for President (the undervote ballots) violates the equal protection or due process guaranteed by the Fourteenth Amendment. None of these issues is difficult to describe or to resolve.

A

The 3 U. S. C. §5 issue is not serious. That provision sets certain conditions for treating a State's certification of Presidential electors as conclusive in the event that a dispute over recognizing those electors must be resolved in the Congress under 3 U. S. C. §15. Conclusiveness requires selection under a legal scheme in place before the election, with results determined at least six days before the date set for casting electoral votes. But no State is required to conform to §5 if it cannot do that (for whatever reason); the sanction for failing to satisfy the conditions of §5 is simply loss of what has been called its "safe harbor." And even that determination is to be made, if made anywhere, in the Congress.

B

The second matter here goes to the State Supreme Court's interpretation of certain terms in the state statute governing election "contests," Fla. Stat. §102.168 (2000); there is no question here about the state court's interpretation of the related provisions dealing with the antecedent process of "protesting" particular vote counts, §102.166, which was involved in the previous case, *Bush v. Palm Beach County Canvassing Board.* The issue is whether the judgment of the state supreme court has displaced the state legislature's provisions for election contests: is the law as declared by the court different from the provisions made by the legislature, to which the national Constitution commits responsibility for determining how each State's Presidential electors are chosen? See U. S. Const., Art. II, §1, cl. 2. Bush does not, of course, claim that any judicial act interpreting a statute of uncertain meaning is enough to displace the legislative provision and violate Article II; statutes require interpretation, which does not without more affect the legislative character of a statute within the meaning of the Constitution. Brief for Petitioners 48, n. 22, in *Bush v. Palm Beach County Canvassing Bd.*, et al., 531 U. S. ___ (2000). What Bush does argue, as I understand the contention, is that the interpretation of §102.168 was so unreasonable as to transcend the accepted bounds of statutory interpretation, to the point of being a nonjudicial act and producing new law untethered to the legislative act in question.

The starting point for evaluating the claim that the Florida Supreme Court's interpretation effectively re-wrote §102.168 must be the language of the provision on which Gore relies to show his right to raise this contest: that the previously certified result in Bush's favor was produced by "rejection of a number of legal votes sufficient to change or place in doubt the result of the election." Fla. Stat. §102.168(3)(c) (2000). None of the state court's interpretations is unreasonable to the point of displacing the legislative enactment quoted. As I will note below, other interpretations were of course possible, and some might have been better than those adopted by the Florida court's majority; the two dissents from the majority opinion of that court and various briefs submitted to us set out alternatives. But the majority view is in each instance within the

bounds of reasonable interpretation, and the law as declared is consistent with Article II.

1. The statute does not define a "legal vote," the rejection of which may affect the election. The State Supreme Court was therefore required to define it, and in doing that the court looked to another election statute, §101.5614(5), dealing with damaged or defective ballots, which contains a provision that no vote shall be disregarded "if there is a clear indication of the intent of the voter as determined by a canvassing board." The court read that objective of looking to the voter's intent as indicating that the legislature probably meant "legal vote" to mean a vote recorded on a ballot indicating what the voter intended. *Gore v. Harris*, ___ So. 2d ___ (slip op., at 23-25) (Dec. 8, 2000). It is perfectly true that the majority might have chosen a different reading. See, e.g., Brief for Respondent Harris et al. 10 (defining "legal votes" as "votes properly executed in accordance with the instructions provided to all registered voters in advance of the election and in the polling places"). But even so, there is no constitutional violation in following the majority view; Article II is unconcerned with mere disagreements about interpretive merits.

2. The Florida court next interpreted "rejection" to determine what act in the counting process may be attacked in a contest. Again, the statute does not define the term. The court majority read the word to mean simply a failure to count. ____ So. 2d, at___ (slip op., at 26-27). That reading is certainly within the bounds of common sense, given the objective to give effect to a voter's intent if that can be determined. A different reading, of course, is possible. The majority might have concluded that "rejection" should refer to machine malfunction, or that a ballot should not be treated as "reject[ed]" in the absence of wrongdoing by election officials, lest contests be so easy to claim that every election will end up in one. Cf. id., at ____ (slip op., at 48) (Wells, C. J., dissenting). There is, however, nothing nonjudicial in the Florida majority's more hospitable reading.

3. The same is true about the court majority's understanding of the phrase "votes sufficient to change or place in doubt" the result of the election in Florida. The court held that if the uncounted ballots were so numerous that it was reasonably possible that they contained enough "legal" votes to swing the election, this contest would be authorized by the statute. While the majority might have thought (as the trial judge did) that a probability, not a possibility, should be necessary to justify a contest, that reading is not required by the statute's text, which says

nothing about probability. Whatever people of good will and good sense may argue about the merits of the Florida court's reading, there is no warrant for saying that it transcends the limits of reasonable statutory interpretation to the point of supplanting the statute enacted by the "legislature" within the meaning of Article II.

In sum, the interpretations by the Florida court raise no substantial question under Article II. That court engaged in permissible construction in determining that Gore had instituted a contest authorized by the state statute, and it proceeded to direct the trial judge to deal with that contest in the exercise of the discretionary powers generously conferred by Fla. Stat. §102.168(8) (2000), to "fashion such orders as he or she deems necessary to ensure that each allegation in the complaint is investigated, examined, or checked, to prevent or correct any alleged wrong, and to provide any relief appropriate under such circumstances." As Justice Ginsburg has persuasively explained in her own dissenting opinion, our customary respect for state interpretations of state law counsels against rejection of the Florida court's determinations in this case.

C

It is only on the third issue before us that there is a meritorious argument for relief, as this Court's Per Curiam opinion recognizes. It is an issue that might well have been dealt with adequately by the Florida courts if the state proceedings had not been interrupted, and if not disposed of at the state level it could have been considered by the Congress in any electoral vote dispute. But because the course of state proceedings has been interrupted, time is short, and the issue is before us, I think it sensible for the Court to address it.

Petitioners have raised an equal protection claim (or, alternatively, a due process claim, see generally *Logan v. Zimmerman Brush Co.*, 455 U. S. 422 (1982)), in the charge that unjustifiably disparate standards are applied in different electoral jurisdictions to otherwise identical facts. It is true that the Equal Protection Clause does not forbid the use of a variety of voting mechanisms within a jurisdiction, even though different mechanisms will have different levels of effectiveness in recording voters' intentions; local variety can be justified by concerns about cost, the potential value of innovation, and so on. But evidence in the record here suggests that a different order of disparity obtains under rules for determining a voter's intent that have been applied (and could continue to be applied) to identical types of ballots used in identical brands of machines and exhibiting identical physical characteristics (such as "hanging" or "dimpled" chads). See, e.g., Tr., at 238-242 (Dec. 2-3, 2000) (testimony of Palm Beach County Canvassing Board Chairman Judge Charles Burton describing varying standards applied to imperfectly punched ballots in Palm Beach County during precertification manual recount); id., at 497-500 (similarly describing varying standards applied in Miami-Dade County); Tr. of Hearing 8-10 (Dec. 8, 2000) (soliciting from county canvassing boards proposed protocols for determining voters' intent but declining to provide a precise, uniform standard). I can conceive of no legitimate state interest served by these differing treatments of the expressions of voters' fundamental rights. The differences appear wholly arbitrary.

In deciding what to do about this, we should take account of the fact that electoral votes are due to be cast in six days. I would therefore remand the case to the courts of Florida with instructions to establish uniform standards for evaluating the several types of ballots that have prompted differing treatments, to be applied within and among counties when passing on such identical ballots in any further recounting (or successive recounting) that the courts might order.

Unlike the majority, I see no warrant for this Court to assume that Florida could not possibly comply with this requirement before the date set for the meeting of electors, December 18. Although one of the dissenting justices of the State Supreme Court estimated that disparate standards potentially affected 170,000 votes, *Gore v. Harris*, supra, ___ So. 2d, at ___ (slip op., at 66), the number at issue is significantly smaller. The 170,000 figure apparently represents all uncounted votes, both undervotes (those for which no Presidential choice was recorded by a machine) and overvotes (those rejected because of votes for more than one candidate). Tr. of Oral Arg. 61-62. But as Justice Breyer has pointed out, no showing has been made of legal overvotes uncounted, and counsel for Gore made an uncontradicted representation to the Court that the statewide total of undervotes is about 60,000. Id., at 62. To recount these manually would be a tall order, but before this Court stayed the effort to do that the courts of Florida were ready to do their best to get that job done. There is no justification for denying the State the opportunity to try to count all disputed ballots now.

I respectfully dissent.

Justice Ginsburg, with Whom Justice Stevens Joins, and with Whom Justice Souter and Justice Breyer Join as to Part I, Dissenting

◆ I

The Chief Justice acknowledges that provisions of Florida's Election Code "may well admit of more than one interpretation." Ante, at 3. But instead of respecting the state high court's province to say what the State's Election Code means, The Chief Justice maintains that Florida's Supreme Court has veered so far from the ordinary practice of judicial review that what it did cannot properly be called judging. My colleagues have offered a reasonable construction of Florida's law. Their construction coincides with the view of one of Florida's seven Supreme Court justices. *Gore v. Harris*, __ So. 2d __, __ (Fla. 2000) (slip op., at 45-55) (Wells, C. J., dissenting); *Palm Beach County Canvassing Bd. v. Harris*, __ So. 2d __, __ (Fla. 2000) (slip op., at 34) (on remand) (confirming, 6-1, the construction of Florida law advanced in Gore). I might join The Chief Justice were it my commission to interpret Florida law. But disagreement with the Florida court's interpretation of its own State's law does not warrant the conclusion that the justices of that court have legislated. There is no cause here to believe that the members of Florida's high court have done less than "their mortal best to discharge their oath of office," *Sumner v. Mata*, 449 U. S. 539, 549 (1981), and no cause to upset their reasoned interpretation of Florida law.

This Court more than occasionally affirms statutory, and even constitutional, interpretations with which it disagrees. For example, when reviewing challenges to administrative agencies' interpretations of laws they implement, we defer to the agencies unless their interpretation violates "the unambiguously expressed intent of Congress." *Chevron U. S. A. Inc. v. Natural Resources Defense Council, Inc.*, 467 U. S. 837, 843 (1984). We do so in the face of the declaration in Article I of the United States Constitution that "All legislative Powers herein granted shall be vested in a Congress of the United States." Surely the Constitution does not call upon us to pay more respect to a federal administrative agency's construction of federal law than to a state high court's interpretation of its own state's law. And not uncommonly, we let stand state-court interpretations of federal law with which we might disagree. Notably, in the habeas context, the Court adheres to the view that "there is 'no intrinsic reason why the fact that a man is a federal judge should make him more competent, or conscientious, or learned with respect to [federal law] than his neighbor in the state courthouse.'" *Stone v. Powell*, 428 U. S. 465, 494, n. 35 (1976) (quoting Bator, Finality in Criminal Law and Federal Habeas Corpus For State Prisoners, 76 Harv. L. Rev. 441, 509 (1963)); see *O'Dell v. Netherland*, 521 U. S. 151, 156 (1997) ("[T]he Teague doctrine validates reasonable, good-faith interpretations of existing precedents made by state courts even though they are shown to be contrary to later decisions.") (citing *Butler v. McKellar*, 494 U. S. 407, 414 (1990)); O'Connor, Trends in the Relationship Between the Federal and State Courts from the Perspective of a State Court Judge, 22 Wm. & Mary L. Rev. 801, 813 (1981) ("There is no reason to assume that state court judges cannot and will not provide a 'hospitable forum' in litigating federal constitutional questions.").

No doubt there are cases in which the proper application of federal law may hinge on interpretations of state law. Unavoidably, this Court must sometimes examine state law in order to protect federal rights. But we have dealt with such cases ever mindful of the full measure of respect we owe to interpretations of state law by a State's highest court. In the Contract Clause case, *General Motors Corp. v. Romein*, 503 U. S. 181 (1992), for example, we said that although "ultimately we are bound to decide for ourselves whether a contract was made," the Court "accord[s] respectful consideration and great weight to the views of the State's highest court." Id., at 187 (citation omitted). And in *Central Union Telephone Co. v. Edwardsville*, 269 U. S. 190 (1925), we upheld the Illinois Supreme Court's interpretation of a state waiver rule, even though that interpretation resulted in the forfeiture of federal constitutional rights. Refusing to supplant Illinois law with a federal definition of waiver, we explained that the state court's declaration "should bind us unless so unfair or unreasonable in its application to those asserting a federal right as to obstruct it." Id., at 195.1

In deferring to state courts on matters of state law, we appropriately recognize that this Court acts as an ""outside[r]' lacking the common exposure to local law which comes from sitting in the jurisdiction." *Lehman Brothers v. Schein*, 416 U. S. 386, 391 (1974). That recognition has sometimes prompted us to resolve doubts about the meaning of state law by certifying issues to a State's highest court, even when federal rights are at stake. Cf. *Arizonans for Official English v. Arizona*, 520 U. S. 43, 79 (1997) ("Warnings against premature adjudication of constitutional questions bear heightened attention when a federal court is asked to invalidate a State's law, for the federal tribunal risks friction-generating error when it endeavors to construe a novel state Act not yet reviewed by the State's highest court."). Notwithstanding our authority to decide issues of state law underlying federal claims, we have used the certification devise to afford state high courts an opportunity to inform us on matters of their own State's law because such restraint "helps build a cooperative judicial federalism." Lehman Brothers, 416 U. S., at 391.

Just last Term, in *Fiore v. White*, 528 U. S. 23 (1999), we took advantage of Pennsylvania's certification procedure. In that case, a state prisoner brought a federal habeas action claiming that the State had failed to prove an essential element of his charged offense in violation of the Due Process Clause. Id., at 25-26. Instead of resolving the state-law question on which the federal claim depended, we certified the question to the Pennsylvania Supreme Court for that court to "help determine the proper state-law predicate for our determination of the federal constitutional questions raised." Id., at 29; id., at 28 (asking the Pennsylvania Supreme Court whether its recent interpretation of the statute under which Fiore was convicted "was always the statute's meaning, even at the time of Fiore's trial"). The Chief Justice's willingness to reverse the Florida Supreme Court's interpretation of Florida law in this case is at least in tension with our reluctance in Fiore even to interpret Pennsylvania law before seeking instruction from the Pennsylvania Supreme Court. I would have thought the "cautious approach" we counsel when federal courts address matters of state law, Arizonans, 520 U. S., at 77, and our commitment to "build[ing] cooperative judicial federalism," Lehman Brothers, 416 U. S., at 391, demanded greater restraint.

Rarely has this Court rejected outright an interpretation of state law by a state high court. *Fairfax's Devisee v. Hunter's Lessee*, 7 Cranch 603 (1813), *NAACP v. Alabama ex rel. Patterson*, 357 U. S. 449 (1958), and *Bouie v. City of Columbia*, 378 U. S. 347 (1964), cited by The Chief Justice, are three such rare instances. See ante, at 4, 5, and n. 2. But those cases are embedded in historical contexts hardly comparable to the situation here. Fairfax's Devisee, which held that the Virginia Court of Appeals had misconstrued its own forfeiture laws to deprive a British subject of lands secured to him by federal treaties, occurred amidst vociferous States' rights

attacks on the Marshall Court. G. Gunther & K. Sullivan, Constitutional Law 61-62 (13th ed. 1997). The Virginia court refused to obey this Court's Fairfax's Devisee mandate to enter judgment for the British subject's successor in interest. That refusal led to the Court's pathmarking decision in *Martin v. Hunter's Lessee*, 1 Wheat. 304 (1816). Patterson, a case decided three months after *Cooper v. Aaron*, 358 U. S. 1 (1958), in the face of Southern resistance to the civil rights movement, held that the Alabama Supreme Court had irregularly applied its own procedural rules to deny review of a contempt order against the NAACP arising from its refusal to disclose membership lists. We said that "our jurisdiction is not defeated if the nonfederal ground relied on by the state court is without any fair or substantial support." 357 U. S., at 455. Bouie, stemming from a lunch counter "sit-in" at the height of the civil rights movement, held that the South Carolina Supreme Court's construction of its trespass laws—criminalizing conduct not covered by the text of an otherwise clear statute—was "unforeseeable" and thus violated due process when applied retroactively to the petitioners. 378 U. S., at 350, 354.

The Chief Justice's casual citation of these cases might lead one to believe they are part of a larger collection of cases in which we said that the Constitution impelled us to train a skeptical eye on a state court's portrayal of state law. But one would be hard pressed, I think, to find additional cases that fit the mold. As Justice Breyer convincingly explains, see post, at 5-9 (dissenting opinion), this case involves nothing close to the kind of recalcitrance by a state high court that warrants extraordinary action by this Court. The Florida Supreme Court concluded that counting every legal vote was the overriding concern of the Florida Legislature when it enacted the State's Election Code. The court surely should not be bracketed with state high courts of the Jim Crow South.

The Chief Justice says that Article II, by providing that state legislatures shall direct the manner of appointing electors, authorizes federal superintendence over the relationship between state courts and state legislatures, and licenses a departure from the usual deference we give to state court interpretations of state law. Ante, at 5 ("To attach definitive weight to the pronouncement of a state court, when the very question at issue is whether the court has actually departed from the statutory meaning, would be to abdicate our responsibility to enforce the explicit requirements of Article II."). The Framers of our Constitution, however, understood that in a republican government, the judiciary would construe the legislature's enactments. See U. S. Const., Art. III; The Federalist No. 78 (A. Hamilton). In light of the constitutional guarantee to States of a "Republican Form of Government," U. S. Const., Art. IV, §4, Article II can hardly be read to invite this Court to disrupt a State's republican regime. Yet The Chief Justice today would reach out to do just that. By holding that Article II requires our revision of a state court's construction of state laws in order to protect one organ of the State from another, The Chief Justice contradicts the basic principle that a State may organize itself as it sees fit. See, e.g., *Gregory v. Ashcroft*, 501 U. S. 452, 460 (1991) ("Through the structure of its government, and the character of those who exercise government authority, a State defines itself as a sovereign."); *Highland Farms Dairy, Inc. v. Agnew*, 300 U. S. 608, 612 (1937) ("How power shall be distributed by a state among its governmental organs is commonly, if not always, a question for the state itself."). Article II does not call for the scrutiny undertaken by this Court.

The extraordinary setting of this case has obscured the ordinary principle that dictates its proper resolution: Federal courts defer to state high courts' interpretations of their state's own law. This principle reflects the core of federalism, on which all agree. "The Framers split the atom of sovereignty. It was the genius of their idea that our citizens would have two political capacities, one state and one federal, each protected from incursion by the other." *Saenz v. Roe*, 526 U. S. 489, 504, n. 17 (1999) (citing *U. S. Term Limits, Inc. v. Thornton*, 514 U. S. 779, 838 (1995) (Kennedy, J., concurring)). The Chief Justice's solicitude for the Florida Legislature comes at the expense of the more fundamental solicitude we owe to the legislature's sovereign. U. S. Const., Art. II, §1, cl. 2 ("Each *State* shall appoint, in such Manner as the Legislature *thereof* may direct," the electors for President and Vice President) (emphasis added); ante, at 1-2 (Stevens, J., dissenting). Were the other members of this Court as mindful as they generally are of our system of dual sovereignty, they would affirm the judgment of the Florida Supreme Court.

◆ II

I agree with Justice Stevens that petitioners have not presented a substantial equal protection claim. Ideally, perfection would be the appropriate standard for judging the recount. But we live in an imperfect world, one in which thousands of votes have not been counted. I cannot agree that the recount adopted by the Florida court, flawed as it may be, would yield a result any less fair or precise than the certification that preceded that recount. See, e.g., *McDonald v. Board of Election Comm'rs of Chicago*, 394 U.S. 802, 807 (1969) (even in the context of the right to vote, the state is permitted to reform "one step at a time") (quoting *Williamson v. Lee Optical of Oklahoma, Inc.*, 348 U.S. 483, 489 (1955)).

Even if there were an equal protection violation, I would agree with Justice Stevens, Justice Souter, and Justice Breyer that the Court's concern about "the December 12 deadline," ante, at 12, is misplaced. Time is short in part because of the Court's entry of a stay on December 9, several hours after an able circuit judge in Leon County had begun to superintend the recount process. More fundamentally, the Court's reluctance to let the recount go forward—despite its suggestion that "[t]he search for intent can be confined by specific rules designed to ensure uniform treatment," ante, at 8—ultimately turns on its own judgment about the practical realities of implementing a recount, not the judgment of those much closer to the process.

Equally important, as Justice Breyer explains, post, at 12 (dissenting opinion), the December 12 "deadline" for bringing Florida's electoral votes into 3 U. S. C. §5's safe harbor lacks the significance the Court assigns it. Were that date to pass, Florida would still be entitled to deliver electoral votes Congress must count unless both Houses find that the votes "ha[d] not been… regularly given." 3 U. S. C. §15. The statute identifies other significant dates. See, e.g., §7 (specifying December 18 as the date electors "shall meet and give their votes"); §12 (specifying "the fourth Wednesday in December"—this year, December 27—as the date on which Congress, if it has not received a State's electoral votes, shall request the state secretary of state to send a certified return immediately). But none of these dates has ultimate significance in light of Congress' detailed provisions for determining, on "the sixth day of January," the validity of electoral votes. §15.

The Court assumes that time will not permit "orderly judicial review of any disputed matters that might arise." Ante, at 12. But no one has doubted the good faith and diligence with which Florida election officials, attorneys for all sides of this controversy, and the courts of law have performed their duties. Notably, the Florida Supreme Court has produced two substantial opinions within 29 hours of oral argument. In sum, the Court's conclusion that a constitutionally adequate recount is impractical is a prophecy the Court's own judgment will not allow to be tested. Such an untested prophecy should not decide the Presidency of the United States.

I dissent.

Justice Breyer, with Whom Justice Stevens and Justice Ginsburg Join Except as to Part I—A-1, and with Whom Justice Souter Joins as to Part I, Dissenting

The Court was wrong to take this case. It was wrong to grant a stay. It should now vacate that stay and permit the Florida Supreme Court to decide whether the recount should resume.

◆ I

The political implications of this case for the country are momentous. But the federal legal questions presented, with one exception, are insubstantial.

A

1

The majority raises three Equal Protection problems with the Florida Supreme Court's recount order: first, the failure to include overvotes in the manual recount; second, the fact that all ballots, rather than simply the undervotes, were recounted in some, but not all, counties; and third, the absence of a uniform, specific standard to guide the recounts. As far as the first issue is concerned, petitioners presented no evidence, to this Court or to any Florida court, that a manual recount of overvotes would identify additional legal votes. The same is true of the second, and, in addition, the majority's reasoning would seem to invalidate any state provision for a manual recount of individual counties in a statewide election.

The majority's third concern does implicate principles of fundamental fairness. The majority concludes that the Equal Protection Clause requires that a manual recount be governed not only by the uniform general standard of the "clear intent of the voter," but also by uniform subsidiary standards (for example, a uniform determination whether indented, but not perforated, "undervotes" should count). The opinion points out that the Florida Supreme Court ordered the inclusion of Broward County's undercounted "legal votes" even though those votes included ballots that were not perforated but simply "dimpled," while newly recounted ballots from other counties will likely include only votes determined to

be "legal" on the basis of a stricter standard. In light of our previous remand, the Florida Supreme Court may have been reluctant to adopt a more specific standard than that provided for by the legislature for fear of exceeding its authority under Article II. However, since the use of different standards could favor one or the other of the candidates, since time was, and is, too short to permit the lower courts to iron out significant differences through ordinary judicial review, and since the relevant distinction was embodied in the order of the State's highest court, I agree that, in these very special circumstances, basic principles of fairness may well have counseled the adoption of a uniform standard to address the problem. In light of the majority's disposition, I need not decide whether, or the extent to which, as a remedial matter, the Constitution would place limits upon the content of the uniform standard.

2

Nonetheless, there is no justification for the majority's remedy, which is simply to reverse the lower court and halt the recount entirely. An appropriate remedy would be, instead, to remand this case with instructions that, even at this late date, would permit the Florida Supreme Court to require recounting all undercounted votes in Florida, including those from Broward, Volusia, Palm Beach, and Miami-Dade Counties, whether or not previously recounted prior to the end of the protest period, and to do so in accordance with a single-uniform substandard.

The majority justifies stopping the recount entirely on the ground that there is no more time. In particular, the majority relies on the lack of time for the Secretary to review and approve equipment needed to separate undervotes. But the majority reaches this conclusion in the absence of any record evidence that the recount could not have been completed in the time allowed by the Florida Supreme Court. The majority finds facts outside of the record on matters that state courts are in a far better position to address. Of course, it is too late for any such recount to take place by December 12, the date by which election disputes must be decided if a State is to take advantage of the safe harbor provisions of 3 U. S. C. §5. Whether there is time to conduct a recount prior to December 18, when the electors are scheduled to meet, is a matter for the state courts to determine. And whether, under Florida law, Florida could or could not take further action is obviously a matter for Florida courts, not this Court, to decide. See ante, at 13 (per curiam).

By halting the manual recount, and thus ensuring that the uncounted legal votes will not be counted under any standard, this Court crafts a remedy out of proportion to the asserted harm. And that remedy harms the very fairness interests the Court is attempting to protect. The manual recount would itself redress a problem of unequal treatment of ballots. As Justice Stevens points out, see ante, at 4 and n. 4 (Stevens, J., dissenting opinion), the ballots of voters in counties that use punch-card systems are more likely to be disqualified than those in counties using optical-scanning systems. According to recent news reports, variations in the undervote rate are even more pronounced. See Fessenden, No-Vote Rates Higher in Punch Card Count, N. Y. Times, Dec. 1, 2000, p. A29 (reporting that 0.3% of ballots cast in 30 Florida counties using optical-scanning systems registered no Presidential vote, in comparison to 1.53% in the 15 counties using Votomatic punch card ballots). Thus, in a system that allows counties to use different types of voting systems, voters already arrive at the polls with an unequal chance that their votes will be counted. I do not see how the fact that this results from counties' selection of different voting machines rather than a court order makes the outcome any more fair. Nor do I understand why the Florida Supreme Court's recount order, which helps to redress this inequity, must be entirely prohibited based on a deficiency that could easily be remedied.

B

The remainder of petitioners' claims, which are the focus of the Chief Justice's concurrence, raise no significant federal questions. I cannot agree that the Chief Justice's unusual review of state law in this case, see ante, at 5-8 (Ginsburg, J., dissenting opinion), is justified by reference either to Art. II, §1, or to 3 U. S. C. §5. Moreover, even were such review proper, the conclusion that the Florida Supreme Court's decision contravenes federal law is untenable.

While conceding that, in most cases, "comity and respect for federalism compel us to defer to the decisions of state courts on issues of state law," the concurrence relies on some combination of Art. II, §1, and 3 U. S. C. §5 to justify the majority's conclusion that this case is one of the few in which we may lay that fundamental principle aside. Ante, at 2 (Opinion of Rehnquist, C. J. The concurrence's primary foundation for this conclusion rests on an appeal to plain text: Art. II, §1's grant of the power to appoint Presidential electors to the State "Legislature." Ibid. But

neither the text of Article II itself nor the only case the concurrence cites that interprets Article II, *McPherson v. Blacker*, 146 U. S. 1 (1892), leads to the conclusion that Article II grants unlimited power to the legislature, devoid of any state constitutional limitations, to select the manner of appointing electors. See id., at 41 (specifically referring to state constitutional provision in upholding state law regarding selection of electors). Nor, as Justice Stevens points out, have we interpreted the Federal constitutional provision most analogous to Art. II, §1—Art. I, §4—in the strained manner put forth in the concurrence. Ante, at 1-2 and n. 1 (dissenting opinion).

The concurrence's treatment of §5 as "inform[ing]" its interpretation of Article II, §1, cl. 2, ante, at 3 (Rehnquist, C. J., concurring), is no more convincing. The Chief Justice contends that our opinion in *Bush v. Palm Beach County Canvassing Bd.*, ante, p. ___, (per curiam) (Bush I), in which we stated that "a legislative wish to take advantage of [§5] would counsel against" a construction of Florida law that Congress might deem to be a change in law, id., (slip op. at 6), now means that this Court "must ensure that post-election state court actions do not frustrate the legislative desire to attain the 'safe harbor' provided by §5." Ante, at 3. However, §5 is part of the rules that govern Congress' recognition of slates of electors. Nowhere in Bush I did we establish that this Court had the authority to enforce §5. Nor did we suggest that the permissive "counsel against" could be transformed into the mandatory "must ensure." And nowhere did we intimate, as the concurrence does here, that a state court decision that threatens the safe harbor provision of §5 does so in violation of Article II. The concurrence's logic turns the presumption that legislatures would wish to take advantage of § 5's "safe harbor" provision into a mandate that trumps other statutory provisions and overrides the intent that the legislature did express.

But, in any event, the concurrence, having conducted its review, now reaches the wrong conclusion. It says that "the Florida Supreme Court's interpretation of the Florida election laws impermissibly distorted them beyond what a fair reading required, in violation of Article II." Ante, at 4-5 (Rehnquist, C. J, concurring). But what precisely is the distortion? Apparently, it has three elements. First, the Florida court, in its earlier opinion, changed the election certification date from November 14 to November 26. Second, the Florida court ordered a manual recount of "undercounted" ballots that could not have been fully completed by the December 12 "safe harbor" deadline. Third, the Florida court, in the opinion now under review, failed to give adequate deference to the determinations of canvassing boards and the Secretary.

To characterize the first element as a "distortion," however, requires the concurrence to second-guess the way in which the state court resolved a plain conflict in the language of different statutes. Compare Fla. Stat. §102.166 (2001) (foreseeing manual recounts during the protest period) with §102.111 (setting what is arguably too short a deadline for manual recounts to be conducted); compare §102.112(1) (stating that the Secretary "may" ignore late returns) with §102.111(1) (stating that the Secretary "shall" ignore late returns). In any event, that issue no longer has any practical importance and cannot justify the reversal of the different Florida court decision before us now.

To characterize the second element as a "distortion" requires the concurrence to overlook the fact that the inability of the Florida courts to conduct the recount on time is, in significant part, a problem of the Court's own making. The Florida Supreme Court thought that the recount could be completed on time, and, within hours, the Florida Circuit Court was moving in an orderly fashion to meet the deadline. This Court improvidently entered a stay. As a result, we will never know whether the recount could have been completed.

Nor can one characterize the third element as "impermissibl[e] distort[ing]" once one understands that there are two sides to the opinion's argument that the Florida Supreme Court "virtually eliminated the Secretary's discretion." Ante, at 9 (Rehnquist, C. J, concurring). The Florida statute in question was amended in 1999 to provide that the "grounds for contesting an election" include the "rejection of a number of legal votes sufficient to … place in doubt the result of the election." Fla. Stat. §§102.168(3), (3)(c) (2000). And the parties have argued about the proper meaning of the statute's term "legal vote." The Secretary has claimed that a "legal vote" is a vote "properly executed in accordance with the instructions provided to all registered voters." Brief for Respondent Harris et al. 10. On that interpretation, punchcard ballots for which the machines cannot register a vote are not "legal" votes. Id., at 14. The Florida Supreme Court did not accept her definition. But it had a reason. Its reason was that a different provision of Florida election laws (a provision that addresses damaged or defective ballots) says that no vote shall be disregarded "if there is a clear indica-

tion of the intent of the voter as determined by the canvassing board" (adding that ballots should not be counted "if it is impossible to determine the elector's choice"). Fla. Stat. §101.5614(5) (2000). Given this statutory language, certain roughly analogous judicial precedent, e.g., *Darby v. State ex rel. McCollough*, 75 So. 411 (Fla. 1917) (per curiam), and somewhat similar determinations by courts throughout the Nation, see cases cited infra, at 9, the Florida Supreme Court concluded that the term "legal vote" means a vote recorded on a ballot that clearly reflects what the voter intended. *Gore v. Harris*, ___ So. 2d ___, ___ (2000) (slip op., at 19). That conclusion differs from the conclusion of the Secretary. But nothing in Florida law requires the Florida Supreme Court to accept as determinative the Secretary's view on such a matter. Nor can one say that the Court's ultimate determination is so unreasonable as to amount to a constitutionally "impermissible distort[ion]" of Florida law.

The Florida Supreme Court, applying this definition, decided, on the basis of the record, that respondents had shown that the ballots undercounted by the voting machines contained enough "legal votes" to place "the results" of the election "in doubt." Since only a few hundred votes separated the candidates, and since the "undercounted" ballots numbered tens of thousands, it is difficult to see how anyone could find this conclusion unreasonable-however strict the standard used to measure the voter's "clear intent." Nor did this conclusion "strip" canvassing boards of their discretion. The boards retain their traditional discretionary authority during the protest period. And during the contest period, as the court stated, "the Canvassing Board's actions [during the protest period] may constitute evidence that a ballot does or does not qualify as a legal vote." Id., at *13. Whether a local county canvassing board's discretionary judgment during the protest period not to conduct a manual recount will be set aside during a contest period depends upon whether a candidate provides additional evidence that the rejected votes contain enough "legal votes" to place the outcome of the race in doubt. To limit the local canvassing board's discretion in this way is not to eliminate that discretion. At the least, one could reasonably so believe.

The statute goes on to provide the Florida circuit judge with authority to "fashion such orders as he or she deems necessary to ensure that each allegation … is *investigated, examined, or checked,*… and to provide any relief appropriate." Fla. Stat. §102.168(8) (2000) (emphasis added). The Florida Supreme

Court did just that. One might reasonably disagree with the Florida Supreme Court's interpretation of these, or other, words in the statute. But I do not see how one could call its plain language interpretation of a 1999 statutory change so misguided as no longer to qualify as judicial interpretation or as a usurpation of the authority of the State legislature. Indeed, other state courts have interpreted roughly similar state statutes in similar ways. See, e.g., In re Election of U. S. Representative for Second Congressional Dist., 231 Conn. 602, 621, 653 A. 2d 79, 90-91 (1994) ("Whatever the process used to vote and to count votes, differences in technology should not furnish a basis for disregarding the bedrock principle that the purpose of the voting process is to ascertain the intent of the voters"); *Brown v. Carr*, 130 W. Va. 401, 460, 43 S. E.2d 401, 404-405 (1947) ("[W]hether a ballot shall be counted ... depends on the intent of the voter.... Courts decry any resort to technical rules in reaching a conclusion as to the intent of the voter").

I repeat, where is the "impermissible" distortion?

◆ **II**

Despite the reminder that this case involves "an election for the President of the United States," ante, at 1 (Rehnquist, C. J., concurring), no preeminent legal concern, or practical concern related to legal questions, required this Court to hear this case, let alone to issue a stay that stopped Florida's recount process in its tracks. With one exception, petitioners' claims do not ask us to vindicate a constitutional provision designed to protect a basic human right. See, e.g., *Brown v. Board of Education*, 347 U. S. 483 (1954). Petitioners invoke fundamental fairness, namely, the need for procedural fairness, including finality. But with the one "equal protection" exception, they rely upon law that focuses, not upon that basic need, but upon the constitutional allocation of power. Respondents invoke a competing fundamental consideration—the need to determine the voter's true intent. But they look to state law, not to federal constitutional law, to protect that interest. Neither side claims electoral fraud, dishonesty, or the like. And the more fundamental equal protection claim might have been left to the state court to resolve if and when it was discovered to have mattered. It could still be resolved through a remand conditioned upon issuance of a uniform standard; it does not require reversing the Florida Supreme Court.

Of course, the selection of the President is of fundamental national importance. But that importance is political, not legal. And this Court should resist the temptation unnecessarily to resolve tangential legal disputes, where doing so threatens to determine the outcome of the election.

The Constitution and federal statutes themselves make clear that restraint is appropriate. They set forth a road map of how to resolve disputes about electors, even after an election as close as this one. That road map foresees resolution of electoral disputes by state courts. See 3 U. S. C. §5 (providing that, where a "State shall have provided, by laws enacted prior to [election day], for its final determination of any controversy or contest concerning the appointment of ... electors ... by judicial or other methods," the subsequently chosen electors enter a safe harbor free from congressional challenge). But it nowhere provides for involvement by the United States Supreme Court.

To the contrary, the Twelfth Amendment commits to Congress the authority and responsibility to count electoral votes. A federal statute, the Electoral Count Act, enacted after the close 1876 Hayes-Tilden Presidential election, specifies that, after States have tried to resolve disputes (through "judicial" or other means), Congress is the body primarily authorized to resolve remaining disputes. See Electoral Count Act of 1887, 24 Stat. 373, 3 U. S. C. §§5, 6, and 15.

The legislative history of the Act makes clear its intent to commit the power to resolve such disputes to Congress, rather than the courts:

"The two Houses are, by the Constitution, authorized to make the count of electoral votes. They can only count legal votes, and in doing so must determine, from the best evidence to be had, what are legal votes.... The power to determine rests with the two Houses, and there is no other constitutional tribunal." H. Rep. No. 1638, 49th Cong., 1st Sess., 2 (1886) (report submitted by Rep. Caldwell, Select Committee on the Election of President and Vice-President).

The Member of Congress who introduced the Act added:

"The power to judge of the legality of the votes is a necessary consequent of the power to count. The existence of this power is of absolute necessity to the preservation of the Government. The interests of all the States in their relations to each other in the Federal Union demand that the ultimate tribunal to decide upon the election of President should be a constituent body, in which the States in their federal relationships and the people in their sovereign capacity should be represented." 18 Cong. Rec. 30 (1886).

"Under the Constitution who else could decide? Who is nearer to the State in determining a question of vital importance to the whole union of States than the constituent body upon whom the Constitution has devolved the duty to count the vote?" Id., at 31.

The Act goes on to set out rules for the congressional determination of disputes about those votes. If, for example, a state submits a single slate of electors, Congress must count those votes unless both Houses agree that the votes "have not been … regularly given." 3 U. S. C. § 15. If, as occurred in 1876, one or more states submits two sets of electors, then Congress must determine whether a slate has entered the safe harbor of §5, in which case its votes will have "conclusive" effect. Ibid. If, as also occurred in 1876, there is controversy about "which of two or more of such State authorities … is the lawful tribunal" authorized to appoint electors, then each House shall determine separately which votes are "supported by the decision of such State so authorized by its law." Ibid. If the two Houses of Congress agree, the votes they have approved will be counted. If they disagree, then "the votes of the electors whose appointment shall have been certified by the executive of the State, under the seal thereof, shall be counted." Ibid.

Given this detailed, comprehensive scheme for counting electoral votes, there is no reason to believe that federal law either foresees or requires resolution of such a political issue by this Court. Nor, for that matter, is there any reason to that think the Constitution's Framers would have reached a different conclusion. Madison, at least, believed that allowing the judiciary to choose the presidential electors "was out of the question." Madison, July 25, 1787 (reprinted in 5 Elliot's Debates on the Federal Constitution 363 (2d ed. 1876)).

The decision by both the Constitution's Framers and the 1886 Congress to minimize this Court's role in resolving close federal presidential elections is as wise as it is clear. However awkward or difficult it may be for Congress to resolve difficult electoral disputes, Congress, being a political body, expresses the people's will far more accurately than does an unelected Court. And the people's will is what elections are about.

Moreover, Congress was fully aware of the danger that would arise should it ask judges, unarmed with appropriate legal standards, to resolve a hotly contested Presidential election contest. Just after the 1876 Presidential election, Florida, South Carolina, and Louisiana each sent two slates of electors to Washington. Without these States, Tilden, the Democrat, had 184 electoral votes, one short of the number required to win the Presidency. With those States, Hayes, his Republican opponent, would have had 185. In order to choose between the two slates of electors, Congress decided to appoint an electoral commission composed of five Senators, five Representatives, and five Supreme Court Justices. Initially the Commission was to be evenly divided between Republicans and Democrats, with Justice David Davis, an Independent, to possess the decisive vote. However, when at the last minute the Illinois Legislature elected Justice Davis to the United States Senate, the final position on the Commission was filled by Supreme Court Justice Joseph P. Bradley.

The Commission divided along partisan lines, and the responsibility to cast the deciding vote fell to Justice Bradley. He decided to accept the votes by the Republican electors, and thereby awarded the Presidency to Hayes.

Justice Bradley immediately became the subject of vociferous attacks. Bradley was accused of accepting bribes, of being captured by railroad interests, and of an eleventh-hour change in position after a night in which his house "was surrounded by the carriages" of Republican partisans and railroad officials. C. Woodward, Reunion and Reaction 159-160 (1966). Many years later, Professor Bickel concluded that Bradley was honest and impartial. He thought that "'the great question' for Bradley was, in fact, whether Congress was entitled to go behind election returns or had to accept them as certified by state authorities," an "issue of principle." The Least Dangerous Branch 185 (1962). Nonetheless, Bickel points out, the legal question upon which Justice Bradley's decision turned was not very important in the contemporaneous political context. He says that "in the circumstances the issue of principle was trivial, it was overwhelmed by all that hung in the balance, and it should not have been decisive." Ibid.

For present purposes, the relevance of this history lies in the fact that the participation in the work of the electoral commission by five Justices, including Justice Bradley, did not lend that process legitimacy. Nor did it assure the public that the process had worked fairly, guided by the law. Rather, it simply embroiled Members of the Court in partisan conflict, thereby undermining respect for the judicial process. And the Congress that later enacted the Electoral Count Act knew it.

This history may help to explain why I think it not only legally wrong, but also most unfortunate, for the

Court simply to have terminated the Florida recount. Those who caution judicial restraint in resolving political disputes have described the quintessential case for that restraint as a case marked, among other things, by the "strangeness of the issue," its "intractability to principled resolution," its "sheer momentousness,… which tends to unbalance judicial judgment," and "the inner vulnerability, the self-doubt of an institution which is electorally irresponsible and has no earth to draw strength from." Bickel, supra, at 184. Those characteristics mark this case.

At the same time, as I have said, the Court is not acting to vindicate a fundamental constitutional principle, such as the need to protect a basic human liberty. No other strong reason to act is present. Congressional statutes tend to obviate the need. And, above all, in this highly politicized matter, the appearance of a split decision runs the risk of undermining the public's confidence in the Court itself. That confidence is a public treasure. It has been built slowly over many years, some of which were marked by a Civil War and the tragedy of segregation. It is a vitally necessary ingredient of any successful effort to pro-

tect basic liberty and, indeed, the rule of law itself. We run no risk of returning to the days when a President (responding to this Court's efforts to protect the Cherokee Indians) might have said, "John Marshall has made his decision; now let him enforce it!" Loth, Chief Justice John Marshall and The Growth of the American Republic 365 (1948). But we do risk a self-inflicted wound—a wound that may harm not just the Court, but the Nation.

I fear that in order to bring this agonizingly long election process to a definitive conclusion, we have not adequately attended to that necessary "check upon our own exercise of power," "our own sense of self-restraint." *United States v. Butler*, 297 U. S. 1, 79 (1936) (Stone, J., dissenting). Justice Brandeis once said of the Court, "The most important thing we do is not doing." Bickel, supra, at 71. What it does today, the Court should have left undone. I would repair the damage done as best we now can, by permitting the Florida recount to continue under uniform standards.

I respectfully dissent.

President George W. Bush addresses the nation from the Oval Office on September 11, 2001, following the terrorist attacks earlier in the day. (AP Photo/Doug Mills)

George W. Bush's Address to the Nation on September 11, 2001

"We will make no distinction between the terrorists who committed these acts and those who harbor them."

Overview

At 8:30 in the evening on September 11, 2001, President George W. Bush addressed the nation on television and radio. His five-minute address was delivered in response to terrorist attacks on the nation that had taken place some twelve hours earlier. The attacks would become a defining moment in the Bush presidency and for the nation, leading ultimately to changes in American foreign policy, military interventions in Afghanistan and Iraq, and years of controversy about appropriate and legal ways to combat terrorism at home and abroad. In his address, the president attempted to rally the nation to fight terrorism, to reassure people that the U.S. government was still functioning, to enlist the support of other nations in opposing terrorism, and to vow to bring to justice those responsible for the attacks.

Context

At approximately 8:30 in the morning on September 11, 2001, what had begun as a normal day on the sunny East Coast quickly turned into a day of confusion and tragedy. Working in teams, nineteen men hijacked four commercial airliners departing from Logan Airport in Boston; Dulles International Airport in Washington, D.C.; and Newark International Airport in New Jersey. All of the planes were bound for California.

At 8:46 AM hijackers deliberately flew one of the planes into the North Tower of the World Trade Center in New York City, though many observers who witnessed the event believed that the crash was a horrible accident. Then, at about 9:03, a second plane crashed into the Trade Center's South Tower—an event that was captured on film by journalists and citizens whose cameras were trained on the North Tower after the first crash. As smoke rose from the burning buildings in Lower Manhattan, at 9:37 a third plane crashed into the west side of the Pentagon building in Arlington, Virginia, just outside Washington, D.C. A fourth airliner turned around over Ohio, and although its target remains unknown, authorities are reasonably certain that the hijackers intended to crash it into the White House, the Capitol, or a similar target in the nation's capital. However, passengers and crew, who had learned about the earlier crashes through cell-phone conversations and knew that those hijackings had been suicide missions, attempted to regain control of the aircraft. In the struggle with the hijackers that ensued, the plane crashed in a field near Shanksville, Pennsylvania, killing all aboard.

These attacks were not the first on the World Trade Center. On February 26, 1993, a car bomb had exploded in the parking garage under the Trade Center's North Tower, killing six and injuring more than one thousand people. The attack was the work of Islamic terrorists, who apparently believed that the building would collapse if its structure was weakened by the blast, but the building survived the damage done to it. In the hours after the 2001 attacks, suspicion immediately fell on Islamic extremists, particularly on the terrorist organization known as al Qaeda. These suspicions were ultimately confirmed.

Terrorism, particularly terrorism emanating from Middle Eastern nations, had become a widespread and seemingly intractable problem during the 1980s and 1990s—and indeed the history of Arab terrorism directed against the United States dates all the way back to the nineteenth century, when President Thomas Jefferson had to deal with the terrorist actions of the Barbary Coast pirates in the Mediterranean Sea in America's first war, the Tripolitan War. In April 1983 the U.S. embassy in Beirut, Lebanon, was bombed, killing sixty-three people. Later that year, in October, 241 were killed in a suicide bombing of the U.S. Marine base in Beirut. Over the next two decades, military installations, embassies, nightclubs, cruise ships, and commercial airliners were all targets of terrorist attacks, culminating in the August 1998 bombings of U.S. embassies in Nairobi, Kenya, and in Dar es Salaam, Tanzania, killing 263 people and injuring more than five thousand. In response to those attacks, President Bill Clinton, on August 20, 1998, ordered cruise missile bombings of four al Qaeda training sites in Afghanistan. Two years later, on October 12, 2000, al Qaeda operatives attacked the USS *Cole* while it was docked at the port of Aden in Yemen. The attack killed seventeen sailors and injured thirty-nine others while destroying the ship.

1993

■ **February 26**
Arab extremists detonate a car bomb in the parking garage under New York City's World Trade Center.

1998

■ Osama bin Laden, the leader of the Arab terrorist group al Qaeda, issues a fatwa, or a binding religious decree, declaring that it is the duty of Muslims to kill Americans and their allies.

2001

■ **January 20**
George W. Bush takes office as the forty-third president of the United States.

■ **September 11**
Nineteen members of al Qaeda hijack four American jetliners and crash them into the World Trade Center in New York and the Pentagon outside Washington, D.C. The target of the fourth, which crashed in a Pennsylvania field, was likely the White House or the Capitol in Washington, D.C. President Bush addresses the nation that evening.

■ **September 27**
The Federal Bureau of Investigation releases photos of the nineteen hijackers.

■ **October 4**
The British government releases information linking Osama bin Laden and his al Qaeda organization with the Taliban, the ruling Islamic government in Afghanistan that provided al Qaeda with safe haven.

■ **October 7**
Forces led by the United States invade Afghanistan to oust the Taliban and begin the hunt for Osama bin Laden.

2003

■ **March 19**
U.S.-led forces launch an invasion of Iraq to oust the dictator Saddam Hussein.

The chief challenge that authorities in the United States and other nations faced was that these acts of terrorism were carried out by nonstate actors. That is, they were the work not of identifiable governments but of groups of people acting on their own. In some instances, terrorists were given safe haven and material support in various countries, such as Libya, Pakistan, and Afghanistan; Afghanistan had become a particular focus, for the Islamic Taliban regime in that country gave protection to the al Qaeda network. In other cases, the terrorists lived as fugitives, often in highly isolated parts of the Middle East, where it was difficult to track them down. Further, it was difficult to trace the money used to finance their operations. Much of that money was filtered through front organizations that claimed to serve religious and charitable purposes. It was also challenging to locate the individuals who were planning such attacks. In many cases, they entered or remained illegally in Western nations, where they joined with others in planning and executing acts of terrorism.

The first reports of the September 11, 2001, attacks were broadcast at 8:48 AM, just minutes after the first airliner crash. When the second plane hit, it seemed clear that the crash was no accident. As much of the nation watched on television, the burning jet fuel from the airliners weakened the structure of the World Trade Center towers. The South Tower collapsed at 9:59 and the North Tower at 10:28. It is likely that the hijackers deliberately chose cross-country flights because the planes would be filled to capacity with fuel. Suddenly, Lower Manhattan was turned into a dust-choked war zone as emergency personnel tried to deal with the crisis.

Throughout North America, the airlines worked feverishly to get all airplanes back on the ground. International flights were denied entry into American airspace, and many had to land in Canada. President Bush was first informed of the attacks at 9:03 as he was addressing a class of schoolchildren in Sarasota, Florida. Because of uncertainty about the possibility of subsequent attacks and where and when they might occur, officials kept the president on the move throughout the day. He arrived back in Washington, D.C., early in the evening and addressed the nation at 8:30 PM.

In all, 2,999 people died as a direct result of the attacks. This figure includes the crew and passengers in the airliners, all of whom perished, and over one hundred people on the ground at the Pentagon. The bulk of the casualties were people who were working in or visiting the World Trade Center towers at the time of the attacks and who were unable to escape the buildings. Some, faced with the prospect of a fiery death, chose to leap out of windows to their deaths. More than four hundred of the dead were emergency workers, such as firefighters and police officers who responded to the initial fires caused by the airliners striking the World Trade Center and who were killed when the towers collapsed. In addition to the human cost, the 9/11 attacks had severe economic implications for the country, as airline travel was curtailed, investments lost

---

value, and economic activity slowed, worsening an economic recession that was already under way.

About the Author

George Walker Bush was born in New Haven, Connecticut, on July 6, 1946, the oldest son and first child of George Herbert Walker Bush, the forty-first president of the United States, and his wife, Barbara. Bush was raised in Midland and Houston, Texas, with his four siblings, Jeb, Neil, Marvin, and Dorothy. His grandfather, Prescott Bush, was a U.S. senator from Connecticut.

Bush attended Phillips Academy in Andover, Massachusetts, and Yale University, where he received a bachelor's degree in history in 1968. As a college senior, Bush became a member of the secretive Skull and Bones society. By his own characterization, he was an average student.

In 1968, during the Vietnam War, Bush was accepted into the Texas Air National Guard. After training, he was assigned to duty in Houston. Critics argue that Bush was given preferential treatment because of his father's political standing and that his attendance was irregular. Bush took a transfer to the Alabama Air National Guard in 1972 to work on a Republican Senate campaign, and in October 1973 he received a discharge from the Texas Air National Guard to attend Harvard Business School.

After obtaining a master of business administration degree from Harvard, Bush entered the oil industry in Texas. In 1977 he was introduced to Laura Welch, a schoolteacher and librarian, whom he married; the two settled in Midland and had two children. In 1978 Bush ran unsuccessfully for the U.S. House of Representatives from the Nineteenth Congressional District. He returned to the oil industry as a senior partner or chief executive officer of several ventures, which suffered from the general decline of oil prices in the 1980s.

Bush moved to Washington, D.C., in 1988 to campaign for his father, who successfully ran for president. He then returned to Texas and in 1989 purchased a share in the Texas Rangers baseball franchise, serving as managing general partner for five years. However, in 1994 he returned to politics and was elected governor of Texas. Bush won the presidency in 2000 as the Republican candidate in a close and controversial contest over Vice President Al Gore. In that election, Gore won the nationwide popular vote, but Bush won the electoral vote. The outcome of the election was in doubt for weeks as charges were made of voting irregularities in Florida. Ultimately, the U.S. Supreme Court stopped a recount of the Florida vote, Bush carried the state by a razor-thin margin, and the state's electoral votes went into his column, securing him the win.

As president, Bush pushed through a $1.3 trillion tax cut program and the No Child Left Behind Act, an education initiative. Following the 9/11 attacks, Bush announced a global war on terrorism and ordered an invasion of Afghanistan to overthrow the Taliban regime, destroy al Qaeda, and capture its leader, Osama bin Laden. In March 2003 Bush ordered the invasion of Iraq, asserting that Iraq was in violation of United Nations Security Council Resolution 1441, a resolution, passed unanimously in 2002, in which the United Nations found Iraq and its leader, Saddam Hussein, in violation of ten previous resolutions regarding disarmament.

Bush was reelected in 2004 over the Democrat John Kerry, despite controversy over Bush's handling of the Iraq War and of the economy. After his reelection, he was the target of increasingly heated criticism. His domestic approval declined from 90 percent (the highest ever recorded by the Gallup Organization) immediately after the September 11, 2001, attacks to a low of 26 percent (in a *Newsweek* poll taken in June 2007), the lowest level for any sitting president in thirty-five years. Only Harry S. Truman and Richard M. Nixon scored lower.

Explanation and Analysis of the Document

Bush's Address to the Nation on September 11, 2001, was brief, lasting just five minutes. The president used simple language to reach a broad audience. While the speech does not outline policy in detail, it hints at a significant change in America's response to the terrorism of the 1990s and into the new millennium.

Bush opens his remarks by stating that the nation has been attacked by yet unidentified terrorists and that the victims were largely innocent civilians. He notes that thousands of lives were suddenly ended by "evil, despicable acts of terror" and then recalls the images seen in the media of "airplanes flying into buildings." He characterizes the events as "acts of mass murder" intended to frighten the nation.

Bush states that even such acts of terror cannot shake the resolve of the nation, and in paragraph 3 he remarks that while such attacks can dent the steel of a building, they cannot dent the "steel of American resolve." In paragraph 4 he develops the metaphor of the United States as a beacon of light for freedom and democracy and states that America was attacked because of that role. This paragraph is brief, but it establishes that America was targeted largely because it stands for freedom, opportunity, and values that are antithetical to those held by the terrorist organizations responsible for the 9/11 attacks.

In paragraph 5 Bush notes that the initial response to the attacks was by rescue workers representing "the best of America" as well as others who gave blood, housing, and other forms of support to their fellow Americans in a time of disaster. Here the president contrasts this heroism with the "worst of human nature" displayed by the terrorists. He goes on to explain that he has implemented the government's emergency response plan, mentioning that the nation's military is "powerful" and "prepared" and that emergency teams are working with local rescue efforts in New York and Washington, D.C.

In paragraph 7 Bush continues the theme of an immediate response to the aftermath of the attacks, stating that the nation's first priority is to help those who are injured and to protect the nation from further attack. It was also vital for the president to reassure a stunned and grieving nation that essential government functions would continue without interruption and that people could rely on these services. In paragraph 8 he comments that federal agencies that had to be evacuated during the crisis would reopen the following day. He also assures the American people that the nation's financial institutions would be "open for business" as well.

At the time of this address, it was not yet known who was responsible for the attacks. In paragraph 9 Bush states that the search is under way for those responsible and that he has directed the full resources of the "intelligence and law enforcement communities to find those responsible and to bring them to justice." At the end of this paragraph he makes a short but highly significant policy declaration that "we will make no distinction between the terrorists ... and those who harbor them." Because terrorists are generally nonstate actors, Bush holds countries that harbor them equally responsible for their actions.

Bush recognizes that he cannot act alone and needs support from both Congress at home and governments around the world. In paragraph 10 he thanks those members of Congress who have already joined in condemning the attacks and those foreign leaders who have called him to offer their condolences and support. Paragraph 11 continues this theme as Bush calls upon those who seek "peace and security in the world" to join in a common war against terrorism. This brief initial statement is the call to arms for what would soon become the global war on terror and the hallmark of Bush's presidency. Bush concludes this paragraph with a religious theme, praying for help from a "greater power" and closing the paragraph with the often-quoted Psalm 23: "Even though I walk through the valley of the shadow of death, I fear no evil, for You are with me."

In the final substantive paragraph, Bush concludes his address by stating his conviction that September 11 was a day when all Americans "from every walk of life" were united in their resolve for justice and peace. He reiterates that America has "stood down enemies before" and will "do so this time" as well. He notes that "none of us will ever forget this day." He concludes this paragraph by stating that the nation will "go forward to defend freedom and all that is good and just in our world." Bush then closes the address with his thanks and calls on God's blessing for America.

Audience

As with any presidential address, particularly in response to a national crisis, this one had many audiences. The nominal audience was the American people in general, and the purpose of the address was to provide the public with reassurance. Within that general audience, though, were more particular audiences.

One audience was the people in New York City and Washington, D.C., who were directly affected by the attacks. The president wanted those people to know that the federal government was doing everything it could to ensure their safety, that rescue operations were under way, and that authorities were making every effort to locate people who were missing in the chaos and debris. Further, the president wanted to provide a measure of comfort for those who had lost loved ones in the attacks.

For the broader American public, the president wanted to assure people that the federal government was taking all possible steps to protect the country from further attacks. Thus, the address informed the public that the U.S. military was in a high state of readiness and that all federal agencies, including federal law enforcement agencies, such as the Federal Bureau of Investigation and the Central Intelligence Agency, had been mobilized to deal with further threats. While no further attacks materialized in the hours, days, and weeks following the September 11 attacks, many Americans were apprehensive. Thus, in large part the address was designed to provide reassurance to the American people.

An additional domestic audience, one that is probably always in a president's mind when he is addressing the nation, included members of the U.S. Congress. In speaking directly to the American public, the president began to mobilize support for actions that he believed he needed to take to respond to the attacks and to ward off future attacks. Some of those actions would require the backing of Congress, either in approving the actions or in providing funding. Bush was thus gathering public support—and indeed his approval rating with the public was high in the period following the attacks.

An implied audience was the terrorists themselves as well as those who aided and supported them, including foreign governments. The president did not begin his address with the customary "My fellow Americans." He knew that people around the world would be listening. By vowing to take firm action, he put terrorists on notice that he would take steps to bring them to justice. Additionally, he put nations that harbored terrorists on notice that he would hold them to account. This principle became known as the Bush Doctrine, which was that nations that harbored or supported terrorists would meet with the same response from America as the terrorists themselves. The language of the address was concise and clear. The president did not use the language of diplomacy, which often relies on hints and ambiguity. He wanted the address, when it was translated into foreign languages, to leave no room for doubt or uncertainty.

Finally, the president was addressing foreign governments and their people, whose interests were allied with those of the United States. The address was a first step in enlisting the support of foreign governments, especially those of nations that had themselves been the victims of terrorism, in the effort to hunt down the terrorists and bring them to justice. Thus, with this address, Bush began the process of building a coalition of nations, along with their law enforcement agencies, in the global war on terror.

"*A great people has been moved to defend a great nation. Terrorist attacks can shake the foundations of our biggest buildings, but they cannot touch the foundation of America. These acts shattered steel, but they cannot dent the steel of American resolve.*"

(Paragraph 3)

"*America was targeted for attack because we're the brightest beacon for freedom and opportunity in the world. And no one will keep that light from shining.*"

(Paragraph 4)

"*Today, our nation saw evil, the very worst of human nature. And we responded with the best of America.*"

(Paragraph 5)

"*We will make no distinction between the terrorists who committed these acts and those who harbor them.*"

(Paragraph 9)

"*America and our friends and allies join with all those who want peace and security in the world, and we stand together to win the war against terrorism.*"

(Paragraph 11)

"*America has stood down enemies before, and we will do so this time. None of us will ever forget this day. Yet, we go forward to defend freedom and all that is good and just in our world.*"

(Paragraph 12)

Impact

Assessing the impact of the speech itself is difficult, given that on the evening of September 11, 2001, the nation was still in a state of confusion, uncertainty, and fear. The identities of the hijackers had not yet been determined, and at this point Americans in general were only vaguely familiar, if at all, with the name al Qaeda. The president's extremely high approval rating in the days and weeks following the attacks suggests that the impact of his words and actions was regarded as favorable and that the president was showing firm leadership in response to the crisis.

An issue that arose in the aftermath of the attacks was the effectiveness of federal law enforcement agencies, including the Federal Bureau of Investigation and the Central Intelligence Agency. Many observers believe that if these agencies had had a more cooperative, integrated relationship, the attacks could have been prevented, for there were numerous clues that the attacks were impending. Unfortunately, no one was able to assemble the clues into a coherent picture because federal agencies were not sharing information with each other. However, after the attacks, federal, state, and local counterterrorism agencies began to work together not only to carry out search-and-rescue operations at "Ground Zero," the World Trade Center site, but also to investigate the attacks and determine who was responsible. Ultimately, this effort led to a major restructuring of U.S. intelligence operations, the creation of the Department of Homeland Security, and the establishment of new counterterrorism centers.

The chief impact of the speech had to do with its initial expression of what came to be known as the Bush Doctrine; the phrase echoes similar doctrines in America's past, such as the Monroe Doctrine articulated by President James Monroe in 1823. The Bush Doctrine stated that the United States was justified in taking military action against any nation that supported or harbored terrorist organizations. After al Qaeda was identified as the perpetrator of the attacks, the president ordered U.S. military forces to strike terrorist bases in Afghanistan and to overthrow the Taliban regime that had supported al Qaeda. Later Bush articulated a policy of preemption, expanding the doctrine such that the United States was justified in attacking terrorists or terrorist-harboring nations before they might act against the country rather than merely waiting to respond to an attack. Bush referenced the doctrine in part in 2003 when he initiated a war in Iraq, overthrowing the regime of Saddam Hussein on the ground that the dictator was a state sponsor of terrorism and a threat to other nations. In the diplomatic arena he identified other nations as supporters and sponsors of terrorism, particularly nations he called the "axis of evil" (first mentioned in his 2002 State of the Union address), a trio that included Iraq, Iran, and North Korea (http://www.whitehouse.gov/news/releases/2002/01/20020129-11.html). While he stopped short of overt military actions in some cases, he sought sanctions and other actions in an effort to bring about changes in either policy or regime.

The president's call to other nations to join in the fight against terrorism was in many respects successful. The president's goal was to build an international coalition to fight the war on terror, and many nations agreed to contribute resources. Many provided intelligence resources, military forces, and economic and diplomatic support for the war on terror. Many of those same nations did not support the U.S.-led war in Iraq and in fact were sharply critical of the president both for launching the war and for his handling of it. Nevertheless, U.S. and foreign intelligence agencies continued to cooperate in hunting down terrorists and preempting terrorist attacks. There have been failures, notably the train bombing of March 2004 in Madrid, Spain, and the London train bombing in July 2005, but there were many successes as well, notably the absence of further terrorist attacks on U.S. soil from 9/11 through the end of 2007.

Related Documents

"Address to a Joint Session of Congress and the American People," White House Web site. http://www.whitehouse.gov/news/releases/2001/09/20010920-8.html. Accessed on March 10, 2008. In this address, the president reports on progress; identifies Osama bin Laden as the mastermind behind the 9/11 attacks; reassures Muslims in America and throughout the world that the issue is terrorism, not religion; and steels the nation for a long, sometimes frustrating fight.

"Congressional Reports: Joint Inquiry into Intelligence Community Activities before and after the Terrorist Attacks of September 11, 2001." GPO Access Web site. http://www.gpoaccess.gov/serialset/creports/911.html. Accessed on March 10, 2008. This publication summarizes the official congressional investigation of the attacks.

The 9/11 Commission Report: Final Report of the National Commission on Terrorist Attacks upon the United States. New York: Norton, 2004. This report was issued by a special bipartisan commission appointed by President Bush to study the attacks.

"President Bush Salutes Heroes in New York." White House Web site. http://www.whitehouse.gov/news/releases/2001/09/20010914-9.html. Accessed on March 10, 2008. This brief address was delivered to cheer the rescue workers at the site of the World Trade Center.

"President Delivers State of the Union Address." White House Web site. http://www.whitehouse.gov/news/releases/2002/01/20020129-11.html. Accessed on March 10, 2008. This address reports progress in the war on terror, particularly the success of U.S. military operations in Afghanistan. It marked Bush's first use of the phrase *axis of evil*.

"President's Remarks at National Day of Prayer and Remembrance." White House Web site. http://www.whitehouse.gov/news/releases/2001/09/20010914-2.html. Accessed on March 10, 2008. These remarks were a slightly more prayerful version of the president's September 11 address, noting that by this time Americans were learning the names of those killed.

"September 11, 2001: Attack on America. Text of a Letter from the President to the Speaker of the House of Representatives; September 12, 2001." The Avalon Project at Yale Law School Web site. URL: http://www.yale.edu/lawweb/avalon/sept_11/letter01_091201.htm. Accessed on March 10, 2008. The purpose of this letter was to request the House to pass emergency funding legislation to finance the war on terror.

Bibliography

■ **Books**

Ball, Howard. *Bush, the Detainees, and the Constitution: The Battle over Presidential Power in the War on Terror.* Lawrence: University Press of Kansas, 2007.

Cronin, Audrey Kurth, and James M. Ludes, eds. *Attacking Terrorism: Elements of a Grand Strategy*. Washington, D.C.: Georgetown University Press, 2004.

Hoge, James F., Jr., and Gideon Rose, eds. *Understanding the War on Terror*. New York: Foreign Affairs, 2005.

Kuypers, Jim A. *Bush's War: Media Bias and Justifications for War in a Terrorist Age*. Lanham, Md.: Rowman and Littlefield, 2006.

Wheelan, Joseph. *Jefferson's War: America's First War on Terror, 1801–1805*. New York: Carroll & Graf, 2003.

■ **Web Sites**

"America's War against Terrorism." University of Michigan "Documents Center" Web site.
   http://www.lib.umich.edu/govdocs/usterror.html. Accessed on March 10, 2008.

"A Call to Arms: A Symposium on Bush's Speech to Congress." National Review Online Web site.
   http://www.nationalreview.com/comment/comment-symposium092101.shtml. Accessed on March 10, 2008.

"United States of America: National Security." White House Web site.
   http://www.whitehouse.gov/infocus/nationalsecurity/. Accessed on March 10, 2008.

"The War on Terrorism." The Atlantic Online Web site.
   http://www.theatlantic.com/waronterror/. Accessed on March 10, 2008.

—By Michael J. O'Neal

Questions for Further Study

1. How have other U.S. presidents responded to attacks on the United States? For example, how did President Jefferson respond to the attacks of the Barbary Coast pirates during his administration? How did President Franklin D. Roosevelt respond to the Japanese attack on Pearl Harbor that brought America into World War II?

2. In September 1901, a single terrorist killed President William McKinley. McKinley's successor, President Theodore Roosevelt, declared that he would rid the world of terrorists. In what he called "Big Stick Diplomacy" or the "Big Stick Policy," he claimed that the United States had the right to intervene in the affairs of foreign nations, particularly in the Western Hemisphere. How is this change in U.S. foreign policy similar to the Bush Doctrine? How is it different?

3. In his Address to the Nation on September 11, 2001, Bush describes America as an example for the world, the "brightest beacon for freedom and opportunity in the world." Many observers, though, have sharply criticized the president for various actions and policies in the war on terror. Some of these include suspension of the writ of habeas corpus for those arrested for terrorist activities (meaning that they can be held without formal charges) and various abuses of constitutionally protected freedoms. Is there an inconsistency between the president's words and actions? If so, how? Should suspected terrorists be treated in a way different from ordinary criminals? Why or why not? Do you agree with the argument that terrorists are in effect soldiers in a war and therefore can be held as prisoners of war rather than as criminals? Why or why not?

Glossary

financial institutions	banks, stock exchanges, and brokerage firms
intelligence community	federal agencies charged with intelligence operations, including the Central Intelligence Agency, the National Security Agency, the Defense Intelligence Agency, and several others
law enforcement community	federal agencies charged with investigating criminal activities, including the Federal Bureau of Investigation and numerous others
terrorism	premeditated, politically motivated violence perpetrated against noncombatant targets by subnational groups or clandestine agents

George W. Bush's Address to the Nation on September 11, 2001

Good evening. Today, our fellow citizens, our way of life, our very freedom came under attack in a series of deliberate and deadly terrorist acts. The victims were in airplanes, or in their offices; secretaries, businessmen and women, military and federal workers; moms and dads, friends and neighbors. Thousands of lives were suddenly ended by evil, despicable acts of terror.

The pictures of airplanes flying into buildings, fires burning, huge structures collapsing, have filled us with disbelief, terrible

sadness, and a quiet, unyielding anger. These acts of mass murder were intended to frighten our nation into chaos and retreat. But they have failed; our country is strong.

A great people has been moved to defend a great nation. Terrorist attacks can shake the foundations of our biggest buildings, but they cannot touch the foundation of America. These acts shattered steel, but they cannot dent the steel of American resolve.

America was targeted for attack because we're the brightest beacon for freedom and opportunity in the world. And no one will keep that light from shining.

Today, our nation saw evil, the very worst of human nature. And we responded with the best of America—with the daring of our rescue workers, with the caring for strangers and neighbors who came to give blood and help in any way they could.

Immediately following the first attack, I implemented our government's emergency response plans. Our military is powerful, and it's prepared. Our emergency teams are working in New York City and Washington, D.C. to help with local rescue efforts.

Our first priority is to get help to those who have been injured, and to take every precaution to protect our citizens at home and around the world from further attacks.

The functions of our government continue without interruption. Federal agencies in Washington which had to be evacuated today are reopening for essential personnel tonight, and will be open for business tomorrow. Our financial institutions remain strong, and the American economy will be open for business, as well.

The search is underway for those who are behind these evil acts. I've directed the full resources of our intelligence and law enforcement communities to find those responsible and to bring them to justice. We will make no distinction between the terrorists who committed these acts and those who harbor them.

I appreciate so very much the members of Congress who have joined me in strongly condemning these attacks. And on behalf of the American people, I thank the many world leaders who have called to offer their condolences and assistance.

America and our friends and allies join with all those who want peace and security in the world, and we stand together to win the war against terrorism. Tonight, I ask for your prayers for all those who grieve, for the children whose worlds have been shattered, for all whose sense of safety and security has been threatened. And I pray they will be comforted by a power greater than any of us, spoken through the ages in Psalm 23: "Even though I walk through the valley of the shadow of death, I fear no evil, for You are with me."

This is a day when all Americans from every walk of life unite in our resolve for justice and peace. America has stood down enemies before, and we will do so this time. None of us will ever forget this day. Yet, we go forward to defend freedom and all that is good and just in our world.

Thank you. Good night, and God bless America.

Jay S. Bybee (AP Photo, Evan Vucci)

"Pain amounting to torture must be equivalent ... to the pain accompanying serious physical injury, such as organ failure ... or even death."

Overview

In the spring of 2004, the world discovered that prisoners held in Abu Ghraib prison, just west of Baghdad, Iraq, were being mistreated and tortured by U.S. personnel. In the midst of the resulting scandal, a document that has become known as the Bybee Torture Memo came to light. The memo, dated August 1, 2002, carries the official name "Standards of Conduct for Interrogation under 18 U.S.C. §§2340–2340A." It was written by the Office of Legal Counsel of the Justice Department and addressed to Alberto R. Gonzales, who was then counsel to the president. The stated purpose of the memo was to set forth the views of the Office of Legal Counsel regarding the standards of conduct to be followed by U.S. interrogators under the international Convention against Torture and Other Cruel, Inhuman or Degrading Treatment or Punishment, as implemented through the U.S. Code.

The memo's narrow definition of *torture* caused further scandal and was officially repudiated by the George W. Bush administration in June 2004. The Justice Department itself did not effectively rescind the memo until December 30, 2004, on the eve of the confirmation hearings of Alberto Gonzales for attorney general of the United States.

Context

The United States ratified the Convention against Torture and Other Cruel, Inhuman or Degrading Treatment or Punishment in October 1994. All members of the United Nations are parties to the treaty, which defines *torture* as

> any act by which severe pain or suffering, whether physical or mental, is intentionally inflicted on a person for such purposes as obtaining from him or a third person information or a confession, punishing him for an act he or a third person has committed or is suspected of having committed, or intimidating or coercing him or a third person, or for any reason based on discrimination of any kind, when such pain

> or suffering is inflicted by or at the instigation of or with the consent or acquiescence of a public official or other person acting in an official capacity. It does not include pain or suffering arising only from, inherent to or incidental to lawful sanctions. (http://www.hrweb.org/legal/cat.html)

Article 2 of the convention mandates that "no exceptional circumstances whatsoever, whether a state of war or a threat of war, internal political instability or any other public emergency, may be invoked as a justification of torture."

Congress implemented the Convention against Torture in 1994 by amending the federal criminal code—Title 18 of the U.S. Code—to provide that anyone outside the United States who "commits or attempts to commit torture shall be fined under this title or imprisoned not more than 20 years, or both, and if death results to any person from conduct prohibited by this subsection, shall be punished by death or imprisoned for any term of years or for life." Section 2340 of the criminal code defines *torture* as "an act committed by a person acting under the color of law specifically intended to inflict severe physical or mental pain or suffering (other than pain or suffering incidental to lawful sanctions) upon another person within his custody or physical control" (http://www.law.cornell.edu/uscode/18/usc_sec_18_00002340—-A000-.html).

On September 11, 2001, terrorists flew hijacked passenger jets into the twin towers of the Word Trade Center, in New York City, and into the Pentagon, in Washington, D.C. In response, President George W. Bush declared the so-called War on Terror. In October 2001 the U.S. military invaded Afghanistan in an effort to destroy and capture members of the terrorist organization al Qaeda and upend the ruling Taliban regime. In January 2002 the Justice Department advised the president that the Third Geneva Convention, on the treatment of prisoners of war, did not apply to the conflict with al Qaeda. In a memo dated February 7, 2002, President Bush accepted the Justice Department's legal conclusion that the Third Geneva Convention did not apply to al Qaeda or Taliban detainees.

On March 19, 2003, the U.S. military invaded Iraq. In the spring of 2004, the media reported that prisoners captured in the hostilities were being mistreated and tortured

Time Line

1994

■ **October 21**
Convention against Torture and Cruel, Inhuman or Degrading Treatment or Punishment is ratified by the United States.

■ **June 4**
Congress amends the U.S. Code to implement the Convention against Torture.

2001

■ **October 7**
U.S. military invades Afghanistan.

2002

■ **January 9**
Memorandum written by John Yoo, deputy assistant attorney general, and Robert J. Delahunty, a special counsel in the Justice Department, to William J. Haynes II, general counsel of the Department of Defense, with subject "Application of Treaties and Laws to al Qaeda and Taliban Detainees."

■ **January 25**
Draft memorandum written by Alberto Gonzales, the White House counsel, to President George W. Bush with subject "Decision Re Application of the Geneva Convention on Prisoners of War to the Conflict with al Qaeda and the Taliban."

■ **January 26**
Memorandum written by Colin Powell, secretary of state, to Gonzales with subject "Draft Decision Memorandum for the President on the Applicability of the Geneva Convention to the Conflict in Afghanistan."

■ **February 7**
Memorandum written by President Bush to other administration figures and government leaders with subject "Humane Treatment of al Qaeda and Taliban Detainees."

■ **August 1**
Memorandum written by Jay Bybee, from the Office of Legal Counsel, to Gonzales with subject "Standards of Conduct for Interrogation under 18 U.S.C. §§2340–2340A"; a letter is also written by John Yoo to Gonzales summarizing the conclusions of the Bybee Torture Memo.

by U.S. personnel in Abu Ghraib prison, just west of Baghdad, Iraq. In the midst of the ensuing scandal, several internal executive branch memos became public. One was the Bybee Torture Memo, dated August 1, 2002, which interprets section 2340 of the criminal code as it applies to American personnel conducting interrogations outside the United States. A letter of the same date written by John C. Yoo, one of the memo's authors, to Alberto Gonzales summarizes the memo's conclusions. He advises that interrogation methods in compliance with sections 2340 and 2340A, as interpreted, would not violate the obligations of the United States under the Convention against Torture and would not provide a basis for prosecution before the International Criminal Court.

About the Author

The Bybee Torture Memo is signed by Jay S. Bybee, who was then assistant attorney general in the Office of Legal Counsel and was later appointed to the U.S. Court of Appeals for the Ninth Circuit. However, a deputy assistant attorney general at the time, John C. Yoo, has acknowledged that he was also an author. Yoo had clerked for the U.S. Supreme Court justice Clarence Thomas and was working for the Office of Legal Counsel while on a leave of absence from his professorship at the law school at University of California, Berkeley. He later returned to the law school. Yoo, who has written with skepticism on the impact of international law on the obligations of the United States, has explained, "There was no book at the time you could open and say, 'under American law, this is what torture means'" (Slevin, *Washington Post*, December 26, 2003). He has also opined that the president has the authority to order the torture of detainees. Reportedly, David Addington, who was Vice President Dick Cheney's counsel at the time, was also a drafter of the memo.

Explanation and Analysis of the Document

The Bybee Torture Memo is broken up into six basic parts, with numerous subparts. The authors begin with an introduction that states their understanding that a question regarding standards of conduct under the Convention against Torture, as implemented in the U.S. Code, "has arisen in the context of the conduct of interrogations outside of the United States." They then summarize their conclusions that the criminal code "proscribes acts inflicting, and that are specifically intended to inflict, severe pain or suffering, whether mental or physical"; that those acts must be "of an extreme nature"; and that "certain acts may be cruel, inhuman, or degrading, but still not produce pain and suffering" that would be illegal under section 2340A. They explain that at the end of the memo, they examine possible defenses "that would negate any claim that certain interrogation methods violate the statute."

Part I of the memo provides an interpretation of what is required to convict an interrogator of torture under sections 2340–2340A of the criminal code, which is Title 18 of the U.S. Code. Section 2340A defines as a crime an act by which any person "outside the United States commits or attempts to commit torture." Section 2340 defines *torture* as "an act committed by a person acting under the color of law specifically intended to inflict severe physical or mental pain or suffering (other than pain or suffering incidental to lawful sanctions) upon another person within his custody or physical control." Section 2340's definition of torture is almost identical to that in article 1 of the Convention against Torture, except that the criminal code loosely substitutes "specifically intended to inflict" for the convention's phrasing of "intentionally inflicted."

Part I summarizes that a conviction under section 2340A requires that the torture take place outside the United States, that the interrogator act under the color of law, that the victim be within the interrogator's custody or control, that the interrogator specifically intend to cause severe physical or mental pain or suffering, and that the act in fact inflict severe physical or mental pain or suffering. The memo notes that Gonzales had requested interpretations only of the phrases "specific intent" and "the infliction of severe pain or suffering"; those phrases are then examined.

◆ A. "Specifically Intended"

Where section 2340 requires that an act be "specifically intended" to inflict severe pain or suffering, the authors opine that the phrase requires that the act be done with specific intent as defined in criminal law. They rely on select criminal case law and *Black's Law Dictionary* to define *specific intent* to require that the interrogator "must expressly intend to achieve the forbidden act." They conclude that, therefore, a defendant might lack the requisite specific intent even while knowing that severe pain will result from an act.

◆ B. "Severe Pain or Suffering"

To interpret "severe pain or suffering" in section 2340, the authors rely on a definition of *severe* in *Webster's New International Dictionary* as well as on the use of the phrase "severe pain" elsewhere in the U.S. Code. They find that the phrase appears in several places in the defining of emergency medical conditions for the purpose of providing health benefits. Those statutes define an emergency condition as a condition that is serious enough that a "prudent lay person" could expect that lack of immediate medical care would put the health of the patient "in serious jeopardy" or would cause "serious impairment to bodily functions" or "serious dysfunction of any bodily organ or part."

The memo's authors conclude that the statutes therefore "suggest" that "severe pain" as used in section 2340 must rise to a similarly high level—a level "that would ordinarily be associated with a sufficiently serious physical condition or injury such as death, organ failure, or serious impairment of body functions."

2003

■ **March 19**
U.S. military invades Iraq.

■ **April 4**
Pentagon issues "Working Group Report on Detainee Interrogations in the Global War on Terrorism: Assessment of Legal, Historical, Policy, and Operational Considerations."

2004

■ **December 30**
Memorandum sent from the Office of Legal Counsel to James B. Comey with subject "Legal Standards Applicable under 18 U.S.C. §§2340–2340A," explicitly superseding the Bybee Torture Memo.

◆ C. "Severe Mental Pain or Suffering"

The authors next acknowledge that section 2340 distinguishes severe mental pain and suffering from severe physical pain and suffering. The criminal code here defines "severe mental pain or suffering" as

the prolonged mental harm caused by or resulting from—(A) the intentional infliction or threatened infliction of severe physical pain or suffering; (B) the administration or application, or threatened administration or application, of mind-altering substances or other procedures calculated to disrupt profoundly the senses or the personality; (C) the threat of imminent death; or (D) the threat that another person will imminently be subjected to death, severe physical pain or suffering, or the administration or application of mind-altering substances or other procedures calculated to disrupt profoundly the senses or personality.

The memo's authors discuss the various components of this definition separately.

First consulting dictionary definitions of *prolong*, the authors conclude that section 2340 requires that the acts giving rise to harm have some lasting damage. They distinguish "prolonged mental harm" from the mental stress experienced during a lengthy and intense interrogation. The authors also conclude that the list of proscribed acts in section 2340 is exhaustive. In other words, if prolonged mental harm is caused by an act that is not described in section 2340, it is not "torture." Furthermore, to commit torture under the statute, the defendant must "specifically intend to cause prolonged mental harm by one of the listed acts. It is not sufficient to merely intend the acts that caused the harm." They also advise that a defense against an accusation of specific intent to cause harm could consist of a demonstration that the defendant acted in good faith. In other words, in the authors' opinion, a defendant would not be guilty under section 2340 if he or she believed, in good faith, that his or her conduct was not prohibited by the statute.

The memo next looks at each of the four categories of predicate acts listed in section 2340 as causing prolonged mental harm. The first, "the intentional infliction or threatened infliction of severe physical pain or suffering," is defined as requiring the defendant to "intentionally inflict severe physical pain or suffering with the specific intent of causing prolonged mental harm." The memo notes that a threat, either "implicit or explicit," is a predicate act under the statute. The authors opine that the existence of such a threat "should be assessed from the standpoint of a reasonable person in the same circumstances."

The second predicate act is "the administration or application, or threatened administration or application, of mind-altering substances or other procedures calculated to disrupt profoundly the senses or the personality." The authors conclude that the term "mind-altering substances" refers to drugs and that under the statute they must produce an "extreme effect." They advise that the acts must "penetrate to the core of an individual's ability to perceive the world around him, substantially interfering with his cognitive abilities, or fundamentally alter his personality." The examples they provide are a brief psychotic disorder, the onset of behavior associated with obsessive-compulsive disorder, and "pushing someone to the brink of suicide."

The authors define the third predicate act, "the threat of imminent death," as requiring that the threatened death be immediate. Examples include mock executions or the playing of Russian roulette. The fourth predicate act is any threat that any of the other predicate acts will be performed on a third person. The authors devote only two sentences to this act, advising that the statute "does not require any relationship between the prisoner and the third party."

The authors next include a short section on the legislative history of sections 2340 and 2340A of Title 18 of the U.S. Code. They note that Congress criminalized torture to fulfill the nation's obligations under article 4 of the Convention against Torture, which requires all signatories to "ensure that all acts of torture are offenses under criminal law." They conclude that the only light shed by the scant legislative history is that "Congress intended section 2340's definition of torture to track the definition set forth in [the Convention against Torture], as elucidated by the United States' reservations, understandings, and declarations submitted as part of its ratification." Part I is concluded with a summary in which the authors opine that their interpretations of sections 2340 and 2340A comport with the common meaning of the term *torture* and that the act covers only "extreme acts."

◆ **Part II**

The second part of the memo examines the U.N. Convention against Torture and Other Cruel, Inhuman or Degrading Treatment or Punishment, abbreviated as CAT. (The United Nations has designated that acronym as refer-

ring to an associated body called the Committee against Torture.) The authors explain that because Congress enacted sections 2340 and 2340A to implement the Convention against Torture, the treaty's text and history should be examined to put the statutes in context. They quote the definition of *torture* from the convention and conclude that it reinforces their reading of section 2340 that torture must be an extreme act. They also note that the convention distinguishes "torture" from "other acts of cruel, inhuman, or degrading treatment or punishment." Article 16 of the convention requires parties to "undertake to prevent … other acts of cruel, inhuman or degrading treatment or punishment which do not amount to torture." The memo's authors conclude that, therefore, the United States need not actually criminalize those acts.

◆ **A. Ratification History**

The authors next examine the ratification history of the Convention against Torture, beginning with their opinion that the executive branch's interpretation of a treaty is to be accorded the "greatest weight" in understanding its "intent and meaning." In their view, the executive branch's interpretation of the convention supports their interpretation. They note that the administration of Ronald Reagan submitted the Convention against Torture to the Senate under the following terms: "The United States understands that, in order to constitute torture, an act must be a deliberate and calculated act of an extremely cruel and inhuman nature, specifically intended to inflict excruciating and agonizing physical or mental pain or suffering." The memo's authors note, however, that the Senate did not, in fact, give its advice and consent to the treaty until the George H. W. Bush administration, which had resubmitted the treaty under differently worded terms. Those terms read, in part, "The United States understands that, in order to constitute torture, an act must be specifically intended to inflict severe physical or mental pain or suffering." The terms also included a list of actions that would constitute mental pain or suffering.

The authors opine that George H. W. Bush administration's understanding accomplished two things: First, the term "intentionally" as used in the convention's definition of torture was understood to require "specific intent," and, second, form and substance were added to the term *mental pain or suffering*. They note that the Senate ratified the Convention against Torture with this understanding and that Congress codified the convention almost verbatim in the criminal statute. They admit that the Bush understanding used "less vigorous rhetoric" than the Reagan understanding but detect little difference otherwise, as both "emphasize the extraordinary or extreme acts required to constitute torture."

◆ **B. Negotiating History**

The authors advise that the negotiating history of the Convention against Torture supports their conclusions. Relying on the history set forth in *The United Nations Convention against Torture: A Handbook on the Convention against Torture and Other Cruel, Inhuman, or Degrading Treatment or Punishment*, by J. Herman Burgers and Hans Danelius, they reach two conclusions: First, the injury caused by the acts of torture need not be permanent to constitute torture. Second, the parties to the treaty rejected a proposal that would have made the use of truth drugs, where no physical harm or mental suffering was evident, part of the definition of torture.

In a short conclusion to part II, the authors summarize that the text, ratification history, and negotiation history of the Convention against Torture support their conclusion that section 2340A is meant to address only the "most egregious conduct."

◆ Part III

The third part of the Bybee Torture Memo examines interpretations of torture by U.S. courts. The authors begin by noting that, at the time, no cases of prosecution under section 2340A had been reported. They note that the Torture Victim's Protection Act provides a civil tort remedy for victims of torture by foreigners outside the United States and that it contains a definition of *torture* that is almost identical to that in the Convention against Torture. While the act's definition requires that the physical or mental pain be "intentionally inflicted," among other noted differences, the authors conclude that those differences are not significant for their purposes.

The memo's authors conclude that the courts have not engaged in analyses of the term *torture* because the alleged acts in question have been so extreme in nature. They note seven acts that "consistently reappear" in cases and that are so barbaric that courts would likely find them to constitute torture:

(1) severe beatings using instruments such as iron [bars], truncheons, and clubs; (2) threats of imminent death, such as mock executions; (3) threats of removing extremities; (4) burning, especially burning with cigarettes; (5) electric shocks to genitalia or threats to do so; (6) rape or sexual assault, or injury to an individual's sexual organs, or threatening to do any of these sorts of acts; and (7) forcing the prisoner to watch the torture of others.

The authors also opine that "courts will more likely examine the totality of the circumstances, rather than engage in careful parsing of the statute."

◆ Part IV

The fourth part of the memo examines international decisions. The authors opine that decisions by foreign and international judicial bodies do not have binding authority on the United States but can provide guidance regarding how the rest of the world will view U.S. actions. Considering a decision by the European Court of Human Rights and a decision by the Israeli Supreme Court, they conclude that both bodies recognize acts that fall in the category of "cruel, inhuman, or degrading treatment or punishment" but do

An undated photo of John Yoo, who cowrote the Bybee Torture Memo. (AP Photo/University of California, Berkeley)

not amount to torture. They conclude that, therefore, international law "permits" a limited definition of torture.

Noting that "an analogue to [the Convention against Torture's] provisions can be found in the European Convention on Human Rights and Fundamental Freedoms," the authors analyze the 1978 interpretation of the European convention by the European Court of Human Rights in *Ireland v. United Kingdom*. In that case, the court found that methods used by the British military on Irish Republican Army prisoners were inhuman and degrading but did not amount to torture. The authors recite the methods at issue: wall standing, hooding, subjection to noise, sleep deprivation, and deprivation of food and drink.

The authors also consider *Public Committee against Torture in Israel v. Israel*, a 1999 decision by the Israeli Supreme Court. The case was a challenge against the use by the General Security Service of five interrogation methods: shaking, the "Shabach" (seating the prisoner, hooded, in an uncomfortable position and playing loud music for prolonged periods of time), the "frog crouch," the excessive tightening of handcuffs, and sleep deprivation. The authors concede that the Israeli court did not have to decide whether the methods constituted torture or merely cruel and inhuman treatment because the General Security Service is prohibited from using either type of method. Nevertheless, the authors note that "the court did not expressly find that" the acts in question "amounted to torture," and they thus cite the decision as support for their advice that such acts do not amount to torture.

The authors further note that the Israeli Supreme Court stated that in certain circumstances, General Security Service officers could assert a necessity defense. The authors opine that this would in fact be contrary to article 2, paragraph 2, of the Convention against Torture, which provides that "no exceptional circumstance whatsoever, whether a state of war or a threat of war, internal political instability or any other public emergency may be invoked as a justification of torture."

◆ Part V

The fifth part of the memo begins with the premise that even if a particular interrogation method were to constitute torture under section 2340A, the statute would be unconstitutional if it were to thus encroach on the president's constitutional power as commander in chief. The authors opine that the president's authority as commander in chief includes the detention and interrogation of "enemy combatants" as he sees fit.

◆ A. The War with al Qaeda

The authors next set forth a description of the nature of the threat posed to the United States by al Qaeda. They describe the events of September 11, 2001, and state that those events were part of a violent campaign against the United States that began with the ambush of U.S. servicemen in Somalia in 1993. They state that, in response, the U.S. government "has engaged in a broad effort at home and abroad to counter terrorism." They also point to earlier memoranda in which they reviewed the president's constitutional power to use force abroad in response to the September 11 attacks, as well as to the Patriot Act, which was passed on October 26, 2001.

The authors opine that regardless of this legislation, the United States had failed to capture many leaders of al Qaeda and the Taliban who yet retained access to active terrorist cells and other resources. They conclude that the capture and interrogation of such individuals is "imperative to our national security and defense" because they may provide information concerning the nature of terrorist plans and the identities of other operatives. As an example, they cite the case of José Padilla, a U.S. citizen who at the time was suspected of terrorist activities but was being held by the government without charge.

◆ B. Interpretation to Avoid Constitutional Problems

The authors conclude that section 2340A does not apply to the president's detention and interrogation of enemy combatants pursuant to his authority as commander in chief. They rely on the canon of statutory construction whereby statutes can and should be construed in alternative manners so as to avoid violations of the Constitution, provided that such alternative constructions are reasonable and available. Applying that canon, they state that they will not read section 2340A, a criminal statute, to infringe on the president's power as commander in chief.

◆ Part VI

The last part of the Bybee Torture Memo begins with the premise that even if an interrogation method "might arguably cross the line drawn in Section 2340" and even if the application of that statute to interrogations of enemy combatants was deemed constitutional, the current circumstances might provide certain justification defenses that could negate any criminal liability. Two possible defenses are addressed: necessity and self-defense.

◆ A. Necessity

The authors acknowledge that no federal statute establishes a defense of necessity and so instead rely on a definition found in the Model Penal Code. Section 3.02 of the Model Penal Code provides that

> conduct that the actor believes to be necessary to avoid a harm or evil to himself or another is justifiable, provided that: (a) the harm or evil sought to be avoided by such conduct is greater than that sought to be prevented by the law defining the offense charges; and (b) neither the Code nor other law defining the offense provides exceptions or defenses dealing with the specific situation involved; and (c) a legislative purpose to exclude the justification claimed does not otherwise plainly appear.

The authors opine that because any detainee might have information that would help the United States prevent further attacks like those on September 11, the necessity defense would be available to the interrogator, as any harm that might occur during the interrogation would be insignificant in comparison to the harm potentially avoided in preventing such an attack. In the authors' opinion, the necessity defense would not be available if Congress had clearly stated that a violation of the torture statute could never be outweighed by the harm to be avoided. They note that Congress did not include in the statute either the purposes for infliction of severe pain and suffering found in article 1, paragraph 1, of the Convention against Torture or the statement that "no exceptional circumstances" can justify torture, contained in article 2, paragraph 2, of the convention and that therefore the necessity defense might be available.

◆ B. Self-Defense

Regarding self-defense, the authors opine that the doctrine permitting "the use of force to prevent harm to another person" is not precluded by section 2340A. They advise that four essential elements of self-defense could be met in the case of an interrogation of an enemy combatant: First, the use of force could be necessary. Second, the interrogator's

"Physical pain amounting to torture must be equivalent in intensity to the pain accompanying serious physical injury, such as organ failure, impairment of bodily function, or even death."

(Introduction)

"For purely mental pain or suffering to amount to torture under Section 2340, it must result in significant psychological harm of significant duration, e.g., lasting for months or even years."

(Introduction)

"As Commander-in-Chief, the President has the constitutional authority to order interrogations of enemy combatants to gain intelligence information concerning the military plans of the enemy."

(Part IV)

belief in the need to use force could be reasonable. Third, the threat could be "imminent" in the sense that a defensive response might be "immediately necessary." Fourth, the amount of force could be proportional to the threat.

◆ **Conclusion and Appendix**

In the memo's closing paragraphs, the authors reiterate the conclusions set forth at the beginning, stating that the statutes in question, sections 2340–2340A of Title 18 of the U.S. Code, cover "only extreme acts." The authors attach an appendix summarizing select cases in which U.S. courts have determined that the defendant tortured the plaintiff.

Audience

The Bybee Torture Memo is an internal document written from the Office of Legal Counsel, of the Justice Department, to Alberto R. Gonzales, then counsel to the president. The Office of Legal Counsel assists the attorney general in providing legal advice to the White House and other executive branch agencies on constitutional questions. Although the memo was addressed only to Gonzales, ample evidence suggests that it was widely distributed. For example, much of the memo is repeated in an April 4, 2003, report on detainee interrogations written by a Defense Department working group. The report relies on the Bybee Torture Memo's legal conclusions to recommend interrogation techniques.

Impact

While the full impact of the Bybee Torture Memo within the U.S. government and military may remain unknown, ample evidence indicates that it influenced decision making with regard to the advisability of using coercive forms of interrogation on detainees. For example, in the report dated April 4, 2003, the working group created by the Department of Defense to look at detainee interrogation not only adopted the memo's rationale but also quoted select portions. On April 16, 2003, Donald Rumsfeld, the secretary of defense, relied on the report to issue a list of approved interrogation techniques. He stressed that the techniques could be used only on unlawful combatants held by the United States at Guantanamo Bay, Cuba. He directed that four of the techniques be used only in case of military necessity and only after he was notified.

After the Bybee Torture Memo came to light, both the general public and legal community were outraged. Harold Koh, the dean of Yale Law School and former attorney-adviser at the Office of Legal Counsel, wrote and testified that the legal opinion therein is perhaps the most clearly erroneous one he has ever read. He noted that under the memo's narrow definition of torture, many of the techniques used by Saddam Hussein's regime that have been cited as atrocities by the Bush administration would not qualify as torture. Alberto Mora, then general counsel of the U.S. Navy, also registered his belief that the opinion was profoundly in error.

On December 30, 2004, as the Senate Judiciary Committee was preparing to hold hearings on the nomination of Alberto Gonzales for the position of attorney general, the Office of Legal Counsel issued a second memorandum on the legal interpretation of sections 2340 and 2340A. That memo, with the subject "Re: Legal Standards Applicable under U.S.C. §§2340–2340A," revealed that the Bybee Torture Memo had been withdrawn in June 2004 and asserted that the new memo superseded the prior memo. Specifically, the new memo states that the Office of Legal Counsel no longer finds it useful to parse the precise definition of "specific intent," as used in section 2340, and acknowledges that even under U.S. criminal law the term has been found to have various meanings. It then opines that the "specific intent" element "would be met if a defendant performed an act and 'consciously desire[d]' that act to inflict severe physical or mental pain or suffering." The new memo also disagrees with the Bybee Torture Memo's conclusion that "severe pain" is limited to "excruciating pain" or pain "equivalent in intensity to the pain accompanying serious physical injury, such as organ failure, impairment of bodily functions, or even death" (http://www.us doj.gov/olc/18usc23402340a2.htm).

Related Documents

American Bar Association. "Report to the House of Delegates." In *The Torture Papers: The Road to Abu Ghraib*, eds. Karen J. Greenberg and Joshua L. Dratel. New York: Cambridge University Press, 2005. This report and its recommendations, adopted by the American Bar Association by voice vote on August 9, 2004, urge the U.S. government to stop the torture and abuse of detainees, to investigate and prosecute violations of laws prohibiting such abuse, and to assure compliance with the U.S. Constitution, laws, treaties, and related customary international law. It also criticizes the Bybee Torture Memo.

"Convention against Torture and Other Cruel, Inhuman or Degrading Treatment or Punishment." Human Rights Web Web site. http://www.hrweb.org/legal/cat.html. Accessed on March 11, 2008. This international convention prohibits the use of torture under all circumstances. The United States ratified the convention, and all members of the United Nations are parties to it.

"Legal Standards Applicable under 18 U.S.C. §§2340–2340A." U.S. Department of Justice "Office of Legal Council" Web site. http://www.usdoj.gov/olc/18usc23402340a2.htm. Accessed on March 11, 2008. This memorandum, signed by Daniel Levin, the acting assistant attorney general in the Office of Legal Counsel, was issued a few days before the Senate was to begin confirmation hearings of Alberto Gonzales's nomination for the post of attorney general. It explicitly repudiates the Bybee Torture Memo.

"U.S. Code Collection: § 2340A. Torture." Cornell University Law School "Legal Information Institute" Web site. http://www.law.cornell.edu/uscode/18/usc_sec_18_00002340—-A000-.html. Accessed on March 11, 2008. This statute, part of the United States' implementation of its obligations under the Convention against Torture, makes it a crime to torture someone outside the United States.

Bibliography

■ Articles

Golden, Tim. "A Junior Aide Had a Big Role in Terror Policy." *New York Times*, December 23, 2005.

Koh, Harold Hongju. "A World without Torture." *Columbia Journal of Transnational Law* 43 (2005): 641–661.

Mayer, Jane. "The Memo: How an Internal Effort to Ban the Abuse and Torture of Detainees Was Thwarted." *New Yorker*, February 27, 2006.

Slevin, Peter. "Scholar Stands by Post 9/11 Writings on Torture, Domestic Eavesdropping." *Washington Post*, December 26, 2003.

■ Books

Burgers, J. Herman, and Hans Danelius. *The United Nations Convention against Torture: A Handbook on the Convention against Torture and Other Cruel, Inhuman, or Degrading Treatment or Punishment*. Boston: M. Nijhoff, 1988.

Danner, Mark. *Torture and Truth: America, Abu Ghraib, and the War on Terror*. New York: New York Review Books, 2004.

Goldsmith, Jack L. *The Terror Presidency: Law and Judgment inside the Bush Administration*. New York: W. W. Norton, 2007.

Greenberg, Karen J., and Joshua L. Dratel, eds. *The Torture Papers: The Road to Abu Ghraib*. New York: Cambridge University Press, 2005.

—By Renee Colette Redman

Questions for Further Study

1. The Bybee Torture Memo, in accord with the thinking of some pundits and scholars, suggests that in certain circumstances, torture can be justified. Do you believe that torture can ever be justified on a moral or practical basis? If so, under what circumstances? Can and should torture ever be legally justified?

2. The memo suggests that the president has some constitutional power to torture prisoners. What are the arguments for and against a finding of such authority?

3. Extreme interrogation techniques and harsh treatment of prisoners have been used throughout the world over the centuries. Compare and contrast the methods and rationales employed in ancient Rome, medieval Europe, and the United States in the early 2000s.

4. Many U.S. allies, including the Council of Europe, have condemned the torture of prisoners held by the United States in Guantánamo Bay and elsewhere. What are the grounds for the criticisms? Compare and contrast definitions of the term *torture* used throughout the world.

Glossary

degrading	humiliating
explicit	spelled out; made plain
imminent	about to happen
implicit	not directly stated but implied or understood
interrogation	formal questioning
parse	analyze role of a word in a phrase or sentence
proscribe	forbid

BYBEE TORTURE MEMO

Memorandum for Alberto R. Gonzales, Counsel to the President

Re. Standards of Conduct for Interrogation under 18 U.S.C. §§ 2340-2340A

You have asked for our Office's views regarding the standards of conduct under the Convention Against Torture and Other Cruel, Inhuman and Degrading Treatment or Punishment as implemented by Sections 2340-2340A of title 18 of the United States Code. As we understand it, this question has arisen in the context of the conduct of interrogations outside of the United States. We conclude below that Section 2340A proscribes acts inflicting, and that are specifically intended to inflict, severe pain or suffering, whether mental or physical. Those acts must be of an extreme nature to rise to the level of torture within the meaning of Section 2340A and the Convention. We further conclude that certain acts may be cruel, inhuman, or degrading, but still not produce pain and suffering of the requisite intensity to fall within Section 2340A's proscription against torture. We conclude by examining possible defenses that would negate any claim that certain interrogation methods violate the statute.

In Part I, we examine the criminal statue's text and history. We conclude that for an act to constitute torture as defined in Section 2340, it must inflict pain that is difficult to endure. Physical pain amounting to torture must be equivalent to intensity to the pain accompanying serious physical injury, such as organ failure, impairment of bodily function, or even death. For purely mental pain or suffering to amount to torture under Section 2340, it must result in significant psychological harm of significant duration, e.g., lasting for months or even years. We conclude that the mental harm also must result from one of the predicate acts listed in the statute, namely: threats of imminent death; threats of infliction of the kind of pain that would amount to physical tor-

ture; infliction of such physical pain as a means of psychological torture; use of drugs or other procedures designed to deeply disrupt the senses, or fundamentally alter an individual's personality; or threatening to do any of these things to a third party. The legislative history simply reveals that Congress intended for the statute's definition to track the Convention's definition of torture and the reservations, understandings, and declarations that the United States submitted with its ratification. We conclude that the statute, taken as a whole, makes plain that it prohibits only extreme acts.

In Part II, we examine the text, ratification history, and negotiating history of the Torture Convention. We conclude that the treaty's text prohibits only the most extreme acts by reserving criminal penalties solely for torture and declining to require such penalties for "cruel, inhuman, or degrading treatment or punishment." This confirms our view that the criminal statute penalizes only the most egregious conduct. Executive branch interpretations and representations to the Senate at the time of ratification further confirm that the treaty was intended to reach only the most extreme conduct.

In Part III, we analyze the jurisprudence of the Torture Victims Protection Act, 28 U.S.C. §§ 1350 note (2000), which provides civil remedies for torture victims, to predict the standards that courts might follow in determining what actions reach the threshold of torture in the criminal context. We conclude from these cases that courts are likely to take at totality-of-the-circumstances approach, and will look to an entire course of conduct, to determine whether certain acts will violate Section 2340A. Moreover, these cases demonstrate that most often torture involves cruel and extreme physical pain. In Part IV, we examine international decisions regarding the use of sensory deprivation techniques. These cases make clear that while many of these techniques may amount to cruel, inhuman and degrading treatment, they do not produce pain or suffering of the necessary intensity to meet the definition of torture. From these decisions, we conclude that there is a wide range of such techniques that will not rise to the level of torture.

In Part V, we discuss whether Section 2340A may be unconstitutional if applied to interrogations undertaken of enemy combatants pursuant to the President's Commander-in-Chief powers. We find that in the circumstances of the current war against al Qaeda and its allies, prosecution under Section 2340A may be barred because enforcement of the statute would represent an unconstitutional infringement of the President's authority to conduct war. In Part VI, we discuss defenses to an allegation that an interrogation method might violate the statute. We conclude that, under the current circumstances, necessity or self-defense may justify interrogation methods that might violate Section 2340A.

I. 18 U.S.C. §§ 2340-2340A

Section 2340A makes it a criminal offense for any person "outside the United States [to] commit or attempt to commit torture."(1) Section 2340 defines the act of torture as an: act committed by a person acting under the color of law specifically intended to inflict severe physical or mental pain or suffering (other than pain or suffering incidental to lawful sanctions) upon another person with his custody or physical control.

18 U.S.C.A. §§ 2340(1); see id. §§ 2340A. Thus, to convict a defendant of torture, the prosecution must establish that (1) the torture occurred outside the United States; (2) the defendant acted under the color of law; (3) the victim was within the defendant's custody or physical control; (4) the defendant specifically intended to cause severe physical or mental pain or suffering, and (5) that the act inflicted severe physical or mental pain or suffering. See also S. Exec. Rep. No. 101-30, at 6 (1990) ("For an act to be 'torture,' it must … cause severe pain and suffering, and be intended to cause severe pain and suffering.") You have asked us to address only the elements of specific intent and the infliction of severe pain or suffering. As such, we have not addressed the elements of "outside the United States," "color of law," and "custody or control." (2) At your request, we would he happy to address these elements in a separate memorandum.

◆ A. "Specifically Intended"

To violate Section 2340A, the statute requires that severe pain and suffering must be inflicted with specific intent. See 18 U.S.C. § 2340(1). In order for a defendant to have acted with specific intent, he must expressly intend to achieve the forbidden act. See *United States v. Carter*, 530 U.S. 255, 269 (2000); Black's Law Dictionary at 814 (7th ed. 1999) (defining specific intent as "[t]he intent to accomplish the precise criminal act that one is later charged with"). For example, in *Ratzlaf v. United States*, 510 U.S. 135, 141 (1994), the statute at issue was construed to require that the defendant act with the "specific intent to commit the crime." (Internal quotation marks and citation omitted). As a result, the defendant had to act with the express "purpose to disobey the law" in order for the mens rea element to be satisfied. Ibid. (internal quotation marks and citation omitted)

Here, because Section 2340 requires that a defendant act with the specific intent to inflict severe pain, the infliction of such pain must be the defendant's precise objective. If the statute had required only general intent, it would be sufficient to establish guilt by showing that the defendant "possessed knowledge with respect to the actus reus of the crime." Carter, 530 U.S. at 268. If the defendant acted knowing that severe pain or suffering was reasonably likely to result from his actions, but no more, he would have acted only with general intent. See id. at 269; Black's Law Dictionary 813 (7th ed. 1999) (explaining that general intent "usu[ally] takes the form of recklessness (involving actual awareness of a risk and the culpable taking of that risk) or negligence (involving blameworthy inadvertence)"). The Supreme Court has used the following example to illustrate the difference between these two mental states:

[A] person entered a bank and took money from a teller at gunpoint, but deliberately failed to make a quick getaway from the bank in the hope of being arrested so that he would be returned to prison and treated for alcoholism. Though this defendant knowingly engaged in the acts of using force and taking money (satisfying "general intent"), he did not intend permanently to deprive the bank of its possession of the money (failing to satisfy "specific intent").

Carter, 530 U.S. at 268 (citing 1 W. LaFave & A. Scott, Substantive Criminal Law § 3.5, at 315 (1986)).

As a theoretical matter, therefore, knowledge alone that a particular result is certain to occur does not constitute specific intent. As the Supreme Court explained in the context of murder, "the ... common law of homicide distinguishes ... between a person who knows that another person will be killed as a result of his conduct and a person who acts with the specific purpose of taking another's life[.]"*United States v. Bailey*, 444 U.S. 394, 405 (1980). "Put differently, the law distinguishes actions taken 'because of' a given end from actions taken in spite of their unintended but foreseen consequences." *Vacco v. Quill*, 521 U.S. 793, 802-03 (1997). Thus, even if the defendant knows that severe pain will result from his actions, if causing such harm is not his objective, he lacks the requisite specific intent even though the defendant did not act in good faith. Instead, a defendant is guilty of torture only if he acts with the express purpose of inflicting severe pain or suffering on a person within his custody or physical control. While as a theoretical matter such knowledge does not constitute specific intent, juries are permitted to infer from the factual circumstances that such intent is present. See, e.g., *United States v. Godwin*, 272 F.3d 659, 666 (4th Cir. 2001); *United States v. Karro*, 257 F.3d 112, 118 (2d Cir. 2001); *United States v. Wood*, 207 F.3d 1222, 1232 (10th Cir. 2000); *Henderson v. United States*, 202 F.2d 400, 403 (6th Cir. 1953). Therefore, when a defendant knows that his actions will produce the prohibited result, a jury will in all likelihood conclude that the defendant acted with specific intent.

Further, a showing that an individual acted with a good faith belief that his conduct would not produce the result that the law prohibits negates specific intent. See, e.g., *South Atl. Lmtd. Ptrshp. of Tenn. v. Riese*, 218 F.3d 518, 531 (4th Cir. 2002). Where a defendant acts in good faith, he acts with an honest belief that he has not engaged in the proscribed conduct. See *Cheek v. United States*, 498 U.S. 192, 202 (1991); *United States v. Mancuso*, 42 F.3d 836, 837 (4th Cir. 1994). For example, in the context of mail fraud, if an individual honestly believes that the material transmitted is truthful, he has not acted with the required intent to deceive or mislead. See, e.g., *United States v. Sayakhom*, 186 F.3d 928, 939-40 (9th Cir. 1999). A good faith belief need not be a reasonable one. See Cheek, 498 U.S. at 202.

Although a defendant theoretically could hold an unreasonable belief that his acts would not constitute the actions prohibited by the statute, even though they would as a certainty produce the prohibited effects, as a matter of practice in the federal criminal justice system it is highly unlikely that a jury would acquit in such a situation. Where a defendant holds an unreasonable belief, he will confront the problem of proving to the jury that he actually held that belief. As the Supreme Court noted in Cheek, "the more unreasonable the asserted beliefs or misunderstandings are, the more likely the jury ... will find that the Government has carried its burden of proving" intent. Id. at 203-04. As we explained above, a jury will be permitted to infer that the defendant held the requisite specific intent. As a matter of proof, therefore, a good faith defense will prove more compelling when a reasonable basis exists for the defendant's belief.

◆ B. "Severe Pain or Suffering"

The key statutory phrase in the definition of torture is the statement that acts amount to torture if they cause "severe physical or mental pain or suffering." In examining the meaning of a statute, its text must be the starting point. See *INS v. Phinpathya*, 464 U.S. 183, 189 (1984) ("This Court has noted on numerous occasions that in all cases involving statutory construction, our starting point must be the language employed by Congress,... and we assume that the legislative purpose is expressed by the ordinary meaning of the words used.") (internal quotations and citations omitted). Section 2340 makes plain that the infliction of pain or suffering per se, whether it is physical or mental, is insufficient to amount to torture. Instead, the text provides that pain or suffering must be "severe." The statute does not, however, define the term "severe." "In the absence of such a definition, we construe a statutory term in accordance with its ordinary or natural meaning." *FDIC v. Meyer*, 510 U.S. 471, 476 (1994). The dictionary defines "severe" as "[u]nsparing in exaction, punishment, or censure" or "[I]nflicting discomfort or pain hard to endure; sharp; afflictive; distressing; violent; extreme; as severe pain, anguish, torture." Webster's New International Dictionary 2295 (2d ed. 1935); see American Heritage Dictionary of the English Language 1653 (3d ed. 1992) ("extremely violent or grievous: severe pain"); IX The Oxford English Dictionary 572 (1978) ("Of pain, suffering, loss, or the like: Grievous, extreme" and "of circumstances ... hard to sustain or endure"). Thus, the adjective "severe" conveys that the pain or suffering must be of such a high level of intensity that the pain is difficult for the subject to endure.

Congress's use of the phrase "severe pain" elsewhere in the United States Code can shed more light on its meaning. See, e.g., *West Va. Univ. Hosps., Inc. v. Casey*, 499 U.S. 83, 100 (1991) ("[W]e construe [a statutory term] to contain that permissible meaning which fits most logically and comfortably into the body of both previously and subsequently enacted law."). Significantly, the phrase "severe pain" appears in statutes defining an emergency medical condition for the purpose of providing health benefits. See, e.g., 8 U.S.C. § 1369 (2000); 42 U.S.C. § 1395w-22 (2000); id. § 1395x (2000); id. § 1395dd (2000); id. § 1396b (2000); id. § 1396u-2 (2000). These statutes define an emergency condition as one "manifesting itself by acute symptoms of sufficient security (including severe pain) such that a prudent lay person, who possesses an average knowledge of health and medicine, could reasonably expect the absence of immediate medical attention to result in—placing the health of the individual … (i) in serious jeopardy, (ii) serious impairment to bodily functions, or (iii) serious dysfunction of any bodily organ or part." Id. § 1395w-22(d)(3)(B). Although these statutes address a substantially different subject from Section 2340, they are nonetheless helpful for understanding what constitutes severe physical pain. They treat severe pain as an indicator of ailments that are likely to result in permanent and serious physical damage in the absence of immediate medical treatment. Such damage must rise to the level of death, organ failure, or the permanent impairment of a significant body function. These statutes suggest that "severe pain," as used in Section 2340, must rise to a similarly high level—the level that would ordinarily be associated with a sufficiently serious physical condition or injury such as death, organ failure, or serious impairment of body functions—in order to constitute torture.

◆ C. "Severe Mental Pain or Suffering"

Section 2340 gives further guidance as to the meaning of "severe mental pain or suffering," as distinguished from severe physical pain and suffering. The statute defines "severe mental pain or suffering" as:

The prolonged mental harm caused by or resulting from—(A) the intentional infliction or threatened infliction of severe physical pain or suffering; (B) the administration or application, or threatened administration or application, of mind-altering substances or other procedures calculated to disrupt profoundly the senses or the personality; (C) the threat of imminent death; or (D) the threat that another person will imminently be subjected to death, severe physical pain or suffering, or the administration or application of mind-altering substances or other procedures calculated to disrupt profoundly the senses or personality.

18 U.S.C. § 2340(2). In order to prove "severe mental pain or suffering," the statute requires proof of "prolonged mental harm" that was caused by or resulted from one of four enumerated acts. We consider each of these elements.

1. "Prolonged Mental Harm"

As an initial matter, Section 2340(2) requires that the severe mental pain must be evidenced by "prolonged mental harm." To prolong is to "lengthen in time" or to "extend the duration of, to draw out." Webster's Third New International Dictionary 1815 (1988); Webster's New International Dictionary 1980 (2d ed. 1935). Accordingly, "prolong" adds a temporal dimension to the harm to the individual, namely, that the harm must be one that is endured over some period of time. Put another way, the acts giving rise to the harm must cause some lasting, though not necessarily permanent, damage. For example, the mental strain experienced by an individual during a lengthy and intense interrogation—such as one that state or local police might conduct upon a criminal suspect—would not violate Section 2340(2). On the other hand, the development of a mental disorder such as posttraumatic stress disorder, which can last months or even years, or even chronic depression, which also can last for a considerable period of time if untreated, might satisfy the prolonged harm requirement. See American Psychiatric Association, Diagnostic and Statistical Manual of Mental Disorders 426, 439-45 (4th ed. 1994) ("DSM-IV"). See also Craig Haney & Mona Lynch, Regulating Prisons of the Future: A Psychological Analysis of Supermax and Solitary Confinement, 23 N.Y.U. Rev. L. & Soc. Change 477, 509 (1997) (noting that posttraumatic stress disorder is frequently found in torture victims); cf. Sana Loue, Immigration Law and Health § 10:46 (2001) (recommending evaluating for post-traumatic stress disorder immigrant-client who has experienced torture). (4) By contrast to "severe pain," the phrase "prolonged mental harm" appears nowhere else in the U.S. Code nor does it appear in relevant medical literature or international human rights reports.

Not only must the mental harm be prolonged to amount to severe mental pain and suffering, but also it must be caused by or result from one of the acts listed in the statute. In the absence of a catchall provision, the most natural reading of the predicate acts listed in Section 2340(2)(A)-(D) is that Congress intended it to be exhaustive. In other words, other acts not included within Section 2340(2)'s enumeration are not within the statutory prohibition. See *Leatherman v. Tarrant County Narcotics Intelligence & Coordination Unit*, 507 U.S. 163, 168 (1993) ("Expressio unius est excluio alterius."); Norman Singer, 2A Sutherland on Statutory Construction § 47.23 (6th ed. 2000) ("[W]here a form of conduct, the manner of its performance and operation, and the persons and things to which it refers are designated, there is an inference that all omissions should be understood as exclusions.") (footnotes omitted). We conclude that torture within the meaning of the statute requires the specific intent to cause prolonged mental harm by one of the acts listed in Section 2340(2).

A defendant must specifically intend to cause prolonged mental harm for the defendant to have committed torture. It could be argued that a defendant needs to have specific intent only to commit the predicate acts that give rise to prolonged mental harm. Under that view, so long as the defendant specifically intended to, for example, threaten a victim with imminent death, he would have had sufficient mens rea for a conviction. According to this view, it would be further necessary for a conviction to show only that the victim factually suffered prolonged mental harm, rather than that the defendant intended to cause it. We believe that this approach is contrary to the text of the statute. The statute requires that the defendant specifically intend to inflict severe mental pain or suffering. Because the statute requires this mental state with respect to the infliction of severe mental pain, and because it expressly defines severe mental pain in terms of prolonged mental harm, that mental state must be present with respect to prolonged mental harm. To read the statute otherwise would read the phrase "the prolonged mental harm caused by or resulting from" out of the definition of "severe mental pain or suffering."

A defendant could negate a showing of specific intent to cause severe mental pain or suffering by showing that he had acted in good faith that his conduct would not amount to the acts prohibited by the statute. Thus, if a defendant has a good faith belief that his actions will not result in prolonged mental harm, he lacks the mental state necessary for his actions to constitute torture. A defendant could show that he acted in good faith by taking such steps as surveying professional literature, consulting with experts, or reviewing evidence gained from past experience. See, e.g., Ratzlaf, 510 U.S. at 142 n.10 (noting that where the statute required that the defendant act with the specific intent to violate the law, the specific intent element "might be negated by, e.g., proof that defendant relied in good faith on advice of counsel.") (citations omitted). All of these steps would show that he has drawn on the relevant body of knowledge concerning the result proscribed that [by] the statute, namely prolonged mental harm. Because the presence of good faith would negate the specific intent element of torture, it is a complete defense to such a charge. See, e.g., *United States v. Wall*, 130 F.3d 739, 746 (6th Cir. 1997); *United States v. Casperson*, 773 F.2d 216, 222-23 (8th Cir. 1985).

2. Harm Caused by or Resulting from Predicate Acts

Section 2340(2) sets forth four basic categories of predicate acts. First in the list is the "intentional infliction or threatened infliction of severe physical pain or suffering." This might at first appear superfluous because the statute already provides that the infliction of severe physical pain or suffering can amount to torture. This provision, however, actually captures the infliction of physical pain or suffering when the defendant inflicts physical pain or suffering with general intent rather than the specific intent that is required where severe physical pain or suffering alone is the basis for the charge. Hence, this subsection reaches the infliction of severe physical pain or suffering when it is but the means of causing prolonged mental harm. Or put another way, a defendant has committed torture when he intentionally inflicts severe physical pain or suffering with the specific intent of causing prolonged mental harm. As for the acts themselves, acts that cause "severe physical pain or suffering" can satisfy this provision.

Additionally, the threat of inflicting such pain is a predicate act under the statute. A threat may be implicit or explicit. See, e.g., *United States v. Sachdev*, 279 F.3d 25, 29 (1st Cir. 2002). In criminal law, courts generally determine whether an individual's words or actions constitute a threat by examining whether a reasonable person in the same circumstances would conclude that a threat had been made. See, e.g., *Watts v. United States*, 394 U.S. 705, 708 (1969) (holding that whether a statement constituted a threat against the president's life had to be determined in light of all the surrounding circumstances); Sachdev, 279 F.3d at 29 ("a reasonable person in defendant's position would perceive there to be a threat, explicit, or implicit, of physical injury"); *United States v. Khorrami*, 895 F.2d 1186, 1190 (7th Cir. 1990) (to establish that a threat was made, the statement must be made "in a context or under such circumstances wherein a reasonable person would foresee that the statement would be interpreted by those to whom the maker communicates a statement as a serious expression of an intention to inflict bodily harm upon [another individual]") (citation and internal quotation marks omitted); *United States v. Peterson*, 483 F.2d 1222, 1230 (D.C. Cir. 1973) (perception of threat of imminent harm necessary to establish self-defense had to be "objectively reasonable in light of the surrounding circumstances"). Based on this common approach, we believe that the existence of a threat of severe pain or suffering should be assessed from the standpoint of a reasonable person in the same circumstances.

Second, Section 2340(2)(B) provides that prolonged mental harm, constituting torture, can be caused by "the administration or application or threatened administration or application, of mind-altering substances or other procedures calculated to disrupt profoundly the senses or the personality." The statute provides no further definition of what constitutes a mind-altering substance. The phrase "mind-altering substances" is found nowhere else in the U.S. Code nor is it found in dictionaries. It is, however, a commonly used synonym for drugs. See, e.g., *United States v. Kingsley*, 241 F.3d 828, 834 (6th Cir.) (referring to controlled substances as "mind-altering substance[s]") cert. denied, 122 S.Ct. 137 (2001); *Hogue v. Johnson*, 131 F.3d 466, 501 (5th Cir. 1997) (referring to drugs and alcohol as "mind-altering substance[s]"), cert. denied, 523 U.S. 1014 (1998). In addition, the phrase appears in a number of state statutes, and the context in which it appears confirms this understanding of the phrase. See, e.g., Cal. Penal Code § 3500(c) (West Supp. 2000) ("Psychotropic drugs also include mind-altering… drugs.…"); Minn. Stat Ann. § 260B201(b) (West Supp. 2002) ("chemical dependency treatment" define as programs designed to "reduc[e] the risk of the use of alcohol, drugs, or other mind-altering substances").

This subparagraph, however, does not preclude any and all use of drugs. Instead, it prohibits the use of drugs that "disrupt profoundly the senses or the personality." To be sure, one could argue that this phrase applies only to "other procedures," not the application of mind-altering substances. We reject this interpretation because the terms of Section 2340(2) expressly indicate that the qualifying phrase applies to both "other procedures" and the "application of mind-altering substances." The word "other" modifies "procedures calculated to disrupt profoundly the senses." As an adjective, "other" indicates that the term or phrase it modifies is the remainder of several things. See Webster's Third New International Dictionary 1598 (1986) (defining "other" as "the one that remains of two or more") Webster's Ninth New Collegiate Dictionary 835 (1985) (defining "other" as "being the one (as of two or more) remaining or not included"). Or put another way, "other" signals that the words to which it attaches are of the same kind, type, or class as the more specific item previously listed. Moreover, where statutes couple words or phrases together, it "denotes an intention that they should be understood in the same general sense." Norman Singer, 2A Sutherland on Statutory Construction § 47:16 (6th ed. 2000); see also *Beecham v. United States*, 511 U.S. 368, 371 (1994) ("That several items in a list share an attribute counsels in favor of interpreting the other items as possessing that attribute as well."). Thus, the pairing of mind-altering substances with procedures calculated to disrupt profoundly the senses or personality and the use of "other" to modify "procedures" shows that the use of such substances must also cause a profound disruption of the senses or personality.

For drugs or procedures to rise to the level of "disrupt[ing] profoundly the senses or personality," they must produce an extreme effect. And by requiring that they be "calculated" to produce such an effect, the statute requires for liability the defendant has consciously designed the acts to produce such an effect. 28 U.S.C. § 2340(2)(B). The word "disrupt" is defined as "to break asunder; to part forcibly; rend," imbuing the verb with a connotation of violence. Webster's New International Dictionary 753 (2d ed. 1935); see Webster's Third New International Dictionary 656 (1986) (defining disrupt as "to break apart: Rupture" or "destroy the unity or wholeness of"); IV The Oxford English Dictionary 832 (1989) (defining disrupt as "[t]o break or burst asunder, to break in pieces; to separate forcibly"). Moreover, disruption of the senses or personality alone is insufficient to fall within the scope of this subsection; instead, that disruption must be profound. The word "profound" has a number of meanings, all of which convey a significant depth. Webster's New International Dictionary 1977 (2d ed. 1935) defines profound as: "Of very great depth; extending far below the surface or top; unfathomable[;]... [c]oming from, reaching to, or situated at a depth or more than ordinary depth; not superficial; deep-seated; chiefly with reference to the body; as a profound sigh, wound, or pain[;]... [c]haracterized by intensity, as of feeling or quality; deeply felt or realized; as, profound respect, fear, or melancholy; hence, encompassing; thoroughgoing; complete; as, profound sleep, silence, or ignorance." See Webster's Third New International Dictionary 1812 (1986) ("having very great depth: extending far below the surface ... not superficial"). Random House Webster's Unabridged Dictionary 1545 (2d ed. 1999) also defines profound as "originating in or penetrating to the depths of one's being" or "pervasive or intense; thorough; complete" or "extending, situated, or originating far down, or far beneath the surface." By requiring that the procedures and the drugs create a profound disruption, the statute requires more than that the acts "forcibly separate" or "rend" the senses or personality. Those acts must penetrate to the core of an individual's ability to perceive the world around him, substantially interfering with his cognitive abilities, or fundamentally alter his personality.

The phrase "disrupt profoundly the senses or personality" is not used in mental health literature nor is it derived from elsewhere in U.S. law. Nonetheless, we think the following examples would constitute a profound disruption of the senses or personality. Such an effect might be seen in a drug-induced dementia. In such a state, the individual suffers from significant memory impairment, such as the inability to retain any new information or recall information about things previously of interest to the individual. See DSM-IV at 134. 5 This impairment is accompanied by one or more of the following: deterioration of language function, e.g., repeating sounds or words over and over again; impaired ability to execute simple motor activities, e.g., inability to dress or wave goodbye; "[in]ability to recognize [and identify] objects such as chairs or pencils" despite normal visual functioning; or "[d]isturbances in executive level functioning," i.e., serious impairment of abstract thinking. Id. at 134-35. Similarly, we think that the onset of "brief psychotic disorder" would satisfy this standard. See id. at 302-03. In this disorder, the individual suffers psychotic symptoms, including among other things, delusions, hallucinations, or even a catatonic state. This can last for one day or even one month. See id. We likewise think that the onset of obsessive-compulsive disorder behaviors

would rise to this level. Obsessions are intrusive thoughts unrelated to reality. They are not simple worries, but are repeated doubts or even "aggressive or horrific impulses." See id. at 418. The DSM-IV further explains that compulsions include "repetitive behaviors (e.g., hand washing, ordering, checking)" and that "[b]y definition, [they] are either clearly excessive or are not connected in a realistic way with what they are designed to neutralize or prevent." See id. Such compulsions or obsessions must be "time-consuming." See id. at 419. Moreover, we think that pushing someone to the brink of suicide, particularly where the person comes from a culture with strong taboos against suicide, and it is evidenced by acts of self-mutilation, would be a sufficient disruption of the personality to constitute a "profound disruption." These examples, of course, are in no way intended to be exhaustive list. Instead, they are merely intended to illustrate the sort of mental health effects that we believe would accompany an action severe enough to amount to one that "disrupt[s] profoundly the senses or the personality."

The third predicate act, listed in Section 2340(2) is threatening a prisoner with "imminent death." 18 U.S.C. § 2340(2)(C). The plain text makes clear that a threat of death alone is insufficient; the threat must indicate that death is "imminent." The "threat of imminent death" is found in the common law as an element of the defense of duress. See Bailey, 444 U.S. at 409. "[W]here Congress borrows terms of art in which are accumulated the legal tradition and meaning of centuries of practice, it presumably knows and adopts the cluster of ideas that were attached to each borrowed word in the body of learning from which it was taken and the meaning its use will convey to the judicial mind unless otherwise instructed. In such case, absence of contrary direction may be taken as satisfaction with widely accepted definitions, not as a departure from them." *Morissette v. United States*, 342 U.S. 246, 263 (1952). Common law cases and legislation generally define imminence as requiring that the threat be almost immediately forthcoming. 1 Wayne R. LaFave & Austin W. Scott, Jr, Substantive Criminal Law § 5.7, at 655 (1986). By contrast, threats referring vaguely to things that might happen in the future do not satisfy this immediacy requirement. See *United States v. Fiore*, 178 F.3d 917, 923 (7th Cir. 1999). Such a threat fails to satisfy this requirement not because it is too remote in time but because there is a lack of certainty that it will occur. Indeed, timing is an indicator of certainty that the harm will befall the defendant. Thus, a vague threat that someday the prisoner might be killed would not suffice. Instead, subjecting a prisoner to mock executions or playing Russian roulette with him would have sufficient immediacy to constitute a threat of imminent death. Additionally, as discussed earlier, we believe that the existence of a threat must be assessed from the perspective of a reasonable person is the same circumstances.

Fourth, if the official threatens to do anything previously described to a third party, or commits such an act against a third party, that threat or action can serve as the necessary predicate for prolonged mental harm. See 18 U.S.C. § 2340(2)(D). The statute does not require any relationship between the prisoner and the third party,

3. Legislative History

The legislative history of Sections 2340-2340A is scant. Neither the definition of torture nor these sections as a whole sparked any debate. Congress criminalized this conduct to fulfill U.S. obligations under the U.N. Convention Against Torture and Other Cruel, Inhuman or Degrading Treatment or Punishment ("CAT"), adopted Dec. 10, 1984, S. Treaty Doc. No. 100-20 (1988), 1465 U.N.T.S. 85 (entered into force June 26, 1987), which requires signatories to "ensure that all acts of torture are offenses under its criminal law." CAT art. 4. These sections appeared only in the Senate version of the Foreign Affairs Authorization Act, and the conference bill adopted them without amendment. See H. R. Conf. Rep. No. 103-482, at 229 (1994). The only light that the legislative history sheds reinforces what is already obvious from the texts of Section 2340 and CAT: Congress intended Section 2340's definition of torture to track the definition set forth in CAT, as elucidated by the United States' reservations, understandings, and declarations submitted as part of its ratification. See S. Rep. No. 103-107, at 58 (1993) ("The definition of torture emanates directly from article 1 of the Convention."); id. at 58-59 ("The definition for 'severe mental pain and suffering' incorporates the understanding made by the Senate concerning this term.").

4. Summary

Section 2340's definition of torture must be read as a sum of these component parts. See *Argentine Rep. v. Amerada Hess Shipping Corp.*, 488 U.S. 428, 434-35 (1989) (reading two provisions together to determine statute's meaning); *Bethesda Hosp. Ass'n v. Bowen*, 485 U.S. 399, 405 (1988) (looking to "the language and design of the statute as a whole" to ascertain a statute's meaning). Each component of the definition emphasizes that torture is not the mere infliction of pain or suffering on another, but is instead a step well removed. The victim must experience intense pain or suffering of the kind that is equivalent to the pain that would be associated with serious physical injury so severe that death, organ failure, or permanent damage resulting in a loss of significant body function will likely result. If that pain or suffering is psychological, that suffering must result from one of the acts set forth in the statute. In addition, these acts must cause long-term mental harm. Indeed, this view of the criminal act of torture is consistent with the term's common meaning. Torture is generally understood to involve "intense pain" or "excruciating pain," or put another way, "extreme anguish of body or mind." Black's Law Dictionary at 1498 (7th Ed. 1999); Random House Webster's Unabridged Dictionary 1999 (1999); Webster's New International Dictionary 2674 (2d ed. 1935). In short, reading the definition of torture as a whole, it is plain that the term encompasses only extreme acts.

II. U.N. Convention against Torture and Other Cruel, Inhuman or Degrading Treatment or Punishment

Because Congress enacted the criminal prohibition against torture to implement CAT, we also examine the treaty's text and history to develop a fuller understanding of the context of Sections 2340-2340A. As with the statute, we begin our analysis with the treaty's text. See *Eastern Airlines Inc. v. Floyd*, 499 U.S. 530, 534-35 (1991) (When interpreting a treaty, we begin with the text of the treaty and the context in which the written words are used.) (quotation marks and citations omitted). CAT defines torture as:

> Any act by which severe pain or suffering, whether physical or mental, is intentionally inflicted on a person for such purposes as obtaining from him or a third person information or a confession, punishing him for an act he or a third person has committed or is suspected of having committed, or intimidating or coercing him or a third person, or for any reason based on discrimination of any kind, when such pain or suffering is inflicted by or at the instigation of or with the consent or acquies-

cence of a public official or other person acting in an official capacity.

Article 1(1) Unlike Section 2340, this definition includes a list of purposes for which such pain and suffering is inflicted. The prefatory phrase "such purposes as" makes clear that this list is, however, illustrative rather than exhaustive. Accordingly, severe pain or suffering need not be inflicted for those specific purposes to constitute torture; instead, the perpetrator must simply have a purpose of the same kind. More importantly, like Section 2340, the pain and suffering must be severe to reach the threshold of torture. Thus, the text of CAT reinforces our reading of Section 2340 that torture must be an extreme act.

CAT also distinguishes between torture and other acts of cruel, inhuman, or degrading treatment or punishment. Article 16 of CAT requires state parties to "undertake to prevent ... other acts of cruel, inhuman or degrading treatment or punishment which do not amount to torture as defined in article 1." CAT thus establishes a category of acts that are not to be committed and that states must endeavor to prevent, but that states need not criminalize, leaving those acts without the stigma of criminal penalties. CAT reserves criminal penalties and the stigma attached to those penalties for torture alone. In so doing, CAT makes clear that torture is at the farthest end of impermissible actions, and that it is distinct and separate from the lower level of "cruel, inhuman, or degrading treatment or punishment." This approach is in keeping with CAT's predecessor, the U.N. Declaration on the Protection from Torture. That declaration defines torture as "an aggravated and deliberate form of cruel, inhuman or degrading treatment or punishment." Declaration on Protection from Torture, UN Res. 3452, Art. 1(2) (Dec. 9, 1975).

◆ A. Ratification History

Executive branch interpretation of CAT further supports our conclusion that the treaty, and thus Section 2340A, prohibits only the most extreme forms of physical or mental harm. As we have previously noted, the "division of treaty-making responsibility between the Senate and the President is essentially the reverse of the division of law-making authority, with the President being the draftsman of the treaty and the Senate holding the authority to grant or deny approval." Relevance of Senate Ratification History to Treaty Interpretation, 11 Op. O.L.C. 28, 31 (Apr. 9, 1987) ("Sofaer Memorandum"). Treaties are negotiated by the President in his

capacity as the "sole organ of the federal government in the field of international relations." *United States v. Curtiss-Wright Export Corp.*, 299 U.S. 304, 320 (1936). Moreover, the President is responsible for the day-to-day interpretation of a treaty and retains the power to unilaterally terminate a treaty. See *Goldwater v. Carter*, 617 F.2d 697, 707-08 (D.C Cir.) (en banc) vacated and remanded with instructions to dismiss on other grounds, 444 U.S. 996 (1979). The Executive's interpretation is to be accorded the greatest weight in ascertaining a treaty's intent and meaning. See, e.g., *United States v. Stuart*, 489 U.S. 353, 369 (1989) ("the meaning attributed to treaty provisions by the Government agencies charged with their negotiation and enforcement is entitled to great weight") (quoting *Sumitomo Shoji America, Inc. v. Avagliano*, 457 U.S. 176, 184-85 (1982)); *Kolovrat v. Oregon*, 366 U.S. 187, 194 (1961) ("While courts interpret treaties for themselves, the meaning given them by the department of government particularly charged with their negotiation and enforcement is given great weight."); *Charlton v. Kelly*, 229 U.S. 447, 468 (1913) ("A construction of a treaty by the political departments of the government, while not conclusive upon a court..., is nevertheless of much weight.").

A review of the Executive branch's interpretation and understanding of CAT reveals that Congress codified the view that torture included only the most extreme forms of physical or mental harm. When it submitted the Convention to the Senate, the Reagan administration took the position that CAT reached only the most heinous acts. The Reagan administration included the following understanding:

> The United States understands that, in order to constitute torture, an act must be a deliberate and calculated act of an extremely cruel and inhuman nature, specifically intended to inflict excruciating and agonizing physical or mental pain or suffering.

S. Treaty Doc. No. 100-20, at 4-5. Focusing on the treaty's requirement of "severity," the Reagan administration, concluded, "The extreme nature of torture is further emphasized in [this] requirement." S. Treaty Doc. No. 100-20, at 3 (1988); S. Exec. Rep. 101-30, at 13 (1990). The Reagan administration also determined that CAT's definition of torture fell in line with "United States and international usage, [where it] is usually reserved for extreme deliberate and unusually cruel practices, for example, sustained systematic beatings, application, of electric currents to sensitive parts of the body and tying up or hanging in positions that cause extreme pain." S. Exec. Rep. No. 101-30, at 14 (1990). In interpreting CAT's definition of torture as reaching only such extreme acts, the Reagan administration underscored the distinction between torture and other cruel, inhuman, or degrading treatment or punishment. In particular, the administration declared that article 1's definition of torture ought to be construed in light of article 16. See S. Treaty Doc. No. 100-20, at 3. Based on this distinction, the administration concluded that: "'Torture' is thus to be distinguished from lesser forms of cruel, inhuman, or degrading treatment or punishment, which are to be deplored and prevented, but are not so universally and categorically condemned as to warrant the severe legal consequences that the Convention provides in case of torture." S. Treaty Doc. 100-20, at 3. Moreover, this distinction was "adopted in order to emphasize that torture is at the extreme end of cruel, inhuman and degrading treatment or punishment." S. Treaty Doc. No. 100-20, at 3. Given the extreme nature of torture, the administration concluded that "rough treatment as generally falls into the category of 'police brutality,' while deplorable, does not amount to 'torture.'" S. Treaty Doc. No. 100-20, at 4.

Although the Reagan administration relied on CAT's distinction between torture and "cruel, inhuman, or degrading treatment or punishment," it viewed the phrase "cruel, inhuman, or degrading treatment or punishment" as vague and lacking in a universally accepted meaning. Of even greater concern to the Reagan administration was that because of its vagueness this phrase could be construed to bar acts not prohibited by the U.S. Constitution. The administration pointed to Case of *X v. Federal Republic of Germany* as the basis for this concern. In that case, the European Court of Human Rights determined that the prison officials' refusal to recognize a prisoner's sex change might constitute degrading treatment. See S. Treaty Doc. No. 100-20, at 15 (citing European Commission on Human Rights, Dec. on Adm., Dec. 15, 1977, Case of *X v. Federal Republic of Germany* (No. 6694/74), 11 Dec. & Rep. 16)). As a result of this concern, the Administration added the following understanding:

"The United States understands the term, 'cruel, inhuman or degrading treatment or punishment,' as used in Article 16 of the Convention, to mean the cruel, unusual, and inhumane treatment or punishment prohibited by the Fifth, Eighth and/or Fourteenth Amendments to the Constitution of the United States."

S. Treaty Doc. No. 100-20, at 15-16. Treatment or punishment must therefore rise to the level of action that U.S. courts have found to be in violation of the U.S. Constitution in order to constitute cruel, inhuman, or degrading treatment or punishment. That which fails to rise to this level must fail, a fortiori, to constitute torture under Section 2340.

The Senate did not give its advice and consent to the Convention until the first Bush administration. Although using less vigorous rhetoric, the Bush administration joined the Reagan administration in interpreting torture as only reaching extreme acts. To ensure that the Convention's reach remained limited, the Bush administration submitted the following understanding:

The United States understands that, in order to constitute torture, an act must be specifically intended to inflict severe physical or mental pain or suffering and that mental pain or suffering refers to prolonged mental pain caused by or resulting from (1) the intentional infliction or threatened infliction of severe physical pain or suffering; (2) administration or application, or threatened administration or application, of mind altering substances or other procedures calculated to disrupt profoundly the senses or the personality; (3) the threat of imminent death; or (4) the threat that another parson will imminently be subjected to death, severe physical pain or suffering, or the administration or application of mind-altering substances or other procedures calculated to disrupt profoundly the senses or personality.

S. Exec. Rep. No. 101-30, at 36. This understanding accomplished two things. First, it ensured that the term "intentionally" would be understood as requiring specific intent. Second, it added form and substance to the otherwise amorphous concept of mental pain or suffering. In so doing, this understanding ensured that mental torture would rise to a severity seen in the context of physical torture. The Senate ratified CAT with this understanding, and as is obvious from the text, Congress codified this understanding almost verbatim in the criminal statute.

To be sure, it might be thought significant that the Bush administration's language differs from the Reagan administration understanding. The Bush administration said that it had altered the CAT understanding in response to criticism that the Reagan administration's original formulation had raised the bar for the level of pain necessary for the act or acts to constitute torture. See Convention Against Torture: Hearing Before the Senate Comm. On Foreign Relations, 101st Cong. 9-10 (1990) ("1990 Hearing") (prepared statement of Hon. Abraham D. Sofaer, Legal Adviser, Department of State). While it is true that there are rhetorical differences between the understandings, both administrations consistently emphasize the extraordinary or extreme acts required to constitute torture. As we have seen, the Bush understanding as codified in Section 2340 reaches only extreme acts. The Reagan understanding, like the Bush understanding, ensured that "intentionally" would be understood as a specific intent requirement. Though the Reagan administration required that the "act be deliberate and calculated" and that it be inflicted with specific intent, in operation there is little difference between requiring specific intent alone and requiring that the act be deliberate and calculated. The Reagan understanding also made express what is obvious from the plain text of CAT: torture is an extreme form of cruel and inhuman treatment. The Reagan administration's understanding that the pain be "excruciating and agonizing" is in substance not different from the Bush administration's proposal that the pain must be severe.

The Bush understanding simply took a rather abstract concept—excruciating and agonizing mental pain—and gave it a more concrete form. Executive branch representations made to the Senate support our view that there was little difference between these two understandings and that the further definition of mental pain or suffering merely sought remove the vagueness created by concept of "agonizing and excruciating" mental pain. See 1990 Hearing, at 10 (prepared statement of Hon. Abraham D. Sofaer, Legal Adviser, Department of State) ("no higher standard was intended" by the Reagan administration understanding than was present in the Convention or the Bush understanding); id. at 13-14 (statement of Mark Richard, Deputy Assistant Attorney General; Criminal Division, Department of Justice) ("In an effort to overcome this unacceptable element of vagueness [in the term 'mental pain'], we have proposed an understanding which defines severe mental pain constituting torture with sufficient specificity ... to protect innocent persons and meet constitutional due process requirements.")

Accordingly, we believe that the two definitions submitted by the Reagan and Bush administrations had the same purpose in terms of articulating a legal standard, namely, ensuring that the prohibition against torture reaches only the most extreme acts. Ultimately, whether the Reagan standard would have been even higher is a purely academic question because the Bush understanding clearly established a very high standard.

Executive branch representations made to the Senate confirm that the Bush administration maintained the view that torture encompassed only the most extreme acts. Although the ratification record, i.e., testimony, hearings, and the like, is generally not accorded great weight in interpreting treaties, authoritative statements made by representatives of the Executive Branch are accorded the most interpretive value. See Sofaer Memorandum, at 35-36. Hence, the testimony of the executive branch witnesses defining torture, in addition to the reservations, understandings and declarations that were submitted to the Senate by the Executive branch, should carry the highest interpretive value of any of the statements in the ratification record. At the Senate hearing on CAT, Mark Richard, Deputy Assistant Attorney General, Criminal Division, Department of Justice, offered extensive testimony as to the meaning of torture. Echoing the analysis submitted by the Reagan administration, he testified that "[t]orture is understood to be that barbaric cruelty which lies at the top of the pyramid of human rights misconduct," 1990 Hearing, at 16 (prepared statement of Mark Richard). He further explained, "As applied to physical torture, there appears to be some degree of consensus that the concept involves conduct, the mere mention of which sends chills down one's spine[.]" Id. Richard gave the following examples of conduct satisfying this standard: "the needle under the fingernail, the application of electrical shock to the genital area, the piercing of eyeballs, etc." Id. In short, repeating virtually verbatim the terms used in the Reagan understanding, Richard explained that under the Bush administration's submissions with the treaty "the essence of torture" is treatment that inflicts "excruciating and agonizing physical pain." Id.

As to mental torture, Richard testified that "no international consensus had emerged [as to] what degree of mental suffering is required to constitute torture[,]" but that it was nonetheless clear that severe mental pain or suffering "does not encompass the normal legal compulsions which are properly a part of the criminal justice system[:] interrogation, incarceration, prosecution, compelled testimony against a friend, etc,—notwithstanding the fact that they may have the incidental effect of producing mental strain." Id. at 17. According to Richard, CAT was intended to "condemn as torture intentional acts such as those designed to damage and destroy the human personality." Id. at 14. This description of mental suffering emphasizes the requirement that any mental harm be of significant duration and lends further support for our conclusion that mind-altering substances must have a profoundly disruptive effect to serve as a predicate act.

Apart from statements from Executive branch officials, the rest of a ratification record is of little weight in interpreting a treaty. See generally Sofaer Memorandum. Nonetheless, the Senate understanding of the definition of torture largely echoes the administrations' views. The Senate Foreign Relations Committee Report on CAT opined: "[f]or an act to be 'torture' it must be an extreme form of cruel and inhuman treatment, cause severe pain and suffering and be intended to cause severe pain and suffering." S. Exec. Rep. No. 101-30, at 6. Moreover, like both the Reagan and Bush administrations, the Senate drew upon the distinction between torture and cruel, inhuman or degrading treatment or punishment in reaching its view that torture was extreme. Finally, the Senate concurred with the administrations' concern that "cruel, inhuman, or degrading treatment or punishment" could be construed to establish a new standard above and beyond that which the Constitution mandates and supported the inclusion of the reservation establishing the Constitution as the baseline for determining whether conduct amounted to cruel, inhuman, degrading treatment or punishment. See 136 Cong. Rec. 36,192 (1990); S. Exec. Rep. 101-30, at 39.

◆ B. Negotiating History

CAT's negotiating history also indicates that its definition of torture supports our reading of Section 2340. The state parties endeavored to craft a definition of torture that reflected the term's gravity. During the negotiations, state parties offered various formulations of the definition of torture to the working group, which then proposed a definition based on those formulations. Almost all of these suggested definitions illustrate the consensus that torture is an extreme act designed to cause agonizing pain. For example, the United States proposed that torture be defined as "includ[ing] any act by which extremely severe pain or suffering … is deliberately and mali-

ciously inflicted on a person." J. Herman Burgees & Hans Danelius, The United Nations Convention Against Torture: A Handbook on the Convention Against Torture and Other Cruel Inhuman and Degrading Treatment or Punishment 41 (1988) ("CAT Handbook"). The United Kingdom suggested an even more restrictive definition, i.e., that torture be defined as the "systematic and intentional infliction of extreme pain or suffering rather than intentional infliction of severe pain or suffering." Id. at 45. Ultimately, in choosing the phrase "severe pain," the parties concluded that this phrase "sufficient[ly]… convey[ed] the idea that only acts of a certain gravity shall … constitute torture." Id. at 117.

In crafting such a definition, the state parties also were acutely aware of the distinction they drew between torture and cruel, inhuman, or degrading treatment or punishment. The state parties considered and rejected a proposal that would have defined torture merely as cruel, inhuman or degrading treatment or punishment. See Id. at 42. Mirroring the Declaration on Protection From Torture, which expressly defined torture as an "aggravated and deliberate form of cruel, inhuman or degrading treatment or punishment," some state parties proposed that in addition to the definition of torture set out in paragraph 2 of article 1, a paragraph defining torture as "an aggravated and deliberate form of cruel, inhuman or degrading treatment or punishment" should be included. See Id. at 41; see also S. Treaty Doc. No. 100-20, at 2 (the U.N. Declaration on Protection from Torture (1975) served as "a point of departure for the drafting of [CAT]"). In the end, the parties concluded that the addition, of such a paragraph was superfluous because Article 16 "impl[ies] that torture is the gravest form of such treatment or punishment." CAT Handbook at 80; see S. Exec. Rep. No. 101-30, at 13 ("The negotiating history indicates that [the phrase 'which do not amount to torture'] was adopted in order to emphasize that torture is at the extreme end of cruel, inhuman and degrading treatment or punishment and that Article 1 should be construed with this in mind").

Additionally, the parties could not reach a consensus about the meaning of "cruel, inhuman, or degrading treatment or punishment." See CAT Handbook at 47. Without a consensus, the parties viewed the term as simply "too vague to be included in a convention which was to form the basis for criminal legislation in the Contracting States." Id. This view evinced by the parties reaffirms the interpretation of CAT as purposely reserving criminal penalties for torture alone.

CAT's negotiating history offers more than just support for the view that pain or suffering must be extreme to amount to torture. First, the negotiating history suggests that the harm sustained from the acts of torture need not be permanent. In fact, "the United States considered that it might be useful to develop the negotiating history which indicates that although conduct resulting in permanent impairment of physical or mental faculties is indicative of torture, it is not an essential element of the offence." Id. at 44. Second, the state parties to CAT rejected a proposal to include in CAT's definition of torture the use of truth drugs, where no physical harm or mental suffering was apparent. This rejection at least suggests that such drugs were not viewed as amounting to torture per se. See Id. at 42.

◆ C. Summary

The text of CAT confirms our conclusion that Section 2340A was intended to proscribe only the most egregious conduct. CAT not only defines torture as involving severe pain and suffering, but also it makes clear that such pain and suffering is at the extreme end of the spectrum of acts by reserving criminal penalties solely for torture. Executive interpretations confirm our view that the treaty (and hence the statute) prohibits only the worst forms of cruel, inhuman, or degrading treatment or punishment. The ratification history further substantiates this interpretation. Even the negotiating history displays a recognition that torture is a step far-removed from other cruel, inhuman or degrading treatment or punishment. In sum, CAT's text, ratification history and negotiating history all confirm that Section 2340A reaches only the most heinous acts.

III. U.S. Judicial Interpretation

There are no reported cases of prosecutions under Section 2340A. See Beth Stephens, Corporate Liability: Enforcing Human Rights Through Domestic Litigation, 24 Hastings Int'l & Comp. L. Rev. 401, 408 & n.29 (2001); Beth Van Schaack, In Defense of Civil Redress: The Domestic Enforcement of Human Rights Norms in the Context of the Proposed Hague Judgments Convention, 42 Harv. Int'l L. J. 141, 148-49 (2001); Curtis A. Bradley, Universal Jurisdiction and U.S. Law, 2001 U. Chi. Legal F. 323, 327-28. Nonetheless, we are not without guidance as to how United States courts would approach the question of what conduct constitutes torture. Civil suits filed under the Torture Victim Protection Act ("TVPA"), 28 U.S.C. § 1350 note (2000), which supplies a tort remedy for victims of torture, provide insight into what acts U.S. courts would conclude constitute torture under the criminal statute.

The TVPA contains a definition similar in some key respects to the one set forth in Section 2340. Moreover, as with Section 2340, Congress intended for the TVPA's definition of torture to follow closely the definition found in CAT. See *Xuncax v. Gramajo*, 886 F. Supp. 162, 176 n.12 (D. Mass. 1995) (noting that the definition of torture in the TVPA tracks the definitions in Section 2340 and CAT). The TVPA defines torture as: (1)... any act, directed against an individual in the offender's custody or physical control, by which severe pain or suffering (other than pain or suffering arising only from or inherent in, or incidental to, lawful sanctions), whether physical or mental, is intentionally inflicted on that individual for such purposes as obtaining from that individual or a third person information or a confession, punishing that individual for an act that individual or a third person has committed or is suspected of having committed, intimidating or coercing that individual or a thud person, or for any reason based on discrimination of any kind; and (2) mental pain or suffering refers to prolonged mental harm caused by or resulting from—(A) the intentional infliction or threatened infliction of severe physical pain or suffering; (B) the administration or application, or threatened administration or application, of mind altering substances or other procedures calculated to disrupt profoundly the senses or the personality; (C) the threat of imminent death; or (D) the threat that another individual will imminently be subjected to death, severe physical pain or suffering, or the administration or application of mind altering substances or other procedures calculated to disrupt profoundly the senses or personality.

28 U.S.C. § 1350 note § 3(b). This definition differs from Section 2340's definition in two respects. First, the TVPA definition contains an illustrative list of purposes for which such pain may have been inflicted. See id. Second, the TVPA includes the phrase "arising only from or inherent in, or incidental to lawful sanctions"; by contrast, Section 2340 refers only to pain or suffering "incidental to lawful sanctions," Id. Because the purpose of our analysis here is to ascertain acts that would cross the threshold of producing "severe physical or mental pain or suffering," the list of illustrative purposes for which it is inflicted, generally would not affect this analysis.

Similarly, to the extent that the absence of the phrase "arising only from or inherent in" from Section 2340 might affect the question of whether pain or suffering was part of lawful sanctions and thus not torture, the circumstances with which we are concerned here are solely that of interrogations, not the imposition of punishment subsequent to judgment. These differences between the TVPA and Section 2340 are therefore not sufficiently significant to undermine the usefulness of TVPA cases here.

In suits brought under the TVPA, courts have not engaged in any lengthy analysis of what acts constitute torture. In part, this is due to the nature of the acts alleged. Almost all of the cases involve physical torture, some of which is of an especially cruel and even sadistic nature. Nonetheless, courts appear to look at the entire coarse of conduct rather than any one act, making it somewhat akin to a totality-of-the-circumstances analysis. Because of this approach, it is difficult to take a specific act out of context and conclude that the act in isolation would constitute torture. Certain acts do, however, consistently reappear in these cases or are of such a barbaric nature, that it is likely a court would find that allegations of such treatment would constitute torture: (1) severe beatings using instruments such as iron barks {sic: bars}, truncheons, and clubs; (2) threats of imminent death, such as mock executions; (3) threats of removing extremities; (4) burning, especially burning with cigarettes; (5) electric shocks to genitalia or threats to do so; (6) rape or sexual assault, or injury to an individual's sexual organs, or threatening to do any of these sorts of acts; and (7) forcing the prisoner to watch the torture of others. Given the highly contextual nature of whether a set of acts constitutes torture, we have set forth in the attached appendix the circumstances in which courts have determined that the plaintiff has suffered torture, which include the cases from which these seven acts are drawn. While we cannot say with certainty that acts falling short of these seven would not constitute torture under Section 2340, we believe that interrogation techniques would have to be similar to these in their extreme nature and in the type of harm caused to violate the law.

Despite the limited analysis engaged in by courts, a recent district court opinion provides some assistance in predicting how future courts might address this issue. In *Mehinovic v. Vuckovic*, 198 F. Supp. 2d 1322 (N.D. Ga. 2002), the plaintiffs, Bosnian Muslims, sued a Bosnian Serb, Nikola Vuckovic, for, among other things, torture and cruel and inhumane treatment. The court described in vivid detail the treatment the plaintiffs endured. Specifically, the plaintiffs experienced the following:

Vuckovic repeatedly beat Kemal Mehinovic with a variety of blunt objects and boots, intentionally delivering blows to areas he knew to already be badly injured, including Mehinovic's genitals. Id. at 1333-34. On some occasions he was tied up and hung against windows during beatings. Id. Mehinovic was subjected to the game of "Russian roulette" See id. Vuckovic, along with other guards, also forced Mehinovic to run in a circle while the guards swung wooden planks at him. Id.

Like Mehinovic, Muhamed Bicic was beaten repeatedly with blunt objects, to the point of loss of consciousness. See id. at 1335. He witnessed the severe beatings of other prisoners, including his own brother. "On one occasion, Vuckovic ordered Bicic to get on all fours while another soldier stood or rode on his back and beat him with a baton—a game the soldiers called 'horse.'" Id. Bicic, like Mehinovic, was subjected to the game of Russian roulette. Additionally, Vuckovic and the other guards forcibly extracted a number of Bicic's teeth. Id. at 1336.

Safet Hadzialijagic was subjected to daily beatings with "metal pipes, bats, sticks, and weapons." Id. at 1337. He was also subjected to Russian roulette. See id. at 1336-37. Hadzialijagic also frequently saw other prisoners being beaten or heard their screams as they were beaten. Like Bicic, he was subjected to the teeth extraction incident On one occasion, Vuckovic rode Hadzialijagic like a horse, simultaneously hitting him in the head and body with a knife handle. During this time, other soldiers kicked and hit him. He fell down during this episode and was forced to get up and continue carrying Vuckovic. See id. "Vuckovic and the other soldiers [then] tied Hadzialijagic with a rope, hung him upside down, and beat him. When they noticed that Hadzialijagic was losing consciousness, they dunked his head in a bowl used as a toilet." Id. Vockovic then forced Hadzialijagic to lick the blood off of Vnckovic's boots and kicked Hadzialijagic as he tried to do so. Vuckovic then used his knife to carve a semi-circle in Hadzialijagic's forehead. Hadzialijagic went into cardiac arrest just after this incident and was saved by one of the other plaintiffs. See id.

Hasan Subasic was brutally beaten and witnessed the beatings of other prisoners, including the beating and death of one of his fellow prisoners and the beating of Hadzialijagic in which he was tied upside down and beaten. See id. at 1338-39. Id. at 1338.

Subasic also was subjected to the teeth pulling incident. Vuckovic personally beat Subasic two times, punching him and kicking him with his military boots. In one of these beatings, "Subasic had been forced into a kneeling position when Vuckovic kicked him in the stomach." Id.

The district court concluded that the plaintiffs suffered both physical and mental torture at the hands of Vuckovic. With respect to physical torture, the court broadly outlined with respect to each plaintiff the acts in which Vuckovic had been at least complicit and that it found rose to the level of torture. Regarding Mehinovic, the court determined that Vuckovic's beatings of Mehinovic in which he kicked and delivered other blows to Mehinovic's face, genitals, and others body parts, constituted torture. The court noted that these beatings left Mehinovic disfigured, may have broken ribs, almost caused Mehinovic to lose consciousness, and rendered him unable to eat for a period of time. As to Bicic, the court found that Bicic had suffered severe physical pain and suffering as a result of Vuckovic's repeated beatings of him in which Vuckovic used various instruments to inflict blows, the "horse" game, and the teeth pulling incident. See id. at 1346. In finding that Vuckovic inflicted severe physical pain on Hadzialijagic, the court unsurprisingly focused on the beating in which Vuckovic tied Hadzialijagic upside down and beat him. See id. The court pointed out that in this incident, Vuckovic almost killed Hadzialijagic. See id. The court further concluded that Subasic experienced severe physical pain and thus was tortured based on the beating in which Vuckovic kicked Subasic in the stomach. See id.

The court also found that the plaintiffs had suffered severe mental pain. In reaching this conclusion, the court relied on the plaintiffs' testimony that they feared they would be killed during beatings by Vuckovic or daring the "game" of Russian roulette. Although the court did not specify the predicate acts that caused the prolonged mental harm, it is plain that both the threat of severe physical pain and the threat of imminent death were present and persistent. The court also found that the plaintiffs established the existence of prolonged mental harm as each plaintiff "continues to suffer long-term psychological harm as a result of [their] ordeals." Id. In concluding that the plaintiffs had demonstrated the necessary "prolonged mental harm," the court's description of that harm as ongoing and "long-term" confirms that, to satisfy the prolonged mental harm requirement, the harm must be of a substantial duration.

The court did not, however, delve into the nature of psychological harm in reaching its conclusion. Nonetheless, the symptoms that the plaintiffs suffered and continue to suffer are worth noting as illustrative of what might in future cases be held to constitute mental harm. Mehinovic had "anxiety, flashbacks, and nightmares and has difficulty sleeping." Id. at 1334. Similarly, Bicic, "suffers from anxiety, sleeps very little, and has frequent nightmares" and experiences frustration at not being able to work due to the physical and mental pain he suffers. Id. at 1336. Hadzialijagic experienced nightmares, at times required medication to help him sleep, suffered from depression, and had become reclusive as a result of his ordeal. See id. at 1337-38. Subasic, like the others, had nightmares and flashbacks, but also suffered from nervousness, irritability, and experienced difficulty trusting people. The combined effect of these symptoms impaired Subasic's ability to work. See id. at 1340. Each of these plaintiffs suffered from mental harm that destroyed his ability to function normally, on a daily basis, and would continue to do so into the future.

In general, several guiding principles can be drawn from this case. First, this case illustrates that a single incident can constitute torture. The above recitation of the case's facts shows that Subasic was clearly subjected to torture in a number of instances, e.g., the teeth pulling incident, which the court finds to constitute torture in discussing Bicac. The court nevertheless found that the beating in which Vuckovic delivered a blow to Subasic's stomach while he was on his knees sufficed to establish that Subasic had been tortured. Indeed, the court stated that this incident "caus[ed] Subasic to suffer severe pain." Id. at 1346. The court's focus on this incident, despite the obvious context of a course of torturous conduct, suggests that a course of conduct is unnecessary to establish that an individual engaged in torture. It bears noting, however, that there are no decisions that have found an example of torture on facts that show the action was isolated, rather than part of a systematic course of conduct. Moreover, we believe that had this been an isolated instance, the court's conclusion that this act constituted torture would have been in error, because this single blow does not reach the requisite level of severity.

Second, the case demonstrates that courts may be willing to find that a wide range of physical pain can rise to the necessary level of "severe pain or suffering." At one end of the spectrum is what the court calls the "nightmarish beating" in which Vuckovic hung Hadzialijagic upside down and beat him, culminating in Hadzialijagic going into cardiac arrest and narrowly escaping death. Id. It takes little analysis or insight to conclude that this incident constitutes torture. At the other end of the spectrum, is the court's determination that a beating in which "Vuckovic hit plaintiff Subasic and kicked him in the stomach with his military boots while Subasic was forced into a kneeling position" constituted torture. Id. To be sure, this beating caused Subasic substantial pain. But that pain pales in comparison to the other acts described in this case. Again, to the extent the opinion can be read to endorse the view that this single act and the attendant pain, considered in isolation, rose to the level of "severe pain or suffering," we would disagree with such a view based on our interpretation of the criminal statute.

The district court did not attempt to delineate the meaning of torture. It engaged in no statutory analysis. Instead, the court merely recited the definition and described the acts that it concluded constituted torture. This approach is representative of the approach most often taken in TVPA cases. The adoption of such an approach suggests that torture generally is of such an extreme nature—namely, the nature of acts are so shocking and obviously incredibly painful—that courts will more likely examine the totality of the circumstances, rather than engage in a careful parsing of the statute. A broad view of this case, and of the TVPA cases more generally, shows that only acts of an extreme nature have been redressed under the TVPA's civil remedy for torture. We note, however, that Mehinovic presents, with the exception of the single blow to Subasic, facts that are well over the line of what constitutes torture. While there are cases that fall far short of torture, see infra app., there are no cases that analyze what the lowest boundary of what constitutes torture. Nonetheless, while this case and the other TVPA cases generally do not approach that boundary, they are in keeping with the general notion that the term "torture" is reserved for acts of the most extreme nature.

IV. International Decisions

International decisions can prove of some value in assessing what conduct might rise to the level of severe mental pain or suffering. Although decisions by foreign or international bodies are in no way binding authority upon the United States, they provide guidance about how other nations will likely react to our interpretation of the CAT and Section 2340. As this Part will discuss, other Western nations have generally used a high standard in determining whether interrogation techniques violate the international prohibition on torture. In fact, these decisions have found various aggressive interrogation methods to, at worst, constitute cruel, inhuman, and degrading treatment, but not torture. These decisions only reinforce our view that there is a clear distinction between the two standards and that only extreme conduct, resulting in pain that is of an intensity often accompanying serious physical injury, will violate the latter.

◆ A. European Court of Human Rights

An analogue to CAT's provisions can be found in the European Convention on Human Rights and Fundamental Freedoms (the "European Convention"). This convention prohibits torture, though it offers no definition of it. It also prohibits cruel, inhuman, or degrading treatment or punishment. By barring both types of acts, the European Convention implicitly distinguishes between them and further suggests that torture is a grave act beyond cruel, inhuman, or degrading treatment or punishment. Thus, while neither the European Convention nor the European Court of Human Rights decisions interpreting that convention would be authority for the interpretation of Sections 2340-2340A, the European Convention decisions concerning torture nonetheless provide a useful barometer of the international view of what actions amount to torture.

The leading European Court of Human Rights case explicating the differences between torture and cruel, inhuman, or degrading treatment or punishment is *Ireland v. the United Kingdom* (1978). In that case, the European Court of Human Rights examined interrogation techniques somewhat more sophisticated than the rather rudimentary and frequently obviously cruel acts described in the TVPA cases. Careful attention to this case is worthwhile not just because it examines methods not used in the TVPA cases, but also because the Reagan administration relied on this case in reaching the conclusion that the term torture is reserved in international usage for "extreme, deliberate, and unusually cruel practices." S. Treaty Doc. 100-20, at 4.

The methods at issue in Ireland were: (1) Wall Standing. The prisoner stands spread eagle against the wall, with fingers high above his head, and feet back so that he is standing on his toes such that his all of his weight falls on his fingers. (2) Hooding. A black or navy hood is placed over the prisoner's head and kept there except during the interrogation. (3) Subjection to Noise. Pending interrogation, the prisoner is kept in a room with a loud and continuous hissing noise. (4) Sleep Deprivation. Prisoners are deprived of sleep pending interrogation. (5) Deprivation of Food and Drink. Prisoners receive a reduced diet during detention and pending interrogation.

The European Court of Human Rights concluded that these techniques used in combination, and applied for hours at a time, were inhuman and degrading but did not amount to torture. In analyzing whether these methods constituted torture, the court treated them as part of a single program. See Ireland, § 104. The court found that this program caused "if not actual bodily injury, at least intense physical and mental suffering to the person subjected thereto and also led to acute psychiatric disturbances daring the interrogation." Id. § 167. Thus, this program "fell into the category of inhuman treatment[.]" Id. The court further found that "[t]he techniques were also degrading since they were such as to arouse in their victims feeling of fear, anguish and inferiority capable of humiliating and debasing them and possible [sic] breaking their physical or moral resistance." Id. Yet, the court ultimately concluded:

> Although the five techniques, as applied in combination, undoubtedly amounted to inhuman and degrading treatment, although their object was the extraction of confession, the naming of others and/or information and although they were used systematically, they did not occasion suffering of the particular intensity and cruelty implied by the word torture....

Id. Thus, even though the court had concluded that the techniques produce "intense physical and mental suffering" and "acute psychiatric disturbances," they were not sufficient intensity or cruelty to amount to torture.

The court reached this conclusion based on the distinction the European Convention drew between torture and cruel, inhuman, or degrading treatment or punishment. The court reasoned that by expressly distinguishing between these two categories of treatment, the European Convention sought to "attach a special stigma to deliberate inhuman treatment causing very serious and cruel suffering." Id. § 167. According to the court, "this distinction derives principally from a difference in the intensity of the suffering inflicted." Id. The court further noted that this distinction paralleled the one drawn in the U.N. Declaration on the Protection From Torture, which specifically defines torture as "an aggravated and deliberate form of cruel, inhuman or degrading treatment or punishment." Id. (quoting UN. Declaration on the Protection From Torture).

The court relied on this same "intensity/cruelty" distinction to conclude that some physical maltreatment fails to amount to torture. For example, four detainees were severely beaten and forced to stand spread eagle up against a wall. See id. § 110. Other detainees were forced to stand spread eagle while an interrogator kicked them "continuously on the inside of the legs." Id. § 111. Those detainees were beaten, some receiving injuries that were "substantial" and others received "massive" injuries. See id. Another detainee was "subjected to ... 'comparatively trivial' beatings" that resulted in a perforation of the detainee's eardrum and some "minor bruising." Id. § 115. The court concluded that none of these situations "attain[ed] the particular level [of severity] inherent in the notion of torture." Id. § 174.

◆ **B. Israel Supreme Court**

The European Court of Human Rights is not the only other court to consider whether such a program of interrogation techniques was permissible. In Public Committee Against Torture in *Israel v. Israel*, 38 LLM 1471 (1999), the Supreme Court of Israel reviewed a challenge brought against the General Security Service ("GSS") for its use of five techniques. At issue in Public Committee Against Torture In Israel were: (1) shaking, (2) the Shabach, (3) the Frog Crouch, (4) the excessive tightening of handcuffs, and (5) sleep deprivation. "Shaking" is "the forceful shaking of the suspect's upper torso, back and forth, repeatedly, in a manner which causes the neck and head to dangle and vacillate rapidly." Id. § 9. The "Shabach" is actually a combination of methods wherein the detainee is seated on a small and low chair, whose seat is tilted forward, towards the ground. One hand is tied behind the suspect, and placed inside the gap between the chair's seat and back support. His second hand is tied behind the chair, against its back support. The suspect's head is covered by an opaque sack, failing down to his shoulders. Powerfully loud music is played in the room. Id. § 10.

The "frog crouch'" consists of "consecutive, periodical crouches on the tips of one's toes, each lasting for five minute intervals." Id. § 11. The excessive tightening of handcuffs simply referred to the use {of} handcuffs that were too small for the suspects' wrists. See id. § 12. Sleep deprivation occurred when the Shabach was used during "intense non-stop interrogations." Id. § 13.

While the Israeli Supreme Court concluded that these acts amounted to cruel, and inhuman treatment, the court did not expressly find that they amounted to torture. To be sure, such a conclusion was unnecessary because even if the acts amounted only to cruel and inhuman treatment the GSS lacked authority to use the five methods. Nonetheless, the decision is still best read as indicating that the acts at issue did not constitute torture. The court's descriptions of and conclusions about each method indicate that the court viewed them as merely cruel, inhuman or degrading but not of the sufficient severity to reach the threshold of torture. While its descriptions discuss necessity, dignity, degradation, and pain, the court carefully avoided describing any of these acts as having the seventy of pain or suffering indicative of torture. See id. at §§ 24-29. Indeed, in assessing the Shabach as a whole, the court even relied upon the European Court of Human Right's Ireland decision, for support and it did not evince disagreement with that decision's conclusion that the acts considered therein did not constitute torture. See id. § 30.

Moreover, the Israeli Supreme Court concluded that in certain circumstances GSS officers could assert a necessity defense. CAT, however, expressly provides that "[n]o exceptional circumstance whatsoever, whether a state of war or a threat of war, internal political instability or any other public emergency may be invoked as a justification of torture." Art 2(2). Had the court been of the view that the GSS methods constituted torture, the Court could not permit this affirmative defense under CAT. Accordingly, the court's decision is best read as concluding that these methods amounted to cruel and inhuman treatment, but not torture.

In sum, both the European Court on Human Rights and the Israeli Supreme Court have recognized a wide array of acts that constitute cruel, inhuman, or degrading treatment or punishment, but do not amount to torture. Thus, they appear to permit, under international law, an aggressive interpretation as to what amounts to torture, leaving that label to be applied only where extreme circumstances exist.

V. The President's Commander-in-Chief Power

Even if an interrogation method arguably were to violate Section 2340A, the statute would be unconsti-

tutional if it impermissibly encroached on the President's constitutional power to conduct a military campaign. As Commander-in-Chief, the President has the constitutional authority to order interrogations of enemy combatants to gain intelligence information concerning the military plans of the enemy. The demands of the Commander-in-Chief power are especially pronounced in the middle of a war in which the nation has already suffered a direct attack. In such a case, the information gained from interrogations may prevent future attacks by foreign enemies. Any effort to apply Section 2340A in a manner that interferes with the President's direction of such core war matters as the detention and interrogation of enemy combatants thus would be unconstitutional.

◆ A. The War with Al Qaeda

At the outset, we should make clear the nature of the threat presently posed to the nation. While your request for legal advice is not specifically limited to the current circumstances, we think it is useful to discuss this question in the context of the current war against the al Qaeda terrorist network. The situation in which these issues arise is unprecedented in recent American history. Four coordinated terrorist attacks, using hijacked commercial airliners as guided missiles, took place in rapid succession on the morning of September 11, 2001. These attacks were aimed at critical government buildings in the Nation's capital and landmark buildings in its financial center. These events reach a different scale of destructiveness than earlier terrorist episodes, such as the destruction of the Murrah Building in Oklahoma City in 1994. They caused thousands of deaths. Air traffic and communications within the United States were disrupted; national stock exchanges were shut for several days; and damage from the attack has been estimated to run into the tens of billions of dollars. Moreover, these attacks are part of a violent campaign against the United States that is believed to include an unsuccessful attempt to destroy an airliner in December 2001; a suicide bombing attack in Yemen on the U.S.S. Cole in 2000; the bombings of the United States Embassies in Kenya and in Tanzania in 1998; a truck bomb attack on a U.S. military housing complex in Saudi Arabia in 1996; an unsuccessful attempt to destroy the World Trade Center in 1993; and the ambush of U.S. servicemen in Somalia in 1993. The United States and its overseas personnel and installations have been attacked as a result of Usama Bin Laden's call for a "jihad against the U.S.

government, because the U.S. government is unjust, criminal and tyrannical."

In response, the Government has engaged in a broad effort at home and abroad to counter terrorism. Pursuant to his authorities as Commander-in-Chief, the President in October, 2001, ordered the Armed Forces to attack al Qaeda personnel and assets in Afghanistan, and the Taliban militia that harbored them. That military campaign appears to be nearing its close with the retreat of al Qaeda and Taliban forces from their strongholds and the installation of a friendly provisional government in Afghanistan. Congress has provided its support for the use of forces against those linked to the September 11 attacks, and has recognized the President's constitutional power to use force to prevent and deter future attacks both within and outside the United States. S. J. Res. 23, Pub. L. No. 107-40, 115 Stat. 224 (2001). [The next 12 lines of type are crossed out on the original memo.] The Justice Department and the FBI have launched a sweeping investigation in response to the September 11 attacks, and last fall Congress enacted legislation to expand the Justice Department's powers of surveillance against terrorists. See The USA Patriot Act, Pub. L. No. 107-56, 115 Stat. 272 (Oct. 26, 2001). This spring, the President proposed the creation of a new cabinet department for homeland security to implement a coordinated domestic program against terrorism.

Despite these efforts, numerous upper echelon leaders of al Qaeda and the Taliban, with access to active terrorist cells and other resources, remain at large. It has been reported that the al Qaeda fighters are already drawing on a fresh flow of cash to rebuild their forces. See Paul Haven, U.S.: al-Qaida Trying to Regroup, Associated Press, Mar. 20, 2002. As the Director of the Central Intelligence Agency has recently testified before Congress, "Al-Qa'ida and other terrorist groups will continue to plan to attack this country and its interests abroad. Their modus operandi is to have multiple attack plans in the works simultaneously, and to have al-Qa'ida cells in place to conduct them." Testimony of George J. Tenet, Director of Central Intelligence, Before the Senate Armed Services Committee at 2 (Mar. 19, 2002). Nor is the threat contained to Afghanistan. "Operations against US targets could be launched by al-Qa'ida cells already in place in major cities in Europe and the Middle East. Al-Qa'ida can also exploit its presence or connections to other groups in such countries as Somalia, Yemen, Indonesia, and the Philippines." Id. at 3. It appears that al Qaeda continues to enjoy information and resources that allow it to organize and direct active hostile forces against this country, both domestically and abroad.

Al Qaeda continues to plan further attacks, such as destroying American civilian airliners and killing American troops, which have fortunately been prevented. It is clear that bin Laden and his organization have conducted several violent attacks on the United States and its nationals, and that they seek to continue to do so. Thus, the capture and interrogation of such individuals is clearly imperative to our national security and defense. Interrogation of captured al Qaeda operatives may provide information concerning the nature of al Qaeda plans and the identities of its personnel, which may prove invaluable in preventing further direct attacks on the United States and its citizens. Given the massive destruction and loss of life caused by the September 11 attacks, it is reasonable to believe that information gained from al Qaeda personnel could prevent attacks of a similar (if not greater) magnitude from occurring in the United States. The case of Jose Padilla, a.k.a. Abdullah Al Mujabir, illustrates the importance of such information. Padilla allegedly had journeyed to Afghanistan and Pakistan, met with senior al Qaeda leaders, and hatched a plot to construct and detonate a radioactive dispersal device in the United States. After allegedly receiving training in wiring explosives and with a substantial amount of currency in his position {sic: possession}, Padilla attempted in May, 2002, to enter the United States to further his scheme. Interrogation of captured al Qaeda operatives allegedly allowed U.S. intelligence and law enforcement agencies to track Padilla and to detain him upon his entry into the United States.

◆ B. Interpretation to Avoid Constitutional Problems

As the Supreme Court has recognized, and as we will explain further below, the President enjoys complete discretion in the exercise of his Commander-in-Chief authority and in conducting operations against hostile forces. Because both "[t]he executive power and the command of the military and naval forces is vested in the President," the Supreme Court has unanimously stated that it is "the President alone who is constitutionally invested with the entire charge of hostile operations." *Hamilton v. Dillin*, 88 U.S. (21 Wall.) 73, 87 (1874). That authority is at its height in the middle of a war.

In light of the President's complete authority over the conduct of war, without a clear statement otherwise, we will not read a criminal statute as infringing on the President's ultimate authority in these areas. We have long recognized, and the Supreme Court has established a canon of statutory construction that statutes are to be construed in a manner that avoids constitutional difficulties so long as a reasonable alternative construction is available. See, e.g., *Edward J. DeBartolo Corp. v. Florida Gulf Coast Bldg. & Constr. Trades Council*, 485 U.S. 568, 575 (1988) (citing *NLRB v. Catholic Bishop of Chicago*, 440 U.S. 490, 499-501, 504 (1979)) ("[W]here an otherwise acceptable construction of a statute would raise serious constitutional problems, [courts] will construe [a] statute to avoid such problems unless such construction is plainly contrary to the intent of Congress."). This canon of construction applies especially where an act of Congress could be read to encroach upon powers constitutionally committed to a coordinate branch of government. See, e.g., *Franklin v. Massachusetts*, 505 U.S. 788, 800-1 (1992) (citation omitted) ("Out of respect for the separation of powers and the unique constitutional position of the President, we find that textual silence is not enough to subject the President to the provisions of the [Administrative Procedure Act]. We would require an express statement by Congress before assuming it intended the President's performance of his statutory duties to be reviewed for abuse of discretion."); *Public Citizen v. United States Dep't of Justice*, 491 U.S. 440, 465-67 (1989) (construing Federal Advisory Committee Act not to apply to advice given by American Bar Association to the President on judicial nominations, to avoid potential constitutional question regarding encroachment on Presidential power to appoint judges).

In the area of foreign affairs, and war powers in particular, the avoidance canon has special force. See, e.g., *Dep't of Navy v. Egan*, 484 U.S. 518, 530 (1988) ("unless Congress specifically has provided otherwise, courts traditionally have been reluctant to intrude upon the authority of the Executive in military and national security affairs."); *Japan Whaling Ass'n v. American Cetacean Soc'y*, 478 U.S. 221, 232-33 (1986) (construing federal statutes to avoid curtailment of traditional presidential prerogatives in foreign affairs). We do not lightly assume that Congress has acted to interfere with the President's constitutionally superior position as Chief Executive and Commander in Chief in the area of military operations. See Egan, 484 U.S. at 529 (quoting *Haig v. Agee*, 453 U.S. 280, 293-94 (1981)). See also Agee, 453 U.S. at 291 (deference to Executive Branch is "especially" appropriate "in the area … of … national security").

In order to respect the President's inherent constitutional authority to manage a military campaign against al Qaeda and its allies, Section 2340A must be construed as not applying to interrogations undertaken pursuant to his Commander-in-Chief authority. As our Office has consistently held during this Administration and previous Administrations, Congress lacks authority under Article I to set the terms and conditions under which the President may exercise his authority as Commander in Chief to control the conduct of operations daring a war. See, e.g., Memorandum for Daniel J. Bryant, Assistant Attorney General, Office of Legislative Affairs, from Patrick F. Philbin, Deputy Assistant Attorney General, Office of Legal Counsel, Re: Swift Justice Authorization Act (Apr. 8, 2002); Memorandum for Timothy E. Flanigan, Deputy Counsel to the President, from John C. Yoo, Deputy Assistant Attorney General, Office of Legal Counsel, [Two lines of type are crossed out here in the original memo.] Memorandum for Andrew Fois, Assistant Attorney General, Office of Legislative Affairs, from Richard L. Shiffrin, Deputy Assistant Attorney General, Office of Legal Counsel, Re: Defense Authorization Act (Sep. 15, 1995). As we discuss below, the President's power to detain and interrogate enemy combatants arises out of his constitutional authority as Commander in Chief. A construction of Section 2340A that applied the provision to regulate the President's authority as Commander-in-Chief to determine the interrogation and treatment of enemy combatants would raise serious constitutional questions. Congress may no more regulate the President's ability to detain and interrogate enemy combatants than it may regulate his ability to direct troop movements on the battlefield. Accordingly, we would construe Section 2340A to avoid this constitutional difficulty, and conclude that it does not apply to the President's detention and interrogation of enemy combatants pursuant to his Commander-in-Chief authority.

This approach is consistent with previous decisions of our Office involving the application of federal criminal law. For example, we have previously construed the congressional contempt statute not to apply to executive branch officials who refuse to comply with congressional subpoenas because of an assertion of executive privilege. In a published 1984 opinion, we concluded that

if executive officials were subject to prosecution for criminal contempt whenever they carried out the President's claim of executive privilege, it would significantly burden and immeasurably impair the President's ability to fulfill his constitutional duties. Therefore, the separation of powers principles that underlie the doctrine of executive privilege also would preclude an application of the contempt of Congress statute to punish officials for aiding the President in asserting his constitutional privilege.

Prosecution for Contempt of Congress of an Executive Branch Official Who Has Asserted A Claim of Executive Privilege, 8 Op. O.L.C. 101, 134 (May 30, 1984). Likewise, we believe that, if executive officials were subject to prosecution for conducting interrogations when they were carrying out the President's Commander-in-Chief powers, "it would significantly burden and immeasurably impair the President's ability to fulfill his constitutional duties." These constitutional principles preclude an application of Section 2340A to punish officials for aiding the President in exercising his exclusive constitutional authorities. Id.

◆ C. The Commander-in-Chief Power

It could be argued that Congress enacted 18 U.S.C. § 2340A with full knowledge and consideration of the President's Commander-in-Chief power, and that Congress intended to restrict his discretion in the interrogation of enemy combatants. Even were we to accept this argument, however, we conclude that the Department of Justice could not enforce Section 2340A against federal officials acting pursuant to the President's constitutional authority to wage a military campaign.

Indeed, in a different context, we have concluded that both courts and prosecutors should reject prosecutions that apply federal criminal laws to activity that is authorized pursuant to one of the President's constitutional powers. This Office, for example, has previously concluded that Congress could not constitutionally extend the congressional contempt statute to executive branch officials who refuse to comply with congressional subpoenas because of an assertion of executive privilege. We opined that "courts... would surely conclude that a criminal prosecution for the exercise of a presumptively valid, constitutionally based privilege is not consistent with the Constitution." 8 Op. O.LC. at 141 Further, we concluded that the Department of Justice could not bring a criminal prosecution against a defendant who had acted pursuant to an exercise of the President's constitutional power. "The President, through a United States Attorney, need not, indeed may not, prosecute criminally a subordinate for asserting on his behalf a claim of executive privilege. Nor could

the Legislative Branch or the courts require or implement the prosecution of such an individual." Id. Although Congress may define federal crimes that the President, through the Take Care Clause, should prosecute, Congress cannot compel the President to prosecute outcomes taken pursuant to the President's own constitutional authority. If Congress could do so, it could control the President's authority through the manipulation of federal criminal law.

We have even greater concerns with respect to prosecutions arising out of the exercise of the President's express authority as Commander-in-Chief than we do with prosecutions arising out of the assertion of executive privilege. In a series of opinions examining various legal questions arising after September 11 we have explained the scope of the President's Commander-in-Chief power. We briefly summarize the findings of those opinions here. The President's constitutional power to protect the security of the United States and the lives and safety of its people must be understood in light of the Founders' intention to create a federal government "cloathed with all the powers requisite to the complete execution of its trust," The Federalist No. 23, at 147 (Alexander Hamilton) (Jacob E. Cooke ed. 1961). Foremost among the objectives committed to that trust by the Constitution is the security of the nation. As Hamilton explained in arguing for the Constitution's adoption, because "the circumstances which may affect the public safety" are not "reducible within certain determinate limits," it must be admitted, as a necessary consequence, that there can be no limitation of that authority, which is to provide for the defence and protection of the community, in any matter essential to its efficacy.

Id. at 147-48. Within the limits that the Constitution itself imposes, the scope and distribution of the powers to protect national security must be construed to authorize the most efficacious defense of the nation and its its interests in accordance "with the realistic purposes of the entire instrument." *Lichter v. United States*, 334 U.S. 742, 782 (1948).

The text, structure and history of the Constitution establish that the Founders entrusted the President with the primary responsibility, and therefore the power, to ensure the security of the United States in situations of grave and unforeseen emergencies. The decision to deploy military force in the defense of United States interests is expressly placed under Presidential authority by the Vesting Clause, U.S. Const. Art. I, § 1. cl. 1, and by the

Commander-in-Chief Clause, id., § 2, cl. 1. This Office has long understood the Commander-in-Chief Clause in particular as an affirmative grant of authority to the President. See, e.g., Memorandum for Charles W. Colson, Special Counsel to the President, from William H. Rehnquist, Assistant Attorney General, Office of Legal Counsel, Re: The President and the War Power: South Vietnam and the Cambodian Sanctuaries (May 22, 1970) ("Rehnquist Memorandum"). The Framers understood the Clause as investing the President with the fullest range of power understood at the time of the ratification of the Constitution as belonging to the military commander. In addition, the structure of the Constitution demonstrates that any power traditionally understood as pertaining to the executive—which includes the conduct of warfare and the defense of the nation—unless expressly assigned in the Constitution to Congress, is vested in the President. Article II, Section 1 makes this clear by stating that the "executive Power shall be vested in a President of the United States of America." That sweeping grant vests in the President an unenumerated "executive power" and contrasts with the specific enumeration of the powers—those "herein"—granted to Congress in Article I. The implications of constitutional text and structure are confirmed by the practical consideration that national security decisions require the unity in purpose and energy in action that characterize the Presidency rather than Congress.

As the Supreme Court has recognized, the Commander-in-Chief power and the President's obligation to protect the nation imply the ancillary powers necessary to their successful exercise. "The first of the enumerated powers of the President is that he shall be Commander-in-Chief of the Army and Navy of the United States. And, of course, the grant of war power includes all that is necessary and proper for carrying those powers into execution." *Johnson v. Eisentrager*, 339 U.S. 763, 788 (1950). In wartime, it is for the President alone to decide what methods to use to best prevail against the enemy. See, e.g., Rehnquist Memorandum; Flanigan Memorandum at 3. The President's complete discretion in exercising the Commander-in-Chief power has been recognized by the courts. In the Prize Cases, 67 U.S. (2 Black) 635, 670 (1862), for example, the Court explained that whether the President "in fulfilling his duties as Commander in Chief" had appropriately responded to the rebellion of the southern states was a question "to be decided by him" and which the Court could not question, but

must leave to "the political department of the Government to which this power was entrusted."

One of the core functions of the Commander in Chief is that of capturing detaining, and interrogating members of the enemy. See, e.g., Memorandum for William J. Haynes, II, General Counsel, Department of Defense, from Jay S. Bybee, Assistant Attorney General, Office of Legal Counsel, Re: The President's Power as Commander in Chief to Transfer Captured Terrorists to the Control and Custody of Foreign Nations at 3 (March 13, 2002) ("the Commander-in-Chief Clause constitutes an independent grant of substantive authority to engage in the detention and transfer of prisoners captured in armed conflicts"). It is well settled that the President may seize and detain enemy combatants, at least for the duration of the conflict, and the laws of war make clear that prisoners may be interrogated for information concerning the enemy, its strength, and its plans. Numerous Presidents have ordered the capture, detention, and questioning of enemy combatants during virtually every major conflict in the Nation's history, including recent conflicts such as the Gulf, Vietnam, and Korean wars. Recognizing this authority, Congress has never attempted to restrict or interfere with the President's authority on this score. Id.

Any effort by Congress to regulate the interrogation of battlefield combatants would violate the Constitution's sole vesting of the Commander-in-Chief authority in the President. There can be little doubt that intelligence operations, such as the detention and interrogation of enemy combatants and leaders, are both necessary and proper for the effective conduct of a military campaign. Indeed, such operations may be of more importance in a war with an international terrorist organization than one with the conventional armed forces of a nation-state, due to the former's emphasis on secret operations and surprise attacks against civilians. It may be the case that only successful interrogations can provide the information necessary to prevent the success of covert terrorist attacks upon the United States and its citizens. Congress can no more interfere with the President's conduct of the interrogation of enemy combatants than it can dictate strategic or tactical decisions on the battlefield. Just as statutes that order the President to conduct warfare in a certain manner or for specific goals would be unconstitutional, so too are laws that seek to prevent the President from gaining the intelligence he believes necessary to prevent attacks upon the United States.

VI. Defenses

In the foregoing parts of this memorandum, we have demonstrated that the ban on torture in Section 2340A is limited to only the most extreme forms of physical and mental harm. We have also demonstrated that Section 2340A, as applied to interrogations of enemy combatants ordered by the President pursuant to his Conmander-in-Chief power would be unconstitutional. Even if an interrogation method, however, might arguably cross the line drawn in Section 2340, and application of the statute was not held to be an unconstitutional infringement of the President's Commander-in-Chief authority, we believe that under the current circumstances certain justification defenses might be available that would potentially eliminate criminal liability. Standard criminal law defenses of necessity and self-defense could justify interrogation methods needed to elicit information to prevent a direct and imminent threat to the United States and its citizens.

◆ **A. Necessity**

We believe that a defense of necessity could be raised, under the current circumstances, to an allegation of a Section 2340A violation. Often referred to as the "choice of evils" defense, necessity has been defined as fellows:

Conduct that the actor believes to he necessary to avoid a harm or evil to himself or to another is justifiable, provided that:

(a) the harm or evil sought to be avoided by such conduct is greater than that sought to be prevented by the law defining the offense charged; and (b) neither the Code nor other law defining the offense provides exceptions or defenses dealing with the specific situation involved; and (c) a legislative purpose to exclude the justification claimed does not otherwise plainly appear.

Model Penal Code § 3.02. See also Wayne R. LaFave & Austin W. Scott, 1 Substantive Criminal Law § 5.4 at 627 (1986 & 2002 supp.) ("LaFave & Scott"). Although there is no federal statute that generally establishes necessity or other justifications as defenses to federal criminal laws, the Supreme Court has recognized the defense. See *United States v. Bailey*, 444 U.S. 394, 410 (1980) (relying on LaFave & Scott and Model Penal Code definitions of necessity defense).

The necessity defense may prove especially relevant in the current circumstances. As it has been described in the case law and literature, the purpose behind necessity is one of public policy. According to LaFave and Scott, "the law ought to promote the achievement of higher values at the expense of lesser values, and sometimes the greater good for society will be accomplished by violating the literal language of the criminal law." LaFave & Scott, at 629. In particular, the necessity defense can justify the intentional killing of one person to save two others because "it is better that two lives be saved and one lost than that two be lost and one saved." Id. Or, put in the language of a choice of evils, "the evil involved in violating the terms of the criminal law (… even taking another's life) may be less than that which would result from literal compliance with the law (… two lives lost)." Id.

Additional elements of the necessity defense are worth noting here. First, the defense is not limited to certain types of harms. Therefore, the harm inflicted by necessity may include intentional homicide, so long as the harm avoided is greater (i.e., preventing more deaths). Id. at 634. Second, it must actually be the defendant's intention to avoid the greater harm: intending to commit murder and then learning only later that the death had the fortuitous result of saving other lives will not support a necessity defense. Id. at 635. Third, if the defendant reasonably believed that the lesser harm was necessary, even if, unknown to him, it was not, he may still avail himself of the defense. As LaFave and Scott explain, "if A kills B reasonably believing it to be necessary to save C and D, he is not guilty of murder even though, unknown to A, C and D could have been rescued without the necessity of killing B." Id. Fourth, it is for the court, and not the defendant to judge whether the harm avoided outweighed the harm done. Id. at 636. Fifth, the defendant cannot rely upon the necessity defense if a third alternative is open and known to him that will cause less harm.

It appears to us that under the current circumstances the necessity defense could be successfully maintained in response to an allegation of a Section 2340A violation. On September 11, 2001, al Qaeda launched a surprise covert attack on civilian targets in the United States that led to the deaths of thousands and losses in the billions of dollars. According to public and governmental reports, al Qaeda has other sleeper cells within the United States that may be planning similar attacks. Indeed, al Qaeda plans apparently include efforts to develop and deploy chemical, biological and nuclear weapons of mass destruction. Under these circumstances, a detainee may possess information that could enable the United

States to prevent attacks that potentially could equal or surpass the September 11 attacks in their magnitude. Clearly, any harm that might occur during an interrogation would pale to insignificance compared to the harm avoided by preventing such an attack, which could take hundreds or thousands of lives.

Under this calculus, two factors will help indicate when the necessity defense could appropriately be invoked. First, the more certain that government officials are that a particular individual has information needed to prevent an attack, the more necessary interrogation will be. Second, the more likely it appears to be that a terrorist attack is likely to occur, and the greater the amount of damage expected from such an attack, the more that an interrogation to get information would become necessary. Of course, the strength of the necessity defense depends on the circumstances that prevail, and the knowledge of the government actors involved, when the interrogation is conducted. While every interrogation that might violate Section 2340A does not trigger a necessity defense, we can say that certain circumstances could support such a defense.

Legal authorities identify an important exception to the necessity defense. The defense is available "only in situations wherein the legislature has not itself, in its criminal statute, made a determination of values." Id. at 629. Thus, if Congress explicitly has made clear that violation of a statute cannot be outweighed by the harm avoided, courts cannot recognize the necessity defense. LaFave and Israel provide as an example an abortion statute that made clear that abortions even to save the life of the mother would still be a crime; in such cases the necessity defense would be unavailable. Id. at 630. Here, however, Congress has not explicitly made a determination of values vis-a-vis torture. In fact, Congress explicitly removed efforts to remove torture from the weighing of values permitted by the necessity defense.

◆ B. Self-Defense

Even if a court were to find that a violation of Section 2340A was not justified by necessity, a defendant could still appropriately raise a claim of self-defense. The right to self-defense, even when it involves deadly force, is deeply embedded in our law, both as to individuals and as to the nation as a whole. As the Court of Appeals for the D.C. Circuit has explained:

More than two centuries ago, Blackstone, best known of the expositors of the English common law, taught that "all homicide is malicious, and of course amounts to murder, unless… excused on the account of accident or self-preservation…." Self-defense, as a doctrine legally exonerating the taking of human life, is as viable now as it was in Blackstone's time.

United States v. Peterson, 483 F.2d 1222, 1228-29 (D.C. Cir. 1973). Self-defense is a common-law defense to federal criminal law offenses, and nothing in the text, structure or history of Section 2340A precludes its application to a charge of torture. In the absence of any textual provision to the contrary, we assume self-defense can be an appropriate defense to an allegation of torture.

The doctrine of self-defense permits the use of force to prevent harm to another person. As LaFave and Scott explain, "one is justified in using reasonable force in defense of another person, even a stranger, when he reasonably believes that the other is in immediate danger of unlawful bodily harm from his adversary and that the use of such force is necessary to avoid this danger." Id. at 663-64. Ultimately, even deadly force is permissible, but "only when the attack of the adversary upon the other person reasonably appears to the defender to be a deadly attack." Id. at 664. As with our discussion of necessity, we will review the significant elements of this defense. According to LaFave and Scott, the elements of the defense of others are the same as those that apply to individual self-defense.

First, self-defense requires that the use of force be necessary to avoid the danger of unlawful bodily harm. Id. at 649. A defender may justifiably use deadly force if he reasonably believes that the other person is about to inflict unlawful death or serious bodily harm upon another, and that it is necessary to use such force to prevent it. Id. at 652. Looked at from the opposite perspective, the defender may not use force when the force would be as equally effective at a later time and the defender suffers no harm or risk by waiting. See Paul H. Robinson, 2 Criminal Law Defenses § 131(c) at 77 (1984). If, however, other options permit the defender to retreat safely from a confrontation without having to resort to deadly force, the use of force may not be necessary in the first place. LaFave and Scott at 659-60.

Second, self-defense requires that the defendant's belief in the necessity of using force be reasonable. If a defendant honestly but unreasonably believed force was necessary, he will not be able to make out a successful claim of self-defense. Id. at 654. Conversely, if a defendant reasonably believed an attack was to occur, but the facts subsequently showed no attack was threatened he may still raise self-defense. As LaFave and Scott explain, "one may be justified in shooting to death an adversary who, having threatened to kill him, reaches for his pocket as if for a gun, though it later appears that he had no gun and that he was only reaching for his handkerchief." Id. Some authorities, such as the Model Penal Code, even eliminate the reasonability element, and require only that the defender honestly believed—regardless of its unreasonableness—that the use of force was necessary.

Third, many legal authorities include the requirement that a defender must reasonably believe that the unlawful violence is "imminent" before he can use force in his defense. It would be a mistake, however, to equate imminence necessarily with timing—that an attack is immediately about to occur. Rather, as the Model Penal Code explains, what is essential is that, the defensive response must be "immediately necessary." Model Penal Code § 3.04(1). Indeed, imminence may be merely another way of expressing the requirement of necessity. Robinson at 78. LaFave and Scott, for example, believe that the imminence requirement makes sense as part of a necessity defense because if an attack is not immediately upon the defender, the defender has other options available to avoid the attack that do not involve the use of force. LaFave and Scott at 656. If, however, the fact of the attack becomes certain and no other options remain, the use of force may be justified. To use a well-known hypothetical, if A were to kidnap and confine B, and then tell B he would kill B one week later, B would be justified in using force in self-defense, even if the opportunity arose before the week had passed. Id. at 656; see also Robinson at § 131(c)(1) at 78. In this hypothetical, while the attack itself is not imminent, B's use of force becomes immediately necessary whenever he has an opportunity to save himself from A.

Fourth, the amount of force should be proportional to the threat. As LaFave and Scott explain, "the amount of force which [the defender] may justifiably use must be reasonably related to the threatened harm which he seeks to avoid." LaFave and Scott at 651. Thus, one may not use deadly force in response to a threat that does not rise to death or serious bodily harm. If such harm may result, however, deadly force is appropriate. As the Model Penal Code § 3.04(2)(b) states, "[t]he use of deadly force is not justifiable … unless the actor believes that such force is necessary to protect himself against death,

serious bodily injury, kidnapping or sexual intercourse compelled by force or threat."

Under the current circumstances, we believe that a defendant accused of violating Section 2340A could have, in certain circumstances, grounds to properly claim the defense of another. The threat of an impending terrorist attack threatens the lives of hundreds if not thousands of American citizens. Whether such a defense will be upheld depends on the specific context within which the interrogation decision is made. If an attack appears increasingly likely, but our intelligence services and armed forces cannot prevent it without the information from the interrogation of a specific individual, then the more likely it will appear that the conduct in question will be seen as necessary. If intelligence and other information support the conclusion that an attack is increasingly certain, then the necessity for the interrogation will be reasonable. The increasing certainty of an attack will also satisfy the imminence requirement. Finally, the fact that previous al Qaeda attacks have had as their aim the deaths of American citizens, and that evidence of other plots have had a similar goal in mind, would justify proportionality of interrogation methods designed to elicit information to prevent such deaths.

To be sure, this situation is different from the usual self-defense justification, and, indeed, it overlaps with elements of the necessity defense. Self-defense as usually discussed involves using force against an individual who is about to conduct the attack. In the current circumstances, however, an enemy combatant in detention does not himself present a threat of harm. He is not actually carrying out the attack; rather, he has participated in the planning and preparation for the attack, or merely has knowledge of the attack through his membership in the terrorist organization. Nonetheless, leading scholarly commentators believe that interrogation of such individuals using methods that might violate Section 2340A would be justified under the doctrine of self-defense, because the combatant by aiding and promoting the terrorist plot "has culpably caused the situation where someone might get hurt. If hurting him is the only means to prevent the death or injury of others put at risk by his actions, such torture should be permissible, and on the same basis that self-defense is permissible." Michael S. Moore, Torture and the Balance of Evils, 23 Israel L. Rev. 280, 323 (1989) (symposium on Israel's Landau Commission Report). Thus, some commentators believe that by helping to create the threat of loss of life, terrorists become culpable for the threat even though they do not actually carry out the attack itself. They may be hurt in an interrogation because they are part of the mechanism that has set the attack in motion, id. at 323, just as is someone who feeds ammunition or targeting information to an attacker. Under the present circumstances, therefore, even though a detained enemy combatant may not be the exact attacker—he is not planting the bomb, or piloting a hijacked plane to kill civilians—he still may be harmed in self-defense if he has knowledge of future attacks because he has assisted in their planning and execution.

Further, we believe that a claim by an individual of the defense of another would be further supported by the fact that, in this case, the nation itself is under attack and has the right to self-defense. This fact can bolster and support an individual claim of self-defense in a prosecution, according to the teaching of the Supreme Court in In re Neagle, 135 U.S. 1 (1890). In that case, the State of California arrested and held deputy U.S. Marshal Neagle for shooting and killing the assailant of Supreme Court Justice Field. In granting the writ of habeas corpus for Neagle's release, the Supreme Court did not rely alone upon the marshal's right to defend another or his right to self-defense. Rather, the Court found that Neagle, as an agent of the United States and of the executive branch, was justified in the killing because, in protecting Justice Field, he was acting pursuant to the executive branch's inherent constitutional authority to protect the United States government. Id. at 67 ("We cannot doubt the power of the president to take measures for the protection of a judge of one of the courts of the United States who, while in the discharge of the duties of his office, is threatened with a personal attack which may probably result in his death."). That authority derives, according to the Court, from the President's power under Article II to take care that the laws are faithfully executed. In other words, Neagle as a federal officer not only could raise self-defense or defense of another, but also could defend his actions on the ground that he was implementing the Executive Branch's authority to protect the United States government.

If the right to defend the national government can be raised as a defense in an individual prosecution, as Neagle suggests, then a government defendant, acting in his official capacity, should be able to argue that any conduct that arguably violated Section 2340A was undertaken pursuant to more than just individual self-defense or defense of another. In addition, the defendant could claim that he was fulfilling the Executive Branch's authority to protect the federal government, and the nation, from attack. The September 11 attacks have already triggered that authority, as recognized both, under domestic and international law. Following the example of In re Neagle, we conclude that a government defendant may also argue that his conduct of an interrogation, if properly authorized, is justified on the basis of protecting the nation from attack.

There can be little doubt that the nation's right to self-defense has been triggered under our law. The Constitution announces that one of its purposes is "to provide for the common defense." U.S. Const., Preamble. Article I, § 8 declares that Congress is to exercise its powers to "provide for the common Defence." See also 2 Pub. Papers of Ronald Reagan 920, 921 (1988-89) (right of self-defense recognized by Article 51 of the U.N. Charter) The President has a particular responsibility and power to take steps to defend the nation and its people. In re Neagle, 135 U.S. at 64. See also U.S. Const., art. IV, § 4 (The United States shall ... protect [each of the States] against Invasion"). As Commander-in-Chief and Chief Executive, he may use the armed forces to protect the nation and its people. See, e.g., *United States v. Verdugo-Urquidez*, 494 U.S. 259, 273 (1990). And he may employ secret agents to aid in his work as Commander-in-Chief. *Totten v. United States*, 92 U.S. 105, 106 (1876). As the Supreme Court observed in The Prize Cases, 67 U.S. (2 Black) 635 (1862), in response to an armed attack on the United States "the President is not only authorized but bound to resist force by force ... without waiting for any special legislative authority." Id. at 668. The September 11 events were a direct attack on the United States, and as we have explained above, the President has authorized the use of military force with the support of Congress.

As we have made clear in other opinions involving the war against al Qaeda, the nation's right to self-defense has been triggered by the events of September 11. If a government defendant were to harm an enemy combatant during an interrogation in a manner that might arguably violate Section 2340A, he would be doing so in order to prevent further attacks on the United States by the al Qaeda terrorist network. In that case, we believe that he could argue that his actions were justified by the executive branch's constitutional authority to protect the nation from attack. This national and international version of the right to self-defense could supplement and bolster the government defendant's individual right.

Conclusion

For the foregoing reasons, we conclude that torture as defined in and proscribed by Sections 2340-2340A, covers only extreme acts. Severe pain is generally of the kind difficult for the victim to endure. Where the pain is physical, it must be of an intensity akin to that which accompanies serious physical injury such as death or organ failure. Severe mental pain requires suffering not just at the moment of infliction but it also requires lasting psychological harm, such as seen in mental disorders like posttraumatic stress disorder. Additionally, such severe mental pain can arise only from the predicate acts listed in Section 2340. Because the acts inflicting torture are extreme, there is significant range of acts that though they might constitute cruel, inhuman, or degrading treatment or punishment fail to rise to the level of torture.

Further, we conclude that under the circumstances of the current war against al Qaeda and its allies, application, of Section 2340A to interrogations undertaken pursuant to the President's Commander-in-Chief powers may be unconstitutional. Finally, even if an interrogation method might violate Section 2340A, necessity or self-defense could provide justifications that would eliminate any criminal liability.

Please let us know if we can be of further assistance.

Jay S. Bybee, Assistant Attorney General

Justice Anthony M. Kennedy wrote the majority opinion in **Lawrence v. Texas.** (AP Photo/Dan Loh)

LAWRENCE V. TEXAS

"The liberty protected by the Constitution allows homosexual persons the right to make this choice."

Overview

In 1986, in *Bowers v. Hardwick* the U.S. Supreme Court upheld as constitutional a Georgia law criminalizing sodomy between consenting adults. The defendant in the case was a gay man who had been convicted under the statute. He argued that he had a constitutional right to privacy that extended to private, consensual sexual conduct. Reframing the legal question as whether the Constitution created "a fundamental right to engage in homosexual sodomy," the Court rejected the defendant's arguments and answered that the Constitution provided no such right.

Seventeen years later, in *Lawrence v. Texas*, the Supreme Court faced a direct challenge to the holding of *Bowers*. In *Lawrence*, two men convicted of illegal sexual intercourse under a Texas statute criminalizing oral and anal sex by consenting same-sex couples argued that the Texas law was unconstitutional for the very reasons rejected by the court in *Bowers*. In its decision in *Lawrence*, the Court took the unusual step of overruling itself and striking down the Texas statute. Writing for the majority, Justice Anthony M. Kennedy declared *Bowers* to have been wrongly decided and held that the defendants were free as adults to engage in private sexual conduct in the exercise of their liberty rights as guaranteed by the due process clause of the Fourteenth Amendment.

Context

The social and political landscape for gays and lesbians in the United States in 2003, when *Lawrence* was decided, was significantly different from merely seventeen years earlier, when the Court heard *Bowers*. Those seventeen years saw significant shifts in the country's treatment of gay men and women as well as important changes in the composition of the Supreme Court.

In 1986, the year *Bowers* was decided, most gay men and lesbian women maintained their sexual orientation as a closely guarded secret. The public revelation of homosexual orientation was unusual and often harmful to those exposed. Reports that gay men and lesbian women were publicly subjected to vitriol, discrimination, and outright violence were not uncommon, and the law offered little protection. In fact, twenty-four states and the District of Columbia deemed sex between members of the same sex to be criminal activity. Only Wisconsin outlawed discrimination on the basis of sexual orientation. The military prohibited gay men and lesbians from service, and no state offered legal recognition of same-sex unions.

By 2003, lesbians and gay men had become a visible presence in American society unlike at any other time in history. Politicians, teachers, judges, athletes, and movie stars had made public their attractions to people of the same sex. Gay and lesbian couples lived openly in many communities, raising children and serving in civic organizations. Universities and high schools saw the formation of gay student unions, in which young people made their sexual orientations a matter of public record. Gay characters appeared as protagonists on television and in movies. Gay rights activists organized large, public, and effective advocacy campaigns.

Some of these changes were, somewhat paradoxically, a result of the AIDS crisis of the 1980s. *Bowers v. Hardwick* made its way through the courts at the height of the HIV/AIDS epidemic in the United States, an epidemic that decimated the gay community physically and socially. In the 1980s, HIV infection—originally dubbed the "gay cancer"—was widely believed to be transmitted primarily, if not exclusively, by sex between men. Infection with the virus was essentially a death sentence. As a result, HIV stigmatized gay men as potential predators and sex between men as a threat to health and safety. By 2003 medical advances in the treatment of HIV/AIDS had transformed HIV infection from a veritable death sentence into a treatable condition. Educational efforts had successfully informed the public that the virus infected across genders, ages, and sexual orientations, lessening the stigma of the disease. More important, the political activism generated in response to the AIDS epidemic brought gay rights, and the people seeking them, into mainstream U.S. culture.

Laws reflected the social evolution. By 2003, Vermont had recognized legal civil unions between same-sex couples, and California and New York City had adopted domestic

1891

■ **May 25**
In *Union Pacific Railway Co. v. Botsford*, the Supreme Court rejects the right of a defendant in a civil action to require the plaintiff to submit to physical examination, explaining, "No right is held more sacred, or is more carefully guarded by the common law, than the right of every individual to the possession and control of his own person, free from all restraint or interference of others" (http://supreme.justia.com/us/141/250/case.html).

1965

■ **June 7**
In *Griswold v. Connecticut*, the Supreme Court holds that the constitutional right of privacy encompasses the right of married persons to use contraceptives.

1972

■ **March 22**
In *Eisenstadt v. Baird*, the Supreme Court, specifically citing the right of privacy, holds that a statute prohibiting the use of contraception by unmarried couples but allowing the provision of contraceptives to married adults violates the equal protection clause of the Fourteenth Amendment.

1973

■ The American Psychiatric Association removes homosexuality from its official list of mental disorders.

■ **January 22**
In *Roe v. Wade*, the Supreme Court holds that the right to privacy encompasses the right to choose to terminate a pregnancy, that restrictions on access to abortion must be narrowly tailored to serve a compelling state interest, and that the state's interest in protecting fetal life is compelling only after the fetus is viable.

1983

■ **July**
The Massachusetts representative Gerry Studds makes a speech on the floor of Congress through which he becomes the first openly homosexual member of Congress.

partnership laws. A historic case that would ultimately give gay couples the right to marry in Massachusetts was winding its way through the state courts. Many states allowed same-sex couples to adopt children, and half of the states with sodomy statutes on the books in 1986 had decriminalized homosexual behavior. Municipalities and states throughout the country were making it illegal to discriminate on the basis of sexual orientation in housing, education, and employment. The military, in turn, permitted gay men and lesbians to serve. To be sure, many antigay laws remained on the books, including the one at issue in *Lawrence v. Texas*, but the changes in the political climate and the social status of gay men and women were undeniable.

In addition to the shifts in the social and legal standing of homosexuality, the composition of the Supreme Court changed dramatically in the seventeen years between the decisions in *Lawrence* and *Bowers*. Of the five justices who joined or concurred with the *Bowers* majority opinion (Byron White, Warren Burger, Lewis F. Powell, William Rehnquist, and Sandra Day O'Connor) and the four dissenters (Harry Blackmun, William J. Brennan, Thurgood Marshall, and John Paul Stevens), only O'Connor, Rehnquist, and Stevens were on the bench when the Court heard *Lawrence*. In the years between the decisions in *Bowers* and *Lawrence*, O'Connor, who would concur with the majority in *Lawrence*, and Kennedy, who would be the author of *Lawrence*, cast pivotal votes reaffirming the existence of a constitutional right to privacy, which was in doubt at the time *Bowers* was decided. The other justices who joined the majority in *Lawrence*—David Souter, Ruth Bader Ginsberg, and Steven Breyer—were all new to the Court.

About the Author

Justice Anthony M. Kennedy was born on July 23, 1936, in Sacramento, California. He attended Stanford University from 1954 to 1958, with a period of study at the London School of Economics. After receiving his BA from Stanford, he entered Harvard Law School, where he graduated with a bachelor of laws in 1961. Kennedy then entered the private practice of law, meanwhile coming to serve as a professor of constitutional law at the University of the Pacific's McGeorge School of Law. In 1975, President Gerald Ford nominated Kennedy to serve on the U.S. Court of Appeals for the Ninth Circuit, to which he was appointed. In 1988 President Ronald Reagan nominated him to the U.S. Supreme Court, and he took office as an associate justice on February 18, 1988.

Considered a crucial "swing vote" on the Supreme Court, Justice Kennedy cast the decisive vote in decisions ranging from one that upheld the Republican congressional map in Texas to one invalidating planned military tribunals for suspected terrorists. Through the turn of the twenty-first century, his voting record was not predictably partisan; although he was appointed by a conservative Republican, he tended to vote with the liberal bloc of the Court almost as often as with the conservatives.

◆ **Majority Opinion**

Justice Anthony Kennedy's majority opinion, which was joined by Justices Stevens, Souter, Ginsburg, and Breyer, starts with a philosophical description of the concepts of liberty and freedom. Without reference to law, Kennedy notes that liberty protects people from government intrusions in their homes but also reaches beyond the home, to other spheres where the state does not belong. "Freedom," he states, "extends beyond spatial bounds. Liberty presumes an autonomy of self that includes freedom of thought, belief, expression, and certain intimate conduct. The instant case involves liberty of the person both in its spatial and more transcendent dimensions."

Unlike the introduction, part I is all business. Kennedy first defines the specific issue confronting the court: the validity of a Texas statute criminalizing certain sexual conduct between members of the same sex. He then describes the factual situation that gave rise to the case. The petitioners, he explains, are two men who were arrested for deviate sexual intercourse after being observed by two police officers engaging in consensual anal sex in the bedroom of one man's home. Kennedy lists the three questions the Court would consider: Whether the Texas statute was in violation of equal protection, whether convictions for "adult consensual sexual intimacy in the home" violated Fourteenth Amendment due process protections, and whether the 1986 decision in *Bowers v. Hardwick* should be overruled.

In framing the issues, Kennedy emphasizes that the petitioners were adults at the time of the offense and that the conduct occurred in private and was consensual. These emphases—repeated throughout the opinion—may limit the extent to which the liberty interest identified in *Lawrence* applies; that is, it would not necessarily apply to relationships involving minors or to public or nonconsensual acts.

In part II, Kennedy declares that resolving the case requires a rethinking of the analysis applied by the Court in *Bowers v. Hardwick*. In *Bowers*, the Court had rejected the claim that the due process clause protected individuals from criminal sodomy statutes as "at best, facetious." The decision to reevaluate the analytic framework applied in *Bowers* was a marked departure from typical Supreme Court decision making. In the normal course, justices apply established rules and distinguish new cases from older ones by finding that differences in the facts of the cases require new results or reinterpretations of old rules. The Court rarely engages in a wholesale reevaluation of a prior decision.

In this case, Justice Kennedy begins the reevaluation by tracing the "substantive reach of liberty under the Due Process Clause" in relevant circumstances. He finds most instructive the cases that arose in the context of state attempts to regulate human reproductive activity. Collectively, those cases, *Pierce v. Society of the Sisters of the Holy Names of Jesus and Mary*, *Meyer v. Nebraska*, *Griswold v. Connecticut*, *Eisenstadt v. Baird*, *Roe v. Wade*, and *Carey v. Population Services International*, firmly establish a right to

Time Line

1983

■ **July 4**
The Reverend Jerry Fallwell, leader of the Moral Majority, describes AIDS as the "gay plague" in a rally in Cincinatti.

1986

■ **June 30**
Supreme Court issues its decision in *Bowers v. Hardwick*.

1987

■ **March 20**
The Food and Drug Administration approves azidothymidine, a powerful new drug for AIDS patients that prolongs lives by reducing infection.

1992

■ **June 29**
In *Planned Parenthood of Southeastern Pa. v. Casey*, the Supreme Court reaffirms the existence of a constitutional right to privacy that encompasses a woman's right to terminate a pregnancy.

1993

■ The U.S. military institutes its "Don't ask, don't tell" policy, which allows gay men and lesbians to serve in the military for the first time; homosexual activity by active service members remains banned.

1994

■ The American Medical Association denounces supposed cures for homosexuality.

1996

■ Patients become able to delay the onset of AIDS by taking a combination of as many as sixty drugs called an "AIDS cocktail."

■ **May 20**
In *Romer v. Evans*, the Supreme Court strikes down a Colorado law denying gays and lesbians legal protection against discrimination.

2000

■ **July 1, 2000**
Vermont becomes the first state in the country to legally recognize civil unions between same-sex partners.

2003

■ **June 26**
In *Lawrence v. Texas*, the Supreme Court strikes down a Texas statute criminalizing oral and anal sex by consenting adults and holds that the right to liberty under the due process clause gives consenting adults the full right to engage in private sexual conduct without the interference of government.

■ **November 18**
In *Goodridge v. Department of Public Health*, the Massachusetts Supreme Judicial Court rules that the prohibition of same-sex couples from marrying violates their constitutional rights and denies them their dignity and equality.

2004

■ Eleven states ban same-sex marriage through referendum.

■ **May 17**
Same-sex marriage becomes legal in Massachusetts.

■ **August 23**
In *United States v. Marcum*, the U.S. Court of Appeals for the Armed Forces rejects the argument that *Lawrence* invalidated a military rule prohibiting consensual sodomy.

2005

■ **October 21**
In *State v. Limon*, the Supreme Court of Kansas applies *Lawrence* to find unconstitutional a state "Romeo and Juliet" statute imposing harsher sentences for unlawful voluntary sexual conduct between members of the same sex than for conduct between members of the opposite sex.

privacy that includes the right of married and unmarried individuals to make decisions regarding sexual conduct.

Kennedy writes that although *Bowers v. Hardwick* was decided under the law enunciated in the reproductive freedom cases, the Court's analysis was skewed because it misapprehended the issue at hand. By casting *Bowers* as a case turning on whether the "Federal Constitution confers a fundamental right upon homosexuals to engage in sodomy," the Court failed "to appreciate the extent of the liberty at stake." The liberty at stake when laws criminalize private sexual conduct, Kennedy asserts, concerns not only the sexual act

but also the private personal relationships to which individuals are entitled as part of the greater liberty protected by the Constitution. The state, says Kennedy, should avoid setting boundaries on relationships "absent injury to a person or abuse of an institution the law protects."

Having established that the Court that heard *Bowers* addressed too narrow a question, Kennedy attacks the reasoning used by that Court. He asserts that the historical foundation used in *Bowers* was not correct. Here, Kennedy recharacterizes common history as not definitively opposed to "homosexual" or same-sex conduct until the last third of the twentieth century. He notes that sodomy is seldom prosecuted even in the remaining states that make it a criminal act and that most states have moved to abolish the criminal prohibitions altogether. Kennedy acknowledges the condemnation of same-sex conduct by "powerful voices" but dismisses that condemnation, quoting *Planned Parenthood of Southeastern Pa. v. Casey*: "The issue is whether the majority may use the power of the State to enforce [its] views on the whole society through operation of the criminal law. 'Our obligation is to define the liberty of all, not to mandate our own moral code.'"

Kennedy directly challenges the conclusion drawn in *Bowers* that sodomy has been condemned throughout the history of Western civilization. He cites the nonenforcement of sodomy laws and the reduction in the number of sodomy laws from twenty-five to thirteen in the years following *Bowers*. Then, in one of the more controversial parts of the decision, he turns to evidence of shifting mores from other countries and from international law. For example, he notes that the European Court of Human Rights held that laws proscribing consensual homosexual conduct were invalid under the European Convention on Human Rights, thus showing that foreign court holdings are at odds with the "the premise in *Bowers* that the claim put forward was insubstantial in our Western civilization."

Kennedy goes on to show that two cases decided after *Bowers* cast its holding into even further doubt. He cites *Planned Parenthood of Southeastern Pa. v. Casey*, a case challenging certain Pennsylvania abortion laws, which confirmed that the constitutional protections of the autonomy of a person to make personal choices considered "central to personal dignity and autonomy, are central to the liberty protected by the Fourteenth Amendment." That case, he reasons, requires the Court to recognize for the first time constitutional rights for gays and lesbians: "Persons in a homosexual relationship may seek autonomy for these purposes, just as heterosexual persons do." This pronouncement of substantive due process rights is presented in language traditionally used in equal protection cases. Kennedy further supports the Court's reassessment with the second relevant post-*Bowers* case, *Romer v. Evans*. In that case the Court cited the equal protection clause in striking down legislation disallowing the protection of gays from discrimination. Kennedy writes that the holding of *Romer* that laws "born of animosity toward [a] class of persons" fulfilled no legitimate government interest applies equally in the due process analysis: "Equality of treatment and the due process right to demand respect for conduct protected by the substantive guarantee of liberty are linked."

Kennedy next rejects the notion that *Bowers* remains viable. *Bowers*, he states, does not reflect "values we share with a wider civilization." He notes that the values established by that case have been rejected around the world, including by the European Court of Human Rights, and that the right at issue in this case has been accepted as an "integral part of human freedom in many other countries." As a last justification of the Court's reassessment of the holdings of *Bowers*, Kennedy explains that the present Court need not apply the doctrine of stare decisis (a policy of following principles set forth in previous judicial decisions) because no one has relied on *Bowers* to protect his or her individual rights in taking a given action. Accordingly, no individual will be disadvantaged if it is overruled.

With the Court free, then, to decide the issue anew, Justice Kennedy offers what is an almost shockingly thin analysis. Most significantly, he does not complete the threshold step taken in other due process cases, which is to identify the degree of scrutiny applicable to the law at issue. That step normally frames the rest of the analysis by dictating how essential the government's purpose must be to justify the law. Instead, Kennedy makes reference to Justice Stevens's dissent from *Bowers*, which recognizes a liberty interest in intimate conduct and rejects the notion that a state's view of a practice as immoral is sufficient to uphold the practice, without fitting the conclusion into a traditional analytic framework.

Thus, Kennedy declares, "*Bowers* was not correct when it was decided, and it is not correct today.… *Bowers v. Hardwick* should be and now is overruled." He concludes that the "petitioners are entitled to respect for their private lives. The State cannot demean their existence or control their destiny by making their private sexual conduct a crime."

Beyond its specific holding, the meaning and reach of *Lawrence* is unclear. While the Court adopted a fundamental invalidation through substantive due process, an open question remains as to the standard used by the Court to invalidate the statute: strict scrutiny appropriate for fundamental constitutional rights under due process or rational-basis scrutiny requiring only a legitimate state interest. An interpretation in favor of strict scrutiny is supported by the number of times the Court uses substantive due process in its argument—and rejects "mere" equal protection—and by the way liberty is discussed in the context of the due process clause throughout.

An interpretation favoring rational-basis scrutiny is supported by the failure of the Court to explicitly state the standard in question or use the words *fundamental right* with respect to the liberty interest identified in *Lawrence*. In addition, Kennedy states that "the Texas statute furthers no legitimate state interest which can justify its intrusion into the personal and private life of the individual." This statement indicates that the Texas statute does not even further a *legitimate* state interest, much less the compelling interest required under substantive due process.

A third interpretation of the decision holds that Kennedy applied some form of intermediate scrutiny, by which the government is required to show more than a rational basis but not so much as a compelling state interest to justify laws regulating private sexual conduct.

The uncertainty in the analysis presented by Kennedy cannot be viewed as anything but deliberate. In fact, the dissent takes the majority to task for having "laid waste the foundations of our rational-basis jurisprudence" by refusing to classify the importance of the right at issue. Justice Kennedy had the opportunity to perhaps respond to the criticism, modify his opinion, or clarify the analytic structure; his decision to leave the threshold questions to another day undermines the usefulness and clarity of an otherwise momentous decision. Of greatest import in the decision, then, is the majority's rejection of morality as a legitimate basis for law, a concept echoed by Justice O'Connor in her concurrence.

◆ **Concurrence**

Justice Sandra Day O'Connor wrote separately to concur with the Court's judgment. She does not join the majority to explicitly overrule *Bowers* but finds the Texas statute unconstitutional as a matter of equal protection, in that it applies to sodomy between members of the same sex but not the opposite sex.

Most critically, O'Connor expressly identifies and applies "a more searching form of rational basis review" than the Court has applied in relevant cases involving economic or tax legislation. Reviewing a series of cases, she correctly observes, "When a law exhibits such a desire to harm a politically unpopular group, we have applied a more searching form of rational basis review to strike down such laws under the Equal Protection Clause."

In scrutinizing the Texas statute and the rationale proffered in its defense by the state of Texas, she finds no basis for the statute other than moral disapproval of sodomy. Echoing the sentiments of the majority in its due process analysis, O'Connor rejects moral disapproval alone as a legitimate basis for a law that discriminates among groups of persons. The Texas law discriminates, she says, because it "serves more as a statement of dislike and disapproval against homosexuals than as a tool to stop criminal behavior." A law "branding one class of persons as criminals solely based on the State's moral disapproval of that class and conduct associated with that class" cannot stand.

O'Connor goes out of her way to limit the scope of her opinion. She notes, for example, that preserving the traditional institution of marriage is a legitimate state interest. Nevertheless, she admonishes that "other reasons exist to promote the institution of marriage beyond mere moral disapproval of an excluded group."

◆ **Dissents**

As joined by Justices Rehnquist and Clarence Thomas, Justice Antonin Scalia takes issue with every part of the majority's analysis in a caustic dissent. His introduction accuses the majority of hypocrisy for its willingness to over-

www.milestonedocuments.com

www.milestonedocuments.com

Justice Antonin Scalia wrote a dissenting opinion in
Lawrence v. Texas. (AP Photo/University of Missouri, Chapman
Rackaway)

rule this particular seventeen-year-old precedent when it had
refused to reconsider *Roe v. Wade* just the previous year.
Scalia then mocks the majority for lacking the courage to
identify the liberty interest at stake as fundamental, which,
Scalia suggests, might have been wrong but would have at
least justified the result reached. He also warns that the
majority used an "unheard-of form of rational-basis review,"
an approach that would have far-reaching implications.

In part I of the dissent, Scalia rants against "the Court's
surprising readiness to reconsider a decision rendered a
mere 17 years ago in *Bowers v. Hardwick*." Of note in this
section is the degree to which Scalia renews old battles.
Specifically, he engages in a step-by-step analysis of the
legitimacy of the *Roe v. Wade* abortion decision using the
analytic framework employed by Justice Kennedy in the
majority opinion. Accusing the majority of "manipulating"
the analytic framework employed in *Planned Parenthood of
Southeastern Pa. v. Casey*, Scalia argues that *Roe* should be
overruled. The majority's hypocrisy, he says, has "exposed
Casey's extraordinary deference to precedent for the result-
oriented expedient that it is."

Part I also sets forth one of the two main threads of argument winding their way through the lengthy dissent: The

majority's holding that moral reproach is not a rational basis
for regulation will wreak havoc with the law. In Scalia's view,
"a governing majority's belief that certain sexual behavior is
'immoral and unacceptable' constitutes a rational basis for
regulation." The majority's decision, he claims, calls into
question laws against bigamy, same-sex marriage, incest,
prostitution, adultery, bestiality, and obscenity.

Part II develops the second main theme of the dissent:
The majority's failure to expressly overrule the part of *Bowers* rejecting a claim to a fundamental right in the case of
same-sex sodomy renders the rest of the majority opinion's
conclusions untenable. Here, Scalia sets forth a primer on
substantive due process analysis. While the due process
clause "prohibits States from infringing fundamental liberty interests, unless the infringement is narrowly tailored to
serve a compelling state interest," something is only a "fundamental right" if it is, as stated in the 1997 case *Washington v. Glucksberg*, "deeply rooted in this Nation's history
and tradition." All other liberty interests must merely be
rationally related to a legitimate state interest. Scalia
declares that the due process clause is not implicated in
this case because, as the Court found in *Bowers*, with the
majority here seeming to agree, homosexual sodomy is not
a fundamental right. That the majority "does not have the
boldness to reverse" the conclusion reached in *Bowers* on
the fundamental right point, then, means that the only logical conclusion is that the Texas law does not infringe on a
constitutionally protected liberty interest. Meanwhile, a
rational basis exists here, just as it does with respect to laws
criminalizing prostitution or the recreational use of heroin.

In part III, Scalia addresses "some aspersions that the
Court casts upon *Bowers* conclusion that homosexual
sodomy is not a fundamental right." In particular, Scalia
quarrels with the historical analysis conducted by the
majority. He states that the conclusion in *Bowers* that
"homosexual sodomy is not a fundamental right 'deeply
rooted in this Nation's history and tradition' is utterly unassailable" and that the majority's emphasis on proceedings
from only the last fifty years is inappropriate. An "emerging
awareness," he says, citing a term used in the majority
opinion, does not create a fundamental right.

Part IV returns to the moral slippery slope argument.
Here, Scalia asserts that the majority opinion "effectively
decrees the end of all morals legislation," thus calling into
question "criminal laws against fornication, bigamy, adultery, adult incest, bestiality, and obscenity."

In part V, Scalia responds to Justice O'Connor's concurrence by arguing that the law in question indeed applies
equally to all people. The Texas statute, he asserts, merely
distinguishes "between the sexes insofar as concerns the
partner with whom the sexual acts are performed: men can
violate the law only with other men, and women only with
other women." Such treatment, he says, does not violate
the equal protection clause because it is the same distinction used to justify same-sex marriage prohibitions and
laws against adultery.

Scalia's rhetoric intensifies in his conclusion. He characterizes the majority ruling thus: "Today's opinion is the

"Freedom extends beyond spatial bounds. Liberty presumes an autonomy of self that includes freedom of thought, belief, expression, and certain intimate conduct. The instant case involves liberty of the person both in its spatial and more transcendent dimensions."

(Justice Anthony Kennedy, Majority Opinion)

"When sexuality finds overt expression in intimate conduct with another person, the conduct can be but one element in a personal bond that is more enduring. The liberty protected by the Constitution allows homosexual persons the right to make this choice."

(Justice Anthony Kennedy, Majority Opinion)

"Bowers was not correct when it was decided, and it is not correct today. It ought not to remain binding precedent. Bowers v. Hardwick should be and now is overruled."

(Justice Anthony Kennedy, Majority Opinion)

"Times can blind us to certain truths and later generations can see that laws once thought necessary and proper in fact serve only to oppress. As the Constitution endures, persons in every generation can invoke its principles in their own search for greater freedom."

(Justice Anthony Kennedy, Majority Opinion)

"We have never held that moral disapproval, without any other asserted state interest, is a sufficient rationale under the Equal Protection Clause to justify a law that discriminates among groups of persons."

(Justice Sandra Day O'Connor, Concurrence)

"It is clear from this that the Court has taken sides in the culture war, departing from its role of assuring, as neutral observer, that the democratic rules of engagement are observed."

(Justice Antonin Scalia, Dissent)

product of a Court, which is the product of a law-profession culture, that has largely signed on to the so-called homosexual agenda, by which I mean the agenda promoted by some homosexual activists directed at eliminating the moral opprobrium that has traditionally attached to homosexual conduct." The majority, he says, has departed from its role as neutral observer and imposed its own view of morality on the entire nation, even though "many Americans do not want persons who openly engage in homosexual conduct as partners in their business, as scoutmasters for their children, as teachers in their children's schools, or as boarders in their home."

Justice Clarence Thomas wrote an additional dissent to state that the Constitution does not actually provide a right to privacy, and therefore the Texas law, while "uncommonly silly"—a quote from the dissent of Potter Stewart from the 1965 case *Griswold v. Connecticut*—should stand.

Audience

As with most Supreme Court cases, the majority opinion in *Lawrence v. Texas* was written for several audiences. Its immediate purpose, of course, was to resolve the dispute between the parties before the Court—here, the two men convicted of deviate sexual intercourse under Texas's homosexual conduct law and the state attorney who prosecuted them. Thus, the opinion is written for and to the parties and their lawyers; nevertheless, it was certainly intended to reach a much broader audience than John Lawrence, Tyrone Garner, and the various counsels. Indeed, the authoring justices wrote their opinions to endure, addressing the broader legal community, members of the public, and, in some important ways, each other.

The majority intended to make clear to practicing judges, lawmakers, and prosecutors that convictions under state laws criminalizing private consensual conduct were no longer tenable. Justices Kennedy and O'Connor spoke directly to judges and advocates in limiting the scope of their opinions. For example, both warn advocates and judges that their decisions should not be read to support same sex-marriage, with O'Connor going so far as to announce that "preserving the traditional institution of marriage" is a "legitimate state interest" despite the fact that the legitimacy of bans on same-sex marriage was not before the Court.

The various opinions also contain conversations among the justices. Scalia criticizes O'Connor's departure from stare decisis, the principle that drove her opinion in the *Casey* abortion case. Scalia offers scathing and direct derision of the majority's failure to place the case in an established due process framework by declaring whether the right at issue is fundamental or not.

The opinions also speak to the public at large. With the exception of Thomas's supplemental dissent, all of the opinions are ripe with sound bites. Both Kennedy and O'Connor show some sensitivity to the gay and lesbian community through their choice of language. For example,

Kennedy's characterization of individuals as "persons in homosexual relationships" contrasts directly with the Court's use of the term "homosexuals" in the *Bowers* decision, suggesting recognition of the fact that people's sexual choices do not define their identities. Justice Thomas actually expressly offers something of an apology to the gay and lesbian community for his vote, stating in his brief dissent that he would oppose anti-sodomy laws if he were given the opportunity as a legislator.

Impact

The *Lawrence v. Texas* decision was greeted by gay rights activists and civil libertarians as monumental, even earthshaking. Gay rights activists predicted that no law penalizing gays and lesbians, even indirectly, such as by limiting the availability of social benefits like marriage and adoption, could stand in the wake of *Lawrence*. Whether that excitement was justified remained to be seen within the half decade after the decision.

Critically, the majority opinion in *Lawrence* did not explicitly recognize private sexual activity as a fundamental right. Indeed, one reading of the case is that a state need only offer a rational basis for regulating such activity. As such, *Lawrence* may not serve as the foundation for a gay rights revolution in the same way that, for example, *Brown v. Board of Education* did for race. That its proponents may have overestimated its impact when it was first issued proved to be the case in the legal decisions rendered in the first five years after the decision. For example, in the face of challenges based on *Lawrence*, courts have upheld the ban on homosexual conduct in the military and Florida's ban on adoption by same-sex couples, finding rational bases to support both.

Nevertheless, *Lawrence* remains an important decision, as it immediately made illegal the thirteen remaining state sodomy laws. The Court recognized a constitutional right with regard to private, consensual sexual conduct by adults. More significantly, the decision calls into question laws founded on the moral disapproval of private actions that do no harm to others. Whether rational bases beyond moral disapproval exist for laws banning a wide range of personal behavior remains to be seen.

Related Documents

Anderson v. Morrow, 371 F.3d 1027 (9th Cir. 2004). This decision states that the liberty interest identified in *Lawrence* does not apply to invalidate a state's "rape shield" law, because states have a legitimate interest to prosecute when consent is in doubt.

Bowers v. Hardwick, 478 U.S. 186 (1986). This case upheld a state law criminalizing sodomy; it was later overruled by *Lawrence*.

Eisenstadt v. Baird, 405 U.S. 438 (1972). The case established the right of unmarried people to possess means of contraception just like married couples and thus upheld the right of unmarried couples to engage in potentially procreative sexual acts.

Griswold v. Connecticut, 381 U.S. 479 (1965). This decision held that the U.S. Constitution protected a right to privacy, in this case the right to marital privacy.

Limon v. Kansas, 539 U.S. 955 (2003). A companion case to *Lawrence*, this case suggested that even where conduct does not fall within the *Lawrence* liberty interest and can be generally prohibited, claims based on equal protection may be valid to prohibit disparate punishments for sodomy based on the sex of the actors.

Loomis v. United States, 68 Fed. Cl. 503 (2005). It was the finding in this case that the military's "Don't ask, don't tell" policy was not affected by the liberty interest identified in *Lawrence* because *Lawrence* applied only to criminal prohibitions.

Planned Parenthood of Southeastern Pa. v. Casey, 505 U.S. 833 (1992). This decision upheld *Roe's* holding of a woman's right to privacy with respect to abortion but allowed regulation of abortion where the state has not put an excessive burden on the exercise of the woman's right to choose to have an abortion.

Roe v. Wade, 410 U.S. 113 (1973). This case found that a woman's right to privacy was sufficiently broad to embrace a woman's decision whether or not to end her pregnancy.

United States v. Marcum, 60 M.J. 198 (C.A.A.F. 2004). The court applied the *Lawrence* liberty interest to the military's prohibition of sodomy.

Bibliography

■ Articles

Gardner, Martin R. "Adoption by Homosexuals in the Wake of *Lawrence v. Texas*." *Journal of Law and Family Studies* 6, no. 1 (2004): 19–58.

Gonzalez, Jessica A. "Decriminalizing Sexual Conduct: The Supreme Court Ruling in *Lawrence v. Texas*." *St. Mary's Law Journal* 35, no. 3 (2004): 685–706.

Greene, Jamal. "Beyond *Lawrence*: Metaprivacy and Punishment." *Yale Law Journal* 115, no. 8 (June 2006): 1862–1928.

Hassel, Diana. "Sex and Death: *Lawrence's* Liberty and Physician-Assisted Suicide." *University of Pennsylvania Journal of Constitutional Law* 9 (2007): 1003–1032.

Katyal, Sonia K. "Sexuality and Sovereignty: The Global Limits and Possibilities of *Lawrence*." *William and Mary Bill of Rights Journal* 14 (April 2006): 1429–1492.

Krotoszynski, Ronald J., Jr. "Dumbo's Feather: An Examination and Critique of the Supreme Court's Use, Misuse, and Abuse of Tradition in Protecting Fundamental Rights." *William and Mary Law Review* 48, no. 3 (2006): 923–1023.

Marcus, Nancy C. "Beyond *Romer* and *Lawrence*: The Right to Privacy Comes Out of the Closet." *Columbia Journal of Gender and Law* 15 (2006): 355–436.

Sharum, Jerald A. "Controlling Conduct: The Emerging Protection of Sodomy in the Military." *Albany Law Review* 69, no. 4 (2006): 1195–1236.

Strasser, Mark. "Monogamy, Licentiousness, Desuetude, and Mere Tolerance: The Multiple Misinterpretations of *Lawrence v. Texas*." *Southern California Review of Law and Women's Studies* 15, no. 1 (2005): 95–144.

Susstein, Cass R. "What Did *Lawrence* Hold? Of Autonomy, Desuetude, Sexuality, and Marriage." *Supreme Court Review* 2003 (2003): 27–74.

Tribe, Laurence H. "*Lawrence v. Texas*: The 'Fundamental Right' That Dare Not Speak Its Name." *Harvard Law Review* 117, no. 6 (2004): 1893–1955.

■ Books

Andersen, Ellen Ann. *Out of the Closets and into the Courts: Legal Opportunity Structure and Gay Rights Litigation*. Ann Arbor: University of Michigan Press, 2006.

Richards, David A. J. *The Case for Gay Rights: From* Bowers *to* Lawrence *and Beyond*. Lawrence: University Press of Kansas, 2005.

Roosevelt, Kermit. *The Myth of Judicial Activism: Making Sense of Supreme Court Decisions*. New Haven, Conn.: Yale University Press, 2006.

Walzer, Lee. *Gay Rights on Trial: A Sourcebook with Cases, Laws, and Documents*. Indianapolis: Hackett Publishing, 2002.

■ Web Sites

"ACLU Brief in Lawrence, et al v. Texas." American Civil Liberties Union Web site.
http://www.aclu.org/lgbt/crimjustice/11887lgl20030626.html. Accessed on March 11, 2008.

"*Lawrence v. Texas*." Lambda Legal Web site.
http://www.lambdalegal.org/our-work/in-court/cases/lawrence-v-texas.html. Accessed on March 11, 2008.

"Supreme Court Collection: Anthony M. Kennedy." Cornell University Law School "Legal Information Institute" Web site.
http://www.law.cornell.edu/supct/justices/kennedy.bio.html. Accessed on March 11, 2008.

Union Pacific Railway Co. v. Botsford, 141 U.S. 250 (1891). Justia.com Web site.
http://supreme.justia.com/us/141/250/case.html. Accessed on March 11, 2008.

"Washington v. Glucksberg." U.S. Supreme Court Media "Oyez" Web site.
  http://www.oyez.org/cases/1990-1999/1996/1996_96_110/.
  Accessed on March 11, 2008.

—By Alicia R. Ouellette

Questions for Further Study

1. Which justice presents the best-reasoned analysis in the opinions from *Lawrence v. Texas*? Does Kennedy adequately answer the critiques of his logic put forth by Scalia?

2. Among the most important holdings in *Lawrence* is that moral judgments can no longer serve as a legitimate basis for legislation; other public-interest motivations must be advanced if morality-based legislation is to sustain constitutional attack. What laws might this holding affect? Is there more than a moral basis for outlawing polygamy? Same-sex marriage? Sodomy in the military? Incest? Prostitution? Bestiality? Adoption by gay parents? Obscenity? Recreational drug use?

3. Compare the analysis employed by Justice Kennedy in the majority opinion with that employed by Justice William Rehnquist in *Washington v. Glucksberg* (1997), which rejected the claim that the right to privacy included the right to direct the course of one's own death through physician-assisted suicide. In *Glucksberg* the Court reasoned that access to physician-assisted suicide is not a right deeply rooted in our nation's history and traditions and thus is not protected by the due process clause. Does that analysis withstand scrutiny after *Lawrence*?

Glossary

amicus briefs	briefs by friends of the court, submitted by interest groups or others who are not parties to a case but have special knowledge about or a special interest in the case
compelling state interest	an interest of public concern that is so important as to justify limiting fundamental rights
fundamental rights	rights that are enumerated in the Bill of Rights or are inherent in the national concept of liberty; government cannot interfere with the exercise of fundamental rights without demonstrating that the regulation serves a compelling state interest
plea of *nolo contendere*	plea of no contest—no admission of guilt
rational-basis test	a test, employed in determining the constitutionality of most legislation, that asks if the legislation at issue is reasonably related to a legitimate state interest, such as public safety or the provision of services
stare decisis	the principle holding that courts should follow precedent in the interest of consistency and certainty in the law
substantive due process	the legal theory that rights implicit in the concept of liberty are fundamental and protected under the due process clause of the Constitution even if they are not explicitly mentioned in the Constitution
trial *de novo*	a form of appeal in which the appeals court holds a trial as if no other trial had been held

LAWRENCE V. TEXAS

Responding to a reported weapons disturbance in a private residence, Houston police entered petitioner Lawrence's apartment and saw him and another adult man, petitioner Garner, engaging in a private, consensual sexual act. Petitioners were arrested and convicted of deviate sexual intercourse in violation of a Texas statute forbidding two persons of the same sex to engage in certain intimate sexual conduct. In affirming, the State Court of Appeals held, *inter alia*, that the statute was not unconstitutional under the Due Process Clause of the Fourteenth Amendment. The court considered *Bowers v. Hardwick*, 478 U. S. 186, controlling on that point.

Held: The Texas statute making it a crime for two persons of the same sex to engage in certain intimate sexual conduct violates the Due Process Clause. Pp. 3-18.

(a) Resolution of this case depends on whether petitioners were free as adults to engage in private conduct in the exercise of their liberty under the Due Process Clause. For this inquiry the Court deems it necessary to reconsider its *Bowers* holding. The *Bowers* Court's initial substantive statement—"The issue presented is whether the Federal Constitution confers a fundamental right upon homosexuals to engage in sodomy ...," 478 U. S., at 190—discloses the Court's failure to appreciate the extent of the liberty at stake. To say that the issue in *Bowers* was simply the right to engage in certain sexual conduct demeans the claim the individual put forward, just as it would demean a married couple were it said that marriage is just about the right to have sexual intercourse. Although the laws involved in *Bowers* and here purport to do not more than prohibit a particular sexual act, their penalties and purposes have more far-reaching consequences, touching upon the most private human conduct, sexual behavior, and in the most private of places, the home. They seek to control a personal relationship that, whether or not

entitled to formal recognition in the law, is within the liberty of persons to choose without being punished as criminals. The liberty protected by the Constitution allows homosexual persons the right to choose to enter upon relationships in the confines of their homes and their own private lives and still retain their dignity as free persons. Pp. 3-6.

(b) Having misapprehended the liberty claim presented to it, the *Bowers* Court stated that proscriptions against sodomy have ancient roots. 478 U. S., at 192. It should be noted, however, that there is no longstanding history in this country of laws directed at homosexual conduct as a distinct matter. Early American sodomy laws were not directed at homosexuals as such but instead sought to prohibit nonprocreative sexual activity more generally, whether between men and women or men and men. Moreover, early sodomy laws seem not to have been enforced against consenting adults acting in private. Instead, sodomy prosecutions often involved predatory acts against those who could not or did not consent: relations between men and minor girls or boys, between adults involving force, between adults implicating disparity in status, or between men and animals. The longstanding criminal prohibition of homosexual sodomy upon which *Bowers* placed such reliance is as consistent with a general condemnation of nonprocreative sex as it is with an established tradition of prosecuting acts because of their homosexual character. Far from possessing "ancient roots," *ibid.*, American laws targeting same-sex couples did not develop until the last third of the 20th century. Even now, only nine States have singled out same-sex relations for criminal prosecution. Thus, the historical grounds relied upon in *Bowers* are more complex than the majority opinion and the concurring opinion by Chief Justice Burger there indicated. They are not without doubt and, at the very least, are overstated. The *Bowers* Court was, of course, making the broader point that for centuries there have been powerful voices to condemn homosexual conduct as immoral, but this Court's obligation is to define the liberty of all, not to mandate its own moral code, *Planned Parenthood of Southeastern Pa. v. Casey*, 505 U. S. 833, 850. The Nation's laws and traditions in the past half century are most relevant here. They show an emerging awareness that liberty gives substantial protection to adult persons in deciding how to conduct their private lives in matters pertaining to sex. See *County of Sacramento v. Lewis*, 523 U. S. 833, 857. Pp. 6-12.

(c) *Bowers'* deficiencies became even more apparent in the years following its announcement. The 25 States with laws prohibiting the conduct referenced in Bowers are reduced now to 13, of which 4 enforce their laws only against homosexual conduct. In those States, including Texas, that still proscribe sodomy (whether for same-sex or heterosexual conduct), there is a pattern of nonenforcement with respect to consenting adults acting in private. *Casey, supra*, at 851—which confirmed that the Due Process Clause protects personal decisions relating to marriage, procreation, contraception, family relationships, child rearing, and education—and *Romer v. Evans*, 517 U. S. 620, 624—which struck down class-based legislation directed at homosexuals—cast *Bowers'* holding into even more doubt. The stigma the Texas criminal statute imposes, moreover, is not trivial. Although the offense is but a minor misdemeanor, it remains a criminal offense with all that imports for the dignity of the persons charged, including notation of convictions on their records and on job application forms, and registration as sex offenders under state law. Where a case's foundations have sustained serious erosion, criticism from other sources is of greater significance. In the United States, criticism of *Bowers* has been substantial and continuing, disapproving of its reasoning in all respects, not just as to its historical assumptions. And, to the extent *Bowers* relied on values shared with a wider civilization, the case's reasoning and holding have been rejected by the European Court of Human Rights, and that other nations have taken action consistent with an affirmation of the protected right of homosexual adults to engage in intimate, consensual conduct. There has been no showing that in this country the governmental interest in circumscribing personal choice is somehow more legitimate or urgent. *Stare decisis* is not an inexorable command. *Payne v. Tennessee*, 501 U. S. 808, 828. *Bowers'* holding has not induced detrimental reliance of the sort that could counsel against overturning it once there are compelling reasons to

do so. *Casey, supra*, at 855-856. *Bowers* causes uncertainty, for the precedents before and after it contradict its central holding. Pp. 12-17.

(d) *Bowers'* rationale does not withstand careful analysis. In his dissenting opinion in *Bowers* Justice Stevens concluded that (1) the fact a State's governing majority has traditionally viewed a particular practice as immoral is not a sufficient reason for upholding a law prohibiting the practice, and (2) individual decisions concerning the intimacies of physical relationships, even when not intended to produce offspring, are a form of "liberty" protected by due process. That analysis should have controlled *Bowers*, and it controls here. *Bowers* was not correct when it was decided, is not correct today, and is hereby overruled. This case does not involve minors, persons who might be injured or coerced, those who might not easily refuse consent, or public conduct or prostitution. It does involve two adults who, with full and mutual consent, engaged in sexual practices common to a homosexual lifestyle. Petitioners' right to liberty under the Due Process Clause gives them the full right to engage in private conduct without government intervention. *Casey*, supra, at 847. The Texas statute furthers no legitimate state interest which can justify its intrusion into the individual's personal and private life. Pp. 17-18.

Justice Kennedy Delivered the Opinion of the Court

Liberty protects the person from unwarranted government intrusions into a dwelling or other private places. In our tradition the State is not omnipresent in the home. And there are other spheres of our lives and existence, outside the home, where the State should not be a dominant presence. Freedom extends beyond spatial bounds. Liberty presumes an autonomy of self that includes freedom of thought, belief, expression, and certain intimate conduct. The instant case involves liberty of the person both in its spatial and more transcendent dimensions.

◆ I

The question before the Court is the validity of a Texas statute making it a crime for two persons of the same sex to engage in certain intimate sexual conduct.

In Houston, Texas, officers of the Harris County Police Department were dispatched to a private residence in response to a reported weapons disturbance. They entered an apartment where one of the petitioners, John Geddes Lawrence, resided. The right of the police to enter does not seem to have been questioned. The officers observed Lawrence and another man, Tyron Garner, engaging in a sexual act. The two petitioners were arrested, held in custody over night, and charged and convicted before a Justice of the Peace.

The complaints described their crime as "deviate sexual intercourse, namely anal sex, with a member of the same sex (man)." App. to Pet. for Cert. 127a, 139a. The applicable state law is Tex. Penal Code Ann. §21.06(a) (2003). It provides: "A person commits an offense if he engages in deviate sexual intercourse with another individual of the same sex." The statute defines "[d]eviate sexual intercourse" as follows:

"(A) any contact between any part of the genitals of one person and the mouth or anus of another person; or

"(B) the penetration of the genitals or the anus of another person with an object." §21.01(1).

The petitioners exercised their right to a trial *de novo* in Harris County Criminal Court. They challenged the statute as a violation of the Equal Protection Clause of the Fourteenth Amendment and of a like provision of the Texas Constitution. Tex. Const., Art. 1, §3a. Those contentions were rejected. The petitioners, having entered a plea of *nolo contendere,* were each fined $200 and assessed court costs of $141.25. App. to Pet. for Cert. 107a-110a.

The Court of Appeals for the Texas Fourteenth District considered the petitioners' federal constitutional arguments under both the Equal Protection and Due Process Clauses of the Fourteenth Amendment. After hearing the case en banc the court, in a divided opinion, rejected the constitutional arguments and affirmed the convictions. 41 S. W. 3d 349 (Tex. App. 2001). The majority opinion indicates that the Court of Appeals considered our decision in *Bowers v. Hardwick,* 478 U. S. 186 (1986), to be controlling on the federal due process aspect of the case. *Bowers* then being authoritative, this was proper.

We granted certiorari, 537 U. S. 1044 (2002), to consider three questions:

1. Whether Petitioners' criminal convictions under the Texas "Homosexual Conduct" law—which criminalizes sexual intimacy by same-sex couples, but not identical behavior by different-sex couples—violate the Fourteenth Amendment guarantee of equal protection of laws?

2. Whether Petitioners' criminal convictions for adult consensual sexual intimacy in the home violate their vital interests in liberty and privacy protected by the Due Process Clause of the Fourteenth Amendment?

3. Whether *Bowers v. Hardwick,* 478 U. S. 186 (1986), should be overruled? Pet. for Cert. i.

The petitioners were adults at the time of the alleged offense. Their conduct was in private and consensual.

◆ **II**

We conclude the case should be resolved by determining whether the petitioners were free as adults to engage in the private conduct in the exercise of their liberty under the Due Process Clause of the Fourteenth Amendment to the Constitution. For this inquiry we deem it necessary to reconsider the Court's holding in *Bowers.*

There are broad statements of the substantive reach of liberty under the Due Process Clause in earlier cases, including *Pierce v. Society of Sisters,* 268 U. S. 510 (1925), and *Meyer v. Nebraska,* 262 U. S. 390 (1923); but the most pertinent beginning point is our decision in *Griswold v. Connecticut,* 381 U. S. 479 (1965).

In *Griswold* the Court invalidated a state law prohibiting the use of drugs or devices of contraception and counseling or aiding and abetting the use of contraceptives. The Court described the protected interest as a right to privacy and placed emphasis on the marriage relation and the protected space of the marital bedroom. *Id.,* at 485.

After *Griswold* it was established that the right to make certain decisions regarding sexual conduct extends beyond the marital relationship. In *Eisenstadt v. Baird,* 405 U. S. 438 (1972), the Court invalidated a law prohibiting the distribution of contraceptives to unmarried persons. The case was decided under the Equal Protection Clause, *id.,* at 454; but with respect to unmarried persons, the Court went on to state the fundamental proposition that the law impaired the exercise of their personal rights, *ibid.* It quoted from the statement of the Court of Appeals finding the law to be in conflict with fundamental human rights, and it followed with this statement of its own:

"It is true that in *Griswold* the right of privacy in question inhered in the marital relationship.... If the right of privacy means anything, it is the right of the *individual,* married or single, to be free from unwarranted governmental intrusion into matters so fundamentally affecting a person as the decision whether to bear or beget a child." *Id.*, at 453.

The opinions in *Griswold* and *Eisenstadt* were part of the background for the decision in *Roe v. Wade*, 410 U. S. 113 (1973). As is well known, the case involved a challenge to the Texas law prohibiting abortions, but the laws of other States were affected as well. Although the Court held the woman's rights were not absolute, her right to elect an abortion did have real and substantial protection as an exercise of her liberty under the Due Process Clause. The Court cited cases that protect spatial freedom and cases that go well beyond it. *Roe* recognized the right of a woman to make certain fundamental decisions affecting her destiny and confirmed once more that the protection of liberty under the Due Process Clause has a substantive dimension of fundamental significance in defining the rights of the person.

In *Carey v. Population Services Int'l*, 431 U. S. 678 (1977), the Court confronted a New York law forbidding sale or distribution of contraceptive devices to persons under 16 years of age. Although there was no single opinion for the Court, the law was invalidated. Both *Eisenstadt* and *Carey*, as well as the holding and rationale in *Roe*, confirmed that the reasoning of Griswold could not be confined to the protection of rights of married adults. This was the state of the law with respect to some of the most relevant cases when the Court considered *Bowers v. Hardwick*.

The facts in *Bowers* had some similarities to the instant case. A police officer, whose right to enter seems not to have been in question, observed Hardwick, in his own bedroom, engaging in intimate sexual conduct with another adult male. The conduct was in violation of a Georgia statute making it a criminal offense to engage in sodomy. One difference between the two cases is that the Georgia statute prohibited the conduct whether or not the participants were of the same sex, while the Texas statute, as we have seen, applies only to participants of the same sex. Hardwick was not prosecuted, but he brought an action in federal court to declare the state statute invalid. He alleged he was a practicing homosexual and that the criminal prohibition violated rights guaranteed to him by the Constitution. The Court, in an opinion by Justice White, sustained the Georgia law. Chief Justice Burger and Justice Powell joined the opinion of the Court and filed separate, concurring opinions. Four Justices dissented. 478 U. S., at 199 (opinion of Blackmun, J., joined by Brennan, Marshall, and Stevens, JJ.); *id.*, at 214 (opinion of Stevens, J., joined by Brennan and Marshall, JJ.).

The Court began its substantive discussion in *Bowers* as follows: "The issue presented is whether the Federal Constitution confers a fundamental right upon homosexuals to engage in sodomy and hence invalidates the laws of the many States that still make such conduct illegal and have done so for a very long time." *Id.*, at 190. That statement, we now conclude, discloses the Court's own failure to appreciate the extent of the liberty at stake. To say that the issue in *Bowers* was simply the right to engage in certain sexual conduct demeans the claim the individual put forward, just as it would demean a married couple were it to be said marriage is simply about the right to have sexual intercourse. The laws involved in Bowers and here are, to be sure, statutes that purport to do no more than prohibit a particular sexual act. Their penalties and purposes, though, have more far-reaching consequences, touching upon the most private human conduct, sexual behavior, and in the most private of places, the home. The statutes do seek to control a personal relationship that, whether or not entitled to formal recognition in the law, is within the liberty of persons to choose without being punished as criminals.

This, as a general rule, should counsel against attempts by the State, or a court, to define the meaning of the relationship or to set its boundaries absent injury to a person or abuse of an institution the law protects. It suffices for us to acknowledge that adults may choose to enter upon this relationship in the confines of their homes and their own private lives and still retain their dignity as free persons. When sexuality finds overt expression in intimate conduct with another person, the conduct can be but one element in a personal bond that is more enduring. The liberty protected by the Constitution allows homosexual persons the right to make this choice.

Having misapprehended the claim of liberty there presented to it, and thus stating the claim to be whether there is a fundamental right to engage in consensual sodomy, the Bowers Court said: "Proscriptions against that conduct have ancient roots." *Id.*, at 192. In academic writings, and in many of the scholarly *amicus* briefs filed to assist the Court in this case, there are fundamental criticisms of the historical premises relied upon by the majority and concurring opinions in *Bowers*. Brief for Cato Institute as *Amicus Curiae* 16-17; Brief for American Civil Liberties Union et al. as Amici Curiae 15-21; Brief for Professors of History et al. as *Amici Curiae* 3-10. We need not enter this debate in the attempt to reach a definitive historical judgment, but the following considerations counsel against adopting the definitive conclusions upon which *Bowers* placed such reliance.

At the outset it should be noted that there is no longstanding history in this country of laws directed at homosexual conduct as a distinct matter. Beginning in colonial times there were prohibitions of sodomy derived from the English criminal laws passed in the first instance by the Reformation Parliament of 1533. The English prohibition was understood to include relations between men and women as well as relations between men and men. See, *e.g.,* *King v. Wiseman*, 92 Eng. Rep. 774, 775 (K. B. 1718) (interpreting "mankind" in Act of 1533 as including women and girls). Nineteenth-century commentators similarly read American sodomy, buggery, and crime-against-nature statutes as criminalizing certain relations between men and women and between men and men. See, *e.g.,* 2 J. Bishop, Criminal Law §1028 (1858); 2 J. Chitty, Criminal Law 47-50 (5th Am. ed. 1847); R. Desty, A Compendium of American Criminal Law 143 (1882); J. May, The Law of Crimes §203 (2d ed. 1893). The absence of legal prohibitions focusing on homosexual conduct may be explained in part by noting that according to some scholars the concept of the homosexual as a distinct category of person did not emerge until the late 19th century. See, *e.g.,* J. Katz, *The Invention of Heterosexuality* 10 (1995); J. D'Emilio & E. Freedman, *Intimate Matters: A History of Sexuality in America* 121 (2d ed. 1997) ("The modern terms *homosexuality* and *heterosexuality* do not apply to an era that had not yet articulated these distinctions"). Thus early American sodomy laws were not directed at homosexuals as such but instead sought to prohibit nonprocreative sexual activity more generally. This does not suggest approval of homosexual conduct. It does tend to show that this particular form of conduct was not thought of as a separate category from like conduct between heterosexual persons.

Laws prohibiting sodomy do not seem to have been enforced against consenting adults acting in private. A substantial number of sodomy prosecutions and convictions for which there are surviving records were for predatory acts against those who could not or did not consent, as in the case of a minor or the victim of an assault. As to these, one purpose for the prohibitions was to ensure there would be no lack of coverage if a predator committed a sexual assault that did not constitute rape as defined by the criminal law. Thus the model sodomy indictments presented in a 19th-century treatise, see 2 Chitty, *supra,* at 49, addressed the predatory acts of an adult man against a minor girl or minor boy. Instead of targeting relations between consenting adults in private, 19th-century sodomy prosecutions typically involved relations between men and minor girls or minor boys, relations between adults involving force, relations between adults implicating disparity in status, or relations between men and animals.

To the extent that there were any prosecutions for the acts in question, 19th-century evidence rules imposed a burden that would make a conviction more difficult to obtain even taking into account the problems always inherent in prosecuting consensual acts committed in private. Under then-prevailing standards, a man could not be convicted of sodomy based upon testimony of a consenting partner, because the partner was considered an accomplice. A partner's testimony, however, was admissible if he or she had not consented to the act or was a minor, and therefore incapable of consent. See, *e.g.,* F. Wharton, Criminal Law 443 (2d ed. 1852); 1 F. Wharton, Criminal Law 512 (8th ed. 1880). The rule may explain in part the infrequency of these prosecutions. In all events that infrequency makes it difficult to say that society approved of a rigorous and systematic punishment of the consensual acts committed in private and by adults. The longstanding criminal prohibition of homosexual sodomy upon which the *Bowers* decision placed such reliance is as consistent with a general condemnation of nonprocreative sex as it is with an established tradition of prosecuting acts because of their homosexual character.

The policy of punishing consenting adults for private acts was not much discussed in the early legal literature. We can infer that one reason for this was the very private nature of the conduct. Despite the absence of prosecutions, there may have been periods in which there was public criticism of homosexuals as such and an insistence that the criminal laws be enforced to discourage their practices. But far from possessing "ancient roots," *Bowers,* 478 U. S., at 192, American laws targeting same-sex couples did not develop until the last third of the 20th century. The reported decisions concerning the prosecution of consensual, homosexual sodomy between adults for the years 1880-1995 are not always clear in the details, but a significant number involved conduct in a public place. See Brief for American Civil Liberties Union et al. as *Amici Curiae* 14-15, and n. 18.

It was not until the 1970's that any State singled out same-sex relations for criminal prosecution, and only nine States have done so. See 1977 Ark. Gen.

Acts no. 828; 1983 Kan. Sess. Laws p. 652; 1974 Ky. Acts p. 847; 1977 Mo. Laws p. 687; 1973 Mont. Laws p. 1339; 1977 Nev. Stats. p. 1632; 1989 Tenn. Pub. Acts ch. 591; 1973 Tex. Gen. Laws ch. 399; see also *Post v. State*, 715 P. 2d 1105 (Okla. Crim. App. 1986) (sodomy law invalidated as applied to different-sex couples). Post-*Bowers* even some of these States did not adhere to the policy of suppressing homosexual conduct. Over the course of the last decades, States with same-sex prohibitions have moved toward abolishing them. See, *e.g., Jegley v. Picado*, 349 Ark. 600, 80 S. W. 3d 332 (2002); *Gryczan v. State*, 283 Mont. 433, 942 P. 2d 112 (1997); *Campbell v. Sundquist*, 926 S. W. 2d 250 (Tenn. App. 1996); *Commonwealth v. Wasson*, 842 S. W. 2d 487 (Ky. 1992); see also 1993 Nev. Stats. p. 518 (repealing Nev. Rev. Stat. §201.193).

In summary, the historical grounds relied upon in *Bowers* are more complex than the majority opinion and the concurring opinion by Chief Justice Burger indicate. Their historical premises are not without doubt and, at the very least, are overstated.

It must be acknowledged, of course, that the Court in *Bowers* was making the broader point that for centuries there have been powerful voices to condemn homosexual conduct as immoral. The condemnation has been shaped by religious beliefs, conceptions of right and acceptable behavior, and respect for the traditional family. For many persons these are not trivial concerns but profound and deep convictions accepted as ethical and moral principles to which they aspire and which thus determine the course of their lives. These considerations do not answer the question before us, however. The issue is whether the majority may use the power of the State to enforce these views on the whole society through operation of the criminal law. "Our obligation is to define the liberty of all, not to mandate our own moral code." *Planned Parenthood of Southeastern Pa. v. Casey*, 505 U. S. 833, 850 (1992).

Chief Justice Burger joined the opinion for the Court in *Bowers* and further explained his views as follows: "Decisions of individuals relating to homosexual conduct have been subject to state intervention throughout the history of Western civilization. Condemnation of those practices is firmly rooted in Judeao-Christian moral and ethical standards." 478 U. S., at 196. As with Justice White's assumptions about history, scholarship casts some doubt on the sweeping nature of the statement by Chief Justice Burger as it pertains to private homosexual conduct between consenting adults. See, *e.g.*, Eskridge, Hardwick and Historiography, 1999 U. Ill. L. Rev.

631, 656. In all events we think that our laws and traditions in the past half century are of most relevance here. These references show an emerging awareness that liberty gives substantial protection to adult persons in deciding how to conduct their private lives in matters pertaining to sex. "[H]istory and tradition are the starting point but not in all cases the ending point of the substantive due process inquiry." *County of Sacramento v. Lewis*, 523 U. S. 833, 857 (1998) (Kennedy, J., concurring).

This emerging recognition should have been apparent when *Bowers* was decided. In 1955 the American Law Institute promulgated the Model Penal Code and made clear that it did not recommend or provide for "criminal penalties for consensual sexual relations conducted in private." ALI, Model Penal Code §213.2, Comment 2, p. 372 (1980). It justified its decision on three grounds: (1) The prohibitions undermined respect for the law by penalizing conduct many people engaged in; (2) the statutes regulated private conduct not harmful to others; and (3) the laws were arbitrarily enforced and thus invited the danger of blackmail. ALI, Model Penal Code, Commentary 277-280 (Tent. Draft No. 4, 1955). In 1961 Illinois changed its laws to conform to the Model Penal Code. Other States soon followed. Brief for Cato Institute as *Amicus Curiae* 15-16.

In *Bowers* the Court referred to the fact that before 1961 all 50 States had outlawed sodomy, and that at the time of the Court's decision 24 States and the District of Columbia had sodomy laws. 478 U. S., at 192-193. Justice Powell pointed out that these prohibitions often were being ignored, however. Georgia, for instance, had not sought to enforce its law for decades. *Id.*, at 197-198, n. 2 ("The history of nonenforcement suggests the moribund character today of laws criminalizing this type of private, consensual conduct").

The sweeping references by Chief Justice Burger to the history of Western civilization and to Judeo-Christian moral and ethical standards did not take account of other authorities pointing in an opposite direction. A committee advising the British Parliament recommended in 1957 repeal of laws punishing homosexual conduct. The Wolfenden Report: Report of the Committee on Homosexual Offenses and Prostitution (1963). Parliament enacted the substance of those recommendations 10 years later. Sexual Offences Act 1967, §1.

Of even more importance, almost five years before *Bowers* was decided the European Court of Human Rights considered a case with parallels to

Bowers and to today's case. An adult male resident in Northern Ireland alleged he was a practicing homosexual who desired to engage in consensual homosexual conduct. The laws of Northern Ireland forbade him that right. He alleged that he had been questioned, his home had been searched, and he feared criminal prosecution. The court held that the laws proscribing the conduct were invalid under the European Convention on Human Rights. *Dudgeon v. United Kingdom*, 45 Eur. Ct. H. R. (1981) ¶;52. Authoritative in all countries that are members of the Council of Europe (21 nations then, 45 nations now), the decision is at odds with the premise in *Bowers* that the claim put forward was insubstantial in our Western civilization.

In our own constitutional system the deficiencies in Bowers became even more apparent in the years following its announcement. The 25 States with laws prohibiting the relevant conduct referenced in the Bowers decision are reduced now to 13, of which 4 enforce their laws only against homosexual conduct. In those States where sodomy is still proscribed, whether for same-sex or heterosexual conduct, there is a pattern of nonenforcement with respect to consenting adults acting in private. The State of Texas admitted in 1994 that as of that date it had not prosecuted anyone under those circumstances. *State v. Morales*, 869 S. W. 2d 941, 943.

Two principal cases decided after Bowers cast its holding into even more doubt. In *Planned Parenthood of Southeastern Pa. v. Casey*, 505 U. S. 833 (1992), the Court reaffirmed the substantive force of the liberty protected by the Due Process Clause. The Casey decision again confirmed that our laws and tradition afford constitutional protection to personal decisions relating to marriage, procreation, contraception, family relationships, child rearing, and education. Id., at 851. In explaining the respect the Constitution demands for the autonomy of the person in making these choices, we stated as follows:

"These matters, involving the most intimate and personal choices a person may make in a lifetime, choices central to personal dignity and autonomy, are central to the liberty protected by the Fourteenth Amendment. At the heart of liberty is the right to define one's own concept of existence, of meaning, of the universe, and of the mystery of human life. Beliefs about these matters could not define the attributes of personhood were they formed under compulsion of the State." *Ibid.*

Persons in a homosexual relationship may seek autonomy for these purposes, just as heterosexual persons do. The decision in *Bowers* would deny them this right.

The second post-Bowers case of principal relevance is *Romer v. Evans*, 517 U. S. 620 (1996). There the Court struck down class-based legislation directed at homosexuals as a violation of the Equal Protection Clause. *Romer* invalidated an amendment to Colorado's constitution which named as a solitary class persons who were homosexuals, lesbians, or bisexual either by "orientation, conduct, practices or relationships," *id.*, at 624 (internal quotation marks omitted), and deprived them of protection under state antidiscrimination laws. We concluded that the provision was "born of animosity toward the class of persons affected" and further that it had no rational relation to a legitimate governmental purpose. *Id.*, at 634.

As an alternative argument in this case, counsel for the petitioners and some *amici* contend that *Romer* provides the basis for declaring the Texas statute invalid under the Equal Protection Clause. That is a tenable argument, but we conclude the instant case requires us to address whether *Bowers* itself has continuing validity. Were we to hold the statute invalid under the Equal Protection Clause some might question whether a prohibition would be valid if drawn differently, say, to prohibit the conduct both between same-sex and different-sex participants.

Equality of treatment and the due process right to demand respect for conduct protected by the substantive guarantee of liberty are linked in important respects, and a decision on the latter point advances both interests. If protected conduct is made criminal and the law which does so remains unexamined for its substantive validity, its stigma might remain even if it were not enforceable as drawn for equal protection reasons. When homosexual conduct is made criminal by the law of the State, that declaration in and of itself is an invitation to subject homosexual persons to discrimination both in the public and in the private spheres. The central holding of *Bowers* has been brought in question by this case, and it should be addressed. Its continuance as precedent demeans the lives of homosexual persons.

The stigma this criminal statute imposes, moreover, is not trivial. The offense, to be sure, is but a class C misdemeanor, a minor offense in the Texas legal system. Still, it remains a criminal offense with all that imports for the dignity of the persons charged. The petitioners will bear on their record the history of their criminal convictions. Just this Term we rejected various challenges to state laws requiring the registration of sex offenders. *Smith v. Doe*, 538 U. S. __ (2003); *Connecticut Dept. of Public Safety v. Doe*, 538 U. S. 1 (2003). We are advised that if Texas convicted an adult for private, consensual homosexual conduct under the statute here in question the convicted person would come within the registration laws of a least four States were he or she to be subject to their jurisdiction. Pet. for Cert. 13, and n. 12 (citing Idaho Code §§18-8301 to 18-8326 (Cum. Supp. 2002); La. Code Crim. Proc. Ann., §§15:540-15:549 (West 2003); Miss. Code Ann. §§45-33-21 to 45-33-57 (Lexis 2003); S. C. Code Ann. §§23-3-400 to 23-3-490 (West 2002)). This underscores the consequential nature of the punishment and the state-sponsored condemnation attendant to the criminal prohibition. Furthermore, the Texas criminal conviction carries with it the other collateral consequences always following a conviction, such as notations on job application forms, to mention but one example.

The foundations of *Bowers* have sustained serious erosion from our recent decisions in *Casey* and *Romer*. When our precedent has been thus weakened, criticism from other sources is of greater significance. In the United States criticism of *Bowers* has been substantial and continuing, disapproving of its reasoning in all respects, not just as to its historical assumptions. See, *e.g.*, C. Fried, Order and Law: Arguing the Reagan Revolution—A Firsthand Account 81-84 (1991); R. Posner, Sex and Reason 341-350 (1992). The courts of five different States have declined to follow it in interpreting provisions in their own state constitutions parallel to the Due Process Clause of the Fourteenth Amendment, see *Jegley v. Picado*, 349 Ark. 600, 80 S. W. 3d 332 (2002); *Powell v. State*, 270 Ga. 327, 510 S. E. 2d 18, 24 (1998); *Gryczan v. State*, 283 Mont. 433, 942 P. 2d 112 (1997); *Campbell v. Sundquist*, 926 S. W. 2d 250 (Tenn. App. 1996); *Commonwealth v. Wasson*, 842 S. W. 2d 487 (Ky. 1992).

To the extent Bowers relied on values we share with a wider civilization, it should be noted that the reasoning and holding in *Bowers* have been rejected elsewhere. The European Court of Human Rights has followed not *Bowers* but its own decision in *Dudgeon v. United Kingdom*. See *P. G. & J. H. v. United Kingdom*, App. No. 00044787/98, ¶;56 (Eur. Ct. H. R., Sept. 25, 2001); *Modinos v. Cyprus*, 259 *Eur. Ct. H. R. (1993)*; *Norris v. Ireland*, 142 Eur. Ct. H. R. (1988). Other nations, too, have taken action consistent with an affirmation of the protected right of homosexual adults to engage in intimate, consensual conduct. See Brief for Mary Robinson et al. as Amici Curiae 11-12. The right the petitioners seek in this case has been accepted as an integral part of human freedom in many other countries. There has been no showing that in this country the governmental interest in circumscribing personal choice is somehow more legitimate or urgent.

The doctrine of *stare decisis* is essential to the respect accorded to the judgments of the Court and to the stability of the law. It is not, however, an inexorable command. *Payne v. Tennessee*, 501 U. S. 808, 828 (1991) ("*Stare decisis* is not an inexorable command; rather, it 'is a principle of policy and not a mechanical formula of adherence to the latest decision'") (quoting *Helvering v. Hallock*, 309 U. S. 106, 119 (1940))). In *Casey* we noted that when a Court is asked to overrule a precedent recognizing a constitutional liberty interest, individual or societal reliance on the existence of that liberty cautions with particular strength against reversing course. 505 U. S., at 855-856; see also *id.*, at 844 ("Liberty finds no refuge in a jurisprudence of doubt"). The holding in *Bowers*, however, has not induced detrimental reliance comparable to some instances where recognized individual rights are involved. Indeed, there has been no individual or societal reliance on *Bowers* of the sort that could counsel against overturning its holding once there are compelling reasons to do so. *Bowers* itself causes uncertainty, for the precedents before and after its issuance contradict its central holding.

The rationale of *Bowers* does not withstand careful analysis. In his dissenting opinion in *Bowers* Justice Stevens came to these conclusions:

> "Our prior cases make two propositions abundantly clear. First, the fact that the governing majority in a State has traditionally viewed a particular practice as immoral is not a sufficient reason for upholding a law prohibiting the practice; neither history nor tradition could save a law prohibiting miscegenation from constitutional attack. Second, individual decisions by married persons, concerning the intimacies of their physical relationship, even when not intended to produce offspring, are a form of 'liberty' protected by the Due Process Clause of the Fourteenth Amendment. Moreover, this protection extends to intimate choices by unmarried as well as married persons." 478 U. S., at 216 (footnotes and citations omitted).

Justice Stevens' analysis, in our view, should have been controlling in Bowers and should control here.

Bowers was not correct when it was decided, and it is not correct today. It ought not to remain binding precedent. *Bowers v. Hardwick* should be and now is overruled.

The present case does not involve minors. It does not involve persons who might be injured or coerced or who are situated in relationships where consent might not easily be refused. It does not involve public conduct or prostitution. It does not involve whether the government must give formal recognition to any relationship that homosexual persons seek to enter. The case does involve two adults who, with full and mutual consent from each other, engaged in sexual practices common to a homosexual lifestyle. The petitioners are entitled to respect for their private lives. The State cannot demean their existence or control their destiny by making their private sexual conduct a crime. Their right to liberty under the Due Process Clause gives them the full right to engage in their conduct without intervention of the government. "It is a promise of the Constitution that there is a realm of personal liberty which the government may not enter." *Casey, supra,* at 847. The Texas statute furthers no legitimate state interest which can justify its intrusion into the personal and private life of the individual.

Had those who drew and ratified the Due Process Clauses of the Fifth Amendment or the Fourteenth Amendment known the components of liberty in its manifold possibilities, they might have been more specific. They did not presume to have this insight. They knew times can blind us to certain truths and later generations can see that laws once thought necessary and proper in fact serve only to oppress. As the Constitution endures, persons in every generation can invoke its principles in their own search for greater freedom.

The judgment of the Court of Appeals for the Texas Fourteenth District is reversed, and the case is remanded for further proceedings not inconsistent with this opinion.

It is so ordered.

Justice O'Connor, Concurring in the Judgment

The Court today overrules *Bowers v. Hardwick,* 478 U. S. 186 (1986). I joined *Bowers,* and do not join the Court in overruling it. Nevertheless, I agree with the Court that Texas' statute banning same-sex sodomy is unconstitutional. See Tex. Penal Code Ann. §21.06 (2003). Rather than relying on the sub-stantive component of the Fourteenth Amendment's Due Process Clause, as the Court does, I base my conclusion on the Fourteenth Amendment's Equal Protection Clause.

The Equal Protection Clause of the Fourteenth Amendment "is essentially a direction that all persons similarly situated should be treated alike." *Cleburne v. Cleburne Living Center, Inc.,* 473 U. S. 432, 439 (1985); see also *Plyler v. Doe,* 457 U. S. 202, 216 (1982). Under our rational basis standard of review, "legislation is presumed to be valid and will be sustained if the classification drawn by the statute is rationally related to a legitimate state interest." *Cleburne v. Cleburne Living Center, supra,* at 440; see also *Department of Agriculture v. Moreno,* 413 U. S. 528, 534 (1973); *Romer v. Evans,* 517 U. S. 620, 632-633 (1996); *Nordlinger v. Hahn,* 505 U. S. 1, 11-12 (1992).

Laws such as economic or tax legislation that are scrutinized under rational basis review normally pass constitutional muster, since "the Constitution presumes that even improvident decisions will eventually be rectified by the democratic processes." *Cleburne v. Cleburne Living Center, supra,* at 440; see also *Fitzgerald v. Racing Assn. of Central Iowa, ante,* p. ___; *Williamson v. Lee Optical of Okla., Inc.,* 348 U. S. 483 (1955). We have consistently held, however, that some objectives, such as "a bare ... desire to harm a politically unpopular group," are not legitimate state interests. *Department of Agriculture v. Moreno, supra,* at 534. See also *Cleburne v. Cleburne Living Center, supra,* at 446-447; *Romer v. Evans, supra,* at 632. When a law exhibits such a desire to harm a politically unpopular group, we have applied a more searching form of rational basis review to strike down such laws under the Equal Protection Clause.

We have been most likely to apply rational basis review to hold a law unconstitutional under the Equal Protection Clause where, as here, the challenged legislation inhibits personal relationships. In *Department of Agriculture v. Moreno,* for example, we held that a law preventing those households containing an individual unrelated to any other member of the household from receiving food stamps violated equal protection because the purpose of the law was to "discriminate against hippies." 413 U. S., at 534. The asserted governmental interest in preventing food stamp fraud was not deemed sufficient to satisfy rational basis review. *Id.,* at 535-538. In *Eisenstadt v. Baird,* 405 U. S. 438, 447-455 (1972), we refused to sanction a law that discriminated between married and unmarried persons by prohibiting the distribution of contraceptives to single persons. Likewise, in *Cleburne v. Cleburne Living Center, supra*, we held that it was irrational for a State to require a home for the mentally disabled to obtain a special use permit when other residences—like fraternity houses and apartment buildings—did not have to obtain such a permit. And in *Romer v. Evans*, we disallowed a state statute that "impos[ed] a broad and undifferentiated disability on a single named group"—specifically, homosexuals. 517 U. S., at 632. The dissent apparently agrees that if these cases have *stare decisis* effect, Texas' sodomy law would not pass scrutiny under the Equal Protection Clause, regardless of the type of rational basis review that we apply. See *post*, at 17-18 (opinion of Scalia, J.).

The statute at issue here makes sodomy a crime only if a person "engages in deviate sexual intercourse with another individual of the same sex." Tex. Penal Code Ann. §21.06(a) (2003). Sodomy between opposite-sex partners, however, is not a crime in Texas. That is, Texas treats the same conduct differently based solely on the participants. Those harmed by this law are people who have a same-sex sexual orientation and thus are more likely to engage in behavior prohibited by §21.06.

The Texas statute makes homosexuals unequal in the eyes of the law by making particular conduct—and only that conduct—subject to criminal sanction. It appears that prosecutions under Texas' sodomy law are rare. See *State v. Morales*, 869 S. W. 2d 941, 943 (Tex. 1994) (noting in 1994 that §21.06 "has not been, and in all probability will not be, enforced against private consensual conduct between adults"). This case shows, however, that prosecutions under §21.06 *do* occur. And while the penalty imposed on petitioners in this case was relatively minor, the consequences of conviction are not. As the Court notes, see *ante*, at 15, petitioners' convictions, if upheld, would disqualify them from or restrict their ability to engage in a variety of professions, including medicine, athletic training, and interior design. See, *e.g.*, Tex. Occ. Code Ann. §164.051(a)(2)(B) (2003 Pamphlet) (physician); §451.251 (a)(1) (athletic trainer); §1053.252(2) (interior designer). Indeed, were petitioners to move to one of four States, their convictions would require them to register as sex offenders to local law enforcement. See, *e.g.*, Idaho Code §18-8304 (Cum. Supp. 2002); La. Stat. Ann. §15:542 (West Cum. Supp. 2003); Miss. Code Ann. §45-33-25 (West 2003); S. C. Code Ann. §23-3-430 (West Cum. Supp. 2002); cf. *ante*, at 15.

And the effect of Texas' sodomy law is not just limited to the threat of prosecution or consequence of conviction. Texas' sodomy law brands all homosexuals as criminals, thereby making it more difficult for homosexuals to be treated in the same manner as everyone else. Indeed, Texas itself has previously acknowledged the collateral effects of the law, stipulating in a prior challenge to this action that the law "legally sanctions discrimination against [homosexuals] in a variety of ways unrelated to the criminal law," including in the areas of "employment, family issues, and housing." *State v. Morales*, 826 S. W. 2d 201, 203 (Tex. App. 1992).

Texas attempts to justify its law, and the effects of the law, by arguing that the statute satisfies rational basis review because it furthers the legitimate governmental interest of the promotion of morality. In *Bowers*, we held that a state law criminalizing sodomy as applied to homosexual couples did not violate substantive due process. We rejected the argument that no rational basis existed to justify the law, pointing to the government's interest in promoting morality. 478 U. S., at 196. The only question in front of the Court in *Bowers* was whether the substantive component of the Due Process Clause protected a right to engage in homosexual sodomy. *Id.*, at 188, n. 2. *Bowers* did not hold that moral disapproval of a group is a rational basis under the Equal Protection Clause to criminalize homosexual sodomy when heterosexual sodomy is not punished.

This case raises a different issue than *Bowers*: whether, under the Equal Protection Clause, moral disapproval is a legitimate state interest to justify by itself a statute that bans homosexual sodomy, but not heterosexual sodomy. It is not. Moral disapproval of this group, like a bare desire to harm the group, is an interest that is insufficient to satisfy rational basis review under the Equal Protection Clause. See, *e.g.*, *Department of Agriculture v. Moreno, supra*, at 534; *Romer v. Evans*, 517 U. S., at 634-635. Indeed, we have never held that moral disapproval, without any other asserted state interest, is a sufficient rationale under the Equal Protection Clause to justify a law that discriminates among groups of persons.

Moral disapproval of a group cannot be a legitimate governmental interest under the Equal Protection Clause because legal classifications must not be "drawn for the purpose of disadvantaging the group burdened by the law." *Id.*, at 633. Texas' invocation of moral disapproval as a legitimate state interest proves nothing more than Texas' desire to criminalize homosexual sodomy. But the Equal Protection

Clause prevents a State from creating "a classification of persons undertaken for its own sake." *Id.*, at 635. And because Texas so rarely enforces its sodomy law as applied to private, consensual acts, the law serves more as a statement of dislike and disapproval against homosexuals than as a tool to stop criminal behavior. The Texas sodomy law "raise[s] the inevitable inference that the disadvantage imposed is born of animosity toward the class of persons affected." *Id.*, at 634.

Texas argues, however, that the sodomy law does not discriminate against homosexual persons. Instead, the State maintains that the law discriminates only against homosexual conduct. While it is true that the law applies only to conduct, the conduct targeted by this law is conduct that is closely correlated with being homosexual. Under such circumstances, Texas' sodomy law is targeted at more than conduct. It is instead directed toward gay persons as a class. "After all, there can hardly be more palpable discrimination against a class than making the conduct that defines the class criminal." *Id.*, at 641 (Scalia, J., dissenting) (internal quotation marks omitted). When a State makes homosexual conduct criminal, and not "deviate sexual intercourse" committed by persons of different sexes, "that declaration in and of itself is an invitation to subject homosexual persons to discrimination both in the public and in the private spheres." *Ante*, at 14.

Indeed, Texas law confirms that the sodomy statute is directed toward homosexuals as a class. In Texas, calling a person a homosexual is slander per se because the word "homosexual" "impute[s] the commission of a crime." *Plumley v. Landmark Chevrolet, Inc.*, 122 F. 3d 308, 310 (CA5 1997) (applying Texas law); see also *Head v. Newton*, 596 S. W. 2d 209, 210 (Tex. App. 1980). The State has admitted that because of the sodomy law, *being* homosexual carries the presumption of being a criminal. See *State v. Morales*, 826 S. W. 2d, at 202-203 ("[T]he statute brands lesbians and gay men as criminals and thereby legally sanctions discrimination against them in a variety of ways unrelated to the criminal law"). Texas' sodomy law therefore results in discrimination against homosexuals as a class in an array of areas outside the criminal law. See *ibid*. In *Romer v. Evans*, we refused to sanction a law that singled out homosexuals "for disfavored legal status." 517 U. S., at 633. The same is true here. The Equal Protection Clause "neither knows nor tolerates classes among citizens." *Id.*, at 623 (quoting *Plessy v. Ferguson*, 163 U. S. 537, 559 (1896) (Harlan, J., dissenting)).

A State can of course assign certain consequences to a violation of its criminal law. But the State cannot single out one identifiable class of citizens for punishment that does not apply to everyone else, with moral disapproval as the only asserted state interest for the law. The Texas sodomy statute subjects homosexuals to "a lifelong penalty and stigma. A legislative classification that threatens the creation of an underclass ... cannot be reconciled with" the Equal Protection Clause. *Plyler v. Doe*, 457 U. S., at 239 (Powell, J., concurring).

Whether a sodomy law that is neutral both in effect and application, see *Yick Wo v. Hopkins*, 118 U. S. 356 (1886), would violate the substantive component of the Due Process Clause is an issue that need not be decided today. I am confident, however, that so long as the Equal Protection Clause requires a sodomy law to apply equally to the private consensual conduct of homosexuals and heterosexuals alike, such a law would not long stand in our democratic society. In the words of Justice Jackson:

"The framers of the Constitution knew, and we should not forget today, that there is no more effective practical guaranty against arbitrary and unreasonable government than to require that the principles of law which officials would impose upon a minority be imposed generally. Conversely, nothing opens the door to arbitrary action so effectively as to allow those officials to pick and choose only a few to whom they will apply legislation and thus to escape the political retribution that might be visited upon them if larger numbers were affected." *Railway Express Agency, Inc. v. New York*, 336 U. S. 106, 112-113 (1949) (concurring opinion).

That this law as applied to private, consensual conduct is unconstitutional under the Equal Protection Clause does not mean that other laws distinguishing between heterosexuals and homosexuals would similarly fail under rational basis review. Texas cannot assert any legitimate state interest here, such as national security or preserving the traditional institution of marriage. Unlike the moral disapproval of same-sex relations—the asserted state interest in this case—other reasons exist to promote the institution of marriage beyond mere moral disapproval of an excluded group.

A law branding one class of persons as criminal solely based on the State's moral disapproval of that class and the conduct associated with that class runs contrary to the values of the Constitution and the Equal Protection Clause, under any standard of review. I therefore concur in the Court's judgment that Texas' sodomy law banning "deviate sexual intercourse" between consenting adults of the same sex, but not between consenting adults of different sexes, is unconstitutional.

Justice Scalia, with Whom the Chief Justice and Justice Thomas Join, Dissenting

"Liberty finds no refuge in a jurisprudence of doubt." *Planned Parenthood of Southeastern Pa. v. Casey*, 505 U. S. 833, 844 (1992). That was the Court's sententious response, barely more than a decade ago, to those seeking to overrule *Roe v. Wade*, 410 U. S. 113 (1973). The Court's response today, to those who have engaged in a 17-year crusade to overrule *Bowers v. Hardwick*, 478 U. S. 186 (1986), is very different. The need for stability and certainty presents no barrier.

Most of the rest of today's opinion has no relevance to its actual holding—that the Texas statute "furthers no legitimate state interest which can justify" its application to petitioners under rational-basis review. *Ante*, at 18 (overruling Bowers to the extent it sustained Georgia's anti-sodomy statute under the rational-basis test). Though there is discussion of "fundamental proposition[s]," *ante*, at 4, and "fundamental decisions," *ibid.* nowhere does the Court's opinion declare that homosexual sodomy is a "fundamental right" under the Due Process Clause; nor does it subject the Texas law to the standard of review that would be appropriate (strict scrutiny) if homosexual sodomy were a "fundamental right." Thus, while overruling the *outcome* of *Bowers*, the Court leaves strangely untouched its central legal conclusion: "[R]espondent would have us announce ... a fundamental right to engage in homosexual sodomy. This we are quite unwilling to do." 478 U. S., at 191. Instead the Court simply describes petitioners' conduct as "an exercise of their liberty"—which it undoubtedly is—and proceeds to apply an unheard-of form of rational-basis review that will have far-reaching implications beyond this case. *Ante*, at 3.

◆ I

I begin with the Court's surprising readiness to reconsider a decision rendered a mere 17 years ago in *Bowers v. Hardwick*. I do not myself believe in rigid adherence to *stare decisis* in constitutional cases; but I do believe that we should be consistent rather than manipulative in invoking the doctrine. Today's opinions in support of reversal do not bother to distinguish—or indeed, even bother to mention—the paean to *stare decisis* coauthored by three Members of today's majority in *Planned Parenthood v. Casey*. There, when *stare decisis* meant preservation of judicially invented abortion rights, the widespread criticism of *Roe* was strong reason to *reaffirm* it:

"Where, in the performance of its judicial duties, the Court decides a case in such a way as to resolve the sort of intensely divisive controversy reflected in *Roe[,]*... its decision has a dimension that the resolution of the normal case does not carry.... [T]o overrule under fire in the absence of the most compelling reason ... would subvert the Court's legitimacy beyond any serious question." 505 U. S., at 866-867.

Today, however, the widespread opposition to *Bowers*, a decision resolving an issue as "intensely divisive" as the issue in *Roe*, is offered as a reason in favor of *overruling* it. See *ante*, at 15-16. Gone, too, is any "enquiry" (of the sort conducted in *Casey*) into whether the decision sought to be overruled has "proven 'unworkable,'" *Casey, supra*, at 855.

Today's approach to *stare decisis* invites us to overrule an erroneously decided precedent (including an "intensely divisive" decision) *if*: (1) its foundations have been "eroded" by subsequent decisions, *ante*, at 15; (2) it has been subject to "substantial and continuing" criticism, *ibid.*; and (3) it has not induced "individual or societal reliance" that counsels against overturning, *ante*, at 16. The problem is that *Roe* itself—which today's majority surely has no disposition to overrule—satisfies these conditions to at least the same degree as *Bowers*.

(1) A preliminary digressive observation with regard to the first factor: The Court's claim that *Planned Parenthood v. Casey, supra*, "casts some doubt" upon the holding in *Bowers* (or any other case, for that matter) does not withstand analysis. *Ante*, at 10. As far as its holding is concerned, *Casey* provided a less expansive right to abortion than did *Roe*, which was already on the books when Bowers was decided. And if the Court is referring not to the holding of *Casey*, but to the dictum of its famed sweet-mystery-of-life passage, ante, at 13 ("At the heart of liberty is the right to define one's own concept of existence, of meaning, of the universe, and of the mystery of human life"): That "casts some doubt" upon either the totality of our jurisprudence or else (presumably the right answer) nothing at all. I have never heard of a law that attempted to restrict one's "right to define" certain concepts; and if the passage calls into question the government's power to regulate actions based on

one's self-defined "concept of existence, etc.," it is the passage that ate the rule of law.

I do not quarrel with the Court's claim that *Romer v. Evans*, 517 U. S. 620 (1996), "eroded" the "foundations" of *Bowers'* rational-basis holding. See *Romer, supra*, at 640-643 (Scalia, J., dissenting).) But *Roe* and *Casey* have been equally "eroded" by *Washington v. Glucksberg*, 521 U. S. 702, 721 (1997), which held that *only* fundamental rights which are "deeply rooted in this Nation's history and tradition" qualify for anything other than rational basis scrutiny under the doctrine of "substantive due process." *Roe* and *Casey*, of course, subjected the restriction of abortion to heightened scrutiny without even attempting to establish that the freedom to abort *was* rooted in this Nation's tradition.

(2) *Bowers*, the Court says, has been subject to "substantial and continuing [criticism], disapproving of its reasoning in all respects, not just as to its historical assumptions." *Ante*, at 15. Exactly what those nonhistorical criticisms are, and whether the Court even agrees with them, are left unsaid, although the Court does cite two books. See *ibid.* (citing C. Fried, Order and Law: Arguing the Reagan Revolution—A Firsthand Account 81-84 (1991); R. Posner, Sex and Reason 341-350 (1992)). Of course, *Roe* too (and by extension *Casey*) had been (and still is) subject to unrelenting criticism, including criticism from the two commentators cited by the Court today. See Fried, *supra*, at 75 ("*Roe* was a prime example of twisted judging"); Posner, *supra*, at 337 ("[The Court's] opinion in *Roe* … fails to measure up to professional expectations regarding judicial opinions"); Posner, Judicial Opinion Writing, 62 U. Chi. L. Rev. 1421, 1434 (1995) (describing the opinion in *Roe* as an "embarrassing performanc[e]").

(3) That leaves, to distinguish the rock-solid, unamendable disposition of *Roe* from the readily overrulable *Bowers*, only the third factor. "[T]here has been," the Court says, "no individual or societal reliance on *Bowers* of the sort that could counsel against overturning its holding.…" *Ante*, at 16. It seems to me that the "societal reliance" on the principles confirmed in *Bowers* and discarded today has been overwhelming. Countless judicial decisions and legislative enactments have relied on the ancient proposition that a governing majority's belief that certain sexual behavior is "immoral and unacceptable" constitutes a rational basis for regulation. See, *e.g., Williams v. Pryor*, 240 F. 3d 944, 949 (CA11 2001) (citing *Bowers* in upholding Alabama's prohibition on the sale of sex toys on the ground that "[t]he

crafting and safeguarding of public morality … indisputably is a legitimate government interest under rational basis scrutiny"); *Milner v. Apfel*, 148 F. 3d 812, 814 (CA7 1998) (citing *Bowers* for the proposition that "[l]egislatures are permitted to legislate with regard to morality … rather than confined to preventing demonstrable harms"); *Holmes v. California Army National Guard* 124 F. 3d 1126, 1136 (CA9 1997) (relying on *Bowers* in upholding the federal statute and regulations banning from military service those who engage in homosexual conduct); *Owens v. State*, 352 Md. 663, 683, 724 A. 2d 43, 53 (1999) (relying on *Bowers* in holding that "a person has no constitutional right to engage in sexual intercourse, at least outside of marriage"); *Sherman v. Henry*, 928 S. W. 2d 464, 469-473 (Tex. 1996) (relying on *Bowers* in rejecting a claimed constitutional right to commit adultery). We ourselves relied extensively on *Bowers* when we concluded, in *Barnes v. Glen Theatre, Inc.*, 501 U. S. 560, 569 (1991), that Indiana's public indecency statute furthered "a substantial government interest in protecting order and morality," *ibid.*, (plurality opinion); see also *id.*, at 575 (Scalia, J., concurring in judgment). State laws against bigamy, same-sex marriage, adult incest, prostitution, masturbation, adultery, fornication, bestiality, and obscenity are likewise sustainable only in light of *Bowers'* validation of laws based on moral choices. Every single one of these laws is called into question by today's decision; the Court makes no effort to cabin the scope of its decision to exclude them from its holding. See *ante*, at 11 (noting "an emerging awareness that liberty gives substantial protection to adult persons in deciding how to conduct their private lives *in matters pertaining to sex*" (emphasis added)). The impossibility of distinguishing homosexuality from other traditional "morals" offenses is precisely why Bowers rejected the rational-basis challenge. "The law," it said, "is constantly based on notions of morality, and if all laws representing essentially moral choices are to be invalidated under the Due Process Clause, the courts will be very busy indeed." 478 U. S., at 196.

What a massive disruption of the current social order, therefore, the overruling of *Bowers* entails. Not so the overruling of *Roe*, which would simply have restored the regime that existed for centuries before 1973, in which the permissibility of and restrictions upon abortion were determined legislatively State-by-State. *Casey*, however, chose to base its *stare decisis* determination on a different "sort" of reliance. "[P]eople," it said, "have organized intimate relationships and made choices that define their views of themselves and their places in society, in reliance on the availability of abortion in the event that contraception should fail." 505 U. S., at 856. This falsely assumes that the consequence of overruling *Roe* would have been to make abortion unlawful. It would not; it would merely have *permitted* the States to do so. Many States would unquestionably have declined to prohibit abortion, and others would not have prohibited it within six months (after which the most significant reliance interests would have expired). Even for persons in States other than these, the choice would not have been between abortion and childbirth, but between abortion nearby and abortion in a neighboring State.

To tell the truth, it does not surprise me, and should surprise no one, that the Court has chosen today to revise the standards of *stare decisis* set forth in *Casey*. It has thereby exposed *Casey's* extraordinary deference to precedent for the result-oriented expedient that it is.

◆ **II**

Having decided that it need not adhere to *stare decisis*, the Court still must establish that *Bowers* was wrongly decided and that the Texas statute, as applied to petitioners, is unconstitutional.

Texas Penal Code Ann. §21.06(a) (2003) undoubtedly imposes constraints on liberty. So do laws prohibiting prostitution, recreational use of heroin, and, for that matter, working more than 60 hours per week in a bakery. But there is no right to "liberty" under the Due Process Clause, though today's opinion repeatedly makes that claim. *Ante*, at 6 ("The liberty protected by the Constitution allows homosexual persons the right to make this choice"); *ante*, at 13 ("These matters … are central to the liberty protected by the Fourteenth Amendment"); *ante*, at 17 ("Their right to liberty under the Due Process Clause gives them the full right to engage in their conduct without intervention of the government"). The Fourteenth Amendment *expressly allows* States to deprive their citizens of "liberty," *so long as "due process of law" is provided*:

"No state shall … deprive any person of life, liberty, or property, *without due process of law*." Amdt. 14 (emphasis added).

Our opinions applying the doctrine known as "substantive due process" hold that the Due Process Clause prohibits States from infringing *fundamental* liberty interests, unless the infringement is narrowly tailored to serve a compelling state interest. *Washing-*

ton v. Glucksberg, 521 U. S., at 721. We have held repeatedly, in cases the Court today does not overrule, that *only* fundamental rights qualify for this so-called "heightened scrutiny" protection—that is, rights which are "deeply rooted in this Nation's history and tradition," *ibid*. See *Reno v. Flores*, 507 U. S. 292, 303 (1993) (fundamental liberty interests must be "so rooted in the traditions and conscience of our people as to be ranked as fundamental" (internal quotation marks and citations omitted)); *United States v. Salerno*, 481 U. S. 739, 751 (1987) (same). See also *Michael H. v. Gerald D.*, 491 U. S. 110, 122 (1989) ("[W]e have insisted not merely that the interest denominated as a 'liberty' be 'fundamental' … but also that it be an interest traditionally protected by our society"); *Moore v. East Cleveland*, 431 U. S. 494, 503 (1977) (plurality opinion); *Meyer v. Nebraska*, 262 U. S. 390, 399 (1923) (Fourteenth Amendment protects "those privileges *long recognized at common law* as essential to the orderly pursuit of happiness by free men" (emphasis added)). All other liberty interests may be abridged or abrogated pursuant to a validly enacted state law if that law is rationally related to a legitimate state interest.

Bowers held, first, that criminal prohibitions of homosexual sodomy are not subject to heightened scrutiny because they do not implicate a "fundamental right" under the Due Process Clause, 478 U. S., at 191-194. Noting that "[p]roscriptions against that conduct have ancient roots," *id.*, at 192, that "[s]odomy was a criminal offense at common law and was forbidden by the laws of the original 13 States when they ratified the Bill of Rights," *ibid.*, and that many States had retained their bans on sodomy, *id.*, at 193, *Bowers* concluded that a right to engage in homosexual sodomy was not "deeply rooted in this Nation's history and tradition," *id.*, at 192.

The Court today does not overrule this holding. Not once does it describe homosexual sodomy as a "fundamental right" or a "fundamental liberty interest," nor does it subject the Texas statute to strict scrutiny. Instead, having failed to establish that the right to homosexual sodomy is "deeply rooted in this Nation's history and tradition," the Court concludes that the application of Texas's statute to petitioners' conduct fails the rational-basis test, and overrules *Bowers'* holding to the contrary, see *id.*, at 196. "The Texas statute furthers no legitimate state interest which can justify its intrusion into the personal and private life of the individual." *Ante*, at 18.

I shall address that rational-basis holding presently. First, however, I address some aspersions that the

Court casts upon Bowers' conclusion that homosexual sodomy is not a "fundamental right"—even though, as I have said, the Court does not have the boldness to reverse that conclusion.

◆ **III**

The Court's description of "the state of the law" at the time of *Bowers* only confirms that *Bowers* was right. *Ante,* at 5. The Court points to *Griswold v. Connecticut,* 381 U. S. 479, 481-482 (1965). But that case expressly disclaimed any reliance on the doctrine of "substantive due process," and grounded the so-called "right to privacy" in penumbras of constitutional provisions other than the Due Process Clause. *Eisenstadt v. Baird,* 405 U. S. 438 (1972), likewise had nothing to do with "substantive due process"; it invalidated a Massachusetts law prohibiting the distribution of contraceptives to unmarried persons solely on the basis of the Equal Protection Clause. Of course *Eisenstadt* contains well known dictum relating to the "right to privacy," but this referred to the right recognized in Griswold—a right penumbral to the specific guarantees in the Bill of Rights, and not a "substantive due process" right.

Roe v. Wade recognized that the right to abort an unborn child was a "fundamental right" protected by the Due Process Clause. 410 U. S., at 155. The *Roe* Court, however, made no attempt to establish that this right was "deeply rooted in this Nation's history and tradition"; instead, it based its conclusion that "the Fourteenth Amendment's concept of personal liberty … is broad enough to encompass a woman's decision whether or not to terminate her pregnancy" on its own normative judgment that anti-abortion laws were undesirable. See *id.,* at 153. We have since rejected *Roe's* holding that regulations of abortion must be narrowly tailored to serve a compelling state interest, see *Planned Parenthood v. Casey,* 505 U. S., at 876 (joint opinion of O'Connor, Kennedy, and Souter, JJ.); id., at 951-953 (Rehnquist, C. J., concurring in judgment in part and dissenting in part)— and thus, by logical implication, *Roe's* holding that the right to abort an unborn child is a "fundamental right." See 505 U. S., at 843-912 (joint opinion of O'Connor, Kennedy, and Souter, JJ.) (not once describing abortion as a "fundamental right" or a "fundamental liberty interest").

After discussing the history of antisodomy laws, *ante,* at 7-10, the Court proclaims that, "it should be noted that there is no longstanding history in this country of laws directed at homosexual conduct as a distinct matter," *ante,* at 7. This observation in no way casts into doubt the "definitive [historical] conclusion," *id.,* on which *Bowers* relied: that our Nation has a longstanding history of laws prohibiting *sodomy in general*—regardless of whether it was performed by same-sex or opposite-sex couples:

"It is obvious to us that neither of these formulations would extend a fundamental right to homosexuals to engage in acts of consensual sodomy. Proscriptions against that conduct have ancient roots. *Sodomy* was a criminal offense at common law and was forbidden by the laws of the original 13 States when they ratified the Bill of Rights. In 1868, when the Fourteenth Amendment was ratified, all but 5 of the 37 States in the Union had *criminal sodomy laws.* In fact, until 1961, all 50 States outlawed *sodomy,* and today, 24 States and the District of Columbia continue to provide criminal penalties for *sodomy* performed in private and between consenting adults. Against this background, to claim that a right to engage in such conduct is 'deeply rooted in this Nation's history and tradition' or 'implicit in the concept of ordered liberty' is, at best, facetious." 478 U. S., at 192-194 (citations and footnotes omitted; emphasis added).

It is (as *Bowers* recognized) entirely irrelevant whether the laws in our long national tradition criminalizing homosexual sodomy were "directed at homosexual conduct as a distinct matter." *Ante*, at 7. Whether homosexual sodomy was prohibited by a law targeted at same-sex sexual relations or by a more general law prohibiting both homosexual and heterosexual sodomy, the only relevant point is that it *was* criminalized—which suffices to establish that homosexual sodomy is not a right "deeply rooted in our Nation's history and tradition." The Court today agrees that homosexual sodomy was criminalized and thus does not dispute the facts on which *Bowers actually* relied.

Next the Court makes the claim, again unsupported by any citations, that "[l]aws prohibiting sodomy do not seem to have been enforced against consenting adults acting in private." *Ante*, at 8. The key qualifier here is "acting in private"—since the Court admits that sodomy laws *were* enforced against consenting adults (although the Court contends that prosecutions were "infrequent," *ante*, at 9). I do not know what "acting in private" means; surely consensual sodomy, like heterosexual intercourse, is rarely performed on stage. If all the Court means by "acting in private" is "on private premises, with the doors closed and windows covered," it is entirely unsurprising that evidence of enforcement would be hard to come by. (Imagine the circumstances that would enable a search warrant to be obtained for a residence on the ground that there was probable cause to believe that consensual sodomy was then and there occurring.) Surely that lack of evidence would not sustain the proposition that consensual sodomy on private premises with the doors closed and windows covered was regarded as a "fundamental right," even though all other consensual sodomy was criminalized. There are 203 prosecutions for consensual, adult homosexual sodomy reported in the West Reporting system and official state reporters from the years 1880-1995. See W. Eskridge, Gaylaw: Challenging the Apartheid of the Closet 375 (1999) (hereinafter Gaylaw). There are also records of 20 sodomy prosecutions and 4 executions during the colonial period. J. Katz, Gay/Lesbian Almanac 29, 58, 663 (1983). Bowers' conclusion that homosexual sodomy is not a fundamental right "deeply rooted in this Nation's history and tradition" is utterly unassailable.

Realizing that fact, the Court instead says: "[W]e think that our laws and traditions in the past half century are of most relevance here. These references show *an emerging awareness* that liberty gives substantial protection to adult persons in deciding how to conduct their private lives *in matters pertaining to sex*." *Ante*, at 11 (emphasis added). Apart from the fact that such an "emerging awareness" does not establish a "fundamental right," the statement is factually false. States continue to prosecute all sorts of crimes by adults "in matters pertaining to sex": prostitution, adult incest, adultery, obscenity, and child pornography. Sodomy laws, too, have been enforced "in the past half century," in which there have been 134 reported cases involving prosecutions for consensual, adult, homosexual sodomy. Gaylaw 375. In relying, for evidence of an "emerging recognition," upon the American Law Institute's 1955 recommendation not to criminalize "consensual sexual relations conducted in private," *ante*, at 11, the Court ignores the fact that this recommendation was "a point of resistance in most of the states that considered adopting the Model Penal Code." Gaylaw 159.

In any event, an "emerging awareness" is by definition not "deeply rooted in this Nation's history and tradition[s]," as we have said "fundamental right" status requires. Constitutional entitlements do not spring into existence because some States choose to lessen or eliminate criminal sanctions on certain behavior. Much less do they spring into existence, as the Court seems to believe, because *foreign nations*

decriminalize conduct. The *Bowers* majority opinion never relied on "values we share with a wider civilization," *ante*, at 16, but rather rejected the claimed right to sodomy on the ground that such a right was not "deeply rooted in *this Nation's* history and tradition," 478 U. S., at 193-194 (emphasis added). *Bowers'* rational-basis holding is likewise devoid of any reliance on the views of a "wider civilization," see *id.*, at 196. The Court's discussion of these foreign views (ignoring, of course, the many countries that have retained criminal prohibitions on sodomy) is therefore meaningless dicta. Dangerous dicta, however, since "this Court ... should not impose foreign moods, fads, or fashions on Americans." *Foster v. Florida*, 537 U. S. 990, n. (2002) (Thomas, J., concurring in denial of certiorari).

◆ **IV**

I turn now to the ground on which the Court squarely rests its holding: the contention that there is no rational basis for the law here under attack. This proposition is so out of accord with our jurisprudence—indeed, with the jurisprudence of *any* society we know—that it requires little discussion.

The Texas statute undeniably seeks to further the belief of its citizens that certain forms of sexual behavior are "immoral and unacceptable," *Bowers*, *supra*, at 196—the same interest furthered by criminal laws against fornication, bigamy, adultery, adult incest, bestiality, and obscenity. *Bowers* held that this was a legitimate state interest. The Court today reaches the opposite conclusion. The Texas statute, it says, "furthers *no legitimate state interest* which can justify its intrusion into the personal and private life of the individual," *ante*, at 18 (emphasis addded). The Court embraces instead Justice Stevens' declaration in his Bowers dissent, that "the fact that the governing majority in a State has traditionally viewed a particular practice as immoral is not a sufficient reason for upholding a law prohibiting the practice," *ante*, at 17. This effectively decrees the end of all morals legislation. If, as the Court asserts, the promotion of majoritarian sexual morality is not even a legitimate state interest, none of the above-mentioned laws can survive rational-basis review.

◆ **V**

Finally, I turn to petitioners' equal-protection challenge, which no Member of the Court save Justice O'Connor, *ante*, at 1 (opinion concurring in judgment), embraces: On its face §21.06(a) applies equally to all persons. Men and women, heterosexuals and homosexuals, are all subject to its prohibition of deviate sexual intercourse with someone of the same sex. To be sure, §21.06 does distinguish between the sexes insofar as concerns the partner with whom the sexual acts are performed: men can violate the law only with other men, and women only with other women. But this cannot itself be a denial of equal protection, since it is precisely the same distinction regarding partner that is drawn in state laws prohibiting marriage with someone of the same sex while permitting marriage with someone of the opposite sex.

The objection is made, however, that the antimiscegenation laws invalidated in *Loving v. Virginia*, 388 U. S. 1, 8 (1967), similarly were applicable to whites and blacks alike, and only distinguished between the races insofar as the *partner* was concerned. In *Loving*, however, we correctly applied heightened scrutiny, rather than the usual rational-basis review, because the Virginia statute was "designed to maintain White Supremacy." *Id.*, at 6, 11. A racially discriminatory purpose is always sufficient to subject a law to strict scrutiny, even a facially neutral law that makes no mention of race. See *Washington v. Davis*, 426 U. S. 229, 241-242 (1976). No purpose to discriminate against men or women as a class can be gleaned from the Texas law, so rational-basis review applies. That review is readily satisfied here by the same rational basis that satisfied it in *Bowers*—society's belief that certain forms of sexual behavior are "immoral and unacceptable," 478 U. S., at 196. This is the same justification that supports many other laws regulating sexual behavior that make a distinction based upon the identity of the partner—for example, laws against adultery, fornication, and adult incest, and laws refusing to recognize homosexual marriage.

Justice O'Connor argues that the discrimination in this law which must be justified is not its discrimination with regard to the sex of the partner but its discrimination with regard to the sexual proclivity of the principal actor.

"While it is true that the law applies only to conduct, the conduct targeted by this law is conduct that is closely correlated with being homosexual. Under such circumstances, Texas' sodomy law is targeted at more than conduct. It is instead directed toward gay persons as a class." *Ante*, at 5.

Of course the same could be said of any law. A law against public nudity targets "the conduct that is closely correlated with being a nudist," and hence "is targeted at more than conduct"; it is "directed toward nudists as a class." But be that as it may. Even if the Texas law *does* deny equal protection to "homosexuals as a class," that denial *still* does not need to be justified by anything more than a rational basis, which our cases show is satisfied by the enforcement of traditional notions of sexual morality.

Justice O'Connor simply decrees application of "a more searching form of rational basis review" to the Texas statute. *Ante*, at 2. The cases she cites do not recognize such a standard, and reach their conclusions only after finding, as required by conventional rational-basis analysis, that no conceivable legitimate state interest supports the classification at issue. See *Romer v. Evans*, 517 U. S., at 635; *Cleburne v. Cleburne Living Center, Inc.*, 473 U. S. 432, 448-450 (1985); *Department of Agriculture v. Moreno*, 413 U. S. 528, 534-538 (1973). Nor does Justice O'Connor explain precisely what her "more searching form" of rational-basis review consists of. It must at least mean, however, that laws exhibiting "a ... desire to harm a politically unpopular group," *ante*, at 2, are invalid *even though* there may be a conceivable rational basis to support them.

This reasoning leaves on pretty shaky grounds state laws limiting marriage to opposite-sex couples. Justice O'Connor seeks to preserve them by the conclusory statement that "preserving the traditional institution of marriage" is a legitimate state interest. *Ante*, at 7. But "preserving the traditional institution of marriage" is just a kinder way of describing the State's *moral disapproval* of same-sex couples. Texas's interest in §21.06 could be recast in similarly euphemistic terms: "preserving the traditional sexual mores of our society." In the jurisprudence Justice O'Connor has seemingly created, judges can validate laws by characterizing them as "preserving the traditions of society" (good); or invalidate them by characterizing them as "expressing moral disapproval" (bad).

* * * *

Today's opinion is the product of a Court, which is the product of a law-profession culture, that has largely signed on to the so-called homosexual agenda, by which I mean the agenda promoted by some homosexual activists directed at eliminating the moral opprobrium that has traditionally attached to homosexual conduct. I noted in an earlier opinion the fact that the American Association of Law Schools (to which any reputable law school *must* seek to belong) excludes from membership any school that refuses to ban from its job-interview facilities a law firm (no matter how small) that does not wish to hire as a prospective partner a person who openly engages in homosexual conduct. See *Romer, supra,* at 653.

One of the most revealing statements in today's opinion is the Court's grim warning that the criminalization of homosexual conduct is "an invitation to subject homosexual persons to discrimination both in the public and in the private spheres." *Ante,* at 14. It is clear from this that the Court has taken sides in the culture war, departing from its role of assuring, as neutral observer, that the democratic rules of engagement are observed. Many Americans do not want persons who openly engage in homosexual conduct as partners in their business, as scoutmasters for their children, as teachers in their children's schools, or as boarders in their home. They view this as protecting themselves and their families from a lifestyle that they believe to be immoral and destructive. The Court views it as "discrimination" which it is the function of our judgments to deter. So imbued is the Court with the law profession's anti-anti-homosexual culture, that it is seemingly unaware that the attitudes of that culture are not obviously "mainstream"; that in most States what the Court calls "discrimination" against those who engage in homosexual acts is perfectly legal; that proposals to ban such "discrimination" under Title VII have repeatedly been rejected by Congress, see Employment Non-Discrimination Act of 1994, S. 2238, 103d Cong., 2d Sess. (1994); Civil Rights Amendments, H. R. 5452, 94th Cong., 1st Sess. (1975); that in some cases such "discrimination" is *mandated* by federal statute, see 10 U. S. C. §654(b)(1) (mandating discharge from the armed forces of any service member who engages in or intends to engage in homosexual acts); and that in some cases such "discrimination" is a constitutional right, see *Boy Scouts of America v. Dale,* 530 U. S. 640 (2000).

Let me be clear that I have nothing against homosexuals, or any other group, promoting their agenda through normal democratic means. Social perceptions of sexual and other morality change over time, and every group has the right to persuade its fellow citizens that its view of such matters is the best. That homosexuals have achieved some success in that enterprise is attested to by the fact that Texas is one of the few remaining States that criminalize private, consensual homosexual acts. But persuading one's fellow citizens is one thing, and imposing one's views in absence of democratic majority will is something else. I would no more *require* a State to criminalize homosexual acts—or, for that matter, display *any*

moral disapprobation of them—than I would *forbid* it to do so. What Texas has chosen to do is well within the range of traditional democratic action, and its hand should not be stayed through the invention of a brand-new "constitutional right" by a Court that is impatient of democratic change. It is indeed true that "later generations can see that laws once thought necessary and proper in fact serve only to oppress," *ante,* at 18; and when that happens, later generations can repeal those laws. But it is the premise of our system that those judgments are to be made by the people, and not imposed by a governing caste that knows best.

One of the benefits of leaving regulation of this matter to the people rather than to the courts is that the people, unlike judges, need not carry things to their logical conclusion. The people may feel that their disapprobation of homosexual conduct is strong enough to disallow homosexual marriage, but not strong enough to criminalize private homosexual acts—and may legislate accordingly. The Court today pretends that it possesses a similar freedom of action, so that that we need not fear judicial imposition of homosexual marriage, as has recently occurred in Canada (in a decision that the Canadian Government has chosen not to appeal). See *Halpern v. Toronto,* 2003 WL 34950 (Ontario Ct. App.); Cohen, Dozens in Canada Follow Gay Couple's Lead, Washington Post, June 12, 2003, p. A25. At the end of its opinion—after having laid waste the foundations of our rational-basis jurisprudence—the Court says that the present case "does not involve whether the government must give formal recognition to any relationship that homosexual persons seek to enter." *Ante,* at 17. Do not believe it. More illuminating than this bald, unreasoned disclaimer is the progression of thought displayed by an earlier passage in the Court's opinion, which notes the constitutional protections afforded to "personal decisions relating to *marriage,* procreation, contraception, family relationships, child rearing, and education," and then declares that "[p]ersons in a homosexual relationship may seek autonomy for these purposes, just as heterosexual persons do." *Ante,* at 13 (emphasis added). Today's opinion dismantles the structure of constitutional law that has permitted a distinction to be made between heterosexual and homosexual unions, insofar as formal recognition in marriage is concerned. If moral disapproval of homosexual conduct is "no legitimate state interest" for purposes of proscribing that conduct, *ante,* at 18; and if, as the Court coos (casting aside all pretense of neutrality), "[w]hen sexuality finds overt expression in intimate conduct with another person, the conduct can be but one element in a personal bond that is more enduring," *ante*, at 6; what justification could there possibly be for denying the benefits of marriage to homosexual couples exercising "[t]he liberty protected by the Constitution," *ibid*.? Surely not the encouragement of procreation, since the sterile and the elderly are allowed to marry. This case "does not involve" the issue of homosexual marriage only if one entertains the belief that principle and logic have nothing to do with the decisions of this Court. Many will hope that, as the Court comfortingly assures us, this is so.

The matters appropriate for this Court's resolution are only three: Texas's prohibition of sodomy neither infringes a "fundamental right" (which the Court does not dispute), nor is unsupported by a rational relation to what the Constitution considers a legitimate state interest, nor denies the equal protection of the laws. I dissent.

Justice Thomas, Dissenting

I join Justice Scalia's dissenting opinion. I write separately to note that the law before the Court today "is … uncommonly silly." *Griswold v. Connecticut*, 381 U. S. 479, 527 (1965) (Stewart, J., dissenting). If I were a member of the Texas Legislature, I would vote to repeal it. Punishing someone for expressing his sexual preference through noncommercial consensual conduct with another adult does not appear to be a worthy way to expend valuable law enforcement resources.

Notwithstanding this, I recognize that as a member of this Court I am not empowered to help petitioners and others similarly situated. My duty, rather, is to "decide cases 'agreeably to the Constitution and laws of the United States.'" *Id.*, at 530. And, just like Justice Stewart, I "can find [neither in the Bill of Rights nor any other part of the Constitution a] general right of privacy," *ibid.*, or as the Court terms it today, the "liberty of the person both in its spatial and more transcendent dimensions," *ante*, at 1.

Essays, Reports, and Manifestos
Declaration of Rights of the Stamp Act Congress (1765)
Boston Non-Importation Agreement (1768)
Declaration and Resolves of the First Continental Congress (1774)
Common Sense (1776)
Virginia Declaration of Rights (1776)
Declaration of Independence (1776)
James Madison's Memorial and Remonstrance against Religious Assessments (1785)
Federalist Papers 10, 14, and 51 (1787)
Jefferson's and Hamilton's Opinions on the Constitutionality of the Bank of the United States (1791)
William Lloyd Garrison's First *Liberator* Editorial (1831)
Seneca Falls Convention Declaration of Sentiments (1848)
South Carolina Declaration of Causes of Secession (1860)
Emancipation Proclamation (1863)
Niagara Movement Declaration of Principles (1905)
Southern Manifesto (1956)
Martin Luther King, Jr.'s "Letter from Birmingham Jail" (1963)
Kerner Commission Report Summary (1968)
Bybee Torture Memo (2002)

Legal
Marbury v. Madison (1803)
Martin v. Hunter's Lessee (1816)
McCulloch v. Maryland (1819)
Gibbons v. Ogden (1824)
Dred Scott v. Sandford (1857)
Plessy v. Ferguson (1896)
The Insular Cases: *Downes v. Bidwell* (1901)
Muller v. Oregon (1908)
Hammer v. Dagenhart (1918)
United States v. Curtiss-Wright (1936)
Youngstown Sheet and Tube Co. v. Sawyer (1952)
Brown v. Board of Education (1954)
Miranda v. Arizona (1966)
Roe v. Wade (1973)
Regents of the University of California v. Bakke (1978)
Bush v. Gore (2001)
Lawrence v. Texas (2003)

Legislative
Quartering Act (1765)
Intolerable Acts (1774)
Articles of Confederation (1777)
Pennsylvania: An Act for the Gradual Abolition of Slavery (1780)
Northwest Ordinance (1787)
Constitution of the United States (1787)
Bill of Rights (1791)
Alien and Sedition Acts (1798)
An Act to Prohibit the Importation of Slaves (1807)
Missouri Compromise (1820)
South Carolina Ordinance of Nullification and Andrew Jackson's Proclamation regarding Nullification (1832)

Legislative (cont.)

Joint Resolution of Congress for the Annexation of Texas (1845)
Compromise of 1850
Kansas-Nebraska Act (1854)
Homestead Act (1862)
Morrill Act (1862)
Black Code of Mississippi (1865)
Thirteenth Amendment to the U.S. Constitution (1865)
Civil Rights Act of 1866
Articles of Impeachment of Andrew Johnson (1868)
Fourteenth Amendment to the U.S. Constitution (1868)
Fifteenth Amendment to the U.S. Constitution (1870)
Act Establishing Yellowstone National Park (1872)
Chinese Exclusion Act (1882)
Pendleton Civil Service Act (1883)
Interstate Commerce Act (1887)
Dawes Severalty Act (1887)
Sherman Antitrust Act (1890)
Sixteenth Amendment to the U.S. Constitution (1913)
Nineteenth Amendment to the U.S. Constitution (1920)
Tennessee Valley Authority Act (1933)
National Industrial Recovery Act (1933)
National Labor Relations Act (1935)
Social Security Act (1935)
Lend-Lease Act (1941)
Servicemen's Readjustment Act (1944)
Marshall Plan (1947)
Taft-Hartley Act (1947)
Senate Resolution 301: Censure of Senator Joseph McCarthy (1954)
Federal-Aid Highway Act (1956)
Civil Rights Act of 1964
Gulf of Tonkin Resolution (1964)
Voting Rights Act of 1965
Equal Rights Amendment (1972)
Articles of Impeachment of William Jefferson Clinton (1998)

Military

Quartering Act (1765)
Treaty of Fort Pitt (1778)
War Department General Order 143 (1863)
Gettysburg Address (1863)
Articles of Agreement Relating to the Surrender of the Army of Northern Virginia (1865)
Treaty of Fort Laramie (1868)
Zimmermann Telegram (1917)
Woodrow Wilson: Joint Address to Congress Leading to a Declaration of War against Germany (1917)
Franklin D. Roosevelt's "Pearl Harbor" Speech (1941)
Executive Order 8802 (1941)
Executive Order 9066 (1942)
Dwight D. Eisenhower's Order of the Day (1944)
Servicemen's Readjustment Act (1944)
Executive Order 9981 (1948)
Gulf of Tonkin Resolution (1964)
George H. W. Bush's Address to Congress on the Persian Gulf Crisis (1990)
Bybee Torture Memo (2002)

Presidential/Executive

George Washington's First Inaugural Address (1789)
George Washington's First Annual Message to Congress (1790)
George Washington's Farewell Address (1796)
Thomas Jefferson's First Inaugural Address (1801)
Thomas Jefferson's Message to Congress about the Lewis and Clark Expedition (1803)
Monroe Doctrine (1823)
Andrew Jackson: On Indian Removal (1830)
Andrew Jackson's Veto Message regarding the Bank of the United States (1832)
South Carolina Ordinance of Nullification and Andrew Jackson's Proclamation regarding Nullification (1832)
Abraham Lincoln's "House Divided" Speech (1858)
Abraham Lincoln's First Inaugural Address (1861)
Jefferson Davis's Inaugural Address to the Confederacy (1861)
Emancipation Proclamation (1863)
Gettysburg Address (1863)
Abraham Lincoln's Second Inaugural Address (1865)
Rutherford B. Hayes's Inaugural Address (1877)
William McKinley's Message to Congress about Cuban Intervention (1898)
Roosevelt Corollary to the Monroe Doctrine (1905)
Woodrow Wilson: Joint Address to Congress Leading to a Declaration of War against Germany (1917)
Woodrow Wilson's Fourteen Points (1918)
Franklin D. Roosevelt's First Inaugural Address (1933)
Franklin D. Roosevelt's Campaign Address at Madison Square Garden (1936)
Franklin D. Roosevelt's Four Freedoms Message to Congress (1941)
Executive Order 8802 (1941)
Franklin D. Roosevelt's "Pearl Harbor" Speech (1941)
Executive Order 9066 (1942)
Dwight D. Eisenhower's Order of the Day (1944)
Truman Doctrine (1947)
Press Release Announcing U.S. Recognition of Israel (1948)
Executive Order 9981 (1948)
Executive Order 10730 (1957)
Dwight D. Eisenhower's Farewell Address (1961)
John F. Kennedy's Inaugural Address (1961)
Executive Order 10924 (1961)
John F. Kennedy's Civil Rights Address (1963)
Ronald Reagan's "Evil Empire" Speech (1983)
George H. W. Bush's Address to Congress on the Persian Gulf Crisis (1990)
Bill Clinton's Radio Address on the Welfare Reform Act (1996)
George W. Bush's Address to the Nation on September 11, 2001

Royal

Proclamation of 1763
Proclamation by the King for Suppressing Rebellion and Sedition (1775)

Scientific

Thomas Edison's Patent Application for the Incandescent Light Bulb (1880)
John Glenn's Official Communication with the Command Center (1962)

Speeches/Addresses

Patrick Henry's "Liberty or Death" Speech (1775)
George Washington's First Inaugural Address (1789)
George Washington's First Annual Message to Congress (1790)
George Washington's Farewell Address (1796)
Thomas Jefferson's First Inaugural Address (1801)

Speeches/Addresses (cont.)

Thomas Jefferson's Message to Congress about the Lewis and Clark Expedition (1803)

Andrew Jackson: On Indian Removal (1830)

Andrew Jackson's Veto Message regarding the Bank of the United States (1832)

Frederick Douglass's "Fourth of July" Speech (1852)

Abraham Lincoln's "House Divided" Speech (1858)

Jefferson Davis's Inaugural Address to the Confederacy (1861)

Abraham Lincoln's First Inaugural Address (1861)

Gettysburg Address (1863)

Abraham Lincoln's Second Inaugural Address (1865)

Rutherford B. Hayes's Inaugural Address (1877)

Booker T. Washington's Atlanta Exposition Address (1895)

William Jennings Bryan's "Cross of Gold" Speech (1896)

William McKinley's Message to Congress about Cuban Intervention (1898)

Woodrow Wilson: Joint Address to Congress Leading to a Declaration of War against Germany (1917)

Woodrow Wilson's Fourteen Points (1918)

Franklin D. Roosevelt's First Inaugural Address (1933)

Franklin D. Roosevelt's Campaign Address at Madison Square Garden (1936)

Franklin D. Roosevelt's Four Freedoms Message to Congress (1941)

Franklin D. Roosevelt's "Pearl Harbor" Speech (1941)

Dwight D. Eisenhower's Farewell Address (1961)

John F. Kennedy's Inaugural Address (1961)

John F. Kennedy's Civil Rights Address (1963)

Martin Luther King, Jr.'s "I Have a Dream" Speech (1963)

Richard Nixon's Smoking Gun Tape (1972)

Ronald Reagan's "Evil Empire" Speech (1983)

César Chávez's Commonwealth Address (1984)

George H. W. Bush's Address to Congress on the Persian Gulf Crisis (1990)

Bill Clinton's Radio Address on the Welfare Reform Act (1996)

George W. Bush's Address to the Nation on September 11, 2001

Volume numbers are indicated before each page number. Bold page numbers indicate the primary entry about the topic.

Cicero 3:1100, 3:1106

Civil Aeronautics Act of 1938 3:1497

Civilian Conservation Corps 3:1271, 3:1279, 3:1299, 3:1324

Civil Rights Act of 1866 2:882, **2:886–897**, 2:933, 2:934, 2:935, 2:938, 2:941, 3:1159, 4:1948

Civil Rights Act of 1871 2:938, 3:1061

Civil Rights Act of 1875 2:861, 2:892, 2:893, 2:938, 3:1073, 3:1074, 3:1076, 3:1081, 3:1159, 4:1759, 4:1762, 4:1763

Civil Rights Act of 1957 4:1757, 4:1758, 4:1762, 4:1763, 4:1766, 4:1772, 4:1773, 4:1774, 4:1775, 4:1812, 4:1813

Civil Rights Act of 1960 4:1758, 4:1762, 4:1766, 4:1775, 4:1813

Civil Rights Act of 1964 3:1162, 3:1435, 3:1436, 4:1683, 4:1717, 4:1729, 4:1736, 4:1745, 4:1749, **4:1756–1787**, 4:1760, 4:1799, 4:1800, 4:1803, 4:1806, 4:1813, 4:1857, 4:1859, 4:1878, 4:1883, 4:1885–1886, 4:1888, 4:1889, 4:1931 4:1933, 4:1935, 4:1936, 4:1938, 4:1940, 4:1942, 4:1943, 4:1944, 4:1950

Civil Rights Act of 1968 4:1862

Civil Rights Cases 2:892, 2:938, 2:950, 3:1061, 3:1074, 3:1076, 3:1085, 3:1086, 4:1759, 4:1761, 4:1763

Civil Service Commission 2:1006, 2:1007, 2:1009, 2:1012, 2:1013

Civil War, U.S. 1:200, 1:245, 1:419, 1:425, 1:427, 1:443, 1:491, 1:495, 2:560, 2:562, 2:612, 2:615, 2:639, 2:640, 2:658, 2:684, 2:738–751, 2:752–763, 2:764–775, 2:776–789, 2:791, 2:794, 2:796, 2:803, 2:805, 2:806, 2:808, 2:814–825, 2:826–835, 2:836–845, 2:846–855, 2:856–865, 2:877, 2:881, 2:899, 2:904, 2:916, 2:933, 2:937, 2:946, 2:947, 2:955, 2:960, 2:967, 2:996, 2:1005, 2:1020, 2:1037, 3:1051, 3:1052, 3:1061, 3:1064, 3:1073, 3:1074, 3:1076, 3:1078, 3:1080, 3:1159, 3:1160, 3:1164, 3:1165, 3:1195, 3:1197, 3:1241, 3:1258, 3:1260, 3:1406, 3:1412, 3:1509, 3:1515, 3:1561, 4:1607, 4:1649, 4:1729, 4:1884, 4:1909, 4:1934, 4:1936, 4:1938, 4:1947, 4:2059

Clagett, William H. 2:957

Clark, Bennett Champ 3:1303

Clark, Jim 4:1800

Clark, Kenneth 3:1588

Clark, Tom 3:1573, 4:1816, 4:1819, 4:1840

Clark, William 1:386, 1:389, 1:390, 1:391

Clarke, John H. 3:1244

Clarkson, Thomas 2:661, 2:673

Classification Act of 1923 2:1010, 3:1309, 3:1333, 3:1334, 3:1488, 3:1543, 3:1549

Clay, Henry 1:259, 1:492, 1:493, 1:501, 2:513, 2:544, 2:568, 2:572, 2:592, 2:609, 2:678, 2:685, 2:699, 2:739, 2:741, 2:1005

    Compromise of 1850 **632–655**

Clayton Antitrust Act 3:1054, 3:1057, 3:1212, 3:1230, 3:1241

Clean Air Act 4:1991

Clean Water Act of 1972 4:1899

Clemenceau, Georges 3:1213, 3:1235

Cleveland, Grover 2:1010, 2:1019, 2:1023, 3:1097, 3:1098, 3:1111, 3:1131, 3:1195, 3:1273, 3:1274

Clifford, Clark 3:1498, 3:1499, 3:1554, 3:1555

Clinton, Bill 1:265, 2:904, 2:906, 3:1273, 3:1274, 3:1567, 3:1576, 4:1654, 4:1668, 4:1680, 4:1903, 4:1910, 4:1975, 4:1991, 4:2061

    Articles of Impeachment of William Jefferson Clinton **4:2014–2025**

    Radio Address on the Welfare Reform Act **4:2003–2013**

Clinton, DeWitt 2:513

Clinton, George 1:263, 1:341

Clinton, Hillary Rodham 4:1889, 4:2005

Clinton, Roger, Sr. 4:2005

Clinton, Virginia 4:2005

Coastal Trade and Fisheries Act of 1793 2:517, 2:519

Cobb, Thomas 1:491

Cody, "Buffalo Bill" 2:960

Coercive Acts. *See* Intolerable Acts.

Coffee, Linda 4:1907

Cohen, Ben 3:1421

Cohn, Roy 3:1600

Cold war 3:1424, 3:1475, 3:1494–1507, 3:1508–1519, 3:1524, 3:1551, 3:1554, 3:1562, 3:1564, 3:1567, 3:1596–1605, 4:1956–1971, 4:1992

Cole, Cornelius 2:957

Coles, Edward 1:426

Colfax, Schuyler 2:861, 2:896

Colson, Charles W. (Chuck) 4:1901, 4:1905, 4:2101

Colter, John 2:955

Columbian Exposition 3:1062

Colvin, Reynold H. 4:1941

Commager, Henry Steele 4:1608

Committee on Economic Security 3:1339, 3:1341, 3:1343

Committee to Re-Elect the President (CREEP) 4:1895, 4:1897, 4:1899, 4:1900, 4:1901

Commons, John 3:1340

Common Sense **1:114–145**

Commonwealth Club of California 4:1973, 4:1975, 4:1979

Communist Party 3:1497, 3:1524, 3:1538, 3:1598, 3:1599, 3:1604, 4:1661, 4:1778

Compact of 1802 2:542

Compromise of 1850 2:557, 2:560, 2:612, 2:614, **632–655**, 2:657, 2:661, 2:677, 2:678, 2:685, 2:696, 2:702, 2:739, 2:766, 2:777, 2:779

Comstock, Anthony 4:1907

Comstock Act 4:1907

Conant, James B. 3:1478

Confederate States of America 2:754, 2:755, 2:764–775, 2:774, 2:796, 2:805, 2:815, 2:817, 2:828, 2:833, 2:863, 2:879, 2:899, 2:935, 2:937, 2:938, 2:940, 2:949, 2:965, 3:1561

Confiscation Acts 2:816, 2:829, 2:878, 2:888

Congress of the Confederation 1:171

Congress of Industrial Organizations (CIO) 3:1329, 3:1519, 3:1526, 3:1528

Glorious Revolution 1:107
Goldberg, Arthur 4:1815, 4:1841
Golden, Harry 4:1716, 4:1724
Goldmark, Josephine 3:1185, 3:1187, 3:1189
Goldwater, Barry 4:1790, 4:1793, 4:1794, 4:1959
Gong Lum v. Rice 3:1593, 4:1611, 4:1616
Gonzales, Alberto R. 4:2071, 4:2072, 4:2073, 4:2077, 4:2078, 4:2080
Goodell, William 2:674
Good Neighbor League 3:1374
Goodwin, Doris Kearns 2:820, 2:841
Gorbachev, Mikhail 4:1959, 4:1962, 4:1991, 4:1992, 4:1998, 4:1999
Gore, Albert, Jr. 4:2063
    Bush v. Gore **4:2026–2059**
Gore, Albert, Sr. 4:1619–1621
Gore, Thomas P. 3:1217
Gore v. Harris 4:2038, 4:2040, 4:2045, 4:2049, 4:2050, 4:2051, 4:2055
Gorham, Nathaniel 1:240, 1:423
Gorsuch, Edward 2:657
Gotcher, Emma 3:1184
Gould, Jay 2:861
Graduation Act 2:792
Graham, Catherine Macaulay 1:295
Gramm-Rudman-Hollings Act 4:1989, 4:1993
Granger Laws 2:1019
Grant, Hannah Simpson 2:859
Grant, Josiah Root 2:859
Grant, Julia Dent 2:859
Grant, Ulysses S. 2:779, 2:837, 2:838, 2:847; 2:880, 2:888, 2:899, 2:900, 2:901, 2:902, 2:904, 2:917, 2:921, 2:934, 2:947, 2:957, 2:965, 2:969, 2:976, 2:1005, 2:1006, 3:1122, 3:1124
    Articles of Agreement Relating to the Surrender of the Army of Northern Virginia 2:856–865
Grattan, John 2:915
Gray, Horace 3:1129, 3:1131
Gray, L. Patrick 4:1899, 4:1900, 4:1904
Grayson, William 1:148
Great Depression 1:245, 1:443, 1:471, 2:939, 3:1267, 3:1268, 3:1269, 3:1270, 3:1279, 3:1284, 3:1299, 3:1323, 3:1325, 3:1329, 3:1338–1367, 3:1371, 3:1372, 3:1476, 3:1405, 3:1407, 3:1419, 3:1423, 3:1431, 3:1442, 3:1453, 3:1473, 3:1474, 3:1478, 3:1554, 3:1563, 3:1598, 4:1619, 4:1883, 4:1958, 4:1973, 4:1978
Great Sioux War 2:915
Greeley, Horace 2:706, 2:740, 2:744, 2:792, 2:795, 2:829, 2:888
Green, Ernest 4:1655
Green, William 3:1300, 3:1301
Greene, Harold 4:1758
Grenville, George 1:17, 1:18, 1:21, 1:24, 1:37, 1:107
Grider, Henry 2:935
Grier, Robert C. 2:702, 2:703, 2:706
Griggs, John 3:1132
Grimes, James W. 2:935, 2:937

Grimké, Angelina 2:622
Grimké, Sarah 2:622, 3:1258
Grinnell, George Bird 2:960
Grissom, Virgil 4:1701
Griswold, Estelle 4:1907
Griswold v. Connecticut 2:939, 4:1907, 4:1912, 4:1918, 4:1924, 4:1925, 4:1926, 4:2111, 4:2116, 4:2117, 4:2121, 4:2122, 4:2133, 4:2137
Gromyko, Andrey 3:1555
Grossman, Marc 4:1974, 4:1979
Grow, Galusha A.
    Homestead Act 2:790–801
Gruening, Ernest 4:1794
Guelzo, Allen 2:821
Guinn & Beal v. United States 2:949, 2:950
Guiteau, Charles 2:1006
Gulf of Tonkin Resolution **4:1788–1797**
Gwinnett, Button 1:173

H
Haas, Francis J. 3:1436
Haas, Robert 4:1692
Hadzialijagic, Safet 4:2093, 4:2094, 4:2095
Haldeman, H. R. 4:1895, 4:1896, 4:1897, 4:1899, 4:1900, 4:1901, 4:1904, 4:1905
Halleck, Charles 3:1520
Halleck, Henry 2:838
Hallford, James Hubert 4:1908, 4:1909, 4:1915, 4:1916, 4:1917, 4:1928
Hamilton, Alexander 1:179, 1:213, 1:241, 1:244, 1:246, 1:257, 1:258, 1:259, 1:263, 1:293, 1:295, 1:301–305, 1:308, 1:339, 1:345, 1:346, 1:358, 1:373, 1:375, 1:389, 1:397, 1:401, 1:436, 1:465, 1:472, 2:514, 2:567, 2:574, 2:575, 2:741, 3:1389, 3:1577, 4:2053, 4:2100
    Federalist 31 1:470
    Federalist 33 1:304, 1:470
    Federalist 78 1:403
    Opinion as to the Constitutionality of the Bank of the United States 1:312–326
Hamilton, James 2:590
Hammer, W. C. 3:1241, 3:1243
Hammer v. Dagenhart **3:1240–1255**
Hammerback, John C. 4:1975, 4:1978, 4:1980
Hammett, Dashiell 3:1598
Hancock, John 1:51
Handlin, Oscar and Lilian 2:842
Haney, Craig 4:2083
Harding, Warren G. 3:1267, 3:1387, 3:1432, 4:1883
Harlan, John Marshall 3:1132, 3:1133, 3:1189, 3:1590, 3:1591, 4:1734, 4:1737, 4:1740
    Plessy v. Ferguson, 3: **1072–1095**
Harlan, John Marshall, II 4:1816, 4:1819, 4:1841, 4:1848, 4:1946
Harney, William S. 2:915, 2:917, 2:918, 2:925, 2:929
Harold (king of England) 1:117
Harper, Ida Husted 2:624
Harper, Robert Goodloe 1:360

Indian Peace Commission 2:914–931
Indian Removal Act 2:541–549
Indian Reorganization Act 2:1042
Infant Life (Preservation) Act 4:1919
Ingalls, John J. 2:960
Ingles, William 3:1520
Ingraham, Patricia 2:1005
Insular Cases: *Downes v. Bidwell* **3:1128–1157**, 3:1399
Internal Revenue Code of 1954 4:1622, 4:1626, 4:1636, 4:1643, 4:1644
Interstate Commerce Act **2:1018–1035**, 3:1052, 3:1057
Intolerable Acts 1:23, 1:24, **1:54–79**, 1:81, 1:106, 1:187. *See also* Administration of Justice Act, Boston Port Act, Massachusetts Government Act, Quartering Act (1774).
Iran-Contra scandal 4:1903, 4:1959
Iran hostage crisis 4:1989, 4:1992
Iredell, James 1:364
Iroquois Confederacy 1:188
Irving, Washington 2:955
Iserman, Theodore 3:1520
Iwo Jima, battle of 3:1469

J

Jackson, Andrew 1:245, 1:399, 1:443, 2:609, 2:615, 2:634, 2:703, 2:794, 2:1005, 2:1043, 3:1100, 3:1106, 3:1122–1123, 3:1372
    On Indian Removal **2:540–553**
    Proclamation regarding Nullification **2:588–607**
    Veto Message regarding the Second Bank of the United States **2:566–587**
Jackson, Howell Edmunds 3:1250
Jackson, Mahalia 4:1744
Jackson, Rachel Donelson Robards 2:568
Jackson, Robert H. 3:1390–1391, 3:1571, 3:1573, 3:1575
Jackson, William Henry 2:957
Jacobson, Edward 3:1553, 3:1554
Jagow, Gottlieb von 3:1205
James I (king of England) 1:435
James Madison's Memorial and Remonstrance against Religious Assessments **1:210–223**
Japanese-American Evacuation Claims Act 3:1458
Jay, John 1:82, 1:85, 1:173, 1:179, 1:213, 1:246, 1:257, 1:258, 1:259, 1:294, 1:373, 1:436, 1:472, 3:1577
Jay Treaty of 1794 1:373, 1:375, 1:435, 1:436, 1:439, 1:440, 1:459, 1:503, 3:1389, 3:1396
Jefferson, Thomas 1:62, 1:81, 1:88, 1:96, 1:100, 1:110, 1:115, 1:147, 1:148, 1:150, 1:157, 1:158, 1:178, 1:197, 1:200, 1:214, 1:218, 1:226, 1:227, 1:228, 1:245, 1:259, 1:294, 1:300–305, 1:307–308, 1:329, 1:330, 1:331, 1:357, 1:358, 1:359, 1:361, 1:363, 1:364, 1:368, 1:372–383, 1:397, 1:402, 1:420, 1:425, 1:427, 1:435, 1:437, 1:443, 1:465, 1:466, 1:467, 1:490, 1:494, 1:495, 1:496, 1:501, 1:502, 2:514, 2:515, 2:541, 2:549, 2:555, 2:569, 2:574, 2:575, 2:593, 2:625, 2:662, 2:674, 2:746, 2:755, 2:765, 2:791, 2:794, 2:796, 2:1043, 3:1141, 3:1173, 3:1389,
3:1391, 4:1678, 4:1716, 4:1724, 4:1725, 4:1901, 4:1959, 4:1966, 4:2061
    Act for Establishing Religious Freedom 1:211, 1:213, 1:217, 1:375
    First Inaugural Address **1:372–383**
    Message to Congress about the Lewis and Clark Expedition **1:384–395**
    Notes on the State of Virginia 1:387
    Opinion on the Constitutionality of a National Bank 1:310–313
    Summary View of the Rights of British America 1:62, 1:84, 1:375, 1:419
Jefferson Davis's Inaugural Address to the Confederacy **2:764–775**
Jefferson's and Hamilton's Opinions on the Constitutionality of the Bank of the United States **300–327**
Jenckes, Thomas Allen 2:1005
Jenkins, Herbert 4:1859
Jenkins, W. A. 4:1711
Jensen, Richard J. 4:1975, 4:1978, 4:1980
Jim Crow laws 2:870, 2:871, 2:882, 3:1340, 3:1431, 3:1434, 3:1435, 3:1436, 3:1562, 3:1583, 3:1588, 4:1611, 4:2052
John (king of England) 1:84
John F. Kennedy's Civil Rights Address **4:1729–1741**
John F. Kennedy's Inaugural Address 3:1274, **4:1674–1685**
John Glenn's Official Communication with the Command Center **4:1698–1709**
John Kill Buck, Jr., Captain 1:189
Johnson, Andrew 1:265, 2:755, 2:791, 2:831, 2:861, 2:864, 2:867, 2:870, 2:879, 2:880, 2:882, 2:887, 2:888, 2:889, 2:890, 2:891; 2:933, 2:935, 2:936, 2:937, 2:938, 2:941, 2:946, 2:947, 4:1903, 4:2016, 4:2021, 4:2022
    Articles of Impeachment **2:898–913**
Johnson, Edwin C. 3:1600
Johnson, Hugh Samuel 3:1300, 3:1301, 3:1302, 3:1303, 3:1304, 3:1305
Johnson, Lyndon B. 3:1435, 3:1585, 4:1679, 4:1690, 4:1692, 4:1700, 4:1701, 4:1713, 4:1731, 4:1736, 4:1749, 4:1757, 4:1758, 4:1761, 4:1789, 4:1790, 4:1791, 4:1793, 4:1794, 4:1795, 4:1796, 4:1801, 4:1804, 4:1805, 4:1857–1858, 4:1859, 4:1862, 4:1863, 4:1864, 4:2003
Johnson, Reverdy 2:935
Johnson, Samuel 1:197, 1:202
Johnson, William (American jurist) 1:436, 1:437, 1:440–442, 1:457, 2:513, 2:515, 2:517–519, 2:521
    Gibbons v. Ogden **2:533–538**
Johnson, William (British general) 1:4, 1:7, 1:9, 1:10
Johnson, William Samuel 1:228, 1:241
Johnston, Joseph E. 2:742, 2:858, 2:860, 2:861, 2:863
Joint Resolution of Congress for the Annexation of Texas **2:608–619**
Jones, Anson 2:610, 2:613, 2:614
Jones, Clarence 4:1712

Otis, Harrison Gray 1:360
Otis, James 1:37, 1:39, 1:48, 1:49
Owens, Jack B. 4:1941

P

Pacific Railway Act 2:793
Padilla, José 4:2076, 4:2098
Page, Walter Hines 3:1204, 3:1218
Paine, Thomas 1:47, 1:257, 1:263, 1:330, 2:661, 4:1962, 4:1970
    Case of the Officers of Excise 1:116
    An American Crisis 1:199
    Common Sense 1:47, 1:52, 1:88, 1:114, 1:164
      1:114–145, 1:157, 1:188, 1:199, 1:329, 1:346
    The Age of Reason 1:121
    "Royal Brute" 1:108
Painter, Nell Irvin 2:797
Palestine Liberation Organization (PLO) 4:2005
Panama Canal Zone 3:1464
Panic of 1819 1:489, 2:791
Panic of 1837 2:567, 2:572, 2:792, 2:794
Panic of 1893 3:1097
Pankhurst, Christabel 4:1886
Papandreou, George 3:1498
Papen, Franz von 3:1216
Parks, Rosa 4:1884
Passenger Cases 2:519
Pasteur, Louis 4:1923
Patent and Trademark Office, U.S. 2:978–989
Paterson, William 1:241
Patrick Henry's "Liberty or Death" Speech **1:94–103**, 2:986
Patriot Act 3:1459, 4:2076, 4:2098
Patterson, Robert 4:1608
Patton, George S. 3:1469
Paul, Alice 3:1261, 3:1263, 4:1882, 4:1883, 4:1886–1888
Peabody, George H. 3:1370
Pearl Harbor attack 3:1419, 3:1421, 3:1422, 3:1423, 3:1425, 3:1432, 3:1440–1449, 3:1452, 3:1453
Peckham, Rufus 3:1130, 3:1132, 3:1133, 3:1135
Peden, Katherine Graham 4:1859
Pelham, Henry 1:118
Pendergast, James M. 3:1554
Pendergast, Tom 3:1496, 3:1497
Pendleton, Edmund 1:82
Pendleton, George Hunt 2:1004–1017
Pendleton Civil Service Act **2:1004–1017**, 3:1052
Penn, William 4:1959, 4:1966
Pennsylvania: An Act for the Gradual Abolition of Slavery. *See* Act for the Gradual Abolition of Slavery (Pennsylvania).
Pennsylvania Society for the Abolition of Slavery 1:198
Pentagon Papers 3:1573, 3:1575, 4:1896
People's Party 3:1097, 3:1102
Perkins, Frances 3:1326, 3:1339–1341
Perot, Ross 2:575, 4:1991, 4:2005

Perret, Geoffrey 3:1466
Pershing, John J. 3:1204, 3:1205, 3:1212, 3:1510, 4:1651
Persian Gulf crisis 4:1988–2001, 4:2101
Personal Responsibility and Work Opportunity Reconciliation Act of 1996 3:1378. *See also* Bill Clinton's Radio Address on the Welfare Reform Act.
Peter the Hermit 3:1100, 3:1105
Peterson, William 2:955
Petition of Right 1:22
Petticoat Affair 2:548
Petty, William. *See* Shelburne, 2nd Earl of.
Phelps, John W. 2:828
Philbin, Patrick F. 4:2099
Phillips, Wendell 2:557, 2:560, 2:948
Pichel, Irving 4:1706
Pierce, Franklin 2:639, 2:677, 2:742, 2:767, 2:793
Pillsbury, Parker 2:560, 2:624, 2:828
Pinckney, Charles 1:228, 1:240, 1:241, 1:293, 1:374, 1:375, 1:422, 2:514
Pinckney, Charles Cotesworth 1:422–423, 1:424
Pinckney's Treaty 1:385
Pine, David A. 3:1571, 3:1573
Pipe, Captain 1:189
Pitt, William (the elder). *See* Chatham, 1st Earl of.
Pitt, William (the younger) 1:107
Planned Parenthood of Southeastern Pa. v. Casey 4:1912, 4:2112, 4:2114, 4:2116, 4:2117, 4:2120, 4:2124, 4:2125, 4:2126, 4:2127, 4:2130, 4:2131, 4:2132, 4:2133
Plan for Settlements 1:5
Plato 4:1918
Platt, Orville H. 3:1176
Platt Amendment 3:1130, 3:1136, 3:1176, 3:1180
Plessy v. Ferguson 2:939, 2:950, 3:1061, **3:1072–1095**, 3:1131, 3:1132, 3:1159, 3:1164, 3:1166, 3:1188, 3:1434, 3:1583, 3:1586, 3:1587, 3:1588, 3:1589, 3:1590, 3:1591, 3:1592, 3:1593, 3:1594, 4:1607, 4:1611, 4:1616, 4:1649, 4:1729, 4:1734, 4:1816, 4:1936, 4:1947, 4:2129
Polenberg, Richard 3:1433, 3:1436
Polk, Frank L. 3:1204
Polk, James K. 2:609, 2:610, 2:613, 2:662, 2:741
Pollock, Charles 3:1195
Pomeroy, Clarke 2:957
Pontiac's Rebellion 1:3, 1:5, 1:7, 1:9, 1:17, 1:187
Poole, William 1:7
Poor, Salem 1:197
Pope Leo XIII 4:1974
Populist Party 2:880, 2:888
Porter, David 2:858, 2:863
Posner, Richard 4:2017, 4:2021
Potsdam Conference 3:1495, 3:1497
Potter, Clarkson N. 2:971
Potter, David 2:639
Powell, Colin 4:1997
Powell, Lewis F. 4:1908, 4:1909, 4:2110, 4:2122, 4:2129
    Regents of the University of California v. Bakke **4:1930–1955**

Pownall, John 1:5, 1:7
Pownall, Thomas 1:5, 1:6, 1:10, 1:18
Pratt, Richard 2:1042
Preemption Act 2:792
Preservation of American Antiquities Act of 1906 4:1622, 4:1636
President's Committee on Equal Employment Opportunity 4:1931, 4:1938
Press Release Announcing U.S. Recognition of Israel **3:1550–1559**
Pringle, Thomas 2:558, 2:565
Proclamation by the King for Suppressing Rebellion and Sedition **104–113**, 1:115
Proclamation of 1763 **1:2–15**, 1:17, 1:105, 1:161, 1:187
Progressive Era 2:1027, 3:1370, 3:1405, 3:1584
Progressive Party 3:1212, 3:1497
Protestant Reformation 1:118, 1:133
Provost, Samuel 1:278
Public Health Service, U.S. 3:1342, 3:1358
Public Welfare Amendments Act of 1962 4:2003
Public Works Administration 3:1279, 3:1299, 3:1303, 3:1304, 3:1405
Pulitzer, Joseph 3:1067
Pullman Strike 3:1054, 3:1057, 3:1064, 3:1098
Punitive Expedition 3:1204, 3:1206
Pure Food and Drug Act 3:1241, 3:1249, 3:1253
Putin, Vladimir 4:1706
Putnam, Samuel 1:437

Q

Quartering Act of 1765 **1:16–35**, 1:48
Quartering Act of 1774 1:57, 1:60, 1:75, 1:332
Quasi-War of 1798–1800 1:375
Quebec Act of 1774 1:6, 1:11, 1:24, 1:55, 1:60–61, 1:62, 1:75–79, 1:83, 1:85, 1:106, 1:162, 1:211
Quillian, Benjamin F. 2:803

R

Rabin, Yitzhak 4:2005
Railroad Unemployment Insurance Act 3:1491
Railway Labor Act 3:1301, 3:1326, 3:1332, 3:1525, 3:1532, 3:1546
Randolph, A. Philip 3:1431, 3:1432, 3:1433, 3:1434, 3:1435, 3:1436, 3:1438, 3:1562, 4:1652, 4:1743, 4:1744
Randolph, Edmund 1:100, 1:240, 1:277, 1:289, 1:303, 1:305, 1:339
Randolph, Peyton 1:82
Rankin, Jeanette 3:1218
Rankin, J. Lee 3:1586
Rankin, John 3:1436, 3:1474–1476
Rauh, Joseph L. 3:1432, 3:1433
Rayburn, Sam 3:1421
Raymond, Jack 4:1666
Raymond, Robert R. 2:661
Raynolds, William F. 2:955

Read, George 1:173
Reagan, John H. 2:1019, 2:1020
Reagan, Ronald 3:1273, 3:1274, 3:1458, 3:1473, 3:1478, 3:1501, 4:1886, 4:1903, 4:1910, 4:1973, 4:1975, 4:1977, 4:1990, 4:1991, 4:2004, 4:2006, 4:2008, 4:2074, 4:2088, 4:2089, 4:2090, 4:2091, 4:2096, 4:2105, 4:2110
    "Evil Empire" Speech **4:1957–1971**
    Radio address of February 15, 1986, on welfare reform 4:2011
Reagan Bill 2:1020
Reconstruction 2:847, 2:852, 2:861, 2:862, 2:864, 2:866–875, 2:876–885, 2:886–897, 2:899, 2:904, 2:932–943, 2:944–953, 2:967, 2:970, 2:972, 2:975, 3:1051, 3:1061, 3:1073, 3:1076, 3:1078, 3:1080, 3:1081, 3:1159, 3:1241, 3:1260, 3:1435, 3:1587, 3:1588, 4:1649, 4:1651, 4:1757, 4:1762, 4:1859, 4:2009
Reconstruction Finance Corporation 3:1303, 3:1320
Red Cloud 2:916, 2:917, 2:920, 2:921, 2:923
Red Cloud's War 2:915, 2:916, 2:918, 2:921
Redress Act of 1988 3:1458
Reed, James A. 3:1218
Reed, Merl E. 3:1436
Reed, Thurlow 2:851
Reeder, Andrew 2:684
Regents of the University of California v. Bakke **4:1930–1955**
Rehabilitation Act of 1973 4:1968
Rehnquist, William H. 1:397, 2:520, 4:1821, 4:1908, 4:1933, 4:1935, 4:1936, 4:1937, 4:1941, 4:1942, 4:2030, 4:2031, 4:2034, 4:2042, 4:2055, 4:2057, 4:2101, 4:2110, 4:2113, 4:2118, 4:2130, 4:2133
Reich, Robert B. 4:2009
Reidhaar, Donald L. 4:1941
Reilly, Gerald 3:1520, 3:1521
Reno, Janet 4:2015
Report by the President's Committee on Civil Rights 3:1566
Republican Party 1:159, 1:245, 1:259, 1:357–359, 1:373, 1:397, 1:399, 2:592, 2:634, 2:639, 2:677, 2:684, 2:685, 2:702, 2:706, 2:739, 2:744, 2:745, 2:751, 2:754, 2:777, 2:778, 2:779, 2:780, 2:793, 2:794, 2:803, 2:804, 2:816, 2:830, 2:837, 2:838, 2:847, 2:848, 2:870, 2:879, 2:880, 2:881, 2:882, 2:887, 2:888, 2:890, 2:899, 2:900, 2:901, 2:906, 2:934, 2:937, 2:938, 2:940, 2:965, 2:966, 2:967, 2:968, 2:969, 2:970, 2:972, 3:1062, 3:1074, 3:1101, 3:1129, 3:1134, 3:1175, 3:1241, 3:1260, 3:1369, 3:1370, 3:1372, 3:1373, 3:1374, 3:1376, 3:1378, 3:1380, 3:1403, 3:1405, 3:1408, 3:1432, 3:1436, 3:1453, 3:1497, 3:1499, 3:1512, 3:1519, 3:1520, 3:1526, 3:1552, 3:1554, 3:1584, 3:1585, 3:1601, 4:1651, 4:1821, 4:1895, 4:1896, 4:1897, 4:1898, 4:1908, 4:1910, 4:1931, 4:1959, 4:1979, 4:1984, 4:1985, 4:1990, 4:1991, 4:1994, 4:2000, 4:2003, 4:2004, 4:2005, 4:2007, 4:2009, 4:2010, 4:2015, 4:2016, 4:2017, 4:2019, 4:2058, 4:2110

Reuss, Henry 4:1687. 4:1688
Reuther, Walter 3:1528
Revenue Act of 1861 3:1199
Revenue Act of 1926 3:1318, 3:1319, 3:1360, 3:1363
Revenue Act of 1932 3:1317, 3:1319
Revenue Act of 1934 3:1343, 3:1359, 3:1360
Revolution, American 1: 11, 1:37, 1:42, 1:52, 1:55, 1:96,
    1:115, 1:116, 1:121, 1:162, 1:165, 1:174, 1:176,
    1:178, 1:187, 1:189, 1:190, 1:191, 1:197, 1:200,
    1:201, 1:202, 1:204, 1:211, 1:217, 1:220, 1:225,
    1:226, 1:231, 1:239, 1:244, 1:257, 1:273, 1:279,
    1:292, 1:295, 1:301, 1:303, 1:329, 1:331, 1:332,
    1:339, 1:357, 1:359, 1:361, 1:419, 1:425, 1:435,
    1:437, 1:466, 1:502, 2:595, 2:257, 2:659, 2:767,
    3:1101, 3:1153, 3:1257, 3:1455, 3:1567, 4:1883,
    4:1962
Reynolds, Terry S. 2:808
Richard, John K. 3:1132
Richard, Mark 4:2090, 4:2091
Richard Nixon's Smoking Gun Tape 4:1895–1905
Richberg, Donald 3:1300, 3:1301, 3:1305
Ritchie, Thomas 1:436
Roane, Spencer 1:435, 1:436, 1:438, 1:443, 1:444,
    1:471, 1:472
Roaring Twenties 3:1267
Robbins, Jonathan 3:1389
Robbins, Roy 2:791
Roberts, Owen 3:1452
Roberts v. City of Boston 3:1586, 3:1590, 4:1611, 4:1616
Robespierre, Maximilien 3:1100, 3:1106
Robinson, Edward G. 3:1598
Robinson, Paul H. 4:2103, 4:2104
Rochester Ladies' Anti-Slavery Society 2:657, 2:658
Rockefeller, John D. 3:1051, 3:1052, 3:1195
Rockingham, 2nd Marquess of (Charles Watson-
    Wentworth) 1:107
Rockwell, Norman 3:1403, 3:1409, 3:1410
Rodino, Pete 4:2016, 4:2017
Rodney, Caesar 1:82
Roe, Jane 4:1907, 4:1908, 4:1909, 4:1914, 4:1916,
    4:1925. *See also* McCorvey, Norma.
Roe v. Wade 2:939, 4:1906–1929, 4:1961, 4:2111,
    4:2114, 4:2117, 4:2122, 4:2130, 4:2131, 4:2132,
    4:2133
Rogers, Andrew P. 2:935
Rölvaag, Ole Edvart 2:797
Romer v. Evans 4:2112, 4:2120, 4:2125, 4:2126, 4:2127,
    4:2128, 4:2129, 4:2131, 4:2135, 4:2136
Rommel, Erwin 3:1466
Ronald Reagan's "Evil Empire" Speech 4:1957–1971
Roosevelt, Eleanor 3:1329, 3:1370, 3:1372, 3:1375,
    3:1404, 3:1409, 3:1431, 3:1432, 3:1438, 4:1883,
    4:1885, 4:1888
Roosevelt, Franklin D. 1:245, 2:519, 2:980, 3:1177,
    3:1196, 3:1279, 3:1280, 3:1281, 3:1284, 3:1285,
    3:1286, 3:1299, 3:1300, 3:1301, 3:1303, 3:1305,
    3:1323, 3:1325, 3:1328, 3:1329, 3:1385, 3:1389,
    3:1390, 3:1393, 3:1497, 3:1499, 3:1510, 3:1552,

3:1554, 3:1561, 3:1563, 3:1572, 3:1573, 3:1599,
    4:1651, 4:1677, 4:1729, 4:1743, 4:1883, 4:1897,
    4:1901, 4:1932, 4:1973, 4:2003, 4:2007, 4:2011,
    4:2068
    "Arsenal of Democracy" speech 3:1407, 3:1410,
        3:1420, 3:1421, 3:1433
    Campaign Address at Madison Square Garden
        3:1368–1383
    Executive Order 8802 3:1430–1439, 3:1561
    Executive Order 9066 3:1450–1461
    First Inaugural Address 3:1266–1277, 3:1376,
        3:1378
    Four Freedoms Message to Congress 3:1402–1417
    Fourth Inaugural Address 3:1405, 3:1446, 3:1447
    Lend-Lease Act 3:1418–1429
    "Pearl Harbor" Speech 3:1440–1449
    Servicemen's Readjustment Act 3:1472–1493
    Social Security Act 3:1338–1367
    State of the Union Address (1944) 3:1446
Roosevelt, Sara Delano 3:1370
Roosevelt, Theodore 1:245, 1:506, 2:1010, 2:1012,
    3:1051, 3:1054, 3:1067, 3:1103, 3:1129, 3:1130,
    3:1134, 3:1136, 3:1195, 3:1212, 3:1217, 3:1218,
    3:1241, 3:1242, 3:1267, 3:1340, 3:1370, 3:1404,
    3:1432, 3:1441, 3:1474, 4:2068
    Roosevelt Corollary to the Monroe Doctrine
        3:1172–1181
Roosevelt Corollary to the Monroe Doctrine
    3:1172–1181
Root, Elihu 3:1175
Rosenberg, Julius and Ethel 3:1599
Ross, John 2:546
Ruffner, Louis 3:1063
Ruffner, Viola 3:1063
Rumsey, James 2:513
Rumsfeld, Donald 4:2077
Rundstedt, Gerd von 3:1465
Runte, Alfred 2:957
Rush, Benjamin 1:116, 1:120, 1:121, 1:198, 1:199
    *An Address to the Inhabitants of the British
        Settlements in America, upon Slave-Keeping*
        1:199
Rusk, Dean 4:1790, 4:1793, 4:1796
Russell, Richard B., Jr. 4:1609, 4:1610, 4:1617, 4:1655
Russell, William 3:1100
Russian Revolution 3:1216, 3:1597
Rustin, Bayard 4:1743
Rutherford B. Hayes's Inaugural Address 2:964–977
Rutledge, Edward 1:173
Rutledge, John 1:241, 1:421

S
Salem, Peter 1:197
Sanborn, John B. 2:917, 2:918, 2:925, 2:929
Sandburg, Carl 2:745
Sanford, John F. A. 2:698–737
Sargent, Aaron A. 2:624, 2:991, 3:1257, 3:1259, 3:1260

Turnbull, Robert J. 2:590
Turner, Henry McNeal 2:829
Turner, Nat 2:560
Turtle Heart 1:7
Twain, Mark 3:1052
Twelfth Amendment to the U.S. Constitution 4:1925,
    4:2057
Twenty-fourth Amendment to the U.S. Constitution
    2:950, 4:1885
Twenty-second Amendment to the U.S. Constitution
    4:1925
Twenty-sixth Amendment to the U.S. Constitution 2:945
Tydings, Millard 3:1602
Tyler, John 1:374, 2:610, 2:661, 2:702

U

Underwood-Simmons Tariff 3:1212
Unemployment Trust Fund 3:1341, 3:1362
Uniform Abortion Act of 1972 4:1922
United Auto Workers 3:1433, 3:1528
United Farm Workers of America 4:1973, 4:1974,
    4:1977, 4:1978, 4:1979, 4:1983, 4:1984
United Mine Workers 3:1528
United Nations Charter 4:2105
United Nations Convention against Torture and Other
    Cruel, Inhuman or Degrading Treatment or
    Punishment (CAT) 4:2071, 4:2072, 4:2073, 4:2074,
    4:2075, 4:2076, 4:2078, 4:2080, 4:2087, 4:2088,
    4:2089, 4:2090, 4:2091, 4:2092, 4:2095
United Nations Declaration of Human Rights 1:150,
    1:152
United Nations Declaration on Protection from Torture
    4:2088, 4:2091, 4:2096
United Nations Security Council Resolution 1441
    (regarding Saddam Hussein and Iraq) 4:2063
United Nations Universal Declaration of Human Rights
    3:1403, 3:1409, 3:1562, 3:1566
United States v. Brown 3:1524, 3:1529
United States v. Curtiss-Wright **3:1384–1401**, 3:1577,
    4:2088
United States v. Nixon 3:1575, 3:1577, 4:1901
Upshur, Abel 2:609

V

Vafiades, Markos 3:1498
Van Buren, Martin 2:544, 2:567, 2:568, 2:609, 2:615,
    3:1123
Vancouver, George 1:386
Vandenberg, Arthur 3:1496, 3:1497
Vanderbilt, Cornelius 3:1052
Van Schaack, Beth 4:2092
Van Zandt, Isaac 2:610
Vardaman, James K. 3:1217
Vesey, Denmark 2:589
Vest, George G. 2:960
Veterans Administration 3:1475, 3:1476, 3:1478, 3:1481

Victory Liberty Loan Act 3:1317
Viereck, George Sylvester 3:1206–1207
Vietnam War 3:1478, 3:1499, 3:1501, 3:1573, 4:1713,
    4:1745, 4:1749, 4:1791, 4:1857, 4:1862, 4:1886,
    4:1895, 4:1898, 4:1899, 4:1901, 4:1931, 4:1959,
    4:2003, 4:2063, 4:2101
Vilas, William F. 3:1098–1100
Villa, Francisco "Pancho" 3:1204, 3:1205, 3:1212
Vinson, Frederick M. 3:1584, 3:1575
Virgil 2:516, 2:517
Virginia Declaration of Rights **1:146–155**
Virginia and Kentucky Resolutions of 1798 2:593, 2:594,
    2:755, 4:1612
Voltaire 2:661
Voorhis, Jerry 4:1897
Voting Rights Act of 1965 2:950, 3:1166, 3:1435,
    4:1620, 4:1713, 4:1736, 4:1745, 4:1757, 4:1759,
    4:1762, 4:1763, 4:1765, **4:1798–1813**, 4:1857,
    4:1859, 4:1885, 4:1950, 4:2036
Voting Rights Acts of 1970, 1975, 1982, and 2006 2:950
Vuckovic, Nikola 4:2093, 4:2094, 4:2095
Vyshinsky, Andrei 3:1501

W

Wabash, St. Louis & Pacific Railroad Co. v. Illinois 2:519,
    2:1019
Wade, Henry 4:1907, 4:1908
Wade-Davis Bill 2:847
Wagner, Robert F. 3:1300, 3:1301, 3:1323, 3:1324,
    3:1339, 3:1379
Wagner Act. *See* National Labor Relations Act.
Wagner-Lewis Bill 3:1339
Waite, Morrison 3:1132
Walker, David 2:555
Walker, Robert J. 2:611
Walker, Wyatt T. 4:1712
Wallace, George C. 4:1716, 4:1725, 4:1729, 4:1731,
    4:1746
Wallace, Henry A. 3:1339, 3:1497, 3:1500, 3:1501,
    3:1503, 3:1556
Walpole, Horace 1:9
Walters, Vernon A. 4:1899, 4:1900, 4:1901, 4:1904,
    4:1905
Ward, Hamilton 2:901
War Department General Order 143 **2:826–835**
War of 1812 1:176, 1:202, 1:213, 1:259, 1:436, 1:442,
    1:501, 1:502, 1:503, 1:504, 1:506, 3:1412, 3:1567
War Hawks 2:634
War of Independence (American). *See* Revolution,
    American.
War of Independence (Israel) 3:1556
War Labor Disputes Act 3:1519, 3:1526
War Manpower Commission 3:1436
War and National Defense Acts 3:1455
War on Poverty 4:1983
War Relocation Authority 3:1455, 3:1456, 3:1457,
    3:1458

War of the Roses 1:117

Warren, Earl 4:1607, 4:1677, 4:1803, 4:1805, 4:1931, 4:1933

    Brown v. Board of Education 3:1582–1595

    Miranda v. Arizona 4:1814–1855

Warren, Mercy Otis 3:1257

Warren Commission 3:1454, 3:1585

War on Terror 4:1965, 4:1994, 4: 2060–2069, 4:2070–2107

Washburn, Henry Dana 2:956

Washburne, Elihu B. 2:935

Washington, Booker T. 3:1060–1070, 3:1159, 3:1160, 3:1161, 3:1162, 3:1163, 3:1164, 3:1165, 3:1166, 4:1751, 4:1860

    Atlanta Exposition Address 3:1060–1071, 4:1751

Washington, Bushrod 2:514

Washington, George 1:8, 1:55, 1:82, 1:96, 1:116, 1:147, 1:148, 1:157, 1:174, 1:175, 1:190, 1:197, 1:228, 1:239, 1:240, 1:244, 1:245, 1:259, 1:300, 1:301, 1:303, 1:307, 1:358, 1:361, 1:373, 1:375, 1:387, 1:389, 1:397, 1:436, 1:465, 1:467, 1:501, 1:502, 2:514, 2:541, 2:659, 3:1406, 4:1677, 4:1901, 4:1959, 4:1966

    Farewell Address **1:338–355**

    First Annual Message to Congress **1:288–299**

    First Inaugural Address **1:276–287**, 1:289, 1:292, 1:293, 1:296, 1:379, 4:1677, 4:1679

Watergate affair 3:1344, 3:1577, 4:1894–1905, 4:2003, 4:2016, 4:2021

Watergate Hotel 4:1895, 4:1896

Watkins, Arthur V. 3:1600, 3:1601, 3:1602, 3:1604

Watson-Wentworth, Charles. *See* Rockingham, 2nd Marquess of.

Watts riot of 1965 4:1749

Webster, Daniel 1:228, 2:513, 2:515, 2:519, 2:520, 2:570, 2:572, 2:574, 2:593, 2:633, 2:636, 2:638, 2:639, 2:640, 2:1005

Weddington, Sarah 4:1907

Weinberg, Gerhard L. 3:1509

Weitze, Godfrey 2:858

Weizmann, Chaim 3:1554, 3:1556

Welch, Joseph 3:1600

Weld, Theodore Dwight 2:660

Welfare Reform Act **4:2002–2013**

Welles, Orson 3:1598

Wells, Robert 2:701

West, Andrew Fleming 3:1212

Wetmore, William 1:228

Wheeler, Burton 3:1408

Whig Party 2:544, 2:546, 2:634, 2:639, 2:677, 2:678, 2:684, 2:739, 2:766, 2:778, 2:793, 2:805, 2:816, 2:838, 2:848, 2:862, 2:970, 3:1052

White, Byron 4:1816, 4:1819, 4:1841, 4:1848, 4:1908, 4:1918, 4:1924, 4:1925, 4:1933, 4:1936, 4:1941, 4:1942, 4:1948, 4:1955, 4:2110, 4:2122, 4:2124

White, Edward 3:1129, 3:1131, 3:1132, 3:1133, 3:1134, 3:1136, 3:1137, 3:1215, 3:1241

White Citizens' Council 4:1608

White Eyes, Captain 1:189, 1:190

White House Special Investigations Unit (the "plumbers") 4:1900

White-Slave Traffic Act 3:1243, 3:1249, 3:1253

Whitewater scandal 4:2015, 4:2016

Whittier, John Greenleaf 2:660, 3:1064

Wiggins, Warren W. 4:1688

Wilberforce, William 2:661, 2:673

Wilder, Laura Ingalls 2:797, 2:798

Wilhelm II (German kaiser) 3:1174, 3:1205

Wilkins, Roy 4:1859

Willey, Kathleen 4:2015, 4:2017

William, S. Clay 3:1305

William III (king of England) 1:67, 1:68

William the Conqueror 1:117, 1:129, 1:132, 1:140

William Jennings Bryan's "Cross of Gold" Speech **3:1096–1109**

William Lloyd Garrison's First *Liberator* Editorial **2:554–565**

William McKinley's Message to Congress about Cuban Intervention **3:1110–1127**

Williams, Edward Bennett 3:1600

Williams, George H. 2:935

Williams, Jim 2:961

Williams, John Sharp 3:1216

Williams, Thomas F. 2:903

Williamson, Hugh 1:240

Willis, Albert 2:992

Willkie, Wendell 3:1408

Wills, Garry 2:840, 2:842

Wilmot, David 2:614, 2:677, 2:794

Wilmot Proviso 2:614, 2:633, 2:635, 2:636, 2:685, 2:739, 2:765, 2:794

Wilson, Edmund 3:1272

Wilson, Henry 2:947, 2:948

Wilson, James 1:241, 1:423, 1:424

Wilson, James F. 2:878, 2:879, 2:900–901

Wilson, Pete 4:1975

Wilson, Woodrow 1:158, 1:245, 2:1025, 3:1177, 3:1184, 3:1204, 3:1205, 3:1206, 3:1207, 3:1208, 3:1241, 3:1242, 3:1247, 3:1257, 3:1259, 3:1261, 3:1267, 3:1270, 3:1279, 3:1280, 3:1370, 3:1371, 3:1387, 3:1403, 3:1405, 3:1410, 3:1419, 3:1432, 3:1442, 3:1444, 3:1453, 3:1499, 3:1501, 3:1503, 3:1554, 4:1886

    Congressional Government: A Study in American Politics 3:1230

    Fourteen Points 3:1213, **3:1228–1239**

    Joint Address to Congress Leading to a Declaration of War against Germany **3:1210–1227**

Wilson-Gorman Tariff Act 3:1195, 3:1197, 3:1199

Winthrop, John 4:1694

    "A Modell of Christian Charity" 4:1694

Wirt, William 2:513, 2:516–517

Witherspoon, Jonathan 1:213

Witte, Edwin 3:1340–1345

Wolfe, Thomas 4:1704

Wollstonecraft, Mary 3:1257, 3:1262

    A Vindication of the Rights of Woman 3:1257

Wolverton, Charles 3:1190

Woman's Peace Party 3:1231

Woodford, Stewart 3:1114, 3:1120, 3:1121

Woodrow Wilson: Joint Address to Congress Leading to a Declaration of War against Germany **3:1210–1227**

Woodrow Wilson's Fourteen Points 3:1213, **3:1228–1239**

Woods, Randall 4:1609

Woodward, Bob 4:1899

Woolman, John 1:199

Worcester v. Georgia 1:192, 1:399, 2:548

Works Progress Administration 3:1304

World Anti-Slavery Convention 2:622, 2:623

World Bank 3:1454

World Trade Center attack (1993) 4:2097

World Trade Center attack (2001). *See* September 11, 2001, terrorist attacks.

World War I 3:1177, 3:1197, 3:1203, 3:1211, 3:1212, 3:1220, 3:1229, 3:1230, 3:1231, 3:1232, 3:1243, 3:1257, 3:1259, 3:1260, 3:1261, 3:1302, 3:1403, 3:1406, 3:1407, 3:1408, 3:1412, 3:1419, 3:1443, 3:1444, 3:1473, 3:1474, 3:1510, 3:1512, 3:1552, 3:1554, 3:1563, 3:1567, 3:1572, 3:1584, 3:1597, 4:1619, 4:1663, 4:1743, 4:1860, 4:1866, 4:1883

World War II 3:1279, 3:1284, 3:1323, 3:1344, 3:1371, 3:1381, 3:1402–1417, 3:1418–1429, 3:1430–1439, 3:1440–1449, 3:1450–1461, 3:1462–1471, 3:1472–1493, 3:1495, 3:1499, 3:1506, 3:1507, 3:1509, 3:1511, 3:1515, 3:1551, 3:1552, 3:1556,
3:1558, 3:1562, 3:1564, 3:1567, 3:1571, 3:1572, 3:1583, 3:1587, 3:1598, 4:1611, 4:1619, 4:1654, 4:1663, 4:1671, 4:1675, 4:1676, 4:1678, 4:1679, 4:1687, 4:1688, 4:1730, 4:1731, 4:1733, 4:1789, 4:1859, 4:1860, 4:1883, 4:1884, 4:1895, 4:1897, 4:1932, 4:1957, 4:1958, 4:1974, 4:1995, 4:2068

World Woman's Party 4:1887

Wright, Martha 2:621, 2:622, 2:623

Wright, Susan Webber 4:2020

Wyndham, Charles 1:5

Wythe, George 1:375

X-Y-Z

XYZ Affair 1:398, 2:514

Yalta Conference 3:1495, 3:1499, 3:1506

Yates, Abraham 1:228

Yellowstone National Park, Act Establishing. *See* Act Establishing Yellowstone National Park.

Yellowstone Park Improvement Company 2:960

Yoo, John C. 4:2072, 4:2075, 4:2099

Yosemite Land Grant of 1864 2:957, 2:959, 2:961

Youngstown Sheet and Tube Co. v. Sawyer 3:1388, 3:1390, 3:1391, 3:1392, **3:1570–1581**

Zenger, John Peter 1:359

Zhou Enlai 4:1678

Zimmermann, Arthur 3:1203, 3:1204–1205

Zimmermann Telegram **3:1202–1209**, 3:1211, 3:1216, 3:1217

Zompetti, Joseph P. 4:1975